ARISTOTLE'S

CONSTITUTION OF ATHENS

A REVISED TEXT
WITH AN INTRODUCTION
CRITICAL AND EXPLANATORY NOTES
TESTIMONIA AND INDICES

BY

JOHN EDWIN SANDYS

Elibron Classics
www.elibron.com

Elibron Classics series.

ISBN 1-4212-2957-9 (paperback)
ISBN 1-4212-2956-0 (hardcover)

This Elibron Classics Replica Edition is an unabridged facsimile of the edition published in 1893 by Macmillan and Co., London and New York.

ARISTOTLE'S
CONSTITUTION OF ATHENS

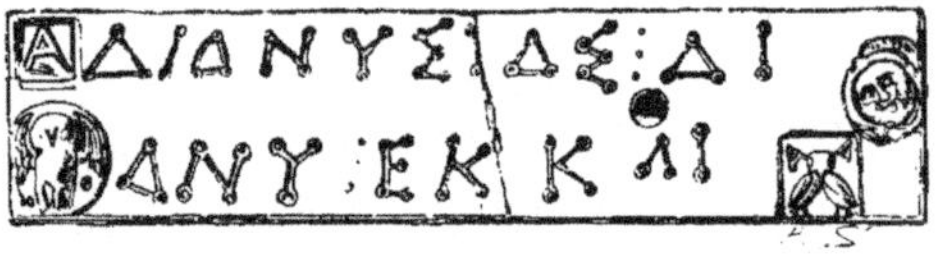

(1) ΠΙΝΑΚΙΟΝ ΔΙΚΑΣΤΙΚΟΝ (c. 63 § 4)

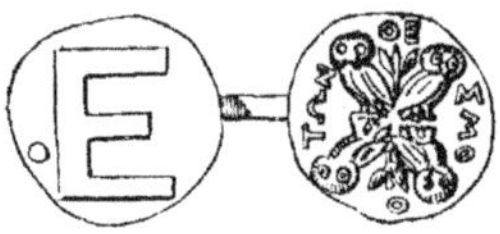

(2)

(3)

(2) and (3) ΚΛΗΡΟΙ ΘΕΣΜΟΘΕΤΩΝ (c. 63 § 5)

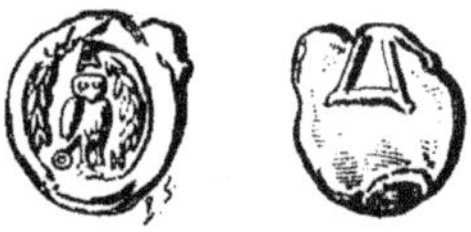

(4)

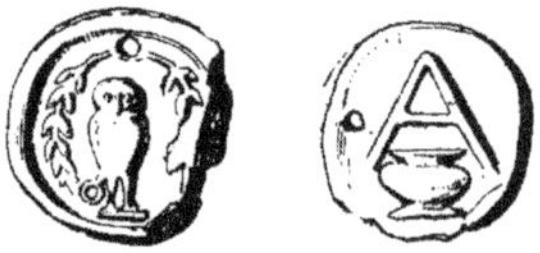

(5)

(4) and (5) ΣΥΜΒΟΛΑ ΔΙΚΑΣΤΙΚΑ (col. 32, 14)

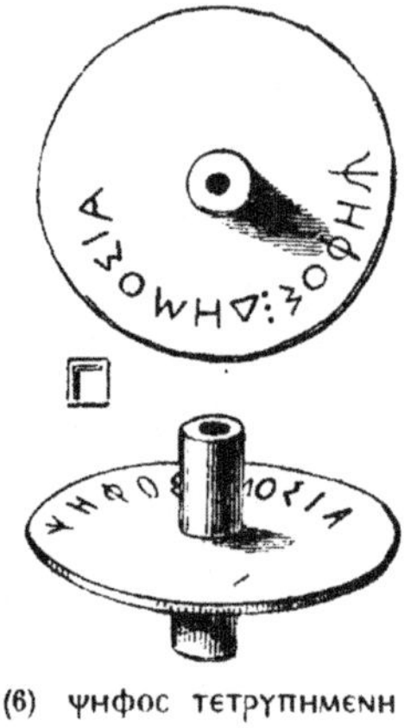

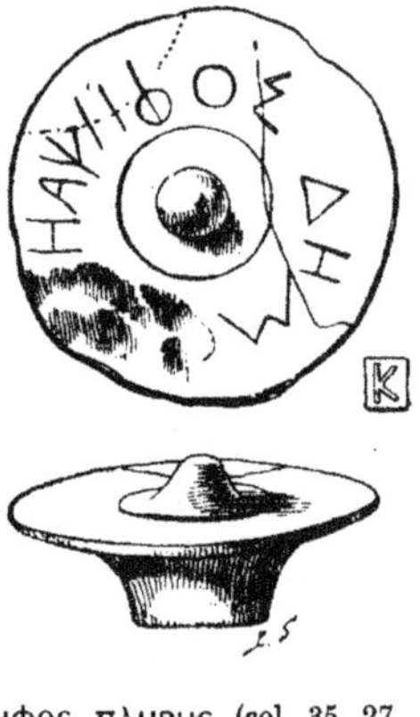

(6) ΨΗΦΟΣ ΤΕΤΡΥΠΗΜΕΝΗ (7) ΨΗΦΟΣ ΠΛΗΡΗΣ (col. 35, 27—29)

ΣΚΕΥΗ ΔΙΚΑΣΤΙΚΑ

(*See description on p.* lxxvi)

ΑΡΙΣΤΟΤΕΛΟΥΣ ΑΘΗΝΑΙΩΝ ΠΟΛΙΤΕΙΑ

ARISTOTLE'S CONSTITUTION OF ATHENS

A REVISED TEXT
WITH AN INTRODUCTION
CRITICAL AND EXPLANATORY NOTES
TESTIMONIA AND INDICES

BY

JOHN EDWIN SANDYS, LITT. D.,
FELLOW AND TUTOR OF ST JOHN'S COLLEGE,
AND PUBLIC ORATOR IN THE UNIVERSITY OF CAMBRIDGE;
HON. LITT. D. DUBLIN.

Tetradrachm of Athens, C. 590—525 B.C. (*See note on page* 39.)

London:
MACMILLAN AND CO.
AND NEW YORK.
1893

Cambridge:
PRINTED BY C. J. CLAY, M.A. AND SONS
AT THE UNIVERSITY PRESS.

PREFACE.

THE preparation of the present volume was planned not long after the memorable publication of Mr Kenyon's *editio princeps* on Friday, the thirtieth of January, 1891. In that important work much was happily done by its able editor to facilitate the study of the newly discovered treatise by a skilful decipherment of the *papyrus*, by a careful comparison of the text with that of the existing fragments, by a judicious restoration of a large number of passages imperfectly preserved in the manuscript, and by an eminently readable commentary on many interesting points of constitutional history. The *editio princeps* was also the *editoris primitiae;* and, considering the brief limits of time within which it was prepared, and notwithstanding certain superficial blemishes which have since been removed, it was undoubtedly a remarkable achievement.

In the opinion, however, of competent critics there appeared to be room, by the side of Mr Kenyon's work, for an edition in which closer attention might fitly be paid to matters of scholarship and verbal criticism, together with a more minute comparison of the fresh evidence with that already familiar to us in two closely allied departments of Classical learning, (1) the Constitutional History, and (2) the Legal Antiquities of Athens. There was also at that time an acknowledged need of an *Index Graecitatis;* and lastly there was a call for a fuller and clearer statement of the evidence on the text so far as it could be derived from quotations in later Greek literature. It has been the aim of the present writer to endeavour to supply such an edition.

The *Introduction* begins with a slight sketch of the political literature of Greece before the time of Aristotle, so far as it was directly concerned with theories of government. This is followed by a brief notice of the *Politics* of Aristotle and of the lost political works ascribed to the same author. The external evidence as to the authorship of the Πολιτεῖαι is next reviewed in chronological order, showing that, according to testimony extending over fifteen centuries from the age immediately succeeding that of Aristotle, the work, as a whole, was ascribed to Aristotle and to none beside. A brief account of the later literature of the subject is succeeded by a description of the Berlin Fragments, and the British Museum papyrus, of the Ἀθηναίων πολιτεία. The date of the treatise is placed between 328 and 325 B.C., which corresponds to the latter part of Aristotle's life; and, after a discussion of its relation to the *Politics*, and an examination of its style and language, it is accepted as being substantially the work of Aristotle himself; due regard is, however, paid to the considerations that have been urged on the other side by several eminent scholars. The discussion of the authorship is followed by an indication of the authorities either certainly or probably used by the writer. This is succeeded by an abstract of the contents, which (excepting a few dates added for the sake of clearness, with one or two items supplementary to the lost beginning of the treatise), is strictly confined to the author's own statements, any extraneous matter being carefully distinguished as such. The rest of the Introduction is mainly devoted to a conspectus of the Bibliography of the treatise, showing that, apart from editions and translations and separate works, the number of writers of signed contributions to the literature of the subject, in the department of periodical publications alone, already exceeds one hundred and thirty. Many of these papers were not published until after the present edition was already in type, the Commentary on the first forty-one chapters and the first draft of the Critical Notes and Testimonia having been written during the Long Vacation of 1891, while the greater part of the Introduction was prepared for delivery in the form of College Lectures in the autumn of the same year. An abstract of the contents of some of the more recent literature is included in the conspectus, wherever it seemed to be desirable. Professor Bruno Keil's important volume of nearly 250 pages on the *Solonian Constitution* as described in the Ἀθηναίων πολιτεία, with many interesting criticisms on the treatise in general, did not appear until the present edition was nearly ready for publication; but it has been found possible to include a few references to it in the *Addenda* and in the *English Index*.

In settling the *Text* I have constantly used the *facsimile* published by the Trustees of the British Museum; and, on nearly all points of special difficulty, I have also endeavoured to form an opinion of my own by consulting the *papyrus* itself. In the case of passages imperfectly preserved in the MS, I have considered it safer to accept Mr Kenyon's testimony as to the exact number of letters still visible, than that of other editors who, without having had the advantage of inspecting the MS, much less of having constant access to it, have not unfrequently indicated letters as actually visible which (at the best) are represented only by the faintest traces in the facsimile on which their texts are confessedly founded. Where the reading is uncertain, or the MS defective, I have freely admitted conjectures that commended themselves to my judgment as sound restorations of the text. My own conjectures, so far as they are here put forward for the first time, are always distinguished by an asterisk whenever they are included in the text; but even of these, several must be regarded as merely provisional and tentative restorations. Others are only suggested in the notes. References to all of them may be readily found in the English Index, under the heading 'Conjectures.'

In the *Critical Notes* the readings of the MS are for convenience recorded in a distinctive type. No one, however, who is familiar with the facsimile as a whole, or with the specimen published in Mr Kenyon's Translation, will regard these 'small uncials' as intended to represent the actual characters used by any one of the four copyists employed on the work. I have also indicated the readings or conjectures adopted in the principal critical editions that have already appeared; the Dutch edition, by van Herwerden and van Leeuwen; the two German editions, by Kaibel and von Wilamowitz-Moellendorff, and by Blass respectively; and the third (and carefully revised) edition by Mr Kenyon. Where Mr Kenyon has himself withdrawn the reading proposed in his first edition, I have not thought it desirable to record the reading so withdrawn, unless it helped to explain some of the earlier conjectures which in themselves appeared deserving of mention. I have therefore said nothing about such purely provisional readings as καρδίᾳ καὶ κοινῇ in c. 40 l. 17. It was clear that καρδίᾳ could not be right, and more than one scholar (for example, Professor Blass, Professor Mayor, and Mr Bywater) saw at once that καὶ ἰδίᾳ καὶ κοινῇ was a necessary correction;

but, now that it is admitted that this is virtually the reading of the *papyrus*, in which ΚΑΙΔΙΑ is corrected into ΚΑΙΙΔΙΑ, it is no longer necessary to record the text of the first edition. At the time, however, when the above suggestion was made, it had every right to be described as an 'emendation'; and it may be interesting to add that, as such, it attracted the notice of the late Mr Freeman, who observes in the preface to the third volume of his *History of Sicily*:—'such an emendation as this is not conjecture at all; it is the keen instinct of the true expert seeing his way straight to the right thing.' Again, it has not been deemed desirable to record *all* the conjectures that have been proposed since the publication of the *editio princeps*, many of them, however attractive at first sight, being excluded by our present knowledge of the actual readings of the papyrus, or by other considerations.

The *Testimonia*, printed immediately below the critical notes, contain further evidence on the text, in the form of quotations in Greek Lexicographers, Scholiasts, and others. Many, but by no means all, of these, had already been recorded in the various editions of the Fragments. In the present volume, a good deal of pains has been spent on the endeavour to trace in the Scholiasts, and in authors such as Aristides, tacit quotations or paraphrases of our text, which had hitherto escaped detection owing to their source having been unacknowledged. In the case of these quotations, it has been thought best not to remain content with giving references alone, but (as a general rule) to print the passages in full. It is only thus that their exact value in relation to the text can be readily seen.

In the *Explanatory Notes* considerable space has naturally been assigned to the quotation of parallel passages, especially from the *Politics*; and on every point an endeavour has been made to compare the new evidence with the old. In the historical notes to the first part (c. 1—41) much had already been accomplished by Mr Kenyon; but the second part (c. 42 to the end) was comparatively new ground. Throughout the work special attention has been given to the evidence of Greek Inscriptions.

The *Greek Index* gives a complete list of the vocabulary, with full citations of the phraseology of the treatise, including that of the passages quoted from the poems of Solon and the decrees of Athens, which are duly distinguished from citations from the body of the work. Words not recorded in the *Index Aristotelicus*, and words hitherto unknown, are indicated by distinctive marks. In checking the items in this Index, much help has been derived from the two Greek Indices, the *Index Dictionis* and the *Index Nominum et Rerum*, of the Dutch edition; but in the present work it has been thought best to have only one Greek Index, and to adopt a more convenient mode of reference. The preparation of this Index has been a laborious task and has considerably delayed the publication of the volume.

The *Archaeological Illustrations* in the frontispiece are borrowed from Daremberg and Saglio's *Dictionnaire des Antiquités* (Hachette, Paris): the Aeginetan and Attic coins on p. 39, from Baumeister's *Denkmäler des Klassischen Alterthums* (Oldenbourg, Munich). To the publishers of both of these important works, the best thanks are due for the readiness with which they have accorded the use of these illustrations.

Among those who in other ways have aided me in preparing the present work, I gladly mention in the first place Mr Kenyon, who, with his able colleagues in the department of MSS at the British Museum, has afforded me every facility for studying the *papyrus;* and, at times when my daily duties in Cambridge made it impossible for me to visit the Museum, has readily given me the fullest information on any point on which I had occasion to consult him. It is a pleasure to add that for a large number of valuable notes and references I am indebted to the kindness of two whose names have long been eminent in the world of scholars:—Mr W. L. Newman, Fellow of Balliol College, Oxford, and editor of Aristotle's *Politics;* and the Rev. John Eyton Bickersteth Mayor, Senior Fellow of St John's, and Professor of Latin in the University of Cambridge. I am similarly indebted in no less degree to a scholar of more recent reputation, Mr W. Wyse, late Fellow of Trinity, and now Professor of Greek in University College, London, whose felicitous emendations of the text, founded mainly on a minute acquaintance with the Attic Orators, and proposed at a time when he was resident in his College rooms in Cambridge, are one more proof that the spirit of Dobree still happily dwells in its ancient home. Lastly, in response to a request conveyed by Mr George Macmillan, Secretary of the Hellenic Society and a member of the firm by which this volume is published, his Excellency the Minister for Greece, whose recent departure from England is regretted by all lovers of Hellenic learning, was good enough to lend me his own copy of the admirable emendations proposed by his brother, Anastasios Gennadios, in the columns of an Athenian newspaper taking its name from the Acropolis.

He also kindly allowed me the use of a number of a Greek philological magazine, Ἀθηνᾶ, containing valuable articles on the textual criticism of the treatise by G. A. Papabasileios, and K. S. Kontos. This magazine was not to be found in the Library of the British Museum, and is practically inaccessible in England except to its annual subscribers. While engaged in exploring the scattered literature of such a subject as the present, one feels in such a case, no less than in that of the *Sitzungsberichte* of the Berlin Academy, the full force of the complaint made not long ago by the late Mr Freeman. 'No man can undertake to find out every pamphlet and every article. And, when one has found what is wanted, it is sometimes forbidden to buy the number that one wants, unless one chooses to buy a whole volume that one does not want.' I can only add that I shall be grateful to writers of similar articles for any separate copies of their papers that happen to be available; and, if in this way I become possessed of any duplicates, I propose to present the duplicate to a Library where it will be readily accessible to many who are interested in the subject.

I owe much besides to the principal editions of the treatise, especially to Mr Kenyon's third edition, more particularly for details connected with the readings in the *papyrus*. The study of the MS and of the facsimile alike has been considerably facilitated by the convenient plan adopted in the Dutch edition of Professors Van Herwerden and Van Leeuwen, in which the contents of the MS are indicated, not merely column by column, but also line by line. The edition of the text by Professors Kaibel and von Wilamowitz-Moellendorff has been of much use in revising the text and the *testimonia*, and in dealing with the fragments. In this last particular, as in some others, a still further advance has been made in the very useful Teubner text recently edited by Professor Blass, the results of whose subsequent examination of the *papyrus* have, by his own kindness, reached me in time to be included in the *Addenda*.

My obligations to other published works are acknowledged as they arise, and are also expressed in general terms at the close of the bibliographical part of the Introduction. It may here be noticed that several of the most important of the books of reference to which I am thus indebted, are already attesting in their new editions the value of the evidence on the Constitutional History and the Public Antiquities of Athens which is contained in the treatise that, little more than two years ago, was so unexpectedly restored to us from the tombs of Egypt.

Up to the time of that fortunate event, the student was compelled to satisfy his curiosity with the scattered fragments that, in successive generations, first in Italy and France, and afterwards in Holland and Germany, had been diligently sought by the industry of scholars, and collected into one by those 'friends of Truth,' who (in Milton's phrase) 'imitating the carefull search that Isis made for the mangl'd body of Osiris, went up and down gathering limb by limb still as they could find them.' Even now, when in place of these *disiecta membra*, the actual body of the work has been happily recovered in an approximately complete condition, the 'friends of Truth' have made much ado over many minor details of the great discovery. After all that has been found, the quest continues still; but it is no longer limited, as it was two years ago, to the enterprise of a single scholar, enjoying all the privileges, and, at the same time, encountering not a few of the perils of a solitary pioneer. On the contrary, it is shared by a goodly number of eager investigators in many lands; and the very number of those who are joining in the quest is almost a source of embarrassment to any one of them who attempts to gather up the main results of their research and to combine them with his own. The last two years have led to many points connected with the new treatise being viewed in a more sober light and with a more fitting sense of proportion: the exaggerated expectations that were at first aroused have been followed by a natural reaction, which is now succeeded in its turn by the prevalence of an intermediate state of settled contentment. Meanwhile, the excitement of that earlier time is over; and those who are still engaged on the quest must be content to continue their patient toil unstimulated and unrewarded by any such general and public interest as that which justly awaited the first announcement of an event which has enabled men of letters to realise in the present day some of the joyous surprises of the age of the Renaissance. In the feeling language lately used in Cambridge by a learned prelate belonging to both of the two oldest Universities of the United Kingdom, 'the dignity and nobility of a scholar's life lie in this, that it claims no recognition, and asks for no reward. It seldom admits of excitement; it has no prospect of great encouragement; it looks forward to no definite achievement.' There are times, however, when a student, while attempting to restore and explain some imperfectly recorded remnant of the past, may take a quiet pleasure in obeying the precept of George Herbert:—

'If studious, copie fair what Time hath blurr'd'.

And at last there is a moment when, in the spirit of thankfulness that comes with the completion of an arduous undertaking, he may, as at present, offer to the kindly criticism and to the use of others a work which, however long delayed by lack of leisure, and however inadequate in itself, has at least been the result of the most unsparing labour and the most strenuous endeavour.

December 27, 1892.

CONTENTS.

PAGES

INTRODUCTION

§ 1. *The political literature of Greece before the time of Aristotle* . . . ix—xii
§ 2. *Political works ascribed to Aristotle* . . . . . xii—xix
§ 3. *Evidence of ancient authorities on the authorship of the* Πολιτεῖαι . . . . xix—xxix
§ 4. *The later literature of the* Πολιτεῖαι . . . . . xxix—xxxi
§ 5. *The Berlin Fragments of the* Ἀθηναίων πολιτεία . . xxxi—xxxiii
§ 6. *The British Museum Papyrus* . . . . . . xxxiv—xxxix
§ 7. *Date and Authorship of the treatise* . . . . . . xxxix—liv
§ 8. *Authorities followed in it* . . . . liv—lviii
§ 9. *Abstract of its contents* . . . . lix—lxvii
§ 10. *Conspectus of the Literature of the subject* . . . . lxvii—lxxv
§ 11. *List of Abbreviations used in the critical notes* . . . lxxvi
§ 12. *List of Illustrations* lxxvi

CORRIGENDA lxxvi

ADDENDA . . . . lxxvii—lxxx

TEXT AND NOTES, including 'Fragmenta ex papyri paginis ultimis' (237—249) . . . . 1—249

HERACLIDIS EPITOMA 250

FRAGMENTA ex prima libri parte 251—3; dubia 253—4; aliena 254—5 251—5

FRAGMENTORUM IN PAPYRO LONDINENSI INVENTORUM INDEX . 256

GREEK INDEX . . . . 257—296

ENGLISH INDEX . . . . 297—302

INTRODUCTION.

§ 1. *The political literature of Greece before the time of Aristotle.*

In a brief preliminary survey of the political literature of Greece[1], it is unnecessary to dwell on the names of representatives of the pre-Socratic schools of philosophy, such as Pythagoras of Samos and Protagoras of Abdera, although the former is said to have written a πολιτικὸν σύγγραμμα (Diog. Laert. viii 6), and the latter a treatise περὶ πολιτείας (*ib.* ix 55). The work ascribed to Pythagoras was undoubtedly spurious; like that of Protagoras, it has been lost to posterity.

The earliest extant specimen of this branch of literature is the treatise preserved among the works of Xenophon under the title of Ἀθηναίων πολιτεία. Among modern scholars Cobet stands almost alone in being content to accept it as Xenophon's (*Nov. Lect.* p. 706). Its authorship is in fact uncertain: it has been attributed to Alcibiades[2], and also to Critias[3], who is known to have written on the πολιτεῖαι of Sparta, Thessaly and Athens. It may fairly be regarded as emanating from the oligarchical party at Athens, and as primarily intended for the perusal of readers at Sparta who sympathised with their aims. It was probably written between B.C. 426 and 413. It is in any case the earliest Greek political treatise that has come down to us. More than this, it is the 'oldest extant specimen of literary Attic prose[4]'; it is also 'the oldest extant specimen of a political pasquinade'. The real or imputed abuses of the Athenian Democracy are attacked in a tone of bitter sarcasm or insidious irony, relieved by acute remarks on interesting points of national economy, such as the relations of Athens to her subjects and rivals, and the comparative strength and weakness of her naval and military establishments[5].

The Λακεδαιμονίων πολιτεία, though regarded as spurious by Deme-

[1] Cf. Henkel, *Studien zur Geschichte der Griechischen Lehre vom Staat*, esp. pp. 1—17, *die politischen Schriften der Philosophen*.

[2] W. Helbig, *Rhein. Mus.*, xvi 511 ff.

[3] *e.g.* by Boeckh, *Public Economy of Athens*, III v, vol. i p. 390 Fränkel.

[4] Jebb, *Primer of Gk. Lit.*, p. 114.

[5] Col. Mure's *Literature of Greece*, v 422—5. See also A. Kirchhoff, in the *Abhandlungen* of the Berlin Academy for 1874.

trius of Magnesia (Diog. Laert. ii 57), is accepted as the work of Xenophon by Plutarch (*Lyc.* 1) and others in ancient times, and among the moderns by Cobet (*Nov. Lect.* p. 705—724) and many others. Its date is possibly later than the battle of Leuctra (371); but is more probably between 403 and 401. It is a work inspired throughout by admiration of Spartan institutions. The Κύρου παιδεία is later than the death of Socrates (*Cyrop.* III i 38—40), and was probably written after Xenophon's return from exile, or about 369. While professing to describe the education of the founder of the Persian empire, it is really a historical and political romance, an idealised biography with a didactic purpose, being practically an encomium on Socratic principles and Spartan practice. It is prompted by the author's experience of Hellenic political and social life, especially the instability and vicissitudes of various forms of government[1].

The pamphlet entitled πόροι [ἢ περὶ προσόδων] was probably not the work of Xenophon, but was written about 346 B.C. as a manifesto of the party who held that the commercial prosperity of Athens depended on peace with Philip. It suggests several expedients for enlarging the revenue, especially by means of taxes levied on resident aliens, as well as profits derived from the labour of 10,000 public slaves who were to be employed in the mines of Laurium.

Passing from 'Xenophon' to Plato, we have in the *Republic* the most memorable of all delineations of an Ideal State. In the first four books the description of the State is in harmony with Hellenic notions of religion and morality; in the remainder, the Hellenic State is transformed into an ideal kingdom of philosophy, of which all other governments are perversions[2]. In the eighth book[3] all conceivable forms of constitutions are reduced to five classes, represented by aristocracy, timocracy, oligarchy, democracy and despotism or tyranny, corresponding to five leading types of individual character. In the portraits of the typical 'timocrat', tyrant, and democrat, and in the account of the successive changes which they represent, we have a sequence of transformations that is not entirely in accordance with historical facts, but nevertheless supplies us with something of the nature of a philosophy of history. The author is clearly no lover of democracy, or indeed of any of the existing varieties of government. His gaze is fixed on something above and beyond the horizon of his time. In his view, as expressed in the closing words of the ninth book, the man of understanding is little likely to be a politician in the land of his birth, though he will certainly be a politician in an ideal city which is all his own;

[1] Introduction to Holden's ed.
[2] Jowett, *Introd.* to the *Republic*, p. 3.
[3] p. 544, compared with IV *ult.*

a city whose pattern is laid up in heaven, and he who desires may look on that pattern and in the vision find indeed his home. But whether there really is, or ever will be, such a city, is of no concern to him; for he will do all things in obedience to the laws of that city and of no other.

The *Republic* is almost always called the Πολιτεία, but sometimes bears the plural name, Πολιτεῖαι. Thus Themistius (ii 32 C) associates with the name of Plato, Πολιτεῖαί τε αἱ κλειναὶ καὶ οἱ θεσπέσιοι Νόμοι. The dialogue on the *Laws* was composed after the *Republic* (Ar. *Pol.* ii 3, 1), and was published after the author's death (Diog. Laert. iii 37). It sets forth in minutest fulness the details of an Ideal Code; and, in the absence of any actual code of the institutions of Athens, the indications of the existing laws therein contained are often of special value[1]. The lofty conception of the 'rule of Philosophers' is here abandoned, and the state described is the best which is practically possible under the existing limitations of Greek life. In the third book the author reviews the constitutions of Sparta, Persia and Athens, noting the causes of the success and failure of each; and then proceeds to develop his own constitution. In the Platonic dialogue, entitled the Πολιτικός, or an inquiry into the definition of a Ruler, there is much affinity with the *Laws* of Plato and the *Politics* of Aristotle. In contrast to the doubtless earlier scheme in the *Republic*, with its five types of constitution, we here find a series of seven, in which, apart from the ideal and only perfect type, we have six existing forms of government. These six are obtained by dividing the rule of the One (μοναρχία), of the Few (ἡ ὑπὸ τῶν ὀλίγων δυναστεία), and of the Many (δημοκρατία) into two varieties each, (1) into kingship and tyranny, and (2) into aristocracy and oligarchy, while the two varieties of democracy ('constitutional government' and 'simple democracy') are undistinguished by any differences of name. The distinction in each of these three pairs turns upon the question whether Law is observed or not[2]. In its political views, and probably in its date, this dialogue occupies an intermediate position between the *Republic* and the *Laws*; and its classification of typical forms of government reappears, with slight differences of terminology, in the *Ethics* and *Politics* of Aristotle[3]. Of the other political dialogues bearing Plato's name, the *Epinomis* is an appendix to the *Laws*, and is mainly concerned with Education; the *Minos* dis-

[1] See esp. K. F. Hermann, *De vestigiis institutorum veterum, imprimis Atticorum, per Platonis de Legibus libros indagandis*, 1836.

[2] *Politicus*, pp. 291, 302.

[3] *Eth.* viii 10; *Pol.* iii 7 and vi (iv) 2. Cf. Newman's *Politics*, i 430—433, and Prof. Sidgwick in *Class. Rev.* vi 141—4.

cusses the definition of Law; but neither of these can be reckoned among the genuine works of Plato.

The above summary has been purposely confined to writings strictly concerned with politics, to the exclusion of historical works in which political discussion only plays a subordinate part. Otherwise, we might have recalled the debate on the relative merits of monarchy, oligarchy and democracy, which is ascribed to the Persian grandees in the pages of Herodotus (iii 80—82); and the reflexions on the effects of party spirit in Grecian politics, to which Thucydides is prompted by the narrative of the vengeance of the victorious *demos* on the oligarchs of Corcyra (iii 82 f). As it is, in the limited field of purely political literature, we have noted the rise of the polemical pamphlet, and the historical romance, while in Plato's delineation of an Ideal State and an Ideal Code, we have seen the prototype of writings such as Sir Thomas More's *Utopia* and Bacon's *New Atlantis*. The setting forth of such ideals became a favourite medium for the expression of political criticism; but it is characteristic of Aristotle that, while following this fashion, he succeeded in bringing the political speculations of philosophy into closer relation with the facts of history. In the language of one of the foremost authorities on the political writings of Aristotle, "political science 'begins' for Aristotle 'in History', no less than in Ethics"[1]. 'The vision of an ideal State did not make Aristotle indifferent to the problems and difficulties of the actual State. The age which dreams of ideal States is often on the point of losing its interest in politics; but this was far from being the case with Aristotle[2]'.

§ 2. *Political works ascribed to Aristotle.*

Among the political writings ascribed to Aristotle by far the most important is, of course, the *Politics*. The imperfect form in which it has come down to us has been variously explained. The earlier view, supported by Spengel[3], was that the work of Aristotle was originally completed by himself, and that important portions of it were afterwards lost. The later view, which is more probable in itself, and is accepted by almost all Aristotelian scholars in modern times, regards the *Politics* as a work that was left unfinished. This view is corroborated by the fact that in later writers we have no reference to the *Politics* which cannot be traced to the existing work. The latest event mentioned in it is the death of Philip, B.C. 336 (viii (v) 8, 10, p. 1311 *b* 2). As to

[1] Mr W. L. Newman's *Politics*, vol. i p. 15.

[2] *ib.* p. 89.

[3] *Ueber die Pol. des Ar.*, pp. 44 ff.

the order of the books, it can hardly be doubted that, owing to the nature of their contents, books vii and viii should come immediately after iii, while it is not quite certain that books v and vi should be transposed. The order adopted by Susemihl is as follows: i, ii, iii, vii, viii, iv, vi, v. Thus books iv—viii of the new order correspond to vii, viii, iv, vi, v, of the old[1]. In the *Politics* Aristotle discusses the origin of the household, the village and the state, and examines the nature of property, and in particular of property in slaves (Bk. I). The citizen is defined as one who shares in the judicial or deliberative administration of a state. In the next book, Aristotle criticises the *Republic* and the *Laws* of Plato, the constitutions framed by Phaleas and Hippodamus, and the actual forms of government prevailing in Sparta, Crete and Carthage, closing with some (possibly interpolated) criticisms on Solon and Pericles (II). The various types of government are thereupon described in turn, Monarchy, Aristocracy and a mixed constitutional system called πολιτεία, together with the three forms into which they respectively degenerate, Tyranny, Oligarchy and Democracy (III). The author next delineates his Ideal State, and deals with the subject of Marriage and of Education, Bk IV (VII). The latter should be national and also liberal; its two main branches are 'music' and 'gymnastic', Bk V (VIII). The types of government are then discussed in detail. Of the three perversions, Tyranny, the perversion of Monarchy, which is itself the best and most divine, is necessarily the worst. Oligarchy, the perversion of Aristocracy, is not so bad as Tyranny; the last, and the least bad, is Democracy. The different kinds of government are then further discriminated, with the forms assumed by the deliberative and the executive power in each, Bk VI (IV). The basis of democracy is defined to be liberty, which includes the principle that 'all should rule and be ruled in turn'. The characteristics of democracy are then described:—all officers of state are appointed 'by all, and out of all'; all rule over each, and each in turn rules over all; the appointment is by lot, except in cases where special knowledge is required; there is little or no qualification; office is held for a short time only, and rarely (if ever) twice, except in the case of military offices; all men, or at least persons selected out of all, sit in judgment in all causes, or at any rate on the most important; the public Assembly is supreme, not the officers of state; when the citizens are paid, even the Council loses its

[1] In the present work, whenever the books of the *Politics* are specified, the number in the new order is given first, followed (in parenthesis) by that of the old order. As a general rule, however, the references are solely to the pages and lines of the Berlin ed.—Among the most recent discussions of the order of the books may be mentioned Shute's *History of the Aristotelian Writings*, pp. 164—176; and Newman's *Politics*, vol. i 292, vol. ii pp. xxi—xxiv.

power, as the Assembly and the Lawcourts take all the business to themselves. Then follow the various kinds of oligarchies; and the consideration of the due coordination of offices in the state, Bk VII (VI). The author's design is now nearly completed. He has still to speak of the motives, objects and occasions of revolutions in states. Revolutions begin in trifling matters but involve important issues. They are brought about either by force or by fraud. The author next considers how revolutions may be avoided, and tyrannies and monarchies preserved; he describes a despot of a virtuous and beneficent type; and adds some reflexions on the short duration of tyrannies and oligarchies. Lastly, he attacks the views put forward in the *Republic* as to the cycle through which states are described as passing in the course of their decline. Thus the work ends (as it began) with a criticism on Plato.

Among the lost writings of Aristotle was one entitled Πολιτικός, a dialogue in two books, expressly mentioned by Diogenes Laertius (v 22), and vaguely noticed by Cicero[1]. The anonymous list of his works, now ascribed to Hesychius, includes the περὶ ῥήτορος ἢ πολιτικοῦ. That of Diogenes Laertius, a work entitled περὶ βασιλείας, said to have been addressed to Alexander[2]; and a dialogue on colonisation under the name of Ἀλέξανδρος ἢ ὑπὲρ ἀποικιῶν α'[3]. In closer connexion with contemporary history, the δικαιώματα πόλεων ascribed to Aristotle are said to have contained the formal pleas on the points of difference submitted by the Greek states to the arbitration of Philip[4]. A work of far wider scope was that known as the νόμιμα, or νόμιμα βαρβαρικά, of Aristotle. This was a comprehensive account of the institutions of various non-hellenic peoples, including the Etruscans, under the head of νόμιμα Τυρρηνῶν. An abstract of this existed at one time under the name of νομίμων βαρβαρικῶν συναγωγή[5].

Lastly, there was the work entitled the Πολιτεῖαι, or sketches of the constitutional history of a large number of Hellenic states. Constitutional history, however, was far from forming the sole subject of this extensive work. The numerous fragments that have survived give abundant proof that local legends, national proverbs, and even anecdotes of social life found a place in its pages[6]. It is generally supposed

[1] *De Fin.* V 4, 11, 'cumque uterque eorum (Aristoteles et Theophrastus) docuisset, qualem in republica principem esse conveniret'—; *ad Quintum fratrem*, iii 5, 1, 'Aristotelem, quae de republica et praestante viro scribat, ipsum loqui.' Cf. Bernays, *die Dialoge des Ar.* pp. 53, 153.

[2] Cf. Bernays, *l. c.*, pp. 53, 154; published by Lippert (1891) from an Arabic translation.

[3] Bernays, *l. c.*, pp. 56, 156.

[4] Rose, *Aristotelis qui ferebantur librorum fragmenta*, (Teubner) 1886, frag. 612—614.

[5] *ib.* frag. 604—610. Diels (Berlin Academy, 30 July, 1891) suggests that pap. ix p. 29 of the Flinders Petrie *papyri* is an excerpt from the νόμιμα βαρβαρικά.

[6] Rose, *Aristoteles Pseudepigraphus*, p. 395; *Fragmenta*, 381—603, ed. 1886.

that the great collection of facts comprised in the Πολιτεῖαι formed the materials for the composition of the *Politics*. It will be shewn at a later point that the Ἀθηναίων πολιτεία in particular was not completed until about nine years after the latest date recorded in the *Politics;* but this fact is not inconsistent with the materials collected for the Πολιτεῖαι being used in the *Politics* even before they had themselves been reduced into their present form. As regards the comparative value of the two works, the general character of the fragments of the Πολιτεῖαι shews that it would be going too far to say that we could wish that the Πολιτεῖαι were 'preserved, even at the expense of the extant book on the theory of politics', especially when we reflect that, in the words of the writer just quoted, 'the *Politics* are confessed on all hands to be the ripest and fullest outcome of Greek political experience'[1].

The treatise known as the Ἀθηναίων πολιτεία formed part of the vast collection of Πολιτεῖαι which the unanimous voice of antiquity ascribed to the pen of Aristotle. In tracing the literary history of the Πολιτεῖαι we must necessarily begin with the well-known story of the fate of Aristotle's library, which is told in full by Strabo (p. 608—9), and more briefly touched upon by Plutarch (*Sulla*, 26). On the death of Aristotle, in 322 B.C., his library passed into the possession of his pupil, Theophrastus, who presided over the Peripatetic school at Athens until his death in 287. The library of Theophrastus, including that of Aristotle, was bequeathed to a pupil of both, named Neleus, who removed it to Scêpsis, an inland town of Asia Minor, in the S.E. of the Troad. From Neleus it passed to his descendants, who were men of neither literary accomplishments nor philosophic tastes. They are described by Strabo as ἰδιῶται. They were, however, sufficiently conscious of the value of the manuscripts to prevent their being appropriated by the kings of Pergamos, who began to form their famous library about thirty or forty years after the death of Theophrastus. The manuscripts were accordingly concealed in a cellar, where they were exposed to injury from the effects of damp and the depredations of worms. It was probably after the death of the last of the Pergamene Kings in B.C. 133, that they were sold to Apellicon of Teôs, a wealthy adherent of the Peripatetic school at Athens. On examination they were found to contain many compositions which were unknown to the successors of Theophrastus at the head of the Lyceum. Their owner caused them to be copied; but, as he was 'more of a *bibliophile* than a philosopher', the transcripts published under his care proved to be far from accurate. In 86 B.C. Athens was captured by Sulla, and the library of Apellicon was taken to Rome. It was there placed under the charge of a librarian, by whose

[1] Mahaffy's *Hist. of Classical Gk. Literature*, ii 414.

permission it was properly arranged by a learned Greek, a friend of Cicero and a preceptor of Strabo (p. 548), named Tyrannion. Copies were obtained from Tyrannion by Andronicus of Rhodes, who classified the works according to subjects[1], published them, and drew up the lists which were current in the time of Plutarch[2].

On the strength of this last statement it has been supposed that all the extant lists of Aristotelian writings are to be ultimately traced to Andronicus[3]. But, even before his time, the successors of Theophrastus possessed copies of a few at least of the works of Aristotle, chiefly of the exoteric or popular class[4]. As examples of these, the list suggested by Grote[5] includes the dialogues; the legendary and historical collections; and the constitutional histories of various Hellenic cities. Thus, the Πολιτεῖαι may have been known to the successors of Theophrastus even before the library of Aristotle was for a time restored to Athens more than two centuries after the owner's death. But, to show that the fate of Aristotle's writings did not entirely depend on the fortunes of the library buried in the vault at Scêpsis, we have abundant proof of some of them being familiar to the philosophic world during the interval in which his library itself was lost to view[6]; and it is probable that many of them, including those of more general interest, were at an early date transcribed at Athens and thence transmitted to the great library at Alexandria.

In the case of Theophrastus, we know for certain that lists of his works were drawn up, not only by Andronicus of Rhodes, but also by Hermippus of Smyrna, who lived till about the end of the third century B.C. and was a pupil of Callimachus, the chief librarian of the Alexandrian Museum[7]. Such a list is preserved by Diogenes Laertius[8], with the titles arranged in alphabetical order. The corresponding list of the writings of Aristotle is not in the order of the alphabet, but is arranged with a certain degree of method under 146 titles as follows. "First we have the dialogues and other exoteric works, then two or three early abstracts of Platonic lectures or writings, then we come to a part of the list in which logical works seem to predominate; ethical, political and

[1] Porphyry, *life of Plotinus*, c. 24, p. 117 Didot.

[2] Plut. *Sulla*, 26; cf. Grote's *Aristotle*, i pp. 50—54, and Shute's *History of the Aristotelian Writings*, p. 29—39.

[3] Rose, *Ar. Pseud.*, p. 8; *Frag.* (1886) p. 1.

[4] Strabo, p. 609, *συνέβη δὲ τοῖς ἐκ τῶν περιπάτων τοῖς μὲν πάλαι τοῖς μετὰ Θεόφραστον οὐκ ἔχουσιν ὅλως τὰ βιβλία πλὴν ὀλίγων, καὶ μάλιστα τῶν ἐξωτερικῶν.*

[5] *Aristotle*, p. 55.

[6] Zeller, *Phil. d. Griechen*, II ii p. 145—153[3].

[7] Schol. in Theophr. *Met.* *τοῦτο τὸ βιβλίον Ἀνδρόνικος μὲν καὶ Ἕρμιππος ἀγνοοῦσιν. οὐδὲ γὰρ μνείαν αὐτοῦ ὅλως πεποίηνται ἐν τῇ ἀναγραφῇ τῶν Θεοφράστου.* Heitz, *die Verlorenen Schriften des Ar.*, p. 47. Susemihl, *Ar. über die Dichtkunst*, 1865, p. 17; and *Gr. Litt. in der Alexandrinerzeit*, i 492, 494 note 11.

[8] v 21—27.

rhetorical works predominate towards the middle; then come physical and zoological works; last in order we have works designed in all probability for Aristotle's own use ('hypomnematic works'), letters and poems[1]". The arrangement seems hardly sufficiently precise to be that of Andronicus, who is said to have introduced the plan of grouping the writings according to their subject-matter[2]; and this is not the only reason for regarding it as independent of Andronicus[3]. It has in fact been conjecturally ascribed to Hermippus, and has been generally supposed to be founded on the catalogue of Aristotle's works in some great library like that of Alexandria. In a subsequent passage (v 34) Diogenes observes that the books enumerated were nearly 400 in number. He even adds that their genuineness was not contested by any one[4].

There is a second list, ascribed to Hesychius and containing only 127 titles, 27 of those in Diogenes being here omitted and 8 added in their place[5].

A third list, ascribed to 'Ptolemy the philosopher,' is found in an Arabic translation only. This includes 92 titles. It is certainly later than the time of Andronicus, as one of the titles relates to certain treatises found in the library of *Almikun* (*Ablikun* or *Atlikun*), the Arabic form of Apellicon.

In all three lists the Πολιτεῖαι are included. In I they appear as the 143rd item:—*πολιτεῖαι πόλεων δυοῖν δεούσαιν ρ̅ξ̅* (*sc.* 158), *<κοιναὶ> καὶ ἴδιαι, δημοκρατικαί, ὀλιγαρχικαί, ἀριστοκρατικαί, τυραννικαί.*

In II 135 the title is *πολιτείας πόλεων ἰδιωτικῶν καὶ δημοκρατικῶν καὶ ὀλιγαρχικῶν <καὶ> ἀριστοκρατικῶν καὶ τυραννικῶν ρ̅ν̅η̅* (158).

In III 81 the Arabic description is translated as follows: 'liber quem inscripsit de regimine civitatum et nominatur *bulitija*, et est liber in quo commemoravit regimen populorum et civitatum plurium e civitatibus Graecorum et aliorum earumque relationem (originem? cognationem?); numerus vero populorum et civitatum quarum meminit [in eo] CLXXI [civitates magnae][6]'.

In III the number of the *πολιτεῖαι* is given as 171; whereas I and II agree in making it 158. The ancient Latin Version of the life of Aristotle states the number as 250; while, among the early expositors of Aristotle, Elias twice gives the same number, and Ammonius has

[1] Mr W. L. Newman's ed. of Ar. *Pol.* vol. i p. vi.

[2] Porphyry, ref. on p. xvi, note 1.

[3] Zeller, II ii, 51 f.

[4] Grote's *Ar.* i 40.

[5] First published by Ménage on Diog. vol. ii 201. The same list was found by Rose in two MSS in the Ambrosian library at Milan (*A. P.* p. 709). All the lists are given by Rose in the Berlin *Ar.*, vol. v 1463—1473, and in the Teubner text of the *Fragmenta*, pp. 3—22.

[6] Rose, *Frag.* pp. 8, 16, 21[3].

250. The higher estimate is either a mere mistake, or has arisen from including among the πολιτεῖαι certain of the νόμιμα βαρβαρικά. The latter view is confirmed by the fact that one of our authorities for the larger number[1] mentions it in immediate connexion with the statement that Aristotle accompanied Alexander on his expedition to the East, even as far as 'the land of the Brahmins,' where (according to this imaginative commentator) he actually compiled 'the 255 πολιτεῖαι'; while the estimates of Elias are in both cases given in a similar connexion. We may therefore discard the larger number, and accept 158 as resting on better authority[2].

The total number of πολιτεῖαι included in modern collections of their fragments is 99. In 51 of these the name of Aristotle and the title of the πολιτεία are expressly mentioned, generally thus: Ἀριστοτέλης ἐν τῇ —ων πολιτείᾳ. In 16 others, Aristotle is cited, but the name of the state is not given, though it can be inferred from the contents of the passage. Lastly, out of the total number of 80 states mentioned in the *Politics*, there are 32 that are not named in the fragments already enumerated, but which may fairly be assumed to have been included in the original work. Thus we have a list of 51 + 16 + 32, or 99 states, more than half of which (51) are represented by fragments in which the title of the work, as well as the name of Aristotle, is mentioned, while in more than two-thirds (67 out of 99) the name of Aristotle occurs. The three classes are as follows:

I (51)			II (16)	III (32)	
Ἀθηναίων	Ἱμεραίων	Μηλιέων	Ἀντανδρίων	Ἀμφιπολιτῶν	Καρχηδονίων
Αἰγινητῶν	Κείων	Ναξίων	Ἀτραμυτηνῶν	Ἀντισσαίων	Καταναίων
Αἰτωλῶν	Κερκυραίων	Νεοπολιτῶν	Ἐπιδαυρίων	Ἀπολλωνιατῶν	Κλαζομενίων
Ἀκαρνάνων	Κιανῶν	Ὀπουντίων	Θηβαίων	Ἀπολλωνιατῶν	Κνιδίων
Ἀκραγαντίνων	Κολοφωνίων	Ὀρχομενίων	Ἰασέων	ἐν Πόντῳ	Κώων
Ἀμβρακιωτῶν	Κορινθίων	Παρίων	Κρητῶν	Ἀρυδηνῶν	Λαρισσαίων
Ἀργείων	Κυθνίων	Πελληνέων	Κροτωνιατῶν	Ἀφυταίων	Λεοντίνων
Ἀρκάδων	Κυμαίων	Σαμίων	Κυθηρίων	Βυζαντίων	Μαγνήτων
Ἀχαιῶν	Κυπρίων	Σαμοθρᾴκων	Μηλίων	Ἐπιδαμνίων	Μαντινείων
Βοττιαίων	Κυρηναίων	Σικυωνίων	Μιλησίων	Ἐρετριέων	Μολοσσῶν
Γελῴων	Λακεδαιμονίων	Σινωπέων	Ῥηγίνων	Ἐρυθραίων	Μυτιληναίων
Δελφῶν	Λευκαδίων	Συρακοσίων	Ῥοδίων	Ἑστιαιέων	Ῥοδίων
Δηλίων	Λοκρῶν	Ταραντίνων	Σολέων	Ζαγκλαίων	Φαρσαλίων
Ἠλείων	Λυκίων	Τεγεατῶν	Συβαριτῶν	Ἡραιέων	Χαλκιδέων
Ἠπειρωτῶν	Μασσαλιωτῶν	Τενεδίων	Τηνίων	Ἡρακλεωτῶν	Χίων
Θετταλῶν	Μεγαρέων	Τροιζηνίων	Χαλκηδονίων.	Θηραίων	Ὠρειτῶν.
Ἰθακησίων	Μεθωναίων	Φωκαιέων.		Ἰστριέων	

[1] *Vita Ar. vulg.*, Rose, *Frag.* p. 258³.

[2] A division of the πολιτεῖαι into genuine and spurious seems to be implied by Simplicius, *in Ar. Categ.* p. 27 *a* 43 Brandis, ἐν ταῖς γνησίαις αὐτοῦ πολιτείαις. But it has been proposed either

The πολιτεῖαι are said to have been arranged in the order of the alphabet[1]. Some have seen indications of this in the reading preserved in a single MS of Harpocration, s.v. θεσμοθέται :—'Αριστοτέλης ἐν τῇ ᾱ 'Αθηναίων πολιτείᾳ, and also in the phrase in Photius, s.v. σκυτάλη :—ὡς 'Αριστοτέλης ἐν τῇ 'Ιθακησίων πολιτείᾳ μβ̄. Here the πολιτεία of Ithaca appears to be described as 42nd in the series. If we test this by taking the 99 extant titles of πολιτεῖαι as the basis of our calculation, Ithaca, which is 37th in the list of 99, would have been 58th in the complete list of 158; if, again, we take the 67 titles in which Aristotle is named, Ithaca, which is 21st of the 67, would have been 50th in the complete list; if the 51 in which the name of the particular πολιτεία is specified, Ithaca, which is 17th of the 51, would have been 52nd, not 42nd. This calculation, of course, assumes that in the longer list, the names in alphabetical order are distributed in the same proportion as in the shorter lists. But it is highly probable that μβ̄ is a corruption of either μέμνηται or (as proposed by Bergk) μαρτυρεῖ. If so, we cannot rely on this phrase as proof of an alphabetical order. Besides, if the order was alphabetical, it was unnecessary to specify the number of any particular treatise. Such an arrangement, however, although not attested with any certainty, is natural in itself, and the constitution of Athens would in any case have occupied the first place.

§ 3. *On the evidence of ancient authorities as to the authorship of the* Πολιτεῖαι.

We may now proceed to review in chronological order the successive quotations from the Πολιτεῖαι which are preserved in ancient authorities.

Firstly, there is reason to believe that the historian PHILOCHORUS, writing before 306 B.C., or less than 20 years after the composition of the 'Αθηναίων πολιτεία, quoted that work as Aristotle's. The grounds which have been suggested for this belief are as follows :—

(1) The Scholium on Arist. *Vesp.* 1223 includes a quotation from 'Αθ. πολ. 13, ll. 16—20; the latter part of that Scholium coincides with one on *Lys.* 58 which is proved by Strabo, p. 392 c, to come from Philochorus. Hence it is possible that the whole of the Schol. on *Vesp.* 1223 really comes from Philochorus, and that Philochorus is our real authority for the citation from the 'Αθ. πολ. (2) In the term ἀποψηφισθῆναι τὸ ἄχθος (*frag.* 57), Philochorus appears to be correcting or explaining the phrase τὸ ἄχθος ἀποσείσασθαι,—probably a reminiscence of ἀποσεισάμενοι τὸ βάρος in 'Αθ. πολ. 6 § 1. (3) In Plutarch's *Life of Themistocles*, 10, Aristotle is cited as

to alter πολιτείαις into ἐπιστολαῖς (Ideler, in Ar. *Meteor.* I xii n. 40), or (with greater probability) to regard γνησίαις as a corruption of the number ρνη̄ (158); Heitz, *Frag. Ar.* p. 223 *a*.

[1] κατὰ στοιχεῖα, Elias, ap. Rose, *Frag.* p. 258[3], l. 29.

authority for a statement respecting the action of the Areopagus immediately before the battle of Salamis ('Αθ. πολ. 23 § 1). Cleidemus, the author of an 'Ατθίς, is next quoted as asserting that this action was due to the wiles of Themistocles. Then follows the story of the dog of Xanthippus which, in Aelian, *de Natura Animalium*, xii 35, is attributed to 'Aristotle and *Philochorus*.' It has been plausibly suggested that Aelian had read an extract, ultimately derived from Philochorus, on the events immediately preceding the battle of Salamis, in which the name of Aristotle may have occurred in connexion with the account of the action of the Areopagus, and in which the story of the dog of Xanthippus was also related. This may have lead Aelian to make the mistake of quoting Aristotle, as well as Philochorus, as authorities for the story about the dog. If, as is not improbable, the whole of the narrative in Plutarch comes from Philochorus, then Philochorus, and not Plutarch, is our authority for attributing to Aristotle the quotations from the 'Αθ. πολ. respecting the action of the Areopagus. This implies that 'a careful historical student and critic, who lived and wrote at Athens in the generation immediately following Aristotle's,' accepted the 'Αθηναίων πολιτεία as the work of Aristotle himself[1].

An early notice of the Πολιτεῖαι may also be traced in the attack made by TIMAEUS on Aristotle's account of the origin of the Greek colony of Locri Epizephyrii. Timaeus was born about 352 B.C. (or 30 years before the death of Aristotle), was banished from Tauromenium in 310, and from about that time resided in Athens for more than 50 years, dying about 256 B.C. The evidence for this attack on the part of Timaeus is to be found in Polybius, who rejects the view of Timaeus, and emphatically supports the account given by Aristotle[2]. From a subsequent passage it appears that the attack of Timaeus was directed against Theophrastus as well. We are not told in which of Aristotle's works the description of the origin of Locri was to be found, but it is reasonable to suppose that it was the Πολιτεῖαι. The only other possible work would have been the 'Αλέξανδρος περὶ ἀποικιῶν, which is now represented by its title only. Now Timaeus was in Athens for 23 out of the 35 years during which Theophrastus presided over the Lyceum as the successor of Aristotle. He had thus exceptional opportunities for becoming acquainted with Aristotle's writings, and with the traditional knowledge of them preserved by the Peripatetic School; and he may fairly be quoted to prove that within 66 years of the death of Aristotle, one of the Πολιτεῖαι was attributed to that author.

The Πολιτεῖαι appear to have been also quoted by PHILOSTEPHANUS of Cyrene, the author of works entitled περὶ εὑρημάτων and περὶ νήσων, who lived under Ptolemy Philopator (B.C. 222—206). 'Aristotle' and Philostephanus are quoted by Varro (apud Servium ad Verg. *Georg.* i 19) and by Pliny (*N. H.* vii 57); and it has been conjectured

[1] Abridged from Prof. J. H. Wright's article in the *American Journ. of Philology*, xii 3, 310—318.

[2] Polyb. *Excerpta libri* xii 5—8, and 11; Rose, *Frag.* 547[3]; cf. Heitz, *Verl. Schr.* p. 243, and Shute, *l. c.*, p. 39.

that Varro and Pliny took their quotations of Aristotle at second-hand from Philostephanus[1].

It was probably in the middle of the second century B.C. that excerpts from the Πολιτεῖαι were made by HERACLEIDES LEMBOS, who appears to have followed his original with an almost slavish fidelity. We have only fragments of these excerpts under the title ἐκ τῶν Ἡρακλείδου περὶ πολιτειῶν[2].

CICERO refers as follows to the Πολιτεῖαι and νόμιμα βαρβαρικά of Aristotle, as well as to the work of Theophrastus περὶ νόμων:—*omnium fere civitatum non Graeciae solum sed etiam barbariae ab Aristotele mores instituta disciplinas; a Theophrasto leges etiam cognovimus* (*de Fin.* v 4 § 11); but there is no proof of any direct acquaintance with the text of the Πολιτεῖαι[3]. In the *de Officiis*, ii 18, he quotes, as from Theophrastus, the account of the liberality of Cimon which we find in c. 27 of the Ἀθηναίων πολιτεία. In the *de Senectute* § 72 he tells an anecdote about Solon and Peisistratus without showing any knowledge of c. 14 of that treatise. Similarly, in *de Officiis*, i 75, he writes of Solon and Themistocles with reference to the Areopagus without betraying any close acquaintance with chapters 23 and 25. Whatever knowledge he possessed as to the contents of those chapters was probably obtained second-hand from his authority, Panaetius, who, as we know from Cicero himself (*de Fin.* iv 28 § 79), constantly quoted from Plato, Aristotle, Xenocrates, Theophrastus and Dicaearchus. About Dicaearchus in particular Cicero writes to Atticus in glowing terms:—in his Tusculan villa he has been reading with admiration that author's account of the constitution of Pellene, while he fancies that his library at Rome contains a copy of the Constitutions of Corinth and of Athens[4]. These

[1] Rose, *A. P.*, pp. 410, 534; Susemihl, *Gr. Litt. in der Alexandrinerzeit*, i 476.

[2] Heracleides Lembos, probably born at Kallatis in Pontus, was the author of an extensive compilation called Ἱστορίαι. He flourished under Ptolemy VI, Philometor (181—146). Cf. Susemihl, *u. s.*, i 503—5. (Rühl even supposes that he was the editor of the Ἀθ. πολ. in its present form.)

The author of the excerpts is, however, regarded by Rose (in his *A. P.*, p. 532) as far later in date, and as having borrowed his excerpts from Didymus (who was born B.C. 63). But the part played by Didymus in transmitting the knowledge of the Πολιτεῖαι to a later time has been much exaggerated, and the form in which the excerpts from Heracleides have reached us is hardly worthy of the industrious and intelligent critic from whom they are supposed to have been derived.—See also Prof. Wright in *Harvard Studies*, iii 15, and Holzinger in *Philologus*, vol. 50, p. 436. *Infra*, p. 250.

[3] See also Shute, *l. c.*, p. 72.

[4] *Ad Att.* ii 2, 'Πελληναίων in manibus tenebam et hercule magnum acervum Dicaearchi mihi ante pedes exstruxeram. O magnum hominem! et unde multo plura didiceris quam de Procilio. Κορινθίων et Ἀθηναίων puto me Romae habere. Mihi crede, leges;...mirabilis vir est.' Heitz, *Verl. Schr.*, p. 244, considers that these may have formed part of the βίος Ἑλλάδος of Dicaearchus. Bergk, *Rhein. Mus.* 1881, p. 113 *n.* 2, suggests that the reference is to the Πολιτεῖαι of Aristotle. He would alter *Dicaearchi* into *Dicaearchiae* (*i.e.* 'at Puteoli'); but his suggestion (with the textual alteration which it involves) seems very improbable.

Constitutions may well have been written in imitation of the earlier work ascribed to Aristotle; and the imitation may have been sufficiently close to lead to the contents of the Πολιτεῖαι of Aristotle becoming known to later writers through the medium of Dicaearchus[1].

It has been conjectured that many of the quotations from the Πολιτεῖαι in later authors were taken second-hand from the works of Alexandrian scholars such as Didymus Chalcenterus, and his successor, Pamphilus[2]. Didymus was born in 63 B.C. and compiled a Lexicon of Tragic and Comic Diction, while among the lexicographical works of Pamphilus, who flourished in 20 B.C., was one entitled Ἀττικαὶ λέξεις. The scholiast on Aristophanes, *Aves* 471, quotes Aristotle ἐν τῇ Σαμίων πολιτείᾳ, as well as the comic poet, Plato; and such a scholium may readily have been derived from Didymus[3]; but the indebtedness of later writers to this able and industrious compiler has been greatly overrated; and, now that we know of the actual existence of copies of the Ἀθηναίων πολιτεία at a time when it was supposed to have been hopelessly lost, there is less reason for attributing to the interposition of Didymus a knowledge of the Πολιτεῖαι which may easily have been derived from the work itself. It has further been supposed that some of the accounts of remarkable phenomena found in later collections, such as the Θαυμάσια Ἀκούσματα of various writers, may have been originally borrowed from the Πολιτεῖαι. Thus, Antigonus of Carystus, who probably lived in the time of Ptolemy Philadelphus, in his Ἱστοριῶν Παραδόξων Συναγωγή (144), quotes from Callimachus a description by Aristotle of the two fountains of the Sun in the temple of Zeus Ammon. This description may have been derived from the Πολιτεία of Cyrene[4].

In the age of Augustus, the Πολιτεῖαι are not quoted by DIONYSIUS of Halicarnassus, who, however, refers to the Τυρρηνῶν Νόμιμα, which formed part of the Νόμιμα Βαρβαρικὰ ascribed to Aristotle[5].

STRABO (who belongs to the same age) refers in general terms to Aristotle in connexion with Elis (Rose, *Frag.* 493^3), Argos (482), Epidaurus (491), Tenedos (594), and Chalcis (601, 603). In a single passage (on p. 321—2), after stating that the migrations of the Leleges are attested by αἱ Ἀριστοτέλους πολιτεῖαι, he appeals to no less than four of them as his authorities, *viz.* those of the Acarnanians, Opuntians, Megarians and Leucadians. When we remember that the story of the recovery of the lost library of Aristotle is told by Strabo (doubtless on

[1] Heitz, *Verl. Schr.*, p. 244.
[2] Rose, *A. P.*, p. 400; Heitz, *Verl. Schr.* p. 244, and *Ar. Frag.* p. 219.
[3] Rose, *A. P.*, p. 521.
[4] Rose, *Frag.* 531^3; *A. P.* p. 487; Heitz, *Verl. Schr.* p. 245.
[5] Rose, *Frag.* 609^3.

the authority of his preceptor Tyrannion), we are not surprised at finding in his pages not a few traces of a first-hand acquaintance with the Πολιτεῖαι. Nevertheless, the fact that only a comparatively small number of the πολιτεῖαι are noticed in Strabo has led to the supposition that he had no direct knowledge of that work[1].

PLINY the elder (23—79 A.D.) names Aristotle as his authority mainly on the geography of several of the Greek islands (Tenos, Delos, Melos and Samos), and also in connexion with Argos, Thebes and Chalcis. One of his references may be traced to the Νόμιμα Βαρβαρικά. He also states that, according to Aristotle, the art of painting was introduced into Greece by *Euchir*, *Daedali cognatus* (Rose, *Frag.* 382[3]); but there is no sufficient warrant for referring this to a lost passage of the Ἀθηναίων πολιτεία. Pliny's references to Aristotle may safely be regarded as taken at second hand[2]. This has also been assumed, but with perhaps less justice, in the case of Plutarch (c. 46—120 A.D.).

PLUTARCH repeatedly mentions Aristotle as his authority:—five times in the life of *Lycurgus*[3]; once in that of *Cleomenes*[4]; and twice in that of *Pericles*[5], in passages that may perhaps be traced to the Σαμίων πολιτεία. In five instances Aristotle is named in connexion with Naxos, Tegea (twice), Troezen and Ithaca[6]; and in two others we may trace the reference to the Νόμιμα Βαρβαρικά[7]. The Ἀθηναίων πολιτεία may fairly be regarded as the source of Plutarch's references to Aristotle in the lives of *Theseus*[8], *Solon*[9], *Themistocles*[10], *Cimon*[11], *Pericles*[12] and *Nicias*[13]; as also of certain passages in which Aristotle is not actually named[14]. At this point it may be interesting to notice two good examples of tacit quotation from the Ἀθηναίων πολιτεία in the pages of Plutarch. In c. 14 § 4 of the πολιτεία we read that, with the aid of Φύη, Megacles restored the exiled Peisistratus ἀρχαϊκῶς (or ἀρχαίως) καὶ λίαν ἁπλῶς: in Plutarch's *Solon* (3 § 5) we find the phrase ἁπλοῦς...λίαν καὶ ἀρχαῖος. Again, in c. 5 § 2 of the πολιτεία, we are told of Solon, εἵλοντο κοινῇ διαλλακτὴν καὶ ἄρχοντα Σόλωνα: in the *Amatorius* of Plutarch (18 § 14), a passage that has not hitherto been noticed in this connexion, we find five consecutive words applied to Solon, which are identical with those

[1] Heitz, *Verl. Schr.* p. 244.

[2] *e.g.* through Philostephanus of Cyrene.

[3] cc. 1, 5, 6, 28, 31; Rose, *Frag*[3]. 533—538.

[4] c. 9; *Frag*[3]. 539.

[5] cc. 26, 28; *Frag*[3]. 577—8.

[6] *Frag*[3]. 559, 592, 507, 597.

[7] *Camill.* 22, and *De Cohibenda Ira* 11; *Frag*[3]. 610, 608.

[8] c. 25 (*Frag.* 384).

[9] c. 25 (*Frag.* 390 = Ἀθ. πολ. c. 7 § 1, κύρβεις).

[10] c. 10 (*Frag.* 398).

[11] c. 10 (*Frag.* 402).

[12] c. 9, 10 (*Frag.* 403, 405).

[13] c. 2 (*Frag.* 407).

[14] *Solon*, c. 20 (*Frag.* 391), c. 25 (*Frag.* 416).

just quoted,—τοῦτον εἵλοντο κοινῇ διαλλακτὴν καὶ ἄρχοντα καὶ νομοθέτην.

In view of such instances it seems difficult to maintain the theory that Plutarch had only a second-hand knowledge of the Ἀθηναίων πολιτεία[1]. He has even been charged with the incredible carelessness of keeping words such as νῦν unchanged in copying from the intermediate authorities which he is supposed to have followed. Thus, in *Solon*, c. 25, his statement that fragments of the wooden tablets on which the laws of Solon were inscribed were still to be seen in his own day (ἔτι καθ' ἡμᾶς) in the Athenian πρυτανεῖον, was regarded by Rose as a careless transcript from some such phrase in Polemon as διασώζονται δ' ἐν τῷ Πρυτανείῳ[2]. Similarly, in *Lycurgus*, c. 28, ἔτι καὶ νῦν was held to refer to the age of Plutarch's authority Ephorus[3]. In the former case, at any rate, the statement of Plutarch is corroborated by the evidence of Pausanias (i 18 § 3) who, even at a later date, observes that in the πρυτανεῖον the laws of Solon εἰσὶ γεγραμμένοι. Other quotations in Plutarch are ascribed by Rose to the *Eclogae* and *Collectanea* of previous writers, such as Didymus; but this ascription is not supported by the context of the quotations themselves. Plutarch places the Πολιτεῖαι of Aristotle in the same category as the works of Herodotus, Xenophon, Eudoxus and Aristoxenus, implying that all these writers dealt with important and interesting events in a style that was at once vigorous and graceful[4]. Such is not the language of one whose knowledge of

[1] Prof. J. H. Wright, *The Date of Cylon*, p. 25, observes: 'Most of Plutarch's statements on the affair of Cylon are traceable to Aristotle's *Respub. Ath.* A comparison of Plutarch's account of pre-Solonian affairs with that of Aristotle shows, however, first, that this dependance is not immediate, and, secondly, that there is much admixture of foreign matter'...In the note he refers to 38 passages in Plutarch's *Solon* which bear resemblance to passages in Aristot. *Respub. Ath.*, and are evidently traceable to the latter work. Only once, however, is Aristotle here named (*Sol.* 25 *ad init.*) 'A minute comparison of the wording of these parallel passages, and a consideration of the order in which they occur in the two writers, as also of extraneous matter inserted and of important and illuminating facts omitted, show that Plutarch was certainly not intimately acquainted with the *Respub. Ath.* The resemblances, the dissimilarities, and the discrepancies alike are intelligible only on the supposition that Plutarch was transcribing from some work in which an abridgment of these parts of the *Respub. Ath.* was embodied. In transcribing from this abridgment he interpolates foreign matter, which is inconsistent with the unabridged Aristotle. The abridgment omitted the main part of cc. 2—4, also c. 13 [§§ 2, 3], as well as many minor statements. The poetical quotations of Plutarch are from a different collection; such as coincide are in a different order...Plutarch's otherwise unaccountable omission in his *Them.* of the characteristic anecdote of Themistocles, Ephialtes, and the Areopagus (*Respub. Ath.* c. 25) may be explained on the hypothesis that the copy of Aristotle's work used by Plutarch did not contain this story. In *Pericles*, Aristotle is cited, but immediately there follow statements as to Pericles which directly contradict Aristotle (cf. Ad. Bauer, *Forschungen*, p. 77, who believes, however, in a first-hand use of *Respub. Ath.* by Plutarch).'

[2] Preller on Polemon, p. 87.

[3] Rose, *A. P.*, pp. 413, 491.

[4] *Non posse suaviter vivi sec. Epicurum*, c. 10, ὅταν δὲ μηδὲν ἔχουσα λυπηρὸν ἡ

the Πολιτεῖαι was mainly or solely derived from second-hand sources of information.

ZENOBIUS, who flourished in the time of Hadrian (117—138 A.D.), refers to c. 28 of the Ἀθηναίων πολιτεία, and mentions the πολιτεῖαι of Corcyra, Samos, Delphi and Methone (*Frag.*[3] 513, 576, 487, 552). He also names Aristotle as his authority for facts relating to Cythnus and Thebes (*Frag.*[3] 523, 502).

AULUS GELLIUS (115—180 A.D.) names Aristotle in connexion with Solon's law against neutrality. The law is found in Ἀθ. πολ. c. 8 § 5.

ARISTIDES, one of the most celebrated rhetoricians of the 2nd century (117 or 129—180 A.D.) never mentions the Ἀθηναίων πολιτεία, but the only poems of Solon which he quotes are extracted from those preserved in that treatise; he also paraphrases other passages from those poems and from the text of Aristotle[1].

DIOGENES LAERTIUS (towards the close of the 2nd century A.D.) twice appeals to Aristotle for facts connected with Corinth (*Frag.*[3] 516, 517). In the first of these passages he couples him with Ephorus. In a third passage he refers to Aristotle ἐν τῇ Δηλίων πολιτείᾳ (*Frag.*[3] 489); but, as the vague plural φασὶν occurs in the previous context, there is no certain proof of first-hand acquaintance with the work in question. In this author, however, we have several parallels to the account of Solon given in the Ἀθηναίων πολιτεία[2].

POLLUX of Naucratis (*fl.* 180—238 A.D.), who dedicated his Ὀνομαστικόν to Commodus (Emp. 180—192), quotes largely from the Πολιτεῖαι, especially from that of Athens. The latter is his main authority on all points of Athenian law and antiquities[3]. Many consecutive lines are either transcribed or paraphrased from its pages, *e.g.* the epigram about Diphilus and a large part of its context in c. 7 § 4. But his debt to the Ἀθηναίων πολιτεία, though vast, is invariably unacknowledged, while the only passage in which he mentions the name of Aristotle in connexion with a term of Attic law, is not

βλαβερὸν ἱστορία καὶ διήγησις, ἐπὶ πράξεσι καλαῖς καὶ μεγάλαις προσλάβῃ λογον ἔχοντα δύναμιν καὶ χάριν, ὡς τὸν Ἡροδότου τὰ Ἑλληνικά, καὶ Περσικὰ τοῦ Ξενοφῶντος, ὅσα δὲ Ὅμηρος ἐθέσπισε θέσκελα εἰδώς, ἢ τὰς περιόδους Εὔδοξος, ἢ κτίσεις καὶ πολιτείας Ἀριστοτέλης, ἢ βίους ἀνδρῶν Ἀριστόξενος ἔγραψεν, οὐ μόνον μέγα καὶ πολὺ τὸ εὐφραῖνον, ἀλλὰ καὶ καθαρὸν καὶ ἀμεταμελητόν ἐστιν.

[1] Cf. Aristides ii 360, 361 Dind., with Ἀθ. πολ. 5 § 2, 11 § 2, 12 § 5; also p. 535—538 with Ἀθ. πολ. c. 12; and lastly i p. 765, (Σόλωνα) φασι τῆς πολιτείας καταλυθείσης λαβόντα ἀσπίδα καὶ δόρυ καθῆσθαι πρὸ τῆς οἰκίας, βοηθεῖν μὲν οὐκ ἔχοντα, οἶμαι, ἐνδεικνύμενον δὲ ὡς ἔχει γνώμης, with Ἀθ. πολ. c. 14 § 2.

[2] Diog. Laert. i §§ 45, 50, 58.

[3] Even before the discovery of the Ἀθ. πολ. this fact had been partially ascertained by comparing the language of Pollux with that quoted from the Ἀθ. πολ. in the lexicographers. Cf. Stojentin, *De Iulii Pollucis in publicis Atheniensium antiquitatibus enarrandis auctoritate*, (Breslau) 1875; and Stoewer, *in quibus nitantur auctoribus Iulii Pollucis rerum iudicialium enarrationes*, (Münster) 1888.

found in that treatise, so far as it has been preserved[1]. Several of the other πολιτεῖαι are, however, expressly mentioned, viz. that of Acragas (twice in *Frag.*[3] 476), Himera (twice in 510), Tarentum (590), Orchomenus (566), and Sicyon (580). In other passages, where Aristotle is named, the information may have been ultimately derived from the Constitutions of Cyprus (527), Rhegium (568), Syracuse (585, 589), Cyrene (529) and Argos (481), or from the Τυρρήνων νόμιμα (608).

ATHENAEUS, who, like Pollux, was a native of Naucratis (*fl. c.* 200 A.D.) expressly mentions the πολιτεῖαι of Aegina (*Frag.*[3] 472), Delos (490), Naxos (558), Troezen (596), Thessaly (499), Methone (551), Colophon (515), Massalia (549), Croton (583), Sybaris (584) and Syracuse (588). The name of Aristotle is also mentioned in connexion with Miletus (557); and that of Timaeus with reference to Aristotle's account of Locri (547), which has already been noticed[2]. Aristotle ἐν Τυρρήνων νομίμοις is also quoted (607). It has been conjectured that these quotations may have been taken second-hand from lexicographical works, such as the lexicon to the Comic poets compiled by Pamphilus from that of his predecessor Didymus. This is supported by the fact that on p. 499 Athenaeus twice quotes the comic poet Diphilus; and, between the two quotations, inserts a reference to Aristotle ἐν τῇ Θετταλῶν πολιτείᾳ to prove that the Thessalians used a feminine form ἡ λάγυνος[3]. But a native of a country, in which, as we now know, copies of the Ἀθηναίων πολιτεία were actually in existence at the time, may well have derived much of his information from the original work. Apart from the British Museum papyrus and the fragments of the Berlin papyrus, both of which came from Egypt, we know of a third copy, which is mentioned in the catalogue of an Egyptian library of the third century A.D.[4].

HARPOCRATION of Alexandria, the lexicographer of the Attic Orators, who is doubtfully ascribed either to the second, or (less probably) to the fourth century of our era, expressly quotes Ἀριστοτέλης ἐν Ἀθηναίων πολιτείᾳ in no less than 50 places. A lost passage in the same treatise is less precisely cited with the phrase ὡς Ἀριστοτέλης φησί (381). There are nine other πολιτεῖαι which he mentions by name, those of Arcadia, Elis, Thessaly, Cythnus, Cyprus, Sparta, Massalia, Opus and Pellene. The quotations from the Ἀθηναίων πολιτεία are so numerous and so precise, that it may fairly be assumed that they were taken at first-hand from the treatise itself.

CLEMENT of Alexandria (*ob.* 220 A.D.) quotes the πολιτεῖαι of

[1] Pollux viii 62, παράβολον (*Frag.*[3] 456); cf. iii 17, τριτοπάτωρ (*Frag.*[3] 415).
[2] p. xx.
[3] Rose, *A. P.*, p. 471, *Frag.* 499[3].
[4] Zündel in *Rhein. Mus.* 1866, p. 432.

Phocaea and Locri, and refers in more general terms to that of Sparta (*Frag.* 599, 548, 535); while AELIAN (*fl.* 250 A.D.) tells the story of the usurpation of Peisistratus in language almost identical with that of c. 14 of the Ἀθηναίων πολιτεία.

HESYCHIUS of Alexandria, who belongs to the end of the fourth century, or (more probably) to the fifth, is a compiler from earlier authorities, the best of whom is Diogenianus of Heraclea (of the time of Hadrian). The lexicon of Hesychius expressly quotes the Constitution of the Opuntians (*Frag.*[3] 563), and names Aristotle as the authority for statements respecting Cyrene (528), Corcyra (513) and Sparta (541). The second of these items may, however, be traced back to Zenobius. Not a few articles are ultimately founded on the Ἀθηναίων πολιτεία, though neither the work is named, nor its author. Such are the articles on ἀδύνατοι (Ἀθ. πολ. 49 § 4), ἀπὸ συμβόλων δικάζειν (59 § 6), Βουζύγης (*Frag.* 386), βουλεύσεως ἔγκλημα (Ἀθ. πολ. 57 § 3), δήμαρχοι (21 § 5), διαμεμετρημένην ἡμέραν (col. 35, 3), ἱππάς (7 § 4), and ἵππου τροχός (49 § 1). To the same source may be traced the articles on Διονύσου γάμος and Ἐπιλύκειον (3 § 5), and also on ἕδραι βουλῆς (30 § 4), and χαλκοῦν πινάκιον (63 § 4).

PHOTIUS, the patriarch of Constantinople (815—891 A.D.), states that excerpts from the πολιτεῖαι of Aristotle, viz. from those of Thessaly, Achaia, Paros, Lycia and Ceos, were included in the twelfth book of the historical selections of Sopater (sixth cent.)[1]. In his *Lexicon*, the Ἀθηναίων πολιτεία is mentioned in the articles on ναυκραρία (Ἀθ. πολ. 8 § 3), and ὑπὲρ τὰ Καλλικράτους (28 § 3): the latter may, however, be traced back to Zenobius. The πολιτεῖαι of Sparta, Samos and Ithaca are expressly cited (*Frag.*[3] 586, 575, 509); and Aristotle is named in several articles[2], including one on πελάται (Ἀθ. πολ. 2 § 2). During the embassy 'to the Assyrians' the patriarch perused and epitomised no less than 280 volumes, many of which are now lost; but there is nothing to prove that the Ἀθηναίων πολιτεία was included among them.

TZETZES of Constantinople (born c. 1120 A.D.) refers to the πολιτεῖαι of Orchomenus (*Frag.*[3] 505) and Ithaca (504 and 508). Of the last two references the former is also found in the *Etymologicum Magnum;* so that possibly all three may have been borrowed from earlier sources. The lexicon last named, *s.v.* ἱεροποιοί, expressly quotes Aristotle ἐν τῇ Ἀθηναίων πολιτείᾳ (c. 54 § 6), and has a short article as δατητής (*Frag.* 422) which may be traced to Harpocration (c. 56 § 6). It also names Aristotle in connexion with Cumae (*Frag.* 525), and we know that this article comes ultimately from the Πολιτεῖαι.

[1] Phot. *Bibl. Cod.* 161, p. 104 *b* 38, quoted by Rose, *A. P.* p. 401, *Frag.*[3] p. 258.
[2] *Frag.*[3] 496, 541, 593, 554.

Eustathius of Constantinople, archbishop of Thessalonica (who died c. 1198) refers to the πολιτεῖαι of Sparta (545) and Ithaca (506), and names Aristotle in a passage which comes from the πολιτεία of Thessaly (437). But there is no proof of direct acquaintance with any of the πολιτεῖαι. His only notice of the Ἀθηναίων πολιτεία (c. 44 § 1) is borrowed from Telephus of Pergamos who lived under Hadrian and (among other works) wrote on the Laws and Customs, and on the Lawcourts of Athens.

Thus far we have surveyed in chronological order the writers who, either at first or second hand, quote from the Πολιτεῖαι of Aristotle. We have still to notice a few anonymous citations.

(1) The unknown author of the ὑπόθεσις to the *Areopagiticus* of Isocrates, a Christian writer of perhaps the sixth century, is the only person who quotes the anecdote in c. 25 respecting the part ascribed to Themistocles in the overthrow of the Areopagus[1].

(2) The *Scholia* to Aristophanes refer to the Ἀθ. πολ. in no less than thirteen places[2]. They also expressly quote the πολιτεῖαι of Sparta and Samos, and name Aristotle in connexion with Orchomenos, Corcyra and Cyrene. Many of the Scholia on Aristophanes are derived from Aristophanes of Byzantium and his pupils Callistratus, Aristarchus and Didymus; as well as from the Pergamene scholars, Herodicus and Asclepiades. The earlier Scholia were drawn up in the 3rd century A.D.; while the later Scholia go down as far as the age of Thomas Magister and Triclinius (end of 13th cent.).

The *Scholia* on Sophocles cite Aristotle for a fact mentioned in Ἀθ. πολ. 60 § 2; those on Euripides quote from the πολιτεῖαι of Sparta (*Frag.* 544) and Thessaly (498), and name Aristotle in connexion with terms relating to the πολιτεία of Cumae (524—5). Those on Homer give us evidence as to the πολιτεῖαι of Iasos and Samos (503 and 571); those on Pindar cite the πολιτεῖαι of Sparta, Syracuse and Gela (*Frag.* 532, 587, 486), and name Aristotle in connexion with Aegina, Rhodes, Crete, Acarnania, Opus and Locri. Those on Plato quote Aristotle for facts which may be traced to the πολιτεῖαι of Athens (385) and Thessaly (498). Those on Apollonius Rhodius refer to the πολιτεῖαι of Samos and Samothrace, Sinope and Tegea, Corcyra and Kios in Mysia; those of Theocritus refer to Croton, Ceos and Crete[3]. The *Scholia* on

[1] Rose, *A. P.*, p. 423, no. 359; *Frag.* 404[3].

[2] Ἀθ. πολ. 7 § 1 (**Av.* 1354); 15 § 3 (**Ach.* 234); 19 § 3 (**Lys.* 665), § 4 (*Lys.* 1153), § 6 (*Vesp.* 502); 21 § 5 (*Nub.* 37); c. 28 § 3? (*Vesp.* 684); 34 § 1 (*Ran.* 1532), § 3 (*Vesp.* 157); 34 ult. (*Vesp.* 157); 54 § 2 (*Vesp.* 691); col. 32, 8—15 (**Plut.* 278); col. 36, 3—9 (*Eq.* 1150). In four of these places (marked with an asterisk) the title is given in full: Ἀρ. ἐν Ἀθ. πολ.; in two (*Vesp.* 157, 684) the form is Ἀρ. ἐν πολιτείαις.

[3] In the Schol. on Theocr. iv 7 we are told that the Olympic crown ἐκ τῆς καλλιστοῦς ἢ καλλιστεφάνου ἐλαίας γενόμενος δίδοται, ἥτις ἀπέχει σταδίων ὀκτὼ ὥς φασιν (sic) Ἀριστότελης. This is less

Aeschines contain no express mention of Aristotle, but they include several items of information ultimately derived from the Ἀθηναίων πολιτεία[1].

It will be observed that the references to the Πολιτεῖαι, which have now been enumerated, extend over a period of no less than fifteen centuries, and attest different degrees of acquaintance with the work in many parts of the ancient world, chiefly in great centres of learning, such as Alexandria and Constantinople. In the case of the Ἀθηναίων πολιτεία, the exact degree to which the text of the treatise was known to those who refer to it, may in general be traced in the *Testimonia* which are printed below the critical notes in the present edition. All the external evidence is in favour of ascribing the Πολιτεῖαι to Aristotle.

§ 4. *The later literature of the* Πολιτεῖαι.

After the revival of learning in Italy it was Francesco Patrizzi who, in the course of a calumnious attack on the personal character and philosophical authority of Aristotle, unconsciously did some little service to the cause which he impugned by investigating the earlier sources of information as to the lost works of Aristotle. In his *Discussiones Peripateticae*, published in 1571 at Venice, and reprinted ten years later at Basel, he made the first attempt to collect their fragmentary remains[2]. Patrizzi's collection was included in Casaubon's Aristotle (1590), and in 1593 a more comprehensive edition was promised by Casaubon himself[3]. The lost πολιτεῖαι are also mentioned by the learned Selden[4], but meanwhile Casaubon's promise remained unfulfilled. The importance of the fragments was noticed by Niebuhr[5] and others.

It was not until 1827 that C. F. Neumann, then living at Munich, published his *Aristotelis Rerumpublicarum Reliquiae*, including fragments from 50 of the πολιτεῖαι, the number traced to the Ἀθηναίων πολιτεία being 59 in all. In 1843 a similar collection was published by H. A. Van Dyck at Utrecht. These were superseded by Carl Müller's edition in the *Fragmenta Historicorum Graecorum*, Paris (Didot), 1848, in which the editor says of Neumann's work: *qui quidem libellus nullius nobis usus esse potuit: tam supina est auctoris negligentia.* The total number of πολιτεῖαι in this new collection is 95, and the fragments of the Ἀθηναίων πολιτεία have now risen in number to 74.

This collection served as the foundation for a still more extensive

likely to have been derived from the θαυμάσια ἀκούσματα than from the πολιτεία of Elis.

[1] Ἀθ. πολ. 28 § 3, 57 § 3, 59 §§ 1, 2.

[2] Hallam, *Lit. of Europe*, ii 6, ed. 1854; Heitz, *Verl. Schr.*, p. 1.

[3] Note on Diog. Laert. p. 76, ed. 1615.

[4] *De jure naturali &c.*, *Opera* 1 i 74—5.

[5] *Hist. Rom.* i 20, p. 12 of 3rd Eng. ed.

work by Valentine Rose. In his *Aristoteles Pseudepigraphus* (1863), we have 213 fragments, 89 of which are assigned to the Ἀθ. πολ. Rose's second edition of these fragments was included in Vol. v of the Berlin edition of Aristotle (1870), with three new fragments (445, 470, 511) from the πολιτεῖαι of Delphi, Corcyra and Methone published by a French scholar from a MS of Zenobius discovered on Mount Athos[1]. Lastly, in 1886 Rose's third edition was published by Teubner; the number of fragments is now 223, and of these 91 are traced to the Ἀθ. πολ., the two new fragments being no. 413 and 429 (corresponding to c. 3 § 5 and 52 § 1).

Meanwhile, in 1869, the fragments had been edited by Emil Heitz, the able author of *Die Verlorenen Schriften des Aristoteles* (1865). This edition was practically simultaneous with the second edition by Rose which, although printed in 1867, was not published until 1870.

In the case of the more important πολιτεῖαι and especially in that of Athens, the substance of these fragments has been not unfrequently set forth by modern scholars in various degrees of fulness. Thus Carl Müller (FHG ii 104) supplies an epitome of the Fragments on Athens; and Rose, a brief digest in the form of a table of contents[2]. But the most successful endeavour to give life to these fragmentary remains is to be found in the Appendix to the important work of Oncken on the political teaching of Aristotle[3]. The fragments are there discussed in their historical bearing, and the scattered facts contained in them presented in a consecutive order and in an interesting form. The introduction to the analysis of the fragments closes with some valuable criticisms to the following effect:—

> The method of dealing with the history of Athens which was pursued by Aristotle and his pupils must be regarded as marking the beginning of a new epoch. Without in any way undervaluing the influence of the contemporary school of Isocrates, as represented by Ephorus, Theopompus and Androtion, we may say without exaggeration that the picture, not only of the political life of Athens down to the overthrow of her freedom, but also of most of her statesmen, which became permanent in the literary tradition of later ages, was in its leading traits first delineated by the school of Aristotle and his followers.

The analysis concludes with the following remarks on the second part of the Ἀθηναίων πολιτεία :—

> Even a hasty glance at all these details gives one an impression of the extraordinarily valuable store of authentic facts here gathered by the industry of Aristotle. He has presented us with a description of the very subjects which the Athenians themselves did not deem worth the trouble of describing, since the knowledge of these de-

[1] E. Miller, *Mélanges de littérature grecque*, Paris, 1868; p. 369.

[2] *A. P.*, p. 402.

[3] *Die Staatslehre des Aristoteles in Historisch-Politischen Umrissen*, vol. ii (1875), pp. 410—528.

tails of every-day life was for themselves the merest matter of course. In Aristotle the scientific instinct of the genuine investigator was blended with the natural curiosity of the foreigner; and this double interest served to add a fresh keenness to his perception of what posterity would deem to be best worth knowing. For later generations his πολιτεία became a veritable treasure-house of accumulated learning. Things that are only incidentally noticed by the orators and poets of the time, as being perfectly familiar to every one, are here narrated, described and elucidated by Aristotle for the benefit of all of those to whom this information was unknown. It was an important and an imperishable service. It was also one which was the natural result of his peculiar method as an investigator. To display the various members of the living body of definite fact, to separate all the complex framework into its component parts, to trace the sequence of a series of results as they came into being, to describe for after ages what was regarded by contemporaries as no less obvious than their daily meat and drink,—to do all this was thoroughly characteristic of Aristotle. It is more than enough to prove the truth of the opinion that Aristotle is above all others the scientific investigator of the Hellenic idea of political life.

Thus far we have dealt with laborious collections of the merest fragments of the Πολιτεῖαι, and with one vivid commentary upon the most important of the series. Meanwhile, the original work was deemed to have vanished as completely as the lost decads of Livy. Neumann, in the *Prolegomena* to his edition of the fragments, laments the loss in the following terms: *eheu amissum est in sempiternum praeclarum opus, nisi e palimpsestis quibusdam fortasse eruatur.* In the *Bibliothèque Orientale* of Herbelot (p. 971), mention is made of an Arabic translation of the work, but the hope inspired by this statement remained unfulfilled[1]. To cherish such a hope, even for a moment, was in 1865 denounced as folly[2].

§ 5. *The Berlin Fragments of the* Ἀθηναίων πολιτεία.

In the year 1880 the interest of scholars was aroused by the announcement that, among the fragments of *papyrus* found in the Fayoom near the ancient Arsinoe, and acquired for the Egyptian Museum at Berlin, there were two small pages with writing on both sides. They were skilfully deciphered by Blass, and a comparison with other *papyri* led

[1] The title of the alleged translation is *Ketab Siassat Almoden* (the book of the government of States). Herbelot's authority is Haji Khalfa, who died in 1658. In Fluegel's ed., vol. v p. 97, no. 10, 203, Haji Khalfa says that, in the book on 'the Government of States,' Aristotle mentions 171 great States. He distinguishes this book from the *Politics*, and says that the latter was translated into Arabic, which perhaps implies that the 'Government of States' was not. Part of this statement is doubtless derived from the list of Aristotle's writings in Ibn Abi Useibia, which includes 'a book about the Government of States and the number of the nations, in which he mentions 151 great States' (ed. Müller, 1884, p. 68). As this list is confessedly taken from a Greek catalogue by Ptolemy (see *supra* p. xvii), we have no right to assume that the Arabs possessed the book. It is not at all the kind of book that was likely to interest them. For the substance of this note I am indebted to Prof. W. Robertson Smith.

[2] Heitz, *Verl. Schr.*, p. 230.

to their being provisionally assigned to the second century A.D. The first fragment contained on one side (I *a*) the long passage in Iambic verse quoted by Aristides from the poems of Solon; on the other (I *b*), a passage in prose on the archonship of Damasias. The second fragment had on one side (II *a*) an account of the reforms of Cleisthenes; and on the other (II *b*), a passage on the ostracism of Megacles and Xanthippus, with some mention of the mines at Maroneia. So imperfect were the indications given by the context that Blass identified Damasias as the archon of 639—8, instead of the archon of 582—1 and 581—0. The institution of the nine archons seemed to be mentioned *after* the extract from Solon. It thus appeared impossible to attribute the fragments to a historical work written in chronological order, such as that of Ephorus or one of the writers of Ἀτθίδες. But Theopompus was known to have closed the tenth book of his *Philippica* with an excursus on the demagogues of Athens. This (as Blass thought) might well have begun with some account of Dracon and Solon, followed by a digression on the early history of the archonship and by notices of various statesmen such as Megacles, together with some observations on the institution of Ostracism and the reforms of Cleisthenes. It was accordingly conjectured that the newly discovered fragments belonged to Theopompus.

Here the matter rested for a very short time. The article by Blass was published in *Hermes* in October, 1880. The very next number of the *Rheinisches Museum* contained a brilliant contribution by the veteran scholar Bergk, who was then in his 69th year and had just completed the fourth edition of his *Poetae Lyrici Graeci*, and whose attention was perhaps mainly drawn to the fragments because they included fresh evidence on the poems of Solon. Bergk pointed out that the passage on Cleisthenes corresponded with a scholium on Aristophanes, *Nubes*, 37. The papyrus as deciphered by Blass had the following letters:

— — — ΑΘΗΝΑΙΟΙϹ
— — ΧΟ̣ · · · Ε̣Δ̣Ε̣Κ̣ · ΔΗΜ̣Ο̣Ι̣
— — Ε̣Π̣Ο̣ΜΕΝΠ̣ΑΝΤ · Ϲ̣ · [Ν̣Α̣
— Τ̣Ο · Ϲ̣ ΔΗΜΟΥϹΑΝΑ · · ΩΝ

With the help of the *Scholium* Bergk restored the second and following lines thus:

κατ]έσ[τησ]ε δὲ κ[αὶ] δημαρ-
χοὺς τὴν αὐτὴν ἔχοντας] ἐπίμελειαν τ[οῖ]ς πρ[ό-
τερον ναυκράροις καὶ τοὺ]ς δήμους ἀντ]ὶ τῶν
ναυκραριῶν ἐποίησε]

This *Scholium*, although introduced by the words Ἀριστοτέλης δὲ περὶ Κλεισθένους φησί, had not found its way into either of Rose's previous editions of the fragments, its place having been taken by a less accurate transcript in the lexicon of Harpocration (Rose, 359[2]); but it is duly cited in the edition by Heitz (no. 19 = 388).

In addition to the proof supplied by this citation, the internal evidence of the style of these scanty fragments was enough to convince Bergk that the prose portions could not have come from any other work than the lost πολιτεῖαι of Aristotle[1]. But Bergk could not believe that so long a passage of poetry as the fragment of Solon could have been cited in the Ἀθηναίων πολιτεία. He accordingly suggested two alternative solutions: either the poem was an interpolation inserted in a complete copy of the Ἀθηναίων πολιτεία by a copyist who desired to illustrate the reforms of Solon by transcribing the poem, or the work consisted of selections from various writers on the constitution of Athens.

The Berlin fragments were further discussed by Landwehr, who published a transcript and a restoration of the text in 1883; which he afterwards revised and corrected in the *Philologus* (Suppl. Bd. v 195). They were also the subject of an able paper by Diels in 1885[2]. According to his view the fragments are simply two loose pages of papyrus filled with transcripts from the Ἀθηναίων πολιτεία by some schoolboy of Arsinoe. Damasias is rightly identified as Damasias II, and many other points are discussed in a masterly manner. It is also maintained for the first time that all the four pages belong to the same work, and that the Ἀθ. πολ. of Aristotle. The paper includes a convenient reprint of the various restorations of the fragments, and also a lithographed facsimile.

[1] p. 90, 'Wohl aber erinnert die Behandlungsweise an Aristoteles: selbst ein blödes Auge wird erkennen, dass der Verfasser vollkommen mit seinem Gegenstande vertraut ist, dass er zwischen Wesentlichem und Unwichtigem sehr wohl zu scheiden weiss, dass hier nicht ein buchgelehrter Grammatiker zu uns spricht, sondern ein erfahrener Mann, der mit scharfen Blicke das politische Leben zu betrachten gewohnt war, der sein historischer Sinn vor jeder Befangenheit des Urtheils bewahrte. Nicht minder erinnert die schlichte und schmucklose, nur auf die Sache gerichtete Darstellung an die Weise des Begründers der Staatswissenschaft. Auf mich wenigstens machten diese Bruchstücke sofort den Eindruck, als hätte ich Reste der Aristotelischen Politie der Athener vor mir.'

[2] *Philos. u. Hist. Abhandlungen*, Berlin Acad., 1886, ii pp. 1—57.

§ 6. *The British Museum papyrus.*

Thus far the student of Aristotle's Πολιτεῖαι had to found his conclusions as to the character of the work solely on meagre fragments laboriously collected from many sources, and on two barely legible and most imperfect scraps of *papyrus* in the Museum at Berlin, when suddenly, on the morning of Monday, Jan. 19, 1891, the readers of *The Times* were startled by the announcement that a MS containing the greater portion of Aristotle's *Constitution of Athens* had been acquired by the British Museum as part of a collection of papyrus rolls from a place in Egypt which, for adequate reasons, it was not expedient to specify more particularly. It was not until the rolls had been examined at the British Museum that it was found that three of them contained what was identified as the text of the Ἀθηναίων πολιτεία.

The secret of the discovery had been well kept: and by its first public announcement the interest of scholars at home and abroad was roused to a high pitch of expectation. Only eleven days later, on Friday, Jan. 30th, the printed text appeared under the editorship of Mr F. G. Kenyon, Fellow of Magdalen College, Oxford, Assistant in the Department of MSS, British Museum. It was soon discovered that, although the text was described in the preface to the *editio princeps* as 'in good condition' and requiring 'little emendation', there was a still deeper truth in the editor's fuller statement on a later page :—'There remain not a few passages which still require emendation by conjecture, in some of which the reading of the MS is completely lost, while in others a few faint traces of letters remain, which will serve as tests of the accuracy of any proposed emendation'. A vast number of conjectures of very various degrees of merit were accordingly proposed by English scholars in the pages of the *Athenaeum*, and the *Academy*, and the substance of these, together with the criticisms of continental scholars, were reprinted, with many other suggestions, in successive numbers of the *Classical Review* (March to July, 1891). Many further contributions to the criticism and elucidation of the treatise have since appeared. A conspectus of the literature of the subject is reserved for a later section (§ 10).

Early in March the Trustees of the British Museum published a Facsimile of the *papyrus*. The immediate, and indeed the permanent, result of this publication was a widely expressed recognition of the remarkable skill with which Mr Kenyon had accomplished the task of deciphering the MS. In those portions of the MS which are most easily read in the original, the facsimile is an adequate substitute for the *papyrus*. It is mainly, though by no means exclusively, in the places where the papyrus is rubbed, and the remains of the letters only faintly visible, that it is absolutely necessary to resort to the original.

The MS consists of four separate rolls with the letters A, B, Γ, written at the beginning of the first three:

I	7 feet, 2½ inches, in length, by about 11 inches in height, including Columns	1—11
II	5 ,, 5½ ,, ,, ,, ,, ,,	12—24
III	3 ,, ,, ,, ,, ,, ,,	25—30
IV	about 3 feet (originally) in length, by about 10 inches in height, including remains of Columns	31—37

Total length about 18 feet, 8 inches[1].

The MS is written in four hands: (1) extends over Columns 1—12, and is described as 'a small semi-cursive hand, employing a large number of abbreviations of common syllables.'

(2) begins with Col. 13 and ends in the middle of Col. 20. This is described as an 'uncial of fair size,' plain but not ornamental, employing no contractions, and making a large number of blunders in matters of spelling.

(3) is a 'straggling' and often ill-formed semi-cursive hand, of larger size than the first. This extends from the middle of Col. 20 to the end of Col. 24; and also includes the mutilated remains of Cols. 31—37.

(4) closely resembles (1), and 'employs many of the same abbreviations,' but is generally finer and more upright, and possesses some distinctive forms of letters. This extends over Cols. 25—30[2].

Abbreviations are not used uniformly by all the four hands. They are chiefly confined to hands (1) and (4), while they are very sparingly used by (3), and not at all by (2). Hence it is obvious that, in restoring the text, it is solely in Cols. 1—12, and 25—30, that we can assume the existence of abbreviations. They can only be admitted within very narrow limits in Cols. 20—24, and 31—37; while they cannot be admitted at all in Cols. 13—20.

(1) and (4) have many abbreviations in common; but at the same time each of the two has some that are characteristic of itself alone. This will be made clear by the following classified list[3].

[1] According to Pliny (*N. H.* xiii § 78) the two best kinds of papyrus were thirteen digits in height (13 × ·72821 = 10·4653 inches), rather less tall than rolls I—III, but rather taller than IV.

[2] Mr Kenyon's *Introduction*, p. xi. The proposal to identify hands (1) and (4), and hands (2) and (3), made by Kaibel and Wilamowitz on pp. v—vi of their preface, is refuted by Mr Kenyon (ed. 3 p. xii) whose opinion is justly confirmed by Blass (*Praef.* iv—vii).

[3] Mr Kenyon has already given a general list on the last page of his *Introd.* I have endeavoured to classify this list, and to represent approximately the shapes of the letters used in the *papyrus*.

hands (1) and (4)		hand (1) only
ϯ = γάρ	ⲡ = παρά and παρα-	° = -οι, -ου, -ον, οις, -ους
δ′ = δέ and -δε-	π′ = περί	π′ = περ
δ = διά and δια-	ϲ́ = σύν and συν-	ϲ^{θ} = -σθαι
＼ = εἶναι	τϛ = -ται	χ = χρόνος, -ου, -ον, -ων, -οις
∕ = ἐστί	† = τήν and -την	ω = -εως
κ́ = καί and -και-	τ᾿ = τῆς and -της	**hand (4) only**
μ′ = μέν and -μεν-	τ′ = τῶν and -των	α᾿ = ἀνα-
μ\ = μετά and (in 1) μετα-	ω = -ων	⇛ = εἰσί
° = -ος		ϲθ = -σθαι
ό = οὖν and -ουν-		ϒ\` = ὑπό and ὑπο-

hand (3) only	hands (3) and (4) only
ϒ᾿ = ὑπέρ	κ = -καί- and in (3) καί

Hands (1) and (4) have not only certain distinctive abbreviations, but they also use with different degrees of frequency the abbreviations that are common to both. Thus the symbol for εἶναι is found fourteen times in (1), and only five times in (4); that for ἐστί four times in (1), and twenty-eight times in (4); that for συν- seventy times in (1), and six times in (4); that for -ουν- three times in (1), and sixteen times in (4); that for -ται twenty-four times in (1), and fifty-seven times in (4); and that for -ος is far more frequent in (1) than in (4)[1]. These considerations prevent us from identifying the two hands. There are also certain distinctive differences in the shapes of the letters used by each; and the same remark applies to hands (2) and (3)[2].

Final syllables are often omitted in (1) and (4). Thus φυ^{λ} is found in both hands for φυλῆς and φυλήν, and βου^{λ} is used for all the cases of βουλή in the singular. Hand (3) has χωρ̀ for χώραν (col. 22, 2); τρὸ for τρόπον (*ib.* 11) and απογρὰ for ἀπογραφάς (*ib.* 35). An abbreviation for αυ is exceptionally used for αὐτήν (in col. 9, 8); and a symbol for δραχμή, found in cols. 21, 35 and 26, 54, is common to hands (2) and (4). Numerals are denoted by the ordinary symbols in all hands alike[3].

[1] For the details of these statistics, see van Leeuwen's *Observationes Palaeographicae* in the Dutch edition, pp. 170—7.

[2] See the alphabets reproduced in *Class. Rev.* v 183.

[3] The use of the above abbreviations, and their distribution over the several hands, may be illustrated by the following examples. For convenience, ordinary type is here used, and the words are separated from one another.

Abbreviations in (1), also found in (4):—σ́εβη (col. 1, 3); π̀χωρησαντ (1, 20); τα μ́ ό π́ τασ αρχασ (1, 35); τ′ τ̀ χρεων αποκοπησ (2, 31); ατιμον \ κ′ τ′ πολεω (3, 32); δ′κα εϯ ου γ′ οιεσθαι δικ́ον \ (4, 6); μεμνητϛ π′ αυτ′ (4, 15); π′ τ′ δ′νεμεσθ τ̀ γην (4, 21); μ̀ τ̀ τ′ νομων θεσιν (5, 23); ου γ′ ενδεχετϛ (7, 2); μ̀πεμπομ́οσ (7, 14); αρμοδι° (7, 25); σ′παντα σ′ οισ (8, 21); δ′κα μ́ τ′ π′ το αστυ (9, 4); κ′ τ′ σ′μαχ^{ω} (10, 12); \ κ′ δικ′οσ (11, 1), \ τωι π′κλει (11, 27); επει δ′ μ̀ τ̀ εν σικε^{λ} γενομ́ην δ′φοραν (11, 46); σ γραψεινάανηγωντϛ, *i.e.* συγγράψειν ἃ ἂν ἡγῶνται (12, 3).

In (4), also found in (1):—κ̀βαλλετϛ (25, 25); δραχμ^{ω} (27, 1); αρχοντ° (27, 23); π′αιρειται (29, 18); δ̀τιθησι (29, 23); μ̀ τ′ βου^{λ} (29, 50); π̀τιθενται (30, 41).

In (1) alone:—° = ου in 15 places, *e.g.*

Iota adscriptum is hardly ever omitted in (1); hardly ever inserted in (2); (3) and (4) do not follow any fixed rule[1].

ει and ι are frequently interchanged, especially in (2); some of these mistakes are however corrected by hand (1). But even in (1) we sometimes have ι for ει, *e.g.* πισιστρατος in three places (Col. 5, 28, 33, 37), besides four other instances. In (2) there are as many as 41, *e.g.* αφιλον for ἀφεῖλον (Col. 16, 4); in (3) and (4) there are only four and five respectively. Conversely we have ει for ι in all the four hands, the number of instances being 14, 11, 15 and 2 respectively. Both of these mistakes are combined in πολειτιαν (Col. 13, 3) and πολειτιας (14, 1; 16, 26)[2].

There is nothing resembling a mark of punctuation, except the short horizontal line in the margin (Cols. 1, 40; 2, 4; 7, 15, 30; 11, 5, 31; 13, 15). In some cases this may be a true παραγραφή, as in Col. 1, 40 and 8, 21 f, where it coincides with the natural end of a chapter; in others (as suggested by Blass[3]) it may denote a corruption; at any rate this appears more probable than van Leeuwen's[4] opinion that it draws attention to an important or striking statement.

There are no breathings or accents, except in εκμαρτυρῶν (Col. 3, 9), νομοφυλακεῖν (3, 26), δῆμον? (4, 29), ἀ (12, 3) ἡγῶνται (13, 11) and αὖτου (29, 46). In some of these cases they are apparently added to prevent ambiguity of meaning[5].

Blunders made by hand (2) are occasionally corrected, apparently by hand (1), or possibly (4). It has been suggested that the transcript was begun by some one who desired a copy for his own use, and, after writing out the first twelve columns, entrusted to others the task of copying the remainder, being content to revise their work and to correct their misspellings and their other mistakes[6]. The editors of the first German edition, Kaibel and von Wilamowitz[7], hold that all the corrections are due to hand (1) which they identify with (4). To account for the fact that many blunders are left uncorrected, they assume that the

αρειᵒ παγᵒ, (2, 9); =ον in 44 places, *e.g.* θητικᵒ, (3, 3); =οι in 8 places, *e.g.* δισχιλιᵒ (10, 17); =οις once, αλλᵒ (2, 33); =-ους in 16 places, *e.g.* κλεισθενᵒ, (12, 8); κ́ π (8, 9).

In (4) alone:—//=εἰσί (in 20 places, *e.g.* twice in 27, 11 and 28, 41); ὑ=ὑπό (26, 19, 30; 27, 20; 28, 24); σθ′=-σθαι in 16 places, *e.g.* δυνασθ′ (26, 9); ὑ=ὑπό in 26, 19 and 30; 27, 20; 28, 24; also =ὑπο- in ὑζυγιων (26, 52); ἀ=ἀνα- in 13 places, *e.g.* ἀβηναι 30, 3.

In (3) alone: ὑ=ὑπέρ twice 21, 24 and 23, 22 (cf. 22, 44). (3) κ=καί (22, 13 *bis*; 23, 22;) =-και- in αναγκον (23, 14). χωρ̀ =χώραν (22, 2); τρο=τρόπον (22, 11); απογρὰ=ἀπογραφάς 22, 35. Final ν above last letter of word, seven times, cf. p. 151, *n.c.* κ also=-και- in (4), 27, 17.

1 Van Leeuwen, *l. c.* p. 165.

2 Van Leeuwen, *l. c.* p. 166.

3 *Praef.* p. xi.

4 l.c. p. 166.

5 Mr Kenyon's *Introd.* last page; and van Leeuwen, *l. c.* p. 167.

6 Mr Kenyon's *Introduction*, p. xi.

7 *Praef.* p. vii.

text depends on two earlier MSS, one of them much more accurate than the other[1]. Blass however, holds, with apparently greater probability, that there are several correctors: all the four hands correct some of their own mistakes; and one or more of them correct the work of the rest, not to mention the possibility of a revision independent of all the four. The same critic divides the 'corrections' into five groups, the most important of which he prefers to regard as *variae lectiones* which were recorded as such in the MS from which our *papyrus* was copied[2].

The process by which the *papyrus* plant was made into material for writing was as follows: the tall stem had its rind stripped off and the pith cut with a sharp instrument into broad slices of extreme thinness and considerable length. These were laid in long strips on a flat board; across these were placed in the opposite direction and touching one another, a number of short strips corresponding in length to the proposed height of the roll. The upper and lower surfaces were made to adhere to one another by means of the slightly glutinous sap of the pith or (failing that) by means of paste. The long scroll thus formed was thereupon smoothed down with an ivory instrument or a shell[3]. The proper side for writing is that on which the horizontal strips allow of the pen running freely without traversing the frequent joinings of the successive parallel strips of papyrus. Thus, the British Museum papyrus of the first three speeches of Hyperides is written entirely on what may be called the 'horizontal' side, *i.e.* that on which the strips of *papyrus* run in a horizontal direction. If any writing is added on the back, it may be described as written on the 'vertical' side, that on which the strips run vertically and overlap one another at their edges. After the front of a scroll has been filled, the back is not unfrequently used for some other writing on a totally different subject. For example, the British Museum papyrus of the Funeral Oration of Hyperides has a Greek horoscope on one side, and that the 'horizontal,' or right side; while the speech of Hyperides is written on the 'vertical,' or wrong side. Similarly the Ἀθηναίων πολιτεία is written on the vertical, or wrong side, technically called *verso* (or 'reverse') as opposed to *recto*. It may be inferred that the text of any author so inscribed on the back of the scroll is not only later in date than that on the other side; but also that it has been copied solely for the private use of the owner, and not for publication or for preservation in a public library[4].

On the horizontal side of the papyrus of the Ἀθηναίων πολιτεία are

1 *Praef.* p. ix.

2 Blass, *Praef.* pp. viii—xi.

3 Martial xv 209, 'Levis ab aequorea cortex Mareotica concha Fiat: inoffensa currit harundo via.' Cf. Blümner's *Technologie*, i 308—325.

4 U. Wilcken, *Hermes* 1887, p. 487—492, *Recto oder Verso*.

the accounts of receipt and expenditure drawn up by a bailiff on a private estate in the eleventh year of Vespasian (from Aug. 78 to June 79 A.D.)[1]. After (but probably not very long after) the time when the accounts had ceased to be valuable, the other side was used to the extent of a column and a half for the transcription of an argument to the *Midias* of Demosthenes[2]; the latter was then struck out, the roll turned upside down and the Ἀθηναίων πολιτεία written on it, beginning at the other end of the roll. The MS has been assigned to 'the end of the first century of our era or, at latest, the beginning of the second,' and this opinion is confirmed by several dated documents of the first and second centuries which have come to light since the first publication of the *papyrus*[3].

§ 7. *Date and Authorship of the* Ἀθηναίων πολιτεία.

The date of the original composition of the treatise is determined by internal evidence. The system of electing *Strategi* for special departments of military duty, which is recognised in c. 61 § 1, was introduced after B.C. 334. Hence the work was written later than that date. The latest date expressly quoted in it is the archonship of Cephisophon, B.C. 329—8 (c. 54 § 7). Again, since in c. 46 § 1 mention is made of triremes and quadriremes, and not of quinqueremes, it has been inferred that it was written before B.C. 325—4, the earliest date at which quinqueremes are named in connexion with the navy of Athens[4]. Further, it is clear that the treatise could not have been composed after 322 B.C.; because, in that case, we should certainly have had some account of the change in the constitution of Athens which was brought about by Antipater in that year[5]. Lastly, the treatise describes the Athenians as still sending officials to Samos (c. 62, 16); in the autumn of B.C. 322 that island ceased to be under the control of Athens. B.C. 322 is also the year of the death of Aristotle: hence, the evidence derived from the treatise itself shews that it was written while Aristotle was still alive; and the reasons above assigned enable us to place its date between B.C. 328 and 325.

We have already traced in chronological order the evidence of all

[1] ἔτους ἐνδεκάτου αὐτοκράτορος Καίσαρος Οὐεσπασιάνου Σεβαστοῦ ἀργυρικὸς λόγος Ἐπιμάχου Πολυδεύκους λημμάτων καὶ ἀναλωμάτων τῶν δι' ἐμοῦ Διδύμου Ἀσπασίου χειριζομένων (in the original there are no accents).

[2] Printed in the Dutch ed. of the Ἀθ. πολ., pp. 180—185; and in Mr Kenyon's 3rd ed., pp. 215—219.

[3] Mr Kenyon's *Introd.* to ed. 3, p. xvi.

[4] Mr Cecil Torr in *Athenaeum*, Feb. 7, 1891; Bruno Keil, *Berl. Phil. Woch.* 1891, p. 614; J. H. Lipsius, *Verhandlungen der Sächs. Gesellschaft der Wissenschaften*, 28 Feb. 1891, p. 45. See note on 46 § 1.

[5] Bruno Keil, *u. s.* p. 613.

the ancient authorities who quote the Πολιτεῖαι. We have seen that the work as a whole is assigned to Aristotle by the unanimous voice of antiquity; and it has just been shewn that the Ἀθηναίων πολιτεία was certainly completed while Aristotle was still alive. In such a case we must necessarily accept the work as Aristotle's, unless internal evidence is conclusive on the other side. The consideration of that evidence turns partly on questions of style, partly on the relations subsisting between the Ἀθηναίων πολιτεία and the *Politics*. Let us consider the latter point first.

The latest event mentioned in the *Politics* is the death of Philip in B.C. 336. Had the *Politics* been finished even as early as seven years after that date, it would have been completed before the Ἀθηναίων πολιτεία. But, according to the opinion now prevalent among Aristotelian scholars, it was left incomplete by its author and was not given to the world in his lifetime. Books vii (iv) and viii (v) are more carefully composed than the rest, being specially marked by the avoidance of *hiatus*. It is possible that these two books represent the author's finished style; it is also possible that they owe their polish to the skill of a pupil of the Peripatetic school[1]. But in either case they are not of the nature of a popular work, and there is nothing to prove that they were in general circulation during the author's lifetime.

Probably the greater part of the *Politics* had already been written by the year 336. It has sometimes been supposed that the vast collection of facts relating to the πολιτεῖαι of various Greek states was formed to serve as materials for the theoretical treatment of the subject in the *Politics*. The *Politics*, however, were never completed, whereas the Ἀθηναίων πολιτεία assumed a finished form more than three years before the death of Aristotle. But it is quite possible that the *materials* for the Ἀθηναίων πολιτεία, and for the rest of the series, were collected before the larger part of the *Politics* was reduced to writing. The same materials would serve for both; but, in the case of the Πολιτεῖαι, they were embodied in a finished work for popular perusal; in the case of the *Politics*, they formed part of the preliminary studies for courses of lectures probably confined to the philosopher's immediate circle. Now, as the *Politics* may have continued to supply the theme for such lectures in and after 334, while the Ἀθηναίων πολιτεία was not ready for public perusal until 6 or 8 years later, we need not be surprised to find in the *Politics* no reference whatsoever to the Πολιτεῖαι. At a time when only fragments of the latter were known to scholars, this fact used to be quoted in proof of the spuriousness of the work. But now that

[1] Shute's *History of the Aristotelian Writings*, pp. 164—170.

nearly the whole of one of the Πολιτεῖαι has been recovered, and its date determined to be later than the latest event noticed in the *Politics*, no argument against its genuineness can be founded on the fact that the author of the unfinished work says nothing of a popular treatise that had not yet been published while the theoretical work was still in course of preparation.

The question arises whether the Πολιτεῖαι are ever mentioned in the undisputed works of Aristotle. At the close of the *Ethics*, when about to state the theme of the ensuing discussion in the *Politics*, Aristotle speaks of τῶν πολιτειῶν αἱ συναγωγαὶ and also of τῶν συνηγμένων πολιτειῶν (x 9 §§ 21, 23). The sense of the context of the latter phrase may be expressed as follows: 'First then let us endeavour to review whatever is to some extent valuable in the statements of our predecessors, and then to learn from the constitutions which have been collected (or put into juxtaposition with one another), the causes which are apt to preserve or to destroy states, and the causes which have this effect on the several constitutions.' This promise is sufficiently fulfilled by the review of the various constitutions in Book II, their classification in Books III-VI[1], and the discussion of the ways in which revolutions may be caused or prevented in Book VIII (V).

Rose, however, in his *Aristoteles Pseudepigraphus*, while regarding the πολιτειῶν συναγωγαὶ as existing collections of facts forming materials for the *Politics*, insists at the same time that Aristotle had not himself written any such work or expressed any intention of writing it[2]. The *Politics* of Aristotle, he adds, were supplemented in due time by the works on νομοθεσία written by his pupil Theophrastus; but neither Aristotle nor Theophrastus, he contends, ever wrote any work on πολιτεῖαι. The Πολιτεῖαι, attributed to Aristotle, are ascribed by Rose to some anonymous Peripatetic who was less of a philosopher than a historian and philologist. Such was Demetrius Phalereus who wrote works περὶ τῆς Ἀθήνησι νομοθεσίας and περὶ τῶν Ἀθήνησι πολιτειῶν. Such, again,

[1] Cf. Newman, Ar. *Pol.* vol. i pp. 2, 214—220.

[2] Rose, *A. P.* p. 396.

Camerarius and Victorius understood πολιτεῖαι συνηγμέναι as a reference to Aristotle's historical work, a view supported by Grant and Stahr, Ar. *Pol.* (1860) p. 66. Heitz, *Verl. Schr.* p. 232, quotes the paraphrase of Andronicus: εἶτα συναγαγόντες τὰς πολιτείας θεωρῶμεν ἐν αὐταῖς ἅ τε φθείρει καὶ ἃ σῴζει τὰς πόλεις. From the use of συναγωγαί in *Pol.* vii (vi) *init.*, p. 1316 *b* 40, ἔτι δὲ τὰς συναγωγὰς αὐτῶν τῶν εἰρημένων ἐπισκεπτέον πάντων τῶν τρόπων, and συνακτέον εἰς ὀλίγα in 1319 *b* 23, he infers that they are *die unter eine gewisse Anzahl von Rubriken vertheilten, verschiedenen Verfassungsformen.* But the meaning of συναγωγαὶ in the former of these two passages is determined by Aristotle himself by the use of the word συνδυαζόμενα in the very next line, and συνδυασμοί in the subsequent context. It refers to constitutions which exceptionally *combine* oligarchic and democratic elements; and this sense has nothing to do with the interpretation of the passage in the Ethics proposed by Heitz. Susemihl (followed by Mr J. A. Stewart) brackets *Eth.* x 9 §§ 22, 23.

was Dicaearchus, whose πολιτεῖαι were known to Cicero. The author of the Πολιτεῖαι was (according to Rose) inspired, like Dicaearchus, by the example of Aristotle who, in his *Politics*, touches on the constitutions of a large number of states. Now that we know that the Ἀθηναίων πολιτεία was completed several years before the death of Aristotle, while the *Politics* was still unfinished, the suggestion that the unknown author of the Πολιτεῖαι was inspired by the *Politics* falls to the ground, unless indeed we are to assume that the author was one of the pupils of Aristotle who attended his course on the *Politics* at some date after his return to Athens (334). If so, it is singular that the name of this remarkably prolific writer should not have been preserved. On the contrary, the name has completely vanished, and in its place we find everywhere the name of Aristotle and of none beside.

The only two that have been seriously suggested as authors of the Ἀθηναίων πολιτεία are Demetrius Phalereus and Dicaearchus. The former is suggested by Rose in his *Aristoteles Pseudepigraphus*, p. 398. Two of the fragments seemed to imply a more aristocratic type of constitution than any that prevailed at Athens before about 317 B.C.; and, on the other hand, the work must have been composed before the number of the Attic tribes was increased from ten to twelve (B.C. 307). The fragments in question are those on θεσμοθετῶν ἀνάκρισις (414^3) and στρατεία ἐν τοῖς ἐπωνύμοις (469^3). The inference drawn by Rose is not supported by the context in which we find those fragments in the present work (c. 55 § 1 and c. 53 § 7); and we now know that the treatise was written not between 317 and 307, but between 328 and 325. Rose's suggestion has been recently revived by Schvarcz[1]. If any detailed refutation of this view is necessary, it may be noticed that, of all the passages attributed to the work of Demetrius περὶ τῆς Ἀθήνησι νομοθεσίας (either by Harpocration, *s.v.* σκαφηφόροι, Ζεὺς ἕρκειος and παράστασις, or by Plutarch, *Sol.* 23, or by the Scholiast on Arist. *Nubes* 37, or by other authorities mentioned in Müller's FHG), not one is to be found in the πολιτεία. Indeed, in the very first fragment of the work of Demetrius, the account of κυρία ἐκκλησία is described by Harpocration as less satisfactory than that of 'Aristotle' which is found in c. 43 § 4. Similarly Harpocration, *s.v.* παράστασις, prefixes to a quotation from Demetrius περὶ νομοθεσίας, a quotation from 'Aristotle' ἐν τῇ Ἀθηναίων πολιτείᾳ which is found in c. 59 § 3; and the Scholiast on Arist. *Nubes* 37 quotes from both treatises, his quotation from 'Aristotle' being found in c. 21 § 5. (From the other work, περὶ τῶν Ἀθήνησι πολιτειῶν or πολιτῶν, named in Diog. Laert. v 80, not a single fragment has

[1] *Ar. und die* Ἀθ. πολ., pp. *c*, *d*.

survived.) To meet these difficulties Schvarcz suggests that, at the time of writing the *περὶ τῶν Ἀθήνησι πολιτειῶν*, which he practically identifies with the *Ἀθηναίων πολιτεία*, Demetrius was unacquainted with the facts which he afterwards ascertained by further study in the archives of Athens and embodied in his later work *περὶ τῆς Ἀθήνησι νομοθεσίας*. And yet, strange to say, the account of *κυρία ἐκκλησία* in this 'later work' is in the judgment of Harpocration inferior to that in the treatise which Schvarcz identifies with the 'earlier work' of Demetrius.

It is equally impossible to assign it to Aristotle's pupil, Dicaearchus, for not a single fragment attributed to him by ancient authorities is to be found in the *Ἀθηναίων πολιτεία*. Nothing is quoted from his *πολιτεῖαι* of Pellene and Corinth, or Sparta and Athens; and the few remains of his antiquarian works *περὶ μουσικῶν ἀγώνων*, *περὶ Διονυσιακῶν ἀγώνων* and *Παναθηναϊκός*, have nothing in common with the treatment of those topics in the treatise ascribed to Aristotle.

While in the *Politics* there is no allusion to the *Πολιτεῖαι*, there are many passages in the *Ἀθ. πολ.* which, either in thought or expression, are so closely parallel to the *Politics*, as to suggest a common authorship. Such coincidences might of course be due to the retentive memory of a pupil attending the master's lectures on his unfinished and unpublished work; but it seems more natural to ascribe them to a common author. Let us first consider the more general coincidences of thought.

(1) The *Ἀθηναίων πολιτεία* is the work of one who displays a certain predilection for an aristocratic form of government.

In the *Politics* there is no question as to the author's general sympathies being on the side of an aristocratic government. *Aristocracy* is to Aristotle an *ἀρίστη πολιτεία*. It is marked by election for merit; it is distinguished from the perfect state as being a government of men who are only good relatively to the constitution; it is so called because the best rule, or because the best interests of the state are consulted; it is analogous to royalty as a government of the best: it is even preferable to royalty, because under it the good are more than one. *Oligarchy*, the perverted form of Aristocracy, is inferior to constitutional government (*πολιτεία*), and to its perverted form, Democracy.

Democracy is described in the *Politics* as the government of the many in their own interests; it is the perversion of constitutional government; it is akin to tyranny; in its extreme form it is peculiarly apt to pass into tyranny; it is, however, the only possible form of government in large states; and it is more stable than oligarchy. 'Liberty and equality', as well as the 'use of the lot', are dispassionately described as characteristic of democracy; and suggestions are propounded for the improvement of this form of government[1].

The author of the Ἀθηναίων πολιτεία dwells on the importance of the services rendered by the Areopagus in the times of Dracon (c. 4) and Solon (c. 9), and in the sixteen years immediately succeeding the formation of the confederacy of Delos (c. 23). Cleon is regarded as a demagogue who corrupted the people (c. 28). Nicias, Thucydides (son of Melesias), and Theramenes, are counted among the best statesmen of Athens (c. 28). The writer shows the greatest interest in the constitutional measures proposed by the Four Hundred (c. 29—32); at the same time he does not disguise the atrocities committed by the Thirty (c. 35 end). The restoration of the democracy is described in dispassionate and unenthusiastic terms (c. 38). The defeat of a proposal to reward all who had aided in its restoration is mentioned in language implying that the author did not disapprove of the result.

On the other hand, the transfer of judicial functions from the βουλή to the ἐκκλησία is commended on the ground that 'small bodies are more open to corruption than large ones' (c. 41, l. 28); but this approval is expressed in the mildest terms and does not imply sympathy with democracy as such. It has been quoted[2] as inconsistent with the *Politics*; but the reason given for the writer's approval of the transfer is in perfect accord with a passage in the *Politics* (1286 *a* 30, quoted in note on c. 41 l. 28). There are two periods in which Athens enjoyed a good government:— (1) the 16 years during which the Areopagus was supreme; and (2) the time immediately after the Four Hundred. The only phrase that does not remind one of the writer of the *Politics* is the reference to the 'forgiving spirit' of democracy in c. 22 § 4:—χρώμενοι τῇ εἰωθυίᾳ τοῦ δήμου πρᾳότητι. I am not aware of anything like it in the *Politics*, but I may observe that it recalls a notable passage in the *Republic*, and may possibly be a reminiscence of it[3].

The attitude of the author of the πολιτεία towards Peisistratus and Theramenes is in harmony with what we should expect from the author of the *Politics*. Both agree that Peisistratus rose to power by attacking the men of the Plain[4]; unless a certain passage in the *Politics* is interpolated, both observe that he was summoned before the Areopagus,

[1] For the reff. as to all these points, see Index to Jowett's *Politics* s. v. Aristocracy and Democracy.

[2] Cauer, *Hat Ar. die Schrift vom Staate der Athener geschrieben?* p. 49.

[3] p. 558 B (of the 'forgiving spirit' of democracy), ἡ συγγνώμη καὶ οὐδ' ὁπωστιοῦν σμικρολογία αὐτῆς. The term πρᾳότης happens to be used just before, but it is there applied to the 'calmness' with which condemned criminals go about the world like heroes under a democratical government:—ἡ πρᾳότης ἐνίων τῶν δικασθέντων οὐ κομψή;

[4] *Pol.* 1305 *a* 23.

and that he was twice exiled from Athens[1]. When recommending 'the constitution that gives predominance to the moderately wealthy class' (1296 *a* 38), Aristotle adds that 'only one of those who had played a leading part in the affairs of Greece had encouraged the introduction of this form'. As to the person meant there is much diversity of opinion; but whether (with Mr Newman) we identify him with Theramenes, or (as Dr Jowett prefers) with Solon, we have in either case a complete agreement with the Ἀθηναίων πολιτεία, though this does not exhaust the question. Again, the description of Ostracism and its object is 'to a considerable extent in harmony with that given in the *Politics*'[2]. The account of the policy of Aristides is less favourable than we should expect (see c. 24), 'inasmuch as he is said to have converted a citizen-body largely consisting of peasants into an urban citizen-body subsisting on pay and exercising a despotic authority over the subject states, and thus to have contributed to the establishment of an extreme democracy'. We are taught, however, in the *Politics* (1292 *b* 41—1293 *a* 6) to 'connect the establishment of a τελευταία δημοκρατία with a great increase in the size of the city and with the provision of pay'; and we also know that the opinion of Aristotle's pupil, Theophrastus, on the policy of Aristides, 'was not an altogether favourable one' (Plut. *Aristid.* c. 25)[3].

While the two works are in general agreement on the points above mentioned, there are certain apparent discrepancies that must now be noticed. (1) The 'Draconian Constitution' of the πολιτεία is in conflict with the passage in the *Politics* (1274 *b* 15) which states that Dracon 'adapted his laws to a constitution that already existed'; but the 'Draconian Constitution' has been vigorously attacked on its own merits, while the passage in the *Politics* is of doubtful genuineness. Again, the πολιτεία states that Peisistratus reigned for 19 years; the *Politics* (1315 *b* 31) makes his reign last for 17, but the whole of the context of the latter passage is bracketed by Susemihl in his 2nd and 3rd editions. In a disputed passage of the πολιτεία, Themistocles co-operates with Ephialtes for the curtailment of the power of the Areopagus: in a possibly interpolated chapter of the *Politics* (ii 12), the place of Themistocles is taken by Pericles, but not without protest on the part of critics, even before the discovery of the πολιτεία. In the πολιτεία (c. 21 § 6) we are told that Cleisthenes 'allowed every one to retain his γένος and φρατρία and his (hereditary) priesthood according to his ancestral rights'; in a perfectly genuine passage of the *Politics* (1319 *b* 23) it is implied that Cleisthenes 'increased the number of the phratries' and 'converted a number of private worships into a few

[1] *Pol.* 1315 *b* 21, 31.
[2] Mr Newman in *Class. Rev.* v 162 *b*.
[3] *Ibid.*

public ones'. But these passages may be readily reconciled with one another if we consider that the passage in the πολιτεία refers to those who were already citizens; that in the *Politics* to the νεοπολῖται.

It has been pointed out by Mr Macan that 'the ideas underlying the second part of the work are conspicuously Aristotelian. The distinction beween ἄρχειν and ἄρχεσθαι and its relation to the franchise; the definition and essence of citizenship (1275 *a* 22, and *b* 22)...; the theory of citizenship in the *Politics*, especially in Bk III *ad init.* might seem to be presupposed in the treatment of the ἀρχαὶ in the work under consideration''[1].

The comparison we have endeavoured to draw between the Ἀθηναίων πολιτεία and the *Politics* cannot perhaps be better concluded than by a striking example of identity of thought and language in the two works. In Ἀθ. πολ. c. 16 we read of Peisistratus: τοῖς ἀπόροις προεδάνειζε χρήματα πρὸς τὰς ἐργασίας, ὥστε διατρέφεσθαι γεωργοῦντας. τοῦτο δ' ἐποίει δυοῖν χάριν, ἵνα μήτε ἐν τῷ ἄστει διατρίβωσιν ἀλλὰ διεσπαρμένοι κατὰ τὴν χώραν, καὶ ὅπως εὐποροῦντες τῶν μετρίων καὶ πρὸς τοῖς ἰδίοις ὄντες μήτ' ἐπιθυμῶσι μήτε σχολάζωσιν ἐπιμελεῖσθαι τῶν κοινῶν. In the *Politics* we are told that (even under a democracy) it is advisable to provide the poor (τοὺς ἀπόρους) with capital, and encourage them to work (τρέπειν ἐπ' ἐργασίας 1320 *b* 8); and that it is characteristic of an oligarchy and a tyranny to drive the people out of the city and disperse them (1311 *a* 14). We learn elsewhere that the best material for a democracy is an agricultural population; for being poor they have no leisure (ἄσχολος), and therefore seldom attend the assembly; and, not having the necessaries of life, they are always at their work (πρὸς τοῖς ἔργοις διατρίβουσι καὶ τῶν ἀλλοτρίων οὐκ ἐπιθυμοῦσι, 1318 *b* 14); lastly, that while mechanics or traders or labourers are apt to frequent the city and find it easy to attend the assembly, the agricultural class (οἱ γεωργοῦντες) do not attend meetings, or equally feel the need of assembling together, because they are scattered over the country (διὰ τὸ διεσπάρθαι κατὰ τὴν χώραν, 1319 *a* 30). It would be difficult to imagine a more complete series of parallelisms in expression as well as thought.

Next, as to the *language and style* of the treatise. The vocabulary includes nine words that are not found elsewhere: these fall into two groups, (1) technical expressions, viz. ἐπιζημίωσις (45, 9, quoted from a law), ἑπτετηρίς (54, 29), ἑπτάχους (col. 34, 32), προδρομεύω (49, 6), and προεδρικός (59, 6); (2) words compounded with two prepositions, viz. ἐπεισκαλῶ and ἐπείσκλητος (30, 22—23); προσαναζητῶ (29, 16); προδιασπείρω (14, 23). The technical terms need no defence; ἑπτετηρὶς is exactly analogous to

[1] *J. H. S.* 1891, p. 21.

τριετηρὶς and πεντετηρίς, and ἑπτάχους to δίχους and ἑξάχους which occur elsewhere. Of the compound words the first three occur in quotations from public documents, and the last is supported by the analogy of προδιαβάλλειν, προδιασύρειν and προδιαχωρεῖν in the undisputed works. Double compounds are in fact characteristic of Aristotle; in the *Index Aristotelicus*, out of nine words compounded with ἐπεισ- one is found in Aristotle alone, and two others are first found in his pages; while, among the compounds with προσανα- and προσαπο-, two are found in Aristotle alone, and five are used by no earlier writer[1].

Among words that are not found in the *Index Aristotelicus* may be mentioned: κυαμεύειν, ἀνακράζειν, βῆμα, ἀντιστασιώτης, ὁμοφρονήσαντες (14, 8), ἀγηλατεῖν (20, 8). Of these ἀγηλατεῖν is obviously quoted from Herodotus; and ὁμοφρονήσαντες, which occurs four times in Herodotus (though not in the same historical connexion), comes immediately after a word borrowed from that historian. The rest are part of the necessary vocabulary of the subject, and their non-appearance in the undisputed works is merely accidental. Exception has been taken to συμβουλεύειν (c. 30, 14) as non-Aristotelian, and τούτων χάριν (29, 25) and ἐντὸς τριῶν μνῶν (49, 26) have been described as apparently un-Aristotelian[2]; but the last of these is cited from a law, and the other two are also in quotations; so that here at any rate we have no right to demand adherence to Aristotelian usage.

Among the compound verbs that are not found in any contemporary writer are καταφατίζειν, ἐπιδιανέμειν, ἐξαπορεῖν, συναρέσκεσθαι and παραστρατηγηθῆναι; and, among technical terms, ζευγίσιον, ὀστρακοφορία, ἀφέσιμος (ἡμέρα), εὐσημία, βάλανος, ἐμπήκτης, ἐπιστύλιον, ἐκθύματα (?), and ἐναγίσματα. The word προδανείζειν, which has been quoted as only used by later writers, is actually found in contemporary decrees[3]; and τριακοντόριον, which has been described as an 'entirely new word', is to be seen in contemporary inscriptions[4]. μεμψιμοιρία is not found in Aristotle, but he uses μεμψίμοιρος.

Lists of 'un-Aristotelian words and phrases' have been collected by various scholars in the *Classical Review*[5]; and many of the items in such a list will call for notice in the course of the commentary. Attention has also been drawn to the absence of certain turns of expression characteristic of the undisputed writings of Aristotle: thus in the πολιτεία

[1] Gomperz, *Anzeiger der phil.-hist. Classe*, Wien, 1891, no. xi.

[2] *Class. Rev*, v 273.

[3] The decree of Stratocles preserved in [Plut.] 852 B; and another inscr. relating to Lycurgus in CIA ii 162 *c* 7 and 9 (cf. *Class. Rev*. vi 255 *a*).

[4] Besides the inscr. of B.C. 325/4 quoted on 56, 20, we have one of 330/29 in which the word occurs twice:—cf. Boeckh's *Seeurkunden*, p. 393.

[5] v 123 (J. B. Mayor), 184 and 272 (H. Richards); 'rare words', *ib*., 229 (E. J. Chinnock). See also *Greek Index*.

'there is a good deal about democracy, but we miss the technical terms ἐσχάτη, ὑστάτη, τελευταία, ἄκρατος, δημοκρατία. Nothing is ἄτοπον, and no person or thing is either σπουδαῖος or φαῦλος'[1]. But, however acute such criticism may be, and undoubtedly is, much of its point is removed, and its edge appreciably blunted, by a frank recognition of the necessary distinction that separates the style of a popular manual like the πολιτεία from that of a philosophical investigation like the *Politics*.

To a similar cause we may ascribe the differences which may be noticed in the degree to which certain particles and conjunctions are used in the πολιτεία as compared with the undisputed works already known to us. Of the *particles*, γε is not used at all, and consequently γοῦν does not occur, τοι occurs only once in μέντοι (28, 35) where its existence is solely due to a probable, but not perfectly certain, emendation. περ is found only in καθάπερ, καίπερ, ὅσπερ, ὅσοσπερ and ὥσπερ. μὴν is only used in οὐ μὴν followed by ἀλλά. δή is rather rare, but is sometimes found after a demonstrative pronoun, once after a superlative (κάλλιστα δή 40, 17); and in several instances where τε is followed by καὶ δὴ καί; ἐπειδὴ is rare, while ἐπειδὰν is common. Of the *conjunctions*, οὖν is never used except in μὲν οὖν (hence it cannot be accepted in c. 43, 15, where καθ' ἣν οὖν καθίζει has been conjecturally proposed). ἄρα, τοίνυν, τοίγαρ, and τε γάρ, are not found. ἀλλὰ occurs some thirty times, but always after a negative. καὶ always follows διό, and nearly always follows ὅθεν, when used in the sense of διό; ἵνα is found about ten times; ὅπως seventeen times; and ὅπως ἂν twice[2].

In the undisputed works, γε and οὖν and τε γὰρ are common; ἄρα is rare in the *Politics;* τοίνυν, μέντοι and καίτοι frequent in the *Metaphysics*, *Physics* and *Politics;* yet, in the *Rhetoric*, μέντοι is found only four times; καίτοι only five. μὴν is used not only after οὐ (as in the πολιτεία), but also after ἀλλά; οὐ μὴν ἀλλά, though only found once (except in quotations) in the *Rhetoric* (1361 *a* 29), is not infrequent in the *Politics* (*e.g.* 1284 *b* 4, 1262 *a*, 1264 *a*, 1290 *b*) as in the πολιτεία. The argumentative sense of δὴ is common, but δὴ is never found after a superlative (as once in the πολιτεία); as a variation on καὶ δὴ καὶ (which also occurs in the πολιτεία) we have καὶ followed (but never *immediately* followed) by δή; ὅθεν is followed by καὶ in *Pol.* 1384 *a* 11, ὅθεν δῆλον ὅτι καί; and διὸ by καὶ in 1301 *b* 39. After final conjunctions, such as ἵνα and ὅπως, whether the tense of the principal verb be present or not, the optative is hardly ever used, but almost invariably the subjunctive[3]. Now that ἵνα μὴ συμμιγεῖέν τι has been withdrawn from

[1] *Class. Rev.* v 273 *b* (H. Richards).

[2] Cf. van Herwerden's *Index Dictionis*, s.v. 'Particulae.'

[3] The exceptions are *Pol.* 1320 *a* 35, and *Eth.* 1117 *b* 9—12. See Eucken, *De Particularum usu*, p. 53. This work

the text of c. 42, 35, the only exception to this rule in the πολιτεία is in c. 18, 30, ἵνα ἀσεβήσαιεν ἅμα καὶ γένοιντο ἀσθενεῖς, which may possibly be a quotation, as suggested by the introductory phrase, ὥς οἱ δημοτικοί φασιν. In the undisputed works ὅπως ἂν generally has a relative sense, which it does not entirely lose even when the sense appears to be final[1]; in the πολιτεία, the only instances of ὅπως ἂν are in quotations from decrees of the fifth century, in which ὅπως with the subjunctive is never found without ἂν[2]; all the other instances of ὅπως in the πολιτεία are in strict accordance with Aristotle's usage.

In the above statement such divergences as have been noticed may be fairly attributed to the different character of the works compared. There is clearly less scope for a multiplicity of particles, or of illative conjunctions (such as οὖν and τοίνυν and ἄρα), in a consecutive exposition of constitutional history and antiquities, than in the course of a philosophic discussion.

In a review of the πολιτεία it has been well observed by the latest editor of the *Politics*, that 'the style differs much from the style of the recognised works of Aristotle. It is a clear and precise, though a rather bald style, a style which has not the pregnancy which we associate with the style of Aristotle, and is also comparatively free from the ambiguities and irregularities which beset it'. But 'the work before us is a narrative and descriptive work addressed apparently...to the world at large, not to the pupils for whom the recognised works of Aristotle were probably designed, and it is not likely that it would be written in the same style'[3]. The treatise is in fact the sole representative of the more popular class of writings attributed to Aristotle, and it enables us for the first time to appreciate the justice of some of the ancient encomiums on Aristotle's style, which have hitherto been hard to reconcile with that of his abstruser works. Thus Cicero speaks of his *flumen orationis aureum*[4], and his *dicendi incredibilis copia* and *suavitas*[5]; and similar phrases are found in Dionysius of Halicarnassus and Quintilian[6]. The encomium in Cicero's *Academica* in particular may indeed owe its exaggerated form to a desire to point the contrast between the style of Aristotle and the style of the Stoics; but the general purport of these eulogies is enough to prove that, at a time when the abstruser writings of Aristotle were imperfectly known, his style enjoyed the reputation of being marked by a singular charm and

has also been used for other details in this paragraph.

[1] Eucken, p. 55.

[2] Meisterhans, *Gr. d. Att. Inschriften*, p. 212.

[3] Mr Newman in *Class. Rev.* v 159.

[4] *Acad. Prior.* ii 119.

[5] *Topica* i 3.

[6] Grote's *Ar.* i 43—47; the passages are quoted at length in my note on the *Orator* of Cic., § 62.

richness and variety. This language has been generally explained as applicable to the lost dialogues of Aristotle; but there seems no sufficient reason for refusing to recognise it as holding good in the case of other popular works, ascribed to the same author. Such a work was the Ἀθηναίων πολιτεία, and the style of that work may be fairly described as on the whole smooth and flowing, and severely graceful.

It is perhaps even more than this. It is observed by Blass that its composition is marked by a high degree of attention to laws of rhythm similar to those adopted by Isocrates, and generally approved in the third book of the *Rhetoric*. Within the compass of a single sentence we repeatedly find a series of five to twelve or more syllables immediately followed by another of identical, or nearly identical, rhythm. Many examples of this have been noticed[1] but a single instance of an exceptionally striking character may perhaps suffice for the present purpose (c. 55 § 4):—

(ἐπειδὰν) δὲ παράσχηται τοὺς μάρτυρας
ἐπ-ερωτᾷ, 'τούτου βούλεταί τις κατηγορεῖν;'
κἂν μὲν ᾖ τις κατήγορος κτλ.

Here the first word is followed by a double series of nine syllables, passing off into a double series of eight; and, within each pair of sequences, the quantities of all the syllables correspond.

The general avoidance of *hiatus* in this treatise implies that it is a finished work prepared for popular perusal and not a mere series of memoranda (or ὑπομνήματα) for personal use. This point was observed by Blass even in the scanty remains preserved in the Berlin fragments, and also by Mr Newman in the case of the work as a whole. It has since been investigated more minutely by Mr J. W. Headlam in the *Classical Review*.

He shows (1) that a definite principle is observed throughout the greater part of the work. (α) as a general rule *hiatus* occurs only after the article, after numerals, after καί, διά and περί[2], and after words in which the last vowel is readily elided *e.g.* δέ, τε, τινα, ἔπειτα, εἶτα, ἀλλά, μηδέ, μήτε, πάντα, σφόδρα, μάλιστα. *Hiatus* is avoided at a pause, as well as in the middle of a sentence. (β) In quoted documents the rule does not hold (contrast c. 28 with latter part of c. 29). Nor (γ) in certain technical expressions, such as indications of dates, *e.g.* εὐθὺς δὲ τῷ ὑστέρῳ ἔτει ἐπὶ Τελεσίνου ἄρχοντος (22, 21); constitutional terms, *e.g.* ἡ βουλὴ ἡ ἐξ Ἀρείου πάγου (4, 20); and legal phrases, *e.g.* περὶ τοῦ δοῦναι τὰ ἑαυτοῦ ᾧ ἂν ἐθέλῃ (35, 14) and μὴ εἶναι ἐλεύθερον (42, 8). To these may be added ᾗ (or ᾧ) ὄνομα (14, 27; 17, 13).

(2) The exceptions are very unevenly distributed. A list of all that occur in the first part (cc. 1—41) shows that, at the beginning, clear and undoubted exceptions are very rare: in cc. 1—14 § 3 (omitting c. 7, 21—30), there are only five. In the second part, the first few pages are as free as any in the first part; then cases become more

[1] Blass, *Praef.* xvi—xxv.

[2] Also after ἤ, εἰ and μή.

frequent, and at the end the rule is almost completely neglected. The author had to insert so many technical expressions that he gave up troubling about the matter. In the first part the more striking exceptions often occur directly after a quotation (c. 32 § 1). In the first part at least, no conjectural emendation should be accepted which violates *hiatus*.

The rule is much laxer than that of the school of Isocrates. Hence the work was not written by any member of that school. On the other hand there is considerable evidence that it is from the hand of Aristotle himself, for the usage in this matter is very nearly the same as that of some of his best authenticated works[1].

While it cannot have been written by any of the Isocratean school it exhibits the same familiarity with the works of Isocrates as that displayed by Aristotle himself[2]. A passage that reminds us of the *Gorgias* is introduced by the characteristic τινες, which is Aristotle's favourite way of referring to Plato in the *Politics*[3].

Thus far I have endeavoured to state the internal evidence in favour of accepting the treatise as being substantially the work of Aristotle. It is impossible, however, to ignore the fact that not a few highly competent scholars at home and abroad hesitate to accept it as such[4]. Doubtless, in its manner of dealing with matters of history and particularly of chronology, side by side with much minuteness of detail on the subject of dates, there is evidence of occasional carelessness. There is sometimes a certain lack of intellectual force and vigour. And, further, there is an absence of those long and tangled sentences in which Aristotle, as we have hitherto known him, reviews and discusses a rapid succession of difficulties, doubts, and contradictions amid frequent irregularities of construction and amid repeated violations of his own rule against the use of parenthesis (*Rhet.* iii 5 § 7).

Much, perhaps too much, has been made of such points, and in consequence some have been disposed to regard the treatise as simply a product of the Peripatetic School, the work of some pupil writing with or without the general guidance and direction of Aristotle. It must, however, be remembered that, even in the case of works which are without question accepted as Aristotle's, it is extremely difficult to determine how far they were actually composed by him in the form in which they have reached us; how far they are merely notes of his oral teaching, not given to the world in his lifetime, but revised and edited after his death by the industry and devotion of his pupils and successors. Of the usually accepted works of Aristotle it is doubtful whether any one, as a whole, passed beyond the limits of the lecture-room during

[1] *Class. Rev.* v 270—2.

[2] See notes on 26 § 2 ult., and 35 § 4 ult., and Newman in *Class. Rev.* v 160—1.

[3] See note on 26, 23 χείρους γενέσθαι.

[4] *e. g.* the Dutch editors; also F. Cauer and F. Rühl; and in England Mr H. Richards and several other contributors to the *Classical Review*.

the life of its author. 'Portions of the *Metaphysics* and *de Caelo*, some at least of the *Parva Naturalis*, the two books περὶ φιλίας, now included in the Nicomachean *Ethics*, and the two books on the ideal state, *Politics* vii (iv) and viii (v), may have first seen the light in some other form during the lifetime of Aristotle.[1]' On the other hand, the Πολιτεῖαι (like the *Dialogues*) 'would have been very likely to see the light early, for they were on a subject of far greater general interest than most of Aristotle's works...It could only be through his *Dialogues* and Πολιτεῖαι that he could hope to be immediately known to a wide circle of non-philosophic readers. If he were during his lifetime something more than the revered teacher of a limited circle of pupils, we may safely assume that the publication took place.[2]'

The above remarks are quoted from the work of an Aristotelian scholar of the highest promise, whose *History of the Aristotelian Writings* was published in 1888, after his own death, and several years before the discovery of the Ἀθηναίων πολιτεία. The inference there drawn on grounds of *a priori* probability, as regards the Πολιτεῖαι in general, is conclusively confirmed by the internal evidence of the date of the Ἀθηναίων πολιτεία in particular. It was certainly written, and probably published, before the death of Aristotle.

I may also appeal to the same unimpeachable testimony as to the exact degree of value to be attached to the evidence afforded by the avoidance of *hiatus*:—

> 'Wherever it occurs, we have a work, or a portion of a work, in exactly the state which was given to it by the author who threw it into its present form. As to whether this author was or was not Aristotle himself, a good deal may be said on either side.'
>
> On the one hand, 'the Aristotle whom we know shows the most absolute contempt for all matters of style,' and seems little likely to have adopted the Isocratean rule of avoiding *hiatus*. On the other, there is 'nothing wonderful or difficult in keeping one style for oral lectures and another for published books. Still less wonderful would it be if there was a wide difference to be found between mere notes for such lectures and deliberately finished publications[3].'

Assuming, as we fairly may, that the Ἀθηναίων πολιτεία was a work of Aristotelian origin, it may still remain uncertain whether it was prepared for publication by the great teacher himself, or by some unknown and unnamed pupil who was skilled in certain graces of style that were apt to win the popular ear. The latter hypothesis might help to account for certain divergencies from the diction of the generally accepted works of Aristotle. To the interposition of such an editor we might perhaps attribute the general smoothness of style that marks its composition.

[1] Shute, *History of the Aristotelian Writings*, p. 23.

[2] Shute, p. 23.

[3] Shute, p. 165 f.

To the same source we might possibly trace certain inaccuracies of historical statement that tend to impair the authority of the work. But even Aristotle himself may have been quite capable of making a mistake in matters of history. The 'master of those who know' was not necessarily omniscient.

It must also be admitted that works like the Πολιτεῖαι, owing to the miscellaneous character of their contents, were, in their transmission from age to age, peculiarly liable to interpolation. It has even been suggested that, like the *History of Animals* and the ἱστορίαι generally, 'they represent not any fixed work of Aristotle or of anyone else, but merely a continuously open note-book'[1]. The Ἀθηναίων πολιτεία may have suffered to some extent from this cause of corruption.

The difficulties as to the authorship of the treatise appear to be fairly met by an eminent Transatlantic scholar who expresses his opinion as follows:

'We are compelled to believe, from many indications, that it was written mainly by Aristotle, with perhaps the help of a pupil who prepared certain of the less important passages, the padding as it were; the work was then revised, but not rewritten, by him. If we are ready to maintain—a proposition by no means self-evident—that the main body of the writings current as Aristotle's are the genuine works of the master in their original form, and that, accordingly, they are the only norm by which everything else is to be tested, we may still account for the "non-Aristotelian" peculiarities of the language of the Ἀθηναίων πολιτεία as due, in part, to the fact that the historical sources (epigraphic and literary) are often given in verbal quotations, or at least in paraphrases that retain original forms of expression; due in part, perhaps, to tne stylistic idiosyncrasies of an assistant whose work was incorporated with the master's, and finally to the most significant fact that the work was intended not for the scientific inner circle, but for the general reader'...

'The evidence, internal and external, of essentially Aristotelian authorship, as well as authority, seems so overwhelming, that, as between the two alternatives, one should prefer to modify his conceptions of Aristotle than reject this treatise. As Diels[2] has pointedly phrased it:—*Diese* Ἀθηναίων πολιτεία [*ist*] *nicht nur echt aristotelisch sondern aristotelischer als die meisten der uns erhaltenen Lehrbücher an welcher sich jene Skeptiker halten*'[3].

If we now revert to the evidence of ancient writers who, either directly or indirectly, quote the Ἀθηναίων πολιτεία as the work of Aristotle, we find that, out of 56 fragments in which the Ἀθηναίων πολιτεία is expressly mentioned, 53 are found in our MS; of the remaining three, one (*Frag*[8]. 385) belongs to the lost beginning, one (463) to the mutilated end; the third (447) is an inaccurate transcript of c. 54 § 2. Of the 35 fragments in which Aristotle is named without any express mention of the work, 25 are found in the MS; of the remainder, three belong to the lost beginning (381, 384, and the new fragment on p. 253,

[1] Shute, p. 72.
[2] *Archiv f. Gesch. d. Philos.*, iv, p. 479.
[3] Prof. J. H. Wright, *The Date of Cylon*, p. 22 f.

l. 50); seven probably do not come from this work at all (382, 386, 392, 399, 401, 415, and part of 394); one (456) may possibly have come from the mutilated end of the work; and one (396) is a misquotation of the text, which can readily be brought into harmony with it. Thus, of the total number of 93 fragments (of which 86 are probably genuine references to this work), 78 are found in the MS, and all the rest are satisfactorily accounted for[1]. More than 50 of the fragments of the πολιτεία are preserved by Harpocration alone, and all of these are found in the MS.

Lastly, the Berlin fragments are all here. These fragments correspond to the following passages in the text:

I *a* begins before δουλευόντων and ends with ἀνδρῶν, c. 12, 26—52.

I *b* begins before ἄρχοντα and ends with χρέα, c. 13, 4—22.

II *a* begins before Ἀθηναῖοι and ends after φυλῆς ἑκάστης, c. 21, 18—c. 22, 10.

II *b* begins before Ἵππαρχος and ends after τριήρεις, c. 22, 19—37.

In I *a* the long Iambic passage is written as consecutive prose, and I *b* is less complete than II *a* and *b*. Hence it is difficult to found any calculation on leaf I. But the contents of leaf II are equivalent to 44 lines of print in the present edition. Hence one page is equivalent to about 22 (say 24) lines of print. The number of lines of print now lost between the bottom of leaf I and the top of leaf II is 240 (4 + 30 + 26 + 44 + 18 + 38 + 39 + 23 + 18). Thus it is not improbable that the lost portion is equivalent to 10 pages, and that the MS was made up of gatherings of 12 pages each. The number of lines in our printed text preceding I *a* is 245, which would take up only 10 pages. Hence the first two pages of the lost MS to which the Berlin fragments belong, were either left blank, or they actually contained the beginning of the treatise. If the latter, then the amount of the Ἀθ. πολ. which is now lost is equivalent to about 44 to 48 lines of the present edition.

§ 8. *Authorities followed in the* Ἀθηναίων πολιτεία.

The only authors actually named by the writer are Solon and Herodotus. From SOLON he quotes a large number of verses, most of them already familiar to us through Aristides, who shows no proof of any acquaintance with the poems of Solon, beyond that which he derived from the present work. The writer's debt to HERODOTUS is far larger than appears at first sight. He only mentions the historian once (c. 14), but he closely follows him in the account of Peisistratus and Cleisthenes (cc. 14, 15, 20), though not without interesting variations. He also borrows from THUCYDIDES, while deliberately differing from him on several important points in the story of Harmodius and Aristogeiton (c. 18). He coincides with the historian in many parts of his narrative of the revolution of the Four Hundred (cc. 29, 33); but the

[1] The same facts have been duly stated by Mr Kenyon in his *Introduction*, p. xv; revised in ed. 3, p. xvi.

coincidence is not complete, and the writer quotes original documents which are not quoted by the historian. As regards XENOPHON, we find a close resemblance in the account of the speech of Theramenes (c. 36) and elsewhere; at the same time, the divergences are sufficiently numerous to suggest that the authority followed here was the same as that followed at a later date by Diodorus Siculus. This authority has sometimes been supposed to have been the *Hellenica* of Theopompus[1]; it has also been suggested that the writer owes to another work of Theopompus, the tenth book of his *Philippica*, his list of the Athenian demagogues, and his portrait of Cleon. It is just possible that the exaggerated account of the generosity of Cimon, which appeared in that work, is tacitly corrected in c. 27 § 3. But there is reason to believe that Theopompus did not publish his work until 324, after Alexander's departure from India; if so, it was later than the *πολιτεία*. The common source, followed by Diodorus as well as the writer, was more probably EPHORUS, who is expressly mentioned by Diodorus[2].

As regards the writer's relation to the various writers of Ἀτθίδες, there is no trace of any indebtedness to Hellanicus, whose carelessness on points of chronology[3] would have been enough to prevent his being trusted by a writer who usually aims at being precise in matters of chronological detail. To CLEIDEMUS, the next in order of time, we may probably attribute the Ionism in c. 14 § 4, where the form *παραιβατούσης* appears to be an echo of *παραιβατήσασαν* in Cleidemus' description of the stately woman who assumed the garb of Athene and rode in the chariot of Peisistratus on the occasion of his first restoration to Athens. The account of the disciplinary powers entrusted to the Areopagus (c. § 6), bears some resemblance to a passage attributed to PHANODEMUS; but a statement to the same effect is attributed to a writer of the next generation to that of Aristotle, namely Philochorus, who may, however, have borrowed his phraseology from Phanodemus. In any case, the resemblance between the passage in the *πολιτεία* and that attributed to 'Phanodemus and Philochorus' is not sufficiently close to make it quite certain that the writer was following Phanodemus[4].

ANDROTION may be identified with the person attacked in the 22nd speech of Demosthenes; he may therefore be placed earlier than the age of Aristotle. If so, he is closely followed in the account of the ostracism of Hipparchus son of Charmus (22 § 3); and the statement as to the number of the *συγγραφεῖς* in c. 29 § 2 is in accordance

[1] Th. Reinach's *Transl.* of 'Αθ. πολ., p xxiv.

[2] xiv 11 and 22; Bauer, *Forschungen*, p. 155. Theopompus, in Pollux, v 43.

[3] Thuc. i 97, *βραχέως τε καὶ τοῖς χρόνοις οὐκ ἀκριβῶς*.

[4] See note on p. 12 *a*.

with that of Androtion. But the writer differs from Androtion as to the nature of Solon's σεισάχθεια, without going out of his way to controvert it. Here, as sometimes elsewhere, he is only tacitly polemical.

The most famous of the writers of Ἀτθίδες, Philochorus, belongs to the age after that of Aristotle, and has several points in common with the writer of the πολιτεία. As has been shown by Professor Wright, it is not improbable that he actually quoted the latter and accepted it as the work of Aristotle[1].

On the relations subsisting between the Ἀθηναίων πολιτεία and the *Atthidographi*, I may be allowed to quote some criticisms for which I am indebted to the kindness of Mr W. L. Newman.

It is remarkable that while, in the *Politics*, there is little to remind us of the writings of the *Atthidographi*, in the πολιτεία there is much. This indeed holds good of the Πολιτεῖαι generally. No doubt it is not unnatural that the 'Constitutions' ascribed to Aristotle, containing as they do sketches of local history, should follow the model furnished by local histories like the *Atthides;* still it is strange that, if Aristotle was the author of these 'Constitutions,' he should be so little influenced by the *Atthides* in the *Politics*, if indeed he is so at all. Readers of the πολιτεία, on the contrary, find it hard to avoid the suspicion that some *Atthis* has been largely used by the writer, very possibly the *Atthis* of Androtion. We may note the following resemblances between the Ἀθ. πολ. and the other Πολιτεῖαι ascribed to Aristotle on the one hand, and the writings of the *Atthidographi* on the other:—

(1) The Ἀθ. πολ. is up to the mark of the last new historical fashion in respect of chronological exactitude. No doubt the effort to be chronologically exact is traceable early in the development of Greek historical literature. Thucydides knows the date of the fall of Troy (i 12), and the approximate date of the founding of Melos (v 112). Still the passion for chronological exactitude increased during the fourth century B.C. and later; for instance, Ephorus (*Frag.* 9 *a*) and Callisthenes knew that Troy was taken on the 23rd of Thargelion. As to Timaeus see Diod. v 1 and Polyb. xii 10. Nothing of this care for exactness in dates appears in the *Politics* or in other recognised writings of Aristotle. The writer of the Ἀθ. πολ., again, often dates by archons, but Aristotle never does so in the *Politics*. This dating by archons was perhaps no new thing in historical writing; some think that Hellanicus reckoned by archons, but here again we have an Atthidographic feature. Androtion and Philochorus reckoned by archons (Busolt, *Gr. Gesch.* i 363, note 4); see also Philoch. *Frag.* 52 (where Philochorus knows in whose archonship at Athens Homer flourished) and Androt. *Frag.* 46.

(2) The Ἀθ. πολ. and other Constitutions ascribed to Aristotle resemble the *Atthides* in the interest they show in the origin of words and familiar phrases. See Ἀθ. πολ. c. 2, 5; 6, 12; 13, 25; 21, 6 and 21; 45, 7 &c.; and Aristotle's Constitutions (*Frag*³. 477, 484, 488, 491, 495, 512, 514, 519, 536, 562, 580, 582, 595, 596); and compare Androtion, *Frag.* 28—29, 33: Phanodem. *Frag.* 1, 13, 14: Ister, *Frag.* 28, 32, 35, 39, 43, 52, 57: Philoch. *Frag.* 4, 5, 6, 7, 10, 12, 16, 42, 48 and many others. The interest which the Ἀθ. πολ. and the other Constitutions show in these matters is a good deal more marked than that which we trace in Aristotle's recognised works, and the same may be said of

[1] *American Journal of Philology*, xii 310 f.; *supra*, p. xix f.

(3) the interest which the Ἀθ. πολ. and other Constitutions share with the *Atthides* in (A) the origin of institutions and the like, and (B) the explanation of proverbs.

As to (A), compare Ἀθ. πολ. c. 8, 3 and *passim*, and Aristotle's Constitutions, *Frag*.[3] 475, 479, 501, 511, 519, with Philoch. *Frag*. 51, 56, 66, 189.

As to (B), see Ἀθ. πολ. c. 16, 18; 21, 6 &c., and Aristotle's Constitutions, *Frag*.[3] 487, 505, 513, 523, 528, 545, 558, 559, 571, 584, 591, 592. Demon, one of the *Atthidographi*, wrote a book about Proverbs (Müller, FHG i 379).

In choosing his authorities and in deciding between them when they differ, the author is guided by the consideration of the comparative probability of the accounts before him. He repels the calumnies against Solon (6) and Theramenes (28); and, in the story of Harmodius and Aristogeiton, gives an adequate reason for not accepting an opinion sanctioned by Thucydides (18 § 4). On the other hand, he is himself far from infallible as a historian. There is much confusion in the chronology of the years between the archonship of Solon and that of Damasias II (p. 50); and in that of the times of Peisistratus (p. 56). The presence of Themistocles in Athens in 462 seems impossible to reconcile with the chronology of his later years suggested by the *data* in Thucydides (p. 101); and there are several grave inaccuracies in the brief allusion to the trial of the generals after the battle of Arginusae (p. 129).

Besides relying on the testimony of Solon's poems, the writer draws inferences from popular poetry such as the *scolium* in honour of Cedon and that on the baffled heroes of Leipsydrium (cc. 19, 20). He quotes archaeological evidence derived from the κύρβεις of Solon (7 § 1), from the prae-Solonian coinage (c. 10), and from a relief and inscription on the Acropolis (7 § 4). He alludes to proverbial phrases, χωρίον ἀτελές (16 § 6) and μὴ φυλοκρινεῖν (21 § 2). He also takes special pains in quoting official documents[1].

The decrees proposed by Aristion (14 § 1) and Themistocles (22 § 7) are noticed in general terms; that proposed by Pericles in 451—0 (26 ult.), is expressly quoted. The official documents cited *in extenso* are those connected with the revolution of the Four Hundred in 413; viz. the motion of Pythodorus for the appointment of 30 συγγραφεῖς, with the amendment by Cleitophon; the formal record of the preliminary

[1] In these quotations we find a minute but not uninteresting proof of his fidelity: in the whole work, out of 17 instances of ὅπως with subjunctive or with future indicative, we have only two of ὅπως ἂν with the subjunctive (29, 24, and 30, 20); both of these occur in decrees of the fifth century, and the inscriptions of that century give us 16 instances of ὅπως ἄν, and none of ὅπως with the subjunctive. In view of this fact it is clear that in 29, 18 ὅπως ἀκούσαντες is only a copyist's mistake for ὅπως ἄν. This is noticed by Prof. Wright in *The Nation*, 1 May, 1891, p. 383. It must not, however, be inferred that ὅπως c. fut. is not found in inscriptions: on the contrary it is very common (Meisterhans, note 1705[2]).

proposals and of the constitution drawn up by the συγγραφεῖς (c. 29); with the ultimate and the provisional constitutions drawn up by the hundred Commissioners (cc. 30, 31). We have also the terms of the reconciliation effected between the oligarchical and democratic parties in 403 (c. 39). These documents were presumably preserved among the archives of the State in the *Metroon;* but they probably owed their publication not only to their historical importance, but also to their including typical forms of oligarchical constitutions which afforded suitable themes for discussion among students of the theory of politics. The writer's evident interest in the detailed history of the period between B.C. 413 and 403 is one of the considerations in favour of identifying him with the author of the *Politics*. In the latter Aristotle selects the Revolution of the Four Hundred as a typical instance of a revolution effected by fraud on the part of those who, when the deception is over, still endeavour to retain the government by force (1304 *b* 12, quoted on c. 29, 8). Elsewhere, while discussing revolutions in oligarchies arising within the governing class, he mentions, as first of the two types of the oligarchical demagogue, 'one who practises on the oligarchs themselves; for, although the oligarchy are quite a small number, there may be a demagogue among them, as at Athens the party of Charicles predominated among the Thirty, that of Phrynichus in the Four Hundred' (1305 *b* 24—27). It is, however, only fair to add that neither Phrynichus nor Charicles is mentioned in the πολιτεία.

In the absence of direct historical evidence, the writer's favourite form of argument is that indicated by Mr Macan in an interesting contribution to the *Journal of Hellenic Studies*. 'The author has a source of knowledge, or rather a method of reconstruction, to take the place of direct testimony, tradition or evidence. This method consists in a process of inference from the present to the past, from existing circumstances to their presumable antecedents, from a given state of institutions to a former condition of the same'.[1] As instances in which the author mentions the employment of this method by others, we have (1) the oaths of the nine Archons (3 § 3); and (2) the property qualification of the ἱππεῖς (7 § 4). He uses it himself in cases such as the following: (1) the sacral marriage of the βασίλιννα (3 § 5); (2) the Solonian method of appointing officials (8 § 1); (3) the institution of the οἱ κατὰ δήμους δικασταί by Peisistratus (16 § 5); and (4) the motive for the institution of ostracism by Cleisthenes (22 § 3)[2].

[1] *J. H. S.* 1891, p. 37.

[2] *ib.* p. 38. For some of the 'signals of this method,' cf. note on 8 § 1, p. 30, ὅθεν ἔτι διαμένει.

§ 9. *Abstract of the* Ἀθηναίων πολιτεία.

The work is divided into two parts, (I) a Sketch of the Constitutional History of Athens down to the Restoration of the Democracy in 403 B.C. (cc. 1—41); and (II) a detailed analysis of the machinery of the Constitution between 328 and 325 B.C. (c. 42 to the end). The first has been well described as a 'Primer of Constitutional History'; the second, as a 'Citizen's Handbook.'[1]

Part I, in its complete form, comprised an account of the 'original constitution' of Athens, and of the eleven changes through which it successively passed (c. 41). Accordingly, in the following abstract, we have to deal with a series of twelve constitutions.

(1) *The constitution in the time of Ion.* The original constitution of Athens was an absolute monarchy. In process of time, owing to some of the hereditary line of kings being feeble in war, ION, the son of Apollo by the daughter of an Attic king, was summoned to their aid, and invested with military command. Such was the origin of the office of *Polemarch*, which was second to that of *Basileus* in order of date (3 § 2). In the days of Ion, the people were divided into four tribes, with four φυλοβασιλεῖς or 'tribal kings' (41, 6—9). To Apollo's son, the first Polemarch, the Athenians owed the name of Ionians and the worship of Apollo πατρῷος (frag. 381[3]).

(2) *The constitution in the time of Theseus.* Under THESEUS, we are simply told that the constitution exhibited a slight divergence from absolute monarchy (41, 10; and frag. 384[3]).

[About 1088 B.C., on the death of Codrus, and the accession of his son Medon, the kingly power ceased to be hereditary. Henceforth the kings were elected for life from members of the royal house.][2] By the side of the King, the *Polemarch* was already in existence as commander in the time of war; and in the reign either of Medon, or his son Acastus, a third office, that of *Archon*, came into being, and was endowed with some of the royal prerogatives by the descendants of Codrus (3 § 3). In process of time the name of Archon was transferred from the third officer of State to the first [c. 753/2 B.C.]. The chief Archon was elected [from the royal house], but his term of office was limited to ten years (3 § 1 end), while the title of King, with the privilege of attending to certain religious duties, was assigned to another archon, called the *Basileus*. It was not until the three primary offices of State, those of Archon, Polemarch and Basileus, had become annual [c. 683/2 B.C.], that their number was increased by the institution of the six *Thesmothetae*, whose duty it was to record and preserve all legal decisions with a view to their being enforced against transgressors of the law (3 § 4). In the course of time the Archons were elected by the Council of the Areopagus (8 § 2) under qualifications of birth and wealth (3 § 1), while the Areopagus itself was composed of those who had filled the office of Archon.

[1] *Cambridge Review*, 20 Feb. 1891, p. 212 *a*.

[2] Throughout this abstract, dates and other items derived from sources extraneous to the treatise itself are distinguished by being placed within brackets. Such items generally represent the traditional accounts of Attic history accepted (whether rightly or wrongly) by the Athenians themselves.—The dates in this paragraph depend mainly on the *Marmor Parium* (Busolt, *Gr. Gesch.*, i 404[1]).

It was the duty of the Areopagus to maintain the supremacy of law, to inflict personal punishments and fines, and to administer the State in general (3 § 6).

[In an Olympic year between 636 and 624 B.C.] an attempt to seize despotic power was made by a young nobleman named Cylon [who had been a victor in the Olympic games of 640]. The attempt was unsuccessful: the adherents of Cylon were put to death under the authority of the Archon Megacles, of the house of the Alcmaeonidae, who violated their right of sanctuary and thus brought a curse on Athens and his descendants (*Heracl. Epit.* § 4).

The constitution at this time was thoroughly oligarchical. There was a conflict between the various orders in the State: the land was in the hands of a few; discontent prevailed among the poor, who, if they failed to pay their rent, became the slaves of the rich (c. 2).

(3) *The Constitution of Dracon.* It was with a view to providing a remedy for these evils that (in 621 B.C.) the first code of law was drawn up by DRACON (41, 11). The franchise was at this time possessed by all who could provide their own equipment for war. It was these who elected the Archons and other principal officers of State; and out of their own body a Council of 401 members was appointed by lot from among those who had attained the age of 30. Members of the Council were liable to fines varying with their social status. The Council of the Areopagus continued to maintain the supremacy of law and the efficient discharge of the duties assigned to the officers of State; it also received formal complaints from persons aggrieved by the infringement of any statute (c. 4).

In due time the friends of the exiled members of Cylon's party acquired sufficient power to compel the Alcmaeonidae to submit to a trial before a special court of 300 citizens selected from the noblest families of Athens. They were found guilty; the dead bodies of the offenders were cast out, and their surviving relatives condemned to perpetual exile. Athens was further purified from the curse of sacrilege by Epimenides (c. 1).[1]

(4) *The Constitution of Solon.* Dracon's legislation having failed to remedy the wrongs of the poor, the conflict of the orders broke out afresh and was not allayed until [c. 594 B.C.] both parties agreed on choosing SOLON as mediator and as Archon (5 § 2). Solon cancelled all existing debts, whether public or private; and for the future he made it illegal to lend money on the security of the person of the debtor (6 § 1). With the exception of the laws on homicide, the code of Dracon was repealed, and a new code published. The people were divided into four classes, *Pentacosiomedimni*, *Hippeis*, *Zeugitae*, and *Thetes;* the various offices of State being now assigned to the first three classes in proportion to the amount at which they were severally rated, while the fourth class had only the right of taking part in the public Assembly and in the Law-courts (c. 7). The nine Archons were now appointed by lot, out of forty selected candidates, nominated to the number of ten by each of the four tribes. A Council of 400 was also constituted, 100 from each tribe. The Areopagus, which still retained the duty of supervising the laws and maintaining the constitution in general, was now empowered to try cases of treason (c. 8). In Solon's constitution the specially democratical elements were:—(1) the prohibition of loans on the security of the person; (2) the privilege of every citizen to claim legal satisfaction on behalf of any one who was wronged; and (3) the right of appeal to the law-courts. The power of voting in the law-courts made the com-

[1] On the date of Epimenides, see p. 3, and cf. Prof. Wright's *Date of Cylon*, pp. 70 and 74, where the visit of Epimenides, as well as the trial of the Alcmaeonidae, is conjecturally assigned to 615 B.C.

mons master of the constitution (c. 9). Solon also introduced a new standard of coinage, and of weights and measures (c. 10). His legislation, however, did not prove acceptable to either of the two great parties in the State. Finding himself beset and harassed by both, and declining to make himself despot at the expense of either, he withdrew for ten years to Egypt (c. 11).

When he had gone abroad, although the State was still disturbed by divisions, they lived in peace for four years; but, in the next year, and again four years later, their divisions prevented the election of an Archon. After another term of four years(?), the choice fell on Damasias [582], who succeeded in remaining in office for two years and two months. The interval of civil strife was closed by an agreement to elect ten Archons from the several orders in the State, five from the *Eupatridae*, three from the *Agroeci*, and two from the *Demiurgi*. But the general discontent was not allayed. Some of the rich had lost their wealth; others had lost their political power; a few besides were inspired by personal ambition. At this time the three parties of the Shore, the Plain and the Highlands, representing the moderate, the oligarchical and the democratic spirit respectively, were under the leadership of Megacles, Lycurgus, and Peisistratus. The party of Peisistratus was reinforced by those whom Solon's legislation had deprived of the debts due to them, and also by persons whose dubious birth gave them an uncertain claim to the rights of citizenship (c. 13). These struggles found their issue in the tyranny of Peisistratus and his sons.

(5) *The tyranny of Peisistratus and his sons.* PEISISTRATUS, who had won distinction in the war against Megara, persuaded the people to grant him the protection of a body-guard, and with the aid of the latter seized the Acropolis (560 B.C.). He ruled in a constitutional spirit; but, five years later, he was expelled by a coalition between the parties of Megacles and Lycurgus. Eleven(?) years afterwards he was restored by the aid of Megacles on condition of marrying his daughter (14). This condition was only nominally fulfilled; and, about six years later, he was once more expelled. He withdrew to Macedonia, where he acquired money and mercenary troops. Ten years subsequently, with the help of Thebes, of Lygdamis of Naxos, and the Knights of Eretria, he recovered his power and disarmed his subjects (15). His rule, however, was mild and humane. To encourage agriculture he advanced money to the poorer classes, with a view to their staying in the country and looking after their own affairs instead of coming into the town and taking part in public business. With the same object he instituted 'local justices,' and himself visited various parts of the country, thus making it unnecessary for the tenants to neglect their farms by bringing their grievances to Athens. Besides this, the cultivation of the soil promoted an increase in his revenues (16).

Peisistratus died in 527/6 B.C., having held actual possession of his power for nineteen out of the thirty-three years that had elapsed since he had originally established himself as 'tyrant' (c. 17). He was succeeded by his sons Hippias and Hipparchus, who at first ruled in their father's spirit; but, when Hipparchus had been slain in the conspiracy of Harmodius and Aristogeiton (c. 18), the rule of Hippias became more severe. Three years afterwards (c. 19 § 2) he was expelled by Cleomenes, king of Sparta (in the spring of 510 B.C.).

(6) *The Reforms of Cleisthenes.* After the overthrow of the tyranny the rival leaders in the State were Isagoras, an adherent of the tyrants, and CLEISTHENES, of the house of the Alcmaeonidae. Isagoras invited the aid of Cleomenes. Thereupon Cleisthenes withdrew, while Cleomenes vainly endeavoured to supersede the Council and to set up a body of 300 partisans of Isagoras in its place. Cleisthenes soon returned, and became leader of the people (c. 20). In 508 B.C. he distributed the population

into ten tribes instead of the existing four; and instituted a Council of 500 (fifty out of each of the ten new tribes), in place of that of 400 (100 out of each of the four tribes). He also made the deme the unit of his social organisation, combined the demes into groups (τριττύες), and assigned these groups to the several tribes in such a manner that each tribe had three groups allotted to it, one from the urban or suburban district, one from the coast, and one from the interior (c. 21). The reforms of Cleisthenes made the constitution more democratic than that of Solon. Among the laws now passed was that concerning Ostracism, which was at first intended to serve as a safeguard against the reestablishment of a tyranny. In 504 B.C. [or, more probably, in 501], the oath, which was still in use in the writer's time, was first imposed on the Council. The Generals were elected according to tribes, one from each tribe (22 § 2). The law of Ostracism was enforced for the first time in 488/7, two years after Marathon, the person ostracised being Hipparchus son of Charmus (§ 4); he was followed in 487/6 by Megacles [a nephew of Cleisthenes], by Xanthippus [the father of Pericles] in 485/4, and about 484/3 by Aristides. Meanwhile, in 487/6, for the first time since the establishment of the tyranny, the nine Archons were appointed by lot out of 500 [or more probably, 100] candidates selected by the demes. In 483/2, on the discovery of certain silver mines in Attica, Themistocles persuaded the people to lend the proceeds to the hundred wealthiest men in Attica, and thus brought about the building of the hundred triremes, with which the battle of Salamis was won [480].

(7) *The supremacy of the Areopagus.* Thus far the growth of the democracy had been advancing with the gradual growth of Athens; but, after the Persian wars, the Council of the Areopagus once more assumed the control of the State. It owed this high position, however, not to any formal decree, but to the spirited action it had taken in connexion with the battle of Salamis. When the Generals were unable to cope with the crisis, it was the Areopagus that provided pay for the crews, and thus ensured the manning of the fleet and the gaining of the victory (23 § 1). The leaders of the people at this time were ARISTIDES and THEMISTOCLES. On the establishment of the Confederacy of Delos, Aristides assessed the amount to be paid to the common fund by the allies of Athens, beginning with the year 478/7 (§ 5). By his advice the inhabitants of Attica left the rural districts and settled in the city, on the assurance that all of them would be able to maintain themselves by the discharge of military duties or by taking part in public affairs, and would thus secure the control of the league. Thus it was that Athens came to adopt the policy of oppressing her allies, from which Chios, Lesbos and Samos alone were exempt.

(8) *The restored and developed democracy.* The supremacy of the Areopagus lasted for about seventeen years (478 to 462 inclusive). The power of the people was meanwhile increasing, and EPHIALTES, on becoming their leader, attacked the Areopagus, by depriving it of all the more recent privileges by which it had attained the control of the constitution, transferring some of them to the Council of Five Hundred, and others to the Assembly and the Law-courts (462 B.C.). In this revolution he was aided by Themistocles (25).

Thereupon the administration of the State became more and more lax owing to the rivalries that arose between successive aspirants for popular favour. At this time the aristocratical party had no real chief, although their leader was Cimon, who was comparatively young for that position, and had been rather late in entering on public life. In 457/6 the office of Archon was thrown open to the *Zeugitae.* In 453/2 the thirty 'local justices' were restored; and in 451/0, on the proposal of PERICLES, it was enacted that the franchise should be limited to those who were of citizen blood by both parents (26). Under Pericles, the constitution became still more democratic. He deprived the Areopagus of some of its ancient privileges, and also prompted Athens to aim at the empire of the sea (27 § 1). The Peloponnesian war (B.C. 431—) inured the people to military service, and led to their assuming the administration of the State (§ 2). Pericles was also the first to provide pay for serving in the Law-courts (§ 3).

So long as he was leader of the people, public affairs were managed comparatively well; at his death there was a great change for the worse (28 § 1). It was then that, for the first time, in the person of Cleon, the people had for their leader one who was of no reputation among the upper classes (§ 2); on the other side, the leader of the aristocracy was Nicias. These two were succeeded by Cleophon and Theramenes respectively. It was Cleophon who was the first to provide each citizen with the grant of two obols for a seat in the theatre (§ 3); and the series of demagogues, who succeeded him, owed their position to their recklessness of language, and to their readiness to gratify the immediate desires of the populace (§ 4). Of the leaders of the aristocratical party, Nicias and Thucydides (son of Melesias) are justly esteemed as statesmen. Concerning Theramenes there is a conflict of opinion; but, on calm reflexion, it is clear that, so far from subverting every kind of constitution, he really supported each in turn, so long as it was faithful to the laws; thus proving that, like a good citizen, he was capable of living in contentment under any form of government, while he could never be a party to unconstitutional conduct, but on the contrary was always its resolute foe (§ 5)[1].

(9) *The revolution of the Four Hundred.* After the failure of the Sicilian expedition [Sept. 413], when the power of Sparta had been increased by her alliance with Persia, Athens was compelled to abolish her democracy and to accept the oligarchical revolution of the Four Hundred. At this crisis it was proposed by Pythodorus that the popular Assembly should elect a Committee of thirty in all, to draw up proposals for the public safety; and that any other person might make such proposals as he pleased, so that the people might decide on whatever course it thought fit (29 §§ 1, 2). An amendment moved [and probably carried] by Cleitophon made it an instruction to the Committee to take into consideration the constitution of Cleisthenes in drawing up their report (§ 3). The Committee reported in favour of the Prytanes being compelled to put to the vote any motion for the public safety (instead of exercising their own discretion in the matter). They also proposed the abolition of all indictments for illegal motions, all impeachments before the Council or the Assembly, and all citations before the Law-courts, so that nothing should hinder any citizen from offering such counsel as he thought fit. If any person attempted, either by fine or citation or prosecution, to prevent such counsel being given, he was to be summarily brought before the Generals and delivered up to execution (§ 4). They further drew up the following form of constitution:—The revenues were to be spent solely on the conduct of the war. So long as the war lasted, no officers of State were to receive any pay except the nine Archons and the Prytanes. The franchise (including the right of making treaties) was to be entrusted to not less than Five Thousand of the citizens who were best able to serve the State. The list of the Five Thousand was to be drawn up by a Commission of one hundred formed by electing ten out of each of the tribes (§ 5).

When these proposals had been ratified, the [provisionally acting body of] 'Five Thousand' elected from among their own members the hundred Commissioners for

[1] There is a monograph on Theramenes by Dr Carl Pöhlig (Teubner, 1877). On the party of 'moderate oligarchs' to which Theramenes belonged, see Dr Jackson's article on *Socrates* in *Encycl. Brit.* ed. 9.

drawing up the constitution. The Commissioners proposed for the future a Council, which was to be in power for a year at a time, and to include certain officers of State (about 100 in all) as members *ex officio*. The Council was to appoint these out of a larger number of selected candidates chosen out of the members of the Council for the time being. All other offices were to be filled by lot (30 § 2). There were to be four Councils of four hundred each, such four Councils serving in turn, for a year each, in an order to be determined by lot (§ 3). Members of the Council absent without leave were to be fined (§ 6).

For the immediate present, there was to be a Council of Four Hundred (as in the constitution of Solon), forty from each tribe, appointed out of a larger number selected by the members of the several tribes. This Council was to appoint the officers of State, and to have complete discretion in questions of legislation, official audits, &c.; but was to have no power to alter the new constitution (31 § 1). Military officers were to be elected provisionally by the 'Five Thousand,' but ultimately by the Council (§ 2). No office, except that of a General or a member of the Council, was to be held more than once (§ 3).

About the end of May, 411, the existing Council was dissolved; and on June 7 the Four Hundred entered on office. An oligarchical constitution was thus established nearly a century after the expulsion of the tyrants (510). The leaders of the Revolution were Peisander, Antiphon and Theramenes. The Four Hundred sent envoys to Sparta, proposing the termination of the war on the basis of *uti possidetis*; but, as the envoys declined to surrender the maritime supremacy of Athens, Sparta refused to come to terms (c. 32).

(10) *The restored Democracy.* The defeat of Athens in the naval battle of Eretria, and the consequent loss of Euboea, led the people to depose the Four Hundred, after they had been in power for four months (May to August, 411); and to entrust the management of affairs to the Five Thousand, a body consisting of all citizens capable of providing a military equipment. No pay was to be given for any public office. This revolution was led by Aristocrates and Theramenes, both of whom disapproved of the Four Hundred for keeping all the power in their own hands, and not referring anything to the Five Thousand. The constitution at this time appears to have worked excellently, inasmuch as it was a time of war and the franchise was entrusted to those who provided a military equipment (c. 33).

[After the victories in the Hellespont in 410] the people soon deprived the Five Thousand of their exclusive right to the franchise. In 406 the victory of Arginusae was won, but that victory was attended with the following results: (1) Under the misleading influence of passionate appeals to the feelings of the people, all the Generals who had won that victory had their fate sealed by a single verdict (see note on pp. 129—130); and (2), when Sparta proposed to evacuate Decelea, Cleophon protested that she should be required to surrender all the cities that owed allegiance to her (34 § 1). Athens soon had good reason to regret her mistake. In 405 she was vanquished at Aegospotami; and Lysander became master of Athens and established the rule of the Thirty (§ 2).

(11) *The despotic government of the Thirty and of the Ten.* The THIRTY, instead of framing a constitution, appointed a Council of five hundred, out of a large number of selected candidates; associated with themselves ten officials in the Peiraeus, eleven superintendents of the prison, and three hundred attendants; and, with the help of these, kept the city completely under their own control. At first they acted with moderation: they professed to restore the ancient constitution; repealed the laws of Ephialtes curtailing the privileges of the Areopagus; and abolished the limitations to the right of bequest granted by Solon. But, as soon as they had established themselves in power, they proceeded to put to death those who were eminent for wealth or birth or reputation; and, within a short time, the number of their victims rose to 1,500 (c. 35). Alarmed, however, by the indignant protests and the ever increasing popularity of Theramenes, they offered to draw up a list of 3,000 who were to receive the franchise. Theramenes was still dissatisfied; the list was withheld, and, when published, was constantly liable to arbitrary alterations (c. 36).

Meanwhile, winter set in, and the Thirty were repulsed in their attack on Thrasybulus, who, with the exiles of the democratic party, had taken possession of the fort of Phyle. The Thirty now resolved on disarming the people and getting rid of Theramenes. For the latter purpose they compelled the Council to pass two proposals, (1) giving the Thirty power to put to death any person not included in the list of the 3,000; (2) preventing any one from enjoying the franchise if he had taken part in demolishing the fort of Eetioneia or had in any way opposed the Four Hundred. Theramenes had done both. After putting him to death, they disarmed all the people except the 3,000; and proceeded to further extremities of cruelty and crime (37).

After this, Thrasybulus and his soldiers occupied Munichia and defeated the partisans of the Thirty. The party of the city retreated to Athens; and, on the next day, held a meeting in the market-place, deposed the Thirty and elected Ten of the citizens as commissioners with full powers to bring the war to a conclusion. The Ten did nothing of the kind; they sent to Sparta to ask for aid and to borrow funds. Finding that this was resented by those who possessed the franchise, and fearing they might be deposed in consequence, they arrested a citizen of the highest repute and put him to death. They thus strengthened their position, and they were further supported by the Spartan harmost Callibius and his Peloponnesians, and by certain of the Knights. The party of the Peiraeus, however, were soon joined by all the people, and began to get the upper hand in the struggle. Thereupon, the party of the city deposed the Ten, and elected in their place another body of the same number, consisting of men of the highest character, among whom was Rhinon (who was afterwards elected one of the Generals). Under the management of this new body of Ten, and with the aid of Pausanias and ten Commissioners from Sparta, terms of reconciliation were drawn up and the democratic party returned to Athens (c. 38).

The terms were as follows: All who had remained in Athens might reside at Eleusis, while retaining their property and their full rights as citizens (35 § 1). The temple at Eleusis was to be common ground for both parties; but, except at the season of the Mysteries, the settlers at Eleusis were not to enter Athens, or the residents in Athens to visit Eleusis. The settlers at Eleusis were to contribute their share to the federal fund (§ 2). If any one killed or wounded another, trials for homicide were to be held, as of old (§ 5). Lastly, there was to be a general amnesty towards all persons, except the Thirty, the Ten (who immediately succeeded them), the Eleven, and the Ten who had ruled in the Peiraeus; and even these were not to be excluded, if they rendered an account of their office (§ 6).

A prominent part was played at this time by Archinus:—(1) He accelerated the date for the closing of the list of settlers at Eleusis (40 § 1); (2) he successfully resisted the proposal of Thrasybulus to confer the franchise on all who had aided in the restoration of the democracy; and (3) he insisted on the penalty of death being inflicted on one who attempted to violate the amnesty (§ 2). The funds which the Thirty had borrowed from Sparta for their own purposes, were repaid out of the public treasury (§ 3). A further reconciliation was effected with the settlers at Eleusis in B.C. 401/0 (§ 4).

(12) *The restored and extreme Democracy.* The constitution established in B.C. 403 remained in force until the time when the work was written (B.C. 328—325) with ever-increasing accessions to the power of the people. The people had made itself master of everything, and administered all the affairs of State by means of the decrees of the Assembly and the decisions of the Law-courts. In the latter, no less than in the former, the people ruled supreme. Even the judicial decisions formerly in the hands of the Council were transferred to the people, a course which the writer approves on the ground that small bodies are more liable to corruption than large ones (41 § 2). At first it was decided not to provide pay for attendance at the Assembly; but, as its members were habitually absent, an allowance of one obol a day was introduced by Agyrrhius, to be increased to two obols by Heracleides, and to three by Agyrrhius himself (§ 3).

Part II, which describes the machinery of the 'existing Constitution,' under the general heads of (i) the Franchise (c. 42), (ii) Legislature (43—45), (iii) Administration (46—62), and (iv) Judicature (63 to end), may from one point of view be regarded as entirely concerned with a single subject, being an account of αἱ ἀρχαί, the 'posts of power or service, honour or emolument, for which the Athenian citizen becomes eligible or qualified sooner or later,' when once the franchise is conferred on him. It may be divided into four sections (i) the conditions of the franchise (c. 42); (ii) the exercise of the full franchise in the ἐγκύκλιοι ἀρχαί (cc. 43—62), first the κληρωταί, the Council with sundry other authorities (43—54), and the Archons (55—59). From these may be detached (iii) the χειροτονηταὶ ἀρχαί, or ἀρχαὶ πρὸς πόλεμον (61), and (iv) the Dikasteria (63 to end), placed here because they are permanent and not concerned with administration (ἡ διοίκησις), although recruited by the Lot (Mr Macan, *J. H. S.*, xii 21). Or, again, we may for convenience use ἀρχαὶ in the narrower sense, and divide the second part into three main portions under the head of (i) πολιτεία (c. 42); (ii) ἀρχαί (cc. 42—62); (iii) δικαστήρια (cc. 62 to end).

In (i) we have first an account of the method of enrolling citizens, with interesting details as to the military training of youthful citizens between the ages of 18 and 20 (c. 42). In (ii) the foremost place is occupied by the administrative functions of the Council and of the officials who act in concert with it (43—49); while the ἐκκλησία is only briefly dealt with in connexion with the πρυτάνεις and πρόεδροι in c. 43 and c. 44. Then follow certain other officials appointed by lot, with some account of the public Arbitrators (50—54), and the nine Archons (55—59), with a detailed statement of the duties of the Archon (56), the Basileus (57), the Polemarch (58) and the Thesmothetae (59) respectively. Next come the ἀθλοθέται, with some notice of the Sacred Olives (60). Thus far for officials appointed by lot. Next in order we have the military officers (61), who have already been briefly mentioned with other officials elected by show of hands (43 § 1). This portion of the work closes with a chapter on Salaries (62). The remainder is entirely concerned with the Law-courts, and, in particular, with the way by which the dicasts were allotted to the several courts, the method of voting, the measurement of time during the proceedings, and lastly the arrangements for paying the dicasts when their duties were over.

A large amount of the contents of the Second Part was already known to us in a fragmentary way, through the quotations preserved by grammarians and lexicographers; but it is a signal advantage to have before us the source of all these quotations with the opportunity of testing every statement by the light of its immediate context. We are thus at last able to deal with a first-hand authority for the Constitutional Antiquities of Athens. Whatever hesitation there may necessarily be as to the historic value of certain details in the First Part of the treatise, especially in cases where the writer is describing the institutions of a distant past, which had left behind it no contemporary records except a single chapter from the code of Dracon, with the laws and poems of Solon; or where his account refuses to be reconciled with that of writers such as Thucydides and Xenophon; there can be no question as to the great importance and the completely trustworthy character of the Second Part, with its terse and clear description of the machinery of the State towards the close of the third quarter of the fourth century B.C. And the value of all this is unimpaired by any doubts that have been entertained as to the authorship of the work.

§ 10. *Conspectus of the Literature of the* Ἀθηναίων πολιτεία.

(The order in each division is mainly chronological except in **B** III and IV, where it is alphabetical.)

(A) *Published before the discovery of the Papyrus in the British Museum.*

(1) Aristotelis rerum publicarum reliquias collegit **C. F. Neumann**. Heidelberg, 1827.

(2) Heraclidis politiarum quae extant recensuit **F. G. Schneidewin**. Göttingen, 1847.

(3) Fragmenta historicorum Graecorum collegit **C. Müller**; vol. II pp. 102—107; Heraclides, *ib.* 208—224; Paris (Didot), 1848.

(4) **Valentini Rose** Aristoteles Pseudepigraphus, Leipzig, 1863, [quoted in this book as Rose, *A. P.*].

(5) Die verlorenen Schriften des Aristoteles, von **Emil Heitz**, Leipzig (Teubner), 1865.

(6) Fragmenta Aristotelis collegit disposuit illustravit **Aemilius Heitz**, Paris (Didot), Nov. 1868.

(7) Aristotelis Opera; edidit Academia Regia Borussica. vol. V Aristotelis qui ferebantur librorum *Fragmenta* collegit **Valentinus Rose**, pp. 1535—1571 [quoted as Rose, 343^2 to 568^2],—Index Aristotelicus, Bonitz. Berlin (Reimer), 1870.

(8) **W. Oncken**, *Die Staatslehre der Ar. in historisch-politischen Umrissen*, vol. 2, esp. pp. 410—528 (Engelmann) Leipzig, 1875.

(9) Aristotelis qui ferebantur librorum Fragmenta collegit **Valentinus Rose**, pp. 258—386 [quoted as Rose, 381^3 to 611^3], Leipzig (Teubner), 1886.

On the Berlin Fragments.

(10) **F. Blass**, *Hermes*, 1880, xv 366. (11) **Th. Bergk**, *Rheinisches Museum*, 1881, xxxvii p. 87. (12) **H. Landwehr**, (*a*) *de papyro Berolinensi*, no. 163, Berlin, 1883; (*b*) *papyrum Berol. commentario adiecto edidit*, Gotha, 1883; and (*c*) in *Philologus* Suppl. v 100—196. (13) **H. Diels**, *Abhandlungen der Berliner Akademie, mit* 2 *Tafeln*, Mai 1885, ii pp. 1—57.

(**B**) *Published after the discovery of the Papyrus.*

(I) EDITIONS.

(1) Aristotle On the Constitution of Athens, edited by **F. G. Kenyon**, M.A., Fellow of Magdalen College, Oxford; Assistant in the Department of MSS, British Museum. Printed by Order of the Trustees of the Museum (Preface dated 31 Dec. 1890), 1st ed. Jan. 30, 1891; 2nd ed. Feb.; 3rd and revised ed. 25 Jan. 1892.

Preliminary notice of discovery in the *Times*, 19 *Jan.* (reprinted in *Classical Review*, v 70); Reviews of 1st or 2nd ed.:—in *Times*, 30 Jan. '91; *Athenaeum*, 4 April, p. 434—6; *Saturday Review*, 21 March, p. 358; *Edinburgh Rev.*, April, p. 470—494; *Revue de l'Instruction Publique en Belgique*, pp. 133—9; and elsewhere: also in signed (or acknowledged) articles by Mr Macan, Mr F. T. Richards, Prof. Tyrrell, Prof. Gildersleeve and Prof. J. H. Wright; M. Dareste, M. Haussoullier and M. Weil; Prof. Blass, Prof. Diels, Prof. Bruno Keil, P. Meyer, and G. J. Schneider (see under their respective names in B III). Review of 3rd ed. in *Academy*, 8 June '92. Descriptive article (signed K) in *Review of Reviews*, 14 Feb. '91, with reduced facsimile of col. 29 and 30.

(2) Aristotle on the Constitution of Athens. Autotype **Facsimile** ed. 22 Plates, 20 × 15 inches. Folio; ed. 1, March, '91; ed. 2 in the same year.

Reviews in *Times*, 4 March, '91; *Athenaeum*, 4 April, p. 434—436, and elsewhere.

(3) Ἀθηναίων πολιτεία ἐκδιδομένη ἐπὶ τῇ βάσει τῆς δευτέρας ἀγγλικῆς τοῦ K. Κένυον ἐκδόσεως. **A. Ἀγαθόνικος.** (Barth and Christ) Athens; 1891.

(4) Aristotele, la Costituzione degli Ateniesi, testo greco, versione italiana, introduzione e note di **C. Ferrini.** (Hoepli) Milan [rev. in *Athenaeum*, 5 Sept. '91, p. 317].

(5) Aristotelis Πολιτεία Ἀθηναίων, ediderunt **G. Kaibel** et **U. de Wilamowitz-Moellendorff**, '91. ed. 1, July; ed. 2, September (Weidmann) Berlin [reviewed in *Berl. Philol. Wochenschr.*, 1892, p. 453 (F. Cauer); *Neue Philol. Rundschau*, '92, p. 210 (P. Meyer); *Lit. Centralblatt*, '92, n. 2, p. 56; *Revue des études grecques* iv 405 (Weil); *Deutsche Litteraturzeitung*, '91, p. 1639 (Gomperz); and elsewhere].

(6) Aristotelis quae fertur Ἀθηναίων πολιτεία. Post Kenyonem recensuerunt **H. van Herwerden** et **J. van Leeuwen**; accedunt MSTI Apographum, Observationes Palaeographicae cum Tabulis iv, Indices Locupletissimi; (Sijthoff) Leyden, '91 [reviewed in *Berl. Philol. Wochenschr.*, 1892, pp. 613, 649; *Class. Rev.* vi 20—24; *Neue Philol. Rundschau*, '92, p. 210 (P. Meyer); and elsewhere].

(7) Aristotelis Πολιτεία Ἀθηναίων, edidit **F. Blass** (Teubner) Leipzig, Jan. 1892 [reviewed in *Wochenschr. f. klass. Philol.* no. 38; and elsewhere].

(8) a school-edition of c. 1—41, by **Karl Hude** of Copenhagen (Teubner, Leipzig, Dec. 1892).

Editions have also been promised by

(9) **H. Diels** (Berlin); (10) **B. Haussoullier** (Paris).

(II) TRANSLATIONS.

English. (1) with Introduction and Notes (and Facsimile of first eleven lines of col. 10) by **F. G. Kenyon**, M.A. (Bell) London, July, 1891. (2) **E. Poste**, M.A., Fellow of Oriel Coll., Oxford; (Macmillan) London, July, '91; ed. 2, Dec. '92. (3) **T. J. Dymes**, B.A., late Scholar of Lincoln Coll., Oxford; (Seeley) London, 1891.

German. (4) **G. Kaibel** u. **A. Kiessling**, two editions in 1891; (Trübner) Strassburg. (5) **F. Poland** (Langenscheidt) Berlin, '91. (6) **M. Erdmann** (Neumann) Leipzig, 1892. (7) **H. Hagen** see in III (31).

French. (8) **Th. Reinach** (Hachette) Paris; (9) **B. Haussoullier** (Bouillon) Paris, Nov. 1891.

Italian. (10) **C. Ferrini** (Hoepli) Milan; (11) **C. O. Zuretti** (Loescher) Turin.

Russian. (12) **Belajew**, Kasan; (13) anonymous translation in *Journ. d. kais. russ. Ministeriums d. Volksaufklärung*, Jul.—Aug. '91.

Polish. (14) **L. Cwiklinski**, Krakau, Nov. '92.

(Several of the above Translations are reviewed in the *Athenaeum*, 5 Sept. '91, p. 316, and by Mr F. T. Richards in the *Academy*, 15 Aug., '91, p. 137.)

(III) SIGNED (OR ACKNOWLEDGED) CONTRIBUTIONS TO PERIODICAL PUBLICATIONS &c.

(ems. = emendations)

(1) **Adam, J.**, On Solon in c. 12 § 5 πρὶν ἀνταράξας πῖαρ ἐξεῖλεν γάλα. *Academy*, 14 March, '91, p. 259. (2) **Allen, F. D.**, Prof. Wright's paper in 1888, on the date of Cylon; *The Nation*, 5 March, '91, p. 197. (3) **Bauer, A.**, (*a*) Vortrag in Graz, 18 Feb.; *Wissenschaftliche Rundschau der Münchner Neuesten Nachrichten*, no. 97, 103, 109. (*b*) *Preussische Jahrbücher*, vol. 68, part 1. See also IV (1). (4) **Bernardakis, G.**, 'Επιστολὴ περὶ τῆς πολ. 'Αθ. τοῦ 'Αρ., ἀνατύπωσις τῆς 'Εφημερίδος, Athens, '91. (5) **Benn, A. W.**, On c. 25, *Academy*, 14 March, '91, p. 259. (6) **Blass, F.**, Review in *Litterarische Centralblatt*, 28 Feb. 301—4 (with numerous emendations, reprinted in *Class. Rev.* v 175). See also ed. in I (7). (7) **Brieger, A.**, die Verfassungsgeschichte von Athen, nach Aristoteles' neu angefundener Schrift, *Unsere Zeit*, ii 18—36, '91. (8) **Brooks, E. H.**, ems. in *Class. Rev.* v 182. (9) **Burnet, J.**, ems. in *Class. Rev.* v 107, 117. (10) **Bury, J. B.**, ems. in *Academy*, 7 March, '91, p. 234; *Athenaeum*, p. 344; (= *Class. Rev.* v 175). (11) **Busolt, G.**, 'zur Gesetzgebung Drakons,' *Philologus*, vol. 50, pp. 393—400. (12) **Butcher, S. H.**, c. 13, 21, *Class. Rev.* v 178. (13) **Bywater, I.**, ems. in *Academy*, 14 Feb. '91, p. 163-4 (= *Class. Rev.* v 105—). (14) **Campbell, Lewis**, ems. in *Class. Rev.* v 105—, 119. (15) **Chinnock, E. J.**, 'Rare Words,' *Class. Rev.* v 229. (16) **Cholodniak, J.**, General article in *Journal d. k. Russ. Min. der Volksaufklärung*, May '91, p. 58—70 (in Russian). (17) **Comparetti, D.**, *Nuova Antologia*, xxvi 3, vol. 34, fasc. 13. (18) **Cox, Rev. Sir G. W.**, 'Aristotle as an Historian,' *Academy*, July—Aug. '92, pp. 52, 111, 152, 171. (19) **Crusius, O.**, 'die Schrift vom Staate der Athener, und Aristoteles über die Demokratie,' *Philologus*, vol. 50, pp. 173—8. (20) **Curtius, E.**, *Berl. Arch. Gesellschaft* (*Berl. Philol. Wochenschrift*, '91, p. 27). (21) **Dareste, R.**, (*a*) *Séances et travaux de l'Acad. des Sciences Morales et Politiques*, '91, p. 341—364 (abstract of Part ii); (*b*) *Journal des Savants*, May, '91, p. 257—273. (22) **De-Sanctis, G.**, 'Studi sull' 'Αθ. πολ.,' *Rivista di filologia*, vol. xx p. 147—163. (23) **Diels, H.**, (*a*) *Deutsche Litteraturzeitung*, '91, no. 7, p. 239—242; no. 24, p. 878; (*b*) *Archiv f. Geschichte der Philosophie*, iv 478; (*c*) On Epimenides, *Sitzungsberichte der Berliner Akademie*, '91, p. 387. (24) **Ellis, Robinson**, ems. in *Class. Rev.* v 181—2. (25) **Fraenkel, M.**, (*a*) *Zeitschrift f. Geschichtswissenschaft*, '91, p. 164—7; (*b*) *Rh. Mus.* xlvii 473. (26) **Gennadios, A.**, 'Ακρόπολις, Athens, 18 March—2 April (*Class. Rev.* v 274). (27) **Gertz, M. C.**, (*a*) *Filologiske Tidskrift*, '91, p. 252—5; (*b*) *Jahrb. f. Philologie*, '91, p. 192. (28) **Gildersleeve, B.**, Rev. in *American Journal of Philology*, xii 97, cf. *ib.* i 458, iv 92, on Solon in c. 12 § 5, πρὶν ἀναταράξας. (29) **Giles, P.**, *English Historical Review*, April, '92. (30) **Gomperz, Th.**, (*a*) 'Aristoteles u. seine neuentdeckte Schrift.'

Deutsche Rundschau, xvii 219, May, '91; (*b*) 'Ueber das neuentdeckte Werk des Ar., U. die Verdächtiger seiner Echtheit,' *Anzeiger der Wiener Akademie*, no. xi (3) [both printed separately]; (*c*) *Deutsche Litteraturzeitung*, '91, no. 24, p. 877; no. 45, p. 1639. See also IV (5). (31) **Hagen, H.**, trans. in *Schweizerische Rundschau*, '91, no. 4—6. (32) **Harberton, Lord**, On c. 35 § 1, *Class. Rev.* vi 123. (33) **Hardie, W. R.**, 'The διαιτηταί' (c. 53), *Class. Rev.* v 164. (34) **Hartman, J. J.**, general descriptive article in *De Nederlandsche Spectator*, 14 March, '91. (35) **Haskins, C. E.**, em. (20, 5) *Class. Rev.* v 111 *b*. (36) **Haussoullier, B.**, (*a*) *Revue des Études Grecques*, no. 12 (belated no. for Dec. 1890), p. 475; (*b*) *Revue Critique*, '91, no. 10, p. 181—6; '92, no. 10, p. 179—183; (*c*) *Acad. des Inscr. et Belles Lettres*, '91, Feb. 13 and 20; (*d*) *Revue de Philologie*, xv 2, p. 98 f. (37) **Havell, H. L.**, 'The Great Discovery,' *Macmillan's Mag.*, March, '91, p. 392—400. (38) **Headlam, J. W.**, (*a*) 'The Constitution of Draco' (c. 4), *Class. Rev.* v 166—9; (*b*) 'On the use of the *hiatus* in the Πολιτεία,' *ib.* 270—2; (*c*) 'Notes on Early Athenian History (i) The Council: ἐφέται and ναύκραροι,' *ib.* vi 249—253, and (ii) 'The Council,' *ib.* 293—8. See also IV (8). (39) **Herwerden, H. van**, (*a*) *Berl. Philol. Wochenschrift*, '91, pp. 322, 418, 610; (*b*) *Mnemosyne*, '91, p. 168. See also ed. in I (6). (40) **Hicks, R. D.**, ems. *Camb. Philol. Soc. Proc.*, 12 Feb. '91, p. 10; *Class. Rev.* v 111 *a*, 116 *b*. (41) **Hill, G. F.**, c. 25, *Class. Rev.* v 169; 176. (42) **Holzinger**, 'Aristoteles' athenische Politie und die Heraklidischen Excerpte,' *Philologus*, vol. 50, p. 436—446. (43) **Houseman, A. E.**, em. in *Class. Rev.* v 110 *a*. (44) **Houtsma, E. O.**, *Berl. Philol. Wochenschr.*, 27 Jun. '91, p. 801. (45) **Hude, C.**, 'Coniecturae Aristotelicae,' *Filologiske Tidskrift*, '91, p. 248—251. (46) **Hultsch, F.**, 'Das Pheidonische Masssystem,' *Jahrb. für Philol.*, '91, p. 262—4. (47) **Immisch, O.**, On c. 41, *Berl. Philol. Wochenschr.*, '91, p. 707. (48) **Jackson, H.**, ems. in *Camb. Philol. Soc. Proc.*, 12 Feb. '91; *Class. Rev.* v 105—, 122. (49) **Kaibel, G.**, article in *Nord und Süd*, Apr. '91, p. 80—92; cf. I (5). (50) **Keil, Bruno**, (*a*) rev. of Mr Kenyon's ed. in *Berl. Philol. Wochenschr.*, '91, 25 April—16 May; also separately printed, pp. 56; (*b*) rev. of van Herwerden and van Leeuwen's ed., *ib.* '92, pp. 613, 649. Cf. IV (10). (51) **Kenyon, F. G.**, (*a*) 'New Readings,' *Class. Rev.* v 269—; (*b*) 'Recent Literature,' *ib.* 332. See also edd. in I (1). (52) **Kontos, K. S.**, (*a*) *Le Spectateur* (Athens), 13 Apr. '91; (*b*) 'Αθηνᾶ, iii 289—400; (*c*) Στοά, i 44. (53) **Lacon, B.**, 'Ημέρα (Athens). (54) **Lean, W. S.**, *Academy*, 7 March, '91, p. 234. (55) **Leeuwen, J. van**, (*a*) *Mnemosyne*, xix 2, April, '91, reprinted in *Class. Rev.* v 224; (*b*) *Verslagen en Medeelingen der Kon. Acad. v. Wett. afd. Letterkunde*, 1891 (May), p. 154—176. See also ed. in I (6). (56) **Lipsius, J. H.**, *Verhandlungen d. k. Sächs. Gesellschaft d. Wissenschaften*, '91, p. 41—69 (also printed separately). (57) **Macan, R. W.**, (*a*) Review of Mr Kenyon's first ed. in *Oxford Magazine*, 4 Feb. '91; (*b*) *Journal of Hellenic Studies*, April, xii 17—40 (on the historical aspect of the 'Αθ. πολ., 11 March, '91). (58) **Maehly, G.**, Review in *Rivista di Filologia*, '91, p. 551—7. (59) **Marchant, E. C.**, (*a*) 'The Deposition of Pericles' (c. 44), *Class. Rev.* v 165—6; (*b*) Emendations, *ib.* v 105—. (60) **Marindin, G. E.**, *Class. Rev.* v 176, 177, 181. (61) **Mayor, John E. B.**, (*a*) ems. &c. in *Camb. Univ. Reporter*, 3 March, '91, p. 607; *Class. Rev.* v p. 105—; (*b*) references on subject-matter, *ib.* 120—2; also in *Proceedings of the Camb. Philological Society*, 17 and 26 Feb. '91, pp. 10—15. (62) **Mayor, Joseph B.**, (*a*) on c. 7 § 4, and c. 17 § 4, *Academy*, 28 March, '91, p. 304; (*b*) 'Unaristotelian words and phrases,' *Class. Rev.* v 122—185; (3) em. *ib.* 175. (63) **Murray, A. S.**, on c. 7 § 4, *Class. Rev.* v 108. (64) **Newman, W. L.**, (*a*) Review of Mr Kenyon's ed. in *Class. Rev.* v 155—164; (*b*) em. *ib.* 105—. (65) **Nicklin, T.**, ems. in *Class. Rev.* v 227, 228. (66) **Niemeyer, K.**, *Jahrb. für Philol.* '91, p. 405—

415. (67) **Oman, C. W.**, paper read at meeting of Historical Society, 19 Nov. '91 (*Academy*, 28 Nov., p. 483). (68) **Pais, E.**, *Rivista di Filologia*, xix 557—569. (69) **Pantazidis**, *φιλολογικὸν παράρτημα τῆς Ἑστίας*, 1891. (70) **Papabasileios**, Ἀθηνᾶ, ii 278—288. (71) **Paton, W. R.**, (*a*) *Athenaeum*, 21 Feb. '91, p. 251, and *Class. Rev.* v 105—, 175—, 225; (*b*) 'The Attic Phratries,' *ib.* 221. (72) **Platt, A.**, ems. in *Class. Rev.* v 109, 175—, 185. (73) **Poland, F.**, *Jahrb. für Philol.* '91, p. 259—262. (74) **Radinger, C.**, *Philologus*, vol. 50, pp. 229, 400, 468. (75) **Reinach, Th.**, (*a*) 'Trois Passages du livre d'A. &c.' (on cc. 4, 8, 25) *Académie des Inscr. &c.*, 5 June, '91; *Revue Critique*, n. 24; (*b*) 'La Constitution de Dracon et la Constitution de l'an 411,' *Revue des Études Grecques*, '91, p. 82; (*c*) 'Aristote ou Critias ?,' *ib.* 143—158. (76) **Richards, F. T.**, (*a*) Rev. of Mr Kenyon's ed. in *Academy*, 14 Feb. '91, p. 165—7; (*b*) Rev. of Bauer's *Forschungen* and of Mr Kenyon's and Mr Poste's Translations, *ib.* 15 Aug. '91, p. 137—8; (*c*) Letter, *ib.* 13 Aug. '92, p. 133, mainly on discrepancies between *Politics* and Ἀθ. πολ. (77) **Richards, Herbert** [quoted in critical notes by surname only], (*a*) ems. in *Academy*, 14 Feb. '91, p. 163—4; and 18 Apr. p. 371; (*b*) ems. in *Class. Rev.* v 105—, 122, 175, 224, 334; (*c*) 'Unaristotelian words and phrases,' *ib.* 184, 272. (78) **Ridgeway, W.**, *Academy*, 21 Feb. '91, p. 186—7 (*Class. Rev.* v 109). See also *Origin of Metallic Currency and Weight Standards*, pp. 306, 324. (79) **Ruehl, F.**, (*a*) *Rhein. Mus.*, '91, p. 426—464; (*b*) *Wochenschr. für klass. Philol.*, '92, no. 1; cf. (128). (80) **Rutherford, G.**, (*a*) 'The New Aristotle Papyrus in its bearings on Textual Criticism,' *Class. Rev.* v 89—91; (*b*) ems. *ib.* 105—, 175. (81) **Saint-Hilaire, B.**, *Revue Bleue*, 21 March, '91. (82) **Sandys, J. E.**, (*a*) ems. in *Academy*, 7 Feb. '91, p. 137 (*Class. Rev.* v 105—); (*b*) ems. &c. *Camb. Phil. Soc. Proc.*, 26 Feb. '91, p. 14 (with additions in *Class. Rev.* v 119—120). (83) **Schneider, G. J.**, Review of Mr Kenyon's ed. in *Wochenschr. für klass. Philol.*, 29 Apr.—20 May, '91, pp. 371, 498, 528, 544. (84) **Schoell, R.**, *Münchener Allgemeine Zeitung*, Beilage, no. 106—109; Sonderabdruck der 41 Philol.-Versammlung in München, Mai '91 (J. G. Cotta) Munich. (85) **Schvarcz, J.**, *Ungarische Revue*, Apr. '91. See also IV (12). (86) **Sidgwick, A.**, ems. in *Class. Rev.* v 105—. (87) **Stewart, J. A.**, em. in *Academy*, 7 March, '91, p. 234 (*Class. Rev.* v 179). (88) **Smith, Cecil**, Ostracism of Xanthippus, *Class. Rev.* v 277. (89) **Smith, J. A.**, em. in *Academy*, 14 Feb. (*Class. Rev.* v 118). (90) **Szanto, E.**, *Wochenschr. für klass. Philol.*, '91, p. 761. (91) **Thompson, E. S.**, (*a*) em. in *Class. Rev.* v 223, 224—; 277; (*b*) The Draconian Constitution, *ib.* 336; (*c*) Date of the Expulsion of the Pisistratids, *ib.* vi 181; (*d*) Age of the διαιτηταί, *ib.* 182. (92) **Torr, Cecil**, (*a*) on the date, *Athenaeum*, 7 Feb. (*Class. Rev.* v 119 note); (*b*) on 51 § 4, *Class. Rev.* v 117; (*c*) on the στρατηγοὶ in c. 61, *ib.* p. 119; (*d*) on c. 54, the Delian festival, *ib.* 277. (93) **Tyrrell, R. Y.**, (*a*) ems. in *Academy*, 28 Feb. '91, p. 210; 7 March, p. 234 (*Class. Rev.* v 175—); (*b*) 'The New Papyri,' *Quarterly Review*, April, '91, p. 320—350. (94) **Vanderkindere**, *Revue Belgique*, March, '91. (95) **Wachsmuth, C.**, 'zur Topographie von Athen,' *Rheinisches Museum*, '91, Heft 2. (96) **Walker, E. M.**, Chronology of 462—445 B.C., *Class. Rev.* vi 95. (97) **Wardale, J. R.**, *Class. Rev.* v 273. (98) **Weil, H.**, *Journal des Savants*, April, '91, p. 197. (99) **Whibley, L.**, (*a*) on cc. 22, 23, 28, *Class. Rev.* v 168—9; (*b*) em. *ib.* 180; (*c*) on the Authorship, *ib.* 223. (100) **Wright, J. H.**, (*a*) Review of Mr Kenyon's ed. in *The Nation*, 7 May, '91; (*b*) 'Did Philochorus quote the Ἀθ. πολ. as Aristotle's?', *American Journal of Philology*, xii 3, 310—318. (*c*) 'The Date of Cylon,' a Study in early Athenian history, *Harvard Studies in Classical Philology*, iii 1892. Also reprinted, pp. 80 (Ginn and Co.) Boston. (101) **Wyse, W.**, (*a*) ems. in *Camb. Phil. Soc. Proc.* for Feb. 12, '91; also in *Athenaeum*, Feb. 14

and 21, and *Academy*, 21 Feb. p. 186 (*Class. Rev.* v 105—); (*b*) ems. in *Class. Rev.* v 225—; (*c*) notes, *ib.* 122, 224, 274—6, 335—6; (*d*) on προδανείζειν, 16 § 2, *ib.* vi 254—7.

Many of the following articles appeared at a later date than the above:—

(102) **Bérard, J.**, *Aristote, La Constitution d'Athènes*, (Extrait) Paris. (103) **Betge**, popular article in *Gegenwart*, '91, no. 29. (104) **Buseskul**, (*a*) on cc. 4 and 25, *Journ. d. Min. der Volksaufkl.*; noticed in *Berl. Phil. Woch.*, 8 Oct. '92, p. 1289; (*b*) in *Russ. hist. Rundschau*, ii 221—239 (both in Russian). (105) **Cauer, Paul**, *Aristoteles Urteil über die Demokratie*, Fleckeisen's *Jahrb.* '92, p. 581—593. (106) **Cavazza, P.**, *Discorso* in *Annuario dell' Istituto di studi superiori in Firenze*, pp. 20, '92. (107) **Derewizki, A.**, (in Russian) Charkow, '91. (108) **Dimitsas, M. G.**, 'Ελλάς, iii 4 p. 357—379. (109) **Duemmler, F.**, *Die* 'Αθ. πολ. *des Kritias*, in *Hermes*, '92, p. 260—280. (110) **Ferrini, C.**, *Rendiconto dell' Ist. lombardo*, ser. ii, vol. xxiv, fasc. 8—9. (111) **Fontana, G.**, On Aristides in 'Αθ. πολ., pp. 26, (Tedeschi) Verona. (112) **Fraccaroli, G.**, *due versi di Solone* (c. 12, 28), in *Rivista di Filologia*, xxi, p. 49—50. (113) **Goodell, T. W.**, 'Ar. on the Athenian Arbitrators' in *Amer. Journ. of Philology*, xii 319—326. (114) **Grunzel, J.**, (Friedrich) Leipzig. (115) **Hertz, M. C.**, On c. 38, *Jahrb. f. Philol.*, '91, p. 192. (116) **Hude, K.**, On the murder of Hipparchus (where Ar. differs from Thuc. he is probably following Androtion), *Jahrb. f. Philol.*, '92, p. 171—6. (117) **Knoke, F.**, popular article in *Grenzboten*, '91, no. 43—44. (118) **Köhler, U.**, (A) On Heracleides of Clazomenae, *Hermes*, '92, p. 68 f. (B) *Die Zeiten der Herrschaft des Peisistratos; Sitzungsberichte* of the Berlin Academy, 7 April, '92, pp. 339—343; a not entirely accurate abstract in *Berl. Phil. Woch.*, 13 Aug. p. 1053—6. [(*a*) The account of Peisistratus in cc. 14, 15 is primarily derived from Hdt. i 59—64, combined (but not harmonised) with other sources of information. The second exile lasted 10 years; the first τυραννίς 5; and the first exile and the second and third τυραννίς, 6 years each. This result was probably obtained by deducting the 10 years of the second exile from the 33 years of c. 17, and dividing the remainder (23) into four approximately equal parts, thus making the τυραννίς last for 17 years in all, and the exile for 16 years. The 19 years of τυραννίς in c. 17 § 1, which are inconsistent with this, are obtained (as already suggested on p. 76 *a*) by deducting the 17 years of the rule of the Peisistratidae (c. 19 ult.) from the 36 years assigned by Hdt. to the rule of Peisistratus and his sons. (The connexion of Peisistratus with Rhaecelus explains the offer of Amyntas I to allow Hippias to settle at the neighbouring town of Anthemûs, Hdt. v 94.) (*b*) The author's method of combining different sources of information is further illustrated by comparing his account of Cleisthenes (c. 20—21) with that of Hdt. (The beginning of the στάσις is placed by Köhler before 508/7, and the reforms of Cleisthenes in 507/6.) (*c*) In the figures given in c. 24 the main stress is laid on the total, 20,000 (cf. Arist. *Vesp.* 706—8), not on the details; it is an exaggeration to put the number of the ἀρχαὶ ἔνδημοι and ὑπερόριοι at 700 each; and the estimate of 2500 hoplites and 20 guardships properly belongs to the time of the battle of Tanagra. A body as numerous as the 2,000 φρουροὶ must have held office for more than a year. (*d*) c. 25 describes the censorial powers of the Areopagus as ἐπίθετα, whereas, in cc. 3, 4, 8, these powers are described as having belonged to it from the earliest times. Hence we may infer that c. 25 is founded on a different account of the historical development of the powers of the Areopagus to that followed in the previous chapters. Further, it is more probable that Ephialtes, in his attack on the Areopagus, cooperated with Pericles than with Themistocles. The story about the latter in c. 25 is a *läppische, chronologische unmögliche Erzählung*, probably borrowed from some such writer as Stesimbrotus.]

(119) **Kurze, F.**, *Westermann's Monatshefte*, Nov. '91, p. 281—4. (120) **Mahaffy, J. P.**, *obiter dicta* in *Problems in Greek History*, pp. 84, 87, 89, 96, 122, 128. (121) **Melber, J.**, *Aristoteles* Ἀθηναίων πολιτεία *u. die bisher darüber erschienene Litteratur* in *Blätter für das bayerische Gymnasialwesen* xxviii 1, p. 29—44 (*Class. Rev.* vi 375). (122) **Meyer, P.**, (*a*) *der neue Ar. u. die Schule*, in *Gymnasium*, '92, no. 2—3; (*b*) Reviews in *Zeitschr. f. d. Gymnasialwesen*, XLVI 144—155. (123) **Muller, H. C.**, in Ἑλλὰς iv, pp. 76 ff, and **Kenyon**, *ibid.* 137, Leyden, '92. (124) **Munro, J. A. R.**, 'The Chronology of Themistocles' career,' *Class. Rev.* vi 333 f. (125) **Nissen, H.**, *die Staatschriften des Ar.* in *Rhein. Mus.* '92, vol. 47, pp. 161—206 (holds that the Πολιτεῖαι were intended to lead up to the publication of a code for the dominions of Alexander, and also to serve as a series of hand-books for the use of Macedonian diplomatists. The article is ably criticised by Bruno Keil, *die Solonische Verfassung*, p. 127—150). (126) **Piccolomini, Aeneas**, *In Aristot. et Herodam animadv. criticae*, in *Rivista di filologia*, xx p. 456—264, Turin, 1892. (127) **Postgate, J. P.**, em. ἠλάσατε for ἀάσατε, in c. 5, 16 (*Class. Rev.* v 109). (128) **Ruehl, F.**, *Der Staat der Athener und kein Ende*, in *Jahrb. f. class. Philol. Suppl. Bd.*, 18, pp. 675—706; also reprinted (Teubner) Leipzig. [Rev. in *Neue Philol. Rundschau*, '92, no. 15, p. 229 (P. Meyer); *Woch. f. kl. Philol.* '92, no. 35, p. 949 (G. J. Schneider); *Berl. Phil. Woch.* 15 Oct. p. 1317 (Schöffer). 'Fassen wir des Ergebniss meines ersten Aufsatzes (79) und das der vorstehenden weiteren Ausführungen zusammen, so ergibt sich die neue Schrift als ein Werk, das sich sehr nahe an die aristotelische Ἀθ. πολ. anschloss, stellenweise fast oder ganz wörtlich, das ihr manche feine, echt aristotelische Wendung verdankte, das sie aber einerseits an vielen Stellen zusammenzog, anderseits dagegen auch erweiterte und möglicherweise auch einzelne Partien durch andere ersetzte' (p. 700). He holds that the editor of the work was 'Herakleides Lembos' (p. 701 f.).] (129) **Schöffer, Val. von,** (*a*) On the date of the Ἀθ. πολ. in Introd. to *Bürgerschaft u. Volksversammlung zu Athen*, I, Moscow, '91 (in Russian), *Berl. Phil. Woch.* 8 Oct. '92, p. 1290; (*b*) Reviews in *Berl. Phil. Woch.* 8 and 15 Oct. '92. (130) **Schultz, H.**, *Russ. Phil. Rundschau*, ii p. 33—44 (in Russian). (131) **Stern, E. v.**, *die neuentdeckte* Ἀθ. πολ. *des Ar.* pp. 42 (Abdruck aus B. II der Annal. der hist.-phil. Ges.), in Russian, Odessa, '92; [attacks the views of Schvarcz, Rühl and Cauer, *Berl. Phil. Woch.* 8 Oct. '92, p. 1291]. (132) **Szanto, E.**, *zur drakonischen Gesetzgebung*, in *Arch.-epigr. Mittheilungen aus Oesterreich*, XV 2, p. 180—2. (133) **Tacchi-Venturi**, *Civiltà Cattolica*, xii no. 995—6. (134) **Zielinski, Th.**, on c. 4, in *Russ. Phil. Rundschau*, i 2, p. 125 f. (in Russian). (135) **Zingerle, A.**, *Zeitschrift f. d. Oesterr. Gymn.* xliii 207 f.

(IV) SEPARATE WORKS.

(1) **Bauer, A.**, *Litterarische u. historische Forschungen zu Aristoteles'* Ἀθ. πολ. (C. H. Beck) Munich, pp. 190, May '91. (Rev. in *Athenaeum*, 5 Sept. '91, p. 317; *Academy*, 15 Aug. '91, p. 137; *Berl. Phil. Woch.* 15 Oct. '92, p. 1321, Schöffer; and elsewhere.) [In three parts: (1) On the relations of Ar. to the historical literature of Greece; (2) historical results derived from the Ἀθ. πολ.; (3) Chronological tables, drawn up in accordance with the dates given in the Ἀθ. πολ.]

(2) **Cassel, Paulus**, Vom neuen Aristoteles u. seiner Tendenz (Bibliograph. Bureau) Berlin, '91. (Rev. in *Berl. Phil. Woch.* 15 Oct. '92, p. 1320, Schöffer; and elsewhere.) [An unscholarly pamphlet, describing the ideal of the author of the Ἀθ. πολ. as 'die alte, erbliche, patriarchalische, gewissenhafte, königliche Verfassung.']

(3) **Cauer, Fr.**, '*Hat Aristoteles die Schrift vom Staate der Athener geschrieben?*

ihr Ursprung und ihr Wert für die ältere athenische Geschichte,' (Göschen) Stuttgart, pp. 78, '91. (Rev. in *Academy*, 6 June '91, p. 540; *Athenaeum*, 5 Sept. '91, p. 317; *Deutsche Litteratur-Zeitung*, p. 878, Diels; *Litt. Centralblatt*, p. 1120; *Wochenschr. f. kl. Phil.* no. 28, Szanto; *Gymn.* p. 567, P. Meyer; *Berl. Phil. Woch.* '92, p. 1288, Schöffer; and elsewhere.) [Argues against the treatise being the work of Aristotle.]

(4) **Droysen, H.**, *Vorläufige Bemerkungen zu Aristoteles'* 'Αθ. πολ., Oster Programm des königstädt. Gymn. (Gärtner) Berlin, '91. [Mainly chronological.]

(5) **Gomperz, Th.**, *Die Schrift vom Staatswesen der Athener und ihr neuester Beurtheiler*, (Holder) Vienna, '91. [A polemical pamphlet directed mainly against Dr Franz Rühl's article in *Rheinisches Museum*, xlvi 426.]

(6) **Hagfors, E.**, *de praepositionum in Ar. Politicis et in* 'Αθ. πολ. *usu*, Helsingfors Dissertation, pp. 130 (Mayer u. Müller, Berlin, '92). [Rev. in *Woch. f. kl. Philol.* '92, p. 997. The net result of this elaborate statistical investigation is that, in the prepositions, the writer finds nothing in the 'Αθ. πολ. divergent from the usage in the *Politics*. On the other hand, there is little in the use of prepositions in the former that is distinctively characteristic of Aristotle. This is limited to the use of ἐξ ἀρχῆς (for ἐν ἀρχῇ), ἐξ ὑπαρχῆς, and οἱ περί τινα. The conclusion is:—'quantum ex praepositionum usu concludere licet, ille liber ab Aristotele *potest* esse conscriptus.']

(7) **Hammond, B. E.**, *Greek Constitutions*, (a sketch including fresh details from the 'Αθ. πολ.) pp. 68 (E. Johnson) Cambridge, '91.

(8) **Headlam, J. W.**, Appendix to Historical Essay, *Election by Lot at Athens*, pp. 183—190, (University Press) Cambridge, '91. See also III (38).

(9) **Herzog, E.**, *Zur Litteratur über den Staat der Athener*, pp. 83 (Fues) Tübingen, Nov. '92. (1) On [Xen.] 'Αθ. πολ.; (2) on Ar. 'Αθ. πολ. c. 4.

(10) **Keil, Bruno**, *Die Solonische Verfassung nach Aristoteles*, pp. 248 (Gärtner) Berlin, Nov. '92. [Ar. was engaged in the preparation of the *Politics* from about 350 to 335 B.C. It was apparently after this that he put into shape the materials collected for his Πολιτεῖαι, the redaction of the 'Αθ. πολ. falling between 329 and 325. In its polemical passages and elsewhere, it shows the influence of the 'Ατθίς of Androtion, besides other traces of further research subsequent to the preparation of the *Politics*. It was intended for publication, as is proved by the elaborate style of certain portions, by the attention paid to rhythm at the ends of the sentences, by the avoidance of *hiatus*, and by other indications of deliberate purpose and methodical plan. The work did not, however, receive the author's finishing touches, and was probably not given to the world until after his death.—The text of chaps. 5—13 is printed with critical notes, followed by a commentary on each chapter, together with many valuable remarks on the work as a whole. Among the restorations of the text here proposed are c. 9, 11 ὅπως π(ερὶ) τῆς κρίσε[ως ὁ δ]ῆ[μος ᾖ κ]ύριος, c. 10, 5 παρ' ὀ[λί]γον, c. 11, 10 γενέσθαι τὴν [νέαν] τάξιν, c. 11, 12 ἢ σ[χεδὸν ἀ]παράλλα[κτον].]

(11) **Meyer, Peter**, Des Aristoteles' Politik u. die 'Αθ. πολ., nebst einer Litteratur-Uebersicht, pp. 72 (Cohen) Bonn, '91. (Rev. in *Berl. Phil. Woch.* 8 Oct. '92, p. 1291, Schöffer; and elsewhere.) [Gives some useful parallel passages from the *Politics*; but goes too far in contending that *Politics* ii 12 and c. 4 of 'Αθ. πολ. are both equally authoritative.]

(12) **Schvarcz, Julius**, '*Aristoteles u. die* 'Αθ. πολ.,' 1 Abtheilung des Werkes *Die Demokratie*, pp. 25 (Friedrich) Leipzig, '91. [Ascribes the treatise to Demetrius Phalereus.]

(13) **Schjott, P.** *Aristoteles om Athens Statsforfatning*. Christiania, '91, Dybwad. (Rev. by B in *Lit. Centralblatt*, no. 29, p. 1025.)

(14) **Wright, J. H.** *The Date of Cylon*, (Reprint of III (100 *c*), 1892); noticed

in *Academy*, 11 June, '92, p. 570; *Class. Rev.* vi 457; *Berl. Phil. Woch.* '92, p. 1555; and elsewhere. [Places the attempt of Cylon between 636 and 624 B.C., and the trial and banishment of the Alcmaeonidae, and the visit of Epimenides, in 615.]

The principal books of reference used in preparing the commentary are: (*a*) the *Corpus Inscriptionum Atticarum*, quoted as CIA; with E. L. Hicks, *Gk. Historical Inscriptions*, and Dittenberger's *Sylloge*; also von Hartel's *Studien über Attisches Staatsrecht u. Urkundenwesen* (1878), and Meisterhans, *Grammatik der Attischen Inschriften*, ed. 2 (1888).

(*b*) the *Index Aristotelicus* of Bonitz; and the editions (or translations) of the *Politics* by Susemihl, Jowett, Newman and others; also the various editions of the *Fragments*.

(*c*) the Greek lexicographers, esp. Bekker's *Anecdota*, vol. i; Etymologicum Magnum (Gaisford); Harpocration (Dindorf); Hesychius (Schmidt); Photius (ed. Porson, revised by Dobree, 1822, who printed as Appendix the *Lexicon Rhetoricum Cantabrigiense*; Dobree's transcript of the latter was also published posthumously in 1834); also id. (ed. Naber, 1864—5); Pollux (Bekker); and Suidas (Bernhardy).

(*d*) in Gk. History:—Herodotus, Thucydides, Xenophon, also C. Müller's *Fragmenta Historicorum Graecorum*, quoted as FHG:—among modern writers, Thirlwall, Grote (ed. 1862 in 8 vols), Curtius (ed. Ward), Duncker, Busolt, Holm, Abbott; also Gilbert's *Beiträge*. In Chronology, Eusebius (ed. Schoene, 1866—75); and the *Marmor Parium* in Müller's FHG; also Clinton's *Fasti*, and Peter's *Zeittafeln*.

(*e*) in Antiquities and Law: (1) **Boeckh**, *Die Staatshaushaltung der Athener*, ed. 2, 1851, ed. 3 (by Fränkel) 1886; also the translations of ed. 1 by Sir Geo. Cornewall Lewis 1828, 1842; of ed. 2 by Lamb, Boston, U.S., 1857. (2) the new edition of **K. F. Hermann's** *Lehrbuch der Griechischen Antiquitäten*[1]. (3) **Meier u. Schoemann**, *der Attische Process*, 1824, ed. Lipsius 1881—6; also **Lipsius**, in *Verhandlungen d. k. Sächs. Gesellschaft d. Wissenschaften*, '91, p. 41—69. (4) **G. F. Schoemann**, *Antiquities of Greece*, vol. i translated by Hardy and Mann, 1880. (5) **Gilbert**, *Griechische Staatsalterthümer*, 1881—5 (new ed., and English trans. of vol. i in preparation). (6) **Busolt**, *Die Griechischen Alterthümer*, 1887 (ed. 2, '92), and **Stengel**, *Sakralalterthümer*, 1890, both in Iwan Müller's *Handbuch*. (7) **A. Mommsen**, *Heortologie*, 1864. (8) **Smith**, *Dict. of Gk. and Roman Antiquities*, ed. Wayte and Marindin (with Appendix on 'Αθ. πολ.). (9) **Daremberg et Saglio**, *Dict. des Antiquités*. (10) **Haussoullier**, *la Vie Municipale en Attique*, 1884; **Hauvette-Besnault**, *les Stratèges Athéniens*, 1885; **A. Martin**, *les Cavaliers Ath.*, 1887; **Dürrbach**, *L'Orateur Lycurgue*, 1890, and other monographs in the same series. (11) **Philippi**, *Beiträge zu einer Geschichte des Attischen Bürgerrechtes* (1870), and *Der Areopag und die Epheten*, 1874. (12) **Fraenkel**, *die attischen Geschworenengerichte*, 1877. (13) **Schulthess**, *Vormundschaft*, 1886. (14) **U. von Wilamowitz-Moellendorff**, *Aus Kydathen*, in 'Philol. Untersuchungen,' 1880. (15) Dissertations by **Thumser**, *de Civium Atheniensium muneribus*, 1880; **Kornitzer**, *De Scribis Publicis*, 1883; **Haederli**, *Astynomen u. Agoranomen*, 1886; **Panske**, *de Magistratibus Atticis, qui saeculo A. C. quarto pecunias publicas curabant*, i, 1890; and others. (16) Articles in Philological Journals, &c.

[1] Vol. I, Part ii, *Der Athenische Staat und seine Geschichte*, edited by **Thumser**, was published in Nov. 1892, too late to be of use in the present work.

§ 11. *Abbreviations used in the critical notes, &c.*

SIGLARIUM.

Papyri Londinensis lectiones litterae 'unciales' indicant;
[ ] quae in papyro prius, ut videtur, fuerunt, nunc autem evanuerunt;
< > quae in papyro per errorem omissa, propter sensum addenda sunt;
⟦ ⟧ quae in papyro scripta, ut aliena omittenda sunt:
† obelus lectionem corruptam designat;
* asteriscus coniecturas non antea ab editore prolatas.

Editiones.

K^1 = Kenyonis ed. prima; K^2 secunda; K^3 tertia;
K-W^1 = Kaibel et von Wilamowitz-Moellendorff, ed. prima; K-W^2, ed. altera;
H-L = van Herwerden et van Leeuwen;
B = Blass.

§ 12. *List of Illustrations.*

In Frontispiece. Fig. 1; Heliastic πινάκιον, from Daremberg and Saglio's *Dict. des Antiquités*, iii 190, fig. 2410; first published by M. Rayet, *Annuaire de l'Association des Études Grecques*, 1878, p. 206. See note on p. 235.

Fig. 2 and 3; two bronze counters, probably used in the allotment of citizens to the several heliastic divisions. On the obverse, four owls and two sprays of olive, encircled with the word ΘΕϹΜΟΘΕΤΩΝ. On the reverse, fig. 2 (from the Berlin Museum) bears the letter Ε; fig. 3 (published in *Parnassos*, Athens, 1883), the letter Α. From Daremberg and Saglio, *l.c.*, fig. 2411, 2412. See note on p. 236 *b*.

Fig. 4 and 5; heliastic σύμβολα. On the obverse, a copy of the design on a τριώβολον,—an owl surrounded with two sprays of olive, and ΑΘΗ in fig. 4, Θ only in fig. 5. On the other side, a letter, probably denoting one of the heliastic sections. See note on p. 240 *b*. From Daremberg and Saglio, *l.c.*, fig. 2413, 2414.

Fig. 6 and 7; bronze ψῆφοι used for voting, found at Athens (*Bull. de Corr. Hellén.* 1887, xi 210). From Daremberg and Saglio, *l.c.*, fig. 2415—6. See note on p. 246.

On p. 39; Aeginetan Didrachmon; Berlin Cabinet, Friedländer u. Sallet, *Beschreibung*, no. 2. From Baumeister's *Denkmäler*, fig. 1010.

Ibid. and *Title-page.* Early Attic Tetradrachmon; Berlin Cabinet, *u.s.*, no. 54. From Baumeister's *Denkmäler*, fig. 1013.

CORRIGENDA.

p. 2 *b*, l. 17 from end: *read* 'either as early as 636 or as late as **624**.'
p. 7, l. 3: *dele* asterisk.
p. 133, in critical note on 35, 5: *read* Πειραιέως K, K-W.

ADDENDA.

Introduction, p. xii. The sketch on pp. ix—xii is perhaps needlessly limited to the literature of the theory of government. A survey of 'political literature', if interpreted in its wider sense, might have included some account of the *de Pace* and the *Areopagiticus* of Isocrates. Of these two political pamphlets the first advises Athens to abandon the Empire of the Sea; the second commends the earlier mode of appointing the officers of State by election (*αἵρεσις*) rather than by lot (*κλήρωσις*), and pleads for the restoration of the censorial power once wielded by the Council of the Areopagus. Both of these works may be ascribed to the year 355 B.C., and both have important points of contact with the *'Αθηναίων πολιτεία*, which was written nearly 30 years later. Some of these points are noticed in Bruno Keil's *Solon. Verf.*, pp. 78 ff, 215 &c.

p. l. The observations of Blass on the *rhythm* of the *'Αθηναίων πολιτεία* are perhaps unduly fanciful. In the extreme case quoted in the text the metrical correspondence is possibly due to accident alone. The central clause of the sentence is a quotation, *τούτου βούλεται τις κατηγορεῖν*; and it is difficult to believe that, in the language used immediately before and after this clause, the writer was consciously guided by the metrical value of the successive syllables of the quotation itself. One may also fairly mistrust a theory which leads its exponent to print the trisyllabic Πειραιῶς in c. 35 § 1, while everywhere else he prefers the quadrisyllabic Πειραιέως. A more cautious and sober view is that of Bruno Keil, *l.c.*, p. 36, who observes:—'die Unfertigkeit des Aristotelischen Buches lässt eine Rhythmik in dem Umfange, wie Blass sie annimmt, m. E. überhaupt gar nicht suchen'. Elsewhere, p. 33, he makes the interesting remark: 'das *Tempo* der Sprache unseres Buches ist im ganzen ein schnelles'.

Commentary, p. 9 (c. 3, 25): **βουκολεῖον** *κτλ*] Cf. Bruno Keil, in *Berl. Phil. Woch.* 21 May, 1892, p. 652 f.

p. 14 (c. 4, 6): **ταμίας**] The earliest inscription in which the *ταμίαι* are mentioned belongs to the first half of the sixth century, CIA iv 373[238], p. 199, *οἱ ταμίαι τάδε χαλκία κτλ*. Cf. *J. H. S.* ix 125.

p. 28 (c. 7, 23): **Διφίλου 'Ανθεμίων**] Bruno Keil, *Solon. Verf.*, p. 67, identifies with this monument a work of art mentioned in CIA, ii 742 A 12 (*Catalogi signorum ex aere factorum*), early in the second half of the 4th century:—*ἀνάθημα 'Ανθεμίων[ος....] κυνῆν ἔχει καὶ λό[γχην] vel λό[φον]*. He accordingly infers that the monument may be described as *ἀνάθημα 'Ανθεμίωνος, εἰκὼν Διφίλου*. Köhler describes the age of these *Catalogi* as *ultimis decenniis saeculi quarti non multo antiquior*. But the work of art itself may easily have been very much older, some of the rest in the list having certain portions missing. Cf. Boeckh, ii 311[2], 279[3].

p. 79 f (c. 21, 12): **διένειμε**]. Add, Milchhoefer's *Untersuchungen über die Demenordnung des Kleisthenes*, with Map, Reimer, Berlin, Oct. '92; and Szanto, *Hermes*, '92, p. 312.

p. 134 *a* (c. 35, 9): **'Εφιάλτου καὶ 'Αρχεστράτου**] Bruno Keil, *Solon. Verf.*, p. 54, proposes to identify Archestratus with the mover of the last amendment in the decree concerning Chalcis, CIA iv 1, p. 12 n. 27 *a*, 70, *'Αρχέστρατο[ς] εἶπε τὰ μὲν ἄλλα καθάπερ ['Α]ντικλῆς· τὰς [δ]ὲ εὐθύνας Χαλκιδεῦ[σ]ι κατὰ σφῶν αὐτῶν εἶναι ἐν Χαλκίδι καθάπερ 'Αθήνησιν 'Αθηναίοις, πλὴν φυγῆς καὶ θανάτου καὶ ἀτιμίας. περὶ δὲ τούτων ἔφεσιν εἶναι 'Αθήναζε ἐς τὴν ἡλιαίαν τῶν θεσμοθετῶν κατὰ τὸ ψήφισμα τοῦ δήμου.* The spirit of this proposal harmonises with the policy of Ephialtes.

Addenda Notulis Criticis. Bm = **Blass**, *Mitteilungen aus Papyrus-handschriften*, in Fleckeisen's *Jahrbücher*, Oct. 1892, pp. 571—5. Lectionum harum ipsa papyro inspecta prolatarum exemplar Blassii ipsius benevolentiae acceptum refero; ex eisdem nonnullas ab eodem impertitas in editione capitum 1—41 in textum nuperrime recepit **Hude**. Recensentur infra etiam coniecturae quaedam, quas nuper proposuit Bruno **Keil**.

2, 2 ἦν γὰρ [τότε]: ἦν γὰρ αὐτ(ῶν) Bm (Hude).

3, 6 ἐξ [ἀρχ]ῆ[ς ἦν] a J W Headlam prolatum accepi et defendi: καὶ π[άτ]ριος [ἦν] Bm (Hude). **10** [τὴν ἀρχήν· σημεῖον] δ': [ταύτ(ην)]· τεκμήρι(ον) δ' Bm (Hude). **11** ὀμνύουσι [καθάπερ]: ὀμνύουσι[ν ὥσ]περ Wessely et Bm (Hude). **14** ὁποτέρως ποτ' ἔχει μικρόν, ἐγένετο γὰρ ἐν τούτοις τοῖς χρόνοις: ὁποτέρως ποτ' ἔχει, μικρὸν ἂν παραλλάττοι τοῖς χρόνοις Bm (Hude). **17** [μόνον τὰ ἐπίθ]ετα: π[ερ] . . . . . ἐπ[ί]θετα (περ[αίνειν] ἐπίθετα?) Bm. **22** πλείων [ἢ] ἐνιαύσιος. [οὗτοι] μὲν οὖν χρ(όνον): πλείων ἐνιαυσίας. [τ]ῷ μὲν οὖν χρ(όνῳ) Bm, coll. Pl. *Leg.* 779 D οὐκ ἐλάττων ἐνιαυσίας (Hude).

4, 10 διε[γγυ]ᾶ[σθαι]: διε[γγυ]ᾶν, *cautionem* (vel *sponsionem*) *exigere*, Bm (Hude); idem coniecerat Fränkel, *Rhein. Mus.* xlvii 473, sed alio sensu, *spondere*. **12** π(αρα)σχομένους* cum Blassio conieceram: δεχομένους K, K-W, (participio cum ἔνους constructo) Bm (Hude). **13** οὗπερ <εἰσὶν> Hude.

5, 8 ἐσορῶντ' Naber (Hude). **9** καὶ γὰρ †ἐπελαύνει καὶ πρὸς: 'καινομένην' (de Attica, *pereuntem*), ἐν ᾗ (HI) πρὸς Bm (Hude). **17** ἐν μετρίοισι τ[ρέφεσθε]: ἐν μετρίοισι τι . . . θε Bm; recte igitur τίθεσθε proposuerat Platt. **21** τήν τε φι[λοχρημ]ατίαν (quod coniecerat Kontos) Bm, qui usitatam lectionem φιλαργυρίαν cum litterarum vestigiis non congruere arbitratur, sed spatium litteris tribus PHM paullo angustius esse confitetur.

6, 15 ἀπεχθέσθαι <ἑλέσθαι> Hude, hiatu sine causa admisso. **18** καταρρυπαίν[ε]ιν: καταρρυπῆναι Gertz (Hude), hiatu admisso.

7, 7 κατεκύρωσεν (δὲ τοὺς νόμους): κατέκλησεν (ICEN iam antea Wessely) Bm; 'machte fest', 'gab Geltung', Hude; sed explicandum potius *leges suas intra centum annorum spatium inclusit.* **9** τιμήμα[τα δι]εῖλεν: τιμήματι [δι]εῖλεν Wessely, Bm (Hude). **11** τὰς μ[ὲν οὖ]ν ἀρχὰς: κ(αὶ) τὰς μὲν ἀρχὰς (spatio inter ME et N vacuo relicto) Bm (Hude).

8, 21 [καὶ] τά τε ἄλλα: [ἢ] τά τε ἄλλα Bm (Hude). **24** [τοῦ *πράττ]εσθαι: [τοῦ ἐ]κτ[ίν]εσθ(αι) Bm (Hude); idem coniecerat Tyrrell.

9, 11 ὅπως π(ερὶ) τῆς κρίσε[ως ὁ δ]ῆ[μος ᾖ κ]ύριος Keil.

10, 2 ποιῆσαι K; ποιῆσα[ι] Bm. **5** παρ' ὀ[λί]γον Keil. **6** ἦν δ' ὁ ἀρχαῖος χαρακτὴρ διδράχμου. ἐποίησε δὲ καὶ <τὰ> σταθμὰ πρὸς τ[ὸ] νόμισμα, τ[ρ]εῖς καὶ <τετταράκοντα ἐπαυξήσας εἰς τὰς> ἑξήκοντα μνᾶς τὸ τάλαντον ἀγούσας Keil, *Solon. Verf.* p. 166. **8** ἑξήκοντα: ὀγδοήκοντα Gertz (Hude). **9** [αἱ] μναῖ: [αἱ γ'] μναῖ Bm, supra versum hastam numeri signum prodentem cerni posse testatus: αἱ τρεῖς καὶ εἴκοσι (κγ' Gertz) μναῖ Hude.

11, 10 An γενέσθαι τὴν [νέαν] τάξιν? Keil. **12** ἢ σ[χεδὸν ἀ]παράλλακτον Keil; ἢ μ[ικ]ρ[ὸ]ν παραλλάξ[ειν Bm, et deinceps ὅθε]ν [ἀ]μφοτέρους. **13** συστά[ντι]: συστά[ντ]α Bm (Hude).

12, 14 ὅσοις: ὅτοις Hude. **51** φρασαίατ' ἂν Hude. **54** πολλαῖσιν: πολλῇισ[ι]ν Bm. (πολλῇσιν Hude).

16, 17 τὰ: τὸ H-L (Bm). **18** πα[ττά]λῳ: ἐπιμελῶς Hude, quod obiter conieceram. **27** ἐθ[ρυ]λλ[εῖ]το: ἐνθύμ(ιον) ἦν Bm (Hude), qui lectionem novam idem ac ἐνεθυμοῦντο valere dicit, sed exspectares potius ἐνεκωμιάζετο. **31** [προῃρεῖτο]: [ἐ]β[ούλ]ε[το] Bm (Hude). **35** ἔμεινεν <ἐν> [τῇ ἀρχῇ, κ(αὶ)] ὅτ' ἐκπέσοι: ἔμεινεν, [κ(αὶ) δὴ] κ(αὶ) ὅτ' ἐκπέσοι Bm (Hude). **42** Ἀθηναίω[ν] K (Bm).

17, 4 ἔφ[ευγ]εν γὰρ: ἔφ[ευ]γε γ(ὰρ) Bm. **18, 19** τ(ῶν) [λοιπῶν]: τ(ῶν) [ἄλλ]ων K (Bm).

19, 20 ὅθεν εὐπόρησαν κτλ: ὅτι εὔποροι ἦσαν χρημάτων, <ἀποβλέποντες> hiatu bis admisso Hude.

21, 3 <τὴν πολιτείαν ὧδε κατέστησεν>. ※ ※ πρῶτον μὲν οὖν <συν>ένειμε Hude.

22, 42 ἀτίμους: ἀτίμοις Hude. **24, 11** τῶν τελῶν ⟦καὶ⟧ <τῶν ἀπὸ> τῶν συμμάχων Hude. **19** ἄλλαι δὲ <δέκα> νῆες αἱ τοὺς φόρους ἄγουσαι, <ἔχουσαι> Hude.

28, 16 ταῖς ὁρμαῖς <χαριζόμενος> J B Mayor (Hude).

29, 7 το[ῦ Ἐπι]ζ[ήλου]: το[ῦ Ἀναφλ]υ[σ]τίου Bm (Hude), demi potius quam patris nomine etiam alias usurpato, c. 28, 22, c. 34, 27, c. 38, 22; Pythodorum igitur non Epizeli filium tribus Aegeidis sed Anaphlystium quendam tribus Antiochidis fuisse censet B. **8** τ(ὸν) βασιλέα Bm.

31, 19 ⟦τοῖς⟧ αὐτοῖς: τοῖς ἀστοῖς K[3] (Bm). **32, 16** ὑπακου[σά]ντων: ὑποκουόντων (H-L) Bm.

36, 13 πολὺν μὲν χρόνον ὑπερεβάλλοντο <ἐκφέρειν Gertz>—, ὅτε δὲ καὶ ἔδοξεν αὐτοῖς ⟦ἐκφέρειν⟧, τοὺς μὲν ἐξήλειψαν τῶν <ἐγ>γεγραμμένων, τοὺς δ' ἀντενέγραψαν τῶν ἔξωθεν Hude.

38, 7 *ἐπέ[στελλον]—μεταπε[μπόμ]ενοι: ἔπε[μ]πο[ν]—μεταπεμπόμενοι Bm (Hude).

39, 24 τοὺς δ' ἐν τῷ ἄστει ἐν τοῖς <ἐν τῷ ἄστει τοῖς> τὰ <αὐτὰ> τιμήματα παρεχομένοις Gertz (Hude).

41, 3 ※ ※ δοκοῦσι δὲ δικαίως ⟦τοῦ δήμου⟧ λαβεῖν τὴν πολιτείαν (π[ο]λιτ[ι]αν Bm), Hude. **27** <ἀν>εληλύθασιν Hude.

42, 11 ἐὰν: HAN (deleto H) Bm. **43, 15** καθίζειν: KAΘIZEI Bm.

47, 12 τὰ εἰς <γ'> ἔ[τη] πεπραμένα: τὰ εἰς [ι' ἔτ]η π. Bm. **14** [ὀφειλε]τῶν ἐν[αντίον]: AΛ[ΛE]N[......], ἄλλ(ων) ἐναντίον Bm. **17** [ὅσου] ἂν πρίηται: ἃ ἂν πρίηται Bm. **30** τὰ γραμματ[εῖα τὰ] τὰς καταβολὰς ἀναγεγραμμένα: τὰ γραμματεῖα K (*i.e.* K̀=κατὰ) τὰς καταβολὰς ἀναγεγραμμένα Bm, coll. v. 20.

48, 5 διπλ[οῦν ἀ]νάγκη: διπλά[σιον ἀ]νάγκη Bm. **8** τὰ χρ[ήματα]: τὰς τ[ιμὰ]ς Bm. **16** ἀ[γορ]αῖς: AN .... AIC (ante AIC vinculi vestigium litteram K vel Λ vel X indicantis) Bm, qui ἀν[αδικί]αις, *appellationum causa*, dubitanter conicit. **21** τό <τε>[αὐτοῦ]: τό [θ' αὐτοῦ], αὐτοῦ per se spatium non implet, Bm. **25** ἐπι]γράφει: ἀ]ναγράφει Bm. **27** [τὴν] εὔθυναν: [ταύτ(ην) τ(ὴν)] εὔθυναν Bm, spatio sex litteris apto.

49, 1 f καλὸν ἵ[ππον ἔχ]ων: καλ[ῶ]ν [τροφεὺ]ς ὢν Bm, numero plurali cum contextu congruente. Cf. Pl. *Leg.* 735 B τροφεὺς ἵππων.

54, 32 [νῦν] δ(ὲ) πρόσκειται (Π superscr. POC, deinde KEITAI) [κ(αὶ) Ἡ]φαίσ[τι]α, ἐπὶ Κηφισοφῶντος ἄρχοντος Bm, confessus Ἡφαιστίων in πεντετηρίδα mutationem nusquam alias commemorari. **36** καὶ τοὔ[ν]ομα.

55, 2 [πραγμάτ]ων, spatio non sufficiente: [ἁπάντ]ων Bm. **3** [εἴρη]ται: [προε]ίρητα[ι mavult Bm.

56, 21 [τῆς τε]: [τῆ]ς (littera producta) Bm. **30** εἰς τ[ὸ δι]καστήριον: εἰς δ[ι]καστήριον Bm.

57, 2 [τῶν ἐπιμελητῶν οὓς] ὁ δῆμος χειροτονεῖ: τῶν ἐπ. ὧ]ν ὁ δ. χ. Bm. **25** καὶ δικάζο[υσιν] ἐν ἱερ[ῶι] καὶ ὑπαί[θ]ριοι, coll. v. 29 εἰς τὸ ἱερόν, Bm, notas quasdam fallaces, non litterarum vestigia vera, superesse arbitratus. **28** δ[ίκαιον ἐ]μβαλεῖν: ν[όμος ἐ]μβαλεῖν Bm.

61, 27 καὶ ἄλλον τῆς [τοῦ Ἄ]μμωνος: καὶ ν[ῦν] τῆς (superscr.) [τοῦ Ἄ]μμωνος mavult Bm.

62, 5 δ[ημότ]ας: δήμ[ου]ς Bm. **63, 18** πινάκιον: [καὶ] πινάκιον, suadente spatio, Bm.

Pag. 31, 18 κα[λεῖ εἰς τὸ κ]ληρωτήριον: κληρ[οῖ κατὰ κ]ληρωτήριον Bm. **24** [ἄρχων]: literae primae hasta superest, legendum igitur [κῆρυξ], Bm. ὑπάρχει—**25** εἰς [ὃ]ν [αὐτῷ]ν: ὑπάρχει—εἰς τὸν (Wessely) κ[λῆρο]ν, *sortitioni iam antea paratus est*, aut *sortem iam antea duxit*, Bm, εἰς τὸν [ἀριθμὸ]ν sensui magis congruere confessus. **26** εἰλη]χ[ὼς ἕλ[κ]ει [βάλανο]ν ἐκ τῆς ὑδρίας: ΕΙΛΚΥϹ..... ΕΙ κτλ, supra quattuor litteras primas ΕΛΚ (ut videtur) scriptum, Bm, cui nihil sensui aptum obtigit: scribendum fortasse ἑλκύσ[ας αἱρ]εῖ. **27** καὶ ὀρ[έ]ξας αὐτῇ[ν, οὐκ ἰδ]ὼν τὸ γράμμα, δ[εί]κνυσιν πρ[ῶτον αὐτὸ] τῷ ἄρχοντι Bm. **30** ὅπου: ΟΙΟΥ Bm, coll. v. 32. **36** ὅσ' ἂν ἀεὶ [μ]έλλῃ: ΟϹΑΝΠΕΡ (deleto Ν) κτλ, ὅσαπερ [ἂν μ]έλλῃ Bm, quod exspectabant K-W.

Pag. 32, 1 ἑκάσ|του] ΕΙΧ: ἑκάσ|του εἴληχ[ό]ς Bm. **4** post γράμμα ΕΙ, coniciendum igitur ἔ[στιν], Bm. **17—27** τοῖς δ' ἀπο|λα]γ[χ]ανουσ[ι]ν ἀποδιδ[όασιν] οἱ ἐμπ[η]κτ[αι (ΕΜΠΕΠ.ΚΤ.. fortasse per errorem scripto) | τὰ] πινάκια. οἱ δὲ ὑπη[ρέται] οἱ δημοσια[κοὶ (?) | τῆ]ς φυλῆς ἑκάστης π[αραδι]δόασιν τὰ κ[ι|βώτια ἓν ἐπὶ τὸ δικα[στήρ]ιον ἕκαστον, ἐ[ν] οἷ[ς] | ἔνεστιν τὰ ὀνόματ[α τῆς] φυλῆς τὰ ὄντ[α | ἐν ἑκάστῳ τ[ῶν δι]κα[στηρί]ων. παραδιδόασι | δὲ τοῖς εἰληχ[όσιν ἀποδ]ιδόναι τοῖς δικασ|ταῖς ἐν ἑκάστῳ [δ]ικα[στηρί]ῳ ἀριθμῷ τὰ | πινάκια, [ἵν'? (post πινάκια Τ, ut videtur, superscriptum) ἐ]κ τού[των σκο]ποῦντες ἀπο[δι|δῶσι τὸν [μισ]θόν. Bm. In v. 22 τὰ [ὀνόμ]α[τα quondam conieceram, sed postea τὰ [πιν]ά[κια] praetuli. **28—35** κατὰ δικαστήριον (ΡΙΝ littera Ο super Ι scripta). τί[θεται δ'] ἐν τῷ πρ[ώτῳ τ]ῶν | δικαστηρ[ίων κ(αὶ)] κλ[ηρωτή]ρια καὶ κ[ύβ]οι [χ]αλκοῖ | ἐν οἷς ἐπιγέγραπται [τὰ χρώ]ματα τῶν δικ[αστηρίων] | καὶ ἕτεροι κύ[βοι], ἐν οἷ[ς ἐστιν] τῶν ἀρ[χῶ]ν τ[ὰ ὀ]νό[μα|τα ἐπι[γεγ]ρ[α]μμέ[να. οἱ λαχ]όντες [δὲ] τῶν [θεσμ]ο|θετῶν χωρὶς ἑκα[τέρο]υς τοὺς κύ[βους ἐμ|β[ά]λλουσιν, ὁ μὲν τ[ῶν δικαστ]ηρ[ίων εἰς ἓν κληρω|τ[ή]ριον, ὁ δὲ τῶν ἀρχ[ῶν εἰς ἕτερ]ον — — —

Pag. 33; 33^a et 33^b, composita a K-W (B), vix revera coniuncta fuisse putat Bm; 33^a et 34^c potius componenda: cumque primum 34^c et 35^a, deinde 35^a et 35^b, denique 35 et 36 coniuncta sint, fragmenta in hunc ordinem redigenda:—32, 33^b, 34^{ab} (cum 33^b coniunctum), $33^a + 34^c$, 35, 36, 37.

Pag. 35, 1 τῶν λ]όγων B: Ν]ΟΜΟΝ K[3]; ΝΟΜΟΝ (itaque in v. 2 ἢ μαρ[τυρίαν]) Bm. **7—8** Ποσε[ι|δεῶνος Bm. **12—13** κατηγ]οροι ἐσ|πενδο[ν Bm.

Pag. 36, 5 [μ]ή [τινε]ς ὑπο[β]άλλωνται non recte: [μ]ὴ [πρ]οϋπο[βάλλωνται (K-W) substitui potest, Bm. **17** πιέ[ζει]: πιέ[ζ]ων satis clare apparet, Bm. **23** λαβόντες [ὑ]πηρέτ[ας (non iam inserto δύ') Bm. **24** [ἐξε]ρῶσι ἐ[πὶ] ἄβα|κα Bm. Cf. Arist. *Vesp.* 993, φέρ' ἐξεράσω (τὰς ψήφους). **27** [καὶ] τὰ πλήρη δῆλ(α), λ supra ΔΗ scriptum, Bm.

ΑΡΙΣΤΟΤΕΛΟΥΣ
ΑΘΗΝΑΙΩΝ ΠΟΛΙΤΕΙΑ.

1. — — [Μ]ύρωνος καθ' ἱερῶν ὀμόσαντες ἀριστίνδην. καταγνωσθέντος δὲ τοῦ ἄγο[υ]ς [αὐτ]οὶ μὲν ἐκ τῶν τάφων ἐξεβλήθησαν,

θαρθεν

I 1 καταγνωϲθεντοϲ. Sensui repugnat *καθαρθέντος*, etenim tunc temporis erat *τὸ ἄγος καταγνωσθὲν* tantum, nondum autem *καθαρθέν*. **2** *αὐτοὶ* scripsi; quod cum verbis in altero membro (*τὸ γένος αὐτῶν*) satis apte quadrat; cf. Paus. i 25, 3 *αὐτοί τε οἱ ἀποκτείναντες ἐνομίσθησαν καὶ οἱ ἐξ ἐκείνων ἐναγεῖς τῆς θεοῦ*. Idem scripserunt K–W et K[3] Kirchhoffium et Kontum secuti. *νεκροὶ* quondam K, *οἱ νεκροὶ* H-L, sed articulo quem desideramus spatium non sufficit, et in ipsa papyro litterae τ potius quam ρ apparet vestigium.

Testimonia. **1** Capitis primi partem deperditam in compendium redactam conservat Heraclidis epitoma (Rose, Frag. 611, 2[3]): *τοὺς μετὰ Κύλωνος* (Κύκλωπος codices meliores) *διὰ τὴν τυραννίδα ἐπὶ τὸν βωμὸν τῆς θεοῦ πεφευγότας οἱ περὶ Μεγακλέα ἀπέκτειναν, καὶ τοὺς δράσαντας ὡς ἐναγεῖς ἤλαυνον.*

I. *Cylon's attempt to establish a tyranny, and its consequences.*

Μύρωνος] Myron of Phlya is mentioned by Plutarch alone, *Sol.* 12, as the accuser of the Alcmaeonidae who were involved in the curse of Cylon. At a later time one of the Alcmaeonidae, named *Λεωβώτης*, had his revenge for this act of a member of the deme of Phlya by bringing a charge of high treason against a distinguished member of that deme, Themistocles (Plut. *Them.* 23; cf. *ib.* 1 § 3). Busolt, *Griechische Geschichte*, 1885, i 508.

καθ' ἱερῶν ὀμόσαντες] Cf. decree quoted in c. 29 (at end), *ὀμόσαντες καθ' ἱερῶν τελείων*.

ἀριστίνδην] cannot be taken with *καθ' ἱερῶν ὀμόσαντες*, but must go with some such verb as *ἐδίκαζον* in the earlier part of the sentence. We may perhaps infer from Plutarch *Sol.* 12 that the sentence ran as follows: [*ἐδίκαζον δὲ τριακόσιοι κατηγοροῦντος*] *Μύρωνος καθ' ἱερῶν ὀμόσαντες ἀριστίνδην*. According to Plutarch the Alcmaeonidae were tried by a court consisting of 300 persons selected from the noblest families (*δικαζόντων ἀριστίνδην*). The number is confirmed by its being identical with that of the *Boule* of the partisans of Isagoras which Cleomenes king of Sparta endeavoured to establish at Athens in a subsequent attack on the Alcmaeonidae (Hdt. v 72). For *ἀριστίνδην* cf. c. 3, l. 2.

καταγνωσθέντος—τοῦ ἄγους] 'The charge of sacrilege having been made good' by the sentence of condemnation passed by the court.

ἐκ τῶν τάφων ἐξεβλήθησαν] The same incident is mentioned in Plutarch *l. c.*, and Thuc. *l. c.* In the latter it seems to be more closely connected with the second expulsion of the *ἐναγεῖς* (in 508 B.C.), than with the first.

The principal ancient authorities on the affair of Cylon are as follows. Hdt. v 71, *ἦν Κύλων τῶν Ἀθηναίων ἀνὴρ Ὀλυμπιονίκης. οὗτος ἐπὶ τυραννίδι ἐκόμησε, προσποιησάμενος δὲ ἑταιρηίην τῶν ἡλικιωτέων καταλαβεῖν τὴν ἀκρόπολιν ἐπειρήθη, οὐ δυνάμενος δὲ ἐπικρατῆσαι ἱκέτης ἵζετο πρὸς τὸ ἄγαλμα. τούτους ἀνιστᾶσι μὲν οἱ πρυτάνιες τῶν ναυκράρων* (*al.* *ναυκραριέων*), *οἵπερ ἔνεμον τότε τὰς Ἀθήνας, ὑπεγγύους*

3 τὸ δὲ γένος αὐτῶν ἔφυγεν ἀειφυγίαν. Ἐ[πι]μενίδης δ᾽ ὁ Κρὴς ἐπὶ τούτοις ἐκάθηρε τὴν πόλιν.

πλὴν θανάτου· φονεῦσαι δὲ αὐτοὺς αἰτίη ἔχει Ἀλκμεωνίδας. ταῦτα πρὸ τῆς Πεισιστράτου ἡλικίης ἐγένετο. The above account is unduly favourable to the Alcmaeonidae. It is materially corrected by Thucydides, i 126 § 2, Κύλων ἦν Ὀλυμπιονίκης, ἀνὴρ Ἀθηναῖος τῶν πάλαι εὐγενής τε καὶ δυνατός...ὁ δὲ...κατέλαβε τὴν ἀκρόπολιν ὡς ἐπὶ τυραννίδι... § 6 οἱ δὲ μετὰ τοῦ Κύλωνος πολιορκούμενοι φλαύρως εἶχον σίτου τε καὶ ὕδατος ἀπορίᾳ. ὁ μὲν οὖν Κύλων καὶ ὁ ἀδελφὸς αὐτοῦ ἐκδιδράσκουσιν· οἱ δ᾽ ἄλλοι ὡς ἐπιέζοντο καί τινες καὶ ἀπέθνησκον ὑπὸ τοῦ λιμοῦ, καθίζουσιν ἐπὶ τὸν βωμὸν ἱκέται τὸν ἐν τῇ ἀκροπόλει. ἀναστήσαντες δὲ αὐτοὺς οἱ τῶν Ἀθηναίων ἐπιτετραμμένοι τὴν φυλακήν, ὡς ἑώρων ἀποθνήσκοντας ἐν τῷ ἱερῷ ἐφ᾽ ᾧ μηδὲν κακὸν ποιήσουσιν ἀπαγαγόντες ἀπέκτειναν. § 7 καθεζομένους δέ τινας καὶ ἐπὶ τῶν σεμνῶν θεῶν [ἐν τοῖς βωμοῖς] ἐν τῇ παρόδῳ διεχρήσαντο. καὶ ἀπὸ τούτου ἐναγεῖς καὶ ἀλιτήριοι τῆς θεοῦ ἐκεῖνοί τε ἐκαλοῦντο καὶ τὸ γένος τὸ ἀπ᾽ ἐκείνων. ἤλασαν μὲν οὖν καὶ οἱ Ἀθηναῖοι τοὺς ἐναγεῖς τούτους, ἤλασε δὲ καὶ Κλεομένης ὁ Λακεδαιμόνιος ὕστερον μετὰ Ἀθηναίων στασιαζόντων (B.C. 508), τούς τε ζῶντας ἐλαύνοντες καὶ τῶν τεθνεώτων τὰ ὀστᾶ ἀνελόντες ἐξέβαλον. Plutarch, *Solon* 12, supplies us with the following narrative, which has several points of contact with the account in the text. τὸ δὲ Κυλώνειον ἄγος ἤδη μὲν ἐκ πολλοῦ διετάραττε τὴν πόλιν, ἐξ οὗ τοὺς συνωμότας τοῦ Κύλωνος ἱκετεύοντας τὴν θεὸν Μεγακλῆς ὁ ἄρχων ἐπὶ δίκῃ κατελθεῖν ἔπεισεν· ἐξάψαντας δὲ τοῦ ἕδους κρόκην κλωστὴν καὶ ταύτης ἐχομένους, ὡς ἐγένοντο περὶ τὰς σεμνὰς θεὰς καταβαίνοντες, αὐτομάτως τῆς κρόκης ῥαγείσης, ὥρμησε συλλαμβάνειν ὁ Μεγακλῆς καὶ οἱ συνάρχοντες, ὡς τῆς θεοῦ τὴν ἱκεσίαν ἀπολεγομένης· καὶ τοὺς μὲν ἔξω κατέλευσαν, οἱ δὲ τοῖς βωμοῖς προσφυγόντες ἀπεσφάγησαν· μόνοι δ᾽ ἀφείθησαν οἱ τὰς γυναῖκας αὐτῶν ἱκετεύσαντες. ἐκ τούτου δὲ κληθέντες ἐναγεῖς ἐμισοῦντο· καὶ τῶν Κυλωνείων οἱ περιγενόμενοι πάλιν ἦσαν ἰσχυροὶ καὶ στασιάζοντες ἀεὶ διετέλουν πρὸς τοὺς ἀπὸ τοῦ Μεγακλέους. ἐν δὲ τῷ τότε χρόνῳ τῆς στάσεως ἀκμὴν λαβούσης μάλιστα καὶ τοῦ δήμου διαστάντος, ἤδη δόξαν ἔχων ὁ Σόλων παρῆλθεν εἰς μέσον ἅμα τοῖς ἀρίστοις τῶν Ἀθηναίων, καὶ δεόμενος καὶ διδάσκων ἔπεισε τοὺς ἐναγεῖς λεγομένους δίκην ὑποσχεῖν καὶ κριθῆναι τριακοσίων ἀριστίνδην δικαζόντων. Μύρωνος δὲ τοῦ Φλυέως κατηγοροῦντος ἑάλωσαν οἱ ἄνδρες, καὶ μετέστησαν οἱ ζῶντες· τῶν δ᾽ ἀποθανόντων τοὺς νεκροὺς ἀνορύξαντες ἐξέρριψαν ὑπὲρ τοὺς ὅρους. ταύταις δὲ ταῖς ταραχαῖς καὶ Μεγαρέων συνεπιθεμένων ἀπέβαλόν τε Νίσαιαν οἱ Ἀθηναῖοι καὶ Σαλαμῖνος ἐξέπεσον αὖθις. καὶ φόβοι τινὲς ἐκ δεισιδαιμονίας ἅμα καὶ φάσματα κατεῖχε τὴν πόλιν, οἵ τε μάντεις ἄγη καὶ μιασμοὺς δεομένους καθαρμῶν προφαίνεσθαι διὰ τῶν ἱερῶν ἠγόρευον. οὕτω δὴ μετάπεμπτος αὐτοῖς ἧκεν ἐκ Κρήτης Ἐπιμενίδης ...ἐλθὼν δὲ καὶ τῷ Σόλωνι χρησάμενος φίλῳ πολλὰ προσυπειργάσατο καὶ προωδοποίησεν αὐτῷ τῆς νομοθεσίας...τὸ δὲ μέγιστον, ἱλασμοῖς τισι καὶ καθαρμοῖς καὶ ἱδρύσεσι κατοργιάσας καὶ καθοσιώσας τὴν πόλιν ὑπήκοον τοῦ δικαίου καὶ μᾶλλον εὐπειθῆ πρὸς ὁμόνοιαν κατέστησε.

The date of the Olympic victory of Cylon is 640 B.C. Sex. Julius Africanus (early in 3rd century A.D.), as quoted in the Chronicon of Eusebius, i p. 145=198, has, under *Ol.* 35, 1=B.C. 640, *Recursum Cylon Atheniensis, is qui tyrannidem affectavit.* Plutarch *l. c.* implies that Epimenides visited Athens, in connexion with the expiation of the curse of Cylon, shortly before the legislation of Solon (archon 594 B.C.). Hence the attempt of Cylon has generally been placed after the date of Dracon (621 B.C.). Thucydides, i 126, 3, places Cylon's attempt to seize the tyranny in an Olympic year. It has therefore been assigned to the Olympic years 620 (Clinton and Peter), 616 (Duncker), 612 (Corsini). But Herodotus *l. c.* describes the partisans of Cylon as an ἑταιρηίη τῶν ἡλικιωτέων, which points to a company of young men. Hence it has been suggested that the attempt was made at an earlier date, before the time of Dracon. It has accordingly been assigned to various Olympic years between 640 and 620 B.C., either as early as 636 or as late as 620 (Busolt, *Griechische Geschichte*, 1885, i 498 note 8, and 505). The same opinion was maintained by Prof. John H. Wright as reported in the *Proceedings of the American Philological Association*, 1888, p. xxvi. His arguments were drawn from the language of Herodotus, Thucydides and the other authorities on this incident; from considerations of the probable age of Megacles and the date of Cylon's father-in-law, Theagenes of Megara. He also urged that 'the adoption of the earlier date lent unexpected coherence and significance to certain phenomena in early Attic history, the episode thus being one of the important steps in the social

2. *μετὰ δὲ ταῦτα συνέβη στασιάσαι τούς τε γνωρίμους καὶ τὸ*

II 1 ϹΤΑϹΙΑϹΑΙ fortasse in ΔΙΑϹΤΗϹΑΙ mutandum, idem suspicantur H-L coll. Arist. *Vesp.* 41 τὸν δῆμον ἡμῶν βούλεται διιστάναι; alioqui τὸν δῆμον secludendum.

---

and political development of Athens, and not an unrelated event.' This opinion is confirmed by the text which clearly implies that the affair of Cylon preceded the date of Dracon.

ἔφυγεν ἀειφυγίαν] Plat. *Leg.* 871 D, 877 C, 881 BD, φευγέτω ἀειφυγίαν, 877 E, (ὅταν) ἐν ἀειφυγίᾳ τις φεύγῃ. Plut. *Sol.* 24, τοῖς φεύγουσιν ἀειφυγίᾳ τὴν ἑαυτῶν. Photius, *s. v.* μαστῆρες: τῶν ἀειφυγίαν φυγαδευθέντων.

Ἐπιμενίδης] The purification of Athens by Epimenides is generally assigned to B.C. 596—5, shortly before the archonship of Solon in 594—3 (Clinton, *Fasti*, and Busolt, i 509). These dates are consistent with the account in Plutarch and were possibly suggested by it, or derived from some common source, such as Hermippus of Alexandria, quoted in Plut. *Sol.* 11. The chronology of the life of Epimenides is however extremely uncertain. Diogenes Laertius, i 111, quotes Phlegon as stating that Epimenides returned to Crete and died not long after at the age of 157. He adds that Xenophanes made him die at the age of 154, and the Cretans at 299. (But the Cretans, as we know on the authority of Epimenides himself, 'are always liars.') Suidas puts his birth in Ol. 30 (about 659 B.C.), and describes him as an old man at the time of the purification, which he places in Ol. 44 (B.C. 604—), corrected by Bernhardy into Ol. 46 (B.C. 596—). At the latter date he would have been 63.

On the other hand, Plato, *Leg.* 642 D, 698 C, describes him as coming to Athens and offering expiatory sacrifices in 500 B.C. This account is rejected by Bentley and Grote. The former says of Plato: 'that great Man did not tie himself in his Discourses to Exactness of Time' (*Phalaris*, p. 58); the latter regards the statement in the *Laws* as 'a remarkable example of carelessness in chronology' (*H. G.*, c. 10, ii 294). The sacrifices ascribed to Epimenides by Plato may, indeed, be connected with the outbreak of a plague attested by an inscription of about 500 B.C. (CIA i 475, Busolt i 509), but this is not enough to warrant our placing the prophet a century later than the age of Solon.

Thus we have two accounts of the date of Epimenides, (1) that represented by Plato, placing him about 500 B.C.; (2) that represented hitherto by no earlier authority than Hermippus, placing him about 600 B.C. (2) is supported by the text, which mentions his visit immediately after an account of a trial assigned by Plutarch to the time of Solon. The discrepancy between the two accounts is explained by Diels as arising from the fact that Plato is referring to the Epimenides of literature and not to the Epimenides of history. The Theogony ascribed to Epimenides was written under Orphic influence shortly before the Persian wars; and the story of the protracted sleep of Epimenides, which lasted for a whole century, was a fiction designed at the same time to give currency to the poetical fabrications ascribed to him. The curse of Cylon was originally expiated through the banishment of the Alcmaeonidae and the purification of Athens by Epimenides about 600 B.C. In the following century the Alcmaeonidae returned and about 508 B.C., after the expulsion of the Peisistratidae, when Cleisthenes, the Alcmaeonid, was the foremost man in the state, the influence of the exiles led to a revival of the memory of the ancient crime. At such a time as this the story of Epimenides was naturally revived by the opponents of Cleisthenes, and his oracles invented as part of their machinations against the guilty race of the Alcmaeonidae (Diels, *Sitzungsberichte* of the Berlin Academy, April 16, 1891, part xxi; abstract in *Berliner Philologische Wochenschrift*, p. 766).

ἐπὶ τούτοις] either 'thereupon,' or 'besides.' Ἐπὶ τούτοις in the former sense = μετὰ ταῦτα has hitherto been found only in the spurious works (Eucken, *Sprachgebrauch des Ar.*, p. 51). The latter sense (*praeterea*) is on the whole preferable, and is found in *Rhet.* ii 6, 1384 *a* 9. Cf. *Pol.* ii 9, 1271 *a* 39, ἐπὶ τοῖς βασιλεῦσιν ἡ ναυαρχία ἑτέρα βασιλεία καθέστηκεν.

ἐκάθηρε] For the details of this purification, see Plut. *Sol.* 12 *ad fin.* (καθαρμοῖς), and Diogenes Laertius i 110.

II. *The conflict of the classes before the times of Dracon and Solon.*

μετὰ ταῦτα] *i.e.* after the affair of Cylon, which must have been the main πλῆθος πολὺν χρόνον [[τὸν δῆμον]]. ἦν γὰρ [τότε] ἡ πολιτεία τ[οῖς 2 τε] ἄλλοις ὀλιγαρχικὴ πᾶσι, καὶ δὴ καὶ ἐδούλευον οἱ πένητε[ς τ]οῖς πλουσίοις καὶ αὐτοὶ [καὶ τ]ὰ τέκνα καὶ αἱ γυναῖκες, καὶ ἐκαλοῦντο πελάται καὶ ἑκτημόροι· κατὰ ταύτην γὰρ τὴν μίσθωσιν [εἰ]ργά-

2 τὸν δῆμον secluserunt K, K-W, H-L, B: defendit J E B Mayor. **5** ΚΙΤΑΥΤΓ ΤΜΙCΘ^{ωσ} ἀντὶ ταύτης γὰρ τῆς μισθώσεως H-L. εἰργάζοντο H-L.

TESTIMONIA. **5** πελάται καὶ ἑκτημόροι. *Photius s. v. πελάται 2 Aristotelem nominat. Cf. schol. in Plat. *Euthyphr.* p. 327; Pollux iv 165 ἑκτημόριοι (ἑκτημόριον codices, emendavit Jungermann; ἑκτημόροι Cobet Pollucis sui in margine) δὲ παρὰ τοῖς Ἀττικοῖς, id. iii 82; Plut. *Sol.* 13 (Rose, Ar. Frag. 351^2, 389^3).

---

subject of the previous chapter; although, in the part that has been preserved, the narrative of its consequences is brought down to the time of Epimenides (and Solon).

For the general sense, cf. Plut. *Sol.* 13 *init.*, οἱ δ' Ἀθηναῖοι τῆς Κυλωνείου πεπαυμένης ταραχῆς καὶ μεθεστώτων...τῶν ἐναγῶν, τὴν παλαιὰν αὖθις στάσιν ὑπὲρ τῆς πολιτείας ἐστασίαζον, ὅσας ἡ χώρα διαφορὰς εἶχεν, εἰς τοσαῦτα μέρη τῆς πόλεως διαστάσης.

In the *editio princeps* τὸν δῆμον was regarded as 'superfluous,' and as 'probably a gloss upon τὸ πλῆθος.' The text was thereupon defended by Professor Mayor as follows: 'when Cobet removes glosses from late texts, he can appeal to *scholia*, in which even common words are explained. Readers and scribes in Egypt, say 100 A.D., needed no such helps: again πλῆθος is not coextensive with δῆμος, and is elsewhere found in close connexion with it (20 § 1; 21 § 1). Here οἱ γνώριμοι and τὸ πλῆθος are the factions whose struggles convulse τὸν δῆμον. For στασιάζω is here transitive. Otherwise πολὺν χρόνον must have been placed just before or just after στασιάσαι. In the manuscript reading it separates the complex subject of the verb from the object and keeps the reader in suspense.' Mr Kenyon, in his third ed., replies that 'δῆμος does not seem to be used in this treatise as denoting the whole state except with the collateral sense that the state was a democracy.' Even in c. 14 § 1, ἐπαναστὰς ...τῷ δήμῳ, and 15 § 3, παρελόμενος τοῦ δήμου τὰ ὅπλα, 'there is the sense of an attack on the democracy by a despot.' He also modifies his view respecting τὸν δῆμον, suggesting that the words were 'written as a correction of τὸ πλῆθος, not as an explanation.'

The transitive use of στασιάζειν, above suggested, is very rare. In [Dem.] 11 § 18, p. 157, 10, τῶν ἐκείνου πραγμάτων οὐδὲν στασιάζειν παρασκευάζομεν (quoted in L and S) really means 'we do not cause faction in any of his affairs' (see Weil *ad loc.*). The intrans. sense is also clearly marked in Lysias 18 § 18, τοῖς θεοῖς ηὔχεσθε εἰς ὁμόνοιαν καταστῆναι τὴν πόλιν μᾶλλον ἢ [ἐπὶ τιμωρίαν τῶν παρεληλυθότων τραπόμενοι] τὴν μὲν πόλιν στασιάσαι τοὺς δὲ λέγοντας ταχέως πλουτῆσαι. The trans. use is found in 'Anon. apud Stobaeum 510, 1 οἴκους'; but the *Indices* to Plato and Aristotle supply no example of this use. To express the trans. Isocrates uses ποιεῖν στασιάζειν, p. 68 B, and 279 D. στασιάζειν is intrans. twice in 8 § 5, twice in 13 § 2, also in 20 § 1, and elsewhere. Hence we must either take it as intrans. here, and strike out τὸν δῆμον (which I prefer), or regard ΣΤΑΣΙΑΣΑΙ as having taken the place of a trans. verb ΔΙΑΣΤΗΣΑΙ. Cf. Hdt. ix 1 § 2, πέμπε χρήματα εἰς τοὺς δυναστεύοντας ἄνδρας ἐν τῇσι πόλισι, πέμπων δὲ τὴν Ἑλλάδα διαστήσεις· ἐνθεῦτεν δὲ τοὺς μὴ τὰ σὰ φρονέοντας ῥηιδίως μετὰ τῶν στασιωτέων καταστρέψει. Xen. *Hell.* ii 4 § 35, διΐστη δὲ καὶ τοὺς ἐν τῷ ἄστει. Plut. *Sol.* 13 (of the same period) τῆς πόλεως διαστάσης. Ar. *Pol.* 1321 *a* 15, ὅταν διαστῶσι, and *ib.* 19 ταύτῃ δὲ ἐπικρατοῦσιν ἐν ταῖς διαστάσεσιν οἱ δῆμοι τῶν εὐπόρων. As a possible alternative one might suggest διαστασιάσαι, 'to form into separate factions,' *Pol.* 1303 *b* 26, ὅθεν προσλαμβάνοντες τοὺς ἐν τῷ πολιτεύματι διεστασίασαν πάντας, and 1306 *a* 3, διεστασίασεν αὐτοὺς πρὸς τοὺς εὐπόρους.

§ 2. **τοῖς τε ἄλλοις...καὶ δὴ καὶ**] 16 §§ 2, 10. In 18 § 2 and 19 § 3 we have καὶ alone in the second clause. It is exceptional for τε to be omitted, as in Lycurg. *Leocr.* 95, ἐπὶ τὴν ἄλλην χώραν καὶ δὴ καὶ (where Baiter prefers ἐπί τε).

πελάται] used by Plutarch in eight passages as an equivalent for the Roman *clientes* (*Romulus* 13, *Poplicola* 5, *Coriolanus* 13 and 21 § 4, *Marius* 5 § 5, *Crassus*

ζοντο τῶν πλουσίων τοὺς ἀγρούς (ἡ δὲ πᾶσα γῆ δι' ὀλίγων ἦν),
καὶ εἰ μὴ τὰς μισθώσεις [ἀπ]οδιδοῖεν, ἀγώγιμοι καὶ αὐτοὶ καὶ οἱ
παῖδες ἐγίγνοντο, καὶ [οἱ δανεισμοὶ π]ᾶσιν ἐπὶ τοῖς σώμασιν
ἦσαν μέχρι Σόλωνος· οὗτος δὲ πρῶτος ἐγέν[ετο τοῦ] δή[μου] προ-
3 στάτης. χαλεπώτατον μὲν οὖν καὶ πικρότατον ἦν τοῖς πολλοῖς τῶν
κατὰ τὴν πολιτείαν τὸ [δουλεύ]ειν. οὐ μὴν ἀλλὰ καὶ ἐπὶ τοῖς
ἄλλοις ἐδυσχέραινον· οὐδενὸς γάρ, ὡς εἰπεῖν, ἐτύγχανον μετέ-
χοντες.

8 ΕΓΙΝΟΝΤΟ (K-W): ἐγίγνοντο (H-L, K[3]); in titulis Atticis annorum 445—292 A.C. quadraginta tribus locis inventum est γίγνομαι, nusquam γίνομαι (Meisterhans, *Grammatik der Attischen Inschriften*, p. 141[2]); itaque ubique praetuli γίγνομαι. καὶ οἱ δανεισμοὶ πᾶσιν Blass (K[3] p. LXIV): καὶ [δε]δ[εμένοι τοῖς δανείσ]ασιν K, καὶ γὰρ κτλ. K-W; ὑπόχρεῳ γὰρ H-L repugnante papyro. 11 δουλεύειν K-W (K[3], B): [τὸ τῆς γῆς μὴ κρατ]εῖν H-L Blassii coniecturam secuti.

---

21 § 5, *Cato Minor* 34 § 3, *Tib. Gracchus* 13 § 2); also in *Agis* 6 § 5, and *Quaest. Conviv.* ii 10, (ὁ κιττὸς) Βοιωτίου θεοῦ πελάτης καὶ παράσιτος ὤν.

ἑκτημόροι] (1) Plut., *Sol.* 13, states that these tenants paid their landlords a sixth part of the produce (ἕκτα τῶν γινομένων τελοῦντες). Similarly, Hesychius, *s. v.* ἐπίμορτος. (2) Photius, *s. v.* πελάται, says that they cultivated the soil in return for a sixth part of the produce (ἕκτῳ μέρει τῶν καρπῶν εἰργάζοντο τὴν γῆν). Similarly, Hesychius, *s. v.* ἑκτημόροι, and the Scholiast on Plato, *Euthyphron* 4 C. Thus Plutarch makes them pay 1/6 and retain 5/6 for their own maintenance; while Photius makes them pay 5/6 and retain 1/6. The former view is preferable and it is supported by Oncken (*Staatslehre*, ii 437 n) who observes that a tax of 1/6 was sufficiently severe to imply a considerable amount of distress, and by Gomperz (in Appendix III to his polemical pamphlet, *Die Schrift vom Staatswesen der Athener*, pp. 45—48).

μίσθωσιν] 'rent' (not 'wages'). *Inf.* μισθώσεις ἀποδιδοῖεν. Dem. 28 § 12, ἀποδέδωκε τὴν μίσθωσιν, and 43 § 58 (*lex*) τοὺς μὴ ἀποδιδόντας τὰς μισθώσεις τῶν τεμενῶν.

δι' ὀλίγων ἦν] c. 4 *ad fin.* The sense is not materially different in *Pol.* viii (v) 6, 1306 *a* 16, τῆς πολιτείας δι' ὀλίγων οὔσης, and *infra* c. 29 l. 9, δι' ὀλίγων ποιήσωνται τὴν πολιτείαν, also *Pol.* 1318 *b* 34, αἵ τε γὰρ ἀρχαὶ ἀεὶ διὰ τῶν βελτίστων ἔσονται, 1301 *b* 12, τὴν μὲν κατάστασιν προαιροῦνται τὴν αὐτήν, δι' αὑτῶν δ' εἶναι βούλονται, 1293 *a* 28, δι' αὑτῶν ἔχειν (Eucken, *Sprachgebrauch des Ar.*, p. 38).

ἀγώγιμοι] Plut. *Sol.* 13, χρέα λαμβάνοντες ἐπὶ τοῖς σώμασιν ἀγώγιμοι τοῖς δανείζουσιν ἦσαν, 15 § 8, τῶν ἀγωγίμων πρὸς ἀργύριον γεγονότων πολιτῶν.

Diod. Sic. i 79, 16 (of an Egyptian lawgiver) τῶν ὀφειλόντων τὴν ἔκπραξιν τῶν δανείων ἐκ τῆς οὐσίας μόνον ἐποιήσατο, τὸ δὲ σῶμα κατ' οὐδένα τρόπον εἴασεν ὑπάρχειν ἀγώγιμον.

δανεισμοὶ κτλ.] c. 4 *ad fin.*, c. 9 § 1 δανείζειν ἐπὶ τοῖς σώμασιν. Dion. Halic. *Ant. Rom.* iv 9, p. 658, 6 Reiske (of Servius Tullius), νόμον θήσομαι, μηδένα δανείζειν ἐπὶ σώμασιν ἐλευθέροις, and v 53, p. 970, 4 (οἱ δανείζοντες) εἰς δεσμοὺς τὰ τῶν ὑποχρέων ἀπῆγον σώματα. The word δανεισμὸς occurs in *Eth.* 1131 *a* 3, Plat. *Rep.* 473 E, *Leg.* 842 D, 921 C.

τοῦ δήμου προστάτης] In Plut. *Sol.* 13 *ad fin.*, the oppressed citizens resolve on choosing ἕνα προστάτην ἄνδρα, and the choice falls on Solon. The same term is applied *infra* c. 28 to Solon, Peisistratus, Cleisthenes, Xanthippus, Themistocles and Aristides, Ephialtes and Pericles, Cleon and Cleophon. According to Grote's definition, which is mainly applicable to a time later than that of Solon, the term 'denotes the leader of a popular party, as opposed to an oligarchical party (see Thuc. iii 70, 82, iv 66, vi 35) in a form of government either entirely democratical, or at least in which the public assembly is frequently convoked and decides on many matters of importance' (*Hist. of Gr.* vii p. 304 n). See Dr Hager's article in Smith's *Dict. of Ant.* ii 504.

§ 3. **οὐδενὸς...ὡς εἰπεῖν**] An example of the normal use of ὡς εἰπεῖν, to modify a numerical exaggeration. To the passages quoted in my note on Dem. *Lept.* § 140, the following may be added, from Aristotle's *Politics*. ὡς εἰπεῖν is used with πᾶς in 1263 *b* 4, 1273 *b* 17, 1282 *a* 5,

3. ἦν δ' ἡ τάξις τῆς ἀρχαίας πολιτείας τῆς πρὸ Δράκοντος [τοιάδε]. τὰς μὲν ἀρχὰς [καθί]στασαν ἀριστίνδην καὶ πλουτίνδην· ἦρχον δὲ [τὸ] μὲν πρῶτ[ον διὰ βίου], μετὰ δὲ ταῦτα

III 3 διὰ βίου K-W, H-L (K³, B): ἀεὶ quondam K.

1314 *a* 14, 1319 *a* 30, 1323 *a* 20, 1328 *b* 16; also with numbers in 1285 *b* 34 σχεδὸν δύο ἐστὶν ὡς εἰπεῖν, 1302 *a* 19 σχεδὸν ὡς εἰπεῖν τρεῖς. ὡς ἐπὶ τὸ πλεῖστον εἰπεῖν occurs in 1297 *b* 33, 1335 *a* 8. ὡς ἁπλῶς εἰπεῖν, in 1293 *b* 34, 1299 *a* 25, 1310 *a* 37.

ὡς εἰπεῖν is less frequently used to modify a strong metaphor or other emphatic phrase unconnected with number: 1263 *a* 36 τοῖς δούλοις χρῶνται τοῖς ἀλλήλων, ὡς εἰπεῖν ἰδίοις, 1268 *a* 23 τὰς κυριωτάτας ἀρχὰς ὡς εἰπεῖν, 1324 *b* 6 τῶν πλείστων νομίμων χύδην ὡς εἰπεῖν κειμένων, 1301 *b* 5 ἀρχαὶ μὲν οὖν ὡς εἰπεῖν [bracketed by Susemihl, transferred after πηγαὶ by others] αὗται καὶ πηγαὶ τῶν στάσεών εἰσιν, 1304 *b* 5, οἱ κατ' ἀρετὴν διαφέροντες οὐ ποιοῦσι στάσιν ὡς εἰπεῖν, 1312 *b* 23 εὐθὺς ὡς εἰπεῖν. ὡς ἔπος εἰπεῖν is combined with πᾶς, 1252 *b* 29; also *infra* c. 57 § 1, and with πλεῖστα in 49 § 5. It is quite unnecessary to substitute it for ὡς εἰπεῖν here.

III. *The Athenian Constitution before the time of Dracon.*

According to the current account the title of king was abolished on the death of Codrus. His son Medon, and twelve successors, beginning with Acastus and ending with Alcmaeon, were archons for life. In the second year of Alcmaeon (752 B.C.) the life archonships of the Medontidae were reduced to the duration of ten years. The names of seven decennial archons have been preserved. In 712 B.C., with this limitation in the tenure of the office, the archonship was thrown open to all the Eupatridae. Lastly, in the archonship of Creon (683 B.C.), or on the expiration of that of Eryxias (682, Duncker, *Hist. of Greece*, ii 135 E. T.), the single decennial archon was abolished, and his duties were distributed over nine officials who held office for a year only, and were elected by the Eupatridae out of their own body (Grote, *H.G.*, ii chap. 10 *init.*). The legend that it was out of gratitude for the heroism of Codrus that the title of king was abolished has no earlier authority than that of Justin (ii 7). It is not recognised by Plato or Aristotle, or by any early writer. Plato describes Codrus as meeting his doom in quest of glory and in the interests of the royal status of his descendants, *Symp.* 208 D, ὑπὲρ τῆς βασιλείας τῶν παίδων. Aristotle, *Pol.* viii (v) 10, p. 1310 *b* 37, implies that he was one of those who earned their royal power by their services to their country (κατὰ πόλεμον κωλύσαντες δουλεύειν). The life-archons were elected from the royal house, and bore the title of βασιλεύς (Pausanias i 3 § 3). This title was never formally abolished, but survived even in later times in the name of the ἄρχων βασιλεύς. The institution of the office of life-archon is described by Pausanias, iv 5 § 10, as a change ἀντὶ βασιλείας ἐς ἀρχὴν ὑπεύθυνον. In explanation of this phrase it has been suggested that the life-archon was 'responsible to the general body of the Eupatridae' (*See* ARCHON, p. 166 *a*, in Smith's *Dict. Ant.*); but it seems more probable that Pausanias used a phrase which was an obvious antithesis to an irresponsible monarchy without having any real knowledge of the nature of the responsibility attaching to the holder of a life-archonship (Busolt, i pp. 400 f).—Cf. Lugebil, *Jahrb. f. class. Philol.*, suppl. Bd v 539—564.

ἀριστίνδην καὶ πλουτίνδην] *inf.* § 6. *Pol.* 1273 *a* 23, οὐ γὰρ μόνον ἀριστίνδην ἀλλὰ καὶ πλουτίνδην οἴονται δεῖν αἱρεῖσθαι τοὺς ἄρχοντας, 1293 *b* 10, ὅπου γε μὴ μόνον πλουτίνδην ἀλλὰ καὶ ἀριστίνδην αἱροῦνται τὰς ἀρχάς, 1272 *b* 36, ταύτην δ' αἱροῦνται τὴν ἀρχὴν ἀριστίνδην. =κατ' ἀρετὴν 1273 *a* 26. Isocr. *Paneg.* 146, οὐκ ἀρ. ἐπειλεγμένους. Plat. *Leg.* 855 C, ἀρ. ἀπομερισθὲν δικαστήριον. In Andoc. *de Pace* 30, πολλοὺς Ἀθηναίων ἀπολέσαντες ἀριστίνδην καὶ τῶν συμμάχων, I should prefer to read ἄρδην, which is combined with ἀπολλύναι in Plato *Rep.* 421 A. The adverb is defined by Timaeus as meaning κατ' ἀνδραγαθίαν αἱρετόν. Prof. Mayor adds to lexicons the following examples of ἀριστίνδην: 'Dem. p. 1069, 7, Plut. *Sol.* 12 § 2, *Lysand.* 13 § 7 (where also πλουτίνδην, as in *Septem Sap. Conv.* 11 pr. p. 154). Euseb. *Ecl. Proph.* iv 4 p. 177, 18. CIA i 61, App. *Bell. Civ.* i 35. Aelian in Suid., Διονυσίων σκωμμάτων, has πλουτίνδην' (*Class. Rev.* v 120).

διὰ βίου] *Pol.* 1270 *b* 39, 1272 *a* 37, 1285 *a* 15; *inf.* at end of § 6.

2 [δεκ]αετίαν. μέγισται δὲ καὶ πρῶται τῶν ἀρχῶν ἦσαν βασ[ιλεὺς καὶ πολ]έμαρχος καὶ ἄρ[χων]· τούτων δὲ πρ[ώτ]η μὲν ἡ τοῦ βασιλέως, αὕτη γὰρ *ἐξ [ἀρχ]ῆ[ς ἦν]. δευτέρα δ' ἐπικατέστη [ἡ πολε]μαρχία διὰ τὸ γε[ν]έσθαι τινὰς τῶν βασιλέων τὰ πολεμικὰ μαλ[ακούς, ὅθεν καὶ] τὸν Ἴωνα μετε[πέμ]ψαντο χρεία[ς κ]αταλαβούσης.
3 τελευταία δ' ἡ [τοῦ ἄρχο]ντος· [οἱ] μὲν γὰρ πλείους [ἐ]πὶ Μέδοντος, ἔνιοι δ' ἐπὶ Ἀκάστου φασὶ γενέσθαι [τὴν ἀρχήν· σημεῖον] δ' ἐπιφέρουσιν [ὅτι] οἱ ἐννέα ἄρχοντες ὀμνύουσι [καθάπερ] ἐπὶ Ἀκάστου τὰ ὅρκια ποι[ή]σειν, ὡς ἐπὶ τού[το]υ τῆς βασιλείας παραχωρησάντων τῶν Κοδ[ριδῶν], *ἀνταποδοθεισῶν τῷ ἄρχοντι δωρεῶν.

6 ἐξ ἀρχῆς ἦν J W Headlam, quod accepi coll. 16 § 1, 28 § 1, 55 § 1, *Pol.* 1297 *b* 17 ἡ πρώτη δὲ πολιτεία ἐν τοῖς Ἕλλησιν ἐγένετο μετὰ τὰς βασιλείας ἐκ τῶν πολεμούντων, ἡ μὲν ἐξ ἀρχῆς ἐκ τῶν ἱππέων, et Ar. frag. 611 (1) R[3] Ἀθηναῖοι τὸ μὲν ἐξ ἀρχῆς ἐχρῶντο βασιλείᾳ. ἐν ἀρχῇ ἦν hiatu sine causa admisso K[3]; ἐν [ἀρχῇ κατέστη] K-W, πάτριος ἐγένετο H-L, sed lectioni neutri spatium sufficit. ἡ inseruit J B Mayor (H-L, K[3]). **7** γενέσθαι K-W, B. ΠΟΛΕΜΙΑ K (K-W, H-L): πολεμικὰ Blass; cf. 23, 14. **8** ὅθεν καὶ K (H-L), litteras ΟΘ aliquatenus cerni posse arbitratus: [πρῶτον] δὲ K-W, B. **10** ἐπ' H-L. τὴν ἀρχὴν K (H-L): ταύτην K-W: [βασιλέ]ως B. [σημεῖον] K, K-W, H-L: τ[ούτῳ] B. **12** τὰ ὅρκια ποιήσειν (litteris primis quinque incertis) K[3]; τὰ ἄρτια ποιήσειν e papyro eruerat Wessely. [τῆς πόλεως ἀρχ]ειν K[1], [τῆς] πόλ[εως ἄ]ρξειν KW, [βασιλέως ἄρξ]ειν Platt (H-L). τούτου τῆς H-L (K[3]): τῆς ἐ[κείνου] K[1] (K-W). **13** ἀντὶ τῶν δοθεισῶν, litteris evanidis scripta, K[3], B: τ]ῶν [ὑπεξῃρημένων] K-W: pro ἀντὶ τῶν δοθεισῶν (ΑΝΤΙΤ'ΔΟΘΕΙϹΩΝ), quod litteris valde obscuris scriptum esse dicitur, scripserim aut ἀντιπαραδοθεισῶν (ΑΝΤΙΠ̓ΔΟΘΕΙϹΩΝ) aut (quod usitatius est) ἀνταποδοθεισῶν; litteris fere tredecim spatium sufficit.

---

§ 2. **πολεμαρχία]** This account of the original relation of the πολέμαρχος to the βασιλεὺς is illustrated by the Schol. on Plat. *Phaedr.* 235 D, where the former is described as ὥσπερ λοχαγὸς τοῦ βασιλέως (Wyse in *Class. Rev.* v 224). Similarly in certain semi-savage tribes the institution of a 'war-king' has grown up beside that of the regular hereditary monarch. Cf. Post, *Bausteine*, ii p. 84.

μαλακούς] Heraclidis epitoma, Rose, Frag. 611, 1, ἀπὸ δὲ Κοδριδῶν οὐκέτι βασιλεῖς ᾑροῦντο διὰ τὸ δοκεῖν τρυφᾶν καὶ μαλακοὺς γεγονέναι.

Ἴωνα] Ion, the son of Creusa, daughter of Erechtheus, was summoned to the aid of Athens against Eleusis and was entrusted with the conduct of the war. Hdt. viii 44, Paus. vii 5, 1, and esp. i 31 § 3, Ἀθηναίων ἐπὶ τοῦ πολέμου τοῦ πρὸς Ἐλευσινίους ἐπολεμάρχησε. Cf. Schol. on Arist. *Aves* 1527, πατρῷον δὲ τιμῶσιν Ἀπόλλωνα Ἀθηναῖοι, ἐπεὶ Ἴων ὁ πολέμαρχος Ἀθηναίων ἐξ Ἀπόλλωνος καὶ Κρεούσης τοῦ Ξούθου (γυναικὸς) ἐγένετο (Rose, Frag. 343[2] = 381[3]). This scholium may have been derived either from the present passage, or from another in which Ion was mentioned near the beginning of the treatise.

τελευταία—ἄρχοντος] It is uncertain whether the president of the board of nine magistrates bore the title of Archon before the time of Solon. Probably up to that time the members of the board were called πρυτάνεις and their president retained the ancient title of βασιλεύς. It was the βασιλεὺς that presided over the archons when assembled as a judicial body (Busolt, i 408). On the other side, see Gilbert's *Gr. St.*, i 117—118.

§ 3. **Μέδοντος]** son of Codrus. **Ἀκάστου**, successor of Medon (Busolt, i 403).

ὀμνύουσι] The oath of the archons is also mentioned in 7 § 1 and in 55 *ad fin.*, but this particular clause is not cited elsewhere.

παραχωρησάντων] For the constr. cf. Dem. p. 38, 24, ἀξιῶ ὑμᾶς μὴ παραχωρεῖν τῆς τάξεως, p. 655, 17, π. τῆς ἀρχῆς. For the sense, *Pol.* 1285 *b* 14, τὰ μὲν αὐτῶν παριέντων τῶν βασιλέων, τὰ δὲ τῶν ὄχλων παραιρουμένων, ἐν μὲν ταῖς ἄλλαις πόλεσιν, αἱ πάτριοι θυσίαι κατελείφθησαν τοῖς βασιλεῦσι μόνον.

ἀνταποδοθεισῶν——δωρεῶν] 'corre-

τοῦτο μὲν οὖν ὁποτέρως ποτ' ἔχει μικρόν, ἐγένετο γὰρ ἐν τούτοις
τοῖς χρόνοις· ὅτι δὲ τελευταία τούτων ἐγένετο τῶν ἀρχῶν, [ση]μεῖον
καὶ [τὸ] μη[δ]ὲν [τῶν π]ατρίων τὸν ἄρχοντα διοικεῖν ὥσπερ ὁ
βασιλεὺς καὶ ὁ πολέμαρχος, ἀλλὰ [μόνον τὰ ἐπίθ]ετα. διὸ
καὶ νεωστὶ γέγονεν ἡ ἀρχὴ μεγάλη, τοῖς ἐπ[ι]θέτοις αὐξηθ[εῖσα.
θεσ]μοθέται δὲ πολλο[ῖ]ς ὕστερον ἔτεσιν ᾑρέθησαν, ἤδη κατ' 4
ἐνιαυτὸν αἱρ[ουμένων] τὰς ἀρχάς, ὅπως ἀναγράψαντες τὰ θέσμια
φυλάττωσι πρὸς τὴν τῶν [παρανομού]ντων κρίσιν· διὸ καὶ μόνη
τῶν ἀρχῶν οὐκ ἐγένετο πλείων [ἢ] ἐνιαύσιος. [οὗτοι] μὲν οὖν 5
χρόνον τοσοῦτον προέχουσιν *ἀλλήλων. ᾤκησαν* δ' οὐχ ἅμα πάντες

14 μικρὸν [διαφέρει, ἅτε δὴ ἐν ἀτάκ]τοις τοῖς χρόνοις Paton, μικρὸν διαφέρει ἐν τούτοις <τοῖς> χρόνοις H-L; μικρόν, ἀλλ' [οὖν ἐγένε]το ἐν τούτοις <τοῖς> χρόνοις K-W; μικρὸν ἃ[ν διαλλάτ]τοι τοῖς χρόνοις, vel μικρόν γε π[αρα]λλάττει τοῖς χρόνοις, B. ἐγένετο γὰρ ἐν τούτοις τοῖς, litteris evanidis scripta, K^3. **16** πατρίων Wyse, Blass, K-W, H-L (K^3), coll. 57 § 1 τὰς πατρίους θυσίας διοικεῖ οὗτος (ὁ βασιλεὺς) πάσας. **17** ἀλλὰ [μόνον τὰ ἐπίθ]ετα K^3, B; an μᾶλλον? ἀλλὰ καινά τινα ἐπίθετα H-L; ἀλλ' [ὅλως μηδὲν μ]έγα K-W. **20** αἱρουμένων Wyse, Blass, K-W, H-L, K^3. **21** παρανομούντων K (K-W, B): ἀκοσμούντων H-L spatio vix expleto. **22** ΠΛΕΙΩΝ K: πλεῖον K-W, B; πλεῖν H-L. πλὴν ἤ, vel πλὴν εἰ, H Richards. **23** ΑΛΛΗΩΝΗϹΑΝ: ἄλλων. ᾤκησαν K: ἀλλήλων. ἦσαν Jackson, Blass (K-W, H-L); malui ἀλλήλων. ᾤκησαν: ἀλλήλων. ἐδίκαζον Herwerden coll. Suid. s. v. ἄρχων: καθῖζον Gennadios, συνῆσαν Kontos.

sponding privileges being (at the same time) assigned to the archon.' ἀντὶ τῶν δοθεισῶν, suggested by Mr Kenyon, is confessedly a somewhat remarkable expression, and is interpreted to mean 'in consideration of the privileges which were surrendered to the archon'; but this is hardly satisfactory in point of sense. What we expect is ἀντιπάλων δοθεισῶν τῷ ἄρχοντι δωρεῶν.

ὁποτέρως ποτ' ἔχει] *De Physica Auscult.* 252 *b* 35, ὁποτέρως ποτ' ἔχει. *De Sensu*, 446 *a* 21, ὁποτέρως ποτὲ γίνεται. περὶ ζωῆς 467 *b* 17, ὁποτέρως ποτὲ δεῖ καλεῖν (*Index Ar.*).

§ 4. **θεσμοθέται**, literally 'legislators,' from θεσμοί, the old term for νόμοι. The name was 'probably applied to them as the judges who determined the great variety of causes which did not fall under the cognizance of their colleagues; because, in the absence of a written code, those who declare and interpret the laws may be properly said to make them' (Thirlwall, ii 17). According to the text, the object of their appointment was to secure that the enactments of the law should be publicly recorded and duly preserved, with a view to their being enforced against transgressors. In the absence of a code of law, such as Dracon afterwards gave to Athens, the θέσμια of the text were presumably 'judicial decisions' recorded as precedents for similar cases in the future. See also Holm, *Gr. Gesch.* i 516.

κατ' ἐνιαυτὸν—τὰς ἀρχάς] B.C. 683.

ἀναγράψαντες] not exactly to 'commit to writing' (Poste), but to engrave on a tablet and set up in a public place (this is the force of ἀνα-); in brief, 'to record publicly.'

διὸ] does not appear to refer to the immediately preceding clause, but to the beginning of the previous sentence. It was because the *thesmothetae* were not instituted until the time when magistrates were appointed annually that, unlike the three senior archons in former days, they never held office for more than a year.

§ 5. **οὗτοι—ἀλλήλων**] 'Such then is the order of precedence which these magistrates have over one another in point of date,' *i.e.* (1) βασιλεύς, (2) πολέμαρχος, (3) ἄρχων, (4) θεσμοθέται. **ἀλλήλων** is somewhat loosely used.

ᾤκησαν δ' οὐχ ἅμα πάντες κτλ.] With reference to the lexicographical articles quoted above, in the *Testimonia*, it was remarked by Schömann (*Ant. Gr.* p. 412 E. T.) that 'before the time of Solon, as we are assured by evidence which, it must be admitted, is exceedingly apocryphal in character, the nine Archons were not permitted to sit in judgment all to-

οἱ ἐννέα ἄρχοντες, ἀλλ' ὁ μὲν βασιλεὺς ε[ἶ]χε τὸ νῦν καλούμενον βουκολεῖον, πλησίον τοῦ πρυτανείου (σημεῖον δέ· ἔτι καὶ νῦν γὰρ

25 ΒΟΥΚΟΛΙΟΝ (K, H-L, B): *βουκολεῖον* K-W.

TESTIM. **23—33.** Bekk. *Anecd.* 449, 19 et Suidas s. v. *ἄρχων*: ...*πρὸ μὲν τῶν Σόλωνος νόμων οὐκ ἐξῆν αὐτοῖς ἅμα δικάζειν, "ἀλλ' ὁ μὲν βασιλεὺς" καθῆστο παρὰ τῷ καλουμένῳ βουκολείῳ, τὸ δὲ ἦν "πλησίον τοῦ πρυτανείου," "ὁ δὲ πολέμαρχος" ἐν Λυκείῳ καὶ ὁ ἄρχων παρὰ τοὺς ἐπωνύμους, οἱ δὲ* (om. Suidas) *θεσμοθέται παρὰ τὸ θεσμοθέσιον. κύριοί τε ἦσαν ὥστε "τὰς δίκας αὐτοτελεῖς" ποιεῖσθαι, ὕστερον δὲ Σόλωνος οὐδὲν ἕτερον αὐτοῖς τελεῖται ἢ μόνον ἀνακρίνουσι* (*ὑποκρ.* Suid., *ἀνακρ.* Pearson et Matthiae) *τοὺς ἀντιδίκους.*

---

gether. They were, however, equally precluded from doing this in the times better known to us, and the statement must therefore be based on some kind of misapprehension.' It was also noticed that, before the time of Solon, the archon could not have had his official residence *παρὰ τοὺς ἐπωνύμους*, as the statues of the *ἐπώνυμοι*, or national heroes that gave their names to the ten Attic tribes, could not have existed before the institution of those tribes by Cleisthenes (508 B.C.). Hence it was inferred by K. F. Hermann (*Gr. Staatsalt.*, p. 407, note 14) that the information referred to the post-Solonian time. But at that time the official residence of the Archon-Basileus was the *Stoa Basileios*, not the *Basileion*. Accordingly it was suggested by Wecklein (*Monatsber. der München. Akad.*, 1873, 5. 38) that the *Basileion*, which he supposed was the residence of the *φυλοβασιλεῖς*, had been confounded with that of the Archon-Basileus.

We now see that the main source of the information, so far as it is correct, was the present passage. The information really refers to the time before Solon; but the lexicographers commit an anachronism, for which they are themselves responsible, in placing the office of the archon near the *Eponymi*, instead of in the *Prytaneum*, in the neighbourhood of which the statues of the *Eponymi* were afterwards set up.

βουκολεῖον] We are here told that the official residence of the Archon-Basileus was the building which, in the time of the writer, was called the *βουκολεῖον*. This explains the otherwise obscure passage quoted in Athenaeus, p. 235, from the law relating to the Archon-Basileus: *τοὺς δὲ παρασίτους ἐκ τῆς βουκολίας ἐκλέγειν ἐκ τοῦ μέρους τοῦ ἑαυτῶν ἑκτέα κριθῶν κτλ.* In Telfy's *Corpus Iuris Attici* § 358 the words *ἐκ τῆς* (or *ἐκτὸς*) *βουκολίας* are strangely rendered *absque dolo*. It is now, however, clear that they must refer to the residence of the Archon-Basileus and are used in the same sense as *ἐκ τοῦ βουκολείου*, which was perhaps the original reading.

The *βουκολεῖον* is possibly connected with the *βουζύγιον*, or field of sacred ox-ploughing, described by Plutarch (*Coniugalia Praecepta*, xlii) as below the Acropolis: *Ἀθηναῖοι τρεῖς ἀρότους ἱεροὺς ἄγουσι...τρίτον ὑπὸ πόλιν τὸν καλούμενον βουζύγιον* (Miss Harrison, *Mythology and Monuments of Ancient Athens*, p. 166). It has been suggested that a black-figured vase-painting on a *hydria* in the Berlin Museum, where an ox is standing within a small Doric shrine, not bound as for sacrifice, but free and stately, is a representation of the sacred ox in his *βουκολεῖον*, whether it be the building below the Acropolis or some other shrine of *Ζεὺς Πολιεύς* (*ib.* p. 428). It is more probable, however, that the *βουκολεῖον* was connected with the worship of Dionysus, who was often represented in the form of an ox (cf. Eur. *Bacchae*, 100, 920—922, 1017, 1159). There was a play of Cratinus called the *Βουκόλοι*, which began with a dithyramb, and it has been inferred from Aristoph. *Vesp.* 10, *τὸν αὐτὸν ἄρ' ἐμοὶ βουκολεῖς Σαβάζιον*, that the votaries of the Thracian Dionysus, *ὁ ταυρόμορφος*, were called *βουκόλοι* (O. Crusius, in *Philologus*, xlvii 34). It will be observed that in the text the *βουκολεῖον* is mentioned in connexion with Dionysus. Curtius is content to regard it as having been in primitive times a royal farmhouse, including a slaughter-house for the royal sacrifices (*Stadtgeschichte von Athen*, 1891, p. 51).

πρυτανείου] The position of the *Prytaneion* is disputed, and it is sometimes supposed that there was more than one building of the name. Pausanias tells us (i 18 § 3) that near the *Agrauleion* is 'the *Prytaneion*, in which are inscribed the laws of Solon.' By this is probably meant the original *Prytaneion*, the centre of the ancient city and the site of the hearth of the state. This *Prytaneion* was probably τῆς τοῦ βασιλέως γυναικὸς ἡ σύμμειξις ἐνταῦθα γίγνεται τῷ Διονύσῳ καὶ ὁ γάμος), ὁ δὲ ἄρχων τὸ πρυτανεῖον, ὁ δὲ πολέμαρχος τὸ Ἐπιλύκειον· ὃ πρότερον μὲν ἐκαλεῖτο πολεμαρχεῖον, ἐπεὶ δὲ Ἐπίλυκος ἀνῳκοδόμησε καὶ κατεσκεύασεν αὐτὸ πολεμα[ρχή]σας, Ἐπιλύκειον ἐκλήθη· θεσμοθέται δ' εἶχον τὸ θεσμοθετεῖον. ἐπὶ δὲ

26 ΣΥΜΜΙΞΙΣ *σύμμειξις* K-W, H-L, K³, coll. Meisterhans, p. 144². ΓΙΝΕΤΑΙ (K-W). **27** *καὶ ὁ γάμος* delet Rutherford (H-L). **28** ΕΠΙΛΥΚΙΟΝ: *-ειον* K etc. **29** *πολεμαρ[χῶν]* H-L, invita papyro.

TESTIM. **26** Hesych. *Διονύσου γάμος: τῆς τοῦ βασιλέως γυναικὸς καὶ θεοῦ γίνεται γάμος.* **28** Hesych. *Ἐπιλύκ(ε)ιον* (cod. *ἐπιλύκιον*): *ἀρχεῖον τοῦ πολεμάρχου Ἀθήνησιν.*

---

a little to the east of the ground beneath the northern, or north-eastern, cliff of the Acropolis, somewhat high up the slope (Miss Harrison, *l. c.*, p. 165). Before reaching it Pausanias had seen (i 5 § 1) the statues of the *ἐπώνυμοι* 'above the *Bouleuterion*' or Council Chamber of the Five Hundred. Near the latter he sees 'what is called the Θόλος, where the Prytanes offer sacrifice.' It was apparently for this reason that the Θόλος was sometimes called the *πρυτανεῖον*, *e.g.* in Schol. on Aristoph. *Pax* 1183, *τόπος Ἀθήνησιν παρὰ πρυτανεῖον ἐν ᾧ ἑστήκασιν ἀνδριάντες οὓς ἐπωνύμους καλοῦσιν* (*ib.* p. 171 note 106). Curtius places the original *Prytaneion* in the Old Agora which, according to his view, was S. of the Acropolis; he recognises a second *Prytaneion* in the *Tholos* situated in the Agora of the Cerameicus; while he regards the *Prytaneion* of Pausanias, on the northern slope of the Acropolis, as a building belonging to Roman times (*Stadtgeschichte*, p. 302). Wachsmuth (*Stadt Athen*, i 465) accepts the *Prytaneion* of Pausanias as the original building and regards the *Tholos* in the Cerameicus as a 'dépendance' in which the *Prytanes* had their public meals in the democratic days of Athens. Round the original *Prytaneion* rose the official residences of an earlier age. First among these was the *βασίλειον*, or official residence of the kings, which may be identified with the building in which the four *φυλοβασιλεῖς* performed their religious rites (Pollux viii 111, *ἐν τῷ βασιλείῳ τῷ παρὰ τὸ βουκολεῖον*) and with the residence of the Archon-Basileus (Wachsmuth, p. 468). See also Busolt, i 407 note 4.

ἔτι καὶ—γάμος] Either on the second day of the *Anthesteria* at the beginning of March, or at the Greater *Dionysia* at the end of that month, there was a procession representing the entry of Dionysus *Ἐλευθερεὺς* 'from without the city into the little temple of the Cerameicus,' 'and his incorporation into the city by union with the noblest woman of the land, the wife of the king.' On this occasion the *Basilinna* was accompanied by fourteen venerable priestesses, and was solemnly and secretly betrothed to the god. In the temple in Limnae she administered a vow to the priestesses, offered a mystic sacrifice, wherein she prayed for all blessings for the state, and then remained for the night in the interior of the temple. Cf. [Dem.] *c. Neaeram*, §§ 74—78, and Mommsen's *Heortologie*, pp. 358—360, quoted by Mr Purser on *Dionysia* in Smith, *Dict. Ant.* i 639 *a*. The passage in the *c. Neaeram* § 76 speaks of the law relating to the *βασίλιννα* as inscribed on a tablet in the temple of Dionysus *ἐν Λίμναις* opened only once a year on the second day of the *Anthesteria*. It also describes her as *τὴν θεῷ γυναῖκα δοθησομένην*, but says nothing of her spending the night in the temple.

Ἐπιλύκειον] Suidas, *s. v.* *ἄρχων*, describes the official residence of the Polemarch as *ἐν Λυκείῳ*, and accordingly it is generally held that 'the Polemarch had his office outside the walls, but quite close to the city, beside the Lyceum, a shrine consecrated to Apollo and frequently mentioned on account of a gymnasium existing there' (Schömann, *Antiquities*, p. 412 E. T.; see also Curtius, *Stadtgeschichte*, p. 58). The office was doubtless *ἐπὶ Λυκείῳ* (not *ἐν Λυκείῳ*), and this is what is meant by the name *Ἐπιλύκειον*. This is far more probable than the story about the 'polemarch Epilycus,' which is justly rejected by Mr Kenyon.

θεσμοθετεῖον] Suidas, *s. v.* *ἄρχων*, on the authority doubtless of the present passage, says that the *θεσμοθέται* held their court *παρὰ τὸ θεσμοθέσιον* (Bekker, *Anecd.* 449, 23, *παρὰ τὸ θεσμοθέσιον*). Cf. Hyperides, *Eux.* xxii, *θεσμοθετῶν συνέδριον*. It was there also that they dined at the public expense: Schol. Plato, *Phaedr.* 235 D,

Σόλωνος ἅ[π]αντες εἰς τὸ θεσμοθετεῖον συνῆλθον. κύριοι δ' ἦσαν καὶ τὰς δίκας αὐτοτελεῖς [κρίν]ειν, καὶ οὐχ ὥσπερ νῦν προανακρίνειν. τὰ μὲν οὖν [περὶ] τὰς ἀρχὰς τοῦτον εἶχε τὸν τρόπον.
6 *ἡ δὲ τῶν Ἀρεοπαγιτῶν βουλὴ τὴν μὲν τάξιν εἶχε τοῦ διατηρεῖν*

32 *αὐτοτελ[ῶς]* J B Mayor (H-L). **34, 38** ΑΡΕΟΠΑΓΕΙΤ

οἱ δὲ θεσμοθέται ἕξ εἰσι τὸν ἀριθμόν, ἀφ' ὧν καὶ ὁ τόπος, ὅπου συνῄεσαν καὶ ἐσιτοῦντο, θεμίστιον (*leg.* *θεσμοθέσιον vel θεσμοθετεῖον*) *ἐκαλεῖτο.* Its position is unknown, but it was not improbably near the *πρυτανεῖον*, though there is nothing to prevent its being placed in the *ἀγορά*, as (from the very first) the *θεσμοθέται* had judicial duties to discharge. Köhler conjectures that it was near the *βουλευτήριον*, but the evidence for this is inconclusive (Wachsmuth, *l. c.* i p. 482—3, ii 353—4).

ἐπὶ δὲ Σόλωνος—συνῆλθον] Diog. Laert. i 58 (of Solon), *καὶ πρῶτος τὴν συναγωγὴν τῶν ἐννέα ἀρχόντων ἐποίησεν, εἰς τὸ συνειπεῖν, ὡς Ἀπολλόδωρός φησιν ἐν δευτέρῳ περὶ νομοθετῶν.* The text confirms the conjecture of Schömann (*Ant.*, p. 412 E. T.) that the 'Thesmothesium' was used by the whole board of the nine archons. It also favours the view that as early as the time of Solon all the nine archons were called *Thesmothetae* (K. F. Hermann, *Staatsalt.* § 138, n. 3, and Bergk in *Rheinisches Museum* xiii 449, quoted by Wachsmuth, *l. c.*, ii 354).

αὐτοτελεῖς κρίνειν] c. 53 § 2.

κρίνειν...προανακρίνειν] *Pol.* 1298 *a* 31, *τέταρτος δὲ τρόπος τὸ πάντας περὶ πάντων βουλεύεσθαι συνιόντας, τὰς δ' ἀρχὰς περὶ μηδενὸς κρίνειν ἀλλὰ μόνον προανακρίνειν, ὅνπερ ἡ τελευταία δημοκρατία νῦν διοικεῖται τρόπον.* This is in favour of *κρίνειν*, as against *ποιεῖν* (suggested by Suidas).—'In the later and better-known times of Athenian law, we find these archons deprived in great measure of their powers of judging and deciding and restricted to the task of first hearing the parties and collecting the evidence; next, of introducing the matter for trial into the appropriate dikastery, over which they presided' (Grote, *H. G.* chap. 10, ii 283 ed. 1862).

§ 6. **ἡ τῶν Ἀρεοπαγιτῶν βουλή**] The first establishment of the senate of Areopagus is sometimes ascribed to Solon. Thus Plutarch, *Sol.* 19 *init.*, says of Solon *συστησάμενος τὴν ἐν Ἀρείῳ πάγῳ βουλὴν ἐκ τῶν κατ' ἐνιαυτὸν ἀρχόντων.* But in Ar. *Pol.* ii 12 1274 *a*, it is stated that the Council of the Areopagus was already in existence: *ἔοικε δὲ Σόλων ἐκεῖνα μὲν ὑπάρχοντα πρότερον οὐ λῦσαι, τήν τε βουλὴν καὶ τὴν τῶν ἀρχῶν αἵρεσιν.* On the other hand, Cicero, *de Off.* i 22 § 75, speaks of it as the *senatus, qui a Solone erat constitutus*; and Pollux, viii 125, describes it as established by Solon as a tribunal of homicide, in addition to that of the Ephetae. 'But there can be little doubt' says Grote, ii p. 281, 'that this is a mistake, and that the senate of Areopagus is a primordial institution, of immemorial antiquity, though its constitution as well as its functions underwent many changes. It stood at first alone as a permanent and collegiate authority, originally by the side of the Kings and afterwards by the side of the archons. It would then of course be known by the title of *The* Boulê—*The* senate or council; its distinctive title, "Senate of Areopagus" (borrowed from the place where its sittings were held), would not be bestowed until the formation by Solon of the second senate or council, from which there was need to discriminate it.' The Areopagus appears to represent the Homeric *βουλὴ γερόντων* (Meier and Schömann p. 10), and is probably as early as the time of the Attic kings; but, if so, its number must have been very limited. By modern writers its number is sometimes supposed to have been either **300** (Schömann, *Jahrb. f. kl. Philol.* 1875, p. 154, Hermann, *Staatsalt.* § 102, 17, Lange, *Ephet. u. Areop.* p. 27, Duncker, *Gesch. des Alterth.* v 473 = *H. G.* ii 141 E. T.); or **360**, representing the 360 *γένη* (Philippi, *Areop. u. Epheten*, p. 206); or **60**, *i.e.* 15 nominated by each of the four tribes, and including the 9 archons, the remaining 51 being those known as the Ephetae (Busolt, i 418). As soon as it became customary for the archons to be added to the Areopagus at the end of their year of office, the number would cease to be fixed; but we do not know at what time this method of recruiting the Areopagus was first adopted. Mr Kenyon suggests that 'the automatic process of forming it from all ex-archons was probably put into operation from the date of the establishment of the annual archonship.'

τὴν μὲν τάξιν *κτλ.*] This confirms Grote's statement that 'the functions of *τοὺς νόμους, διῴκει δὲ τὰ πλεῖστα καὶ τὰ μέγιστα τῶν ἐν τῇ πόλει, καὶ κολάζουσα καὶ ζημ[ιο]ῦσα πάντας τοὺς ἀκοσμοῦντας κυρίως. ἡ γὰρ αἵρεσις τῶν ἀρχόντων ἀριστίνδην καὶ πλουτίνδην ἦν, ἐξ ὧν οἱ Ἀρεοπαγῖται καθίσταντο. διὸ καὶ μόνη τῶν ἀρχῶν αὕτη μεμένηκε διὰ βίου καὶ νῦν.*

4. *ἡ μὲν οὖν πρώτη πολιτεία ταύτην ε[ἶ]χε τὴν ὑπο[γρα]φήν. μετὰ δὲ ταῦτα, χρόνου τινὸς οὐ πολλοῦ διελθόντος, ἐπ' Ἀρι-*

36 *καὶ κολάζουσα* : *καὶ* delet Gennadios (H-L). **37** *γὰρ* : *δὲ* mavult Gennadios, ante *ἡ γὰρ* aliquid excidisse putat Keil.

---

the Areopagus were originally of the widest senatorial character, directive generally as well as judicial.' With the context, cf. Isocr. *Areop.* § 37, *τὴν ἐξ Ἀρείου πάγου βουλὴν ἐπέστησαν ἐπιμελεῖσθαι τῆς εὐκοσμίας, ἧς οὐχ οἷόν τ' ἦν μετασχεῖν πλὴν τοῖς καλῶς γεγονόσι καὶ πολλὴν ἀρετὴν ἐν τῷ βίῳ καὶ σωφροσύνην ἐνδεδειγμένοις*, and §§ 30—55, esp. § 46, *τοὺς ἀκοσμοῦντας ἀνῆγον εἰς τὴν βουλήν.* Athen. iv 19 p. 168 A: *ὅτι δὲ τοὺς ἀσώτους καὶ τοὺς μὴ ἔκ τινος περιουσίας ζῶντας τὸ παλαιὸν ἀνεκαλοῦντο οἱ Ἀρεοπαγῖται καὶ ἐκόλαζον, ἱστόρησαν Φανόδημος καὶ Φιλόχορος* (FHG i 394, cf. 387, 17).

διατηρεῖν τοὺς νόμους] Aeschin. 3 § 6, *ὅταν διατηρηθῶσιν οἱ νόμοι τῇ πόλει, σῴζεται καὶ ἡ δημοκρατία.*

γὰρ] The Areopagus was entrusted with all these powers, *because* it consisted of archons who had themselves been elected under special qualifications of birth and wealth.

The constitution of the Areopagus is the subject of a fragment of Philochorus (frag. 58 in Müller's *Frag. Hist. Gr.*, i 394): *ἐκ γὰρ τῶν ἐννέα καθισταμένων ἀρχόντων Ἀθήνησι τοὺς Ἀρεοπαγίτας ἔδει συνεστάναι δικαστάς, ὥς φησιν Ἀνδροτίων ἐν δευτέρᾳ τῶν Ἀτθίδων· ὕστερον δὲ πλειόνων γέγονεν ἡ ἐξ Ἀρείου πάγου βουλή· τουτέστιν ἐξ ἀνδρῶν περιφανεστέρων πεντήκοντα καὶ ἑνός* (this implies an identification of the Ephetae and the Areopagus). *οὐ παντὸς ἀνδρὸς ἦν εἰς τὴν ἐξ Ἀρείου πάγου βουλὴν τελεῖν· ἀλλ' οἱ παρ' Ἀθηναίοις πρωτεύοντες ἔν τε γένει καὶ πλούτῳ καὶ βίῳ χρηστῷ, ὡς ἱστορεῖ Φιλόχορος διὰ τῆς τριτῆς τῶν αὐτῶν Ἀτθίδων.*

διὸ—καὶ νῦν] 'This is also the reason why it is the only office which has continued to be held for life down to the present day.' For **διὰ βίου**, cf. 2 § 1.

IV. *The Draconian Constitution.*

τὴν ὑπογραφήν] 'outline', 'sketch'. Ar. *de Gen. Anim.* ii 6, 743 *b* 20—25, esp. *οἱ γραφεῖς ὑπογράψαντες ταῖς γραμμαῖς οὕτως ἐναλείφουσι τοῖς χρώμασι τὸ ζῷον. De Anima*, ii 1, 413 *a* 10, *τύπῳ ..ταύτῃ διωρίσθω καὶ ὑπογεγράφθω περὶ ψυχῆς. Pol.* ii 5, 1263 *a* 31, *ἔστιν ἐν ἐνίαις πόλεσιν οὕτως ὑπογεγραμμένον.*

χρόνου—διελθόντος] A vague note of time, the event from which the writer reckons being apparently the affair of Cylon and its more immediate consequences (c. 1).

Ἀρισταίχμου ἄρχοντος] The name of this archon (*Ἀρίσταιχμος*) is now known for the first time. It follows that Dracon was not the *ἄρχων ἐπώνυμος* of the year, as has been sometimes supposed (*e.g.* Busolt, i 510). Cf. Pausanias, ix 36 § 8, *Δράκοντος Ἀθηναίοις θεσμοθετήσαντος ἐκ τῶν ἐκείνου κατέστη νόμων, οὓς ἔγραφεν ἐπὶ τῆς ἀρχῆς, ἄλλων τε ὁπόσων ἄδειαν εἶναι χρή, καὶ δὴ καὶ τιμωρίας μοιχοῦ.* It may fairly be assumed that he was one of the *θεσμοθέται*, in the narrower sense of the term. Hence Grote is right in describing him as 'the thesmothet Drako.' His legislation may be assigned to B.C. 621 (Clinton's *Fasti*, *sub anno*; Busolt, i 510).

θεσμοὺς ἔθηκεν] This confirms the view that he was one of the *θεσμοθέται* at the time. *θεσμοί* was the term generally applied to the laws of Dracon: Andocides, *de Myst.* § 81, *χρῆσθαι τοῖς Σόλωνος νόμοις καὶ τοῖς Δράκοντος θεσμοῖς.* But even the laws of Solon were by himself called *θεσμοί.* Plutarch, *Sol.* 19, quotes from one of them the words *ὅτε θεσμὸς ἐφανὴ ὅδε*, and the word occurs in his own poems c. 12 § 4, line 18, *θεσμοὺς...ἔγραψα.* The same ancient term was preserved in the oath of the *περίπολοι* in Pollux viii 106, *καὶ τοῖς θεσμοῖς τοῖς ἱδρυμένοις πείσομαι*, which in later Greek would have been expressed *τοῖς νόμοις τοῖς κειμένοις* (cf. Grote, c. 10, ii p. 283, note).

§ 2. **ἡ δὲ τάξις** *κτλ.*] To identify the *τάξις*, or constitution, with the *θεσμοί*, or *σταίχμου ἄρχοντος Δρά[κω]ν τοὺς θεσμοὺς ἔθηκεν· ἡ δὲ τάξις* 2

legislation, is inconsistent with the distinction drawn by Aristotle in *Pol.* 1289 *a* 15, πολιτεία μὲν γάρ ἐστι τάξις ταῖς πόλεσιν ἡ περὶ τὰς ἀρχὰς...νόμοι δὲ κεχωρισμένοι τῶν δηλούντων τὴν πολιτείαν, καθ' οὓς δεῖ τοὺς ἄρχοντας ἄρχειν κτλ. Cf. also 1286 *a* 3. This distinction is maintained in cc. 7 and 9, but not in c. 34. The term θεσμοί has a distinctive meaning and can only refer to a code, not to a constitution (*Class. Rev.* v 167 *a*).

Dracon has hitherto been recognised as a legislator alone. There is a well-known passage respecting him in Ar. *Pol.* ii 12, p. 1274 *b* 15, Δράκοντος δὲ νόμοι μέν εἰσι, πολιτείᾳ δ' ὑπαρχούσῃ τοὺς νόμους ἔθηκεν κτλ. This passage, which describes Dracon as adapting his laws to a constitution already in existence, is inconsistent with the present chapter, which almost ignores the legislation of Dracon and represents him as the framer of a constitution.

The passage in question comes from a chapter which, in the opinion of Zeller, Susemihl and other Aristotelian scholars, has suffered from considerable interpolation. Thus Mr W. L. Newman conjectures 'that Aristotle may have left only the fragment about Solon and a few rough data for insertion after the notice of the Carthaginian constitution, and that some member of the school, not very long after his death, completed them as best he could' (Newman's ed. ii 373, 377). Accordingly it is possible that the passage about Dracon in the *Politics* was not written by Aristotle himself.

In *Rhet.* ii 23 § 29, 1400 *b* 21, Ar. quotes Herodicus (the physician) as saying of Dracon (ὁ νομοθέτης), ὅτι οὐκ ἀνθρώπου οἱ νόμοι ἀλλὰ δράκοντος· χαλεποὶ γάρ. Of the actual legislation of Dracon little is known, since his laws (with the exception of those on homicide) were repealed by Solon (c. 7 § 1 πλὴν τῶν φονικῶν and Plut. *Sol.* 17 there quoted). This is possibly a sufficient reason for the absence of any reference to it in the constitutional part of this treatise, except in the words τοὺς θεσμοὺς ἔθηκε. All that survived is sufficiently described in the second part of the work, in the account of the procedure in cases of homicide (c. 57).

According to the text the main points in the constitution of Dracon's time are (1) a hoplitic franchise, already in existence; (2) those who had this franchise elected the Archons, the *Tamiae*, the *Strategi*, the *Hipparchi* and the *Prytanes* (unless, indeed, these are identical with the Archons) from among those who were duly qualified by a property-qualification. (3) A Council of 401, elected by lot from among those who had the franchise, and were over 30 years of age. The same limitation held good for other offices filled by casting lots, and no one was to hold office twice till every one else had had his turn. (4) Members of the Council were fined for not attending meetings of the Council or Assembly, and the fine varied with their status.

This 'Draconian constitution' has, not unnaturally, been viewed with suspicion. It tells us of a Council of 401, of which we never hear elsewhere, and (which is more serious) of certain property-qualifications which have hitherto been regarded as part of the subsequent legislation of Solon, and which the author himself minutely describes in connexion with Solon (c. 7). A writer in the *Athenaeum*, 1891, p. 435 *b*, denounces it as 'the amazing Draconian constitution.' It has also been attacked by Weil (*Journal des Savants*, Avril, 1891), and Cauer; also by Mr Macan in the *Journ. of Hellenic Studies*, April, 1891, pp. 24, 27, and in detail by Mr J. W. Headlam in an article in the *Class. Rev.*, v 166—168; followed by valuable criticisms by Mr E. S. Thompson, *ib.* p. 336, and by M. Théodore Reinach in the *Revue Critique*, p. 143—5.

Mr Headlam's main points are these: (1) No other writer knows anything of a constitution attributed to Dracon. Plutarch, when speaking of the θεσμοί of Dracon, mentions nothing but a code of law. (2) Other passages in the πολιτεία itself support the view taken by Plutarch and in the *Politics*. (*a*) In chap. vii the writer speaks of the θεσμοί of Dracon in connexion with the new code of laws made by Solon, but makes no reference to Dracon in speaking of the constitutional innovations of Solon. (*b*) The recapitulation in c. 41 states that the characteristic feature of Dracon's legislation was the publication of the law. This is inconsistent with chap. 4 and its very remarkable constitution. (3) Among the provisions of the constitution at least one could not possibly have been devised in Dracon's time, the property-qualification for the archonship being expressed in terms of money that probably belong to a later age; nearly all of them are very difficult to reconcile with what we know of the state of Athens at the time; and several of them inconsistent with other αὕτη τόνδε τὸν τρόπον εἶχε. ἀπεδέδοτο μὲν ἡ πολιτεία τοῖς ὅπλα παρεχομένοις· ᾑροῦντο δὲ τοὺς μὲν ἐννέα ἄρχοντας [καὶ τ]οὺς [τ]αμίας οὐσίαν κεκτημένους οὐκ ἐλάττω δέκα μνῶν ἐλευθέραν,

IV 4 ΑΥΤ' (= αυτης): correxit K. μὲν per compendium, ut videtur, scriptum (K-W, K^3, B): mihi quidem Δ' (δὲ) potius quam Μ' (μὲν) videtur scriptum: om. H-L. **5** ΑΡΧΟΝΤΕC **6** ἔλαττον ἢ K-W. ΔΕΚΑ: ἑκατὸν Thompson; διακοσίων Weil (*Journal des Savants*, p. 10); 'maiorem censum nemo non expectet' H-L.

---

statements in this book. (4) None of the provisions, some of them very remarkable, are ever quoted by later writers. (5) The whole constitution is exactly like those afterwards described in connexion with the aristocratic revolutions in 411. The details connected with the above criticism will be noticed as they occur in the following notes.

Dr P. Meyer (*Des Aristoteles Politik und die* Ἀθηναίων πολιτεία, pp. 31—44) regards the passage in the *Politics* and the present chapter as, both of them, equally genuine, and vainly endeavours to reconcile the two. He holds that the 'Draconian constitution' does not differ materially from the constitution which preceded it, the ἀρχαία πολιτεία of c. 3. If so, the writer of the present chapter has not succeeded in making the points of resemblance clear. The 'Draconian constitution' is defended with greater success by Prof. Gomperz (*Die Schrift vom Staatswesen der Athener*, p. 43). He holds that, in distributing the citizens of Attica into four classes, Solon availed himself of existing social divisions, and gave them a new definition. This may hold good in the case of the ἱππεῖς, the ζευγῖται and the θῆτες. But it is difficult to accept it in the case of the πεντακοσιομέδιμνοι. The term is used without any explanation in the present chapter; but, in the description of Solon's constitution, it is defined with precision as though it were then used for the first time. One would be glad to believe with Mr Kenyon, in his note on this chapter, p. 13 ed. 3, that 'a sober historical judgment will probably in the end find its statements not so startling as they at first appear'; but at present the contents of the greater part of the chapter seem to require the most careful scrutiny before they can be finally accepted.

Considerations in favour of the account are urged by Busolt, in *Philol.* 1891, vol. 50, pp. 393—400. He points out that the Pseudoplatonic *Axiochus*, which has several points of contact with this treatise (cf. c. 18 § 1, 34 § 1, 42 § 2), uses the phrase ἐπὶ τῆς Δράκοντος ἢ Κλεισθένους πολιτείας (p. 365). While admitting the coincidences with the oligarchical constitutions of 411, he holds that the oligarchs professed to aim at the restoration of the πάτριος πολιτεία, which may fairly be identified with the pre-Solonian constitution. (1) The term πεντακοσιομέδιμνος must originally have referred to measures of corn: Solon extended its meaning to measures of wine and oil, and gave it a different value by changing the standard. (2) Fines in money may have been exacted by the State at a time when private transactions were settled by the transfer of oxen. (3) We know little of the early history of the στρατηγία, but it is possible that the fears inspired by the affair of Cylon may have led the aristocracy to limit the authority of the polemarch by means of four στρατηγοὶ appointed from the wealthier class.

ἀπεδέδοτο κτλ.] not ἀπεδόθη. The tense implies that the franchise had already been given and that this was not part of the alleged constitution of Dracon. This point is brought out by Mr Poste who translates: 'Sovereign power was already wielded by the class of persons capable of providing its own equipment for war.' He adds in a note: 'This agrees with the statement of Aristotle, *Pol.* ii 12, that Drakon made no change in the constitution. The revolution had already taken place. Drakon's task was to adjust the laws to the changed centre of political power.' Mr Kenyon's rendering is here less exact: 'The franchise was given &c.' (see, however, *Class. Rev.* v 467 *b*).—The same kind of franchise is to be found in the constitution proposed by the party of Theramenes in 411, c. 33 at end, Thuc. viii 97, and Xen. *Hell.* ii 3 (*Class. Rev.* v 168 *a*).

δέκα μνῶν] We have to notice (1) the nature, no less than (2) the amount of the property-qualification required of archons.

(1) At this time property was reckoned not in money but in corn. Now, the qualification of a ζευγίτης was to possess land capable of producing 200 μέδιμνοι: a

[Col. 2.] *τὰς δ' ἄλλας ἀρχὰς || <τὰς> ἐλάττους ἐκ τῶν ὅπλα παρεχ[ομένων], στρατηγοὺς δὲ καὶ ἱππάρχους οὐσίαν ἀποφαίνοντας οὐκ ἔλαττον ἢ ἑκατὸν μνῶν ἐλευθέραν καὶ παῖδας ἐ[κ] γαμετῆς γυναικὸς γνησίους ὑπὲρ δέκα ἔτη γεγονότας· τούτους δ' ἔδει διε[γγυ]ᾶ[σθαι] τοὺς πρυτάνεις καὶ τοὺς στρατηγοὺς καὶ τοὺς ἱππάρχους τοὺς ἕνους*

7 <τὰς> ἐλάττους Richards, Blass, K-W, H-L, K[3]. 8 ἔλαττον Marchant coll. Dobr. Adv. in Thuc. ii 13: ἐλάττον' olim K. 9 ἢ ἑκατὸν in ἕκαστον η' (= ὀκτὼ) mutabat Marindin (Smith, *Dict. Ant.* ii 1071 *b*). ἢ delet Thompson, utpote ex numerali H (= ἑκατὸν) natum. ΕΛΕΥΘΕΡΩΝ: corr. Wyse etc. 10 Δ'ΔΙ (supra scr. ΔΕΙ)...δ' ἔδει διατηρεῖν H-L; διεγγυᾶν Schulthess deletis verbis καὶ τοὺς στρατηγοὺς καὶ τοὺς ἱππάρχους; δι......K-W; δ' ἔδει διεγγυᾶσθαι K[3], B. 11 τοῦ γένους K[1]: τοὺς ἕνους Paton et van Leeuwen (edd.), quod et in papyro scriptum et unice verum est, cf. [Dem.] 25 § 20 τὰς ἕνας ἀρχὰς ταῖς νέαις ἐκούσας ὑπεξιέναι, et Ar. *Pol.* 1322 *a* 11 τὰς τῶν ἕνων (Scaliger) μᾶλλον τὰς νέας (ἀρχάς).

μέδιμνος of corn was worth at this time about a drachma (Plut. *Sol.* 23). Land of this extent must thus have been worth not less than 2000 drachmas. According to this, men were eligible to the archonship who were excluded by Solon from all office (*Class. Rev.* v 167 *b*).

(2) In the constitution described in c. 29, the archons and prytanes alone were to receive pay, 2 obols a day, implying that no high property-qualification was required. The comparatively high qualification for the generals, 100 minae (if the text is sound), would be natural in 411 but not in 621 (*ib.* 168 *a*).

Busolt, however, points out that the two qualifications of 100 and of 10 minae respectively correspond to the relative values of gold and silver in ancient times, 10 : 1. He supposes that a piece of land valued at 1000 Aeginetan drachmae might produce a return of 120—130 Aeginetan or 166—180 Attic drachmae; and if we assume that in those early days, when money was scarcer than in Solon's time, a medimnus was worth only 2 to 3 Aeginetan obols, the yearly produce would be from 360 (or 390) to 250 medimni. This would correspond to the census of a ἱππεὺς under the Solonian constitution (*Philol.* 1891, pp. 393—400).

l. 6. **ἐλευθέραν**, 'unencumbered.' Isaeus 10 § 17, ὁ μὲν κλῆρος ἐλεύθερος ἦν, contrasted with ὑπόχρεως. Dem. 35 § 21, ὑποτιθέασι ταῦτ' ἐλεύθερα, and § 22, ἐπ' ἐλευθέροις τοῖς χρήμασι δανειζόμενοι. Dittenberger, *Sylloge*, no. 344, 38; 294, 10; 126, 20, 28. Cf. c. 12, 34.

l. 8. **στρατηγοὺς**] It is urged by Mr Headlam that (*a*) We have no other record of στρατηγοὶ at this time: in the list in c. vii § 3 they are not mentioned. (*b*) The clause about their children is entirely new. (*c*) If there were such officers, they held an inferior position, and the comparatively high property-qualification is unaccountable (*Class. Rev.* 167 *b*). Qualifications of a similar character may, however, be noticed at a much later date, in Deinarchus, *contr. Dem.*, § 71, τοὺς νόμους προλέγειν τῷ ῥήτορι καὶ τῷ στρατηγῷ (τῷ) τὴν παρὰ τοῦ δήμου πίστιν ἀξιοῦντι λαμβάνειν, παιδοποιεῖσθαι κατὰ τοὺς νόμους, γῆν ἐντὸς ὅρων κεκτῆσθαι, πάσας τὰς δικαίας πίστεις παρακαταθέμενον, οὕτως ἀξιοῦν προεστάναι τοῦ δήμου.

διεγγυᾶσθαι] If this is the right reading, it must presumably be rendered 'should have security given on their behalf.' The accepted meaning of the word in the passive is 'to be bailed' by any one, *e.g.* Thuc. iii 70, ὀκτακοσίων ταλάντων τοῖς προξένοις διηγγυημένοι.

τοὺς πρυτάνεις] Here mentioned for the first time, whereas the form of the sentence (so far as the text is sound) implies they have already been referred to. If so, they must either be included among the ἄλλας ἀρχὰς τὰς ἐλάττους, or they are identical with the ἐννέα ἄρχοντες. As to the latter alternative, it is probable that up to the time of Solon the archons were called πρυτάνεις. This is inferred by Busolt, i 408, from the term for court-fees, πρυτανεῖα, which cannot be explained with the help of anything in the post-Solonian constitution, and from the analogy of Greek states in Asia, where the king was succeeded by a πρύτανις. It will be remembered that the official residence of the Archon was the πρυτανεῖον, c. 3 § 5. This appears better than identifying them with 'the president of the Council and Assembly in later days.'

μέχρι εὐθυνων, ἐγγυητὰς τέτταρας ἐκ τοῦ αὐτοῦ τέλους *παρασχο-
μένους οὗπερ οἱ στρατηγοὶ καὶ οἱ ἵππαρχοι. βουλεύειν δὲ τετρακο- 3
σίους καὶ ἕνα τοὺς λαχόντας ἐκ τῆς πολιτείας· κληροῦσθαι δὲ καὶ ταύ-
την καὶ τὰς ἄλλας ἀρχὰς τοὺς ὑπὲρ τριάκοντα ἔτη γεγονότας, καὶ δὶς
τὸν αὐτὸν μὴ ἄρχειν πρὸ τοῦ πάντας *[δι]ελθεῖν· τότε δὲ πάλ[ιν] ἐξ

12 ΕΓ̣Γ̣..ΤΑC ἐγγυητὰς K[3], K-W, B; ἐπιμελητὰς H-L. δ' K[1]; δ̄ (=τέτταρας) K-W, H-L etc. Δ' (?supra scr. ΟΔ?) ΧΟΜ'ΟΥC; δεχομένους K, K-W, H-L: παρεχομένους Rutherford, ΠCΧΟΜΕΝΟΥC fortasse volebat corrector; idem conicit Blass qui in ectypo ΠΕ (supra scr. ΟΥ=οὗπερ) ΧΟΜΕΝΟΥC in ΠCΧΟΜΕΝΟΥC correctum agnoscit. **15** ΤΡΙΑΚΟΝΘΕΤΗ. **16** περιελθεῖν K[1]. Expectares potius aut εἰς πάντας περιελθεῖν aut διὰ πάντων διελθεῖν τὴν ἀρχήν: quod ad illud attinet, cf. Plut. *Arist.* 5 ὡς περιῆλθεν εἰς αὐτὸν ἡ ἀρχή; quod ad hoc, Ar. *Pol.* 1298 *a* 17 et 1300 *a* 25 ἕως ἂν διελθῇ διὰ πάντων: etiam πάντας ἑξῆς λαχεῖν conicere in promptu est, coll. [Xen.] *Rep. Ath.* i 6 μὴ ἐᾶν λέγειν πάντας ἑξῆς μηδὲ βουλεύειν. ἐξελθεῖν K-W, H-L, K[3], B; διελθεῖν malui: praestaret διεξελθεῖν (K-W[2]), sed spatium non sufficit.

μέχρι εὐθυνῶν] 'until the audit.' At Athens, according to the evidence of later times, all officials were ὑπεύθυνοι. Aeschin. *Ctes.* § 17, οὐδείς ἐστιν ἀνυπεύθυνος τῶν καὶ ὁπωσοῦν πρὸς τὰ κοινὰ προσεληλυθότων.

παρασχομένους] Often used in middle with μάρτυρας, *Pol.* 1269 *a* 2, παρασχέσθαι πλῆθος μαρτύρων, and Ant. 5 §§ 20, 22, 24, 28, 30, &c. Cf. Aeschin. *c. Ctes.* 199, συνηγόρους παρασχέσθαι. The usual verb with ἐγγυητὰς is καθιστάναι, Dem. 24 §§ 39, 40, 55, and esp. 144, ὃς ἂν ἐγγυητὰς τρεῖς καθιστῇ τὸ αὐτὸ τέλος τελοῦντας.

§ 3. **βουλεύειν**] This is the only mention of a Draconian council of 401. In c. 8 we are told of Solon βουλὴν δὲ ἐποίησε τετρακοσίους, *i.e.* 'he set up a council of 400.' Had the writer already mentioned a council of 401 he would probably have expressed himself differently in c. 8. The addition of the 'one' is a common device to prevent the votes being exactly equal. But it is a device mainly characteristic of later times, *e.g.* the δικαστήρια consisting of 501, or 1001, δικασταί. On the other hand, we have the 51 Ephetae who are generally ascribed to the time of Dracon.

ἐκ τῆς πολιτείας = ἐκ τῶν πολιτῶν.

κληροῦσθαι] the first mention of election by lot in this treatise. Hitherto, it has been generally agreed that, even in Solon's time, the Council was not appointed by lot, and this view is accepted by Thirlwall, Grote, Schömann (*Antiq.* p. 331 E. T.), and others. The introduction of the lot for this purpose has been usually ascribed to the time of Cleisthenes (508 B.C.). But the present passage implies that the use of the lot was as early as the time of Dracon. This, if true, supports the opinion of Fustel de Coulanges (*la Cité Antique*, p. 212—4, ed. 1883), that the lot is an institution of religious origin and therefore of great antiquity. See Mr J. W. Headlam's *Election by Lot at Athens*, esp. pp. 183—, and note on c. 8 § 1 *infra*.

ταύτην] τὴν ἀρχήν, *sc.* τὸ βουλεύειν.

τὰς ἄλλας ἀρχάς, exclusive of the Archons, Strategi and Hipparchi, already mentioned, but probably not exclusive of the ἄλλας ἀρχὰς τὰς ἐλάττους.

τριάκοντα ἔτη] This is the age at which an Athenian citizen could become a βουλευτής (Xen. *Mem.* i 2 § 35) or a δικαστής (c. 63 § 3, cf. document quoted in Dem. *Timocr.* 151, and Pollux, viii 122). It has already been inferred (Meier and Schömann, *Att. Proc.*, p. 240 Lipsius) that the same requirement of age held good for other officials, the ἄλλαι ἀρχαί of the text. (The Ephetae and the public Envoys were, however, required to be 50 years of age; the Diaetetae 59.)

δὶς τὸν αὐτὸν μὴ ἄρχειν κτλ.] *Pol.* 1299 *a* 10, μὴ τὸν αὐτὸν δὶς ἀλλ' ἅπαξ μόνον (ἄρχειν) and 1317 *b* 23 τὸ μὴ δὶς τὸν αὐτὸν ἄρχειν μηδεμίαν ἢ ὀλιγάκις ἢ ὀλίγας ἔξω τῶν κατὰ πόλεμον. Of officials in general we read in Dem. *Timocr.* 150 (document quoted as ὅρκος ἡλιαστῶν) οὔτε δὶς τὴν αὐτὴν ἀρχὴν τὸν αὐτὸν ἄνδρα οὔτε δύο ἀρχὰς ἄρξαι τὸν αὐτὸν ἐν τῷ αὐτῷ ἐνιαυτῷ. The same citizen could be a βουλευτὴς more than once, as is shewn by the case of Timarchus and that of Demosthenes (*adv. Mid.* 114 and Aeschin., *F. L.* 17); and is stated in c. 62 *ad fin.* It is doubted by Boeckh (*Staatsh.* ii 763) whether the same citizen could be a βουλευτὴς for two years in succession, but this is purely conjectural (Hermann's ὑπαρχῆς κληροῦν. εἰ δέ τις τῶν βουλευτῶν, ὅταν ἕδρα βουλῆς ἢ ἐκκλησίας ᾖ, ἐκλείποι τὴν σύνοδον, ἀπέτινον ὁ μὲν πεντακοσιο- 18

18 ἐκλίποι H-L.

Staatsalt. § 125, 1). The ἐπιστάτης τῶν πρυτάνεων was not allowed to hold that office more than once (c. 44 § 1).

The rotation of all in office was a well-known device of later times (cf. Headlam's *Election by Lot*, p. 88): but it may well be asked how far it was applicable to a large body of citizens, most of whom lived at a considerable distance from Athens. It was in fact the work of a developed democracy (*Class. Rev.* v 168 *a*). Ar. *Pol.* vi (iv) 14, 1298 *a* 14, ἐν ἄλλαις δὲ πολιτείαις βουλεύονται αἱ συναρχίαι συνιοῦσαι, εἰς δὲ τὰς ἀρχὰς βαδίζουσι πάντες κατὰ μέρος ἐκ τῶν φυλῶν καὶ τῶν μορίων τῶν ἐλαχίστων παντελῶς, ἕως ἂν διεξέλθῃ διὰ πάντων. *ib.* p. 1300 *a* 23, ἢ γὰρ πάντες (οἱ πολῖται τὰς ἀρχὰς καθιστᾶσιν) αἱρέσει, ἢ πάντες ἐκ πάντων κλήρῳ (καὶ [ἢ] ἐξ ἁπάντων ἢ ὡς ἀνὰ μέρος, οἷον κατὰ φυλὰς καὶ δήμους καὶ φατρίας, ἕως ἂν διέλθῃ διὰ πάντων τῶν πολιτῶν κτλ.). It is characteristic of the oligarchical spirit μὴ ἐᾶν λέγειν πάντας ἑξῆς μηδὲ βουλεύειν ([Xen.] *Rep. Ath.* i 6).

διελθεῖν] τὴν ἀρχήν. Cf. βίον διελθεῖν. It would, however, be more natural to say διὰ πάντων διελθεῖν or διεξελθεῖν (τὴν ἀρχήν), as in *Pol.* 1273 *b* 17, διὰ πάντων ...διελήλυθε τὸ ἄρχειν καὶ τὸ ἄρχεσθαι, and the passages quoted in last note.

For ἐξελθεῖν *ex urna* (van Leeuwen) cf. Horace's *sors exitura*, but this use of ἐξελθεῖν is doubtful. In *Pol.* ii 11, 1273 *a* 16, the word is applied otherwise, to the 'going out of office' (of certain officials in the Carthaginian constitution), καὶ γὰρ ἐξεληλυθότες ἄρχουσι καὶ μέλλοντες.

ἕδρα βουλῆς] c. 30 § 4.

ἐκκλησίας] Of the general assembly of the citizens, in or before the times of Dracon, nothing is known. 'The people must have had some power' (says Mr Abbott, *History of Greece*, i 230[1]), 'or the Draconian laws would not have been published, and Solon would not have been chosen to reform the constitution. We do not know that the officers were elected by, or responsible to, the assembly, and of legislative and judicial authority the people had none. Perhaps we may assume that war could not easily be proclaimed without their consent, as they formed the bulk of the soldiers. If that were the case, the safety and power of the State depended, in the last resort, upon the General Assembly.'

εἰ δέ τις...ἐκλείποι...ἀπέτινον] Goodwin's *Moods and Tenses*, § 462.

ἐκλείποι τὴν σύνοδον] Xen. *Hell.* v 2 § 22, εἰ δέ τις τῶν πόλεων ἐκλίποι τὴν στρατειάν, ἐξεῖναι Λακεδαιμονίοις ἐπιζημιοῦν στατῆρι κατὰ τὸν ἄνδρα τῆς ἡμέρας. The phrase is not found in Aristotle, although in *Pol.* 1331 *b* 10 we have πρὸς ἀγορᾷ...καὶ συνόδῳ τινὶ κοινῇ. σύνοδος is applied to an ἐκκλησία in 1319 *a* 32, οἱ δὲ γεωργοῦντες διὰ τὸ διεσπάρθαι κατὰ τὴν χώραν οὔτ' ἀπαντῶσιν οὔθ' ὁμοίως δέονται τῆς συνόδου ταύτης, and to the συσσίτια in 1271 *a* 28, ἔδει γὰρ ἀπὸ κοινοῦ μᾶλλον εἶναι τὴν σύνοδον, καθάπερ ἐν Κρήτῃ. ἐκλείπειν is generally intrans. in Ar.—Fines for non-attendance are mentioned in *Pol.* 1297 *a* 17 (among the devices by which oligarchies deceive the people), περὶ ἐκκλησίαν μὲν τὸ ἐξεῖναι πᾶσιν ἐκκλησιάζειν, ζημίαν δὲ ἐπικεῖσθαι τοῖς εὐπόροις ἐὰν μὴ ἐκκλησιάζωσιν..., and (among the counter-devices on the part of democracies) 1297 *a* 37, τοῖς μὲν γὰρ ἀπόροις μισθὸν πορίζουσιν ἐκκλησιάζουσι καὶ δικάζουσιν, τοῖς δ' εὐπόροις οὐδεμίαν τάττουσι ζημίαν. 1294 *a* 38, ἐν μὲν γὰρ ταῖς ὀλιγαρχίαις τοῖς εὐπόροις ζημίαν τάττουσιν, ἂν μὴ δικάζωσιν, τοῖς δὲ ἀπόροις οὐδένα μισθόν, ἐν δὲ ταῖς δημοκρατίαις τοῖς μὲν ἀπόροις μισθόν, τοῖς δὲ εὐπόροις οὐδεμίαν ζημίαν.

Mr Headlam observes that the only Athenian instance of a law inflicting a fine for non-attendance at the Council is to be found in the constitution of the 400 in c. 30 *ult.*

There is no evidence as to fines for non-attendance at official duties in the earlier part of Athenian history. The fines inflicted by Solon's legislation are of a completely different character.

In the laws of Dracon fines were levied in terms of so many head of oxen: Pollux ix 61, κἀν Δράκοντος νόμοις ἐστὶν ἀποτίνειν εἰκοσάβοιον. This may have been the compensation paid to a man's relatives in a case of unintentional homicide. But (as observed by Busolt, *Philol.* 1891, p. 399) fines paid to the public chest in the form of oxen would be very inconvenient, and in such cases the payment was probably exacted in money.

ἀπέτινον] Ar. *Pol.* ii 12, 1274 *b* 20, ζημίαν ἀποτίνειν (in an interpolated chapter).

πεντακοσιομέδιμνος, ἱππεύς, ζευγίτης] see c. 7 § 4. All these have hitherto been

μέδιμνος τρεῖς δραχμάς, ὁ [δὲ ἱ]ππεὺς δύο, ζευγίτης δὲ μίαν. ἡ δὲ 4
βουλὴ ἡ ἐξ Ἀρείου πάγου φύλαξ ἦν τῶν νόμων καὶ διετήρ[ει τὰ]ς ἀρχὰς ὅπως κατὰ τοὺς νόμους ἄρχωσιν. ἐξῆν δὲ τῷ ἀδικουμένῳ πρὸ[ς τὴν τῶν] Ἀρεοπαγιτ[ῶν] βουλὴν εἰσαγγέλλειν ἀποφαίνοντι παρ' ὃν ἀδικεῖται νόμον. ἐπὶ δὲ τοῖς σώ[μα]σιν ἦσαν οἱ δανεισμοί, 5
καθάπερ εἴρηται, καὶ ἡ χώρα δι' ὀλίγων ἦν.

5. *τοιαύτης δὲ τῆς τάξεως οὔσης ἐν τῇ πολιτείᾳ καὶ τῶν*

19 <ὁ> *ζευγίτης* H-W, H-L; sed exspectares *ὁ δὲ ζ.* **22** ΑΡΕΟΠΑΓΕΙΤ. **23—4** *ἐπὶ—ἦν* spuria putant Richards et Keil. *δεδεμένοι* quondam dubitanter K (K-W); *δεδανεισμένοι* Richards, H-L; *οἱ δανεισμοὶ* Blass (K³ p. LXIV).

regarded as characteristic results of Solon's legislation; but some sort of property classification, even before the time of Dracon, is implied in c. 3 § 1, where magistrates are described as chosen *πλουτίνδην*.

We here reach the end of that part of the chapter which is open to most dispute. Its possible origin is thus indicated by Mr Headlam:

'The constitution described betrays the thought of a particular party; the reformers of this school used to advocate their policy by maintaining that it really would restore Athens to the condition in which it was before the democratic changes began. Many as we know looked on Solon as the originator of the changes which they deplored (Ar. *Polit.* ii 12). They would then recommend a constitution of this kind by saying it was like that which prevailed in Athens before the time of Solon. This has misled some transcriber or editor. After the words *τοὺς θεσμοὺς ἔθηκεν*, influenced by the expression at the beginning of chap. iii he desiderated some account of the constitution in the time of Draco and inserted this passage out of some other book' (*Class. Rev.* v 168 *b*).

§ 4. **φύλαξ τῶν νόμων**] Plut. *Sol.* 19, *τὴν δ' ἄνω βουλὴν ἐπίσκοπον πάντων καὶ φύλακα τῶν νόμων ἐκάθισεν*, *inf.* 8 § 4.

τῶν νόμων] esp. the *θεσμοί* of Draco mentioned in l. 3 immediately before the disputed passage.

εἰσαγγέλλειν] 'to impeach,' or 'lay an information' or 'denunciation.' The first known instance of the verb belongs to an inscr. soon after 446 B.C. (*Bull. de Corresp. hellén.* 1880, p. 225). The use of the term here does not correspond precisely with any of the technical senses which it afterwards bears in a more highly developed stage of Attic law. An *εἰσαγγελία* could be brought before the Archon or the Polemarch in certain cases, or before the *Boule* or the *Ecclesia*, but not before the Council of the Areopagus. See Dr Hager in Smith, *Dict. Ant. s.v.*

§ 5. **ἐπὶ δὲ** κτλ.] c. 2 § 2. In spite of the advantage of being able to appeal to the Areopagus against acts of injustice, the people had the standing grievance of having their persons mortgaged to their creditors &c. The statement follows naturally from the previous sentence and leads up to the account of the rebellion of the poor against the rich in the next. It is therefore unnecessary to accept the view of a writer in the *Edinburgh Review*, 1891, 479: "the statement is quite superfluous; the conjunction does not link it with the preceding sentence, which is concerned with a wholly different subject, and the form, 'as has been said,' shows clearly that it is a marginal comment made by some one who wished to impress the fact on his memory." So far from wishing to strike out this passage, we should be grateful for its preservation, as it has made it possible to restore the sense in the previous mention of the same facts in chap. 2. It has already been shewn that it is quite in harmony with the context.

V—XII. *The legislation of Solon.*

V § 1. **τάξεως**] If in the previous chapter, the description of the *τάξις* is an interpolation, and the mention of the *θεσμοί* in relation to the Areopagus and the economic condition of the poorer classes is alone to be regarded as genuine, the use of *τάξεως* here becomes open to suspicion, unless we are content to regard the powers of the Areopagus and the right of bringing grievances before them as sufficient to constitute a *τάξις*, or constitutional order of things.

ἐν τῇ πολιτείᾳ] almost equivalent to *τῆς πολιτείας*, the gen. being avoided because of the gen. preceding. Cf. *De Gen. Anim.* 1, 1, 715 *a* 1, *ἐπεὶ δὲ περὶ τῶν ἄλλων μορίων εἴρηται τῶν ἐν τοῖς ζῴοις*.

[π]ολλῶν δουλευόντων τοῖς ὀλίγοις, ἀντέστη τοῖς γνωρίμοις ὁ
2 δῆμος. ἰσχυρᾶς δὲ τῆς στάσεως οὔσης καὶ πολ[ὺν] χρόνον ἀντικαθημένων ἀλλήλοις, εἵλοντο κοινῇ διαλλακτὴν καὶ ἄρχοντα Σόλωνα, καὶ τ[ὴν πολι]τεί[α]ν ἐπέτρεψαν αὐτῷ ποιήσαντι τὴν ἐλεγείαν ἧς ἐστὶν ἀρχὴ

γιγνώ[σκω], καί μοι φρενὸς ἔνδοθεν ἄλγεα κεῖται,
πρεσβυτάτην ἐσορῶν γαῖαν Ἰαονίας.

καὶ γὰρ †ἐπελαύνει καὶ πρὸς ἑκατέρους ὑπὲρ ἑκατέρων μάχεται

V 2 an ἐπανέστη? Wyse. **7** ΓΙΝΩ[ΣΚΩ] K, K-W, H-L: γιγνώσκω certe usque ad annum 325 A.C. in titulis Atticis scriptum fuisse constat (Meisterhans, p. 142²): an οἰμώζω? H-L. **8** Ἰαονίην Richards (*Class. Rev.* v 334 *a*). **9** ΕΠΕΛΑΥΝΕΝ legit K (ἐπήλαυνεν K¹ sed tempus praesens flagitat contextus). ἐπαλλάττει J B Mayor, Richards, cf. *Pol.* 1255 *a* 13, 1257 *b* 35, 1295 *a* 9. ἐπιλεαίνει quondam tentabam, sed desideratur accusativus velut τοὺς τραχυνομένους; ἐπελαύνει K³, sed sensus in obscuro. [συμβουλεύων πολλὰ] πρὸς H-L. πολι[τικώ-

---

§ 2. **ἀντικαθημένων**] a metaphor implying two forces watching one another. The literal sense is found in Thuc. v 6 § 3, and similarly with ἀντικαθίζεσθαι *ib.* iv 124 § 2.

διαλλακτὴν καὶ ἄρχοντα] Plut. *Sol.* 14, ὁμοῦ καὶ διαλλακτὴς καὶ νομοθέτης, *Praec. Ger. Reip.* 10 § 16 p. 805, οὐδενὶ γὰρ ἐμμίξας ἑαυτὸν ἀλλὰ κοινὸς ὢν πᾶσι καὶ πάντα λέγων καὶ πράττων πρὸς ὁμόνοιαν, ᾑρέθη νομοθέτης ἐπὶ τὰς διαλύσεις, *ib.* p. 825 D ἥμερον διαλλακτήν, and esp. *Amatorius* 18 § 14, 763 D, τοῦτον εἵλοντο κοινῇ διαλλακτὴν καὶ ἄρχοντα καὶ νομοθέτην. The last passage supports the opinion that Plutarch had a first-hand acquaintance with this treatise.

The archonship of Solon is assigned to B.C. 594 (Clinton *F. H.*, ii p. 298 = 363³; Busolt, i 524, note 2). Cf. note on 13 § 1.

τὴν ἐλεγείαν] here, and in l. 3 from end of chapter, 'the elegiac poem.' The fem. form is found in Theophrastus, *Hist. Plant.* ix 15, 1, and also in late authors (*e.g.* Plut. *Sol.* 26, *Cimon* 10). Aristotle uses τὰ ἐλεγεῖα in *Poet.* 1, διὰ τριμέτρων ἢ ἐλεγείων, *Rhet.* i 15, ἐλεγεῖα Σόλωνος, iii 2, ἐλεγεῖα Διονυσίου (cf. *Class. Rev.* v 334 *a*).

The lines quoted have been hitherto unknown. They may fairly be accepted as the opening couplet of the poem cited in Dem. *de Falsa Leg.*, p. 421, § 255, sometimes called Ὑποθῆκαι εἰς Ἀθηναίους. The passage as there quoted begins with the words:

ἡμετέρα δὲ πόλις κατὰ μὲν Διὸς οὔποτ' ὀλεῖται
αἶσαν καὶ μακάρων θεῶν φρένας ἀθανάτων.

Voemel saw no difficulty in regarding the passage quoted by Dem. as the actual beginning of the poem: "Particula δὲ non obstat initio....Similia initia Tyrtaei, Mimnermi, Callini. Imo optime convenit commoto atque elato Solonis animo relictâ sententiâ 'Aliae quidem urbes interierunt et interibunt,' sic incipere: '*sed* Athenae sunt perpetuae'." But, if the couplet quoted in the text comes from the same poem at all, we now have the true beginning of that composition. The poet begins in a strain of sorrow and dejection due to the sad condition of his country, mingled with fear of the consequences of the avarice and pride of the wealthy (*infra*, τήν τε φιλαργυρίαν τήν θ' ὑπερηφανίαν). Afterwards (in the passage preserved by Dem.) he changes his tone to one of exultant trust in the overruling power of the patron-goddess of Athens. He then dwells on the injustice, the insolence, and the greed of the δήμου ἡγεμόνες; and insists on the evils caused by bad legislation and the blessings brought about by good. Thus far we have only an attack against one of the two parties in the state. The other topics may have found a place in the lost portions of the poem.

Ἰαονίας] Ἰαονίην is proposed by Mr H. Richards on the ground that Solon is not likely to have used *Ionia* for 'all lands where Ionians dwell.' The Ionic form may have been wrongly written Ἰαονίαν, and then altered into Ἰαονίας in consequence of the superlative. Considering, however, that it was a fixed belief of the Athenians that Ion had been their own πολέμαρχος, and was the father of the four progenitors of the Ionian tribes, Attica may well be called the oldest land in all the Ionian world.

ἐπελαύνει] apparently intransitive; used elsewhere of military movements

καὶ διαμφισβητεῖ, καὶ μετὰ ταῦτα κοινῇ παραινεῖ [κατα]παύειν
τὴν ἐνεστῶσαν φιλονικίαν. ἦν δ' ὁ Σόλων τῇ μὲν [φύ]σει καὶ τῇ 3
δόξῃ τῶν πρώτων, τῇ δ' οὐσίᾳ καὶ τοῖς πράγμασι τῶν μέσων, ὡς ἔκ
τε τῶν ἄλλων ὁμολογεῖται καὶ αὐτὸς ἐν τοῖσδε τοῖς ποιήμασιν
μαρτυρεῖ, παραινῶν τοῖς πλουσίοις μὴ πλεονεκτεῖν·

ὑμεῖς δ' ἡσυχάσαντες ἐνὶ φρεσὶ καρτερὸν ἦτορ,
οἱ πολλῶν ἀγαθῶν ἐς κόρον [ἠλ]άσατε,
ἐν μετρίοισι τ[ρέφεσθ]ε μέγαν νόον· οὔτε γὰρ ἡμεῖς
πεισόμεθ', οὔθ' ὑμῖν ἄρτια πά[ντ'] ἔσεται.

καὶ ὅλως ἀεὶ τὴν αἰτίαν τῆς στάσεως ἀνάπτει τοῖς πλουσίοις· διὸ καὶ ἐν ἀρχῇ τῆς ἐλεγείας δεδοικέναι φησὶ

τατα] ? K-W, qui legi posse existimant ΚΑΙΓΑΡΠΟΛΙ...ΕΤΑΙΚΑΙΠΡΟΣ; quae si revera olim exstabant, licet conicere *καὶ γὰρ πολι[τεύ]εται καὶ πρὸς*, quod confirmat aliquatenus Aristides ii 361 Dind. in commentario exscriptus, qui in loco nostro suos in usus convertendo verbum *ἐπολιτεύετο* bis usurpavit. **11** ΦΙΛΟΤΙΜΙΑΝ superscr. ΝΙΚΙ. *φύσει* Richards, Wyse (edd.): *ῥήσει* olim K. **16** *ἀάσατε* K[1] sensu intransitivo usurpatum: correxit Postgate coll. Tyrtaei loco infra allato; idem conicit Naber (edd.). **17** *τ[ίθεσθε]* Platt (H-L); *μετρίοις τέρπεσθε* Kontos. **18** *ἄρτια*: *ἄρθμια* Tyrrell, coll. Theogn. 1312 *ἄρθμιος ἠδὲ φίλος*, adde Hdt. vi 83 *τέως μὲν δή σφι ἦν ἄρθμια εἰς ἀλλήλους*: *ἄρκια* Kontos (H-L). *πά[ντ']* K-W quod locis infra laudatis confirmatur; *τἆλλ'* K[1] qui ΤΑ potius quam ΠΑ in papyro legit; *ταῦτ'* H-L (K[3], B); *πόλλ'* quondam Blass. **19** ΑΙΕΙ (K, K-W, B): *ἀεὶ* (H-L). Formam utramque usurpant decreta

---

such as 'charging' (Hdt. ix 49), or 'marching against' (i 17); here perhaps of 'attacking.' This sense would lead up to the next verb *μάχεται*. Another suggestion, *ἐπαλλάττει*, as observed by one of its proposers, 'seems suitable to describe the attitude of a man who sees and takes both sides of a question at once, who is at home in both camps' (H. Richards in *Class. Rev.* v 107 *a*). But we should expect *δυσχεραίνει* or *ἀντιτείνει*.

πρὸς ἑκατέρους ὑπὲρ ἑκατέρων] The purport of this part of the poem must have been the same as that of the *λόγοι* of Solon described in Aristides, ii 361, who probably had this passage in view: *καίτοι Σόλων τὰ μὲν εἰς Μεγαρέας ἔχοντα ᾆσαι λέγεται, τοὺς δὲ νόμους οὐκ ᾖδε περιιὼν οὐδὲ τοὺς λόγους τοὺς ὑπὲρ τῶν εὐπόρων πρὸς τὸν δῆμον, οὐδὲ τοὺς ὑπὲρ τῶν πολλῶν πρὸς τοὺς πλουσίους οὐκ ᾖδεν, οὐδ' ὅσα ἄλλα ἐπολιτεύετο, οὐκ ᾄδων οὐδ' ἐν μέτροις ἐπολιτεύετο, ἀλλὰ τῷ τῆς ῥητορικῆς τύπῳ καθαρῶς χρώμενος.*

§ 3. **τῇ μὲν φύσει** *κτλ.*] Plut. *Sol.* 1, *ἀνδρὸς οὐσίᾳ μέν, ὥς φασι, καὶ δυνάμει μέσου τῶν πολιτῶν, οἰκίας δὲ πρώτης κατὰ γένος.*

τῶν μέσων *κτλ.*] Ar. *Pol.* vi (iv) 11, 1296 *a* 19, *σημεῖον δὲ δεῖ νομίζειν καὶ τὸ τοὺς βελτίστους νομοθέτας εἶναι τῶν μέσων πολιτῶν· Σόλων τε γὰρ ἦν τούτων* (*δηλοῖ δ' ἐκ τῆς ποιήσεως*). This statement is proved by the verses here quoted. *τῶν μέσων* must not be confounded with our 'middle classes.' It refers rather to the moderately wealthy citizens (see Newman's *Politics* of Ar., i p. 500). Cf. *Pol.* 1295 *b*, 1296 *a* 7, 13, 1289 *b* 29 f.

ἡσυχάσαντες] The vb is transitive in this tense alone. Plat. *Rep.* 572 A, *ἡσυχάσας μὲν τὼ δύο εἴδη, τὸ τρίτον δὲ κινήσας.* These four lines have been hitherto unknown.

οἳ—ἐς κόρον ἠλάσατε] 'ye that plunged into surfeit of many good things.' Tyrtaeus 11 (7), 10, *ἀμφοτέρων δ' εἰς κόρον ἠλάσατε*, Hdt. ii 124, *ἐς τοσοῦτον ἤλασαν* (*τὸ πρᾶγμα*), 'they drove it thus far'; v 50, *ἐς πᾶσαν κακότητα ἐλάσας.*

οὔτε γὰρ ἡμεῖς—ἔσεται] neither shall we (who are oppressed) continue to obey you, nor will you (who are wealthy) find all things perfect.

ἄρτια πάντ'] Solon 4 (13) 35, *εὐνομία δ' εὔκοσμα καὶ ἄρτια πάντ' ἀποφαίνει*, and *ib.* 40, *ἔστι δ' ὑπ' αὐτῇ πάντα κατ' ἀνθρώπους ἄρτια καὶ πινυτά.* Theognis 946, *εἶμι παρὰ στάθμην ὀρθὴν ὁδόν, οὐδετέρωσε | κλινόμενος· χρὴ γάρ μ' ἄρτια πάντα νοεῖν.*

τὴν αἰτίαν...ἀνάπτει] 'ascribes the origin' (K). Rare in Aristotle; *Met.* 12, 4, τήν τε φ[ιλαργυρ]ίαν τήν θ' ὑπερηφανίαν,

ὡς διὰ ταῦτα τῆς ἔχθρας ἐνεστώ[σ]ης.

6. κύριος δὲ γενόμενος τῶν πραγμ[άτ]ων Σόλων τόν τε δῆμον ἠλευθέρωσε καὶ ἐν τῷ παρόντι καὶ εἰς τὸ μέλλον, κωλύσας δ[ανεί]ζειν ἐπὶ τοῖς σώμασιν, καὶ νόμους ἔθηκε καὶ χρεῶν ἀ[πο]κοπὰς ἐπ[ο]ίησε καὶ τῶν ἰδίων καὶ τῶν δημοσίων, ἃς σεισάχθειαν καλοῦσιν, ὡς ἀποσεισαμένων τὸ βάρος. ἐν οἷς πειρῶνταί τι[νες] δια-
2 βάλλειν αὐτόν· συνέβη γὰρ τῷ Σόλωνι μέλλοντι ποιεῖν τὴν

publica usque ad annum 361 A.C., ex quo anno ἀεὶ tantum inventum est, quamquam θιασωτῶν in titulis diu duravit αἰεὶ (Meisterhans, p. 25^2); itaque ἀεὶ ubique scripsi; quod autem inter Aristotelis editores nonnulli modo hanc, modo illam formam malunt, velut in *Pol.* 1276 *a* 36, 38 ubi inter trium versuum spatium καίπερ αἰεὶ et καίπερ ἀεὶ legitur, vix credibile est scriptorem eundem formam utramque usurpasse.
21 τήν τε φ[ιλαργυρ]ίαν K, K-W, H-L; τὴν φ[ιλοχρηματ]ίαν Kontos, Bernardakis: τήν τε ἀ[χρημ]ατίαν B. τήν τε ὑπερ. (K, K-W); τήν θ' ὑπερ. J B Mayor, Jackson, H-L; et metrum et τε iteratum poetae versum produnt.
VI 1 <ὁ> Σόλων K-W. **3** καὶ νόμους ἔθηκε secl. K-W, Reinach. C
4 ΑCΕΙCΑΧΘΙΑ: ἃς σεισάχθειαν K etc. καλοῦσιν: 'fort. ἐκάλουν scribendum' (K-W).
5 ΑΠΟCΙCΑΜΕΝΟΙ: ἀποσεισάμενοι K, H-L; ἀποσεισαμένων J B Mayor, K-W, B. ΒΑΡΟC K etc.: [ἄχθ]ος H-L.

TESTIMONIA. **VI 3** Heraclidis epitoma: νομοθετῶν Ἀθηναίοις καὶ χρεῶν ἀποκοπὰς ἐποίησε, τὴν σεισάχθειαν λεγομένην (Rose, Frag. 611, 3^3). Hesych. σεισάχθεια· Σόλων χρεῶν ἀποκοπὴν δημοσίων καὶ ἰδιωτικῶν ἐνομοθέτησεν, ἥνπερ σεισάχθειαν ἐκάλεσε παρὰ τὸ ἀποσείσασθαι τὸ βάρος τῶν δανείων. Photius (= Suidas) σεισάχθεια, = Apostolius 17, 52.

3, ὧν τοὺς λόγους εἰς ἀριθμοὺς ἀνῆπτον, 'to ascribe or refer to.' Common in Plutarch, *e.g. Lycurg.* 6, τὴν ἀρχὴν καὶ τὴν αἰτίαν τῆς πολιτείας εἰς τὸν Πύθιον ἀνῆψε, 13 § 3, τὸ δὲ ὅλον καὶ πάσης νομοθεσίας ἔργον εἰς τὴν παιδείαν ἀνῆψε, *Numa* 12 § 1, εἰς μιᾶς δύναμιν θεοῦ τὰ περὶ τὰς γενέσεις καὶ τὰς τελευτὰς ἀνάπτοντες. Cf. ἀναφέρειν. Mr Poste and Mr H. Richards (*Class. Rev.* v 466 *a*) understand it 'imputes the blame.' This might be defended by Od. ii 86 μῶμον ἀνάψαι (Schol. περιποιῆσαι, περιθεῖναι), where Ameis prefers ἐκ μῶμον ἀνάψαι. But in Attic Gk we should expect περιάπτει in this sense (Dem. *Lept.* 10). **τῆς ἐλεγείας**, § 2.

δεδοικέναι κτλ.] Plut. *Sol.* 14, δεδοικὼς τῶν μὲν τὴν φιλοχρηματίαν τῶν δὲ τὴν ὑπερηφανίαν. The double τε is far more common in verse than in prose (Kühner, § 520).

VI § 1. **κωλύσας δανείζειν** κτλ.] Plut. *Sol.* 15, Σόλωνος...τὴν τῶν χρεῶν ἀποκοπὴν σεισάχθειαν ὀνομάσαντος. τοῦτο γὰρ ἐποιήσατο πρῶτον πολίτευμα, γράψας τὰ μὲν ὑπάρχοντα τῶν χρεῶν ἀνεῖσθαι, πρὸς δὲ τὸ λοιπὸν ἐπὶ τοῖς σώμασι μηδένα δανείζειν. Diog. Laert. i 45. The phrase χρεῶν ἀποκοπαὶ is found in Dem. 17 § 15, 24 § 149, Andoc. *de Myst.* 88, Plut. ii 226 B, Cic. *ad Att.* vii 11 § 1, χ. ἀποκοπὴ in Plato, *Legg.* 736 C.

σεισάχθειαν] (1) Most of our ancient authorities understood this to imply a complete remission of debts; this is the view of the text, and of Philochorus, frag. 57, and it is accepted by Schömann, *Ant.* p. 328 E. T.; Gilbert i 130; Landwehr, *Philol. Suppl. Bd* v (1884) 131 ff.; and Busolt, i 525. (2) Others, including Androtion (see note on 10 § 1), held that Solon relieved the debtors, partly by a diminution in the rate of interest, partly by the introduction of a new money-standard; this is accepted by Boeckh; Hermann, *Staatsalt.* § 106; E. Curtius; and (in the main) by Duncker, *Gesch. d. Alt.* vi ed. 5, 158. (3) Grote (c. 11, ii 304) assumes a total remission of debts, but limits it to the case of debts secured on the debtor's person or his land.

§ 2. **συνέβη—ἐπλούτουν**] Plut. *Sol.* 15, πρᾶγμα δ' αὐτῷ συμπεσεῖν λέγεται πάντων ἀνιαρότατον ἀπὸ τῆς πράξεως ἐκεί-

*σεισάχ[θ]ειαν προειπεῖν τισὶ τῶν [γνω]ρίμω[ν], ἔπειθ', ὡς μὲν οἱ
δημοτικοὶ λέγουσι, παραστρατηγηθῆναι διὰ τῶν φίλων, ὡς δ' οἱ
[βουλ]όμενοι βλασφημεῖν, καὶ αὐτὸν κοινωνεῖν. δανεισάμενοι γὰρ
οὗτοι συνεπρίαντο πολλὴν χώραν, [μετὰ δ'] οὐ πολὺ τῆς τῶν
χρεῶν ἀποκοπῆς γενομένης ἐπλούτουν· ὅθεν φασὶ γενέσθαι τοὺς
ὕστερον δο[κο]ῦντας εἶναι παλαιοπλούτους. οὐ μὴν ἀλλὰ πιθ[ανώ-]* 3
*τερος [ὁ] τῶν δημοτικῶ[ν λ]όγος· οὐ γὰρ [εἰκ]ὸς ἐν μὲν τοῖς ἄλλοις
οὕτω μέτριον γενέσθαι καὶ κοινὸν [ὥσ]τ', ἐξὸν αὐτῷ [τ]οὺς [ἑτ]έ[ρο]υς
ὑποποιησάμενον τυραννεῖν τῆς πόλεως, ἀμφοτέροις ἀπεχ[θ]έσθαι
καὶ περὶ πλείονος [ποι]ήσασθαι τ[ὸ κα]λὸν καὶ τὴν τῆς πόλεως
σωτηρίαν ἢ τὴν αὑτοῦ πλεονεξίαν, ἐν [οὕτ]ω δὲ μικροῖς [καὶ]
ἀν[αξίο]ις καταρρυπαίν[ε]ιν ἑαυτόν. ὅτι δὲ ταύτην ἔσχε τὴν* 4
ἐξουσίαν, τά τε πράγματα νοσοῦντα μα[ρτυ]ρεῖ [τοῦ]το, καὶ ἐν τοῖς

8 Δ', διὰ K etc.: ὑπὸ K-W. **10** *μετὰ δ'* K etc. (cf. *Magn. Mor.* 1211 *b* 1, *μετ' οὐ πολύ*); *εἶτα μετ'* H-L. **11** ΓΙΝΟΜΕΝΗϹ (K[1]): *γενομένης* Rutherford, K-W, H-L, K[3]. **14** *ὥστ'* Richards, Jackson, Blass (edd.): *ἅμα τ'* olim K. [*νόμ*]*ους* K, K-W: [*ἑτ*]*έ*[*ρο*]*υς* (ει) Blass (H-L) coll. c. 11, 13. **19** Μ....ΡΟ...ΤΟ litteris obscure scriptis. *μαρτυρεῖ* legunt Wessely et Blass, quod mihi quoque in mentem venerat. *τοῦτο* mecum coniecerunt K-W[2], *ἃ ἰάσατο* Wessely, quod vel propter hiatum vix tolerari potest. *μετεχειρίσατο* quod olim protuli (coll. Plat. *Rep.* 408 C *ἰατροὶ νοσώδεις μετεχειρίσαντο*, et 346 E *τὰ ἀλλότρια κακὰ μεταχειρίζεσθαι ἀνορθοῦντα*) acceperunt H-L, sed repugnat papyrus. *μαρτύρ*[*ι*]*ο*[*ν μέ*]*γα* Blass, sed ΤΟ potius quam ΓΑ in papyro apparet.

νης. ὡς γὰρ ὥρμησεν ἀνιέναι τὰ χρέα καὶ λόγους ἁρμόττοντας ἐζήτει καὶ πρέπουσαν ἀρχήν, ἐκοινώσατο τῶν φίλων οἷς μάλιστα πιστεύων καὶ χρώμενος ἐτύγχανε, τοῖς περὶ Κόνωνα καὶ Κλεινίαν καὶ Ἱππόνικον, ὅτι γῆν μὲν οὐ μέλλει κινεῖν, χρεῶν δὲ ποιεῖν ἀποκοπὰς ἔγνωκεν. οἱ δὲ προλαβόντες εὐθὺς καὶ φθάσαντες ἐδανείσαντο συχνὸν ἀργύριον παρὰ τῶν πλουσίων καὶ μεγάλας συνεωνήσαντο χώρας. εἶτα τοῦ δόγματος ἐξενεχθέντος τὰ μὲν κτήματα καρπούμενοι, τὰ δὲ χρήματα τοῖς δανείσασιν οὐκ ἀποδιδόντες εἰς αἰτίαν τὸν Σόλωνα μεγάλην καὶ διαβολήν, ὥσπερ οὐ συναδικούμενον, ἀλλὰ συναδικοῦντα, κατέστησαν. ἀλλὰ τοῦτο μὲν εὐθὺς ἐλύθη τὸ ἔγκλημα τοῖς πέντε ταλάντοις· τοσαῦτα γὰρ εὑρέθη δανείζων, καὶ ταῦτα πρῶτος ἀφῆκε κατὰ τὸν νόμον. ἔνιοι δὲ πεντεκαίδεκα λέγουσιν, ὧν καὶ Πολύζηλος ὁ Ῥόδιός ἐστι. τοὺς μέντοι φίλους αὐτοῦ χρεωκοπίδας καλοῦντες διετέλεσαν (the story of the five talents comes from some other source than the text). *Praecept. Ger. Reip.* 13 § 10 p. 807, *τοῦτο γὰρ καὶ Σόλωνα κατῄσχυνε καὶ διέβαλε πρὸς τοὺς πολίτας· ἐπεὶ γὰρ ἐν νῷ λαβὼν τὰ ὀφλήματα κουφίσαι, καὶ τὴν σεισάχθειαν (τοῦτο δ' ἦν ὑποκόρισμα χρεῶν ἀποκοπῆς) εἰσενεγκεῖν, ἐκοινώσατο τοῖς φίλοις· οἱ δ' ἔργον ἀδικώτατον ἔπραξαν· ἐδανείσαντο γὰρ ὑποφθάσαντες ἀργύριον πολύ, καὶ μετ' ὀλίγον χρόνον εἰς φῶς τοῦ νόμου προαχθέντος, οἱ μὲν ἐφάνησαν οἰκίας τε λαμπρὰς καὶ γῆν συνεωνημένοι πολλὴν ἐξ ὧν ἐδανείσαντο χρημάτων· ὁ δὲ Σόλων αἰτίαν ἔσχε συναδικεῖν ἠδικημένος.*

παλαιοπλούτους] Lys. 19 § 49.

§ 3. **καταρρυπαίνειν**] To the passages from Isocr. and Plato, quoted in L and S, may be added Plut. *de Cohibenda Ira* 6, ii p. 456, *καταρρυπαίνει καὶ πίμπλησιν ἀδοξίας*, *de Profectibus in Virt.* 17, ii p. 85 F, *οὐ δ' ὁπωσοῦν ἀξιῶν ῥυπαίνεσθαι*. The word is not found in Ar.

§ 4. **ταύτην τὴν ἐξουσίαν**] *sc. τοῦ τυραννεῖν*. Plut. *Sol.* 14 and Solon fragm. 33, *οὐκ ἔφυ Σόλων βαθύφρων κτλ.*, there quoted: also fragm. 32.

τά τε πράγματα νοσοῦντα *κτλ.*] Prof. Tyrrell (*Class. Rev.* v 177) defends *μετεκρούσατο* (K[1]) as follows: "The idea of a balance underlies the word, as in *παρακρούεσθαι*, and 'he shifted the balance of affairs' would be a not unnatural way of saying 'he changed the face of politics.' But, even if *μετεκρούσατο* were defensible in itself, one could hardly justify such a mixture of metaphors as 'adjusting the ποιήμασιν αὐτὸς πολλαχοῦ μέμνηται, καὶ οἱ ἄλλοι συνομολογοῦσι πάν[τες]. ταύτην μὲν οὖν χρὴ νομίζειν ψευδῆ τὴν αἰτίαν εἶναι.

7. πολιτείαν δὲ κατέστησε καὶ νόμους ἔθηκεν ἄλλους, τοῖς δὲ Δράκοντος θεσμοῖς ἐπαύσαντο χρώμενοι πλὴν τῶν φονικῶν. ἀναγράψαντες δὲ τοὺς νόμους εἰς τοὺς κύρβεις ἔστησαν ἐν τῇ στοᾷ τῇ

TESTIMONIA. **VII 3** *Harp. *κύρβεις*: "*ἀναγράψαντες—ἐν τῇ στοᾷ τῇ βασιλείᾳ* (*βασιλίδι* cod. D et Photius)." *Plut. *Sol.* 25 (*οἱ ξύλινοι ἄξονες*) *προσηγορεύθησαν, ὡς Ἀριστοτέλης φησί, κύρβεις.* *Schol. Arist. *Av.* 1354 (=Lexicon Dem. Patmiacum, p. 150 Sakkelion) *κύρβεις...κατὰ δὲ ἐνίους ἄξονες τρίγωνοι* (*κατασκευάσματά τινα ξύλινα τρίγωνα* Lex. Patm.) *ἐν οἷς ἦσαν οἱ τῶν πόλεων νόμοι γεγραμμένοι...καθάπερ καὶ Ἀρ. ἐν τῇ Ἀθ. πολ. φησὶ καὶ Ἀπολλόδωρος* (Rose, Frag. 352^2, 390^3).

---

balance of the maladies of the state.' My former suggestion *νοσοῦντα μετεχειρίσατο* is defended in point of expression by the passages of Plato quoted in the critical notes. It is also incidentally confirmed in point of sense by a passage in Grote's *History of Greece* (ii 327), where he speaks of the 'discontents of the miserable Athenian population' experiencing Solon's 'disinterested and *healing management*.' The *τε* in this case would mean 'and accordingly' (being armed with this authority), as often in Herodotus and Thucydides, and not seldom in Xenophon (Kühner, § 519, 3). The usage of Ar. does not differ in this from that of other writers (Eucken, *De Ar. dicendi ratione*, i p. 13).

The suggestion that the sense required is '*docet et res publica aegrotans et*' (K-W[1]) admits of being carried out by proposing *τά τε πράγματα νοσοῦντα μαρτυρεῖ τοῦτο.* The sequence *μαρτυρεῖ...μέμνηται...συνομολογοῦσι* would in this case find its parallel in c. 5 § 3, *ἔκ τε τῶν ἄλλων ὁμολογεῖται καὶ αὐτὸς ἐν τοῖσδε τοῖς ποιήμασιν μαρτυρεῖ*, and 12 § 1. Cf. *Pol.* 1334 *a* 5 *ὅτι δὲ δεῖ...μαρτυρεῖ τὰ γιγνόμενα τοῖς λόγοις*, *Metaphysica* 282 *b* 22 *ὁ λόγος μαρτυρεῖ*, *De Anima* 410 *a* 29, *ὡς* —, *μαρτυρεῖ τὸ νῦν λεχθέν*, *Eth.* ii 1, 1103 *b* 2 *μαρτυρεῖ δὲ καὶ τὸ γιγνόμενον ἐν ταῖς πολεσιν*, &c. Since this note was written *μαρτυρεῖ* has been conjectured in K-W[2], and this is the reading which I now prefer.

νοσοῦντα] c. 13 § 3, *στασιάζοντες* followed by *νοσοῦντες* metaphorically used in the same sense. Plat. *Rep.* 470 C, *νοσεῖν...καὶ στασιάζειν*, and 556 E, *νοσεῖ τε καὶ αὐτὴ αὑτῇ μάχεται* (*ἡ πόλις*).

μέμνηται] 'makes mention of,' usually c. gen.; here *ὅτι* is due partly to the influence of *συνομολογοῦσι*, and still more to *μαρτυρεῖ*, if that be accepted. Cf. 12 § 1, *ὅτι—συμφωνοῦσι—μέμνηται.*

VII § 1. **Δράκοντος θεσμοῖς**] c. 4 § 1.

πλὴν τῶν φονικῶν] Plut. *Sol.* 17 *init.* *πρῶτον μὲν οὖν τοὺς Δράκοντος νόμους ἀνεῖλε πλὴν τῶν φονικῶν ἅπαντας διὰ τὴν χαλεπότητα καὶ τὸ μέγεθος τῶν ἐπιτιμίων.* Cf. Dem. 23 § 66, Aelian *V. H.* viii 10, Josephus *Apion.* i 4, *τῶν δημοσίων γραμμάτων ἀρχαιοτάτους τοὺς ὑπὸ Δράκοντος αὐτοῖς περὶ τῶν φονικῶν γραφέντας νόμους.* On the revision of the laws of Athens, after the restoration of the democracy in the summer of 411 B.C., the laws of Dracon respecting homicide were once more retained. An inscr. of 409 B.C. records a decree authorizing the *γραμματεὺς* of the *βουλὴ* to give the *ἀναγραφῆς*, or recorders of the laws, a true copy of Dracon's law. *Δράκοντος νόμον τὸν περὶ τοῦ [φόν]ου [ἀ]ν[α]γραψά[ν]τ[ων οἱ ἀ]ν[αγρα]φῆς τῶν νόμων—ἐ στήλῃ λιθίνῃ κ[αὶ κ]α[τ]α[θέν]τ[ων πρόσθεν τ]ῆ[ς] στοᾶς τῆς βασιλείας.* (Cf. Andoc. i 84, 85)... Then follows a copy of the *πρῶτος ἄξων* of Solon, containing Dracon's law on involuntary homicide (CIA i 61; Dittenberger, p. 87; Hicks, *Greek Hist. Inscr.* p. 112).

κύρβεις] Rectangular wooden tablets painted white and arranged in sets of four, each set forming a 'pillar' about the height of a man. This pillar revolved on an upright axis; hence the *κύρβεις* were called *ἄξονες*, the *axes ligneae* of Gellius ii 12. The *κύρβεις* are mentioned in a fragment of Cratinus, quoted by Plutarch *Sol.* 25. An inscr. of 409 B.C. cites the *πρῶτος ἄξων* (see note on *πλὴν τῶν φονικῶν*). Lysias, Or. 30, *c. Nicomachum* (B.C. 399), § 17 *τὰς θυσίας τὰς ἐκ τῶν κύρβεων.* In Dem. *Aristocr.* p. 629 § 28, the law of homicide is found *ἐν τῷ α´* (*i.e. πρώτῳ*) *ἄξονι* (as emended by Cobet).

Aristotle is said to have written a treatise in five books *περὶ τῶν Σόλωνος ἀξόνων* (see list of his works, ascribed to Hesychius, in Rose, *Fragm. Ar.* p. 16, l. 140). Eratosthenes supposed that the several tablets were triangular in shape. This *βασιλείῳ καὶ ὤμοσαν χρήσεσθαι πάντες· οἱ δ' ἐννέα ἄρχοντες*

---

mistake was corrected by Polemon of Ilium, who, on the strength of his own observation, insists on the quadrangular shape of the tablets (Harpocr. *s. v.* ἄξονι: οἱ Σόλωνος νόμοι ἐν ξυλίνοις ἦσαν ἄξοσι γεγραμμένοι...ἦσαν δέ, ὥς φησι Πολέμων ἐν τοῖς πρὸς Ἐρατοσθένην, τετράγωνοι τὸ σχῆμα, διασῴζονται δὲ ἐν τῷ Πρυτανείῳ, γεγραμμένοι κατὰ πάντα τὰ μέρη· ποιοῦσι δ' ἐνίοτε φαντασίαν τρίγωνον, ὅταν ἐπὶ τὸ στενὸν κλιθῶσι τῆς γωνίας. Polemo fragm. 48, Müller, FHG iii 130). A pupil of Eratosthenes, the famous critic Aristophanes of Byzantium, gives a clear account of their shape: Etymologicum Magn. p. 547, ἀμφοτέρων δὲ (*sc.* τῶν κύρβεων καὶ τῶν ἀξόνων) τὸ κατασκεύασμα τοιοῦτον· πλινθίον τι μέγα ἀνδρόμηκες, ἡρμοσμένα ἔχον ξύλα τετράγωνα, τὰς πλευρὰς πλατείας ἔχοντα καὶ γραμμάτων πλήρεις, ἑκατέρωθεν δὲ κνώδακας ('pivots'), ὥστε κινεῖσθαι καὶ περιστρέφεσθαι ὑπὸ τῶν ἀναγιγνωσκομένων. The 'grammarians' Didymus (Plut. *Sol.* 1) and Seleucus (Suidas, *s. v.* ὀργεῶνες) wrote monographs on the ἄξονες. Plutarch, in his life of Solon, refers to the first, the thirteenth and the sixteenth ἄξων (c. 24, 19, 23), and states that some small fragments of the ἄξονες were still to be seen in his own day in the Prytaneum (c. 25).

Some of the Greek lexicographers erroneously distinguished between the κύρβεις and ἄξονες in respect to shape, material and contents (cf. Schol. on Apollonius Rhodius iv 280). The distinction assumes the following form in Tzetzes, *Chiliades*, xii 349:

> οἱ ἄξονες τετράγωνοι, τρίγωνοι δὲ αἱ κύρβεις,
> εἶχον δὲ οἱ μὲν ἄξονες νόμους τοὺς ἰδιώτας,
> αἱ κύρβεις εἶχον νόμους δὲ τοὺς περὶ δημοσίων.
> καὶ ἔτι οἱ μὲν ἄξονες ὑπῆρχον ἀπὸ ξύλων,
> αἱ κύρβεις ἦσαν δὲ χαλκαί.

But the identity of the ἄξονες and κύρβεις has been proved by Hulleman, *Miscellanea Philol.* (Amsterdam, 1850), and is now generally accepted. Cf. Preller on Polemon, p. 87; Frohberger's *Lysias*, III p. 23; Rose, *Ar. Pseudepigraphus*, 414; and Oncken, *die Staatslehre des Ar.*, 422. In view of the text, it is no longer possible to regard the κύρβεις (placed in the στοὰ) as later copies of the ἄξονες in the Prytaneum (so Busolt, i 539, and Müller, *Handbuch*, IV i 118).

τῇ στοᾷ τῇ βασιλείῳ] called ἡ στοὰ ἡ βασιλεία in CIA i 61 (quoted in n. on πλὴν τῶν φονικῶν). Harpocr. *s. v.* βασίλειος στοά: δύο εἰσὶ στοαὶ παρ' ἀλλήλας, ἥ τε τοῦ Ἐλευθερίου Διὸς καὶ ἡ βασίλειος.

In literature it is known as ἡ τοῦ βασιλέως στοά (Plat. *Euthyphron* 2 A, *Theaet.* 210 D) or ἡ στοιὰ ἡ βασίλειος (Aristoph. *Eccl.* 684). Cf. Pausan. i 3, 1, καλουμένη στοὰ βασίλειος ἔνθα καθίζει βασιλεὺς ἐνιαυσίαν ἄρχων ἀρχὴν καλουμένην βασιλείαν. Pausanias, entering the inner Cerameicus from the north, sees the στοὰ βασίλειος as the first building on his right, *i.e.* on the W. side of the Cerameicus. Apparently he did not go inside, and he tells us nothing of the altar outside, where the Archons took their oath. (See esp. Wachsmuth, *Stadt Athen*, ii 344—351; Curtius, *Stadtgeschichte von Athen*, p. xc *b*, and p. 294; and cf. Miss Harrison's *Mythology* &c. *of Athens*, p. 24.)

The use of this στοὰ as a place for keeping a record of the laws of Athens is attested in Andoc. *De Myst.* 82, 85, ἀναγράψαι ἐν τῇ στοᾷ, and 84, εἰς τὸν τοῖχον ἵνα περ πρότερον ἀνεγράφησαν. The statement of Anaximenes (in Harpocration, *s. v.* ὁ κάτωθεν νόμος), that Ephialtes transferred τοὺς ἄξονας καὶ τοὺς κύρβεις from the Acropolis to the βουλευτήριον and the ἀγορά, is inconsistent with the text, and is probably a mere flourish of rhetoric. The κύρβεις were apparently always in the ἀγορά. Cf. Oncken, *Staatslehre*, ii 422. Secret meetings of the Areopagus were sometimes held ἐν τῇ βασιλείῳ στοᾷ, Dem. 25, *Aristog.* A, § 23.

ὤμοσαν κτλ.] Plut. *Solon* 25, κοινὸν μὲν οὖν ὤμνυεν ὅρκον ἡ βουλὴ τοὺς Σόλωνος νόμους ἐμπεδώσειν, ἴδιον δ' ἕκαστος τῶν θεσμοθετῶν ἐν ἀγορᾷ πρὸς τῷ λίθῳ, καταφατίζων, εἴ τι παραβαίη τῶν θεσμῶν, ἀνδριάντα χρυσοῦν ἰσομέτρητον ἀναθήσειν ἐν Δελφοῖς. On the oath of the Archons, cf. c. 55 § 5, and Plato *Phaedr.* 235 D, καί σοι ἐγώ, ὥσπερ οἱ ἐννέα ἄρχοντες, ὑπισχνοῦμαι χρυσῆν εἰκόνα ἰσομέτρητον εἰς Δελφοὺς ἀναθήσειν.

The word ἰσομέτρητον is omitted in the text and in Pollux viii 86. It is ingeniously explained by Bergk (*Rhein. Mus.* xiii 448) as virtually equivalent to ἰσοστάσιον and as implying that the statue in gold was to be equivalent in weight to the amount of silver received as a bribe. This, he urges, is suggested by Deinarchus i 60, ii 17, where the δεκαπλοῦν τίμημα may be explained with reference to the relative value of gold to silver at Athens in the time of Solon, being 10 : 1. According to this view the archons swore that they would pay a fine equivalent to ten times the value of any bribe they

ὀμνύντες πρὸς τῷ λίθῳ κατεφάτιζον ἀναθήσειν ἀνδριάντα χρυσοῦν, ἐάν τινα παραβῶσι τῶν νόμων· ὅθεν ἔτι καὶ νῦν οὕτως ὀμνύουσι.
2 κατεκύρωσεν δὲ τοὺς νόμους εἰς ἑκατὸν [ἔ]τη καὶ διέταξε τὴν πολιτείαν τόνδε <τὸν> τρόπον.

3 τιμήμα[τα δι]εῖλεν εἰς τέτταρα τέλη, καθάπερ διῄρητο καὶ πρότερον, εἰς πεντακοσιομ[έδιμ]ν[ον καὶ ἱππέα] καὶ ζευγίτην καὶ

8 τόνδε <τὸν> τρόπον edd.; cf. c. 29 § 5, 37 § 1. **9** <τὰ> τιμήματα Blass (H-L); ante τιμήματα lacunam indicant K-W, 'velut <τὸ πᾶν πλῆθος ἐκ> τιμημάτων διεῖλεν,' coll. Hesych. et Harp.

TESTIMONIA. **5** *Harp. λίθος:...ἐοίκασι δ' Ἀθηναῖοι πρός τινι λίθῳ τοὺς ὅρκους ποιεῖσθαι, ὡς Ἀρ. ἐν τῇ Ἀθ. πολ. καὶ Φιλόχορος ἐν τῷ γ' ὑποσημαίνουσιν.
9 *Harp. ἱππάς:...Ἀρ. ἐν Ἀθ. πολ. φησὶν ὅτι Σόλων εἰς τέτταρα διεῖλε τέλη

---

received. In the text, however, we have no reference to receiving bribes and no mention of the bulk of the statue; nor again have we either here, or in the excerpts of Heraclides or in Pollux, any mention of Delphi. Suidas (as observed by Thompson on Pl. *Phaedr. l. c.*) 'makes the statues three instead of one and represents them as portrait-statues of the delinquent' (χρυσῆ εἰκών: ὤμνυον οἱ Ἀθήνῃσιν ἄρχοντες, ἄν τι παρέλθωσιν ἐφ' οἷς ἂν ἄρχωσιν, χρυσῆν εἰκόνα αὐτῶν ἀναθήσειν ἐν ἄστει, ἐν Πυθοῖ, ἐν Ὀλυμπίᾳ). But portrait-statues were not in use in Solon's time, and 'it is very unlikely that the Delphians would have allowed their sacred peribolus to be defiled by the statue of a detected criminal. And if the penalty was intended to be enforced, the offering must needs have been of much more limited dimensions. It is therefore conceivable that both ἰσομέτρητον and αὐτοῦ were introduced by late writers into the text of the original oath, in order to make it conformable to the supposed meaning of Plato.' The text shews that this conjecture is right, and also that the insertion of ἐν Δελφοῖς has no warrant in the original form of the oath.

The λίθος was possibly identical with the altar of Ζεὺς ἀγοραῖος (Wachsmuth, *Stadt Athen*, ii 352[2]).

§ 2. **εἰς ἑκατὸν ἔτη**] Plut. *Sol.* 25 init., ἰσχὺν δὲ τοῖς νόμοις πᾶσιν εἰς ἑκατὸν ἐνιαυτοὺς ἔδωκε.

§ 3. **τιμήματα** κτλ.] Hitherto it has been universally held that the classification of citizens according to property was first devised by Solon. Plut. *Sol.* 18, δεύτερον δὲ Σόλων τὰς μὲν ἀρχὰς ἁπάσας, ὥσπερ ἦσαν, τοῖς εὐπόροις ἀπολιπεῖν βουλόμενος, τὴν δ' ἄλλην μῖξαι πολιτείαν, ἧς ὁ δῆμος οὐ μετεῖχεν, ἔλαβε τὰ τιμήματα τῶν πολιτῶν, καὶ τοὺς μὲν ἐν ξηροῖς ὁμοῦ καὶ ὑγροῖς μέτρα πεντακόσια ποιοῦντας πρώτους ἔταξε καὶ πεντακοσιομεδίμνους προσηγόρευσε· δευτέρους δὲ τοὺς ἵππον τρέφειν δυναμένους ἢ μέτρα ποιεῖν τριακόσια· καὶ τούτους ἱππάδα τελοῦντας ἐκάλουν· ζευγῖται δ' οἱ τοῦ τρίτου τιμήματος ὠνομάσθησαν, οἷς μέτρον ἦν συναμφοτέρων διακοσίων. οἱ δὲ λοιποὶ πάντες ἐκαλοῦντο θῆτες, οἷς οὐδεμίαν ἄρχειν ἔδωκεν ἀρχήν, ἀλλὰ τῷ συνεκκλησιάζειν καὶ δικάζειν μόνον μετεῖχον τῆς πολιτείας. The quotations in Harpocration are to the same effect. They ignore the 'Draconian constitution,' and they lend no support to the phrase: καθάπερ διῄρητο καὶ πρότερον. Those who decline to accept the 'Draconian constitution' must necessarily omit the words just quoted. Mr Kenyon suggests that the statements in c. 4 can only be reconciled with the general ascription of the classes in question to Solon, by supposing that the latter brought them into a new relation to the political constitution. Solon began his reforms by repealing all of Dracon's laws except those relating to homicide. This implies that 'Solon made a clean sweep of all the laws relating to the constitution, so as to have a free hand in reconstructing it according to his own ideas. He then re-introduced the property classes, as well as the Council of Four hundred and the Areopagus.' This explanation is skilful and ingenious and may possibly be right.

On Solon's τιμήματα, see Boeckh, Book iv c. v; Grote, c. 11, vol. ii 318; Busolt i 527. The term τίμημα occurs first in CIA i 31.

ζευγίτην] from ζεῦγος, 'a team,' applied to one who kept a pair of mules (Isaeus 5 § 43; 6 § 33), or of working horses, or a yoke of oxen.

θῆτα. τὰς μ[ὲν οὖ]ν ἀρχὰς ἀπένειμεν || ἄρχειν ἐκ πεντακοσιομε- [Col. 3.] δίμνων καὶ ἱππέων καὶ ζευγιτῶν, τοὺς ἐννέα ἄρχοντας καὶ τοὺς ταμίας καὶ τοὺς πωλη[τὰς] καὶ τοὺς ἕνδεκα καὶ τοὺς κωλακρέτας, ἑκάστοις ἀνάλογον τῷ μεγέθει τοῦ τιμ[ή]μ[ατο]ς ἀποδιδοὺς τ[ὴν ἀρ]χήν. τοῖς δὲ τὸ θητικὸν τελοῦσιν ἐκκλησίας καὶ δικαστηρίων

11 τὰς μὲν οὖν ἀρχὰς K, K-W, H-L: [καὶ] τὰς ⟦με[γίστ]ας⟧ ἀρχὰς Blass, qui aut μεγίστας (quod legi posse concedit K) delendum, aut in sequentibus complura mutanda putat.

τὸ πᾶν πλῆθος Ἀθηναίων, πεντακοσιομεδίμνους καὶ ἱππέας καὶ ζευγίτας καὶ θῆτας. *Id. πεντακοσιομέδιμνον:...ὅτι δ̄ τέλη ἐποίησεν Ἀθηναίων ἁπάντων Σόλων, ὧν ἦσαν καὶ οἱ πεντακοσιομέδιμνοι, δεδήλωκεν Ἀρ. ἐν Ἀθ. πολ. *Id. θῆτες:...εἰς τέσσαρα διῃρημένης παρ' Ἀθηναίοις τῆς πολιτείας οἱ ἀπορώτατοι ἐλέγοντο θῆτες καὶ θητικὸν τελεῖν κτλ. Pollux viii 130 τιμήματα δ' ἦν τέτταρα κτλ. Hesych. ἐκ τιμημάτων:...διῄρητο γὰρ ἡ πολιτεία κατὰ Σόλωνα εἰς τέσσαρα, πεντακοσιομέδιμνον... Id. ζευγίσιον:...ἦν δὲ διῃρημένη ἡ πολιτεία εἰς τέσσαρα τιμήματα. (Cf. Rose, Frag. 350^2, 388^3.)

15 Schol. Arist. *Eq.* 627 (οἱ θῆτες), οἷς οὐδὲ ἄρχειν ἐφεῖτο, ἢ δικάζειν καὶ ἐκκλησιάζειν μόνον.

τὰς ἀρχὰς ἀπένειμεν ἄρχειν] This does not mean that the members of all the three highest classes were eligible for the office of archon. The first part of the sentence must be read in the light of the second, which implies that there was a kind of scale of eligibility according to the class in which the citizen was placed. Those in the first class alone would be eligible for the archonship. Cf. Plut. *Aristides* 1, τὴν ἐπώνυμον ἀρχήν, ἣν ἦρχε τῷ κυάμῳ λαχὼν ἐκ τῶν γενῶν τῶν τὰ μέγιστα τιμήματα κεκτημένων, οὓς πεντακοσιομεδίμνους προσηγόρευον. The same class supplied the ταμίαι c. 8 § 1. On the **ταμίαι** and the **πωληταί**, see c. 47; on the **ἕνδεκα**, c. 52.

κωλακρέτας] The form given by Photius and Suidas: κωλαγρέτης in the Ravenna MS of Aristoph. and in the lexicon of Timaeus; lit. 'collectors of hams,' so called from receiving the prime parts of the victims to aid them in providing the public meals in the *prytaneum*. They are said to have had the control of financial matters in the time of the kings; in later times they acted as treasurers of the *naucrariae*. They were left untouched by the legislation of Solon, in connexion with which they are mentioned in the text; but in the reforms of Cleisthenes they lost the charge of the finances, which was then transferred to new officers called *Apodectae* (48). Under Pericles they were assigned the duty of paying the dicasts, and they were considered officials of some importance in the time of Aristophanes (Schol. on *Vesp.* 695, 727, *Av.* 1541). There is no documentary proof of their existence after the Archonship of Euclides (403 B.C.). Cf. Boeckh, ed. Fränkel, note 302, and Schömann's *Antiquities*, i 327 E. T.; also Mr Wayte's article in Smith's *Dict. Ant.*, *s.v.*, Gilbert, i 119 and Busolt, i 159.

ἑκάστοις—τὴν ἀρχήν] *Pol.* 1291 *b* 38 ἓν μὲν οὖν εἶδος δημοκρατίας τοῦτο, τὸ τὰς ἀρχὰς ἀπὸ τιμημάτων εἶναι κτλ.

τοῖς δὲ τὸ θητικὸν τελοῦσιν—μόνον] *Pol.* ii 12, 1274 *a* 15, Σόλων γε ἔοικε τὴν ἀναγκαιοτάτην ἀποδιδόναι τῷ δήμῳ δύναμιν, τὸ τὰς ἀρχὰς αἱρεῖσθαι καὶ εὐθύνειν..., τὰς δ' ἀρχὰς ἐκ τῶν γνωρίμων καὶ τῶν εὐπόρων κατέστησε πάσας, ἐκ τῶν πεντακοσιομεδίμνων καὶ ζευγιτῶν καὶ [τρίτου τέλους] τῆς καλουμένης ἱππάδος· τὸ δὲ τέταρτον τὸ θητικόν, οἷς οὐδεμιᾶς ἀρχῆς μετῆν. Cf. end of this chapter, τοὺς δὲ ἄλλους θητικόν, οὐδεμιᾶς μετέχοντας ἀρχῆς.

τὸ θητικὸν τελοῦσιν] 'those who belonged to the thetic census.' It will be observed that they are not here called θῆτες. Of those who were placed in the fourth class Grote (ii 321) observes: 'It is said that they were all called *Thêtes*, but this appellation is not well sustained and cannot be admitted: the fourth compartment in the descending scale was indeed termed the Thetic census, because it contained all the *Thêtes*, and because most of its members were of that humble description, but it is not conceivable that a proprietor whose land yielded to him a clear annual return of 100, 120, 140 or 180 drachms, could ever have been designated by that name.' See, however, l. 11. τελεῖν does not necessarily mean *actual*

4 μετέδωκε μόνον. ἔδει δὲ τελεῖν πεντακοσιομέδιμνον μὲν ὃς ἂν ἐκ τῆς οἰκείας ποιῇ πεντακόσια μέτρα τὰ συνάμφω ξηρὰ καὶ ὑγρά, ἱππάδα δὲ τοὺς τριακόσια ποιοῦντας (ὡς δ' ἔνιοί φασι τοὺς ἱπποτροφεῖν δυναμένους. σημεῖον δὲ φέρουσι τό τε ὄνομα το[ῦ] τέλους, ὡς ἂν ἀπὸ τοῦ πράγ[μ]ατος κείμενον, καὶ τὰ ἀναθήματα τῶν

17 τῆς : γῆς Bywater; τῆς defendit Kontos (*Athena* iii 321—2). ξηρῶν καὶ ὑγρῶν H-L coll. Plut. *Sol.* 18 (ἐν ξηροῖς ὁμοῦ καὶ ὑγροῖς). **19** δ' ἐπιφέρουσι H-L coll. c. 3, 11. **20** ὡς ἂν—κείμενον delent H-L; ἂν delet B.

TESTIM. **16—19** Pollux viii 130 οἱ μὲν ἐκ τοῦ πεντακόσια μέτρα ξηρὰ καὶ ὑγρὰ ποιεῖν κληθέντες...οἱ δὲ τὴν ἱππάδα τελοῦντες ἐκ μὲν τοῦ δύνασθαι τρέφειν ἵππους κεκλῆσθαι δοκοῦσιν, ἐποίουν δὲ μέτρα τριακόσια (cf. Schol. in Plat. *Rep.* 415). Bekk. *Anecd.* 298, 20 πεντακοσιομέδιμνοι: οἱ ἐκ τῆς οἰκείας γῆς ποιοῦντες πεντακόσια μέτρα συνάμφω ξηρὰ καὶ ὑγρά. Id. 267, 13 ἱππάς:...οἱ ποιοῦντες τριακόσια μέτρα.
18 Schol. Arist. *Eq.* 627...ἱππεῖς δὲ αὐτοὺς ὠνόμαζον διὰ τὸ δύνασθαι...ἵππον ἕκαστον αὐτῶν τρέφειν. Etym. cod. Vossianus, p. 1170, Gaisford, ζευγίσιον :...δευτέρους δὲ τοὺς ἱπποτροφεῖν δυναμένους καὶ τοὺς τοὺς ἵππους δὲ (leg. καὶ τοὺς ἱππάδα) τελοῦντας ἐκάλουν.

---

payment, but 'the being included in a class with a certain aggregate of duties and liabilities,'—equivalent to *censeri*, 'to rank as'; Boeckh, p. 36, Grote, p. 321 n.

ἐκκλησίας—μόνον] *Pol.* 1281 *b* 30, λείπεται δὴ τοῦ βουλεύεσθαι καὶ κρίνειν μετέχειν αὐτούς κτλ.

§ 4. **ποιῇ**] [Dem.] *Phaenipp.* 42 § 20, p. 1045, πλουτεῖς εἰκότως ἐπειδὰν ποιῇς σίτου μὲν μεδίμνους πλέον ἢ χιλίους, οἴνου δὲ μετρητὰς ὑπὲρ ὀκτακοσίους. **πεντακόσια κτλ.** Hitherto, it has been sometimes supposed that one who obtained from his land a net return of 500 measures of dry produce, such as corn or barley, together with 500 measures of liquid produce, such as oil or wine, ranked in the first class (Bruno Keil in *Berl. Phil. Woch.* 1891, p. 521 n.). It has also been held that a net return of either 500 dry measures or 500 liquid measures constituted a claim to that class (Busolt, i 527). It is now clear that the 500 measures could be made up of dry and liquid produce taken together, and this is also the purport of some of the evidence previously known to us, *e.g.* the article in Bekker's *Anecd.* 298, 20, which, it now appears, was taken from the present passage. By μέτρα is meant either a μέδιμνος (=six ἑκτεῖς=six *modii* =about 12 imperial gallons, or a bushel and a half) of dry measure, or a μετρητής in liquid measure. The latter is the standard ἀμφορεὺς of 12 χόες=69·33 pints, or slightly over 8⅔ gallons, and therefore three-fourths of the standard dry measure, the μέδιμνος.

ἱππάδα] (τελεῖν). Isaeus 7 § 39, ἀπεγράψατο μὲν τίμημα μικρόν, ὡς ἱππάδα δὲ τελῶν ἄρχειν ἠξίου τὰς ἀρχάς. In the Lex. of Photius, the first article on ἱππὰς (followed by Suidas) makes the curious mistake of distinguishing the ἱππεῖς and the ἱππάς and treating the latter as a fifth class; the second article, with the help of Harpocration's quotation from ll. 9, 10 of this chapter, corrects this mistake, adding τῶν οὖν ἱππέων οἱ (*sic*) ἱππάδες.

ὡς δ' ἔνιοί φασι] There is no real discrepancy between the two views, all whose land produced a net return of 300 μέδιμνοι being deemed to have enough property to enable them to keep a horse for military purposes and to serve in the cavalry. Suidas, *s. v.* ἱππεῖς, following Schol. on Aristoph. *Eq.* 627, says: ἱππεῖς δὲ αὐτοὺς ὠνόμαζον διὰ τὸ δύνασθαι, εἴποτε χρεία γένοιτο, ἵππον ἕκαστον αὐτῶν τρέφειν. In addition to the war-horse (ἵππος πολεμιστήριος), a horse would be required for the servant of the ἱππεύς, and those who belonged to this class would also need a team for agricultural purposes (Boeckh, p. 639, Lamb, p. 579, Fränkel).

ὡς ἂν—κείμενον] 'as though' (or implying that') 'the name was derived from the fact just mentioned.' Ar. *Analytica Posteriora*, Γ 3, 72 *b* 9, ὡς οὐκ ἂν ἐπισταμένους. περὶ ἀκουστῶν 803 *b* 5, ἕκαστον τῶν μορίων προσπῖπτον, ὡς ἂν ἀπὸ πληγῆς ἑτέρας ὄν, and 804 *b* 25, φωνοῦσιν, ὡς ἂν τὸ πνεῦμα βιαζόμενον. **κείμενον**, used, as often, for the perf. pass. part. of τίθημι. Isaeus 3 § 32, εἴ τις ᾔδει τοῦθ' ὑπὸ τοῦ πατρὸς κείμενον, *nomen a patre impositum* (Cobet, *V. L.* 311, *N. L.* 703). Similarly in the next few lines, ἀναθήματα...ἀνάκειται...ἀνέθηκε.

ἀναθήματα] Polemon, a contemporary

ἀρχαίων· ἀνάκειται γὰρ ἐν ἀκροπόλει εἰκὼν [[*Διφίλου*]], *ἐ*[*φ' ᾗ ἐπ*]*ι-γέγραπται τάδε·*

Διφίλου Ἀνθεμίων τήνδ' ἀνέθηκε θεοῖς,
θητικοῦ ἀντὶ τέλους ἱππάδ' ἀμειψάμενος.

καὶ παρέστηκεν ἵππος [[*ἐκμαρτυρῶν*]], *ὡς τὴν ἱππάδα τοῦτο σημα*[*ί*]-

21 Διφίλου secl. Thompson, K-W, B. **23** καὶ τὸ ἐπίγραμμα Διφίλου Ἀνθεμίων ἵππον τόνδ' ἀνέθηκε θεοῖς Pollucis codices, ubi viderunt critici aut Διφίλου et ἐπίγραμμα coniungenda esse aut cum Bekkero legendum Διφίλου Ἀνθεμίων τόνδ' ἵππον θεοῖς ἀνέθηκεν. Pollucis vero e codicibus unus habet Διφίλου Ἀνθεμίων τόνδ' ἀνέθηκε θεοῖς. Nostro autem in loco versum hexametrum nonnulli restituerunt, velut <ἵππον> Διφίλου Ἀνθεμίων ἀνέθηκε θεοῖσι Tyrrell; Διφίλου Ἀνθεμίων τήνδ' <εἰκόν'> ἔθηκε θεοῖσι numerosius J B Mayor, ἀνέθηκε ex ονεθηκε ortum fuisse arbitratus (*Class. Rev.* v 177 *a*); Διφίλου Ἀνθεμίων τήνδ' <εἰκόνα> θεοῖς ἀνέθηκε Thompson (ib. 225 *b*). Sed Pollucis codices, non minus quam papyrus nostra, testantur versum priorem pentametrum fuisse. **25** ЄΚΜΑΡΤΥΡῶΝ (K): †ἐκμαρτυρῶν (K-W): ἐπιμαρτυρῶν Tyrrell et olim Blass (H-L); etiam ἐκ τῶν ἀριστερῶν Blass, sed exspectares ἐξ ἀριστερᾶς. Equidem ΤЄΚΜΗΡΙΟΝ ad explicandum sensum quondam adscriptum postea in ЄΚΜΑΡΤΥΡΩΝ mutatum fuisse crediderim; ΤΥ in litura. εἰς μαρτύριον ed. Blass.

TESTIMONIA. **21—24** Pollux viii 131 Ἀνθεμίων δὲ ὁ Διφίλου καλλωπίζεται δι' ἐπιγράμματος ὅτι ἀπὸ τοῦ θητικοῦ τέλους εἰς τὴν ἱππάδα μετέστη, καὶ εἰκών ἐστιν ἐν ἀκροπόλει ἵππος ἀνδρὶ παρεστηκώς· καὶ τὸ ἐπίγραμμα | Διφίλου Ἀνθεμίων τόνδ' ἀνέθηκε θεοῖς | θητικοῦ ἀντὶ τέλους ἱππάδ' ἀμειψάμενος (Falckenburgii codex).

---

of Ptolemy Epiphanes (B.C. 204—181) devoted four books of his *περιήγησις* to the *ἀναθήματα* on the Acropolis (Strabo, ix 396). If the present passage was inserted at a later date than the time of Aristotle, it may possibly have been borrowed from the work of Polemon; but the only reason for doubting whether it is by the same hand as the rest of the treatise is the exceptionally frequent occurrence of *hiatus*, *ἀκροπόλει εἰκὼν Διφίλου ἐφ' ᾗ ἐπιγέγραπται.* The passage was known to Pollux (viii 131), but whether his quotations from this treatise are taken at first hand or not, is uncertain.

Διφίλου] The statue was dedicated by Anthemion son of Diphilus. Diphilus himself had apparently belonged to the *θητικὸν τέλος* and would therefore have had no claim to be represented with a horse beside him. Mr A. S. Murray is therefore probably right in regarding the statue as that of the son, Anthemion (*Class. Rev.* v 108). Anthemion probably owed his promotion from the lowest to the second class either to a legacy or some other stroke of fortune which suddenly made him a wealthy man (Boeckh, p. 641 Lamb).

It is very improbable that an inscription of such a date consisted of two pentameter lines. 'Vix crediderim inscriptionem vetustam ex duobus pentametris constitisse. Exempla quidem id genus titulorum quae Kaibel in ind. [*Epigr. Gr.*] p. 702 affert, sunt recentissima' (Preger, *Inscr. Gr. Metricae*, 1891, no. 74). The lines happen to give a consecutive sense but are possibly selected from two successive couplets of the original set of verses, the intermediate hexameter being omitted. '*ἄνδρα παρεστηκότα* in versibus omitti non mirum... In anaglyphis saepius equi ad ordinem equestrem significandum additi sunt, cf. Goettling, *Opusc. Acad.* 243' (Preger, *l. c.*).

ἐκμαρτυρῶν] *ἐκμαρτυρῶ* = *palam testificor* in Aesch. *Eum.* 461, *λουτρῶν ἐξεμαρτύρει φόνον*, and Aeschin. p. 15, 19, *Or.* I § 107, *ὧν οὐδένα ἐγὼ παρακαλῶ δεῦρο τὴν ἑαυτοῦ συμφοράν, ἣν εἵλετο σιγᾶν, εἰς πολλοὺς ἐκμαρτυρῆσαι.* This sense is just tolerable in the present passage, though the word is perhaps needlessly strong for the context. It would be clearly out of place to give it the technical sense corresponding to that of *ἐκμαρτυρία* (*Class. Rev.* v 177 *a*), *i.e.* a deposition made by a witness who, by reason of illness or absence abroad, was unable to attend in court. The horse in this case may metaphorically indeed be described as giving evidence; but (so far from being either absent abroad or on the point of leaving the country) it is standing in the very νουσ[α]ν. οὐ μὴν ἀλλ' εὐλογώτερον τοῖς μέτροις διῃρῆσθαι καθάπερ τοὺς πεντακοσιομεδίμνους)· ζευγίσιον δὲ τελεῖν τοὺς διακόσια τὰ συνάμφω ποιοῦντας· τοὺς δ' ἄλλους θητικόν, οὐδεμιᾶς μετέχοντας ἀρχῆς. διὸ καὶ νῦν ἐπειδὰν ἔρηται τὸν μέλλοντα κληροῦσθαί τιν' ἀρχήν, ποῖον τέλος τελεῖ, οὐδ' ἂν εἷς εἴποι θητικόν.

8. τὰς δ' ἀρχὰς ἐποίησε κληρωτὰς ἐκ προκρίτων, [ο]ὓς

26 ΜΕΤΡΙΟΙC. **27** *δ' ἔδει τελεῖν* Kontos (H-L).
VIII 1 Τ'ΔΑΡΧΗC (=*τῆς δ' ἀρχῆς*) frustra tueri conatus est Bury: emendavit K.

TESTIMONIA. **27—29** Pollux viii 130 *οἱ δὲ τὸ ζευγήσιον* (codd., Hesych., Phot., Schol. Plat., Bekk. *An.* 260 ult.: *ζευγίσιον* Etym. Magn.) *τελοῦντες ἀπὸ διακοσίων μέτρων κατελέγοντο...οἱ δὲ τὸ θητικὸν οὐδεμίαν ἀρχὴν ἦρχον.* *Harp. *θῆτες:...οὗτοι δὲ οὐδεμιᾶς μετεῖχον ἀρχῆς, ὡς καὶ 'Αρ. δηλοῖ ἐν 'Αθ. πολ.* Etym. Mag. p. 452, 15 *θητικόν: οὗτοι δὲ οὐδὲ μιᾶς μετεῖχον ἀρχῆς.*

---

centre of Athens, on the platform of the Acropolis. The technical sense is therefore out of place, and the word is probably corrupt.

ὡς—σημαίνουσαν] For the participle used as an accusative absolute after ὡς, cf. c. 29 § 3, *ὡς οὐ δημοτικὴν ἀλλὰ παραπλησίαν οὖσαν τὴν...πολιτείαν*, and *Pol.* v (viii) 4, 1338 *b* 13, (*οἱ Λάκωνες*) *θηριώδεις ἀπεργάζονται τοῖς πόνοις, ὡς τοῦτο πρὸς ἀνδρίαν μάλιστα συμφέρον.* Kühner, *G. G.* § 488 *d*; Maetzner *ad Lycurgum*, § 90, p. 231; Rehdantz, *Ind. Dem. s. v.* Participium. Trans. 'implying that this was the meaning of the status of Knight.'

ζευγίσιον] This form is supported by the Etymologicum Magnum (and Gudianum) alone. The *codex Sorbonicus* of the latter, p. 1170 D Gaisford, has *ζευγίσιον: τῷ χαρακτῆρι τῶν διὰ τοῦ ισιον, οἷον, 'Αφροδίσιον, 'Ατρεμίσιον* (*sic*), *Προβαλίσιον. οὕτως οὖν καὶ ζευγίσιον.* 'Per ῑ scribendum docet Choeroboscus in Crameri Anecd. ii p. 215, 10.' Fränkel (n. 805 to Boeckh) urges that *ζευγήσιον* is the right form, and is better accredited than *ζευγίσιον*.

διακόσια] The property qualification of the *ζευγῖται* has hitherto been a matter of dispute. Boeckh, p. 641 Lamb, fixes it at 150 medimni. This he infers from a law quoted in [Dem.] *Macart.* 43 § 54, p. 1067, according to which a *πεντακοσιομέδιμνος* was to pay the *ἐπίκληρος* a dowry of 500 drachmae, a *ἱππεὺς* 300, and a *ζευγίτης* 150. From the correspondence of the first and second of these sums to the annual income of members of the first and second class, he infers that the dowry required of a *ζευγίτης* is identical in amount with his annual income. But he admits that all the positive evidence is in favour of 200 medimni. This view, which is adopted by Grote (ii 320 note), is supported by the authority of the text.

διὸ καὶ νῦν *κτλ.*] 'Hence it is that even now, when one who is about to draw lots for any office is asked to what rank he belongs, no one would say that he belonged to the rank of the Thetes.' The subject of *ἔρηται* is the officer superintending the drawing of lots for an appointment. The same vague use of the verb occurs in c. 55, *ἐπερωτῶσιν* and *φησίν*. As it was under the superintendence of the *Thesmothetae* that officials were appointed by lot (Schömann, *Antiquities*, p. 402 E. T.), the subject is probably *ὁ θεσμοθέτης*.

At first it was only the *πεντακοσιομέδιμνοι* who were eligible to the office of archon; next the *ἱππεῖς*; the *ζευγῖται* became eligible in 457 B.C. (see c. 26). The present passage, as observed by Mr Kenyon, is interesting as shewing that the property qualification can never have been entirely abolished by law.

VIII § 1. **κληρωτὰς ἐκ προκρίτων**] 'appointed by lot, out of candidates selected by each of the (four) tribes.' Each of the 4 tribes nominated 10, and, out of these 40, the 9 archons were appointed by lot. The archons had formerly been elected by the Areopagus; and, whatever may have been the rule under Dracon, it was Solon who, with a view to extending the political power of the people, devised the combination of selection and sortition described in the text. It has hitherto been sometimes supposed that appointment by lot was not used in Athens before the time of Cleisthenes. This is the view of Grote, C. F. Hermann, Busolt, Gilbert, Duncker and others. Grote in fact cannot believe [ἑκάσ]τῃ προκρίνειε τῶν φυλῶν. προὔκρινεν δ' εἰς τοὺς ἐννέα ἄρχοντας ἑκάστη δέκα, καὶ τού[τοις] ἐ[πεκ]λήρουν· ὅθεν ἔτι δια-

2 προκρίνειε Gertz (K-W, K³, B); ΠΡΟΚΡΙΝΕΙ (K¹); προὔκρινε olim B (H-L). **3** τούτοις ἐπεκλήρουν K³ coll. 59 § 5, 'litterae unius tantum spatio inter ΤΟΥ et Є relicto, ubi ΤΟΥϹ (ut videtur) in ΤΟΥΤΟΙϹ correctum.' τούτους ἐκλήρουν K¹ (H-L); aut τούτων aut <ἐκ> τούτων ἐκλήρουν (B) K-W; κἀκ τούτων ἐκλήρουν Gomperz.

---

it was introduced as early as the time of Cleisthenes (c. 31, iii 123 n.). Curtius (i 478 E. T.) assigns it to this time. Schömann, in his criticisms on Grote (*Const. Hist. of Athens*, p. 73 E. T.), shews that an earlier date was not improbable; while Fustel de Coulanges (*La Cité Antique*, p. 212—4, ed. 1883) claims it as an institution of religious origin and therefore of great antiquity. The evidence of this treatise is in favour of its having been introduced at an early date.

The text enables us to understand the statement in Isocrates that, 'in the times of Solon and Cleisthenes,' they did not apply the lot to filling up offices out of the whole body of citizens, but selected those who were the best and the most suitable candidates for each office: *Areop.* § 22, οὐκ ἐξ ἁπάντων τὰς ἀρχὰς κληροῦντες ἀλλὰ τοὺς βελτίστους καὶ τοὺς ἱκανωτάτους ἐφ' ἕκαστον τῶν ἔργων προκρίνοντες. Elsewhere, *Panath.* 145, he describes the constitution that the Athenians maintained 'for 1000 years' down to the age of Solon and the rule of Peisistratus, and says of the Athenians of old time that they ἐν ὀλίγαις ἡμέραις ἑώρων τοὺς νόμους ἀναγεγραμμένους (this can only refer to the legislation of Dracon). He then adds: περὶ τοὺς αὐτοὺς χρόνους καθίστασαν ἐπὶ τὰς ἀρχὰς τοὺς προκριθέντας ὑπὸ τῶν φυλετῶν καὶ δημοτῶν. [Dem.] *Neaer.* 59 § 75 says of the ἄρχων βασιλεὺς in the times after the συνοικισμὸς of Theseus: τὸν μὲν βασιλέα...ὁ δῆμος ᾑρεῖτο ἐκ προκρίτων κατ' ἀνδραγαθίαν χειροτονῶν, where however we have mention of election by show of hands instead of appointment by lot. The use of the lot in the time of Solon is implied by Dem. *Lept.* § 90 (after mentioning Solon), τοὺς θεσμοθέτας τοὺς ἐπὶ τοὺς νόμους κληρουμένους, but too great stress must not be laid on this phrase, as the orators sometimes ascribe to Solon institutions which really belonged to a later date.

The natural interpretation of the present passage is that Solon introduced a new principle by combining selection with sortition. In this respect it is not perhaps inconsistent with the statement in *Pol.* ii 12, 1273 *b* 41, ἔοικε δὲ Σόλων ἐκεῖνα μὲν ὑπάρχοντα πρότερον οὐ καταλῦσαι, τήν τε βουλὴν (*i.e.* the Areopagus) καὶ τὴν τῶν ἀρχῶν αἵρεσιν, τὸν δὲ δῆμον καταστῆσαι, τὰ δικαστήρια ποιήσας ἐκ πάντων. Aristotle had just before remarked that some had singled out, as an aristocratic element in Solon's constitution, τὸ τὰς ἀρχὰς αἱρετὰς (εἶναι). He adds that Solon did not abolish this principle, for αἵρεσις is not the 'manner of electing the magistrates,' but simply their election. They were still elected, but the details of the method of election were partly new; the new element being apparently the selection by the tribes. Aristotle approves of this method in *Pol.* viii (v) 5, 1305 *a* 28, μεταβάλλουσι δὲ καὶ ἐκ τῆς πατρίας δημοκρατίας εἰς τὴν νεωτάτην· ὅπου γὰρ αἱρεταὶ μὲν αἱ ἀρχαί, μὴ ἀπὸ τιμημάτων δέ, αἱρεῖται δὲ ὁ δῆμος, δημαγωγοῦντες οἱ σπουδαρχιῶντες εἰς τοῦτο καθιστᾶσιν ὡς κύριον εἶναι τὸν δῆμον καὶ τῶν νόμων. ἄκος δὲ τοῦ ἢ μὴ γίνεσθαι ἢ τοῦ γίνεσθαι ἧττον τὸ τὰς φυλὰς φέρειν τοὺς ἄρχοντας, ἀλλὰ μὴ πάντα τὸν δῆμον.

In *Pol.* vi (iv) 14, 1298 *b* 9, while discussing oligarchies, he mentions some non-oligarchical elements: ἐὰν δὲ ἐνίων μὲν αἱρετοὶ ἐνίων δὲ κληρωτοί, καὶ κληρωτοὶ ἢ ἁπλῶς ἢ ἐκ προκρίτων, ἢ κοινῇ αἱρετοὶ καὶ κληρωτοί, τὰ μὲν πολιτείας ἀριστοκρατικῆς ἐστι τούτων, τὰ δὲ πολιτείας αὐτῆς. Cf. 1266 *a* 8; Plat. *Leg.* 945 B, 753; *Rep.* 537 D.

ὅθεν ἔτι διαμένει] This passage and its context are among the many in which the author argues from survivals, or infers a fact from a reason.

'The signals of this method,' as remarked by Mr Macan (*J. H. S.* xii 38), 'are the innocent γάρ (c. 2 l. 5, c. 3 l. 6 *et alibi*), the more elaborate ὅθεν or ὅθεν καί (c. 3 l. 8, c. 8 l. 3), the suspicious διό, διὸ καί (c. 3 l. 17, c. 8 l. 16) and above all the term σημεῖον. Wherever these signals occur the critical reader will beware of danger ahead. It may not be necessary in every case to reject the supposed evidence and inference, but it will always be expedient carefully to examine before admitting them.' The writer is here arguing that the method of appointing archons

μένει ταῖς φυλαῖς τὸ δέκα κληροῦν ἑκάστην, εἶτ' ἐκ τούτων κυαμεύε[ιν]. σημεῖον δ' ὅτι κληρωτὰς ἐποίησεν ἐκ τῶν τιμημάτων ὁ περὶ τῶν ταμιῶν νόμος, ᾧ χρώμενοι [διατελο]ῦσιν ἔτι καὶ νῦν·
2 κελεύει γὰρ κληροῦν τοὺς ταμίας ἐκ πεντακοσιομεδίμνω[ν. Σόλ]ων μὲν οὖν οὕτως ἐνομοθέτησεν περὶ τῶν ἐννέα ἀρχόντων. τὸ γὰρ ἀρχαῖον ἡ ἐν 'Αρ[είῳ πάγῳ βουλ]ὴ ἀνακαλεσαμένη καὶ κρίνασα καθ' αὑτὴν τὸν ἐπιτήδειον ἐφ' ἑκάστῃ τῶν ἀρχῶν ἐπ' [ἐνι]α[υτ]ὸν
3 [διατάξα]σα ἀπέστελλεν. φυλαὶ δ' ἦσαν τέτταρες καθάπερ πρότερον καὶ φυλοβασιλεῖς τέτταρες. ἐκ δὲ [τῆς] φυ[λῆς ἑκ]άστης

5 ΕΠΟΙΗCΑΝ (Κ): ἐποίησεν Bury, Hude, K-W, H-L, B. **8** περὶ τῶν ἐννέα ἀρχόντων secl. K-W^2. **10** ἑκάστην H-L. **11** διατάξασα K, H-L: καθιστᾶσα K-W. ἦσαν τέτταρες: ΗCΑΝΔ. **12** ΤΕCCΑΡΕC. ΕΚ: ἐπὶ H-L, sed spatium non sufficit.

TESTIMONIA. **11—14** *Photius *ναυκραρία:...ναυκραρία μὲν ὁποῖόν τι ἡ συμμορία καὶ ὁ δῆμος, ναύκραρος δὲ ὁποῖόν τι ὁ δήμαρχος, Σόλωνος οὕτως ὀνομάσαντος, ὡς καὶ 'Αρ. φησί...ἐκ δὲ τῆς 'Αριστοτέλους πολιτείας ὃν τρόπον διέταξε τὴν πόλιν ὁ Σόλων* "*φυλαί—ἑκάστην*" (cf. Pollux viii 108; Rose, Frag. 349^2, 387^3). Hesych. *ναύκλαροι*.

---

adopted in his own day is a survival from that in the times of Solon. The intervention of the tribes is the point in common between the two methods: but, whereas in the earlier method they select, in the later they only appoint by lot. In the former, the lot is resorted to in the second stage only; in the latter, in both.

κυαμεύειν] is synonymous with *κληροῦν*, the *κύαμος*, or bean, being employed in the process of appointment by lot. The procedure was as follows: Two jars were set up; in one of these was placed a number of white and coloured beans, in the other the small tablets with the names of the candidates. Then a tablet and a bean were drawn simultaneously and the candidate whose name came out along with the white bean was nominated (Schömann, *Antiquities*, p. 402 E. T.).

κυαμεύειν occurs in the *ὅρκος ἡλιαστῶν* in Dem. 24 § 150, *ὅσαι (ἀρχαὶ) μετὰ τῶν ἐννέα ἀρχόντων κυαμεύονται*, cf. Xen. *Mem.* i 2 § 9 (Socrates) *λέγων ὡς μῶρον εἴη τοὺς μὲν τῆς πόλεως ἄρχοντας ἀπὸ κυάμου καθιστάναι, κυβερνήτῃ δὲ μηδένα ἐθέλειν χρῆσθαι κυαμευτῷ*. c. 22 § 5.

σημεῖον δ' ὅτι κτλ.] The law requiring the *ταμίαι* to be elected from among the *πεντακοσιομέδιμνοι* is quoted to prove that Solon regulated the allotment of office according to the property classes. The law existed in the writer's time but was practically unenforced, as appears from c. 47. *Pol.* 1282 *a* 29, *τῆς μὲν ἐκκλησίας μετέχουσι καὶ βουλεύουσι καὶ δικάζουσιν ἀπὸ μικρῶν τιμημάτων καὶ τῆς τυχούσης ἡλικίας, ταμιεύουσι δὲ καὶ στρατηγοῦσι καὶ τὰς μεγίστας ἀρχὰς ἄρχουσιν ἀπὸ μειζόνων*.

§ 2. **ἡ ἐν 'Αρείῳ πάγῳ βουλή**] This passage gives us definite authority for the manner in which the public officials were elected in earlier times at Athens. Heretofore it could only be conjectured that they were elected by the Areopagus. *τὸ ἀρχαῖον* is vague, and may either mean up to the time of Solon, or up to that of Dracon. In c. 4 we have been told that, under Dracon, the officials were elected by *οἱ ὅπλα παρεχόμενοι*, but the Draconian constitution is much disputed.

ἀνακαλεσαμένη] 'having summoned,' without any necessary allusion to the fact that the *βουλή* of the Areopagus was *ἡ ἄνω βουλή*. Cf. Aeschines, *F. L.* 17, *ἔπεισε τὴν βουλὴν* (the 500) *ἀνακαλέσασθαι τὸν 'Αριστόδημον*.

§ 3. **φυλαί**] The successive names of the four tribes in the early history of Athens are quoted by Pollux viii 109. In the time of Erechtheus they took their names (*Γελέοντες, Ὅπλητες, Αἰγικόρεις, 'Αργάδεις*) from the sons of Ion. Cf. Hdt. v 66 (of Cleisthenes) *τῶν Ἴωνος παίδων Γελέοντος καὶ Αἰγικόρεος καὶ 'Αργάδεω καὶ Ὅπλητος ἀπαλλάξας τὰς ἐπωνυμίας*. Eur. *Ion* 1579, *Γελέων* (Canter: *Τελέων* vulg.) *μὲν ἔσται πρῶτος· εἶτα δεύτερον Ὅπλητες 'Αργαδῆς τ', ἐμῆς δ' ἀπ' αἰγίδος ἓν φῦλον ἕξουσ' Αἰγικορῆς*. (Schömann, *On Grote*, § 2, and *Antiquities*, p. 317 f. E. T.; Philippi, *Att. Bürgerrecht*, pp. 233—296.)

φυλοβασιλεῖς] These officials are iden-

ἦσαν νενεμημέναι τριττύες μὲν τρεῖς, ναυκραρίαι δὲ δώδεκα καθ' ἑκάστην. [ἐπὶ δὲ τῶν] ναυκραριῶν ἀρχὴ καθεστηκυῖα ναύκραροι, τεταγμένη πρός τε τὰς ε[ἰσ]φορὰς καὶ τὰς δαπ[άνας] τὰς γιγνο-

13 ΝΑΥΚΡΑΙ|ΡΑΙ. **14** *ἐπὶ δὲ τῶν* Blass; *ἦν δὲ τῶν* K; *ἦν δ' ἐπὶ τῶν* K-W, H-L, sed spatium vix sufficit. **15** ΓΙΝΟΜΕΝΑC (K-W).

---

tical with those called *βασιλεῖς* (1) in the 13th Axon of Solon, quoted by Plutarch, *Sol.* 19, *ἐπιτίμους εἶναι πλὴν ὅσοι ἐξ 'Αρείου πάγου ἢ ὅσοι ἐκ τῶν 'Εφετῶν ἢ ἐκ Πρυτανείου καταδικασθέντες ὑπὸ τῶν βασιλέων ἐπὶ φόνῳ ἢ σφαγαῖσιν ἢ ἐπὶ τυραννίδι ἔφευγον*, and also (2) in the decree of Patrocleides, Andocides, *de Myst.* § 78 (founded on the language of the law just quoted), *ἢ ἐξ 'Αρείου πάγου ἢ τῶν 'Εφετῶν ἢ ἐκ Πρυτανείου ἢ Δελφινίου ἐδικάσθη ἢ ὑπὸ τῶν βασιλέων, ἢ ἐπὶ φόνῳ τίς ἐστι φυγή, ἢ θάνατος κατεγνώσθη, ἢ σφαγεῦσιν ἢ τυράννοις*. In the context of the first passage they are called *πρυτάνεις*; in that of the second, they are distinguished from the Archon-Basileus. The identity of the *βασιλεῖς* of Solon with the *φυλοβασιλεῖς* of Pollux (viii 111, 120) is supported by the connexion of both with the *Πρυτανεῖον*. The *βασιλεῖς* apparently dealt with cases of persons who aimed at a *τυραννίς*. They also presided over the Ephetae in the court of homicide at the Prytaneum (cf. 57 end). They probably represented 'the priestly functions of the ancient chieftains of the several separate tribes which were ultimately fused into a single community' (Prof. Ridgeway in Smith, *Dict. Ant. s. v.*). The fact that they were four in number was already known from the quotation of the present passage in Photius, *s. v. ναυκραρία*. Cf. Pollux viii 111, as emended by Wecklein, *οἱ δὲ φ. ἐξ εὐπατριδῶν τέσσαρες* ($\bar{\delta}$ for *δὲ*) *ὄντες κτλ.* In the *Bulletin de Correspondance Hellénique*, iii 69, we have an inscr. found on the Acropolis respecting a fund called *τὰ φυλοβασιλικά*, part of which was spent on celebrating a religious festival.

τριττύες ... ναυκραρίαι] The plupf. shews that these divisions had existed before the time of Solon. Photius, *s. v. ναυκραρία*, carelessly quotes Aristotle as his authority for ascribing to *Solon* the origin of the term *ναύκραρος* (*Σόλωνος οὕτως ὀνομάσαντος, ὡς καὶ 'Αριστοτέλης φησί*). That he had the present passage in view is indicated by his quoting it *verbatim* at the end of his article.

The existence of the *ναυκραρίαι* before the time of Solon is proved by Hdt. v 71, where their *πρυτάνεις* are described as holding an important position in the government of Athens at the time of the conspiracy of Cylon: *οἱ πρυτάνιες τῶν ναυκράρων* (*al.* *ναυκραριέων*) *οἵπερ ἔνεμον τότε τὰς 'Αθήνας*; but Thuc. i 126 § 5 corrects this account and substitutes for them the nine Archons, adding *τότε δὲ τὰ πολλὰ τῶν πολιτικῶν οἱ ἐννέα ἄρχοντες ἔπρασσον*. Schömann (*Ant.* p. 326 E. T.) endeavours to reconcile both narratives by assigning to the nine Archons a place on the board of Prytaneis.

The *Naucrari* were the presidents of the *Naucrariae*, and the latter were the administrative districts into which the country was then divided. There were 12 in each tribe or 48 in all. Every four of these districts formed a group called a *τριττύς*, or third part of a tribe. In Photius p. 196 Porson, and in Bekk. *Anec.* p. 275, mention is made of a *ναυκραρία* called *Κωλιάς* which is the name of a strip of coast and cliffs near Phalerum. The term *ναυκραρία* has reference to the duty imposed on these districts of equipping a ship of war, in addition to that of providing two horsemen (Pollux viii 108). Grote, c. 10, ii 264 n., thinks 'the statement that each Naukrary was obliged to furnish one ship can hardly be true of the time before Solon.' The actual expense probably fell on the wealthier inhabitants of the district, and it would naturally be from their number that the *ναύκραροι*, or presidents of the *ναυκραρίαι*, were chosen. There was one president for each *ναυκραρία*, or 12 for each tribe. Hesychius *s. v. ναύκλαροι* (*sic*)·...*τινὲς δὲ ἀφ' ἑκάστης φυλῆς δώδεκα, οἵτινες ἀφ' ἑκάστης χώρας τὰς εἰσφορὰς ἐξέλεγον. ὕστερον δὲ δήμαρχοι ἐκλήθησαν* (Schömann, *Antiquities*, p. 326 E. T.; Duncker, *H. G.* ii 144 E. T.; Gilbert, *Gr. St.* i 135; *Jahrb. f. cl. Phil.* 1875, pp. 9 and 452). *ναύκρᾱρος* is formed from *ναῦς* and the root *κᾰρ* (by metathesis *κρᾱ*) which appears in *κραίνω* 'to complete or accomplish' (G. Meyer in Curtius, *Studien*, vii 175).

τὰς εἰσφοράς] Pollux viii 108, *τὰς δ' εἰσφορὰς τὰς κατὰ δήμους διεχειροτόνουν οὗτοι* (*sc.* *οἱ ναύκραροι*) *καὶ τὰ ἐξ αὐτῶν ἀναλώματα.*

*μένας· διὸ καὶ ἐν τοῖς νόμοις τοῖ[ς Σ]όλωνος, οἷς οὐκέτι χρῶνται,
πολλαχ[οῦ] γέγραπται τοὺς ναυκράρους εἰσπράττειν καὶ ἀνα-*
4 *λίσκειν ἐκ τοῦ ναυκραρικοῦ ἀργυρ[ίου. βουλ]ὴν δ' ἐποίησε
τετρακοσίο[υς], ἑκατὸν ἐξ ἑκάστης φυλῆς, τὴν δὲ τῶν Ἀρεοπαγιτῶν
ἔταξεν ἐ[πὶ τὸ] νομοφυλακεῖν, ὥσπερ ὑπῆρχεν καὶ πρότερον ἐπί-
σκοπος ο[ὖ]σα τῆς πολιτείας· καὶ τά τε ἄλλα τὰ πλεῖστα καὶ τὰ
μέγιστα τῶν πολιτ<ικ>ῶν διετήρει καὶ τοὺς ἁμαρτάνοντας ηὔθυνεν
κυρί[α] οὖσα [καὶ ζη]μι[οῦν] καὶ κολάζειν, καὶ τὰς ἐκτίσεις ἀνέ-
φερεν εἰς πόλιν οὐκ ἐπιγράφουσα τὴν πρόφασι[ν τοῦ *πράττ]εσθαι,
καὶ τοὺς ἐπὶ καταλύσει τοῦ δήμου συν[ι]σταμένους ἔκρινεν, Σόλω-*
5 *νος θέν[τος] νόμον εἰσα[γγ]ελ[ίας] περὶ αὐτῶν. ὁρῶν δὲ τὴν μὲν*

17 *πολλαχοῦ* Wessely (K³, B, litteris incertis ΑΧ); *πολλαχόθι* Paton (H-L), sed spatium vix sufficit; *πολλ[άκι]ς* K-W. **20** *ἐπὶ τὸ* Paton, Gennadios (K-W, H-L, K³, B): *ἔτι* K¹. **21** *καὶ εἰς τὰ ἄλλα* H-L. **22** Τ(ΩΝ) ΠΟΛΙΤΩ(Ν): *τῶν πολιτικῶν* Richards, Hude (K-W, H-L, K³, B), cf. 3, 35 *τὰ πλεῖστα καὶ μέγιστα τῶν ἐν τῇ πόλει*; *τῶν <περὶ τῶν> πολιτῶν* satis probabiliter conicit K. **23** *καὶ ζημιοῦν* Blass (H-L, K³); *τοῦ ζημιοῦν* K¹ (K-W). *ἐκτείσεις* B. **24** *τοῦ πράττεσθαι* (exigendi) scripsi, coll. Plat. *Leg.* 762 B *τὴν διπλασίαν (ζημίαν) πραττέσθω τὸν ὑποφεύγοντα*: *τοῦ κολάζεσθαι* K¹; (hiatu admisso) *τοῦ εὐθύνεσθαι* Blass (H-L, K³); *τοῦ εἰσπράττεσθαι*? K-W; *τοῦ ἐκτίνεσθαι* Tyrrell. **26** *νόμον εἰσαγγελίας* Wessely et K³; *νόμον*......... K-W, B; *ὁ μὲν [οὖν ταῦτ' ἔταξε]* K¹ (H-L).

ἐν τοῖς νόμοις *κτλ.*] Phot. *Lex. ναυκραρία*: *καὶ ἐν τοῖς νόμοις δὲ "ἐάν τις ναυκραρίας ἀμφισβητῇ," καὶ "τοὺς ναυκράρους τοὺς κατὰ τὴν ναυκραρίαν."*

§ 4. **βουλὴν δ' ἐποίησε τετρακοσίους**] A new council of 400 is here contrasted with the previously existing council of the Areopagus. There is nothing in the phrase to shew that the writer has made any mention of a previous council under Dracon. Cf. Plut. *Sol.* 19, *συστησάμενος δὲ τὴν ἐν Ἀρείῳ πάγῳ βουλὴν...δευτέραν προσκατένειμε βουλὴν ἀπὸ φυλῆς ἑκάστης, τεττάρων οὐσῶν, ἑκατὸν ἄνδρας ἐπιλεξάμενος.*

Ἀρεοπαγιτῶν] Philippi, *Areop. u. Epheten*, pp. 199—246; Gilbert, i 136. Duncker, *Gesch. d. Alt.* (XII 12) vol. vi 187—194.

ἐπίσκοπος οὖσα *κτλ.*] Plut. *l.c.*, *τὴν δ' ἄνω βουλὴν ἐπίσκοπον πάντων καὶ φύλακα τῶν νόμων ἐκάθισεν.*

τὰ πλεῖστα καὶ τὰ μέγιστα *κτλ.*] c. 3 § 6, *διῴκει δὲ τὰ πλεῖστα καὶ τὰ μέγιστα τῶν ἐν τῇ πόλει, καὶ κολάζουσα καὶ ζημιοῦσα πάντας τοὺς ἀκοσμοῦντας κυρίως.*

ἀνέφερεν] Dem. 41 § 8, *τὴν τιμὴν οὔτ' ἐκείνῳ διέλυσεν οὔτε νῦν εἰς τὸ κοινὸν ἀνενήνοχεν.*

εἰς πόλιν] = *εἰς ἀκρόπολιν* (cf. c. 60 § 3). Thuc. ii 15, *καλεῖται δὲ ἡ ἀκρόπολις μέχρι τοῦδε ἔτι ὑπ' Ἀθηναίων πόλις.* Aristoph. *Nub.* 69, *Eq.* 267, *Lys.* 245. 'In inscriptions *ἐν ἀκροπόλει* is first found in B.C. 387—6, according to *Bull. d. Corr. Hell.* 1888 p. 149. In *fourth* century *prose* the use of *πόλις* is preserved in certain familiar and unambiguous combinations: [Xen.] *De Red.* v 12, *χρήματα εἰς τὴν πόλιν ἀνενεχθέντα.* Schol. Aristoph. *Lys.* 273, *ἔστησαν ἐν πόλει παρὰ τὸν ἀρχαῖον νεών* (possibly quoted from one of the writers of *Ἀτθίδες* or from Craterus). For other references see Maetzner on Antiph. 6 § 39 *ἐν τῇ πόλει.* On the other hand Andoc. 3 § 7, and Aeschin. 2 § 175, have *ἀναφέρειν εἰς τὴν ἀκρόπολιν*' (Wyse).

ἐπὶ καταλύσει τοῦ δήμου—νόμον εἰσαγγελίας] *εἰσαγγέλλειν* has already been used in a general sense in 4 § 4. We now find a definite *νόμος εἰσαγγελίας* ascribed for the first time to Solon. The special case here mentioned corresponds to the first of the three classes of crimes which, according to Hyperides, were included in the *νόμος εἰσαγγελτικός*, *pro Eux.* 22, *ἐάν τις τὸν δῆμον τὸν Ἀθηναίων καταλύῃ ἢ συνίῃ ἐπὶ καταλύσει τοῦ δήμου ἢ ἑταιρικὸν συναγάγῃ* (Isocr. *de Big.* 6; Dinarch. *c. Dem.* 94). Cf. Theophr. apud Lex. Rhet. Cantab. *s.v. εἰσαγγελία*: *ἐάν τις καταλύῃ τὸν δῆμον.* The text implies that the definition given by Theophrastus applies to a far earlier date than the time πόλιν πολλάκις στασιάζουσαν, τῶν δὲ πολιτῶν ἐνίους δ[ιὰ] τὴν ῥᾳθυμ[ία]ν [ἀγαπῶ]ντας τὸ αὐτόματον, νόμον ἔθηκε πρὸς αὐτοὺς ἴδιον, ὃς ἂν στασιαζούσης τῆς πόλ[εω]ς μ[ὴ θ]ῆται τὰ ὅπλα μηδὲ μεθ' ἑτέρων, ἄτιμον εἶναι καὶ τῆς πόλεως μὴ μετέχειν.

9. τὰ μὲν οὖν [περὶ τὰ]ς ἀρχὰς τ[οῦτ]ον εἶχε τὸν τρόπον. δοκεῖ δὲ τῆς Σόλωνος πολιτείας τρία ταῦτ' εἶναι τὰ δημοτικώτατα·

28 ἀγαπῶντας K-W et Kontos: ἀποκνοῦντας Rutherford; περιμένοντας (J E B Mayor, Marchant, Blass, Gennadios, H-L) quondam conieci, coll. Plut. *Sol.* 20 περιμένειν ἀκινδύνως τὰ τῶν κρατούντων, sed ωΝΤ potius quam ΟΥΝΤ in papyro apparet. περιορῶντας Bury coll. Thuc. iv 71 τὸ μέλλον περιιδεῖν (B). Fortasse περιορῶντας τὸ ἀποβαῖνον scribendum. **29** θῆται H-L (K^3, B); τιθῆται Richards, Blass, K-W, sed spatium vix sufficit.

IX 1 ειχε litteris evanidis (K, B): ἔταξε K-W, H-L. **2** τρια ταῦτ' papyrum secutus K; τρια τάδ' H-L, $K\text{-}W^2$. τὰ om. H-L.

Testimonia. **28—30.** *Gellius, ii 12: In legibus Solonis illis antiquissimis quae Athenis axibus ligneis incisae sunt quasque latas ab eo Athenienses ut sempiternae manerent poenis et religionibus sanxerunt, legem esse *Aristoteles* refert scriptam ad hanc sententiam: 'si ob discordiam dissensionemque seditio atque discessio populi in duas partes fiet et ob eam causam irritatis animis utrimque arma capientur pugnabiturque, tum qui in eo tempore in eoque casu civilis discordiae non alterutrae parti sese adiunxerit, sed solitarius separatusque a communi malo civitatis secesserit, is domo patria fortunisque omnibus careto, exul extorrisque esto' (Rose, Frag. 353^2, 391^3).

---

after Eucleides, to which it has been assigned by Fränkel, *Att. Geschworenenger.*, p. 77.

There is a vague reference to εἰσαγγελίαι in the time of Solon in Pollux viii 53, χίλιοι δὲ κατὰ μὲν Σόλωνα τὰς εἰσαγγελίας ἔκρινον, κατὰ δὲ τὸν Φαληρέα καὶ πρὸς πεντακόσιοι, cf. Philochorus, 155 Müller, εἰσήγγειλαν, ὡς μὲν Φιλόχορος, χιλίων καθεζομένων, ὡς δὲ Δημήτριος ὁ Φαληρεὺς χιλίων πεντακοσίων (cf. Duncker, *G. d. A.* vi 179 n). The special case mentioned in the text came before the Areopagus.

§ 5. **νόμον ἔθηκε κτλ.**] Plut. *Sol.* 20 *init.* τῶν δ' ἄλλων αὐτοῦ νόμων ἴδιος μὲν μάλιστα καὶ παράδοξος ὁ κελεύων ἄτιμον εἶναι τὸν ἐν στάσει μηδετέρας μερίδος γενόμενον. βούλεται δ', ὡς ἔοικε, μὴ ἀπαθῶς μηδ' ἀναισθήτως ἔχειν πρὸς τὸ κοινόν, ἐν ἀσφαλεῖ θέμενον τὰ οἰκεῖα καὶ τῷ μὴ συναλγεῖν μηδὲ συννοσεῖν τῇ πατρίδι καλλωπιζόμενον, ἀλλ' αὐτόθεν τοῖς τὰ βελτίω καὶ δικαιότερα πράττουσι προσθέμενον συγκινδυνεύειν καὶ βοηθεῖν μᾶλλον ἢ περιμένειν ἀκινδύνως τὰ τῶν κρατούντων. *Praec. Ger. Reip.* 32 § 1, ii 823 F, ἀπορήσει...καὶ θαυμάσει τί παθὼν ἐκεῖνος ὁ ἀνὴρ ἔγραψεν ἄτιμον εἶναι τὸν ἐν στάσει πόλεως μηδετέροις προσθέμενον, *De Sera Numinis Vindicta* 4, ii 550 B—C, παραλογώτατον δὲ τὸ τοῦ Σόλωνος, ἄτιμον εἶναι τὸν στάσει μηδετέρᾳ μερίδι προσθέμενον μηδὲ συστασιάσαντα. Cic. *ad Atticum* x 1, 2, ego vero Solonis... legem neglegam, qui capite sanxit, si quis in seditione non alterius utrius partis fuisset. (Cf. Grote, c. 11, ii 341.) Prof. Mayor (*Class. Rev.* v 120 *b*) also refers to Cantacuzen. iv 13, and Nicephorus Gregora ix 6 *fin.*

θῆται τὰ ὅπλα] metaphor from taking up a position in the face of an enemy. Plato, *Rep.* 440 E, ἐν τῇ τῆς ψυχῆς στάσει τίθεσθαι τὰ ὅπλα πρὸς τοῦ λογιστικοῦ. The phrase is frequent in Xenophon's *Anabasis* in several military senses, *e.g.* εἰς τάξιν τὰ ὅπλα τίθεσθαι ii 2, 21 and v 4, 11 (Krüger's *Lexikon*, or Vollbrecht's *Wörterbuch*).

μηδὲ μεθ' ἑτέρων] Also in Thuc. ii 67 § 5, cf. v 48, οὐδ' ὑφ' ἑτέρων. vi 44 § 4, οὐδὲ μεθ' ἑτέρων. vii 59 § 1, μηδὲ μεθ' ἕτερα.

IX § 1. **τῆς Σόλωνος πολιτείας—τὰ δημοτικώτατα**] Isocr. 7 § 16, ἐκείνην τὴν δημοκρατίαν, ἣν Σόλων μὲν ὁ δημοτικώτατος γενόμενος ἐνομοθέτησε. Dem. 18 § 6, Σόλων, εὔνους ὢν ὑμῖν καὶ δημοτικός. For Solon's relations to democracy see *Pol.* ii 12, 1273 *b* 35. In the language of Mr Newman's excellent paraphrase in vol. i p. 373, we are there told that 'certain persons regarded Solon as the destroyer of an extreme oligarchy, on the ruins of which he constructed the πάτριος δημοκρατία, a wisely mixed constitution: they took him to have founded *πρῶτον μὲν καὶ μέγιστον τὸ μὴ δανείζειν ἐπὶ τοῖς σώμασιν, ἔπειτα τὸ ἐξεῖναι τῷ βουλομένῳ [τιμωρεῖν] ὑπὲρ τῶν ἀδικουμένων, τρίτον δὲ (<ᾧ> μάλιστά φασιν ἰσχυκέναι τὸ πλῆθος) ἡ εἰς τὸ δικ[αστή-ριον] ἔφ[εσι]ς· κύριος γὰρ ὢν ὁ δῆμος τῆς ψήφου, κύριος γίγνεται τῆς*

4 *τιμωρεῖν* Paton, K-W (K^3, B), cf. 19, 2; *τιμωρεῖσθαι* Wyse, H-L; *δικάζεσθαι* K^1; *δίκην λαβεῖν* (hiatu vitato) J W Headlam et Lipsius, coll. Plut. *Sol.* 18. **5** *ᾧ* ins. H-L (K^3, B); *ᾧ καὶ* K-W; *ᾗ* K^1. **6, 9, 13** ΓΙΝ (K-W).

---

the Areopagus, to have introduced the system of filling magistracies by election, and to have created the popular dicastery, thus as it were equipping the State with a complete set of new institutions....To this view of Solon's work Aristotle objects: he says that Solon would seem to have found the council of the Areopagus, and the system of filling the magistracies by election, already established, and that he...left them as he found them, whereas he did institute the popular element in the constitution by founding the popular dicasteries. He appeals in support of his contention to the opinion of a second set of critics, who made Solon responsible for the existing extreme democracy. They complained that, so far from being the author of a mixed constitution, he overpowered the oligarchical element by the democratic, inasmuch as he gave supreme power to the popular dicastery. Armed with this judicial authority, the people became masters of the State; one statesman after another had to play into their hands, and so the extreme democracy gradually came into being. Aristotle, however, holds that these inquirers ascribed to Solon's institution of popular dicasteries consequences which would not have resulted from it, if it had not been for accidental circumstances. Solon was far from intending to found an extreme democracy; he gave, in fact, only a modicum of power to the people—enough to content them and no more—and reserved office for the better-to-do classes. On the other hand, he was not the contriver of an elaborate mixed constitution, but rather the founder of the beginnings of popular liberty; still less was he the undoer of the power of the Few. He left office in their hands, and gave the people only just enough power to make the holders of office govern well.'

μὴ δανείζειν *κτλ.*] 6 § 1. **τὸ ἐξεῖναι—ἀδικουμένων**] Plut. *Sol.* 18, *οἰόμενος δεῖν ἐπαρκεῖν τῇ τῶν πολλῶν ἀσθενείᾳ, παντὶ λαβεῖν δίκην ὑπὲρ τοῦ κακῶς πεπονθότος ἔδωκε· καὶ γὰρ πληγέντος ἑτέρου ἢ βλαβέντος ἐξῆν τῷ δυναμένῳ καὶ βουλομένῳ γράφεσθαι τὸν ἀδικοῦντα καὶ διώκειν, ὀρθῶς ἐθίζοντος τοῦ νομοθέτου τοὺς πολίτας ὥσπερ ἑνὸς μέρους συναισθάνεσθαι καὶ συναλγεῖν ἀλλήλοις. τούτῳ δὲ τῷ νόμῳ συμφωνοῦντα λόγον αὐτοῦ διαμνημονεύουσιν. ἐρωτηθεὶς γάρ, ὡς ἔοικεν, ἥτις οἰκεῖται κάλλιστα τῶν πόλεων, "ἐκείνῃ," εἶπεν, "ἐν ᾗ τῶν ἀδικουμένων οὐχ ἧττον οἱ μὴ ἀδικούμενοι προβάλλονται καὶ κολάζουσι τοὺς ἀδικοῦντας."*

ἡ εἰς τὸ δικαστήριον ἔφεσις] The constr. changes from the substantival use of the infinitive to an ordinary substantive. The eulogists of Solon, referred to in *Pol.* ii 12, 1273 *b* 41, recognise the *δικαστήριον* as the element which is *δημοτικὸν* in his constitution; while his critics describe him as having subordinated the oligarchical element, *κύριον ποιήσαντα τὸ δικαστήριον πάντων, κληρωτὸν ὄν*. Aristotle himself subsequently mentions as one of the two elements in the necessary modicum of political power assigned to the people that of *εὐθύνειν*, *i.e.* calling the officials to account in the law-courts, *μηδὲ γὰρ τούτου κύριος ὢν ὁ δῆμος δοῦλος ἂν εἴη καὶ πολέμιος.* Plut. *Sol.* 18 (after saying of the *θῆτες* that *τῷ συνεκκλησιάζειν καὶ δικάζειν μόνον μετεῖχον τῆς πολιτείας*) adds: *ὃ κατ' ἀρχὰς μὲν οὐδέν, ὕστερον δὲ παμμέγεθες ἐφάνη· τὰ γὰρ πλεῖστα τῶν διαφόρων ἐνέπιπτεν εἰς τοὺς δικαστάς. καὶ γὰρ ὅσα ταῖς ἀρχαῖς ἔταξε κρίνειν, ὁμοίως καὶ περὶ ἐκείνων εἰς τὸ δικαστήριον ἐφέσεις ἔδωκε τοῖς βουλομένοις.* Grote (ii 325) holds that the popular dicasteries were not established by Solon, a view which is not in accordance with the text. He also points out (p. 326) that, although Solon laid the foundation of the Athenian democracy, his institutions were not democratical (as compared with those of Cleisthenes and Pericles). The dicasteries doubtless became more highly developed in later times, but of their existence in Solon's time for certain purposes, such as the control of officials, there can be no reasonable doubt. See Duncker, *Gesch. d. Alt.* vi 179, 180.

πολιτείας. ἔτι δὲ καὶ διὰ τὸ μὴ γεγρ[ά]φθ[αι το]ὺς νόμους ἁπλῶς 2
μηδὲ σαφῶς, ἀλλ' ὥσπερ ὁ περὶ τῶν κλήρων καὶ ἐπικλήρων, ἀν[άγ]κ[η πο]λλὰς ἀμφισβητήσεις γίγνεσθαι καὶ πάντα βραβεύειν καὶ τὰ κοινὰ καὶ τὰ ἴδια τὸ δικα[στ]ήρ[ιον]. οἴονται μὲν οὖν τινὲς ἐπίτηδες ἀσαφεῖς αὐτὸν ποιῆσαι τοὺς νόμους, ὅπως ῇ τῆς κρίσεως [ὁ δ]ῆ[μος κ]ύριος. οὐ μὴν εἰκός, ἀλλὰ διὰ τὸ μὴ δύνασθαι καθόλου

9 *πολλὰς* Paton, Blass, K-W, K^{3}; *ἦν τὰς* K^{1}; *ἦν πολλὰς* H-L sed deest spatium. **10** *τὸ δικαστήριον* K-W, K^{3}, papyri lectio incerta (B): *τὰ δικαστήρ[ια]* K^{1} (H-L), sed propter tot generis neutri vocabula pluralia in contextu cumulata numerus singularis videtur elegantior. **11** *ῇ* K^{3} (B); *τι* K-W (in papyro utrumvis legi potest). *ὅπως τι τῆς κρίσεως ὁ δῆμος ῇ κύριος* K-W^{1}; 'aut *τι* delendum aut *ὅπως ῇ τῆς κρίσεως ὁ δῆμος κύριος* (B) legendum' K-W^{2}; *ὅπως τῆς κρίσεως ὁ δῆμος ῇ κύριος* H-L. **12—13** ΠΕΡΙΛΑΒΕΙΝ etiam ante ΚΑΘΟΛΟΥ scriptum et deinde deletum; *πανταχοῦ* sine causa legendum suspicantur H-L.

---

§ 2. **ἁπλῶς...σαφῶς**] Dem. *Lept.* § 93, *ἁπλᾶ καὶ σαφῆ*, Isaeus 11 § 32, *ἁπλᾶ καὶ γνώριμα μαθεῖν*, Dem. 24 § 68, *ἁπλῶς καὶ πᾶσι γνωρίμως γεγράφθαι.* In all these passages perspicuity is described as a merit in legislative enactments. Here the obscurity of some of Solon's laws is said to have increased the powers of the people as interpreters of the law in the dicasteries.

ὁ περὶ τῶν κλήρων] The reference is to the law of intestate succession quoted in Dem. *Macart.* 43 § 51, p. 1067. Parts of this law are paraphrased or expressly cited in Isaeus 11 §§ 1, 2, and 7 § 20. The law of the **ἐπίκληρος** is quoted in Dem. 43 §§ 16, 54, and 46 § 22, ending with the words *ἀνεπίδικον μὴ ἐξεῖναι ἔχειν μήτε κλῆρον μήτε ἐπίκληρον.* This law is referred to in Isaeus 3 §§ 64, 74 and elsewhere. Both laws may be fairly ascribed to Solon, and students of Isaeus will admit the ambiguity of certain clauses in them. The greater part of Plutarch's *Sol.* 20 is devoted to details of the law of the *ἐπίκληρος*, but the points there touched upon are curious rather than obscure. In the time of Aristophanes the decision of rival claims to the hand of an 'heiress' was one of the most cherished privileges of the Athenian dicast (*Vesp.* 583—587). Cf. *inf.* 42 § 5, *περὶ κλήρου καὶ ἐπικλήρου*, 50 § 6 *ἐπικλήρου κακώσεως*, and *κλήρων καὶ ἐπικλήρων ἐπιδικασίαι*, also 43 § 4.

ἀνάγκη] *sc. ἦν. Rhet.* i 1 § 8 *ἀνάγκη ἐπὶ τοῖς κριταῖς καταλείπειν*, *Eth.* 1137 *b* 15, *ἀνάγκη μὲν εἰπεῖν καθόλου, μὴ οἷόν τε δὲ ὀρθῶς.*

οἴονται κτλ.] Plut. *Sol.* 18, *λέγεται δὲ καὶ τοὺς νόμους ἀσαφέστερον γράψας καὶ πολλὰς ἀντιλήψεις ἔχοντας αὐξῆσαι τὴν τῶν δικαστηρίων ἰσχύν· μὴ δυναμένους γὰρ ὑπὸ τῶν νόμων διαλυθῆναι περὶ ὧν διεφέροντο συνέβαινεν ἀεὶ δεῖσθαι δικαστῶν καὶ πᾶν ἄγειν ἀμφισβήτημα πρὸς ἐκείνους, τρόπον τινὰ τῶν νόμων κυρίους ὄντας.* 'It is hardly just to Plutarch' (says Grote) 'to make him responsible for the absurd remark that Solon rendered his laws intentionally obscure... We may well doubt whether it was ever seriously intended even by its author, whoever he may have been' (Grote, c. 11, ii 330). We now see that Plutarch quotes from the text, where the authors of this opinion are not specified. The opinion is only quoted to be rejected. The real cause for the obscurity of some of Solon's laws is introduced with the words *οὐ μὴν εἰκὸς κτλ.*

διὰ τὸ μὴ δύνασθαι (sc. Σόλωνα) **καθόλου περιλαβεῖν τὸ βέλτιστον**] 'owing to his being unable to attain the perfection of legislative expression while drawing up his laws in general terms.' It is characteristic of a legislator to deal with *τὸ καθόλου*, leaving the dicast to deal with the details. *Rhet.* i 1 § 7, *ἡ μὲν τοῦ νομοθέτου κρίσις οὐ κατὰ μέρος ἀλλὰ περὶ μελλόντων τε καὶ καθόλου ἐστίν*, 13 § 13, *συμβαίνει δὲ τοῦτο (τὸ ἐπιεικὲς) τὰ μὲν ἀκόντων τὰ δὲ ἑκόντων τῶν νομοθετῶν, ἀκόντων μὲν ὅταν λάθῃ, ἑκόντων δ' ὅταν μὴ δύνωνται διορίσαι, ἀλλ' ἀναγκαῖον μὲν ῇ καθόλου εἰπεῖν, μὴ ῇ δέ, ἀλλ' ὡς ἐπὶ τὸ πολύ.* *Eth. Nic.* v 14, 1137 *b* 15, *Pol.* iii 11, 1282 *b* 2, (those in authority must be) *κυρίους περὶ ὅσων ἐξαδυνατοῦσιν οἱ νόμοι λέγειν ἀκριβῶς διὰ τὸ μὴ ῥᾴδιον εἶναι καθόλου δηλῶσαι περὶ πάντων*, *Pol.* 1268 *b* 39, 1269 *a* 9, 1286 *a* 10.

περιλαβεῖν, here 'to define strictly, determine in express words, draw up in a legal form' (L and S), Plat. *Leg.* 823 B, *θήρα* περιλαβεῖν τὸ βέλτιστον· οὐ γὰρ [δ]ίκ[αιον] ἐκ τῶν νῦν γιγνομένων ἀλλ' ἐκ τῆς ἄλλης πολιτείας θεωρεῖν τὴν ἐκείνου βούλησιν.

10. ἐν [μὲν οὖν τ]οῖς νόμοις ταῦτα δοκεῖ θεῖναι δημοτικά, πρὸ δὲ τῆς νομοθεσίας ποιῆσαι τὴν τῶν χρεῶ[ν ἀπο]κοπήν, καὶ μετὰ ταῦτα τήν τε τῶν μέτρων καὶ σταθμῶν καὶ τὴν τοῦ νομίσματος αὔξησιν.
2 ἐπ' ἐκείνου γὰρ ἐγένετο καὶ τὰ μέτρα μείζω

X 2 'aut ποιῆσαι fuit aut ποιήσας, certe non ποιήσασθαι' K-W; ποιήσας K-W, B; ποιῆσαι H-L. **4** ΑΥΞΗϹΙΝ littera Ξ incerta (K), non ΕΠΑΥΞΗϹΙΝ (K-W) nec ΚΑΤΑϹΤΑϹΙΝ (H-L). ΜΕΙΖΩ (K, K-W), non ΜΕΙΩ (H-L).

γὰρ πάμπολύ τι πρᾶγμά ἐστι, περιειλημμένον ὀνόματι νῦν σχεδὸν ἑνί. Ar. *Eth. Nic.* v 4, 1130 *b* 3, ἑνὶ ὀνόματι περιλαβεῖν (embrace, include) ταῦτα πάντα, iii 12, 1117 *b* 21, τύπῳ περιλαβεῖν. *Pol.* iii 16, 1287 *b* 19, τὰ μὲν ἐνδέχεται τοῖς νόμοις περιληφθῆναι, vi 5, 1320 *a* 1, νόμοι οἳ περιλήψονται τὰ σῴζοντα τὰς πολιτείας.

οὐ γὰρ δίκαιον—βούλησιν] One of the writer's favourite methods of reconstruction is 'inference from the present to the past, from existing circumstances to their presumable antecedents, from a given state of institutions to a former condition of the same.' We here find 'part of a formula for the critical application of this method,' or rather for the limitations under which it may be applied (Mr Macan, *J. H. S.*, xii 37 f.).

X § 1. **πρὸ δὲ τῆς νομοθεσίας** κτλ.] Solon's general legislation falls between the σεισάχθεια and the alteration of the currency. There is thus no direct connexion between the change in the coinage and the famous 'disburdening' ordinance. It was not by a modification of the monetary standard that Solon relieved the oppressed debtors; it was by an absolute cancelling of the debt. The opposite view was held by Androtion, whose opinion is quoted by Plutarch only to be rejected: *Sol.* 15, καίτοι τινὲς ἔγραψαν, ὧν ἐστιν 'Ανδροτίων, οὐκ ἀποκοπῇ χρεῶν, ἀλλὰ τόκων μετριότητι κουφισθέντας ἀγαπῆσαι τοὺς πένητας, καὶ σεισάχθειαν ὀνομάσαι τὸ φιλανθρώπευμα τοῦτο καὶ τὴν ἅμα τούτῳ γενομένην τῶν τε μέτρων ἐπαύξησιν καὶ τοῦ νομίσματος τιμήν. ἑκατὸν γὰρ ἐποίησε δραχμῶν τὴν μνᾶν πρότερον ἑβδομήκοντα καὶ τριῶν οὖσαν, ὥστ' ἀριθμῷ μὲν ἴσον, δυνάμει δ' ἔλαττον ἀποδιδόντων, ὠφελεῖσθαι μὲν τοὺς ἐκτίνοντας μεγάλα μηδὲν δὲ βλάπτεσθαι τοὺς κομιζομένους. οἱ δὲ πλεῖστοι πάντων ὁμοῦ τῶν συμβολαίων ἀναίρεσιν γενέσθαι τὴν σεισάχθειαν, καὶ τούτοις συνᾴδει μᾶλλον τὰ ποιήματα.

τῶν μέτρων καὶ σταθμῶν καὶ...τοῦ νομίσματος αὔξησιν] 'the augmentation of the measures and weights and of the currency.' Andoc. *De Myst.* 83 (the decree of Tisamenus), πολιτεύεσθαι 'Αθηναίους κατὰ τὰ πάτρια, νόμοις δὲ χρῆσθαι τοῖς Σόλωνος καὶ μέτροις καὶ σταθμοῖς. It was held by Boeckh (*Metrologie*, 1838, xv § 2) that Solon 'not only debased the coin but also altered the weights and measures.' Grote dissented from this opinion on the latter point, giving his reasons in the *Classical Museum*, i p. 25: 'I believe that the statement of Androtion...has no reference to the *medimnus* and *metretes*, and that we cannot even deduce from it the vague inference...that Solon made *some* new arrangement of the measures.' He interprets the words τῶν μέτρων ἐπαύξησιν (Plut.) of the monetary standard alone, referring them to the 'increased number of drachmae, which every mina and every talent were now made to contain.' He even adds that 'we know positively that Solon did not meddle with the weights.' He holds that it was 'for the express purpose of affording relief to debtors, that Solon degraded the monetary standard, and maintains that Solon 'would not choose such a moment for rearranging the liquid and dry measures.' The present passage conclusively confirms the opinion held by Boeckh.

τὴν τοῦ νομίσματος αὔξησιν] refers to the fact that 73 old Aeginetan drachmas were replaced by 100 Attic drachmas, so that the same amount of silver was represented by a larger number of coins.

§ 2. **τὰ μέτρα μείζω τῶν Φειδωνείων**] Hdt. vi 127, Φείδωνος τοῦ 'Αργείου τυράννου...τοῦ τὰ μέτρα ποιήσαντος τοῖς Πελοποννησίοισι. The date of Pheidon is disputed. He is sometimes placed in Ol. 8 = B.C. 748 (Pausan. vi 22, 2, followed by Unger, Duncker, and Busolt, i 140 n); sometimes (by altering the text of Pausanias) in Ol. 28 = B.C. 668 (Weissenborn, followed by Curtius). Hdt. *l.c.* mentions a τῶν Φειδωνείων, καὶ ἡ μνᾶ πρότερον [ἄγο]υσα παρα[πλήσ]ιον ἑβδομήκοντα δραχμὰς ἀνεπληρώθη ταῖς ἑκατόν. || ἦν δ' ὁ ἀρχαῖος [Col. 4.]

5 ἕλκουσα K-W, H-L, K^3; ἄγουσα B; aut ἕλκουσα aut ἄγουσα, quorum hoc usitatius sit, legendum putat Wyse; cf. c. 51 § 3 *τὸν σταθμὸν ἄγοντας*. παρα[πλήσ]ιον K; παρὰ [μικρ]όν K-W; *τρεῖς καὶ* H-L; *τὰς γ' καὶ* B. **6** *ταῖς*: *τότ' εἰς* H-L; *εἰς* (hiatu admisso) coniecerat Mahaffy (*Athenaeum*, 1891, p. 344), sed numerum omnibus notum indicat articulus.

---

son of Pheidon among the suitors of the daughter of Cleisthenes, despot of Sicyon, which would make Pheidon's date shortly before 600 B.C. The first of these dates is half a century before the beginning of Greek coinage, which may be placed about B.C. 700 (Busolt, i 355). The earliest authority for the statement that silver *coins* were first struck by Pheidon at Aegina is Ephorus, quoted by Strabo p. 376, Ἔφορος δ' ἐν Αἰγίνῃ ἄργυρον πρῶτον κοπῆναί φησιν ὑπὸ Φείδωνος, cf. *ib.* 358, μέτρα ἐξεῦρε τὰ Φειδώνια καλούμενα καὶ σταθμοὺς καὶ νόμισμα κεχαραγμένον τό τε ἄλλο καὶ τὸ ἀργυροῦν (cf. Busolt, i 144 n). This last is the only passage which describes Pheidon as an inventor of *weights*; and even here the epithet 'Pheidonian' is applied to the μέτρα alone. The *Marmor Parium*, ep. 30, connects him with silver coinage as well as with a reform in the measures of capacity: Φείδων ὁ Ἀργεῖος ἐδήμευσε τὰ μέτρα...καὶ ἀνεσκεύασε ('reformed them') καὶ νόμισμα ἀργυροῦν ἐν Αἰγίνῃ ἐποίησεν. The Etymologicum Magnum, *s. v.* ὀβελίσκος, mentions his coinage, but implies that he made no change in standards of *weight*: πάντων δὲ πρῶτος Φείδων Ἀργεῖος νόμισμα ἔκοψεν ἐν Αἰγίνῃ· καὶ δοὺς τὸ νόμισμα καὶ ἀναλαβὼν τοὺς ὀβελίσκους (spits, or small bars, of metal), ἀνέθηκε τῇ ἐν Ἄργει Ἥρᾳ, ἐπειδὴ δὲ τότε οἱ ὀβελίσκοι τὴν χεῖρα ἐπλήρουν, τουτέστι τὴν δράκα (the grasp), ἡμεῖς, καίπερ μὴ πληροῦντες τὴν δράκα τοῖς ἓξ ὀβολοῖς, δραχμὴν αὐτὴν λέγομεν παρὰ τὸ δράξασθαι. ὅθεν ἔτι καὶ νῦν λέγομεν ὀβολοστάτην τὸν τοκιστήν, ἐπειδὴ σταθμοῖς [τοὺς ὀβελίσκους *addit* Orion p. 118 'qui Heraclidis Pontici auctoritate utitur,' Gaisford] παρεδίδουν οἱ ἀρχαῖοι. The text mentions him solely in connexion with μέτρα, or 'measures of capacity,' and not in connexion with coinage or weights, the present section dealing in order with three topics (1) measures, (2) coinage, (3) weights, which must not be confounded with one another. Similarly, in another of the πολιτεῖαι, that of Argos (Rose, Frag. 480, 3, Pollux 10, 179) μέτρα alone are mentioned in connexion with Pheidon; εἴη δ' ἂν καὶ φείδων τι ἀγγεῖον ἐλαιηρὸν ἀπὸ τῶν Φειδωνίων μέτρων ὠνομασμένον, ὑπὲρ ὧν ἐν Ἀργείᾳ πολιτείᾳ Ἀριστοτέλης λέγει.

The present passage tells us for the first time that the Pheidonian measures of capacity were smaller than the corresponding Attic measures. The Pheidonian scale of measures may be identified with the Babylonian, and the ratio of the Pheidonian to the Solonian measures may accordingly be 12 : 13. Thus, in liquid measure, the Solonian μετρητής is already known to have contained about 39 *litres*, or 8½ gallons: the Pheidonian μετρητής would therefore contain about 36 *litres*, or rather less than 8 gallons, and be identical with the Babylonian *epha* and the old Egyptian *artabe*. Similarly, in dry measure, the Solonian μέδιμνος contained about 52 *litres*, or about 12 gallons; and the Pheidonian, 48 *litres*, or about 11 gallons (Hultsch, *Neue Jahrb. für Philologie*, 1891, pp. 263—4). For the opinion held hitherto, that the Pheidonian measures were larger than the Solonian, cf. Duncker, *Hist. Gr.* Bk II, c. ii, vol. ii 26 E. T.

ἡ μνᾶ—ἑκατόν] According to the statement of Androtion in Plut. *Sol.* 15, Solon, in introducing a new standard for silver coin, lowered the standard to the extent of 27 per cent. 100 drachmas of the new standard contained no more silver than 73 of the old. Thus the new mina was equivalent in weight to 73 unreduced drachmas. As 73 : 100 :: 100 : 137; hence, 100 drachmas of the old standard would be equivalent in weight to 137 of the new. 73 to 100 is precisely the proportion between the Attic drachmas of 67·5 *grs.* and average Aeginetan drachmas of rather over 90 *grs.* (73 : 100 :: 67·5 : 92·4), the Attic mina being to the Aeginetan as 100 : 137 (Head's *Historia Numorum*, p. 309). If, however, instead of taking Aeginetan coins of average weight, we take those of actual maximum weight, the stater of two drachmae weighs 194 *grs.* The corresponding Attic coin weighs 135 *grs.* Then as 194 : 135 :: 100 : $69\frac{57}{97}$. Hence the number of drachmas of the Aeginetan χαρακτὴρ δίδραχμον. ἐποίησε δὲ καὶ σταθμὰ πρὸς τ[ὸ] νόμισμα 7

7 χαρακτὴρ διδράχμου <βοῦς> ? Wyse, coll. Poll. ix 60; χαρακτὴρ <βοῦς καὶ τὸ νόμισμα> δίδραχμον J B Mayor. σταθμὰ K-W, K[3], B; σταθμὸν K[1]; πρὸς τὸν σταθμὸν τὸ νόμισμα ? H-L.

---

standard, which would be equivalent in weight to 100 Attic drachmas, would be about 69½. Thus, according as we take average or maximum weights, Mr Kenyon's text, παραπλήσιον ἑβδομήκοντα δραχμάς, will mean either 73 or 69½.—The reading proposed by Blass gives us exactly 73 drachmas.

The new standard introduced by Solon in place of the Aeginetan has been convincingly proved by Mommsen (*Röm. Münzwesen*, p. 43 *sq.*, *Mon. Rom.* ed. Blacas, i 29 *sqq.*, 73 *sq.*) to have been the Euboic, and henceforth Euboean coins would circulate freely in Attica, side by side with the new Attic money (Head, p. 310, cf. 302 and xxxviii—xlii). Thus Solon's reform of the currency was not necessarily due to economic reasons connected with the debts of the poorer citizens. It had a commercial object and was intended to facilitate trade with the neighbouring island of Euboea (especially with Chalcis and Eretria), and with other Greek cities (for example, Cyrene), where the Euboic standard prevailed. It would also promote trade with Corinth, where a similar standard was in use (Busolt, i p. 525), and with the Greek colonies in Chalcidice and Sicily (Köhler, in *Mittheil. d. d. arch. Inst.* 1885, x 151—157). It has further been suggested by Mr R. S. Poole (*Dict. of the Bible*, art. 'Weights and Measures') that the new Solonian standard was borrowed from Egypt. The Egyptian unit of weight was 140 grains, and the Solonian didrachm weighed 135 grains. Thus, whether the standard was actually borrowed from Egypt or Euboea, the Solonian coinage would facilitate intercourse with Egypt as well as with the countries where the Euboic standard was in use.

In this connexion it is interesting to notice that, after reforming the currency, and thus facilitating trade with countries employing either the Euboic or the Egyptian standard, Solon set out for Egypt, where he stayed for ten years, one of his avowed objects being the pursuit of commerce.

ἀνεπληρώθη] 'was raised to the full number of a hundred drachmas.'

ἦν—δίδραχμον] 'the primitive type of coin was the two-drachma piece.' χαρακτὴρ means (1), as here, τὸ κεχαραγμένον, that which has a stamp impressed upon it, cf. Plato, *Politicus*, 289 B, ἡ τοῦ νομίσματος ἰδέα καὶ σφραγίδων καὶ παντὸς χαρακτῆρος: (2) the stamp itself, as in Ar. *Pol.* i 9, 1257 *a* 40 χαρακτῆρα ἐπιβαλόντων, ἵν' ἀπολύσῃ τῆς μετρήσεως αὐτούς· ὁ γὰρ χαρακτὴρ ἐτέθη τοῦ πόσου σημεῖον. *Oecon.* ii 5 (of Hippias), τὸ δὲ νόμισμα τὸ ὂν Ἀθηναίοις ἀδόκιμον ἐποίησεν· τάξας δὲ τιμὴν ἐκέλευσε πρὸς αὐτὸν ἀνακομίζειν· συνελθόντων δὲ ἐπὶ τῷ κόψαι ἕτερον χαρακτῆρα ἐξέδωκε τὸ αὐτὸ ἀργύριον.

Before the time of Solon, the only money current in Attica, as well as in Boeotia and Peloponnesus, seems to have been the Aeginetan didrachm of about 194 grains; but there are no Athenian coins extant of Aeginetan weight. Thus, apart from mere tradition (Plut. *Thes.* 25 ἔκοψε δὲ καὶ νόμισμα βοῦν ἐγχαράξας), there is no proof of any coins having been struck at Athens before Solon (Head, p. xlii). The text must therefore refer to the old Aeginetan didrachms in circulation in Attica before the time of Solon. These coins had on the obverse a tortoise with a plain shell and a row of dots down the middle of its back; and, on the reverse, an incuse square divided into eight triangular compartments, of which four or more are deeply hollowed out (Head, *l.c.*, p. 332, fig. 220).

From the time of Solon the standard coin of Athens was the tetradrachm of the

full Euboic weight of 270 grains. The common type is a head of Athena of rude

8 τ[ρ]εῖς καὶ ἑξήκοντα μνᾶς τὸ τάλαντον ἀγούσας, καὶ ἐπιδιενεμήθησαν [αἱ] μναῖ τῷ στατῆρι καὶ τοῖς ἄλλοις σταθμοῖς.

8 *τρεῖς καὶ* seclusit K; ante *ἑβδομήκοντα* (v. 6) posuerunt H-L, alii; defendit Ridgeway, retinuerunt K-W, B.

---

archaic style with large prominent eye, wearing a round earring and close-fitting crested helmet: on the obverse is an owl with head facing and wings closed; also an olive-spray and the letters Α Θ Ε (*ib.* p. 310, fig. 209). *After* the time of Solon, coins of Eretria, stamped with the head of a bull, together with other Euboean coins, may have circulated in Attica, side by side with the Solonian 'owls.' But there is no authority earlier than Philochorus (in the generation after Aristotle), for stating that the early didrachms, which preceded the Solonian 'owls,' were impressed with the figure of an ox (Head, *l.c.* p. 309). Cf. Schol. on Arist. *Av.* 1106, *ἡ γλαῦξ ἐπὶ χαράγματος ἦν τετραδράχμου, ὡς Φιλόχορος· ἐκλήθη δὲ τὸ νόμισμα τὸ τετράδραχμον τότε [ἡ] γλαῦξ. ἦν γὰρ γλαῦξ ἐπίσημον καὶ πρόσωπον Ἀθηνᾶς, τῶν πρότερον διδράχμων ὄντων ἐπίσημον δὲ βοῦν ἐχόντων.* Pollux, ix 60, *δίδραχμον· τὸ παλαιὸν δὲ τοῦτ' ἦν Ἀθηναίοις νόμισμα, καὶ ἐκαλεῖτο βοῦς, ὅτι βοῦν εἶχεν ἐντετυπωμένον.* We cannot, however, ignore the fact that archaic coins of Euboea, bearing the bull's head, have repeatedly been found in Attica (cf. Koehler, *Mittheilungen*, ix 357—9).

ἐποίησε—ἀγούσας] 'He also instituted standard weights corresponding to the coinage, 63 minae weighing the talent,' *i.e.* 'at the rate of 63 minae to the weight of a talent.' Cf. c. 51, *τὸν σταθμὸν ἄγοντας ὅσον ἂν αὐτοὶ τάξωσιν.*

Much difficulty has been felt respecting these 63 minae, on the ground that, in every standard, a talent invariably consists of 60 minae. Thus it is ingeniously suggested by Mr Kenyon and others that *τρεῖς καὶ* 'was written as an explanation of *παραπλήσιον* above, and was subsequently inserted in the text in the wrong place,' and this suggestion has been regarded with considerable favour. But the text, as it stands, admits of a ready explanation if we regard it as stating the *weight* of the Solonian currency as compared with the average weight of the corresponding coins of the Euboic standard.

The average weight for the Solonian silver coinage was slightly higher than that of the Euboic. Solon made his new talent consist of 63 old minae of the average Euboic weight; and this talent was, like all other talents, divided into 60 minae. As the post-Solonian mina weighed about 6750 grains, the talent must have weighed 60 times that amount, or 405,000 grains. To obtain the weight of the mina superseded by the Solonian mina, we divide by 63 and the result is $6428\frac{4}{7}$ grains. A stater, or fiftieth part of this, is $128\frac{4}{7}$ grains. In other terms, 63 : 60 : 135 : $128\frac{4}{7}$. This is in sufficiently close agreement with the actual weights of the coins of Euboea, as compared with those of Attica. The two-drachma piece of the former weighs 130 grains (only one grain and three-sevenths more than the weight above mentioned); that of the latter, 135 grains. The substance of this explanation is due to Prof. Ridgeway, who also shews that, while the Aeginetan standard was used for *silver*, the Euboic was used for gold and silver, being in fact the only standard used for *gold*. Solon framed for the coinage of Athens a standard founded on that already in use for all transactions in gold. Possibly to adjust his silver currency to the standard gold unit, he augmented the silver standard, making 63 old minas go to his new talent of 60 minae. Thus, while about 70 Aeginetan drachmas are equal in weight to 100 Attic drachmas, rather less than 63, or, strictly speaking, $62\frac{3}{8}$ Euboic minas are equal in weight to 60 of the Solonian standard.

The above note refers to the *average* weight of coins of the Euboic standard. In the case of coins of *full* weight, that standard is practically identical with the Solonian, the staters of *both* weighing 135 grains (see Head's *Brit. Mus. Cat. of Coins of Corinth*, 1889, p. xix).

ἐπιδιενεμήθησαν] 'The minae were divided into fractions consisting of (*lit.* 'were apportioned out by') the *stater* and the other weights.' *ἐπιδιανέμω*, "'to distribute besides,' Philo 2, 651; *τινί τι* Josephus, *B. J.* 2, 6, 3" (L and S).

στατὴρ is the general term for a standard unit of weight and (more frequently) of money. It here denotes the weight of a fiftieth part of a mina. The weights here meant are probably coin-weights alone, market-weights being apparently left out of consideration. Solon made no change in the *weights used in com-*

11. διατάξας δὲ τὴν πολιτείαν ὅνπερ εἴρηται τρόπον, ἐπειδὴ
προσιόντες αὐτῷ περὶ τῶν νόμων ἠνώχλουν, τὰ μὲν ἐπιτιμῶντες
τὰ δὲ ἀνακρίνοντες, βουλόμενος μήτε ταῦτα κινεῖν μήτ' ἀπεχ-
θάνεσθαι παρών, ἀποδημίαν ἐποιήσατο κατ' ἐμπορί[αν] ἅμα καὶ
θεωρίαν εἰς Αἴγυπτον, [εἰπ]ὼν ὡς οὐ[χ ἥξ]ει δέκα ἐτῶν· οὐ γὰρ
οἴεσθαι δίκαιον εἶναι [το]ὺς νόμους ἐξηγεῖσθαι παρὼν ἀλλ' ἕκαστον
2 τὰ γεγραμμένα ποιῆσαι. ἅμα δὲ καὶ συνέβαιν[εν] αὐτῷ τῶν τε
γνωρίμων διαφόρους γεγενῆσθαι πολλοὺς διὰ τὰς τῶν χρεῶν
ἀποκοπά[ς, κ]αὶ τὰς στάσεις ἀμφοτέρας μεταθέσθαι διὰ τὸ παρὰ
δόξαν αὐτοῖς γενέσθαι τὴν κατάστασιν. ὁ μὲν γὰρ δῆμος ᾤετο

XI 2 ΕΝΩΧΛΟΥΝ (K[1], K-W, B): *ἠνώχλουν* J B Mayor (H-L, K[3]); verbum in codicibus optimis augmentum duplex habere constat. **3** ΚΕΙΝΕΙΝ. **5** *εἰπὼν ὡς οὐχ ἥξει* Wessely (K[3], B); *λέγων ὡς οὐχ ἥξει* coniecerat van Leeuwen; [*περὶ Κα*]*νώπου* [*πόλ*]*ει* K[1]. **6** *δίκαιος* Jackson (H-L). **7** *ποιῆσαι* K, H-L: *ποιεῖν* K-W, B.
Κ...CΤΑCΙΝ
10 ΤΗΝΙC ΑΝΤΑΞΙΝ: *τὴν οὖσαν κατάστασιν* K[1]; *τὴν κατάστασιν* K-W, B; *τὴν οὖσαν τάξιν* H-L.

TESTIMONIA. **2—5** Heraclidis Epitoma, Rose, Frag. 611, 3[3], *ὡς δὲ διώχλουν* (codd.; *δ' ἐνώχλουν* K-W) *αὐτῷ τινὲς περὶ τῶν νόμων, ἀπεδήμησεν εἰς Αἴγυπτον.*

---

merce, the Aeginetan mina being still retained unaltered (see Dr Percy Gardner on *Pondera*, in Smith's *Dict. Ant.* ii p. 449 *b*).

XI § 1. **διατάξας—ποιῆσαι**] Plut. *Sol.* 25, *ἐπεὶ δὲ τῶν νόμων εἰσενεχθέντων ἔνιοι τῷ Σόλωνι καθ' ἑκάστην προσῄεσαν ἡμέραν ἐπαινοῦντες ἢ ψέγοντες ἢ συμβουλεύοντες ἐμβάλλειν τοῖς γεγραμμένοις ὅ τι τύχοιεν ἢ ἀφαιρεῖν, πλεῖστοι δ' ἦσαν οἱ πυνθανόμενοι καὶ ἀνακρίνοντες καὶ κελεύοντες αὐτὸν ὅπως ἕκαστον ἔχει καὶ πρὸς ἣν κεῖται διάνοιαν ἐπεκδιδάσκειν καὶ σαφηνίζειν, ὁρῶν, ὅτι ταῦτα καὶ τὸ πράττειν ἄτοπον καὶ τὸ μὴ πράττειν ἐπίφθονον, ὅλως δὲ ταῖς ἀπορίαις ὑπεκστῆναι βουλόμενος καὶ διαφυγεῖν τὸ δυσάρεστον καὶ φιλαίτιον τῶν πολιτῶν (ἔργμασι γὰρ ἐν μεγάλοις πᾶσιν ἁδεῖν χαλεπόν, ὡς αὐτὸς εἴρηκε), πρόσχημα τῆς πλάνης τὴν ναυκληρίαν ποιησάμενος ἐξέπλευσε δεκαετῆ παρὰ τῶν Ἀθηναίων ἀποδημίαν αἰτησάμενος. ἤλπιζε γὰρ ἐν τῷ χρόνῳ τούτῳ καὶ τοῖς νόμοις αὐτοὺς ἔσεσθαι συνήθεις. πρῶτον μὲν οὖν εἰς Αἴγυπτον ἀφίκετο καὶ διέτριψεν, ὡς αὐτός φησι,*
Νείλου ἐπὶ προχοῇσι Κανωβίδος ἐγγύθεν ἀκτῆς.

ἠνώχλουν] This form is found in Xen. *Cyr.* v 3, 56, Isocr. 5 § 53, Aeschin. 1 § 58, Dem. *Lacr.* 16, *Olymp.* 19. In *Lacr.* 30 the MSS vary between *ἐνωχλοῦμεν* (Σ and other MSS), *ἐνοχλοῦμεν* (Aug. 1), *ἠνωχλοῦμεν* (*vulgo*). The *Rhet. ad Alex.* 1445 *b* 2 has *ἠνώχλησαν*. In Aeschin. 3 § 44 the MSS vary between *ἠνωχλεῖτο* (Bekker, Franke, Schultz), and *ἐνωχλεῖτο*. Voemel, *Proleg. Dem.* § 67, quotes Photius: *ἠνείχετο καὶ ἠνώχλει... κοινὸν τῶν Ἀττικῶν ἰδίωμα.* See also Lobeck's *Phrynichus*, p. 154.

ἀποδημίαν ἐποιήσατο] c. 13 *init.*

δέκα ἐτῶν] For the fact cf. Hdt. i 29, *ἀπεδήμησε ἔτεα δέκα.* For the construction, cf. *ib.* vi 58, *ἐπεὰν θάψωσι, ἀγορὴ δέκα ἡμερέων οὐκ ἵσταταί σφι.* Xen. *Anab.* i 7, 18, *οὐ μαχεῖται δέκα ἡμερῶν.* Plat. *Gorg.* 516 D, *ἵνα αὐτοῦ δέκα ἐτῶν μὴ ἀκούσειαν τῆς φωνῆς* (of Cimon's exile).

οὐ γὰρ οἴεσθαι δίκαιον εἶναι—παρών] The nom. c. inf. after *δίκαιον εἶναι* may perhaps be defended (1) by Dem. 15 § 16, *ὧν οὐδενὸς αὐτοὶ δοῦναι δίκην δίκαιον ἂν εἶναι* (where, however, several editors prefer *δίκαιοι ἄν*, which involves a *hiatus*); (2) by Dem. *Prooem.* p. 1439, 14, *ἐγὼ μὲν δὴ δίκαιον ὑπείληφα πρῶτον ἁπάντων αὐτὸς εἰπεῖν.* In the text the construction after *δίκαιον εἶναι* is apparently identical with that often found after *δεῖν* (Rehdantz, *Ind. Dem. s. v. οἴεσθαι*).

§ 2. **ἅμα δὲ καὶ** *κτλ.*] Plut. *Sol.* 16 *init.*, *ἤρεσε δ' οὐδετέροις, ἀλλ' ἐλύπησε καὶ τοὺς πλουσίους ἀνελὼν τὰ συμβόλαια καὶ μᾶλλον ἔτι τοὺς πένητας, ὅτι γῆς ἀναδασμὸν οὐκ ἐποίησεν ἐλπίσασιν αὐτοῖς.*

μεταθέσθαι] 'changed their opinion with regard to him,' *i.e.* 'were alienated from him.'

ὁ μὲν γὰρ δῆμος *κτλ.*] Plut. *Sol.* 14, *Φανίας ὁ Λέσβιος αὐτὸν ἱστορεῖ τὸν Σόλωνα* *πάντ' ἀνάδαστα ποιήσειν αὐτόν, οἱ δὲ γνώριμοι [πά]λιν ἢ τὴν αὐτὴν τάξιν ἀποδώσειν ἢ [μικρὸν] παραλλάξ[ειν. ὁ δὲ ἀ]μφοτέροις ἠναντιώθη, καὶ ἐξὸν αὐτῷ μεθ' ὁποτέρων ἐβούλετο συστά[ντι] τυραννεῖν, εἵλετο πρὸς ἀμφοτέρους ἀπεχθέσθαι σώσας τὴν πατρίδα καὶ τὰ βέ[λτι]στα νομοθετήσας.*

12. *ταῦτα δ' ὅτι τοῦτον <τὸν> τρόπον ἔσχεν οἵ τ' ἄλλοι συμφωνοῦσι πάντες, καὶ αὐτὸς ἐν τῇ ποιήσει μέ[μν]ηται περὶ αὐτῶν ἐν τοῖσδε·*

δήμῳ μὲν γὰρ ἔδωκα τόσον γέρας ὅσσον ἀπαρ[κεῖ],
τιμῆς οὔτ' ἀφελὼν οὔτ' ἐπορεξάμενος.
οἳ δ' εἶχον δύναμιν καὶ χρήμασιν ἦσαν ἀγητο[ί],
καὶ τοῖς ἐφρασάμην μηδὲν ἀ[ει]κὲς ἔχειν.
ἔστην δ' ἀμφιβαλὼν κρατερὸν σάκος ἀμφοτέροισι,
ν[ι]κᾶν δ' οὐκ εἴασ' οὐδετέρους ἀδίκως.

πάλιν δ' ἀποφαινόμενος περὶ τοῦ πλήθους, ὡς α[ὐτ]ῷ δεῖ χρῆσθαι· 2

δῆμος δ' ὧδ' ἂν ἄριστα σὺν ἡγεμόνεσσιν ἕποιτο,
μήτε λίαν ἀν[ε]θεὶς μήτε βιαζόμενος.

11 ἢ scrips. K-W[2], cf. *Pol.* 1296 *a* 40 ταύτην ἀποδοῦναι τὴν τάξιν: ΕΙC (K, H-L), secl. K-W[1], B. **12** ἢ σ[μικρὸν] παραλλάξ[ειν· ὁ δὲ] Blass (K-W, H-L, K[3]); lacuna in altera ρ discerni putat K, in altera spatium plurium litterarum capax superesse. μικρὸν K-W. **13** ΗΒΟΥΛΕΤΟ (K-W, B), quod in titulis Atticis ante annum 300 A.C. non apparet, Meisterhans, p. 134[2]. **14** ΑΠΕΧΘΕCΘΗΝΑΙ.

XII 1 <τὸν> propter homoeoteleuton exciderat. εἶχεν K-W. **4** ΔΗΜΟΙ. γέρας: κράτος Plut. ἀπαρκεῖ: ἐπαρκεῖ Plut. (B), ubi ἀπαρκεῖ coniecerat Coraës: ἀπαρκεῖν H-L (nisi forte ἀπήρκει legendum). **5—6** ΑΠΟΡΕΞΑΜΕΝΟCΟCΟΙ. **7** τοῖσ' H-L. **12** λίην Plut. βιαζόμενος: πιεζόμενος Plut.

TESTIMONIA. **XII 4—9** Plut. *Sol.* 18. **11—14** Plut. *Comp. Sol. et Popl.* 2.

χρησάμενον ἀπάτῃ πρὸς ἀμφοτέρους ἐπὶ σωτηρίᾳ τῆς πόλεως ὑποσχέσθαι κρύφα τοῖς μὲν ἀπόροις τὴν νέμησιν, τοῖς δὲ χρηματικοῖς βεβαίωσιν τῶν συμβολαίων.

ἀνάδαστα] Dem. 24 § 149, γῆς ἀναδασμόν, Plat. *Leg.* 684.

ἐξὸν αὐτῷ κτλ.] Paraphrased by Aristides, ii 360 Dind., παρὸν αὐτῷ στασιαζούσης τῆς πόλεως ὁποτέρων βούλοιτο προστάντι τυραννεῖν, ἀπεχθάνεσθαι μᾶλλον ἀμφοτέροις εἵλετο ὑπὲρ τοῦ δικαίου.

XII § 1. **δήμῳ—ἀδίκως**] These six lines are quoted in Plut. *Sol.* 18 = frag. 5 Bergk.

l. 4. **ἀπαρκεῖ**] 'is sufficient,' as in Aesch. *Pers.* 474, Soph. *O. C.* 1769, Eur. frag. 892, 4 Nauck[2], ὧν οὐκ ἀπαρκεῖ πλησμονή, Arist. frag. 395 οὐκ ἀπήρκει, 'it was not enough' (L and S). Grote (ii 326), who had before him Plutarch's reading ἐπαρκεῖ, translates: 'I gave to the people as much strength as sufficed for their needs'; but ἐπαρκεῖν must mean either (*a*) 'to supply' or (*b*) 'to be strong enough' (whether to help or to hinder). Plutarch's ἐπαρκεῖ is the only instance of the absolute use of the verb given in L and S, except Soph. *Ant.* 612, ἐπαρκέσει νόμος ὅδ', 'this law shall prevail' or 'hold good,' = διαρκέσει. Such is the satisfactory explanation given by Professor Jebb, who adds that in the only other instance, *i.e.* in Plutarch's quotation from Solon, 'we must surely read ἀπαρκεῖ with Coraës.' This opinion is conclusively confirmed by the reading given us by the papyrus.

§ 2. **δῆμος—βιαζόμενος**] quoted in Plut. *Solonis et Poplicolae comparatio*, c. 2; frag. 6 Bergk.

τίκτει γὰρ κόρος ὕβριν, ὅταν πολὺς ὄλβος ἕπητ[αι]
ἀνθρώποισιν ὅσοις μὴ νόος ἄρτιος ᾖ.

3 *καὶ πάλιν δ' [ἑτέρ]ωθί που λέγει περὶ τῶν διανείμασθαι τὴν γῆν βουλομένων·*

οἳ δ' ἐφ' ἁρπαγαῖσιν ἦλθον, ἐλπί[δ' εἶ]χον ἀφνεάν,
κἀδόκουν ἕκαστος αὐτῶν ὄλβον εὑρήσειν πολύν,
καί με κωτίλλοντα λείως τραχὺν ἐκφανεῖν νόον.
χαῦνα μὲν τότ' ἐφράσαντο, νῦν δέ μοι χολούμενοι
λο[ξὸν ὀ]φθαλ[μοῖ]ς ὁρῶσι πάντες ὥστε δήϊον.
οὐ χρεών· ἃ μὲν γὰρ εἶπα σὺν θεοῖσιν ἤνυ[σα],
[ἄλλα δ' ο]ὐ μ[ά]την ἔερδ[ο]ν, οὐδέ μοι τυραννίδος
ἁνδάνει βίᾳ τι [ῥέζ]ειν, οὐδὲ πιε[ίρα]ς χθονὸς
πατρίδος κακοῖσιν ἐσθλοὺς ἰσομοιρίαν ἔχειν.

13 ΠΟΛΥΣ: *κακῷ* Theognis 153. **14** *ἀνθρώπῳ καὶ ὅτῳ* Theognis 154. **15** *καὶ* secl. K-W. *δ' ἑτέρωθί που* R D Hicks, Wyse, Sidgwick, idem ego quoque conieceram (K-W, K[3], B); *δ' ἄλλοθί που* J B Mayor, Bywater, Blass; *ἀλλαχόθι που* Naber (H-L); *διαγνῶθι ποῦ* K[1]. *διανέμεσθαι* H-L. **17** *οἳ δ' ἐφ' ἁρπαγαῖσιν ἐλπίδ' ἤλιθ' εἶχον?* K-W. **18** 'Fortasse *αὐτὸς*' Richards. **21** *ὀφθαλμοῖσ'* B. ΔΗΙΟΝ (K-W, K[3], B): *δήιοι* in Plutarcho Reiskium secutus Bergk (K[1], H-L). **22** *ἃ μὲν γὰρ ἄελπτα* Aristidis (ii 536) codices ΓΘ; *ἅμα γὰρ ἄελπτα* Stephanus, S Jebb; *ἃ μὲν ἄελπτα* coniecit Gaisford, recepit Bergk, versus initium arbitrati. **23** In Aristidis loco *ἄλλα* coniecit Gaisford; legebatur *ἅμα*. *οὐ* Bury, H-L, K-W, K[3], B: *αὖ* in Aristide Bergk (K[1]). **24** *ἁνδάνει κτλ.*: *ἥνδανεν* (Richards) *βίαια λήματ'* H-L.

TESTIMONIA. **20, 21** Plut. *Sol.* 16. **22—23** Aristid. ii 536.

τίκτει—ἕπηται] quoted as Solon's by Clemens Alexandrinus (*Stromateus*, vi 740): *Σόλωνος δὲ ποιήσαντος· τίκτει γὰρ* (*v. l.* *τοι*) *κτλ. ἄντικρυς ὁ Θέογνις γράφει· τίκτει τοι κόρος ὕβριν ὅταν κακῷ ὄλβος ἕπηται* (Theognis 153, followed by the line *ἀνθρώπῳ, καὶ ὅτῳ μὴ νόος ἄρτιος ᾖ*). The Schol. on Pindar *Ol.* xiii 12 cites the first line as 'Homer's.' In the Proverbs of Diogenianus, viii 22, it appears in the form *τίκτει τοι—κακῷ ἀνδρὶ παρείη*.

Diog. Laert. i 59 quotes, among the apophthegms of Solon; *καὶ τὸν μὲν κόρον ὑπὸ τοῦ πλούτου γεννᾶσθαι, τὴν δὲ ὕβριν ὑπὸ τοῦ κόρου.*

§ 3. **καὶ πάλιν δ'**] *καὶ—δὲ* is common in Ar.; *e.g.* *Pol.* 1252 *a* 13, 1254 *b* 24, 1287 *a* 7, 1297 *b* 16; and especially in *Ethics* iv, viii, ix, x; 'adjungit autem *καὶ—δὲ* rem novam, saepe tam leni modo, ut idem fere valeat atque *τέ*. Etiam saepius quam Aristoteles Theophrastus iis particulis utitur' (In the *Historia Plantarum* there are about 100 instances; in the *Characters* more than 70)—Eucken, *De Ar. dicendi ratione*, i 32.

ἑτέρωθί που λέγει] Ar. *de Anima* i 2, 404 *b* 2 ('Αναξαγόρας), *πολλαχοῦ μὲν γὰρ τὸ αἴτιον τοῦ καλῶς καὶ ὀρθῶς τὸν νοῦν λέγει, ἑτέρωθι δὲ τοῦτον εἶναι τὴν ψυχήν*, *De Partibus Animalium*, iii 2, 663 *b* 3, *ἑτέρωθί που τοῦ σώματος*. Plut. *Sol.* 2, *ἀλλ' ἑτέρωθι λέγει* (of Solon).

ll. 17—25. **οἳ δ' ἐφ' ἁρπαγαῖσιν—ἔχειν**] Lines 17—19, 24 and 25 are entirely new; 20 and 21 are quoted by Plutarch *Sol.* 16; part of 22, 23 by Aristides, ii 536 Dind., *ὁ δὲ δὴ Σόλων καὶ βιβλίον ἐξεπίτηδες πεποίηκεν...εἰς αὐτὸν καὶ τὴν ἑαυτοῦ πολιτείαν, ἐν ᾧ ἄλλα τε δὴ λέγει καὶ ταῦτα· ἃ μὲν—ἔρδον.* Two other fragments in the same metre are assigned by Bergk to the same poem. The first of these is described in Plut. *Sol.* 14 as addressed *πρὸς Φῶκον*; the second is quoted by Plutarch immediately afterwards, beginning with *οὐκ ἔφυ Σόλων βαθύφρων*.

l. 19. **καί με κωτίλλοντα—νόον**] 'and that I, though smoothly glozing, would reveal my rude intent.' *ἐκφανεῖν* cannot be translated as though it were synonymous with *κρύψαι*. For **κωτίλλοντα λείως**, cf. Theognis 852, *ὃς τὸν ἑταῖρον μαλθακὰ κωτίλλων ἐξαπατᾶν ἐθέλει*.

26 [πάλιν] δὲ καὶ περὶ τῆς ἀπ[οκ]οπῆς τῶν χ[ρε]ῶν καὶ τῶν δουλευόν- 4
των μὲν πρότερον ἐλευθερωθέντων δὲ διὰ τὴν σεισάχθει[αν]·

ἐγὼ δὲ τῶν μὲν οὕνεκα ξυνήγαγον

26 ἀποκοπῆς τῶν χρεῶν Wessely (K[3], B): ἀπο[ρί]ας τῆς τῶν [πενήτ]ων K[1] (H-L); ἀπ[ορίας] τῆς τῶν [ὑπόχρε]ων K-W[2]. **26—52** δουλευόντων—ἐχηρώθη πόλις in fragmenti Berolinensis pagina prima continentur. **27** <τότε> διὰ H-L. **28** οὕνεκα, in poetis Atticis a criticis suspectum, saeculi quinti et sexti in titulis legitur, CIA iv *b* 491, 8 ἀρετῆς οὕνεκα καὶ φιλίας (saec. v), CIA i 487, 1 οὕνεκα πιστὸς ἔφυς (saec. vi—v). Meisterhans, p. 177[2]. εἵνεκ' K-W. εἵνεκα ξυνήγαγον Platt, coll. *Pol.* 1285 *b* 7 διὰ τὸ συναγαγεῖν (τὸ πλῆθος) ἐγίγνοντο βασιλεῖς ἑκόντων. οὕνεκα ξ.νήγαγον H-L. Equidem ΟΥΝΕΚΑΞΥΝΗΓΑΓΟΝ in papyro cerni posse puto, recte tamen animadvertit K supra litteram Ξ scriptum esse O, et litteras ΓΑΓ litteris ΛΑΤ aut CΑΤ prorsus esse similes. οὕνεκ' ἀξονήλατον K[1]; εἵνεκ' ἀξονήλατον K-W[1], ἀξονηλατῶν K-W[2]. οὕνεκα ξενήλατον Jackson et Tyrrell (cf. Plut. *Sol.* 13 ἐπὶ τὴν ξένην πιπρασκόμενοι, *ib.* 15 ἀνήγαγεν ἀπὸ ξένης, et inf. vv. 36—39). οὕνεκ' ἐξανήγαγον van Leeuwen. Aut ζυγήλατον (quod nusquam adhuc inventum est) aut ζυγηφόρον (quod a papyri scriptura nimis remotum est) Marindin. τῶν μὲν οὕνεκ' ἀξονηλάτουν δῆμον, τί τούτων πρὶν τυχεῖν ἐπαυσάμην; quondam Blass, coll. ἁρματηλατεῖν (Hdt. Xen.), ζευγηλατεῖν (Xen.), πόλιν ναυκληρεῖν (Aesch. *S. C. T.* 652, Soph. *Ant.* 994); eadem fere Crusius (*Philol.* L p. 177). τῶν μὲν οὕνεκα ξυνήγαγον δῆμον, τί τούτων πρὶν τυχεῖν ἐπαυσάμην; R C Jebb, cuius interpretationem unice veram esse patet. ξυνήγαγον etiam Blassio postea placuit.

---

§ 4. l. 28. The doubtful reading ἀξονήλατον is found in Aesch. *Suppl.* 181, σύριγγες...ἀξονήλατοι, 'whirling on the axle' (L and S); 'the sockets (in the naves) *pressed* by the axle, or through which the axle is driven' (Tucker). It seems impossible to interpret it (with Mr Kenyon) as a metaphor indicating 'a torture such as that of Ixion.' Much less can we understand it as an allusion to the ἄξονες of Solon.—ἀξονηλάτουν, impf. of ἀξονηλατεῖν, has been suggested; this is supported by O. Crusius (*Philologus* l, 177) as a metaphor from the race-course which he considers characteristic of Solon, comparing l. 47 κέντρον...λαβών, and fragm. 23 Bergk, which merely mentions μώνυχες ἵπποι. ξενήλατον, 'driven from the country as strangers,' though not found elsewhere, is implied in ξενηλατεῖν, and might be defended by Plut. *Sol.* 13, ἐπὶ τὴν ξένην πιπρασκόμενοι, and *ib.* 15 ἀνήγαγον ἀπὸ ξένης followed by a quotation of ll. 38—41, γλῶσσαν—ἔχοντας.

On the whole, I prefer accepting in the first line ξυνήγαγον. For the second I gladly adopt a suggestion due to Professor Jebb, who makes the sentence interrogative. He adds that the rhetorical emphasis obtained by placing the relative clause (τῶν μὲν) before the antecedent (τούτων) seems to confirm the view that this is a question. 'But, as to the ends for which I formed the popular party, or (less probably) gathered the people into one (by healing the divisions which separated the various orders in the state), why did I desist before I had attained those ends?' (With ἐπαυσάμην, cf. l. 63 in fragment at the end of this chapter: 'anyone else would *not* have restrained the people' οὐδ' ἐπαύσατο κτλ.) Solon is here quoting the question addressed to him by some of his opponents who held that he had not carried his reforms far enough. He is in fact putting in his own words the complaint which elsewhere he gives in the words of the malcontents, περιβαλὼν δ' ἄγραν ἀγασθεὶς οὐκ ἐπέσπασεν μέγα | δίκτυον (frag. 33 Bergk[4], l. 3). In the triumphant συμμαρτυροίη κτλ., he seems to say, 'Earth is the best witness whether I had cause enough τοῦ τὸν δῆμον συναγαγεῖν, *without* going on to do those things which I am blamed for not doing.' Prof. Jebb further points out that it is probable that the first two lines formed a separate sentence, as Aristides does not quote them, and it is unlikely that he would have begun his quotation with the third line, συμμαρτυροίη, κτλ., if it had been in the middle of a sentence. I may add that the sense thus gained is confirmed by a subsequent line, l. 44, in which Solon protests that he has performed all that he has promised: διῆλθον ὡς ὑπεσχόμην. Cf. l. 22, ἃ μὲν γὰρ εἶπα σὺν θεοῖσιν ἤνυσα.

δῆμον, τί τούτων πρὶν τυχεῖν ἐπαυσάμην;
συμμαρτυρ[οί]η ταῦτ' ἂν ἐν δίκῃ χρόνου
μήτηρ μεγίστη δαιμόνω[ν Ὀλυ]μπίων
ἄριστα, Γῆ μέλαινα, τῆς ἐγώ ποτε
[ὅ]ρους ἀνεῖλον πολλαχῇ πεπηγότα[ς],

29 δῆμον τι τούτων πρὶν τυχῶν ἐπαυσάμην, K[1]. δῆμόν τι τούτων πρὶν τυχ[εῖ]ν ἐπαυσάμην, K-W, alii; τοιούτων Sidgwick, τοιούτων πρὶν τυχὼν van Leeuwen. τί τούτων πρὶν τυχεῖν ἐπαυσάμην; recte Blass et Jebb. **30** χρόνου etiam Aristides habet: Κρόνου μήτηρ Clavigerus apud Bergk[2], qui ibidem ipse conicit ἐν Δίκης θρόνῳ. Κρόνου μήτηρ μεγίστη δαιμόνων τ' Ὀλυμπίων Poste. **33** πολλαχῇ: an πολλ' ἔτη? J B Mayor.

TESTIMONIA. **30—54** Aristid. ii 536—8. **33, 34** Plut. *Sol.* 15.

---

ll. 30—54. **συμμαρτυροίη — λύκος**] Quoted by Aristides, ii 536—8, in two portions, (*a*) ll. 30—49 ending *οὐκ ἂν κατέσχε δῆμον*, and (*b*) *εἰ γὰρ ἤθελον* to the end. (*b*) is introduced with the words: *εἶτα τί φησὶν ὁ Σόλων;*

l. 30. **ἐν δίκῃ χρόνου**] possibly (1) 'before the tribunal of time,' a bold expression, but less bold than that in Eur. *Bacch.* 889, *δαρὸν χρόνου πόδα*. Or, less probably, (2) 'in the justice of time,' *i.e.* 'justice which time eventually brings.' *συμμαρτυρεῖν* is combined with *χρόνος* in Xen. *Hell.* iii 3 § 2, *συνεμαρτύρησε δὲ ταῦτ' αὐτῷ καὶ ὁ ἀληθέστατος λεγόμενος χρόνος εἶναι*. Solon appeals to Earth to bear witness before the tribunal of Time that he had attained the ends he had in view.

l. 31. **μήτηρ—Γῆ**] Even the Attic land set free from its encumbrances is boldly personified as Mother Earth. Cf. Plato, *Leg.* 740 A, *δεῖ τὸν λαχόντα τὴν λῆξιν ταύτην νομίζειν μὲν κοινὴν αὐτὴν τῆς πόλεως ξυμπάσης, πατρίδος δὲ οὔσης τῆς χώρας θεραπεύειν αὐτὴν δεῖ μειζόνως ἢ μητέρα παῖδας, τῷ καὶ δέσποιναν θεὸν αὐτὴν οὖσαν θνητῶν ὄντων γεγονέναι*, and 741, *τῆς γῆς ἱερᾶς οὔσης τῶν πάντων θεῶν*.

ll. 33, 34. **ὅρους—ἐλευθέρα**] These lines, and part of ll. 38—41, are quoted in Plut. *Sol.* 15, *σεμνύνεται γὰρ Σόλων ἐν τούτοις, ὅτι τῆς τε προϋποκειμένης γῆς*

ὅρους ἀνεῖλε—νῦν ἐλευθέρα·

καὶ τῶν ἀγωγίμων πρὸς ἀργύριον γεγονότων πολιτῶν τοὺς μὲν ἀνήγαγεν ἀπὸ ξένης

γλῶσσαν οὐκέτ' Ἀττικὴν—ἔχοντας.

l. 33. **ὅρους**] Sir George Cox, *Hist. of Greece*, i 201, has suggested that this means *boundaries*, and similarly in the *Edinburgh Review*, 1891, p. 493, 'These *boundary stones* were the marks of the religious ownership of the Eupatrids.' This view is refuted in Mr Evelyn Abbott's *History of Greece*, i 407.

As regards the meaning of *ὅρος* and cognate words in early Greek literature, the ambiguity in *Il.* xii 421, *ἀμφ' οὔροισι δύ' ἀνέρε δηριάασθον*, is made clear by other passages, which prove that the *οὖρα* are 'stones (xxii 405) marking off the allotments, and are easily moveable by a fraudulent neighbour (xxi 489),' Leaf *ad loc.* In Hdt. i 93 *οὖροι* is used of stones bearing inscriptions. In the present passage we have the earliest instance of *ὅροι* in the sense of 'mortgage pillars,' '*stone-slabs* or *tablets set up on mortgaged property*, to serve as a bond or register of the debt' (L and S). This use is common in the time of Demosthenes, *e.g.* Or. 31 § 1, *τίθησιν ὅρους ἐπὶ μὲν τὴν οἰκίαν δισχιλίων, ἐπὶ δὲ τὸ χωρίον ταλάντου*, 42 § 5, *οὐδεὶς ὅρος ἔπεστιν ἐπὶ τῇ ἐσχατιᾷ*, and § 28, *ἐκέλευον δεῖξαι ὅρον εἴπου ἔπεστι*, 49 § 13, *τοὺς ὅρους ἀνέσπακε*, 'has (illicitly) removed the tablets,' and § 11, *ἡ οὐσία ὑπόχρεως ἦν ἅπασα καὶ ὅροι αὐτῆς ἕστασαν*, *ib.* § 61, *ὅσοις αὐτοῦ ἡ οὐσία ἀφωρισμένη ἦν*, 25 § 69, *οἱ τεθέντες ὅροι ἑστηκότες*, 41 § 6, *ὅρους ἐπιστῆσαι χιλίων δραχμῶν ἐμοὶ τῆς προικὸς ἐπὶ τὴν οἰκίαν*. Isaeus 6 § 36, *ὅπως . . ὅροι τεθεῖεν*. In Theophrastus (*Char.* 10 = 24 Jebb) it is characteristic of the *μικρολόγος* to inspect the *ὅροι* day by day. Harpocr. *s. v.* *ὅρος· οὕτως ἐκάλουν οἱ Ἀττικοὶ τὰ ἐπόντα ταῖς ὑποκειμέναις οἰκίαις καὶ χωρίοις γράμματα, δηλοῦντα ὅτι ὑπόκεινται δανειστῇ*.

Originally the *ὅρος* was doubtless a boundary-stone or land-mark. In the absence of other means of registration, it became customary to inscribe on these boundary-stones a notice of the charges on the property. Solon, by his *σεισάχθεια*, released the poorer classes from the burden of their debts, and set the land, which was security for these debts, free from encumbrances. No sooner was the debt itself abolished, than the stones in-

[πρόσθ]εν δὲ δουλεύουσα, νῦν ἐλευθέρα.
πολλοὺς δ' Ἀθήνας, πατρίδ' εἰς θεόκτιτ[ον],
[ἀνή]γαγον πραθέντας, ἄλλον ἐκδίκως,
ἄλλον δικαίως, τοὺς δ' ἀναγκαίης ὕπο
χρειοῦς φυγόντας, γλῶσσαν οὐκέτ' Ἀττικὴν
ἱέντας, ὡς ἂν πολλαχῇ πλαν[ωμένους],
τοὺς δ' ἐνθάδ' αὐτοῦ δ[ουλί]ην ἀεικέα
[ἔ]χοντας, ἤθη δεσποτῶν τρομευμέν[ους],

34 δὲ: γε J B Mayor (H-L). νῦν δ' H-L. **35** ΘΕΟΚΤΙϹΤΟΝ: idem habent Aristidis codices prope omnes. **38** χρησμὸν λέγοντας (quod intelligi nequit) Aristides. **41** ἤδη Aristides, correxit Bergk.

---

scribed with the record of the security were removed, and the land set free. (Cf. Blass in *Hermes*, xv 286 ff.)

Many exx. of these inscribed ὅροι have been found. Those of Attica are published in CIA ii, the ordinary boundary-stones forming nos. 1062—1102 and the *termini fundorum pigneratorum* nos. 1103—1153. A specimen is figured in Duruy's *Histoire des Grecs*, i 385; and all the extant Greek inscriptions of this kind are collected and classified in the *Inscriptions Juridiques Grecques* by MM. Dareste, Haussoullier and Th. Reinach, 1891, i p. 107—142. Classes A and B are securities (ἀποτιμήματα) for money belonging either to minors (1—9) or married women (10—24). Class C (25—59), records of sale with right of redemption, 'ostensibly a purchase, but really a loan of money secured by the conveyance of property.' 'The debtor continues to occupy it, paying interest on the purchase-money and possessing the power of redemption within a certain time' (Hager in Smith's *Dict. Ant. s. v.* HORI). The following are some of the more interesting dated examples: A 5 (CIA ii 1138) ἐπὶ Νικοκλέους ἄρχοντος (B.C. 302/1)· ὅρος χωρίων καὶ οἰκίας καὶ τοῦ ὕδατος τοῦ προσόντος τοῖς χωρίοις κλήρων δυεῖν ἀποτετιμημένων παισὶν ὀρφανοῖς τοῖς Χαρίου ἰσοτελοῦς Χαιρίππῳ καὶ Χαρίᾳ. B 17 (CIA ii 1137) ἐπὶ Εὐξενίππου ἄρχοντος (B.C. 305/4)· ὅρος χωρίων καὶ οἰκιῶν ἀποτιμημάτων προικὸς Ξεναρίστει Πυθοδώρου Γαργηττίου θυγατρί, τὸ κατὰ τὸ ἥμισυ καὶ τὸ ἐκ τούτου γιγνόμενον αἰτεῖ εἰς Λεώστρατον ἄρχοντα XXΓHH... C 49 (CIA ii 1133) ἐπὶ Πραξιβούλου ἄρχοντος (B.C. 315/4)· ὅρος οἰκίας πεπραμένης ἐπὶ λύσει. D 61 (CIA ii 1134) ἐπὶ Θεοφράστου ἄρχοντος (B.C. 313/2)· ὅρος χωρίου τιμῆς ἐνοφειλομένης Φανοστράτῳ Παιανεῖ XX = 2000 dr.

All these inscriptions belong to the latter part of the fourth century. It cannot be supposed, however, that lending money on mortgage was unknown in the previous century. Under the Second Athenian Confederation (CIA ii 17), the Athenians were forbidden to purchase lands or houses in the territory of their allies or to lend money on mortgage. This implies that, under the First Confederation, lending money on these terms was not forbidden. But it would appear that for some centuries the Athenians, while still employing boundary-stones for their public or sacred domains, gave up using them as records of mortgages. It has been suggested that 'in the early times, which followed the reforms of Solon, no one had recourse to recording his claims on the detested tablets of stone whose removal from the land had been celebrated with such enthusiasm by the legislator himself' (*Inscr. Juridiques*, i 122). —For a similar reform among the Jews in the latter part of the fifth century, see *Nehemiah* v, 1—13.

πεπηγότας] Lycurg. *Leocr.* § 73, ὅρους τοῖς βαρβάροις πήξαντες. Thuc. iv 92, 4, τοῖς μὲν ἄλλοις οἱ πλησιόχωροι περὶ γῆς ὅρων τὰς μάχας ποιοῦνται, ἡμῖν δὲ ἐς πᾶσαν, ἢν νικηθῶμεν, εἷς ὅρος οὐκ ἀντίλεκτος παγήσεται.

l. 36. **πραθέντας**] Solon ap. Dem. *F. L.* p. 421, τῶν δὲ πενιχρῶν | ἱκνοῦνται πολλοὶ γαῖαν ἐς ἀλλοδαπὴν | πραθέντες κτλ. Cf. Grote, c. 11, ii 310 n.

l. 37. **ἀναγκαίης ὕπο χρειοῦς**] Cf. *Il.* viii 57, χρειοῖ ἀναγκαίῃ.

l. 38—41. **γλῶσσαν—ἔχοντας**] quoted by Plut. *Sol.* 15.

l. 40. **δουλίην**] Ionic forms are characteristic of Solon's verses: cf. l. 41, τρομευμένους, and in Plut. *Sol.* 14, αἰδεῦμαι and δοκέω.

l. 41. **ἤθη—τρομευμένους**] 'trembling at each mood of their masters.'

[ἐλ]ευθέρους ἔθηκα. ταῦτα μὲν κράτει
νόμου, βίαν τε καὶ δίκην συναρμόσας,
[ἔρ]εξα, καὶ διῆλθον ὡς ὑπεσχόμην.
θεσμοὺς δ' ὁμοίως τῷ κακῷ τε κἀγαθῷ,
εὐθεῖαν εἰς ἕκαστον ἁρμόσας δίκην,
ἔγραψα. κέντρον δ' ἄλλος ὡς ἐγὼ λαβών,
[κακ]οφραδής τε καὶ φιλοκτήμων ἀνήρ,
οὐκ ἂν κατέσχε δῆμον· εἰ γὰρ ἤ[θε]λον
ἃ τοῖς ἐναντίο[ισι]ν ἥνδανεν τότε,
αὖθις δ' ἃ τοῖσιν οὔτεροι φρασαίατο,
πολλῶν ἂν ἀνδρῶν ἥδ' ἐχηρώθη πόλις.
τῶν οὕνεκ' ἀλκὴν πάντοθεν ποιεύμενος

42 ΚΡΑΤΕΕΙ: *κράτει* (*κράτη* cod. Θ, Bergk) Aristides: *κρ.τη* Papyrus Berol. **43** ΝΟΜΟΥ (K, H-L): *ὁμοῦ* Aristides, Plut., Papyrus Berol. (K-W, B). **44** *ἔρεξα* Aristides. *διῆλθον*: *διήνυσ'*? Herwerden. **45** ΤΕ, ut videtur, correctum in *θ'* (K): *δ'* Aristides (Wyse, K-W, H-L, B). *ὁμοίους* Bergk, Aristidis codices duos secutus. **49** ΔΗΜΟΝ: idem habent Aristides et Plut. *Sol.* 16: *θυμὸν* hic et infra v. 63 legendum suspicantur H-L; idem olim Cantero et Reiskio placuerat. **50** *ἃ τοῖς*: ΑΥΤΟΙΣ. *τότε*: *ποεῖν* Sidgwick (H-L). **51** *ἃ τοῖσιν οὔτεροι φρασαίατο* Platt, K-W, K³, B. ΑΥΤΟΙΣΙΝΟΥΤΕΡΟΙ(vel ΑΙ)ΦΡΑΣΑΙΑΤΟ. *ἃ τοῖσιν ἀτέροις δρᾶσαι, διὰ* (*κακὰ* Valckenaer, *βίᾳ* Schaefer, *δίχα* O Schneider et Ahrens, *δρᾶσαι δίχα* Bergk) Aristides. *ἃ τοῖσι θἀτέρᾳ δρᾶσαι δίχα* Ellis. *ἃ τοῖσιν οὑτέρᾳ* (=*οἱ ἑτέρᾳ*) *φρασαίατο* quondam Blass. *ἃ χωρὶς ἅτεροι φρασαίατο* Sidgwick (H-L). *ἃ τοῖσδ' ἂν ἅτεροι φρασαίατο* Tyrrell. **52** *ἐχειρώθη* Aristides, correxit Valckenaer. **53** ΟΥΝΕΚ (K, H-L): *εἵνεκ'* K-W (cf. v. 28). *ἀλκήν*: *ἀρχὴν* Arist., *ὀργὴν* Bergk. ΠΟΙΟΥΜΕΝΟΣ (K¹): *ποιεύμενος* Platt, K-W, H-L, K³; *κυκεύμενος* Arist.

TESTIMONIA. **38—41, 43** Plut. *Sol.* 15.

---

l. 45. **θεσμοὺς**] In Plut. *Sol.* 19 end, *θεσμὸς ἐφάνη ὅδε* is quoted from one of Solon's laws. Cf. note on c. 4 § 1.

l. 47. **κέντρον**] the 'goad' is here the symbol of strong control, as in Soph. *Frag.* 606 (of sovereignty), *λαβὼν δὲ χερσὶ κέντρα κηδεύει πόλιν*.

l. 49. **οὐκ ἂν κατέσχε δῆμον**] With these words the first quotation in Aristides ends. Plutarch, however (*Sol.* 16), cites two lines with the following introduction: *καίτοι φησίν, ὡς, εἴ τις ἄλλος ἔσχε τὴν αὐτὴν δύναμιν,*

οὔτ' ἂν κατέσχε δῆμον οὔτ' ἐπαύσατο
πρὶν ἂν ταράξας πῖαρ ἐξέλῃ γάλα.

Hence in Bergk's ed. of frag. 36 these two lines are added to the passage quoted by Aristides; and the passage *εἰ γὰρ ἤθελον—λύκος*, quoted subsequently by Aristides, is treated as a separate fragment (37). But the text makes it clear that this last passage followed immediately after his first quotation, while the couplet in Plutarch comes from a subsequent portion of the same poem quoted near the end of this chapter.

l. 51. **τοῖσιν οὔτεροι φρασαίατο**] 'what their foes devised within their hearts' (K.). This does not explain the construction; *τοῖσι* cannot go with *οὔτεροι*, for 'their foes' would be *τῶν οὔτεροι*, 'those different from these.' *τοῖσι* must be dative after *φρασαίατο*. '*φράζεσθαι* c. dat. and inf. = to tell one to do so and so,' but the inf. is sometimes omitted, as in Hom. *Od.* x 549, *ἀλλ' ἴομεν· δὴ γάρ μοι ἐπέφραδε πότνια Κίρκη*. The sense seems to be 'whatever at any time the other party would devise for their opponents,' or perhaps, 'urge their opponents (*τοῖσι* = *ἐναντίοισι*) to do.' The *ἐναντίοι* are the party opposed to Solon's remedial measures. The *οὔτεροι* are the popular party. With *φρασαίατο* cf. *ποιοίατο* at end of next quotation.

l. 52. **ἀνδρῶν—ἐχηρώθη**] Hdt. vi 83, *Ἄργος ἀνδρῶν ἐχηρώθη*.

l. 53. **ποιεύμενος**] An Ionism; cf. note

ὡς ἐν κυσὶν πολλαῖσιν ἐστράφην λύκος.
καὶ πάλιν ὀνειδίζων πρὸς τὰς ὕστερον αὐτ[ῶν] μεμψιμοιρίας ἀμφοτέρων·
δήμῳ μὲν εἰ χρὴ διαφάδην ὀνειδίσαι,
ἃ νῦν ἔχουσιν οὔποτ' ὀφθαλμοῖσιν ἂν
εὕδοντες εἶδον·
ὅσοι δὲ μείζους καὶ βίαν ἀμείνονες
αἰνοῖεν ἄν με καὶ φίλον ποιοίατο.
εἰ γάρ τις ἄλλος, φησί, ταύτης τῆς τιμῆς ἔτυχεν,
οὐκ ἂν κατέσχε δῆμον οὐδ' ἐπαύσατο,
πρὶν ἀνταράξας πῖαρ ἐξεῖλεν γάλα. ||
ἐγὼ δὲ τούτων ὥσπερ ἐν μεταιχμίῳ [Col. 5.]
ὅρος κατέστην.

54 ΕΤΡΑΦΗΝ vel ΕΓΡΑΦΗΝ: *ἐστράφην* Arist. (K, K-W, H-L, B). **55** *αὐτῶν* Blass (K-W, K³): *αὖθις* H-L. **57** ΔΙΑΦΡΑΔΗΝ: *διαφάδην* Kontos et K-W (K³, B): *μ' ἀμφάδην* Platt (H-L). **64** ΠΡΙΝΑΝΤΑΡΑΞΑΣΠΥΑΡΕΞΕΙΛΕΝ: *πρὶν ἂν ταράξας πῖαρ ἐξέλῃ γάλα* Plut. (et K-W¹), unde Adam ad Plat. *Crit.* 44 D coniecerat *πρὶν ἀνταράξας—ἐξεῖλεν*, etiam Gildersleeve *ἀνταράξας* legendum esse olim viderat; eadem postea protulerunt Sidgwick, Blass, H-L (K³). *πρὶν ἢ ταράξας πῖαρ ἐξεῖλεν γάλα* K-W².

TESTIMONIA. **63, 64** Plut. *Sol.* 16. **65—66** Cf. Aristid. infra exscriptum.

on l. 40, *δουλίην*. In Soph. *O. C.* 459, *ἀλκὴν ποιεῖσθαι* means 'to succour.'

l. 54. **ὡς ἐν κυσὶν—ἐστράφην λύκος**] A reminiscence of Homer, *Il.* 12, 42, *ἔν τε κύνεσσι...κάπριος ἠὲ λέων στρέφεται.* Cf. Solon 15, 23, *ταῦτα μὲν ἐν δήμῳ στρέφεται κακά.*

§ 5. **διαφάδην**] *διαφράδην* is unknown. *διαφραδέως* means 'distinctly' (of sound) in Hippocrates 408. *διαφάδην*, 'openly,' is here accepted. This is found in Pollux ii 129, *ἀρρήδην, διαρρήδην, διαφάδην.*

l. 59. **εὕδοντες**] 'even in their dreams.' Dem. *F. L.* 275, *ἃ μηδ' ὄναρ ἤλπισαν πώποτε.*

l. 60. **ὅσοι**] *sc. εἰσί.* The last two lines refer to the rich, the first three to the poor. The whole of this passage (57—61) is new.

l. 62. **εἰ γάρ τις** *κτλ.*] Plut. *Sol.* 16, quoted in note on l. 49.

l. 64. **πρὶν—γάλα**] *πρὶν* c. subj. aor. (or *πρὶν ἂν* in Attic Gk) is properly only used after negative clauses, to denote a point in *future* time before which something else must happen; or (as Goodwin puts it, *Moods and Tenses*, § 638), 'when a clause with *πρίν*, *until*, refers to the future, and depends on a *negative* clause of future time (*not* containing an optative), *πρίν* takes the subjunctive.' Such a construction is out of place here, where we require *πρὶν* c. indic. With the text, as emended, cf. Plat. *Meno* 86 D, *οὐκ ἂν ἐπεσκεψάμεθα πρότερον εἴτε διδακτὸν εἴτε οὐ διδακτὸν ἡ ἀρετή, πρὶν ὅ τι ἔστι πρῶτον ἐζητήσαμεν* (*ib.* 84 C and *Theaet.* 165 D: Goodwin, § 637).

ἀνταράξας] In Ionic (as well as Doric poetry) *ἀν-* and *ἀμ-* stand for *ἀνα-*. *Od.* i 440, *ἀγκρεμάσασα*, and elsewhere *ἀνστήσων, ἀνστήτην, ἀνστήμεναι*; *Il.* xxiv 756, *ἀνστήσεις*; *Od.* v 320, *ἀνσχεθέειν*; *ἀνσχήσεσθαι, ἄνσχεο, ἀνσχετός.*

πῖαρ] (*πίων*) lit. 'fat,' an Epic and Ionic word; *Il.* xi 550, xvii 659, *βοῶν ἐκ πῖαρ ἑλέσθαι*, of *cream* in Solon; also used metaphorically of 'the cream' of a thing, the choicest and best (L and S). Hesychius, *πῖαρ: τὸ κράτιστον.* This suits the context better than *πῦαρ*, which is 'the first milk after calving,' 'beestings,' or the rennet made from it. The sense requires not a particular kind of milk, such as 'beestings'; but the best part of the milk, the 'cream.' The constr. is either *πρὶν ἀνταράξας γάλα ἐξεῖλεν πῖαρ*, or else *γάλα* is acc. after the complex verb *πῖαρ ἐξεῖλεν.*

l. 65. **ἐγὼ—κατέστην**] 'I set myself as

13. τὴν μὲν οὖν ἀποδημίαν ἐποιήσατο διὰ ταύτας τὰς αἰτίας. Σόλωνος δ' ἀποδημήσαντος, ἔτι τῆς πόλεως τεταραγμένης, ἐπὶ μὲν ἔτη τέτταρα διῆγον [ἐ]ν ἡσυχίᾳ· τῷ δὲ πέμπτῳ μετὰ τὴν Σόλωνος

---

a landmark between two armed hosts.' Hdt. viii 140, 2 (of debateable land), *δειμαίνω ὑπὲρ ὑμέων ἐν τρίβῳ τε μάλιστα οἰκημένων τῶν συμμάχων πάντων αἰεί τε φθειρομένων μούνων, ἐξαίρετον μεταίχμιόν τε τὴν γῆν ἐκτημένων.* *ὅρος*, 'landmark,' or 'wall,' seems a harsh metaphor, except perhaps in one who, like Solon, had the *ὅροι*, the boundaries as well as the mortgage-tablets, of Attica much in his mind. The passage is paraphrased in Aristides, ii 360 (of Solon), *ἔστη δ' ἐν μεθορίῳ πάντων ἀνδρειότατα καὶ δικαιότατα, ὥσπερ τινὰς ὡς ἀληθῶς ἐκ γεωμετρίας περιγραπτοὺς φυλάττων ὅρους.*

XIII § 1. **ἀποδημίαν ἐποιήσατο**] c. 11 § 1.

Σόλωνος—τεταραγμένης *κτλ.*] 'When S. had gone abroad, although the state was still disturbed by divisions, yet for four years they lived in peace, but in the fifth year' &c. *ἀποδημεῖν* has two meanings (1) to be abroad, and (2) to go abroad. (1) is found in *Pol.* 1303 *b* 23, and *Poet.* 17, 1455 *b* 17, *ἀποδημοῦντος*: (2) in the present passage. The fact that *τεταραγμένης* precedes, accounts for the article in *τὴν στάσιν.*

τῷ δὲ πέμπτῳ μετὰ τὴν Σόλωνος ἀρχὴν] The archonship of Solon is usually placed in B.C. 594/3 = *Ol.* 46, 3. This is the date given by Diog. Laert. i 62 on the authority of Sosicrates of Rhodes, the author of a work on the *History of Crete* and on the *Succession of Philosophers*, who flourished between 200 and 128 B.C. The archons about this time are given by Clinton as follows:

Ol.	B.C.	
46, 2	= 595	Philombrotus
3	= 594	Solon
4	= 593	Dropides
47, 1	= 592	Eucrates?
2	= 591	Simon
3	= 590	[Simon, in *Marmor Parium*]

Jerome places Solon in 592: and the Armenian version of Eusebius in 590. 592 is already occupied by Eucrates, and 590 (in the *Marmor Parium*, see § 2 n) possibly by Simon. The text of c. 14 § 1 appears to place Solon 31 years before the archonship of Comeas (B.C. 560), *i.e.* in 591. But if Solon is placed in 591, Philombrotus and Dropides must be placed in 592 and 590, which are already assigned to other archons. Again, if Comeas is (by another method of reckoning) assigned to 561, Solon falls in 592, the year assigned to Eucrates. Eucrates, however, may really belong to a later date. Sosicrates (*ap.* Diog. Laert. i 101) places him in Ol. 47 (592—589) and makes Anacharsis visit Solon during the archonship of Eucrates. But Solon left Athens for ten years when his own archonship was over, so that, if Sosicrates (our only authority for Eucrates) is right about the date of the visit of Anacharsis, Eucrates cannot be earlier than 583. On the year of Solon's archonship, cf. Clinton, *Fasti*, ii 298; Fischer's *Gr. Zeittafeln*, p. 114; and Busolt, i 524.

If Solon was archon in 594, and if 'in the fifth year' means four years after Solon, then the first year of anarchy falls in 590, and the second in 586. Then, if *διὰ τῶν αὐτῶν χρόνων* is retained in the sense, 'after the same interval of time,' *i.e.* four years later, the archonship of Damasias begins in 582. This is Mr Kenyon's view. In this calculation the first period of four years of peace must include either the year of Solon's archonship or the first year of anarchy; and the second period must include one of the years of anarchy.

On the other hand, if the first 'four years' extend from B.C. 593 to 590, then the first year of anarchy is 589; again, if *ἔτει πέμπτῳ* is taken as meaning 'five years afterwards,' the second year of anarchy is 584. Further, if *διὰ τῶν αὐτῶν χρόνων* is regarded as an interpolation, the beginning of the rule of Damasias follows at once in 583. This is the view of Bauer, and of Kaibel and Wilamowitz. But the first year of Damasias coincides with that in which the Pythian festival was transformed into an *ἀγὼν στεφανίτης*, and the festival was held in the third year of each Olympiad, whereas 583 is the second year. The opinion that it fell in the second year of the Olympiad, which has been inferred from Thuc. iv 117 and v 1, is refuted in Clinton's *Fasti*, ii p. 195 = 245[3].

Again, if the archonship of Solon is placed in 591, the years of anarchy may be put at intervals of four years in 587 and 583. Then, if *διὰ τῶν αὐτῶν χρόνων*

ἀρχὴν οὐ κατέστησαν ἄρχοντα διὰ τὴν στ[άσ]ιν, καὶ πάλιν ἔτει
πέμπτῳ < διὰ > τὴν αὐτὴν αἰτίαν ἀναρχίαν ἐποίησαν. μετὰ δὲ 2
ταῦτα διὰ τῶν αὐτῶν χρόνων Δ[αμ]α[σίας αἱρε]θεὶς ἄρχων ἔτη

XIII 4 ΟΥΚΑΤΕϹΤΗϹΑΝ (K-W, K^3): *οὐκ ἐπέστησαν* K^1 (H-L). **4** *ἄρχοντα*—**18** *διώκειν* continentur fragmenti Berolinensis in pagina secunda. **5** <*διὰ*> add. e papyro Berol. ΑΙΤΙΑΝΑΡΧΑΙΑΝ: *αἰτίαν ἀναρχίαν* Campbell, Jackson, Housman, Burnet, K-W, H-L, K^3. **6** *διὰ τῶν αὐτῶν χρόνων* secl. K-W; *διὰ τοῦ αὐτοῦ χρόνου*? Herwerden.

---

be omitted, we get 582 as the first year of Damasias. This is the view of T. Reinach and of Poland. It has the advantage of leaving the text in c. 14 § 1 untouched, and it gives a date for Damasias which is consistent with Pausanias x 7, 5, where the first Pythian *ἀγὼν στεφανίτης*, which coincided with the first year of Damasias, is placed in 582. If so, the archonship of Simon which, according to the Scholiasts on Pindar, was five years before Damasias, may provisionally be placed in 587, instead of 590, the year assigned to it by the Parian Marble; but 587 was on this view a year of anarchy; hence it is not improbable that Simon was really archon in 586.

All the above views agree in placing the beginning of the archonship of Damasias later than 586 B.C., in or about 582. The following is a conspectus of the views above mentioned.

	Mr Kenyon	Bauer and K-W.	Reinach and Poland
Solon, archon	594	594	591
First period of 4 years	594–1 / 593–0	593–590	591–588
First year of anarchy	590	589	587
Second period of 4 years	590–87 / 589–86	588–585	586–583
Second year of anarchy	586	584	583
Third period of 4 years	586–3 / 585–2	nil	nil
Damasias, archon	582	583	582

A space of 13 years, 594 to 582 inclusive, does not allow of three periods of four years, and four years besides. It only admits of three periods of three years (and four years over). But these can only be obtained by altering *τέτταρα* into *τρία* and *πέμπτῳ* twice into *τετάρτῳ*. This, however, would perhaps be going too far.

§ 2. **Δαμασίας**] On the discovery of the Berlin fragments, much controversy arose respecting the Damasias there mentioned. It was at first proposed to identify him with Damasias I, the archon of 639 B.C. This opinion was conclusively refuted by Diels (*Berlin Acad.* 1885, p. 12); and, now that we have the context of the fragment before us, it is obvious that Damasias II can alone be meant.

Hitherto the determination of the date of Damasias II has depended on a mutilated passage in the Parian Marble. (This important chronological document was bought in Smyrna by an agent of Thomas Howard, Earl of Arundel and Surrey, 1585—1646, and sent to Arundel House in 1627. It was first edited by Selden, 1628. In 1667, at the instance of John Evelyn, *Letters*, Aug. 4, 1667, *Diary*, Sept. 19, Oct. 8, 17, 25, it was presented by the Earl's grandson to the University of Oxford, and in 1676 it was edited once more by Prideaux. After being preserved for many years in the Ashmolean Museum, it was removed to the University Galleries in 1889. It has been edited by Boeckh, CIG ii 2374, and C. Müller, FHG i 535—590. The authority for the chronology recorded in this Marble is probably Phanias of Eresos, a pupil of Aristotle. The dates are reckoned by the number of years that had elapsed before the archonship of Diognetus, B.C. 264—3.)

δύο καὶ δύο μῆνας ἦρξεν, ἕως ἐξηλάθη βίᾳ τῆς ἀρχῆς. εἶτ' ἔδοξε[ν] αὐτοῖς διὰ τὸ στασιάζειν ἄρχοντας ἐλέσθαι δέκα, πέντε μὲν εὐπατριδῶν, τρεῖς δὲ ἀ[γρ]οίκων, δύο δὲ δημιουργῶν, καὶ οὗτοι

7 ΕΞΗΛΑϹΘΗ: correxerunt Richards, K-W, H-L (K[3]). <*ἐκ*>*τῆς ἀρχῆς* H-L. **9** *ἀποίκων* Berol.; litterae ρ partem inferiorem cerni posse putat K.

TESTIMONIA. **9** Hes. *ἀγροιῶται· ἄγροικοι* (locus infra exscriptus).

The passage, with which we are concerned, is restored as follows: ll. 53—54, [*ἀφ' οὗ Ἀμφικτύονες ἐνίκησαν ἑλ*]*όντες Κύρραν, καὶ ὁ ἀγὼν ὁ γυμνικὸς ἐτέθη χρηματίτης ἀπὸ τῶν λαφύρων, ἔτη* HH[H]ΔΔΠII (327), *ἄρχοντος Ἀθήνησι Σίμωνος. ἀφ' οὗ* [*ἐν Δελφοῖς στεφ*]*ανίτης ἀγὼν πάλιν ἐτέθη, ἔτη* HHHΔ..II, *ἄρχοντος Ἀθήνησι Δαμασίου τοῦ δευτέρου.* The interval between the year of Diognetus and that of Damasias is here denoted by the symbols HHHΔ..II (312). (*a*) Boeckh and C. Müller insert ΠI (6), thus making the number 318; (*b*) Chandler and Clinton, Δ (10), making it 322; while Dopp (the latest editor) proposes ΔI (11), making it 323. The corresponding dates B.C. are: (*a*) 582/1 or 581/0, according as we reckon exclusively or inclusively; or (*b*) 586/5, according as we reckon inclusively with 323 or exclusively with 322. But the archonship of Damasias coincides with a Pythian festival; this excludes 581 and leaves us the choice between 586 and 582.

It has been urged in favour of 586/5 that Diog. Laert. I i 22 describes Thales and the other Wise Men of Greece as flourishing in the archonship of Damasias; and that 586/5 would be an appropriate year to mark their epoch, because the eclipse predicted by Thales took place on May 28, 585 B.C. (Cf. Busolt, i 493.)

On the other hand, 582/1 is supported by Pausanias (x 7, 4—5), who implies that the first *ἀγὼν στεφανίτης* was in 582/1, and the last *ἀγὼν χρηματίτης* in 586/5.

It may here be suggested, that probably the first year of Damasias coincided with the first celebration of the Pythian games after their transformation into an *ἀγὼν στεφανίτης*, *i.e.* with 582. Subsequently, a confusion may have arisen between the year of that celebration and the actual year in which the change was made (586). The archonship of Damasias was thus put four years too early. If the archonship of Simon coincided with the last *ἀγὼν χρηματίτης* and if that *ἀγὼν* was four years earlier than the change in the Pythian games (586), it follows that the archonship of Simon must be put in 590. Simon is placed in that year in the Parian Marble; and the evidence of the text, which gives at least 10 years between the year of Solon and that of Damasias, points to 582 as the year of Damasias.

If Damasias was archon in 582, Solon would by that date have returned to Athens after his absence of ten years (593—584 inclusive). This may be held to favour the conjecture of Diels (*Berl. Acad.* 1885, p. 13 f.) that Solon refers to the usurpation of Damasias in fragm. 32 and 33, quoted in Plut. *Sol.* 14, *εἰ δὲ γῆς ἐφεισάμην κτλ.*, and *οὐκ ἔφυ Σόλων βαθύφρων.* The trochaic passage quoted above in c. 12 has been ascribed to the same poem, *πρὸς Φῶκον.*

ἐξηλάθη] The form *ἐξηλάσθη* is given in the papyrus and in the restoration of the Berlin fragment by Blass *ἐξηλά*[*σ*]*θη*. For *ἠλάσθην* Veitch, *s.v. ἐλαύνω*, quotes Diod. Sic. 20, 51, *συν-* Plut. *Caes.* 17. Gaisford, however, edits *ἀπ-* and *ἐξηλάσθην* in Hdt. iii 54, vii 6 &c [Hdt. vii 6 *ἐξηλάσθη ὑπὸ Ἱππάρχου...ἐξ Ἀθηνέων. ἐξηλάσθη* cod. Florentinus: *ἐξηλάθη al.* iii 51 and i 173, *ἐξελασθείς*, in the latter passage the *cod. Parisinus* has *ἐξελαθείς*].

ἄρχοντας—δέκα] Owing to a lacuna in the Berlin fragment, which only mentions the three archons elected by the second class and the two by the third, it was supposed that the first class elected four, making nine archons in all. It now appears that in this particular year the number was ten. This election was a reactionary measure. It implied an abandonment of the classification by assessment which was the cardinal point of Solon's constitution.

ἀγροίκων] The Berlin fragment has *ἀποίκων*. There is a similar confusion in l. 2 of the poems of Herondas, where ΑΠΟΙΚΙΗϹ was first written and then corrected into ΑΓΡΟΙΚΙΗϹ. The usual name for this class is *γεωμόροι* (Plut. *Thes.* 25; Bekker's *Anecd. Gr.* 257, 7; Etym. Mag. p. 395, 50, &c), or *γεωργοί*

τὸν μετὰ Δαμασίαν [ἦ]ρξα[ν ἐ]νιαυτόν. ᾧ καὶ δῆλον ὅτι μεγίστην
εἶχεν δύναμιν ὁ ἄρχων· φαίνονται γὰρ ἀεὶ στ[α]σιάζοντες περὶ
ταύτης τῆς ἀρχῆς. ὅλως δὲ διετέλουν νοσοῦντες τὰ πρὸς ἑαυτούς, 3
οἱ μὲν ἀρχὴν καὶ πρόφασιν ἔχοντες τὴν τῶν χρεῶν ἀποκοπήν,
συνεβεβήκει γὰρ αὐτοῖς γεγονέναι πένησιν, οἱ δὲ τῇ πολιτείᾳ
δυσχεραίνοντες διὰ τὸ μεγάλην γεγονέναι μεταβολήν, ἔνιοι δὲ
δ[ιὰ τὴν] πρὸς ἀλλήλους φιλονικίαν. ἦσαν [δ'] αἱ στάσεις τρεῖς, 4
μία μὲν τῶν παραλίων, ὧν προειστήκει Μεγακλῆς ὁ Ἀλκμέωνος,
ο[ἵ]περ ἐδόκουν μάλιστα διώκειν τὴν μέσην πολιτείαν· ἄλλη δὲ
τῶν πεδια[κῶν], οἳ τὴν ὀλιγαρχίαν ἐζήτουν, ἡγεῖτο δ' αὐτῶν Λυκοῦργος· τρίτη δ' ἡ τῶν διακρίων, ἐφ' ᾗ τεταγμένος ἦν Πεισίστρα-

11 *δύναμιν εἶχεν* Berol. *ἀεὶ* Berol. (H-L): ΑΙΕΙ (K, K-W, B). **12** *νοσοῦντες* om. Berol. **15** *δὲ*: *μὲν* Berol. **16** *ἦσαν* [*δ'*] K, H-L: *ἦσαν δὲ* Berol. (K-W, B). **18** *οἵπερ*: *οἱ δὲ* (ut videtur) Berol. *δὲ*: 'an *δ' ἡ*?' Blass. **19** *ἐζήτουν*: *ἐζήλουν* hic et c. 34 § 3 coniecit Bury (H-L).

TESTIMONIA. **16—20** Schol. Arist. *Vesp.* 1223...*κατὰ γὰρ τοὺς Σόλωνος νόμους τρεῖς ἦσαν αἱ τάξεις* (sic), *μία μὲν τῶν παραλίων, ὧν προειστήκει Μεγακλῆς, ἑτέρα δὲ τῶν πεδιέων, ὧν προειστήκει Λυκοῦργος, τρίτη δὲ τῶν διακρίων, ὧν προειστήκει Πεισίστρατος.*

(Schol. on Plat. *Axioch.* p. 253, Moeris, *s. v. γεννηταί*). But *ἄγροικοι* is the term used in Dion. Halic. ii 8 (after mentioning the *εὐπατρίδαι*), *ἀγροίκους δὲ* (*ἐκάλουν*) *τοὺς ἄλλους πολίτας οἳ τῶν κοινῶν οὐδενὸς ἦσαν κύριοι· σὺν χρόνῳ δὲ καὶ οὗτοι προσελήφθησαν ἐπὶ τὰς ἀρχάς.* Cf. Hesych. *s. v. ἀγροιῶται· ἄγροικοι. καὶ γένος Ἀθήνησιν, οἳ ἀντιδιεστέλλοντο πρὸς τοὺς Εὐπατρίδας. ἦν δὲ τῶν γεωργῶν. καὶ τρίτον τὸ τῶν δημιουργῶν.* (Landwehr in *Philologus*, Suppl. v, 1889, p. 139—155, *Die drei Stände in Attika.*)

§ 3. **νοσοῦντες**] of faction, c. 6 near end.

οἱ μὲν...οἱ δὲ...ἔνιοι δὲ] The first two are different sections of the Eupatridae, some of whom resented the loss of money involved in Solon's *σεισάχθεια*, while others lamented the loss of political influence; besides these, a few were actuated by the mere spirit of factious rivalry.

§ 4. **στάσεις τρεῖς...τῶν παραλίων ...τῶν πεδιακῶν...τῶν διακρίων**] Hdt. i 59, (Peisistratus) *στασιαζόντων τῶν παράλων καὶ τῶν ἐκ τοῦ πεδίου Ἀθηναίων, καὶ τῶν μὲν προεστεῶτος Μεγακλέος τοῦ Ἀλκμέωνος τῶν δὲ ἐκ τοῦ πεδίου Λυκούργου Ἀριστολαΐδεω, καταφρονήσας τὴν τυραννίδα ἤγειρε τρίτην στάσιν, συλλέξας δὲ στασιώτας καὶ τῷ λόγῳ τῶν ὑπερακρίων, προστὰς μηχανᾶται τοιάδε.* (Dion. Hal. i 13, *ὡς ὑπερακρίους τινὰς καὶ παραλίους Ἀθήνησιν.*) Plut. *Sol.* 29, *οἱ δὲ ἐν ἄστει ἐστασίαζον ἀποδημοῦντος τοῦ Σόλωνος· καὶ προειστήκει τῶν μὲν Πεδιέων Λυκοῦργος, τῶν δὲ Παράλων Μεγακλῆς ὁ Ἀλκμαίωνος, Πεισίστρατος δὲ τῶν Διακρίων, ἐν οἷς ἦν ὁ θητικὸς ὄχλος καὶ μάλιστα τοῖς πλουσίοις ἀχθόμενος.* *ib.* 13 (of the *στάσεις* just before the legislation of Solon), *τὴν παλαιὰν αὖθις στάσιν ὑπὲρ τῆς πολιτείας ἐστασίαζον, ὅσας ἡ χώρα διαφορὰς εἶχεν, εἰς τοσαῦτα μέρη τῆς πόλεως διαστάσης· ἦν γὰρ τὸ μὲν τῶν Διακρίων γένος δημοκρατικώτατον, ὀλιγαρχικώτατον δὲ τὸ τῶν Πεδιέων· τρίτοι δ' οἱ Πάραλοι μέσον τινὰ καὶ μεμιγμένον αἱρούμενοι πολιτείας τρόπον ἐμποδὼν ἦσαν καὶ διεκώλυον τοὺς ἑτέρους κρατῆσαι* (*Moralia* 805 D *τῶν Διακρίων...τῶν Πεδιέων ...τῶν Παραλίων*, 763 D *Παράλων, Ἐπακρίων, Πεδιέων*). *Πεδιεῖς* is the form found in Diog. Laert. i 58, and Schol. on Arist. *Vesp.* 1223, a confused account (founded on this passage, see *Testimonia*), in which the *τάξεις*, as they are there called, are apparently regarded as the *result* of Solon's legislation. Suidas *s. v.* *Πάραλοι* mentions the *Πεδιάσιοι* and *Διάκριοι.*

On these three parties, cf. Schömann, *Ant.* p. 327 f., E. T.; Gilbert, i 126 f.; Duncker, 6, 447 f.

For the form **πεδιακῶν**, cf. *Pol.* viii (v) 1305 *a* 21—24, *πάντες δὲ τοῦτο ἔδρων ὑπὸ τοῦ δήμου πιστευθέντες, ἡ δὲ πίστις ἦν ἡ*

5 τος, δημ[οτ]ι[κ]ώτατος εἶναι δοκῶν. προσεκεκόσμηντο δὲ τούτοις οἵ τε ἀφ[η]ρημένοι τὰ χρέα διὰ τὴν ἀπορ[ί]αν, καὶ οἱ τῷ γένει μὴ καθαροὶ διὰ τὸν φόβον· σημεῖον δ', ὅτι μετὰ τὴν <τῶν> τυράννων κατάλυσιν ἐποίησαν διαψηφισμὸν ὡς πολλῶν κοινωνούντων τῆς πολιτείας οὐ προσῆκον. εἶχον δ' ἕκαστοι τὰς ἐπωνυμίας ἀπὸ τῶν τ[ό]πων ἐν οἷς ἐγεώργουν.

21 προσεκεκόλληντο H-L, Kontos, Gennadios; προσενενέμηντο Butcher, coll. Dem. *Ol.* ii 29 προσνενέμησθε οἱ μὲν ὡς τούτους, οἱ δὲ ὡς ἐκείνους, *Ep.* iii 2 ταῖς τοῦ δήμου προαιρέσεσι προσένειμεν ἑαυτόν, *Aristog.* i 43 προσνέμοντες αὐτοὺς τούτῳ. **23** τῶν addiderunt Rutherford, Blass, Gennadios, K-W, H-L (K[3]). **24** ΔΙΑΦΗΜΙCΜΟΝ: διαψηφισμὸν scripsi, idem scripserunt Blass, K-W, H-L (K[3]).

ἀπέχθεια ἡ πρὸς τοὺς πλουσίους, οἷον Ἀθήνησί τε Πεισίστρατος στασιάσας πρὸς τοὺς πεδιακούς.

δημοτικώτατος] 14 § 1; 16 § 8; 22 § 3.

§ 5. **προσεκεκόσμηντο**] 'had joined their ranks'; the compound verb is not found elsewhere in this sense.

οἵ τε—φόβον] The faction of Peisistratus was joined by those whom Solon's legislation had deprived of the debts due to them. The allegiance of these was prompted by their losses. Peisistratus was also joined by those who were not of pure descent. The latter were afraid of the oligarchical faction gaining the ascendency and depriving them of the privileges of citizenship in consequence of their inferior birth. Landwehr, who doubts whether the parties really existed before the time of Solon (*Philol.* Suppl. v 155), suggests that οἱ ἀφῃρημένοι τὰ χρέα are the capitalists belonging to the παράλιοι who had lost their money, whereas the πεδιακοί still had their land.

σημεῖον δ'—προσῆκον] The writer infers that the party of Peisistratus included persons of dubious origin from the fact that, after the rule of the Peisistratidae was brought to an end, there was a revision of the list of citizens. Cf. note on 8 § 1, ὅθεν ἔτι διαμένει.

διαψηφισμόν] The word occurs in Athenaeus, 218 A, διαψηφισμὸς ὁ γενόμενος κατὰ τῶν Ἐρασινίδην στρατηγῶν. The verb is used in c. 42 § 1, l. 4, διαψηφίζονται. The admission of citizens took place in their 18th year, when, if their title to citizenship was sufficiently proved, they were entered on the register called ληξιαρχικὸν γραμματεῖον and (probably two years afterwards) in the πίναξ ἐκκλησιαστικός. The lists of citizens were revised on special occasions, particularly when there was reason for suspecting that a number of persons had been improperly registered. The names were then read one by one from the register, and, as each was read, it was asked whether any objections were to be made to it. Such objections were discussed and evidence brought forward, so that the matter could not be despatched in one assembly, but required several meetings of the members of the deme (Dem. *Eubulides* § 9 seq.). If, finally, a vote was taken, and the result was unfavourable, the name was struck out (Schömann, *Ant.* 368 f. E. T.). See esp. Dem. *Eubul.* (an appeal against the vote of the δημόται, who had struck the speaker off their list) § 7, ἐν τοῖς δημόταις—τὴν διαψήφισιν γενέσθαι, § 15, περὶ ἁπάντων τῶν δημοτῶν διαψηφίσασθαι, § 62 τῇ προτέρᾳ διαψηφίσει. Hitherto, the earliest known revision of the roll of citizens has been that in the archonship of Lysimachides B.C. 445/4 (Philochorus in Schol. on Ar. *Vesp.* 718; Plut. *Pericles* 37. Philippi, however, contends that the procedure of διαψήφισις was not resorted to on this occasion, *Bürgerrecht*, pp. 34—49). The next was in the archonship of Archias, 346 B.C. Cf. Harpocr. *s. v.* διαψήφισις: ἰδίως λέγεται ἐπὶ τῶν ἐν τοῖς δήμοις ἐξετασέων, αἳ γίγνονται περὶ ἑκάστου τῶν δημοτευομένων, εἰ τῷ ὄντι πολίτης καὶ δημότης ἐστὶν ἢ παρεγγέγραπται ξένος ὤν· Αἰσχίνης κατὰ Τιμάρχου (§ 77, γεγόνασι διαψηφίσεις ἐν τοῖς δήμοις, καὶ ἕκαστος ὑμῶν ψῆφον δέδωκε περὶ τοῦ σώματος, ὅστις Ἀθηναῖος ὄντως ἐστὶ καὶ ὅστις μή). ἐντελέστατα δὲ διείλεκται περὶ τῶν διαψηφίσεων, ὡς γεγόνασιν ἐπὶ Ἀρχίου ἄρχοντος, Ἀνδροτίων ἐν τῇ Ἀτθίδι καὶ Φιλόχορος ἐν ϛ' τῆς Ἀτθίδος. Cf. Schol. Aeschin. 1 §§ 77, 114; Hermann, *Staatsalt.* § 121, 19, and Meier and Schömann, p. 989 Lips.

εἶχον δ' ἕκαστοι—ἐγεώργουν] 'These parties derived their respective designations from the districts in which they held their lands,' the Plain, the Shore

14. δημοτικώτατος δ' εἶναι δοκῶν ὁ Πεισίστρατος, καὶ σφόδρ' εὐδοκιμηκὼς ἐν τῷ πρὸς Μεγαρέας πολέμῳ, κατατραυματίσας ἑαυτὸν συνέπεισε τὸν δῆμον, ὡς [ὑ]π[ὸ] τῶν ἀντιστασιωτῶν ταῦτα πεπονθ[ώ]ς, φυλακὴν ἑαυτῷ δοῦναι τοῦ σώματος, 'Αριστίωνος [γ]ρ[ά]ψαντος τὴν γνώμην. λαβὼν δὲ τοὺς κορυνηφόρους καλου-

XIV 2 ηὐδοκιμηκὼς H-L. **3** ὑπὸ K-W (K[3], B): παρὰ K[1].

---

and the Mountain (or Highlands). The men of the *Mountain* led a hard life in the uplands of Parnes which afforded pasturage for sheep and goats, and were scantily supplied with the fruits of the field or of trees. (2) The men of the *Shore* enjoyed more abundant means of support in the building of boats, in ferrying and fishing, and in the manufacture of salt. (3) The men of the *Plain* formed the wealthiest class, with their groves of olives in the valley of the Cephisus and their fields of corn stretching inland from Eleusis. (Cf. Curtius, *H. G.*, i 311 E. T.) Grote, c. 11, ii p. 300 n, observes that Plutarch's description of the men of the Plain, as representing the oligarchical tendency, and the men of the Mountain, the democratical, is 'not quite accurate when applied to the days of Solon. Democratical pretensions, as such, can hardly be said to have existed.' Plutarch (or the authority he follows in c. 13) possibly makes these parties come into existence too early; elsewhere, c. 29, he places them after Solon's time, probably on the authority of the text, which distinctly describes the men of the Plain as oligarchical in spirit.

XIV § 1. **εὐδοκιμηκὼς—πολέμῳ**] Hdt. i 59, *πρότερον εὐδοκιμήσας ἐν τῇ πρὸς Μεγαρέας γενομένῃ στρατηγίῃ, Νίσαιάν τε ἑλὼν καὶ ἄλλα ἀποδεξάμενος μεγάλα ἔργα.* Plut., *Sol.* 8, mentions the long and distressing war with Megara for the possession of Salamis, and describes Peisistratus as taking the lead in supporting Solon in his endeavour to rouse the people to fight once more for the recovery of the island. At the end of c. 9 he says of Solon, *ἐνίκησε τοὺς Μεγαρέας.* He implies that the war for the possession of Salamis was the origin of Solon's influence in Athens; if so, it can hardly be put later than 600 B.C. But Daimachus of Plataea (third century B.C., quoted in Plut. *Sol. et Popl. comp.* 4) denied that Solon acted as general in the war against Megara. That Peisistratus took any prominent part in a war as early as 600 B.C. is improbable, as he lived to 527 B.C. (Abbott, *H. G.*, i 400 n). Solon, who was some 30 years older than Peisistratus, took a leading part in the conquest of Salamis before he was archon, *i.e.* possibly about 600 B.C.; Peisistratus in the capture of Nisaea, probably about 570 B.C. (Busolt, i 521 n). Curtius (i 672, note 135) places the capture of Nisaea in 565, and Holm (i 481) shortly before the tyranny. In c. 17 we are told that the relative ages of Solon and Peisistratus make it impossible to accept the story that the latter was *στρατηγὸς* in the war with Megara for the possession of Salamis (*i.e.* the *first* Megarian war), in which Solon was concerned. Salamis and Nisaea were, however, recaptured by the Megarians (Plut. *Sol.* 12); and Pesistratus may have distinguished himself in a subsequent war with the Megarians for the recovery of the island.

κατατραυματίσας κτλ.] Hdt. i 59, *τρωματίσας ἑωυτόν τε καὶ ἡμιόνους ἤλασε ἐς τὴν ἀγορὴν τὸ ζεῦγος ὡς ἐκπεφευγὼς τοὺς ἐχθρούς, οἵ μιν ἐλαύνοντα ἐς ἀγρὸν ἠθέλησαν ἀπολέσαι δῆθεν, ἐδέετό τε τοῦ δήμου φυλακῆς τινὸς πρὸς αὐτοῦ κυρῆσαι... ὁ δὲ δῆμος ὁ τῶν 'Αθηναίων ἐξαπατηθείς, ἔδωκέ οἱ τῶν ἀστῶν καταλέξας ἄνδρας τούτους οἳ δορυφόροι μὲν οὐκ ἐγένοντο Πεισιστράτου κορυνηφόροι δέ· ξύλων γὰρ κορύνας ἔχοντες εἵποντό οἱ ὄπισθε· συνεπαναστάντες δὲ οὗτοι ἅμα Πεισιστράτῳ ἔσχον τὴν ἀκρόπολιν.* Plut. *Sol.* 30 § 1, *κατατρώσας αὐτὸς ἑαυτὸν ὁ Πεισίστρατος.* Polyaen. i 21 § 3 and Diogen. Laert. i 60 have *κατατρώσας*, or *κατέτρωσεν*, *ib.* § 66 *ἑαυτῷ τραύματα ποιήσας.* Diod. Sic. xiii 95 end, (of P.) *ἑαυτὸν κατατραυματίσαντα προελθεῖν. κατατραυματίζω* is also found in Polyb. xv 13 § 1, Dion. Halic. and Dio Cass.

'Αριστίωνος κτλ.] Plut. *Sol.* 30 § 2, *'Αρίστωνος* (*sic*) *δὲ γράψαντος, ὅπως δοθῶσι πεντήκοντα κορυνηφόροι τῷ Πεισιστράτῳ φυλακὴ τοῦ σώματος.*

κορυνηφόρους] Plat. *Rep.* 566 B, *τὸ δὴ τυραννικὸν αἴτημα τὸ πολυθρύλητον...αἰτεῖν τὸν δῆμον φύλακάς τινας τοῦ σώματος.* Ar. *Rhet.* i 2, 19, *Πεισίστρατος ἐπιβουλεύων ᾔτει φυλακὴν καὶ λαβὼν ἐτυράν-*

μένους, ἐπαναστὰς μετὰ τούτων τῷ δήμῳ κατέσχε τὴν ἀκρόπολιν ἔτει †δευτέρῳ† καὶ τριακοστῷ μετὰ τὴν τῶν νόμων θέσιν, ἐπὶ
2 Κ[ωμ]έου ἄρχοντος. λέγεται δὲ Σόλωνα, Πεισιστράτου τὴν φυλακὴν αἰτοῦντος, ἀντιλέξαι καὶ εἰπεῖ[ν ὅ]τι τῶν μὲν εἴη σοφώτερος, τῶν δ' ἀνδρειό[τερο]ς· ὅσοι μὲν γὰρ ἀγνοοῦσι Πεισίστρατον ἐπιτιθέμενον τυραν[νίδι], σοφώτερος εἶναι τούτων, ὅσοι δ' εἰδότες κατασιωπῶσιν, ἀνδρειότερος. ἐπεὶ δὲ λέγων [οὐκ ἔπει]θεν, ἐξαράμενος τὰ ὅπλα πρὸ τῶν θυρῶν αὐτὸς μὲν ἔφη βεβοηθηκέναι

7 *δευτέρῳ*: δ′ (=*τετάρτῳ*) K-W et Bauer (B). **8** ΠΙCΙCΤΡΑΤΟΥ ut saepe: Πεισ. ubique K[3] etc. **12** ΚΑΤΑCΙΩΠΩΝΤΕC: correxit K. *οὐκ ἔπειθεν* R D Hicks (K-W, H-L, K[3]). **13** ΕΞΑΙΡΑΜΕΝΟC: *ἐξαράμενος* K (K-W, H-L).

TESTIMONIA. **8—15.** Verbis fere isdem rem narrat Aelianus, *Var. Hist.* viii 16: ...(Σόλων) ἔφη ὅτι τῶν μέν ἐστι σοφώτερος, τῶν δὲ ἀνδρειότερος· ὁπόσοι μὲν μὴ γινώσκουσιν ὅτι φυλακὴν λαβὼν περὶ τὸ σῶμα τύραννος ἔσται, ἀλλὰ τούτων μέν ἐστι σοφώτερος· ὁπόσοι δὲ γινώσκοντες ὑποσιωπῶσι, τούτων ἀνδρειότερός ἐστιν. ὁ δὲ λαβὼν τὴν δύναμιν τύραννος ἦν. καθεζόμενος δὲ Σόλων πρὸ τῆς οἰκίας, τὴν ἀσπίδα καὶ τὸ δόρυ παραθέμενος ἔλεγεν ὅτι ἐξώπλισται καὶ βοηθεῖ τῇ πατρίδι ᾗ δύναται.

νευσε. *Pol.* viii (v) 9, 1310 *b* 15, σχεδὸν γὰρ οἱ πλεῖστοι τῶν τυράννων γεγόνασιν ἐκ δημαγωγῶν ὡς εἰπεῖν, πιστευθέντες ἐκ τοῦ διαβάλλειν τοὺς γνωρίμους, and *ib.* 30, οἷον ...Πεισίστρατος Ἀθήνησι...ἐκ δημαγωγίας τύραννος κατέστη.

κατέσχε τὴν ἀκρόπολιν] Plut. *Sol.* 30 § 4, τὴν ἀκρόπολιν κατέσχε. Phaedrus i 2, 5, *arcem tyrannus occupat Pisistratus.* The political importance of the citadel in revolutions is exemplified in Juv. x 307 n, Lucan viii 490, Diod. Sic. xvi 70 § 4, Plut. *Timol.* 20 § 1 (Mayor).

ἔτει—τριακοστῷ] As Comeas was archon in 560 B.C., it would follow from the manuscript text that Solon was archon in 591. But, as Solon was more probably archon in 594, δευτέρῳ should be altered into τετάρτῳ, the former being possibly a corruption of δ̄. We thus get an interval of 33 years and keep the usual date for Solon's archonship (Bauer, p. 45 f).

ἐπὶ Κωμέου] Plut. *Sol.* 32, ἐπεβίωσε δ' οὖν ὁ Σόλων ἀρξαμένου τοῦ Πεισιστράτου τυραννεῖν, ὡς μὲν Ἡρακλείδης ὁ Ποντικὸς ἱστορεῖ, συχνὸν χρόνον, ὡς δὲ Φανίας ὁ Ἐρέσιος ἐλάττονα δυοῖν ἐτῶν. ἐπὶ Κωμίου ἄρχοντος μὲν γὰρ ἤρξατο τυραννεῖν Πεισίστρατος, ἐφ' Ἡγεστράτου δὲ Σόλωνά φησιν ὁ Φανίας ἀποθανεῖν τοῦ μετὰ Κωμίαν ἄρξαντος. (Plutarch is possibly quoting from the work of Phanias, on τυράννων ἀναίρεσις ἐκ τιμωρίας. Oncken, *Staatslehre*, ii 445 n.)

The present treatise and the *Politics*, v 5, 23, agree in stating that Peisistratus lived for 33 years after usurping the government of Athens; the Peisistratidae ruled for 18 years (*Pol. l.c.*), and the interval between their expulsion and the battle of Marathon was 19 years (Thuc. vi 59). Thus the rule of Peisistratus began 70 years before B.C. 490, *i.e.* in 560. The year given by the Parian Marble (297 + 264/3 =) 561/0 (as well as by Jerome and the Armenian version of Eusebius) must be corrected to 560 (Clinton's *Fasti*, *sub anno*).

§ 2. **εἰπεῖν ὅτι τῶν—ἀνδρειότερος**] Plut. *Sol.* 30, ὁρῶν δὲ τοὺς μὲν πένητας ὡρμημένους χαρίζεσθαι τῷ Πεισιστράτῳ καὶ θορυβοῦντας, τοὺς δὲ πλουσίους ἀποδιδράσκοντας καὶ ἀποδειλιῶντας, ἀπῆλθεν εἰπών, ὅτι τῶν μέν ἐστι σοφώτερος, τῶν δὲ ἀνδρειότερος· σοφώτερος μὲν τῶν μὴ συνιέντων τὸ πραττόμενον, ἀνδρειότερος δὲ τῶν συνιέντων μέν, ἐναντιοῦσθαι δὲ τῇ τυραννίδι φοβουμένων. Cf. Diog. Laert. i 49—50, 65; Aelian *Var. Hist.* viii 16 (who tells the story in almost the same words as the text); and Aristid. i 765 Dind. The story is also told in Valer. Max. v 3 E 3, viii 9 E 1.

ἐξαράμενος τὰ ὅπλα] Plut. *Sol.* 30, οὐδενὸς δὲ προσέχοντος αὐτῷ διὰ τὸν φόβον ἀπῆλθεν εἰς τὴν οἰκίαν τὴν ἑαυτοῦ καὶ λαβὼν τὰ ὅπλα καὶ πρὸ τῶν θυρῶν θέμενος εἰς τὸν στενωπόν, "ἐμοὶ μὲν" εἶπεν "ὡς δυνατὸν ἦν βεβοήθηκα τῇ πατρίδι καὶ τοῖς νόμοις." *Moralia* 794 E, ὁ δὲ Σόλων, τῆς Πεισιστράτου δημαγωγίας ὅτι τυραννικὸν ἦν μηχάνημα φανερᾶς γενομένης, μηδενὸς

τῇ πατρίδι καθ' ὅσον ἦν δυνατός (ἤδη γὰρ σφόδρα πρεσβύτης ἦν), ἀξιοῦν δὲ καὶ τοὺς ἄλλους ταὐτὸ τοῦτο ποιεῖν. Σόλων [μὲν οὖν 3
οὐ]δὲν ἤνυσεν τότε παρακαλῶν· Πεισίστρατος δὲ λαβὼν τὴν ἀρχὴν διῴκει τὰ κοινὰ πολιτικῶς μᾶλλον ἢ τυραννικῶς. οὔπω δὲ τῆς ἀρχῆς ἐρριζωμένης ὁμοφρονήσαντες [οἱ] περὶ τὸν Μεγακλέα καὶ τὸν Λυκοῦ[ργο]ν ἐξέβαλον αὐτὸν ἕκτῳ ἔτει μετὰ τὴν πρώτην

16 ἤνυσε H-L.

ἀμύνεσθαι μηδὲ κωλύειν τολμῶντος, αὐτὸς ἐξενεγκάμενος τὰ ὅπλα καὶ πρὸ τῆς οἰκίας θέμενος, ἠξίου βοηθεῖν τοὺς πολίτας. Diod. Sic. ix 29 Bekker, *οὐδενὸς δὲ αὐτῷ προσέχοντος ἀναλαβὼν τὴν πανοπλίαν προῆλθεν εἰς τὴν ἀγορὰν γεγηρακώς, καὶ τοὺς θεοὺς ἐπιμαρτυρόμενος ἔφησε καὶ λόγῳ καὶ ἔργῳ τῇ πατρίδι κινδυνευούσῃ βεβοηθηκέναι τὸ κατ' αὐτὸν μέρος.* Grote, ii 352, says of this incident, as related by Plutarch: 'As a last appeal, he put on his armour and *planted himself* in military posture before the door of his house.' *θέμενος*, however, is not used absolutely, but must be construed with *ὅπλα.*

§ 3. **πολιτικῶς μᾶλλον ἢ τυραννικῶς**] Cf. *inf.* c. 16 § 8. Hdt. i 59, *οὔτε τιμὰς τὰς ἐούσας συνταράξας οὔτε θέσμια μεταλλάξας, ἐπί τε τοῖσι κατεστεῶσι ἔνεμε τὴν πόλιν κοσμέων καλῶς τε καὶ εὖ.* Thuc. vi 54. For *πολιτικῶς*, cf. (with Mr Wyse) Isocr. iv 79, 151; ix 46, *Ep.* ii 3.

οὔπω δὲ—ἐξέβαλον αὐτόν] Hdt. i 60, *μετὰ δὲ οὐ πολλὸν χρόνον τὠυτὸ φρονήσαντες οἵ τε τοῦ Μεγακλέος στασιῶται καὶ οἱ τοῦ Λυκούργου, ἐξελαύνουσί μιν. οὕτω μὲν Πεισίστρατος ἔσχε τὸ πρῶτον Ἀθήνας, καὶ τὴν τυραννίδα οὔκω κάρτα ἐρριζωμένην ἔχων ἀπέβαλε.*

ἕκτῳ ἔτει] The sixth year from 560/59 would be 555/4.

The following are the notes of time given in the manuscript text for the chronology of Peisistratus:

14 § 1. Beginning of rule. *ἐπὶ Κωμέου.*

14 § 3. First exile. *ἕκτῳ ἔτει.*

14 § 4. First return. *ἔτει δωδεκάτῳ μετὰ ταῦτα.*

15 § 1. Second exile. *ἔτει μάλιστα ἑβδόμῳ.*

15 § 2. Second return. *ἑνδεκάτῳ... ἔτει.*

17 § 1. Total duration of rule. (*ἔτη*) *ἑνὸς δέοντα εἴκοσι.*

ib. Death, 33 years from beginning of rule. *ἐπὶ Φιλονέω ἄρχοντος..ἔτη τριάκοντα καὶ τρία.*

The above data alone account for a total of at least (5 + 11 + 6 + 10 =) 32 years; and, as Peisistratus lived for 33 years after usurping the government, they leave only one year for the third period of rule. But c. 17 § 1 tells us that he ruled for 19 years in all; if so, his third period of rule must have lasted (19 − 5 − 6 =) 8 years. On the other hand, the passage in *Pol.* v 9 § 23, p. 1315 *b* 32, gives 17 years for the total duration of his rule, thus leaving 6 years for the third period. The chronology has been much discussed both before and after the discovery of this treatise. The following table gives a conspectus of some of the arrangements proposed. As typical instances, before the discovery of this treatise, I have selected Clinton (*Fasti*, vol. ii, Appendix 11) and Busolt (i 551). To these I have added the years as arranged by Bauer (*Forschungen zu Ar.* Ἀθ. πολ.), and Poland (in the notes to his German transl.). Thus far the chronology proposed accords, in the total number of years of rule and exile, with the data in the *Politics*. The other two estimates, those of Mr Kenyon and M. Th. Reinach, adhere more closely to the data of the present treatise.

	Clinton	Busolt	Bauer	Poland	Kenyon	Reinach
1st *τυραννίς*	**6**	**5**	**5**	**5**	**5**	**5**
1st exile	6	5	6	6	4	3
2nd *τυραννίς*	**1**	**1**	**1**	**6**	**6**	**6**
2nd exile	10	11	10	10	10	10
3rd *τυραννίς*	**10**	**11**	**11**	**6**	**8**	c.**9**
years of *τυραννίς*	**17**	**17**	**17**	**17**	**19**	c.**20**
years of exile	16	16	16	16	14	c.13

It will be observed that there is a general consensus as to the duration of the first *τυραννίς* and the second exile. The greatest discrepancies are in the duration of the second and third *τυραννίς*.

4 κατάστασιν, ἐφ' Ἡγησίου ἄρχοντος. ἔτει δὲ †δωδεκάτῳ† μετὰ ταῦτα περιελαυνόμενος ὁ Μεγακλῆς τῇ στάσει, πάλιν ἐπικηρυκευσάμενος πρὸς [τὸ]ν Πεισίστρατον ἐφ' ᾧ τε τὴν θυγατέρα αὐτοῦ λήψεται, κατήγαγεν αὐτὸν ἀρχαϊκῶς καὶ λίαν ἁπλῶς. προδιασπείρας γὰρ λόγον ὡς τῆς Ἀθηνᾶς καταγούσης Πεισίστρατον, καὶ γυναῖκα μεγάλην καὶ καλὴν ἐξευρών, ὡς μὲν Ἡρόδοτός φησιν ἐκ τοῦ δήμου τῶν Παιανιέων, ὡς δ' ἔνιοι λέγουσιν ἐκ τοῦ Κολλυτοῦ στεφανόπωλιν Θρᾶτταν, ᾗ ὄνομα Φύη, τὴν θεὸν ἀπομιμησάμενος τῷ κόσμῳ συν[εισή]γαγε[ν] μετ' αὐτοῦ, καὶ ὁ μὲν Πεισίστρατος

20 δωδεκάτῳ (K, H-L): τετάρτῳ Thompson (K-W[1]); πέμπτῳ K-W[2]. 21 ταῦτα: ταύτην Bauer. 23 ΑΡΧΑΙ^{ως}ΚΩC ἀρχαϊκῶς (K, H-L, B), cf. *Met.* 1089 *a* 2 Bonitz ἀρχαϊκῶς ἀπορῆσαι: ἀρχαίως H-W, cf. *Pol.* 1330 *b* 33 λίαν ἀρχαίως ὑπολαμβάνουσι. 25 ⟦καὶ⟧ γυναῖκα K-W[2]. φησιν: ΦΗ. 26 Παιανιῶν H-L. ΚΟΛΥΤΟΥ, etiam altera Τ, et fortasse altera λ, suprascripta. 28 συνεισήγαγεν (H-L, K[3]) potius quam κατήγαγεν (K[1], K-W) in papyro legi putat K; εἰσήγαγε coniecerat Richards.

23 Plut. *Sol.* 3 § 5 (de alia re) ἁπλοῦς ἐστι λίαν καὶ ἀρχαῖος, unde apparet hanc narrationem Plutarcho fuisse notam.

In the first exile, Bauer and Poland assume that ἔτει δωδεκάτῳ (14 § 4) is reckoned from the beginning of the usurpation and that μετὰ ταῦτα is to be either omitted or altered into μετὰ ταύτην; while Mr Kenyon and M. Reinach alter δωδεκάτῳ into τετάρτῳ. In the second τυραννίς, Bauer alters ἔτει...ἑβδόμῳ (15 § 1) into μηνὶ...ἑβδόμῳ. For the length of the third τυραννίς we have no data except those gained by subtracting the two earlier periods of rule from the total duration of actual rule. Of the above arrangements, Mr Kenyon's alone strictly adheres to the total of 19 years. The 19 years of this treatise do not seem to admit of being reconciled with the 17 years of the *Politics*. It is suggested by Bauer that the difference may be obtained by supposing that the fractions of the years in the three periods of rule were excluded in one reckoning and included in the other. This would imply that each of the three periods of rule, as estimated in the present treatise, extended to an average of two-thirds of a year beyond the duration stated in the *Politics*. This is possible, but not probable. It may be added that the genuineness of the passage in the *Politics* is not certain. Susemihl, in his 2nd and 3rd editions, brackets the whole of the paragraph in which it occurs; and, even if both passages are equally due to Aristotle, the present treatise may possibly represent his latest views.

§ 4. **ἔτει δωδεκάτῳ μετὰ ταῦτα**] This would naturally mean 'eleven years after the first exile.' But the sum of the two periods of exile was (according to 17 § 1) 33 – 19, or 14 years; and the second exile lasted 10 years (15 § 2), leaving only four years for the first exile. Such a number of years may perhaps be obtained by altering δωδέκατῳ into τετάρτῳ (see *N. C.*), and by assuming that the symbol δ̄ followed by the erroneous explanation δεκάτῳ led to the reading δωδεκάτῳ. Another alternative (adopted in Kaibel and Kiessling's transl.) is to count the eleven years from the beginning of the rule of Peisistratus. This involves either omitting μετὰ ταῦτα or altering it into μετὰ ταύτην (τὴν πρώτην κατάστασιν). See Bauer, p. 50 f.

περιελαυνόμενος κτλ.] Hdt. i 60, περιελαυνόμενος δὲ τῇ στάσει ὁ Μεγακλῆς ἐπεκηρυκεύετο Πεισιστράτῳ, εἰ βούλοιτό οἱ τὴν θυγατέρα ἔχειν γυναῖκα ἐπὶ τῇ τυραννίδι.

θυγατέρα] Κοισύραν, Schol. Arist. *Nub.* 49, 800, and Suidas, *s. v.*

Ἡρόδοτος] i 60 *ad fin.*, ἐν τῷ δήμῳ τῷ Παιανιέι. This is the only passage in which any writer of prose is named in this treatise. The only poet quoted by name is Solon.

Κολλυτοῦ] Wachsmuth, *Stadt Athen*, ii 262 f.

Φύη] The Schol. on Arist. *Eq.* 449 calls her Μυρρίνη.

ἐφ' ἅρματος εἰσήλαυνε παραιβατούσης τῆς γυναικός, οἱ δ' ἐν τῷ ἄστει προσκυνοῦντες ἐδέχοντο θαυμάζοντες.

15. ἡ μὲν οὖν πρώτη κάθοδος ἐ[γέν]ετο τοιαύτη. μετὰ δὲ ταῦτα, ὡς ἐξέπεσε τὸ δεύτερον ἔτει μάλιστα ἑβδόμῳ μετὰ τὴν κάθοδον,—οὐ γὰρ πολὺν χρόνον κατεῖχεν, ἀλλ[ὰ] διὰ τὸ μὴ βούλεσθαι τῇ τοῦ Μεγακλέους θυγατρὶ συγγίγνεσθαι φοβηθεὶς ἀμφοτέρας τὰς στάσεις ὑπεξῆλθεν· καὶ πρῶτον μὲν συνῴκισε περὶ 2
τὸν Θερμαῖον κόλπον χωρίον ὃ καλεῖται Ῥαίκηλος, ἐκεῖθεν δὲ παρῆλθεν εἰς τοὺς περὶ Πάγγαιον τόπους, ὅθεν χρηματισά-

30 *προσκυνοῦντες* delet Gennadios *τοῦ θαυμάζοντες* interpretamentum arbitratus. *θαυμάζοντες* delet Richards (H-L), defendit Gennadios coll. Xen. *Hell.* i 6, 11.
XV 2 ΤΑΥΤΑΩϹΕΞ (K, B): *ταῦτ' ἐξέπεσε* K-W. *ταῦτ' αὖθις ἐξέπεσε* Gennadios (H-L). *ἑβδόμῳ*: *τρίτῳ* coni. K-W. **3** ΚΑΤΕϹΧΕΝ, *κατεῖχεν* Wyse (K-W, H-L, K[3]): *διακατέσχεν* B. **4** ϹΥΓΓΙΝ (K-W).
ι λ
5 *συνῴκισε*: *ᾤκισε* coni. Gennadios, Hude (H-L, B). **6** ΡΑΚΗΛΟϹ.

παραιβατούσης] A noteworthy Ionism, but not derived from the account in Hdt. The same word is used as a reference to the same incident in Cleidemus, *ap.* Athenaeum, 609 C, *στεφανόπωλις δὲ ἦν, καὶ αὐτὴν ἐξέδωκε πρὸς γάμου κοινωνίαν ὁ Πεισίστρατος Ἱππάρχῳ τῷ υἱῷ, ὡς Κλείδημος ἱστορεῖ ἐν ὀγδόῳ νόστων· "ἐξέδωκε δὲ καὶ Ἱππάρχῳ τῷ υἱεῖ τὴν παραιβατήσασαν αὐτῷ γυναῖκα Φύην, τὴν Σωκράτους θυγατέρα"* (Müller, FHG i 364). Cleidemus, who wrote an *Ἀτθίς* (Athen. 235 A), has been identified with Cleitodemus, mentioned by Pausanias (x 15, 5) as the most ancient writer of Athenian history. Plutarch (*Arist.* 19) refers to his account of the battle of Plataea; so that his date is after 479 B.C. The story is also told in Polyaen. i 21, 1; Val. Max. i 3, 3; Hermogenes *de Invent.* ii 185, 21 Spengel, with Schol.; and Phylarchus *ap.* Athen. 609 C (Mayor).

XV § 1. **ἔτει μάλιστα ἑβδόμῳ**] It has been urged by Bauer (p. 51) and Rühl (*Rhein. Mus.* 1891, p. 442), that it is improbable that Megacles waited so long as six years to avenge the neglect of his daughter by her husband, Peisistratus; and the text implies that the duration of the second *τυραννίς* was short. Bauer accordingly suggests that *ἔτει* should be altered into *μηνί*, and for similar reasons K-W alter *ἑβδόμῳ* into *τρίτῳ*. On the other hand it is plausibly suggested by Gomperz (p. 23 n) that the compact between Megacles and Peisistratus was made before the daughter of the former had attained a marriageable age.

τῇ τοῦ Μεγακλέους θυγατρί] Hdt. i 61, *οἷα δὲ παίδων τέ οἱ ὑπαρχόντων νεηνιέων καὶ λεγομένων ἐναγέων εἶναι τῶν Ἀλκμεωνιδέων, οὐ βουλόμενός οἱ γενέσθαι ἐκ τῆς νεογάμου γυναικὸς τέκνα ἐμίσγετό οἱ οὐ κατὰ νόμον.*

ὑπεξῆλθεν] Hdt. i 61, *ἀπαλλάσσετο ἐκ τῆς χώρας τὸ παράπαν, ἀπικόμενος δὲ ἐς Ἐρέτριαν ἐβουλεύετο ἅμα τοῖς παισί.* Herodotus mentions the help offered by the Thebans and Argives, and by Lygdamis of Naxos, and then continues: *ἐξ Ἐρετρίης δὲ ὁρμηθέντες διὰ ἑνδεκάτου ἔτεος ἀπίκοντο ὀπίσω.* Eretria alone is there mentioned in connexion with this period of exile.

§ 2. **Ῥαίκηλος**] The Schol. on Lycophron, 1236, states that this was the old name of *Αἶνος* in Macedonia. It is identical with the *Αἴνεια* of Hdt. vii 123, and is situated to the S. of the promontory at the extreme west of Chalcidice, opposite the mouth of the Axius and Ludias. (There was another *Αἶνος* in Thrace, near the mouth of the Hebrus.)

τοὺς περὶ Πάγγαιον τόπους] the region near the mouth of the Strymon. Though Herodotus says nothing of this region in connexion with the second exile of Peisistratus, the account in the text is illustrated by the passage in which the historian says of the tyrant on his final restoration: (i 64), *ἐρρίζωσε τὴν τυραννίδα ἐπικούροισί τε πολλοῖσι, καὶ χρημάτων συνόδοισι, τῶν μὲν αὐτόθεν, τῶν δὲ ἀπὸ Στρυμόνος ποταμοῦ συνιόντων.* Here *τῶν μὲν* and *τῶν δὲ* naturally refer to *χρημάτων* alone, and *συνιόντων* in the second clause echoes

μενος καὶ στρατιώτας μισθωσάμενος, ἐλθὼν εἰς Ἐρέτριαν ἑνδεκάτῳ πάλιν ἔτει τό<τε> πρῶτον ἀνασῴσασθαι βίᾳ τὴν ἀρχὴν ἐπεχείρει, συμπροθυμουμένων αὐτῷ πολλῶν μὲν καὶ ἄλλων, μάλιστα δὲ Θηβαίων καὶ Λυγδάμιος τοῦ Ναξίου, ἔτι δὲ τῶν
3 ἱππέων τῶν ἐχόντων ἐν Ἐρετρίᾳ τὴν πολιτείαν. || νικήσας δὲ τὴν
[Col. 6.]

9 τό<τε> Blass (K-W, H-L, K³). ΑΝΑCΩCΑCΘΑΙ, ἀνασῴσασθαι K³, B: ΑΝΑ(C)ΚΤΗCΑCΘΑΙ?, ἀνακτήσασθαι Herwerden (K-W).

TESTIMONIA. **12—13** *Schol. Arist. *Ach.* 234 Παλλήναδε: οἱ Παλληνεῖς δῆμός ἐστι τῆς Ἀττικῆς, ἔνθα Πεισιστράτῳ βουλομένῳ τυραννεῖν καὶ Ἀθηναίοις ἀμυνομένοις αὐτὸν συνέστη πόλεμος...μέμνηται δὲ τούτου καὶ Ἀνδροτίων καὶ Ἀρ. ἐν Ἀθ. πολ. (Rose, Frag. 355², 393³).

συνόδοισι (=προσόδοισι) in the first. We may therefore agree with Thirlwall (ii p. 61), as against Grote (iii 92 n), who refers τῶν μὲν to χρημάτων and τῶν δὲ to ἐπικούροισι. Thirlwall had said of Peisistratus that he 'possessed lands on the Strymon in Thrace, which yielded him a large revenue.' Grote thought this improbable, adding: 'If Peisistratus had established any settlement at the mouth of the Strymon, we must surely have heard something of it afterwards.' The text does not indeed tell us that Peisistratus made an actual settlement near that river, but it supplies us with exactly the kind of evidence which would have removed Grote's hesitation in accepting Thirlwall's inference from the account in Herodotus. The text tells us more than the historian. It informs us definitely that Peisistratus visited the region near the mouth of the Strymon, and thence drew his supplies of men, as well as of money.

It is interesting to notice these details respecting Rhaecelos and the country around Mount Pangaeus. The Pangaean Mount is plainly visible across the gulf of the Strymon from the neighbourhood of Stageira; and the bold promontory, north of Rhaecelus, is in full view across the plains that extend to the mouth of the Ludias from the Macedonian capital at Pella. These topographical considerations may serve to support the ascription of the treatise to the authorship of Aristotle, who was a Macedonian by birth and spent the first seventeen years of his life, and seven years besides, at his native town of Stageira. In the *Historia Animalium*, pp. 592 *a* 7, 597 *a* 10, Aristotle makes special mention of the eels and the pelicans of the Strymon.

πάλιν] confirms the account of Hdt., implying that Peisistratus had in the first instance retired to Eretria, though we are not expressly told so in the text.

ἀνασῴσασθαι...τὴν ἀρχήν] Hdt. i 73, ἀνασῴσασθαι τὴν ἀρχήν, and in the same chapter ἀναλαβεῖν and ἀνακτᾶσθαι τὴν ἀρχήν.

Θηβαίων] Hdt. i 61, πολλῶν δὲ μεγάλα παρασχόντων χρήματα, Θηβαῖοι ὑπερεβάλοντο τῇ δόσι τῶν χρημάτων.

Λυγδάμιος] Hdt. *l.c.*, καὶ γὰρ Ἀργεῖοι μισθωτοὶ ἀπίκοντο ἐκ Πελοποννήσου, καὶ Νάξιός σφι ἀνὴρ ἀπιγμένος ἐθελοντής, τῷ οὔνομα ἦν Λύγδαμις. Ar. *Pol.* viii (v) 5, 1305 *a* 42, ὅταν ἐξ αὐτῆς συμβῇ τῆς ὀλιγαρχίας γίνεσθαι τὸν ἡγεμόνα, καθάπερ ἐν Νάξῳ Λύγδαμις, ὃς καὶ ἐτυράννησεν ὕστερον τῶν Ναξίων. The story of the way in which Lygdamis became tyrant of Naxos is quoted in Athen. viii 348, from 'Aristotle ἐν τῇ Ναξίων πολιτείᾳ.' In consequence of the wrongs done by some Naxian youths to the wealthy and popular Telestagoras and his two daughters, ἀγανακτήσαντες οἱ Νάξιοι καὶ τὰ ὅπλα ἀναλαβόντες ἐπῆλθον τοῖς νεανίσκοις· καὶ μεγίστη τότε στάσις ἐγένετο, προστατοῦντος τῶν Ναξίων Λυγδάμιδος, ὃς ἀπὸ ταύτης τῆς στρατηγίας τύραννος ἀνεφάνη τῆς πατρίδος. (Frag. 558 Rose³.)

τῶν ἱππέων—πολιτείαν] 'the Knights who held the supreme power in the constitution of Eretria' (K.). πολιτεία is here *ius civitatis*, *potestas in civitate*, often used in the *Politics* in the phrase μετέχειν τῆς πολιτείας (*Index Ar. s. v.* 3). Eretria was under the rule of an oligarchy of Knights, which was overthrown by one Diagoras, probably not long before the Persian wars, *Pol.* viii (v) 6, 1306 *a* 35, τὴν ἐν Ἐρετρίᾳ δ' ὀλιγαρχίαν τὴν τῶν ἱππέων Διαγόρας κατέλυσεν ἀδικηθεὶς περὶ γάμων, and vi (iv) 3, 1289 *b* 36, ἐπὶ τῶν ἀρχαίων χρόνων ὅσαις πόλεσιν ἐν τοῖς ἵπποις ἡ δύναμις ἦν, ὀλιγαρχίαι παρὰ τούτοις ἦσαν·

ἐπὶ Παλληνίδι [μάχη]ν καὶ λαβὼν [τὴν ἀρχὴ]ν καὶ παρελόμενος
τοῦ δήμου τὰ ὅπλα κατεῖχεν ἤδη τὴν τυραννίδα βεβαίως, καὶ
Νάξον ἑλὼν ἄρχοντα κατέστησε Λύγδαμιν. παρεῖλε[το] δὲ τοῦ 4
δήμου τὰ ὅπλα τόνδε τὸν τρόπον. ἐξοπλισίαν ἐν τ[ῷ] Θησείῳ

13 ἀναλαβὼν? Richards. **14—15** *καὶ γὰρ Νάξον ἑλὼν* K-W: *καὶ Νάξον ἑλὼν* K[3], B; *καὶ εἰς Νάξον ἐλθὼν* K[1] (H-L). **15** *παρείλετο* Rutherford, K-W, H-L, K[3]: *παρεῖλεν* K[1]. **16** ΕΞΟΠΛΑΣΙΑΝ retinuerunt Kontos, K-W, B, titulis nonnullis freti (Dittenberger 158, 11, titulo Iliensi post Alexandri mortem scripto, *τῶν ἐξοπλασιῶν*, et 349, 40, lapide in insula Ceo invento, *ἐν τῇ ἐξοπλασίᾳ ἐξετάζειν*; eadem scriptura etiam in Diodori Siculi codicibus servata est). ΘΗΣΕΙΩΙ nunc in papyro legit K (B): Α|ΝΑΚΕΙΩΙ legunt K-W, quod ex Polyaeno quondam sumpserat K[1] (H-L).

ἐχρῶντο δὲ πρὸς τοὺς πολεμίους ἵπποις πρὸς τοὺς ἀστυγείτονας, οἷον Ἐρετριεῖς καὶ Χαλκιδεῖς κτλ. An inscription preserved in the temple of Artemis, about a mile from the city, recorded that the Eretrians used to march to that temple with 3000 hoplites, 600 horsemen, and 60 chariots (Strabo, p. 448). Cf. Gilbert, *Gr. St.*, ii 67 n.

§ 3. **τὴν ἐπὶ Παλληνίδι μάχην**] On the way from Marathon to Athens. Hdt. i 62, *ἐπὶ Παλληνίδος Ἀθηναίης ἱρόν*. The deme Pallene lay near Gargettos, between Pentelicus and the northern spurs of Hymettus. It has been proposed to place it S.E. of Hymettus, near *Koropi* (*Ath. Mittheilungen*, xvi 200—234); but this appears to have been the site of Sphettos, and the proposed identification does not suit the data in Hdt.; while the name of Pallene survives in *Ballána* between *Kantza* and *Hieraka* (Milchhöfer in *Berl. Phil. Wochenschr.*, 1892, no. 1 and 2). Cf. Arist. *Ach.* 233 *βλέπειν Βαλλήναδε*. In the Austrian map the name *Balánas* is given to a stream which rises near *Kantza* and falls into the sea at Araphen, after flowing in a direction parallel to the route by which Peisistratus marched to Athens round the S. of Pentelicus.

Νάξον—Λύγδαμιν] Hdt. i 64, *καὶ γὰρ ταύτην ὁ Πεισίστρατος κατεστρέψατο πολέμῳ καὶ ἐπέτρεψε Λυγδάμι.* Schol. Aristoph. *Vesp.* 355, *Νάξος ἑάλω ἐπὶ Πεισιστράτου.*

As Polycrates came to the end of his rule of 16 years in B.C. 521, having been aided in its establishment by Lygdamis, it follows that Lygdamis was in power at Naxos in 537 (Duncker, *G. d. A.* vi 465 and 512). As Peisistratus, who restored Lygdamis, died in 527, it would follow that the third *τυραννίς* probably lasted 10 or 11 years. The only alternative is to suppose that Lygdamis aided Polycrates before he himself needed the aid of Peisistratus.

§ 4. **παρείλετο—τὰ ὅπλα**] characteristic of a *τυραννίς*. *Pol.* viii (v) 10, 1311 *a* 12, *τὸ τῷ πλήθει μηδὲν πιστεύειν (διὸ καὶ τὴν παραίρεσιν ποιοῦνται τῶν ὅπλων).*

ἐξοπλισίαν] Cf. Xen. *Anab.* i 7 § 10, *ἐν τῇ ἐξοπλισίᾳ*, of an armed mustering of troops in preparation for a battle, the only passage in which the word is used by Xenophon. *Cyrop.* viii 5 § 9 *ἐξόπλισις*. *ἐξοπλίζεσθαι* occurs in *Anab.* i 8 § 3, ii 1 § 2, iv 6 § 7, v 9 § 11, *ἐξωπλισμένος* iii 1 § 28, iv 3 § 3. Diodorus xix 3 *ἐν ταῖς ἐξοπλισίαις φέρειν πανοπλίαν.*

The story is told as follows in Polyaenus i 21 § 2, *Πεισίστρατος Ἀθηναίων τὰ ὅπλα βουλόμενος παρελέσθαι, παρήγγειλεν ἥκειν ἅπαντας εἰς τὸ Ἀνάκειον μετὰ τῶν ὅπλων. οἱ μὲν ἧκον· ὁ δὲ προῆλθε βουλόμενος δημηγορῆσαι, καὶ σμικρᾷ τῇ φωνῇ λέγειν ἤρχετο. οἱ δὲ ἐξακούειν μὴ δυνάμενοι, προελθεῖν αὐτὸν ἠξίωσαν εἰς τὸ προπύλαιον, ἵνα πάντες ἀκούσειαν. ἐπεὶ δὲ ὁ μὲν ἡσυχῇ διελέγετο, οἱ δ' ἐντείναντες τὰς ἀκοὰς προσεῖχον, οἱ ἐπίκουροι προελθόντες ἀράμενοι τὰ ὅπλα κατήνεγκαν εἰς τὸ ἱερὸν τὸ Ἀγραύλου. Ἀθηναῖοι δὲ γυμνοὶ καταλειφθέντες, τότε ᾔσθοντο τῆς Πεισιστράτου βραχυφωνίας, ὅτι ἄρα ἦν τέχνασμα κατὰ τῶν ὅπλων.*

The *Ἀνάκειον*, or temple of the *Dioscuri* or *Ἄνακες* (Plut. *Thes.* 33, Cic. *Nat. Deor.* iii 53), mentioned by Polyaenus, stood S.E. of the market of the Ceramicus (Curtius, *Text der Sieben Karten*, p. 53; *Stadtgeschichte von Athen*, pp. XLVI and 82). It was probably some way up the northern slope of the Acropolis. Lucian, *Piscator*, 42, humorously describes the philosophers 'planting their ladders against the *Ἀνάκειον*, and swarming up' the Acropolis. Andocides, *De Myst.* i 45, mentions a cavalry muster at the *Ἀνάκειον*, and Thucydides, viii 93, says that the hoplites who had destroyed the *ποιησάμενος ἐκκλησιάζειν ἐπεχείρει, [τῆς δὲ φωνῆς ἐχάλ]ασεν μικρόν· οὐ φασκόντων δὲ κατακούειν ἐκέλευσεν αὐτοὺς προσαν[α]βῆ[ναι] πρὸς τὸ πρόπυλον τῆς ἀκροπόλεως ἵνα γεγώνῃ μᾶλλον. ἐν ᾧ δ' ἐκεῖνος διέτριβε δημηγορῶν, ἀνελόντες οἱ ἐπὶ τούτῳ*

17 *τῆς δὲ φωνῆς ἐχάλασεν* coniecit Kontos (laudant H-L in praefatione, accepit K[3]): [*φθέγγεσθαι δ' ἐσπούδ*]*ασεν* K-W; *ἐπιτηδὲς δ' ἐφώνησε* Tyrrell et Gertz (H-L in textu). **20** ΔΙΕΤΡΕΙΒΕ. **20—21** ΤΟΥΤ(ΩΝ). ΤΕΤΑΓ: *τούτῳ* Rutherford et J E B Mayor, coll. Plut. *Sulla* 14 § 10 *Κουρίωνος ἐπὶ τούτῳ τεταγμένου* (K[3], B), *τοῦτο* K-W, *τοῦτ' ἐπιτεταγμένοι* H-L.

---

fort of Eetioneia *ἔθεντο ἐν τῷ 'Ανακείῳ τὰ ὅπλα* (Miss Harrison, *Mythology etc. of Athens*, 152).

The precinct of Agraulos, also mentioned by Polyaenus, may be placed below the ancient stone staircase in the N. cliff of the Acropolis, some 60 yards W. of the N. Porch of the Erechtheum. (Cf. Curtius, *Stadtgeschichte*, pp. XLIV, 37.)

The *Θησεῖον* is mentioned in the text. Its position is approximately determined by the description of Pausanias. After leaving the Gymnasium and the *Θησεῖον*, which are near one another and 'not far from the Agora,' he passes from the *Θησεῖον* to the *'Ανάκειον*, and adds that above the latter is the precinct of Agraulos (i 17 § 2, 18 §§ 1, 2). The *Θησεῖον* was probably E. of the Agora and is not to be confounded with the building on the 'hill of Colonus' within the walls, popularly called the 'Theseum,' but now generally identified as the temple of Hephaestus (Miss Harrison, *l. c.* 145, 118). According to Polyaenus, the weapons are at first left in the *'Ανάκειον* and transferred to the *'Αγραύλιον*. According to the text, they are left in the *Θησεῖον* and are then locked up *εἰς τὰ πλησίον οἰκήματα τοῦ Θησείου*, not 'the buildings near the Theseum,' as we might have expected, but 'the neighbouring buildings of the Theseum.' The latter phrase suggests that some other building than the *Θησεῖον* has already been mentioned, and this (so far as it goes) is in favour of *ἐν τῷ 'Ανακείῳ*, although it is not in the MS. If *ἐν τῷ 'Ανακείῳ* is accepted, it proves that the *Theseum* is near the *Anaceum*, below the N. cliff of the Acropolis (C. Wachsmuth, *Rheinisches Museum*, xlvi 327).

τῆς δὲ φωνῆς ἐχάλασεν μικρόν] Lucian, *Bis Accus.* 21, *χαλῶντες τοῦ τόνου*, Aelian, *Hist. Anim.* xii 46.

With *φθέγγεσθαι δ' ἐσπούδασεν μικρόν*, printed by K-W, may be compared Dem. *F. L.* 206, *φθέγγεσθαι μέγιστον ἁπάντων*, 216, *καλὸν καὶ μέγα οὗτος φθέγξεται,*... *φαῦλον ἐγώ*, 337, *καλὸν φθεγγομένῳ*, *Pant.* 37 § 52, *μέγα φθέγγεται*, *Steph.* 45 § 77, *λαλεῖν μέγα*, Lysias 16 § 19, *μικρὸν διαλεγόμενοι*. *ἐσπούδασεν* is not, however, convincing.

τὸ πρόπυλον] Apparently used on purpose to avoid the grander term *προπύλαια*, which would have been an anachronism in so far as it would have suggested the Propylaea of the time of Pericles. *πρόπυλον* itself is seldom used in the singular. Cic. *ad Att.* vi 1, 26, *audio Appium πρόπυλον Eleusine facere*, Plut. *Mor.* 363 F, *ἐν τῷ προπύλῳ τοῦ ἱεροῦ τῆς 'Αθηνᾶς* (at Sais); Plin. *N. H.* xxxv 101, *Minervae delubri propylon*, xxxvi 32, *in propylo Atheniensium*. Pliny may have borrowed this exceptional form from Heliodorus, who possibly lived under Ptolemy Epiphanes, and wrote a work on the Acropolis (Wachsmuth, *Stadt Athen*, i 36). The word is found (in pl.) in Hdt., Hippocrates, and in an inscription from Smyrna. Mr H. Richards accordingly suggests that it may be an Ionism. But the word is also found in an inscr. of the 5th century from the Peiraeus, CIA ii 521 *e*, p. 122, *προπύλου δημοσίου ὅρος*.

Traces of the foundations of this ancient portal have been noticed S. of the E. hall of the Propylaea. It faced S.W. (Milchhöfer in Baumeister, *Denkm.* i 201 *a*).

γεγώνῃ] Ar. *De Anima* ii 8, 420 *a* 1, *διὰ τὸ ψαθυρὸς εἶναι ὁ ἀὴρ οὐ γεγωνεῖ*. *περὶ ἀκουστῶν*, 804 *b* 24, *φθέγγονται μὲν ἀλλ' οὐ δύνανται γεγωνεῖν, ἀλλὰ μόνον φωνοῦσιν*, cf. 802 *b* 6, *a* 23. *Probl.* 917 *b* 21, *ὁ αὐτὸς τῇ αὐτῇ φωνῇ πορρωτέρω γεγωνεῖ μετ' ἄλλων ᾄδων ἢ μόνος*, cf. 901 *b* 31 *γεγώνασι*, 904 *b* 35 *γεγωνώς* (*Index Ar.*). Antiphon, *de caede Herod.* 44, *πολλῷ πλέον γεγωνεῖν ἔστι νύκτωρ ἢ μεθ' ἡμέραν* (Cobet, *Mnem.* iv 153). *γεγωνεῖν* is the normal form in Attic prose, but the word is far from common.

τεταγμένοι τὰ ὅπλα [καὶ κατα]κλήσαντες εἰς [τὰ] πλησίον οἰ-
κήματα τοῦ Θησείου διεσήμηναν ἐλθόντες πρὸς τὸν Πεισίστρα-
τον· ὁ δέ, [ἐπεὶ τ]ὸν ἄλλον λόγον ἐπετέλεσεν, εἶπε καὶ περὶ τῶν 5
ὅπλων, τὸ γεγονὸς [ὡς οὐ] χρὴ θαυμάζειν οὐ[δ' ἀ]θυμεῖν, ἀλλ'
ἀπελθόντας ἐπὶ τῶν ἰδίων εἶναι, τῶν δὲ κοινῶν [αὐτὸς ἐπι]με-
λήσεσθαι πάντων.

16. [ἡ μὲν οὖν Πει]σιστράτου τυραννὶς ἐξ ἀρχῆς τε κατέστη
[τοῦτον] τὸν τρόπον καὶ [μεταβο]λὰς ἔσχε τοσαύτας. διῴκει δ' ὁ 2
Πεισίστρατος, ὥσπερ εἴρηται, [τὰ κατὰ] τὴν πόλιν μετρίως καὶ
μᾶλλον πολιτικῶς ἢ τυραννικῶς· ἔν τε γὰρ τοῖς ἄλλοις [φι]λάν-
θρωπος ἦν καὶ πρᾶος καὶ τοῖς ἁμαρτάνουσι συγγνωμονικός, καὶ δὴ
καὶ τοῖς ἀ[πό]ροι[ς] προεδάνειζε χρ[ήμα]τα πρὸς τὰς ἐργασίας, ὥστε
διατρέφεσθαι γεωργοῦντας. τοῦτο δ' ἐποίει δυοῖν [χά]ριν, ἵν[α] 3
μήτε ἐν τῷ ἄστει διατρίβωσιν ἀλλὰ διεσπαρμένοι κατὰ τὴν χώραν,

21 αὐτῶν [καὶ συγ]κλήσαντες K (K-W, H-L), sed αὐτῶν quidem in papyro abesse, partem autem notae quae κατά significaret apparere, indicavit Blass. **24** [καὶ ὡς οὐ χρὴ] H-L (K³), [ὡς οὐ] χρὴ B, [λέγων ὡς οὐ χρὴ] K¹; [ἔφη δ' οὐ δεῖν] K-W. ἀθυμεῖν K-W (K³, B): [ἀγανακτ]εῖν H-L. **25** εἶναι add. Marchant coll. Aesch. 3 § 8, Dem. 15 § 11, 6 § 4, 26 § 33 et infra 16 § 3 πρὸς τοῖς ἰδίοις ὄντες. Compendium quod verbum εἶναι exprimit \ in papyro inesse divinavit Wyse, invenit K. αὐτὸς ἐπιμελήσεσθαι Blass, K-W, K³: αὐτὸς νῦν ἐπ. H-L.

XVI 3 εἴρηται [τὰ κατὰ] B: εἴρηται [ἤδη] (K³, K-W): εἰρήκαμεν (K¹, H-L). **4** τοῖς ἄλλοις (K³, K-W): τοῖς θ[εσμοῖς] K¹, ταῖς ὁμιλίαις H-L. **5** ΠΡΑΟϹ (K, B), cf. Voemel, *Prolegomena Grammatica ad Dem. Contiones*, § 29: πρᾶος K-W, H-L. **6** προσεδάνειζε Rutherford et quondam Wyse. **7** ΔΙΑ...ΦΕϹΓΕΩΡΓΟΥΝΤΑϹ (ΘΓ supra) litteris incertis scripta (K-W, K³, B): διαμπερὲς ἐγεωργοῦντο quondam K, διανεκὲς ἐγεωργοῦντο H-L. **8** διεσπαρμένοι <ὦσι> Kontos (H-L).

τεταγμένοι] *Pol.* 1298 *a* 23, τὰς ἀρχὰς τὰς ἐφ' ἑκάστοις τεταγμένας. τετάχθαι may have ἐπὶ with the dat. or acc., the former is found in Xen., and both in Plato. Plat. *Rep.* 345 D, ἐφ' ᾧ τέτακται, *Crit.* 50 D, οἱ ἐπὶ τούτῳ τεταγμένοι νόμοι, *Leg.* 952 E, τοὺς ἐπὶ τούτοις ἄρχοντας τεταγμένους, *ib.* 772 B, ἐπὶ πάντα καὶ ἕκαστα ταχθεὶς (χρόνος), *Tim.* 47 C, λόγος ἐπ' αὐτὰ ταῦτα τέτακται. The gen. is comparatively rare.

§ 5. **ἀθυμεῖν**] *Met.* iii 5, 1009 *b* 37, πῶς οὐκ ἄξιον ἀθυμῆσαι. δυσθυμεῖν (Hdt. viii 10) is not found in Ar.

ἐπὶ τῶν ἰδίων εἶναι] c. 16 § 3. *Pol.* viii (v) 8, 1309 *a* 6, οἱ γὰρ ἄποροι οὐ βουλήσονται ἄρχειν τῷ μηδὲν κερδαίνειν, ἀλλὰ πρὸς τοῖς ἰδίοις εἶναι μᾶλλον, οἱ δὲ εὔποροι δυνήσονται διὰ τὸ μηδενὸς προσδεῖσθαι τῶν κοινῶν.

XVI § 2. **εἴρηται**] 14 § 3.

καὶ δὴ καὶ] § 10.

τοῖς ἀπόροις—γεωργοῦντας] In the same spirit, we read in Plut. *Sol.* 31, ὡς δὲ Θεόφραστος ἱστόρηκε, καὶ τὸν τῆς ἀργίας νόμον οὐ Σόλων ἔθηκεν, ἀλλὰ Πεισίστρατος, ᾧ τήν τε χώραν ἐνεργεστέραν καὶ τὴν πόλιν ἠρεμαιοτέραν ἐποίησεν. For διατρέφεσθαι Mr Wyse compares Xen. *de Red.* i 1; iv 49; Schol. Aristoph. *Vesp.* 1446, ἐργαζόμενοι διατρέφοιντο. For the general sense, cf. *Pol.* 1320 *b* 7, (even under a democracy) χαριέντων ἐστὶ καὶ νοῦν ἐχόντων γνωρίμων καὶ διαλαμβάνοντας τοὺς ἀπόρους ἀφορμὰς διδόντας τρέπειν ἐπ' ἐργασίας.

προεδάνειζε] In this verb πρὸ does not mean 'beforehand,' but 'in advance.' προδανείζειν, originally 'to make an advance,' develops the meaning 'to lend without interest.' The conjecture προσεδάνειζε, 'he *also* lent money,' is withdrawn. It rested on the assumption that προεδάνειζε meant 'he lent beforehand,' a sense unsuitable to the context (Wyse in *Class. Rev.* vi 254.

§ 3. **μήτε...ἀλλὰ**] *Pol.* viii (v) 8, 1308

καὶ ὅπως [εὐπο]ροῦντες τῶν μετρίων καὶ πρὸς τοῖς [ἰ]δίοις ὄντες
μήτ' ἐπιθυμῶσι μήτε σχολάζ[ωσιν] ἐπιμελεῖσθαι τῶν κοινῶν.
4 *ἅμα δὲ συνέβαινεν αὐτῷ καὶ τὰς προσόδους γίγνεσθαι μ[είζο]υς*
ἐξεργαζομένης τῆς χώρας· ἐπράττετο γὰρ ἀπὸ τῶν γιγνομένων
5 *δεκάτην. διὸ καὶ τοὺς κατὰ [δήμ]ους κατεσκεύαζε δικαστὰς καὶ*
αὐτὸς ἐξῄει πολλάκις εἰς τὴν χώραν ἐπισκοπῶν [καὶ] διαλ[ύ]ων
τοὺς διαφερομένους, ὅπως μὴ καταβαίνοντες εἰς τὸ ἄστυ παρα-
6 *μελῶσι τῶν [ἀγρ]ῶν. τοιαύτης γάρ τινος ἐξόδου τῷ Πεισιστράτῳ*

11 ΓΙΝ (K-W) sed in versu proximo ΓΙΓΝ (K-W etc.). **12** *ἐξ ἐργαζομένης* H-L. **13** ΚΑΤΕϹΚΕΥΑΖΕ (K, H-L): *κατεσκεύασε* K-W, B. **14** *διαλύων* (K^3, K-W, B): *διαλλάττων* K^1 (H-L); lacuna vix quattuor litterarum capax.

---

b 11, *μήτ' αὐξάνειν λίαν μηδένα παρὰ τὴν συμμετρίαν, ἀλλὰ μᾶλλον πειρᾶσθαι.* *Rhet.* i 4, 1359 *b* 6. For the general sense, *Pol.* viii (v) 10, 1311 *a* 14, *τὸ ἐξ ἄστεος ἀπελαύνειν καὶ διοικίζειν ἀμφοτέρων κοινόν, καὶ τῆς ὀλιγαρχίας καὶ τῆς τυραννίδος.*

διεσπαρμένοι κατὰ τὴν χώραν] *Pol.* vii (vi) 4, 1319 *a* 30, *διὰ τὸ περὶ τὴν ἀγορὰν καὶ τὸ ἄστυ κυλίεσθαι πᾶν τὸ τοιοῦτον γένος ὡς εἰπεῖν ῥᾳδίως ἐκκλησιάζει. οἱ δὲ γεωργοῦντες διὰ τὸ διεσπάρθαι κατὰ τὴν χώραν οὔτ' ἀπαντῶσιν οὔθ' ὁμοίως δέονται τῆς συνόδου ταύτης.* vi (viii) 5, 1292 *b* 25, *ὅταν μὲν οὖν τὸ γεωργικὸν καὶ τὸ κεκτημένον μετρίαν οὐσίαν κύριον ᾖ τῆς πολιτείας, πολιτεύονται κατὰ νόμους· ἔχουσι γὰρ ἐργαζόμενοι ζῆν, οὐ δύνανται δὲ σχολάζειν, ὥστε τὸν νόμον ἐπιστήσαντες ἐκκλησιάζουσι τὰς ἀναγκαίας ἐκκλησίας.* vii (vi) 4, 1318 *b* 9, *βέλτιστος γὰρ δῆμος ὁ γεωργικός ἐστιν...διὰ μὲν γὰρ τὸ μὴ πολλὴν οὐσίαν ἔχειν ἄσχολος, ὥστε μὴ πολλάκις ἐκκλησιάζειν.* Diogenes Laert. i 98 says of Periander, on the authority of Ephorus and Aristotle, *οὐκ εἴα ἐν ἄστει ζῆν τοὺς βουλομένους.* Similarly, in the abstract of Aristotle, by Heracleides, *οὐκ ἐπιτρέπων ἐν ἄστει ζῆν* (Rose, Frag.[3] 611, 20).

Cf. Aelian *V. H.* ix 25; Max. Tyr. xxix 3; and Dion Chrys. *Or.* 7 i p. 257 f. R., i 520—1 R. (Mayor).

τῶν μετρίων] 27 § 3.

πρὸς τοῖς ἰδίοις ὄντες] See note on 15 § 5, *ἐπὶ τῶν ἰδίων εἶναι.*

μήτε σχολάζωσιν] Similarly in *Pol.* viii (v) 11, 1313 *b* 23, the object of the Peisistratidae, in beginning the building of the Olympieum, was *ἀσχολίαν (καὶ πενίαν) τῶν ἀρχομένων.* Cf. *ib.* 19 ff.

§ 4. **δεκάτην]** Hitherto, the main evidence for this has been the spurious letter of Peisistratus to Solon, Diog. Laert. i 53. The present passage supports the view of Boeckh (iii 6), Arnold (on Thuc. vi 54 § 5) and Thirlwall (c. xi, p. 72—74), that Peisistratus levied a tax of ten per cent. Grote demurred to accepting this, on the ground of insufficient evidence. (It is mentioned in Zenobius iv 76, Mantissa Proverb. i 76, and Proverbiorum Appendix, ii 66.) Thuc. *l. c.*, after mentioning Hipparchus, says *ἐπετήδευσαν ἐπὶ πλεῖστον δὴ τύραννοι οὗτοι ἀρετὴν καὶ ξύνεσιν, καὶ Ἀθηναίους εἰκοστὴν μόνον πρασσόμενοι κτλ.*, and the scholars abovementioned accordingly assumed that the tax was reduced by the Peisistratidae. The text implies that this assumption was correct.

§ 5. **τοὺς κατὰ δήμους—δικαστάς]** The origin of these 'district-judges,' who went on circuit through the demes of Attica, is here for the first time ascribed to Peisistratus. Their number is stated as 30 under Pericles (c. 26 § 5). After the time of the Thirty Tyrants the number was changed to 40, four from each tribe (c. 53 § 1).

§ 6. **τοιαύτης γάρ τινος ἐξόδου** *κτλ.*] Zenobius, *Proverb. cent.* iv 76, *καὶ σφάκελοι ποιοῦσιν ἀτέλειαν* (= Suidas *s. v.* *καὶ σφάκελοι* p. 189, *et σφακελισμός*): *Πεισίστρατος, ὥς φασιν, ὁ τύραννος δεκάτην τῶν γεωργουμένων ἀπῄτει τοὺς Ἀθηναίους· παριὼν δέ ποτε, καὶ ἰδὼν πρεσβύτην πέτρας ἐργαζόμενον καὶ τόπους λιθώδεις, ἤρετο τὸν πρεσβύτην, τίνας ἐκ τῶν τόπων κομίζοιτο τοὺς καρπούς. ὁ δὲ ἀπεκρίνατο, Ὀδύνας καὶ σφακέλους, καὶ τούτων δεκάτην Πεισίστρατος φέρει. θαυμάσας δὲ ὁ Πεισίστρατος τὴν παρρησίαν αὐτοῦ τῆς δεκάτης ἀτέλειαν ἔδωκε καὶ ἐκ τούτου οἱ Ἀθηναῖοι τῇ παροιμίᾳ ἐχρήσαντο,* Mantissa Proverb. *cent.* i 76 (= Apostolius x 80 ed. Pontini). Diodorus Sic. ix 57 Bekker, *...ὁ ἐργάτης ἔφησε λαμβάνειν ἐκ τοῦ χωρίου κακὰς ὀδύνας, ἀλλ' οὐθὲν αὐτῷ μέλειν· τού-*

γιγνομένης συμβῆναί φασι τὰ περὶ τὸν ἐν τῷ [Ὑμητ]τῷ γεωργοῦντα τὸ κληθὲν ὕστερον χωρίον ἀτελές. ἰδὼν γάρ τινα πα[ττά]λῳ πέτρας σκάπτοντα καὶ ἐργαζόμενον, ⟦διὰ τὸ θαυμάσαι⟧ τὸν πα[ῖδα] ἐκέλευεν [ἐρ]έσθαι τί γίγνεται ἐκ τοῦ χωρίου· ὁ δ', ὅσα κακὰ καὶ ὀδύναι, ἔφη, καὶ τούτων τῶν κακῶν καὶ τῶν [ὀ]δυνῶν Πεισίστρατον δεῖ λαβεῖν τὴν δε[κά]την. ὁ μὲν οὖν ἄνθρωπος [ἀ]πε[κρί]νατο ἀγνοῶν, ὁ δὲ Πεισίστρατος ἡσθεὶς διὰ τὴν παρρησίαν καὶ τὴν φιλεργίαν [ἀ]τελῆ ἁπάντων ἐποίησεν αὐτόν. οὐδὲν δὲ τὸ πλῆθος 7
οὐδ' ἐν τοῖς ἄλλοις παρώχλει κατὰ τὴν ἀρχήν, ἀλλ' ἀεὶ π[α]ρεσκ[εύ]αζεν εἰρήνην καὶ ἐ[τ]ήρει τὴν ἡσυχίαν· διὸ καὶ πολλάκις ἐθ[ρυ]λλ[εῖ]το, ὡς [ἡ] Πεισιστράτου τυραννὶς ὁ ἐπὶ Κρόν[ου] βίος εἴη· συνέβη γὰρ ὕστερον δια[δεξαμένων] τῶν υἱέων πολλῷ γενέσθαι τραχυτέραν τὴν ἀρχήν. μέγιστον δὲ πάντων ἦν [τῶν 8
ἐπαινου]μένων τὸ δημοτικὸν εἶναι τῷ ἤθει καὶ φιλάνθρωπον. ἔν τε γὰρ τοῖς ἄλλο[ις προῃρεῖτο] πάντα διοικεῖν κατὰ τοὺς νόμους, οὐδεμίαν ἑαυτῷ πλεονεξίαν διδ[ούς, καί ποτ]ε προσκληθεὶς φόνου δίκην εἰς Ἄρειον πάγ[ον] αὐτὸς μὲν ἀπήντησεν ὡς [ἀπολο]γησό-

17 ΤΑ: τὸ H-L. ΥΜΜΗΤΩΙ? **18** πατάλῳ K; π...λω[ς] K-W, παντελῶς Wessely, B; sed exspectares potius ἐπιμελῶς vel ἐπιπόνως: πρεσβύτην invita papyro H-L. **19** πέτρας: ΠΕΤΡΑΙϹ?, [ἐν] πέτραις K-W et Wessely. διὰ τὸ θαυμάσαι secl. K-W, 'θαυμάσας scriptum malis' H-L. παῖδα K-W, H-L, K[3], B: πάτταλον K[1], sed spatium non sufficit. **20** [περι]γίγνεται K-W invita papyro. **21** τῶν κακῶν καὶ τῶν ὀδυνῶν om. H-L; τῶν ante ὀδυνῶν secl. K-W. **23** <αὐτὸν> ἀγνοῶν H-L. **25** ΠΑΡΩΧΛΕΙ (K): παρηνώχλει J B Mayor (K-W, H-L, B). **26** ἐτήρει τὴν ἡσυχίαν (K[3], K-W, H-L, B); ἐπηρείας ἡσυχίαν coniecerat Blass. **27** [παρῳμιάζ]ετο K; [τοῦτ' ἐλέ]γετο K-W, [ὕστερον ἐλέγετο] H-L; ἐθρύλησαν Wessely (litteras priores saltem cum papyri indiciis obscuris congruere existimat K); ἐθ[ρυ]λλ[εῖ]το B. **28** δια[δεξαμένων] E Bruhn (B): διὰ τὴν ὕβριν Sidgwick, Gennadios, K-W, H-L, K[3]. **30** ἐπαινουμένων J B Mayor, Newman, Bury, K-W, H-L (K[3], B). **31** εἰώθει K (H-L); προῃρεῖτο K-W, B.

των γὰρ τὸ μέρος Πεισιστράτῳ διδόναι. ὁ δὲ δυνάστης...γελάσας ἐποίησε τὸ χωρίον ἀτελές, καὶ ἐντεῦθεν ἡ παροιμία 'καὶ σφάκελοι ποιοῦσιν ἀτέλειαν.' Procopius in Villoison, *Anecd.* ii 40.

The story has been traced to Demon, the writer of a work on proverbs, who is probably the same as the writer of an Ἀτθίς, earlier than Philochorus (Zenob. Athous ii 4 quoted by O. Crusius *Anal. ad Paroem.* p. 132 f). But, if this Demon is the same as the nephew of Demosthenes bearing that name, he is later than the date of this treatise.

§ 7. **παρώχλει**] παροχλέω is found in Theophr. *C. P.* iii 10, 5. παρενοχλέω is less uncommon.

ὁ ἐπὶ Κρόνου βίος] 'the golden age.' [Plat.] *Hipparch.* 229 B (after the death of Hipparchus) τρία ἔτη ἐτυραννεύθησαν Ἀθηναῖοι ὑπὸ τοῦ ἀδελφοῦ αὐτοῦ Ἱππίου, καὶ πάντων ἂν τῶν παλαιῶν ἤκουσας, ὅτι ταῦτα μόνα τὰ ἔτη τυραννὶς ἐγένετο ἐν Ἀθήναις, τὸν δ' ἄλλον χρόνον ἐγγύς τι ἔζων Ἀθηναῖοι ὥσπερ ἐπὶ Κρόνου βασιλεύοντος. The same proverbial phrase is applied by Plutarch, *Arist.* 24, to the happy condition of the Athenian allies under the administration of Aristeides, and in *Cimon* 10 to the liberality of Cimon (*inf.* c. 27 § 3).

συνέβη—ἀρχήν] c. 15 § 1.

§ 8. **δημοτικὸν**] c. 14 *init.*

καί ποτε προσκληθεὶς—ἔλιπεν] *Pol.* viii (v) 12, 1315 *b* 21, φασὶ δὲ καὶ Πεισίστρατον ὑπομεῖναί ποτε προσκληθέντα δίκην εἰς Ἄρειον πάγον. Plut. *Sol.* 31, ὅς γε καὶ φόνου προσκληθεὶς εἰς Ἄρειον πάγον ἤδη τυραννῶν ἀπήντησε κοσμίως ἀπολογησόμενος, ὁ δὲ κατήγορος οὐχ ὑπήκουσε.

9 μενος, ὁ δὲ προσκαλεσάμενος φοβηθεὶς ἔλιπεν. διὸ καὶ πολὺν χρόνον ἔμεινεν <ἐν> [τῇ ἀρχῇ, καὶ] ὅτ' ἐκπέσοι πάλιν ἀνελάμβανε ῥᾳδίως. ἐβούλοντο γὰρ καὶ τῶν γνωρίμων καὶ τῶν [δημο]τικῶν οἱ πολλοί· τοὺς μὲν γὰρ ταῖς ὁμιλίαις τοὺς δὲ ταῖς εἰς τὰ ἴδια βοηθείαις προ[σ]ήγετο, καὶ πρὸς ἀμφοτέρους ἐπεφύκει καλῶς.
10 ἦσαν δὲ καὶ τοῖς Ἀθηναίοις οἱ περὶ τῶν [τυ]ράννων νόμοι πρᾷοι κατ' ἐκείνους τοὺς καιροὺς οἵ τ' ἄλλοι καὶ δὴ καὶ ὁ μάλιστα καθ[ήκ]ων πρὸς τὴν <κατάστασιν> τῆς τυραννίδος. νόμος γὰρ αὐτοῖς ἦν ὅδε· θέσμια τάδε Ἀθηναί[οις] καὶ πάτρια· ἐάν [τιν]ες τυραννεῖν ἐπανιστῶ[ν]ται ⟦ἐπὶ τυραννίδι⟧, ἢ τὴν τυραννίδα τις συγκαθιστῇ, ἄτιμο[ν εἶναι καὶ] αὐτὸν καὶ γένος.

17. Πεισίστρατος μὲν οὖν ἐγκατεγήρασε τῇ ἀρχῇ καὶ ἀπ-[έθ]ανε νοσήσα[ς ἐπὶ] Φιλόνεω ἄρχοντος, ἀφ' οὗ μὲν κατέστη τὸ

34 ἐξέλιπεν Richards coll. Dinarch. 3, 98 et Plat. *Leg.* 943 A (H-L). **35** ἐν ἀρχῇ H-L (K³): ἐν τῇ ἀρχῇ quondam Blass, K-W; cf. 17, 3—4. In papyro χ cerni posse putat K et post ἔμεινεν partem inferiorem litterae φ, deinde quinque sexve litterarum spatium. ΕΠΕΛΑΜΒΑΝΕ (K¹); ἀπελάμβανε Wyse, Gennadios, Ferrini, H-L, K³; ἀνελάμβανε K-W (B). **38** ἀμφοτέρας H-L. **39** ΠΡΑΟΙ (K), cf. v. 5. **41** καθήκων K (B): ἀνήκων H-L; κα[θεστώς] K-W. ΤΗΝΤΗΣ: τὰ τῆς H-L. κατάστασιν addidit post τυραννίδος K, post τὴν B; lacunam indicant K-W. **42** Ἀθηναίοις Kontos (B): Ἀθηναί[ων] K etc. ἐστί K (H-L): κατὰ τὰ K-W; κ(αὶ) Blass. **43** ΗΕΠΙΤΥΡΑΝΝΙΔΙΤΙΣΥΝΚΑΘΙΣΤΗΙΤΗΝΤΥΡΑΝΝΙΔΑ: ἢ τὴν τυραννίδα τις συγκαθιστῇ, Blass. ἐπὶ τυραννίδι secluserat K (K-W), utpote quondam supra verbum τυραννεῖν per formulam usitatiorem interpretandi causa scriptum. ἢ ἐπὶ τυραννίδι τις συγκαθιστῇ συνωμοσίαν, ἄτιμον H-L. ἐπι<τιθῆται> τυραννίδι Richards coll. *Pol.* 1108 *a* 22, Lycurg. *Leocr.* 125. ἐάν τις ἐπὶ τυραννίδι ἐπανιστῆται ἢ συγκαθίστῃ τὴν τυραννίδα Hager. <ἢ> τι<ς> K³: cum in papyro ἢ et τι prorsus similia sint, fortasse nihil nisi ἢ legendum suspicatur K; ἢ K-W, B **44** εἶναι καὶ H-L ('fortasse recte' K), B: εἶναι K.

XVII 1 ΕΝΚΑΤΕΓΗΡΑΣΕ (probat Rutherford).

§ 9. **διὸ—ἐπεφύκει καλῶς**] Cf. the sketch of the best means for maintaining a τυραννίς in *Pol.* 1314 *a* 30—1315 *b* 10.

ὅτ' ἐκπέσοι...ἀνελάμβανε] Optative of indefinite frequency, followed by the impf., as in *Pol.* viii (v) 5, 1305 *a* 7, ἐπὶ δὲ τῶν ἀρχαίων, ὅτε γένοιτο ὁ αὐτὸς δημαγωγὸς καὶ στρατηγός, εἰς τυραννίδα μετέβαλλον. For ἀνελάμβανε cf. Hdt. iii 73, (τὴν ἀρχὴν) ἀναλαβεῖν.

§ 10. **καὶ δὴ καί**] as often with οἵ τε ἄλλοι preceding; *supra* § 2.

ἐάν τινες—καὶ γένος] Andocides, *De Mysteriis*, § 97, ἐάν τις τυραννεῖν ἐπαναστῇ ἢ τὸν τύραννον συγκαταστήσῃ. In later times such an offence would be met by a καταλύσεως τοῦ δήμου γραφή, and the penalty would be death and confiscation of property. The decree against the orator Antiphon and Archeptolemus (one of the Four Hundred) required them to be put to death and their property to be confiscated. It also declared each of them to be ἄτιμον...καὶ τὸ γένος τὸ ἐκ τούτοιν (Pseudo-Plut. *vit. Antiph.* § 28).

Cf. Arist. *Thesm.* 338, εἴ τις...τυραννεῖν ἐπινοεῖ ἢ τὸν τύραννον ξυγκαταγεῖν, *Vesp.* 495, 498, 502, *Lys.* 630. The text shews that in Andoc. *l.c.* Dobree's suggestion, <ἐπὶ τῷ> τυραννεῖν, is unnecessary.

XVII § 1. **ἐγκατεγήρασε**] used metaphorically in Dinarchus, *Aristog.* § 3, πονηρίαν ἀρχομένην, contrasted with ἐγκαταγεγηρακυῖαν, 'inveterate.' Plut. *Phocion* 30, πενίαν ἐν ᾗ...ἐγκατεγήρασε. ἐγγηράσκειν is similarly used c. dat.

Cf. Thuc. vi 54, 2, II. γηραιοῦ τελευτήσαντος; Val. Max. viii 9 E 2, 'decrepitum.'

Φιλόνεω ἄρχοντος] B.C. 527. The name of the archon of the year is now ascertained for the first time. The date of the death of Peisistratus was known

πρῶτον τύραννος, ἔτη τριά[κο]ν[τ]α καὶ τρία βιώσας, ἃ δ' ἐν τῇ
ἀρχῇ διέμεινεν, ἑνὸς δέοντα εἴκοσι· ἔφ[ευγ]εν γὰρ τὰ λοιπά. διὸ 2
καὶ φανερῶς ληροῦσιν <οἱ> φάσκοντες ‖ ἐρώμενον εἶναι Πεισί- [Col. 7.]
στρατον Σόλωνος καὶ στρατηγεῖν ἐν τῷ πρὸς Μεγαρέας πολέμῳ
περὶ Σαλαμῖνος· οὐ γὰρ ἐνδέχεται ταῖς ἡλικίαις, ἐάν τις ἀναλογί-
ζηται τὸν ἑκατέρου βίον καὶ ἐφ' οὗ ἀπέθανεν ἄρχοντος. τελευτή- 3
σαντος δὲ Πεισιστράτου, κατεῖχον οἱ υἱεῖς τὴν ἀρχήν, προάγοντες
τὰ πράγματα τὸν αὐτὸν τρόπον. ἦσαν δὲ δύο μὲν ἐκ τῆς γαμετῆς,
Ἱππίας καὶ Ἵππαρχος, δύο δ' ἐκ τῆς Ἀργείας, Ἰοφῶν καὶ Ἡγησί-
στρατος, ᾧ παρωνύμιον ἦν Θετταλός. ἔγημεν γὰρ Πεισίστρατος ἐξ 4

4 ἔφευγεν J B Mayor, Rutherford, K-W, H-L, K[3]: ΕΦ.ΓΕΝ: ἔφυγεν K[1], B. 5 ΛΗΡΟΥCΙ: ληροῦσιν οἱ K-W, H-L, Lacon, Hude (K[3], B). 7 CΑΛΑΜΕΙΝΟC. 9 ΠΡΟΑΓΑΓΟΝΤΕC: corr. Rutherford, J B Mayor, Blass, K-W, H-L (K[3]). 10 <'Αττικῆς> γαμετῆς H-L.

TESTIMONIA. 3 Heraclidis epitoma (Rose, Ar. Frag. 611, 4[3]) Πεισίστρατος λγ̄ ἔτη τυραννεύσας γηράσας ἀπέθανεν.

---

already. He died in the beginning of B.C. 527, the latter half of Ol. 63, 1. The date is fixed by Ar. *Pol.*, quoted below, and by Thuc. vi 59 § 5. The former makes the rule of the Peisistratidae last 18 years; the latter says that the battle of Marathon was in the 20th year after the expulsion of Hippias. 490 + 18 + 19 = 527 (Clinton, *Fasti*, ii 254).

ἔτη τριάκοντα καὶ τρία] *Pol.* viii (v) 12, 1315 *b* 30, ἡ τῶν Πεισιστρατιδῶν (ἀρχὴ) Ἀθήνησιν. οὐκ ἐγένετο δὲ συνεχής· δὶς γὰρ ἔφυγε Πεισίστρατος τυραννῶν· ὥστ' ἐν ἔτεσι τριάκοντα καὶ τρισὶν ἑπτακαίδεκα ἔτη τούτων ἐτυράννευσεν, ὀκτωκαίδεκα δὲ οἱ παῖδες, ὥστε τὰ πάντα ἐγένετο ἔτη τριάκοντα καὶ πέντε. The passage is part of a paragraph regarded as an interpolation by Susemihl, ed. 2 and 3.

ἑνὸς δέοντα εἴκοσι] In *Pol.* quoted above, the rule of Peisistratus is said to have lasted 17 years. It has been proposed to reconcile the two accounts by supposing that fractions of a year are included here, and excluded in the *Politics*. See, however, note on 14 § 3.

§ 2. **ἐρώμενον**] Ael. *V. H.* viii 16, λέγεται γὰρ αὐτοῦ παιδικὰ γενέσθαι.

Μεγαρέας] c. 14 § 1.

ἀπέθανεν] Solon died not long after 560 B.C. (Plut. *Sol.* 12); Peisistratus, in 527.

§ 3. **τὸν αὐτὸν τρόπον**] Thuc. vi 54 §§ 4 f. 6.

ἐκ τῆς γαμετῆς] The name is not known.

ἐκ τῆς Ἀργείας] Hdt. v 94, Πεισίστρατος...κρατήσας αὐτοῦ (sc. Σιγείου) κατέστησε τύραννον εἶναι παῖδα τὸν ἑωυτοῦ νόθον Ἡγησίστρατον, γεγονότα ἐξ Ἀργείας γυναικός. "Herodotus calls Hegesistratus νόθον, because after the middle of the fifth century (c. 26 *ad fin.*) women of foreign blood certainly could not occupy at Athens the position of a lawful wife: the children of a ξένη were both νόθοι and ξένοι. The same distinction is present to the writer: he contrasts 'the wedded wife' of Athenian birth with the 'Argive woman.' The reading need not be altered. Thucydides (vi 55 § 1) seems to include Thessalus among the legitimate sons of Peisistratus, τῶν γνησίων ἀδελφῶν" (Wyse, *Class. Rev.* v 226 *b*). In i 20 § 2, after stating that Hippias was the eldest son, he adds that Hipparchus and Thessalus were his brothers. The name of Thessalus was probably given him out of compliment to the Thessalian allies of the house of Peisistratus. The Thessalians ineffectually sent 1000 horse to defend Hippias shortly before his expulsion (Hdt. v 63). Plutarch, *Cato major* 24, calls Thessalus the son of Peisistratus and Timonassa, but we now know for the first time that this was another name for Hegesistratus. As regards the nationality of his mother it will be remembered that Peisistratus was aided, during his second exile, by mercenary troops from Argos (Hdt. i 61).

παρωνύμιον] = ἐπωνυμία (c. 45 § 1).

Ἄργους ἀνδρὸς Ἀργείου θυγατέρα, ᾧ ὄνομα ἦν Γοργίλος, Τιμώνασσαν, ἣν πρότερον ἔσχεν γυναῖκα Ἀρχῖνος ὁ Ἀμπρακιώτης τῶν Κυψελιδῶν· ὅθεν καὶ ἡ πρὸς τοὺς Ἀργείους ἐνέστη φιλία, καὶ συνεμαχέσαντο χίλιοι τὴν ἐπὶ Παλληνίδι μάχην Ἡγησιστράτου κομίσαντος. γῆμαι δέ φασι τὴν Ἀργείαν οἱ μὲν ἐκπεσόντα τὸ πρῶτον, οἱ δὲ κατέχοντα τὴν ἀρχήν.

18. ἦσαν δὲ κύριοι μὲν τῶν πραγμάτων διὰ τὰ ἀξιώματα καὶ διὰ τὰς ἡλικίας Ἵππαρχος καὶ Ἱππίας, πρεσβύτερος δ' ὢν ὁ

14 ἔσχε H-L. **15** ΕΝΕϹΤΗ: συνέστη H-L. **16** Ἡγησιστράτου primus detexit J B Mayor (K-W, H-L, K[3], B): Πεισιστράτου K[1].
XVIII 1 ΤΩΝ ΜΕΝ: μὲν τῶν Blass, Richards, edd.

Plat. *Soph.* 228 C. The adj. παρωνύμιος is found in Plat. *Leg.* 757 D, and the corresponding verb in Ar. *Phys.* vii 3, 245 *b* 11, 28, παρωνυμιάζοντες λέγομεν, and *Eth. Eud.* iii 1, 1228 *a* 35, παρωνυμιάζεσθαι = παρωνύμως παρά τι λέγεσθαι. The ordinary form of the adj. in Ar. is παρώνυμος.

§ 4. **Ἀρχῖνος ὁ Ἀμπρακιώτης τῶν Κυψελιδῶν**] Cypselus (tyrant of Corinth for 30 years from B.C. 658 or 655) was succeeded by his son Periander. Among the contemporaries of the latter was another Periander, son of Gorgus, who was either a son or a brother of Cypselus. This second Periander was a tyrant of *Ambracia*. The establishment of a branch of the Cypselidae in Ambracia was in accordance with the ambitious policy of that dynasty. They attempted to occupy the coast of the Ionian sea as far as Illyria (Müller, *Dor.* i 8 § 3). Periander was deposed probably after the death of the Corinthian tyrant of the same name (B.C. 585). *Pol.* viii (v) 10, 1311 *a* 39, Περιάνδρῳ τῷ ἐν Ἀμβρακίᾳ τυράννῳ, and 4, 1304 *a* 31, ἐν Ἀμβρακίᾳ ... Περίανδρον συνεκβαλὼν τοῖς ἐπιθεμένοις ὁ δῆμος τὸν τύραννον εἰς ἑαυτὸν περιέστησε τὴν πολιτείαν. Ambracia was colonised in the reign of Cypselus (Strabo, p. 452) either by that tyrant's brother, Torgus, or his son Gorgus. Strabo, p. 328, describes Ambracia as Τόλγου (*sic*) τοῦ Κυψέλου κτίσμα (Clinton's *Fasti*, sub anno 612 B.C.). In the *Politics* the affair of Harmodius and Aristogeiton is mentioned just before the fall of the Ambracian tyrant, Periander: here it is narrated shortly after a reference to another member of the Ambracian branch of the Cypselidae.—On Ambracia see Duncker, *H. G.* ii 353 E.T.

ἐπὶ Παλληνίδι] 15 § 3.

ἐκπεσόντα...κατέχοντα] If Peisistratus married Timonassa on his first usurpation of the government in 560 B.C., Hegesistratus may have been either 21, 23, 24 or 26 years of age at the battle of Pallene according as we place that event in 539 (Bauer), 536 (Reinach), 535 (Kenyon) or 533 (Poland). If he married her on his first expulsion, the son may have been four years younger (17 to 22) in the year of the battle. The latter view seems preferable, as his marriage with the 'Argive woman' is more likely to have taken place, when it was to his interest to secure the aid of Argos, than on his first usurpation, when her presence in the palace would not have ingratiated him with his Athenian subjects or with his wedded wife. The beginning of the second tyranny, four to six years later, is out of the question, partly because Peisistratus was then in alliance with Megacles, while Timonassa was probably no longer alive; and partly because this would make the son 15 at the most on the occasion of the battle.

Within about eight years of this time Hegesistratus was old enough to be placed in charge of Sigeum (Hdt. v 94). He was 'much younger' than Hipparchus (c. 18 § 2). Hipparchus, again, was younger than Hippias, and Hippias was an old man in B.C. 490 (Thuc. vi 59 § 5). If Hippias was more than 70 in 490, he was born before 560. Hippias and Hipparchus were already 'young men' (Hdt. i 61) when their father married the daughter of Megacles, either 8, 9 or 11 years after 560. All these considerations are in favour of placing the marriage at the time of the first exile.

XVIII. *Harmodius and Aristogeiton.*

§ 1. **πρεσβύτερος—ὁ Ἱππίας**] Thuc. i

Ἱππίας καὶ τῇ φύσει πολιτικὸς καὶ ἔμφρων ἐπεστάτει τῆς
ἀρχῆς. ὁ δὲ Ἵππαρχος παιδιώδης καὶ ἐρωτικὸς καὶ φιλόμουσος
ἦν, καὶ τοὺς περὶ Ἀνακρέοντα καὶ Σιμωνίδην καὶ τοὺς ἄλλους
ποιητὰς οὗτος ἦν ὁ μεταπεμπόμενος· Θετταλὸς δὲ νεώτερος πολὺ 2
καὶ τῷ βίῳ θρασὺς καὶ ὑβριστής. ἀφ' οὗ καὶ συνέβη τὴν ἀρχὴν

6—7 Θετταλὸς—ὑβριστὴς delet Herwerden: defendit Heraclides infra laudatus.

TESTIMONIA. **4—7** Heraclidis epitoma (Rose, Ar. Frag. 611, 4[3]) Ἵππαρχος ὁ υἱὸς Πεισιστράτου παιδιώδης ἦν καὶ ἐρωτικὸς καὶ φιλόμουσος, Θεσσαλὸς δὲ νεώτερος καὶ θρασύς. τοῦτον τυραννοῦντα μὴ δυνηθέντες ἀνελεῖν Ἵππαρχον ἀπέκτειναν τὸν ἀδελφὸν αὐτοῦ.

20, 2, Ἀθηναίων γοῦν τὸ πλῆθος Ἵππαρχον οἴονται ὑφ' Ἁρμοδίου καὶ Ἀριστογείτονος τύραννον ὄντα ἀποθανεῖν, καὶ οὐκ ἴσασιν ὅτι Ἱππίας μὲν πρεσβύτατος ὢν ἦρχε τῶν Πεισιστράτου υἱέων, Ἵππαρχος δὲ καὶ Θεσσαλὸς ἀδελφοὶ ἦσαν αὐτοῦ, and vi 54 § 2; 55 §§ 1, 2.

In [Plato], *Hipparchus*, 228 B, Hipparchus is wrongly described as the eldest son.

φιλόμουσος] Hipparchus is said to have set up in the demes of Attica Hermae inscribed with verses. *Hipparch.* 229 A, μνῆμα τόδ' Ἱππάρχου· στεῖχε δίκαια φρονῶν...ἔστι δὲ τῶν ποιημάτων καὶ ἄλλα ἐν ἄλλοις Ἑρμαῖς πολλὰ καὶ καλὰ ἐπιγεγραμμένα. The Homeric recitations introduced by Peisistratus at the Panathenaea were improved in certain respects by Hipparchus (*ib.* 228 B, Aelian, *V. H.* viii 2).

τοὺς περὶ] 'Formula οἱ περί τινα...interdum ita usurpatur, ut ab ipso personae nomine non multum differat, οἱ περὶ Ἐμπεδοκλέα καὶ Δημόκριτον *de Caelo* ii 7, 305 *b* 1 (cf. Ἐμπεδοκλῆς καὶ Δημόκριτος 305 *a* 34). οἱ περὶ Ἱπποκράτην *Meteor.* i 6, 342 *b* 35 (cf. Ἱπποκράτης 343 *a* 28). ἡ τῶν περὶ Γέλωνα τυραννὶς καὶ νῦν ἡ τῶν περὶ τὸν Διονύσιον, ἡ μὲν Γέλωνος *Pol.* v 10, 1312 *b* 10. Cf. *de Gener. et Corrupt.* 314 *a* 25, *Pol.* v 6, 1305 *b* 26', *Index Aristotelicus*. In such cases the proper name has no article (Eucken, *Sprachgebrauch*, *Praep.* p. 66).

Ἀνακρέοντα καὶ Σιμωνίδην] *Hipparch.* 228 C, (Hipparchus) ἐπ' Ἀνακρέοντα τὸν Τήϊον πεντηκόντορον στείλας ἐκόμισεν εἰς τὴν πόλιν· Σιμωνίδην δὲ τὸν Κεῖον ἀεὶ περὶ αὑτὸν εἶχε, μεγάλοις μισθοῖς καὶ δώροις πείθων.

Simonides (born 556 B.C.) was 29 years of age on the death of Peisistratus in 527. It was probably after the expulsion of the Peisistratidae that he wrote the epitaph on Archedice, daughter of Hippias, quoted in Thuc. vi 59. Cf. Plat. *Protag.* 346 B. He also celebrated the death of his patron Hipparchus (ἦ μέγ' Ἀθηναίοισι φόως γένεθ' ἡνίκ' Ἀριστο-γείτων Ἵππαρχον κτεῖνε καὶ Ἁρμόδιος, 134 Bergk). After spending some years at the court of the Aleuadae in Thessaly, he returned to Athens and there commemorated in verse some of the great events of the Persian wars. See also Freeman's *Sicily*, ii 258—264.

There is no evidence of intimate relations between Simonides and Anacreon, unless we ascribe to Simonides the epitaphs on Anacreon in *Anthol. Pal.* vii 24, 25, which are assigned with greater probability to a later poet, Leonidas.

Anacreon lived for many years at the court of Polycrates of Samos (Hdt. iii 121, Strabo, xiv 638), who was put to death in 522. The death of his patron and the unpopular rule of his successor would prompt him to accept the invitation of Hipparchus. At Athens he made the acquaintance of various members of noble families, such as Critias, son of Dropides (Plat. *Charmides*, 157 E) and Xanthippus, afterwards the victor of Mycale and the father of Pericles. On the death of Hipparchus, he probably went (like Simonides) to the court of the Aleuadae.

τοὺς ἄλλους ποιητὰς] *e.g.* the founder of the Athenian school of Dithyrambic poetry, and the teacher of Pindar, Lasus of Hermione, one of the rivals of Simonides (Aristoph. *Vesp.* 1410 Schol.). His detection of the forgeries of Onomacritus led to the banishment of the latter by Hipparchus (Hdt. vii 6).

§ 2. **Θετταλὸς**] Diodorus Sic., x 16, 1, gives him a character for wisdom: ἀπείπατο τὴν τυραννίδα.

ἀφ' οὗ] Whether οὗ is neuter or (more probably) masculine, it is clear that the troubles of the Peisistratidae are here ascribed to the ὕβρις of Thessalus, who is naturally the subject of the next sentence

αὐτοῖς γενέσθαι πάντων τῶν κακῶν. ἐρασθεὶς γὰρ τοῦ Ἁρμοδίου καὶ διαμαρτάνων τῆς πρὸς αὐτὸν φιλίας, οὐ κατεῖχε τὴν ὀργήν, ἀλλ' ἔν τε τοῖς ἄλλοις ἐνεσημαίνετο πικ[ρ]ῶς, καὶ τὸ τελευταῖον μέλλουσαν αὐτοῦ τὴν ἀδελφὴν κανηφορεῖν Παναθηναίοις ἐ[κώ]λυσεν, λοιδορήσας τι τὸν Ἁρμόδιον ὡς μαλακὸν ὄντα, ὅθεν συνέβη παροξυνθέντα τὸν Ἁρμόδιον καὶ τὸν Ἀριστογείτονα πράττειν τὴν πρᾶξιν μετεχόντων πολλῶν.
3 ἤδη δὲ [παρατη]ροῦντες ἐν ἀκροπόλει

10 πικρῶς K-W (K^3, B); ἐνεσήμαινε τὸ πικρὸν K^1, ἐνεσημαίνετο τὸ πικρόν Richards (H-L). **13** παροξυνθέντας H-L, sed 'spatium deest.' **14** μετεχόντων πολλῶν 'satis clare legitur' Blass: μετὰ πολιτῶν πολλῶν K; μετὰ πολιτῶν οὐ πολλῶν Gennadios; μετὰ συνει<δό>των <οὐ> πολλῶν J B Mayor (K-W); μετὰ συνωμοτῶν οὐ πολλῶν Thompson; μετ' ὀλίγων ἄλλων Richards; μετ' [ἄλλων οὐ] πολλῶν H-L.

ἐρασθεὶς γὰρ κτλ. This is so completely at variance with the account in Thucydides that Mr Kenyon in his first ed. felt constrained to throw the description of Thessalus into a parenthesis. But the writer does not hesitate to disagree with Thucydides in several of his details, and he may have deliberately disagreed with him in this important point. It does not follow that Thucydides is wrong. The whole of the episode on Harmodius and Aristogeiton is apparently written with extreme care to refute a popular error. It must also be remembered that (according to Hermippus, in Marcellinus, *Vit. Thuc.* p. ix, and Schol. on i 20) the historian was related to the Peisistratidae. Cf. vi 55 § 1, *εἰδὼς...καὶ ἀκοῇ ἀκριβέστερον ἄλλων*. On the other hand, the writer of this treatise shews in the latter part of c. 17 that he knows more than Thucydides about Thessalus, and Thucydides himself tacitly corrects in book i 20 some of the details in the account in book vi (Weil, *Journal des Savants*, avril 1891).

ἐρασθεὶς τοῦ Ἁρμοδίου] This is reported of Hipparchus by Diod. Sic. x 16 § 2, Plut. *Amator.* 16 § 27, p. 760, Athen. p. 602 A (Mayor).

ἐνεσημαίνετο πικρῶς] On the other hand, Thuc. (vi 54 § 4), with greater partiality towards the Peisistratidae, says of Hipparchus, *βίαιον μὲν οὐδὲν ἐβούλετο δρᾶν*. For *ἐνσημαίνεσθαι*, cf. Isocr. 20 § 22, *ἐνσημανεῖσθε...τὴν ὀργήν*.

μέλλουσαν—ἐκώλυσεν] Thuc. vi 56 § 1, *ἀδελφὴν γὰρ αὐτοῦ κόρην, ἐπαγγείλαντες ἥκειν κανοῦν οἴσουσαν ἐν πομπῇ τινί, ἀπήλασαν, λέγοντες οὐδὲ ἐπαγγεῖλαι τὴν ἀρχὴν διὰ τὸ μὴ ἀξίαν εἶναι.* Ar. *Pol.* viii (v) 10, 1311 *b* 36, (the rule of the Peisistratidae was attacked) *διὰ τὸ προπηλακίσαι μὲν τὴν Ἁρμοδίου ἀδελφὴν ἐπηρεάσαι δ' Ἁρμόδιον (ὁ μὲν γὰρ Ἁρμόδιος διὰ τὴν ἀδελφήν, ὁ δὲ Ἀριστογείτων διὰ τὸν Ἁρμόδιον).* The text connects this incident with the approaching Panathenaic festival, at which Hipparchus was put to death. The Panathenaea are mentioned in connexion with the sister of Harmodius by Aelian *V. H.* xi 8, and Max. Tyr. 24, 2. The year was B.C. 514.

On **κανηφορεῖν**, cf. Aristoph. *Eccl.* 732, *Av.* 1551, and Harpocr. s. v. *κανηφόροι...Φιλόχορος ἐν β' Ἀτθίδος φησὶν ὡς Ἐριχθονίου βασιλεύοντος πρῶτον κατέστησαν αἱ ἐν ἀξιώματι παρθένοι φέρειν τὰ κανᾶ τῇ θεῷ, ἐφ' οἷς ἐπέκειτο τὰ πρὸς τὴν θυσίαν, τοῖς τε Παναθηναίοις καὶ ταῖς ἄλλαις πομπαῖς* (for other authorities, see Michaelis, *Parthenon*, p. 329 f.). The Panathenaea had been revived by Peisistratus, but even in 566 B.C., six years before his first usurpation, it was attended by a large concourse in consequence of the institution of gymnastic contests at that date (Marcellinus, *Vit. Thuc.* i). The Scholiast on Aristides, iii 323 Dind., says of the great Panathenaea, *Πεισίστρατος ἐποίησε.*

μαλακὸν] 'effeminate,' opp. to *καρτερικός* in *Eth.* 1147 *b* 23, 1150 *a* 14, 33; *Eth. Eud.* 1229 *b* 7, *πρὸς τὸν θάνατον μαλακὸς ἢ περίφοβος.* Cf. c. 3 l. 7.

μετεχόντων πολλῶν] This contradicts Thuc. vi 56 § 3, *ἦσαν δὲ οὐ πολλοὶ οἱ ξυνομωμοκότες ἀσφαλείας ἕνεκα.*

§ 3. **ἐν ἀκροπόλει]** Thucydides (vi 57 § 1) describes Hippias as marshalling the procession outside Athens in the (outer) Cerameicus, and adds that, on noticing one of the conspirators conversing with him, Harmodius and Aristogeiton, fearing that the plot was discovered, rushed *within the gates* (*εἴσω τῶν πυλῶν*), found Hipparchus near the Leocorium and stabbed him to death. Hippias, meanwhile, had remained outside the

τοῖς Παναθηναίοις Ἱππίαν (ἐτύγχανεν γὰρ οὗτος μὲν [δ]εχόμενος, ὁ δ' Ἵππαρχος ἀποστέλλων τὴν πομπήν), ἰδόντες τινὰ τῶν κοινωνούντων τῆς πρά[ξ]εως φιλανθρώπως ἐντυγχάνοντα τῷ Ἱππίᾳ, καὶ νομίσαντες μηνύειν, βουλόμενοί τι δρᾶσαι πρὸ τῆς συλλήψεως, καταβάντες καὶ προεξαναστάντες τῶν [λοιπῶν], τὸν μὲν Ἵππαρχον διακ[οσ]μοῦντα τὴν πομπὴν παρὰ τὸ Λεωκόρειον ἀπέκτειναν, [τὴν δ' ὅ]λην ἐλυμήναντο πρᾶξιν. αὐτῶν δ' ὁ μὲν Ἁρμόδιος εὐθέως 4
ἐτελεύτησεν ὑπὸ τῶν δ[ορυφό]ρων, ὁ δ' Ἀριστο[γε]ίτων ὕστερον συλληφθεὶς καὶ πολὺν χρόνον αἰκισθείς. κατηγόρησεν δ' ἐν [τ]αῖς ἀνάγκαις πολλῶν οἳ καὶ [τῇ] φύσει τῶν ἐπιφανῶν καὶ φίλοι τοῖς τυράννοις ἦσαν. οὐ [γὰρ ἐ]δύναντο παραχρῆμα λαβεῖν οὐδὲν ἴχνος τῆς πράξεως, ἀλλ' ὁ λεγόμενος λόγος ὡς ὁ Ἱππίας ἀποστήσας

15 *μὲν δεχόμενος* K-W, H-L (K[3], B); *μετερχόμενος* K[1]. **19** *λοιπῶν* B; *ἄλλων* K, K-W[2], H-L; *ἑτέρων* K-W[1]. **20** ΠΑΡΑ: *περὶ* H-L. **21** *τὴν δ'* K-W (K[3], B); [*τὴν μὲν οὖν*] K[1]; *ᾧ τὴν* H-L. *δ'*: *γὰρ* invita papyro K-W.

---

gates, and it was there that he disarmed the citizens. The text describes H and A as waiting for Hippias on the Acropolis. On observing some one conversing with Hippias, they descend (*καταβάντες*) and slay Hipparchus near the Leocorium. The two accounts are impossible to reconcile. In more than one point our author deliberately differs from the historian (*inf.* § 4).

ἰδόντες—συλλήψεως] Thuc. vi 57 § 3, *ὡς εἶδόν τινα τῶν ξυνωμοτῶν σφίσι διαλεγόμενον οἰκείως τῷ Ἱππίᾳ...ἔδεισαν καὶ ἐνόμισαν μεμηνῦσθαί τε καὶ ὅσον οὐκ ἤδη ξυλληφθήσεσθαι. πρὸ τῆς συλλήψεως* confirms Thuc. i 21, *πρὶν συλληφθῆναι*, suspected by Cobet.

προεξαναστάντες τῶν λοιπῶν] 'having begun the attack without waiting for their confederates.'

Ἵππαρχον διακοσμοῦντα τὴν πομπὴν] Thuc. i 21 § 3, *τῷ Ἱππάρχῳ περιτυχόντες περὶ τὸ Λεωκόριον καλούμενον τὴν Παναθηναϊκὴν πομπὴν διακοσμοῦντι ἀπέκτειναν.* In vi 57, the historian mentions Hippias alone as marshalling the procession outside the gates: (Harm. and Ar.) *περιέτυχον τῷ Ἱππάρχῳ παρὰ τὸ Λεωκόριον καλούμενον.*

τὸ Λεωκόρειον] The monument of the three daughters of Leos who, at the command of an oracle, sacrificed themselves for their country, [Dem.] 60 § 29, Cic. *Nat. Deor.* iii 50. Harpocration places it in the midst of the (inner) Cerameicus. It is mentioned in connexion with the *ἀγορά* in Dem. 54 § 7. Cf. Wachsmuth, *Stadt Athen*, ii 417, and Judeich in *Fleckeis. Jahrb.* 1890, p. 756.

§ 4. **πολὺν χρόνον αἰκισθείς**] Thuc. vi 57 § 3, *οὐ ῥᾳδίως διετέθη.*

κατηγόρησεν—ἦσαν] The story is told of Aristogeiton and Hippias by Seneca, *de Ira*, ii 23, and Justin. ii 9 §§ 1—6. Cf. Diod. Sic. x 16 §§ 3, 4. The like story is told of Zeno of Elea, Cic. *Tusc.* ii 52, Val. Max. iii 3 E § 1 (where the tyrant is Phalaris, as in Heraclides Ponticus in Athen. 652 B), Diog. Laert. ix 26, 27, Plut. ii 505 D (Mayor). Polyaenus i 22, *Ἀριστογείτων, ὑπὸ τῶν δορυφόρων στρεβλούμενος περὶ τῶν συνειδότων, τῶν μὲν συνειδότων ὡμολόγησεν οὐδένα, πάντας δὲ τοὺς Ἱππίου φίλους κοινωνῆσαι τῆς ἐπιθέσεως· ὁπότε δὲ τούτους Ἱππίας ἀπέκτεινε, τότε ὁ Ἀριστογείτων ὠνείδισεν αὐτῷ τὸ στρατήγημα τῶν φίλων.*

ταῖς ἀνάγκαις] Hdt. i 116, *Ἀστυάγης δέ μιν οὐκ εὖ βουλεύεσθαι ἔφη ἐπιθυμέοντα ἐς ἀνάγκας μεγάλας ἀπικνέεσθαι, ἅμα τε λέγων ταῦτα ἐσήμαινε τοῖσι δορυφόροισι λαμβάνειν αὐτόν. ὁ δὲ ἀγόμενος ἐς τὰς ἀνάγκας οὕτω δὴ ἔφαινε τὸν ἐόντα λόγον.* Antiphon, *de Chor.* 25. Thuc. i 99 § 1, *προσάγοντες τὰς ἀνάγκας.*

φύσει] 'in birth', as in c. 5 § 3.

ἴχνος] met. as in Antiphon, *Tetral.* A γ 10, *φανερῶς δὲ τὰ ἴχνη τῆς ὑποψίας εἰς τοῦτον φέροντα*, and A δ 10, *τὰ ἴχνη τοῦ φόνου.* Ar. *Hist. An.* 8, 588 *a* 33, *ἐν τοῖς παισὶ τῶν ὕστερον ἕξεων ἐσομένων ἔστιν ἰδεῖν οἷον ἴχνη καὶ σπέρματα*, *a* 19; 9, 608 *b* 4.

ὁ λεγόμενος λόγος] Thuc. vi 58, (Hippias) *ἐκέλευσεν αὐτούς, δείξας τι χωρίον,*

ἀπὸ τῶν ὅπλων τοὺς πομπεύοντας ἐφώρασεν τοὺς τὰ ἐγχειρίδια ἔχοντας οὐκ ἀληθής ἐστιν· οὐ γὰρ ἔπεμπον τό<τε> μεθ' ὅπλων,
5 ἀλλ' ὕστερον τοῦτο κατεσκεύασεν ὁ δῆμος. κατηγόρει δὲ τῶν τοῦ τυράννου φίλων, ὡς μὲν οἱ δημοτικοί φασιν, ἐπίτηδες ἵνα ἀσεβήσαιεν ἅμα καὶ γένοιντο ἀσθενεῖς ἀνελόντες τοὺς ἀναιτίους καὶ φίλους ἑαυτῶν, ὡς δ' ἔνιοι λέγουσιν, οὐχὶ πλαττόμενος ἀλλὰ τοὺς
6 συνειδότας ἐμήνυεν. καὶ τέλος ὡς οὐκ ἐδύνατο πάντα ποιῶν ἀποθανεῖν, ἐπαγγειλάμενος ὡς ἄλλους μηνύσων πολλούς, καὶ πείσας αὐτῷ τὸν Ἱππίαν δοῦναι τὴν δεξιὰν πίστεως χάριν, ὡς ἔλαβεν ὀνειδίσας ὅτι τῷ φονεῖ τοῦ ἀδελφοῦ τὴν δεξιὰν δέδωκεν, οὕτω παρώξυνε τὸν Ἱππίαν ὥσθ' ὑπὸ τῆς ὀργῆς οὐ κατεῖχεν ἑαυτὸν ἀλλὰ σπασάμενος τὴν μάχαιραν διέφθειρεν αὐτόν.

19. μετὰ δὲ ταῦτα συνέβαινεν πολλῷ τραχυτέραν εἶναι τὴν τυραννίδα· καὶ γὰρ διὰ τὸ τιμωρεῖν τῷ ἀδελφῷ καὶ διὰ τὸ πολλοὺς

27 ΕΦΩΡΑΣΕΝ B: *-σε* K *etc.* **28** ΑΛΗΘΕΣ. ΕΠΕΜΠΟΝΤΟ: *ἔπεμπον τό<τε>* correxi cum H-L, K-W, *etc.* (K[3]); *ἔπεμπόν πω* Papabasileios (B). **31** *-σειαν* H-L. ΑΣΘΕΝΕΙΣ, litteris ΣΘΕΝ obscure scriptis, super *ἀνελόντες* additum (K[3], K-W, B); *ἀγεννεῖς* K[1], *ἐναγεῖς* H-L, *etc.* **33** *ἐδύνατο* H-L: ΗΔΥΝΑΤΟ (K, K-W, B), quod in titulis non nisi post annum 300 A.C. invenitur, Meisterhans, p. 134[2]. **35** *αὐτῷ* H-L. **36** ΤΑΔΕΛΦΟΥ (retinent K-W, B). ΔΕΔΩΚΕ (K, K-W, H-L, B). **37** ΚΑΤΕΣΧΕΝ correctum in -ΕΙΧΕΝ.

XIX 2 ΤΙΜΩΡΕΙΝ *τιμωρῶν* K-W. ΤΑΔΕΛΦΩΙ (K-W, B). *καὶ διὰ τὸ* secl. K-W.

ἀπελθεῖν ἐς αὐτὸ ἄνευ τῶν ὅπλων. καὶ οἱ μὲν ἀνεχώρησαν οἰόμενοί τι ἐρεῖν αὐτόν, ὁ δὲ τοῖς ἐπικούροις φράσας τὰ ὅπλα ὑπολαβεῖν ἐξελέγετο εὐθὺς οὓς ἐπῃτιᾶτο καὶ εἴ τις εὑρέθη ἐγχειρίδιον ἔχων· μετὰ γὰρ ἀσπίδος καὶ δόρατος εἰώθεσαν τὰς πομπὰς ποιεῖν. The conspirators purposely selected the festival of the Panathenaea (about Aug. 13), *ἐν ᾗ μόνον ἡμέρᾳ οὐχ ὕποπτον ἐγίγνετο ἐν ὅπλοις τοὺς τὴν πομπὴν πέμψοντας ἀθρόους γενέσθαι.* (The passage in Lysias 13 § 80, *συνηκολούθει γὰρ λαβὼν τὰ ὅπλα καὶ συνέπεμπε τὴν πομπὴν μετὰ τῶν πολιτῶν πρὸς τὸ ἄστυ*, quoted in Michaelis, *Parthenon*, 332, does not refer to the *Panathenaea*, but to the festal procession on the restoration of the democracy, on Sept. 21, 403.) The statement in the text is intended as a deliberate correction of the account in Thucydides, but we have now no means of ascertaining the ultimate authority for the correction. The first line of the famous scolium of Callistratus (probably written not long after the Persian war), implies that Harmodius and Aristogeiton concealed their daggers in branches of myrtle (*ἐν μύρτου κλαδὶ τὸ ξίφος φορήσω*), but says nothing about spear or shield.

§ 5. **ἀσεβήσαιεν** indicates the consequence of their destroying the innocent; *γένοιντο ἀσθενεῖς*, that of their destroying their own friends.

§ 6. **πάντα ποιῶν**] [Lys.] 8 § 5, *ἐφάσκετε...πάντα ποιοῦντες οὐκ ἔχειν ὅπως ἀπαλλαγῆτέ μου.* Lys. 12 § 84, *πάντα ποιοῦντες δίκην παρ' αὐτῶν οὐκ ἂν δύναισθε λαβεῖν.* Dem. 21 § 2, *πάντα ποιοῦντος τούτου (ὁ δῆμος) οὐκ ἐπείσθη.*

ὀνειδίσας] Cf. Polyaen. quoted on § 4. 'The narrative of the end of Aristogiton betrays the same liking for sensational stories as we trace, for instance, in Phylarchus' (W. L. Newman in *Class. Rev.* v 161 *b*).

XIX. *Hippias.* § 1. **τραχυτέραν**] Hdt. v 62 (of Hippias), *ἐμπικραινομένου Ἀθηναίοισι διὰ τὸν Ἱππάρχου θάνατον.* Thuc. vi 59 § 1, *τοῖς δ' Ἀθηναίοις χαλεπωτέρα μετὰ τοῦτο ἡ τυραννὶς κατέστη, καὶ ὁ Ἱππίας διὰ φόβου ἤδη μᾶλλον ὢν τῶν τε πολιτῶν πολλοὺς ἔκτεινε κτλ.*

ἀνῃρηκέναι καὶ ἐκβεβληκέναι πᾶσιν ἦν ἄπιστος καὶ πικρός. ἔτει 2
δὲ τετάρτῳ μάλιστα μετὰ τὸν Ἱππάρχου θάνατον, ἐπεὶ κακῶς
εἶχεν τὰ ἐν τῷ ἄστει, τὴν Μουνιχίαν ἐπεχείρησε τειχίζειν, ὡς
ἐκεῖσε μεθιδρυσόμενος. ἐν τούτοις δ' ὢν ἐξέπεσεν ὑπὸ Κλεομένους
τοῦ Λακεδαιμονίων βασιλέως, χρησμῶν γιγνομένων ἀεὶ τοῖς Λάκωσι
καταλύειν τὴν τυραννίδα διὰ τοιάνδ' α[ἰτίαν]. οἱ φυγάδες, ὧν οἱ 3
Ἀλκμεωνίδαι προειστήκεσαν, αὐτοὶ μὲν δι' αὐτῶν οὐκ ἐδύναντο
ποιήσασθαι τὴν κάθοδον, ἀλλ' ἀεὶ προσέπταιον· || ἔν τε γὰρ τοῖς [Col. 8.]
ἄλλοις οἷς ἔπραττον διεσφάλλοντο, καὶ τειχίσαντες ἐν τῇ χώρᾳ
Λειψύδριον τὸ ὑπὲρ Πάρνηθος, εἰς ὃ συνεξῆλθόν τινες τῶν ἐκ τοῦ

3 ΠΙ·ΣΤΟ: *πικρός* K *etc.* **4** *κακῶς*: ΕΝΚΑΚΩΙ, postea correctum. **5** *εἶχε* H-L. *τῷ* a correctore additum abesse propter numeros mavult Blass. ΜΟΥΝΥΧΙΑΝ passim: *Μουνιχίαν* K-W, H-L (K[3], B), cf. Meisterhans, p. 23[2]. **6** *ἐκεῖσε* J B Mayor, Sidgwick (H-L, B): ΕΚΕΙ K, K-W. **7** *Λακεδαίμονος* K[1], K-W[1]. ΓΙΝ (K-W). ΑΕΙ (edd.). **9** *ἐδύναντο* K, H-L: ΗΔΥΝΑΝΤΟ (K-W, B); cf. 18, 33. **10** ΑΙΕΙ (K, K-W, B); cf. 5, 19. **12, 15** ΛΙΨΥΔΡΙΟΝ, idem habet Suidae cod. Mediceus. ΥΠΕΡ: *ὑπό*? J H Wright, in Herodoto *ὑπὲρ Παιονίης ὑπὸ Πάρνηθος* scriptum fuisse arbitratus.

TESTIM. **3** *πικρός*. Heraclidis epitoma (611, 4[3]) *Ἱππίας δὲ πικρότατα ἐτυράννει.* **8—18** Etym. M. p. 361, 32 Gaisf. (=Suidas, Eustath.) *ἐπὶ Λειψυδρίῳ μάχη: χωρίον ἦν ὑπὸ τῆς Πάρνηθος ὃ ἐτείχισαν οἱ φυγάδες τῶν τυράννων ὧν οἱ Ἀλκμαιωνίδαι προεστήκεσαν. ἐκπολιορκηθέντων δ' αὐτῶν ὑπὸ τῶν περὶ Πεισίστρατον, σκόλιον εἰς αὐτοὺς ᾔδετο "αἰαῖ—εὐπατρίδας," οἳ τότ'* (Etym. M. ed. Gaisf.; idem habent Athen. 695 et Suidas; *ὁπότ'* Etym. M. codex Dorvillii Bodleianus, et Apostolius vii 70) *ἔδειξαν οἵων πατέρων ἔσαν.* Cf. Rose, Frag. 356[2], 394[3].
12 *Schol. Arist. *Lys.* 666: *Λειψύδριον: χωρίον τῆς Ἀττικῆς περὶ τὴν Πάρνηθον* (ita codex Ravennas, *τὸ ὑπὲρ Πάρνηθος* Suid., *ὑπὸ τὴν Πάρνηθον* Et. M.), *εἰς ὃ συνῆλθόν τινες* (cod. L et Suidas) *τῶν ἐκ τοῦ ἄστεος, ὥς φησιν Ἀρ. ἐν Ἀθ. πολ.* *Ib.* 665 ... *(οἱ Ἀλκμαιωνίδαι) πόλεμον ἀράμενοι πρὸς Ἱππίαν τὸν τύραννον καὶ τοὺς Πεισιστρατίδας ἐτείχισαν τὸ Λειψύδριον.* Hesych. *Λειψύδριον: χωρίον τι ὑπὲρ Πάρνηθος ὃ ἐτείχισαν Ἀλκμαιωνίδαι.* Cf. Rose, *l.c.*

πικρός] Hdt. *l. c.*, *ἐμπικραινομένου.*

§ 2. **ἔτει—τετάρτῳ**] B.C. 511/0.

τὴν Μουνιχίαν—τειχίζειν] Plut. *Sol.* 12, *λέγεται δὲ* (Epimenides) *τὴν Μουνιχίαν ἰδὼν καὶ καταμαθὼν πολὺν χρόνον εἰπεῖν πρὸς τοὺς παρόντας, ὡς τυφλόν ἐστι τοῦ μέλλοντος ἄνθρωπος· ἐκφαγεῖν γὰρ ἂν Ἀθηναίους τοῖς αὑτῶν ὀδοῦσιν, εἰ προῄδεσαν, ὅσα τὴν πόλιν ἀνιάσει τὸ χωρίον* (Diog. Laert. i 114). The height of Munichia, which commanded the harbours of Munichia and Zea, is 255 Paris feet above the sea, whereas the highest part of the Peiraeus is only 191. It was an important point in the fortification of the harbours, instituted by Themistocles; and its importance is also shewn by the fact that in 411 B.C. we read of the commander *τῶν περιπόλων τῶν Μουνιχίασι τεταγμένων* (Thuc. viii 92, 3); it was fortified by Thrasybulus in 403 (Xen. *Hell.* ii 4, 11—12; Diodor. Sic. xiv 33, M. *λόφον ἔρημον καὶ καρτερόν*). In the time of Alexander (325/4) one of the *στρατηγοί* was specially appointed to guard this point (c. 61 § 1). In 322 it was occupied by a Macedonian garrison (Plut. *Phocion* 27, 28; Curtius, *Stadtgeschichte*, p. 222); in 307 the fort was destroyed by Demetrius Poliorcetes (Plut. *Demetr.* 10), but was soon restored in the Macedonian interest, to be evacuated in 229. It was probably destroyed by Sulla. By the time of Strabo (p. 395 c) it was in ruins (C. Wachsmuth, *Stadt Athen*, ii 42—45).

ὑπὸ Κλεομένους] Hdt. v 64, 65. **χρησμῶν**] *ib.* 63 (quoted on § 4).

§ 3. **οἱ φυγάδες—προσέπταιον**] Hdt. v 62, (the Alcmeonidae) *ἅμα τοῖσι ἄλλοισι Ἀθηναίων φυγάσι πειρωμένοισι κατὰ τὸ ἰσχυρὸν οὐ προεχώρεε κάτοδος, ἀλλὰ προσέπταιον μεγάλως πειρώμενοι κατιέναι τε καὶ ἐλευθεροῦν τὰς Ἀθήνας, Λειψύδριον τὸ ὑπὲρ Παιονίης τειχίσαντες.* Duncker, *G. d. A.* vi 501, places this incident in B.C. 513. Cf. J. H. Wright, *The date of Cylon*, p. 54.

Λειψύδριον] a 'waterless' spot on the southern flank of Parnes. The site has ἄστεως, ἐξεπολιορκήθησαν ὑπὸ τῶν τυράννων, ὅθεν ὕστερον μετὰ ταύτην τὴν συμφορὰν ᾖδον ἐν τοῖς σκολίοις [[αἰεί]]·

αἰαῖ Λειψύδριον προδωσέταιρον,
οἵους ἄνδρας ἀπώλεσας μάχεσθαι
ἀγαθούς τε καὶ εὐπατρίδας,
οἳ τότ' ἔδειξαν οἵων πατέρων ἔσαν.

4 ἀποτυγχάνοντες οὖν ἐν ἅπ[α]σι τοῖς ἄλλοις, ἐμισθώσαντο τὸν ἐν

13 ΜΕΤΑ: *εἰς* K-W (B) ex Etym. Mag. 361, 33 *σκόλιον εἰς αὐτοὺς ᾖδετο.* **14** *αἰεί* secl. Hude, K-W, H-L, utpote ex dittographia ortum. **16—17** *μάχεσθαί τ' ἀγαθοὺς καὶ* Eustathius; *τ' ἀγαθούς, γένει τ'* Hermann, *El. D. Metr.* 695. *καὶ εὐπατρίδας*, idem habent Athenaeus, Suidas et Etym. Mag.: *κἀξ εὐπατριδᾶν* Tyrrell; *ἀγαθούς, καλούς, εὐπατρίδας* Bury.

19 * Schol. in Arist. *Lys.* 1153: Ἀριστοτέλης φησὶ μετὰ τὸν Ἱππάρχου θάνατον χρησμὸν γενέσθαι τοῖς Λάκωσιν καταλύειν τὴν τυραννίδα, τῆς Πυθίας, ὡς οἱ Ἀλκμαιονίδαι ἐμισθώσαντο τὸν ἐν Δελφοῖς νεὼν οἰκοδομεῖν, συνεχῶς τοῦτο χρώσης αὐτοῖς μαντευομένοις, ἕως πρότερον μὲν Ἀγχίμολον (cod. Rav.) ἔπεμψαν κατὰ θάλασσαν, ἀποκρουσθέντος δὲ αὐτοῦ ὀργισθέντες οἱ Λάκωνες Κλεομένη τὸν βασιλέα σὺν μείζονι ἐξέπεμψαν στόλῳ· καὶ νικήσας τοὺς Θετταλοὺς εἰσῆλθεν εἰς τὴν Ἀττικὴν καὶ τὸν Ἱππίαν συνέκλεισεν εἰς τὸ Πελαργικὸν τεῖχος, ἕως οἱ παῖδες τῶν τυράννων ἐξιόντες ἑάλωσαν (Rose, Frag. 357[2], 395[3]).

---

not been identified. Leake (*Demi*, p. 39), placing Paeonidae at *Menidhi*, regarded the monastery of St Nicolas at the upper end of a long acclivity three or four miles (*drei Stunden*, Kastromenos, *die Demen*, p. 95) to the N. as the site of Leipsydrium. The monastery is 'built in a strong situation upon the summit of a height, backed by the pine woods of Parnes and near the right bank of a remarkable torrent'. But the presence of the torrent is unfavourable to this identification of the 'waterless' spot. Kastromenos, *l.c.*, merely says of this torrent that its water 'has certainly never failed to supply Leipsydrium,' but he does not say clearly that this fact goes against the proposed identification. *Menidhi* is now identified as the site of Acharnae, while Paeonidae may possibly correspond to the ruined village of *Varipompi*, two hours north of *Menidhi* at the southern edge of Parnes, and Leipsydrium may have occupied the same position as the Pyrgos above that village (Hanriot, *Recherches*, p. 55 *sqq.*, quoted in Bursian's *Geographie*, i 334).

ᾖδον ἐν τοῖς σκολίοις] cf. c. 20 at end. On *scolia*, see K. O. Müller's *Lit. of Ancient Greece*, i 249 E. T. 'The rhythms of the extant scolia are very various, though, on the whole, they resemble those of the Aeolic lyric poetry; only that the course of the strophes is broken by an accelerated rhythm, and is in general more animated. This is particularly true of the apt and elegant metre, which occurs in eight Scolia (one of them the Harmodius), and of which there is a comic imitation in Aristoph. *Eccl.* 938.

– ⏒ –́⏑⏑ –⏑ –⏑ –⏑
– ⏒ –́⏑⏑ –⏑ –⏑ –⏑
⏑⏑–́ ⏑– –́⏑⏑–
–́⏑⏑ –⏑– –́⏑⏑ –⏑–

Here the hendecasyllables begin with a composed and feeble tone; but a more rapid rhythm is introduced by the anapaestic beginning of the third verse; and the two expressions are reconciled by the logaœdic members in the last verse.' This scolium is quoted with many others in Athenaeus, xv p. 695.

προδωσέταιρον] a rare epithet appropriate to an impromptu song. It was afterwards used in late prose by Dio Cassius 58, 14. The only other word exactly parallel to it is *προδωσίκομπος* of 'a boaster who breaks his word'. Both words are noticed by Lobeck, *Phryn.* 770 (L and S).

§ 4. **ἐμισθώσαντο—Ἀθήνας**] Hdt. v 62, *παρ' Ἀμφικτυόνων τὸν νηὸν μισθοῦνται τὸν ἐν Δελφοῖσι...ἐξοικοδομῆσαι. οἷα δὲ χρημάτων εὖ ἥκοντες καὶ ἐόντες ἄνδρες δόκιμοι ἀνέκαθεν ἔτι, τόν τε νηὸν ἐξεργάσαντο τοῦ παραδείγματος κάλλιον*...(c. 63) *ὡς οὖν δὴ οἱ Ἀθηναῖοι λέγουσι, οὗτοι οἱ*

Δελφοῖς νεὼν οἰκοδομεῖν, ὅθεν εὐπόρησαν χρημάτων πρὸς τὴν τῶν Λακώνων βοήθειαν. ἡ δὲ Πυθία προὔφερεν ἀεὶ τοῖς Λακεδαιμονίοις χρηστηριαζομένοις ἐλευθεροῦν τὰς Ἀθήνας, εἰς τοῦθ' ἕως προὔτρεψε τοὺς Σπαρτιάτας, καίπερ ὄντων ξένων αὐτοῖς τῶν Πεισιστρατιδῶν· συνεβάλλετο δὲ οὐκ ἐλάττω μοῖραν τῆς ὁρμῆς τοῖς Λάκωσιν ἡ πρὸς τοὺς Ἀργείους τοῖς Πεισιστρατίδαις ὑπάρ-
χουσα φιλία. τὸ μὲν οὖν πρῶτον Ἀγχίμολον ἀπέστειλαν κατὰ 5

20 *οἰκοδομεῖν ὅθεν εὐπόρησαν χρημάτων*, K; *χρησμῶν*? Wyse; commatis signum post *οἰκοδομεῖν* (B) posuerunt H-L ('gravius vitium subesse' arbitrati), et K-W (lacuna post *χρημάτων* indicata). *ηὐπόρησαν* H-L. **21** *προύφερεν* H-L, cf. v. 23 *προὔτρεψε*: ΠΡΟΕΦ (K, K-W, B). ΑΙΕΙ (K, K-W, B); cf. 5, 19. **22** ΕΙCΤΟΥΤΕΥΘΕΩC: correxit Blass e Schol. Arist. *Lys.* 1153 (K-W, H-L, K[3]). **24** CΥΝΕΒΑΛΛΕΤΟ (K, K-W, B): *συνεβάλετο* Richards (H-L).

ἄνδρες ἐν Δελφοῖσι κατήμενοι ἀνέπειθον τὴν Πυθίην, ὅκως ἔλθοιεν Σπαρτιητέων ἄνδρες εἴτε ἰδίῳ στόλῳ εἴτε δημοσίῳ χρησόμενοι, προφέρειν σφι τὰς Ἀθήνας ἐλευθεροῦν, *ib.* ii 180. Schol. Aeschin. 3, 116.

The temple at Delphi was burnt down in B.C. 548; the contract of 300 talents for rebuilding it is assigned by Duncker, *G. d. A.* vi 493, to about 535. Pharaoh Amasis, who contributed to its restoration, died in 526.

Rose, *A. P.*, p. 418, observes, on Schol. Arist. *Lysistr.* 1153, that the writer of the Ἀθ. πολ. must have closely followed Herodotus. But this is no proof of the spuriousness of the treatise, as Ar. frequently refers to Herodotus in his undisputed works: 123 *b* 9, 523 *a* 17, 736 *a* 10, 756 *b* 6, 1343 *a* 20, 1344 *a* 16, 1409 *a* 27, 1451 *b* 2 (Heitz, *Verl. Schriften*, p. 246).

It appears impossible to take *ὅθεν* as = *ἀφ' ὧν* (as proposed by Mr Kenyon). It can only mean: 'hence it was that they had abundance of money'. Similar uses of *ὅθεν* occur in 6 § 2, 7 § 4, 21 §§ 2, 4. We have here a slight divergence from the account in Herodotus. The historian describes the wealth of the Alcmaeonidae as enabling them to undertake the contract for rebuilding the temple, which they carried out in a splendid manner. The text states that, owing to their undertaking the contract, they had large supplies of money. These sums were entrusted to them to enable them to execute their contract, but they were (partly) applied to securing the aid of Sparta against the Peisistratidae. This account is confirmed by a subsequent Atthidographer, Philochorus, *frag.* 70, FHG; 395, ap. Schol. Pind. *Pyth.* vii 9, *λέγεται, ὅτι τὸν Πυθικὸν ναὸν ἐμπρησθέντα, ὥς φασιν, ὑπὸ τῶν Πεισιστρατιδῶν οἱ Ἀλκμαιωνίδαι φυγαδευθέντες ὑπ' αὐτῶν ὑπέσχοντο ἀνοικοδομῆσαι, καὶ δεξάμενοι χρήματα καὶ συναγαγόντες δύναμιν ἐπέθεντο τοῖς Πεισιστρατίδαις, καὶ νικήσαντες μετ' εὐχαριστηρίων πλειόνων ἀνῳκοδόμησαν τῷ θεῷ τὸ τέμενος, ὡς Φιλόχορος ἱστορεῖ.* Isocr. *de Perm.* 232 describes the Alcmaeonid Cleisthenes as having established the democracy, *λόγῳ πείσας τοὺς Ἀμφικτύονας δανεῖσαι τῶν τοῦ θεοῦ χρημάτων αὐτοῦ.* Similarly Dem. *c. Mid.* 144 says of the Alcmaeonidae: *τούτους δέ φασιν ὑπὸ τῶν τυράννων ὑπὲρ τοῦ δήμου στασιάζοντας ἐκπεσεῖν, καὶ δανεισαμένους χρήματ' ἐκ Δελφῶν ἐλευθερῶσαι τὴν πόλιν καὶ τοὺς Πεισιστράτου παῖδας ἐκβαλεῖν.*

προὔφερεν] This defends *προφέρειν* in Hdt. v 63, against *προφαίνειν* (preferred by Bekker and Dindorf).

καίπερ ὄντων ξένων] Hdt. *l. c.*, *καὶ ξεινίους σφι ἐόντας τὰ μάλιστα.*

συνεβάλλετο—μοῖραν] Plat. *Tim.* 47 C, (*λόγος*) *μεγίστην ξυμβαλλόμενος εἰς αὐτὰ μοῖραν*, and often with *μέρος*. Ar. *de Anima* 1, 402 *b* 22, *συμβάλλεται μέγα μέρος πρὸς τὸ εἰδέναι*, *Poet.* 22, 1458 *a* 34; *de Part. Anim.* iii 12, 673 *b* 25, *συμβάλλεται πολὺ μέρος πρὸς ὑγίειαν.* *Pol.* iv (vii) 11, 1330 *b* 13, *ταῦτα πλεῖστον συμβάλλεται πρὸς τὴν ὑγίειαν*, ii 9, 1270 *a* 14, *συμβάλλεσθαί τι πρὸς τὴν φιλοχρηματίαν*, iii 9, 1281 *a* 4, *συμβάλλονται πλεῖστον εἰς—*, vii (vi) 2, 1317 *b* 16, *συμβάλλεται ταύτῃ πρὸς—*.

ἡ πρὸς Ἀργείους—φιλία] c. 17 *ad fin.*

§ 5. **Ἀγχίμολον**] Hdt. v 63, *πέμπουσι Ἀγχιμόλιον — κατὰ θάλατταν πλοίοισι.* *Ἀγχίμολον* is the reading in the Ravenna MS of Schol. on Aristoph. *Lys.* 1153.

θάλατταν ἔχοντα στρατιάν. ἡττη[θέν]τος δ' αὐτοῦ καὶ τελευτήσαντος, διὰ τὸ Κινέαν βοηθῆσαι τὸν Θετταλὸν ἔχοντα χιλίους ἱππεῖς, προσοργισθέντες τῷ γενομένῳ, Κλεομένην ἐξέπεμψαν τὸν βασιλέα στόλον ἔχοντα μείζω κατὰ γῆν, ὃς ἐπεὶ τοὺς τῶν Θετταλῶν ἱππεῖς ἐνίκησεν κωλύοντας αὐτὸν εἰς τὴν Ἀττικὴν παριέναι, κατακλείσας τὸν Ἱππίαν εἰς τὸ καλούμενον Πελαργικὸν τεῖχος ἐπολιόρκει μετὰ τῶν Ἀθηναίων.
6 προσκαθημένου δ' αὐτοῦ συνέπεσεν ὑπεξιόντας ἁλῶναι τοὺς τῶν Πεισιστρατιδῶν υἱεῖς· ὧν ληφθέντων ὁμολογίαν ἐπὶ τῇ τῶν παίδων σωτηρίᾳ ποιησάμενοι, καὶ τὰ ἑαυτῶν ἐν πένθ' ἡμέραις ἐκκομισάμενοι, παρέδωκαν τὴν ἀκρόπολιν τοῖς Ἀθηναίοις ἐπὶ Ἁρπακτίδου ἄρχοντος, κατασχόντες τὴν τυραννίδα

28 ΘΕϹϹΑΛΟΝ (K-W): Θετταλὸν (K, H-L, B), Meisterhans p. 72². **29** προσοργισθέντες (K, K-W?, B): παρ- Naber (H-L) et K-W. **32** -ΚΛΕΙϹΑϹ K, coll. Meisterhans, p. 28²: -κλήσας (K-W, H-L, B). **34** ΕΠΕΞΙΟΝΤΑϹ (with . .Τ. written above): ὑπεξιόντας Wyse (K-W, H-L, K³, B). **37** ΕΠΙΠΑΡΠΑΚΙΔΟΥ, ἐπὶ Ἁρπακτίδου (K, K-W, B, ἐφ' Ἁρπ. H-L).

Κινέαν] Hdt. *l. c.* Θεσσαλοὶ...ἀπέπεμψαν...χιλίην τε ἵππον καὶ τὸν βασιλέα τὸν σφέτερον Κινέην.

Κλεομένην—παριέναι] Hdt. v 64, μέζω στόλον στείλαντες ἀπέπεμψαν ἐπὶ τὰς Ἀθήνας, στρατηγὸν τῆς στρατιῆς ἀποδέξαντες βασιλέα Κλεομένεα τὸν Ἀναξανδρίδεω, οὐκέτι κατὰ θάλασσαν στείλαντες ἀλλὰ κατ' ἤπειρον· τοῖσι ἐσβαλοῦσι ἐς τὴν Ἀττικὴν χώρην ἡ τῶν Θεσσαλῶν ἵππος πρώτη προσέμιξε καὶ οὐ μετὰ πολλὸν ἐτράπετο. Arist. *Lys.* 1150—6.

κατακλείσας—Ἀθηναίων] Hdt. *l. c.* ἅμα Ἀθηναίων τοῖσι βουλομένοισι εἶναι ἐλευθέροισι ἐπολιόρκεε τοὺς τυράννους ἀπεργμένους ἐν τῷ Πελασγικῷ τείχεϊ.

Πελαργικὸν τεῖχος] the ancient fortification surrounding the west end (if not the whole) of the Acropolis; it had nine gates, and was the chief fortress of Athens until the expulsion of the Peisistratidae. It was thereupon destroyed and its site was left unoccupied (Thuc. ii 17). Even in the second century A.D. the blocks of stone from its ruined walls were still to be seen (Lucian, *Piscator* 47). Cf. Bursian, *Geogr.* i 305 and Lolling in I. Müller's *Handbuch*, iii 337. Curtius insists on the literal sense of the passages describing it as surrounding the Acropolis, Hdt. vi 137, τοῦ τείχεος τοῦ περὶ τὴν ἀκρόπολίν ποτε ἐληλαμένου, Dionys. Hal. i 28, Paus. i. 28 3 (*Stadtgeschichte* pp. LXXVI, 47, and map on p. 61). Cf. Holm, ii 341. After the building of the wall of Cimon, the name was probably confined to the west end of the fortification (Judeich in *Fleckeis. Jahrb.* 1890, p. 753 f.).

§ 6. **ὑπεξιόντας**] Hdt. v 65, ὑπεκτιθέμενοι γὰρ ἔξω τῆς χώρης οἱ παῖδες τῶν Πεισιστρατιδέων ἥλωσαν. **ὁμολογίαν κτλ.**] *ib.* παρέστησαν—ὥστε ἐν πέντε ἡμέρῃσι ἐκχωρῆσαι ἐκ τῆς Ἀττικῆς.

ἐπὶ Ἁρπακτίδου ἄρχοντος] The expulsion of the Peisistratidae belongs to the year 511/0 B.C., being placed by Thuc. vi 59 § 5 (παυθεὶς ἐν τῷ τετάρτῳ), in the fourth year of the sole rule of Hippias, which began in 514 B.C. It is also the fourth year before the archonship of Isagoras in B.C. 508/7 (21 § 1). The name of the archon is now known for the first time.

When Thucydides (*l.c.*), as observed by Mr Kenyon, describes Hippias as fighting at Marathon 'in the 20th year' after his expulsion, he is using a round number, as the actual interval was 20 years and a few months. Mr E. S. Thompson (*Class. Rev.* vi 181) connects the Plataean alliance with the expulsion of the Peisistratidae, placing both events in B.C. 511/0. Hence, in Thuc. iii 68, where the fall of Plataea is put in the 93rd year after its alliance with Athens, Mr Thompson proposes to alter the 93rd into the 84th year.

μετὰ τὴν τοῦ πατρὸς τελευτὴν ἔτη μάλιστα ἑπτακαίδεκα, τὰ δὲ σύμπαντα σὺν οἷς ὁ πατὴρ ἦρξεν ἑνὸς δεῖν πεντήκοντα.

20. καταλυθείσης δὲ τῆς τυραννίδος, ἐστασίαζον πρὸς ἀλλ[ήλ]ους Ἰσαγόρας ὁ Τεισάνδρου, φίλος ὢν τῶν τυράννων, καὶ Κλεισθένης τοῦ γένους ὢν τῶν Ἀλκμεωνιδῶν. ἡττώμενος δὲ ταῖς ἑταιρείαις ὁ Κλεισθένης προσηγάγετο τὸν δῆμον, ἀποδιδοὺς τῷ πλήθει τὴν πολιτείαν. ὁ δὲ Ἰσαγόρας ἐπιλειπόμενος τῇ δυνάμει 2
πάλιν ἐπικαλεσάμενος τὸν Κλεομένην, ὄντα ἑαυτῷ ξένον, συνέπεισεν ἐλαύνειν τὸ ἄγος, διὰ τὸ τοὺς Ἀλκμεωνίδας δοκεῖν εἶναι τῶν

39 δεῖν J E B Mayor, Sidgwick, K-W (K[3]): ΔΕΙ hic et 27 § 2 (H-L, B).
XX 2 ΤΙϹΑΝΔΡΟΥ. **3** ΑΛΚΜΕΟΝΙΔΩΝ hic et v. 20. ΗΤΤΗΜΕΝΟϹ (K): ἡττώμενος Blass coll. Hdt. v 66 (K-W, H-L). **5** ΕΠΙΛΕΙΠΟΜΕΝΟϹ (K, K-W, B), cf. 27 § 4, 34 § 3: ἀπολειπόμενος Richards, Kontos, H-L; ὑπο- Haskins. **7—8** ἄγος et ἠγηλάτει K et H-L; ceterum cf. Jebb ad Soph. O. T. 402.

39 Schol. Arist. *Vesp.* 502...δοκεῖ δὲ ἡ τυραννὶς καταστῆναι, ὥς φησιν Ἐρατοσθένης, ἐπὶ ἔτη ν̄ (50), τοῦ ἀκριβοῦς διαμαρτάνων, Ἀριστοτέλους (Bentley; legebatur Ἀριστοφάνους) μὲν τεσσαράκοντα καὶ ἓν (per errorem pro ἐννέα scriptum) φήσαντος, Ἡροδότου δὲ (v 65) ἓξ καὶ τριάκοντα (Rose, Frag. 358[2], 396[3]).

ἔτη μάλιστα ἑπτακαίδεκα—ἑνὸς δεῖν πεντήκοντα] In *Pol.* viii (v) 12, 1315 *b* 31, the rule of the sons lasts 18 years, while from the beginning to the end of the τυραννὶς of the father is 33 years, thus giving a total of 51 years. The 49 years of the text include '*about* 17 years' for the rule of the sons, added to the 33 years assigned to the father in c. 17 § 1. In Hdt. v 65 the actual τυραννὶς of Peisistratus and his sons lasts for 36 years. It is probably by deducting from this number the 17 years here mentioned, that the writer gets 19 years as the duration of the actual rule of Peisistratus in 17 § 1.

σὺν] Rare in Attic prose, except in Xenophon, its place being generally taken by μετὰ with gen. One of the special uses of σὺν in Attic prose is to express numerical addition. According to Eucken, *Sprachgebrauch des Ar.*, p. 29, the following are the only instances of σὺν in the genuine writings of Aristotle. *Met.* 1039 *b* 21, σὺν τῇ ὕλῃ συνειλημμένος, 1044 *b* 15, ἐὰν δὲ προστεθῇ τὸ ὑπὸ γῆς ἐν μέσῳ γινομένης, ὁ σὺν τῷ αἰτίῳ λόγος οὗτος, 1058 *b* 17, σὺν τῇ ὕλῃ οἱ λόγοι αὐτῶν. *Meteor.* 348 *a* 24, φερόμενα σὺν ψόφῳ πολλῷ. *Hist. Anim.* 490 *a* 32, αἱ γὰρ καμπαὶ τέτταρες, ἢ δύο σὺν τοῖς πτερυγίοις, 525 *b* 15—17, πόδας δ' οἱ μὲν κάραβοι ἐφ' ἑκάτερα ἔχουσι πέντε σὺν ταῖς ἐσχάταις χηλαῖς· ὁμοίως δὲ καὶ οἱ καρκίνοι δέκα τοὺς πάντας σὺν ταῖς χηλαῖς. *De partib. anim.* 683 *b* 3, ἑξάποδα δὲ τὰ τοιαῦτα πάντ' ἐστὶ σὺν τοῖς ἀλτικοῖς μορίοις. It will be observed that in several of these exx. the numerical sense is prominent. In the spurious works near the time of Ar. there is no instance of σύν, but it occurs in those of much later date. In the most extensive of the works of Theophrastus it is only found thrice: *Hist. Pl.* ix 20, 4, *Caus. Pl.* ii 17, 8, v 6, 6 (Eucken, p. 30).

δεῖν, not δεῖ, is the right form here, and in c. 27, ἑνὸς δεῖν πεντηκοστῷ ἔτει, as well as in *Rhet.* ii 14 *fin.* To make δεῖν stand for δέον is a barbarism (Kühner, *Gr. Gr.* § 50, 11, p. 216 Blass) and cannot be defended on the analogy of πλεῖν ('more than') which is really for πλεῖον, not for πλέον. It is remarkable that this numerical expression (=*undequinquaginta*) has escaped lexicographers and grammarians (Mayor).

XX—XXII. *The Constitution of Cleisthenes.*

XX § 1. **ἡττώμενος—δῆμον**] Hdt. v 66, (Κλεισθένης καὶ Ἰσαγόρης) ἐστασίασαν περὶ δυνάμιος, ἑσσούμενος δὲ ὁ Κλεισθένης τὸν δῆμον προσεταιρίζεται, *ib.* 69 *fin.* ἦν δὲ τὸν δῆμον προσθέμενος πολλῷ κατύπερθε τῶν ἀντιστασιωτέων. (70) ἐν τῷ μέρεϊ δὲ ἑσσούμενος ὁ Ἰσαγόρης ἀντιτεχνᾶται τάδε. On ἑταιρεῖαι cf. *Pol.* 1313 *a* 39 ff.

§ 2. **ἐπικαλεσάμενος—ξένον**] Hdt. v 70, ἐπικαλέεται Κλεομένεα...γενόμενον ἑωυτῷ ξεῖνον.

ἐλαύνειν τὸ ἄγος] Cf. c. 1.

3 ἐναγῶν. ὑπεξελθόντος δὲ τοῦ Κλεισθένους μετ' ὀλίγων, ἡγηλάτει τῶν Ἀθηναίων ἑπτακοσίας οἰκίας· ταῦτα δὲ διαπραξάμενος, τὴν μὲν βουλὴν ἐπειρᾶτο καταλύειν, Ἰσαγόραν δὲ καὶ τριακοσίους τῶν φίλων μετ' αὐτοῦ κυρίους καθιστάναι τῆς πόλεως. τῆς δὲ βουλῆς ἀντιστάσης καὶ συναθροισθέντος τοῦ πλήθους, οἱ μὲν περὶ τὸν Κλεομένην καὶ Ἰσαγόραν κατέφυγον εἰς τὴν ἀκρόπολιν· ὁ δὲ δῆμος δύο μὲν ἡμέρας προσκαθεζόμενος ἐπολιόρκει, τῇ δὲ τρίτῃ Κλεομένην μὲν καὶ τοὺς μετ' αὐτοῦ πάντας ἀφεῖσαν ὑποσπόνδους, Κλει-
4 σθένην δὲ καὶ τοὺς ἄλλους φυγάδας μετεπέμψαντο. κατασχόντος δὲ τοῦ δήμου τὰ πράγματα, Κλεισθένης ἡγεμὼν ἦν καὶ τοῦ δήμου προστάτης. αἰτιώτατοι γὰρ σχεδὸν ἐγένοντο τῆς ἐκβολῆς τῶν τυράννων οἱ Ἀλκμεωνίδαι, καὶ στασιάζοντες τὰ πολλὰ διετέλεσαν.
5 ἔτι δὲ πρότερον τῶν Ἀλκμεωνιδῶν Κήδων ἐπέθετο τοῖς τυράννοις· διὸ καὶ ᾖδον καὶ εἰς τοῦτον ἐν τοῖς σκολίοις·

ἔγχει καὶ Κήδωνι, διάκονε, μηδ' ἐπιλήθου,
εἰ χρὴ τοῖς ἀγαθοῖς ἀνδράσιν οἰνοχοεῖν.

21. διὰ μὲν οὖν ταύτας τὰς αἰτίας ἐπίστευεν ὁ δῆμος τῷ Κλεισθένει. τότε δὲ τοῦ πλήθους προεστηκώς, ἔτει τετάρτῳ μετὰ
2 τὴν τῶν τυράννων κατάλυσιν, ἐπὶ Ἰσαγόρου ἄρχοντος, πρῶτον μὲν

8 <*ἀφικόμενος ὁ Κλεομένης*> *μετ' ὀλίγων ἡγηλάτει* add. K-W[2] ex Hdt. v 70. *ἀγηλατεῖ* B, coll. Hdt. v 72. **11** ΜΤΟΥ *sc. μετα του.* **15** ΑΦΙΕϹΑΝ: *ἀφεῖσαν* (K-W, B). ΚΛΕΙϹΘΕΝΗΝ (K-W, H-L, B); cf. 22 § 1, et Kühner, *Gr. Gr.* i p. 512[3]. **19** *ἀντιστασιάζοντες* H-L. *πρὸς τούτους* vel *κατὰ τούτων* desiderat Gennadios. **23** *εἰ δὴ χρὴ ἀγαθοῖς* minus bene Athen. 695; *εἰ δὴ χρή σ' ἀγαθοῖς* Bergk.

·o·

XXI 1 ΕΠΙϹΤΕΥΕΝ, cf. 35 § 3 *ἔχαιρον ἡ πόλις. ἐπίστευεν ὁ δῆμος* K, H-L, B: *ἐπίστευον* ⟦*ὁ δῆμος*⟧ Rutherford, Bury, K-W. **3** *ἐπ'* H-L.

§ 3. **ὑπεξελθόντος**] Hdt. v 72, *Κλεομένης δὲ ὡς πέμπων (κήρυκα) ἐξέβαλλε Κλεισθένεα καὶ τοὺς ἐναγέας, Κλεισθένης μὲν αὐτὸς ὑπεξέσχε.* **ἡγηλάτει**] *ib. ἀγηλατέει ἑπτακόσια ἐπίστια Ἀθηναίων.*

ταῦτα δὲ—ὑποσπόνδους] Hdt. v 72, *ταῦτα δὲ ποιήσας δεύτερα τὴν βουλὴν καταλύειν ἐπειρᾶτο, τριηκοσίοισι δὲ τοῖσι Ἰσαγόρεω στασιώτῃσι τὰς ἀρχὰς ἐνεχείριζε. ἀντισταθείσης δὲ τῆς βουλῆς καὶ οὐ βουλομένης πείθεσθαι ὅ τε Κλεομένης καὶ ὁ Ἰσαγόρης καὶ οἱ στασιῶται αὐτοῦ καταλαμβάνουσι τὴν ἀκρόπολιν. Ἀθηναίων δὲ οἱ λοιποὶ τὰ αὐτὰ φρονήσαντες ἐπολιόρκεον αὐτοὺς ἡμέρας δύο· τῇ δὲ τρίτῃ ὑπόσπονδοι ἐξέρχονται ἐκ τῆς χώρης ὅσοι ἦσαν αὐτῶν Λακεδαιμόνιοι.* Isagoras withdrew with the Lacedaemonians (74); the rest of the Athenians who had taken his side were put to death (72 *fin.*).

μετεπέμψαντο] Hdt. v 73, *Κλεισθένεα καὶ τὰ ἑπτακόσια ἐπίστια τὰ διωχθέντα ὑπὸ Κλεομένεος μεταπεμψάμενοι.*

§ 4. **τοῦ δήμου προστάτης**] c. 2 § 2 *ad fin.*

§ 5. **Κήδων**] Nothing else is known of this person. His endeavour to expel the tyrants was doubtless one of the unsuccessful attempts recorded in c. 19 in the general phrase: *ἀεὶ προσέπταιον.*

καὶ εἰς τοῦτον] *i.e.* as well as the baffled heroes of Leipsydrium celebrated in the song recorded in c. 19, and quoted by Athenaeus immediately after this couplet. This juxtaposition seems to shew that both quotations were derived from this work.

XXI § 1. **ἔτει τετάρτῳ...ἐπὶ Ἰσαγόρου ἄρχοντος**] The fourth year after the expulsion of the Peisistratidae (511/0) corresponds to 508/7 B.C. The archonship of Isagoras is placed by Dionysius *συνένειμε πάντας εἰς δέκα φυλὰς ἀντὶ τῶν τεττάρων, ἀναμεῖξαι βουλόμενος ὅπως μετάσχωσι πλείους τῆς πολιτείας· ὅθεν ἐλέχθη*

4 ΟΥΝΕΝΕΙΜΕ: *συνένειμε* Newman, Kontos, Gertz, H-L (K[3] coll. 41 § 2, B); *οὖν συνένειμε* K-W, qui lacunam post *ἄρχοντος* indicatam ope Ar. *Pol.* 1275 *b* 36 explendam censent. *διένειμε* Wyse, *ἀνένειμε* Thompson. *ἀναμεῖξαι* K-W, H-L, K[3]; cf. 3 § 5 *σύμμειξις*: ΑΝΑΜΙΞΑΙ.

Hal., *Ant. Rom.* i 74, in Ol. 68, 1 = 508/7 B.C.; and his second mention of the same date, in v 1, shews that it was an Olympic year.

The text implies that the reforms of Cleisthenes were subsequent to the expulsion of Isagoras and Cleomenes. Cleisthenes begins by *offering* (ἀποδιδούς, 20 § 1) the commons a share in the constitution; Isagoras appeals to Cleomenes for his assistance against Cleisthenes, and is defeated; thereupon Cleisthenes carries out his proposed reforms. Herodotus briefly mentions some of these reforms (v 66 and 69), and describes the calling in of Cleomenes as a counter-move on the part of Isagoras (70). Hence modern historians, *e. g.* Thirlwall, Grote, Curtius and Busolt, place the constitutional reforms of Cleisthenes before the calling in of Cleomenes. This appears improbable, for (as justly observed by Mr Kenyon) 'there was not time to have introduced such extensive constitutional changes before the Spartan invasion; a remark which had already been made by Sauppe, *De Demis Urbanis*, p. 1. The evidence of Herodotus, when carefully examined, is partly in favour of the account in the text. He begins by describing Cl. as courting the aid of the commons (τὸν δῆμον προσεταιρίζεται). He then adds that it was *afterwards* (μετὰ δὲ) that Cl. transformed the four tribes into ten. This part of his narrative is a digression, and the story is resumed in c. 69, ἦν τε τὸν δῆμον προσθέμενος πολλῷ κατύπερθε τῶν ἀντιστασιωτέων. In this view, I find myself in agreement with Lugebil, *Philol.* Suppl. Bd. iv 165.

§ 2. **εἰς δέκα φυλὰς ἀντὶ τῶν τεττάρων κτλ.**] Hdt. v 66, μετὰ δὲ τετραφύλους ἐόντας Ἀθηναίους δεκαφύλους ἐποίησε κτλ. *ib.* 69, τὰς φυλὰς μετωνόμασε καὶ ἐποίησε πλεῦνας ἐξ ἐλασσόνων· δέκα τε δὴ φυλάρχους ἀντὶ τεσσέρων ἐποίησε, δέκα δὲ καὶ τοὺς δήμους κατένειμε ἐς τὰς φυλάς. In the *Politics*, Ar. alludes to these reforms as follows: iii 2, 1275 *b* 37, ἀλλ' ἴσως ἐκεῖνο μᾶλλον ἔχει ἀπορίαν, ὅσοι μετέσχον μεταβολῆς γενομένης πολιτείας (cf. μετάσχωσι...τῆς πολιτείας), οἷον Ἀθήνησιν ἐποίησε Κλεισθένης μετὰ τὴν τῶν τυράννων ἐκβολήν· πολλοὺς γὰρ ἐφυλέτευσε ξένους καὶ δούλους μετοίκους, *i.e.* enrolled (as citizens) in the tribes not only free-born foreigners but also slaves who by emancipation had already become μέτοικοι (cf. Gilbert, *Gr. St.* i 144; Hermann, *Staatsalt.* § 111, 18). The text, as it stands, makes no direct mention of these, though it incidentally names the νεοπολῖται at the end of § 4. Cf. *ib.* vii (vi) 4, 1319 *b* 20, ἔτι δὲ καὶ τὰ τοιαῦτα κατασκευάσματα χρήσιμα πρὸς τὴν δημοκρατίαν τὴν τοιαύτην, οἷς Κλεισθένης τε Ἀθήνησιν ἐχρήσατο βουλόμενος αὐξῆσαι τὴν δημοκρατίαν, καὶ περὶ Κυρήνην οἱ τὸν δῆμον καθιστάντες. φυλαί τε γὰρ ἕτεραι ποιητέαι πλείους καὶ φατρίαι, καὶ τὰ τῶν ἰδίων ἱερῶν συνακτέον εἰς ὀλίγα καὶ κοινά, καὶ πάντα σοφιστέον ὅπως ἂν ὅτι μάλιστα ἀναμιχθῶσι (cf. ἀναμεῖξαι) πάντες ἀλλήλοις, αἱ δὲ συνήθειαι διαζευχθῶσιν αἱ πρότεραι. See Grote, c. 31, ii p. 109—113; and *inf.* p. 83.

ὅθεν—βουλομένους] 'Hence the advice, not to notice the tribe, which was tendered to those who would scrutinise (the lists of) the clans.' This is the interpretation suggested by Mr Kenyon who, in the course of an excellent note, observes that, as the φυλαί, after the reforms of Cleisthenes, 'no longer bore any relation to the γένη, it was useless to enter on an examination of the tribes for the purpose of reviewing the lists of the γένη... A number of persons were admitted to the new tribes who had not been members of the old, and these were not necessarily entered on the rolls of any of the γένη. Formerly, on any review of the citizen-roll, it was no doubt usual to go through it tribe by tribe, following all the subdivisions of the old patriarchal system. Now, the tribe-roll had no relation to that of the γένη, and consequently those persons who wished to examine the latter would have nothing to do with distinctions of tribe.' In the words of Grote, c. 10, ii 273, 'the *gentes* had no connection, as such, with these new tribes, and the members of the same gens might belong to different demes'.

[Col. 9] *καὶ τὸ μὴ φυλοκρινεῖν, ‖ πρὸς τοὺς ἐξετάζειν τὰ γένη βουλομένους.*

3 *ἔπειτα τὴν βουλὴν πεντακοσί[ους] ἀντὶ τετρακοσίων κ[ατ]έστησεν, πεντήκοντα ἐξ ἑκάστης φυλῆς· τότε δ' ἦ[σα]ν ἑκατόν. διὰ τοῦτο δὲ οὐκ εἰς δώ[δε]κα φυλὰς συνέταξεν, ὅπ[ως α]ὐτῷ μὴ συμβαίνῃ μερίζειν κατὰ τὰς προϋπαρχούσας τριττῦς· ἦσαν γὰρ ἐκ τεττάρων φυλῶν δώδεκα τριττύες· ὥστ' οὐ [συν]έπιπτεν <ἂν> ἀναμίσγεσθαι τὸ πλῆθος.*

4 *διένειμε δὲ καὶ τὴν χώραν κατὰ δήμους τριάκοντα μέρη,*

10 ΠΡΟϹ corr. in ΚΑΤΑ. *τεττάρων*: Δ̄. **11** ΟΥϹ'ΕΠΕΙΠΤΕΝ? *οὐκ ἂν συνέπιπτεν* Richards (H-L); *οὐ συνέπιπτεν ἂν* Hude, K-W, K³, B.

TESTIMONIA. **12—15** Michael Psellus *περὶ τῶν ὀνομάτων τῶν δικῶν*, p. 103 Boissonade, p. 1015 § 31 Migne, *ἡ δὲ τριττὺς νεωτέρων ὄνομα παρὰ τοῖς Ἀθηναίοις ἐστί. Κλεισθένης γάρ τις, εἰς τριάκοντα μοίρας τὴν Ἀττικὴν ἅπασαν διανείμας, ἐπειδὴ τὸ μὲν αὐτῆς ἐπιθαλαττίδιον ἦν, τὸ δὲ ἐπὶ τοῦ μέσου καθῆστο τῆς χώρας, τὸ δὲ παρὰ τὸ ἄστυ συνέστρωτο, δέκα μὲν μοίρας τῇ παραλίῳ συντέτευχε, δέκα δὲ κατέστησεν ἐπὶ τὴν μεσόγειον, δέκα δὲ ἀστυνόμους ἐποίησε· καὶ τὸ τριτημόριον τριττὺς ὠνόμαστο* (attulerunt K-W).

φυλοκρινεῖν] 'to draw distinctions between tribes'. The word occurs in Thuc. vi 18 § 2, *εἴγε ἡσυχάζοιεν πάντες ἢ φυλοκρινοῖεν οἷς χρεὼν βοηθεῖν*, where, like *ταμιεύεσθαι* in § 3, and *στορέσωμεν* in § 4, it is a vivid metaphor characteristic of the speaker, Alcibiades. Cf. Lucian, *Abdicatus*, 4, *οὐκ ἐς βάθος ὁρώντων, οὐδ' ἀκριβῶς φυλοκρινούντων* (Schol. *διακρουόντων, δοκιμαζόντων περιέργως*) *τὰς νόσους*, and *Phalaris alter*, 9, *φυλοκρινεῖν τὰ ἀναθήματα καὶ γενεαλογεῖν τὰ πεμπόμενα, ὅθεν καὶ ἀφ' ὅτου καὶ ὁποῖα* (in all these passages there is a *v. l. φιλοκρινεῖν*). In late authors we also have *φυλοκρίνησις*, *φυλοκρινητέον*, and *φυλοκρινητικός* (see L and S). Pollux, viii 110, after recounting the names of the Attic tribes, adds *ἀπὸ δὲ φυλῶν τὸ φυλοκρινεῖν ὠνομάσθη*; and Suidas explains *φυλοκρινεῖ* by *διακρίνει, καταδοκιμάζει περιέργως*. Cf. Phrynichus, p. 71, 8 Bekk. An. *φυλοκρινεῖν· κυρίως μὲν τὸ τὰς φυλὰς τὰς ἐν ταῖς πόλεσι διακρίνειν, σημαίνει δὲ καὶ τὸ ἄλλο τι διατάττειν καὶ διακρίνειν*, id. '*App. Soph.* p. 81, 7, *φιλοκρίνει* (*sic*)· *διακρίνει, δοκιμάζει περιέργως, κατεξετάζει*', quoted by Schmidt on Hesych. *φυλ[λ]οκρινεῖν· τὰς φυλὰς διακρίνειν.*

ἐξετάζειν] Dem. 45 § 82, *τὸν ἡμέτερον πατέρα ἐξήταζες ὅστις ἦν* (of one who was once a slave). Cf. note on Dem. *Lept.* § 5.

§ 3. **τὴν βουλὴν**] From this time forward the Solonian Council of 400 is superseded by that of 500, *ἡ τῶν πεντακοσίων βουλή*, or *ἡ βουλὴ οἱ πεντακόσιοι* (Aeschin. *Ctes.* § 2) as it was sometimes called, to distinguish it from the Council of the Areopagus. The institution of the Council of the Five Hundred has always been attributed to Cleisthenes, in connexion with the introduction of the ten tribes; but this passage is probably the first express statement on the subject in any ancient author.

ὅπως—μὴ συμβαίνῃ] *Inf. ὅπως—μετέχῃ*, and *ἵνα μὴ...ἐξελέγχωσιν.*

τριττῦς] c. 8 § 3.

οὐ συνέπιπτεν ἂν—πλῆθος] 'quod si fecisset, non contigisset ut multitudo misceretur' Hude (placing *ἦσαν—τριττύες* in a parenthesis).

§ 4. **διένειμε—τριάκοντα μέρη**] c. 30 § 3, *διανεῖμαι...τέτταρα μέρη*, Xen. *Cyrop.* vii 5, 3, *τὸ στράτευμα κατένειμε δώδεκα μέρη*, Plato, *Politicus*, p. 283 D *διέλωμεν αὐτὴν δύο μέρη* (Kühner *Gr. Gr.* § 411, 6 *c*).

Cleisthenes divided the whole of Attica into 30 portions, each of them called a *τριττύς*. 10 of these were urban or suburban, 10 on the coast, and 10 in the interior. Each of the 10 tribes had three *τριττῦς* allotted to it, one from each of the above districts. Thus 'the tribe, as a whole, did not correspond with any continuous portion of the territory, nor could it have any peculiar local interest, separate from the entire community' (Grote). In this way the evils that had arisen during the previous century from the factions of the Shore, the Plain and the Mountain, were effectually counteracted.

The number of demes in each *τριττύς* is not known. From the passage in Hdt. v 69, *δέκα δὲ καὶ τοὺς δήμους κατένειμε ἐς τὰς φυλάς*, 'Cleisthenes distributed the demes among the tribes by tens', it has been inferred that he 'at first recognised exactly *δέκα μὲν τῶν περὶ τὸ ἄστυ, δέκα δὲ τῆς παραλίας, δέκα δὲ τῆς μεσογείου, καὶ ταύτας ἐπονομάσας τριττῦς, ἐκλήρωσεν τρεῖς εἰς τὴν φυλὴν ἑκάστην, ὅπως ἑκάστη μετέχῃ πάντων τῶν τόπων. καὶ*

---

100 demes, distributed in equal proportion among his 10 tribes'. This is the view of Schömann (*Ant.* p. 365 E. T.). K. F. Hermann (*Staatsalt.* § 111, 12) held that this is what Herodotus meant to affirm, but he does not accept the account as true. Gilbert, *Gr. St.* i 142, notes that the existence of the Attic demes before Cleisthenes is implied in [Plato], *Hipparch.* p. 228—9. He also quotes Herodian, περὶ μονήρους λέξεως, p. 17, 8, Ἀραφὴν εἷς τῶν ἑκατὸν ἡρώων. *Araphen*, one of the Attic demes, is thus identical in name with one of the 100 κτίσται ἐπώνυμοι of the demes. He therefore accepts the statement of Herodotus. Others again (*e.g.* Corsini, Grote in his first ed., and Dietrich, *de Clisthene*, Halle, 1840, p. 32) connect δέκα with ἐς τὰς φυλάς and contend that such a collocation is not uncommon in Herodotus. Madvig, *Adv. Crit.* i 305, strikes out δέκα δέ. Bake (*Bibliotheca Critica* iv 272) alters it into καὶ δή. Cf. Schömann, *On Grote*, § 6, and *Ant.* pp. 336, 366 E. T.

Even supposing that 100 demes were recognised by Cleisthenes, that number did not remain unaltered. Early in the 2nd century B.C. (in the time of Polemon, quoted by Strabo p. 396) the number was 174. The number known to us from inscriptions is 182, besides 8 doubtful cases (Hermann's *Staatsalt.* ed. 5, p. 797). Out of these 182, there are 14 duplicate names, such as 'upper' and 'lower *Lamptrae*'; so that the number of known names of demes is 168. Landwehr (*Philologus*, Suppl. v, 1889 p. 161—166) holds that 174 was the original number, and that this remained unaltered. The number of τριττῦς was evidently constant and it may be fairly assumed that the demes belonging to each τριττύς were, as a general rule, contiguous. If there were 100 demes, each of the 30 τριττῦς would contain 3 or 4 demes, twenty of them containing only 3 demes each, and the remaining ten as many as 4, $(\overline{20 \times 3} + \overline{10 \times 4} = 100)$. Dividing this number by 10 we get for each tribe $\overline{2 \times 3} + \overline{1 \times 4}$ demes, distributed in such a way that each tribe has one τριττύς consisting of 4 demes, and 2 consisting of 3. In the case of each tribe, one of these τριττῦς would be situated in or near the capital, one near the coast, and one in the interior. The following scheme shows how it would be possible to distribute 100 demes among ten tribes while assigning ten trittyes of 3 or 4 demes each to each of the 3 districts:

	urban or suburban	the coast	the interior
Erechtheis	4	3	3
Aegeis	4	3	3
Pandionis	4	3	3
Leontis	3	4	3
Acamantis	3	4	3
Oeneis	3	4	3
Cecropis	3	3	4
Hippoöntis	3	3	4
Aeantis	3	3	4
Antiochis	3	3	4
	33	33	34

Total: 100 demes.

Out of the 160 demes in Smith's *Dict. Geogr.*, 124 are assigned to certain tribes; no tribe has less than 10, though several have more; *Acamantis*, *Hippothontis*, and *Leontis* having as many as 15, 16 and 17 respectively.

Athens itself, with its immediate neighbourhood, was divided into several demes and those demes assigned to several tribes, as follows: Agryle (*Erechtheis*), Kollytus and Diomeia (*Aegeis*), Kydathenaeon (*Pandionis*), Scambonidae (*Leontis*), Cerameicus (*Acamantis*), Lakiadae (*Oeneis*), Melite (*Cecropis*), Ceiriadae (*Hippothontis*), Phaleron (*Aeantis*), Colonus ἀγοραῖος (*Antiochis*?). The Peiraeus was assigned to the tribe *Hippothontis*. (Lolling in I. Müller's *Handbuch*, iii 306.) In the case of the demes in or near Athens it would be difficult for them to be contiguous with the other demes in the same τριττύς. It is not impossible that less than 3 demes may in some cases have constituted a τριττύς. On the distribution of the demes among the tribes, cf. Wilamowitz, *Aus Kydathen*, i 110; Hug, *Gemeinden und Bürgerrecht in Attika*, 19; Milchhöfer, *Erl. Text zu Curtius und Kaupert, Karten von Attika* i 28, ii 39 n. 3 (Busolt, i 614, n. 5).

ὅπως ἑκάστη μετέχῃ πάντων τῶν τόπων] *Pol.* 1330 *a* 16, ἵνα—ἀμφοτέρων τῶν τόπων πάντες μετέχωσιν. Plat. *Leg.* 745 B–E (Newman).

δημότας ἐποίησεν ἀλλήλων τοὺς οἰκοῦντας ἐν ἑκάστῳ τῶν δήμων, ἵνα μὴ πατρόθεν προσαγορεύοντες ἐξελέγχωσιν τοὺς νεοπολίτας, ἀλλὰ τῶν δήμων ἀναγορεύωσιν· ὅθεν καὶ καλ[οῦ]σιν Ἀθηναῖοι σφᾶς αὐτοὺς τῶν δήμων. κατέστησε δὲ καὶ δημάρχους τὴν αὐτὴν ἔχοντας ἐπιμέλειαν τοῖς πρότερον ναυκράροις· καὶ γὰρ τοὺς δήμους

18 προσαγορεύωσιν Richards. καὶ <νῦν> K-W.

19—21 *Schol. Arist. *Nub.* 37 Ἀρ. δὲ περὶ Κλεισθένους φησὶ "κατέστησε καὶ δημάρχους—ἐποίησεν" (Rose, Frag. 397^3, deerat in ed. 2). *Harp. ναυκραρικά:...Ἀρ. δ' ἐν Ἀθ. πολ. φησὶ "κατέστησαν δὲ δημάρχους—ναυκράροις· δημίους (δημαίους cod. A) ἀντὶ τῶν ναυκράρων ἐποίησαν" (359^2, 397^3). *Harp. δήμαρχος:... τούτους δέ φησιν Ἀρ. ἐν Ἀθ. πολ. ὑπὸ Κλεισθένους κατασταθῆναι τὴν αὐτὴν ἔχοντας ἐπιμέλειαν τοῖς πρότερον ναυκράροις (*ib.*). Hesych. δήμαρχοι: οἱ πρότερον καλούμενοι ναύκραροι...

δημότας—δήμων] Under this arrangement every one originally belonged to the deme in which he lived. His descendants, whether they had property in the deme or not, continued to belong to the same deme. It was only through adoption that a member of one deme became a member of another, by being enrolled in the deme of his adoptive father (Dem. *Leoch.* §§ 22, 34; Schömann, *Antiq.* p. 367, E. T.).

ἵνα μὴ—νεοπολίτας] Many foreigners and resident aliens were added by Cleisthenes to the roll of citizens (*Pol.* 1275 *b* 37, quoted on p. 78). Such a newly enrolled citizen, if called by his father's name alone, would betray his foreign origin; but, by being designated by his deme, he lost the badge of his alien birth and was put on equal terms with the other members of the deme. **πατρόθεν]** Xen. *Oecon.* vii 3, Pausan. vii 7 § 4. **ἐξελέγχωσιν]** Dem. *Eubul.* 57 § 3, τοῖς μὲν ἐξελεγχομένοις ξένοις οὖσι χαλεπαίνειν, and *ib.* § 51.

τῶν δήμων ἀναγορεύωσιν] 'publicly (or officially) call them by their demes.' Cf. τῶν δήμων Πιθεύς, τῶν δήμων Θορίκιος (Plat. *Euthyphro*, 2 B, and Dem. 39 § 30), Lys. 23 § 2, ὁπόθεν δημοτεύοιτο. It may be inferred that before the time of Cleisthenes Athenians were not described by the name of their demes. 'In Athens, at least after the revolution of Kleisthenês, the gentile name was not employed: a man was described by his own single name, followed first by the name of his father and next by that of the deme to which he belonged' (Grote c. 10, ii 274).

§ 5. **κατέστησε—δημάρχους]** Photius, s.v. ναυκραρία, quotes from this treatise (c. 8 § 3), φυλαὶ δὲ ἦσαν—καθ' ἑκάστην. After this quotation should follow the words which have by mistake been placed before it, viz.: ὕστερον δὲ ἀπὸ Κλεισθένους δῆμοί εἰσι, καὶ δήμαρχοι ἐκλήθησαν. At the close of his article he cites Cleidemus (ἐν τῇ τρίτῃ): ὅτι Κλεισθένους δέκα φυλὰς ποιήσαντος ἀντὶ τῶν τεσσάρων, συνέβη καὶ εἰς πεντήκοντα μέρη διαταγῆναι· αὐτοὺς (ταῦτα Müller) δὲ ἐκάλουν ναυκραρίας, ὥσπερ νῦν εἰς τὰ ἑκατὸν μέρη διαιρεθέντα (διαιρεθέντας Siebelis) καλοῦσι συμμορίας (FHG i 361). According to this view, the change in the number of tribes from four to ten involved a change in the number of ναυκραρίαι from 48 (12 × 4) to 50. If the normal number of demes recognised by Cleisthenes was 100, it would follow from this that he combined every two demes into a ναυκραρία (Schömann, *Ant.* p. 370 E.T.); or rather that he transferred the duties of each ναυκραρία to a pair of contiguous demes. The importance of the *Naucrariae* naturally did not remain the same as it had formerly been, and we hear in particular that the business which had once belonged to the *Naucrari* now passed to the Demarchs (*ib.* p. 370, on the authority of quotations from this passage in Harpocration &c.).

In the passage above cited from Photius Mr P. Giles (*English Historical Review*, 1892, p. 331) proposes, instead of πεντήκοντα (i.e. Ν) μέρη, to read τριάκοντα (i.e. Λ) μέρη, and to identify these μέρη with the τριττῦς. He also assumes that this sentence was followed by a clause referring to the δῆμοι. He is doubtless justified in adding that this treatise gives no direct support to the view that the ναυκραρία consisted of two δῆμοι.

The Peripatetic, Demetrius Phalereus (Müller, FHG, ii 363), ascribed the establishment of demarchs not to Cleisthenes but to οἱ περὶ Σόλωνα (Newman).

ἀντὶ τῶν ναυκραριῶν ἐποίησεν. προσηγόρευσε δὲ τῶν δήμων τοὺς μὲν ἀπὸ τῶν [τ]όπ[ων], τοὺς δὲ ἀπὸ τῶν κτισάντων· οὐ γὰρ ἅπαν-
23 *τες ὑπῆρχον ἔτι τοῖς τόποις. τὰ δὲ γένη καὶ τὰς φρατρίας καὶ τὰς* 6

22 ἅπαντες ὑπῆρχον ἔτι (K, K-W); ΕΝ| pro ἔτι Berol. (B, qui etiam in papyro Londin. ΕΝ legendum suspicatur; certe litteris valde obscuris ΕΤΙ indicatur): ἅπασιν κτλ coniecit K (J B Mayor); ἅπασιν ὑπῆρχεν ὀνόματα Bury (H-L); etiam ἅπαντες <οἱ κτίσαντες> ὑπῆρχον ἔτι τοῖς τόποις coniecerat Bury. **23** ΦΑΤΡΙΑC, idem habet corr. Berol.

προσηγόρευσε—κτισάντων] 'He named some of the demes from their localities, and some from their founders.' Demes were already in existence before Cleisthenes; but they were now recognised as component parts in the new constitutional order, and had their names fixed by official sanction. Many of them had *local* designations derived either from natural features (Ποταμός, Κηφισία, Ἐπικηφισία, Δειράδες, Ἁλιμοῦς), or places in their neighbourhood (Οἶον Δεκελεικόν, Οἶον Κεραμεικόν), or plants or trees that grew there (Μαραθών, Ῥαμνοῦς, Μυρρινοῦς, Ἀγνοῦς, Ἀχερδοῦς, Ἰτέα, Ἐλαιοῦς, Ἐρίκεια, Θρία, Πρασίαι, Πτελέα, Φηγοῦς). Among other local designations may be mentioned Οἰνόη, Βῆσα, Λαμπτραί, Ἐλευσίς. Cf. Etym. Magn. s. v. Ἐλεεῖς:...ἢ ἀπὸ τῶν τόπων, ἢ ἀπὸ τῶν παρακειμένων αὐτοῖς, ἢ ἀπὸ τῶν ἐν αὐτοῖς φυτῶν, ἢ ἀπὸ τῶν ἐν αὐτοῖς χειροτεχνῶν, ἢ ἀπὸ τῶν οἰκησάντων (οἰκισάντων Leake) ἀνδρῶν καὶ γυναικῶν, and Schol. Aristoph. *Plut.* 586.

Other demes were named 'from their founders,' *i.e.* from one of the 'hundred heroes' or eponymous founders of the demes (Herodian, quoted on § 3). The names of these are collected by Sauppe, *De Demis Urbanis*, p. 4 ff.; but since many of them are obviously coined from the names of the demes, it is in these cases inaccurate to describe the demes as designated after their founders. Many of the demes were called after distinguished *gentes* who held property in them (*e.g.* Butadae, Thymaetadae, Cothocidae, Perithoedae, Semachidae, Scambonidae, Colleidae). There are as many as 30 such demes (25 of them are given in Grote, c. 10, ii 273 n.); and it has been suggested that all of these were constituted by Cleisthenes. 'It seems that Kleisthenes' (says Grote, *l. c.*) 'recognised a certain number of new demes to which he gave names derived from some important *gens* resident near the spot. It is thus that we are to explain the large number of Kleisthenean demes that bear patronymic names.' If, under Cleisthenes, the number of demes was 100, it follows that before his time 70 demes were already in existence. (Cf. Smith, *Dict. Ant.* s. v. *Demus.*) 'The demes named after *gentes* are situated mainly in that part of the country which has been assigned to the *Phyle* of the Geleontes, and where accordingly the greater number of noble families and the most important of them lived' (Schömann, *Ant.* p. 366 n. E.T.). It is not impossible that τῶν κτισάντων is meant to include the ancestors of these families as well as the 'eponymous heroes'; but the distinction is immaterial, as a deme might readily regard, as its eponymous hero, the founder of the family from which it derived its name.

οὐ γάρ—τοῖς τόποις] 'for (from the time of Cleisthenes) the demes were no longer called in all cases from the localities' (understanding προσαγορευθέντες from προσηγόρευσε); *i.e.* they then ceased to be in every instance designated by 'local' names. These old 'local' names had often been derived from the villages or hamlets included within the limits of the deme as constituted by Cleisthenes. Many of these were superseded by gentile or patronymic or heroic names,—names derived ἀπὸ τῶν κτισάντων. οὐ γὰρ ἔτι is inconsistent in sense with ὑπῆρχον, unless the latter is made to mean little more than ἦν. Possibly the sentence implies that (even in the time of Cl.) the demes had already lost their local designations, and had received names derived from persons instead. Cl. gave official recognition to both classes of names, local and personal. Poland translates as follows: *Denn nicht alle Gaue entsprachen mehr den alten Namen der Örtlichkeiten*, adding in a note, that, in naming the new demes, Cl. availed himself of the old names, but had often, for example, to break up an old deme into several divisions and thus create new names. Blass reads ἐν τοῖς τόποις, with the following interpretation: *non omnes demi erant inter vicos qui iam exstabant; itaque multos ab heroibus appellavit.*

ἱερεωσύνας εἴασεν ἔχειν ἑκάστους κατὰ τὰ πάτρια. ταῖς δὲ φυλαῖς ἐποίησεν ἐπωνύμ[ους] ἐκ τῶν προκριθέντων ἑκατὸν ἀρχηγετῶν οὓς ἀνεῖλεν ἡ Πυθία δέκα.

24 ΙΕΡΩϹΥΝΑϹ (K, H-L, B): *ἱερεωσύνας* K-W, Meisterhans, p. 36[2]. **25** ΕΠΩΝΥΜΟΥϹ Berol.; idem coniecerant J B Mayor, Richards: *ἐπωνυμ[ίας]* K[1].

25—26 Etym. M. *ἐπώνυμοι* (locus infra exscriptus).

---

§ 6. **τὰ δὲ γένη—πάτρια**] The parallel passage in the *Politics*, 1319 *b* 20, quoted on p. 78, implies that Cleisthenes increased the number of the phratries (and it was so understood by Buermann, *Jahrb. f. kl. Phil.* Suppl. Bd. ix 1878, 597 *sqq.*). The text states that he allowed every one to remain in his former phratria. It was once held by Busolt (*Gr. Gesch.* i 394, note 5, after Landwehr, *Philologus*, Suppl. Bd. v 168) that the reference to the phratries in the passage in the *Politics* did not necessarily apply to Athens, but to Cyrene, which is mentioned in the same passage; and with this view Mr W. R. Paton agrees (*Class. Rev.* v 221 *b*). See also Duncker, *G. d. A.* vi 591 note. Busolt, however, has since admitted that the *φρατρίαι* are those of Athens (I. Müller's *Handbuch*, iv 1, p. 144 note 11); he adds that the present passage (as represented in the Berlin fragment) implies that the principle of the organisation of the phratries according to *γένη* remained unchanged. 'Probably the phratries before the time of Cleisthenes were larger bodies which, on the occasion of his reforms, were broken up into smaller portions. The number of the phratries is unknown; but they must have been more than 12' (*ib.*).

The present passage has been held to be 'somewhat out of harmony' with that in the *Politics*, and the question has been asked whether the statement as to priesthoods can be easily reconciled with the fact that Cleisthenes converted a number of private worships into a few public ones' (Mr W. L. Newman, in *Class. Rev.* v 162 *a*). If we are compelled to choose, one would prefer the definite statement in the text to the inference drawn from the less definite statement in the *Politics*, not to mention the disturbing influence of the mention of Cyrene in that passage. The two statements may, however, be reconciled. I take the text to refer to those who were already citizens connected with existing *γένη* and *φρατρίαι*. Cleisthenes allowed all these to continue as of old in their respective *γένη* and *φρατρίαι*, with their religious institutions intact. Among these institutions would be (1) the sacrificial rites performed by the *φυλοβασιλεῖς*, who survived the change from four tribes into ten (8 § 3; 57 end); and (2) the hereditary priesthoods such as those held by the Eumolpidae, Kerykes and Eteobutadae. Cf. Lex. Dem. Patm. p. 152, Sakkelion, (of the 30 *γεννηταί*) *ὧν αἱ ἱερωσύναι ἑκάστοις προσήκουσαι ἐκληροῦντο, οἷον Εὐμολπίδαι καὶ Κήρυκες καὶ Ἐτεοβουτάδαι, ὡς ἱστορεῖ ἐν τῇ Ἀθ. πολ. Ἀριστοτέλης κτλ.* (Rose, Frag. 385[3]).

In contrast to the existing citizens there were a number of other persons who had hitherto not belonged to that body and therefore had no *γένη*. These are the *νεοπολῖται* of § 4. It was for these that Cleisthenes provided new *φρατρίαι*. At the same time he absorbed many of the minor local cults into public festivals held at Athens.

In *Class. Rev.* v 222 *b*, Mr W. R. Paton observes that the *νεοπολῖται* could not be received into the *γένη*, all the members of which were allied (or supposed to be allied) by blood; but he considers that they could be received into the phratries, each of which was a group of *γένη* not claiming a blood-relationship with each other and therefore more elastic. He assumes that Cleisthenes did not increase the number of phratries; whereas it is not improbable that he did, and there is nothing in the present passage to prove that he did not.

ταῖς δὲ φυλαῖς—δέκα] In Etym. M., *s. v.* *ἐπώνυμοι*, after mention of the *ἐπώνυμοι τῶν ἡλικιῶν* (c. 53), we have, contrasted with these, *οἱ δέκα ἀφ' ὧν αἱ φυλαὶ προσηγορεύθησαν, οἷον Ἐρεχθεύς, Αἰγεύς, Πανδίων, Λεώς, Ἀκάμας, Οἰνεύς, Κέκροψ, Ἱπποθόων, Αἴας, Ἀντίοχος· ταῦτα δὲ τὰ δέκα ὀνόματα ἀπὸ ρ'* (=*ἑκατόν*, codices *ἀπόροις*) *ὁ Πύθιος εἵλετο, Κλεισθένους οὕτω διαταξαμένου τὸ πᾶν πλῆθος εἰς δέκα φυλάς.* Cf. Lex. Dem. Patm., p. 15, Sakkelion (*Bull. de corr. hellén.* 1877), *...τοῦ θεοῦ τοῦτο χρήσαντος...τούτους γὰρ ἐξ ὀνομάτων ἑκατὸν ὁ θεὸς ἐξελέξατο*, and Schol. Aristid. iii 331, 20 Dind. This is one of several instances in which the influence

22. τούτων δὲ γενομένων δημοτικωτέρα πολ[ὺ τῆς Σ]όλωνος ἐγένετο ἡ πολιτεία· καὶ γὰρ συνέβη τοὺς μὲν Σόλωνος νόμους ἀφανίσαι τὴν τυραννίδα διὰ τὸ μὴ χρῆσθαι, καινοὺς δ' ἄλλους θεῖναι τὸν Κλεισθένην στοχαζόμενον τοῦ πλήθους, ἐν οἷς ἐτέθη καὶ ὁ περὶ τοῦ ὀστρακισμοῦ νόμος. πρῶτον μὲν οὖν ἔτει †πέμπτῳ† 2
μετὰ ταύτην τὴν κατάστασιν ἐφ' Ἑρμοκρέοντος ἄρχοντος τῇ βουλῇ τοῖς πεντακοσίοις τὸν ὅρκον ἐποίησαν, ὃν ἔτι καὶ νῦν ὀμνύ-

XXII **3** κ(αι)νογς? (και...Berol.), K-W, K[3], B: [νόμ]ους H-L. **4** κλειcθενη (K, K-W, H-L, B). **5** †πεμπτῳ†, an ὀγδόῳ? K. **6** ερμογ|κρεοντος (K).

Testimonia. **XXII 5—39** Heraclidis epitoma (Rose, Frag. 611, 4[3]): καὶ τὸν περὶ ὀστρακισμοῦ νόμον εἰσηγήσατο, ὃς ἐτέθη διὰ τοὺς τυραννιῶντας. καὶ ἄλλοι τε ὠστρακίσθησαν καὶ Ξάνθιππος καὶ Ἀριστείδης.

---

of the Alcmaeonidae with the oracle at Delphi was of important consequences to Athens.

ἀρχηγετῶν] The ἐπώνυμοι are themselves called ἀρχηγέται in Aristoph. Frag. 186 Dind. (παρὰ τοὺς ἀρχηγέτας), ap. Bekk. *Anecd.* i 449: ἀρχηγέται· ἡγεμόνες οἱ ἐπώνυμοι τῶν φυλῶν.

XXII. *Ostracism.*

§ 1. **στοχαζόμενον τοῦ πλήθους**] *Pol.* vi (iv) 12, ἂν...ὀλιγαρχικοὺς τοὺς νόμους τιθῇ στοχάζεσθαι χρὴ τῶν μέσων.

ὀστρακισμοῦ] Our knowledge of the procedure in cases of ostracism is founded on a fragment of Philochorus 79 *b* (FHG i 396), in the Appendix to Photius, p. 675 Porson: προχειροτονεῖ μὲν ὁ δῆμος πρὸ τῆς η' πρυτανείας (see c. 43 § 5), εἰ δοκεῖ τὸ ὄστρακον εἰσφέρειν· ὅτε δὲ δοκεῖ, ἐφράσσετο σανίσιν ἡ ἀγορὰ καὶ κατελείποντο εἴσοδοι δέκα, δι' ὧν εἰσιόντες κατὰ φυλὰς ἐτίθεσαν τὰ ὄστρακα, στρέφοντες τὴν ἐπιγραφήν. ἐπεστάτουν δὲ οἵ τε ἐννέα ἄρχοντες καὶ ἡ βουλή· διαριθμηθέντων δὲ ὅτῳ πλεῖστα γένοιτο καὶ μὴ ἐλάττω ἑξακισχιλίων, τοῦτον ἔδει τὰ δίκαια δόντα καὶ λαβόντα ὑπὲρ τῶν ἰδίων συναλλαγμάτων ἐν δέκα ἡμέραις μεταστῆναι τῆς πόλεως ἔτη δέκα (ὕστερον δὲ ἐγένοντο πέντε) καρπούμενον τὰ ἑαυτοῦ μὴ ἐπιβαίνοντα ἐντὸς Γεραιστοῦ (Dobree's correction of πέρα τοῦ) Εὐβοίας ἀκρωτηρίου· μόνος δὲ Ὑπέρβολος ἐκ τῶν ἀδόξων δοκεῖ ἐξοστρακισθῆναι διὰ μοχθηρίαν τρόπων, οὐ δι' ὑποψίαν τυραννίδος· μετὰ τοῦτον δὲ κατελύθη τὸ ἔθος, ἀρξάμενον νομοθετήσαντος Κλεισθένους, ὅτε τοὺς τυράννους κατέλυσεν, ὅπως συνεκβάλῃ καὶ τοὺς φίλους αὐτῶν. According to Ephorus and Theopompus the object of ostracism was to check ὑπεροχή (cf. Diod. xi 55, Nepos, *Them.* 8, *Cimon* 3; Plut. *Arist.* 7, *Them.* 22, *Nic.* 11, *Alcib.* 13). This opinion is shared by Ar. *Pol.* iii 13, 1284 *a* 17 and 36, and viii (v) 3, 1302 *b* 15. The checking of ὑπεροχή may well have been its original purpose, but in process of time it was made the means of preventing mischief arising from στάσεις by suppressing the leader of the opposition and leaving the majority free to carry out their wishes without hindrance. See Grote, c. 31; Busolt, i 620, and in Müller's *Handbuch*, iv 1, 121; Lugebil, *Das Wesen und die historische Bedeutung des Ostrakismos in Athen*, in *Jahrb. f. cl. Phil.* Suppl. Bd. iv, 119—175; Gilbert, *Gr. St.* i 446–6; Abbott's *Hist. of Gr.* i 481–3; and Smith, *Dict. Ant.* s. v.

§ 2. **ἔτει πέμπτῳ**] The text, as it stands, implies 504/3 B.C., four years after the archonship of Isagoras, 508/7. But the archon of 504/3 is already known, *Acestorides* (Dionys. v 37), and not *Hermocreon*. The year is the 12th before the battle of Marathon 490/489, and must therefore be 501/0, the archon of which year has not hitherto been known. It is just conceivable that the reforms of Cleisthenes may have taken three years to get into complete shape, but nothing is said to this effect in the text, and it seems therefore necessary (as suggested by Mr Kenyon) to alter the 5th year into the 8th (ε̄ into η̄).

τοῖς πεντακοσίοις] So called to distinguish it from the Council of the Areopagus. The addition of these words is not inappropriate here, as the establishment of the Council of 500 was one of the recent reforms.

τὸν ὅρκον] Xen. *Mem.* i 1 § 18, τὸν βουλευτικὸν ὅρκον ὀμόσας, ἐν ᾧ ἦν κατὰ τοὺς νόμους βουλεύσειν. Lys. 31 § 1, ὀμόσας εἰσῆλθον εἰς τὸ βουλευτήριον τὰ βέλτιστα συμβουλεύσειν τῇ πόλει, ἔνεστί τε ἐν τῷ ὅρκῳ ἀποφαίνειν εἴ τίς τινα οἶδε

ουσιν· ἔπειτα τοὺς στρατηγοὺς ᾑροῦντο κατὰ φυλάς, ἐξ ἑκάστης <τῆς> φυλῆς ἕνα, τῆς δὲ ἁπάσης στρατιᾶς ἡγεμὼν ἦν ὁ πολέμαρχος.
3 ἔτει δὲ μετὰ ταῦτα δωδεκάτῳ νικήσαντες τὴν ἐν Μαραθῶνι μάχην ἐπὶ Φαινίππου ἄρχοντος, διαλιπόντες ἔτη δύο μετὰ τὴν νίκην, θαρροῦντος ἤδη τοῦ δήμου, τότε πρῶτον ἐχρήσαντο τῷ νόμῳ τῷ περὶ τὸν ὀστρακισμόν, ὃς ἐτέθη διὰ τὴν ὑποψίαν τῶν ἐν ταῖς δυνά-

8 ἑκάστης <τῆς> φυλῆς B, [...φυ]λῆς ἑκάστ[ης] Berol. **13** τοῦ ὀστρακισμοῦ K-W.

12—17 Harp. Ἵππαρχος (locus infra exscriptus).

τῶν λαχόντων ἀνεπιτήδειον ὄντα βουλεύειν. [Dem.] 59 § 4, ὀμωμοκὼς τὰ βέλτιστα βουλεύσειν τῷ δήμῳ τῶν Ἀθηναίων. In Solon's time the βουλὴ swore τοὺς Σόλωνος νόμους ἐμπεδώσειν (Plut. *Sol.* 25).

The oath included a clause, οὐδὲ δήσω Ἀθηναίων οὐδένα, ὃς ἂν ἐγγυητὰς τρεῖς καθιστῇ τὸ αὐτὸ τέλος τελοῦντας, πλὴν ἐάν τις ἐπὶ προδοσίᾳ τῆς πόλεως ἢ ἐπὶ καταλύσει τοῦ δήμου συνιὼν ἁλῷ, ἢ τέλος τι πριάμενος ἢ ἐγγυησάμενος ἢ ἐκλέγων μὴ καταβάλλῃ (Dem. 24 § 144). Arist. *Thesm.* 943, ἔδοξε τῇ βουλῇ σε δεῖν. Dem. *ib.* 148 refers the ὅρκος βουλευτικὸς to Solon; but it was the Areopagus that had cognisance of high treason assigned to it by Solon (c. 8 § 4), and presumably did not lose it until B.C. 462/1 (c. 25 § 2). The statement that the oath in the times of Cleisthenes was the same as that in the times of the writer seems inconsistent with the account in c. 45, where we are told that the βουλὴ had meanwhile lost the right of imprisoning, &c. (Wyse).

στρατηγοὺς ᾑροῦντο] Grote observes that 'there were now created, for the first time, ten *stratêgi* or generals, one from each tribe ... The ten generals, annually changed, are thus (like the ten tribes) a fruit of the Kleisthenean constitution' (c. 31, iii 116). Plut. *Aristid.* 5, τῶν δέκα καθεστώτων τοῖς Ἀθηναίοις ἐπὶ τὸν πόλεμον στρατηγῶν. *Them.* 6 § 1, τῶν Ἀθηναίων βουλευομένων περὶ στρατηγοῦ, where mention is made of χειροτονία (Busolt, i 616, n. 3). Unless we are prepared to accept the 'Draconian constitution' of c. 4, there is no reason for departing from the ordinary view that the institution of the στρατηγοὶ dates from the time of Cleisthenes.

τῆς ἁπάσης στρατιᾶς ἡγεμὼν—πολέμαρχος] 'Even after the *stratêgi* had been created, under the Kleisthenean constitution, the polemarch still retained a joint right of command along with them —as we are told at the battle of Marathon, where Kallimachus the polemarch not only enjoyed an equal vote in the council of war along with the ten *strategi*, but even occupied the post of honour on the right wing' (Hdt. vi 109—111; Grote, *l. c.*). In still closer accordance with the fresh evidence of the text, Busolt, i 616, observes: *der Polemarchos zog nach wie vor an der Spitze des Heeres aus der Stadt.*

§ 3. **διαλιπόντες ἔτη δύο**] i.e. in B.C. 488/7. *Pol.* 1299 *a* 37, τοὺς μὲν διαλείπειν πολὺν χρόνον, *Hist. Anim.* 523 *a* 8, δ. ἓν ἔτος.

θαρροῦντος—τοῦ δήμου. The connexion here and elsewhere established (cc. 24, 27) 'between moments of elation and self-confidence at Athens and constitutional changes for the worse' may be compared with Isocr. *Areop.* § 3 *sqq.* and *Panath.* § 133 (W. L. Newman, *Class. Rev.* v 161 *a*).

περὶ τὸν ὀστρ.] c. gen. in § 1. 'Ad significandam eam rem, de qua agitur ac disputatur, περὶ etiam c. acc. ita usurpatur ut ab usu praep. περὶ c. gen. non videatur discerni posse, veluti...*Pol.* 1300 *a* 8, 9; 1322 *b* 30, 31, 1286 *b* 34 et 1287 *a* 1; *Rhet.* 1414 *a* 28, 1418 *a* 2' *Ind. Ar.*

ἐτέθη διὰ τὴν ὑποψίαν—Ἵππαρχος Χάρμου] Archon in 496/5. Harpocr. *s. v.* Ἵππαρχος...ἄλλος δέ ἐστιν Ἵππαρχος ὁ Χάρμου, ὥς φησι Λυκοῦργος ἐν τῷ κατὰ Λεωκράτους (§ 117, Ἵππαρχον τὸν Τιμάρχου, who, in his absence, was condemned to death for προδοσία; nothing else is known of him and it is not impossible that Τιμάρχου in Lycurgus may be a mistake for Χάρμου)· περὶ δὲ τούτου Ἀνδροτίων ἐν τῇ β′ (frag. 5) φησὶν ὅτι συγγενὴς μὲν ἦν Πεισιστράτου τοῦ τυράννου καὶ πρῶτος ἐξωστρακίσθη τοῦ περὶ τὸν ὀστρακισμὸν νόμου τότε πρῶτον τεθέντος διὰ τὴν ὑποψίαν τῶν περὶ Πεισίστρατον, ὅτι δημαγωγὸς ὢν καὶ στρατηγὸς ἐτυράννησεν.

It will be observed that language almost identical with the text is quoted

μεσιν, ὅτι Πεισίστρατος δημαγωγὸς καὶ στρατηγὸς ὢν τύραννος
κατέστη· καὶ πρῶτος ὠστρακίσθη τῶν ἐκείνου συγγενῶν Ἵππαρχος 4
Χάρμου Κολλυτεύς, δι' ὃν καὶ μάλιστα τὸν νόμον ἔθηκεν ὁ Κλει-
σθένης, ἐξελάσαι βουλόμενος αὐτόν. οἱ γὰρ Ἀθηναῖοι τοὺς τῶν
τυράννων φίλους, ὅσοι μὴ συνεξημάρτανον ἐν ταῖς ταραχαῖς, εἴων
οἰκεῖν τὴν πόλιν, χρώμενοι τῇ εἰωθυίᾳ τοῦ δήμου πρᾳότητι· ὧν
ἡγεμὼν καὶ προστάτης ἦν Ἵππαρχος. εὐθὺς δὲ τῷ ὑστέρῳ ἔτει 5
ἐπὶ Τελεσίνου ἄρχοντος ἐκυάμευσαν τοὺς ἐννέα ἄρχοντας κατὰ

14 ΟΤΕ: ὅτι (K, H-L, B); ὁ γὰρ K-W. **16** ΚΟΛΥΤΤΕΥΣ. **18** ΣΥΝΕΞ-ΑΜΑΡΤΑΝΟΝ: *συνεξημάρτανον* K, K-W[1], B; *συνεξαμαρτάνοιεν* Poste (H-L, et omisso *ἐν* K-W[2]). **19** ΠΡΑΟΤΗΤΙ (K); cf. 16, 5 et 35. **20** ΥΣΤΕΡΩΙ: *ὕστερον* K-W, B; cf. 34 § 2.

---

by Harpocration from the Ἀτθίς of Androtion. The historian of that name is almost certainly identical with the orator attacked in Dem. *κατὰ Ἀνδροτίωνος*, in 355 B.C. He had then been a prominent politician for 30 years (Dem. *l. c.* § 66). The authorities in favour of this identification are Westermann, and Arnold Schaefer; against it are Ruhnken, Dindorf and C. Müller (FHG, i p. lxxxiii) and recently M. Weil, *Journal des Savants*, 1891, p. 203. All the extant quotations from the Ἀτθίς (except the present) 'just cover the period of Androtion's political career, and a few more years which he may have passed in exile: the latest event noticed is the *διαψήφισις* .. in B.C. 346–5.' He probably left Athens soon after B.C. 355, retired to Megara, and there wrote his Ἀτθίς in the enforced leisure of banishment, Plut. *de exil.* 14, p. 605 C, (*συνέγραψεν*) Ἀνδροτίων Ἀθηναῖος ἐν Μεγάροις (Wayte, Dem. *Androt.* p. xlix, l). If the present work was written about 325 B.C., the passage in the text may well have been borrowed from Androtion, who was probably no longer alive at the time. If he began public life at 30, he must have been born in B.C. 415 (355 + 30 + 30) and, if alive, would have been 90 at the date assumed for the present work.

δημαγωγὸς] *Pol.* 1305 *a* 7, *ἐπὶ δὲ τῶν ἀρχαίων, ὅτε γένοιτο ὁ αὐτὸς δημαγωγὸς καὶ στρατηγός, εἰς τυραννίδα μετέβαλλον· σχεδὸν γὰρ οἱ πλεῖστοι τῶν ἀρχαίων τυράννων ἐκ δημαγωγῶν γεγόνασιν*, and (on Peisistratus in particular) *ib.* 1310 *b* 27; Isocr. *Panath.* 148; Dio Chrys. i 303, 13 D.

§ 4. **πρῶτος ὠστρακίσθη** *κτλ.*] Plut. *Nic.* 11, *πρῶτος δ' (ἐξωστρακίσθη) Ἵππαρχος ὁ Χολαργεὺς* (probably a mistake for Κολλυτεύς, or for Χάρμου) *συγγενής τις ὢν τοῦ τυράννου.* According to Cleitodemus, ap. Athen. 609 C, Hippias had married a daughter of Charmus.

τῇ εἰωθυίᾳ τοῦ δήμου πρᾳότητι] Dem. *Timocr.* 51, *ὁ τὸν νόμον τοῦτον...θεὶς ᾔδει τὴν φιλανθρωπίαν καὶ πρᾳότητα τὴν ὑμετέραν.* It may be doubted whether any such praise as that of *πρᾳότης* is ever ascribed to the *δῆμος* in the extant works of Ar.

§ 5. **τῷ ὑστέρῳ ἔτει**] In 34 § 2 we have *τῷ ὕστερον ἔτει.* In 42 § 4 *τὸν ὕστερον (ἐνιαυτὸν)* is contrasted with *τὸν πρῶτον* and the former is found in 45 § 3.

ἐπὶ Τελεσίνου ἄρχοντος] The last date mentioned having been 488 B.C. (i.e. 'two years after Marathon'), the archonship of T. may be placed in 487/6. The only years after B.C. 496 (down to 292) for which the archons are not already known are 487 and 486. 482 may be assigned to Themistocles, and 481 to Hypsichides (c. 22 end).

ἐκυάμευσαν τοὺς ἐννέα ἄρχοντας *κτλ.*] Under the Solonian constitution (c. 8) the archons had been appointed by lot out of forty candidates nominated by the four tribes. From the close of the *τυραννίς* the archons had been elected (*οἱ δὲ πρότεροι πάντες ἦσαν αἱρετοί*), by whom we do not know, possibly (as Mr Kenyon suggests) by the *ἐκκλησία*. The general principle of the Solonian system was now revived by introducing a combination of selection and sortition.

The successive changes in the method of election to this office (as summed up by Mr Kenyon) were as follows: (1) the archons were originally nominated by the Council of the Areopagus, c. 8 § 2; (2) under the 'Draconian constitution' they were elected by the general body of

φυλάς, ἐκ τῶν προκριθέντων ὑπὸ τῶν δημοτῶν πεντακοσίων, τότε μετὰ τὴν τυραννίδα πρῶτον, (οἱ δὲ πρότεροι πάντες ἦσαν αἱρετοί)·
6 καὶ ὠστρακίσθη Μεγακλῆς Ἱπποκράτους Ἀλωπεκῆθεν. ἐπὶ μὲν

22 τῶν δημοτῶν πεντακοσίων (K, K-W, B): τοῦ δήμου ἐκ τῶν πεντακοσιομεδίμνων J W Headlam, τοῦ δήμου πεντακοσιομεδίμνων H-L. TOIC (πεντεκαιεικοστῷ ἔτει Weil): τότε Blass, K-W, H-L, K[3].

---

citizens (c. 4 § 2); (3) under the Solonian constitution, they were in ordinary course appointed by lot from forty candidates selected by the four tribes (c. 8 § 1); (4) under the *τυραννίς* this system was perhaps practically in abeyance, though nothing had been formally done to repeal appointment by lot (Peisistratus, son of Hippias was archon, Thuc. vi 54, and there was always one of the ruling house holding office); (5) under the constitution of Cleisthenes they were elected by the ecclesia (*οἱ δὲ πρότεροι πάντες ἦσαν αἱρετοί*); (6) from 487 B.C. they were appointed by lot from 100 (or 500) candidates selected by the tribes; (7) subsequently, from an uncertain date down to the time of the writer, the lot was applied to the preliminary nomination by the tribes as well as to the actual appointment (c. 8 § 1).

As appointment to the archonship by lot was apparently done away with by Cleisthenes in 508, and was re-introduced in 487, it follows that the archons in 490 were not appointed by lot, and that Herodotus was therefore mistaken in describing the polemarch of that year as *ὁ τῷ κυάμῳ λαχών* (vi 109). This had already been maintained by Grote (c. 31, iii 126), Busolt (ii 338) and others, and their opinion is now found to be correct. Cf. Lugebil in *Jahrb. f. class. Philol.*, Suppl. Bd. v 564—699; Holm, *Gr. Gesch.* ii 140, note 18.

Aristides was archon in 489 when the office was still elective, yet Demetrius Phal. makes him archon in 478, and, consistently with this, describes him as *κυάμῳ λαχών* (Plut. *Arist.* 1, 5). On the other hand, Idomeneus (fl. B.C. 310—270), having in view the archonship of 489, as it appears correctly, speaks of him as having held office *οὐ κυαμευτὸν ἀλλ' ἑλομένων Ἀθηναίων*. It was Aristides who, shortly after the battle of Plataea, carried a proposal that they should thenceforth choose (*αἱρεῖσθαι*) the *ἄρχοντες* (in the widest sense of the term) from all the Athenians alike. Duncker, *G. d. A.* vi 593, holds that it was on this occasion that appointment by lot was introduced: before it, we find the office of archon filled by leading statesmen; not so, afterwards. He also holds that the reforms of Cleisthenes did not touch the method of appointing the archons.

There is a difficulty as to the persons by whom the preliminary selection was made. The text, as it stands in the MS, speaks of them as 500 selected by the members of the demes. The practice down to the writer's time was for each tribe to nominate ten by lot, or 100 in all (c. 8). Now if each tribe ever nominated 50, it is improbable that its privilege would be reduced to that of nominating 10. Hence Mr Kenyon proposes to alter 500 (φ') into 100 (ρ').

'It seems possible that Demetrius Phal. accepted this date (B.C. 487) for the introduction of the lot: he placed the archonship of Aristides the year after Plataea (Plut. *Arist.* c. 1 and 5) and spoke of *ἡ ἐπώνυμος ἀρχὴ ἣν ἦρξε τῷ κυάμῳ λαχὼν ἐκ τῶν γενῶν τῶν τὰ μέγιστα τιμήματα κεκτημένων οὓς πεντακοσιομεδίμνους προσηγόρευον* (*ib.* c. 1): the admission of *ἱππεῖς* then, according to Demetrius, is after 478. We see now that there is not necessarily any conflict between Idomeneus of Lampsacus and Demetrius, except as to the year when Aristides was archon Idomeneus, like Plutarch, may have assigned Aristides to the year after Marathon (*ib.* c. 5): in which case his statement (*ib.* c. 1 *ἄρξαι γε τὸν Ἀριστείδην οὐ κυαμευτὸν ἀλλ' ἑλομένων Ἀθηναίων*) agrees with the 'Ἀθ. Πολ.' (Wyse).

Μεγακλῆς] son of Hippocrates (Hdt. vi 131), grandson of Megacles (the opponent of Peisistratus c. 14 and 15), and nephew of Cleisthenes. Through his sister, Agariste, he was the uncle of Pericles. There was another Megacles in the same generation (victor in the Pythian games, Pind. *Pyth.* vii 15), a son of Cleisthenes, and grandfather of Alcibiades. The ostracism of this second Megacles is mentioned in Lysias, *Alc.* 14 § 39. According to Pindar (*l. c.*) the house of Megacles was subject to *φθόνος* on account of its *εὐπραγία*.

It is remarkable that an institution

οὖν ἔτη τρία τοὺς τῶν τυράννων φίλους ὠστράκιζον, ὧν χάριν ὁ νόμος ἐτέθη, μετὰ δὲ ταῦτα τῷ τετάρτῳ ἔτει καὶ τῶν ἄλλων εἴ τις δοκοίη μείζων εἶναι μεθίστατο· καὶ πρῶτος ὠστρακίσθη τῶν ἄπωθεν τῆς τυραννίδος Ξάνθιππος ὁ Ἀρίφρονος. ἔτει δὲ τρίτῳ 7

N

27 ΜΕΘΙϹΤΑΤΟ: μεθίστατο B, -ίσταντο ceteri.

---

founded by Cleisthenes should have thus been brought into play against his son and his nephew. According to Aelian, *Var. Hist.* xiii 24, Cleisthenes himself was ostracised, but of this there is no proof. As to the ostracism of the nephew there is no doubt. Even one of the pieces of pottery used in voting on the question has been found. It bears the name of **Μεγακλῆς** [Ἱππο]κράτους Ἀλωπεκῆθεν (published in Benndorf's *Gr. u. Sic. Vasenbilder* p. 50, pl. 29, no. 10). It is a fragment of black-glazed ware, apparently cut into a circular form for the purpose. It was discovered in the pre-Persian stratum to the E. of the Parthenon (*Class. Rev.* v 278 *a*). CIA iv 3 no. 569.

§ 6. **ἔτη τρία**] Mr Kenyon holds that the three years are B.C. 489—87, *i.e.* the two after the battle of Marathon and the year in which Hipparchus son of Charmus was ostracised; but, unless we press the meaning of the imperfect *ὠστράκιζον*, and apply it to the purpose and desire of the people, rather than to their acts, it seems better to consider the period of three years to begin with that in which Hipparchus was banished, *i.e.* 488/7. Thus the three years would be B.C. 488/7, 487/6 and 486/5. Then the ostracism of Xanthippus, *τῷ τετάρτῳ ἔτει*, would be in 485/4 and 'the third year after this,' 483/2, the archonship of Nicodemus, which is in accordance with the chronology adopted in Clinton's *Fasti*. *ἐν τούτοις τοῖς καιροῖς* (*i.e.* not necessarily under Nicodemus, but in the previous year 484/3) Aristides was banished; and, in the 'fourth year after,' he was recalled, 481/0 (Bauer, p. 59).

τῷ τετάρτῳ ἔτει] 485/4.

εἴ τις δοκοίη μείζων εἶναι] *Pol.* 1302 *b* 15, *στάσις* arises *ὅταν τις ᾖ τῇ δυνάμει μείζων*, and the correction of this (says Ar.) was the object of ostracism.

ἄπωθεν τῆς τυραννίδος] *Pol.* ii 3, 1262 *a* 29, *ὧν οὐδὲν ὅσιόν ἐστι γίνεσθαι πρὸς πατέρας καὶ μητέρας καὶ τοὺς μὴ πόρρω τῆς συγγενείας ὄντας, ὥσπερ πρὸς τοὺς ἄπωθεν* (distant in relationship), iii 9, 1280 *b* 9, *γίνεται γὰρ ἡ κοινωνία συμμαχία τῶν ἄλλων τόπῳ διαφέρουσα μόνον τῶν ἄπωθεν συμμαχιῶν* (alliances, of which the members live apart), *ib.* 18, *εἴ τινες οἰκοῖεν χωρὶς μέν, μὴ μέντοι τοσοῦτον ἄπωθεν* (so far off) *ὥστε μὴ κοινωνεῖν*. '*οἱ ἄπωθεν*, syn. *οἱ ἀγνῶτες*, opp. *οἱ γνώριμοι, οἱ συνήθεις, οἱ συγγενεῖς*.' *Rhet.* i 11, 1371 *a* 12 *οἱ συνήθεις καὶ οἱ πολῖται* (*μᾶλλον*) *τῶν ἄπωθεν*: c. gen. in Thuc. iii 111 § 1, *ἄποθεν τῆς Ὄλπης*, Aristoph. *Plut.* 674 *ἄπωθεν τῆς κεφαλῆς*.

Ξάνθιππος ὁ Ἀρίφρονος] During the excavations on the Acropolis in 1886, a fragment of a late black-figured vase was found in the pre-Persian stratum E. of the Parthenon, with the following inscription clearly incised upon it.

ΧΣΑΝΘΙΠΠΟΣ
ΑΡΡΙΦΡΟΝΟΣ

The fragment was published by Studniczka, *Arch. Jahrb.* 1887, p. 161, who observed that the position in which it was found proved that the ostracism of Xanthippus took place before B.C. 480 (*Class. Rev.* v 277 *b*). CIA iv 3, 568. In March, 1891, after the first publication of this treatise, another fragment was found at Athens in the *ὁδὸς Πειραιῶς* with the first five or six letters of the father's name written (with the double *ρ*) above that of the son (CIA iv 3, 571).

Xanthippus impeached Miltiades in 490/89 (Hdt. vi 136; Grote, c. 36, iii 312). The present passage shews that his ostracism falls in 485/4, *before* that of Aristides (484/3). Of its causes we know nothing; but it is natural to suppose that the friends of Miltiades had something to do with it. In 480 Xanthippus left Athens with the other inhabitants at the approach of Xerxes: Plutarch, *Them.* 10, tells the story of his dog, which could not endure to be left behind on this occasion. Xanthippus was the archon of 479 (Diod. xi 27). He commanded the Athenians at Mycale (479, Hdt. ix 114) and at the siege of Sestos (ix 121). By Agariste, daughter of Hippocrates, and sister of the Megacles mentioned above, he became the father *μετὰ ταῦτα Νικοδήμου ἄρχοντος, ὡς ἐφάνη τὰ μέταλλα τὰ ἐν*

29 ΝΙΚΟΜΗΔΟΥΣ (K-W, H-L, B): Ν(ΙΚΟ)ΔΗΜΟ(Υ) Berol. et Dion. Hal. viii 83 (K). ΕΦΑΝΗ: an *ἀπεγράφη*? Wyse (*Class. Rev.* v 112); <*λυσιτελεστέρα*> *ἐφάνη* Richards (*ib.* 226).

---

of Pericles (Hdt. vi 131) and Ariphron (Plut. *Alc.* 1, Plat. *Protag.* 320). The elder of the two legitimate sons of Pericles was named after his grandfather, Xanthippus (Plut. *Per.* 24, 36).

§ 7. **ἔτει...τρίτῳ** after 486, would bring us to 484/3 for the archonship of Nicodemus. It was *ἐν τούτοις τοῖς καιροῖς* that Aristides was ostracised, and in 481/0 all the citizens who had been ostracised were recalled *διὰ τὴν Ξέρξου στρατείαν* (§ 8). But Nicodemus, according to Dionysius Hal. viii 83, p. 1711 Reiske, was archon in the consulship of L. Aemilius Mamercus and K. Fabius, 270 A.U.C. (Cato). In Baiter's *Fasti Consulares* this is identified as A.U.C. 269 = B.C. 484. This would support Mr Kenyon's view. See, however, note on § 6, *ἔτη τρία*.

Νικομήδους is the reading in the papyrus; Ν(*ικο*)ΔΗΜΟ(*υ*) that of the Berlin fragment, and similarly in Dionysius. Mr Kenyon, perhaps rightly, holds that, in this conflict between the two MSS, 'the authority of Dionysius may turn the scale.'

The name *Νικομήδης* ('victor in counsel') is formed from *μήδομαι* on the analogy of *Ἀγαμήδης*, *Ἀλιμήδης*, *Ἀμφιμήδης*, *Ἀνδρομήδης*, *Ἀριστομήδης*, *Ἀστυμήδης*, *Αὐτομήδης*, *Διομήδης*, *Εὐμήδης*, *Εὐρυμήδης*, *Θεομήδης*, *Θρασυμήδης*, *Καλλιμήδης*, *Κλει-* (= *Κλεο*)*μήδης*, *Κλυτομήδης*, *Λαομήδης*, *Λυκομήδης*, *Νεομήδης*, *Ξενομήδης*, *Ὀνασσι-* (*i.e.* *Ὀνασι-*)*μήδης*, *Παλαμήδης*, *Περιμήδης* and *Πολυμήδης* (Pape-Benseler, *Eigennamen*, p. xxx). It cannot be interpreted as 'conqueror of the Medes,' which would be *Μηδόνικος*. Similarly, the alternative name *Νικόδημος* means 'with victorious army or people' *ib. s. v.*

ὡς ἐφάνη τὰ μέταλλα *κτλ.*] Hdt. vii 144, *Ἀθηναίοισι γενομένων χρημάτων μεγάλων ἐν τῷ κοινῷ, τὰ ἐκ τῶν μετάλλων σφι προσῆλθε τῶν ἀπὸ Λαυρείου, ἔμελλον λάξεσθαι ὀρχηδὸν ἕκαστος δέκα δραχμάς. τότε Θεμιστοκλῆς ἀνέγνωσε Ἀθηναίους τῆς διαιρέσιος ταύτης παυσαμένους νέας τούτων τῶν χρημάτων ποιήσασθαι ἐς τὸν πόλεμον, τὸν πρὸς Αἰγινήτας λέγων.* (Plut. *Them.* 4, *τὴν Λαυρεωτικὴν πρόσοδον ἀπὸ τῶν ἀργυρείων μετάλλων ἔθος ἐχόντων Ἀθηναίων διανέμεσθαι κτλ.*) This account, esp. the word *παυσαμένους*, implies that the revenue for the mines had *hitherto* been distributed among the people (to the extent of 10 drachmas a head).

ἐφάνη can only mean 'were discovered,' which may possibly be supported by *εὑρέθη* in Bekker's *Anecdota*, p. 279, *Μαρώνεια: τόπος ἦν τῆς Ἀττικῆς, ὅπου τὰ μέταλλα εὑρέθη.* The mention of the revenue of 100 talents from the works comes somewhat suddenly after the first announcement of the discovery of the mines, and possibly some other word was really written by the author. The author of the tract *περὶ πόρων* implies that they were of immemorial antiquity, but there are indications that they had only recently come into prominence. Aeschylus in the *Persae*, 238, the dramatic date of which is 480 B.C., makes the chorus answer an enquiry of the wife of Darius as to the wealth of Athens by the reply *ἀργύρου πηγή τις αὐτοῖς ἐστι, θησαυρὸς χθονός.* 'At what time they first began to be worked,' says Grote (c. 39, iii 406), 'we have no information; but it seems hardly possible that they could have been worked with any spirit or profitable result, until after the expulsion of Hippias and the establishment of the democratic constitution of Kleisthenes.' It is quite conceivable that a very recent discovery of a very productive mine at one particular place, Maroneia, may have given a new importance to the question of the best disposal of the revenue.—It has even been suggested that the mines had originally belonged to Aegina and had been wrested from her by Athens (Mahaffy, *Rambles and Studies in Greece*, p. 163); but neither the text nor the parallel passages in Hdt. and Plut. lend any support to this. The Athenians had to rely on the revenue from the mines to make way against the Aeginetans.

τὰ ἐν Μαρωνείᾳ] 'The mining district, besides the *demi* Anaphlystus, Besa, Amphitrope, and Thoricus, contained several places which were not *demi*, as Laureium, Thrasyllum [*ἐπὶ Θρασύλλῳ*, Dem. 37 § 25, Aeschin. 1 § 101], Maroneia, Aulon [Aeschin. *l. c.*]' (Leake's *Demi*, p. 274). Laurium may have been the general term for the district, derived from its numerous shafts and tunnels, *λαῦραι*, lit. 'narrow passages'. Maroneia may perhaps be identified with some ruins five miles N. of Sunium. In Dem. *Pant.* 37 § 4, Nicobulus and his partner Euergus

Μαρωνείᾳ καὶ περιεγένετο τῇ πόλει τάλαντα ἑκατὸν ἐκ τῶν ἔργων, συμβουλευόντων τινῶν τῷ δήμῳ διανείμασθαι τὸ ἀργύριον, Θεμι-

30—31 [*περιεγένετο*] | *ἐκ τ[ῶν ἔργων]* (vel *π. τοῖς* | *κεκτη[μένοις]*) *ἑκατ[ὸν τάλαντα, συμβουλευ]όντων τ[ινῶν] τῇ πό[λει διανείμασθαι τὸ ἀρ]γύριον* Berol.

30 Bekk. An. p. 279 Μαρώνεια: *τόπος ἦν τῆς Ἀττικῆς, ὅπου τὰ μέταλλα εὑρέθη.* Harp. s. v.: (Dem. *Pant.* § 4), *τόπος ἐστὶ τῆς Ἀττικῆς.*

---

allege that they lent to Pantaenetus 105 minae, *ἐπ' ἐργαστηρίῳ τε ἐν τοῖς ἔργοις ἐν Μαρωνείᾳ καὶ τριάκοντα ἀνδραπόδοις.* On the silver mines of Laurium, see Boeckh's *Dissertation*, pp. 615—678, printed as Appendix to Boeckh's *Public Economy*, trans. Lewis; K. F. Hermann, *Privatalt.* § 14, 17; Büchsenschütz, *Besitz und Erwerb*, pp. 98—103; *Select Private Orations of Dem.* ed. 2, ii p. 89.

τάλαντα ἑκατὸν κτλ.] Polyaenus, i 30 § 6 (5), *Θεμιστοκλῆς ἐν τῷ πρὸς Αἰγινήτας πολέμῳ μελλόντων Ἀθηναίων τὴν ἐκ τῶν ἀργυρίων πρόσοδον, ἑκατὸν τάλαντα, διανέμεσθαι, κωλύσας ἔπεισεν ἑκατὸν ἀνδράσι τοῖς πλουσιωτάτοις ἑκάστῳ δοῦναι τάλαντον· κἂν μὲν ἀρέσῃ τὸ πραχθησόμενον, τῇ πόλει τὸ ἀνάλωμα λογισθῆναι, ἐὰν δὲ μὴ ἀρέσῃ, τοὺς λαβόντας ἀποδοῦναι. ταῦτα μὲν ἔδοξεν. οἱ δὲ ἑκατὸν ἄνδρες ἕκαστος μίαν τριήρη κατέστησαν, σπουδῇ χρησάμενοι κάλλους καὶ τάχους. Ἀθηναῖοι καινὸν στόλον ποιήσαντες ᾔσθησαν, καὶ οὐ μόνον κατὰ Αἰγινητῶν ταῖς τριήρεσι ταύταις, ἀλλὰ καὶ κατὰ Περσῶν ἐχρήσαντο.*

In Hdt. vii 144 the amount available for distribution is stated as 10 drachmas a head. Elsewhere (in v 97) Hdt. reckons the citizens at 30,000. This gives us 50 talents for distribution. He also speaks of 200 ships. But 50 talents is far too small a sum for a fleet, even if only 100 ships were built at the cost of only one talent each. It has accordingly been suggested that Hdt. founded his calculation on the diminished returns of the mines at a later date, about 430 B.C. (Stein *ad loc.*). Boeckh considers that the population was probably 20,000 at the time meant by the historian. The amount to be distributed, at 10 dr. a head, would in that case be 200,000 dr. = 33⅓ talents.

It was Boeckh's opinion that all the public money arising from the mines was (annually) divided among the members of the community (Dissertation, § 8, p. 652 Lewis ed. 2). Grote himself held that the sum for distribution only formed 'part of a larger sum lying in the treasury, arising from the mines. Themistokles persuaded the people to employ the *whole* sum in ship-building, which of course implied that the distribution was to be renounced. Whether there had been distributions of a similar kind in former years...is a matter on which we have no evidence' (c. 39, iii 407 n.). The evidence of the text supports Grote's view. The date of the building of the fleet is discussed by Busolt, ii 123 f., but the text was then represented by the Berlin fragment only.

Θεμιστοκλῆς was evidently not in the position of archon *eponymus* in the year of the proposal to distribute the revenue from the silver mines. The archon of that year was Nicodemus (483/2). He was in office, however, at the time when he proposed the fortification of the Peiraeus, Thuc. i 93 § 2, *ὑπῆρκτο δ' αὐτοῦ πρότερον ἐπὶ τῆς ἐκείνου ἀρχῆς ἧς κατ' ἐνιαυτὸν Ἀθηναίοις ἦρξεν*, and he may have been archon eponymus at that time. The archon for 481/0 is Hypsichides (*infra* § 8). We may therefore place the archonship of Themistocles in 482/1.

Dionysius Hal., *Ant. Rom.* vi 34, p. 1117 R, makes Themistocles archon in 493 B.C., but (as Mr Kenyon shews) this is very improbable.

The chronology suggested by Bauer is as follows: according to Plutarch (*Them.* 31 and *Cim.* 18) Themistocles died at the age of 65 at the time of Cimon's expedition against Cyprus (448/7). This would give us 513 for his birth. He would be 30 in 483/2, and this was the year in which he brought about the formation of a fleet. His archonship should probably be placed in 482/1, a year that is not yet filled by any name. This is supported by the scholiast on Thuc. *πρὸ δὲ τῶν Μηδικῶν ἦρξεν Θ. ἐνιαυτὸν ἕνα.* Hdt. vii 143 describes him as *ἀνὴρ ἐς πρώτους νεωστὶ παριών*, which is unfavourable to placing his archonship as far back as 493: *νεωστὶ* is more likely to denote an interval of two, than of 13 years. The Themistocles of 493 (Dionysius) would in this case be another of the same name. But there is more probability in Mr Kenyon's second alternative, that Dionysius has simply made a mistake.

In 480/79 he was *στρατηγὸς* of the

στοκλῆς ἐκώλυσεν, οὐ λέγων ὅ τι χρήσεται τοῖς χρήμασιν ἀλλὰ δανεῖσαι κελεύων τοῖς πλουσιωτάτοις Ἀθηναίων ἑκατὸν ἑκάστῳ τάλαντον, εἶτ' ἐὰν μὲν ἀρέσκῃ τὸ ἀνάλωμα, τῆς πόλεως εἶναι τὴν δαπάνην, εἰ δὲ μή, κομίσασθαι τὰ χρήματα παρὰ τῶν δανεισαμένων. λαβὼν δ' ἐπὶ τούτοις ἐνα[υ]πηγήσατο τριήρεις ἑκατόν, ἑκάστου ναυπηγουμένου τῶν ἑκατὸν μίαν, αἷς ἐναυμάχησαν ἐν Σαλαμῖνι πρὸς τοὺς βαρβάρους. ὠστρακίσθη δ' ἐν τούτοις τοῖς

8 καιροῖς Ἀριστείδης ὁ Λυσιμάχου. τετάρτῳ δ' ἔτει κατεδέξαντο πάντας τοὺς ὠστρακισμένους, ἄρχοντος Ὑψιχίδου, διὰ τὴν Ξέρξου στρατείαν· καὶ τὸ λοιπὸν ὥρισαν τοῖς ὀστρακιζομένοις ἐκτὸς

34—35 *ἐὰν μὲν ἀρέσκῃ, τὸ ἀνάλωμα τῆς πόλεως εἶναι*, deletis *τὴν δαπάνην*, H-L., B, coll. Polyaen. i 30 *κἂν μὲν ἀρέσῃ τὸ πραχθησόμενον, τῇ πόλει τὸ ἀνάλωμα λογισθῆναι.* **39** *τετάρτῳ: τρίτῳ* 'corr. e Plut. *Ar.* 8' K-W[2] (B). **40** ΥΨΗΧΙΔΟΥ ante corr. (H-L): *Ὑψιχίδου* (K, K-W, B). **41** ΣΤΡΑΤΙΑΝ: *στρατείαν* (K-W, H-L, K[3]). In titulis (velut etiam in codicibus) et *στρατεία* et *στρατιά* *expeditionem* significat (*στρατεύεσθαι—τὰς στρατείας*, B.C. 325;—*τὰς στρατιὰς* B.C. 330) Meisterhans, p. 43[2]. ΕΝΤΟΣ K, K-W, H-L: *ἐκτὸς* Wyse (B), quod egregie confirmat Philochorus in Lex. Rhet. Cantab. *ὀστρακισμοῦ τρόπος: μὴ ἐπιβαίνοντα ἐντὸς Γεραίστου.*

Athenian troops that marched to Tempe (Hdt. vii 173).

ὅ τι χρήσεται] Plat. *Crit.* 45 C, *οὐκ ἔχω ὅ τι χρήσομαι τῷ ἀργυρίῳ.*

ἐν τούτοις τοῖς καιροῖς] Jerome has, under Ol. 74, 1 (=484/3), *Aristides cum ignominia eicitur.* On the ostracism of Aristides, cf. Plut. *Arist.* 7.

§ 8. **τετάρτῳ ἔτει**] 481/0. This fixes the date of the archonship of Hypsichides, a name that is now known for the first time. Plut., *Arist.* 8, says that the Athenians recalled Aristides, *Ξέρξου διὰ Θετταλίας καὶ Βοιωτίας ἐλαύνοντος*, *i.e.* in the spring of 480 B.C. He adds that the vote for the recall was passed in the *third* year after the banishment. This note of time may be explained by the fact that, if the vote for ostracising Aristides took place at the 6th (or 8th) *πρυτανεία* (c. 43 § 5), this would fall early in B.C. 483, and the corresponding date in 480 would be the end of the third year after.

κατεδέξαντο] Andoc. 1 § 107 (of the same incident), *ἔγνωσαν τούς τε φεύγοντας καταδέξασθαι καὶ τοὺς ἀτίμους ἐπιτίμους ποιῆσαι.*

τὸ λοιπὸν] [Dem.] 26 § 6, *Ἀριστείδην μὲν γάρ φασιν ὑπὸ τῶν προγόνων μετασταθέντα ἐν Αἰγίνῃ διατρίβειν ἕως ὁ δῆμος αὐτὸν κατεδέξατο.* Hdt. viii 79, *ἐξ Αἰγίνης διέβη.* Suidas, *s. v.* *Ἀριστείδης*, *διέτριψεν ἐν Αἰγίνῃ φυγών. Ξέρξου δὲ ὡς αὐτὸν ἐν τῇ φυγῇ πρεσβευσαμένου καὶ τρισχιλίους δαρεικούς...διδόντος, οὐδὲν ἐπιστρέφεσθαι ἔφη τοῦ Περσικοῦ πλούτου κτλ.* The fact that Aristides remained in Aegina explains the provision that henceforth persons ostracised were to reside *outside* Geraestus and the Scyllaean promontory. According to Plutarch (*Cim.* 17), Cimon when ostracised appeared at Tanagra (Wyse in *Class. Rev.* v 274 *b*).

ἐκτὸς] Mr Kenyon, retaining *ἐντὸς*, suggests that the object of the regulation was to keep the ostracised person 'within very narrow boundaries,' so as to obviate the danger of a banished citizen entering into communication with Persia. But, as Aristides had remained within these limits, it is more reasonable to suppose that the line *beyond* which the ostracised person was to withdraw was thenceforward made the subject of special regulation. Banishment had in fact to be defined more strictly. Otherwise the exile might remain within a very short distance of Attica and carry on intrigues against his opponents.

Themistocles, while under ostracism, lived at Argos, Thuc. i 139, *ἔχων δίαιταν μὲν ἐν Ἄργει* (Plut. *Them.* 23 § 1), *ἐπιφοιτῶν δὲ καὶ ἐς τὴν ἄλλην Πελοπόννησον*, and afterwards went to Corcyra, and Epirus, to Pydna in Macedonia, and thence to Naxos and Ephesus. He clearly kept outside the limits described in the text as emended. Hyperbolus, again, lived in Samos (Thuc. viii 73 § 2). Both these cases exemplify the rule. According

Γεραιστοῦ καὶ Σκυλλαίου κατοικεῖν ἢ ἀτίμους εἶναι καθάπαξ.

23. τότε μὲν οὖν μέχρι τούτου προῆλθεν ἡ πόλις, ἅμα τῇ δημοκρατίᾳ κατὰ μικρὸν αὐξανομένη· μετὰ δὲ τὰ Μηδικὰ πάλιν ἴσχυσεν ἡ ἐν Ἀρείῳ πάγῳ βουλὴ καὶ διῴκει τὴν πόλιν, οὐδενὶ δόγματι λαβοῦσα τὴν ἡγ[εμο]νίαν, ἀλλὰ διὰ τὸ γενέσθαι τῆς περὶ Σαλαμῖνα ναυμαχίας αἰτία. τῶν γὰρ στρατηγῶν ἐξαπορησάντων τοῖς πράγμασι καὶ κηρυξάντων σῴζειν ἕκαστον ἑαυτόν, πορίσασα
δραχμὰς ἑκάστῳ ὀκτὼ διέδωκε καὶ ἐνεβίβασεν εἰς τὰς ναῦς. διὰ 2
ταύτην δὴ τὴν αἰτίαν παρεχώρουν αὐτῇ τοῦ ἀξιώματος, καὶ ἐπολι-

XXIII 1 ΤΟΤΕ: τὸ Poste (H-L). **5** διαπορησάντων Richards, coll. Cobet *V. L.* pp. 219—220. **6** ΣΩΖΕΙΝ: σῴζειν (edd.), cf. Meisterhans, p. 142². **7** inter ἑκάστῳ et ὀκτώ lacunam indicat B, coll. Plut. *Them.* 10, ἑκάστῳ τῶν στρατευομένων. **8** ΑΥΤ(ΗΝ)ΤΩΙΑΞΙΩΜΑΤΙ: αὐτῇ τῷ ἀξιώματι K; αὐτῆς ἀξιώματι Rutherford; αὐτῆς τῷ ἀξιώματι Blass (H-L); αὐτῇ τοῦ ἀξιώματος J E B Mayor, K-W.

TESTIMONIA. **XXIII 5—7** * Plut. *Them.* 10 οὐκ ὄντων δὲ δημοσίων χρημάτων τοῖς Ἀθηναίοις Ἀρ. μέν φησι τὴν ἐξ Ἀρείου πάγου βουλὴν πορίσασαν ἑκάστῳ τῶν στρατευομένων ὀκτὼ δραχμὰς αἰτιωτάτην γενέσθαι τοῦ πληρωθῆναι τὰς τριήρεις.

---

to the Schol. on Aristoph. *Vesp.* 947, one of the differences between those who are banished for life and those who are ostracised is that the former 'have no fixed place of abode, no time of return assigned, but the latter have' (καὶ τόπος ἀπεδίδοτο καὶ χρόνος).

Γεραιστοῦ] The cape at the S. W. extremity of Euboea. (Hdt. viii 7, ix 105, Thuc. iii 3 § 4.) **Σκυλλαίου**] the cape at the eastern extremity of the territory of Troezen (Thuc. v 53), the most easterly point of the Peloponnesus, and forming (with the opposite promontory of Sunium) the entrance to the Saronic gulf.

ἀτίμους—καθάπαξ] The penalty is that of perpetual ἀτιμία. For καθάπαξ in this connexion cf. Dem. *Mid.* §§ 32, 87, *Aristog.* i § 30. The various disabilities in such a case are enumerated by Aeschines, *c. Timarch.* § 18 (see Smith, *Dict. Ant.* i 242 *a*).

XXIII, XXIV. *The supremacy of the Areopagus. Aristides and Themistocles.*

XXIII § 1. **μετὰ τὰ Μηδικὰ—βουλὴ**] *Pol.* viii (v) 4, 1304 *a* 20, ἡ ἐν Ἀρείῳ πάγῳ βουλὴ εὐδοκιμήσασα ἐν τοῖς Μηδικοῖς ἔδοξε συντονωτέραν ποιῆσαι τὴν πολιτείαν.

οὐδενὶ δόγματι κτλ.] This is said of the Areopagus to contrast it with the Four hundred (c. 29) and the Thirty (c. 34 end, and Isocr. *Areop.* 67, οἱ...ψηφίσματι παραλαβόντες τὴν πόλιν).

τῆς περὶ Σαλαμῖνα ναυμαχίας] *Pol.* 1304 *a* 22, ὁ ναυτικὸς ὄχλος γενόμενος αἴτιος τῆς περὶ Σαλαμῖνα νίκης καὶ διὰ ταύτης (ταύτην? Susemihl) τῆς ἡγεμονίας διὰ τὴν κατὰ θάλατταν δύναμιν τὴν δημοκρατίαν ἰσχυροτέραν ἐποίησεν.

ἐξαπορησάντων τοῖς πράγμασι] Isocr. *Paneg.* 147, ἀπορήσας τοῖς παροῦσι πράγμασι. For the general sense of the context, cf. Cic *de Off.* i 75, *et Themistocles quidem nihil dixerit, in quo ipse Areopagum adiuverit, at ille vere a se adiutum Themistoclem; est enim bellum gestum consilio senatus eius qui a Solone erat constitutus.*

πορίσασα δραχμὰς] Probably from the sacred treasure on the Acropolis; cf. Philippi, *Areopag.* 293; Oncken, *Staatslehre*, 468.

§ 2. **παρεχώρουν αὐτῇ τοῦ ἀξιώματος**] The most common construction of παραχωρεῖν is *c. dat. pers. et gen. rei vel loci.* Isocr. 118 D, π. τοῖς ἐχθροῖς τῆς ἡμετέρας. Aeschin. 54, 21. Polyb. iv 5, 1 etc., π. τινὶ τῆς πολιτείας, τῆς ἀρχῆς (L and S). Similarly εἴκειν τινὶ τῆς ὁδοῦ (Hdt. ii 80). For ἀξίωμα, cf. Thuc. vi 15 § 2, ὢν ἐν ἀξιώματι ὑπὸ τῶν ἀστῶν, and i 130 § 1.

Mr Kenyon prints παρεχώρουν αὐτῇ τῷ ἀξιώματι, 'gave place (or 'precedence') to it in rank' (or 'reputation'). The simple dat. may here be equivalent to ἐν—. The latter is found in *Magn. Mor.* ii 1, 1198 *b* 28, ὁ ἐν τούτοις παραχωρῶν ἐπιεικής, but I can find no exact parallel for the dative alone.

ἐπολιτεύθησαν—καλῶς] With the sub-

τεύθησαν Ἀθηναῖοι καλῶς καὶ κατὰ τούτους τοὺς καιρούς. συνέβη
γὰρ αὐτοῖς περὶ τὸν χρόνον τοῦτον τά τε εἰς τὸν πόλεμον ἀσκῆσαι
καὶ παρὰ τοῖς Ἕλλησιν εὐδοκιμῆσαι καὶ τὴν τῆς θαλάττης ἡγεμο-
3 νίαν λαβεῖν ἀκόντων τῶν Λακεδαιμονίων. ἦσαν δὲ προστάται τοῦ
δήμου κατὰ τούτους τοὺς καιροὺς Ἀριστείδης ὁ Λυσιμάχου καὶ
Θεμιστοκλῆς ὁ Νεοκλέους, ὁ μὲν τὰ πολεμικὰ δοκῶν, ὁ δὲ τὰ πολι-
τικὰ δεινὸς εἶναι, καὶ δικαιοσύνῃ τῶν καθ᾽ ἑαυτὸν διαφέρειν· διὸ
4 καὶ ἐχρῶντο τῷ μὲν στρατηγῷ, τῷ δὲ συμβούλῳ. τὴν μὲν οὖν τῶν
τειχῶν ἀνοικοδόμησιν κοινῇ διῴκησαν, καίπερ διαφερόμενοι πρὸς

9 *καὶ* (ante *κατὰ*) secl. K, K-W; retinent H-L (B), coll. 33 § 3. **10** Κ(ΑΤΑ) supra scripto ΠΕΡΙ (B). *κατὰ τὸν χρόνον τοῦτον* secl. K-W. **12** ΑΚΟΝΤΩΝ (K, K-W, B): *ἑκόντων* J B Mayor (*Class. Rev.* v 112 *b*), Gennadios; *εἰκόντων* Naber (H-L). **14** ΠΟΛΕΜΙΑ (K, K-W, H-L): *πολεμικὰ* Blass, Richards, Thompson; *πολέμια* defendit K coll. Thuc. i 18 *εὖ παρεσκευάσαντο τὰ πολέμια*, et iv 80 *ἐν τοῖς πολεμίοις γεγενῆσθαι σφίσιν ἄριστοι*. ΑΣΚΩΝ (retinent (K, K-W[1]): *δοκῶν* Richards, Thompson, Kontos (H-L, K-W[2], B); *δοκῶν ἀσκεῖν* conicit K. **14—15** ΠΟΛΕΜΙΚΑΔΕΙΝΟΣ per errorem, corr. K. *δεινὸς εἶναι* <*δοκῶν*> K, K-W[1].

---

sequent context, cf. Isocr. *Areop.* 51 (of the Areopagus), *ἧς ἐπιστατούσης οὐ δικῶν οὐδ᾽ ἐγκλημάτων οὐδ᾽ εἰσφορῶν οὐδὲ πενίας οὐδὲ πολέμων ἡ πόλις ἔγεμεν…παρεῖχον γὰρ σφᾶς αὐτοὺς τοῖς μὲν Ἕλλησι πιστούς, τοῖς δὲ βαρβάροις φοβερούς· τοὺς μὲν γὰρ σεσωκότες ἦσαν κτλ.*, and §§ 80, 82. *Panath.* 151, *τὰς πράξεις τὰς ἐκ τοῦ καλῶς πολιτεύεσθαι* …152, *παρὰ τοῖς Ἕλλησιν εὐδοκίμησαν*. *De Pace*, 75—77, esp. *τῆς πολιτείας τῆς παρὰ πᾶσιν εὐδοκιμούσης*.

καὶ κατὰ τούτους τοὺς καιρούς] *καὶ* is perhaps added because Athens had been well governed when the Areopagus was in power before, cf. § 1, *πάλιν ἴσχυσεν* (Newman).

τὴν τῆς θαλάττης ἡγεμονίαν *κτλ.*] Isocr. *Paneg.* 72 (after the Persian wars), *οὐ πολλῷ δ᾽ ὕστερον τὴν ἀρχὴν τῆς θαλάττης ἔλαβον, δόντων μὲν τῶν ἄλλων Ἑλλήνων, οὐκ ἀμφισβητούντων δὲ τῶν νῦν ἡμᾶς ἀφαιρεῖσθαι ζητούντων*, *de Pace* 30, *παρ᾽ ἑκόντων τῶν Ἑλλήνων τὴν ἡγεμονίαν ἐλάβομεν*, *Panath.* 67, *οἱ σύμμαχοι τὴν ἡγεμονίαν ἡμῖν τὴν κατὰ θάλατταν ἔδοσαν*. Thuc. i 96, *παραλαβόντες οἱ Ἀθ. τὴν ἡγεμονίαν … ἑκόντων τῶν ξυμμάχων διὰ τὸ Παυσανίου μῖσος*. In Xen. *Hell.* vi § 34 a Spartan declares that the Athenians were chosen leaders at sea *τῶν Λακεδαιμονίων συμβουλευομένων*. None of the above passages shews that the Lacedaemonians were really willing to surrender the supremacy; and in Thuc. i 96 the reference is not to the Lacedaemonians, but to the allies of Athens who smarted under the overbearing conduct of Pausanias. Hence *ἀκόντων* should be retained.

§ 3. **προστάται τοῦ δήμου**] c. 2 § 2, and c. 28. Holm, *Gr. Gesch.* ii 43, 110.

Νεοκλέους] Plut. *Them.* 1, N. *οὐ τῶν ἄγαν ἐπιφανῶν Ἀθήνησι*.

τὰ πολεμικὰ] *Pol.* 1305 *a* 14, *ἀπειρία τῶν πολεμικῶν*, 1285 *b* 18, *ἡγεμονία τῶν πολεμικῶν*. *Ind. Ar.* On the other hand, *πολέμιος* is rare in *Ar.* Cf. c. 3 l. 7.

δικαιοσύνῃ] Plut. *Arist.* 3 *fin.*, and 7, *τὸν δίκαιον*.

τῷ μὲν στρατηγῷ, τῷ δὲ συμβούλῳ] Aristotle obviously refers to the rival claims of Themistocles and Aristides in *Pol.* viii (v) 8, 1309 *a* 39, *ἔχει δ᾽ ἀπορίαν, ὅταν μὴ συμβαίνῃ ταῦτα πάντα (φιλίαν πρὸς τὴν καθεστῶσαν πολιτείαν… δύναμιν μεγίστην τῶν ἔργων τῆς ἀρχῆς… ἀρετὴν καὶ δικαιοσύνην) περὶ τὸν αὐτόν, πῶς χρὴ ποιεῖσθαι τὴν αἵρεσιν… ἐν στρατηγίᾳ μὲν (δεῖ βλέπειν) εἰς τὴν ἐμπειρίαν μᾶλλον τῆς ἀρετῆς…ἐν δὲ φυλακῇ καὶ ταμιείᾳ τοὐναντίον*. On the other hand Isocr., *Panath.* 143, strangely maintains that the best *σύμβουλος* will also prove the best general (*Class. Rev.* v 161 *a*).

§ 4. **τειχῶν ἀνοικοδόμησιν**] Thuc. i 89 § 3, *τὴν πόλιν ἀνοικοδομεῖν παρεσκευάζοντο καὶ τὰ τείχη*. Themistocles went as envoy to Sparta to gain time while the walls were being built (*ib.* 90), while Aristides was one of the *ξυμπρέσβεις* who afterwards announced to Themistocles *ἔχειν ἱκανῶς τὸ τεῖχος* (91 § 3). Cf. Busolt, ii 321—9.

ἀλλήλους· ἐπὶ δὲ τὴν ἀπόστασιν τὴν τῶν Ἰώνων ἀπὸ τῆς τῶν Λακεδαιμονίων συμμαχίας Ἀριστείδης ἦν ὁ προτρέψας, τηρήσας τοὺς Λάκωνας διαβεβλημένους διὰ Παυσανίαν. διὸ καὶ τοὺς 5
φόρους οὗτος ἦν ὁ τάξας ταῖς πόλεσιν τοὺς πρώτους ἔτει τρίτῳ μετὰ τὴν ἐν Σαλαμῖνι ναυμαχίαν ἐπὶ Τιμοσθένους ἄρχοντος, καὶ τοὺς ὅρκους ὤμοσεν τοῖς Ἴωσιν ‖ ὥστε τὸν αὐτὸν ἐχθρὸν εἶναι καὶ [Col. 10]
φίλον, ἐφ' οἷς καὶ τοὺς μύδρους ἐν τῷ πελάγει καθεῖσαν.

24. *μετὰ δὲ ταῦτα θαρρούσης ἤδη τῆς πόλεως καὶ χρημάτων ἠθροισμένων πολλῶν, συνεβούλευεν ἀντιλαμβάνεσθαι τῆς ἡγεμονίας καὶ καταβάντας ἐκ τῶν ἀγρῶν οἰκεῖν ἐν τῷ ἄστει· τροφὴν γὰρ ἔσεσθαι πᾶσι, τοῖς μὲν στρατευομένοις, τοῖς δὲ φρουροῦσι, τοῖς δὲ τὰ κοινὰ πράττουσι, εἶθ' οὕτω κατασχήσειν τὴν ἡγεμονίαν.*
πεισθέντες δὲ ταῦτα καὶ λαβόντες τὴν ἀρχὴν τοῖς ⟦τε⟧ *συμμάχοις* 2

18 ΙΩΝΩΝΚ(ΑΙ)Τ(ΗΝ)Τ(ΩΝ)ΛΑΚΕΔ—ΜΑΧΙΑΝ :—*ἀπὸ τῆς—συμμαχίας* Blass, H-L, K-W, K³. **21** *πόλεσι* H-L. **23** *ὤμοσε* H-L, B.

B A
XXIV 2 ΠΟΛΛΩΝΗΘΡΟΙϹΜΕΝΩΝ: *πολλῶν ἠθροισμένων* H-L, B; *ἀθροιζομένων π.* K-W. **5** *πράττουσιν* H-L. **6** *τοῖς τε*: *τοῖς* B.

ἀπόστασιν τὴν τῶν Ἰώνων] Thuc. i 95 § 1, *ἐν τῇδε τῇ ἡγεμονίᾳ ἤδη βιαίου ὄντος αὐτοῦ* (Pausanias) *οἵ τε ἄλλοι Ἕλληνες ἤχθοντο καὶ οὐχ ἥκιστα οἱ Ἴωνες...φοιτῶντές τε πρὸς τοὺς Ἀθηναίους ἠξίουν αὐτοὺς ἡγεμόνας σφῶν γενέσθαι κατὰ τὸ ξυγγενὲς καὶ Παυσανίᾳ μὴ ἐπιτρέπειν.* Plut. *Arist.* 23. On the other hand Hdt. viii 3, *πρόφασιν τὴν Παυσανίεω ὕβριν προϊσχόμενοι ἀπείλοντο τὴν ἡγεμονίαν τοὺς Λακεδαιμονίους.* On Pausanias cf. *Pol.* 1307 *a* 2, 1333 *b* 32.

§ 5. **τοὺς φόρους**] 'tributes.' Thuc. i 96, *ἔταξαν ἅς τε ἔδει παρέχειν τῶν πόλεων χρήματα πρὸς τὸν βάρβαρον καὶ ἃς ναῦς... καὶ ἑλληνοταμίαι τότε πρῶτον Ἀθηναίοις κατέστη ἀρχή, οἳ ἐδέχοντο τὸν φόρον· οὕτω γὰρ ὠνομάσθη τῶν χρημάτων ἡ φορά.* v 18 § 4, *τὰς πόλεις φερούσας τὸν φόρον τὸν ἐπ' Ἀριστείδου.* Plut. *Arist.* 24. Schol. Aeschin. 3 § 258, *Ἀριστείδης ὁ τοὺς φόρους τάξας τοῖς Ἕλλησι.* The *φόρος* was fixed in the first instance at 460 talents.

ἐπὶ Τιμοσθένους] B.C. 478/7.

The commencement of the Athenian ascendancy is placed by Diodorus (xi 41) in the year of Adeimantus (477/6). This is the date accepted by Clinton. Ephorus appears to have placed the first payment of tribute in the spring of 476 (Busolt, *Rhein. Mus.* xxxvii 313), and accordingly this has been the date usually assigned to the formation of the Confederacy of Delos. Dem., *Phil.* iii 23, makes the Athenian ascendancy last 73 years, and the Lacedaemonian 29. The 29 years are reckoned from the battle of Aegospotami (July 405) to the battle of Naxos (Sept. 376). As the first of these battles marked the end of the Athenian empire, it follows that Dem. reckoned the beginning of the Athenian empire from 478, the first year after the Persian wars. For further details, see Clinton's *Fasti*, Appendix, c. 6; and Busolt, ii 345.

τοὺς ὅρκους ὤμοσεν] Plut. *Arist.* 25, *ὁ δ' Ἀριστείδης ὥρκισε μὲν τοὺς Ἕλληνας καὶ ὤμοσεν ὑπὲρ τῶν Ἀθηναίων, μύδρους ἐμβαλὼν ἐπὶ ταῖς ἀραῖς εἰς τὴν θάλατταν.* The same symbol of an irrevocable oath is recorded in Hdt. i 165, *οἱ Φωκαιέες ἐποιήσαντο ἰσχυρὰς κατάρας τῷ ὑπολειπομένῳ ἑωυτῶν τοῦ στόλου· πρὸς δὲ ταύτῃσι καὶ μύδρον σιδήρεον κατεπόντωσαν καὶ ὤμοσαν μὴ πρὶν εἰς Φωκαίην ἥξειν, πρὶν ἢ τὸν μύδρον τοῦτον ἀναφῆναι,* and in Horace, *Epod.* 16, 25.

XXIV § 1. **θαρρούσης**] c. 22 § 3.

καταβάντας ἐκ τῶν ἀγρῶν *κτλ.*] In contrast to Peisistratus who encouraged agriculture with a view to preventing his subjects from living in Athens (c. 16 § 3).

§ 2. **λαβόντες τὴν ἀρχὴν**] The simple verb is similarly used in Isocr. 4 § 72; 5 § 61; 7 § 7; 8 §§ 30, 69, 74, 104; 16 § 103. He has *παραλαβεῖν τὴν ἀρχὴν*

δεσποτικωτέρως ἐχρῶντο πλὴν Χίων καὶ Λεσβίων καὶ Σαμίων· τούτους δὲ φύλακας εἶχον τῆς ἀρχῆς, ἐῶντες τάς τε πολιτείας παρ'
3 *αὐτοῖς καὶ ἄρχειν ὧν ἔτυχον ἄρχοντες. κατέστησαν δὲ καὶ τοῖς πολλοῖς εὐπορίαν τροφῆς, ὥσπερ Ἀριστείδης εἰσηγήσατο. συνέβαινεν γὰρ ἀπὸ τῶν φόρων καὶ τῶν τελῶν* ⟦*καὶ τῶν συμμάχων*⟧

8 <*τὰς*> *παρ'*, Richards, K-W. **9** *ἄρχοντες* <*αὐτοῖς ἐπιτρέποντες, καὶ* — —> 'dictum erat de cleruchis' K-W. **10** *συνέβαινε* H-L. **10—22** 'idoneam sententiam non praebent...certe ipsi auctori tribuenda non videntur' H-L. **11** ΦΟΡΩΝ: *εἰσφορῶν* Whibley (H-L). *καὶ τῶν συμμάχων* secl. K-W, B.

---

in 4 § 100; 8 § 101; *κατασχεῖν* in 4 § 102, 8 § 126.

δεσποτικωτέρως] This comparative of the adverb is not in L and S. *Pol.* iv 10, 3, *τὸ δεσποτικῶς ἄρχειν.*

πλὴν Χίων καὶ Λεσβίων καὶ Σαμίων] Thuc. i 19, (in the interval between the Persian and Peloponnesian wars) *Ἀθηναῖοι δὲ (τοὺς ξυμμάχους ἡγοῦντο) ναῦς τε τῶν πόλεων τῷ χρόνῳ παραλαβόντες, πλὴν Χίων καὶ Λεσβίων, καὶ χρήματα τοῖς πᾶσι τάξαντες φέρειν.* Even when (under Pericles) the confederacy of Delos was transformed into an empire on the part of Athens, with her former confederates degraded into tributary dependencies, Chios, Samos and Lesbos alone remained on their original footing of autonomous allies.

It was after the revolt of *Samos* in 440 B.C. that that state was conquered by an armament under ten generals, including Pericles and Sophocles, and after a prolonged contest disarmed and dismantled (Thuc. i 115—117). Lesbos and Chios still remained in a privileged position (Thuc. iii 10).

Mitylene and the greater part of *Lesbos* revolted in 428 (*ib.* 2), one of the reasons being that the Mitylenæans 'had no security that Athens would not degrade them into the condition of subject-allies like the rest' (*ib.* 10 *fin.*). The fortifications of Mitylene were razed, all her ships of war captured, and the greater part of the island allotted to Athenian settlers (*ib.* 50).

In 425 *Chios* incurred the suspicion of Athens by building a new wall, which implied an intention to revolt (Thuc. iv 51). The Athenians insisted on the destruction of the wall (52). Chios actually revolted in 412 and was much harassed by the Athenians (Thuc. viii 14—61).

It is to the result of these revolts that Aristotle refers in *Pol.* iii 13, 1284 *a* 39, where, after speaking of ostracism as a means of suppressing undue prominence, he adds: *τὸ δ' αὐτὸ καὶ περὶ τὰς πόλεις καὶ τὰ ἔθνη ποιοῦσιν οἱ κύριοι τῆς δυνάμεως, οἷον Ἀθηναῖοι μὲν περὶ Σαμίους καὶ Χίους καὶ Λεσβίους (ἐπεὶ γὰρ θᾶττον ἐγκρατῶς ἔσχον τὴν ἀρχήν, ἐταπείνωσαν αὐτοὺς παρὰ τὰς συνθήκας).* But (as observed by Schlosser) the remark in the *Politics* is untrue of Lesbos, and barely true of Samos and Chios. The account in the text correctly describes the position of privilege at first enjoyed by these three islands. The passage in the *Politics* refers to a later time and is therefore not inconsistent with the text (cf. W. L. Newman, *Class. Rev.* v 162 *b*).

ἐῶντες] The two constructions of **ἐᾶν** are here combined, (1) the acc., as in *Pol.* v 7, 1307 *b* 16, *κινήσαντας τὸν νόμον ἐάσειν τὴν ἄλλην πολιτείαν*, and (2) the inf., as *ib.* 3, 1302 *b* 20, *ἐάσαντας γενέσθαι ἰᾶσθαι ὕστερον.*

ὧν ἔτυχον ἄρχοντες] For Chian possessions on the mainland, cf. Hdt. i 160 (Wyse). On the relations of Athens to Chios, Lesbos and Samos, cf. Wilamowitz, *Aus Kydathen*, pp. 11, 12.

§ 3. **ὥσπερ Ἀριστείδης εἰσηγήσατο**] 'If the policy of Aristides is placed in a less favourable light than we should expect, inasmuch as he is said to have converted a citizen-body largely consisting of peasants into an urban citizen-body subsisting on pay and exercising a despotic authority over the subject states, and thus to have contributed to the establishment of an extreme democracy, we remember that we are taught in the *Politics* (iv 6, 5, 1292 *b* 41 *sqq.*) to connect the establishment of a *τελευταία δημοκρατία* with a large increase in the size of the city and with the provision of pay, and also that Theophrastus' opinion of Aristides was not an altogether favourable one (Plut. *Arist.* c. 25).' (W. L. Newman in *Class. Rev.* v 162 *b.*)

τῶν φόρων] See note on 23 § 5.

τῶν τελῶν] 'taxes.' With the exception of the produce of plunder in war *πλείους ἢ δισμυρίους ἄνδρας τρέφεσθαι. δικασταὶ μὲν γὰρ ἦ[σα]ν ἑξακισχίλιοι, τοξόται δ' ἑξακόσιοι καὶ χίλιοι, καὶ πρὸς τούτοις ἱππεῖς χίλιοι καὶ διακόσιοι, βουλὴ δὲ πεντακόσιοι, καὶ φρουροὶ*

12 ΔΙΚΑϹΤΑΙ: ὁπλῖται? van Leeuwen, Gennadios.

---

and sale of prisoners, the *φόρος* was at this time the only source of revenue from foreigners. (The duty on merchandise passing to or from the Euxine was not levied until 409.) Hence the reference in *τελῶν* is to taxes imposed by the Athenians and levied *at home*, whether (1) ordinary taxes, such as harbour-dues, market-dues, court-fees, and payments made by resident aliens, or (2) extraordinary taxes. The latter were levied for special purposes, viz. the property-tax (*εἰσφορά*) which was practically a war-tax, and the *λῃτουργίαι*, or compulsory services. These last did not contribute towards the support of the citizens except by relieving them of expenses which might otherwise have fallen on the public chest. Lastly, there was the income derived from rents of public lands, and from the mines at Laurium.

In Thuc. vi 91, 6, Alcibiades enumerates some of these sources of revenue, viz. the mines, the public land and the law-courts and the tribute paid by the allies (*τῆς ἀπὸ τῶν ξυμμάχων προσόδου*). There is a fuller enumeration in Aristoph. *Vesp.* 656, *καὶ πρῶτον μὲν λογίσαι φαύλως, μὴ ψήφοις, ἀλλ' ἀπὸ χειρός, τὸν φόρον ἡμῖν ἀπὸ τῶν πόλεων ξυλλήβδην τὸν προσιόντα· κἄξω τούτων τὰ τέλη χωρὶς καὶ τὰς πολλὰς ἑκατοστάς, πρυτανεῖα, μέταλλ', ἀγοράς, λιμένας, μισθοὺς καὶ δημιόπρατα* (making a total of nearly 2000 talents, of which the 6000 *δικασταί* received 150).

As the *σύμμαχοι* contribute no payment except the *φόρος*, it is clear that the mention of them in the text is superfluous.

'The text, as it stands, appears to imply that the citizens of Athens derived maintenance from the allies over and above the *φόροι* and the *τέλη* paid by them; cf. [Xen.] *Rep. Ath.* i 16—18. Fees paid by the allies in lawsuits may be included in the reference, for these helped to maintain the dicasts (Gilbert, i 382, 4). There was also an *ἐπιφορά* (*ib.* 397). The visits of the citizens of the allied states to Athens would be another source of profit' (Newman).

πλείους ἢ δισμυρίους] The numbers actually specified amount to 15,750. If to this we add (with Mr Kenyon) '4000 men for the 20 guard-ships at the usual rate of 200 men to each ship,' we obtain a total of 19,750, not including the orphans and other privileged persons mentioned at the end of the chapter.

δικασταὶ] As these were not paid until the time of Pericles, this must be (as Mr Kenyon notices) an anticipation of the results of the policy initiated by Aristides. **ἑξακισχίλιοι**] *i.e.* 600 for each tribe. This is apparently the number of the dicasts in the times of the democracy after Cleisthenes. The *Heliastae* were instituted by Solon; but their number in his days is unknown, though it was probably not very small.

τοξόται] The context shews that *citizens* serving as bowmen are meant. The figures in the text are partly borrowed from Thuc. ii 13 § 7, where Pericles, on the outbreak of the Peloponnesian war, estimates the number of the *τοξόται* at 1600, and the *ἱππεῖς* at 1200 *ξὺν ἱπποτοξόταις*. In Thuc. vi 25 Nicias requires for the Sicilian expedition *τοξοτῶν τῶν αὐτόθεν καὶ ἐκ Κρήτης*. Gilbert, *Gr. St.*, i 305, quotes CIA i 79, *τοξόται οἱ ἀστικοί*; i 45, (*κατὰ*) *φυλὰς τοχ(σόται δέ)κα*; and i 55, 433, 446; *ib.* i 79, *οἱ τόξαρχοι*. The 1600 freeborn bowmen in the text must be distinguished from the 1200 Scythian bowmen of Andocides (*de Pace*, 7) and Aeschines (*F. L.* §§ 173—4). The latter were a police force instituted in 480 B.C. when 300 were purchased for this purpose by the state (Andoc. *l. c.* 5).

ἱππεῖς] The same number is found in Thuc. ii. 13 § 7, and in Andocides and Aeschines (*l. c.*) In 490 Athens had no cavalry (Hdt. vi 112). The number gradually rose to 1000, Arist. *Eq.* 225, Philochorus *ἐν τετάρτῳ* (B.C. 456—404) ap. Hesych. s. v.; and this number was maintained in the fourth century (Xen. *Hipparch.* 9, 3; Dem. 14 § 13). The number 1200 in Thuc. includes the *ἱπποτοξόται*. As the latter were Scythian slaves, it was a discredit to an Athenian citizen to serve in this force (Lys. 15 § 6). The fact that only 1000, out of the total 1200, are really citizens is apparently overlooked in the text. Gilbert, *Gr. St.*, i 305, n. 5, quotes Philochorus, *l. c.*, *διάφορα γὰρ ἦν ἱππέων πλήθη κατὰ χρόνον Ἀθηναίοις*, but holds *νεωρίων πεντακόσιοι, καὶ πρὸς τούτοις ἐν τῇ πόλει φρουροὶ πεντήκοντα, ἀρχαὶ δ' ἔνδημοι μὲν εἰς ἑπτακοσίους ἄνδρας, ὑπερόριοι δ'*

15 τῇ secl. K-W², B. 16 Μ(ΕΝ) ΗϹΑΝ ΕΙϹ.

---

that little credit can be given to any statements giving 1200 as the total number of the *ἱππεῖς* alone.

φρουροὶ νεωρίων] I cannot find any other passage in which these are expressly mentioned. In Thuc. ii 13 § 6 half the circuit of the Peiraeus and Munichia is described as *ἐν φυλακῇ*, and the total number of *ὁπλῖται τῶν ἐν τοῖς φρουρίοις καὶ τῶν παρ' ἔπαλξιν* is 16,000 (*ib.* § 3). This number is the force employed on the outbreak of war.

ἐν τῇ πόλει φρουροί] The mention of the *νεώρια* in the previous clause might at first sight suggest that these *φρουροὶ* were concerned with the upper *πόλις* in contrast with the Peiraeus: but, if so, we should expect *ἐν τῷ ἄστει* as the normal term to express this contrast. It is therefore probable that *τῇ πόλει* refers to the *Acropolis*, and it is so translated by Th. Reinach. This view (as Mr Wyse suggests to me) is supported by an inscr. of the 5th cent. published in the *Bulletin de Corr. Hellénique*, 1890, 177—180, and ascribed to 447 B.C. in CIA iv 3, 26 *a*, *[τ]ὴν πόλιν . . ο . . . . [ο]ἰκο[δ]ομῆσαι ὅ[πως] ἂν δραπέτης μὴ ἐ[σί]ῃ μηδὲ λωποδύτ[ης]· ταῦτα δὲ ξυγγρ[ά]ψαι μὲν Καλλικρ[ά]τη(ν) ὅπως ἄριστα κα[ὶ] εὐτελέστατα σκ[ε]υά[σ]αιν[τ]ο, μισθῶσα[ι] δὲ τοὺς πωλητὰς ὅπως ἂν ἐντὸς ἑξή[κ]οντα ἡμερῶν ἐπισκ[ε]υασθῇ, φύλακας δὲ [εἶ]ναι τρεῖς μὲν τοξό[τ]ας ἐκ τῆς φυλῆς τῆς [π]ρυτανευούσης.* M. Foucart understands the three *τοξόται* who are to act as *φύλακες* to be *trois Scythes*, on the ground that the police was not recruited from the citizens, but it will be observed that they belong to a *φυλή* and are therefore citizens. They are appointed to guard the approach to a particular part of the *Acropolis* and to prevent runaway slaves from seeking sanctuary in the temples. *πόλις*, or *ἡ πόλις*, is regularly used of the *Acropolis* in the 5th century. Thuc. ii 15 *fin.* (*καλεῖται*) *ἡ ἀκρόπολις μέχρι τοῦδε ἔτι ὑπ' Ἀθηναίων πόλις.* Cf. c. 8 l. 24.

'Aristophanes always uses *ἐν πόλει*, *εἰς πόλιν* (without the article) when he means the Acropolis. In prose writers, however, there are places where the MSS give the article: Xen. *Anab.* vii 1, 27, *ὑπαρχόντων πολλῶν χρημάτων ἐν τῇ πόλει*, Aeschin. 1 § 97, *οἰκίαν ὄπισθεν τῆς πόλεως*, Antiph. 6 § 39, *διηλλάγην τούτοις ἐν τῇ πόλει ἐναντίον μαρτύρων*, [Xen.] *de Red.* 5 § 12, *πολλὰ χρήματα εἰς τὴν πόλιν ἀνενεχθέντα*, Phil. *Per.* 32, *ὅπως...οἱ δὲ δικασταὶ τὴν ψῆφον ἀπὸ τοῦ βωμοῦ φέροντες ἐν τῇ πόλει κρίνοιεν.* *ἐμ πόλει* is no doubt the normal form in CIA i' (Wyse).

ἀρχαὶ...ἔνδημοι] The total number is large, and there is nothing to shew that the higher officers of state are excluded. Schömann (*Ant.* p. 147, E. T.) says: 'so far as our knowledge extends, the offices of government were unpaid.' Again, on p. 402, 'official functionaries,' as contrasted with subordinates, 'served without pay' (cf. *ib.* 436). But in c. 62 the archons receive for maintenance 4 obols a day each, and in c. 29 (under the constitution of 411) the archons and *πρυτάνεις* are excepted from the rule that all offices should be without pay.

ὑπερόριοι] In *Pol.* iii 14, 1285 *b* 14, we have *τὰ κατὰ πόλιν καὶ τὰ ἔνδημα καὶ τὰ ὑπερόρια συνεχῶς ἦρχον*, and the term *ὑπερόριος* occurs again in l. 18. Cf. law quoted in Aeschin. *c. Timarch.* 47, *μηδὲ ἀρχὴν ἀρχέτω μηδεμίαν, μήτε ἔνδημον μήτε ὑπερόριον.* Mr Kenyon's translation distinguishes between magistrates 'within the city' and 'those whose jurisdiction lay outside it'; Mr Poste (more satisfactorily) between 'home' and 'foreign' magistrates. The latter would naturally include the officials in the Athenian *κληρουχίαι*. The first *κληρουχία* was that settled near Chalkis in 510 B.C. The number of cleruchs sent out between 460 and 427 amounted to 9,450, not including those sent to Lemnos, Imbros and Aegina (Gilbert, *Gr. St.* i 421, note 4).

The cleruchs were subject to military orders, and we sometimes hear of civil magistrates being sent out by Athens, *e.g.* *ἄρχοντες* sent to Lesbos (Antiphon, *de Caede Her.* § 47). Cf. the *ἐπίσκοποι* of Aristoph. *Av.* 1022, 1050 (see Wilamowitz, *Aus Kydathen*, p. 75), and the *ἐπιμεληταὶ* sent to Miletus (CIA iv 1, 22ª) and in later times to Delos, Haliartos and Paros (Boeckh, i 508 *a*, and n. 709 Fränkel).

The *ἀρχαὶ ὑπερόριοι* would also include the *φρούραρχοι*, as at Erythrae, CIA i 9 (Ditt. no. 2), and 10. *φρουραρχία* is mentioned in Xen. *Mem.* iv 4, 17, and *φρούραρχοι* possibly in [Xen.] *de Rep.*

εἰς ἑπτακοσίους· πρὸς δὲ τούτοις, ἐπεὶ συνεστήσαντο τὸν πόλεμον ὕστερον, ὁπλῖται μὲν δισχίλιοι καὶ πεντακόσιοι, νῆες δὲ φρουρίδες
19 εἴκοσι, ἄλλαι δὲ νῆες αἱ τοὺς φρουροὺς ἄγουσαι τοὺς ἀπὸ τοῦ

17 *ἑπτακοσίους* e v. 16 male repetitum putant K-W (B). 'an <*τὰ εἰς*> *τὸν πόλεμον*?' K-W; *κατέστησαν ἐς τὸν πόλεμον* Richards. **19** ΦΟΡΟΥϹ K, et (lacuna post *ἄγουσαι* indicata) K-W: *φρουροὺς* van Leeuwen et Blass, coll. 62 § 1; *φόρους* 'vox aperte corrupta,' H-L; *μισθοφόρους*? Herwerden.

Ath. i 18, *τοὺς ἐκπλέοντας Ἀθηναίων ἐτίμων ἂν μόνους, τούς τε στρατηγοὺς καὶ τοὺς φρουράρχους* (MSS *τριηράρχους*) *καὶ τοὺς πρέσβεις* (Wilamowitz, *Aus Kydathen*, pp. 73—76). Cf. inscr. ascribed to the beginning of the Peloponnesian war (CIA iv 3, 27 *c*), *οἵτινες Ἀθηναίων ἄρχουσι ἐν τῇ ὑπερορίᾳ*.

συνεστήσαντο τὸν πόλεμον] The phrase *συστῆσαι* or *συστήσασθαι πόλιν* or *πολιτείαν* is found in the *Politics* and *τὰ πράγματα συνίστασθαι* (of tragic poets) in the *Poetics* 6, p. 1450 *a* 37. Again, in Thuc. i 15 § 2 we find *κατὰ γῆν δὲ πόλεμος... οὐδεὶς ξυνέστη*, and Hdt. vi 108 has *συνεστεῶτας Βοιωτοῖσι* for 'engaged in conflict with' the B. Here, if *τὰ εἰς* were to be inserted, it might mean 'organised,' as in Xen. *Anab.* vii 6 § 26 *ἱππικὸν συνεστηκός*, cf. *τὸ στράτευμα συνεστηκός*, of 'a standing army,' in Dem. p. 93 *fin.*

ὁπλῖται] The number 2,500 is difficult to reconcile with the figures mentioned elsewhere. The number of Athenians who fought at Marathon was 9,000 (Pausan. x 20, 2) or 10,000 (Justin. ii 9); at Plataea, 8,000. In Thuc. ii 13 § 2, Pericles estimates the number of hoplites at 13,000 fit for service in the field, and 16,000 (of the oldest and the youngest of the citizens) as fit to serve on garrison duty and to man the walls. In Thuc. ii 31 § 2, the Athenians march into Megara with a force of not less than 10,000 hoplites who were citizens, and not less than 3,000 who were *μέτοικοι*. Acharnae (the largest of the demes) could put into the field 3,000 hoplites. Possibly these numbers are exceptionally large and represent the maximum number of hoplites available on an emergency; but the number in the text professes to be that of the hoplites on the outbreak of war. The armament for the Sicilian expedition included not less than 4,000 hoplites (Thuc. vi 31, 2). In Thuc. vii 20 the hoplites *ἐκ καταλόγου* number 1,200.

It seems certain that these 2,500 hoplites (as partly implied in *πρὸς τούτοις*) are in *addition* to such of the citizens who were available in time of war. Most of these have already been enumerated under previous headings. Thus, if we add to the 2,500 hoplites the 6,000 dicasts and the 500 members of the *βουλή*, we obtain a total of 9,000, the exact number of Athenians who (according to Pausanias) fought at Marathon. Again, if we further add the 700 home officials, we get a total of 9,700, only 300 less than the 10,000 Athenian hoplites who marched into Megara early in the Peloponnesian war.

Blass understands by *ὁπλῖται* *qui continuo in praesidiis erant.*

νῆες—φρουρίδες] 'guard-ships.' In Thuc. iv 13 § 2 the Athenian fleet at Pylos includes *τῶν φρουρίδων τινὲς τῶν ἐκ Ναυπάκτου*: the ships from Zacynthus are 50 in all; of these 35 were already at that island in c. 5, and 4 ships came from Chios, leaving eleven as the number of guard-ships from Naupactus, which had been an Athenian naval station ever since its capture in 455 B.C. (Thuc. i 103). The only other passages in which 'guard-ships' are mentioned are Xen. *Hell.* i 3, 17, where they form part of the Spartan fleet in the Hellespont, *ναῦς αἳ ἦσαν ἐν τῷ Ἑλλησπόντῳ καταλελειμμέναι φρουρίδες*, and CIA iv 22 *a*, at Miletus, *[ἀπο]στειλάντων [δύο] φρουρίδε*. Cf. Wilamowitz, *Aus Kydathen*, p. 73 f.

The Athenian triremes were generally manned by about 200 each (Boeckh II xxii p. 376 Lamb; Gilbert, i 310).

τοὺς—ἄγουσαι] *φόρους* raises a serious difficulty. It has hitherto been supposed that the 'tributaries' of Athens paid in the money themselves to the Council (Boeckh II vii, p. 177 Lewis; Gilbert, i 398). Pollux (viii 114) inaccurately says that the *ἑλληνοταμίαι* collected the tribute, but this duty (when necessary) was (after 446 ?) performed by the *ἐκλογεῖς*. It was only the collection of *arrears* or *fines* that was enforced by means of *νῆες ἀργυρολόγοι* (Thuc. iii 19; iv 50, 75) under the command of one or more *στρατηγοί* (Gilbert, i 398, and *Beiträge*, p. 67). Further, unless we suppose a lacuna, *τοὺς ἄνδρας* cannot be construed. Hence the suggestion *φρουρούς*, which follows naturally *κυάμου δισχιλίους ἄνδρας, ἔτι δὲ πρυτανεῖον καὶ ὀρφανοὶ καὶ δεσμωτῶν φύλακες· ἅπασι γὰρ τούτοις ἀπὸ τῶν κοινῶν ἡ διοίκησις ἦν.*

25. *ἡ μὲν οὖν τροφὴ τῷ δήμῳ διὰ τούτων ἐγίγνετο. ἔτη δὲ ἑπτὰ καὶ δέκα μάλιστα μετὰ τὰ Μηδικὰ διέμεινεν ἡ πολιτεία προεστώτων τῶν Ἀρεοπαγιτῶν, καίπερ ὑποφερομένη κατὰ μικρόν. αὐξανομένου δὲ τοῦ πλήθους, γενόμενος τοῦ δήμου προστάτης Ἐφιάλ-*

20 'πρυτανεῖον vix verum' K-W. **21** ἅπασιν B. ΔΙΟΙΚΗϹΙϹ: διασίτησις H-L.

XXV 1 ЄΓΙΝ (K-W).

TESTIMONIA. **XXV 4** Heraclidis epitoma (Rose, Frag. 611): Ἐφιάλτης.

---

after *φρουρίδες* and enables us to take *τοὺς ἄνδρας* in apposition with it. In addition to the guard-ships stationed at places like Naupactus, there would be transports to take the *φρουροί* to the places where they were to be stationed. These *φρουροί* were appointed by lot by the demes. Even when changes were made in other appointments, the *βουλευταί* and the *φρουροί* still continued to be thus appointed (c. 62 § 1).

πρυτανεῖον] *i.e.* the persons maintained in the *prytaneum*, *e.g.* citizens who had done good service and were entertained at the public expense, either on a special occasion or for life. Among the latter were victors in the panhellenic games, distinguished generals or statesmen, and the representatives of Harmodius and Aristogeiton. The archons and other officials are not included in this list, as they have already been included in the *ἀρχαὶ ἔνδημοι*; and besides, in historic times, the archons probably dined in the *Thesmothesion* and the prytanes and certain other officials in the *Tholos* (see *Dict. Ant. s. v.*). Cf. Hermann, *Staatsalt.* § 127, 17 f.

ὀρφανοί] The sons of citizens who had fallen in war were maintained during their minority at the public expense. The regular phrase for this was *δημοσίᾳ τρέφειν*. Cf. Thuc. ii 46, *τοὺς παῖδας ἀπὸ τοῦδε δημοσίᾳ ἡ πόλις μέχρι ἥβης θρέψει*. *Pol.* ii 8, 1268 *a* 8 (*τοῖς παισὶ τῶν ἐν τῷ πολέμῳ τετελευτηκότων ἐκ δημοσίου γίνεσθαι τὴν τροφήν*)...*ἔστι δὲ καὶ ἐν Ἀθήναις οὗτος ὁ νόμος νῦν*. Plat. *Menex.* 248 E. The institution is said to have gone back as far as the time of Solon (Diog. Laert. i 54). Cf. Schulthess, *Vormundschaft*, pp. 13—26. '*ὀρφανοὶ* are mentioned in an inscr. said to be not later than 460 B.C. (Dittenberger, no. 384, l. 120), but the latter part is much mutilated' (Wyse).

δεσμωτῶν φύλακες] The Eleven had the management of the prison and had under them subordinates, such as jailers, executioners and torturers; but as these were *δημόσιοι*, or public slaves, the reference may possibly be to the Eleven themselves, who are called *δεσμοφύλακες* in the Schol. on Dem. *Androt.* § 26, *Timocr.* § 210, and on Aristoph. *Plut.* 1108 where the term is corrupted to *θεσμοφύλακες*.

διοίκησις] lit. 'administration.' *Pol.* iii 16, 1287 *a* 6, *ποιεῖν ἕνα κύριον τῆς διοικήσεως*, and 1331 *b* 9, *περὶ γραφὰς δικῶν καὶ τὴν ἄλλην τὴν τοιαύτην διοίκησιν*. iv (vii) 10, 1330 *a* 7 (it is not easy for all the citizens to pay their share in the *συσσίτια*) *καὶ διοικεῖν τὴν ἄλλην οἰκίαν*. The word is often used in the *Politics*, of management or administration. The primary meaning is 'to keep house,' as in Plato *Meno* 91 A, *τάς τε οἰκίας καὶ τὰς πόλεις διοικεῖν*. *διοίκησις* means 'housekeeping' in Dem. *Steph.* 45 § 32, *τῆς καθ' ἡμέραν διοικήσεως*. In the text it includes maintenance (*σίτησις*) and payment of money.

XXV. *Ephialtes.*

§ 1. **ἔτη ἑπτὰ καὶ δέκα μάλιστα**] From 478/7 B.C., the date of the Confederacy of Delos (23 § 5), in the first year after the Persian wars, to 462/1, the archonship of Conon.

προεστώτων τῶν Ἀρεοπαγιτῶν] See c. 23 § 1, and *Politics* there quoted. Isocr. *Areop.* 51 *ἧς ἐπιστατούσης κτλ.*

ὑποφερομένη] c. 36 § 1.

Ἐφιάλτης ὁ Σοφωνίδου] The father's name is given (Σοφ-) in Aelian *Var. Hist.* ii 43; iii 17; xi 9 (*πενέστατος ἦν*). The last of these passages illustrates **ἀδωροδόκητος**. He declined an offer of 10 talents from his friends, saying: *ταῦτά με ἀναγκάσει αἰδούμενον ὑμᾶς καταχαρίσασθαί τι τῶν δικαίων, μὴ αἰδούμενον δὲ μηδὲ χαριζό-*

της ὁ Σοφωνίδου, || καὶ δοκῶν ἀδωροδόκητος εἶναι καὶ δίκαιος [Col. 11] πρὸς τὴν πολιτείαν, ἐπέθετο τῇ βουλῇ. καὶ πρῶτον μὲν ἀνεῖλεν 2 πολλοὺς τῶν Ἀρεοπαγιτῶν, ἀγῶνας ἐπι[φ]έρων περὶ τῶν διῳκημένων· ἔπειτα τῆς βουλῆς ἐπὶ Κόνωνος ἄρχοντος ἅπαντα περιείλετο

5 [[καὶ]] δοκῶν H-L, K-W². 6 ἀνεῖλε H-L. 8 ΠΕΡΙΕΙΛΕ: περιείλετο Richards, K-W, K³, B; παρείλετο H-L.

μενον ὑμῖν ἀχάριστον δόξαι. Cf. Plut. *Cim.* 10. On Ephialtes, see Duncker, *G. d. A.* viii; Holm, *Gr. Gesch.* ii 176—7.

δίκαιος πρὸς τὴν πολιτείαν] The phrase reminds us of the *Politics*; v 9 § 1, 1309 *a* 36, τρίτον δ' ἀρετὴν καὶ δικαιοσύνην ἐν ἑκάστῃ πολιτείᾳ τὴν πρὸς τὴν πολιτείαν (*Class. Rev.* v 160 *a*). Aelian *Var. Hist.* xiii 39, Ἐφ. στρατηγοῦ ὀνειδίσαντος αὐτῷ τινος πενίαν 'τὸ δὲ ἕτερον' ἔφη 'διὰ τί οὐ λέγεις, ὅτι δίκαιός εἰμι;'

§ 2. **ἀγῶνας ἐπιφέρων**] Plut. *Per.* 10 § 6, Ἐφιάλτην...φοβερὸν ὄντα τοῖς ὀλιγαρχικοῖς καὶ περὶ τὰς εὐθύνας καὶ διώξεις τῶν τὸν δῆμον ἀδικούντων ἀπαραίτητον. Ephialtes had made himself feared by his opposition to Cimon in particular; Cimon's party was in a minority, as may be inferred from his being ostracised, probably in the spring of 462 (Busolt, i 454 n).—Cf. Oncken, *Staatslehre*, pp. 492—505, 'Ephialtes und die Gerichtsreform.'

ἐπὶ Κόνωνος] B.C. 462/1, Diod. xi 74. Hitherto the date of this attack on the Areopagus has not been accurately known. It has sometimes been assigned to B.C. 460 (Diodorus xi 77, followed *e.g.* in Peter's *Zeittafeln*) or about 458 (*e.g.* in Smith, *Dict. Ant. s. v.* Areopagus). Cf. Philippi, *Areop.* p. 256—9.

περιείλετο] *Inf.* § 4, περιείλοντο. See note on παραιρεῖσθαι and περιαιρεῖσθαι in 27 § 1.

On the overthrow of the Areopagus by Ephialtes, cf. *Pol.* ii 12, 1274 *a* 7, καὶ τὴν μὲν ἐν Ἀρείῳ πάγῳ βουλὴν Ἐφιάλτης ἐκόλουσε καὶ Περικλῆς (καὶ Π. bracketed by Sauppe). It was not until a later date that Pericles deprived the Areopagus of some of its remaining privileges, c. 27 § 1. The text implies that he was not the leader of the present attack. Philochorus (FHG i 407), Ἐφ. μόνα κατέλιπε τῇ ἐξ Ἀρείου πάγου βουλῇ τὰ ὑπὲρ τοῦ σώματος. Theopompus is supposed to be the authority followed on this point by Plutarch: *Pericles* 7 (Eph.) κατέλυσε τὸ κράτος τῆς ἐξ Ἀρείου πάγου βουλῆς, πολλὴν (κατὰ τὸν Πλάτωνα, *Rep.* 562 C, D) καὶ ἄκρατον τοῖς πολίταις ἐλευθερίαν οἰνοχοῶν, and *ib.* 9 (of the Areop.) ὥστε τὴν μὲν ἀφαιρεθῆναι τὰς πλείστας κρίσεις δι' Ἐφιάλτου. *Cimon* 10, (Cimon) πρὸς Ἐφιάλτην ὕστερον χάριτι τοῦ δήμου καταλύοντα τὴν ἐξ Ἀρείου πάγου βουλὴν διηνέχθη, *ib.* 15, Ἐφιάλτου προεστῶτος ἀφείλοντο τῆς ἐξ Ἀρείου πάγου βουλῆς τὰς κρίσεις πλὴν ὀλίγων ἁπάσας, καὶ τῶν δικαστηρίων κυρίους ἑαυτοὺς ποιήσαντες εἰς ἄκρατον δημοκρατίαν ἐνέβαλον τὴν πόλιν. *Praec. Ger. Reip.* 10 § 15 (II 805), βουλήν τινες ἐπαχθῆ καὶ ὀλιγαρχικὴν κολούσαντες, ὥσπερ Ἐφιάλτης Ἀθήνησι..., δύναμιν ἅμα καὶ δόξαν ἔσχον, *ib.* 15 § 18, ὡς Περικλῆς...δι' Ἐφιάλτου τὴν ἐξ Ἀρείου πάγου βουλὴν ἐταπείνωσε. Pausan. i 29, 15, Ἐφ. ὃς τὰ νόμιμα τὰ ἐν Ἀρείῳ πάγῳ μάλιστα ἐλυμήνατο. Cf. Philippi, *Der Areopag*, pp. 256—271; Busolt, ii 460.

In the *Eumenides* (681—706) we have a well-known defence of the jurisdiction of the Areopagus in matters of homicide, the main point which was left untouched by the reforms of Ephialtes. The date of the play is fixed by the hypothesis to the *Agamemnon* as the archonship of Philocles, Ol. 80, 2 = 459/8; and the list of νῖκαι Διονυσιακαί found on the Acropolis in 1886 describes Aeschylus as exhibiting in that year, *i.e.* in March, 458: Ἐφ. Ἀρχ. 1886, p. 209, quoted in Haigh's *Attic Theatre*, p. 322, [ἐπὶ Φιλο]κλέους...τραγῳδῶν, Ξενοκλῆς Ἀ-φιδναῖ[ος] ἐχορή[γει], Αἰσχύλος ἐδίδασκεν. It was held by Meier, Boeckh and K. O. Müller that even the cognisance of cases of homicide was taken away from the Areopagus by Ephialtes and not restored until after the expulsion of the Thirty. Müller (*Dissertation on Eum.* § 36) went so far as to affirm that the motion of Ephialtes was carried *after* the representation of the *Eumenides*, whereas Diodorus places it two years earlier (460) and the text four years earlier. The fact that they retained their jurisdiction in cases of homicide is clearly stated by Philochorus (*l.c.*) and has been conclusively proved by Forchhammer (1828). The very privilege that the reformers left untouched is prominently brought forward by the poet.

τὰ ἐπίθετα δι' ὧν ἦν ἡ τῆς πολιτείας φυλακή, καὶ τὰ μ[ὲν τ]οῖς πεντακοσίοις, τὰ δὲ τῷ δήμῳ καὶ τοῖς δικαστηρίοις ἀπέδωκεν.
3 ἔπραξε δὲ ταῦτα συναιτίου γενομένου Θεμιστοκλέους, ὃς ἦν μὲν

11 ΕΠΡΑ·Ε?, ἔπραξε B, ἔπραττε K etc. ΓΕΝ: γιν- Richards, γιγν- H-L.

11 *Isocr. Areopagitici argumentum (ed. Benseler, p. lviii; Schol. in Aeschin. etc. Dind. p. 111; Orat. Att. ed. Turicensis, ii p. 6): Ἐφιάλτης τις καὶ Θεμιστοκλῆς χρεωστοῦντες τῃ πόλει χρήματα καὶ εἰδότες ὅτι, ἐὰν δικασθῶσιν (δικάσωσιν Bens.) οἱ Ἀρεοπαγῖται, πάντως ἀποδώσουσι, καταλῦσαι αὐτοὺς ἔπεισαν τὴν πόλιν, οὕτως οὔπως τινὸς μέλλοντος κριθῆναι. "ὁ γὰρ Ἀρ. λέγει ἐν τῇ πολ. τῶν Ἀθ. ὅτι καὶ ὁ Θεμιστοκλῆς αἴτιος ἦν μὴ πάντα (πάντως cod. Mustoxydis) δικάζειν τοὺς Ἀρεοπαγίτας" (Rose, Frag. 366², 404³)· δῆθεν μέν, ὡς δι' αὐτοὺς τοῦτο ποιοῦντες, τὸ δ' ἀληθὲς διὰ τοῦτο πάντα κατασκευάζοντες. εἶτα οἱ Ἀθηναῖοι ἀσμένως ἀκούσαντες τῆς τοιαύτης συμβουλῆς κατέλυσαν αὐτούς.

Cf. Philippi, *Areop.* pp. 264, 290, and Grote, c. 46 (iv 112 n).

τὰ ἐπίθετα] These 'additional privileges' include almost everything except the ancient prerogatives of the Areopagus in connexion with trials for homicide. The legend of Orestes and the history of the first Messenian war (B.C. 743) alike imply that it had jurisdiction in such cases 'from of old,' Pausan. iv 5 § 2 δίκας τὰς φονικὰς...δικάζειν ἐκ παλαιοῦ. Cf. Meier and Schömann, *Att. Process*, ed. Lipsius, p. 11.

Harpocr. *s. v.* ἐπιθέτους ἑορτάς defines them as τὰς μὴ πατρίους (cf. c. 3, 16—18), and adds: ἐλέγετο δὲ παρ' αὐτοῖς καὶ ἄλλα ἐπίθετά τινα, ὁπόσα μὴ πάτρια ὄντα ἡ ἐξ Ἀρείου πάγου βουλὴ ἐδίκαζεν, ὡς σαφὲς ποιεῖ Λυσίας κτλ (cf. Philippi, *Areop.* 157). The reference to Lysias shews that the ἐπίθετα meant by Harpocr. are after the time of the Thirty and are not the same as those meant in the text.

φυλακή] c. 4 § 4 φύλαξ, and 8 § 4, ἐπίσκοπος. Schömann's *Ant.* pp. 332 and 493, E. T. Among the privileges now taken away from the Areopagus would be the general superintendence of education and of public morals, *e.g.* the enforcing of the ancient νόμος ἀργίας. Grote, c. 46, iv 112; Schömann, p. 498; Philippi, *Areop.* pp. 162—170, 268—272.

τῷ δήμῳ] Cic. *de Rep.* i 43, 'Athenienses quibusdam temporibus sublato Areopago nihil nisi populi scitis ac decretis agebant.'

τοῖς δικαστηρίοις] Thus, the jurisdiction in cases of ἀσέβεια seems in general to have been transferred to the law-courts; but certain forms of ἀσέβεια continued to be tried by the Areopagus, esp. the offence of doing damage to the sacred olive-trees (Lys. *Or.* 7). Schömann, p. 498. On the general question, cf. Philippi, *Areop.* pp. 272—289.

§ 3. **συναιτίου γενομένου Θεμιστοκλέους**] Hitherto, the attack on the Areopagus has been generally attributed to Ephialtes and Pericles (*Pol.* 1274 *a* 7); the present passage assigns a prominent part to Themistocles. The only other authority for associating Themistocles with Ephialtes on this occasion is to be found in the argument to the *Areopagiticus* of Isocrates (see *Testimonia*), probably due to a Christian writer in the sixth century (Rose, *A. P.*, p. 423). Duncker, *G. d. A.* viii 258—260, discusses the account just mentioned. He attributes the attack on the part of Themistocles to a change of policy in the Areopagus due to its now containing a large number of ex-archons who had been merely appointed by lot and not by open election.

The text implies that Themistocles was still at Athens in 462 B.C., whereas, according to the current view, he was ostracised in 471 B.C. (Diod. xi 54) and fled to Persia about 466 B.C. In his flight he passed through the Athenian fleet which was besieging Naxos (Thuc. i 137 § 2, and Plut. *Them.* 25 § 1). The reduction of Naxos took place before the battles at the Eurymedon (Thuc. i 100 § 1), which are assigned to 466. Xerxes died in 465 and, according to Thuc. i 137 § 3, Themistocles on his arrival at the Persian court found Artaxerxes νεωστὶ βασιλεύοντα. Besides Thucydides, Charon of Lampsacus, one of the λογογράφοι prior to Herodotus, is quoted by Plutarch, *Them.* 27 § 1, as making Themistocles reach the court after the death of Xerxes. The authorities there quoted, as making him arrive before the king's death, are Ephorus, Deinon, Cleitarchus and Heracleides; but the account of Thuc. is accepted as 'agreeing better with the dates, although these again have not been firmly settled beyond dispute.'

11 τῶν Ἀρεοπαγιτῶν, ἔμελλε δὲ κρίνεσθαι μηδισμοῦ. βουλόμενος δὲ

If the narrative in the text is accepted, Themistocles was at Athens in 462, awaiting his trial on the charge of Medism. This must be the first accusation, prior to his ostracism, and on this charge (according to Diod. xi 54) he was acquitted (Grote, c. 44, iv 36, 37). The second accusation, which is the only one mentioned by Thuc. (i 135 § 1), and Plut. (*Them.* 23), was not brought forward until after his banishment. We should then be compelled to place his ostracism not earlier than 461, and his flight to Persia about 460, when Artaxerxes had been on the throne for about five years. To reconcile this with νεωστὶ in Thuc., Mr Kenyon suggests that 'the fifth year of a king who ruled for forty might well be spoken of as in the beginning of his reign.' But the incident connected with the siege of Naxos makes it impossible to make the narrative in the text agree with the account in Thuc. Mr Kenyon proposes two alternatives: either (1), the story of the flight of Them. should be connected with some operations about 460 B.C. and not with the siege of Naxos; or (2), there were two inconsistent accounts of the latter years of Them., that adopted by Thuc. and that in the present text. We can hardly hesitate in choosing the second alternative, and in following the authority of Thucydides. Cf. Abbott, *Hist. Gr.* ii 386—8.

The chronology of this period has been investigated anew by Bauer, who implicitly accepts the statement in the text, and accordingly alters the date of the siege of Naxos. His dates as compared with those of Clinton are as follows:

	Clinton	Bauer
Siege of Naxos	466	460 (spring)
battle of Eurymedon	,,	,, (autumn)
revolt of Thasos	465	459 (spring)
third Messenian war	464	,, (summer?)
defeat at Drabescus	465	,, (autumn)
Thasos subdued by Cimon	463	457 (spring)
expedition to Egypt	460	456 (spring)
ostracism of Cimon	461	455 (spring)
recall of Cimon	456	452 (winter)
end of Egyptian war	455	450 (spring)
death of Cimon	449	448

These dates involve setting aside the text of Thuc. iv 102 in two points: in § 1 we are told that the defeat at Drabescus was 32 years after the failure of Aristagoras to establish himself on the Strymon, and (*ib.* § 2) 28 years before the founding of Amphipolis (in 437 B.C.), Schol. Aeschines ii 31. It is more in accordance with the narrative in Hdt. v 126 to place the failure of Aristagoras in B.C. 497 than in 491. Again, the alliance with Argos is placed late in 457, whereas the *Eumenides* of Aeschylus, which contains a clear reference to this alliance (l. 290, 757—766), was performed in March, 458, more than a year earlier (*Athenaeum*, 1891, p. 317). See also Mr E. M. Walker in *Class. Rev.* vi 95—99.

It is remarkable that in Plutarch's *Life of Themistocles* not a word is said as to his having taken any part in the attack on the Areopagus. In this connexion Plutarch mentions Ephialtes and Pericles alone (note on § 2, περιείλετο). We must infer either (1), that Plutarch had no first-hand acquaintance with this treatise; or (2), that he carelessly omitted to notice this narrative; or (3), that he had no such narrative in his copy.

Against (1) we may set the fact that in 10 § 3 Plutarch quotes Aristotle as his authority for a statement found in c. 23 § 1, and also for the murder of Ephialtes mentioned at the end of this very chapter. But this makes Plutarch's silence on Themistocles all the more singular. (Cf. Abbott, *Hist. Gr.* ii 518.)

Against (2) it may be remarked that the story would have admirably illustrated the duplicity of Themistocles, and as such would naturally have been welcomed by the biographer. Mr Kenyon suggests that the omission 'can hardly be explained except on the theory that in actually writing his lives he used the notes and extracts he had previously made without having the complete work before him'; but this puts the difficulty only one stage further back, and compels us to ask how Plutarch came to omit to make any note of this narrative. He accepts the statement in Thucydides that Themistocles reached the Persian court after the death of Xerxes as in better agreement with the dates. This implies that the biographer had paid some attention to the chronology of the time. It seems possible therefore that he rejected the narrative on the ground that it did not fit in with the date of the siege of Naxos, which Plutarch, following Thucydides, mentions in connexion with the flight of Themistocles. But even supposing he deliberately rejected the narrative, it is strange that he says nothing about it. His treatment of his authorities is, however, by no means systematic and uniform. In his *Life of Themistocles*, he quotes no less than 30 different authorities of very various degrees of importance. Even Thucydides does not command his

καταλυθῆναι τὴν βουλὴν ὁ Θεμιστοκλῆς πρὸς μὲν τὸν Ἐφιάλτην ἔλεγεν ὅτι συναρπάζειν αὐτὸν ἡ βουλὴ μέλλει, πρὸς δὲ τοὺς Ἀρεοπαγίτας ὅτι δείξει τινὰς συνισταμένους ἐπὶ καταλύσει τῆς πολιτείας. ἀγαγὼν δὲ τοὺς αἱρεθέντας τῆς βουλῆς οὗ διέτριβεν ὁ Ἐφιάλτης, ἵνα δείξῃ τ[οὺ]ς ἀθροιζομένους, διελέγετο μετὰ σπουδῆς αὐτοῖς.
4 *ὁ δ' Ἐφιάλτης ὡς εἶδεν καταπλαγεὶς καθίζει μονοχίτων*

16 ΑΦΑΙΡΕΘΕΝΤΑC (K): *αἱρεθέντας?* K (K-W, B); *αἱρεθέντας ὑπὸ* Richards; *ἐφαιρεθέντας* H-L, coll. Thuc. iv 38; *ἐξ-* Poland. ΟΥ: *οἳ* H-L.

---

undivided allegiance. With regard to the adventures of Themistocles in Asia, while respecting the chronology of Thucydides, Plutarch disdains to reproduce the historian's account of those adventures, following by preference the untrustworthy romance of Phanias of Eresos (Holden's *Introd.* §§ 17, 22). Such a fact detracts considerably from his authority as a judicious critic of the materials which he had before him.

As to (3), Prof. Tyrrell in the *Quarterly Review*, 1891, p. 344, infers from the silence of Plutarch that he 'never read the work before us. But he had certainly read some other treatise ascribed to Aristotle on the *Athenian Constitution*; therefore there must have been other editions of the *Athenian Constitution* circulating under the name of Aristotle.' Yet both the passages, which Plutarch in his *Themistocles* quotes as from this treatise, are to be found in the edition which we possess. Prof. Tyrrell regards the description of this attack on the Areopagus as 'very bald and feeble.' Such a consideration might point to its not being by the same hand as the main bulk of the treatise; and suggest that, without our assuming that it was absent in Plutarch's copy, it might on this ground alone be regarded as an interpolation. But the style of the narrative does not appear to me to differ materially from that of the context, and I should therefore prefer to attribute it to the same author as the rest of the treatise. But, while the narrative may be genuine, we can hardly regard it as authentic. The celebrated story of the proposal of Themistocles to burn the Hellenic fleet at Pagasae is described by Grote (v 27, note 2) as 'probably the invention of some Greek of the Platonic age'; and the present narrative has probably no earlier origin.

ἣν τῶν Ἀρεοπαγιτῶν] He owed this position to the fact that he had been archon in 482/1; see note on c. 22 § 7.

συναρπάζειν] The object of Themistocles perhaps was to inveigle the Areopagus into exposing itself to a charge of attempting to 'pounce upon' an influential citizen. It was one of the things remembered against the Thirty that they 'pounced on' citizens in this way, Lys. 12 § 96 (Newman).

τοὺς αἱρεθέντας] *τοὺς ἀφαιρεθέντας*, if retained, means not 'the persons despatched by the Areopagus,' but 'members of the Council of the Areopagus selected and set apart for the purpose.' *Hist. An.* 6, 22, 576 *b* 23, *ὥρα δ' οὐκ ἀφαιρεῖται οὐδεμία ἀφωρισμένη* (*Class. Rev.* v 164 *a*). *ἀφαιρεῖσθαι*, however, is very rarely used in this sense.

'In Lys. 13 § 23 the *Codex Palatinus* has *οἱ διαιρεθέντες τῶν βουλευτῶν*, where Reiske's correction *οἱ αἱρεθέντες* has been generally accepted; Weidner, however, proposes *οἱ δέκα αἱρεθέντες*' (Wyse).

οὗ διέτριβεν] usually understood as 'the house of' Ephialtes. In c. 16 we have *ἐν τῷ ἄστει διατρίβωσιν*. It need not imply anything so definite as a 'house': it may refer to any public place, such as the precincts of a temple. Ephialtes, on receiving the hint that the Council was intending to arrest him, may well have taken the precaution of being not only in the company of his friends but also within reach of sanctuary in the neighbourhood of a *βωμός*.

§ 4. **καθίζει—ἐπὶ τὸν βωμόν**] On altars as places of refuge, cf. Eur. *Ion*, 1257—1260, *ποῖ φύγω δῆτ';...ποῖ δ' ἂν ἄλλοσ', ἢ 'πὶ βωμόν;* **μονοχίτων**] 'wearing his tunic only,' instead of the *ἱμάτιον* as well. Such a guise would be appropriate to his position as a suppliant. The word is formed on the analogy of *μονόπεπλος* 'wearing but one robe,' 'wearing the tunic only,' Eur. *Hec.* 933 = *ἄπεπλος*, 'without the upper garment'; Pind. *N.* i 74. But, hitherto, it has not been found earlier than Polybius (fragm. xiv 11, 2). It was also quoted from Pythaenetus, *ap.* Athen. 589 F, *Μέλισσα ἀναμπέχονος καὶ μονοχίτων ἦν.* **τὸν βωμόν**] The article is ἐπὶ τὸν βωμόν. θαυμασάντων δὲ πάντων τὸ γεγον[ὸς] καὶ μετὰ ταῦτα συναθροισθείσης τῆς βουλῆς τῶν πεντακοσίων κατηγόρουν τῶν Ἀρεοπαγιτῶν ὅ τ' Ἐφιάλτης καὶ <ὁ> Θεμιστοκλῆς, καὶ πάλιν ἐν τῷ δήμῳ τὸν αὐτὸν τρόπον, ἕως περιείλοντο αὐτῶν τὴν δύναμιν. καὶ <ὁ μὲν Θεμιστοκλῆς — —>, ἀνῃρέθη δὲ καὶ ὁ Ἐφιάλτης δολοφονηθεὶς μετ' οὐ πολὺν χρόνον δι' Ἀριστοδίκου [τ]οῦ Ταναγραίου.

26. ἡ μὲν οὖν τῶν Ἀρεοπαγιτῶν βουλὴ τοῦτον τὸν τρόπον ἀπεστερήθη τῆς ἐπιμελείας. μετὰ δὲ ταῦτα συνέβαινεν ἀνίεσθαι μᾶλλον τὴν πολιτείαν διὰ τοὺς προθύμως δημαγωγοῦντας. κατὰ γὰρ τοὺς καιροὺς τούτους συνέπεσε μηδ' ἡγεμόνα ἔχειν τοὺς ἐπιεικεστέρους, ἀλλ' αὐτῶν προεστάναι Κίμωνα τὸν Μιλτιάδου, †νεώτε-

21 <ὁ> Θεμ. K-W, H-L, B. **22** ΠΕΡΕΙΛΟΝ[ΤΟ]: περιείλοντο K, K-W, B; παρείλοντο H-L. **23** καὶ <ὁ μὲν Θεμιστοκλῆς — —>, ἀνῃρέθη δὲ κτλ K-W. καὶ om. J B Mayor, Blass, (H-L).

XXVI 4 Post ἡγεμόνα adiectivum (velut ἔμπειρον) desiderat Richards, σπουδαῖον Gennadios; an ἡγεμόνα ἔχειν ἱκανόν? **5** νεώτερον: νωθρότερον? Kontos, K-W; idem mavult Herwerden qui ἀνούστερον coniecerat; 'fort. νωθρόν' B; νωθέστερον vel ἐνεώτερον Weil (*Journal des Savants*, Avril, 1891); aliquid eiusmodi desiderabat Wyse; quondam ἀβέλτερον conieci; στρατιωτικώτερον (coll. Polyb. 23, 10, 4 στρατιωτικώτερος ἢ πολιτικώτερος) vel πολεμικώτερον Richards, cf. Plut. *Praec. Ger. Reip.* c. 16 § 22 ἦν γὰρ ὁ μὲν (Περικλῆς) πρὸς πολιτείαν, ὁ δὲ (Κίμων) πρὸς πόλεμον εὐφυέστερος.

TESTIMONIA. **XXV 23, 24** * Plut. *Per.* 10 (infra exscriptum).

---

peculiar. If the 'house' of Eph. is meant, it implies 'the family altar.' Otherwise, some notable altar may be intended, such as the 'altar of the twelve gods' (so Milchhöfer in Curtius, *Stadtgeschichte*, p. cxxi), or that of Ζεὺς ἀγοραῖος. The latter was near the στοὰ βασίλειος where meetings of the Areopagus were sometimes held (Dem. 25 § 23). Cf. Lys. 13 § 4 καθίζουσιν ἐπὶ τὸν βωμὸν Μουνιχίασιν and § 54, ἐπὶ τοῦ βωμοῦ ἐκάθητο.

τῶν πεντακοσίων] added to contrast the βουλὴ of the Five Hundred with that of the Areopagus mentioned in the context.

ἀνῃρέθη] Plut. *Per.* 10 *ad fin.* Ἐφιάλτην ...ἐπιβουλεύσαντες οἱ ἐχθροὶ δι' Ἀριστοδίκου τοῦ Ταναγρικοῦ (*v.l.* -αίου) κρυφαίως ἀνεῖλον, ὡς Ἀριστοτέλης εἴρηκεν. In the same chapter Plutarch quotes and rejects the account of Idomeneus, κατηγοροῦντι τοῦ Περικλέους, ὡς τὸν δημαγωγὸν Ἐφιάλτην φίλον γενόμενον καὶ κοινωνὸν ὄντα τῆς ἐν τῇ πολιτείᾳ προαιρέσεως δολοφονήσαντος διὰ ζηλοτυπίαν καὶ φθόνον τῆς δόξης. Diod. xi 77, 6, τῆς νυκτὸς ἀναιρεθεὶς ἄδηλον ἔσχε τὴν τοῦ βίου τελευτήν. [Plat.] *Axioch.* 368 D, ποῦ δ' Ἐφιάλτης (τέθνηκε); Antiph. 5 § 68, οὐδέπω νῦν εὕρηνται οἱ ἀποκτείναντες.

XXVI. *Cimon.*

§ 1. **ἀνίεσθαι—πολιτείαν**] The metaphorical use of ἀνίεσθαι is common in Ar. *e.g. Rhet.* i 4, 1360 *a* 24, πολιτεῖαι καὶ ἀνιέμεναι καὶ ἐπιτεινόμεναι φθείρονται (with Cope's note), *Pol.* v 1, 1301 *b* 17, ἵνα ἐπιταθῶσιν ἢ ἀνεθῶσιν αἱ πολιτεῖαι, vi (iv) 3, 1290 *a* 28, πολιτεῖαι ἀνειμέναι καὶ μαλακαί (opp. to συντονώτεραι), iv (vii) 4, 1326 *a* 28, πολιτεία ἀνειμένη πρὸς τὸ πλῆθος. The origin of the metaphor (from the strings of a musical instrument) may be seen in *Pol.* v (viii) 7, 1342 *b* 22, ἁρμονίαι ἀνειμέναι opp. to σύντονοι.

For the facts, cf. Plut. *Cimon* 15, ὡς δὲ πάλιν ἐπὶ στρατείαν ἐξέπλευσε, τελέως ἀνεθέντες οἱ πολλοὶ καὶ συγχέοντες τὸν καθεστῶτα τῆς πολιτείας κόσμον τά τε πάτρια νόμιμα, οἷς ἐχρῶντο πρότερον, Ἐφιάλτου προεστῶτος ἀφείλοντο τῆς ἐξ Ἀρείου πάγου βουλῆς τὰς κρίσεις πλὴν ὀλίγων ἁπάσας, καὶ τῶν δικαστηρίων κυρίους ἑαυτοὺς ποιήσαντες εἰς ἄκρατον δημοκρατίαν ἐνέβαλον τὴν πόλιν, ἤδη καὶ Περικλέους δυναμένου καὶ τὰ τῶν πολλῶν φρονοῦντος. The time to which Plutarch refers is later than Cimon's subjugation of Thasos (463 Clinton; 457 Bauer). He is following those who place the beginning of the influence of Pericles at an earlier date than that assumed in the present treatise.

τοὺς—δημαγωγοῦντας] *Pol.* 1274 *a* 14, δημαγωγοὺς ἔλαβε φαύλους.

νεώτερον] possibly means 'rather young'

ρον ὄντα καὶ πρὸς τὴν πόλιν ὀψὲ προσελθόντα, πρὸς δὲ τούτοις ἐφθάρθαι τοὺς πολλοὺς κατὰ πόλεμον· τῆς γὰρ στρατείας γιγνομένης ἐν τοῖς τότε χρόνοις ἐκ καταλόγου, καὶ στρατηγῶν ἐφισ[τ]αμένων ἀπείρων μὲν τοῦ πολεμεῖν τιμωμένων δὲ διὰ τὰς πατρικὰς δόξας, ἀεὶ συνέβαινεν τῶν ἐξιόντων ἀνὰ δισχιλίους ἢ τρισχιλίους ἀπόλλυσθαι, [ὥ]στε ἀναλίσκεσθαι τοὺς ἐπιεικεῖς καὶ τοῦ δήμου καὶ

7 ΓΙΝ (K-W). 10 ΑΙΕΙ (K, K-W).

---

to be the leader of a great political party. But, as Cimon had fought at Salamis 18 years before (Plut. *Cim.* 5), he could hardly have been less than 36 in B.C. 462; and was probably more than 40, if we place his birth in 504 (the date given on p. 39 of Ekker's ed. of Plut. *Cim.*). His birth should probably be placed earlier, as he was *στρατηγὸς* (and therefore over 30) at Eion in 476 (Thuc. i 98). Again, Pericles, who was probably born in B.C. 493, is described as a young man (*νέος ὤν*, 27 § 1), when he made his reputation by accusing Cimon, presumably after the expedition to Thasos, 463. How then can Cimon, who was obviously older than Pericles, and who had won the battle of Eurymedon three years before, be described as 'rather young' shortly after B.C. 462? *νεώτερον* has therefore been generally regarded as corrupt, and various emendations have been suggested, expressive of Cimon's inadequacy for the position of a political leader. The fact that his intellectual development was somewhat tardy is implied in the story preserved by Aristides, ii 203 Dind., according to which his guardians did not allow him to manage his own property until some time after he had come of age (*μέχρι πόρρω τῆς ἡλικίας*), while in Plut. *Cim.* 4 he is said to have resembled his father in *εὐήθεια*. (Cf. Wyse in *Class. Rev.* v 274 *b*.) The combination of *νεώτερον* and *ὀψὲ προσελθόντα* is in itself open to suspicion.

νωθρότερον (which has been suggested) is found in Ameipsias, frag. 16, Pollux ix 138; cf. the description of Chares in Theopompus, frag. 288, *νωθροῦ τ' ὄντος καὶ βραδέος*. See also Schol. to Aristides in iii 515, 8—10 and 517, 28—30 Dind.

νεώτερον is, however, retained by Bauer (p. 101), who suggests that, under the influence of the Areopagus, the leaders of the political parties had generally been elderly men. Mr E. M. Walker (*Class. Rev.* vi 98) holds that the epithet is consistent with c. 25 which implies that Themistocles was at Athens in 462: 'it is only when we recognise that the author ...put the battle of Eurymedon some eight years too late, and that the interval between Tanagra and the five years' truce found no place in his historical retrospect, that we can understand how he came to apply to Cimon in the year 462 those much discussed words *νεώτερον ὄντα καὶ πρὸς τὴν πόλιν ὀψὲ προσελθόντα*.'

πρὸς τὴν πόλιν ὀψὲ προσελθόντα] 'having been rather late in entering on public life.' I am not aware of any exact parallel to this phrase; but we have something like it in c. 27 § 1, *πρὸς τὸ δημαγωγεῖν ἐλθόντος*.

ἐκ καταλόγου] 'from the roll of hoplites,' as contrasted with the mercenary troops that came into vogue at a later date.

πατρικὰς] here 'ancestral.' See c. 28 § 5.

ἀνὰ δισχιλίους—ἀπόλλυσθαι] Isocr. *De Pace* § 87 (of the losses sustained by Athens in her pursuit of supremacy at sea), *τοὺς κατὰ χιλίους καὶ δισχιλίους ἀποθνήσκοντας τίς ἂν ἀριθμήσειεν*; *Pol.* viii (v) 3, 1303 *a* 9, *καὶ ἐν Ἀθήναις ἀτυχούντων πεζῇ οἱ γνώριμοι ἐλάττους ἐγένοντο διὰ τὸ ἐκ καταλόγου στρατεύεσθαι ὑπὸ τὸν Λακωνικὸν πόλεμον*.

ἀπόλλυσθαι] Between 462 and 457 B.C. the Athenians were defeated by the Corinthians at Halieis (458; Thuc. i 105, 1), and by the Lacedaemonians at Tanagra (457; *ib.* 108, 1). The operations in Egypt, which had been begun in 460, came to an unsuccessful conclusion in 455 (*ib.* 110, 1). On the other hand, they were victorious over the Peloponnesians on the sea at Kekryphaleia, and over the Aeginetans in a naval engagement in 458 (Thuc. i 105, 1—2). During the absence of the main body of the Athenian soldiers in Egypt and Aegina, Myronides defeated the Corinthians in the territory of Megara (458, i 105, 4). In 456 the Athenians defeated the Boeotians at Oenophyta, and in the same year Aegina yielded to Athens.

τῶν εὐπόρων. τὰ μὲν οὖν ἄλλα πάντα διῴκουν οὐχ ὁμοίως καὶ 2
πρότερον τοῖς νόμοις προσέχοντες, τὴν δὲ τῶν ἐννέα ἀρχόντων
αἵρεσιν οὐκ ἐκίνουν, ἀλλ' ἕκτῳ ἔτει μετὰ τὸν Ἐφιάλτου θάνατον
ἔγνωσαν καὶ ἐκ ζευγιτῶν προκρίνεσθαι τοὺς κληρωσομένους τῶν
ἐννέα ἀρχόντων, καὶ πρῶτος ἦρξεν ἐξ αὐτῶν Μνησιθείδης. οἱ δὲ
πρὸ τούτου πάντες ἐξ ἱππέων καὶ πεντακοσιομεδίμνων ἦσαν, οἱ
<δὲ> ζευγῖται τὰς ἐγκυκλίους ἦρχον, εἰ μή τι παρεωρᾶτο τῶν ἐν
τοῖς νόμοις. ἔτει δὲ πέμπτῳ μετὰ ταῦτα ἐπὶ Λυσικράτους ἄρχον- 3
τος οἱ τριάκοντα δικασταὶ κατέστησαν πάλιν οἱ καλούμενοι κατὰ
δήμους· καὶ τρίτῳ μετὰ τοῦτον ἐπὶ Ἀντιδότου διὰ τὸ πλῆθος τῶν 4
πολιτῶν, Περικλέους εἰπόντος, ἔγνωσαν μὴ μετέχειν τῆς πόλεως ὃς
ἂν μὴ ἐξ ἀμφοῖν ἀστοῖν ᾖ γεγονώς.

12 *οὐχ* quondam delebat Wyse. **14** ἀλλ' ἢ Blass (H-L). **18** *δὲ* add. K (edd.). post *παρεωρᾶτο* deletum *ὑπὸ τῶν δήμων* retinent H-L. **21** ΜΕΤΑΥΤΟΝ ante corr. (K[1], H-L, B); *μετὰ τοῦτον* post corr. (K-W, K[2]). **23** ΗΝ: corr. K.

---

§ 2. **οὐχ ὁμοίως—προσέχοντες**] The main change was the reduction of the power of the Areopagus. But while, in this and other respects, Athens departed from her previous constitutional arrangements, she retained the limitations under which the archons were appointed from among the first and second classes of citizens. It was not until 457 that the archonship was thrown open to members of the third class.

ἕκτῳ ἔτει] It was in 462 B.C. that Ephialtes overthrew the Areopagus; and 457 is the date of the change in the archonship immediately before the archonship of Mnesitheides. The latter event is 5 years (or in the sixth year) after the former. The change in the archonship is here described as happening in the sixth year 'after the death of Ephialtes.' It follows (as observed by Mr Kenyon) that Ephialtes was put to death in the year in which he overthrew the Areopagus.

ἐκ ζευγιτῶν] Originally the office of archon was open to members of the first class only (cf. c. 7 § 3 and Plut. *Arist.* 1). In course of time it became open to the second class, possibly after the Persian wars, when, according to Plut. *Arist.* 22, the archonship was made accessible to 'all the Athenians,' on the motion of Aristides, who (after the battle at Plataea) *γράφει ψήφισμα κοινὴν εἶναι τὴν πολιτείαν καὶ τοὺς ἄρχοντας ἐξ Ἀθηναίων πάντων αἱρεῖσθαι.* Lastly, in 457 we here have the office open to the third class. It was never *legally* open to the fourth class (c. 7 *ad fin.*). Cf. Abbott, *Hist. Gr.* ii 385—6.

προκρίνεσθαι] 8 § 1; 22 § 5.

κληρωσομένους τῶν ἐννέα ἀρχόντων] *sc.* *ἀρχήν*. Lysias 6 § 4, *ἐὰν ἔλθῃ κληρωσόμενος τῶν ἐννέα ἀρχόντων καὶ λάχῃ βασιλεύς*, and *ib.* 24 § 13, *τί με κωλύει κληροῦσθαι τῶν ἐννέα ἀρχόντων;*

Μνησιθείδης] B.C. 457/6.

τὰς ἐγκυκλίους] *sc.* *ἀρχάς*, 'the ordinary (*i.e.* inferior) offices.' *Pol.* i 7, 1255 *b* 25, *τὰ ἐγκύκλια διακονήματα*, ii 5, 1263 *a* 21, *τὰς διακονίας τὰς ἐγκυκλίους*, ii 9, 1269 *b* 35, *χρησίμου δ' οὔσης τῆς θρασύτητος πρὸς οὐδὲν τῶν ἐγκυκλίων ἀλλ' εἴπερ πρὸς τὸν πόλεμον.* The term had already been similarly used by Isocr. 3 § 22, *ἐν τοῖς ἐγκυκλίοις καὶ τοῖς καθ' ἡμέραν ἑκάστην γιγνομένοις*, and *de Pace* 87. *Inf.* c. 43, l. 3.

εἰ μή τι παρεωρᾶτο] 'assuming the laws were strictly observed'; in other words, the members of the third class were, *strictly speaking*, eligible for the ordinary offices alone; but occasionally by an oversight they were elected to the office of archon. Similarly, in later times even members of the fourth class became archons, although not legally qualified.

§ 3. **ἐπὶ Λυσικράτους**] B.C. 453/2.

οἱ τριάκοντα] 16 § 5.

§ 4. **ἐπὶ Ἀντιδότου**] B.C. 451/0.

Περικλέους εἰπόντος—γεγονώς] *Pol.* iii 5, 1278 *a* 34, *τέλος δὲ μόνον τοὺς ἐξ ἀμφοῖν ἀστῶν πολίτας ποιοῦσιν.* Plut. *Pericles* 37, *ἀκμάζων ὁ Περικλῆς ἐν τῇ πολιτείᾳ πρὸ πάνυ πολλῶν χρόνων καὶ παῖδας ἔχων*

27. μετὰ δὲ ταῦτα πρὸς τὸ δημαγωγεῖν ἐλθόντος Περικλέους, καὶ πρῶτον εὐδοκιμήσαντος ὅτε κατηγόρησε τὰς εὐθύνας Κίμωνος στρατηγοῦντος νέος ὤν, δημοτικωτέραν ἔτι συνέβη γενέσθαι τὴν πολιτείαν· καὶ γὰρ τῶν Ἀρεοπαγιτῶν ἔνια παρείλετο, καὶ μάλιστα προὔτρεψεν τὴν πόλιν ἐπὶ τὴν ναυτικὴν δύναμιν, ἐξ ἧς συνέβη

XXVII 2 ΠΡΩΤΟΥ: *πρὸ τοῦ* Jackson, van Leeuwen; *πρῶτον* Blass, alii (K-W, H-L, K[3]). **4** ΠΑΡΕΙΛΕΤΟ (K, H-L, B): *περιείλετο* K-W, cf. 25 vv. 8, 22. **5** *προύτρεψε* H-L.

...*γνησίους, νόμον ἔγραψε μόνους Ἀθηναίους εἶναι τοὺς ἐκ δυεῖν Ἀθηναίων γεγονότας.* Aelian *Var. Hist.* vi 10, xiii 24, frag. 68. Cf. Isaeus 8 § 19; 12 § 9; Aeschin. 1 § 39. Philippi, *Bürgerrecht*, p. 69 *seq.*

The text places this event early in the public career of Pericles: Plutarch places it later. It has been argued that no such law could have been proposed by Pericles (see Buermann, *Jahrb. f. cl. Phil.* Suppl. Bd ix 624–, 1878; Gilbert, *Gr. St.* i 179; Schenkl, *Wiener Studien*, ii 171; Duncker, *Bericht d. Berl. Akad.*, 1883, p. 935; Busolt in Müller's *Handbuch* IV 1, 141). According to these, the 'law of Pericles' was really a revision of the list of citizens in 445/4 (*Athenaeum*, 1891, 435 *c*). See also Westermann's Introduction to Dem. *Eubulides*.

XXVII. *Pericles.*

§ 1. **κατηγόρησε—Κίμωνος νέος ὤν**] Plutarch, *Cim.* 14, states that Cimon was put on his trial on his return from the reduction of Thasos on the ground that he had been bribed not to follow up his success by an invasion of Macedonia: *δίκην ἔφυγε* (*ἔφευγε*? cf. Plut. *Per.* 10, *ὅτε—δίκην ἔφευγε*) *τῶν ἐχθρῶν συστάντων ἐπ' αὐτόν.* He also quotes from Cimon's contemporary, Stesimbrotus, the story of Cimon's sister Elpinice appealing to Pericles (*οὗτος γὰρ ἦν τῶν κατηγόρων ὁ σφοδρότατος*) in favour of her brother. The result was that Pericles *ἔν γε τῇ δίκῃ πρᾳότατον γενέσθαι τῷ Κίμωνι καὶ πρὸς τὴν κατηγορίαν ἅπαξ ἀναστῆναι μόνον, ὥσπερ ἀφοσιούμενον.* In Plut. *Pericles* 10, he is described as *εἷς τῶν κατηγόρων...ὑπὸ τοῦ δήμου προβεβλημένος*, and as having done less than the rest of the prosecutors to damage the cause of Cimon. Cimon's expedition to Thasos has generally been placed in B.C. 465—3. The date suggested by Bauer for the revolt of Thasos is 459, and for its reduction (*τρίτῳ ἔτει*, Thuc. i 101) 457.

εὐθύνας] 59 § 2, *στρατηγοῖς εὐθύνας.*

τῶν Ἀρεοπαγιτῶν ἔνια παρείλετο] Plutarch, *Pericles* 9, describes Pericles as attacking the Areopagus after he had instituted pay for the law courts at the instance of 'Damonides.' He also states that it was by the aid of Ephialtes that he deprived the Areopagus of the greatest part of its jurisdiction. In the text, which Plutarch professes to follow, by quoting Aristotle as his authority for 'Damonides,' the present attack on the Areopagus is placed *before* the account of the payment of the law courts; and Ephialtes is no longer alive (c. 25 § 4).

παραιρεῖσθαι, in mid., is used of '*disfranchising* persons' in *Pol.* iii 5, 1278 *a* 32, *εὐποροῦντες δὴ ὄχλου κατὰ μικρὸν παραιροῦνται τοὺς ἐκ δούλου πρῶτον ἢ δούλης*, 14, 1285 *b* 16, *τῶν ὄχλων παραιρουμένων* (of the withdrawal of royal privileges on the part of the people), viii (v) 10, 1311 *b* 6, *γυναῖκα παρελέσθαι*, to seduce. In Hdt. ii 109, *π. τί τινος* is used in the general sense of 'taking away from,' 'stealing away from.' In c. 15 §§ 3, 4, and twice in 37 § 2, it is applied to *ὅπλα*.

περιαιρεῖσθαι is similarly used of 'stripping off' and 'taking away,' *e.g.* Dem. p. 246, 23, *ἁπάντων...ἐλευθερίαν περιείλετο*, *Pol.* vii (vi) 2, 1318 *a* 1, (*τὰ τοιαῦτα δημοτικά*)...*ἐὰν δέ τις καταλειφθῇ ἐξ ἀρχαίας μεταβολῆς, τότε περιαιρεῖσθαι τὴν δύναμιν αὐτῆς καὶ ἐξ αἱρετῶν κληρωτοὺς ποιεῖν.* Both words are equally defensible and the MS reading may therefore be retained. We have *περιαιρεῖσθαι τὰ ἐπίθετα* in 25 § 2, and *τὴν δύναμιν* in 25 § 4; we also have *περιαιρεῖσθαι στέφανον* in c. 57 § 4.

ναυτικὴν δύναμιν] *Pol.* vii (vi) 7, 1321 *a* 14, *ἡ δὲ ψιλὴ δύναμις καὶ ναυτικὴ δημοτικὴ πάμπαν.* viii (v) 4, 1304 *a* 22 (immediately after mention of the influence of the Areopagus), *καὶ πάλιν ὁ ναυτικὸς ὄχλος γενόμενος αἴτιος τῆς περὶ Σαλαμῖνα νίκης καὶ διὰ ταύτης* (*ταύτην* *coni.* Susemihl) *τῆς ἡγεμονίας διὰ τὴν κατὰ θάλατταν δύναμιν τὴν δημοκρατίαν ἰσχυροτέραν ἐποίησεν.* The inhabitants of the Peiraeus, consisting mainly of the *ναυτικὸς ὄχλος*, were distinctively democratical.

θαρρήσαντας τοὺς πολλοὺς ἅπασαν τὴν πολιτείαν μᾶλλον ἄγειν
εἰς αὐτούς. μετὰ δὲ τὴν ἐν Σαλαμῖνι ναυμαχίαν ἑνὸς δεῖν πεντη- 2
κοστῷ ἔτει ἐπὶ Πυθοδώρ[ου] ἄρχοντος ὁ πρὸς Πελοποννησίους
ἐνέστη πόλεμος, ἐν ᾧ κατακλῃσθεὶς ὁ δῆμος ἐν τῷ ἄστει καὶ συν-
εθισθεὶς ἐν ταῖς στρατείαις μισθοφορεῖν, τὰ μὲν ἑκὼν τὰ δὲ ἄκων
προῃρεῖτο τὴν πολιτείαν διοικεῖν αὐτός. ἐποίησε δὲ καὶ μισθοφόρα 3
τὰ δικαστήρια Περικλῆς πρῶτος, ἀντιδημαγωγῶν πρὸς τὴν Κίμω-
νος εὐπορίαν. ὁ γὰρ Κίμων, ἅτε τυραννικὴν ἔχων οὐσίαν, πρῶτον
μὲν τὰς κοινὰς λῃτουργίας ἐλῃτούργει λαμπρῶς, ἔπειτα τῶν δημο-

.ᴀ.

6 ΠΑϹΑΝ: πᾶσαν B, ἅπασαν ceteri. 7 ΔΕΙ (H-L, B): δεῖν J E B Mayor, K-W, K[3]. 9 ΕΝΕϹΤΗ: συνέστη H-L: confert K c. 5 vv. 11, 22; 17 v. 15; 41 v. 2, quibus omnibus in locis H-L συνέστη malunt. -ΚΛΙϹΘΕΙϹ: -κλεισθεὶς K, cf. 19, 32; -κλῃσθεὶς K-W, H-L, B. 10 ϹΤΡΑΤΙΑΙϹ.

Testimonia. **14—18** Heraclidis epitoma (Rose, Ar. Frag. 611, 5[3]): τοὺς ἰδίους ἀγροὺς ὀπωρίζειν παρεῖχε τοῖς βουλομένοις, ἐξ ὧν πολλοὺς ἐδείπνιζε. *Plut. *Cim.* 10 (infra exscriptum).

θαρρήσαντας] c. 22 and 24 § 1.

§ 2. **δεῖν**] c. 19 end.

ἐπὶ Πυθοδώρου] B.C. 432/1, 48 years after 480/79. Thuc. ii 2, § 1 fixes the date of the beginning of the war as the Spring of 431, Πυθοδώρου ἔτι δύο μῆνας ἄρχοντος.

ἐνέστη] συνέστη has been proposed, on the ground that ἐνέστη refers to a *bellum instans*, and συνέστη to a *bellum ortum*. Thuc. i 15 § 2, κατὰ γῆν δὲ πόλεμος... οὐδεὶς ξυνέστη. It is true that in Isocr. p. 82 B τὸν πόλεμον τὸν ἐνστάντα...τῇ πόλει refers to an imminent war, but it is equally true that in Dem. 255, 10 (cf. 274, 6) the beginning of a war is expressed by ὁ τότε ἐνστὰς πόλεμος. Cf. Aeschin. *F.L.* 58, ἔτι τοῦ πολέμου...ἐνεστηκότος. The latter phrase is contrasted, in the *Rhet. ad Alex.* 3, 1425 *a* 36, with γίγνεσθαι μέλλων. Ar. *Rhet.* i. 9, 1366 *b* 23, κατὰ τὸν ἐνεστῶτα καιρόν. Φυσικὴ Ἀκρόασις, iv 13, 222 *b* 14, ὁ χρόνος ἐγγὺς τοῦ ἐνεστῶτος νῦν.

κατακλῃσθεὶς—ἄστει] Thuc. ii 13 § 2, (Pericles) παρῄνει τὴν πόλιν εἰσελθόντας φυλάσσειν, *ib.* 14—17.

§ 3. **ἐποίησε—μισθοφόρα τὰ δικαστήρια**] *Pol.* ii 12, τὰ δὲ δικαστήρια μισθοφόρα κατέστησε Περικλῆς. Plut. *Per.* 9. Aristides, ii 192 Dind. Boeckh, II xv; Grote, c. 46, iv 103; Gilbert, *Gr. St.* i 325.

τυραννικὴν—οὐσίαν] Cimon, son of Miltiades, was (on the side of his mother, Hegesipyle) grandson of the Thracian king Olorus (Plut. *Cim.* 4). The fine of 50 talents inflicted on Miltiades was paid by Cimon.

λῃτουργίας ἐλῃτούργει] λητουργεῖν and λητουργὸς are quoted as Attic forms by ancient grammarians (Ammonius 89; Moeris 202; Bekker's *Anecd.* 277, οἱ παλαιοὶ Ἀττικοὶ διὰ τοῦ η ἔλεγον λητουργεῖν); and the forms in λῃ- are found in inscriptions of the fourth century. In 386 B.C. we have [λ]ῃιτουργιῶν, CIA ii add. 554 *b* 14; in the time of Demosthenes and Aristotle, τὰ[ς ἄ]λλας λῃι[τουργ]ίας καλῶς λῃιτου[ργ]εῖ..., *ib.* 557, 5; in 340—332, λῃιτού[ργ]ησαν, *ib.* 172, 4. Meisterhans, *Grammatik d. Attischen Inschriften*, ed. 1888, p. 29, note 174 (Introd. to Dem. *Lept.* p. iii).

τῶν δημοτῶν ἔτρεφε πολλούς κτλ] Plut. *Cim.* 10, τῶν τε γὰρ ἀγρῶν τοὺς φραγμοὺς ἀφεῖλεν, ἵνα καὶ τοῖς ξένοις καὶ τῶν πολιτῶν τοῖς δεομένοις ἀδεῶς ὑπάρχῃ λαμβάνειν τῆς ὀπώρας, καὶ δεῖπνον οἴκοι παρ' αὐτῷ λιτὸν μέν, ἀρκοῦν δὲ πολλοῖς, ἐποιεῖτο καθ' ἡμέραν, ἐφ' ὃ τῶν πενήτων ὁ βουλόμενος εἰσῄει καὶ διατροφὴν εἶχεν ἀπράγμονα, μόνοις τοῖς δημοσίοις σχολάζων. ὡς δ' Ἀριστοτέλης φησίν, οὐχ ἁπάντων Ἀθηναίων, ἀλλὰ τῶν δημοτῶν αὐτοῦ Λακιαδῶν παρεσκευάζετο βουλομένῳ τὸ δεῖπνον. *Pericl.* 9, ἐν ἀρχῇ...πρὸς τὴν Κίμωνος δόξαν ἀντιταττόμενος ὑπεποιεῖτο τὸν δῆμον· ἐλαττούμενος δὲ πλούτῳ καὶ χρήμασιν, ἀφ' ὧν ἐκεῖνος ἀνελάμβανε τοὺς πένητας δεῖπνόν τε καθ' ἡμέραν τῷ δεομένῳ παρέχων Ἀθηναίων καὶ τοὺς πρεσβυτέρους ἀμφιεννύων, τῶν τε χωρίων τοὺς φραγμοὺς ἀφαιρῶν, ὅπως ὀπωρίζωσιν οἱ βουλόμενοι, τούτοις ὁ Περικλῆς καταδημαγωγούμενος τρέπεται πρὸς τὴν τῶν δημοσίων διανομήν. The

τῶν ἔτρεφε πολλούς· ἐξῆν γὰρ τῷ βουλομένῳ Λακιαδῶν καθ' ἑκάστην τὴν ἡμέραν ἐλθόντι παρ' αὐτὸν ἔχειν τὰ μέτρια, ἔτι δὲ τὰ χωρία πάντα ἄφρακτα ἦν, ὅπως ἐξῇ τῷ βουλομένῳ τῆς ὀπώρας
4 ἀπολαύειν. πρὸς δὴ ταύτην τὴν χορηγίαν ἐπιλειπόμενος ὁ Περικλῆς τῇ οὐσίᾳ, συμβουλεύσαντος αὐτῷ Δαμωνίδου τοῦ Οἰῆθεν (ὃς

15 ΤΟΥϹΠΟΛΛΟΥϹ, deleto ΤΟΥϹ. **17** ΕΞΗΝ : ἐξῇ (K-W, H-L, K[3], B). **18** ΕΠΙΛΕΙΠ : ἀπολειπόμενος Richards (H-L). **19** <Δάμωνος> Δαμωνίδου Ὄαθεν Wyse (*Class. Rev.* v 227), cf. Wilamowitz, *Hermes* xiv 320. Οἰῆθεν H-L, K[3] (Meisterhans, 45[2]); Οἴηθεν K-W, B.

19 * Plut. *Per.* 9 (Ar. Frag. 365[2], 403[3]), infra exscriptum.

---

story of Cimon's generosity appears in an exaggerated form in Theopompus, *Philippica* x (FHG ii 293, *ap.* Athen. 533 A), Κίμων ὁ Ἀθηναῖος ἐν τοῖς ἀγροῖς καὶ τοῖς κήποις οὐδένα τοῦ καρποῦ καθίστα φύλακα, ὅπως οἱ βουλόμενοι τῶν πολιτῶν εἰσιόντες ὀπωρίζωνται καὶ λαμβάνωσιν εἴ τινος δέοιντο τῶν ἐν τοῖς χωρίοις. ἔπειτα τὴν οἰκίαν παρεῖχε κοινὴν ἅπασι· καὶ δεῖπνον ἀεὶ εὐτελὲς παρασκευάζεσθαι πολλοῖς ἀνθρώποις, καὶ τοὺς ἀπόρους προσιόντας τῶν Ἀθηναίων εἰσιόντας δειπνεῖν. This exaggerated account is recorded by Plutarch to be corrected on the authority of the present passage. Aristotle's pupil, Theophrastus, was no less careful in adhering to the truth, Cic. *de Off.* ii 64, 'Theophrastus scribit Cimonem Athenis etiam in suos curiales Laciadas hospitalem fuisse: ita enim instituisse et vilicis imperavisse, ut omnia praeberentur, quicumque Laciades in villam suam devertisset.' The excerpts ascribed to Heracleides tell the same story of Ephialtes: Ἐφ. τοὺς ἰδίους ἀγροὺς ὀπωρίζειν παρεῖχε τοῖς βουλομένοις, ἐξ ὧν πολλοὺς ἐδείπνιζε. The text is apparently the authority followed by the Schol. on Aristides, iii 517 l. 30 Dind., τοὺς γὰρ φραγμοὺς ὑπανεῴγνυ τοῖς βουλομένοις ὀπωρίζεσθαι τῶν αὐτοῦ καὶ τὴν οἰκίαν ἀριστοῦσιν αἱρεῖσθαι (?), and *ib.* p. 446 l. 18. Cf. Nepos, *Cimon* 4 § 1.

The various forms which the story of the generosity of Cimon assumed have been examined in *Mnemosyne*, ix 58.

Λακιαδῶν] The δημόται of Cimon, Plut. *Cim.* 4. The deme itself was also called Λακιάδαι.

τὰ μέτρια] 'moderate provision,' Xen. *Lac.* i 3, σῖτος μετριώτατος, *Mem.* ii 6, 22, τὰ μ. κεκτῆσθαι, *Cyr.* v 2, 17, μετριότης τῶν σίτων. *Supra* 16 § 3.

ὅπως ἐξῇ] This implies that Cimon caused his fences to be pulled down *in order to* allow his fellow demesmen to enter his orchards. This constr. is supported by ὅπως ὀπωρίζωνται in Theopompus and ὅπως ὀπωρίζωσιν in Plut. *Per.* 9. ὅπως ἐξῆν would be quite out of place here (Goodwin, *Moods and Tenses*, § 333[2]).

§ 4. **ἐπιλειπόμενος**] ἐπιλείπεσθαι in pass. c. gen., 'to fall short of,' is found in [Plat.] *Epinomis* 978 A. ἐπιλείπειν is far more frequently used in act. in the sense of 'to fail.' In Ar. we have *Eth.* iv 3, 1121 *a* 34, 17, ταχὺ ἐπιλείψει αὐτοὺς τὰ ὑπάρχοντα, and there are several exx. of its intransitive use. ἀπολειπόμενος does not appear to be supported by the usage of Aristotle, as shewn in the *Index Aristotelicus*. More probable than either is ὑπολειπόμενος. Cf. *Pol.* iv (vii) 16, 1334 *b* 39, δεῖ οὔτε λίαν ὑπολείπεσθαι ταῖς ἡλικίαις τὰ τέκνα τῶν πατέρων οὔτε λίαν πάρεγγυς εἶναι, and i 5, 1254 *b* 35, εἰ τοσοῦτον γένοιντο διάφοροι τὸ σῶμα ὅσον αἱ τῶν θεῶν εἰκόνες, τοὺς ὑπολειπομένους (*inferiores*) πάντες φαῖεν ἂν ἀξίους εἶναι τούτοις δουλεύειν.

Δαμωνίδου] Damonides is mentioned in Plut. *Per.* 9, τρέπεται πρὸς τὴν τῶν δημοσίων διανομὴν συμβουλεύσαντος αὐτῷ Δαμωνίδου τοῦ Οἴηθεν (Ὄαθεν Sintenis, collato Steph. Byz. *s. v.* Ὄα: Δημωνίδου τοῦ Ὄαθεν vulg.), ὡς Ἀριστοτέλης ἱστόρηκε. Damon, *ib.* 4, ὁ δὲ Δάμων...τῷ Περικλεῖ συνῆν καθάπερ ἀθλητῇ τῶν πολιτικῶν ἀλείπτης καὶ διδάσκαλος...ἀλλ' ὡς μεγαλόφρων καὶ φιλοτύραννος ἐξωστρακίσθη, *ib.* 14, *Nic.* 6, and *Arist.* 1. Plat. *Alc.* i 118 C, *Lach.* 180 D, *Rep.* 400 B, 424 C. Duncker, *G. d. A.*, ix c. 8; Busolt, ii 443; Holm, ii 345, 17.

Δάμων and Δαμωνίδης appear to be two forms of name belonging to one person (cf. Duncker, *Gesch. des Alt.* ix p. 12, n. 1). As other exx. of double names we have Κλεανδρίδης and Κλέανδρος, Φρασικλείδης and Φρασικλῆς, Εὐβουλίδης and Εὔβουλος, Τευταμίδης and Τεύταμος, Σιμιχίδης and Σίμιχος, Μαιανδρίδης and Μαίανδρος, Θεσπιάδης and Θέσπιος (Hemsterhuys on ἐδόκει τῶν πολλῶν εἰσηγητὴς εἶναι τῷ Περικλεῖ, διὸ καὶ ὠστράκισαν αὐτὸν ὕστερον), ἐπεὶ τοῖς ἰδίοις ἡττᾶτο, διδόναι τοῖς πολλοῖς τὰ αὐτῶν, κατεσκεύασε μισθοφορὰν τοῖς δικασταῖς· ἀφ' ὧν αἰτιῶνταί τινες χείρους γενέσθαι, κληρουμένων ἐπιμελῶς ἀεὶ μᾶλλον τῶν τυχόντων ἢ τῶν ἐπιεικῶν ἀνθρώπων. ἤρξατο δὲ μετὰ ταῦτα καὶ τὸ δεκάζειν, πρώτου καταδείξαντος Ἀνύτου μετὰ τὴν ἐν Πύλῳ

20 ΠΟΛΛΩΝ (K-W, K[3], B): ΠΟΛΕΜΩΝ (K[1]), πολιτικῶν Wyse (H-L). **22** δικαστηρίοις Blass, Richards (H-L), propter ΧΕΙΡΩ in versu proximo positum. ἀφ' οὗ Richards (H-L). **23** ΧΕΙΡΩ (K, H-L): χείρους Newman, Hude, K-W; τὰ πράγματα τὰ κατὰ τὴν πολιτείαν, vel τὴν πόλιν, excidisse putant J B Mayor et Rutherford; τὰ κατὰ τὰ δικαστήρια desiderat Bury. **25** Ἀνύτου: ΑΥΤΟΥ corr. K.

25 * Harp. δεκάζων:...'Αρ. δ' ἐν 'Αθ. πολ. Ἄνυτόν φησι καταδεῖξαι τὸ δεκάζειν τὰ δικαστήρια. Bekk. *An.* p. 211, 31 Ἄνυτος: οὗτος πρῶτος δικαστήριον <δεκάζειν> κατέδειξεν. Schol. Aeschin. i 87 ἐδέκαζεν οὖν διέφθειρεν ἀργυρίῳ τοὺς δικαστάς· ἤρξατο δὲ τοῦ τοιούτου πρῶτος Ἄνυτος. Bekk. *An.* p. 236, 6 (=Etym. M. p. 254, 31) πρῶτος δ' ἐδόκει δεκάσαι Μέλης (leg. Ἄνυτος) τὰς εὐθύνας διδοὺς τῆς ἐν Πύλῳ στρατηγίας ἣν κακῶς ἐστρατήγησεν. Cf. Rose, 371[2], 409[3].

Lucian, *Timon*, p. 157), Καλλιπίδης and Κάλλιππος, Ἀγνωνίδης and *Agnon*, Ἐξηκεστίδης and Ἐξήκεστος, Εὐφρονίδης and Εὐφρόνιος, Μεγακλείδης and Μεγακλῆς, Μνησαρχίδης and Μνήσαρχος, Ξανθιππίδης and Ξάνθιππος (O. Crusius in *N. Jahrb.*, 1891, pp. 385—394, 'Die Anwendung von Vollnamen und Kurznamen bei derselben Person'). Plutarch, *Per.* 4 *init.*, tells us that certain persons said that the first syllable of Δάμων was pronounced short.

Mr Kenyon suggests that Plutarch confused two persons, the musician Damon, son of Damonides of Ὄα, and the politician Damonides of Οἴη, and transferred to the former some of the attributes of the latter. The demonymic of the former would be Ὄαθεν; of the latter, Οἰῆθεν. This has also been suggested by Gomperz, *Deutsche Rundschau*, May 1891, p. 232, and is probably the best solution of the discrepancy.

εἰσηγητής] apparently not found in Ar. Thuc. viii 48, τοὺς καλοὺς κἀγαθοὺς—ποριστὰς ὄντας καὶ εἰσηγητὰς τῶν κακῶν τῷ δήμῳ. *Pol.* ii 8, 1268 *b* 30, εἰσηγεῖσθαι (advise, propose) νόμων λύσιν, and vi (iv) 1, 1289 *a* 1, τοιαύτην εἰσηγεῖσθαι τάξιν, and several times in [Ar.] *Rhet. ad Alex.* Thuc. iv 76, ἐσηγουμένου (τινός), 'on his proposal.'

διδόναι τοῖς πολλοῖς τὰ αὐτῶν] 'to offer the people what was their own'—an easy piece of liberality. In epigrammatic point this phrase is somewhat of an exception to the ordinary style of the treatise and reminds one of Aristotle's manner; but the epigram is ascribed to Damon and the writer does not necessarily claim it as his own. 'The dry way in which the sarcastic counsel of Damonides of Oea, the Ahithophel of his time, is repeated is not unlike Aristotle' (W. L. Newman, *Class. Rev.* v 159 *b*).

χείρους γενέσθαι] The writer is possibly referring to Plato's *Gorgias* 515 E, ταυτὶ γὰρ ἔγωγε ἀκούω, Περικλέα πεποιηκέναι Ἀθηναίους ἀργοὺς καὶ δειλοὺς καὶ λάλους καὶ φιλαργύρους, εἰς μισθοφορίαν πρῶτον καταστήσαντα. Aristotle often refers to Plato in the *Politics* as τινες, *e.g.* in iv (vii) 7, 5, 1327 *b* 38 (W. L. Newman in *Class. Rev.* v 160 *b*).

§ 5. **δεκάζειν**] Lys. 29 § 12, δεδεκασμένοι, Isocr. 8 § 50, θανάτου τῆς ζημίας ἐπικειμένης, ἐάν τις ἁλῷ δεκάζων, Aeschin. 1 § 87, μαρτυρεῖν τὸν μὲν ὡς ἐδέκαζε τὸν δὲ ὡς ἐδεκάζετο. Cf. note on Dem. 46 § 26, ἐάν τις...συνδεκάζῃ τὴν ἡλιαίαν in *Select Private Orations*, ii 139, ed. 1886. Plut. *Pericl.* 9 § 3, συνδεκάσας τὸ πλῆθος.

Ἀνύτου] In 409 B.C. Pylos, which had remained an Athenian post since 425, was retaken by the Lacedaemonians. The Athenians had sent to its relief 30 triremes under Anytus, who however came back without even reaching the place. On his return he was put on his trial for having betrayed the trust confided to him. Diodorus xiii 64. Plut. *Coriolanus* 14, Ἀθήνησι δὲ λέγεται πρῶτος ἀργύριον δοῦναι δικασταῖς Ἄνυτος ὁ Ἀνθεμίωνος προδοσίας περὶ Πύλου κρινόμενος (Grote c. 63, v 465). He is mentioned in c. 34 § 3 as one of the leaders of the moderate section of the oligarchical party. He was afterwards notorious as one of the prosecutors of Socrates (*Anyti reus*).

στρατηγίαν. κρινόμενος γὰρ ὑπό τινων διὰ τὸ ἀποβαλεῖν Πύλον, δεκάσας τὸ δικαστήριον ἀπέφυγεν.

28. ἕως μὲν οὖν Περικλῆς προειστήκει τοῦ δήμου βελτίω τὰ κατὰ τὴν πολιτείαν ἦν, τελευτήσαντος δὲ Περικλέους πολὺ χείρω. πρῶτον γὰρ τότε προστάτην ἔλαβεν ὁ δῆμος οὐκ εὐδοκιμοῦντα παρὰ τοῖς ἐπιεικέσιν· ἐν δὲ τοῖς πρότερον χρόνοις ἀεὶ διετέλουν οἱ
2 ἐπιεικεῖς δημαγωγοῦντες. ἐξ ἀρχῆς μὲν γὰρ καὶ πρῶτος ἐγένετο προστάτης τοῦ δήμου Σόλων, δεύτερος δὲ Πεισίστρατος, τῶν εὐγενῶν καὶ γνωρίμων· καταλυθείσης δὲ τῆς τυραννίδος Κλεισθένης, τοῦ γένους ὢν τῶν Ἀλκμεωνιδῶν, καὶ τούτῳ μὲν οὐδεὶς ἦν ἀντιστασιώτης ὡς ἐξέπεσον οἱ περὶ τὸν Ἰσαγόραν. μετὰ δὲ ταῦτα τοῦ μὲν δήμου προειστήκει Ξάνθιππος, τῶν δὲ γνωρίμων Μιλτιάδης· ἔπειτα Θεμιστοκλῆς καὶ Ἀριστείδης· μετὰ δὲ τούτους Ἐφιάλτης μὲν τοῦ δήμου, Κίμων δ' ὁ Μιλτιάδου τῶν εὐπόρων· εἶτα Περικλῆς μὲν τοῦ δήμου, Θουκυδίδης δὲ τῶν ἑτέρων, κηδεστὴς ὢν Κίμωνος.
3 Περικλέους δὲ τελευτήσαντος τῶν μὲν ἐπιφανῶν προειστήκει Νικίας, ὁ ἐν Σικελίᾳ τελευτήσας, τοῦ δὲ δήμου Κλέων ὁ Κλεαι-

XXVIII 6—7 τῶν εὐγενῶν καὶ γνωρίμων secl. K-W; τῶν εὐγενῶν <ὢν> κτλ Richards (H-L, B).

TESTIMONIA. **XXVIII 15—18** *Schol. in Luciani Timonem 30 (i p. 100 ed. Bipontinae, p. 47 Jacobitz): ὁ δὲ Κλέων δημαγωγὸς ἦν Ἀθηναίων προστὰς αὐτῶν ἑπτὰ

XXVIII. *The successors of Pericles.*

§ 1. **Περικλῆς προειστήκει τοῦ δήμου**] From about B.C. 450 (c. 28 § 1) till his death in the summer of 429. The writer's praise of the policy of Pericles is so briefly expressed, that it hardly arrests our attention. The text implies that the excellence of that policy was not absolute, but relative:—*βελτίω*, as contrasted with that of his successors, which was *χείρω*. The merits of Pericles are here recognised with far less generosity than in the pages of Thucydides. In the text, Pericles is the last leader of the popular party who, owing to his high birth, was acceptable even to his opponents: the decadence begins with his successor, Cleon, who had no such advantages.

πρῶτον—οὐκ εὐδοκιμοῦντα] *Pol.* 1274 *a* 13—15, *ὁ δῆμος...δημαγωγοὺς ἔλαβε φαύλους ἀντιπολιτευομένων τῶν ἐπιεικῶν.*

οἱ ἐπιεικεῖς δημαγωγοῦντες] Schol. Arist. *Pax* 681, *πρότερον δημαγωγούντων τῶν πάνυ λαμπρῶν πολιτῶν.*

§ 2. **προστάτης τοῦ δήμου**] a purely unofficial title, applied to the leader of the popular party. Cf. 2 § 2, and see Whibley's *Political Parties*, p. 51.

τῶν εὐγενῶν καὶ γνωρίμων] We must either insert *ὢν* after *εὐγενῶν*, or understand the words to refer to Solon and Peisistratus, or remove them from the text. In any case Peisistratus, who is described as *δημοτικώτατος* in 13 § 4 and 14 § 1, is to be regarded as a *προστάτης τοῦ δήμου* and not as a *προστάτης τῶν εὐγενῶν καὶ γνωρίμων*. Below, *τῶν γνωρίμων* is contrasted with *τοῦ δήμου*.

ἀντιστασιώτης] Hdt. i 92, iv 164, v 69. Not found in Ar.

Θεμιστοκλῆς καὶ Ἀριστείδης] joint leaders of the popular party, c. 23 § 3.

Θουκυδίδης] son of Melesias, of Alopeke, mentioned below (§ 5) with Nicias and Theramenes. He was ostracised in 444 B.C., and it has been considered worthy of note that the writer says nothing of this fact (*Rhein. Mus.* xlvi 455), but to mention it here would only impede the natural course of the narrative.

τῶν ἑτέρων] 'the opposite party,' used here, and below, to avoid the too frequent repetition of *τῶν γνωρίμων, τῶν εὐπόρων*, or *τῶν ἐπιφανῶν*.

§ 3. **Νικίας—τελευτήσας**] Thuc. vii 86 § 1.

Κλέων] Gilbert, *Beiträge*, pp. 127—146.

νέτου, ὃς δοκεῖ μάλιστα διαφθεῖραι τὸν δῆμον ταῖς ὁρμαῖς, καὶ πρῶτος ἐπὶ τοῦ βήματος ἀνέκραγε καὶ ἐλοιδορήσατο καὶ περιζωσάμενος ἐδημηγόρησε, τῶν ἄλλων ἐν κόσμῳ λεγόντων. εἶτα μετὰ τούτους τῶν μὲν ἑτέρων Θηραμένης ὁ Ἅγνωνος, τοῦ δὲ δήμου Κλεοφῶν ὁ λυροποιός, ὃς καὶ τὴν διωβελίαν ἐπόρισε πρῶτος· καὶ

16 ΟΡΜΑΙϹ, *ἑκάστοτε χαριζόμενος* vel aliquid eiusmodi desiderat J B Mayor. Scribendum fortasse *διανομαῖς*, coll. Plut. *Arist.* 24 (de demagogis post Periclem) *τὸν δῆμον εἰς διανομὰς προαγαγόντες*, *Per.* 9 *μισθῶν διανομάς*, Aeschin. *F. L.* 76 *Κλεοφῶν διεφθαρκὼς νομῇ χρημάτων τὸν δῆμον*, *Eth.* 1130 *b* 31 *ἐν ταῖς διανομαῖς τιμῆς ἢ χρημάτων*, 1131 *b* 30 *ἀπὸ χρημάτων κοινῶν ἐὰν γίγνηται ἡ διανομή*, 1131 *a* 25. **20** ΔΙωΒΟΛΙΑΝ.

ἔτη, ὃς πρῶτος δημηγορῶν ἀνέκραγεν ἐπὶ τοῦ βήματος καὶ ἐλοιδορήσατο... ἐπέστη δὲ καὶ τῇ πρὸς Λακεδαιμονίους εἰρήνῃ, ὡς Φιλόχορος καὶ Ἀριστοφάνης (*Ἀριστοτέλης* Hemsterhuis quem sequitur Rose, Frag. 368², 406³), *προσθεὶς ἄρχοντα Εὔθυνον· Ἀριστοτέλης δὲ καὶ περιζωσάμενον αὐτὸν λέγει δημηγορῆσαι, εἰς τὴν θρασύτητα αὐτοῦ ἀποσκώπτων.* Schol. Aeschin. i 25 "*ἐν τῇ ἀγορᾷ τῇ Σαλαμινίων ἀνάκειται ὁ Σόλων ἐντὸς τὴν χεῖρ' ἔχων*": *ἀνετέθη ἡ Σόλωνος εἰκὼν οὐκ ἐπὶ τῷ ἐν κόσμῳ λέγειν, ὥς φησιν Αἰσχίνης, ἀλλ' ἐπειδὴ οὕτω τὰ ἐλεγεῖα ἀπήγγειλε. Δημοσθένης μέντοι* (Or. 19 § 251) *νεωστί φησι πρὸ πεντήκοντα ἐτῶν ἀνατεθεῖσθαι ταύτην τὴν εἰκόνα. λέγεται δὲ Κλέων ὁ δημαγωγὸς παραβὰς τὸ ἐξ ἔθους σχῆμα περιζωσάμενος δημηγορῆσαι.*

16 Heraclidis epitoma, 611, 6. *Κλέων παραβαλὼν διέφθειρε τὸ πολίτευμα.*

20—23 Locum de pecunia theorica ad iudicum mercedem male transtulerunt interpretes antiqui. *Schol. Arist. *Vesp.* 684 *τοὺς τρεῖς ὀβολούς: τὸν φόρον λέγει,*

ταῖς ὁρμαῖς] hardly 'his wild undertakings' (Kenyon), or even 'his incitations' (Poste), though the latter rendering may be preferred. Better *ses emportements* (Reinach), 'his impulsive ways.' Plut. i 1012, *πρᾳότερος καὶ ταῖς ὁρμαῖς φύσει μαλακώτερος*, *Them.* 2, *ἐν ταῖς πρώταις τῆς νεότητος ὁρμαῖς*. The pl. is found in Ar. *Eth.* i 13, 1102 *b* 21, *ἐπὶ τἀναντία αἱ ὁρμαὶ τῶν ἀκρατῶν*, *Magn. Mor.* i 35, 1197 *b* 39, *ἀρεταὶ φύσει οἷον ὁρμαί τινες ἐν ἑκάστῳ*. In contrast to Cleon, we read of Pericles (Plut. *Per.* 20) *οὐ συνεχώρει ταῖς ὁρμαῖς τῶν πολιτῶν*. But the use of the word in the text is curious, and it is perhaps better to propose *διανομαῖς* which would obviously refer to Cleon's raising the *μισθὸς δικαστικὸς* to three obols.

ἐπὶ τοῦ βήματος ἀνέκραγε] Neither *βῆμα* nor *ἀνακράζω* is found in the *Index Ar.*

The Pnyx was first identified by Chandler in 1765 (*Travels in Greece*, ii 84, ed. 1825) as 'a large semicircular area or terrace, supported by stones of vast size cut into squares, nearly opposite the rock of the Areopagus,' from the centre of which it is distant about a quarter of a mile to the S.W. The excavations directed by Lord Aberdeen in 1822 disclosed a projecting cubic block, hewn out of the rock, and approached on each side by steps. This was identified as the *βῆμα* of the Athenian orators. It has, however, been maintained by Ulrichs (1842), Welcker (1852), E. Curtius (1862, 1868), that this block is an altar, and the semicircular area a *τέμενος* of *Ζεὺς ὕψιστος*. The site of the *βῆμα* is placed by Curtius on the slopes of the 'Museum' hill, due S. of the Areopagus. See his *Att. Studien*, i 23—, and *Stadtgeschichte*, pp. 30 and 61. See also Prof. Crow and Mr Clarke in *Papers of Amer. School*, iv 205—277.

ἀνέκραγε] Arist. *Vesp.* 596, *Κλέων ὁ κεκραξιδάμας*, *Eq.* 137, *Κυκλοβόρου φωνὴν ἔχων*.

περιζωσάμενος] 'with his cloak girt up short about him' (Kenyon), 'with his robes fastened or tucked up, as if he were engaged in some manual labour' (Poste, n). Cf. Plut. *Nic.* 9, *περισπάσας τὸ ἱμάτιον* (with Holden's n), and contrast *Mor.* ii 800 (of Pericles), *τὴν χεῖρα συνέχειν ἐντὸς τῆς περιβολῆς*.

Θηραμένης] *inf.* § 5.

Κλεοφῶν ὁ λυροποιός] He is so styled by Andoc. *de Myst.* § 146; Aesch. *F. L.* § 76; and the Scholiast on Aristoph. *Thesm.* 805, *Ran.* 681 (as restored by Taylor). Cf. Suidas, *s. v.* *φιλοτιμότεραι Κλεοφῶντος*. Aelian, *Var. Hist.* xii 43, says that his father's name was unknown (Mayor). Cf. Lysias 13 §§ 8, 9, 12; 30 §§ 11—13; and *inf.* 34 § 1. For further details see Holden's *Onomasticon* to Aristophanes.

τὴν διωβελίαν] *Pol.* ii 7, 1267 *b* 1,

χρόνον μέν τινα διεδίδοτο, μετὰ δὲ ταῦτα κατέλυσε Καλλικράτης Παιανιεὺς πρῶτος ὑποσχόμενος ἐπιθήσειν πρὸς τοῖν δυοῖν ὀβολοῖν

21 ΔΙΕΔΙΔΟΥ (B): *διεδίδοτο* Wyse, Richards, K-W, H-L (K[2]). ΚΑΤΕΛΥϹΕ edd.: *κατηύξησε* Whibley. **22** *πρῶτον* van Leeuwen.

ἀφ' ὧν ἐδίδοτο τὸ τριώβολον. τοῦτο δὲ ἄλλοτε ἄλλως ἐδίδοτο, τῶν δημαγωγῶν τὰ πλήθη κολακευόντων, ὥς φησιν Ἀρ. ἐν πολιτείαις (adde Schol. *Vesp.* 300, *ἦν μὲν γὰρ ἄστατον τὸ τοῦ μισθοῦ· ποτὲ γὰρ διωβόλου ἦν, ἐγίνετο δὲ ἐπὶ Κλέωνος τριώβολον*, *Vesp.* 88 *ἐδίδοτο χρόνον μέν τινα δύο ὀβολοί, ὕστερον δὲ Κλέων στρατηγήσας τριώβολον ἐποίησεν ἀκμάζοντος τοῦ πολέμου τοῦ πρὸς Λακεδαιμονίους*). Cf. Rose, 421[2], 461[3]. Ceterum Kenyon noster arbitratur schol. ad Arist. *Vesp.* 684 referre partim ad c. 62 § 1 (*τὰ δικαστήρια τρεῖς ὀβολούς*), partim fortasse ad locum tractatus nostri e fine deperditum ubi de iudiciis agitur.

21 *Zenob. vi 29 (Athous iii 151 apud K-W laudatus) *ὑπὲρ τὰ Καλλικράτους* infra exscriptus = *Photius et Suidas, s.v.; fere eadem habet Pseudo-Plut. *Proverbia*, 111. Cf. Boeckh II xv p. 299 Fränkel; Meineke, *Com. Gr.* IV p. 700. Macarius iv 68... *ἐπὶ τῶν καθ' ὑπερβολήν τι ποιούντων, ἢ ἐπὶ τῶν τοὺς πρωτεύοντας ἔν τισιν ὑπεραιρόντων.*

ἡ πονηρία τῶν ἀνθρώπων ἄπληστον, καὶ τὸ πρῶτον μὲν ἱκανὸν διωβολία μόνον, ὅταν δ' ἤδη τοῦτ' ᾖ πάτριον, ἀεὶ δέονται τοῦ πλείονος, ἕως εἰς ἄπειρον ἔλθωσιν. This must refer to the *theoricon*, the fund for paying the price of admission to the theatre at the rate of 2 obols for each of the ordinary seats (Dem. *de Cor.* p. 234, 24, *ἐν τοῖν δυοῖν ὀβολοῖν*). The payment of the *theoricon* out of the treasury of the State is attributed to Pericles in Plutarch, *Pericl.* 9, *ὑπ' ἐκείνου φασὶ τὸν δῆμον ἐπὶ κληρουχίας καὶ θεωρικὰ καὶ μισθῶν διανομὰς προαχθῆναι*, and Ulpian on Dem. *Ol.* i *init.* *τὰ χρήματα ταῦτα τὰ δημόσια θεωρικὰ ἐποίησεν ἐξ ἀρχῆς ὁ Περικλῆς,...βουλόμενος ἀρέσαι τῷ δήμῳ καὶ τοῖς πένησιν.* Cf. Gilbert, i 324.

It cannot refer to the *μισθὸς δικαστικός*, for it was long before the time of Cleophon that Cleon (about 428 B.C.) raised the dicast's fee to three obols: Schol. on Ar. *Plut.* 330; *Vesp.* 80, 300; *Eq.* 51, 255 (425 B.C.); *Vesp.* 607, 682, 688, 797, 1116 (423 B.C.); *Aves* 1540 (415 B.C.). Boeckh, II xv p. 326 Lamb. Probably it was originally one obol and never two. Again, it cannot be the *μισθὸς ἐκκλησιαστικός* as this was introduced by Agyrrhius at the rate of one obol, increased by Heracleides to two obols, and again by Agyrrhius to three (c. 41 end).

διεδίδοτο] '(the fee) continued to be paid.' **κατέλυσε**] either (1) 'overthrew him,' 'ousted him' (K.), 'outbid him' (Reinach); or (2) 'abolished it' (Kaibel and Kiessling, Poland and Haussoullier). (2) is probably right; but we should have expected some notice of the subsequent restoration of the *theoricon*. This omission may, however, be only accidental. Philochorus, ap. Harp. *s. v.* *θεωρικόν*, says that it was restored by Agyrrhius; but this is doubtful. Agyrrhius was certainly concerned with the *μισθὸς ἐκκλησιαστικός* (c. 42 end).

Καλλικράτης] In Zenobius vi 29, and elsewhere (Boeckh, II xv p. 327 Lamb), we read of a proverbial phrase *ὑπὲρ τὰ Καλλικράτους* applied to excessive wealth by the inhabitants of Carystus in Euboea. This explanation of the proverb is quoted from Clearchus. Then follows an inaccurate reminiscence of the present passage in the following form: *Ἀριστοτέλης δέ φησιν ἐν τῇ Ἀθηναίων πολιτείᾳ Καλλικράτην τινὰ πρῶτον τῶν δικαστῶν τοὺς μισθοὺς εἰς ὑπερβολὴν αὐξῆσαι, ὅθεν καὶ τὴν παροιμίαν εἰρῆσθαι.* Possibly the last clause, *ὅθεν—εἰρῆσθαι*, has got displaced and should be placed at the end of the previous sentence, immediately after the mention of the proverb. The first part of the explanation will then run as follows: *φησὶ Κλέαρχος ὅτι Καλλικράτης τις ἐγένετο ἐν Καρύστῳ πλουσιώτατος· εἴ ποτε οὖν ἐθαύμαζόν τινα οἱ Καρύστιοι ἐπὶ πλούτῳ, ὑπερβολικῶς ἔλεγον, ὑπὲρ τὰ Καλλικράτους· ὅθεν καὶ τὴν παροιμίαν εἰρῆσθαι.* In any case it is not absolutely necessary to suppose that the proverb was ever quoted in this treatise. Zenobius misunderstood the passage as referring to the pay of the dicasts, which had been increased to 3 obols about 428 B.C., whereas Cleophon, and *a fortiori* Callicrates, belongs to a much later date.

ὑποσχόμενος—ἄλλον ὀβολόν] If the grant of the fee of two obols a head out of the theoric fund was sufficient to enable all the poorer citizens to attend the theatre, it is not easy to see what object

*ἄλλον ὀβολόν. τούτων μὲν οὖν ἀμφοτέρων θάνατον κατέγνωσαν
ὕστερον· εἴωθεν γάρ, κἂν ἐξαπατηθῇ τὸ πλῆθος, ὕστερον μισεῖν
τούς τι προαγαγόντας ποιεῖν αὐτοὺς τῶν μὴ καλῶς ἐχόντων. ἀπὸ* 4
δὲ Κλεοφῶντος *ἤδη διεδέχοντο συνεχῶς τὴν δημαγωγίαν οἱ
μάλιστα βουλόμενοι θρασύνεσθαι καὶ χαρίζεσθαι τοῖς πολλοῖς
πρὸς τὸ παραυτίκα βλέποντες. δοκοῦσι δὲ βέλτιστοι γεγονέναι* 5
τῶν Ἀθήνησι *πολιτευσαμένων μετὰ τοὺς ἀρχαίους* Νικίας *καὶ*
Θουκυδίδης *καὶ* Θηραμένης· *καὶ περὶ μὲν* Νικίου *καὶ* Θουκυδίδου
*πάντες σχεδὸν ὁμολογοῦσιν ἄνδρας γεγονέναι οὐ μόνον καλοὺς
κἀγαθοὺς ἀλλὰ καὶ πολιτικοὺς καὶ τῇ πόλει πάσῃ πατρικῶς χρω-*

24 εἴωθε H-L. κἂν: ἐὰν H-L. **25** ΠΡΟ.ΑΓΑΓΟΝΤΑϹ. **28** τὸ Kontos, Gennadios (H-L, B qui το etiam in papyro invenit): τὰ K, K-W. ΔΕ ex ΔΕΟΙ corr. βέλτιστοι: praestat fortasse βέλτιστα, coll. 28, 4—et 32, 10. **29** ΑΘΗΝΗΙϹΙ, in titulis ΚΑΛΩϹ semel tantum apparet anno 302 A.C. (Meisterhans, p. 114²). **32** ΠΑΤΡΙΚΩϹ.

28—30 * Plut. *Nic.* 2 (infra exscriptum).

---

there was in increasing it. But the *theoricon* was not confined to the *Dionysia*, it was also paid at the Panathenaea and at all the great festivals (Boeckh, II xiii p. 305 Lamb). Harpocr. *s. v.* θεωρικὰ χρήματα·...ἄλλοτε μέντοι ἄλλως ὡρίσθη τὸ διδόμενον εἴς τε τὰς θέας καὶ εἰς τὰς θυσίας καὶ ἑορτάς, ὡς ἔστι δῆλον ἐκ τοῦ α' Φιλιππικῶν Δημοσθένους (*i.e. Ol.* i).

θάνατον] We know nothing of the death of Callicrates. That of Cleophon is well attested. In 404 B.C., not long before the establishment of the Thirty, he was condemned and put to death on the plea of having neglected his military duty; Lys. 13 § 12, πρόφασιν μὲν ὅτι οὐκ ἦλθεν εἰς τὰ ὅπλα ἀναπαυσόμενος, τὸ δ' ἀληθὲς ὅτι ἀντεῖπεν ὑπὲρ ὑμῶν μὴ καθαιρεῖν τὰ τείχη. The Council, whose temper and proceedings he had denounced, illegally constituted itself part of the tribunal that tried him (*ib.* 30 §§ 10—14). According to Xenophon, *Hell.* i 7 § 35, Callixenus and others, who had prompted the people to put to death the generals who had neglected their duty at Arginusae, made their escape before they could be put on their trial, στάσεώς τινος γενομένης, ἐν ᾗ Κλεοφῶν ἀπέθανεν (Grote, c. 65, v 552).

μισεῖν] Ar. *Rhet.* ii 4. Similarly in Xen. *Hell.* i 7 § 35 Callixenus, the proposer of the motion against the generals who fought at Arginusae, who is there included among those who τὸν δῆμον ἐξηπάτησαν, returned on the restoration of the democracy, and μισούμενος ὑπὸ πάντων λιμῷ ἀπέθανεν.

Mr W. L. Newman suspects a tacit reference to the death of Socrates, cf. Diod. xiv 37, and Diog. Laert. ii 43.

§ 4. **ἀπὸ δὲ Κλεοφῶντος** κτλ.] Isocr. *Panath.* 132 sq.

διεδέχοντο τὴν δημαγωγίαν] Schol. Arist. *Pax* 681, οὗτος (Ὑπέρβολος) μετὰ τὴν τοῦ Κλέωνος δυναστείαν διεδέξατο τὴν δημαγωγίαν (Wyse).

παραυτίκα] Hitherto found only in spurious writings of Ar., esp. in the *De Plantis* and in the *Rhet. ad Alexandrum* (Eucken, *Sprachgebrauch des Ar.*, *Praepositionen*, p. 62, quoted in *Class. Rev.* v 160 *a*). It occurs (without the article) in Thuc. viii 48, 3 and iv 76, 5.

§ 5. **δοκοῦσι—βέλτιστοι γεγονέναι τῶν...πολιτευσαμένων**] This is somewhat carelessly paraphrased in Plut. *Nic.* 2, ἔνεστιν οὖν περὶ Νικίου πρῶτον εἰπεῖν ὃ γέγραφεν Ἀριστοτέλης, ὅτι τρεῖς ἐγένοντο βέλτιστοι τῶν πολιτῶν καὶ πατρικὴν ἔχοντες εὔνοιαν καὶ φιλίαν πρὸς τὸν δῆμον, Νικίας ὁ Νικηράτου καὶ Θουκυδίδης ὁ Μελησίου καὶ Θηραμένης ὁ Ἅγνωνος. The text describes the three as *reputed* to be the best *politicians:* Plutarch describes them as actually being the best *citizens*. The text describes Nicias and Thucydides as ruling the State in a paternal spirit; Plutarch ascribes to them a hereditary affection for it. βέλτιστοι here has a political sense; cf. οἱ ἐπιεικεῖς in § 1, and καλοὺς κἀγαθοὺς in § 5; and see Holm, *Gr. Gesch.* ii 583.

πατρικῶς] 'paternally'; not 'they acted in all their public life in a manner worthy of their ancestry' (Kenyon), but *μένους, περὶ δὲ Θηραμένους διὰ τὸ συμβῆναι κατ' αὐτὸν ταραχώδεις <εἶναι> τὰς πολιτείας ἀμφισβήτησις τῆς κρίσεώς ἐστι. δοκεῖ μέν<τοι> τοῖς μὴ παρέργως ἀποφαινομένοις οὐχ ὥσπερ αὐτὸν διαβάλλουσι πάσας τὰς πολιτείας καταλύειν, ἀλλὰ πάσας προάγειν ἕως μηδὲν παρανομοῖεν, ὡς δυνάμενος πολιτεύεσθαι κατὰ πάσας, ὅπερ ἐστὶν ἀγαθοῦ πολίτου ἔργον, παρανομούσαις δὲ οὐ συγχωρῶν ἀλλ' ἀπεχθανόμενος.*

29. *ἕως μὲν οὖν ἰσόρροπα τὰ πράγματα κατὰ τὸν πόλεμον ἦν, διεφ[ύλαττον] τὴν δημοκρατίαν. ἐπεὶ δὲ μετὰ τὴν ἐν Σικελίᾳ γενομένην συμφορὰν ἰσχυρότερα τὰ τῶν Λακεδαιμονίων ἐγένετο διὰ τὴν πρὸς βασιλέα συμμαχίαν, ἠναγκάσθησαν κ[ινήσα]ντες*

34 <*εἶναι*> *τὰς πολιτείας* K-W: *τὰς πολιτείας* <*εἶναι*> Richards (H-L). **35** Μ(ΕΝ)ΤΟΙϹΜΗ: *μέντοι τοῖς μὴ* K (H-L); *μέντοι μὴ* K-W; *δὲ τοῖς μὴ* B. **38** fortasse aut *ἔργον* secludendum aut *ἔργον ἀγαθοῦ πολίτου* scribendum putat B.

XXIX 1 *πράγματα* secl. H-L. **3** Δ(ΙΑ)ΦΟΡΑΝ: *συμφορὰν* Richards, K-W (e Schol. Ar. *Lys.* 421), H-L (K^3, B). ΙϹΧΥΡΟΤΑΤΑ (K): *ἰσχυρότερα* J B Mayor, Blass, K-W, H-L. **4** *με[ταστήσα]ντες* K; *με[ταβαλό]ντες* Hultsch (H-L); *κι[νήσα]ντες* K-W et B, qui in papyro recte legunt ΚΕ.....ΝΤΕϹ (=*κεινήσαντες*).

TESTIMONIA. **XXIX 3** v. notam proximam.

'they ruled the state as a father rules his household' (Poste). *Pol.* viii (v) 11, 1315 *a* 21, (*δεῖ*) *τὰς κολάσεις πατρικῶς φαίνεσθαι ποιούμενον.*

Similarly Aristides ii 161 Dind. (quoted by Mr Wyse, *Class. Rev.* v 275 *a*) describes Pericles as, in certain respects, *ἐν πατρὸς ὢν τάξει τῷ δήμῳ.*

Cf. *Pol.* iii 14, 1285 *a* 19 (*βασιλεῖαι*) *καὶ κατὰ νόμον καὶ πατρικαί.* i 2, 1253 *b* 10 and 12, 1259 *a* 38, (*οἰκονομία*) *πατρική.*

δοκεῖ μέντοι—ἀπεχθανόμενος] This eulogy of Theramenes is all the more welcome as the traditional opinion respecting him is that he was not much better than an Opportunist. His nickname, *ὁ κόθορνος*, is notorious. He is one of those who have been suggested as the politician referred to in *Pol.* vi (iv) 11, 1296 *a* 38, *εἷς γὰρ ἀνὴρ συνεπείσθη μόνος τῶν πρότερον ἐφ' ἡγεμονίᾳ γενομένων ταύτην ἀποδοῦναι τὴν τάξιν* (*sc. τὴν μέσην πολιτείαν*). See Newman's *Politics*, i p. 470. But it seems more probable that Solon is meant (cf. Susemihl² note 1303).

μὴ παρέργως] *Pol.* (vii) 11, 1330 *b* 11, *ἐπιμέλειάν τινος ἔχειν μὴ παρέργως.* **ἀποφαινομένοις**] *Pol.* i *ad fin.* *πρῶτον ἐπισκεψώμεθα περὶ τῶν ἀποφηναμένων περὶ τῆς ἀρίστης πολιτείας.* vi (iv) 1, 1288 *b* 35, *οἱ πλεῖστοι τῶν ἀποφαινομένων περὶ πολιτείας.* (vii) 14, 1333 *b* 12, *ἀπεφήναντο τὴν αὐτὴν δόξαν.* *Rhet.* ii 21, 1395 *a* 7, *ῥᾳδίως ἀποφαίνονται.*

διαβάλλουσι] Critias is one of those referred to, Xen. *Hell.* ii 3, 30. Cf. Lys. 12 § 78 (Newman).

παρανομούσαις οὐ συγχωρῶν] See Meineke's notes in *Frag. Com. Gr.* ii 867 and 1165, where he quotes Hesych. *τῶν τριῶν ἕν: Θηραμένης ἐψηφίσατο τρεῖς τιμωρίας κατὰ τῶν παράνομόν τι δρώντων.* The text dwells on the kindly feeling of Theramenes towards the whole city: we may contrast with this Lys. 13 § 10 (Newman).

XXIX—XXXIII. *The Revolution of the Four Hundred.*

XXIX § 1. **ἰσόρροπα**] Compare *Eth.* 9, 1, 1164 *b* 4, *τιμή τε ἰσόρροπος οὐκ ἂν γένοιτο*, *De Part. Anim.* iv 12, 695 *a* 12, *ἰσορρόπου ὄντος τοῦ βάρους.* Thuc. i 105, 6, *μάχης γενομένης ἰσορρόπου.*

μετὰ τὴν ἐν Σικελίᾳ—συμφορὰν] Thuc. viii 24, 5, *μετὰ τὴν Σικελικὴν ξυμφοράν* (*ib.* vii 85—87). Dem. *Lept.* 42, Isocr. 16 § 15.

βασιλέα] After the Persian wars *βασιλεύς*, *without* the article, is the ordinary designation of the king of Persia (*e.g.* Hdt. vii 174, Thuc. viii 36). *ὁ βασιλεὺς* is found in this sense in Hdt. i 132, 137 (L and S).

συμμαχίαν] in allusion to the successive treaties with Tissaphernes on behalf τὴν δημοκρατίαν καταστῆσαι τὴν ἐπὶ τῶν τετρακοσίων πολιτείαν, εἰπό[ντο]ς τὸν μὲν πρὸ τοῦ ψηφίσματος λόγον Μηλοβίου, τὴν δὲ γνώμην γράψαντος Πυθοδώρου το[ῦ Ἐπι]ζ[ή]λου, μάλιστα δὲ συμπεισθέντων τῶν πολλῶν διὰ τὸ νομίζειν βασιλέα [μᾶλλο]ν ἑαυτοῖς συμπολεμήσειν ἐὰν δι' ὀλίγων ποιήσωνται τὴν πολιτείαν.‖

ἦν δὲ τὸ ψήφισμα τοῦ Πυθοδώρου τοιόνδε· τὸν δῆμον ἑλέσθαι 2 [Col. 12.]

7 [Πολυζήλ]ου Poland coll. Diog. Laert. ix 8, 5 Πυθόδωρος Πολυζήλου, εἷς τῶν τετρακοσίων (H-L, K^3); ['Επι]ζήλου K-W (B) coll. *Athen. Mittheil.* xiv 398: spatium septem octove litterarum capax, ut nomen utrumque scribi potuerit ΤΟ[Υ ΠΟΛΥ ΕΠΙ]ΖΗΛΟΥ. **8** μᾶλλον J B Mayor (K-W, K^3, B) quod confirmat Thuc. viii 48, 1; θᾶττον H-L; μέλλειν Marchant. [ἄσμενο]ν K^1, vel propter hiatum suspectum, etiam papyri scripturae evanidae minus congruere confitetur K.

10—14 Schol. Arist. *Lys.* 421: πρόβουλοι δὲ πρὸς τοῖς δέκα (τοῖσδε Schol., τοῖς οὖσι Suid., correxit Schoell) ᾑρέθησαν ἄλλοι κ', εἰσηγησόμενοι τὰ δοκοῦντα βέλτιστα (om. Puteanus) τῇ πολιτείᾳ (τῇ πόλει Puteanus) μετὰ τὴν ἐν τῇ Σικελίᾳ συμφοράν (cf. v. 3).

---

of Persia. For the first of these, see Thuc. viii 18: for the second, *ib.* 37; for the third, *ib.* 58 (Grote c. 62, v pp. 330, 346, 373). See also Andoc. 2 § 11—17.

τὴν ἐπὶ τῶν τετρακοσίων πολιτείαν] Thuc. viii 54—97, esp. 67.

πρὸ] either 'in favour of' (Reinach), like ὑπέρ; or 'previous to' (Kenyon). Poste vaguely renders: 'the orator who prepared the public mind for the change.' But, unless sufficient authority can be found for either use of πρὸ in such a context, it may be safer to accept περί, proposed by Mr Wyse.

Μηλοβίου] almost certainly identical with the Melobius who was afterwards one of the Thirty and who joined in the attack on Lysias and his brother Polemarchus, Lysias 12 § 12.

Πυθοδώρου] Pythodorus is the name of the archon in whose year of office the Peloponnesian war began (Thuc. ii 2, 1). It is also the name of a στρατηγός (a son of Isolochus) in B.C. 426/5 etc, Thuc. iii 115, 1, 3; iv 2, 1, and 65, 3, who is described in Plat. *Parm.* 126—130 as entertaining Parmenides and Zeno (*Alc.* i 119 A): this Pythodorus had among his friends one Aristoteles τὸν τῶν τριάκοντα γενόμενον (*Parm.* 127 D): it was hence inferred by Bergk (*Comment. de rel. Com. ant.*, p. 100) that he was identical with the archon of B.C. 404—3. The name of Pythodorus was also borne by a representative of Athens in the treaty of B.C. 421 (Thuc. v 19 and 24). A Πυθόδωρος Ἁλαιεὺς was first ταμίας τῆς θεοῦ in B.C. 418/7 (CIA i 157). The date of the Pythodorus of Thuc. vi 105 (B.C. 414/3) makes it likely that he was identical with the Pythodorus who is mentioned in the text. This Pythodorus, the archon of B.C. 404/3, is identified as the prosecutor of Protagoras, Πυθόδωρος Πολυζήλου, εἷς τῶν τετρακοσίων (Diog. Laert. ix 8, 54). But the name of his father was not Πολύζηλος but Ἐπίζηλος. In an inscription ascribed to the early part of the fourth century Πυθόδωρος Ἐπιζήλου ἐχορήγει (CIA ii 1250); and a pre-Euclidean inscr. at Eleusis bears the name of a ἵππαρχος who was son of Ἐπίζηλος. The confusion between Ἐπίζηλος and Πολύζηλος is paralleled by the corruption of the Ἐπίζηλος of Hdt. vi 117 into the Πολύζηλος of Diog. Laert. i 2, 56 and elsewhere. Cf. *Athen. Mittheil.* xiv 398.

συμπεισθέντων—πολιτείαν] In Thuc. viii 48, 1, Alcibiades assures the Athenian officers who had crossed over to the mainland from Samos, Τισσαφέρνην μὲν πρῶτον, ἔπειτα δὲ καὶ βασιλέα φίλον ποιήσειν, εἰ μὴ δημοκρατοῖντο (οὕτω γὰρ ἂν πιστεῦσαι μᾶλλον βασιλέα). *Ib.* 53 § 2, Peisander asks each of his opponents at Athens εἴ τινα ἐλπίδα ἔχει σωτηρίας...εἰ μή τις πείσει βασιλέα μεταστῆναι παρὰ σφᾶς. On their replying in the negative he says plainly (§ 3) that they cannot hope for any deliverance εἰ μὴ πολιτεύσομέν τε σωφρονέστερον καὶ ἐς ὀλίγους μᾶλλον τὰς ἀρχὰς ποιήσομεν, ἵνα πιστεύῃ ἡμῖν βασιλεύς. *Pol.* viii (v) 4, 1304 *b* 12, (of the 400) τὸν δῆμον ἐξηπάτησαν φάσκοντες τὸν βασιλέα χρήματα παρέξειν πρὸς τὸν πόλεμον κτλ.

μετὰ τῶν προϋπαρχόντων δέκα προβούλων ἄλλους εἴκοσι ἐκ τῶν ὑπὲρ τετταράκοντα ἔτη γεγονότων, οἵτινες, ὀμόσαντες ἦ μὴν συγγράψειν ἃ ἂν ἡγῶνται βέλτιστα εἶναι τῇ πόλει, συγγράψουσι περὶ τῆς σωτηρίας· ἐξεῖναι δὲ καὶ τῶν ἄλλων τῷ βουλομένῳ
3 *γράφειν, ἵν' ἐξ ἁπάντων αἱρῶνται τὸ ἄριστον. Κλειτοφῶν δὲ τὰ μὲν ἄλλα καθάπερ Πυθόδωρος εἶπεν, προσαναζητῆσαι δὲ τοὺς αἱρεθέντας ἔγραψεν καὶ τοὺς πατρίους νόμους οὓς Κλεισθένης ἔθηκεν ὅτε καθίστη τὴν δημοκρατίαν, ὅπως <ἂν> ἀκούσαντες καὶ*

13 *συγγράψουσι*: *συμβουλεύσουσι* Rutherford (H-L). **17** *ἔγραψε* H-L. **18** ΟΠΩC—ΒΟΥΛΕΥCΩΝΤΑΙ (K): *ὅπως—βουλεύσονται* H-L; *ὅπως ἂν—βουλεύσωνται* K-W, B. Cf. v. 24, c. 30, 20, et Meisterhans, p. 212[2].

---

§ 2. **τῶν—δέκα προβούλων**] Thuc. viii 1 § 3, (*ἐδόκει*) *ἀρχήν τινα πρεσβυτέρων ἀνδρῶν ἑλέσθαι, οἵτινες περὶ τῶν παρόντων ὡς ἂν καιρὸς ᾖ προβουλεύσουσι.* Cf. Grote, c. 61, v 318—9. This passage confirms Grote's observation that this 'Board was doubtless merged in the Oligarchy of Four Hundred.' Hermann, *Staatsalt.* § 165, 10 and 11; Curtius, ii 690[6] n. 162 (Germ. ed.). Hagnon, the adoptive father of Theramenes, is described as one of the *πρόβουλοι* in Lysias 12 § 65, and as joining Theramenes in favouring the establishment of the 400. It is implied in Ar. *Rhet.* iii 18, 2 that all of the *πρόβουλοι* lent their countenance to the change in the constitutional government of Athens (Grote c. 62, v 379 n). Cf. Isocr. *Areop.* 58; *Pol.* 1299 *b* 30—38.

The ten *πρόβουλοι* of the present passage are identical with the ten *ξυγγραφεῖς* of Thuc. viii 67, *τὸν δῆμον ξυλλέξαντες εἶπον γνώμην δέκα ἄνδρας ἑλέσθαι ξυγγραφέας αὐτοκράτορας, τούτους δὲ ξυγγράψαντας γνώμην ἐσενεγκεῖν ἐς τὸν δῆμον ἐς ἡμέραν ῥητὴν καθ' ὅ τι ἄριστα ἡ πόλις οἰκήσεται.*

In Bekker's *Anecd.* p. 301, 13, no number is given, but Harpocration, *s.v.* *συγγραφεῖς*, describes that body as numbering 30, and Suidas, *s.v.* *πρόβουλοι*, speaks of 20 being elected in addition to the 10 *πρόβουλοι* to form a body of 30 *συγγραφεῖς*. Hence in the above passage of Thuc. it has been suggested by C. F. Hermann, *Staatsalt.* 165, 11, to alter *δέκα* into *τριάκοντα*. The historian's account is correct so far as it goes, but is less minute than that in the text, which has been followed by Harpocration and Suidas.

Cf. Schol. on Aristoph. *Lysistr.* 421, *πρόβουλοι δὲ πρὸς τοῖς δέκα* (*τοῖσδε* schol., *τοῖς οὖσι* Suidas; correxit Schoell) *ᾑρέθησαν ἄλλοι κ', εἰσηγησόμενοι τὰ δοκοῦντα βέλτιστα τῇ πολιτείᾳ μετὰ τὴν ἐν τῇ Σικελίᾳ συμφοράν.*

The account in the text is in accordance with the statement of Androtion (probably written before it) and of Philochorus (certainly written after it), as recorded by Harpocration *s.v.* *συγγραφεῖς*: *ἦσαν δὲ οἱ μὲν πάντες συγγραφεῖς τριάκοντα οἱ τότε αἱρεθέντες, καθά φησιν Ἀνδροτιών τε καὶ Φιλόχορος, ἑκάτερος ἐν τῇ Ἀτθίδι· ὁ δὲ Θουκυδίδης τῶν ῑ ἐμνημόνευσε μόνων τῶν προβούλων.* Cf. (with Wyse) Schol. *Lysistr.* 609, *τοῖς κ' τοῖς ἐκ τῆς συναρχίας*, and Harpocr. *s. v.* *Ἀπόληξις· εἷς τῶν συγγραφέων ὃν Πλάτων κωμῳδεῖ ἐν Σοφισταῖς* (where Cobet inserts *ι'* after *τῶν*, following Thuc. *l. c.*).

§ 3. **Κλειτοφῶν**] mentioned with Theramenes as a 'pupil' of Euripides, in Arist. *Ran.* 967, *οὑμοὶ δὲ* (*μαθηταί εἰσιν*) *Κλειτοφῶν τε καὶ Θηραμένης ὁ κομψός.* Identified by Holden (*Onomasticon Arist.*) with Cleitophon, son of Aristonymus, who gives the title to one of Plato's dialogues and is mentioned with Thrasymachus in *Rep.* 328 B (where Stallbaum does not identify them). He is named, with Cleon, as *φαῦλος* in Plut. *Mor.* 805, but this is probably a mistake for Cleophon.

τὰ μὲν ἄλλα καθάπερ...εἶπεν...δὲ] This is the regular formula for introducing an amendment to a proposed decree. As examples before the archonship of Eucleides we have CIA i (l. 28), 18, 38, 41, 52[c], 54, 55, 85, 95, 119, 131, 135 (?), 138, 146, 163, 186 (Hartel, *Studien über Attisches Staatsrecht*, p. 221). Swoboda, *Gr. Volksbeschlüsse*, p. 14, shews that amendments are not often found except in Athenian inscriptions. Plato refers to the customary formula in *Gorg.* 451 B, *εἴποιμ' ἂν ὥσπερ οἱ ἐν τῷ δήμῳ συγγραφόμενοι, ὅτι τὰ μὲν ἄλλα καθάπερ ἡ ἀριθμητικὴ ἡ λογιστικὴ ἔχει.*

Κλεισθένης] cc. 21, 22.

τούτων βουλεύσωνται τὸ ἄριστον, ὡς οὐ δημοτικὴν ἀλλὰ παρα-
πλησίαν οὖσαν τὴν Κλεισθένους πολιτείαν τῇ Σόλωνος. οἱ δ' 4
αἱρεθέντες πρῶτον μὲν ἔγραψαν ἐπάναγκες εἶναι τοὺς πρυτάνεις
ἅπαντα τὰ λεγόμενα περὶ τῆς σωτηρίας ἐπιψηφίζειν, ἔπειτα τὰς
τῶν παρανόμων γραφὰς καὶ τὰς εἰσαγγελίας καὶ τὰς προσκλήσεις
ἀνεῖλον, ὅπως ἂν οἱ ἐθέλοντες Ἀθηναίων συμβουλεύωσι περὶ τῶν
προκειμένων· ἐὰν δέ τις τούτων χάριν ἢ ζημιοῖ ἢ προσκαλῆται ἢ

23 ΠΡΟΚΛΗϹΕΙϹ: corr. Wyse, Blass (K-W, H-L, K³). **25—26** ΗΕΙϹΑΓΗΙΗΕΙϹ: corr. K.

ὡς οὐ—Σόλωνος. Isocr., *Areop.* § 16, implies (like Cleitophon) that the constitution of Cleisthenes was identical with, or closely similar to, that of Solon. The text, while correcting the view of Cleitophon, is also a tacit correction of that of Isocr. (*Class. Rev.* v 161 *a*). For ὡς c. acc. of the participle, cf. c. 7 § 4 ὡς—σημαίνουσαν.

For the view that the constitution of Cleisthenes was not democratic, cf. Plut. *Cim.* 15, τοῦ Κίμωνος...πειρωμένου ἄνω τὰς δίκας ἀνακαλεῖσθαι καὶ τὴν ἐπὶ Κλεισθένους ἐγείρειν ἀριστοκρατίαν.

§ 4. **πρῶτον μὲν ἔγραψαν—ζημιῶσαι.** We here find stated in full detail what is briefly summarised in Thuc. viii 67, ἐσήνεγκαν οἱ ξυγγραφῆς ἄλλο μὲν οὐδέν, αὐτὸ δὲ τοῦτο, ἐξεῖναι μὲν ἀζήμιον εἰπεῖν (so Classen, following Wilamowitz in *Hermes*, xii 336 n. 17: Ἀθηναίων ἀνειπεῖν or ἀνατρέπειν, MSS; Ἀθηναίοις Suidas; Ἀθηναίῳ ἀνδρὶ εἰπεῖν Stahl ed. 1874: ἀνατεὶ εἰπεῖν ed. 1883, following Sauppe. The text is in favour of the restoration of Ἀθηναίων or some similar word, instead of accepting the conjecture of Wilamowitz. Ἀθηναίων τοῖς ἐθέλουσιν εἰπεῖν would make good sense, but would involve too great a departure from the MSS) γνώμην ἣν ἄν τις βούληται· ἢν δέ τις τὸν εἰπόντα ἢ γράψηται παρανόμων ἢ ἄλλῳ τῳ τρόπῳ βλάψῃ μεγάλας ζημίας ἐπέθεσαν.

τοὺς πρυτάνεις—ἐπιψηφίζειν] c. 43. The members of the tribe presiding for the time being were thus compelled to put *every* proposition to the vote, undeterred by any risk of penalties falling on the proposer or themselves.

τὰς τῶν παρανόμων γραφάς] The γραφὴ παρανόμων having become recognised as one of the safeguards of the democratic constitution, it was necessary to repeal it before any revolutionary changes could be introduced. Dem. *Timocr.* 24 § 154, ἀκούω...καταλυθῆναι τὴν δημοκρατίαν, παρανόμων πρῶτον γραφῶν καταλυθεισῶν καὶ τῶν δικαστηρίων ἀκύρων γενομένων. Aeschin. 3 § 121, ἡνίκα αὐτὰ ὁ δῆμος κατελύθη, ἐπειδή τινες τὰς γραφὰς τῶν παρανόμων ἀνεῖλον (*Att. Process*, p. 428—437 Lipsius; Hager in Smith's *Dict. Ant. s. v.*).

εἰσαγγελίας] various forms of denunciation, applied to three kinds of legal causes: (1) κατὰ καινῶν καὶ ἀγράφων ἀδικημάτων (Caecilius, in *Lex. Rhet. Cant.* p. 667, possibly referring to the times before Eucleides, see 8 § 4); (2) wrongs done to orphans, heiresses and widows; (3) complaints against διαιτηταί (c. 53 § 6). See Hager in *Dict. Ant. s. v.*; *Att. Proc.* 312 f. Lips.

προσκλήσεις] *inf.* προσκαλῆται. Legal forms of summons to the defendant. *Att. Process*, p. 770—2. In the MS προκλήσεις ('challenges') is a mistake for προσκλήσεις. Similarly in Plat. *Leg.* 936 E, and Dem. *c. Aphob.* iii § 20, προκαλεῖσθαι has been wrongly suggested instead of προσ- (*Att. Process*, p. 884).

οἱ ἐθέλοντες] 'Notetur usus verbi ἐθέλειν pro βούλεσθαι, qui per haec decreta (etiam c. 30) obtinet, ad imitationem veteris linguae, qua vel Solo (c. 35 § 2; Dem. 46 § 14) vel Clisthenes usus erat' (Blass).

τούτων χάριν] *i.e.* for making any proposal which he thought fit.

ζημιοῖ...προσκαλῆται...εἰσάγῃ κτλ.] In all three cases the present here has a *tentative* sense. **ζημιοῖ** implies an attempt to get the speaker fined either by means of a γραφὴ παρανόμων, or an εἰσαγγελία. **προσκαλῆται** refers to the abovementioned προσκλήσεις. **εἰσάγῃ** κτλ. to the fact that, under the first of the three varieties of εἰσαγγελία, the βουλὴ might hand the defendant over for trial by a court, instead of fining him. Cf. *Att. Proc.* p. 45 Lips.

εἰσάγῃ εἰς δικαστήριον, ἔνδειξιν αὐτοῦ εἶναι καὶ ἀπαγωγὴν πρὸς
τοὺς στρατηγούς, τοὺς δὲ στρατηγοὺς παραδοῦναι τοῖς ἕνδεκα
5 θανάτῳ ζημιῶσαι. μετὰ δὲ ταῦτα τὴν πολιτείαν διέταξαν τόνδε
<τὸν> τρόπον· τὰ μὲν χρήματα <τὰ> προσιόντα μὴ ἐξεῖναι
ἄλλοσε δαπανῆσαι ἢ εἰς τὸν πόλεμον, τὰς δ' ἀρχὰς ἀμίσθους
ἄρχειν ἁπάσας ἕως ἂν ὁ πόλεμος ᾖ, πλὴν τῶν ἐννέα ἀρχόντων καὶ
τῶν πρυτανέων οἳ ἂν ὦσιν· τούτους δὲ φέρειν τρεῖς ὀβολοὺς
ἕκαστον τῆς ἡμέρας. τὴν δ' ἄλλην πολιτείαν ἐπιτρέψαι πᾶσαν
Ἀθηναίων τοῖς δυνατωτάτοις καὶ τοῖς σώμασιν καὶ τοῖς χρήμασιν
λητουργεῖν μὴ ἔλαττον ἢ πεντακισχιλίοις, ἕως ἂν ὁ πόλεμος ᾖ·
κυρίους δ' εἶναι τούτους καὶ συνθήκας συντίθεσθαι πρὸς οὓς ἂν

26 *εἰς τὸ* H-L. **29** *<τὸν>* cf. c. 7 v. 8. *<τὰ>* add. K (K-W): *χρήματα* del. Richards (H-L). **33** ΠΑCIN (K): *πᾶσαν* J B Mayor, Newman, K-W, H-L, B. **34** *σώμασι—χρήμασι* H-L. **35** Η ΠΕΝΤΑΚΙCΧΙΛΙΟΙC (ΩΝ written above). Corrector aut *ἢ* non viderat aut delere neglexerat; illud existimat K (*ἢ πεντακισχιλίοις*, H-L et B), hoc K-W (*πεντακισχιλίων*).

δικαστήριον] articulo 'non opus in sententia condicionali' (Blass).

ἔνδειξιν...ἀπαγωγήν] In neither of these forms of procedure was there any summons: hence they were suited to the present emergency, in which *πρόσκλησεις* had been abolished. *ἀπαγωγή* was a summary process, resorted to in certain cases of theft, but also applicable to murderers and adulterers, and to robbers of temples. *ἔνδειξις* was a charge in writing handed over by the prosecutor to the proper authority, who was bound to arrest or hold to bail the person criminated. It was directed against state-debtors, and others who exercised rights while labouring under a disqualification (*Dict. Ant. s. v.*). The text shews that, under the Four Hundred, these forms of procedure were arbitrarily extended to the case of those who attempted to resort to the ordinary legal remedies at a time when they were in abeyance. Cf. *Att. Proc.* pp. 270—280 Lips.

πρὸς τοὺς στρατηγοὺς] In normal cases of *ἀπαγωγή* the delinquent was immediately brought before the *Eleven*; in those of *ἔνδειξις*, generally before the *Thesmothetae*. The Four Hundred departed from those principles in providing that the offender should appear before the *στρατηγοί*, whose jurisdiction was usually limited to military matters. Such a provision may be illustrated by our modern declaration of martial law in cases of emergency.

§ 5. **τὰ μὲν χρήματα** *κτλ.*] Thuc. viii 65, 3, *λόγος τε ἐκ τοῦ φανεροῦ προσείργαστο αὐτοῖς ὡς οὔτε μισθοφορητέον εἴη ἄλλους ἢ τοὺς στρατευομένους, οὔτε μεθεκτέον τῶν πραγμάτων πλείοσιν ἢ πεντακισχιλίοις, καὶ τούτοις οἳ ἂν μάλιστα τοῖς τε χρήμασι καὶ τοῖς σώμασιν ὠφελεῖν οἷοί τε ὦσιν*, and 67, 3, *ἐνταῦθα δὴ λαμπρῶς ἐλέγετο ἤδη μήτε ἀρχὴν ἄρχειν μηδεμίαν ἔτι ἐκ τοῦ αὐτοῦ κόσμου μήτε μισθοφορεῖν, προέδρους τε ἑλέσθαι πέντε ἄνδρας, τούτους δὲ ἑλέσθαι ἑκατὸν ἄνδρας, καὶ τῶν ἑκατὸν ἕκαστον πρὸς ἑαυτὸν τρεῖς· ἐλθόντας δὲ αὐτοὺς τετρακοσίους ὄντας ἐς τὸ βουλευτήριον ἄρχειν ὅπῃ ἂν ἄριστα γιγνώσκωσιν αὐτοκράτορας. καὶ τοὺς πεντακισχιλίους δὲ ξυλλέγειν ὁπόταν αὐτοῖς δοκῇ.* Lys. 20 §§ 13, 16; 30 § 8.

τοῖς δυνατωτάτοις *κτλ.*] The language is almost technical. Cf. (besides Thuc. viii 47, 48, *οἱ δυνατώτατοι*, 63, *δυνάτους* and 65, already quoted) Xen. *Hipparch.* 1 § 9, *τοὺς μὲν τοίνυν ἱππέας...καθιστάναι δεῖ κατὰ τὸν νόμον τοὺς δυνατωτάτους καὶ χρήμασι καὶ σώμασιν.* Also CIG 1845, 44 (inscr. from Corcyra), *ἑλέσθαι δὲ τὰν βουλὰν τοὺς χειριξοῦντας τὸ ἀργύριον ἄνδρας τρεῖς εἰς ἐνιαυτὸν τοὺς δυνατωτάτους χρήμασι* (Gilbert ii 320), and the phrase *ἀσθενὴς χρήμασι* (Wyse).

σώμασιν ...λῃτουργεῖν] Dem. *c. Mid.* 165, *λ. τοῖς σώμασι.*

ἐθέλωσιν· ἑλέσθαι δ' ἐκ τῆς φυλῆς ἑκάστης δέκα ἄνδρας ὑπὲρ τετταράκοντα ἔτη γεγονότας, οἵτινες καταλέξουσι τοὺς πεντακισχιλίους ὀμόσαντες καθ' ἱερῶν τελείων.

30. οἱ μὲν οὖν αἱρεθέντες ταῦτα συνέγραψαν. κυρωθέντων δὲ τούτων εἵλοντο σφῶν αὐτῶν οἱ πεντακισχίλιοι τοὺς ἀναγράψοντας τὴν πολιτείαν ἑκατὸν ἄνδρας. οἱ δ' αἱρεθέντες ἀνέγραψαν καὶ ἐξήνεγκαν τάδε. βουλεύειν μὲν κατ' ἐνιαυτὸν τοὺς ὑπὲρ τριάκοντα 2
ἔτη γεγονότας ἄνευ μισθοφορᾶς· τούτων δ' εἶναι τοὺς στρατηγοὺς

37 δὲ καὶ K, K-W: δ' ἐκ (confusis a librario κ et κ') H-L, B.

ἑλέσθαι...τῆς φυλῆς ἑκάστης δέκα κτλ.] These were the καταλογεῖς appointed to enroll the 5,000 persons to whom the franchise was conceded by the Four Hundred. One of them was Polystratus who is defended in a speech ascribed to Lysias, *Or.* 20, on the 'charge of seeking to abolish the Democracy.' He claims credit for having placed as many as 9,000 on the roll: § 13, ὑμῶν ψηφισαμένων πεντακισχιλίοις παραδοῦναι τὰ πράγματα καταλογεὺς ὢν ἐνακισχιλίους κατέλεξεν. He served for eight days only, shortly before the overthrow of the Four Hundred (§ 14), who in the last resort found themselves compelled to take steps towards enrolling the 5,000. In § 2 it is said of Polystratus: ᾑρέθη ὑπὸ τῶν φυλετῶν. This is explained by the text, in which ten καταλογεῖς are described as elected by each of the tribes. It was supposed by Grote c. 62, v 413, that Polystratus had the sole responsibility of drawing up the list. It is now clear that he was one of a hundred persons charged with this duty.

ὀμόσαντες καθ' ἱερῶν τελείων] cf. Thuc. v 47, 10, ὀμνύντων δὲ τὸν ἐπιχώριον ὅρκον ἕκαστοι (the Athenians on the one part, and the Argives, Mantineans, Eleans and their allies on the other part) τὸν μέγιστον κατὰ ἱερῶν τελείων. Müller, *Handbuch*, v 3, 104. *supra* c. 1.

XXX § 1. **κυρωθέντων**] Cf. 32 l. 2, ἐπικυρωθέντων. The use of the two words in connexion with ψηφίσματα is discussed by Hartel, *Studien*, p. 207 ff., and Swoboda, *Gr. Volksbeschlüsse*, p. 18 ff. The latter has collected a large number of examples from inscriptions (Wyse).

εἵλοντο σφῶν αὐτῶν οἱ πεντακισχίλιοι τοὺς ἀναγράψοντας] Here, and in c. 32 § 1, the existence of the 5,000 is assumed; whereas in 32 § 5 we are told that the 5,000 λόγῳ μόνον ᾑρέθησαν. The latter statement is in accordance with Thuc. viii 92, 11, οἱ τετρακόσιοι...οὐκ ἤθελον τοὺς πεντακισχιλίους οὔτε εἶναι οὔτε μὴ ὄντας δήλους εἶναι. In c. 67 *ad fin.* it had been proposed by Peisander τοὺς πεντακισχιλίους ξυλλέγειν ὁπόταν αὐτοῖς δοκῇ, and this proposal was ratified by the ἐκκλησία in 69 § 1. Mr Kenyon suggests that 'all who could bear arms were provisionally entitled the Five Thousand until a body of that exact number had been drawn up by the board of 100 which was to be appointed for that purpose.' On the fall of the Four Hundred, the government was transferred to a body called the Five Thousand, consisting of all who could furnish arms (Thuc. viii 97, 1). Like the present, this would really be a body of indefinite number; whereas the body of 5,000 contemplated by the oligarchical revolution, though it never came into actual existence, was limited and definite in number. The envoys from the Four Hundred (as observed by Mr Kenyon) assure the army at Samos 'that they will all be members of the Five Thousand *in turn*' (τῶν πεντακισχιλίων πάντες ἐν τῷ μέρει μεθέξουσιν, Thuc. viii 86, 3).

§ 2. **τριάκοντα ἔτη**] This was the age at which an Athenian citizen became capable of belonging to the Council under the regular constitution, Xen. *Mem.* i 2, 35.

ἄνευ μισθοφορᾶς] characteristic of an oligarchy. On the other hand, it is characteristic of a democracy μισθοφορεῖν μάλιστα μὲν πάντας, ἐκκλησίαν δικαστήρια ἀρχάς, εἰ δὲ μή, τὰς ἀρχὰς καὶ τὰ δικαστήρια καὶ <τὴν> βουλὴν καὶ τὰς ἐκκλησίας τὰς κυρίας (*Pol.* vii (vi) 2, 1317 *b* 35). Similarly in the case of the law courts, *Pol.* vi (iv) 8, 1294 *a* 38; 13, 1297 *a* 37; 14, 1298 *b* 18; and of the assembly, 1293 *a* 5—10. One of the causes that led to the fall of democracy in Rhodes was the fact that μισθοφορὰν οἱ δημαγωγοὶ ἐπόριζον (1304 *b* 27).

καὶ τοὺς ἐννέα ἄρχοντας καὶ τὸν ἱερομνήμονα καὶ τοὺς ταξιάρχους καὶ ἱππάρχους καὶ φυλάρχους καὶ ἄρχοντας εἰς τὰ φρούρια καὶ ταμίας τῶν ἱερῶν χρημάτων τῇ θ[εῷ] καὶ τοῖς ἄλλοις θεοῖς δέκα [[καὶ ἑλληνοταμίας]] καὶ τῶν ἄλλων ὁσίων χρημάτων ἁπάντων

XXX 9 *ἑλληνοταμίας—διαχειριοῦσιν* mutila censent K-W. *ἑλληνοταμίας* mutat in *ταμίας* Richards, omisso (ut videtur) *καὶ* quod subsequitur; *καὶ ἑλληνοταμίας* et *οἳ διαχειριοῦσιν*, utpote e v. 13—14 exorta, secludere malui. *καὶ* et *οἳ διαχειριοῦσιν* iure secludit Thompson, sed idem *ἑλληνοταμίας* retinet (*Class. Rev.* v 277 *a*).

τούτων δ' εἶναι *κτλ.*] Here follows a list of official members of the new *βουλή*. They are elected out of the *βουλὴ* for the time being. Mr T. Nicklin (*Class. Rev.* v 228 *b*) suggests that *τούτων* refers to *τοὺς ὑπὲρ τριάκοντα ἔτη γεγονότας*, and that these are the body from which the four councils of 400 each, and the generals &c must come; also that the *ἑλληνοταμίαι* must not at the same time be in the council for the year. This interpretation appears improbable; Mr Kenyon has already pointed out that it involves the insertion of *καὶ* before *τούς*.

στρατηγοὺς] c. 61 §§ 1, 2. **ἄρχοντας**] c. 55. **ἱερομνήμονα**] a recorder or notary. *Pol.* vii (vi) 8, 1321 *a* 34—40, *ἑτέρα δ' ἀρχὴ πρὸς ἣν ἀναγράφεσθαι δεῖ τά τε ἴδια συμβόλαια καὶ τὰς κρίσεις ἐκ τῶν δικαστηρίων...καλοῦνται δὲ ἱερομνήμονες καὶ ἐπιστάται καὶ μνήμονες κτλ.* Hermann-Thumser, *Staatsalt.* p. 99; Gilbert, ii 413.

ταξιάρχους] c. 61 § 3. **ἱππάρχους**] c. 61 § 4. **φυλάρχους**] c. 61 § 5.

ἄρχοντας εἰς τὰ φρούρια] = *φρούραρχοι*, the commanders of Athenian garrisons. c. 24 § 3. Gilbert, *Gr. St.* i 400.

ταμίας τῶν ἱερῶν χρημάτων τῇ θεῷ καὶ τοῖς ἄλλοις θεοῖς δέκα] At Athens the treasures of the various temples were under the charge of officials called *ταμίαι τῶν ἱερῶν χρημάτων* (cf. Ar. *Pol.* vii (vi) 8, 1322 *b* 25). The most important of these treasures was that of Athene on the Acropolis. The officials in charge of this were called *ταμίαι τῆς θεοῦ* or *τῶν τῆς θεοῦ, ταμίαι τῶν ἱερῶν χρημάτων τῆς Ἀθηναίας, ταμίαι τῶν ἱερῶν χρημάτων τῆς θεοῦ*. They are first mentioned in Hdt. viii 51 at the time of the battle of Salamis, *ταμίας τοῦ ἱεροῦ*; also in documents relating to the transfer of the treasure from one body of officials to their successors, from the date of the consecration of the Parthenon to 406 B.C.; in public accounts previous to Euclides; in Dem. *Macart.* p. 1075, 2, and Aeschin. *Timarch.* p. 127 § 110; lastly in inscriptions belonging to B.C. 385, 325 and 300. Similarly, every temple had its special treasurers who, together with its superintendents (*ἐπιστάται*) and sacrificers (*ἱεροποιοί*), had the money of the same under their care.

In 435—4 B.C. (CIA i 32) these several treasurers of the temples, with the exception of those of the temple of Athene, were all united into a single board called *ταμίαι τῶν θεῶν* or *τῶν ἄλλων θεῶν*. From this date all the sacred moneys were kept in the Acropolis, but the treasures of Athene and those of the other divinities were generally under separate officials. Dem. *Timocr.* p. 743, 1, *οἱ ταμίαι ἐφ' ὧν ὁ Ὀπισθόδομος ἐνεπρήσθη, καὶ οἱ τῶν τῆς θεοῦ καὶ οἱ τῶν ἄλλων θεῶν*. Nevertheless we find that both were united for a time as one board of officers, as in the text, and in a decree quoted in Andocides *de Myst.* p. 36, *τοὺς ταμίας τῆς θεοῦ καὶ τῶν ἄλλων θεῶν*. In inscriptions ascribed to B.C. 401, 400, 399—397 they are called *ταμίαι τῶν ἱερῶν χρημάτων τῆς Ἀθηνᾶς καὶ τῶν ἄλλων θεῶν*, and are (as here) in 411 B.C. ten in number. In 385 the treasurers of the goddess again became a separate board of Ten, who were independent of the treasurers of the other deities (see Boeckh II v, 217—220 Lamb, and Gilbert, *Gr. St.* i 234—5).

The *ταμίαι* have been mentioned in c. 4 § 2, c. 7 § 3, c. 8 § 1. They are called *οἱ ταμίαι τῆς Ἀθηνᾶς* in c. 47 § 1, and simply *οἱ ταμίαι* in c. 60 § 3.

ἑλληνοταμίας] obviously corrupt. These officials are immediately afterwards described as excluded from the Council and they could not possibly be here enumerated among its official members.

That portion of the treasures on the Acropolis which, in contrast to the *ἱερὰ χρήματα*, was known as *ὅσια χρήματα*, was according to Suidas (*s. v.* *ταμίαι*, art. 1) entrusted to 'the treasurers chosen by lot who had the care of the statue of Athene.' Thus the public money was ordinarily kept by the *ταμίαι τῆς θεοῦ*, who were often called *ταμίαι* alone (Boeckh εἴκοσι[[ν οἳ διαχειριοῦσιν]] καὶ ἱεροποιοὺς καὶ ἐπιμελητὰς δέκα ἑκατέρους· αἱρεῖσθαι δὲ πάντας τούτους ἐκ προκρίτων, ἐκ τῶν ἀεὶ βουλευόντων πλείους προκρίνοντας, τὰς δ' ἄλλας ἀρχὰς ἁπάσας κληρωτὰς εἶναι καὶ μὴ ἐκ τῆς βουλῆς· τοὺς δὲ ἑλληνοταμίας οἳ ἂν διαχειρίζωσι τὰ χρήματα μὴ συμβουλεύειν. βουλὰς δὲ ποιῆσαι 3

10 διαχειριοῦσι H-L. **13** ΕΑΝ.

Testimonia. **13—14** *Harp. ἑλληνοταμίαι: ... ὅτι ἀρχή τις ἦν οἱ ἑλληνοταμίαι, οἳ διεχείριζον τὰ χρήματα, καὶ 'Αρ. δηλοῖ ἐν τῇ 'Αθ. πολ.

---

l. c. p. 221—2). In the text, with a view to multiplying the official members of the 400, a separate board of 20 is mentioned.

Mr Kenyon infers from the present passage that separate *ταμίαι τῶν ὁσίων χρημάτων* formed part of the ordinary Athenian constitution; in the absence of evidence it is perhaps better to regard them as a special body created by the oligarchical revolution.

ἱεροποιούς] c. 64 § 6. Gilbert, *Gr. St.* i 249. *Pol.* vii (vi) 8, 1322 *b* 22—25, *συμβαίνει τὴν ἐπιμέλειαν ταύτην (τὴν περὶ τοὺς θεοὺς) ἐνιαχοῦ μὲν εἶναι μίαν...ἐνιαχοῦ δὲ πολλὰς καὶ κεχωρισμένας τῆς ἱερωσύνης, οἷον ἱεροποιοὺς καὶ ναοφύλακας καὶ ταμίας τῶν ἱερῶν χρημάτων.*

ἐπιμελητάς] *Pol.* vii (vi) 8, 1322 *b* 19, *ἄλλο δ' εἶδος ἐπιμελείας ἡ περὶ τοὺς θεούς, οἷον ἱερεῖς τε καὶ ἐπιμεληταὶ τῶν περὶ τὰ ἱερὰ τοῦ σῴζεσθαί τε τὰ ὑπάρχοντα καὶ ἀνορθοῦσθαι τὰ πίπτοντα τῶν οἰκοδομημάτων καὶ τῶν ἄλλων ὅσα τέτακται πρὸς τοὺς θεούς.* The *ἱεροποιοί*, the *ναοφύλακες* and the *ταμίαι τῶν ἱερῶν χρημάτων* are in *Pol. l. c.* separate officials entrusted with this *ἐπιμέλεια*. The term *ἐπιμελητής* is vague, but the context implies that the official here meant was connected with matters of public ritual.

αἱρεῖσθαι—ἐκ προκρίτων] 'and that they (the Council, c. 31, 15) should appoint all these officials out of a number of selected candidates, choosing a larger number (than those actually required) out of the members of the Council for the time being.' All the officials enumerated were to be members of the Council of 400, and the Council itself was (1) to nominate candidates out of its own body to succeed these officials and (2) to choose such successors out of the number so nominated.

ἑλληνοταμίας] it is probably this passage, and not the corrupt passage a few lines earlier, that is the source of Harpocration's notice *s. v.* Mr Kenyon leaves both passages as they stand in the MS; he points out the inconsistency between them in his commentary and endeavours to remove it in the notes to his Translation:—"If this is not to be taken as directly contradicting the statement made just above, it must be supposed that the actual handling of the money was confined to a few of the Hellenotamiae (probably in rotation), the duties of the rest being to advise and superintend." The *Hellenotamiae*, or special board for the management of the tributes, existed from the time of the formation of the confederacy of Delos and lasted to the end of the Peloponnesian war. They are frequently mentioned in inscriptions down to the time of the anarchy. On the restoration of the democracy, the office was not revived, as the *ἡγεμονία* of Athens, and the duty of paying tribute on the part of her allies, had come to an end.

In 410/9 we know of eleven Hellenotamiae, three of them from one tribe alone, and two others from another tribe: Two of the tribe Acamantis were Hellenotamiae in the same prytaneia, and the two of the tribe Aeantis were similarly holding office at the same time. Boeckh supposes that in their appointment no regard was paid to the tribes (II vii p. 243 Lamb). Cf. Gilbert, *Gr. St.* i 236.

§ 3. **βουλὰς—τέτταρας**] *i.e.* four Councils of 400 each, each of the four holding office for one year (*εἰς ἐνιαυτὸν inf.*). The order in which they were to hold office was to be decided by lot (cf. *τὸ λαχὸν μέρος*). The one hundred who had drawn up the constitution were to distribute themselves and 'the rest,' *i.e.* the rest of the 5,000 above the age of thirty, into four divisions of 400 each. At the end of c. 31 provision is made for the future 'in order that the 400 may be distributed over the four divisions (*εἰς τὰς τέτταρας λήξεις*),' one hundred being assigned by lot to each of the four divisions of 400.

The total number of the officials above

τέτταρας ἐκ τῆς ἡλικίας τῆς εἰρημένης εἰς τὸν λοιπὸν χρόνον, καὶ τούτων τὸ λαχὸν μέρος βουλεύειν, νεῖμαι δὲ καὶ τοὺς ἄλλους πρὸς τὴν λῆξιν ἑκάστην. τοὺς δ' ἑκατὸν ἄνδρας διανεῖμαι σφᾶς τε αὐτοὺς καὶ τοὺς ἄλλους τέτταρα μέρη ὡς ἰσαίτατα καὶ διακληρῶσαι,
4 καὶ εἰς ἐνιαυτὸν βουλεύειν. <βουλεύεσθαι> δὲ ᾗ ἂν δοκῇ αὐτοῖς ἄριστα ἕξειν περί τε τῶν χρημάτων, ὅπως ἂν σῶα ᾖ καὶ εἰς τὸ δέον ἀναλίσκηται, καὶ περὶ τῶν ἄλλων ὡς ἂν δύνωνται ἄριστα· ἐὰν δέ τι 'θέλωσιν βουλεύσασθαι μετὰ πλειόνων, ἐπεισκαλεῖν ἕκαστον ἐπείσκλητον ὃν ἂν ἐθέλῃ τῶν ἐκ τῆς αὐτῆς ἡλικίας· τὰς δ' ἕδρας ποιεῖν τῆς βουλῆς κατὰ πενθήμερον ἐὰν μὴ δέωνται πλειόνων.

16 ΔΟΥΛΕΥΕΙΝ. **19** βουλεύειν. <βουλεύειν> δὲ K; βουλεύειν <τοὺς λαχόντας· πράττειν> δὲ K-W; βουλεύεσθαι ᾗ ἂν δοκῇ κτλ Richards (H-L). malui βουλεύειν. <βουλεύεσθαι> δὲ scribere. βουλεύειν <τοὺς λαχόντας· βουλεύεσθαι> δὲ Blass. **20** ϹΩΑ; et σῶος et σῶς in titulis Atticis exstant (Meisterhans, pp. 52², 117²): σῷα K-W. **21—22** ΕΑΝΤΙ: κἄν τι K; ἐὰν <δέ> τι J B Mayor, K-W, H-L, B. **22** ἐθέλωσι H-L, K.

23 ΕΠΕΙϹΕΚΛΗΤΟΝ corr. K. **24** ΠΕΝΘΗΜΙΜΕΡΟΝ corr. K.

23—24 Hesych. ἕδραι βουλῆς: αἳ ἐγίνοντο κατὰ πενταήμερον.

---

enumerated is as follows, if we assume that the numbers were in every case the same as usual:

στρατηγοί (10), ἄρχοντες (9), ἱερομνήμων (1), ταξίαρχοι (10), ἵππαρχοι (2, 1 in 31, 14), φύλαρχοι (10), ἄρχοντες εἰς τὰ φρούρια (?), ταμίαι τῶν ἱερῶν χρημάτων (10), ταμίαι τῶν ὁσίων χρ. (20), ἱεροποιοί (10), ἐπιμεληταί (10), making 92 out of a total of perhaps 100.

The ἄρχοντες εἰς τὰ φρούρια were possibly eight in number, in which case they may have represented the 8 tribes not represented by the 2 ἵππαρχοι. Thus η may have dropped out after φρούρια (l. 7). But it is more probable that there was only one ἵππαρχος under this constitution and therefore 9 ἄρχοντες εἰς τὰ φρούρια, in which case θ may be the missing number. This is confirmed by the fact that the number of Attic φρούρια known to us is exactly nine, Eleusis, Anaphlystus, Sunium, Thoricus, Panactum, Oenoe, Phyle, Aphidna and Rhamnus (Boeckh, II x; the evidence for the last two belongs to the times of Philip).

εἰς τὸν λοιπὸν χρόνον] = εἰς τὸν μέλλοντα χρόνον c. 31 § 1.

τοὺς ἄλλους] probably, not the 300 co-opted by the 100 (Thuc. viii 67, 3), but the rest of the 5,000.

διανεῖμαι...τέτταρα μέρη] c. 21 § 4, διένειμε...τριάκοντα μέρη.

ὡς ἰσαίτατα] Plat. *Leg.* 744 C. **διακληρῶσαι**, to 'assign them by lot,' Thuc. viii 30, 1, διακληρωσάμενοι, 'having drawn lots,' vi 42, τρία μέρη νείμαντες ἓν ἑκάστῳ ἐκλήρωσαν.

§ 4. **σῶα**] The evidence of inscriptions shews that σῶος and σῶς were alike in use (Meisterhans, *Gr.* p. 117 ed. 1888). Cf. Dem. *Lept.* § 142 note. The codex Σ of Dem. has nom. masc. **σῶς** in *Mid.* 126, *Aristocr.* 131; neut. σῶν *Lept.* 142; acc. pl. σῶς in *Pac.* 17, *Chers.* 15; gen. sing. σώας *F.L.* 78; pl. **σῶοι** in *F.L.* 57, 153, 326; acc. sing. σώαν *Mid.* 177; pl. nom. **σῶιοι** *Cor.* 49, *Phil.* iii 70, *Timocr.* 106 (Voemel, *Proleg. Gramm. in Dem. Cont.* § 33).

εἰς τὸ δέον ἀναλίσκηται] Aristoph. *Nub.* 859, εἰς τὸ δέον ἀπώλεσα, Dem. *Ol.* 3, 28, ἀνηλώκαμεν εἰς οὐδὲν δέον, Plut. *Per.* 23.

ἐπεισκαλεῖν (to co-opt) and **ἐπείσκλητον** are only found in this passage.

ἕδρας] c. 4 § 3. It is the technical term. CIA i 31, 7; 59, 41; ii 800 *b* 15 cet. (Mayor).

κατὰ πενθήμερον] not 'for five days at a time'; but 'once every five days'; cf. κατ' ἐνιαυτόν ('year by year'), κατὰ μῆνα, καθ' ἡμέραν ('daily,' Thuc. vii 8 § 1 and 50 § 3). Mr Poste extracts *both* senses out of the passage: 'the sessions of the council shall be for five days at a time with intervals of five days.' Under the democracy the βουλή met daily except on public holidays (43 § 3).

πλειόνων, *sc.* ἑδρῶν.

*κληροῦν δὲ τὴν βουλὴν τοὺς ἐννέα ἄρχοντας, τὰς δὲ χειροτονίας
κρίνειν πέντε τοὺς λαχόντας ἐκ τῆς βουλῆς, καὶ ἐκ τούτων ἕνα
κληροῦσθαι καθ' ἑκάστην <τὴν> ἡμέραν τὸν ἐπιψηφιοῦντα. κλη-* 5
*ροῦν δὲ τοὺς λαχόντας πέντε τοὺς ἐθέλοντας προσελθεῖν ἐναντίον
τῆς βουλῆς, πρῶτον μὲν ἱερῶν, δεύτερον δὲ κήρυξιν, τρίτον πρεσ-
βείαις, τέταρτον τῶν ἄλλων· τὰ δὲ τοῦ πολέμου ὅταν δέῃ ἀκληρωτὶ
προσαγαγόντας τοὺς στρατηγοὺς χρηματίζεσθαι. τὸν δὲ μὴ ἰόντα* 6
*εἰς τὸ βουλευτήριον τῶν βουλευόντων τὴν ὥραν τὴν προρρηθεῖσαν
ὀφείλειν δραχμὴν τῆς ἡμέρας ἑκάστης, ἐὰν μὴ εὑρόμενος ἄφεσιν
τῆς βουλῆς ἀπῇ.* ||

25 'an *πλήρουν?*' K-W. **27** *τὴν* addidit B. **29** ΠΡΕϹΒΕΙΑΙ: *πρεσβείαις* Wyse, K-W, H-L, K[3], B. **33** *εὑρόμενος* Tyrrell et Richards (H-L, B); ΕΥΡΙϹΚΟΜΕΝΟϹ (K, K-W).

κληροῦν . . τὴν βουλὴν τοὺς ἐννέα ἄρχοντας] This means either (1) that the Council is to appoint the archons by lot, or (2) the archons are to superintend the sortition of the Council. (1) is followed by Kaibel and Kiessling, and also by Poland; (2) by Mr Poste and Mr Kenyon. In (1) the order is verb, subject, object, just as in § 5 *κληροῦν τοὺς λαχόντας πέντε τοὺς ἐθέλοντας*; and this is supported by the context. We are first told how the Council is constituted, and next what it has to do. But this view is open to a fatal objection. The Council cannot appoint the archons by lot, because under the present constitution the archons are chosen out of a select list (§ 2, l. 11). We must therefore suppose that the archons were to superintend the sortition of the Council. Those of the 5,000, who were over 30 years of age, have already been divided into four groups determined by lot (§ 3). The archons in each year have to draw lots for appointing 400 out of each of these groups to serve on one of the four successive Councils. M. Th. Reinach regards this sentence as an interpolation.

For *πληροῦν*, which has been proposed in place of *κληροῦν*, cf. *δικαστήρια πληροῦν* in Dem. 24 § 92, 21 § 209, and Isaeus 6 § 37; also Arist. *Eccl.* 89, *πληρουμένης ἐκκλησίας*.

χειροτονίας κρίνειν] 'decide divisions taken by show of hands.' The five functionaries act as 'tellers.' One of them is appointed by lot for each of the five days during which the Council sits, 'to put questions to the vote,' *i.e.* to act as president or chairman.

§ 5. **κληροῦν—βουλῆς**] These five persons were to determine by lot the order of precedence among those who wished to appear before the Council.

ἱερῶν ... κήρυξιν ... πρεσβείᾳ ... τῶν ἄλλων] The two alternative constructions are arranged in the order of a *chiasmus* or introverted parallelism, the two nearest and the two furthest terms corresponding in construction. Apart from love of variety there is no apparent reason for this change. Exactly the same order and the same variety of expression is found in the statement of the proceedings in the *ἐκκλησία* in c. 43 § 6, *ἱερῶν...κήρυξιν καὶ πρεσβείαις ... ὁσίων*. Cf. also Aeschin. *Timarch.* 23, *προχειροτονεῖν κελεύει τοὺς προέδρους περὶ ἱερῶν τῶν πατρίων καὶ ὁσίων καὶ κήρυξι καὶ πρεσβείαις*.

§ 6. **τὴν ὥραν**] not 'the hour,' but 'the time'; the use of *ὥρα* for 'hour' is not earlier than the Alexandrine age.

ὀφείλειν δραχμὴν] the infliction of a fine for non-attendance is characteristic of an oligarchy. *Pol.* vi (iv) 9, 1294 *a* 38, (of law courts) *ἐν μὲν γὰρ ταῖς ὀλιγαρχίαις τοῖς εὐπόροις ζημίαν τάττουσιν, ἂν μὴ δικάζωσι, τοῖς δ' ἀπόροις οὐδένα μισθόν*, cf. 1298 *b* 17. It is one of the devices of aristocracies mentioned *ib.* 13, 1297 *a* 17, *ζημίαν ἐπικεῖσθαι τοῖς εὐπόροις, ἐὰν μὴ ἐκκλησιάζωσιν*. Fines for non-attendance at the *βουλὴ* in particular are apparently not mentioned in the *Politics*.

εὑρισκόμενος, 'in the enjoyment of leave of absence,' is less likely to be right than **εὑρόμενος**, 'having obtained for himself leave of absence.'

ἄφεσιν] not found in this sense in Ar. The corresponding adj. *ἀφέσιμος* occurs in c. 43 § 3.

[Col. 13.] **31.** *ταύτην μὲν οὖν εἰς τὸν μέλλοντα χρόνον ἀνέγραψαν τὴν πολιτείαν, ἐν δὲ τῷ παρόντι καιρῷ τήνδε· βουλεύειν μὲν τετρακοσίους κατὰ τὰ πάτρια, τετταράκοντα ἐξ ἑκάστης <τῆς> φυλῆς, ἐκ προκρίτων [ο]ὓς ἂν ἕλωνται οἱ φυλέται τῶν ὑπὲρ τριάκοντα ἔτη γεγονότων. τούτους δὲ τάς τε ἀρχὰς καταστῆσαι καὶ περὶ τοῦ ὅρκου ὅντινα χρὴ ὀμόσαι γράψαι, <καὶ> περὶ τῶν νόμων καὶ τῶν εὐθυ[ν]ῶν καὶ τῶν ἄλλων πράττειν ᾗ ἂν ἡγῶνται [συμ]φέρειν. τοῖς δὲ νόμοις οἳ ἂν τεθῶσιν περὶ τῶν πολιτικῶν χρῆσθαι, καὶ μὴ ἐξεῖναι*
2 *μετακινεῖν μηδ' ἑτέρους θέσθαι. τῶν δὲ στρατηγῶν τὸ νῦν εἶναι τὴν αἵρεσιν ἐξ ἁπάντων ποιεῖσθαι τῶν πεντακισχιλίων, τὴν δὲ βουλήν, ἐπειδὰν καταστῇ, ποιήσασαν ἐξέτασιν <ἐν> ὅπλοις, ἑλέσθαι δέκα ἄνδρας καὶ γραμματέα τούτοις, τοὺς δὲ αἱρεθέντας ἄρχειν τὸν εἰσιόντα ἐνιαυτὸν αὐτοκράτορας, κἄν τι δέωνται συμβουλεύεσθαι μετὰ τῆς βουλῆς. ἑλέσθαι δὲ καὶ ἵππαρχον ἕνα καὶ φυλάρχους δέκα· τὸ δὲ λοιπὸν τὴν αἵρεσιν ποιεῖσθαι τούτων τὴν βουλὴν κατὰ*
3 *τὰ γεγραμμένα. τῶν δ' ἄλλων ἀρχῶν πλὴν τῆς βουλῆς καὶ τῶν στρατηγῶν μὴ ἐξεῖναι μήτε τούτοις μήτε ἄλλῳ μηδενὶ πλέον ἢ*

XXXI 3 *τῆς* addidit B. **6** <*καὶ*> K, K-W, H-L, B. **8** ЄΑΝ. *τεθῶσι* H-L. **11** ΚΑΤΑϹΤΗϹΗΙ corr. Wyse, Blass, etc. ΟΠΛΟΙϹ: <*ἐν*> *ὅπλοις* Wyse, Blass, K-W, H-L; *ὅπλων* K. **13** *ἐξιόντα* H-L. *καὶ ἂν* K, K-W, B; *καὶ ἐάν* H-L. ϹΥΝΒΟΥΛΕΥϹΘΑΙ. **17** ΠΛΕΙΟΝ (K-W, B): *πλέον* H-L, K^3, cf. Meisterhans, p. 120^2, n. 1090.

XXXI § 1. **χρόνον...καιρῷ**] Ar. *Anal. Pr.* i 36 § 6, *ὁ καιρός ἐστι χρόνος δέων*.

ἀνέγραψαν] 'drew up,' c. 2 § 4.

κατὰ τὰ πάτρια] in allusion to the Council of 400 under the Solonian constitution, c. 8 § 4. The phrase is inserted to propitiate those who regarded Solon as the founder of the Athenian democracy.

ἐκ προκρίτων οὓς ἂν ἕλωνται οἱ φυλέται] According to this, the ten tribes were to make a preliminary selection of more than the requisite number; but we are not told how the final choice was made out of those nominated by the tribes. According to Thuc. viii 67, 3, the proposal carried at the *ἐκκλησία* held at Colonus was to choose five *πρόεδροι*; and for these to elect 100 in all, and for each of these 100 to co-opt three others. The historian's account supplies an omission in the text by describing the process by which the requisite number was arrived at. The two accounts may be partly reconciled by supposing that the 100 were limited in their choice to selecting the additional 300 out of those preliminarily selected by the tribes. As regards the method by which the original hundred were appointed, the precise account in Thuc. seems more trustworthy than the vague description of the appointment of the 400 given in the text.

εὐθυνῶν] 'the examination of official accounts,' 'audits.' c. 48 § 4. *Att. Proc.* p. 259 Lips.

§ 2. **τὸ νῦν εἶναι**] Plat. *Rep.* 506 E, Xen. *Cyr.* v 3 § 42.

τὴν αἵρεσιν...ποιεῖσθαι] *inf.* l. 15.

καταστῇ] 32 § 2. Lys. 13 § 34 and 25 § 14, *οἱ τριάκοντα κατέστησαν*.

ἐξέτασιν ἐν ὅπλοις] Xen. *Anab.* v 3, 3, and *Cyrop.* ii 4, 1, *ἐξέτασις ἐν τοῖς ὅπλοις*. Thuc. iv 74 § 3, *ἐξέτασιν ὅπλων ἐποιήσαντο*, vi 45 § 2, *ὅπλων ἐξετάσει καὶ ἵππων*.

εἰσιόντα] during the 'ensuing' year, after the lapse of the two remaining months of the archonship of Callias.

ἵππαρχον ἕνα] The normal number was *two* (c. 61 § 4). **φυλάρχους**, c. 61 § 5.

§ 3. **μὴ ἐξεῖναι—πλέον ἢ ἅπαξ ἄρξαι**] Under the normal constitution of Athens military offices might be repeatedly held by the same person, but none of the others more than once, except in the case of membership of the Council, which *ἅπαξ ἄρξαι τὴν αὐτὴν ἀρχήν. εἰς δὲ τὸν ἄλλον χρόνον, ἵνα νεμηθῶσιν οἱ τετρακόσιοι εἰς τὰς τέτταρας λήξεις, ὅταν ⟦τοῖς⟧ αὐτοῖς γίγνηται μετὰ τῶν ἄλλων βουλεύειν, διανειμάντων αὐτοὺς οἱ ἑκατὸν ἄνδρες.*

32. *οἱ μὲν οὖν ἑκατὸν οἱ ὑπὸ τῶν πεντακισχιλίων αἱρεθέντες ταύτην ἀνέγραψαν τὴν πολιτείαν. ἐπικυρωθέντων δὲ τούτων ὑπὸ τοῦ πλήθους, ἐπιψηφίσαντος Ἀριστομάχου, ἡ μὲν βουλὴ <ἡ> ἐπὶ Καλλίου πρὶν διαβουλεῦσαι κατελύθη μηνὸς Θαργηλιῶνος τετράδι ἐπὶ δέκα, οἱ δὲ τετρακόσιοι εἰσῄεσαν ἐνάτῃ φθίνοντος Θαργηλιῶνος· ἔδει δὲ τὴν εἰληχυῖαν τῷ κυάμῳ βουλὴν εἰσιέναι τετράδι ἐπὶ δέκα*

18—20 *ἵνα* et *ὅταν* locum inter se mutasse putat Hude, qui etiam (cum Thompsono) *ἐγγίγνηται* conicit; *ὅταν νεμηθῶσιν—, ἵνα μὴ—μετὰ τῶν αὐτῶν βουλεύειν, ἄλλως διανειμάντων* nimis audacter Poste. **19** *τοῖς ἀστοῖς* secl. K[3], retinent K-W; *τοῖς αὐτοῖς* Tyrrell (H-L, et B qui etiam in papyro invenit [Α]ΥΤΟΙϹ): mihi quidem [Ε]ΤΕΡΟΙϹ aut simile aliquid scriptum fuisse videtur; malui tamen *αὐτοῖς* accipere, et *τοῖς* secludere, utpote ex interpretamento *τοῖς τ'* (sc. *τοῖς τετρακοσίοις*) exortum.

XXXII 3 <*ἡ*> Rutherford, Blass, K-W, H-L, K[3]. **5** ΕΙϹΗΙΕϹΑΝ: *εἰσῇσαν* K, H-L; *εἰσῄεσαν* K-W, B. **6** *ἔδει δὲ*: ΕΤΙΔΕ corr. K.

---

might be held twice (see c. 62 end, and *Pol.* 1275 *a* 25; 1299 *a* 10; 1317 *b* 24; there quoted).

νεμηθῶσιν...εἰς τὰς...λήξεις] c. 30 § 3, *νεῖμαι...τοὺς ἄλλους πρὸς τὴν λῆξιν ἑκάστην.* 'As regards the future, in order that the 400 may be distributed into the four divisions (above mentioned, 30 § 3), let the hundred make the distribution when it is possible for them (*i.e.* the 400) to sit in council with the rest.'

τῶν ἄλλων refers to the 5,000, as in c. 30 § 3, twice. **αὐτοῖς** refers to the *τετρακόσιοι* aforesaid.

Kaibel and Wilamowitz explain *τῶν ἄλλων* as *τῶν ἐν Σάμῳ*, but (as observed by Mr Kenyon) '*βουλεύειν* is a technical word, and the Athenians with the fleet would not become members of the *βουλὴ* on their return, and there would be no occasion to await their return before arranging the subdivision of the Four Hundred among the four councils.'

In **διανειμάντων** we have a sudden transition from the inf. of *orat. obliqua* to the imperative of *oratio recta.*

XXXII § 1. **ἐπιψηφίσαντος]** 30 § 4 end. **Ἀριστομάχου**, otherwise unknown. 'The absence of the name of father and deme is in accordance with the lapidary style of the 5th century, in which the decrees simply have *ὁ δεῖνα ἐπεστάτει*, *e.g.* CIA I, 32, *ἔδοξεν τῇ βουλῇ καὶ τῷ δήμῳ· Κεκροπὶς ἐπρυτάνευε· Μνησίθεος ἐγραμμάτευε· Εὐπείθης ἐπεστάτει· Καλλίας εἶπε.* On the other hand, the addition of the deme (c. 34 *ult.*, *ἔγραψε τὸ ψήφισμα Δρακοντίδης Ἀφιδναῖος*) or father (29 § 1, *γράψαντος Πυθοδώρου τοῦ Ἐπιζήλου*) of the proposer, is not in the manner of 5th century inscriptions' (Wyse).

ἐπὶ Καλλίου] B.C. 412—411.

πρὶν διαβουλεῦσαι] 'before the completion of its term of office.' The word is not found elsewhere in act. *διαβουλεύεσθαι*, 'to deliberate thoroughly,' is found in Andoc. 2 § 19; and in the sense of 'taking counsel' in Thuc. ii 5 and elsewhere (L and S), *e.g.* vii 50 § 4, 'to discuss.' As appears from the context, the Council was within a month of completing its year of office.

Θαργηλιῶνος τετράδι ἐπὶ δέκα, the 14th of Thargelion (May-June) or about the end of May. **ἐνάτῃ φθίνοντος Θαργηλιῶνος**, the 21st of Thargelion, or about June 7. **τετράδι ἐπὶ δέκα Σκιροφοριῶνος,** the 14th of Scirophorion (June-July), or about the end of June.

ἔδει] 'was bound' in ordinary course, according to the normal constitution.

τὴν εἰληχυῖαν τῷ κυάμῳ βουλὴν] Thuc. viii 66 § 1, *δῆμος μέντοι ὅμως ἔτι καὶ βουλὴ ἡ ἀπὸ τοῦ κυάμου ξυνελέγετο*, *ib.* 69 (of the attack of the Four Hundred and their emissaries on the Council of 412—411), *ἐπέστησαν τοῖς ἀπὸ τοῦ κυάμου βουλευταῖς.* The object of the emphatic mention of *κύαμος* is to point the contrast between the constitutional Council and

2 Σκιροφοριῶνος. ἡ μὲν οὖν ὀλιγαρχία τοῦτον κατέστη τὸν τρόπον ἐπὶ Καλλίου μὲν ἄρχοντος, ἔτεσιν δ' ὕστερον τῆς τῶν τυράννων ἐκβολῆς μάλιστα ἑκατόν, αἰτίων μάλιστα γενομένων Πεισάνδρου καὶ Ἀντιφῶντος καὶ Θηραμένους, ἀνδρῶν καὶ γεγενημένων εὖ καὶ [Col. 14.] 3 συνέσει καὶ γνώμῃ δοκούντων διαφέρειν. || γενομένης δὲ ταύτης τῆς πολιτείας οἱ μὲν πεντακισχίλιοι λόγῳ μόνον ᾑρέθησαν, οἱ δὲ τετρακόσιοι μετὰ τῶν δέκα τῶν αὐτοκρατόρων εἰσελθόντες εἰς τὸ βουλευτήριον ἦρχον τῆς πόλεως, καὶ πρὸς Λακεδαιμονίους πρεσβευσάμενοι κατελύοντο τὸν πόλεμον ἐφ' οἷς ἑκάτεροι τυγχάνουσιν ἔχοντες. οὐχ ὑπακου[σά]ντων δ' ἐκείνων εἰ μὴ καὶ τὴν ἀρχὴν τῆς [θ]αλάττης ἀφήσουσιν, οὕτως ἀπέστησαν.

8 ἔτεσι H-L. **9** μάλιστα ante ἑκατόν temere om. H-L, utpote e verbis proxime sequentibus illapsum. **12** ΗΡΕΘΗCΑΝ (ερη supra scr.) ΗΡΕΘΗCΑΝΟΔΕ (........ supra scr.). **14** ἦρχόν <τε> Hude (K-W). **16** ὑπακου[ό]ντων H-L.

---

that of the Revolution. The latter was *not* appointed by lot out of the general body of citizens. Cf. 31, 4, οὓς ἂν ἕλωνται.

§ 2. **μάλιστα ἑκατόν**] B.C. 510—to end of May 411, or 99 years; hence μάλιστα. Thuc. viii 68, 4, ἐπ' ἔτει ἑκατοστῷ μάλιστα ἐπειδὴ οἱ τύραννοι κατελύθησαν.

Πεισάνδρου] Thuc. viii 49, 53—56, 63—68, esp. 68 § 1 (of the ἐκκλησια held at Colonus), ἦν δὲ ὁ μὲν τὴν γνώμην ταύτην εἰπὼν **Πείσανδρος**, καὶ τἄλλα ἐκ τοῦ προφανοῦς προθυμότατα ξυγκαταλύσας τὸν δῆμον· ὁ μέντοι πᾶν τὸ πρᾶγμα ξυνθεὶς ὅτῳ τρόπῳ κατέστη ἐς τοῦτο καὶ ἐκ πλείστου ἐπιμεληθεὶς **Ἀντιφῶν** ἦν, ἀνὴρ Ἀθηναίων τῶν καθ' ἑαυτὸν ἀρετῇ τε οὐδενὸς δεύτερος καὶ κράτιστος ἐνθυμηθῆναι γενόμενος καὶ ἃ γνοίη εἰπεῖν. In § 3 Thuc. mentions Phrynichus who παρέσχε... ἑαυτὸν πάντων διαφερόντως προθυμότατον ἐς τὴν ὀλιγαρχίαν, and in § 4 **Θηραμένης**, who ἐν τοῖς ξυγκαταλύουσι τὸν δῆμον πρῶτος ἦν, ἀνὴρ οὔτε εἰπεῖν οὔτε γνῶναι ἀδύνατος. ὥστε ἀπ' ἀνδρῶν πολλῶν καὶ ξυνετῶν (cf. **συνέσει**) πραχθὲν τὸ ἔργον οὐκ ἀπεικότως καίπερ μέγα ὂν προὐχώρησε. On Peisander, see also Lys. 12 § 66; 25 § 9; and Andoc. 2 §§ 12—15: on Antiphon, Lys. 12 § 67; on Theramenes, *ib.* 62—78.

§ 3. **λόγῳ μόνον**] Thuc. viii 92 § 11, καὶ οἱ τετρακόσιοι διὰ τοῦτο οὐκ ἤθελον τοὺς πεντακισχιλίους οὔτε εἶναι οὔτε μὴ ὄντας δήλους εἶναι, τὸ μὲν καταστῆσαι μετόχους τοσούτους ἄντικρυς ἂν δῆμον ἡγούμενοι, τὸ δ' αὖ ἀφανὲς φόβον ἐς ἀλλήλους παρέξειν.

οἱ δὲ τετρακόσιοι κτλ.] Thuc. viii 70, οἱ τετρακόσιοι ἐσελθόντες ἐς τὸ βουλευτήριον... τά τε ἄλλα ἔνεμον κατὰ κράτος τὴν πόλιν κτλ.

τῶν δέκα] the ten στρατηγοί of c. 31 § 2.

πρὸς Λακ. κτλ.] Thuc. *ib.* πρός τε Ἆγιν τὸν Λακεδαιμονίων βασιλέα ὄντα ἐν τῇ Δεκελείᾳ ἐπεκηρυκεύοντο, λέγοντες διαλλαγῆναι βούλεσθαι (Grote, v p. 391). 71 § 3, μετὰ δὲ τοῦτο παρά τε τὸν Ἆγιν ἐπρεσβεύοντο οἱ τετρακόσιοι οὐδὲν ἧσσον, κἀκείνου μᾶλλον ἤδη προσδεχομένου καὶ παραινοῦντος ἐκπέμπουσι καὶ ἐς τὴν Λακεδαίμονα περὶ ξυμβάσεως πρέσβεις βουλόμενοι διαλλαγῆναι. 90 § 2, ἀπέστειλαν Ἀντιφῶντα καὶ Φρύνιχον καὶ ἄλλους δέκα κατὰ τάχος... ἐπιστείλαντες παντὶ τρόπῳ ὅστις καὶ ὁπωσοῦν ἀνεκτὸς ξυναλλαγῆναι πρὸς τοὺς Λακεδαιμονίους. Lastly, 91 § 1, οἱ ἐκ τῆς Λακεδαίμονος πρέσβεις οὐδὲν πράξαντες ἀνεχώρησαν τοῖς ξύμπασι ξυμβατικόν. 'We read with astonishment,' says Grote, v 409, 'that the (Lacedaemonians) could not be prevailed upon to contract any treaty and that they manifested nothing but backwardness in seizing the golden opportunity.' But the envoys clearly could not answer for the armament at Samos, and therefore returned without obtaining any terms that would apply to the Athenians at large. The text tells us what we do not learn from Thucydides, viz. that the reason for this failure in the negotiations was due to the envoys declining to surrender the maritime supremacy of Athens. This embassy was afterwards impeached by Theramenes (Lysias 12 §§ 66—68); Antiphon was condemned and executed (Phrynichus had been already assassinated).

κατελύοντο] tentative impf.

33. *μῆνας μὲν οὖν ἴσως τέτταρας διέμεινεν ἡ τῶν τετρακοσίων πολιτεία, καὶ ἦρξεν ἐξ αὐτῶν Μνησίλοχος δίμηνον ἐπὶ Θεοπόμπου ἄρχοντος, <ὃς> ἦρξε τοὺς ἐπιλοίπους δέκα μῆνας. ἡττηθέντες δὲ τῇ περὶ Ἐρετρίαν ναυμαχίᾳ κ[αὶ] τῆς Εὐβοίας ἀποστάσης ὅλης πλὴν Ὠρεοῦ, χαλεπῶς ἐνεγκόντες ἐπὶ τῇ συμφορᾷ μάλιστα τῶν προγεγενημένων (πλείω γὰρ ἐκ τῆς Εὐβοίας ἢ τῆς Ἀττικῆς ἐτύγχανον ὠφελούμενοι), κατέλυσαν τοὺς τετρακοσίους καὶ τὰ πράγματα παρέδωκαν τοῖς πεντακισχιλίοις τοῖς ἐκ τῶν ὅπλων, ψηφισάμενοι μηδεμίαν ἀρχὴν εἶναι μισθοφόρον. αἰτιώτατοι δ'* 2 *ἐγένοντο τῆς καταλύσεως Ἀριστοκράτης καὶ Θηραμένης, οὐ συνα-*

λο

XXXIII 2 ΜΝΑCΙΜΑΧΟC; *Μνασίλοχος* (K, H-L): *Μνησίλοχος* K-W, B. **3** <*ὃς*> K (K-W, B): *ὁ δ'* H-L. *ἡττηθέντες δὲ* <*οἱ Ἀθηναῖοι*>? Herwerden, Richards. **5** ωΡΙΟΥ. **9** ΜΙCΘΟΦΟΡΩΝ: *μισθοφόρον* J B Mayor, Rutherford, Naber, Fränkel, edd.

TESTIMONIA. **1** *Harp. s.v. *τετρακόσιοι*: ... *οἱ τετρακόσιοι πρὸ ἑπτὰ ἐτῶν κατέστησαν τῶν τριάκοντα τυράννων παρ' Ἀθηναίοις· οἵτινες τέτταρας μῆνας ἦρξαν τῆς πόλεως, ὥς φησιν Ἀρ. ἐν Ἀθ. πολ.* (Frag. 372^2, 410^3).

XXXIII § 1. **μῆνας...ἴσως τέτταρας**] The 400 were practically in power from the end of May to the end of June, also for the two months of July and August in the civil year next ensuing (*δίμηνον*). This makes *three* months. Hence the oligarchical revolution began about a month earlier, *i.e.* at the end of April, while the constitutional Council was still nominally in office (Thuc. viii 66, 1), and the four months are May, June, July and and August. Thuc. viii 63, 3, places the fall of the democracy a little earlier than the spring of 411. It has been assigned to March 411, soon after the *Lenaea* in which the *Lysistrata* was produced (Wattenbach, *De Quadr*. p. 29, quoted by Classen, Thuc. *l.c.*). Similarly Grote, c. 63 *init.*, describes the Four Hundred as 'installed in the Senate-House about February or March 411 B.C., and deposed about July of the same year,' and speaks of Athens undergoing '*four or five months* of danger and distraction.' It now appears that these dates are rather too early.

Μνησίλοχος] the archon eponymus selected by the 400. *Μνησίλοχος* is mentioned in the list of the Thirty given in Xen. *Hell.* ii 3, 2 and there is every probability that the two are the same. Cf. CIA iv 3, 179 *d* 1, p. 162, [*Ἀθηναῖ*]*οι ἀνῆλ*[*ωσαν ἐπὶ Μνησιλό*]*χου ἄρχο*[*ντος*]. This expenditure was authorised not (as usual) by vote of the *δῆμος*, but *ψηφισαμένης τῆς βουλῆς*. At the date specified, the 21st of Hecatombaeon, the Four Hundred were still in power.

Θεοπόμπου] the archon eponymus appointed by lot on the restoration of the democracy in the third month of the civil year, B.C. 411—10.

ἐπιλοίπους] not found in the *Index Ar.* In 40 § 1 we have the ordinary word *ὑπολοίπους*. *ἐπίλοιπος* is often used by Plato, *Rep.* 540 B and *Leg.* 728 D, *τὸν ἐπίλοιπον βίον*, *ib.* 628 A, *εἰς τὸν ἐπίλοιπον χρόνον*.

τῇ περὶ Ἐρετρίαν ναυμαχίᾳ] Thuc. viii 95. In Lys. 20 § 14 one of the *καταλογεῖς* sails for Eretria after holding office under the 400 for eight days only. **πλὴν Ὠρεοῦ.** Thuc. *l.c.* § 7, (the Lac.) *Εὔβοιαν ἅπασαν ἀποστήσαντες πλὴν Ὠρεοῦ*.

χαλεπῶς ἐνεγκόντες *κτλ.*] Thuc. viii 96 § 1, *τοῖς δ' Ἀθηναίοις ὡς ἦλθε τὰ περὶ τὴν Εὔβοιαν γεγενημένα, ἔκπληξις μεγίστη δὴ τῶν πρὶν παρέστη.*

πλείω—ὠφελούμενοι] Thuc. viii 96 § 2, (Euboea) *ἐξ ἧς πλείω ἢ τῆς Ἀττικῆς ὠφελοῦντο.* Decelea was at this time in the occupation of Agis.

κατέλυσαν τοὺς τετρακοσίους *κτλ.*] Thuc. viii 97 § 1, *τοὺς τετρακοσίους καταπαύσαντες τοῖς πεντακισχιλίοις ἐψηφίσαντο τὰ πράγματα παραδοῦναι· εἶναι δὲ αὐτῶν ὁπόσοι καὶ ὅπλα παρέχονται· καὶ μισθὸν μηδένα φέρειν μηδεμιᾷ ἀρχῇ.*

§ 2. **Ἀριστοκράτης καὶ Θηραμένης**] Thuc. viii 89, 2 (of the opposition to the ρεσκόμενοι τοῖς ὑπὸ τῶν τετρακοσίων γιγνομένοις· ἅπαντα γὰρ δι' αὐτῶν ἔπραττον, οὐδὲν ἐπαναφέροντες τοῖς πεντακισχιλίοις. δοκοῦσι δὲ καλῶς πολιτευθῆναι κατὰ τούτους τοὺς καιρούς, πολέμου τε καθεστῶτος καὶ ἐκ τῶν ὅπλων τῆς πολιτείας οὔσης.

34. τούτους μὲν οὖν ἀφείλετο τὴν πολιτείαν ὁ δῆμος διὰ τάχους· ἔτει δ' ἑβδόμῳ μετὰ τὴν τῶν τετρακοσίων κατάλυσιν, ἐπὶ Καλλίου τοῦ 'Αγγελῆθεν ἄρχοντος, γενομένης τῆς ἐν 'Αργινούσαις ναυμαχίας, πρῶτον μὲν τοὺς δέκα στρατηγοὺς τοὺς τῇ ναυμαχίᾳ

11 ΓΕΝΟΜΕΝΟΙϹ; γινομένοις K-W; γιγν. H-L, K[3], B. **13** an καίπερ πολέμου? Herwerden.

XXXIV 2 ЄΒΔΟΜΟΙ : ἕκτῳ K-W[2]. ΚΑΤΑΛΥϹΙΝ (ΑΙ) K, H-L, K-W[2], B; κατάστασιν K-W[1]. **3** ΑΡΓΙΝΟΥϹΑϹ : 'Αργινούσσαις B. **4** τὴν ναυμαχίαν Tyrrell. τοὺς—νικῶντας e margine irrepsisse putat Richards.

TESTIMON. **XXXIV 3—12** *Schol. Arist. *Ran.* 1532 Κλεοφῶν δὲ μαχέσθω: παρόσον, ὡς 'Αρ. φησί, μετὰ τὴν 'Αργινούσαις ναυμαχίαν Λακεδαιμονίων βουλομένων ἐκ Δεκελείας ἀπιέναι ἐφ' οἷς ἔχουσιν ἑκάτεροι καὶ εἰρήνην ἄγειν ἐπὶ (τοῦ secl. K-W) Καλλίου, Κλεοφῶν ἔπεισε τὸν δῆμον μὴ προσδέξασθαι, "ἐλθὼν εἰς τὴν ἐκκλησίαν—ἐὰν μὴ πάσας ἀφῶσι τὰς πόλεις οἱ Λακεδαιμόνιοι" (Frag. 370[2], 408[3]).

---

extreme members of the 400), ἔχοντες ἡγεμόνας τῶν πάνυ [στρατηγῶν] τῶν ἐν τῇ ὀλιγαρχίᾳ [καὶ] ἐν ἀρχαῖς ὄντων, οἷον Θηραμένην τε τὸν Ἅγνωνος καὶ 'Αριστοκράτην τὸν Σκελλίου. Lys. 12 § 66, (Theramenes) μετέσχε τῶν 'Αριστοκράτους ἔργων.

Aristocrates had been one of the envoys who negotiated the peace of 421 B.C. (Thuc. v 19 and 24). In 414 B.C. he is represented as a typical 'aristocrat' in Arist. *Aves*, 125, (Ἔποψ) ἀριστοκρατεῖσθαι δῆλος εἶ ζητῶν. (Εὐελπ.) ἐγώ; | ἥκιστα· καὶ τὸν Σκελλίου βδελύττομαι, cf. Plat. *Gorg.* 472 A. He was a ταξίαρχος under the 400 (Thuc. viii 92) and is extolled by the author of the speech against Theocrines, [Dem.] 58 § 67, for taking part in the destruction of the fortress of Eetioneia and restoring the democracy. He was one of the generals at Arginusae (406).

οὐδὲν ἐπαναφέροντες τοῖς πεντακισχιλίοις] In Thuc. *l.c.* the opponents of the 400 insist τοὺς πεντακισχιλίους ἔργῳ καὶ μὴ ὀνόματι χρῆναι ἀποδεικνύναι.

δοκοῦσι δὲ καλῶς πολιτευθῆναι κτλ.] Thuc. viii 97, 2, οὐχ ἥκιστα δὴ τὸν πρῶτον χρόνον ἐπί γ' ἐμοῦ 'Αθηναῖοι φαίνονται εὖ πολιτεύσαντες· μετρία γὰρ ἥ τε ἐς τοὺς ὀλίγους καὶ ἐς τοὺς πολλοὺς ξύγκρασις ἐγένετο καὶ ἐκ πονηρῶν τῶν πραγμάτων τοῦτο πρῶτον ἀνήνεγκε τὴν πόλιν. Grote c. 57, v 430.

ἐκ τῶν ὅπλων] c. 4 § 2, ἀπεδέδοτο ἡ πολιτεία τοῖς ὅπλα παρεχομένοις. *Pol.* 1297 *b* 1, δεῖ δὲ τὴν πολιτείαν εἶναι μὲν ἐκ τῶν τὰ ὅπλα ἐχόντων μόνον.

XXXIV. *Arginusae* and *Aegospotami*.

§ 1. **ἔτει δ' ἑβδόμῳ** κτλ.] The archonship of Theopompus was in B.C. 411/0; that of Callias in 406/5. Thus, the latter was in the *sixth* year after the overthrow of the Four Hundred. Mr Kenyon suggests that 'the calculation was probably made by inadvertence from the *establishment* of the Four Hundred, which was in the official year 412—411 B.C.'

τοῦ 'Αγγελῆθεν] Added to distinguish him from the Callias who was archon in B.C. 412 (c. 32 § 1). Others of the same name were archons in 456 and 377.

It was more usual to remove such ambiguities by adding the archon of the previous year, *e.g. Arg.* to Arist. *Ranae*, ἐπὶ Καλλίου τοῦ μετ' 'Αντιγενῆ (the Callias of the text); Schol. *Ach.* 10, Καλλίου τοῦ μετὰ Μνησίθεον (the Callias of 456). In Schol. *Nub.* 971 Phrynis is said to have been victorious at the Panathenaea ἐπὶ Καλλίου ἄρχοντος, probably B.C. 406, as this was the third year of the Olympiad (Wyse).

'Αργινούσαις] Xen. *Hell.* i 6, 27—38. Cf. Grote, c. 64, v 501—536; Holm, *Gr. Gesch.* ii 573 ff, 585.

τοὺς δέκα στρατηγοὺς] In Xen. *Hell.* i 5, 16 we have the names of the ten generals: Conon, Diomedon, Leon (also mentioned in 6 § 16, but probably a mistake for Lysias, who is mentioned in 6 § 30, and 7 § 1), Pericles, Erasinides, Aristocrates, Archestratus, Protomachus, νικῶντας συνέβη κριθῆναι μιᾷ χειροτονίᾳ πάντας, τοὺς μὲν οὐδὲ

Thrasyllus, Aristogenes. Of these Conon was blockaded in the harbour of Mitylene, and was therefore not present at the battle of Arginusae (*Hell.* 6 §§ 16 ff.). Leon and Erasinides were with Cleon when he first made for Mitylene (*l.c.* § 16) and we hear no more of them until we find Erasinides among those engaged in the battle (§ 29). The other generals engaged in it were Aristocrates, Diomedon, Pericles, Protomachus, Thrasyllus, Lysias, and Aristogenes. We know from Lysias 21 § 8 that Archestratus died at Mitylene, though Xenophon is silent on this point; and Erasinides probably left Mitylene on board the vessel mentioned in the passage of Lysias just quoted: ἀποθανόντος δὲ τούτου (Archestratus) ἐν Μυτιλήνῃ Ἐρασινίδης μετ' ἐμοῦ συνέπλει. (Bauer p. 159, assumes that Leon is the tenth general of whom Xenophon is silent, and that he is not identical with the general who bears the name of Lysias.)

Thus only eight of the ten were engaged in the battle; after the battle, the generals were recalled. Two of them, Protomachus and Aristogenes, declined to come. 'Warned of the displeasure of the people and not confiding in their own case to meet it, they preferred to pay the price of voluntary exile' (Grote v 510, c. 64).

Only six returned to Athens. It was ultimately proposed to the Council by Callixenus (Xen. *Hell.* i 7 § 9) and carried, that the case should be decided by the public assembly voting in their tribes by ballot, and that one single vote was to decide the case of all the generals (§ 34, μιᾷ ψήφῳ ἅπαντας κρίνειν). In the assembly it was moved by Euryptolemus that each of the generals should be tried separately (κρίνεσθαι τοὺς ἄνδρας δίχα ἕκαστον, *ib.*). The assembly first voted by show of hands (διαχειροτονία) in favour of this motion, and then against it; thereupon they condemned all the *eight* generals who had taken part in the battle (κατεψηφίσαντο τῶν ναυμαχησάντων στρατηγῶν, ὀκτὼ ὄντων). The six who had returned were put to death.

If we now turn from the narrative in Xenophon to the description in the text, we find several discrepancies: (1) *all* the ten are put on their trial, not eight alone; (2) they are tried μιᾷ χειροτονίᾳ, whereas it was only the vote on the rival motions (including the decision to try them collectively) that was taken by show of hands, and the final verdict was given by ballot (διαψήφισις). τοὺς μὲν οὐδὲ συνναυμαχήσαντας must refer to Conon who was at Mitylene, and to Archestratus who died there. τοὺς δ' ἐπ' ἀλλοτρίας νεὼς σωθέντας is so far borne out by Xenophon that, according to the statement made in the speech of Euryptolemus (*l.c.* § 32), *one* of the generals was ἐπὶ καταδύσης νεὼς διασωθείς (cf. Diod. xiii 99).

As regards our other authorities, Philochorus (frag. 121) speaks of six generals as having been put to death; Diodorus (xiii 101—2) describes six only as actually condemned. According to Androtion's *Atthis* (quoted by Pausanias vi 7, 7) the decision was limited to the generals who actually took part in the battle. Plut. *Per.* 37 says of Pericles the younger, τοῦτον...ἀπέκτεινεν ὁ δῆμος μετὰ τῶν συστρατηγῶν. The Schol. on Aristoph. *Ran.* 698 describes four of the generals as having escaped and six as having been put to death. This is somewhat fancifully regarded by Bauer (p. 161) as implying that the charge concerned all the ten.

Plato *Apol.* 32 B says: ὅτε ὑμεῖς τοὺς δέκα στρατηγοὺς τοὺς οὐκ ἀνελομένους τοὺς ἐκ τῆς ναυμαχίας ἐβουλεύσασθε ἀθρόους κρίνειν παρανόμως, τότ' ἐγὼ μόνος τῶν πρυτάνεων ἠναντιώθην ὑμῖν. [Plat.] *Axioch.* 368 D states that all the ten στρατηγοί were condemned to death. This account is carelessly followed by Aelian *V. H.* iii 17, οὐκ ἐπεψήφισεν Ἀθηναίοις (Σωκράτης) τὸν τῶν δέκα στρατηγῶν θάνατον. Cf. Valerius Max. iii 8, 3 and Schol. Aristid. iii 245, 24 Dind.

According to Bauer the 'dream of Thrasyllus' (Diod. xiii 97, 6) implies that *seven* of the generals were put to death. The seventh (he suggests) was Leon. Diodorus (xiii 101 § 5) states that Conon also was accused but acquitted. Bauer considers the account in the text too definite in its terms (*zu scharf ausgedrückt*), in so far as it takes no note of Conon's acquittal; but he actually regards it as more correct than the narrative in Xenophon. He suggests that Xenophon passes over the case of Leon who had not been present at the battle, because it would put the injustice of the sentence in too extreme a light. In Bauer's opinion the author can only refer to Leon in the vague plural τοὺς οὐδὲ συνναυμαχήσαντας, which Bauer admits is an exaggeration.

συνναυμαχήσαντας, τοὺς δ' ἐπ' ἀλλοτρίας νεὼς σωθέντας, ἐξαπατηθέντος τοῦ δήμου διὰ τοὺς παροργίσαντας· ἔπειτα βουλομένων Λακεδαιμονίων ἐκ Δεκελείας ἀπιέναι καὶ ἐφ' οἷς ἔχουσιν ἑκάτεροι [Col. 15.] εἰρήνην ἄγειν, ἔνιοι μὲν ἐσπούδαζον, τὸ δὲ πλῆθος || οὐχ ὑπήκουσεν ἐξαπατηθέντες ὑπὸ Κλεοφῶντος, ὃς ἐκώλυσε γενέσθαι τὴν εἰρήνην ἐλθὼν εἰς τὴν ἐκκλησίαν μεθύων καὶ θώρακα ἐνδεδυκώς, οὐ φάσκων

6 ΕΞΑΠΑΤΗΘΕΝΤΕC corr. K. **8** ΑΝΙΕΝΑΙ : ἀπιέναι J B Mayor, Sidgwick, Wyse, Blass, Herwerden, Naber, Gennadios, coll. Schol. Arist. *Ran.* 1532, H-L, K-W, K[3]. ΚΑΙ ΕΦ ΟΙC ΕΧΟΥCΙΝ ΙΡΗΝΗΝ ΕΚΑΤΕΡΟΙ ΑΓΕΙΝ ; καὶ ἐφ' οἷς ἔχουσιν ἑκάτεροι εἰρήνην ἄγειν K (H-L) ;—εἰρήνην ἄγειν ἑκάτεροι Gomperz ; ἐφ' οἷς ἔχουσιν ἑκάτεροι καὶ εἰρήνην ἄγειν K-W e Schol. Arist. (et B, in archetypo ἐφ' οἷς ἔχουσιν ἑκάτεροι supra versum adscriptum fuisse arbitratus). **9** ὑπήκουσαν mavult Herwerden. **10** ἐξαπατηθὲν Rutherford.

7—12 *Schol. Arist. *Ran.* 1532 ; v. Testimonia in p. 129.

ἐξαπατηθέντος τοῦ δήμου] Xen. *Hell.* i 7 § 35, ὕστερον...ἐψηφίσαντο οἵτινες τὸν δῆμον ἐξηπάτησαν, προβολὰς αὐτῶν εἶναι καὶ ἐγγυητὰς καταστῆσαι, ἕως ἂν κριθῶσιν.

παροργίσαντας] in Act. hitherto found only in N. T.

ἐκ Δεκελείας ἀπιέναι] Decelea had been occupied by Agis since the spring of 413 B.C. (Thuc. vii 19 § 1), and it was retained until the end of the Peloponnesian war. On the site, about 15 miles N.E. of Athens, near the entrance of the defile leading between Parnes and Pentelicus from the plain of Athens to Oropus and Tanagra, see Leake's *Demi* p. 18 and plan in Curtius, *Sieben Karten.*

ἐφ' οἷς ἔχουσιν ἑκάτεροι κτλ.] These overtures after the battle of Arginusae are not mentioned by Xenophon or Diodorus. The terms are the same as those proposed, according to Diodorus (xiii 52), after the battle of Cyzicus in 410 B.C., and opposed by Cleophon (*ib.* 53) (see Grote c. 63, v 458—461). The present overtures are in fact 'a second edition' of those put forward four years previously. Xenophon says nothing of them on either occasion. The account in Diodorus led Grote (c. 65 *init.* p. 537 n) to suppose that the Scholiast on Aristoph. *Ranae ult.*, who quotes the present passage, had confounded the two battles. It now appears that the Scholiast's quotation was correct. It is not improbable that Diodorus is wrong. It is to the overtures in the text that we should refer the account in Philochorus, fragm. 117—118 Müller (ap. Schol. ad Eur. *Orest.* 371) :—Λακεδαιμονίων πρεσβευσαμένων περὶ εἰρήνης ἀπιστήσαντες οἱ Ἀθηναῖοι οὐ προσήκαντο. Cf. Schol. on l. 722. Grote v 460 n.

ἐξαπατηθέντες ὑπὸ Κλεοφῶντος] In c. 28 § 4 Cleophon (and Callicrates) are described as having 'deceived the people.' Cleophon's action is described as follows in Lysias 13 § 8, ὅτε γὰρ ἡ πρώτη ἐκκλησία περὶ τῆς εἰρήνης ἐγίγνετο, καὶ οἱ παρὰ Λακεδαιμονίων ἥκοντες ἔλεγον ἐφ' οἷς ἕτοιμοι εἶεν τὴν εἰρήνην ποιεῖσθαι Λακεδαιμόνιοι, εἰ κατασκαφείη τῶν τειχῶν τῶν μακρῶν ἐπὶ δέκα στάδια ἑκατέρου, τότε ὑμεῖς τε, ὦ ἄν. Ἀθ., οὐκ ἠνέσχεσθε ἀκούσαντες περὶ τῶν τειχῶν τῆς κατασκαφῆς, Κλεοφῶν τε ὑπὲρ ὑμῶν πάντων ἀναστὰς ἀντεῖπεν ὡς οὐδενὶ τρόπῳ οἷόν τε εἴη ποιεῖν ταῦτα. Aeschin. *F. L.* 76, Κλεοφῶν...ἀποκόψειν ἠπείλει μαχαίρᾳ τὸν τράχηλον, εἴ τις τῆς εἰρήνης μνησθήσεται, and *F. L.* 151, παντάπασιν ἔκφρων ἐγένετο (with schol. on 150, where εἴ τις εἰρήνη γεννηθήσεται, printed εἰρήνης γεννητὴς ἔσται, is clearly a mistake for εἰρήνης μνησθήσεται). Cf. Arist. *Ran. ad fin.* Κλεοφῶν δὲ μαχέσθω, and Holden's *Onomasticon s. v.*

μεθύων καὶ θώρακα ἐνδεδυκώς] It has been suggested (by Hartman) that we should read θώρακα ἔχων and interpret the latter as a metaphorical phrase equivalent to μεθύων (coll. Aristoph. *Vesp.* 1195 etc). If so, the writer has misinterpreted a phrase borrowed from a comedy and quite out of place here. But there is nothing unreasonable in Cleophon's appearing in armour. His life was not safe, as may be inferred from the animosity with which he was regarded by members of the oligarchical party (Aristoph. *Ran.* 1504, Lys. 13 § 7 ff., 30 § 10 ff.). (Herwerden's n.) It will be remembered that Cicero, at the time of the Catilinarian conspiracy, went down to the *Campus Martius* armed with a *lata insignique lorica* (Cic. *pro Murena*, § 52).

ἐπιτρέψειν ἐὰν μὴ πάσας ἀφῶσι Λακεδαιμόνιοι τὰς πόλεις. οὐ 2
χρησάμενοι δὲ καλῶς τότε τοῖς πράγμα[σι], μετ' οὐ πολὺν χρόνον
ἔγνωσαν τὴν ἁμαρ[τίαν]. τῷ γὰρ ὕστερον ἔτει ἐπ' Ἀλεξίου
ἄρχοντος ἠτύχησαν τὴν ἐν Αἰγὸς ποταμοῖς ναυμαχίαν, ἐξ ἧς
συνέβη κύριον γενόμενον τῆς πόλεως Λύσανδρον καταστῆσαι τοὺς
τριάκοντα τρόπῳ τοιῷδε. τῆς εἰρήνης γενομένης αὐτοῖς ἐφ' ᾧ τε 3
πολιτεύσονται τὴν πάτριον πολιτείαν, οἱ μὲν δημοτικοὶ διασῴζειν
ἐπειρῶντο τὸν δῆμον, τῶν δὲ γνωρίμων οἱ μὲν ἐν ταῖς ἑταιρείαις
ὄντες καὶ τῶν φυγάδων οἱ μετὰ τὴν εἰρήνην κατελθόντες ὀλιγαρχίας
ἐπεθύμουν, οἱ δ' ἐν ἑταιρείᾳ μὲν οὐδεμιᾷ συγκαθεστῶτες [ἄ]λλως
δὲ δοκοῦντες οὐδενὸς ἐπιλείπεσθαι τῶν πολιτῶν τὴν πάτριον
πολιτείαν ἐζήτουν· ὧν ἦν μὲν καὶ Ἀρχῖνος καὶ Ἄνυτος καὶ
Κλειτοφῶν καὶ Φορμίσιος καὶ ἕτεροι πολλοί, προειστήκει δὲ

12 ΑΦΙΩϹΙ (K): ἀφῶσι Naber, Gennadios, Richards, K-W, H-L, B e schol. Arist.
18 ΔΙΑϹΩΖΕΙΝ (C above); -σώσειν K[1]; -σῶσαι hiatu admisso J B Mayor et Wyse; -σῴζειν Blass, K-W, H-L, K[3]. **20** ΑΡΧΙΑΝ corr. J B Mayor, Rutherford, Blass, Fränkel.
22 ΕΠΙΛΙΠΕϹΘΑΙ: ἐπιλείπ. K, B, ('an λείπεσθαι?') K-W; ἀπολειπ. Richards, Gennadios, Kontos, Hultsch (H-L). **23** ΕΖΗΤΟΥΝ (K, K-W, B): ἐζήλουν H-L.

---

§ 2. **ἐπ' Ἀλεξίου**] B.C. 405/4.

ἠτύχησαν τὴν—ναυμαχίαν] an exceptional, but quite intelligible, phrase for expressing 'defeat in the naval engagement.' We have something like it in Aristides ii 334 Dind., *Σοφοκλῆς Φιλοκλέους ἡττᾶτο...τὸν Οἰδίπουν*.

ἐν Αἰγὸς ποταμοῖς] Xen. *Hell.* ii 1, 21—32. Plut. *Lysander*, c. 11—12. Grote c. 65, v 542—7.

Λύσανδρον] Lysias 12 §§ 72—76. Plut. *Lys.* 15, *τριάκοντα μὲν ἐν ἄστει, δέκα δὲ ἐν Πειραιεῖ καταστήσας ἄρχοντας*, Grote c. 65, v 559.

§ 3. **τὴν πάτριον πολιτείαν**] c. 31, l. 3. Xen. *Hell.* ii 3 § 2, *ἔδοξε τῷ δήμῳ τριάκοντα ἄνδρας ἑλέσθαι, οἳ τοὺς πατρίους νόμους ξυγγράψωσι, καθ' οὓς πολιτεύσουσι.* The term (as Mr Kenyon observes) was 'sufficiently vague,' indicating generally the constitution of Solon; but, as the virtue of the constitution depended on its working, it was possible for moderate democrats, extreme oligarchs, and moderate aristocrats alike to hope that it would be modelled according to their views. Diodorus (xiv 3) recounts the arguments of the opposing parties at some length, and describes Theramenes as urging the Athenians to follow *τῇ πατρίῳ πολιτείᾳ*.

τῶν γνωρίμων] 2 § 1, 5 § 1, 16 § 9, 28 § 2.

ἑταιρείαις] Cf. Thuc. iii 82, 8; viii 54, 4. Hermann, *Staatsalt.* 70, 2 and 10; Schömann, *Ant.* p. 363 E. T.

Ἀρχῖνος] Dem. *Timocr.* p. 742 § 135, *Ἀρχίνου...τοῦ καταλαβόντος Φυλὴν καὶ μετά γε τοὺς θεοὺς αἰτιωτάτου ὄντος τῆς καθόδου τῷ δήμῳ καὶ ἄλλα πολλὰ καὶ καλὰ πεπολιτευμένου καὶ ἐστρατηγηκότος πολλάκις.* Isocr. 18 § 2, Aeschin. *c. Ctes.* 187, 195. *Inf.* c. 40 §§ 1, 2.

Ἄνυτος] In the speech made by Theramenes in his defence, in Xen. *Hell.* ii 3 § 42, Anytus is mentioned with Thrasybulus and Alcibiades: *οὐκ αὖ ἐδόκει μοι οὔτε Θρασύβουλον οὔτε Ἄνυτον οὔτε Ἀλκιβιάδην φυγαδεύειν*, and *ib.* § 44, *πότερον οἴεσθε Θρασύβουλον καὶ Ἄνυτον καὶ τοὺς ἄλλους φυγάδας ἃ ἐγὼ λέγω μᾶλλον ἂν ἐνθάδε βούλεσθαι γίγνεσθαι ἢ ἃ οὗτοι πράττουσιν;*

Κλειτοφῶν] the proposer of the rider to the proposal of Pythodorus respecting the establishment of the 400 (29 § 3). Isocr. *Callim.* 11 § 30. He is possibly the same as the son of Aristonymus and pupil of Socrates who gives his name to Plato's *Cleitophon*. In Plut. *Mor.* 805 Κλειτοφῶν (mentioned with Cleon) is probably a mistake for Κλεοφῶν.

Φορμίσιος] Ὑπόθεσις to Lysias *Or.* 34. Dionys. Halic. *de Lysia*, c. 32, *τοῦ γὰρ δήμου κατελθόντος ἐκ Πειραιῶς, καὶ ψηφισαμένου διαλύσασθαι πρὸς τοὺς ἐν ἄστει, καὶ μηδενὸς τῶν γεγενημένων μνησικακεῖν, δέους δὲ ὄντος, μὴ πάλιν τὸ πλῆθος εἰς τοὺς εὐπόρους ὑβρίζῃ τὴν ἀρχαίαν ἐξουσίαν κεκομισμένον, καὶ πολλῶν ὑπὲρ τούτου γινομέ-*

μάλιστα Θηραμένης. Λυσάνδρου δὲ προσθεμένου τοῖς ὀλιγαρχικοῖς καταπλαγεὶς ὁ δῆμος ἠναγκάσθη χειροτονεῖν τὴν ὀλιγαρχίαν. ἔγραψε δὲ τὸ ψήφισμα Δρακοντίδης Ἀφιδναῖος.

35. οἱ μὲν οὖν τριάκοντα τοῦτον τὸν τρόπον κατέστησαν ἐπὶ Πυθοδώρου ἄρχοντος. γενόμενοι δὲ κύριοι τῆς πόλεως τὰ μὲν ἄλλα τὰ δόξαντα περὶ τῆς πολιτείας παρεώρων, πεντακοσίους δὲ βουλευτὰς καὶ τὰς ἄλλας ἀρχὰς καταστήσαντες ἐκ προκρίτων ἐκ τῶν χιλίων, καὶ προσελόμενοι σφίσιν αὐτοῖς τοῦ Πειραιέως

XXXV 1 ΚΑΤΕϹΤΗϹΕ corr. K. **5** *ἐκ τῶν χιλίων* delet Marindin: *πεντακισχιλίων?* K-W, *ἐκ τῶν πεντακισχιλίων* Thompson, H-L; *ἐκ τῶν φυλῶν* Hude. *καὶ τὰς ἄλλας ἀρχὰς καταστήσαντες ἐκ προκρίτων ἐκ τῶν χιλίων* post *μισθοφόρον* in c. 33, 9 ponit Harberton, mutato *χιλίων* in *πεντακισχιλίων* et nostro in loco *προσελόμενοι δὲ* scripto (*Class. Rev.* vi 123). ΠΙΡ^{ε}ΑΙΩϹ: Πειραέως K, K-W; Πειραιῶς H-L, B.

TESTIM. **XXXIV 27** *Schol. Arist. *Vesp.* 157 *Δρακοντίδης:...ἔστι γὰρ οὗτος ὁ τὸ περὶ τῶν τριάκοντα ψήφισμα περὶ ὀλιγαρχίας γράψας, ὡς Ἀρ. ἐν πολιτείαις* (Frag. 373^2, 411^3).
XXXV 5—6 Bekk. *Anecdota*, p. 235 *δέκα τινες εἰσί: δέκα ἦσαν τινες ἐν Πειραιεῖ οἱ ἄρξαντες κατὰ τὴν τυραννίδα τῶν τριάκοντα. ἀλλὰ καὶ προσέταξαν αὐτοῖς εὐθύνας τῆς ἀρχῆς δοῦναι. μὴ ἀγνοῶμεν δὲ ὅτι ἕτεροί εἰσι δέκα, οὓς Ἀθηναῖοι εἵλοντο μετὰ τὴν τῶν τριάκοντα κατάλυσιν* (c. 38, 5).

νων λόγων, Φορμίσιός τις τῶν συγκατελθόντων μετὰ τοῦ δήμου γνώμην εἰσηγήσατο, τοὺς μὲν φεύγοντας κατιέναι, τὴν δὲ πολιτείαν μὴ πᾶσιν, ἀλλὰ τοῖς τὴν γῆν ἔχουσι παραδοῦναι, βουλομένων ταῦτα γενέσθαι καὶ Λακεδαιμονίων. Grote c. 66 vi 4; Schömann, *On Grote*, § 11, holds that it is wrong to regard Phormisius as an adherent of the oligarchical party; at the same time he was no friend to extreme democracy. Schömann's view is supported by the text.

He was sent with Epicrates and others as an envoy to Artaxerxes before the Corinthian war and accepted valuable gifts from the king. The envoys were attacked for this in the *Πρέσβεις* of Plato, ap. Athen. 229 F (*frag.* 119 with Kock's note). He is mentioned in Arist. *Ran.* 965 as an admirer (*μαθητὴς*) of Aeschylus. Didymus, in Schol. *ad loc.*, describes him as *δραστικὸς καὶ τὴν κόμην τρέφων καὶ φοβερὸς δοκῶν εἶναι.*

Λυσάνδρου—τοῖς ὀλιγαρχικοῖς] Diodorus, xiv 3.

ψήφισμα] Isocr. 15 § 67, *οἱ μὲν γὰρ ψηφίσματι παραλαβόντες τὴν πόλιν.*

Δρακοντίδης] Lysias 12 § 73, *Θηραμένης ἐκέλευσεν ὑμᾶς τριάκοντα ἀνδράσιν ἐπιτρέψαι τὴν πόλιν, καὶ τῇ πολιτείᾳ χρῆσθαι ἣν Δρακοντίδης ἀπέφαινεν.* Aristoph. *Vesp.* 157 with Schol. He was himself nominated as one of the Thirty (Xen. *Hell.* ii 3 § 2; Hypereid. ap. Harp. *s.v.*). Cf. Plat. Com. *frag.* 139 Kock.

XXXV—XXXVII. *The Rule of the Thirty.*

XXXV § 1. **οἱ...τριάκοντα**] Diodorus (xix 32 etc) is the first writer who calls them *οἱ τρ. τύραννοι.* The same designation occurs in Plut. *Sull.* 5 and in later writers.

ἐπὶ Πυθοδώρου ἄρχοντος] *ὃν Ἀθηναῖοι, ὅτι ἐν ὀλιγαρχίᾳ ᾑρέθη, οὐκ ὀνομάζουσιν, ἀλλ' ἀναρχίαν τὸν ἐνιαυτὸν καλοῦσιν,* Xen. *Hell.* ii 3 § 1; cf. however Lys. 7 § 9.

τὰ μὲν ἄλλα—βουλευτὰς—καταστήσαντες] Xen. *Hell.* ii 3 § 11, *αἱρεθέντες ἐφ' ᾧτε ξυγγράψαι νόμους, καθ' οὕστινας πολιτεύσοιντο, τούτους μὲν ἀεὶ ἔμελλον ξυγγράφειν τε καὶ ἀποδεικνύναι, βουλὴν δὲ καὶ τὰς ἄλλας ἀρχὰς κατέστησαν, ὡς ἐδόκει αὐτοῖς.* **τὰς ἄλλας ἀρχάς**, *e.g.* that of King-Archon which was filled by Patrocles, Isocr. *Callim.* 18 § 6.

ἐκ προκρίτων ἐκ τῶν χιλίων] 'out of those selected beforehand, *i.e.* out of the 1000.' If *χιλίων* is right, the reference is to the Knights. Cf. Philochorus, fragm. 100, ap. Hesych. *s. v.* *ἱππῆς, ἱππεῖς* (*Ἱππεῦσιν* Schow)· *ἀλλ' εἰσιν ἱππῆς ἄνδρες ἀγαθοὶ χίλιοι* [Aristoph. *Eq.* 225]. *σύστημα πολεμικῶν ἀνδρῶν χιλίων ἵππους τρεφόντων. Φιλόχορος δὲ ἐν τετάρτῳ εἴρηκε, πότε κατεστάθησαν χίλιοι. διάφορα γὰρ ἦν ἱππέων πλήθη κατὰ χρόνον Ἀθηναίοις.* Cf. Gilbert's *Gr. St.* i 305. The Knights were generally credited with oligarchical sympathies. Cf. Martin, *Les Cavaliers Athéniens*, 1886,

ἄρχοντας δέκα καὶ τοῦ δεσμωτηρίου φύλακας ἕνδεκα καὶ μαστιγο-
φόρους τρια[κ]οσίους ὑπηρέτας, κατεῖχον τὴν πόλιν δι' ἑαυτῶν. τὸ 2
μὲν οὖν πρῶτον μέτριοι τοῖς πολίταις [ἦ]σα[ν] καὶ προσεποιοῦντο
διώκειν τὴν πάτριον πο[λιτ]είαν, καὶ τούς τ' Ἐφιάλτου καὶ
Ἀρχεστράτου νόμους τοὺς περὶ τῶν Ἀρεοπαγιτῶν καθεῖλον ἐξ
Ἀρείου [πάγου] καὶ τῶν Σόλωνος θεσμῶν ὅσοι διαμφισβητ[ήσ]εις
εἶχον, καὶ τὸ κῦρος ὃ ἦν ἐν τοῖς δικασταῖς κ[ατέ]λυσαν, ὡς
ἐπανορθοῦντες καὶ ποιοῦντ[ες] ἀναμφισβήτητον τὴν πολιτείαν·

7 *ὑπηρ.* del. Rutherford. ΕΑΥΤΩΝ: *αὐτῶν* J B Mayor sc. *τῶν ὑπηρετῶν* (H-L). **8** *πολιτεύμασι* Poste. **9** ΔΙΟΙΚΕΙΝ (K coll. c. 27, 11): *διώκειν* Kontos, Gertz, K-W, H-L, B, coll. c. 13, 18. **11** ΔΙΑΜΦΙΖΒΗΤ. **13** ΑΝΑΜΦΙΖΒΗΤΗΤΟΝ. Post annum 329 A.C. etiam in titulis Atticis apparet ζ aut σζ pro σ, e.g. *ἐνδέζμους* (329 A.C.). *ψήφιζμα* (paullo post 100 A.C.), Meisterhans, p. 68².

---

pp. 472—480, *Les Cavaliers et les Trente.*

It is improbable however that the select body, out of which the 500 and the other officials were appointed, numbered only 1000. Hence it has been proposed to read *πεντακισχιλίων* (or *ἐκ τῶν π.*), but (as observed by Mr Kenyon) we know of no such body as in existence at this time, unless it is vaguely applied (as under the 400) to all capable of bearing arms.

τοῦ Πειραιέως ἄρχοντας δέκα] Plut. *Lysander* 15, *δέκα δὲ ἐν Πειραιεῖ καταστήσας ἄρχοντας.* Plat. *Epist.* vii p. 324 B. Scheibe, *Oligarchische Umwälzung*, p. 68.

ἕνδεκα] c. 52 § 1. Xen. *Hell.* ii 3 § 54. This new board of Eleven was under the control of Satyrus, one of the most violent partisans of the Thirty.

μαστιγοφόρους] The word occurs in Thuc. iv 47. Xen. *Hell.* ii 3 § 23 mentions certain *νεανίσκοι*, who carried out the orders of the Thirty, but their number is not specified.

§ 2. **μέτριοι**] cf. Xen. *Hell.* ii 3 § 12. The Thirty began by attacking the *συκοφάνται* alone. Plut. *Mor.* ii pp. 959, 998. *Inf.* l. 18.

Ἐφιάλτου] c. 25 § 2.

Ἀρχεστράτου] Possibly the *στρατηγὸς* of that name in the Peloponnesian war, a son of Lycomedes (Thuc. i 57 § 4; Xen. *Hell.* i 5, 16; ii 2, 15). He died at Mitylene (Lys. 21 § 8). In Thuc. viii 74 § 1 we have an Archestratus, who is described as the father of Chaereas.

Mr Kenyon conjectures that 'probably Archestratus was one of the supporters of Ephialtes, and some of the laws curtailing the power of the Areopagus stood in his name.'

καθεῖλον ἐξ Ἀρείου πάγου] This implies that the laws of Ephialtes &c limiting the powers of the Areopagites were actually preserved on the Areopagus and that the Thirty removed them from the hill of Ares and thereby virtually repealed them. The context further implies that the laws of Solon were also preserved on the Areopagus, whereas they were really preserved in the Prytaneum (note on 7 § 1, *κύρβεις*). Possibly we should strike out *ἐξ Ἀρείου πάγου.* As a milder remedy we may remove the comma after *εἶχον*, so as to bring the laws of Solon here referred to under the influence of the verb *κατέλυσαν*: but as the text stands, the laws of Solon are coupled to those of Ephialtes and Archestratus and can only be separated from them by striking out *τ'* before *Ἐφιάλτου.*

Σόλωνος] Schol. Aeschin. 1 § 39, *οἱ λ' τύραννοι...ἐλυμήναντο τοὺς Δράκοντος καὶ Σόλωνος νόμους.*

θεσμῶν] c. 12 § 4 l. 45, in the Iambic lines from Solon.

διαμφισβητήσεις] In c. 9 § 2 it has been remarked that the right of appeal to a lawcourt was one of the strongest points in the democracy as constituted by Solon. In the same passage the ambiguities in the law of property and the law of 'heiresses' are described as giving additional power to the lawcourts. Some of these ambiguities are removed by the Thirty and the power of the lawcourts (and the commons) *pro tanto* diminished.

ἀναμφισβήτητον] an epithet of *κρίσις* in *Pol.* iii 13, 1283 *b* 4, and coupled with *φανερὸν* in 1332 *b* 20 and *Categ.* 5, 3 *b* 4. The adverb is found in *Categ.* 8, 11 *a* 2.

[Col. 16.] οἷο[ν] <τὸν> || περὶ τοῦ δοῦναι τὰ ἑαυτοῦ ᾧ ἂν ἐθέλῃ κύριον ποιή-
σαντες καθάπαξ, τὰς δὲ προσούσας δυσκολίας ‘ἐὰν μὴ μανιῶν ἢ
γήρως <ἕνεκα> ἢ γυναικὶ πιθόμενος’ ἀφεῖλον, ὅπως μὴ ᾖ τοῖς
συκοφάνταις ἔφοδος· ὁμοίως δὲ τοῦτ’ ἔδρων καὶ ἐπὶ τῶν ἄλλων.
3 κατ’ ἀρχὰς μὲν οὖν ταῦτ’ ἐποίουν καὶ τοὺς συκοφάντας καὶ τοὺς
τῷ δήμῳ πρὸς χάριν ὁμιλοῦντας παρὰ τὸ βέλτιστον καὶ κακοπράγ-
μονας ὄντας καὶ πονηροὺς ἀνῄρουν, ἐφ’ οἷς ἔχαιρεν ἡ πόλις
4 γιγνομένοις, ἡγούμενοι τοῦ βελτίστου χάριν ποιεῖν αὐτούς. ἐπεὶ
δὲ τὴν πόλιν ἐγκρατέστερον ἔσχον, οὐδενὸς ἀπείχοντο τῶν πολι-
τῶν, ἀλλ’ ἀπέκτεινον τοὺς καὶ ταῖς οὐσίαις καὶ τῷ γένει καὶ τοῖς

14 οἷον < τὸν > K-W. ἂν < τις > H-L. ΠΟΙΗϹΑΝΤΕϹ: ἐποίησαν ‘emendatio incerta, nec praestat ποιήσαντες καθάπαξ, τὰς προσούσας δυσκολίας’ K-W. **15** ΜΑΝΙΩΝΗΓΗΡΩΝ, μανιῶν ἢ γηρῶν K, K-W: μανιῶν ἢ γήρως <ἕνεκα> Blass et Wyse, coll. [Dem.] 46 § 14; μανιῶν ἢ γήρως <ἢ φαρμάκων ἢ νόσου ἕνεκεν παρανοῶν> Poland; eadem (nisi quod ἕνεκα malunt et παρανοῶν non accipiunt) H-L. **16** ΠΙΘΟΜΕΝΟϹ (edd.): πειθόμενος Wyse et Poland coll. [Dem.] *l.c.* ‘sed praestat aoristus (= πεισθείς)’ H-L. **19** καὶ secl. K-W. **20** ΕΧΑΙΡΟΝ propter participium ἡγούμενοι retineri posse putat K, retinent H-L, B: ἔχαιρεν Sidgwick, Rutherford (K-W, H-L). **21** ΓΙΓΝ (edd.). **23** ΑΠΕΚΤΕΙΝΑΝ (K): ἀπέκτεινον Blass, Kontos, H-L, K-W.

περὶ τοῦ δοῦναι τὰ ἑαυτοῦ ᾧ ἂν ἐθέλῃ] Plut. *Sol.* 21, εὐδοκίμησε δὲ κἀν τῷ περὶ διαθηκῶν νόμῳ· πρότερον γὰρ οὐκ ἐξῆν, ἀλλ’ ἐν τῷ γένει τοῦ τεθνηκότος ἔδει τὰ χρήματα καὶ τὸν οἶκον καταμένειν, ὁ δ’ ᾧ βούλεταί τις ἐπιτρέψας, εἰ μὴ παῖδες ὦσι γνήσιοι, δοῦναι τὰ αὑτοῦ κτλ. οὐ μὴν ἀνέδην γε πάλιν οὐδ’ ἁπλῶς τὰς δόσεις ἐφῆκεν, ἀλλ’ εἰ μὴ νόσων ἕνεκεν ἢ φαρμάκων ἢ δεσμῶν ἢ ἀνάγκῃ κατασχεθεὶς ἢ γυναικὶ πειθόμενος. See note on Dem. *Lept.* § 102.

καθάπαξ] ‘absolutely.’ Under Solon’s law it was only in the event of a man’s having no legitimate children that he could make a will at all. Possibly the Thirty made the right absolute.

τὰς προσούσας δυσκολίας] either ‘the inconvenient limitations *attaching thereto*’ or ‘the *additional* inconvenient limitations’; probably the former.

ἐὰν μὴ μανιῶν—πιθόμενος] [Dem.] 46 § 14, ἐὰν μὴ μανιῶν ἢ γήρως ἢ φαρμάκων ἢ νόσου ἕνεκα, ἢ γυναικὶ πειθόμενος, and § 16, νοσοῦντα η φαρμακῶντα ἢ γυναικὶ πειθόμενον ἢ ὑπὸ γήρως ἢ ὑπὸ μανιῶν ἢ ὑπὸ ἀνάγκης τινος καταληφθέντα. 48 § 56, ἄκυρά γε ταῦτα πάντα ἐνομοθέτησεν εἶναι ὁ Σόλων, ὅ τι ἂν τις γυναικὶ πειθόμενος πράττῃ. Lys. frag. 74, τῆς διαθέσεως...ἣν ἐκεῖνος διέθετο οὐ παρανοῶν οὐδὲ γυναικὶ πεισθείς. Isaeus 6 § 9, ἐὰν μὴ ἄρα μανεὶς ἢ ὑπὸ γήρως κτλ.

§ 3. **τοὺς συκοφάντας** κτλ.] Xen. *Hell.* ii 3, 12, πρῶτον μὲν οὓς πάντες ᾔδεσαν ἐν τῇ δημοκρατίᾳ ἀπὸ συκοφαντίας ζῶντας καὶ τοῖς καλοῖς κἀγαθοῖς βαρεῖς ὄντας συλλαμβάνοντες ὑπῆγον θανάτου· καὶ ἥ τε βουλὴ ἡδέως αὐτῶν κατεψηφίζετο, οἵ τε ἄλλοι, ὅσοι ξυνῄδεσαν ἑαυτοῖς μὴ ὄντες τοιοῦτοι, οὐδὲν ἤχθοντο. Lysias 13 § 5, (οἱ τριάκοντα) φάσκοντες χρῆναι τῶν ἀδίκων καθαρὰν ποιῆσαι τὴν πόλιν. Plato, then a young man of 24, and a nephew of Critias, was at first misled by these splendid professions, *Epist.* 324 BC (Grote, v 562).

πρὸς χάριν] (λέγειν τινι) Xen. *Mem.* iv 4, 4: *Hell.* vi 3, 7; *Rhet.* i 1, 1354 *b* 34, ἀκροᾶσθαι πρὸς χάριν. *Pol.* iii 16, 1287 *a* 38, πολλὰ πρὸς ἐπήρειαν καὶ χάριν πράττειν. *Eth.* 10, 2, 1173 *b* 33, (ὁ φίλος) πρὸς τἀγαθὸν ὁμιλεῖν δοκεῖ, (ὁ κόλαξ) πρὸς ἡδονήν.

Theramenes protested against putting people to death simply because they had enjoyed influence under the democracy: ‘Even you and I (he reminded Kritias) have both said and done many things for the sake of popularity’ Xen. *Hell.* ii 3 § 15 (Grote, v 565).

§ 4. **οὐδενὸς ἀπείχοντο** κτλ.] Xen. *Hell.* ii 3 § 14, οὓς ἐβούλοντο ξυνελάμβανον, οὐκέτι τοὺς πονηρούς τε καὶ ὀλίγου ἀξίους.

ἀπέκτεινον κτλ.] *ib.* § 15 (ὁ Κριτίας) προπετὴς ἦν ἐπὶ τὸ πολλοὺς ἀποκτείνειν, and § 17, ἀποθνησκόντων πολλῶν καὶ ἀδίκως. Among those who were put to death were Strombichides and other officers who were attached to the demo-

ἀξιώμασιν προέχοντας, ὑπεξαιρούμενοί τε τὸν φόβον καὶ βουλόμενοι τὰς οὐσίας διαρπάζειν· καὶ χρόνου διαπεσόντος βραχέος, οὐκ ἐλάττους ἀνῃρήκεσαν ἢ χιλίους πεντακοσίους.

36. *οὕτως δὲ τῆς πόλεως ὑποφερομένης, Θηραμένης ἀγανακτῶν ἐπὶ τοῖς γιγνομένοις τῆς μὲν ἀσελγείας αὐτοῖς παρῄνει παύσασθαι, μεταδοῦναι δὲ τῶν πραγμάτων τοῖς βελτίστοις. οἱ δὲ πρῶτον ἐναντιωθέντες, ἐπεὶ διεσπάρησαν οἱ λόγοι πρὸς τὸ πλῆθος καὶ πρὸς τὸν Θηραμένην οἰκείως εἶχον οἱ πολλοί, φοβηθέντες μὴ προστάτης γενόμενος τοῦ δήμου καταλύσῃ τὴν δυναστείαν καταλέγουσιν τῶν πολιτῶν τρισχιλίους ὡς μεταδώσοντες τῆς πολιτείας. Θηραμένης δὲ πάλιν ἐπιτιμᾷ καὶ τούτοις, πρῶτον μὲν ὅτι, βουλό-* 2
μενοι μεταδοῦναι τοῖς ἐπιεικέσι, τρισχιλίοις μόνοις μεταδιδόασι, ὡς ἐν τούτῳ τῷ πλήθει τῆς ἀρετῆς ὡρισμένης, ἔπειθ᾽ ὅτι δύο τὰ ἐναντιώτατα ποιοῦσιν, βίαιόν τε τὴν ἀρχὴν καὶ τῶν ἀρχομένων ἥττω κατασκευάζοντες. οἱ δὲ τούτων μὲν ὠλιγώρησαν, τὸν δὲ κατάλογον

24 *ἀξιώμασι* H-L. **25** ΔΙΑΠΕϹΟΝΤΟϹ (edd.)?: *διαλιπόντος* J B Mayor, *διελθόντος* Herwerden.
XXXVI 1 *οὕτω* H-L. **2** ΓΙΝ (K-W). **3** ΠΡΩΤΟΙ corr. K. **6** *κατα*-ΚΑ *λέγουσι* H-L. **7** ΔΙϹΧΙΛΙΟΥϹ corr. K. **9** *μεταδιδόασιν* H-L. **12** ΜΕΤΑϹΚΕΥΑΖΟΝΤΕϹ.

XXXV 26 Heraclidis epitoma, Frag. 611, 6[3] (locus infra exscriptus).

---

cracy (Lysias 13 § 13; 30 § 14); Lycurgus who belonged to one of the most eminent sacred *gentes* in the State ([Plut.] *Vit. Orat.* p. 838); a wealthy man named Antiphon; Leon of Salamis (Plat. *Apol.* p. 32); and even Niceratus the son, and Eucrates the brother, of Nicias, Xen. *Hell.* ii 3, 39—41; Lysias 18 §§ 5—8 (Grote v 566).

ὑπεξαιρούμενοι—φόβον] 'cunningly removing (making away with) all whom they had reason to fear.' Plat. *Rep.* 567 B, and in pass. Thuc. viii 70 (of the Four Hundred) *ἄνδρας...ἀπέκτειναν οὐ πολλοὺς οἳ ἐδόκουν ἐπιτήδειοι εἶναι ὑπεξαιρεθῆναι.* Either **τὸν φόβον**, as suggested by Mr W. L. Newman (*Class. Rev.* v 164 *b*), is the 'object of their fear' (a somewhat poetic usage), or we must render the passage 'getting quit of their own apprehension.'

χιλίους πεντακοσίους] Heraclides 9, *καὶ ἀνεῖλον οὐκ ἐλάσσους χιλίων φ'.* Isocr. *Areop.* 67 (of the Thirty), *οἱ μὲν γὰρ ψηφίσματι παραλαβόντες τὴν πόλιν πεντακοσίους μὲν καὶ χιλίους τῶν πολιτῶν ἀκρίτους ἀπέκτειναν*, *Paneg.* 131. Aeschin. *Ctes.* § 235. Cf. Grote v 577 n. The Schol. on Aeschin. 1 § 39 quotes Lysias for the number 2500.

XXXVI § 1. **ὑποφερομένης**] c. 25 § 1.

Θηραμένης *κτλ.*] Xen. *Hell.* ii 3 §§ 15—17.

διεσπάρησαν] *δ. λόγον*, Xen. *Hell.* v 1 § 25.

φοβηθέντες—πολιτείας] Xen. *Hell.* ii 3 § 18, *ἐκ τούτου μέντοι Κριτίας καὶ οἱ ἄλλοι τῶν τριάκοντα, ἤδη φοβούμενοι καὶ οὐχ ἥκιστα τὸν Θηραμένην, μὴ συρρυείησαν πρὸς αὐτὸν οἱ πολῖται, καταλέγουσι τρισχιλίους τοὺς μεθέξοντας δὴ τῶν πραγμάτων.*

προστάτης τοῦ δήμου] c. 2 l. 9; c. 28 § 2.

§ 2. **Θ. πάλιν ἐπιτιμᾷ**] Xen. *Hell.* ii 3 § 19, *ὁ δ' αὖ Θ. καὶ πρὸς ταῦτα ἔλεγεν, ὅτι ἄτοπον δοκοίη ἑαυτῷ γε εἶναι τὸ πρῶτον μὲν βουλομένους τοὺς βελτίστους τῶν πολιτῶν κοινωνοὺς ποιήσασθαι τρισχιλίους, ὥσπερ τὸν ἀριθμὸν τοῦτον ἔχοντά τινα ἀνάγκην καλοὺς κἀγαθοὺς εἶναι, καὶ οὔτ' ἔξω τούτων σπουδαίους οὔτ' ἐντὸς τούτων πονηροὺς οἷόν τε εἴη γενέσθαι· ἔπειτα δ', ἔφη, ὁρῶ ἔγωγε δύο ἡμᾶς τὰ ἐναντιώτατα πράττοντας, βιαίαν τε τὴν ἀρχὴν καὶ ἥττονα τῶν ἀρχομένων κατασκευαζομένους.*

τὸν δὲ κατάλογον *κτλ.*] The narrative in Xenophon (*Hell.* ii 3 § 20) proτῶν τρισχιλίων πολὺν μὲν χρόνον ὑπερεβάλλοντο καὶ παρ' αὐτοῖς ἐφύλαττον τοὺς ἐγνωσμένους, ὅτε δὲ καὶ δόξειεν αὐτοῖς ἐκφέρειν τοὺς μὲν ἐξήλειφον τῶν <ἐγ>γεγραμμένων, τοὺς δ' ἀντενέγραφον τῶν ἔξωθεν.

37. ἤδη δὲ τοῦ χειμῶνος ἐνεστῶτος, καταλαβόντος Θρασυβούλου μετὰ τῶν φυγάδων Φυλήν, καὶ κατὰ τὴν στρατιὰν ἣν ἐξήγαγον οἱ τριάκοντα κακῶς ἀποχωρήσαντες, ἔγνωσαν τῶν μὲν ἄλλων τὰ ὅπλα παρελέσθαι, Θηραμένην δὲ διαφθεῖραι τόνδε <τὸν> τρόπον. νόμους εἰσήνεγκαν εἰς τὴν βουλὴν δύο κελεύοντες ||
[Col. 17.] ἐπιχειροτονεῖν, ὧν ὁ μὲν εἰς αὐτοκράτορας ἐποίει τοὺς τριάκοντα

13 ΥΠΕΡΒΑΛΛ. **14** *συμφέρειν* van Leeuwen. **15** ΓΕΓΡΑΜΜΕΝΩΝ (K): <*ἐγ*>*γεγραμμένων* Herwerden (H-L, K-W, B).
XXXVII 2 *καὶ* secl. K-W. ϹΤΡΑΤΙΑΝ K, H-L, B: *στρατείαν* K-W. **3** *οἱ τριάκοντα* del. Richards (H-L), ante *ἔγνωσαν* ponit J B Mayor. **4** ΠΑΡ^{ε}ΙΕϹΘΑΙ corr. K. **5** <*τὸν*> K-W, H-L, K^3, B, coll. c. 7, 8.

---

ceeds immediately with an account of the review of the 3000 in the *agora* and of the rest (*τῶν ἔξω τοῦ καταλόγου*) elsewhere. The *κατάλογος* is the list of the 3000 referred to by Theramenes in Xen. *Hell.* ii 3 § 52, *ἱκετεύω...μὴ ἐπὶ Κριτίᾳ εἶναι ἐξαλείφειν...ὃν ἂν βούληται, ἀλλ' ὅνπερ νόμον οὗτοι ἔγραψαν περὶ τῶν ἐν τῷ καταλόγῳ, κατὰ τοῦτον...τὴν κρίσιν εἶναι*, *ib.* 4 § 28.

ἀντενέγραφον] The word is used by Dem., but only in the pass.

XXXVII § 1. **τοῦ χειμῶνος ἐνεστῶτος**] the winter of B.C. 404/3.

καταλαβόντος — Φυλήν] Xenophon (*Hell.* ii 3, 23—56) completes the story of the opposition of Theramenes to the proceedings of the Thirty, and his consequent death, before relating the capture of Phyle by Thrasybulus. In ii 4, 1, after the death of Theramenes, the opponents of the Thirty were compelled to withdraw, and many of them went to Megara and Thebes. Thereupon (*ἐκ τούτου* § 2) Thrasybulus *ὁρμηθεὶς ἐκ Θηβῶν ὡς σὺν ἑβδομήκοντα Φυλὴν χωρίον καταλαμβάνει ἰσχυρόν.* In the text the occupation of Phyle, and the defeat of the force sent out by the Thirty against the holders of that fort, are described as the cause of the disarmament of the general body of citizens and the execution of Theramenes.

This implies that Thrasybulus held Phyle for a longer time than has generally been supposed. It was not long after the surrender of Athens, on the 16th of Munychion (end of April), that the Thirty came into power, probably early in May, 404. Cleocritus in Xen. *Hell.* ii 4, 21, speaking immediately after the battle which ensued on the occupation of Munychia, describes the rule of the Thirty as having lasted for eight months. This brings us to the end of December, 404.

It was not until the small force which originally occupied Phyle, variously stated as 30, 60, 70 or over 100 (Grote v 585), had increased to 1000 that Thrasybulus advanced on Athens. Mr Kenyon suggests that 'they probably remained for two or three of the winter months at Phyle.' The fact that it was during the winter that Phyle was in occupation is illustrated by the narrative of the snowstorm which thwarted the Thirty in their attempt to blockade Phyle after their first repulse (Xen. *Hell.* ii 4, 2).

τὰ ὅπλα παρελέσθαι] Xen. *Hell.* ii 3 § 20, *τὰ ὅπλα πάντων πλὴν τῶν τρισχιλίων παρείλοντο*, and *ib.* § 41. *Pol.* 1311 *a* 8 ff.

νόμους εἰσήνεγκαν] asyndeton.

αὐτοκράτορας—τρισχιλίων] Xen. *Hell.* ii 3 § 51 (Critias *loquitur*), *ἔστι δὲ ἐν τοῖς καινοῖς νόμοις τῶν μὲν ἐν τοῖς τρισχιλίοις ὄντων μηδένα ἀποθνήσκειν ἄνευ τῆς ὑμετέρας ψήφου, τῶν δ' ἔξω τοῦ καταλόγου κυρίους εἶναι τοὺς τριάκοντα θανατοῦν. ἐγὼ οὖν, ἔφη, Θηραμένην τουτονὶ ἐξαλείφω ἐκ τοῦ καταλόγου ξυνδοκοῦν ἅπασιν ἡμῖν καὶ τοῦτον, ἔφη, ἡμεῖς θανατοῦμεν.* This implies that there were other *καινοὶ νόμοι*, and the second given in the text, but unrecognised by Xenophon, would be one of them. But if it had already been passed before the meeting of the Council at which Critias denounced Theramenes,

τῶν πολιτῶν ἀποκτεῖναι τοὺς μὴ τοῦ καταλόγου μετέχοντας τῶν τρισχιλίων, ὁ δ' ἕτερος ἐκώλυε κοινωνεῖν τῆς παρούσης πολιτείας ὅσοι τυγχάνουσιν τὸ ἐν Ἠετιωνείᾳ τεῖχος κατασκάψαντες, ἧ τοῖς τετρακοσίοις ἐναντίον τι πράξαντες [[ἧ]] τοῖς κατασκευάσασι τὴν προτέραν ὀλιγαρχίαν· ὧ[ν] ἐτύγχανεν ἀμφοτέρων κεκοινωνηκὼς ὁ Θηραμένης, ὥστε συνέβαινεν ἐπικυρωθέντων τῶν νόμων ἔξω τε γίγνεσθαι τῆς πολιτείας αὐτὸν καὶ τοὺς τριάκοντα κυρίους εἶναι θανατοῦντας. ἀναιρεθέντος δὲ Θηραμένους τά τε ὅπλα παρείλοντο 2
πάντων πλὴν τῶν τρισχιλίων, καὶ ἐν τοῖς ἄλλοις πολὺ πρὸς ὠμότητα καὶ πονηρίαν ἐπέδοσαν.— — πρέσβεις πέμψαντες εἰς

7 *τῶν τρισχιλίων* delere vult B. **9** *τυγχάνουσι* H-L. **10** *ἧ* secl. K-W, H-L. **14** ΘΑΝΑΤΟΥΝΤΑϹ (K, K-W) defendit Kontos coll. Thuc. v 34, Plat. *Leg.* 878 E, Polyb. iii 85, 2 etc.: *θανατοῦν* Lacon, Keil, (+*αὐτόν* Poland), coll. Xen. *Hell.* ii 13, 51. **16** *πρέσβεις* <*δὲ*> J B Mayor, Blass, Hude (H-L, K[3], B): ante *πρέσβεις* lacunam indicant K-W; verba *πρέσβεις—ἐφρούρουν* olim in fine capitis 36 locum habuisse censet van Leeuwen.

---

the latter would obviously have withdrawn from Athens. The only alternative is to suppose, with Mr Kenyon, that Critias proposed the second law on the spot and 'forced it down the throat of the council by the threat of armed force.' This is not inconsistent with striking the name of Theramenes out of the list of the 3000, the only detail recorded by Xenophon, who omits the second law as superfluous, and as therefore marring the dramatic effect of his narrative.

Cf. Isocr. 18 § 16, *οὐδένα φανήσομαι τῶν πολιτῶν οὔτε χρήμασι ζημιώσας οὔτε περὶ τοῦ σώματος εἰς κίνδυνον καταστήσας, οὔτ' ἐκ μὲν τῶν μετεχόντων τῆς πολιτείας ἐξαλείψας εἰς δὲ τὸν μετὰ Λυσάνδρου κατάλογον ἐγγράψας.*

τὸ ἐν Ἠετιωνείᾳ τεῖχος κατασκάψαντες] 'the projecting mole which contracted and commanded, on the northern side, the narrow entrance of Peiraeus,' Grote c. 62, v 403, 408, 412. See Map of Peiraeus in Curtius, *Sieben Karten*, no. 2.

Thuc. viii 90 § 1, *τὸ ἐν τῇ Ἠετιωνείᾳ καλουμένῃ τεῖχος ἐποιοῦντο.* *ib.* 90 § 3, *ἦν δὲ τοῦ τείχους ἡ γνώμη αὕτη, ὡς ἔφη Θηραμένης καὶ οἱ μετ' αὐτοῦ, οὐχ ἵνα τοὺς ἐν Σάμῳ, ἢν βίᾳ ἐπιπλέωσι, μὴ δέξωνται ἐς τὸν Πειραιᾶ, ἀλλ' ἵνα τοὺς πολεμίους μᾶλλον, ὅταν βούλωνται, καὶ ναυσὶ καὶ πεζῷ δέξωνται. χηλὴ γάρ ἐστι τοῦ Πειραιῶς ἡ Ἠετιώνεια, καὶ παρ' αὐτὴν εὐθὺς ὁ ἔσπλους ἐστίν.* *ib.* 92 § 10, *τὸν Θηραμένην ἠρώτων εἰ δοκεῖ αὐτῷ ἐπ' ἀγαθῷ τὸ τεῖχος οἰκοδομεῖσθαι, καὶ εἰ ἄμεινον εἶναι καθαιρεθέν. ὁ δέ, εἴπερ καὶ ἐκείνοις δοκεῖ καθαιρεῖν, καὶ ἑαυτῷ ἔφη ξυνδοκεῖν. καὶ ἐντεῦθεν εὐθὺς ἀναβάντες οἵ τε ὁπλῖται καὶ πολλοὶ τῶν ἐκ τοῦ Πειραιῶς ἀνθρώπων κατέσκαπτον τὸ τείχισμα.* In [Dem.] *Theocr.* § 17 p. 1343, the incident is wrongly referred to the time of the Thirty.

§ 2. **ὅπλα παρείλοντο**] This has already been mentioned as resolved by the Thirty, in § 1. Xenophon places the actual disarmament before the execution of Theramenes, *Hell.* ii 3, 20.

πολὺ πρὸς ὠμότητα—ἐπέδοσαν] Xen. *Hell.* ii 3, 21, *πολλοὺς μὲν ἔχθρας ἕνεκα ἀπέκτεινον, πολλοὺς δὲ χρημάτων.* It was after the disarmament, and before the death of Theramenes, that, according to Xenophon, ten of the *μέτοικοι* became the victims of the Thirty. Among these was Polemarchus, the brother of Lysias (Lys. 12 § 17).—*Categ.* 10, 13 *a* 24 *ἐπιδοίη ἂν εἰς τὸ βέλτιον εἶναι*, *Eth.* 10, 5, 1175 *a* 35, *ἐπιδιδόασιν εἰς τὸ οἰκεῖον ἔργον.* *Magn. Mor.* i 9, 1186 *b* 29, *πρὸς ἃ μᾶλλον ἐπιδίδομεν.* Isocr. 33 B, *ἐ. πρὸς εὐδαιμονίαν.*

πρέσβεις πέμψαντες] This asyndeton is not justifiable on the same grounds as *νόμους εἰσήνεγκαν* in the second sentence of this chapter; and betrays some serious disturbance of the text. 'There is no connexion whatever between the first of these sentences and those that go before them, and the coming of Callibius preceded the final measures taken against Theramenes' (*Edinburgh Review*, 1891 p. 478). Besides, it is too late to accuse Theramenes when he is already executed. There is thus every reason for believing (with van Leeuwen) that this paragraph ought to be transferred to

Λακεδαίμονα τοῦ τε Θηραμένους κατηγόρουν καὶ βοηθεῖν αὐτοῖς ἠξίουν· ὧν ἀκούσαντες οἱ Λακεδαιμόνιοι Καλλίβιον ἀπέστειλαν ἁρμοστὴν. καὶ στρατιώτας ὡς ἑπτακοσίους, οἳ τὴν ἀκρόπολιν ἐλθόντες ἐφρούρουν.

38. *μετὰ δὲ ταῦτα καταλαβόντων τῶν ἀπὸ Φυλῆς τὴν Μουνιχίαν, καὶ νικησάντων μάχῃ τοὺς μετὰ τῶν τριάκοντα βοηθήσαντας, ἐπαναχωρήσαντες μετὰ τὸ[ν] κίνδυνον οἱ ἐκ τοῦ ἄστεως καὶ συναθροισθέντες εἰς τὴν ἀγοράν, τῇ ὑστεραίᾳ τοὺς μὲν τριάκοντα κατέλυσαν, αἱροῦνται δὲ δέκα τῶν πολιτῶν αὐτοκράτορας ἐπὶ τὴν [τοῦ πο]λέμου κατάλυσιν. οἱ δὲ παραλαβόντες τὴν ἀρχὴν ἐφ' οἷς μὲν ᾑρέθησαν οὐκ ἔπραττον, *ἐπέ[στελλον] δ' εἰς Λακεδαίμονα*
2 *βοήθειαν μεταπε[μπόμ]ενοι καὶ χρήματα δανειζόμενοι. χαλεπῶς δὲ [φε]ρόντων ἐπὶ τούτοις τῶν ἐν τῇ πολιτείᾳ, φο[βούμεν]οι μὴ καταλυθῶσιν τῆς ἀρχῆς καὶ βουλόμενοι κατ[απλῆξ]αι τοὺς ἄλλους (ὅπερ ἐγένετο), συλλαβόντες [Δ]ημάρετον οὐδενὸς ὄντα δεύτερον τῶν πολιτῶν ἀπέκτειναν, καὶ τὰ πράγματα βεβαίως εἶχον, συνα-*

17 ΑΥΤΟΙC (K, H-L): *αὐτοῖς* K-W, *ἑαυτοῖς* B.

XXXVIII 2 et **16** ΜΟΥΝΥΧΙΑΝ. Cf. c. 19, 5. **4** CΥΝΑCΘΡΟΙCΘ? **6** ΕΝΟΙC corr. K. **7** *ἐ[πρέσβευ]σ[αν]* K (K-W): *ἔπε[μψαν]* H-L, B; spatium litteras aliquanto plures quam *ἔπεμψαν*, paullo pauciores quam *ἐπρέσβευσαν*, postulare videtur; scripsi *ἐπέστελλον*, coll. Thuc. viii 38 *ἐπιστέλλει—ἐς τὴν Λακεδαίμονα*. **10** *καταλυθῶσι* H-L. **11** *Δημάρετον* Blass (K-W, H-L, K[3]); post hoc nomen *ἀρετῇ* fortasse recte inserit Richards. **12** *συναγωνιζομένων* papyrum habere putabant H-L.

TESTIMONIA. **XXXVIII 5** Bekk. *An.* 235—6 (cf. Testim. ad xxxv 5—6).

---

some such place as the end of c. 36. Xenophon's narrative (*Hell.* ii 3 §§ 13, 14), as noticed by Mr Kenyon, is supported by Diodorus xiv 4, and is in itself more probable than that in the text:—'It would hardly have been possible for the Thirty to have carried on their Reign of Terror without an armed force at their backs, whereas Aristotle represents it as having occurred while the whole body of Athenians was still in possession of weapons.' Part of this objection is removed by transferring the passage to the end of c. 36, but we still have the protests of Theramenes placed after, instead of before, the arrival of the Spartan garrison.

Καλλίβιον] Xen. *l.c.* and Plut. *Lysand.* 15 *ad fin.* In neither of these passages is the number of the garrison mentioned.

XXXVIII—XL. *The Rule of the Ten. The end of the oligarchical revolution and the restoration of the democracy.*

XXXVIII § 1. **καταλαβόντων—Μουνιχίαν** *κτλ.*] Xen. *Hell.* ii 4, 11—19. Andoc. *De Myst.* 80.

ἐπαναχωρήσαντες *κτλ.*] Xen. *l.c.* § 22, *τοὺς μεθ' ἑαυτῶν ἀπήγαγον εἰς τὸ ἄστυ.*

τοὺς τριάκοντα κατέλυσαν *κτλ.*] *ib.* 23, *ἐψηφίσαντο ἐκείνους μὲν καταπαῦσαι, ἄλλους δὲ ἑλέσθαι. καὶ εἵλοντο δέκα, ἕνα ἀπὸ φυλῆς.*

The appointment of the Ten is described by Lysias, *c. Eratosth.* 12 § 54, *ἄρχοντας δὲ τοὺς ἐκείνοις ἐχθίστους εἵλοντο.* Among them were Pheidon, formerly one of the Thirty, with Hippocles and Epichares and others who were regarded as opposed to the extreme party of Charicles and Critias (§ 55). *λαβόντες...τὰς ἀρχὰς καὶ τὴν πόλιν ἀμφοτέροις ἐπολέμουν, τοῖς τε τριάκοντα πάντα κακὰ εἰργασμένοις καὶ ὑμῖν πάντα κακὰ πεπονθόσι* (57). **ἐπέστελλον** *κτλ.*] (Pheidon) *ἐλθὼν εἰς Λακεδαίμονα ἔπειθεν αὐτοὺς στρατεύεσθαι...οὐ δυνάμενος δὲ τούτων τυχεῖν...ἑκατὸν τάλαντα ἐδανείσατο, ἵνα ἔχοι ἐπικούρους μισθοῦσθαι* (58—59). They were appointed soon after the time when *περὶ [τῶν] διαλλαγῶν οἱ λόγοι ἐγίνοντο* (53), but their policy tended *οὐ διαλλάξαι ἀλλ' ἀπολέσαι...τὴν πόλιν* (60). The 100 talents are also mentioned by Xen. *Hell.* ii 4, 28. Suidas and Harp. *s.v. δέκα.*

γωνιζομένου Καλλιβίου τε καὶ τῶν Πελοποννησίων τῶν παρόντων
καὶ πρὸς τού[τοι]ς ἐνίων τῶν ἐν τοῖς ἱππεῦσι· τούτων γάρ τινες
μάλιστα τῶν πολιτῶν ἐσπούδαζον μὴ κατελθεῖν τοὺς ἀπὸ Φυλῆς.
ὡς δ' οἱ τὸν Πειραιέα καὶ τὴν Μουνιχίαν ἔχοντες, ἀποστάντος 3
ἅπαντος τοῦ δήμου πρὸς αὐτούς, ἐπεκράτουν τῷ πολέμῳ, τότε
καταλύσαντες τοὺς δέκα τοὺς πρώτους αἱρεθέντας, ἄλλους εἵλοντο
δέκα τοὺς βελτίστους εἶναι δοκοῦντας, ἐφ' ὧν συνέβη καὶ τὰς
διαλύσεις || γενέσθαι καὶ κατελθεῖν τὸν δῆμον, συναγωνιζομένων καὶ [Col. 18.]
προθυμουμένων τούτων. προειστήκεσαν δ' αὐτῶν μάλιστα Ῥίνων τε
ὁ Παιανιεὺς καὶ Φάϋλλος ὁ Ἀχερδούσιος· οὗτοι γὰρ πρίν <*τε*> ⟦*ἢ*⟧
Παυσανίαν ⟦*τ'*⟧ *ἀφικέσθαι διεπέμ[ποντ]ο πρὸς τοὺς ἐν Πειραιεῖ, καὶ*
ἀφικομένου συνεσπούδασαν τὴν κάθοδον. ἐπὶ πέρας γὰρ ἤγαγε 4
τὴν εἰρήνην καὶ τὰς διαλύσεις Παυσανίας ὁ τῶν Λακεδαιμονίων
βασιλεὺς μετὰ τῶν δέκα διαλλακτῶν τῶν ὕστερον ἀφικομένων ἐκ

ϵ ϵ
16 ΠΙΡΑΙΑ: *Πειραιέα* K, K-W, B; *Πειραιᾶ* H-L: in titulis Atticis *Πειραιέα* saepius quam *Πειραέα* apparet; *Πειραιᾶ* nondum inveni. **17** ΑΠΑΝΤΟϹ Blass (K[3]): ΠΑΝΤΟϹ K[1] (K-W, H-L). ΑΥΤΗΝ (K): *αὐτοὺς* Blass, Kontos, Hude, K-W, H-L. **22** ΑΧΕΡΔΟΥϹΥΙΟϹ corr. Bywater, etc. **22—23** ΠΡΙΝ Η ΠΑΥϹΑΝΙΑΝ ΤΕ *κτλ* (K): *πρὶν ἢ Π.—διεπέμποντό* <*τε*> K-W[1]; *πρὶν* <*τε*> *Π.—διεπέμποντο* Richards (H-L, K-W[2], B). ϵ ϵ **23** ΠΙΡΑΙΙ: *Πειραιεῖ* K, H-L; *Πειραεῖ* K-W, B. *Πειραεῖ* tituli Attici (Meisterhans, p. 25[2]) duodecim in locis habent, e.g. Dittenberger 337, 9, 14, 36 (B.C. 320) *ἐν* vel *ἐμ Πειραεῖ*. **24** ΑΦΙΚΝΟΜΕΝΟΥϹ corr. K. **25** *Παυσανίας* del. H-L; *ὁ—βασιλεὺς* del. Richards, regis nomine iam antea commemorato.

21 Heraclidis epitoma, 611, 6[3], *τούτων δὲ καταλυθέντων Θρασύβουλος καὶ Ῥίνων προειστήκεσαν, ὃς ἦν ἀνὴρ καλὸς καὶ ἀγαθός.*

---

§ 2. **τοῖς ἱππεῦσι**] Xen. *Hell.* ii 4, 24. Lysias *Mantith.* 16 § 3, *οὐχ ἵππευον... ἐπὶ τῶν τριάκοντα.* After the restoration of the democracy there was evidently a prejudice against those who had been *ἱππεῖς* at the time of the Thirty. Mantitheus meets this prejudice by shewing that he was not of the number, and also that many who were, had subsequently become members of the *βουλὴ* or had been elected *στρατηγοὶ* and *ἵππαρχοι* (*ib.* 8).

§ 3. **ἄλλους εἵλοντο δέκα**] These are not mentioned either by Lysias or by Xenophon.

συναγωνιζομένων] with the democratical party. **τούτων** probably refers to the Ten.

Ῥίνων] Isocr. *Callim.* § 7, *εἷς τῶν δέκα γενόμενος*, but Isocrates does not clearly distinguish this board of Ten from those who were elected immediately after the overthrow of the Thirty: § 5, *ἦρχον μὲν γὰρ οἱ δέκα οἱ μετὰ τοὺς τριάκοντα καταστάντες.*

Φάϋλλος] otherwise unknown.

πρὶν] The removal of *ἢ* (proposed by Herwerden) is justified not only by its rarity in Attic Greek, but also by the fact that MSS often vary between *πρὶν* and *πρὶν ἢ* (Wyse).

§ 4. **ἐπὶ πέρας—ἤγαγε**] The phrase *πέρας ἔχειν = περαίνεσθαι* is found in Isocr. 42 B, Lycurg. 155, 34 (§ 60) and elsewhere: and Polybius uses *πέρας λαμβάνειν* (v 31, 2) and *π. ἐπιθεῖναί τινι* (i 41, 2). Ar. *Meteor.* I, 14, 353 *a* 18, *τὸ ἔργον αὐτῶν ἔχει πέρας, ὁ δὲ χρόνος οὐκ ἔχει. πέρας* is a frequent word in Ar., but *ἐπὶ πέρας ἄγειν* is not recorded in the *Index Ar.*, though *ἄγειν ἐπὶ*...occurs in *Pol.* 1313 *a* 19; 1270 *a* 6.

Παυσανίας] Xen. *Hell.* ii 4, 29—39.

τῶν δέκα διαλλακτῶν κτλ.] *l.c.* § 38, *ἐξέπεμψαν πεντεκαίδεκα ἄνδρας εἰς τὰς Ἀθήνας καὶ ἐπέταξαν ξὺν Παυσανίᾳ διαλλάξαι ὅπῃ δύναιντο κάλλιστα.* (It will be observed that Xenophon mentions 15, not 10, and as the number is exceptional it is more likely to be right than not.) *οἱ δὲ διήλλαξαν ἐφ' ᾧτε εἰρήνην μὲν ἔχειν ὡς πρὸς ἀλλήλους, ἀπιέναι δὲ ἐπὶ τὰ ἑαυτῶν*

Λακεδαίμονος, οὓς αὐτὸς ἐσπούδασεν ἐλθεῖν. οἱ δὲ πε[ρὶ] τὸν Ῥίνωνα διά τε τὴν εὔνοιαν τὴν εἰς τὸν δ[ῆμον] ἐπηνέθησαν, καὶ λαβόντες τὴν ἐπιμέλειαν ἐν ὀλιγαρχίᾳ τὰς εὐθύνας ἔδοσαν [ἐ]ν δημοκρατίᾳ, καὶ οὐδεὶς οὐδὲν ἐνεκάλεσε[ν αὐ]τοῖς οὔτε τῶν ἐν ἄστει μεινάντων οὔτε τῶν ἐκ Πειραιέως κατελθόντων, ἀλλὰ διὰ ταῦτα καὶ στρατηγὸς εὐθὺς ᾑρέθη Ῥίνων.

39. Ἐγένοντο δ' αἱ διαλύσεις ἐπ' Εὐκλείδου ἄρχοντος κατὰ τὰς συνθήκας τάσδε. τοὺς βουλομένους Ἀθηναίων τῶν ἐν ἄστει μεινάντων ἐξοικεῖν ἔχειν Ἐλευσῖνα, ἐπιτίμους ὄντας καὶ κυρίους
2 καὶ αὐτοκράτορας ἑ[αυ]τῶν καὶ τὰ αὑτῶν καρπουμένους. τὸ δ' ἱερὸν εἶναι κοινὸν ἀμφοτέρων, ἐπιμελεῖσθαι δὲ Κήρυκας καὶ Εὐμολπίδας κατὰ τὰ πάτρια. μὴ ἐξεῖναι δὲ μήτε τοῖς Ἐλευσίνοθεν εἰς τὸ ἄστυ μήτε τοῖς ἐκ τοῦ ἄστεως Ἐλευσίναδε ἰέναι πλὴν μυστηρίοις ἑκατέρους. συντελεῖν δὲ ἀπὸ τῶν προσιόντων εἰς τὸ

ε

29 post ἐπιμέλειαν .. COYC (εὐθύς ? H-L) deletum. **31** ΠΙΡΑΙΩC: Πειραιέως K, K-W; Πειραιῶς H-L. [Π]ε[ι]ραῶς CIA ii 834 *b* I 64 (B.C. 329).

XXXIX 2 ΑΘΗΝΑΙΩΝ, supra ΤΩΝ additum, retinet K, post τῶν locat K[1], coll. c. 27, 15 τῷ βουλομένῳ Λακιαδῶν et c. 29, 24 οἱ ἐθέλοντες Ἀθηναίων: delent K-W, H-L; ante τῶν ponunt Blass et K[3]. **4** ἑ[αυ]τῶν Jackson, K-W, K[3], B: ἑ[πὶ πᾶσ]ιν K[1]; ἁπάντων Poland (H-L). **8** ἑκατέρους fortasse aut defendi aut excusari posse putat Jackson, sed mavult ἑκατέροις, 'mysteriis maioribus minoribusve'; idem mavult Hude.

ἕκαστον πλὴν τῶν τριάκοντα καὶ τῶν ἕνδεκα καὶ τῶν ἐν τῷ Πειραιεῖ ἀρξάντων δέκα. εἰ δέ τινες φοβοῖντο τῶν ἐξ ἄστεως, ἔδοξεν αὐτοῖς (αὐτοὺς Hartman) Ἐλευσῖνα κατοικεῖν.

XXXIX § 1. **ἐπ' Εὐκλείδου**] B.C. 403/2. The διαλύσεις took place near the end of the summer of 403. Xen. *l.c.* § 25 speaks of the party of the Peiraeus as foraging for ξύλα καὶ ὀπώραν, and Plut. *Mor.* p. 349 F (*de gloria Ath.*) gives the 12th of Boedromion (September) as the date of the return of the exiles.

ἐξοικεῖν ἔχειν] If we retain Ἐλευσῖνα, we should probably have to render the passage: 'should have Eleusis to migrate to.' The words are generally understood to mean: 'should have it in their power to migrate to Eleusis.' This would require Ἐλευσίναδε. Cf. Dem. 29 § 3, Μέγαράδ' ἐξῴκηκε, and Lys. 31 § 19, of an incident of the same date as the present, (Philon) συσκευασάμενος γὰρ τὰ ἑαυτοῦ ἐνθάδε εἰς τὴν ὑπερορίαν ἐξῴκησε.

ἐπιτίμους] in full possession of their rights as citizens; cf. Xen. *Hell.* ii 2, 11 (of an earlier date, when Agis was holding Decelea), τοὺς ἀτίμους ἐπιτίμους ποιήσαντες ἐκαρτέρουν. Xenophon is referring to the ψήφισμα of Patrocleides, quoted in Andoc. *de Myst.* 77—79; *ib.* 73, ἐπεὶ γὰρ αἱ νῆες διεφθάρησαν καὶ ἡ πολιορκία ἐγένετο, ἐβουλεύσασθε περὶ ὁμονοίας καὶ ἔδοξεν ὑμῖν τοὺς ἀτίμους ἐπιτίμους ποιῆσαι. Then follows the *locus classicus* about ἀτιμία in which, among those who were under partial ἀτιμία, are mentioned (in § 75) the soldiers who ἐπέμειναν ἐπὶ τῶν τυράννων ἐν τῇ πόλει (τετρακοσίων may be suggested instead of τυράννων; this suggestion is anticipated by Dobree, and approved by Blass; in any case the Four Hundred are meant; and not the Thirty). **κυρίους καὶ αὐτοκράτορας**] 'possessing full and independent powers of self-government' (K.).

§ 2. **ἱερὸν**] The temple of Demeter at Eleusis. **Κήρυκας καὶ Εὐμολπίδας**] c. 57 § 1.

τοῖς Ἐλευσίνοθεν] *constructio praegnans*, influenced by ἰέναι; similarly below, ἐκ τοῦ ἄστεως.

ἑκατέρους] The constr. changes from the dat. to the acc. with the inf. For a similar change of constr. after ἐξεῖναι, cf. Aeschin. 3 § 2, ἵνα ἐξῇ πρῶτον μὲν τῷ πρεσβυτάτῳ τῶν πολιτῶν...ἐπὶ τὸ βῆμα παρελθόντι τὰ βέλτιστα τῇ πόλει συμβουλεύειν, δεύτερον δ' ἤδη καὶ τῶν ἄλλων

συμμαχικὸν καθάπερ τοὺς ἄλλους Ἀθηναίους. ἐὰν δέ τινες τῶν 3
ἀπιόντων οἰκίαν λαμβάνωσιν Ἐλευσῖνι, συμπείθειν τὸν κεκτη-
μένον· ἐὰν δὲ μὴ συμβαίνωσιν ἀλλήλοις, τιμητὰς ἑλέσθαι τρεῖς
ἑκάτερον, καὶ ἥντιν' ἂν οὗτοι τάξωσιν τιμὴν λαμβάνειν. Ἐλευ-
σινίων δὲ συνοικεῖν οὓς ἂν αὐτοὶ βούλωνται. τὴν δ' ἀπογραφὴν 4
εἶναι τοῖς βουλομένοις ἐξοικεῖν, τοῖς μὲν ἐπιδ[ημ]οῦσιν ἀφ' ἧς ἂν
ὀμόσωσιν τοὺς ὅρκους δ[έκ]α ἡμερῶν, τὴν δ' ἐξοίκησιν εἴκοσι, τοῖς
δ' ἀποδημοῦσιν ἐπειδὰν ἐπιδημήσωσιν κατὰ ταὐτά. μὴ ἐξεῖναι δὲ 5
ἄρχειν μηδεμίαν ἀρχὴν τῶν ἐν τῷ ἄστει τὸν Ἐλευσῖνι κατοικοῦντα
πρὶν ἂν ἀπογράψηται πάλιν ἐν τῷ ἄστει κατοικεῖν. τὰς δὲ || δίκας [Col. 19.]

12 ΕΚΑΤΕΡΩΝ (B): *ἑκάτερον* Bury, Richards, Hude, Papabasilius (K-W, H-L, K[3]). *τάξωσι* H-L. **13** ΟΥΤΟΙ (K, K-W, H-L): *αὐτοὶ* Richards, Herwerden, B qui etiam *οἳ ἂν αὐτοὶ* scribendum suspicatur. **15** *ὀμόσωσι* H-L. *δ[έκ]α* K-W, H-L, K[3], B: *δι'* [*ἕπτ*]*α* K[1]. **16** *ἀποδημοῦσι*<*ν*> K, H-L. **18** ΑΠΟΓΡΑΨΗ|ΨΗΤΑΙ: —*γράψηται* K-W, H-L, B; —*γράφηται* K.

πολιτῶν τὸν βουλόμενον γνώμην ἀποφαίνεσθαι (Kühner, § 475, 2 c, Anm. 1). *ἑκατέρους* is possibly preferred to avoid the ambiguity arising from *ἑκατέροις*, which would naturally agree with *μυστηρίοις* and has actually been proposed in this sense.

συντελεῖν...εἰς] Dem. *Lept.* 28, *συντελοῦσιν εἰς τὸν πόλεμον*.

τὸ συμμαχικὸν] elsewhere of 'the allied forces' (Thuc. iv 77), or of a 'treaty of alliance' (iii 91, v 6): here 'the fund for the common defence.'

§ 3. **συμπείθειν**] not 'shall first obtain the assent of the owner' (Poste), but 'the people would help them to obtain the consent of the owner' (Kenyon).

συνοικεῖν] 'of the inhabitants of Eleusis, those whom the secessionists desired should live in the same community.' Thuc. ii 68, 3, *ἀπὸ τῶν Ἀμπρακιωτῶν ξυνοικησάντων*. In Thuc. vi 64, 3 (the Syracusan horsemen tauntingly ask the Athenians) *εἰ ξυνοικήσοντες σφίσιν αὐτοῖς μᾶλλον ἥκοιεν ἐν τῇ ἀλλοτρίᾳ ἢ Λεοντίνους ἐς τὴν οἰκείαν κατοικιοῦντες*, *ib.* ii 68, 3. The proceedings have an arbitrary air as against the ordinary inhabitants of Eleusis, but it would appear that Eleusis was, subject to certain conditions, handed over to the secessionists.

§ 4. **τὴν ἀπογραφὴν εἶναι**] Those who proposed to secede were required to enter their names in a list (cf. 40 § 1). *ἀπογραφή*, in Attic law, is generally applied to a register of land, property, moneys, rather than of persons. Lys. 25 § 9, *εἰσὶ δὲ οἵτινες τῶν Ἐλευσῖνάδε ἀπογραψαμένων, ἐξελθόντες μεθ' ὑμῶν, ἐπολιορκοῦντο μετ' αὐτῶν* (Westermann, Cobet; *μεθ' αὐτῶν* MS; *ἐπολιόρκουν τοὺς μεθ' αὐτῶν* Scheibe, Frohberger).

τοὺς ὅρκους] 'the oath of pacification' (Poste). Xen. *Hell.* ii 4, 43 (of a slightly later time, after the commanding officers of the party at Eleusis had been put to death and a reconciliation effected with the remainder), *ὀμόσαντες ὅρκους ἦ μὴν μὴ μνησικακήσειν*. **δέκα ἡμερῶν**, 11, 5 *δέκα ἐτῶν*.

§ 5. **πρὶν—ἀπογράψηται**] 'until he shall again register himself in the list with a view to residence in the city.' Lys. 25 § 9 quoted above. *ἀπογράφεσθαι*, mid. to register oneself (*e.g.* as a citizen: *Pol.* vi (iv) 13, 1297 *a* 24, *ἐνιαχοῦ δ' ἔξεστι μὲν πᾶσιν ἀπογραψαμένοις ἐκκλησιάζειν καὶ δικάζειν, ἐὰν δὲ ἀπογραψάμενοι μήτ' ἐκκλησιάζωσι μήτε δικάζωσιν, ἐπίκεινται μεγάλαι ζημίαι τούτοις*). Xen. *Hell.* ii 4 § 8, vi 5 § 29. The passive is found in Plat. *Leg.* 914 C, *ἂν ἀπογεγραμμένον ᾖ παρὰ τοῖς ἄρχουσι τὸ κτῆμα*.

τὰς δὲ δίκας τοῦ φόνου—] This passage does not help us to decide the question whether the Areopagus was suspended or not by the Thirty. Lys. 1 § 30 (delivered after the year of Eucleides) says of this tribunal, *ᾧ καὶ πάτριόν ἐστι καὶ ἐφ' ἡμῶν* (*ὑμῶν* MSS) *ἀποδίδοται* (*ἀποδέδοται* the reading of an inferior MS) *τοῦ φόνου τὰς δίκας δικάζειν*. Grote, Rauchenstein (*Philol.* x 604 ff.) and Curtius (iv 16 note) hold that it was suspended; Schömann (*Ant.* p. 549 E. T.) that it was not. Practically, however, its authority was obviously superseded by the Reign of Terror. See also Philippi, *Areop.* p. 265, 266, and Frohberger's *Lysias* vol. ii 180.

τοῦ φόνου εἶναι κατὰ τὰ πάτρια, εἴ τίς τινα αὐτόχειρ ἀπέκτεινεν, 6 ἢ ἔτρωσεν. τῶν δὲ παρεληλυθότων μηδενὶ πρὸς μηδένα μνησικακεῖν ἐξεῖναι, πλὴν πρὸς τοὺς τριάκοντα καὶ τοὺς δέκα καὶ τοὺς ἕνδεκα καὶ τοὺς τοῦ Πειραιέως ἄρξαντας, μηδὲ πρὸς τούτους, ἐὰν διδῶσιν εὐθύνας. εὐθύνας δὲ δοῦναι τοὺς μὲν ἐν Πειραιεῖ ἄρξαντας ἐν τοῖς ἐν Πειραιεῖ, τοὺς δ' ἐν τῷ ἄστει ἐν τοῖς τὰ τιμήματα παρεχομένοις. εἶθ' οὕτως ἐξοικεῖν τοὺς ἐθέλοντας. τὰ δὲ χρήματα ἃ ἐδανείσαντο εἰς τὸν πόλεμον ἑκατέρους ἀποδοῦναι χωρίς.

40. γενομένων δὲ τοιούτων τῶν διαλύσεων, καὶ φοβουμένων

ε ε
19 ΑΥΤΟΧΙΡΑΕΚΤΙCΙ (CΙ 'ita ut paene Ν legi possit' B) ΕΗΡΩCΑCΤΩΝ ante ρω deletis ΕΗ (B), vel ΟΤ, i.e. *ὁ τρώσας* (K), vel ΟΙC (K-W), vel CΗ (H-L): *αὐτοχειρὶ <ἀπέκτονεν> ἐκτίσει ἱερώσας* K[1], †*αὐτόχειρα ἐκτίσει ἱερώσας*† K[3]; *αὐτοχειρίᾳ ἔκτεινε τρώσας* Wyse; *αὐτοχειρίᾳ ἔκτεινεν ἢ ἔτρωσεν* K-W, H-L; *αὐτόχειρ* (van Leeuwen) *ἀπέκτεινεν ἢ ἔτρωσεν* B.
ε ε ει
22 ΠΙΡΑΙΩC: *Πειραιῶς* H-L. **23** ΠΙΡΑΙΙ. **24** ΠΙΡΑΙΙ. Praestaret *ἐν τοῖς <ἐν τῷ ἄστει* K et Gertz> *τιμήματα (=ἀποτιμήματα) παρεχομένους,* aut *τὰ <αὐτὰ* Gertz> *τιμήματα παρεχομένοις.* Cf. c. 2, 12.
Δ
25 ΤΟΥC ΕΘΕΛΟΝΤΑC: *τοὺς ἀλόντας* B, qui in archetypo litteras ΘΕ deletas, et Α (non Δ) scriptum fuisse putat.

TESTIMONIA. **XXXIX 21—23** Bekk. *An.* 235—6 (cf. Testim. ad xxxv 5—6).

αὐτόχειρ ἀπέκτεινεν] Hdt. i 140 etc. *αὐτοχειρίᾳ κτείνειν. αὐτόχειρ ἔκτεινεν* would be a poetic form of expression, but *αὐτόχειρ* itself is used in prose, as in Dem. p. 321, 18; 549, 5; 552, 18. *τρώσας*, 'by wounding,' gives less good sense than *ἢ ἔτρωσεν*, but might be defended by *ἐάν τις φάρμακον δοὺς ἀποκτείνῃ et similia.* 'Unlawful wounding' comes under the cognisance of the courts that try cases of homicide, c. 57 § 3 *fin.* *κτεῖναι ἢ τρῶσαί τινα.*

§ 6. **μνησικακεῖν**] Xen. *Hell.* ii 4 *ult.*, *ὀμόσαντες ὅρκους ἦ μὴν μὴ μνησικακήσειν, ἔτι καὶ νῦν ὁμοῦ τε πολιτεύονται καὶ τοῖς ὅρκοις ἐμμένει ὁ δῆμος.* Aristoph. *Plut.* 1146, *μὴ μνησικακήσῃς, εἰ σὺ Φυλὴν κατέλαβες, ἀλλὰ ξύνοικον πρὸς θεῶν δέξασθέ με,* with Schol. Andoc. *de Myst.* 90, *καὶ οὐ μνησικακήσω τῶν πολιτῶν οὐδενὶ πλὴν τῶν τριάκοντα καὶ τῶν ἕνδεκα, οὐδὲ τούτων ὃς ἂν ἐθέλοι εὐθύνας διδόναι τῆς ἀρχῆς ἧς ἦρξεν* and *ib.* 81, 91. Aeschin. *F. L.* 176, (Archinus and Thrasybulus) *τὸ μὴ μνησικακεῖν πρὸς ἀλλήλους ἔνορκον ἡμῖν καταστησάντων.* Justin v 10 § 11. Cf. Luebbert, *De Amnestia*, Kiel, 1881.

καὶ τοὺς δέκα] Neither in Xenophon (*Hell.* ii 4, 38) nor in Andocides is this body of Ten described as excluded from the amnesty. Xenophon mentions the 'Ten who ruled in Peiraeus' (c. 35 § 1); Andocides does not mention even these.

ἐν τοῖς ἐν Πειραιεῖ] not 'for all matters coming within the limits of Peiraeus' (Kenyon), but 'before the courts held in the Peiraeus.' 'To the residents in Peiraieus' is Mr Poste's rendering; but such a rendering of an account would be very informal. Some lawfully constituted body is clearly meant.

ἐν τοῖς τὰ τιμήματα παρεχομένοις] 'before a court consisting of those who can produce rateable property' *i.e.* who have property on which they pay taxes. This limitation excludes all paupers or citizens of the lowest class. *παρέχεσθαι*, is 'to have as one's own, to produce as one's own,' 'to bring forward' (L and S); *τοῖς ὅπλα παρεχομένοις* occurs in c. 4, but I can find no instance of *παρέχεσθαι* being coupled with *τιμήματα.*

τιμήματα is here understood of penalties, by Poland, Kaibel and Kiessling, and Haussoullier (*εὐθῦναι* came under the class of *δίκαι τιμηταί*, *Att. Proc.* pp. 226, 264 Lips.). Reinach makes *τίμημα* synonymous with *ἀποτίμημα*, 'a security,' comparing CIA ii 570, 21, [*τιμή*]*ματι ἢ ἐγγυητῇ*, and Lys. ap. Harp. *s.v.* *τίμημα.*

οὕτως] after satisfying all these legal requirements.

ἀποδοῦναι χωρίς] *inf.* c. 40 § 4.

ὅσοι μετὰ τῶν τριάκοντα συνεπολέμησαν, καὶ πολλῶν ἐπινοούντων
μὲν ἐξοικεῖν ἀναβαλλομένων δὲ τὴν ἀπογραφὴν εἰς τὰς ἐσχάτας
ἡμέρας, ὅπερ εἰώθασιν ποιεῖν ἅπαντες, Ἀρχῖνος συνιδὼν τὸ πλῆθος
καὶ βουλόμενος κατασχεῖν αὐτοὺς ὑφεῖλε τὰς ὑπολοίπους ἡμέρας
τῆς ἀπογραφῆς, ὥστε συναναγκασθῆναι μένειν πολλοὺς ἄκοντας
ἕως ἐθάρρησαν. καὶ δοκεῖ τοῦτό τε πολιτεύσασθαι καλῶς Ἀρχῖνος, 2
καὶ μετὰ ταῦτα γραψάμενος τὸ ψήφισμα τὸ Θρασυβούλου παρα-

XL 2 ΜΕΝΕΠΙΝΟΟΥΝΤΩΝ (K, <ἐξοικεῖν> *μὲν ἐπινοούντων*? K-W): *ἐπινοούντων μὲν* Blass (H-L). **3** ΑΝΑΓΡΑΦΗΝ (K): *ἀπογραφὴν* Jackson, Wyse, Bury, Blass, K-W, H-L, B; *ἀνα-γραφὴν* fortasse casu ex *ἀνα-βαλλομένων* ortum. **4** *εἰώθασι* H-L, B.

XL § 1. **Ἀρχῖνος**] mentioned (with Dion) as an orator in Plat. *Menex.* 234 B, and with Cephalus in Dinarchus, 1 § 76. He was the proposer of a law to prevent *συκοφαντία* after the amnesty (Isocr. *c. Callim.* 18 § 2, *ἄν τις δικάζηται παρὰ τοὺς ὅρκους, ἐξεῖναι τῷ φεύγοντι παραγράψασθαι κτλ.*). It was on his motion that the Ionic alphabet was adopted in public documents from the archonship of Eucleides onwards (Suidas *s. v.*). The action recorded in the text is not mentioned elsewhere. He is described as cooperating with Thrasybulus in the restoration of the democracy, *Ἀρχίνου καὶ Θρασυβούλου προστάντων τοῦ δήμου*, Aeschin. *F. L.* 176. It was Archinus who moved the decree on that occasion: *c. Ctes.* 187, *ὁ τὸ ψήφισμα γράψας καὶ νικήσας Ἀρχῖνος ὁ ἐκ Κοίλης, εἷς τῶν καταγαγόντων τὸν δῆμον.* On his opposition to a proposal of Thrasybulus, see below.

συνιδὼν τὸ πλῆθος] 'observing their numbers.'

τὰς ὑπολοίπους ἡμέρας] the remainder of the term of days allowed for the purposes of registration.

§ 2. **γραψάμενος τὸ ψήφισμα τὸ Θρασυβούλου**] This fact is well known owing to its having affected the position of Lysias, who fully deserved promotion from the position of a *μέτοικος* to that of a citizen for his great services towards the restoration of the democracy, and for the losses he had incurred at the hands of the Thirty, who had even put to death his brother Polemarchus (*Or.* 12).

Aeschines, *c. Ctes.* § 195, describes Archinus as having resisted the proposal to confer the distinction of a crown on some of those who had done good service in the restoration of the democracy. The scholia give us further details: *Θρασύβουλος ὁ Στειριεὺς μετὰ τὸ κατελθεῖν τὸν δῆμον ἀπὸ Φυλῆς ἔγραψε ψήφισμα δοθῆναι πολιτείαν Λυσίᾳ τῷ Κεφάλου* (*Κεφάλῳ* MS, correxit Wyse) *τῷ ῥήτορι πολλὰ εὐεργετήσαντι τοὺς εἰς* (*τὴν* MS) *Φυλὴν καταφυγόντας καὶ τοῦτο ἀπροβούλευτον εἰσήνεγκεν εἰς τὸν δῆμον. οὐδέπω γὰρ ἦν καθεσταμένη βουλὴ μετὰ τὴν τῶν λ' κατάλυσιν· τοῦτο τὸ ψήφισμα ἐγράψατο παρανόμων Ἀρχῖνος ὁ ἐκ Κοίλης καὶ εἷλε καὶ ἐτίμησαν τῷ Θρασυβούλῳ οἱ δικασταὶ δραχμῆς μιᾶς. Ἄλλως· ἐπίστευον τοῖς δοκοῦσιν ἀμύνειν τοῖς νόμοις. Ἀρχῖνος γὰρ ὁ ἐκ Κοίλης ἐγράψατο παρανόμων ὅτε κατῆλθεν ὁ δῆμος...Λυσίου τοῦ Συρακοσίου πεντακοσίας μὲν ἀσπίδας δόντος τοῖς μαχεσαμένοις ἐν Φυλῇ, τριακοσίους δὲ* (*Συρακοσίοις* MS, correxit Blass) *στρατιώτας μισθωσαμένου ἐξ Αἰγίνης, ἔγραψε ψήφισμα πολίτην αὐτὸν γενέσθαι Θρασύβουλος. παρανόμων δὲ αὐτὸν Ἀρχῖνος ὁ ἐκ Κοίλης ἐγράψατο, ὅτι οὔπω γενομένης βουλῆς ψήφισμα ἔγραψεν καὶ <οἱ> δικασταὶ κατήνεγκαν αὐτοῦ τὰς ψήφους ὀλιγώρως πρὸ τοῦ βουλὴν ὑπάρξαι* (*ὀλιγώρως—ὑπάρξαι* placed after *ἔγραψεν* by Schultz). *ὁ δὲ ἐν τῇ τιμήσει παρελθών, θανάτου, ἔφη, τιμῶμαι ὅτι ἀχαρίστους Ἀθηναίους ὄντας εὖ ἐποίησα. οἱ δὲ δικασταὶ αἰδεσθέντες τῷ μὲν ἐτίμησαν τὴν καταδίκην δραχμῆς, τὸν δὲ Λυσίαν οὐδ' οὕτως ἐποιήσαντο πολίτην.* Maximus Planudes, Scholia on the *στάσεις* of Hermogenes in Walz, *Rh. Gr.* v 343, *παραπλήσιον καὶ τὸ περὶ Θρασυβούλου ἱστορούμενον, ὃς μετὰ τὴν τῶν τριάκοντα κατάλυσιν ἔγραψε τῷ Λυσίᾳ ψήφισμα περὶ τοῦ δεῖν αὐτὸν γενέσθαι πολίτην καὶ κατηγορηθεὶς ὡς ἀπροβούλευτον ψήφισμα... εἰσενεγκών, οὐ γὰρ ἦν πω καταστᾶσα ἡ βουλή, κατεδικάσθη χρημάτων· ὁ δέ, οὐ μὰ Δία, ἔφη, ἀλλὰ θανάτου· τί γὰρ τοιούτους ἔσωζον;* Cf. [Plut.] 846 A. The proposal was made *μετὰ τὴν κάθοδον ἐπ' ἀναρχίας τῆς πρὸ Εὐκλείδου* (*ib.* 835 EF), *i.e.* between the return from exile and the restoration of the democracy. At that time the *βουλή* had not yet been constituted. See Blass *Att. Ber.* i 340[1],

νόμων, ἐν ᾧ μετεδίδου τῆς πολιτείας πᾶσι τοῖς ἐκ Πειραιέως συγκατελθοῦσι, ὧν ἔνιοι φανερῶς ἦσαν δοῦλοι, καὶ τρίτον, ἐπεί τις ἤρξατο τῶν κατεληλυθότων μνησικακεῖν, ἀπαγαγὼν τοῦτον ἐπὶ τὴν βουλὴν καὶ πείσας ἄκριτον ἀποκτεῖναι, λέγων ὅτι νῦν δείξουσιν εἰ βούλονται τὴν δημοκρατίαν σῴζειν καὶ τοῖς ὅρκοις ἐμμένειν· ἀφέντας μὲν γὰρ τοῦτον προτρέψειν καὶ τοὺς ἄλλους, ἐὰν δ' ἀνέλωσιν παράδειγμα ποιήσειν ἅπασιν. ὅπερ καὶ συνέπεσεν·
3 ἀποθανόντος γὰρ οὐδεὶς πώποτε ὕστερον ἐμνησικάκησεν. ἀλλὰ δοκοῦσιν κάλλιστα δὴ καὶ πολιτικώτατα ἁπάντων καὶ ἰδίᾳ καὶ κοινῇ χρήσασθαι ταῖς προγεγενημέναις συμφοραῖς· οὐ γὰρ μόνον τὰς περὶ τῶν προτέρων αἰτίας ἐξήλειψαν ἀλλὰ καὶ τὰ χρήματα Λακεδαιμονίοις, ἃ οἱ τριάκοντα πρὸς τὸν πόλεμον ἔλαβον, ἀπέδοσαν κοινῇ, κελευουσῶν τῶν συνθηκῶν ἑκατέρους ἀποδιδόναι χωρίς, τούς τ' ἐκ τοῦ ἄστεως καὶ τοὺς ἐκ τοῦ Πειραιέως, ἡγούμενοι τοῦτο πρῶτον ἄρχειν δεῖν τῆς ὁμονοίας· ἐν δὲ ταῖς ἄλλαις πόλεσιν οὐχ ὅτι προστιθέασιν τῶν οἰκείων οἱ δῆμοι κρατήσαντες, ἀλλὰ καὶ

9 ΠΙΡΑΙΟΙϹ (ΕΩϹ above): Πειραιῶς H-L. 13 ϹΩΖΕΙΝ. 17 δοκοῦσι H-L, B. ΚΑΙΔΙΑ (Ε above) ante corr. 22 ΠΙΡΑΙΩϹ: Πειραιῶς H-L. 23 ΔΕΝ correctum in ΔΕΙΝ. 23—24 ΟΥΧ ΟΙΟΝ ΕΤΙ (vel ΕΠΙ): οὐχ οἷον ἔτι K, H-L, B; οὐχ οἷον ἐπιπροστιθέασιν Gennadios (K-W); οὐχ ὅτι προστιθέασιν J B Mayor, ὅτι in ἔτι corruptum atque οἷον deinde per errorem insertum arbitratus. 24 ΟΙΔΗΜΟΚΡΑΤ: οἱ δημοκρατήσαντες K et B cui 'est δημοκρατήσαντες ut μοναρχήσαντες': οἱ δῆμοι κρατήσαντες van Leeuwen, Hude (H-L, K-W), quod unice verum est,—'alibi cum vicerunt populares, spoliare solent divites, non propria etiam bona in publicum commodum absumere' (Herwerden).

349², and Jebb, *Att. Orators*, i 151; cf. Wyse in *Class. Rev.* v 335.

ἤρξατο—μνησικακεῖν] c. 39 § 6. The action of Archinus is the natural sequel of his law against συκοφαντία (Isocr. *c. Callim.* §§ 2, 3). Cf. Curtius, *H. G.* iv 59. But his method of procedure was arbitrary in the extreme. Nevertheless, the author passes no condemnation on it. **ἀπαγαγὼν**] of summary arrest, 29 § 4.

τοῖς ὅρκοις ἐμμένειν] Xen. *Hell.* ii 4 *ult.*, τοῖς ὅρκοις ἐμμένει ὁ δῆμος.

§ 3. **κάλλιστα δὴ**] According to Eucken (*De Aristotelis dicendi ratione; de particularum usu*, p. 49), δὴ is nowhere found in the writings of Aristotle after a superlative (*Class. Rev.* v 160 *a*).

αἰτίας ἐξήλειψαν] Andoc. *de Myst.* 76, ἐξαλεῖψαι πάντα τὰ ψηφίσματα, Lys. 1 § 48, τοὺς κειμένους νόμους ἐξαλεῖψαι, ἑτέρους δὲ θεῖναι, 30 § 5, τὰ μὲν ἐγγράφεις τὰ δ' ἐξαλείφεις. Here probably metaphorical, as in Dem. *Pant.* 37 § 34, τὸ γιγνώσκειν καὶ συνιέναι τὰ δίκαια...ἐξαλεῖψαι. ἐξαλείφειν is not found in the *Index Ar.*; ἀπαλείφειν occurs in c. 47 *fin.* and 48 *init.* and προεξαλείφειν in c. 47 *ult.*

τὰ χρήματα—ὁμονοίας] See note on Dem. *Lept.* p. 460, esp. § 12, τοῦτο πρῶτον ὑπάρξαι τῆς ὁμονοίας σημεῖον, κοινῇ διαλῦσαι τὰ χρήματα, and Isocr. *Areop.* §§ 67, 68 there quoted.

οὐχ ὅτι] οὐχ οἷον is not found in Ar. οὐχ ὅτι...ἀλλὰ καὶ occurs in *Pol.* 1331 *a* 11, *Poet.* 4, 1448 *b* 35. οὐχ ὅτι...ἀλλὰ in *De Gen. Anim.* iv 1, 765 *b* 19, *De Anima* ii 7, 419 *a* 21, *Anal.* i 41, 49 *b* 22.

προστιθέασιν τῶν οἰκείων] 'pay additional sums out of their own property.'

οἱ δῆμοι κρατήσαντες] *Pol.* vi (iv) 8, 1294 *a* 13, ἐν ὀλιγαρχίᾳ καὶ ἐν ἀριστοκρατίᾳ καὶ ἐν δήμοις. viii (v) 10, 1310 *b* 21, οἱ δῆμοι (opp. to αἱ ὀλιγαρχίαι). iii 11, 1282 *a* 28, ἃς (εὐθύνας καὶ ἀρχὰς) ἐν ἐνίαις πολιτείαις...τοῖς δήμοις ἀποδιδόασιν. vii (vi) 4, 1320 *a* 4, οἱ δὲ νῦν δημαγωγοὶ χαριζόμενοι τοῖς δήμοις πολλὰ δημεύουσι διὰ τῶν δικαστηρίων. 7, 1321 *a* 19, ταύτῃ δὲ ἐπικρα-

τὴν ‖ χώραν ἀνάδαστον ποιοῦσιν. διελύθησαν δὲ καὶ πρὸς τοὺς 4 [Col. 20.
[[ἐν]] Ἐλευσῖνι [κατοι]κήσαντας ἔτει τρίτῳ μετὰ τὴν ἐξοίκησιν, ἐπὶ
[Ξεναι]νέτου ἄρχοντος.

41. ταῦτα μὲν οὖν ἐν τοῖς ὕστε[ρο]ν συνέβη γενέσθαι καιροῖς,
τότε δὲ κύριος ὁ δῆμος γενόμενος τῶν πραγμάτων, ἐνεστήσατο τὴν
[νῦν] οὖσαν πολιτείαν, ἐπὶ Πυθοδώρου μὲν ἄρχοντος, [δ]οκοῦντος
δὲ δικαίως τοῦ δήμου λαβεῖν τὴν [ἐξουσί]αν, διὰ τὸ ποιήσασθαι τὴν
κάθοδον δι' αὐτοῦ τὸν δῆμον. ἦν δὲ τῶν μεταβολῶν ἑνδεκάτη τὸ[ν 2
ἀρι]θμὸν αὕτη. πρώτη μὲν γὰρ ἐγένετο [κ]ατάστασις τῶν ἐξ

26 ΕΝ supra scriptum melius abesset (K, coll. Cobet, *Var. Lect.*, pp. 30, 201); retinent K-W, B, delent H-L. Cf. Meisterhans, p. 169². [ἐξοι]κήσαντας K, K-W, H-L: [μετοι]κήσαντας propter hiatum conicit J W Headlam; [κατοι]κήσαντας B, qui ἐξοικ. 'et propter hiatum et propter spatium vestigiaque' condemnat.

XLI 3 Πυθοδώρου: Εὐκλείδου exspectaret B coll. c. 39, 1. Post ἄρχοντος lacunam indicant K-W, 'hiat sententia; damnatae Pythodori memoriae facta erat mentio.' **4—5** δήμου—δῆμον: an Θρασυβούλου—δι' αὐτὸν τὸν δῆμον? K. [ἐξουσί]αν K, K-W, B: [προστασί]αν? K et Kontos (H-L).
Υ
5 ΔΙΑΥΤΟΝ? δι' αὐτὸν K (an ἐφ' αὐτοῦ? H-L): δι' αὐτοῦ B; idem, seclusis τὸν δῆμον, K-W. **6** . . ΑΤΑΤΑCIC: ἡ κατάστασις K, K-W; κατάστασις B. [τῶν κ]ατασ[τάσεων] 'dubitanter van Leeuwen' (H-L).

τοῦσιν ἐν ταῖς διαστάσεσιν οἱ δῆμοι τῶν εὐπόρων. Thuc. iii 82, 1; viii 65, 1.

τὴν χώραν ἀνάδαστον ποιοῦσι] *Pol.* viii (v) 5, 1305 *a* 2, ὁτὲ μὲν γάρ, ἵνα χαρίζωνται, ἀδικοῦντες τοὺς γνωρίμους συνιστᾶσιν, ἢ τὰς οὐσίας ἀναδάστους ποιοῦντες ἢ τὰς προσόδους ταῖς λειτουργίαις, ὁτὲ δὲ διαβάλλοντες, ἵν' ἔχωσι δημεύειν τὰ κτήματα τῶν πλουσίων. 7, 1307 *a* 1 (of the Lacedaemonians about the time of the second Messenian war), θλιβόμενοι γάρ τινες διὰ τὸν πόλεμον ἠξίουν ἀνάδαστον ποιεῖν τὴν χώραν. 8, 1309 *a* 14, δεῖ δ' ἐν μὲν ταῖς δημοκρατίαις τῶν εὐπόρων φείδεσθαι, μὴ μόνον τῷ τὰς κτήσεις μὴ ποιεῖν ἀναδάστους, ἀλλὰ μηδὲ τοὺς καρπούς.

§ 4. **διελύθησαν]** Xen. *Hell.* ii 4, 43, ὑστέρῳ δὲ χρόνῳ ἀκούσαντες ξένους μισθοῦσθαι τοὺς Ἐλευσῖνι, στρατευσάμενοι πανδημεὶ ἐπ' αὐτοὺς τοὺς μὲν στρατηγοὺς αὐτῶν εἰς λόγους ἐλθόντας ἀπέκτειναν, τοῖς δὲ ἄλλοις εἰσπέμψαντες τοὺς φίλους καὶ ἀναγκαίους ἔπεισαν συναλλαγῆναι· καὶ ὀμόσαντες ὅρκους ἦ μὴν μὴ μνησικακήσειν, ἔτι καὶ νῦν ὁμοῦ τε πολιτεύονται, καὶ τοῖς ὅρκοις ἐμμένει ὁ δῆμος.

ἔτει τρίτῳ—ἐπὶ Ξεναινέτου] B.C. 401/0. The final reconciliation is thus placed later than has generally been inferred from Xenophon's phrase ὑστέρῳ χρόνῳ (corresponding to ἐν τοῖς ὕστερον καιροῖς of c. 41 § 1). Grote c. 65 end, v 598—9.

XLI. *Recapitulation.*

§ 1. **ἐνεστήσαντο]** *Probl.* 951 *a* 28, ἐνστήσασθαι τὸ πρᾶγμα. Intrans. 5 § 2, *ib. ult.*, 17 § 4, 27 § 2, 37 § 1. The intrans. parts are those generally used in Ar. On the other hand συνιστάναι (συστῆσαι, συστήσασθαι) πόλιν, πολιτείαν, is found in *Pol.* 1266 *a* 23, 1284 *b* 18, 1288 *a* 40, 1319 *b* 33, also in *Oecon.* 1343 *a* 7.

ἐπὶ Πυθοδώρου] B.C. 404/3. In c. 39 § 1 the formal convention for the restoration of the democracy is placed in the archonship of Euclides (403/2). But the return of Thrasybulus and the other exiles of the democratical party, and the occupation of the Peiraeus, took place about January 403, in the archonship of Pythodorus.

The text implies 'that the subsequent extension of the democracy...was justified by the fact of its having secured its own re-establishment, without the open help of any other nation, and in the face of the opposition of a powerful party at Sparta' (Kenyon). But it is difficult to resist Mr Kenyon's suggestion that the passage is corrupt, and that the position of Thrasybulus as leader of the restored democracy was recognised in the latter part of this sentence.

§ 2. **κατάστασις τῶν ἐξ ἀρχῆς Ἴωνος]** The constitution under Ion (which is, of course, prehistoric) was doubtless described in the early chapters of the treatise. Cf. fragm. 343² = 381³.

ἀρχῆς Ἴωνος καὶ τῶν μετ' αὐτοῦ συνοικησάντων· τότε γὰρ πρῶτον εἰς τὰς τέτταρας συνενεμήθησαν φυλὰς καὶ τοὺς φυλοβασιλεῖς κατέστησαν. δευτέρα δὲ καὶ πρώτη μετὰ ταύτη[ν] ἔχουσα πολιτείας τάξιν ἡ ἐπὶ Θησέως γενομένη, μικρὸν παρεγκλίνουσα τῆς βασιλικῆς. μετὰ δὲ ταύτην ἡ ἐπὶ Δράκοντος, ἐν ᾗ καὶ νόμους ἀνέγραψαν πρῶτον. τρίτη δ' ἡ μετὰ τὴν στάσιν, ἡ ἐπὶ Σόλωνος, ἀφ' ἧς ἀρχὴ δημοκρατίας ἐγένετο. τετάρτη δ' ἡ ἐπὶ Πεισιστράτου τυραννίς. πέμπτη δ' ἡ μετὰ <τὴν> τῶν τυράννων κατάλυσιν, ἡ Κλεισθένους, δημοτικωτέρα τῆς Σόλωνος. ἕκτη δ' ἡ μετὰ τὰ Μηδικά, τῆς ἐξ Ἀρείου πάγου βουλῆς ἐπιστατούσης. ἑβδόμη δ' ἡ μετὰ ταύτην, ἣν Ἀριστείδης μὲν ὑπέδειξεν, Ἐφιάλτης δ' ἐπετέ-

7 συνοικησάντων Blass coll. frag. 381[3], K-W, H-L: συνοικισάντων defendit K[2] coll. c. 15, 7 et Thuc. i 24, vi 5. **8** ΤΕϹϹΑΡΑϹ. **9** ΜΕΤΑ ΤΑΥΤΑ ΕΧΟΥϹΑΙ (HN supra) (deleto ι) ΠΟΛΙΤΕΙΑΝ ΤΑΞΙΝ: μετὰ ταῦτα [ἐξ]έχουσα πολιτείας τάξις K[1], —[μετ]έχουσα J B Mayor, —ὑπάρχουσα Richards; [παρ]έχουσα aut πολιτείαν τάξις (Rutherford) aut πολιτείας τάξιν (Wyse), νέαν ἔχουσα πολιτείας τάξιν Gertz. μετρίαν τιν' ἔχουσα πολιτείας τάξιν H-L; μετὰ ταῦτα .. ἔχουσα πολιτείας τάξιν K-W; μετὰ ταύτην ἔχουσα πολιτείας τάξιν K[3], B. **14** <τὴν> add. K (edd.). **16** ΔΕ ΚΑΙ (K, B coll. vv. 9 et 20—21): δ' ἡ J B Mayor, K-W, H-L. **17** ἐπετέλεσε H-L.

συνοικησάντων] Heraclides *init.*, συνοικήσαντος δὲ Ἴωνος αὐτοῖς.

εἰς τὰς τέτταρας—φυλάς] c. 8 § 3. **συνενεμήθησαν**] cf. 21 § 2, συνένειμε (*al.* διένειμε).

φυλοβασιλεῖς] c. 8 § 3; c. 57 *ult.*

δευτέρα...καὶ πρώτη] *i.e.* the constitution of Theseus was second to that of Ion and was the first of the eleven μεταβολαί.

πολιτείας τάξιν] c. 3 § 1, ἡ τάξις τῆς ἀρχαίας πολιτείας.

μικρὸν παρεγκλίνουσα τῆς βασιλικῆς] The prehistoric 'constitution of Theseus' was treated in an early chapter that is now lost. The lost passage is referred to in Plut. *Thes.* 25, ὅτι δὲ πρῶτος ἀπέκλινε πρὸς τὸν ὄχλον, ὡς Ἀριστοτέλης φησί, καὶ ἀφῆκε τὸ μοναρχεῖν, ἔοικε μαρτυρεῖν καὶ Ὅμηρος ἐν νεῶν καταλόγῳ μόνους Ἀθηναίους δῆμον προσαγορεύσας. παρεγκλίνειν intr. is found in *Hist. Anim.* 498 *a* 16, σκέλη μικρὸν εἰς τὸ πλάγιον παρεγκλίνοντα. ἐγκλίνειν intr. in *Pol.* 1307 *a* 21, ἐφ' ὁπότερον ἂν ἐγκλίνῃ ἡ πολιτεία, and 1266 *a* 7, ἡ τῶν Λακεδαιμονίων πολιτεία μᾶλλον ἐγκλίνειν βούλεται πρὸς τὴν ὀλιγαρχίαν. ἐκκλίνειν intr. in *Pol.* ii 11, 1273 *a* 5, τὰ μὲν εἰς δῆμον ἐκκλίνει μᾶλλον τὰ δ' εἰς ὀλιγαρχίαν.

ἐν ᾗ καὶ νόμους ἀνέγραψαν πρῶτον] The summary does not strictly correspond to the original account in c. 4. Nothing was there stated on the important fact that under Dracon the laws were first reduced to a written code, though it was partly implied in the words: τοὺς θεσμοὺς ἔθηκεν. On the other hand, the remarkable 'Draconian constitution,' which has justly aroused considerable suspicion, finds no recognition in the summary. This supports the view that the description of that constitution is an interpolation.

Σόλωνος] 5—12. **ἀρχὴ δημοκρατίας**] 9 § 1. **Πεισιστράτου**] 14—19. **Κλεισθένους**] 22. **δημοτικωτέρα**] 22 *init.* **τῆς ἐξ Ἀρείου πάγου βουλῆς**] 23.

Ἀριστείδης] Aristides is here described as having *traced the outline* which was completed by his successor Ephialtes. The former admitted the lower classes to a larger share in public life. Though he did not actually throw the archonship open to all the citizens of Athens (as asserted in Plut. *Arist.* 22), he encouraged the rural population to resort to Athens (c. 24 § 1) and thus prompted them to take an interest in political affairs. Ephialtes carried this democratical movement still further by abolishing the supremacy of the Areopagus.

There is no justification for the criticism of Rühl (*Rhein. Mus.* 46, 432) that Aristides is here represented as cooperating with Ephialtes. The absence of the name of Themistocles is, however, worthy of note. As a constitutional reformer he is eclipsed by Aristides. It may even be λεσεν καταλύσας τὴν Ἀρεοπαγῖτιν βουλήν· ἐν ᾗ πλεῖστα συνέβη τὴν πόλιν διὰ τοὺς δημαγωγοὺς ἁμαρτάνειν — — διὰ τὴν τῆς θαλάττης ἀρχήν. ὀγδόη δ' [ἡ] τῶν τετρακοσίων κατάστασις, καὶ μετὰ ταύτην ἐνάτη ⟦δὲ⟧ [δ]ημοκρατία πάλιν. δεκάτη δ' ἡ τῶν τριάκοντα καὶ ἡ τῶν δέκα τυραννίς. ἑνδεκάτη δ' ἡ μετὰ τὴν ἀπὸ Φυλῆς καὶ ἐκ Πειραιέως κάθοδον, ἀφ' ἧς διαγεγένηται μέχρι τῆς νῦν, ἀεὶ προσεπιλαμβάνουσα τῷ πλήθει τὴν ἐξουσίαν. ἁπάντων γὰρ αὐτὸς αὑτὸν πεποίηκεν ὁ δῆμος κύριον καὶ πάντα διοικεῖται ψηφίσμασιν καὶ δικαστηρίοις, ἐν οἷς ὁ δῆμός ἐστιν ὁ κρατῶν. καὶ γὰρ α[ἱ τ]ῆς βουλῆς κρίσεις εἰς τὸν δῆμον ἐληλύθασιν. καὶ τοῦτο

19 διὰ (K, K-W, B): <καὶ> διὰ H-L; — — 'deest fere θαρρήσασαν' K-W coll. *Pol.* 1274 *a* 12. **20** ΟΓΔΟΗΝΔ———ΚΑΤΑΣΤΑΣΤΑΣΙΝ. **21** δὲ secl. J B Mayor (K-W, H-L), retinent K, B. **22** καὶ ⟦ἡ⟧ K-W. **23** ΠΕΙΡΑΙΩΣ (H-L). ΤΗΣ: τοῦ H-L. **24** Locus corruptus, K-W. **26** ψηφίσμασι H-L.

doubted whether he really has any claim to have acted with Ephialtes in overthrowing the Areopagus, as narrated in c. 25 § 3.

17. **ὑπέδειξεν**] with πρῶτος in *Rhet.* iii 2, 1404 *b* 25, and *Poet.* 4, 1448 *b* 37. Cf. Hdt. i 189, Xen. *Oecon.* xi 18. The metaphor is probably derived 'from the tracing of lines *underneath* by a writing-master, for the pupil to follow or write *over*,' *Protag.* 326 D (Cope's *Introd.* to Ar. *Rhet.* p. 284).

Ἐφιάλτης] From the tenour of the earlier part of the work we are prepared to find a prominent place assigned in the summary to Ephialtes, as compared with Pericles. The reforms in the Areopagus due to the latter were of minor importance. But it is singular that so notable a name should find no mention in the present passage. He is here regarded as one of the demagogues whose influence was detrimental to Athens. The slight notice of his policy in 28 § 1 is indeed not unfavourable; but it is certainly far from enthusiastic.

διὰ τὴν τῆς θαλάττης ἀρχήν] Isocr. *de Pace*, 79.

των τετρακοσίων] 29—32. **δημοκρατία**] 34.

ἡ τῶν τριάκοντα—τυραννίς] more accurately described as an oligarchy in 53 *init.*

τῶν δέκα] 38 § 1.

προσεπιλαμβάνουσα τῷ πλήθει τὴν ἐξουσίαν] Schömann, *Ant.* p. 386 E.T.: 'The demagogues found it their interest to extend the activity of the popular assemblies as far as possible, and to establish the principle that the people was, in the most comprehensive sense of the term, lord over everything, and could do what it pleased (*in Neaer.* p. 1375; Xen. *Hell.* i 7, 12). On the other hand, men of keener insight complained that the State was administered by Psephismata—that is, according to the pleasure at any moment of the sovereign people—rather than according to the laws, and that there was only too often a contradiction between the laws and these Psephismata.' *Pol.* vi (iv) 4, 1292 *a* 4—37, ἕτερον εἶδος δημοκρατίας τἆλλα μὲν εἶναι ταὐτά, κύριον δ' εἶναι τὸ πλῆθος καὶ μὴ τὸν νόμον. τοῦτο δὲ γίνεται ὅταν τὰ ψηφίσματα κύρια ᾖ ἀλλὰ μὴ ὁ νόμος. συμβαίνει δὲ τοῦτο διὰ τοὺς δημαγωγούς κτλ. Dem. *Lept.* § 92.

εἰς τὸν δῆμον ἐληλύθασιν] In the department of judicature indictments or informations concerning breaches of the law, which could not be dealt with in the ordinary course, were in the first instance brought before the Council. If the offence were too important for the competency of that body, they passed to the popular assembly. The Council could not inflict any fine beyond 500 *drachmae*. Schömann, *Ant.* 394—5 E. T. Cf. 45 and 49 § 3; *Pol.* 1299 *b* 38 ff.

καὶ τοῦτο κτλ.] This is understood by Cauer (p. 48 f.) as a general eulogy of the fully developed democracy and as inconsistent with the views expressed in the *Politics*. But the eulogy is really limited to one particular point, the transfer of judicial functions from the βουλή to the ἐκκλησία, and both of these bodies are

δοκοῦσι ποιεῖν ὀρθῶς· εὐδιαφθορώτεροι γὰρ <οἱ> ὀλίγοι τῶν πολλῶν
3 *εἰσὶν κ[αὶ] κέρδει κ[αὶ] χάρισιν. μισθοφόρον δ' ἐκκλησίαν τὸ μὲν πρῶτον ἀπέγνωσαν ποιεῖν. οὐ συλλεγομένων δ' εἰς τὴν ἐκκλησίαν, ἀλλὰ πολλὰ σοφιζομένων τῶν πρυτάνεων, ὅπως προσιστῆται τὸ*
[Col. 21.] *πλῆθος πρὸς τὴν ἐπι‖κύρωσιν τῆς χειροτονίας, πρῶτον μὲν Ἀγύρριος ὀβολὸν ἐπόρισεν, μετὰ δὲ τοῦτον Ἡρακλείδης ὁ Κλαζομένιος ὁ βασιλεὺς ἐπικαλούμενος διώβολον, πάλιν δ' Ἀγύρριος τριώβολον.*

42. *ἔχει δ' ἡ νῦν κατάστασις τῆς πολιτείας τόνδε τὸν*

28 ΟΛΙΓΟΝ : *ὀλίγοι* K : <*οἱ*> *ὀλίγοι* Gennadios, Kontos, K-W, H-L, B. **29** *εἰσὶ* H-L. *δ'*: *δὲ* <*τὴν*> K-W, *δὲ* B. **31** CΟ(?)ΦΙΖΟΜΕΝΩΝ Blass, Gomperz, K-W, K[3] : *ψηφιζυμένων* K[1], *ψηφιζομένων* <*μόνων*> H-L.

TESTIMONIA. **XLI 33—34** Hesych. *Κλαζομένιος· οὗτος Ἡρακλείδης ὁ Κλαζομένιός τε καὶ ὁ βαῦς* (ex hoc loco *βασιλεὺς* scripsit Houtsma) *καλούμενος.*

---

distinctly democratic. The text is in fact in perfect accord with a passage in the *Politics*, iii 15, 1286 *a* 30, *διὰ τοῦτο καὶ κρίνει ἄμεινον ὄχλος πολλὰ ἢ εἷς ὁστισοῦν. ἔτι μᾶλλον ἀδιάφθορον τὸ πολύ, καθάπερ ὕδωρ τὸ πλεῖον, οὕτω καὶ τὸ πλῆθος τῶν ὀλίγων ἀδιαφθορώτερον.* Cf. O. Crusius, *Philol.* l, p. 175.

§ 3. **τὸ μὲν πρῶτον**] on the restoration of the democracy.

Ἀγύρριος] a statesman belonging to the deme of Collytus, prominent as a financier in the early part of the fourth century. In 400 B.C. he had a dispute with Andocides about the lease of a tax (Andoc. *De Myst.* 133, with Marchant's note).

Schol. on Arist. *Eccl.* (B.C. 392) 102—5 (*Ἀγύρριος...πράττει τὰ μέγιστ' ἐν τῇ πόλει*): *ὁ Ἀ. στρατηγὸς θηλυδριώδης, ἄρξας ἐν Λέσβῳ. καὶ τὸν μισθὸν δὲ τῶν ποιητῶν συνέτεμε* (cf. Schol. on *Ran.* 367 and Plat. Com. *frag.* 133 Kock) *καὶ πρῶτος ἐκκλησιαστικὸν δέδωκε.* In *Eccl.* 300—310 the poet refers to the time when only one obol was allowed instead of three: *ἡνίκ' ἔδει λαβεῖν ἐλθόντ' ὀβολὸν μόνον*, whereas now *τριώβολον ζητοῦσι λαβεῖν*, *ib.* 380, 392, *Plut.* (ed. 2, B.C. 389) 329 and 171 with the Schol. where, however, the *μισθὸς ἐκκλησιαστικὸς* is confounded with the *μ. δικαστικός*. The text shews that the Schol. on *Eccl.* 102 was right in making Agyrrhius the originator of the fee. Boeckh (II xiv p. 316 Lamb) inferred from the mention of Myronides in *Eccl.* 305 that the fee was introduced some time after the beginning of the influence of Pericles. He was further led to ascribe its origin to one Callistratus, *Append. Vatic. Proverb.* iii, *ὀβολὸν εὗρε Παρνύτης. Καλλίστρατος Ἀθήνησι πολιτευσάμενος, ἐπικαλούμενος δὲ Παρνύτης, μισθὸν ἔταξε τοῖς δικασταῖς καὶ τοῖς ἐκκλησιασταῖς.* Possibly Callicrates, who added an obol to the *διώβολον* of the *θεωρικόν* is really meant (28 § 3). The text also proves that for a short time the fee for the public assembly was two obols, though this was denied by Boeckh, *l. c.*

Agyrrhius also restored the *θεωρικόν* (Philochorus ap. Harpocr. *s.v.*). On the death of Thrasybulus (early in 389) he was elected *στρατηγὸς* (Xen. *Hell.* iv 8, 31; Diod. xiv 99). Plat. Com. *frag.* 185 Kock, *λαβοῦ λαβοῦ τῆς χειρὸς ὡς τάχιστά μου· μέλλω στρατηγὸν χειροτονεῖν Ἀγύρριον.* It was probably after 387 that he was long in prison as a debtor to the State (Dem. 24 § 134).

Ἡρακλείδης ὁ Κλαζομένιος] mentioned in Plat. *Ion*, 541 D (with Phanosthenes of Andros), *οὓς ἥδε ἡ πόλις ξένους ὄντας, ἐνδειξαμένους ὅτι ἄξιοι λόγου εἰσί, καὶ εἰς στρατηγίας καὶ εἰς τὰς ἄλλας ἀρχὰς ἄγει.* Favorinus ap. Athen. 506 A; Aelian, *Var. Hist.* xiv 5. The name *βασιλεὺς* is perhaps due to his belonging to some royal family in Asia Minor (cf. Strabo, p. 632; CIG 2881, 2069, 2157, 2189). Peisistratus was called *βασιλεὺς* in the *Δῆμος* of Eupolis (frag. 123 p. 291 Kock). O. Crusius in *Philol.* l, p. 177. Heracleides is identified by Köhler (*Hermes*, xxvii 68 ff.) with the person of that name mentioned in an inscr. in *Bull. Corr. Hell.* 1888, p. 163.

τρόπον. μετέχουσιν μὲν τῆς πολιτείας οἱ ἐξ ἀμφοτέρων γεγονότες ἀστῶν. ἐγγράφον[ται] δ' εἰς τοὺς δημότας ὀκτωκαίδεκα ἔτη γεγονότες· ὅταν δ' ἐγγράφωνται, διαψηφίζονται περὶ αὐτῶν ὀμόσαντες οἱ δημόται, πρῶτον μὲν εἰ δοκοῦσι γεγονέναι τὴν ἡλικίαν τὴν ἐκ τοῦ νόμου, κἂν μὴ δόξωσι, ἀπέρχονται πάλιν εἰς παῖδα[ς, δ]εύτερον δ' εἰ ἐλεύθερός ἐστι καὶ γέγονε κατὰ [το]ὺς νόμους. ἔπειτ' ἂν μὲν ἀποψηφίσωνται μὴ εἶναι ἐλεύθερον, ὁ μὲν ἐφίησιν εἰς τὸ δικαστή-

XLII 2 μετέχουσι H-L. **3** ΟΚΤΩΚΑΙΔΕΚΑΕΤΕΙϹ ante corr. **4** ΔΕΓΡΑΦ : δ' ἐγγράφ. Wyse, Blass, Herwerden, Naber (K-W, H-L, K[3]). **6** δόξωσιν H-L. **7** ἐὰν μὲν H-L. **8** ΕΠΙΨΗΦ (K) : ἀποψηφ. Wyse, Blass, K-W, H-L; cf. Phot. *l.c.*

Testimonia. **XLII 3—4** *Schol. Arist. *Vesp.* 578 παίδων τοίνυν δοκιμαζομένων· πρὸς τὸ ἔθος. 'Αρ. δέ φησιν ὅτι ψήφῳ οἱ ἐγγραφόμενοι δοκιμάζονται, μὴ νεώτεροι (νεώτεροι μὴ codd., correx. K-W) ιη̄ ἐτῶν εἶεν (Frag. 427[2], 467[3]). ἴσως δ' ἂν περὶ τῶν μὴ κρινομένων παίδων εἰς τοὺς γυμνικοὺς ἀγῶνας λέγει (*sc.* ὁ 'Αριστοφάνης)· οὐχ ὡς ἐν δικαστηρίῳ κρινομένων ἀλλ' ὑπὸ τῶν πρεσβυτέρων.
8 Phot. (et Etym. M.) ἔφεσις: ...ἐγένετο δὲ 'Αθήνησιν ἐπὶ τῶν ἐν τοῖς δήμοις ἀποψηφισθέντων, ἐφεῖσθαι γὰρ αὖθις ἐξῆν αὐτοῖς εἰς δικαστήριον περὶ τῆς πολιτείας· καὶ εἰ μὲν ἑάλωσαν, ἐπωλοῦντο ὡς ξένοι· εἰ δὲ μή, ἐπανῄεσαν εἰς τοὺς ἐξ ὧν ἀπεψηφίσθησαν δήμους.

Part II, c. XLII—LXIII. *The Existing Constitution.*

XLII § 1. *Enrolment on the list of citizens.*

§ 1. **μετέχουσιν τῆς πολιτείας**] *Pol.* 1268 *a* 24, 27; 1275 *b* 31; 1290 *a* 4.

ἐξ ἀμφοτέρων—ἀστῶν] *Pol.* 1278 *a* 34, τέλος δὲ μόνον τοὺς ἐξ ἀμφοῖν ἀστῶν πολίτας ποιοῦσιν. 1275 *b* 21, ὁρίζονται δὲ πρὸς τὴν χρῆσιν πολίτην τὸν ἐξ ἀμφοτέρων πολιτῶν καὶ μὴ θατέρου μόνον, οἷον πατρὸς ἢ μητρός. See note on 26 § 4.

ἐγγράφονται] *Pol.* iii 1, 1275 *a* 14, παῖδας τοὺς μήπω δι' ἡλικίαν ἐγγεγραμμένους. Dem. *Eubul.* 57 § 61, ἡνίκ' ἐνεγράφην ἐγὼ καὶ ὀμόσαντες οἱ δημόται δικαίως πάντες περὶ ἐμοῦ τὴν ψῆφον ἔφερον, οὔτε κατηγόρησεν οὔτ' ἐναντίαν τὴν ψῆφον ἤνεγκεν. Isaeus 7 § 28, ὀμόσαντες καθ' ἱερῶν ἐνέγραψάν με (*sc.* εἰς τὸ ληξιαρχικὸν γραμματεῖον). Lycurg. *Leocr.* 76, ἐπειδὰν εἰς τὸ ληξιαρχικὸν γραμματεῖον ἐγγραφῶσι καὶ ἔφηβοι γένωνται. The earliest ephebic inscr. (B.C. 334–3) mentions οἱ ἔφηβοι οἱ ἐπὶ τοῦ Κτησικλέους ἄρχοντος ἐγγραφέντες. By this registration the youthful citizen entered on the duties of civil life at the same time as he was enrolled on the list of *ephebi*. This was the only list of *ephebi* kept by the demes, and such a phrase as ἐγγράφεσθαι εἰς ἐφήβους (Pseudo-Plat. *Axioch.* 366 E) is an inaccurate equivalent for ἐγγ. εἰς τοὺς δημότας (P. Girard, in Daremberg and Saglio, iii 624).

ὀκτωκαίδεκα ἔτη] Schol. Aeschin. *c. Ctes.* 122, ἀπὸ ὀκτωκαίδεκα ἐτῶν ἐνεγράφοντο εἰς τὸ ληξιαρχικόν, and 1 § 19. ἐπὶ διετὲς ἡβῆσαι (Aeschin. *l. c.*) denoted the close of the two years intervening between the ages of 16 and 18 (A. Schäfer, *Dem.* iii 2, 19—38; Lipsius in *N. Jahrb. f. Philol.*, no. 117, p. 299 ff.; Gilbert, *Gr. St.* i 186).

In Aristoph. *Vesp.* 578 it is regarded as a privilege of the δικασταὶ to take part in ascertaining the physical maturity of Athenian youths on the occasion of the δοκιμασία. In the present passage the preliminary enrolling belongs to the δημόται, while the subsequent δοκιμασία is now for the first time assigned to the βουλή, to which it was perhaps transferred after the time of Aristophanes. According to the text, the δικασταὶ are only concerned in the event of an appeal on the question whether the person enrolled was of free birth or not. (Cf. Meier and Schömann, *Att. Process*, p. 253–4 Lipsius. The doubt there suggested as to the accuracy of the Schol. on *Vesp.* 578 is now withdrawn by Lipsius, in the *Verhandlungen der K. Sächsischen Gesellschaft der Wissenschaften*, Leipzig, 1891, p. 63.) Possibly, in the event of a dispute on the question of age, the matter was similarly referred to a court, but this is not stated in the text.

διαψηφίζονται] The ordinary διαψήφισις here described might be followed by an appeal to a δικαστήριον. The procedure was the same as in the special διαψήφισις described in Dem. 57 § 60, ἔπεισε διαψηφίσασθαι τοὺς 'Αλιμουσίους περὶ αὐτῶν καὶ κατηγορῶν δέκα τῶν δημοτῶν ἐξέβαλεν, οὓς ἅπαντας πλὴν ἑνὸς κατεδέξατο τὸ δικαστήριον.

ριον, οἱ δὲ δημόται κατηγόρους αἱροῦνται πέντε [ἄν]δρας ἐξ αὐτῶν, κἂν μὲν μὴ δόξῃ δι[καί]ως ἐγγράφ[εσ]θαι, πωλεῖ τοῦτον ἡ πόλις· 2 ἐὰν δὲ νικήσῃ, τοῖς [δη]μόταις ἐπάναγκες ἐγγράφειν. μετὰ δὲ ταῦτα δοκιμάζει τοὺς ἐγγραφέντας ἡ βουλή, κἄν τις δόξ[ῃ ν]εώτερος ὀκτωκαίδεκα ἐτῶν εἶναι, ζημιοῖ [τοὺ]ς δημότας τοὺς ἐγγράψαντας. ἐπὰν δὲ δοκιμα[σθ]ῶσιν οἱ ἔφηβοι, συλλεγέντες οἱ πατέρες αὐτῶν κατὰ φυλάς, ὀμόσαντες αἱροῦνται τρεῖς ἐκ τῶν φυλετῶν τῶν ὑπὲρ τετταράκοντα ἔτη γεγονότων, οὓς ἂν ἡγῶνται βελτίστους εἶναι καὶ ἐπιτηδειοτάτους ἐπιμελεῖσθαι τῶν ἐφήβων, ἐκ δὲ τούτων

11 Versus in fine ΕΝΓΡΑΦΕΙ^{N} *ἐγγράφειν* (sc. *ἐπάναγκές ἐστιν αὐτὸν ἐγγράφειν*) recte van Leeuwen (H-L, B): ΕΝΓΡΑΦΕ^{ΑΙ}Τ *ἐγγράφεται* K, K-W; constructio quidem utraque recte se habet; *ἐπάναγκες ἐγγράφειν* defendunt c. 29, 21, *Pol.* 1266 *a* 10, 17, 18 et 1301 *b* 23; *ἐπάναγκες ἐγγράφεται* *Pol.* 1266 *a* 15; sed manus tertia nunquam aut ΤΑΙ contrahit aut ΑΙ supra verbi finem scribit, N autem septies eodem in loco ponit, c. 41, 30 εκκλησια^{ν}, c. 42, 34 λαμβανουσι^{ν}, c. 43, 4 χειροτονουσι^{ν}, 7 πρυτανευει^{ν}, 15 βουλη^{ν}, 17 χειροτονει^{ν}, 29 κελευουσι^{ν}; quorum exemplorum sex in fine versus inventa sunt. **13** *ὀκτωκαίδεκ'* K-W, B. **14** ΕΠΑΝ : *ἐπειδὰν* H-L.

ἀποψηφίσωνται] used absolutely in Dem. 57 §§ 11, 56, 58, 59, 62; followed by *μὴ* in *F. L.* 174, *ἀπεψηφίσαντο μὴ πέμπειν*. *ἐπιψηφίζεσθαι* is found c. acc. in Dion. H., *Ant.* vi 71, and Diod. xix 61; but these passages do not justify the retention of *ἐπιψηφίσωνται*.

ἐφίησιν *κτλ.*] Dem. 57 § 6, *ἀξιῶ... μηδέπω τὴν τῶν δημοτῶν ἀποψήφισιν ποιεῖσθαι τεκμήριον ὑμᾶς, ὡς ἄρ' οὐχὶ προσήκει μοι τῆς πόλεως. εἰ γὰρ ἐνομίζετε τὰ δίκαια δυνήσεσθαι τοὺς δημότας διακρῖναι, οὐκ ἂν ἐδώκατε τὴν εἰς ὑμᾶς ἔφεσιν*. Cf. Etym. M. and Photius, *s. v.* *ἔφεσις*, quoted in *Testim.*

πέντε ἄνδρας] We find a similar procedure in the decree of the *φράτερες* recorded in the Decelean inscr., CIA ii 2, p. 534—6, no. 841 *b*, ll. 30—34, *ἐὰν δέ τις βούληται ἐφεῖναι εἰς Δημοτιωνίδας, ὧν ἂν ἀποψηφίσωνται, ἐξεῖναι αὐτῷ, ἑλέσθαι δὲ ἐπ' αὐτοῖς συνηγόρους τὸν Δεκελεικῶν οἶκον πέντε ἄνδρας ὑπὲρ τριάκοντα ἔτη γεγονότας*. Cf. *Class. Rev.* v 221 *a*.

πωλεῖ] Dionys. on Isaeus, 16 p. 617, *ἐγράφη δή τις ὑπὸ τῶν Ἀθηναίων νόμος· ἐξέτασιν γενέσθαι τῶν πολιτῶν κατὰ δήμους, τὸν δὲ ἀποψηφισθέντα ὑπὸ τῶν δημοτῶν τῆς πολιτείας μὴ μετέχειν, τοῖς δὲ ἀδίκως ἀποψηφισθεῖσιν ἔφεσιν εἰς τὸ δικαστήριον εἶναι, προσκαλεσαμένοις τοὺς δημότας, καὶ ἐὰν τὸ δεύτερον ἐξελεγχθῶσι, πεπρᾶσθαι καὶ τὰ χρήματα εἶναι δημόσια*. Bekker, *Anecd.* (and Suidas) *s. v.* *ἀποψηφισθέντα· εἴ τις ξένος ἔδοξεν εἶναι καὶ οὐ πολίτης, τοῦτον ἐν ταῖς διαψηφίσεσι τῶν δήμων ἀπεψηφίζοντο οἱ δημόται, καὶ ἐλέγετο ἀπεψηφισμένος. εἶτα εἰσήγετο εἰς τὸ δικαστήριον καὶ ἐκρίνετο ξενίας, καὶ εἰ μὲν ἑάλω, ἐπιπράσκετο ὡς ξένος· εἰ δὲ ἐκράτει, ἀνελαμβάνετο εἰς τὴν πολιτείαν. οὕτω Δημοσθένης* (*de Cor.* 132). Cf. Meier and Schömann, p. 440 Lips., n. 705.

§§ 2—5. *On the military training of the Ephebi.* On the *Ephebi*, see Dittenberger, *De Ephebis Atticis*, 1863; Dumont, *Essai sur l'Éphébie Attique*, 1875–6; Grasberger, *Erziehung und Unterricht im Klass. Alterthum*, iii, 1881. Also Capes, *University Life in Ancient Athens*, 1877; Wayte on *Ephebus* in Smith, *Dict. Ant.*; P. Girard, *l'éducation Athénienne*, 1889, pp. 271—327; and esp. the same scholar's article in Daremberg and Saglio, 1891, iii 621—636 (the only account of the subject written since the discovery of this treatise).

§ 2. **δοκιμάζει**] This *δοκιμασία* (like that of adopted sons) probably took place at the time of the *ἀρχαιρεσίαι* (Isaeus 7 § 28; Dem. *c. Leoch.* 44 § 39) at the beginning of the official year (Lys. 21 § 1). Cf. Gilbert, i 187.

ὑπὲρ τετταράκοντα ἔτη] Similarly any *χορηγὸς* who had boys under his superintendence had to have attained the age of 40 (56 § 3).

ὁ δῆμος ἕνα τῆ[ς φ]υλῆς ἑκάστης χειροτονεῖ σωφρονιστήν, καὶ
[κοσ]μητὴν ἐκ τῶν ἄλλων Ἀθηναίων ἐπὶ πάντας. συλλαβόντες δ' 3
οὗτοι τοὺς ἐφήβους, πρῶτον μὲν τὰ ἱερὰ περιῆλθον, εἶτ' εἰς

19 ...ΜΗΤΗΝ?: *κοσμητὴν* Paton, van Leeuwen (H-L), K-W, K[3], B; [*ἐπιμ*]*ελητὴν*K[1]. ΠΑΝΤΑ vel ΠΑΝΤΑϹ ante ϹΥΛΛ: *πάντα. συλλ.* K; *πάντας. συλλ.* K-W, B; *πάντας. παραλ.* H-L.

18—25 Bekk. *Anecd.* 301 (infra exscriptum).

χειροτονεῖ] one of the few exceptions to the general rule by which appointments at Athens were made by lot. Cf. 43 § 1 and Headlam, *On the Lot*, p. 104.

σωφρονιστήν] [Plat.] *Axioch.* 367 A, *πᾶς ὁ τοῦ μειρακίσκου χρόνος* (*v. l.* *πόνος*) *ἐστὶν ὑπὸ σωφρονιστάς.* Dinarchus, *adv. Philocl.* 15, *ὁ μὲν δῆμος ἅπας οὔτ' ἀσφαλὲς οὔτε δίκαιον νομίζων εἶναι παρακαταθέσθαι τοὺς ἑαυτοῦ παῖδας, ἀπεχειροτόνησεν αὐτὸν ἀπὸ τῆς τῶν ἐφήβων ἐπιμελείας.* Philocles, the *στρατηγὸς* here referred to, was a *σωφρονιστής*, not a *κοσμητής* (Gilbert, i 297; Dumont, *Essai sur l'Éphébie Attique*, 1876, p. 169 f.). In Bekker *Anecd.* 301 the *σωφρονισταί* are defined as *ἄρχοντές τινες χειροτονητοί, δέκα τὸν ἀριθμόν, ἑκάστης φυλῆς εἷς. ἐπεμελοῦντο δὲ τῆς σωφροσύνης τῶν ἐφήβων μισθὸν παρὰ τῆς πόλεως λαμβάνοντες ἕκαστος καθ' ἡμέραν δραχμήν* (similarly in Photius and Etym. M. *s. v.*).

They are mentioned in the earliest ephebic inscr. now extant, B.C. 334—3 (*Bull. Corr. Hell.* xiii 253); also in B.C. 320/19 (CIA ii 581); and in B.C. 305/4. This last inscr., as restored, includes the words: *[τοῦ κοσμητοῦ καὶ τ]ῶν σωφρο[νιστῶν καὶ τῶν δι]δασκάλων.* The *κοσμητὴς* also appears to be named near the beginning: *[ἐπειδὴ οἱ ἔφηβοι ... ἐπ]ιμελοῦνται ἐ[....καὶ .. φιλοτ]ιμοῦν[ται....] ιτωσι εὐτάκτως ... τε κοσμη[τ .... τ]ἄλλα τὰ περὶ τὴ[ν ... τοῖς διδα]σκάλοις κτλ.* In the same inscr. the *ἔφηβοι* are described as *ἐγγραφέντες* (Köhler, *Mittheilungen*, 1879, iv 324—7). The latest inscr. belongs to B.C. 303/2, .. *σωφρονιστὴς ὑπὸ τοῦ δήμου χειροτονηθεὶς [τῶν] ἐφήβων τῶν ἐγγραφέντων [τῆς] Πανδιονίδος φυλῆς ἐπὶ Λεωστράτου ἄρχοντος* (B.C. 303) *καλῶς καὶ σωφρόνως καὶ εὐτάκτως ἐ[πιμε]μέληται αὐτῶν καὶ ἀποφ[αίν]ουσιν αὐτὸν εἰς τὴν φυλὴν [οἱ π]ατέρες τῶν ἐφήβων ἐπιμεμ[ελ]ῆσθαι κατὰ τοὺς νόμους τῶν ἐφήβων κτλ.* (*Bull. Corr. Hell.* 1888, xii 149). A relief published in *Rev. Arch.* 1876, ii 185, copied in Daremberg and Saglio, iii 628, represents three *σωφρονισταί* in their robes holding their wands of office in the presence of a divinity who cannot be identified. The office was apparently suppressed early in the third century B.C. to be restored in imperial times. See Dittenberger, *De Ephebis Atticis*, pp. 29, 44; Dumont, *Sur l'Éphébie*, p. 200; Smith, *Dict. Ant.* i 998 *b*; and esp. Girard in Daremberg and Saglio, iii 626.

κοσμητὴν] Erotianus, *Lex. Hipp. s.v.* *κόσμου· κοσμηταὶ οἱ τῶν ἐφήβων εὐταξίας προνοοῦντες.* The word is found in [Plat.] *Axioch.* 363 E (as quoted by Stobaeus), *ἐπειδὰν δ' εἰς τοὺς ἐφήβους ἐγγραφῇ, κοσμητὴς καὶ φόβος χείρων*, and in a general sense in Plat. *Leg.* 372 A. The usual formula for the election of this officer is *χειροτονηθεὶς κοσμητὴς ἐπὶ τοὺς ἐφήβους εἰς τὸν ἐπὶ (τοῦ δεῖνος) ἄρχοντος ἐνιαυτόν*, CIA ii 465, 467, 469: in 471 l. 56 the people *κοσμη[τ]ὴν καθίστησ[ιν ἐκ] τῶν ἄριστα βε[βι]ωκότων.* Hardly any of the inscriptions in which this officer is mentioned are earlier than the second century. The earliest belongs to B.C. 305/4 (quoted in last n.); the next to about B.C. 282 (CIA ii 316, 10 = Dittenberger, *Inscr.* no. 346). It is suggested by Dittenberger (*De Ephebis*, p. 31) that the office was created in the time of Alexander. The inscr. of B.C. 305 (already quoted) shews that for a short time the *κοσμητὴς* and the *σωφρονισταί* existed together. This is confirmed by the text, if the restoration is correct. Cf. Dumont, *Éphébie Attique*, p. 166 ff.; Gilbert, i 299; and Girard in Daremberg and Saglio, iii 626—7.

In literature, one of the earliest passages on the *κοσμητής* is in Teles (fl. middle of 3rd cent.), ap. Stob. 98, 72, *ἔφηβος γέγονεν· ἔμπαλιν τὸν κοσμητὴν φοβεῖται, τὸν παιδοτρίβην, τὸν ὁπλομάχον, τὸν γυμνασίαρχον, ὑπὸ πάντων τούτων μαστιγοῦται, παρατηρεῖται, τραχηλίζεται. ἐξ ἐφήβων ἐστὶ καὶ ἤδη εἴκοσιν ἐτῶν· ἔτι φοβεῖται καὶ παρατηρεῖ καὶ ταξίαρχον καὶ στρατηγόν.*

ἐπὶ πάντας] For *ἐπί*, of persons set over others, cf. Xen. *Cyr.* iv 5, 58, *ἐπὶ τοὺς πεζοὺς καθιστάναι ἄρχοντα*, and *Hell.* iii 4, 20. In this sense it is more common *c. gen.* or *dat.*

§ 3. **τὰ ἱερὰ περιῆλθον**] It was probably at this stage that the *ἔφηβοι* took the oath in the cave of Aglauros (Dem. *F. L.* 303; Lycurgus, *Leocr.* 76; Stobaeus, *Flor.* 43, 48; Pollux viii 105; another clause is quoted in Plut. *Alc.* 15).

Πειραιέα πορεύονται, καὶ φρουροῦσιν οἱ μὲν τὴν Μουνιχίαν οἱ δὲ τὴν Ἀκτήν. χειρο[τονεῖ] δὲ καὶ παιδοτρίβας αὐτοῖς δύο καὶ διδασκάλους, [οἵ]τινες ὁπλομαχεῖν καὶ τοξεύειν καὶ ἀκοντίζειν κ[αὶ] καταπάλτην ἀφιέναι διδάσκουσιν. δίδωσι δὲ καὶ εἰς τρο[φὴν]

21 Πειραιᾶ H-L. ΜΟΥΝΥΧΙΑΝ. Cf. c. 19, 5. **23** [οἵ]τινες K, H-L, B : τ[έτ]τ[α]ρας <οἱ> K-W. **24** ΚΑΤΗΝ ΑΠΕΛΤΗΝ καταπέλτην (K[1], K-W[2]) : —πάλτην K-W[1], H-L, K[3], B, cf. Meisterhans, p. 12[2] (καταπαλτῶν annis A.C. 330—323). διδάξουσιν Rutherford (H-L).

Cobet, *N. L.* 223, regards the formula in Stobaeus and Pollux as a figment of the grammarians; but it can hardly be doubted that some such oath was taken, although it is not mentioned in the text. (Cf. Schömann, *Ant.* p. 359 E. T.; Gilbert, i 296 n.) The taking of the oath is exhibited on a vase in the Hermitage Museum, which shews us an ἔφηβος, armed with shield and spear, holding his right hand over an altar; the oath is being administered by an aged man (probably representing the βουλή) beyond it: behind the ἔφηβος we have a Νίκη holding a helmet (Daremberg and Saglio, iii 624).

Μουνιχίαν] 19 § 2. Even in Roman times, B.C. 100, the *ephebi* περιέπλευσαν ...εἰς Μουνιχίαν (CIA ii 467, 22).

Ἀκτήν] the name given to the southern peninsula of the Peiraeus, the highest point of which is about 180 feet above the sea. Harpocr. *s. v.* ἐπιθαλαττίδιός τις μοῖρα τῆς Ἀττικῆς. Lycurg. *Leocr.* §§ 17, 55; Diod. xx 45; *inf.* 61 § 1. Wachsmuth, *Stadt Athen*, ii 46.

παιδοτρίβας] officials employed to train the *ephebi* in gymnastic exercises. In B.C. 305/4 their number was reduced to one (Köhler, *Mittheilungen*, iv 327, cf. Teles ap. Stob. *Flor.* 98, 72). In the inscriptions this officer generally takes precedence over the other instructors. Dumont, pp. 177—185; Daremberg and Saglio, iii 627 *b*.

διδασκάλους] Down to about B.C. 136 this term is regularly applied to the instructors of the *ephebi*, including the παιδοτρίβης, the ὁπλομάχος and the rest (CIA ii 341, 465, 467, 469): after that date they are usually called παιδευταί. Dumont, p. 176; Daremberg and Saglio, iii 627; Grasberger, iii 167.

The four following verbs describe the functions of the several instructors. The corresponding official titles have hitherto been known to us from the ephebic inscriptions of the 3rd century. The literary evidence of the text is earlier than the earliest inscriptions mentioning these instructors.

ὁπλομαχεῖν] Xen. *Anab.* ii 1, 7; Plat. *Gorg.* 456 E, τοὺς παιδοτρίβας καὶ τοὺς ἐν ὅπλοις διδάσκοντας μάχεσθαι, *Euthyd.* 271 D, *Laches* 179 E, 182 B, *Leg.* 804 D, 813 D, 833 E; Teles ap. Stob. *Flor.* 98, 72; Theophr. περὶ μικροφιλοτιμίας (with Jebb's note on p. 203). In the ephebic inscriptions the ὁπλομάχος, or 'drill-serjeant,' ranks next to the κοσμητής and the παιδοτρίβης (Dumont, pp. 185—9). CIA ii 467 (=Ditt. no. 347) l. 52, B.C. 100, ἐπαινέσαι δὲ καὶ τοὺς διδασκάλους, τόν τε παιδοτρίβην—καὶ τὸν ὁπλομάχον—καὶ τὸν ἀκοντιστήν—καὶ τὸν ἀφέτην. In an inscr. of Teos, the ὁπλομάχος precedes τὸν διδάξοντα τοξεύειν καὶ ἀκοντίζειν and receives a stipend of 300 *dr.*, as against 250 (Ditt. no. 349, 22—27). In the Attic inscriptions the usual order of precedence is ὁπλομάχος, ἀκοντιστής, τοξότης, καταπαλταφέτης, and after these the γραμματεὺς and ὑπηρέτης (CIA ii 316, 465, 467, 469—471, 482). The drill was held in the Lyceum (Grasberger, iii 139).

τοξεύειν] On the τοξότης, see Dumont, p. 152; Daremberg and Saglio, iii 628. He was not necessarily an Athenian (CIA ii 316, ll. 29, 72). Cf. Plat. *Leg.* 813 D.

ἀκοντίζειν] On the ἀκοντιστής, see Dumont, p. 190; Daremberg and Saglio, *l.c.* The same person is repeatedly mentioned in the inscriptions as holding this office for several years (CIA ii 465, 471).

καταπάλτην ἀφιέναι] *Eth.* iii 2, 17, p. 1111 *a* 11, ὃ δὲ πράττει ἀγνοήσειεν ἄν τις, οἷον...δεῖξαι βουλόμενος ἀφεῖναι, ὡς ὁ τὸν καταπέλτην. The instructor in charge of this department was called the ἀφέτης or the καταπαλταφέτης (*le maître de balistique*). The former title is found in B.C. 100; the latter in B.C. 282, CIA ii 316 (=Ditt. 346), 28, ἐπαινέσαι δὲ καὶ τὸν παιδοτρίβην—καὶ τὸν ἀκοντιστήν—[καὶ τὸν καταπ]αλ[τα]φέτην—καὶ τὸν γραμματέα—καὶ τὸν τοξότην (mentioned last in this case because he was not an Athenian, but a Cretan). καταπαλταφέτης, καταπαλταφεσία and καταπάλτης occur in an inscr. of Ceos, Ditt. no. 348, 25, 30, 27. Cf. CIA ii 413 (=Ditt. 196), 15 (after B.C. 200),

τοῖς μὲν σωφρονισταῖς δραχμὴν μίαν ἑκάστῳ, τοῖς δ' ἐφήβοις
τέτταρας ὀβολοὺς ἑκάστῳ· τὰ δὲ τῶν φυλετῶν τῶν αὑτοῦ λαμ-
βάνων ὁ σωφρονιστὴς ἕκαστος ἀγοράζει τὰ ἐπιτήδεια πᾶσιν εἰς τὸ
κοινόν (συσσιτοῦσι γὰρ κατὰ φυλάς), καὶ τῶν ἄλλων ἐπιμελεῖται
πάντων. καὶ τὸν μὲν πρῶτον ἐνιαυτὸν οὕτως διάγουσι· τὸν δ' 4
ὕστερον, ἐκκλησίας ἐν τῷ θεάτρῳ γενομένης, ἀποδειξάμενοι τῷ

25 δραχμὴν μίαν per compendium scriptum < Δ. **28** συσσιτοῦσιν B. **29** οὕτω H-L. **29—30** ΔΥϹΤΕΡΟΝ ; δ' ὕστερον K, H-L, B : δεύτερον K-W, coll. Harpocr. τὸν δεύτερον ἐνιαυτόν. **30** $\overset{ΓΙΓ}{ΓΕΝ}$? γενομένης Blass (K-W, H-L, K^{3}). ΑΠΟΔΕΙΞ K, K-W, B ; ἐπιδειξ. H-L.

§ 4 * Harp. περίπολος:...'Αρ. ἐν 'Αθ. πολ. περὶ τῶν ἐφήβων λέγων φησὶν οὕτως τὸν δεύτερον ἐνιαυτὸν ἐκκλησίας ἐν τῷ θεάτρῳ γενομένης (γιν. CD) ἀποδεξάμενοι (ἀποδειξάμενοι Dittenberger) τῷ δήμῳ περὶ τὰς τάξεις καὶ λαβόντες ἀσπίδα καὶ δόρυ παρὰ τοῦ δήμου περιπολοῦσι τὴν χώραν καὶ διατρίβουσιν ἐν τοῖς φυλακτηρίοις (Frag. 428^{2}, 468^{3}). Schol. Aeschin. 2, 167.

εἰς τοὺς καταπάλτας νευρὰς ἐπέδωκεν. The engine used in this exercise is termed in the inscriptions καταπάλτης, ὄργανον or λιθοβόλος. καταπαλτῶν is the spelling found in B.C. 330 (CIA ii 807 *b* 129, 131, 132); in B.C. 325 (*ib.* 809 *e* 10, 12, 13); and in B.C. 323 (*ib.* 811 *b* 196, 200). Cf. Dumont, p. 191; Daremberg and Saglio, iii 628 *a*; Grasberger, iii 166.

δραχμὴν μίαν κτλ.] Bekker, *Anecd.* 301, quoted on σωφρονιστήν p. 152 *a*. Boeckh, II xvi p. 332 Lamb.

§ 4. **τὸν μὲν πρῶτον ἐνιαυτόν κτλ.**] Aeschines says of himself, *F. L.*, 2 § 167, περίπολος τῆς χώρας ταύτης ἐγενόμην δύ' ἔτη. Hence it has been supposed that the ἔφηβοι served as περίπολοι for two years (Schömann, *Ant.* p. 360 E. T.; Philippi in *Rhein. Mus.* 34, 613). The text describes the first year as spent in military exercises, and the second as devoted to the duties of περίπολοι (this was the view already held by Dittenberger, *De Ephebis*, and Gilbert, i 296). The discrepancy is noticed in Harpocr. *s. v.* περίπολοι ... παρατηρητέον οὖν ὅτι ὁ μὲν Ἀριστοτέλης ἕνα φησὶν ἐνιαυτὸν ἐν τοῖς περιπόλοις γίγνεσθαι τοὺς ἐφήβους, ὁ δὲ Αἰσχίνης δύο (cf. Dumont, p. 28 ff.). The purport of the text is quoted by the Schol. on Aeschin. *l. c.*, οἱ γὰρ ἔφηβοι τὸν δεύτερον ἐνιαυτόν, ἐκκλησίας ἐν τῷ θεάτρῳ γενομένης, λαβόντες ἀσπίδα καὶ δόρυ παρὰ τοῦ δήμου, περιεπόλουν τουτέστι περιήρχοντο τὴν χώραν καὶ διέτριβον ἐν τοῖς φυλακτηρίοις ἢ ἐν τοῖς φρουρίοις ἐνίοτε ἔτος μόνον, ἐνίοτε δύο. The context of the present passage shews that they acted as φρουροί for both years (§ 5), while it is implied that they served as περίπολοι for the second year alone. Girard endeavours to remove the discrepancy by observing that the author 'ne dit pas expressément, en effet, que les éphèbes n'étaient astreints au service de περίπολοι que la seconde année. Il se borne à constater que la première année était remplie par une sorte d'apprentissage du métier de soldat, mais cet apprentissage, qui se faisait au Pirée et à Munychie, avait déjà le caractère de ce que devait être, l'année suivante, la vie éphébique' (Daremberg and Saglio, iii 629, note 174). It seems simpler to suppose that Aeschines was using a popular and only approximately accurate phrase in describing himself as περίπολος for two years.

ἐκκλησίας ἐν τῷ θεάτρῳ] Cf. A. Müller, *Bühnenalterthümer*, p. 74; and Jebb in Smith's *Dict. Ant.* ii 820 *a*. 'Juv. x 128; Plut. *Timol.* 34, 3; 38, 3; Nepos, *Timol.* 4, 2. Athenian decree in Joseph. *Ant.* xiv 8, 5. The inscriptions bearing on this point are collected by Adam Reusch, *de diebus contionum ordinariis ap. Atheni-enses*, diss. phil. Argentor. sel. iii 4' (Mayor).

ἀποδειξάμενοι κτλ.] *i.e.* 'having given public proof of proficiency in military exercises.' Harpocr. has ἀποδεξάμενοι, corrected by Dittenberger, *De Ephebis*, p. 12, n. 10. The ἔφηβοι of B.C. 100 similarly appeared in public, at the *end* of their period of service, ἐποιήσαντο δὲ καὶ ἐπ' ἐξόδῳ τῆς ἐφηβείας τὴν ἀπόδειξιν τῇ βουλῇ, CIA ii 467 (= Ditt. 347, 43); cf. ii 468, 26.

[Col. 22.] δήμῳ ‖ τὰ περὶ τὰς τάξεις, καὶ λαβόντες ἀσπίδα καὶ δόρυ παρὰ τῆς πόλεως, περιπολοῦσι τὴν χώραν καὶ διατρίβουσιν ἐν τοῖς φυλακτηρίοις. φρουροῦσι δὲ τὰ δύο ἔτη, χλαμύδας ἔχοντες, καὶ ἀτελεῖς εἰσὶ πάντων· καὶ δί[κη]ν οὔτ[ε] διδόασιν οὔτε λαμβάνουσιν, ἵνα μὴ π[ρ]ό[φ]ασις ᾖ τ[ο]ῦ ἀπιέναι, πλὴν περὶ κλήρου καὶ ἐπικλή[ρου], κἄν τινι κατὰ τὸ γένος ἱερεωσύνη γένηται. διεξελθόντων δὲ τῶν δυεῖν ἐτῶν, ἤδη μετὰ τῶν ἄλλων εἰσίν. τὰ μὲν οὖν περὶ τὴν τῶν πολιτῶν ἐγγραφὴν καὶ τοὺς ἐφήβους τοῦτον ἔχει τὸν τρόπον.

43. τὰς δ' ἀρχὰς τὰς περὶ τὴν ἐγκύκλιον διοίκησιν ἁπάσας

31 τὰ om. Harp. **32** τῆς πόλεως: τοῦ δήμου Harp. et Schol. Aeschin. **35** π[ρ]ό[φ]ασις ᾖ τ[ο]ῦ ἀπιέναι in ectypo feliciter agnovit Blass (K[3]); legebatur πράγμασι συμμιγεῖέν τι ? K[1]; πρά[γμ]ασι συμμιγνύωνται J B Mayor, Hude (H-L); πράγ[μ]ασι συγγίνωνται Rutherford (K-W). **36** ΚΑΤΑΤΟΓΕΝΟϹ ?, κατὰ τὸ γένος K, H-L, B; κατὰ γένος K-W. ΙΕΡΟϹΥΝΗ; ἱερωσύνη K, H-L, B; ἱερεωσύνη K-W (cf. Meisterhans, p. 36[2]). ΔΙΕ·ΕΛΘΟΙΝΤΩΝ: διελθοντ. H-L. **37** ΔΥΕΙΝ: δυοῖν K-W[1].

ἀσπίδα καὶ δόρυ] These are exhibited on the vase representing the *ephebus* taking the oath, mentioned in note on § 3, τὰ ἱερὰ περιῆλθον.

§ 5. **φρουροῦσι**] The Schol. on Aeschin. *F. L.* 167 quotes the two following lines from Eupolis, οὗτος ἐν τοῖς φρουρίοις κοιτάζεται, and τοὺς περιπόλους ἀπιέναι εἰς τὰ φρούρια. The ἔφηβοι of B.C. 100 (CIA ii 467, 22 and 87) ἐξῆλθον ἐπὶ τὰ φρούρια καὶ τὰ ὅρια τῆς Ἀττικῆς πλεονάκις ἐν ὅπλοις. Among the φρούρια were Anaphlytus, Thoricus, Sunium, Rhamnus, Eleusis, Phyle, Aphidna (Gilbert, i 297).

χλαμύδας] 'short gowns or mantles.' Pollux, x 164, τὸ δὲ τῶν ἐφήβων φόρημα πέτασος καὶ χλαμύς· Φιλήμων ἐν Θυρωρῷ

ἐγὼ γὰρ ἐς τὴν χλαμύδα κατεθέμην ποτέ
καὶ τὸν πέτασον.

Cf. Antidotus, ap. Athen. 240 B, ἐγγραφῆναι καὶ λαβεῖν τὸ χλαμύδιον. Meleager, in *Anth. P.* vii 468, has an epitaph on a youth whom his mother ὀκτωκαιδεκέταν ἐστόλισεν χλαμύδι. ἐκ χλαμύδος = ἐξ ἐφήβου in Plut. ii 752 E, cf. 754 F. It appears on vases as the characteristic dress of young men (L and S), *e.g.* Tischbein, *Vases*, i 14; Hamilton, *Vases*, i 2 (in Smith, *Dict. Ant.* i 416); and esp. on a *lecythus* from Eretria (Studniczka, *Jahrb. des Kais. deutsch. arch. Inst.* ii 163; Daremberg and Saglio, iii 630, fig. 2680). The garb of the ἔφηβοι is sometimes supposed to have been 'yellow or saffron-coloured' (*Dict. Ant. l.c.*), but it was black according to Philostratus, *Vit. Soph.* ii 1, 5, μελαίνας χλαμύδας ἐνημμένοι τὰς ἐκκλησίας περιεκάθηντο καὶ τὰς πομπὰς ἔπεμπον. Herodes Atticus altered it into white and himself defrayed the cost of the change (CIA iii 1132; Capes, *Univ. Life*, p. 9).

ἀτελεῖς—πάντων] This general exemption did not include the τριηραρχία, which was incumbent on all Athenians of a certain *census* from the time of their enrolment on the ληξιαρχικὸν γραμματεῖον (Dem. *Mid.* 154). Even this λῃτουργία was remitted for one year in the case of orphans, Lys. 32 § 24, οὓς ἡ πόλις οὐ μόνον παῖδας ὄντας ἀτελεῖς ἐποίησεν, ἀλλὰ καὶ ἐπειδὰν δοκιμασθῶσιν ἐνιαυτὸν ἀφῆκεν ἁπασῶν τῶν λῃτουργιῶν.

περὶ κλήρου] Thus Demosthenes sued his guardians as soon as he came of age, *Onet.* i 15, 17; *Mid.* 78. **ἐπικλήρου**] At the age of 18, the young Athenian became κύριος τῆς ἐπικλήρου, Isaeus 8 § 31, 10 § 12, *frag.* 90, Hyperid. *frag.* 223 = 194; Suidas, *s. v.* ληξιαρχικὸν γραμματεῖον, B; A. Schäfer, *Dem.* III 2, p. 24 f.

The list of lawsuits in the text is possibly not exhaustive. In Lys. 10 § 4 the speaker, who was 13 at the time when his father was put to death by the Thirty, instituted a prosecution against them before the Areopagus as soon as he came of age, ἐπειδὴ τάχιστα ἐδοκιμάσθην (§ 31, in B.C. 399). The other alternative is to assume that the statement applies only to the time of the writer (Hager in Smith, *Dict. Ant.* ii 1066 *a*).

XLIII § 1. *On officials elected by show of hands.*

§ 1. **τὴν ἐγκύκλιον διοίκησιν**] *Pol.* 1255 *b* 25, ἐγκύκλια διακονήματα, 1263 *a* 21, ἐγκύκλιοι διακονίαι (every-day duties). 1269 ποιοῦσι κληρωτάς, πλὴν ταμίου στρατιωτικῶν καὶ τῶν ἐπὶ τὸ θεωρικὸν καὶ τοῦ τῶν κρηνῶν ἐπιμελητοῦ. ταύτας δὲ χειροτονοῦσιν, καὶ οἱ χειροτονηθέντες ἄρχουσιν ἐκ Παναθηναίων εἰς Παναθήναια. χειροτονοῦσι δὲ καὶ τὰς πρὸς τὸν πόλεμον ἁπάσας.

κ

XLIII 2 ΠΛΗΡΩΤΑΣ (6 ΠΛΗΡΟΥΤΑΙ). <τοῦ> ταμίου <τῶν> στρατιωτικῶν Richards. **3** ΚΡΗΝΩΝ: κοινῶν J W Headlam (H-L).

---

b 35 (of courage), χρήσιμος πρὸς οὐδὲν τῶν ἐγκυκλίων ἀλλ' εἴπερ εἰς τὸν πόλεμον. *Oecon.* 2, 1346 *a* 8, πρόσοδος ἀπὸ τῶν ἐγκυκλίων.

ταμίου—στρατιωτικῶν] The war-fund included the income from the property-tax and the surplus of the yearly revenue, [Dem.] *Neaer.* 4, τὰ περιόντα χρήματα τῆς διοικήσεως. The fund was administered by the ταμίας τῶν στρ. This official provided pay for the troops and defrayed all other military expenses (Smith, *Dict. Ant.* ii 761 *b*). He is first mentioned in B.C. 338, [Plut.] *Lycurg.* 27. In 334 (CIA ii 739) he makes payments to the treasurers of Athene and to the commissioners for restoring the figures of Νίκη and the articles of plate used in processions (see further in Hartel, *Studien über att. Staatsrecht*, pp. 135–6; Gilbert, i 237; Dürrbach, *l'orateur Lycurgue*, pp. 32—33). For some of his other duties cf. *inf.* c. 47 § 2, 49 § 3.

τῶν ἐπὶ τὸ θεωρικὸν] probably instituted under the administration of Eubulus (between B.C. 354 and 339). It has been a moot point whether there was only one official ἐπὶ τὸ θεωρικὸν or more (Gilbert i 229). The text implies that there were several. In B.C. 343/2, CIA ii 114 C 5, a single individual is mentioned ἐπὶ τὸ θεωρικόν, immediately after the γραμματεὺς κατὰ πρυτανείαν and ἐπὶ τὰ ψηφίσματα, and immediately before the βουλῆς ταμίαι; thus he is possibly only a βουλευτὴς charged with looking after that department of business and is not necessarily to be identified with the management of the fund. Aeschines, *c. Ctes.* § 24, mentions the archon of the year in which Dem. was elected treasurer of the θεωρικόν; hence it was inferred by Boeckh (II vii p. 248 Lamb) that the office was annual. The text shews that it was held for four years, from one Panathenaic festival to the next. Cf. 47 § 2.

κρηνῶν ἐπιμελητοῦ] κρηνῶν ἐπιμεληταὶ are mentioned in *Pol.* 1321 *b* 26, where Athens is doubtless in Aristotle's mind, though not expressly named. Plato, *Leg.* 758 E, refers to κρηνῶν ἐπιμελητάς. An inscr. published in the Ἐφημερὶς Ἀρχαιολογική, 1889, pp. 13—16, no. 28, describes the work done by one Pytheas as ἐπιμελητὴς τῶν κρηνῶν in B.C. 333. ἐπειδὴ Πυθέας αἱρεθεὶς ἐπὶ τὰς κρήνας τῶν ἄλλων ἐν τῇ ἀρχῇ ἐπιμελεῖται καλῶς καὶ φιλοτίμως κτλ· ἐπαινέσαι Πυθέαν...ἀρετῆς ἕνεκα καὶ δικαιοσύνης τῆς περὶ τὴν ἐπιμέλειαν τῶν κρηνῶν, ὅπως ἂν οἱ ἄλλοι οἱ ἀεὶ χειροτονούμενοι ἐπὶ τὰς κρήνας φιλοτιμῶνται κτλ.

Cf. Hesych. *s. v.* κρηνάγγη (*sic*)· ἀρχὴ ἐπὶ τῆς ἐπιμελείας ὕδατος, and Pollux viii 113, ἐπιμελητὴς δέ τις...ἐγίνετο, ὃς καὶ ἐκαλεῖτο ἐφ' ὕδωρ, ἦν...καὶ κρηνοφυλάκιον ἀρχή: also Photius, κρηνοφύλαξ· ἦν δὲ καὶ ἀρχή τις Ἀθήνησιν. It is uncertain whether κρηνοφύλαξ was another name for this officer or the title of a subordinate official. The importance of this officer is indicated by his being elected and not appointed by lot. The office of ὑδάτων ἐπιστάτης was held by Themistocles (Plut. *Them.* 31 § 1). Cf. Daremberg and Saglio, *s.v. Epimeletes*, ii p. 668 *b*.

As two of the officials mentioned in the text are connected with finance, some surprise has been felt that no notice is taken of the important financial officer called the ταμίας τῆς κοινῆς προσόδου or ὁ ἐπὶ τῇ διοικήσει. (The latter title is supposed by Fellner to have been introduced about 300 B.C., but the supposition is not approved by Gilbert, i 233. Cf. Dürrbach, *Lycurgue*, pp. 21—38.)

This official, like those in the text, held office for one term of four years only, [Plut.] *vit. Lycurg.* 3. Lycurgus, whose financial activity began in 338, is described as ταχθεὶς ἐπὶ τῇ διοικήσει (Hyper. *frag.* 121 Blass); he probably ceased to hold this office in 334, and this treatise was written about ten years later. Hence, it is suggested by Mr J. W. Headlam to alter κρηνῶν into κοινῶν. It would be safer, however, to suppose that καὶ τοῦ ἐπὶ τῇ διοικήσει had dropped out, than to accept this suggestion. The fact that the κρηνῶν ἐπιμελητὴς was elected at the Panathenaea (about 23—28 Hecatombaeon, before the middle of August) is confirmed by the above decree in honour of Pytheas, which is dated 9 Metageitnion,

2 *βουλὴ δὲ κληροῦται πεντακόσιοι, πεντήκοντα ἀπὸ <τῆς> φυλῆς ἑκάστης. πρυτανεύει δ' ἐν μέρει τῶν φυλῶν ἑκάστη καθ' ὅ τι ἂν λάχωσιν, αἱ μὲν πρῶται τέτταρες ἓξ καὶ τριάκοντα ἡμέρας ἑκάστη,*

6 ΦΝ (K, H-W, B); *πεντακόσιοι, πεντήκοντα* H-L. <*τῆς*> *φυλῆς* B.

TESTIMONIA. **XLIII § 2** *Harp. *πρυτανείας:...ἔστι δὲ ἀριθμὸς ἡμερῶν ἡ πρυτανεία ἤτοι λς ἢ λε, ἃς ἑκάστη φυλὴ πρυτανεύει. διείλεκται δὲ περὶ τούτων Ἀρ. ἐν τῇ Ἀθ. πολ.* Harp. (=Bekk. *An.* 291, 4, Lex. Dem. Patm., Schol. Plat. p. 459) *πρυτάνεις:...ἐπρυτάνευον δὲ...ἐκ διαδοχῆς ἀλλήλαις αἱ δέκα φυλαὶ κλήρῳ λαχοῦσαι.* Schol. Plat. Leg. p. 459: *πρυτανεία δέ ἐστιν ἀριθμός τις ἡμερῶν ἤτοι λς ἢ λε, ἃς ἑκάστη φυλὴ πρυτανεύειν λέγεται...καὶ διῄρηνται εἰς ταύτας αἱ ἡμέραι τοῦ ἐνιαυτοῦ· κατὰ γὰρ σελήνην ἄγουσι τοῦτον, ὡς ἑκάστῃ φυλῇ τῶν δέκα ἐπιβάλλειν λε ἡμέρας, πλεονάζειν δὲ ὀλίγας. διὸ καὶ τὰς λοιπὰς ἀπέδωκαν οἱ Ἀθηναῖοι ταῖς πρώταις λαχούσαις τέσσαρσι φυλαῖς, ἵνα ἐκείνων μὲν ἑκάστη τὰς λς ἡμέρας πρυτανεύῃ, αἱ δὲ λοιπαὶ ἓξ ἀνὰ λε.* Fere eadem Photius, *πρυτανεία*, inter alia *ἐνιαυτὸν δὲ οἱ Ἀθηναῖοι τὸν σεληνιακὸν ἦγον* (Frag. 393[2], 433[3]). Schol. Maximi Planudis ad Hermog. in *Rhet. Gr.* v p. 509, 20 Walz: *ὡρισμέναι ἦσαν ἐκκλησίαι κατὰ πρυτανείαν ἑκάστην τέσσαρες· δέκα δὲ οὐσῶν Ἀθήνησι φυλῶν ἐπρυτάνευον αἱ μὲν πρῶται λαχοῦσαι φυλαὶ τέσσαρες ἀνὰ τριάκοντα ἓξ ἡμέρας, αἱ δὲ λοιπαὶ ἓξ ἀνὰ τριάκοντα πέντε κτλ.*

---

eleven days after the close of the Panathenaea.

ἐκ Παναθηναίων εἰς Παναθήναια] *i.e.* for four years. The phrase (with *ἐς* for *εἰς*) occurs in CIA i 32 A 28, B 27 (Hicks, no. 37); 117, 3; 121; 125; 129; 133; 141, &c; 170; 273 (Hicks, no. 46). The greater Panathenaea were held in every third Olympic year, in the same year as the Pythian games. The *loci classici* are collected in Michaelis, *Parthenon*, Anhang II, 318—333.

τὰς πρὸς τὸν πόλεμον] The offices of *στρατηγοί* and their subordinates, the *ἵππαρχος*, *φύλαρχος* and *ταξίαρχος*. Cf. Gilbert i 220 ff., and Headlam, *On the Lot*, p. 102; *inf.* 61 § 1.

§§ 2, 3. *The Council.* On the subject in general, see Hermann, *Staatsalt.* §§ 125—127; Schömann, *Ant.*, p. 371—9, E. T.; Gilbert, i 251—264; Smith, *Dict. Ant.* i 309.

§ 2. **κληροῦται**] It was appointment by lot that made the Council consistent with the democratical constitution of Athens and prevented its becoming an oligarchical body of higher authority than the public assembly. The power of the old aristocracy had centred in a Council, and this power was broken down by the introduction of the lot. The Council of 400 under the 'Draconian constitution' is described as appointed by lot (4 § 3). The earliest documentary evidence bearing on this subject is an inscr. of Erythrae, the constitution of which was modelled on that of Athens in B.C. 455—450. It is there ordained for Erythrae (as for Athens) **ἀπὸ κυάμων βουλὴν εἶναι** (CIA i 9 = Hicks, no. 23). Cf. Headlam, *On the Lot*, pp. 41—56, 86.

πρυτανεύει] 'presides,' *i.e.* sits as a superintending sub-committee of the Council. Cf. Harpocr. *s. v.* *πρυτάνεις*, Schol. Aeschin. 3 § 3; also Schömann, p. 376, and Gilbert, i 255. Even the order in which the *πρυτάνεις* held office is determined by lot (cf. Headlam, *l. c.*, p. 51). This fact had already been ascertained by Clinton, *Fasti*, ii 344—6 = 415—8.

αἱ μὲν πρῶται κτλ.] The normal Attic year consisting of 354 days, the tenth part would be 35 days, and 4 over. It has been supposed by Gilbert, i 255, that these four days were assigned to the several prytanies by lot. The text states that they were assigned to the first four prytanies, which thus lasted for 36 days, the remaining six lasting for 35 only. This fact was already known to us through Photius, Suidas and the Schol. in Hermogenem, v p. 509; but their authority was set aside on the evidence of the Choiseul Marble, CIA i 188 (Ditt. no. 44), ll. 25—40, B.C. 410/9, where we have express mention of the 36th day of the 8th, 9th, and 10th prytanies. Hence it was inferred by Clinton, *Fasti*, ii 346—418, that the four supernumerary days were assigned to the *last* tribes and not to the *first*. While this was clearly the case in B.C. 410, the text shews that, in the writer's time, the latter plan was adopted instead.

The duration of the *πρυτανεῖαι* is discussed by Unger, *Philol.* 38 p. 425 ff., Usener, *Rhein. Mus.* 34 p. 392 ff., and A. Schmidt, *Gr. Chronologie*, pp. 241, 423 etc.

αἱ δὲ ἓξ αἱ ὕστεραι πέντε καὶ τριάκοντα ἡμέρας ἑκάστη· κατὰ σελήνην γὰρ ἄγουσιν τὸν ἐνιαυτόν. οἱ δὲ πρυτανεύοντες αὐτῶν 3 *πρῶτον μὲν συσσιτοῦσιν ἐν τῇ θόλῳ, λαμβάνοντες ἀργύριον παρὰ τῆς πόλεως, ἔπειτα συνάγουσιν καὶ τὴν βουλὴν καὶ τὸν δῆμον, τὴν μὲν* [[*οὖν*]] *βουλὴν ὅσαι ἡμέραι, πλὴν ἐάν τις ἀφέσιμος ᾖ, τὸν δὲ δῆμον τετράκις τῆς πρυτανείας ἑκάστης. καὶ ὅσ[α] δεῖ χρηματί-*

9—10 *κατὰ σελήνην—ἐνιαυτόν* del. Lipsius, Herwerden. **10** *ἄγουσι* H-L. **12** *συνάγουσι* H-L. ΚΑΙ (vel ΕΙ ?): *καὶ τὴν* K[3], K-W, B: *εἰς τὴν* K[1], *τὴν* H-L. **13** ΟΥΝ om. Harp. (K-W, H-L, B): retinet K coll. Ar. *Poet.* 1458 *a* 25 etc (*Ind. Ar.* p. 540 *b*). ΠΛΗΝΕΝΑΝ corr. K. **14** ΧΡΗΜΑΤΙΖΕΙ corr. K.

§§ **3, 4, 6** Pollux viii 95, *πρυτάνεις: οὗτοι τὴν βουλὴν συνάγουσιν ὁσημέραι, πλὴν ἄν τις ᾖ ἄφετος, "τὸν δὲ δῆμον τετράκις" ἑκάστης πρυτανείας· καὶ προγράφουσι πρὸ τῆς βουλῆς καὶ πρὸ τῆς ἐκκλησίας ὑπὲρ ὧν "δεῖ χρηματίζειν." τῶν δ' ἐκκλησιῶν ἡ μὲν κυρία, ἐν ᾗ τὰς ἀρχὰς ἐπιχειροτονοῦσιν, εἴπερ καλῶς ἄρχουσιν, ἢ ἀποχειροτονοῦσιν· ἐν ᾗ καὶ τὰς εἰσαγγελίας ὁ βουλόμενος εἰσαγγέλλει, "καὶ τὰς ἀπογραφὰς τῶν δημευομένων" ἀναγιγνώσκουσιν οἱ πρὸς ταῖς δίκαις, "καὶ τὰς λήξεις τῶν κλήρων."* 96, *ἡ δὲ δευτέρα ἐκκλησία ἀνεῖται τοῖς βουλομένοις ἱκετηρίαν θεμένοις λέγειν ἀδεῶς περί τε τῶν ἰδίων καὶ τῶν δημοσίων· ἡ δὲ τρίτη "κήρυξι καὶ πρεσβείαις" ἀξιοῖ χρηματίζειν, οὓς δεῖ πρότερον τοῖς πρυτάνεσιν ἀποδοῦναι τὰ γράμματα, ἡ δὲ τετάρτη περὶ ἱερῶν καὶ ὁσίων* (Frag. 394[2], 434[3]). Cf. Schol. in Aeschin. 1 § 104.

§§ **3, 4.** * Harp. *κυρία ἐκκλησία:...τίνες δὲ αἱ κύριαι ἐκκλησίαι 'Αρ. δεδήλωκεν ἐν τῇ 'Αθ. πολ. λέγων τοὺς πρυτάνεις συνάγειν "τὴν βουλὴν καὶ τὸν δῆμον, τὴν μὲν βουλὴν" ὁσημέραι, "πλὴν—ἑκάστης." προγράφουσι δέ φησι καὶ κυρίαν ἐκκλησίαν, ἐν ᾗ δεῖ τὰς ἀρχὰς ἀποχειροτονεῖν οἳ δοκοῦσι μὴ καλῶς ἄρχειν· καὶ περὶ φυλακῆς δὲ τῆς χώρας. "καὶ τὰς εἰσαγγελίας—ποιεῖσθαι" φησι καὶ τὰ ἑξῆς* (Frag. 395[2], 435[3]).

κατὰ σελήνην—ἐνιαυτόν] This explanation is introduced quite as naturally as that in the corresponding passage of Schömann's *Ant.*, p. 376 E. T., where, immediately after defining the duration of a prytany, the writer continues: 'The Athenians, it may be explained, had a legal lunar year consisting of 12 months of 29 and 30 days alternately, and therefore of 354 days altogether.' The phrase reminds one of Arist. *Nub.* 626, *κατὰ σελήνην ὡς ἄγειν χρὴ τοῦ βίου τὰς ἡμέρας*, and Diog. Laert. i 59 (of Solon), *ἠξίωσέ τε 'Αθηναίων τὰς ἡμέρας κατὰ σελήνην ἄγειν.* The explanation (like many others in this treatise) would not be needed by Athenian readers; but it does not necessarily follow that it is an interpolation, as suggested by Lipsius, *Leipzig Verhandl.*, 1891, p. 47 n.

§ 3. **συσσιτοῦσιν ἐν τῇ θόλῳ**] Dem. *F. L.* § 190, *οἱ πρυτάνεις θύουσιν ἑκάστοτε κοινῇ καὶ συνδειπνοῦσιν ἀλλήλοις καὶ συσπένδουσιν.* Ammonius ap. Harpocr. *s. v.* *θόλος,—ὁ δὲ τόπος ὅπου ἑστιῶνται οἱ πρυτάνεις καλεῖται θόλος.* Cf. Pollux viii 155; Bekker, *Anecd.* 264. On a special emergency the *βουλὴ* even passed the night there, Andoc. *de Myst.* 45. It was also called the *σκιάς* (Gilbert, i 256, n. 4). It was near the *βουλευτήριον* (Paus. i 5, 1), to the north of the east end of the Areopagus (Curtius, *Stadtgeschichte*, p. xciii and 171). Thus the *πρυτάνεις* could readily leave the *θόλος* to attend the meetings of the whole body of the Council in the neighbouring *βουλευτήριον*. Cf. Wachsmuth, *Stadt Athen*, ii 315.

συνάγουσιν *κτλ.*] CIA ii 417, 459 and elsewhere (of the *πρυτάνεις*), *ἐπεμελήθησαν δὲ καὶ τῆς συλλογῆς τῆς τε βουλῆς καὶ τοῦ δήμου καὶ τῶν ἄλλων ὧν αὐτοῖς προσέταττον οἱ νόμοι.*

ὅσαι ἡμέραι] The manuscript reading has been retained, 'as it facilitates the following *τις*' (J. B. Mayor). Hitherto our earliest authority for this equivalent to *ὁσημέραι* has been Themistius (A.D. 355), who also has *ὅσαι ὧραι* in p. 192 D. *ὅσοι μῆνες* occurs in Dem. 744, 25 (L and S).

ἀφέσιμος] Aristides i 344 Jebb. The large number of such holidays is noticed in [Xen.] *de Rep. Ath.* 3, 2. Among them were the *Apaturia* (Athen. 171 E), the *Thesmophoria* (Arist. *Thesm.* 79), the *Kronia* (Dem. 24 § 26), and the *ἀποφράδες ἡμέραι* (Plut. *Alc.* 34). Gilbert, i 258, n. 4.

τετράκις] Elsewhere (Photius, *s. v.* *κυρία ἐκκλησία*, Schol. Arist. *Ach.* 19 and Schol. Dem. 24 § 20) we are told of *three*

ζειν τὴν βουλὴν ⟦*καὶ ὅ τι*⟧ *ἐν ἑκάστῃ τῇ ἡμέρᾳ, καὶ ὅπου καθίζειν,*
4 *οὗτοι προγράφουσι. προγράφουσι δὲ καὶ τὰς ἐκκλησίας οὗτοι, μίαν μὲν κυρίαν, ἐν ᾗ δεῖ τὰς ἀρχὰς ἐπιχειροτονεῖν εἰ δοκοῦσι καλῶς ἄρχειν, καὶ περὶ σίτου καὶ περὶ φυλακῆς τῆς χώρας χρηματίζειν, καὶ τὰς εἰσαγγελίας ἐν ταύτῃ τῇ ἡμέρᾳ τοὺς βουλομένους ποιεῖσθαι, καὶ τὰς ἀπογραφὰς τῶν δημευομένων ἀναγιγνώσκειν, καὶ τὰς λήξεις τῶν κλήρων καὶ τῶν ἐπικλήρων* ⟦*ἀναγιγνώσκειν*⟧, [*ὅπω*]*ς*

15 ΚΑΙΟΤΙ (corr. e ΚΑΙΤΟΥ) secl. B. ΟΤΙΟΥΚΑΘ..ΕΙ: *ὅ τι οὐ καθήκει?* K; ΟΤΙΟΥΚΑΘΕΙΖΕΙ? *ὅπου καθίζειν* egregie K-W (B); etiam Herwerden verbum *καθίζει* hic latere suspicabatur. **20, 21** *ἀναγιγνώσκειν* (*bis*) K^3, H-L (Meisterhans, n. 1238^2): ΑΝΑΓΙΝ (K, K-W); verbum in v. 21 secl. K-W, B.

§ **4** *Lex. rhet. Cantab. *κυρία ἐκκλησία :...ἄμεινον οὖν Ἀριστοτέλει* <*πείθεσθαι*>· *τὰς γὰρ ἀρχὰς ἐν ταῖς κυρίαις ἐκκλησίαις φησὶν ἐπιχειροτονεῖσθαι καὶ τὰς εἰσαγγελίας* <*τὸν βουλόμενον εἰσαγγέλλειν* addidit Meier> *καὶ τὰ ἄλλα τῶν ἀναγκαίων χρηματίζειν* "*καὶ περὶ σίτου* <*καὶ*> *φυλακῆς τῆς χώρας, καὶ τὰς ἀπογραφὰς—κλήρων.*"

---

meetings in each month, all of them termed *κυρίαι ἐκκλησίαι*. But the text shews that there was only one *κυρία ἐκκλησία* in each month (§ 4), as already held by Gilbert, i 269, n. 1.

ὅπου καθίζειν] The sessions of the *βουλή*, though ordinarily held in the *βουλευτήριον*, were occasionally transferred to the Eleusinion, the Theseum or the Panathenaic Stadium, or even to the Acropolis (Gilbert, i 259 n. 1). *ὅ τι οὐ καθήκει* could only mean 'what is not suitable'; and such a sense is out of place here. I was once inclined to suggest *ὅταν καθήκῃ*, 'at the proper time,' lit. 'whenever the time arrives.' Dem. p. 399, 6, *ἐκκλησίαν ποιῆσαι, ὅταν ἐκ τῶν νόμων καθήκῃ*. Ar. *Hist. An.* viii 2, 23, *ὁ χρόνος καθήκει*.

προγράφουσι] CIA ii 61, *ἐπειδὰν δὲ ταῦτα παρασκευασθῇ, τοὺς πρυτάνεις προγράψαι περὶ τούτων ἐν βουλευτηρίῳ ὅταν οἷόν τε ᾖ*.

§§ 4—6. *The Public Assembly.*

§ 4. **προγράφουσι—ἐκκλησίας**] Five days notice was given; Bekker, *Anecd.* 296, 8, *πρόπεμπτα* (Gilbert, i 270 n. 1).

μίαν μὲν κυρίαν] see note on *τετράκις*, § 3. The *agenda* for the *κυρία ἐκκλησία* were already known through citations of this passage in Harpocr. (Gilbert, i 282).

ἐπιχειροτονεῖν] 'confirm the election of.' Harpocr. *s. v. καταχειροτονία· ἔθος ἦν Ἀθήνησι κατὰ τῶν ἀρχόντων καὶ κατὰ τῶν συκοφαντῶν προβολὰς ἐν τῷ δήμῳ τίθεσθαι· εἰ δέ τις καταχειροτονηθείη, οὗτος εἰσήγετο εἰς τὸ δικαστήριον*. For this *καταχειροτονία* he refers to Theophrastus, *ἐν δ' Νόμων*. Cf. Schömann, *De Comitiis*, p. 231; *Ant.* 391 E. T. The term *προβολή* is inaccurately applied to the *ἐπιχειροτονία* (Meier and Schömann, note 389 Lips.; and Smith, *Dict. Ant.* ii 492 *b*).

περὶ σίτου] Xen. *Mem.* iii 6, 13, *πόσον χρόνον ἱκανός ἐστιν ὁ ἐκ τῆς χώρας γιγνόμενος σῖτος διατρέφειν τὴν πόλιν, καὶ πόσου εἰς τὸν ἐνιαυτὸν προσδεῖται*.

περὶ φυλακῆς] *ib.* § 10, *περί γε φυλακῆς τῆς χώρας οἶδ' ὅτι ἤδη σοι μεμέληκε, καὶ οἶσθα, ὁπόσαι τε φυλακαὶ ἐπίκαιροί εἰσι καὶ ὁπόσαι μή, καὶ ὁπόσοι τε φρουροὶ ἱκανοί εἰσι κτλ.* This topic of deliberation is mentioned in Ar. *Rhet.* i 4 § 10, *περὶ φυλακῆς τῆς χώρας μὴ λανθάνειν πῶς φυλάττεται κτλ.*: in *Pol.* 1298 *a* 3 it is omitted. Cf. CIA ii 225 and 334, *εἰς φυλακὴν τῆς χώρας* (Gilbert i 282 n. 2).

τὰς εἰσαγγελίας] Such information might either be brought before the *βουλή*, through the *πρυτάνεις*; or (as here) before the *ἐκκλησία*, through the *θεσμοθέται* (c. 59). Cf. Hager in Smith, *Dict. Ant.* i 709, ii 1067.

τὰς ἀπογραφὰς τῶν δημευομένων] 'inventories of confiscated property.' *Pol.* 1298 *a* 3, *περὶ... δημεύσεως*. On *ἀπογραφή* see Meier and Schömann, pp. 304—6 Lips., and *Dict. Ant. s. v.*

τὰς λήξεις τῶν κλήρων καὶ τῶν ἐπικλήρων] *i.e.* the legal claims (or 'lists of suits') for the right of succession to inheritances, and for that of marrying the daughter of a citizen who has left no son to inherit his estate (56 § 6, *κλήρων καὶ ἐπικλήρων ἐπιδικασίαι*). Meier and Schömann, pp. 791—4, 606—8, 616 Lips.; *Dict. Ant. s.v. Heres*, i 947 *a* and *Epiclerus*, p. 747 *a*.

ὅπως—ἔρημον γενόμενον] 'that all may have cognisance of any vacancy in an

μηδένα λάθῃ μηδὲν ἔρημον γενόμενον. ἐπὶ [δὲ] τῆς ἕκτης πρυτα- 5
νείας πρὸς τοῖς εἰρημένοις καὶ περὶ τῆς ὀστρακοφορίας ἐπιχειροτο-
νίαν διδόασιν, εἰ δοκεῖ ποιεῖν ἢ μή, καὶ συκοφαντῶν προβολὰς τῶν
Ἀθηναίων καὶ τῶν μετοίκων μέχρι τριῶν ἑκατέρ[ων, κἄν τι]ς
ὑποσχόμενός τι μὴ ποιήσῃ τῷ δήμῳ. ἑτέραν δὲ ταῖς ἱκετηρίαις, 6

23 ΗΡΗΜΕΝΟΙϹ. ἐπιχειροτονίαν; idem habet lexici rhet. Cantabrig. codex a Dobreo exscriptus (K, H-L, B): προχειροτονίαν K-W quod ibidem a Meiero scriptum est. **25** ΕΚΑΤΕΡΑΝ? κἄν τις Blass, Fränkel (H-L, K[3]); ἐάν τις K[1]; καὶ ἐάν τις K-W. **26** ἑτέραν δὲ K, K-W, B; ἑτέρα δ' ἐστὶ H-L, quod 'spatium non capit' (K[3]).

§ **5** *ib.* "ἐπὶ δὲ τῆς ἕκτης—ἐπιχειροτονίαν" (προχειροτονίαν edd.) δίδοσθαι εἰ δοκεῖ ἢ μή (Frag. 396[2], 436[3]). Hesych. κυρία ἐκκλ.: μία κυρία ἐκκλησία ἤγετο Ἀθήνησιν, ἐν ᾗ τὰς ἀρχὰς ἐπιχειροτονεῖν ἔδει.

---

estate.' This clause refers only to the suits concerning κλῆροι and ἐπίκληροι. ἔρημος is a specially appropriate epithet for an estate deprived of its owner, or for children bereft of their father: Plat. *Leg.* 927, εἰς ὀρφανὰ καὶ ἔρημα ὑβρίζουσιν. The object of this public recital was partly to draw attention to any claims on the estate; partly to give due notice to all who were interested in establishing a right of succession.

§ 5. **ἕκτης πρυτανείας**] In B.C. 410/9, when the Attic year began on July 14, the sixth πρυτανεία began on Jan. 5, B.C. 409 (Clinton, *Fasti*, ii 347 = 418).

ὀστρακοφορίας] On this occasion the point to be determined was whether there was a case for having recourse to ostracism; if so, a day was fixed for the final voting in the eighth πρυτανεία (Lex. Cant. *s. v.* ὀστρακισμός; Schol. Arist. *Eq.* 851, and *fragm. Lex. Dem. Aristocr.*; cf. Blass in *Hermes*, 1882, p. 152).

"A. Schmidt, *Gr. Chronologie*, p. 259, seeks to reconcile Aristotle and Philochorus. The date of the ὀστρακοφορία is explained by the desire to settle a dangerous political struggle before the opening of spring, i.e. before the end of Anthesterion. The 6th prytany in an ordinary year is equivalent in general to Gamelion 1—Anthesterion 5. But Philochorus wished to embrace the case of an intercalary year in which the 7th prytany is equivalent in general to Gamelion 22—end of Anthesterion: 'before the eight prytany' means either in the 6th or 7th, for *if* the principle was that the ostracism was to be proposed in Gamelion or Anthesterion, it might fall in the 7th prytany of an intercalary year. The hypothesis is absurd, for absolutely no reason is suggested why the Athenians should have ostracised men *later* in the year if it chanced to be intercalary,—to say nothing of other obvious objections" (Wyse).

συκοφαντῶν προβολὰς] A προβολή was a preliminary criminal information brought before the public assembly; if the people approved, a trial before an ordinary law-court ensued. This procedure was applied in the case of those who had accused the generals concerned in the battle of Arginusae (Xen. *Hell.* i 7 § 34). The case against Midias began with a προβολή. Cf. Schömann, *De Comitiis*, p. 231 ff., Meier and Schömann, p. 335 Lips., *Dict. Ant.* ii 492 *a*, 732 *a*.

For its application in the case of συκοφάνται, cf. Isocr. *Antid.* 314, κατὰ δὲ τούτων (*sc.* τῶν συκοφαντῶν ἐποίησαν) γραφὰς μὲν πρὸς τοὺς θεσμοθέτας, εἰσαγγελίας δ' εἰς τὴν βουλήν, προβολὰς δ' ἐν τῷ δήμῳ, and Aeschin. *F. L.* 145, τῶν συκοφαντῶν ὡς κακούργων δημοσίᾳ προβολὰς ποιούμεθα, also Pollux viii 46, προβολαὶ δὲ ἦσαν καὶ αἱ τῆς συκοφαντίας γραφαί.

τῶν μετοίκων] This implies that a μέτοικος could be charged with συκοφαντία. Hence it follows that he was entitled to give information against public offenders. Ordinarily this right was confined to citizens (Plut. *Sol.* 18, ἐξῆν τῷ δυναμένῳ καὶ βουλομένῳ κτλ.). A foreigner, who desired to accuse a person of any offence against the people, was required to obtain special permission for that purpose, ἄδεια, Andoc. *De Myst.* § 15. Cf. Meier and Schömann, p. 330 Lips.

κἂν τις ὑποσχόμενος κτλ.] Dem. *Lept.* 100, ἔστι δὲ δήπου νόμος ὑμῖν, ἐάν τις ὑποσχόμενός τι τὸν δῆμον ἢ βουλὴν ἢ δικαστήριον ἐξαπατήσῃ, τὰ ἔσχατα πάσχειν, and *ib.* 135 (where it is called a νόμος ἀρχαῖος and death is named as the penalty). The procedure began either with a προβολή (as in Xen. *Hell.* i 7 § 35) or an εἰσαγγελία, [Dem.] *c. Timoth.* 49 § 67.

§ 6. **ἱκετηρίαις**] 'supplications,' 'formal

[Col. 23.] ἐν ᾗ θεὶς ὁ βουλόμενος ἱκετηρίαν, [ὑπὲρ] ὧν ἂν βούληται ‖ καὶ ἰδίων καὶ δημοσίων διαλέξεται πρὸς τὸν δῆμον. αἱ δὲ δύο περὶ τῶν ἄλλων εἰσίν, ἐν αἷς κελεύουσιν οἱ νόμοι τρία μὲν ἱερῶν χρηματίζειν, τρία δὲ κήρυξιν καὶ πρεσβείαις, τρία δ' ὁσίων. χρηματίζουσιν δ' ἐνίοτε

27 ΟΥΒΟΥΛΟ corr. K. ΩΝ K: περὶ ὧν Kontos, Lipsius, Gertz, K-W, sed spatium vix duarum litterarum capax vacuum relictum; ὑπὲρ (ϒ) ὧν H-L (B). **28** ΔΙΑΛΕΞΕΤΑΙ: διαλέξεται K (K-W, B); διαλέγεται H-L. **30** κήρυξι H-L. ΤΡΙΑΔΟΣΙΩΝ suprascripto ΣΥΡΑΚΟΣΙΩΝ 'corruptumne ex ΣΑΡΑ Δ ΟΣΙΩΝ ut Ar. τέτταρα δ' ὁσίων scripserit?' K-W. χρηματίζουσι H-L.

---

petitions.' For **θεὶς...ἱκετηρίαν** cf. Dem. *de Cor.* 107, οὐχ ἱκετηρίαν ἔθηκε τριήραρχος οὐδεὶς πώποθ' ὡς ἀδικούμενος παρ' ὑμῖν, *c. Timocr.* 12, ἔθεσαν τὴν ἱκ. ὧν ἦσαν τὰ χρήματα ἄνθρωποι, *ib.* 53; Aeschin. *F. L.* 15, ἱκ. θέντες οἱ οἰκεῖοι ἐδέοντο ὑμῶν. The ἱκετηρία (ῥάβδος) was an olive-branch bound with wool (Aesch. *Suppl.* 22, 192), which the 'suppliant,' or petitioner, held in his hand before depositing it on the altar in the place of public assembly. Such an application for the right of petition might also be laid before the βουλή, Aeschin. *c. Timarch.* 104. In Andoc. *De Myst.* 110—116, it is laid before the βουλή on the occasion of its session in the Ἐλευσίνιον, although presenting a petition in that place was forbidden, *ib.* 116. Such petitions might include applications for the recovery of civil rights, or for the remission of sentences; and, in general, for exemption from legal penalties. Cf. Dem. *c. Timocr.* 46, τῆς ἀδείας δοθείσης, and see Schömann, *Ant.* p. 397 E.T.; Gilbert, i 294; *Dict. Ant.* i 24 *b*, 702 *a*.

αἱ δὲ δύο κτλ.] Pollux, who gives in viii 96 a paraphrase of the present passage and its context, describes the hearing of heralds and embassies as the business of the third ἐκκλησία, while that of the fourth is περὶ ἱερῶν καὶ ὁσίων. This distinction is not in accordance with the text. The latter is confirmed by Aeschines 1 § 23, πῶς δὲ κελεύει τοὺς προέδρους χρηματίζειν;—προχειροτονεῖν—περὶ ἱερῶν τῶν πατρίων καὶ κήρυξι καὶ πρεσβείαις καὶ ὁσίων. The statement in Pollux may have originated in some confused and fragmentary reminiscence of the constitution in c. 30 § 5, where, in the order of business before the βουλή, the third place is assigned πρεσβείαις, after which they deliberate περὶ τῶν ἄλλων (= ὁσίων).

τρία] This implies that only three questions under each of the several headings were allowed to be discussed in each πρυτανεία. Similarly in § 5 only three συκοφαντῶν προβολαὶ could be brought against Athenians, and three against resident aliens. These limitations have been hitherto unknown.

Hartel, *Studien über Urkundenwesen*, cites, as examples of business connected with ritual etc., being brought before the people ἐν ἱεροῖς, CIA ii 325, 352 *b*, 373 *b*, and (a decree of the Κήρυκες and Εὐμολπίδαι) 605. On p. 173 ff., he cites the following inscriptions: Ἀθήναιον vi 152 (= Ditt. no. 101, Hicks no. 111) l. 55 (B.C. 347/6 on the πρέσβεις from the sons of Leucon), χρηματίσαι τοὺς προέδρους οἳ ἂν λάχωσι προεδρεύειν ἐν τῷ δήμῳ τῇ ὀγδόῃ ἐπὶ δέκα πρῶτον μετὰ τὰ ἱερά. The privilege of access to the βουλή (and in most cases to the δῆμος) μετὰ τὰ ἱερά was granted to Aretus of Colophon (CIA i 36), to the Νεοπολῖται (*ib.* 51 *Suppl.* p. 17), to the communities of Mytilene, Colophon and Cythnus (CIA ii 52 *c*, 164, 233), and to certain individuals named in 1 *b*, 34, 206, 209, 289, 316. Cf. Dem. 24 § 25 ff.

ἱερῶν...ὁσίων] 'things sacred and profane.' ὅσια, when contrasted with ἱερά, includes all that is untouched by divine law. Thus, in things concrete, ἱερὰ would include temples and their treasures; ὅσια, civic buildings and money belonging to the state. Dem. 24 § 9, τῶν ἱερῶν μὲν χρημάτων τοὺς θεούς, τῶν ὁσίων δὲ τὴν πόλιν ἀποστερεῖ. The same terms are used to contrast religious and civil privileges, Dem. 23 § 65; 39 § 35; as well as the corresponding legal enactments, as in Lys. 30 § 25, τῶν ὁσίων καὶ τῶν ἱερῶν ἀντιγραφεύς (see Frohberger's *Lysias*, iii p. 172, and Ruhnken, *Timaeus*, *s.v.* ὅσια· τὰ ἰδιωτικά, καὶ μὴ ἱερά).

κήρυξιν καὶ πρεσβείαις] The construction changes from gen. to dat., as in Aeschin. 1 § 23, where the order in which the four kinds of business are mentioned is the same as in the text. Foreign envoys were usually introduced to the ἐκκλησία by the βουλή (Aeschin. *F. L.* § 58). Dem. 24 § 150, καὶ κήρυκος καὶ πρεσβείας. Cf. c. 30 § 5.

χρηματίζουσιν—ἄνευ προχειροτονίας]

καὶ ἄνευ προχειροτονίας. προσέρχονται δὲ καὶ οἱ κήρυκες καὶ οἱ πρέσβεις τοῖς πρυτάνεσιν πρῶτον, καὶ οἱ τὰς ἐπιστολὰς φέροντες
33 *τούτοις ἀποδιδόασι.*

44. Ἔστι δ' ἐπιστάτης τῶν πρυτάνεων εἷς ὁ λαχών·

32 πρυτάνεσι H-L, B. **33** ἀποδιδόασιν H-L.

TESTIMONIA. **XLIV §§ 1, 2** * Harp. ἐπιστάτης :...δύο εἰσὶν οἱ καθιστάμενοι ἐπιστάται, ὧν ὁ μὲν ἐκ πρυτάνεων κληρούμενος, ὁ δὲ ἐκ τῶν προέδρων, ὧν ἑκάτερος τίνα διοίκησιν διοικεῖ δεδήλωκεν Ἀρ. ἐν Ἀθ. πολ. Lex. Dem. Patm. p. 13 Sakkelion, ἐπιστάτης : οὗτος ἐκ τῶν πρυτάνεων ἐκληροῦτο καὶ ἐπεστάτει "νύκτα καὶ ἡμέραν" μόνον, καὶ οὐκ ἐξῆν δεύτερον τὸν αὐτὸν γίνεσθαι. τὰς δὲ κλεῖς τῶν "ἱερῶν ἐν οἷς" ἀπέκειτο τὰ χρήματα καὶ τὰ γράμματα τῆς πόλεως... Suidas (e lexico Photiano) ἐπιστάτης : "τῶν πρυτάνεων εἷς ὁ λαχὼν" ἐπιστάτης ἐλέγετο. δὶς δὲ τὸν αὐτὸν ἐπιστατῆσαι οὐκ ἐξῆν. φυλάσσει δὲ τοῦ ἱεροῦ τὰς κλεῖς ἐν ᾧ τὰ δημόσια χρήματα, ἔτι μὴν καὶ τὴν δημοσίαν σφραγῖδα (φυλάσσει—σφραγῖδα Etym. M. p. 364, 41). ἐπειδὰν δὲ οἱ πρυτάνεις "συναγάγωσι τὴν βουλὴν ἢ τὸν δῆμον," ὁ ἐπιστάτης "κληροῖ προέδρους ἐννέα," ἀπὸ "φυλῆς ἑκάστης" ἕνα "πλὴν τῆς πρυτανευούσης. καὶ πάλιν" ἐκ τῶν ἐννέα τούτων ἐπιστάτην ἕνα καὶ τὸ πρᾶγμα (sic) παραδίδωσιν. Telephus ap. Eustath. in Od. ρ 455...γίνεται γάρ φησιν Ἀθήνησιν ἐκ τῶν πρυτάνεων εἷς ὃς "ἐπιστατεῖ νύκτα καὶ ἡμέραν" μίαν, καὶ πλείω χρόνον οὐκ ἔξεστιν οὐδὲ "δὶς τὸν αὐτὸν γενέσθαι, τάς τε κλεῖς <τῶν ἱερῶν> ἐν οἷς τὰ χρήματά εἰσι φυλάττει καὶ τὰ γράμματα τῆς πόλεως καὶ τὴν δημοσίαν σφραγῖδα. κληροῖ δὲ καὶ προέδρους ἐξ ἑκάστης φυλῆς ἕνα "πλὴν τῆς πρυτανευούσης καὶ πάλιν ἐκ τούτων ἐπιστάτην ἕνα" (Frag. 397^2, 437^3). Pollux viii 96: ἐπιστάτης δ' ἐστὶν εἷς τῶν πρυτάνεων, ὁ κλήρῳ λαχών, δὶς δ' οὐκ ἔξεστι γενέσθαι τὸν αὐτὸν ἐπιστάτην. ἔχει δὲ οὗτος τῶν ἱερῶν τὰς κλεῖς ἐν οἷς τὰ χρήματα καὶ τὰ γράμματα. καὶ ὅταν οἱ πρυτάνεις τὸν δῆμον ἢ τὴν βουλὴν συνάγωσιν, οὗτος ἐξ ἑκάστης φυλῆς πρόεδρον ἕνα κληροῖ, μόνην τὴν πρυτανεύουσαν ἀφιείς (Frag. 394^2, 434^3).

'Sometimes the members of the ἐκκλησία take the initiative in bringing forward public business, without a preliminary vote (on the question whether it will discuss a proposal on the part of the βουλή, or accept it without discussion).' Cf. Harpocr. *s.v.* προχειροτονία· ...ὁπόταν τῆς βουλῆς προβουλευσάσης εἰσφέρηται εἰς τὸν δῆμον ἡ γνώμη· πρότερον γίνεται χειροτονία ἐν τῇ ἐκκλησίᾳ πότερον δοκεῖ περὶ τῶν προβουλευθέντων σκέψασθαι τὸν δῆμον, ἢ ἀρκεῖ τὸ προβούλευμα. In Dem. 24 § 12 (after a προβούλευμα) γενομένης ἐκκλησίας προὐχειροτόνησεν ὁ δῆμος. Cf. Aeschin. 1 § 23, and see Gilbert, i 276 n. 3.

The course described in the text would involve a departure from the principle laid down by Solon, μηδὲν ἐᾶν ἀπροβούλευτον εἰς ἐκκλησίαν εἰσφέρεσθαι (Plut. *Sol.* 19). This principle was also virtually set aside when the βουλή, without arriving at any conclusion on its own part, referred a question to the ἐκκλησία direct. Thus, on the memorable evening when the messenger arrived with news of Philip's capture of Elateia, the ἐκκλησία had already begun to assemble before the βουλή had had time to draw up a preliminary decree; and, the business being urgent, the πρυτάνεις brought it immediately before the assembly (Dem. *de Cor.* 170). It was also open to any member of the ἐκκλησία to take the initiative by moving to refer any question to the βουλή with a view to a προβούλευμα being drawn up by the latter (Gilbert, i 278 n. 3).

προσέρχονται—τοῖς πρυτάνεσιν πρῶτον] Aeschin. *F. L.* 58, (the βουλή) ταῖς ξενικαῖς πρεσβείαις τὰς εἰς τὸν δῆμον προσόδους προβουλεύει. On the capture of Elateia, the messenger brought the news ὡς τοὺς πρυτάνεις (*de Cor.* 169). Cf. Arist. *Thesm.* 654, ταῦτα τοῖς πρυτάνεσιν ἀγγελῶ.

XLIV. *The Public Assembly*, continued.

§ 1. **ἐπιστάτης τῶν πρυτάνεων**] In the *fifth* century the ἐπιστάτης τῶν πρυτάνεων actually presided at the meetings of the βουλή and ἐκκλησία, and took the sense of the meeting. Thus, in 415 B.C., we find Nicias addressing the President at the Assembly in the words καὶ σύ, ὦ πρύτανι, ταῦτα...ἐπιψήφιζε (Thuc. vi 14). Again, in 406, on the memorable occasion when Socrates refused to put the illegal proposal that the generals concerned with the battle of Arginusae should have judgment passed upon them collectively, his own tribe was the φυλὴ πρυτανεύουσα (Plat. *Apol.* 32 B), and he

οὗτος δ' ἐπιστατεῖ νύκτα καὶ ἡμέραν, καὶ οὐκ ἔστιν οὔτε πλείω χρόνον οὔτε δὶς τὸν αὐτὸν γενέσθαι. τηρεῖ δ' οὗτος τάς τε κλεῖς τὰς τῶν ἱερῶν ἐν οἷς τὰ χρήματ' ἐστὶν καὶ <τὰ> γράμματα τῇ πόλει, καὶ τὴν δημοσίαν σφραγῖδα, καὶ μένειν ἀναγκαῖον ἐν τῇ θόλῳ τοῦτόν <τ'> ἐστιν καὶ τριττὺν τῶν πρυτάνεων ἣν ἂν οὗτος κελεύῃ.
2 καὶ ἐπειδὰν συναγάγωσιν οἱ πρυτάνεις τὴν βουλὴν ἢ τὸν δῆμον, οὗτος κληροῖ προέδρους ἐννέα, ἕνα ἐκ τῆς φυλῆς ἑκάστης

XLIV 2 οὐκ ἔστι πλείω H-L. **3** ΚΛΕΙϹ (K-W, K^3, B; cf. Meisterhans, p. 28^2): κλῇς K^1, H-L. **4** γράμματα K: <τὰ> γράμματα e gramm. K-W, H-L, B. **6** τοῦτόν <τ'> K-W.

§§ **2, 3** * Harp. *πρόεδροι ἐκληροῦντο τῶν πρυτάνεων καθ' ἑκάστην πρυτανείαν εἷς ἐξ ἑκάστης φυλῆς πλὴν τῆς πρυτανευούσης, οἵτινες τὰ περὶ τὰς ἐκκλησίας διῴκουν.... ὅτι δ' ὁ καλούμενος ἐπιστάτης κληροῖ αὐτούς, εἴρηκεν Ἀρ. ἐν Ἀθ. πολ.* (=Suid. s.v.). Photius (Bekk. *An.* 290) *πρόεδροι: οἱ τὰ περὶ τὰς ἐκκλησίας Ἀθήνησι διοικοῦντες* <*καὶ τῆς εὐταξίας ἐπιμελούμενοι* add. Lex. Dem. Patm. p. 12>. *εἷς ἐκληροῦτο ὑπὸ τῶν πρυτάνεων καθ' ἑκάστην ἐκκλησίαν ἐξ ἑκάστης φυλῆς.*

was ἐπιστάτης for the day (Xen. *Mem.* i 1, 18, ἐπιστάτης ἐν τῷ δήμῳ γενόμενος). Cf. Gilbert, i 257 n. 3.

In the *fourth* century, on the institution of πρόεδροι with an ἐπιστάτης of their own, the duty of presiding in public was transferred to the ἐπ. τῶν προέδρων (Gilbert, *ib.* n. 5), while the ἐπ. τῶν πρυτάνεων discharged the duties stated in the text. As the latter remained in the θόλος for the day and night during which he was in office, he was necessarily precluded from presiding over the ἐκκλησία or the βουλή. On the institution of the πρόεδροι, see § 2.

τάς τε κλεῖς κτλ.] The keys of the public treasure kept in the ὀπισθόδομος on the Acropolis (Boeckh, III xx). The custody of the keys did not involve any responsibility for the actual management of the fund. The Arg. to Dem. *Androt.* p. 590 applies to the ἐπιστάτης language of less precision than that in the text: αὐτὸς τὰς κλεῖς τῆς ἀκροπόλεως ἐπιστεύετο καὶ πάντα τὰ χρήματα τῆς πόλεως. It adds: ἵν' οὖν μὴ ἐρασθῇ τυραννίδος, διὰ τοῦτο μίαν ἡμέραν ἐποίουν αὐτὸν ἄρξαι.

τῶν ἱερῶν does not necessarily imply that the public treasure was kept in more than one temple. Hence the pl. throws no light on the obscure question whether the ὀπισθόδομος of the 'old temple' of Athene between the Erechtheum and Parthenon was at this time still in use, as well as the Parthenon (see Miss Harrison's *Mythology &c of Athens*, p. 505—8). The 'old temple' was burnt in 406 B.C. (Xen. *Hell.* i 6), and the burning of the ὀπισθόδομος mentioned in Dem. 24 § 136 may refer to the same event. In B.C. 353 the priestess transferred to the ἐπιστάται (probably the ἐπ. δημοσίων ἔργων) in the archonship of Thudemus certain 'gold ornaments' which were removed from the 'old temple' to the Parthenon (CIA ii 758 II 7). The public records (**γράμματα**) were preserved in the Μητρῷον near the βουλευτήριον (Aeschin. 3 § 187; Paus. i 3, 5; Lycurg. *Leocr.* 66). Cf. Curtius, *das Metroon*, Gotha, 1868.

δημοσίαν σφραγῖδα] [Xen.] *de Vect.* 4, 21, ἀνδράποδα σεσημασμένα τῷ δημοσίῳ σημάντρῳ. The seal probably represented an owl or a Gorgon's head. Cf. Curtius, *Abh. d. Berlin Akad.* 1874, p. 88 (Gilbert, i p. 256 n. 2). Both the badges above mentioned may be seen on the extant examples of δικαστῶν πινάκια (c. 63 § 4).

§ 2. **προέδρους**] In the *fifth* century it was the πρυτάνεις who presided over the βουλή and ἐκκλησία in the person of one of their own body who was the ἐπιστάτης τῶν πρυτάνεων and was necessarily a member of the πρυτανεύουσα φυλή. Thus, in CIA ii 1 *b*, we have two decrees of the year of Eucleides, B.C. 403—2. (1) was passed in the prytany of the tribe Pandionis, and the ἐπιστάτης was of the deme of Ὄα, which belonged to that tribe; (2) in the prytany of the tribe Erechtheis, and the ἐπιστάτης was of the deme of Κηδαί belonging to that tribe. As a general rule the deme of the ἐπ. τῶν πρυτάνεων is not specified; it necessarily belongs to the presiding tribe.

In the *fourth* century the πρόεδροι came into existence. The ἐπιστάτης τῶν πρυτάνεων was deprived of his preeminence *πλὴν τῆς πρυτανευούσης, καὶ πάλιν ἐκ τούτων ἐπιστάτην ἕνα, καὶ παραδίδωσι τὸ πρόγραμμα αὐτοῖς· οἱ δὲ παραλαβόντες τῆς τ'* 3

10 πρόγραμμα corrupte mutatum in πρᾶγμα habet Suidas s. v. ἐπιστάτης. οἱ K-W, B; οἱ K, H-L.

---

and obtained in its place the privilege of appointing by lot nine προέδροι, one from each of the tribes except his own, and of drawing lots among those nine for one of them to act as the ἐπιστάτης τῶν προέδρων. Under this system, the ἐπ. τῶν προέδρων was necessarily a member of some other than the πρυτανεύουσα φυλή. In CIA ii 17 *b* (Ditt. no. 64), in the archonship of Nausinicus, B.C. 378/7, though the προέδροι are mentioned, the deme of the ἐπιστάτης is uncertain; but in CIA ii 17 (Ditt. no. 63), in the same year, in the prytany of the tribe Hippothontis, the ἐπιστάτης is of the deme Ἄθμονον which belongs to a different tribe, Cecropis. In ii 50 (Ditt. 75), B.C. 368/7, in the prytany of the tribe Aeantis, the ἐπιστάτης belongs to a deme of the tribe Aegeis. In ii 116 (Ditt. 107), B.C. 341/0, in the prytany of the tribe Pandionis, the ἐπιστάτης belongs to another tribe. Between the years 378 and 320 we have in all 24 decrees giving the name of the prytany and the president, and in no case does the deme of the president belong to the φυλὴ πρυτανεύουσα. For the years between Eucleides and Nausinicus (403—378) there is at present no evidence; but it is probable that the change came into force in the latter year, a date of special importance in the financial history of Athens. The aim of the change was clearly to give all the tribes a concurrent share in the superintendence of the βουλή and ἐκκλησία, instead of each tribe having in turn the sole superintendence for the duration of its own prytany. (See esp. Prof. W. W. Goodwin's paper in *Trans. of the American Philol. Association*, 1885, vol. xvi 165—175.)

In the *fifth* century the formula for describing the president was ὁ δεῖνα ἐπεστάτει. From 378 to 347 the same formula is used to denote the ἐπιστάτης τῶν προέδρων, side by side with a new formula, τῶν προέδρων ἐπεψήφιζεν ὁ δεῖνα. From 347 onwards the last alone is found (Gilbert, i 257 n. 5).

It was once supposed that the 50 πρυτάνεις were divided into five groups of ten πρόεδροι holding office for one-fifth of a prytany (generally for seven days) and appointing one of their number to serve as ἐπιστάτης for each day. This supposition rested on the Scholia to Aeschin. *c. Ctes.* 39 and Dem. p. 594, 5, and on the 2nd Arg. to Dem. *Androt.* p. 590. It was accepted in an early work of Schömann (*De Comitiis Ath.*, 1819), where, in the endeavour to reconcile the conflict of evidence, it was suggested that there were two sets of πρόεδροι in existence at the same time, (1) the *proedri contribules*, belonging to the same tribe as the πρυτάνεις, and forming a subdivision of that body; and (2) the *proedri non-contribules*, belonging to a different tribe to that of the πρυτάνεις.

Nearly three centuries earlier it was held by Sigonius (1529—1584) in his *De Atheniensium Republica*, that wherever the πρόεδροι were mentioned, they were the nine who were not of the same tribe. This opinion was accepted by K. F. Hermann (1843), who noticed further that the πρόεδροι are never mentioned until after the time when one of the πρυτάνεις used to preside in the Assembly. Hence the πρόεδροι (*non-contribules*) were a later institution, and the *proedri contribules* were a merely imaginary body. Schömann's earlier view survived in Grote, c. 31, iii 118, but it had meanwhile been abandoned by Schömann himself, in favour of Hermann's view which is conclusively confirmed by the text. See Schömann, *Ant.* p. 377 E.T.

Some confusion has arisen from the fact that Harpocration, *s. v.* πρόεδροι, implies that the πρόεδροι held office during the whole of each prytany, whereas the text, which he professes to follow, really describes them as appointed by lot for each meeting of the βουλή or ἐκκλησία. The most accurate citation of the text is that preserved by Telephus ap. Eustath. on *Od.* 17, 455, and by Suidas, *s. v.* ἐπιστάτης, art. 2. On the general question see Goodwin *l. c.*, and Gilbert i 257 (with the authorities there quoted); also Caillemer on *Boule* in Daremberg and Saglio, i 740—1, and Chavannes on *Epistates, ib.* iii 700; and Wayte in Smith's *Dict. Ant.* i 320—1, and on Dem. *Timocr.* § 21.

ἐπιστάτην] *sc.* τῶν προέδρων. He is mentioned as presiding (1) at the βουλή in Aeschin. *c. Timarch.* 104, βουλευτὴς ὢν καὶ προεδρεύων, and in CIA ii 168 (B.C. 333) τῶν προέδρων ἐπεψήφιζεν, and similarly in ii 179 (B.C. 325) about the time *εὐκοσμίας ἐπιμελοῦνται, καὶ ὑπὲρ ὧν δεῖ χρηματίζειν προτιθέασιν, καὶ τὰς χειροτονίας κρίνουσιν, καὶ τά <τ'> ἄλλα πάντα διοικοῦσιν, καὶ τοῦ ⟦τ'⟧ ἀφεῖναι κύριοί εἰσιν. καὶ ἐπιστατῆσαι μὲν οὐκ ἔξεστιν πλέον ἢ ἅπαξ ἐν τῷ ἐνιαυτῷ, προεδρεύειν δ' ἔξεστιν ἅπαξ ἐπὶ τῆς πρυτανείας ἑκάστης.*

4 *ποιοῦσι δὲ καὶ ἀρχαιρεσίας στρατηγῶν καὶ ἱππάρχων καὶ τῶν ἄλλων τῶν πρὸς τὸν πόλεμον ἀρχῶν ἐν τῇ ἐκκλησίᾳ, καθ' ὅ τι ἂν τῷ δήμῳ δοκῇ· ποιοῦσι δ' οἱ μετὰ τὴν ἕκτην πρυτανεύοντες ἐφ' ὧν*

.ΔΕΙΚ(ΑΙ).

11 ΔΕΙΧΡΗΜΑΤΙΖΕΙΝ: *δεῖ χρηματίζειν* K, H-L, B : *χρηματίζειν δεῖ* K-W. **12** *τά* <*τ'*> K-W. **13** *τ'* delent Richards, Blass, K-W, B; in *δ'* mutat Hude; *τὴν ἐκκλησίαν* Rutherford (H-L). **14** *ἔξεστι* H-L. ΠΛΕΙΟΝ (K-W, B): *πλέον* H-L, K[3], Meisterhans, p. 120[2]. **16** ΔΕΚ(ΑΙ)ΔΕΚΑΡΧ: delevi ΔΕΚ e ΔΕΚ(ΑΙ) male iterato exortum, idem fecerunt Blass, Fränkel, K-W, H-L, K[3]; etiam in versu propinquo (18) dittographiae vitium denuo apparet ΜΕΤΑΤΑΤΗΝ (*μετὰ τὴν*).

---

when this treatise was written; (2) at the *ἐκκλησία*, *id. c. Ctes.* 39, *τὸν δ' ἐπιστάτην τῶν προέδρων διαχειροτονίαν διδόναι τῷ δήμῳ*, *F. L.* 82, (Demosthenes) *λαγχάνει προεδρεύειν* and (84) *ἀναστὰς ἐκ τῶν προέδρων οὐκ ἔφη τὸ ψήφισμ' ἐπιψηφιεῖν*, cf. *ib.* 68.

τὸ πρόγραμμα] 43 § 3, *προγράφουσι.*

§ 3. **εὐκοσμίας ἐπιμελοῦνται**] In the previous century the same duties had been performed by the *πρυτάνεις* with the aid of the *τοξόται*: Arist. *Thesm.* 923, 929—946, and esp. 854, *εἰ μὴ κοσμίως ἕξεις ἕως ἂν τῶν πρυτάνεών τις φανῇ.* The *πρόεδροι* as well as the *πρυτάνεις* are named in Aeschin. *c. Ctes.* 4, *τῆς τῶν ῥητόρων ἀκοσμίας οὐκέτι κρατεῖν δύνανται οὔθ' οἱ νόμοι οὔθ' οἱ πρυτάνεις οὔθ' οἱ πρόεδροι οὔθ' ἡ προεδρεύουσα φυλή.*

The phrase *ἐπιμελεῖσθαι εὐκοσμίας* is found in *Pol.* 1299 *b* 16 and 19 (cf. 1321 *b* 14 and 20); also in Isocr. *Areop.* 37.

προτιθέασιν] 48 § 2; Xen. *Mem.* iv 2, 3, *τῆς πόλεως λόγον προτιθείσης.* In Aeschin. *F. L.* 65 we have the exceptional proposal that, at the first of two *ἐκκλησίαι*, there should be a debate; and that, at the second, the *πρόεδροι* should put the question to the vote, *λόγον δὲ μὴ προτιθέναι.* In the fifth century this was the duty of the *πρυτάνεις.* Thuc. vi 14, *ὦ πρύτανι...γνώμας προτίθει αὖθις*, iii 36, 4; 42, 1.

χειροτονίας] Aeschin. *c. Ctes.* 3, '*ἂν δέ τις τῶν ἄλλων βουλευτῶν ὄντως λαχῇ κληρούμενος προεδρεύειν καὶ τὰς ὑμετέρας χειροτονίας ὀρθῶς ἀναγορεύῃ κτλ.*'

ἀφεῖναι] Arist. *Ach.* 173, *οἱ γὰρ πρυτάνεις λύουσι τὴν ἐκκλησίαν.* Dem. *Timocr.* § 26 (during the *Κρόνια*), *ἀφειμένης τῆς βουλῆς.*

ἐπιστατῆσαι] *sc. τῶν προέδρων.* In Dittenberger, *Inscr.* nos. 98 and 101, we have two decrees in the same prytany of B.C. 347–6, in both of which *Θεόφιλος Ἁλιμούσιος ἐπεστάτει.* It was rightly inferred by A. Schaefer that both were passed at the same meeting of the *ἐκκλησία.* The text shews that no one could be *ἐπιστάτης τῶν προέδρων* more than once in each year.

§ 4. **στρατηγῶν**] 61 § 1. **ἱππάρχων**, 61 § 4. **τῶν ἄλλων**, 61 §§ 3, 5. Cf. Aeschin. *c. Ctes.* 13, (*ἀρχὰς*) *ἃς ὁ δῆμος εἴωθε χειροτονεῖν ἐν ἀρχαιρεσίαις, στρατηγοὺς καὶ ἱππάρχους καὶ τὰς μετὰ τούτων ἀρχάς*, also Xen. *Mem.* iii 4, 1; Dem. 23 § 171; Plut. *Phoc.* 8.

οἱ μετὰ τὴν ἕκτην πρυτανεύοντες] The author of the 2nd Arg. to Dem. *Androt.* p. 590 erroneously states that the *ἀρχαιρεσίαι* fell on the last four days of the Attic lunar year of 354 days. But, as observed by Schömann, *Ant.* 390 E.T., they could not possibly have been held so late in the year: they must necessarily have taken place much earlier, so as to allow time for the *δοκιμασία.* It has been inferred by Köhler (*Monatsb. d. Akad. d. W.*, Berlin, 1866, p. 343), that they were held in the first *ἐκκλησία* of the *ninth* prytany. This inference is drawn from an inscription of the time of the 12 tribes (after B.C. 307), CIA ii 416, in which the *ἀρχαιρεσίαι* are fixed *κατὰ τὴν μαντείαν* for the 22nd day of Munichion (early in May), corresponding (in the time of the 10 tribes) to the beginning of the ninth prytany (see also Gilbert's *Beiträge*, pp. 5—13, and Busolt in Müller's *Handbuch*, IV i 152). The text shews that the election was held in the *seventh* prytany. This would begin *ἂν εὐσημία γένηται. δεῖ δὲ προβούλευμα γενέσθαι καὶ περὶ τούτων.*

45. *ἡ δὲ βουλὴ πρότερον μὲν ἦν κυρία καὶ χρήμασιν ζημιῶσαι καὶ δῆσαι καὶ ἀποκτεῖναι. — — καὶ Λυσίμαχον αὐτῆς ἀγαγούσης*

19 ΓΕΝΕϹΘΑΙ K, H-L, B: *γίνεσθαι* K-W.
XLV 1 *χρήμασι* H-L. **2** post *ἀποκτεῖναι* lacunam indicant K-W.

---

three days before the end of Gamelion (the first six prytanies containing 214 and the first seven months 217 days), and would mainly correspond to the month Anthesterion (middle of February to middle of March).

This statement has a direct bearing on the story of Sophocles being appointed *στρατηγὸς* against Samos &c owing to the success of his *Antigone* (on the authorities for the story, see Jebb's *Introd.* p. xliii). If the play was produced at the Great Dionysia (10—15 Elaphebolion = March—April), *i.e.* late in March, B.C. 441, the ordinary election of *στρατηγοί* for the ensuing official year had already taken place a month before. We must therefore either infer that the story is false; or that the date of the election was exceptionally delayed in that year owing to inauspicious weather; or that, at that time, the *ἀρχαιρεσίαι* fell later than was the case in B.C. 325. If the election of Sophocles took place a month before the Great Dionysia, and was prompted by the success of the *Antigone*, the play must have been performed at the Great Dionysia of the previous year, in which case eleven months must have elapsed before the election. But by that time the impression produced by the play would have become appreciably weaker, and the story would have lost its point. On the bearing of the date of election on the 'deposition of Pericles,' see Mr Marchant in *Class. Rev.* v 165.

εὐσημία] 'on whatsoever days there are *signs of fair weather.*' *εὐσημία* is found in Hippocr. 1170; *εὔσημος* in *Meteor.* p. 363 *a* 27, *γέγραπται τοῦ μᾶλλον εὐσήμως ἔχειν ὁ τοῦ ὁρίζοντος κύκλος.*

The proviso is one of practical importance in the case of a large meeting on an open hill-side like that of the Pnyx. Even when the ordinary *ἐκκλησίαι* came to be held in the theatre of Dionysus (*e.g.* in 290 B.C.), the Pnyx continued to be the scene of the *ἀρχαιρεσίαι* (Pollux viii 133).

When the *δῆμος* was desiring to elect Cleon as *στρατηγός*, there was thunder and lightning, an eclipse of the moon and afterwards one of the sun, Arist. *Nub.* 581—6 (and Schol.). Presumably amid all these portents the election was deferred. In Thuc. v 45 *ult.* an *ἐκκλησία* is adjourned because of an earthquake. Even a drop of rain was sufficient to be regarded as a 'sign from heaven,' *διοσημία 'στι καὶ ῥανὶς βέβληκέ με* (*Ach.* 171). Cf. Suidas, *s.v.*

προβούλευμα κτλ.] In accordance with the general principle ordained by Solon, Plut. *Sol.* 19, *μηδὲν ἐᾶν ἀπροβούλευτον εἰς ἐκκλησίαν εἰσφέρεσθαι.*

XLV—XLIX. *The functions of the Council.*

XLV § 1. **κυρία—ζημιῶσαι**] The *βουλὴ* was not competent to inflict a higher fine than 500 *dr.*, Dem. *c. Euerg.* p. 1152 § 43, (after an *εἰσαγγελία*) *ἐν τῷ διαχειροτονεῖν ἣν ἡ βουλὴ πότερα δικαστηρίῳ παραδοίη ἢ ζημιώσειε ταῖς πεντακοσίαις, ὅσου ἦν κυρία κατὰ τὸν νόμον.* In a decree drawn up about 446 B.C. any encroachment on the *Πελαργικὸν* is punished by a fine of 500 *dr.*, to be inflicted after an *εἰσαγγελία* has been brought before the *βουλὴ* by the archon *βασιλεύς* (Ditt. no. 13, 59).

δῆσαι] Arist. *Thesm.* 943, *ἔδοξε τῇ βουλῇ σε δεῖν.* A limitation to this right is mentioned in the oath taken by the Council in Dem. *c. Timocr.* 144, *οὐδὲ δήσω 'Αθηναίων οὐδένα, ὃς ἂν ἐγγυητὰς τρεῖς καθιστῇ τὸ αὐτὸ τέλος τελοῦντας· πλὴν ἐάν τις ἐπὶ προδοσίᾳ τῆς πόλεως ἢ ἐπὶ καταλύσει τοῦ δήμου συνιὼν ἁλῷ ἢ τέλος τι πριάμενος ἢ ἐγγυησάμενος ἢ ἐκλέγων μὴ καταβάλλῃ.* It is there stated that this oath was in the interest of untried persons to give them every opportunity for preparing for their defence. In § 148 we are told that 'Solon' made the Council *ἄκυρον τοῦ δῆσαι*, *i.e.* did not grant them an absolute right of imprisonment, but a limited right subject to proper bail being found. In certain cases, however, bail was not allowed, and in these the Council's right was not barred. See also 22 § 2 and 48 § 1.

Cleophon was imprisoned by the Council and then handed over to the dicastery (Lys. 30 § 10); he was condemned to death by a court consisting of ὡς τὸν δήμιον *καὶ αὐθημερὸν* ἤδη μέλλοντα ἀποθνῄσκειν Εὐμηλίδης ὁ Ἀλωπεκῆθεν ἀφείλετο, οὐ φάσκων δεῖν ἄνευ δικαστηρίου γνώσεως οὐδένα τῶν πολιτῶν ἀποθνῄσκειν· καὶ κρίσεως ἐν δικαστηρίῳ γενομένης ὁ μὲν Λυσίμαχος ἀπέφυγεν καὶ ἐπωνυμίαν ἔσχεν ὁ ἀπὸ τοῦ τυπάνου, ὁ δὲ δῆμος ἀφείλετο τῆς βουλῆς τὸ θανατοῦν καὶ δεῖν καὶ χρήμασι ζημιοῦν, καὶ νόμον ἔθετο, ἄν τινος ἀδικεῖν ἡ βουλὴ καταγνῷ ἢ ζημιώσῃ, τὰς καταγνώσεις καὶ τὰς ἐπιζημιώσεις εἰσάγειν τοὺς θεσμοθέτας εἰς τὸ δικαστήριον, καὶ ὅ τι ἂν οἱ δικασταὶ ψηφίσωνται, τοῦτο κύριον εἶναι.

[Col. 24.] 2 κρίνει δὲ ‖ τὰς ἀρχὰς ἡ βουλὴ τὰς πλείστας, μάλισθ' ὅσαι χρήματα διαχειρίζουσιν· οὐ κυρία δ' ἡ κρίσις, ἀλλ' ἐφέσιμος εἰς

3 *καθήμενον ἤδη μέλλοντα ἀποθν.* K, K-W, H-L; *καθήμενον ἤδη <καὶ> μέλλοντα ἀποθν.* J B Mayor: legendum fortasse *καὶ αὐθημερὸν ἤδη μέλλοντα ἀποθν.* cf. Aeschin. 1 § 16 (lex) *παραδοθεὶς τοῖς ἕνδεκα τεθνάτω αὐθημερόν.* **3, 5** ΑΠΟΘΝΗϹΚΕΙΝ: *ἀποθνῄσκειν* K-W, H-L, K³, B, cf. Meisterhans, p. 141², n. 1234. **3** ΕΥΜΗΛΕΙΔΗϹ (B coll. *Φιλομηλείδης* Od. ρ 134): *Εὐμηλίδης* K-W, H-L, K³. **4** ΑΛΩΠΕΘΗΚΕΝ corr. K. **5** <*τῷ*> *δικαστηρίῳ* K-W, idem in c. 46, 10 et c. 55, 7 *τῷ* non inserunt. **6** *ἀπέφυγε* H-L. ΕϹΧΕΝ: *ἔσχε* B, *εἶχεν* K. **8** *ἐάν* H-L. **9** *ἐπιζημιώσεις* (nusquam alibi inventum) K, K-W, B: *ζημιώσεις* Wyse, H-L. **13** ΕϹ̣Τ̣ΦΕϹΙΜΟϹ?; *ἐφέσιμος* K, K-W, B; *ἔτ' ἐφέσιμος* H-L.

---

the Council and a dicastery, *ib.* 11, and 13 § 12 (Newman).

Λυσίμαχον] possibly the person of that name mentioned in Xen. *Hell.* ii 4, 8, (the Thirty) *Λυσίμαχον τὸν ἵππαρχον ἐκέλευον ἀναγαγόντα παραδοῦναι αὐτοὺς τοῖς ἕνδεκα.* On the restoration of the democracy his services to the Thirty may well have been remembered against him.

καὶ αὐθημερὸν—ἀποθνῄσκειν] *Hist. An.* 603 *a* 15, *ἀποθνῄσκουσιν αὐθημερόν*, 398 *a* 35, 568 *b* 21.

One Sosias had a similarly narrow escape: Antiphon 5 § 70, *ὁ ἀνὴρ ἀπήχθη* (MSS, *ἀνήχθη* Dobree, *ἀπελύθη* Kayser, *ἀπηλλάχθη* Baiter; *ἀφείλετο*, in the text, suggests *ἀφῃρέθη*) *ὑπὸ τοῦ δήμου τοῦ ὑμετέρου παραδεδομένος ἤδη τοῖς ἕνδεκα.*

Εὐμηλίδης] The only passage where the name is found, as that of an Athenian, is [Dem.] 49 § 11, *τῷ παιδὶ τοῦ Εὐμηλίδου.* The date of the speech is B.C. 362.

ἀφείλετο] here 'rescued him.' It is used below in another sense: 'deprived of the power of.'

ὁ ἀπὸ τοῦ τυπάνου] 'the man who escaped the bastinado.' Schol. Arist. *Plut.* 476, *τύμπανα...ξύλα, δι' ὧν τοὺς καταδίκους ἔτυπτον*, and Photius, *s. v.* *τύμπανον.* Cf. Lys. 13 § 56, *ὡς ἀνδροφόνον ὄντα—τῷ δημίῳ παρέδοτε καὶ ἀπετυμπανίσθη*, *ib.* 67, 68; and Dem. 9 § 61. This form of punishment was inflicted on *κακοῦργοι*, including *ἀνδροφόνοι.* This confirms the conjecture that Lysimachus was arraigned for taking part in causing citizens to be put to death under the Thirty (Xen. *l. c.*). The restriction in the powers of the *βουλὴ* mentioned in this chapter has already been noticed in more general terms in c. 41, *αἱ τῆς βουλῆς κρίσεις εἰς τὸν δῆμον ἐληλύθασιν*, a passage referring to the time subsequent to the archonship of Eucleides. Even before that time the *βουλὴ* did not necessarily enforce its right of inflicting penalties, but sometimes exercised the option of referring the case to a law-court, cf. CIA i 59, (*τὴν βουλὴν*) *κολάζειν τῶν δωροδοκησάντων καταψηφιζομένην, καὶ εἰς δικαστήριον αὐτοὺς εἰσάγειν, καθότι ἂν δοκῇ αὐτῇ.*

ἐπιζημιώσεις] not found elsewhere. *τὰ ἐπιζήμια* is used of 'penalties' in Dem. and Plato; *ἐπιζημιοῦν*, in Xen. *Hell.* v 2 § 22; *ἐπιζημίωμα*, in Pollux viii 149.

θεσμοθέτας] 59.

§ 2. **κρίνει τὰς ἀρχὰς**] Antiphon, 6 § 49, *πυθόμενος αὐτοὺς* (the *πορισταί, πωληταί, πρακτόρες* and *ὑπογραμματεῖς*) *δεινὰ καὶ σχέτλια ἐργάζεσθαι, εἰσῆγον εἰς τὴν βουλήν.*

ἐφέσιμος] [Dem.] 7 § 9, *ταῦτα δὲ κύρια ἔσεσθαι οὐκ ἐπειδὰν ἐν τῷ δικαστηρίῳ τῷ παρ' ὑμῖν κυρωθῇ...ἀλλ' ἐπειδὰν ὡς ἑαυτὸν ἐπανενεχθῇ, ἐφέσιμον τὴν παρ' ὑμῶν γενομένην γνῶσιν ὡς ἑαυτὸν ποιούμενος.* Lucian, *τὸ δικαστήριον. ἔξεστι δὲ καὶ τοῖς ἰδιώταις εἰσαγγέλλειν ἣν ἂν βούλωνται τῶν ἀρχῶν μὴ χρῆσθαι τοῖς νόμοις. ἔφεσις δὲ καὶ τούτοις ἐστὶν εἰς τὸ δικαστήριον, ἐὰν αὐτῶν ἡ βουλὴ καταγνῷ.*

δοκιμάζει δὲ καὶ τοὺς βουλευτὰς τοὺς τὸν ὕστερον ἐνιαυτὸν 3
βουλεύσοντας καὶ τοὺς ἐννέα ἄρχοντας. καὶ πρότερον μὲν ἦν ἀποδοκιμάσαι κυρία, νῦν δὲ <καὶ> τούτοις ἔφεσίς ἐστιν εἰς τὸ δικαστήριον.

τούτων μὲν οὖν ἄκυρός ἐστιν ἡ βουλή. προβουλεύει δ' εἰς τὸν 4
δῆμον, καὶ οὐκ ἔξεστιν οὐδὲν ἀπροβούλευτον οὐδ' ὅ τι ἂν μὴ προγράψωσιν οἱ πρυτάνεις ψηφίσασθαι τῷ δήμῳ· κατ' αὐτὰ γὰρ ταῦτα ἔνοχός ἐστιν ὁ νικήσας γραφῇ παρανόμων.

46. *ἐπιμελεῖται δὲ καὶ τῶν πεποιημένων τριήρων καὶ τῶν σκευῶν καὶ τῶν νεωσοίκων, καὶ ποιεῖται καινὰς [[δὲ]] τριήρεις ἢ*

19 <*καὶ*> *τούτοις* K-W, B. **23** *κατὰ γὰρ ταῦτα* Kontos, H-L; v. Dem. 20 § 96.
XLVI 2 *δὲ* secl. K (edd.).

---

pro Imaginibus 15, *ἐφέσιμον ... δίκην.* Pollux viii 125, (*κρίσιν*) *ἐφέσιμον.*

εἰσαγγέλλειν] probably here used in the general sense of bringing to the knowledge of the Council, without reference to the special process called *εἰσαγγελία.* The procedure in the latter case is described by Dr Hager in *Dict. Ant. s. v.*, i 709 *a.*

§ 3. **δοκιμάζει—βουλευτὰς**] Dem. *Mid.* 111, *βουλεύειν μου λαχόντος δοκιμαζομένου κατηγόρει*, *Neaer.* 3, *λαγχάνει βουλεύειν Ἀπολλόδωρος· δοκιμασθεὶς δὲ καὶ ὀμόσας τὸν νόμιμον ὅρκον κτλ.* Two of the speeches of Lysias are concerned with the *δοκιμασία* of a *βουλευτής*: *Or.* 31, *κατὰ Φίλωνος*. is a speech for the prosecution; *Or.* 16, *ὑπὲρ Μαντιθέου*, for the defence. § 9 of the latter speech shews the wide scope of the scrutiny in such cases: *ἐν δὲ ταῖς δοκιμασίαις δίκαιον εἶναι παντὸς τοῦ βίου λόγον διδόναι.*

ἄρχοντας] Lys. *Or.* 26, *κατ' Εὐάνδρου*, is a speech in accusation of one who was appointed by lot to be First Archon in reserve. The case was heard on the last day but one of the preceding official year (midsummer, B.C. 382). The next day was a public holiday, and, in the event of his rejection, an appeal was impossible: § 6, *δικαστήριον...οὐ δυνατὸν πληρωθῆναι.* Dem. *Lept.* 90 asserts that the junior archons underwent a double *δοκιμασία*:—*τοὺς θεσμοθέτας δὶς δοκιμασθέντας ἄρχειν ἔν τε τῇ βουλῇ καὶ παρ' ὑμῖν ἐν τῷ δικαστηρίῳ.* The *δοκιμασία* before the *βουλὴ* is called an *ἀνάκρισις* in Dem. *Eubul.* 66; it is described as affecting all the archons (*ib.* 70). Cf. c. 55 § 2.

§ 4. **οὐδὲν ἀπροβούλευτον**] Plut. *Sol.* 19, quoted on c. 44 *ult.*

προγράψωσιν] 43 § 3 *ult.*

γραφῇ παρανόμων] Here the illegality turns on a point of form. Among cases in point are the motion of Androtion to award a crown to the outgoing *βουλή* (Dem. *Androt.* 5); and that of Thrasybulus to grant Lysias the citizenship of Athens (note on 40 § 2).

XLVI § 1. **τῶν τριήρων**] Gilbert, i 261 n. 4.

τῶν σκευῶν] esp. of 'naval stores and engines,' and 'the tackling of ships.' [Dem.] 47, *c. Euerg.* § 19, *σκεύη τριηρικά.* Xen. *Oec.* viii 12, *διὰ πολλῶν...ξυλίνων σκευῶν* ('oars,' 'rudders,' 'masts,' 'yards') *καὶ πλεκτῶν* ('cables') *ὁρμίζεται ναῦς καὶ ἀνάγεται, διὰ πολλῶν δὲ τῶν κρεμαστῶν* ('sails' and 'rigging') *καλουμένων πλεῖ.* The specifications of the famous *σκευοθήκη* in the Peiraeus, designed by the architect Philon under the administration of Lycurgus, are still extant (CIA ii 1054 = Ditt. no. 352). This *σκευοθήκη* was intended *τοῖς κρεμαστοῖς σκεύεσιν*, and (though not finished) was probably already in use in B.C. 329, a few years before the text was written. Cf. Dürrbach, *Lycurgue*, pp. 64—73.

τῶν νεωσοίκων] Strictly speaking the *νεώσοικοι* are the sheds in which the ships are laid up, and *νεώρια* the dockyards; but the terms are sometimes interchanged (cf. *Dict. Ant.* ii 206 *a*, and Dürrbach, *l.c.* p. 65, n. 3). In [Xen.] *de Rep. Ath.* iii 2, among the duties of

τετρήρεις, ὁποτέρας ἂν ὁ δῆμος χειροτονήσῃ, καὶ σκεύη ταύταις καὶ νεωσοίκους. χειροτονεῖ δ' ἀρχιτέκτονας ὁ δῆμος ἐπὶ τὰς ναῦς· ἂν δὲ μὴ παραδῶσιν ἐξειργασμένα ταῦτα τῇ νέᾳ βουλῇ, τὴν δωρεὰν οὐκ ἔστιν αὐτοῖς λαβεῖν. ἐπὶ γὰρ τῆς ὕστερον βουλῆς
[Col. 25.] *λαμβάνουσιν.* ‖ *ποιεῖται δὲ τὰς τριήρεις, δέκα ἄνδρας ἐξ ἀ[πάντων]*
2 *ἑλομένη τριηροποιούς. ἐξετάζει δὲ καὶ τὰ οἰκοδομήματα τὰ δημόσια πάντα, κἄν τις ἀδικεῖν αὐτῇ δόξῃ τῷ τε δήμῳ τοῦτον [ἀπ]οφαίνει καὶ καταγνόντος παραδίδωσι δικαστηρίῳ.*

5 ἐὰν H-L. **7** ἀ[πάντων] K, H-L: ἑαυτῆς Wayte, α[ὐτῶν] K-W, B coll. 48, 13. **10** ΚΑΤΑΓΝΟΥϹΑ K, H-L: καταγνόντος K-W, B. <τῷ> δικαστηρίῳ Gennadios, Naber (H-L, idem τῷ non addunt in c. 45, 5 et c. 55, 7).

---

the βουλή we find *νεωρίων ἐπιμεληθῆναι*. From B.C. 347 to 323 an annual property tax amounting to ten talents was raised for the building *τῶν νεωσοίκων καὶ τῆς σκευοθήκης* (CIA ii 270).

καινὰς τριήρεις] Twenty, according to Diod. xi 43. In B.C. 356/5 the Council failed to build the requisite number of new triremes; Androtion nevertheless moved that they should receive the customary compliment of a golden crown; and for this he was attacked under a *γραφὴ παρανόμων* (Dem. *Androt.* 8).

ἢ τετρήρεις] In the list of the fleet for B.C. 330/29 eighteen quadriremes are mentioned: CIA ii 807 *b* 76—79, *τετρήρεις δ' ἐμ μὲν τοῖς νεωρίοις παρέδομεν* ΠΙΙΙ, *ἐμ πλῷ δὲ* Δ. For the three years between B.C. 334/3 (*ib.* 804) and the above date the lists are missing. The earliest notice of quinqueremes is in B.C. 325/4, when seven are mentioned, *ib.* 809 *d* 90, the list for the previous year (*ib.* 808 *d* 36) giving quadriremes, as well as triremes, but no quinqueremes (Boeckh, *Seeurkunden*, p. 76). The archonship of Cephisophon, B.C. 329/8, is mentioned in c. 54 § 7. Hence the date of the treatise falls after B.C. 328, and before 325, the year in which quinqueremes appear for the first time (C. Torr in *Athenaeum*, Feb. 7, 1891; and Lipsius in *Leipzig Verhandlungen*, 1891, p. 45).

ἀρχιτέκτονας] 'naval architects,' or 'master ship-builders.' These are not mentioned elsewhere, but the names of 35 such persons are known to us from inscriptions (Boeckh, *Seeurkunden*, pp. 93—100). The *ἀρχιτέκτων* of Dem. *de Cor.* § 28 is a different kind of official,—the manager of the Theatre of Dionysus.

παραδῶσιν] *οἱ βουλευταί*. **τὴν δωρεὰν**] Dem. *Androt.* § 8, (*νόμου*) *οὐκ ἐῶντος ἐξεῖναι μὴ ποιησαμένῃ τῇ βουλῇ τὰς τριήρεις αἰτῆσαι τὴν δωρεάν* (= *τὸν στέφανον*, *ib.* 36).

τριηροποιούς] In Dem. *Androt.* 17 the treasurer of this body is mentioned: *οὐχ ἡ βουλὴ γέγονεν αἰτία τοῦ μὴ πεποιῆσθαι τὰς ναῦς, ἀλλ' ὁ τῶν τριηροποιῶν ταμίας ἀποδρὰς ᾤχετο ἔχων πένθ' ἡμιτάλαντα*. The reference to the *τριηροποιοί* in Aeschin. *c. Ctes.* 30 implies that they were an *ἀρχὴ αἱρετή*: *οὓς αἱ φυλαὶ καὶ αἱ τριττύες καὶ οἱ δῆμοι ἐξ ἑαυτῶν αἱροῦνται τὰ δημόσια χρήματα διαχειρίζειν*. This last passage suggests that they were chosen by the tribes out of candidates nominated by the demes: the text implies that the choice rested with the βουλή. Probably the latter ratified, as a matter of course, the selection made by the tribes. Among similar commissioners elected by the tribes, may be mentioned the *τειχοποιοί* and the *ταφροποιοί*; the *ἀποστολεῖς* were certainly elected *ἐξ Ἀθηναίων ἁπάντων* (Gilbert, i 250).

§ 2. **οἰκοδομήματα**] The inspection of public buildings has not hitherto been known to be one of the functions of the βουλή. But it is naturally connected with their duty of letting *τεμένη καὶ ἱερὰ καὶ οἰκίας*, [Xen.] *de Vect.* iv 19.

ἀποφαίνει] 'formally denounces,' 'reports.' Ant. *de Chor.* 9, *ἀποφῆνασι καὶ ἐξελέγξασιν*, Lys. 20 § 7 (*οἱ κατήγοροι*) *ἀδικοῦντας ἀποφαίνουσι*, and Dinarch. *c. Dem.* 48, *κἀμοῦ κατέγνω πρότερον ἡ βουλή* (the Areopagus), and *ib.* 49, *ἀπέφηνεν ἡ βουλή*.

παραδίδωσι δικαστηρίῳ] CIA i 59, (B.C. 410), *[τὴν βουλὴν βουλεῦσ]αι ἐν τῇ πρώτῃ ἕδ[ρᾳ ἐν τῷ βουλευτηρί]ῳ καὶ κολάζειν τῶν δωρο[δοκησάντων καταψ]ηφιζομένην, καὶ εἰς δικασ[τήριον αὐτοὺς εἰσάγει]ν, καθότι ἂν δοκῇ αὐτῇ· τ[ῶν δὲ δικαστῶν τοὺς] παρόντας ἀποφαίνειν, κτλ.*

47. *συνδιοικεῖ δὲ καὶ ταῖς ἄλλαις ἀρχαῖς τὰ πλεῖστα. πρῶτον μὲν γὰρ οἱ ταμίαι τῆς Ἀθηνᾶς εἰσὶ μὲν δέκα, κλ[ηροῦται] δ' εἷς ἐκ τῆς φυλῆς, ἐκ πεντακοσιομεδίμνων κατὰ τὸν Σόλωνος νόμ[ον (ἔτι γὰρ ὁ ν]όμος κύριός ἐστιν), ἄρχει δ' ὁ λαχὼν κἂν πάνυ πένης ᾖ. παραλαμβάνου[σι δὲ τ]ό τε ἄγαλμα τῆς Ἀθηνᾶς καὶ τὰς Νίκας καὶ τὸν ἄλλον κόσμον καὶ τὰ χρ[ήματ]α ἐναντίον τῆς βουλῆς.*

XLVII 2 *κληροῦται δ'* Gertz (edd.): *κληρωτοὶ* K[1]. **2, 7** *κληροῦνται δ' εἷς ἐξ ἑκάστης φυλῆς* Wyse coll. 61, 2;—*ἐκ τῆς φυλῆς* <*ἑκάστης*> Bury. **6** '*χρήματα ἱερά τε καὶ δημόσια* Phot. et Bekk. An.' K-W.

TESTIM. **§ 1** * Harp. *ταμίαι*:...*ἀρχή τις παρ' Ἀθηναίοις ἦν οἱ ταμίαι δέκα τὸν ἀριθμόν. παραλαμβάνουσι δ' οὗτοι "τό τε ἄγαλμα—βουλῆς," ὥς φησιν Ἀρ. ἐν Ἀθ. πολ.* Phot. (Bekk. *An.* 306, 7): *ἄρχοντές εἰσιν Ἀθήνησι κληρωτοὶ ἀπὸ τῶν πεντακοσιομεδίμνων, οἳ τὰ ἐν τῷ ἱερῷ τῆς Ἀθηνᾶς ἐν ἀκροπόλει χρήματα ἱερά τε καὶ δημόσια φυλάττουσιν, ἀλλὰ καὶ αὐτὸ τὸ ἄγαλμα τῆς Ἀθηνᾶς* <*καὶ τὸν κόσμον* add. Bekk. *An.* l. c.>. Pollux viii 97: *ταμίαι τῆς θεοῦ κληρωτοὶ μὲν ἐκ πεντακοσιομεδίμνων ἦσαν, τὰ δὲ χρήματα παρελάμβανον τῆς βουλῆς παρούσης.*

XLVII § 1. **οἱ ταμίαι τῆς Ἀθηνᾶς]** The full title is *ταμίαι τῶν ἱερῶν χρημάτων τῆς Ἀθηναίας*. This is found in the inventories of the treasures in the Parthenon, the Hecatompedos and the Pronaos (CIA i 117—175), and in the records of payments from the treasure of Athena for public purposes (*ib.* 179, 180, 188). Cf. Hicks, *Hist. Inscr.* nos. 50, 51, 53, 54. The short title, *ταμίας τῶν τῆς θεοῦ*, is found in inscr. of 325 (Boeckh, *Seeurkunden*, p. 465). See Boeckh II v; Schömann, p. 418; Gilbert, i 234; and cf. note on 30 § 2, *ταμίας τῶν ἱερῶν χρημάτων κτλ.*; also Panske, *de Magistratibus Atticis*, 1890, i pp. 13—46.

Σόλωνος νόμον] 8 § 1, *κληροῦν τοὺς ταμίας ἐκ πεντακοσιομεδίμνων.*

ἄρχει δ' ὁ λαχὼν *κτλ.*] Solon's law regulating the qualification was practically obsolete. Cf. c. 7 *ult.*

παραλαμβάνουσι *κτλ.*] The accounts of the treasures transferred in each year were annually audited; they were also inscribed on blocks of stone once in four years (*ἐκ Παναθηναίων ἐς Παναθήναια*).

τὸ ἄγαλμα] The statue is not mentioned in our inventories; but from B.C. 385 there is proof of the existence of a separate specification respecting it. This was kept in the temple and the treasurers certified in each year that the statue and its appurtenances were all safe *κατὰ τὴν στήλην* (Köhler in *Mittheilungen*, 1879, p. 89, quoted by Hicks, p. 89). The *ἄγαλμα* is incidentally named in CIA ii 652, 42 (B.C. 398).

τὰς Νίκας καὶ τὸν ἄλλον κόσμον] About 435/4 B.C. the treasures of the Parthenon included golden figures of *Νίκη*, CIA i 32, B 2, *τὰς Νί[κας τὰς χρυ]σᾶς καὶ τὰ π[ομπεῖα]*. The number was probably ten. About 407/6 eight of these were melted down and made into gold coin, the *καινὸν χρυσίον* of Arist. *Ran.* 720 (see Schol.). Seven of the pedestals of these figures were still in existence between 377 and 367 (CIA ii 678, 47). In the earliest inventory after the archonship of Eucleides a *χρυσῆ Νίκη* is mentioned (CIA ii 642). This *Νίκη*, which was nearly two talents (52 kilogr. = 115 lb.) in weight, was probably made out of the proceeds of the confiscated property of the Thirty (Michaelis, *Parthenon*, p. 301). The same *Νίκη* is entered in an inventory of the *ταμίαι τῶν ἱερῶν χρημάτων τῆς Ἀθηναίας καὶ τῶν ἄλλων θεῶν*, who existed as a joint body from about 403 to 389 B.C., to be separated again in 385. It is also named in CIA ii 677, B.C. 367.

Under the financial administration of Lycurgus (B.C. 338/7—326/5) part of the surplus of the public revenues was spent on preparing a number of golden *Νῖκαι*, which were set apart among the treasures on the Acropolis. The decree of Stratocles, preserved in [Plut.] ii 852, recites that Lycurgus *αἱρεθεὶς ὑπὸ τοῦ δήμου χρήματα πολλὰ συνήγαγεν εἰς τὴν ἀκρόπολιν καὶ παρασκευάσας τῇ θεῷ κόσμον Νίκας τε ὁλοχρύσους πομπεῖά τε χρυσᾶ καὶ ἀργυρᾶ καὶ κόσμον χρυσοῦν εἰς ἑκατὸν κανηφόρους* (cf. *ib. vit. Lycurg.* § 5, *πομπεῖα τε χρυσᾶ καὶ ἀργυρᾶ τῇ πόλει κατεσκεύασε καὶ Νίκας χρυσᾶς*, and Paus. i 29, 16, *κατεσκεύασε δὲ πομπεῖα τῇ θεῷ καὶ Νίκας χρυσᾶς καὶ παρθένοις κόσμον ἑκατόν*). It was in B.C. 334 that, according to the *λόγος ταμιῶν τῆς θεοῦ* and a special commission acting with them, part of the surplus handed over by the *ταμίας τῶν*

2 ἔπειθ' οἱ πωληταὶ δέκα μέν εἰσι, κληροῦται δ' εἷς ἐκ τῆς φ[υλῆς. μισ]θοῦσι δὲ τὰ μισθώματα πάντα καὶ τὰ μέταλλα πωλοῦσι, καὶ τὰ τέλη [μετὰ τ]οῦ ταμίου τῶν στρατιωτικῶν καὶ τῶν ἐπὶ τὸ θεωρικὸν ᾑρημένων ἐναντίον τῆς [βουλῆς] κατακυροῦσιν ὅτῳ ἂν ἡ βουλὴ χειροτονήσῃ· καὶ τὰ πραθέντα μέταλλα, [τά τ'] ἐργάσιμα τὰ εἰς τρία ἔτη πεπραμένα, καὶ τὰ συγκεχωρημένα τὰ

11 *μέταλλα* [*ὅσα*] K;............*ει* H-L (in papyro scriptum non ει, sed αρ vel αϲ vel αι; *μ. τά τ'* K-W (B), ΜΕΤΑΛΛΑ ΤΑΤΑΡΕΡΓ deletis αρ sec. K-W). In archetypo erat fortasse ΤΑ Τ ΑΡΓΑ Κ̀ ΤΑ ΕΡΓΑCΙΜΑ. **12** *συγκεχωσμένα* Poland, Busolt.

§§ **2, 3** *Harp. *πωληταί: οἱ μὲν πωληταὶ ἀρχή τίς ἐστιν Ἀθήνησι, δέκα τὸν ἀριθμὸν ἄνδρες, εἷς ἐκ φυλῆς ἑκάστης. διοικοῦσι δὲ τὰ πιπρασκόμενα ὑπὸ τῆς πόλεως πάντα, τέλη καὶ μέταλλα καὶ μισθώσεις καὶ τὰ δημευόμενα...διείλεκται δὲ περὶ αὐτῶν καὶ Ἀρ. ἐν Ἀθ. πολ.* Fere eadem in Bekk. *An.* 291, 17 et Lex. Dem. Patm. p. 14. Pollux viii 99: *πωληταὶ τὰ τέλη πιπράσκουσι "μετὰ τῶν ἐπὶ τὸ θεωρικὸν ᾑρημένων," καὶ τὰς "τῶν ἐξ Ἀρείου πάγου" μετὰ τὸν πρότερον λόγον φυγόντων οὐσίας καὶ τὰ δεδημευμένα* (Frag. 401², 441³).

στρατιωτικῶν was spent *εἰς τὰς Νίκ[ας καὶ] τὰ π[ομ]πεῖα* (CIA ii 739). These may be identified with certainty as the *Νῖκαι* of the text. **κόσμος** refers in part to the *κόσμος κανηφορικός* (CIA ii 162, frag. *c* 10), including *δίφροι, ὑποδερίδες* (necklaces), *ἀμφιδέαι* (bracelets), and *στέφανοι* (ii 741 B *c* 3—5). Cf. Michaelis, *Parthenon*, p. 292; Boeckh, note 719 Fränkel; Foucart, *Les Victoires en or de l'Acropole, Bull. de corr. hellén.* xii 283—; and Dürrbach, *Lycurgue*, pp. 80—91.

§ 2. **πωληταί**] Hermann, *Staatsalt.* § 151, 2; Schömann, p. 417; Gilbert, i 227; Panske, *de Magistratibus Atticis*, i p. 10.

μισθοῦσι κτλ.] 'farm out the public contracts.' Thus the contracts for setting up tablets inscribed with public documents (*στῆλαι*) were let out by the *πωληταί* (Ditt. no. 13, 51; 43, 35; 45, 8). The contract for building the walls of Athens in 334—326 is let out by the same body (CIA ii 167).

τὰ μέταλλα πωλοῦσι] By the 'sale of the mines' is meant the sale of the right of working them. The 'purchaser,' who may be more correctly described as the lessee, paid a fixed price together with one twenty-fourth part of the net produce as a perpetual tax. The ordinary price of a share was one talent. See Boeckh, *On the Silver Mines of Laurium*, Appendix to *Publ. Econ.*, ed. Lewis. In CIA ii 780—783, and 782 b (p. 513), we have fragments of *διαγραφαὶ μετάλλων* drawn up by the *πωληταί*.

τὰ τέλη] Most of the tolls, customs and taxes were farmed by *τελῶναι* (Boeckh, III viii; Gilbert, i 335; *Dict. Ant. s.v.*).

τοῦ ταμίου τῶν στρατιωτικῶν] The management of military finances, which, in the fifth century, had been entrusted to the *ἑλληνοταμίαι*, was entrusted in B.C. 338 to a new officer called the *ταμίας τῶν στρατιωτικῶν*. The first to hold this office was Callias, the brother-in-law of Lycurgus ([Plut.] *Vit. Lyc.* § 27). It was supposed by Boeckh (II vii) that it was immediately after the archonship of Eucleides that the *ἑλληνοταμίαι* were superseded by the *ταμίας τῶν στρ.* and the superintendents of the theoric fund. But as late as 347 B.C. we find the *ἀποδέκται* described as making payments *ἐκ τῶν στρατιωτικῶν χρημάτων* (*Ἀθήν.* vi 152), which implies that the *ταμίας τῶν στρ.* was not yet in existence (A. Schaefer in *Rhein. Mus.* xxxiii 431, quoted by Gilbert i 237 n. 3, and *Dem. u. s. Zeit*, II² 307 n. 2). In Boeckh, n. 317, Fränkel assigns 347 as the date when this office was instituted; but he is opposed by Hartel, *Studien*, p. 132 (Dürrbach, *Lycurgue*, p. 32). It is at present therefore impossible to assume any earlier date than 338 for its institution.—The same official took part in superintending the Panathenaic games (49 § 3).

τῶν ἐπὶ τὸ θεωρικὸν] These financial officers were apparently instituted under the administration of Eubulus, between 354 and 339. The plural here decides the question whether there was only one official of the name, or more. Boeckh (II vii, p. 249²) supposed that there were ten. The pl. in Aeschin. *c. Ctes.* 25, *οἱ ἐπὶ τὸ θ. κεχειροτονημένοι* used to be understood of successive holders of the office. Cf. Gilbert, i 230.

τρία ἔτη] It has hitherto been supposed

εἰς <τρία> ἔ[τη] πεπραμένα. καὶ τὰς οὐσίας τῶν ἐξ Ἀρείου
πάγου φευγόντων καὶ τῶν [ὀφειλε]τῶν ἐν[αντίον τῆς] βουλῆς
πωλοῦσιν, κατακυροῦσι δ' οἱ ἐννέα ἄρχοντες· καὶ τὰ τέλη τὰ εἰς
ἐνιαυτ[ὸν] πεπραμένα, ἀναγράψαντες εἰς λελευκωμένα γραμματεῖα
τόν τε πριάμενον καὶ [ὅσου] ἂν πρίηται, τῇ βουλῇ παραδιδόασιν.
ἀναγράφουσιν δὲ χωρὶς μὲν οὓς δεῖ κατὰ πρυ[τ]ανείαν ἑκάστην 3
καταβάλλειν εἰς δέκα γραμματεῖα, χωρὶς δ' οὓς τ[ρὶς τοῦ] ἐνιαυτοῦ,

13 *εἰς . ἔτη* K[3], K-W, '*εἰς γ' ἔτη* dubitanter nunc legit K', *εἰς τρία ἔτη* B: [*εἰς ἀεὶ*] H-L. **14** [*ὀφειλε*]*τῶν*? K[3]: [*ἐξ ἐφε*]*τῶν* dubitanter K-W; *ἀτίμων* (quod quondam conieci) acceperunt H-L; ΑΛΛ (i.e. *ἄλλως* vel *ἄλλοθεν*) post Τ(ΩΝ) agnosci posse putat B qui *τῶν* [*ἄλλοθεν ἐ*]*ν*[*αντίον*] dedit. **17** [*ὁπόσου*] Tyrrell, H-L: *ὅσου* spatio aptius K-W, K[3], B. **18** *τὴν* ante *πρυτανείαν* ins. B. **19** *τ*[*ρὶς τοῦ*] K-W, B; *τ*[*ελοῦντος*] K[1], *τέ*[*λει τοῦ*] K[23]; *πρὸ τέλους* H-L.

---

that the state never let the mines for a term of years, but only granted them on perpetual leases (Boeckh's *Silver Mines of Laurium*, § 7, p. 645).

We have already been told that the *πωληταί* 'sell the mines.' We are now told that they lease for a term of three years, not only the mines that are still workable, but also those that are the subject of special concessions. It is observed by Boeckh, *l. c.* p. 646, that it could 'scarcely have been compulsory upon a tenant to pay to the state the purchase money of a new mine, if, after having expended his trouble and capital, he was unsuccessful in finding any ore.' It may therefore be here suggested that a term of three years was fixed for a provisional letting of the lease, and that the annual payment of $\frac{1}{24}$ was not due until the three years had elapsed. Possibly the original purchase money was in the first instance paid conditionally, and was recovered in the event of no ore being found. In the other event, at the end of the three years the provisional lease would be 'confirmed' in the presence of the *βουλή*.

In connexion with the mines, a period of 'three years' is mentioned in Hyperides, *Eux.* col. xliv, and [Dinarchus] fragm. in Baiter and Sauppe, *Oratores Attici*, ii 325 *b* 4; but it seems to have no bearing on the present passage.

τὰ συγκεχωρημένα] possibly mines 'let under a special agreement' without the previous payment of purchase money. It has been suggested, however, that some word contrasted with *ἐργάσιμα* is needed, such as *συγκεχωσμένα*, exhausted mines with heaps of scoriae accumulated near them. Such mines, if they had reverted in any way to the state, would have to be 'sold' for a very much smaller sum. In CIA ii 782, shortly after the time of Lycurgus, we find mention of a (*μέταλλον*) *παλαιὸν ἀνασάξιμον*, 'an old mine reopened and worked afresh,' which is sold in the second *πρυτανεία* (*ib.* 780) for the small sum of 150 *dr.*

τῶν ἐξ Ἀρείου πάγου φευγόντων] In trials before the Areopagus a person accused of wilful murder might (except in cases of parricide) withdraw from Attica 'after delivering his first speech' (Dem. 23 § 69), and thus avoid the penalty of death (Pollux, viii 117). Such a person was never allowed to return; and, when any decree was passed to sanction the restoration of exiles, there was a special clause excluding *οἱ ἐξ Ἀρείου πάγου φεύγοντες*, Plat. *Leg.* 871 D. Their property was confiscated, Dem. 23 § 45, *τῶν ἀνδροφόνων τῶν ἐξεληλυθότων, ὧν τὰ χρήματα ἐπίτιμα.*

τῶν ὀφειλετῶν] If a debt to the treasury remained unpaid at the ninth prytany, it was doubled and the debtor's property sold (Andoc. *De Myst.* 73; Dem. *c. Nicostr.* p. 1255 § 27; *c. Neaer.* p. 1347 § 7).

λελευκωμένα γρ.] [Dem.] 46 § 11, (*γρ.*) *λελευκωμένον.* Lys. 9 § 6, (of a fine) *γράψαντες εἰς λεύκωμα τοῖς ταμίαις παρέδοσαν.* Dem. 24 *Timocr.* 23, (of a new law) *ἀναγράψας εἰς λεύκωμα.* Bekker, *Anecd.* p. 277, *λεύκωμά ἐστι πίναξ γύψῳ ἀληλιμμένος, πρὸς γραφὴν πολιτικῶν γραμμάτων ἐπιτήδειος.*

§ 3. **καταβάλλειν...καταβολὴν**] of payment by instalments, as in [Dem.] *c. Neaer.* 27, *ἐωνημένος τὴν πεντηκοστὴν τοῦ σίτου...καὶ δέον αὐτὸν καταβάλλειν τὰς καταβολὰς εἰς τὸ βουλευτήριον κατὰ πρυτανείαν*, *c. Timocr.* 98, *αἱ τῶν τελῶν καταβολαί.*

*γραμματεῖον κατὰ τὴν καταβολὴν ἑκάστην ποιήσαντες, χωρὶς δ'
οὓς [ἐπὶ] τῆς ἐνάτης πρυτανείας. ἀναγράφουσι δὲ καὶ τὰ χωρία
καὶ τὰς οἰκίας [τὰ ἀπογραφ]έντα καὶ πραθέντα ἐν τῷ δικαστηρίῳ·
καὶ γὰρ ταῦθ' οὗτοι πωλ[οῦσιν. ἔστι] δὲ τῶν μὲν οἰκιῶν ἐν πέντε
ἔτεσιν ἀνάγκη τὴν τιμὴν ἀποδοῦναι, τῶν δὲ χωρίων ἐν δέκα·*
4 *καταβάλλουσιν δὲ ταῦτα ἐπὶ τῆς ἐνάτης πρυτανείας. εἰσ[φέ]ρει
δὲ καὶ ὁ βασιλεὺς τὰς μισθώσεις τῶν <τε>μενῶν ἀναγράψας ἐν
γραμματε[ίοις λελευκ]ωμένοις. ἔστι δὲ καὶ τούτων ἡ μὲν μίσθωσις*

22 [*τὰ ἀπογραφ*]*έντα* Wyse, K-W, H-L, K[3]; *τἀπογρ.* B; *τ*[*ὰ μισθωθ*]*έντα* K[1]. **23** [*ἔστι*] *δὲ* K-W, K[3], B: *καὶ* H-L. **25** *καταβάλλουσι* H-L. *εἰσφέρει* K-W, K[3], B: *παραδίδωσι* quondam Paton (H-L). **26** Τ(ΩΝ) Μ(ΕΝ)ΩΝ: *τῶν τεμενῶν* Wyse, Blass, (K-W, H-L, K[3]). **27** suppleverunt Jackson, van Leeuwen (edd.).

ἐνάτης πρυτανείας] The time when the purchase-money for the *τέλη* was paid: Dem. *Timocr.* 93, 98.

ἀπογραφέντα] In CIA i 274—281 we have the accounts rendered by the *πωληταί* for property (probably that of the Ἑρμοκοπίδαι) which had been confiscated and sold by the state. See also CIA ii 777, and 779 (*τάδ' ἐπράθη ἐδάφη ἀτίμητα ὄντα*); also 811 col. *c* 183—195, *κατεβλήθη ἐξ ἀπογραφῆς, ἧς ἀπέγραψεν—τοῦτο κατεβλήθη πρὸς πωλητὰς τοὺς ἐφ' Ἡγησίου ἄρχοντος*, B.C. 324/3; cf. Boeckh, *Seeurkunden*, p. 543.

πέντε...δέκα] These details have been hitherto unknown. The only definite statement about the rent of a house is in Isaeus 11 § 42, where a house in Melite worth 30 minas, and another at Eleusis worth 5, jointly produce an annual rent of 3 minas; so that in less than 12 years the occupant would have paid the value of the houses. In the same passage an estate at Thria, worth 150 minas, produces 12 minas per annum; so that in 12½ years the occupant would have paid the value of the estate.

§ 4. **ὁ βασιλεὺς**] The functions of this archon being mainly religious, he is here described as responsible for bringing the leases of sacred enclosures to the knowledge of the Council. Cf. CIA iv *fasc.* 2, 53 *a* (quoted by Wyse, *Class. Rev.* v 275 *a*): (418/7 B.C.) v. 3 *sqq.* *Ἀδούσιο[ς ε]ἶπε· εἶρξαι τὸ ἱερὸν τὸ Κόδρου καὶ τὸ Νηλέως καὶ τῆς Βασίλης* (Plat. *Charm.* 153 A) *κ[α]ὶ μισθῶσαι τὸ τέμενος κατὰ τὰς συνγραφάς, οἱ δὲ πωληταὶ τὴν εἷρξ[ιν] ἀπομισθωσάντων, τὸ δὲ τέμενος ὁ βασιλεὺς ἀπομισθωσάτω κατὰ [τ]ὰς ξυνγραφάς . . . . . τὸ δὲ ἀργύριον ἐς τὴν εἷρξιν ἀπὸ τοῦ τεμένους εἶναι, πρᾶξαι δὲ ταῦτα πρὶν ἢ ἐξιέναι τήνδε τὴν βουλὴν ἢ εὐθύνεσθαι χιλίαισι δραχμῆσι ἕκαστον κατὰ τὰ εἰρημένα.* v. 11 *sqq.*: *Ἀδούσιος εἶπε· τὰ μὲν ἄλλα καθάπερ τῇ βουλῇ· ὁ δὲ βασιλεὺς μ[ι]σθωσάτω καὶ οἱ πωληταὶ τὸ τέμενος τὸ Νηλέως καὶ τῆς Βασίλης κα[τ]ὰ τὰς ξυνγραφὰς εἴκοσι ἔτη. τὸν δὲ μισθωσάμενον εἶρξαι τὸ ἱε[ρ]ὸν τὸ Κόδρου καὶ τὸ Νηλέως καὶ τῆς Βασίλης τοῖς ἑαυτοῦ τέλεσιν. ὁπ[ό]σην δ' ἂν ἄλφῃ μίσ[θ]ωσιν τὸ τέμενος κατὰ τὸν ἐνιαυτὸν ἕκαστον, καταβαλλέτω τὸ ἀργύριον ἐπὶ τῆς ἐνάτης πρυτανείας τοῖς ἀποδέκται[ς], οἱ δὲ ἀποδέκται τοῖς ταμίαισι τῶν ἄλλων θεῶν παραδιδόντων κατὰ τὸν νόμον. ὁ δὲ βασιλεὺς ἐὰν μὴ ποιήσῃ τὰ ἐψηφισμένα ἢ ἄλλος τις οἷς προστέτακται περὶ τούτων, ἐπὶ τῆς Αἰγηίδος πρυτανείας, εὐθυνέσθω μυρίησι δραχμῆσιν. τὸν δὲ ἐ[ω]νημένον τὴν ἰλὺν ἐκκομίσασθαι ἐκ τῆς τάφρου ἐπὶ τῆσδε τῆς βουλῆς ἀποδόντα τὸ ἀργύριον τῷ Νηλεῖ ὅσου ἐπρίατο. ὁ δὲ βασιλεὺς ἐξαλει[ψ]άτω τὸν πριάμενον τὴν ἰλὺν ἐπειδὰν ἀποδῷ τὴμ μίσθωσιν, τὸν δὲ μισθωσάμενον τὸ τέμενος καὶ ὁπόσου ἂν μισθώσηται ἀντενγραψάτω ὁ βασιλεὺς ἐς τὸν τοῖχον καὶ τοὺς ἐγγυητὰς κατὰ τὸν νόμον ὅσπερ κεῖται (περὶ) τῶν τεμενῶν.* Cf. J. R. Wheeler in *American Journal of Archaeology*, iii, nos. 1 and 2.

The *βασιλεὺς* is associated with other officials in an inscr. of B.C. 329, Ἐφ. Ἀρχ. iii, 1883, p. 110 B 29, [*τῶν τεμενῶν*] *ἃ ἐμίσθωσαν ὁ βασιλεὺς καὶ οἱ πάρεδροι καὶ οἱ ἐ[πι]στάτ[αι οἱ Ἐ]λε[υσινόθεν καὶ οἱ ἐπιμεληταὶ τῶν] μυστηρίων.*

τὰς μισθώσεις τῶν τεμενῶν] [Dem.] 43 § 58, *τοὺς μὴ ἀποδιδόντας τὰς μισθώσεις τῶν τεμενῶν.* Didymus ap. Harpocr. *s.v.* *ἀπὸ μισθωμάτων* (Isocr. *Areop.* 11)... *ἐκ τῶν τεμενικῶν προσόδων.* [Xen.] *de Vect.* iv 19, *μισθοῦνται γοῦν καὶ τεμένη καὶ ἱερὰ καὶ οἰκίας, καὶ τέλη ὠνοῦνται παρὰ τῆς πόλεως.* Plat. *Leg.* 759 E.

εἰς ἔτη δέκα, καταβάλλεται δ' ἐπὶ τῆς [ἐνάτης] πρυτανείας· διὸ
καὶ πλεῖστα χρήματα ἐπὶ ταύτης συλλέγεται τῆς πρυ[τα]νείας.
εἰσφέρεται μὲν οὖν εἰς τὴν βουλὴν τὰ γραμματ[εῖα τὰ] τὰς κατα- 5
βολὰς ἀναγεγραμμένα, τηρεῖ δ' ὁ δημόσιος· ὅταν δ' ᾖ χρ[ημάτων
καταβ]ολή, παραδίδωσι τοῖς ἀποδέκταις αὐτὰ ταῦτα καθε[λὼν ἀπὸ
τῶν] ἐπιστυλίων ὧν ἐν ταύτῃ τῇ ἡμέρᾳ δεῖ τὰ χρήματα καταβλη-
[θῆν]αι [καὶ ἀ]παλειφθῆναι· τὰ δ' ἄλλα ἀπόκειται χωρὶς ἵνα μὴ
προεξαλ[ειφθῇ].

48. [εἰσὶ] δ' ἀποδέκται δέκα, κεκληρωμένοι κατὰ φυλάς·

30 κ? ΤΑϹ, καὶ per errorem scriptum putat K : [τὰ] τὰς K-W, B ; πάντων τὰς H-L sed spatium non sinit. **32** καθε[λὼν] ἀπ[ὸ τῶν] van Leeuwen (H-L, K³, B) : καθελ[ὼν] ἐκ [τῶν] K-W sed λ incertum et ἐκ valde dubium putat K. **33** ΔΕΙ, ante τὰ χρήματα K³, K-W, B : om. H-L. καταβληθῆναι καὶ K-W, K³, B : καταβληθέντα δεῖ H-L. **34** ΑΛΕΙΦΗΝΑΙ corr. K. **35** προεξαλ[ειφθῇ] K³, K-W, B : προεξα[λεί-φηται] H-L.

TESTIMONIA. **XLVIII §§ 1, 2** * Harp. ἀποδέκται :...'Αρ. δ' ἐν τῇ 'Αθ. πολ. δεδήλωκεν ὡς δέκα τε εἴησαν καὶ ὡς "παραλαβόντες—χρήματα" τῆς βουλῆς ἐναντίον "ἐν τῷ—δημοσίῳ." καὶ ἁπλῶς ἃ πράττουσι διασαφεῖ. Bekk. *An.* 198, 1 (Etym. M. 124, 41 ;

ἔτη δέκα] CIA ii 1059 (= *Inscr. Brit. Mus.* p. 24 xiii), in B.C. 321, μισθοῦσι Πειραιεῖς Παραλίαν καὶ 'Αλμυρίδα καὶ τἆλλα τεμένη ἅπαντα for a term of ten years. The same term of years is recorded in a lease granted by a φρατρία in B.C. 300 (*ib.* 600), and also in an Attic inscr. relating to some land in Delos and Rheneia belonging to the Delian temple, CIA i 283 (B.C. 434). Wyse (*Class. Rev.* v 275 *b*) quotes a Delian inscr. of B.C. 250 : ἐμισθώσαμεν δὲ καὶ τὰ τεμένη τὰ τοῦ θεοῦ εἰς ἔτη δέκα κατὰ τὴν ἱερὴν συγγραφήν (Homolle, *Les Archives de l'Intendance Sacrée à Délos*, p. 19 n. 1).

πλεῖστα—πρυτανείας] It may further be noticed that all who had not paid their debts to the treasury by this date (the penultimate prytany of the Attic year) had their property sold by the state (see note on ὀφειλετῶν, *supra*, § 2).

§ 5. **ὁ δημόσιος**] 'the public clerk'; slaves were employed as ἀντιγραφεῖς or 'checking-clerks.' *Dict. Ant. s.v.*, and Gilbert, i 323 n. 3.

ἀποδέκταις] 48 § 1. **αὐτὰ ταῦτα**, *sc.* τὰ γραμματεῖα.

ἐπιστυλίων] It has been suggested that this term is metaphorically applied to the 'columns' in the list of accounts (*Class. Rev.* v 181 *b*); but obviously it cannot mean 'columns' at all, but something that rests *upon* them. In architecture the ἐπιστύλιον is generally the 'architrave' (Plut. *Per.* 13 § 5 ; Vitruv. iv 3 § 4, 'supra epistylium conlocandi sunt triglyphi cum suis metopis'; CIG 4608 (A.D. 151), παραστάδας καὶ κιόνια καὶ τὰ ἐπάνω αὐτῶν ἐπιστύλια καὶ ψαλίδας): it is even said to be sometimes used of the whole of the entablature (Smith, *Dict. Ant. s.v. ad fin.*), but I know of no authority for this statement.

In the present passage I should understand it to mean a shelf supporting a series of 'pigeon-holes,' and itself supported by wooden pedestals, in the office of the public clerk. The entablature in Doric architecture, with its originally open metopes alternating between the triglyphs, may well have suggested a metaphorical term for a shelf of 'pigeon-holes' used for the preservation of public documents. K-W translate it *repositorium* or *loculi*. Haussoullier suggests a modern parallel in 'certains bureaux turcs (bureaux de douane ou de santé), où les papiers sont serrés dans les sacs que l'on accroche aux poutres et que l'on décroche au moyen d'un long bâton.'

προεξαλειφθῇ] not found elsewhere. ἐξαλείφειν, however, is found as a synonym of ἀπαλείφειν, being applied to annulling laws and decrees (in Lys. 1 § 48, and Andoc. *De Myst.* 76), and to cancelling debts (in Dem. 25 § 70, ἐξαλήλιπται τὸ ὄφλημα, and CIA i 32, 10, ἀποδόντων τὰ χρήματα καὶ ἐξαλειφόντων). Cf. CIA iv *fasc.* 2, 53 *a*, ἐξαλειψάτω contrasted with ἀντενγραψάτω.

XLVIII § 1. **ἀποδέκται**] 'general receivers.' These officials were instituted

οὗτοι δὲ παραλαβόντες τὰ [γρα]μματεῖα, ἀπαλείφουσι τὰ καταβαλλόμενα χρήματα ἐναντίον [τῆς βουλῆς] ἐν τῷ βουλευτηρίῳ, καὶ πάλιν ἀποδιδόασιν τὰ γραμματεῖα [τῷ δη]μοσίῳ· κἄν τις ἐλλίπῃ καταβολήν, ἐνταῦθ' ἐγγέγραπται, και διπλ[οῦν ἀ]νάγκη τὸ [ἐλλ]ειφθὲν καταβάλλειν ἢ δεδέσθαι, καὶ ταῦτα εἰσπρά[ττειν ἡ
2 βο]υλὴ καὶ δῆσαι [κυρ]ία κατὰ τοὺς νόμους ἐστίν. τῇ μὲν οὖν προτεραίᾳ δέχονται τὰ χρ[ήματα] καὶ μερίζουσι ταῖς ἀρχαῖς, τῇ δ' ὑστεραίᾳ τόν τε μερισμὸν εἰσ[φέρου]σι γράψαντες ἐν σανίδι καὶ καταλέγουσιν ἐν τῷ βουλευτηρίῳ, καὶ π[ροτιθέ]ασιν ἐν τῇ βουλῇ εἴ τίς τινα οἶδεν ἀδικοῦντα περὶ τὸν μερισ[μὸν ἢ ἄρ]χοντα ἢ ἰδιώτην, καὶ γνώμας ἐπιψηφίζουσιν ἐάν τίς τι δοκῇ ἀ[δικεῖν.
3 κ]ληροῦσι δὲ καὶ λογιστὰς ἐξ αὐτῶν οἱ βουλευταὶ δέκα τοὺς

XLVIII 4 ἀποδιδόασι H-L. **5** ΕΝΤΕΥΘΕΝΓΕ, ἐντεῦθεν γέγραπται K : ἐνταῦθ' ἐγγέγραπται Herwerden, Kontos, Gertz (H-L, K-W, B). διπλοῦν ἀνάγκη van Leeuwen (K-W, H-L, K[3], B). **9** εἰσφέρουσι van Leeuwen (K-W, H-L, K[3]). **10** προτιθέασιν olim conieci (H-L), idem habent K-W, K[3], B.

Zonaras 234; Bekk. *An.* 427, 13): ἄρχοντες κληρωτοί, δέκα τὸν ἀριθμὸν κατὰ φυλήν εἰσιν, οἵτινες παρελάμβανον καὶ ἀπεδέχοντο τὰ γραμματεῖα τῶν ὀφειλόντων τῷ δημοσίῳ... εἶτα ἐξήταζον τά τε ὀφειλόμενα καὶ τὰ ἀποδιδόμενα χρήματα σὺν τῇ βουλῇ καὶ ἐμέριζον εἰς ἃ χρὴ ἀναλίσκειν (Frag. 400[2], 440[3]). Schol. in Aeschin. 3 § 25 ἀποδέκται ἦσαν οἱ δεχόμενοι τὰ χρήματα τῶν καταβολῶν κτλ.

§ 3 *Harp. λογισταί:...εἰσὶ δὲ τὸν ἀριθμὸν δέκα (ἑκάστης φυλῆς εἷς Schol. in Aeschin.

by Cleisthenes to take over most of the duties previously performed by the κωλακρέται (Androtion ap. Harpocr. *s. v.*). They are mentioned in Dem. *c. Timocr.* §§ 162, 197, Aesch. *c. Ctes.* 25, *Pol.* 1321 *b* 31, ἄλλη δ' ἀρχὴ πρὸς ἣν αἱ πρόσοδοι τῶν κοινῶν ἀναφέρονται, παρ' ὧν φυλαττόντων μερίζονται (cf. l. 8 **μερίζουσι**) πρὸς ἑκάστην διοίκησιν· καλοῦσι δ' ἀποδέκτας τούτους καὶ ταμίας, also in an inscr. of 418/7 B.C. quoted in note on § 4, ὁ βασιλεύς. See Boeckh, II iv; Schömann, p. 417; Gilbert, i 226; and *Dict. Ant. s. v.*; also Panske, *de Magistratibus Atticis*, i 46—60.

τὰ καταβαλλόμενα χρήματα ἐναντίον τῆς βουλῆς] CIA ii 807 col. *b* 15, τοῦτο κατεβάλομεν ἀποδέκταις in B.C. 330/29; *b* 30, in B.C. 329/8; 803 col. *d* 93 and 138, ὃ εἰς βουλευτήριον κατεβάλομεν, B.C. 360 and 363.

ἐλλίπῃ καταβολήν] 'fail to pay an instalment.' Polyb. iv 60, 2, ἐλλελοιπέναι τινὰ τῶν ὀψωνίων.

ἐνταῦθ' ἐγγέγραπται] 'it is entered in this document'; this seems preferable to ἐντεῦθεν γέγραπται, 'a note is made of it from this record' (K.). ἐγγράφειν is specially applied to entering the names of state-debtors, Dem. 25 § 70 (cf. L and S, II 3).

δῆσαι κυρία] In Dem. *c. Timocr.* 98 the speaker argues that, owing to the law proposed by Timocrates, allowing debtors to the treasury to find securities instead of making prompt payments, the βουλὴ (as well as the δικαστήρια) ceases to be κυρία δῆσαι. Cf. 45 § 1.

§ 2. **μερίζουσι**] CIA ii 38, 18 (not later than Ol. 100 = B.C. 380-), μερίσαι δὲ τὸ ἀργύριον—τοὺς ἀποδέκτας ἐκ τῶν καταβαλλομένων χρημάτων ἐπειδὰν τὰ ἐκ τῶν νόμων μερίσωσι. *Ib.* 181, τοὺς δὲ ἀποδέκτας μερί[σαι τῷ ἀρκε]θεώρῳ ὃς ἂν ἀεὶ ἀρκ[ε]θ[εωρήσῃ τὸ] ἀργύριον. 115 *b* 44, [τὸ ἀργ]ύριον τοῦτο μερίζειν τ[οὺς ἀποδ]έκτας τῷ ταμίᾳ τοῦ δήμ[ου εἰς τὸν] ἐνιαυτὸν ἕκαστον. 834 *b* (B.C. 329/8) col. ii 3, τὸ μερισθὲν εἰς τὰ ἔργα παρ' ἀποδεκτῶν ἐπιστάταις Ἐλευσινόθεν. *Pol.* 1321 *b* 31, quoted above. Cf. Boeckh, i 210 n. *a*, Fränkel.

μερισμὸν] 'the apportionment'; rarely found in this sense. For exx. see Dittenberger, no. 344, 18, 21, 23.

σανίδι] rare in sing. Dem. 25 § 70 (of the record of a debt) ἡ σανὶς ἡ παρὰ τῇ θεῷ κειμένη.

προτιθέασιν] 44 § 3.

§ 3. **λογιστὰς**] These are identical in name and number with those mentioned in 54 § 2. Both bodies are appointed by lot; but the λογισταὶ in the text are a

λογιουμένους τ[αῖς ἀρ]χαῖς κατὰ τὴν πρυτανείαν ἑκάστην. κλη- 4
ροῦσι δὲ καὶ εὐθύνους, ἕνα τῆς φυλῆς ἑκάστης, καὶ παρέδρους δύο ἑκάστῳ τῶν εὐθύνων, οἷς ἀναγκαῖόν ἐστι ταῖς ἀ[γορ]αῖς κατὰ τὸν ἐπώνυμον τὸν τῆς φυλῆς ἑκάστης καθῆσθαι, κἄν τις βού[ληταί] τινι τῶν τὰς εὐθύνας ἐν τῷ δικαστηρίῳ δεδωκότων, ἐντὸς τριῶν ἡ[μερῶν ἀφ'] ἧς ἔδωκε τὰς εὐθύνας, εὔθυναν, ἄν τ' ἰδίαν ἄν τε

16 *ταῖς ἀ[γορ]αῖς* K (K-W): *ταῖς εὐθύναις* H-L et B invita papyro. ΚΑΤΑ (K, B): *παρὰ* van Leeuwen (K-W, H-L). **17** *ἑκάστης* K, K-W; *ἕκαστον* H-L; *ἑκάστο[ι]ς* B; post *τ* prior tantum pars litterae *η* vel *ο* dispici potest. **19** *ἄν τ' ἰδίαν ἄν τε δημοσίαν* optime Gertz (H-W, K[3], *ἐάν τ'—ἐάν τ'*—H-L).

3 § 15; cf. ib. § 9), *οἱ τὰς εὐθύνας τῶν διῳκημένων ἐκλογίζονται ἐν ἡμέραις λ̄, ὅταν τὰς ἀρχὰς ἀποθῶνται οἱ ἄρχοντες...διείλεκται περὶ τούτων Ἀρ. ἐν τῇ Ἀθ. πολ., ἔνθα δείκνυται ὅτι διαφέρουσι τῶν εὐθυνῶν.* Pollux viii 99: *καὶ τούτους ἡ βουλὴ κληροῖ κατ' ἀρχὴν ὡς παρακολουθεῖν τοῖς διοικοῦσιν.*

§ 4 * Harp. *εὔθυνοι:—δέκα τὸν ἀριθμὸν ἦσαν ἄνδρες, παρ' οἷς ἐδίδοσαν οἱ πρεσβεύσαντες ἢ ἄρξαντες ἢ διοικήσαντές τι τῶν δημοσίων τὰς εὐθύνας. διείλεκται περὶ αὐτῶν Ἀρ. ἐν τῇ Ἀθ. πολ.* Phot. *εὔθυνος: ἀρχὴ ἦν τις. ἐξ ἑκάστης δὲ φυλῆς ἕνα κληροῦσι· τούτῳ δὲ δύο παρέδρους* (Frag. 405[2], 445[3]).

---

committee of the Council. They are therefore to be distinguished from the board of *λογισταί*, who, with their *συνήγοροι*, audit the accounts of all officials at the close of their term of office. The officials appointed by lot are enumerated in c. 50—64; c. 54, in which the *λογισταί* are named, is introduced with the words: *κληροῦσι δὲ καὶ τάσδε τὰς ἀρχάς.* This implies that the officials in question have not been mentioned before. The existence of a committee of the Council, side by side with a board of the same name, appears to be supported by the analogy of the committee entitled *οἱ ἐπὶ τὸ θεωρικὸν ᾑρημένοι* (CIA ii 739), and the *βουλευτὴς* described as *ἐπὶ τὸ θεωρικόν* (CIA ii 114 *c* 5), existing by the side of the official board *οἱ ἐπὶ τῷ θεωρικῷ.* The double sense of *λογισταὶ* is confirmed by Pollux viii 99, *λογισταὶ δύο ἦσαν ὁ μὲν τῆς βουλῆς ὁ δὲ τῆς διοικήσεως, καὶ τούτους ἡ βουλὴ κληροῖ κατ' ἀρχὴν ὡς παρακολουθεῖν τοῖς διοικοῦσιν* (Lipsius, *Leipzig Verhandl.* pp. 66, 67). *λογισταὶ δύο* is the reading in Bekker's best MS; the rest have *δύο δ'*, making it refer to the *ἀντιγραφεύς* (see 54 § 3).

τοὺς λογιουμένους—πρυτανείαν ἑκάστην] Lys. 30 § 5, *οἱ μὲν ἄλλοι τῆς αὑτῶν ἀρχῆς κατὰ πρυτανείαν λόγον ἀποφέρουσι* (*ἀναφέρουσι* MSS). The text shews that this passage was rightly understood by Schömann, as referring to the accounts which had to be presented to the *λογισταί*, and not to the *ἐπιχειροτονία τῶν ἀρχῶν* (43 § 4). '*ἀναφέρειν* nihil aliud esse potest quam quod alibi dicitur *λόγον ἐγγράφειν*, hoc est perscriptam rationem ad eos, quibus ea examinanda est, deferre, quemadmodum ipsum Lysiam mox hoc verbo *ἐγγράψαι* uti videmus, et Aeschines quoque *ἀποφέρειν λόγον πρὸς τοὺς λογιστάς* dicit, in Ctesiph. § 22, eodem sensu quo paullo ante, § 20, *λόγον ἐγγράφειν πρὸς τοὺς λογιστὰς* dixerat' (*Opusc. Acad.* i 295).

§ 4. **εὐθύνους**] 'Examiners of accounts.' Harp. in *Testim.* At the audit of accounts by the board of *λογισταί*, the *εὔθυνοι* were entitled to bring charges against the *ὑπεύθυνος*. The assessors of the *εὔθυνοι* are mentioned in Andoc. *De Myst.* 78, *ὅσων εὔθυναί τινές εἰσι κατεγνωσμέναι ἐν τοῖς λογιστηρίοις ὑπὸ τῶν εὐθύνων καὶ* (*ἢ* MSS) *τῶν παρέδρων*, and in CIA 809 *b*, *ὀφειλέτω ὁ μὴ ποιήσας μυρίας δραχμὰς ἱερὰς τῇ Ἀθηνᾷ καὶ ὁ εὔθυνος καὶ οἱ πάρεδροι ἐπάναγκες αὐτῶν καταγιγνωσκόντων ἢ αὐτοὶ ὀφειλόντων.* In CIA ii 571 (B.C. 368), the *εὔθυνος* (of a deme) is mentioned together with his *πάρεδροι*; and *ib.* 578, the *εὔθυνος* (of another deme) with the *λογιστής* and the *συνήγοροι.*

The text shews that, even after the audit had been passed, officials were liable to be prosecuted by private persons in respect to the manner in which they had discharged their duties. Cf. Lipsius in *Leipzig Verhandl.* pp. 66, 67.

ταῖς ἀγοραῖς] *i.e.* at the regular meetings held by the several tribes for the transaction of tribal business. CIA ii 555, *τῇ κυρίᾳ ἀγορᾷ κρύβδην ψηφισαμένων τῶ[ν φυλετῶν] ἐν τῇ ἀκροπόλει,* *δ[ημοσίαν], ἐμβαλέσθαι, γράψας εἰς πινάκιον λελευκωμένον τοὔνομα τό <τε> [αὐτο]ῦ καὶ τὸ τοῦ φεύγοντος καὶ τὸ ἀδίκημ' ὅ τι ἂν ἐγκαλῇ, καὶ τίμημα [ἐπιγραψά]μενος ὅ τι ἂν αὐτῷ δοκῇ, δίδωσιν τῷ εὐθύνῳ· ὁ δὲ λαβὼν τοῦτο καὶ ἀ[νακρίνας], ἐὰν ⟦μὲν⟧ καταγνῷ, παραδίδωσιν τὰ μὲν ἴδια τοῖς δικασταῖς τοῖς κατὰ δ[ήμους, τοῖς] τὴν φυλὴν ταύτην εἰσάγουσιν, τὰ δὲ δημόσια τοῖς θεσμοθέτα[ις ἐπι-]γράφει, οἱ δὲ θεσμοθέται, ἐὰν παραλάβωσιν, πάλιν εἰσάγουσιν [τὴν] εὔθυναν εἰς τὸ δικαστήριον, καὶ ὅ τι ἂν γνῶσιν οἱ δικαστ[αί, τοῦτο κύ]ριόν ἐστι.*

49. *δοκιμάζει δὲ καὶ τοὺς ἵππους ἡ βουλή, κἂν μέν τις καλὸν*

21 *τὸ αὐτοῦ* Blass, Richards, H-L, K^3; *τό τε αὐτοῦ* K-W. **22** *[ἐπιγραφό]μενος* Wyse, Lipsius (K^3); *[ἐπιγραψά]μενος* H-L, B; *ὑ[πογραφ]όμενος* K-W, sed *υ* valde incertum putat K. *δίδωσι* H-L. **23** *ἀ[νακρίνας]* Wayte, Lipsius: *ἀ[ναγνοὺς]* Blass, K-W, H-L, K^3, quamquam vel propter proximum *καταγνῷ* suspectum; *ἀ[κούσας]* K^1. *μὲν* secl. K-W, B. **24** legendum fortasse *τὰ μὲν ἴδια παραδιδῶσιν*, alioqui in altero membro verbum languet. *τοῖς τὴν* B; *οἱ τὴν* cet. **25** ΕΙϹΑΓΟΥϹΙΝ K, H-L, B: *δικάζουσιν* coni. Richards, Thompson (K-W). *[ἀνα]γράφει* K, H-L; *[ἐγ]γράφει* Lipsius; *[ἐπι]γράφει* B; *[τίμημα δ' ὑπο]γράφει* K-W, sed spatium non sinit. **26** *εἰσάγουσι* H-L. **28** *τοῦτο κύριόν ἐστι* van Leeuwen (K-W, H-L, K^3, B).

XLIX 1—2 *καλὸν ἵππον* K-W (K^3, B); *καλ[ῶς ἔχων]* K^1 qui nunc in papyro ONI agnoscit; *κατάστασιν* Wyse (H-L).

---

554 *b*, *ἐν τῇ ἀγορᾷ* (of the tribe Pandionis), 564, *ὅταν ἀγορὰν ποιῶσιν* (Gilbert, i 192).

ἄν τ'...ἄν τε] Kühner, § 541.

ἐμβαλέσθαι] of formally 'putting in' a document, Dem. p. 1014, 25, *ἐμβεβλημένος οὐδεμίαν μαρτυρίαν*, 1104, 6; 1203, 26, *ἐμβαλομένου γὰρ ἐμοῦ τὸν ὅρκον εἰς τὸν ἐχῖνον.*

τίμημα ἐπιγραψάμενος] Arist. *Plut.* 480, *τί δῆτά σοι τίμημ' ἐπεγράψω τῇ δίκῃ;* Lex ap. Aeschin. 1 § 16, *τίμημα ἐπιγραψάμενος.* Dem. 29 § 8, *τῶν ἐπιγεγραμμένων* ('the damages claimed') *ἐτίμησαν.*

§ 5. **ἀνακρίνας—καταγνῷ**] The examination of the accounts by the *λογισταί* and *συνήγοροι* is described as an *ἀνάκρισις*. Ar. ap. *Lex. Rhet. Cant. s.v.* *λογισταί*, (*συνήγοροι*) *συνανακρίνουσι τούτοις* (*sc.* *τοῖς λογισταῖς*). For the general use of *ἀνακρίνω*, as applied to the official conducting an *ἀνάκρισις*, cf. Dem. *Olymp.* 31, *ὁ ἄρχων ἀνέκρινε πᾶσιν ἡμῖν τοῖς ἀμφισβητοῦσιν*, and Isaeus, *Dicaeog.* 32, *ἀνακρίναντες ἡμᾶς πολλάκις οἱ διαιτηταί.* Cf. 56 § 6 (*γραφαί* and *δίκαι*) *ἃς ἀνακρίνας εἰς τὸ δικαστήριον εἰσάγει.* The statement that the *ἀνάκρισις* was also called an *ἀνάγνωσις* rests on a wrong reading in Dem. 53 § 22. The object of an *ἀνάκρισις* was to determine by a preliminary examination, *εἰ ὅλως εἰσάγειν χρή* (Harp. *s.v.*).

δικασταῖς...κατὰ δήμους] 16 § 5; 26 § 3; 53.

τὴν φυλὴν ταύτην εἰσάγουσιν] 53 § 2, *παραδιδόασι...τοῖς τὴν φυλὴν τοῦ φεύγοντος δικάζουσιν*, 58 § 2, *τοὺς τὴν φυλὴν δικάζοντας*, Lys. *Pancl.* 2, *τοὺς τῇ Ἱπποθωντίδι δικάζοντας*, and Isaeus frag. 1, *ὅτι πρὸς τὴν φυλὴν τοῦ κεκτημένου αἱ πρὸς δούλους λαγχάνονται δίκαι* (Meier and Schömann, p. 90 *n.* Lips.).

ἐπιγράφει] Aeschin. 1 § 35, *μέχρι πεντήκοντα δραχμῶν καθ' ἕκαστον ἀδίκημα ἐπιγράφειν τοῖς πράκτορσιν.*

One of the other suggestions, *ἐγγράφει*, is supported by Aeschin. 3 § 20, *λόγον ἐγγράφειν πρὸς τοὺς λογιστάς*, Lys. 30 § 5, Dem. 24 § 199, Arist. *Vesp.* 996 (Lipsius).

The construction is slightly irregular, as a principal verb is not wanted, *παραδίδωσι* being the verb to both clauses—*μὲν* and *δέ*. The irregularity is removed by striking out *μέν*, but this involves a needless hiatus and is not absolutely necessary.

ὅ τι ἂν—κύριόν ἐστι] Cf. c. 45, l. 10.

XLIX § 1. **δοκιμάζει—τοὺς ἵππους**] Xen. *Oec.* ix 15, *ἡ βουλὴ ἵππους καὶ ἱππέας δοκιμάζει*, *Hipparch.* i 8, (*ἡ πόλις*) *προσέταξε τῇ βουλῇ συνεπιμελεῖσθαι τοῦ ἱππικοῦ*, and iii 9—14. A *patera* from Orvieto, now in the Berlin Museum, ἵ[ππον ἔχ]ων κακῶς δοκῇ τρέφειν, ζημιοῖ τῷ σίτῳ, τοῖς δὲ μὴ δυναμένοις [ἀκολ]ουθεῖν, ἢ μὴ 'θέλουσι μένειν ἀναγ<ώγοις> οὖσι, τροχὸν ἐπὶ τὴν γν[άθον ἐπιβάλλει, καὶ ὁ τ]οῦτο παθὼν ἀδόκιμός ἐστι. δοκιμάζει δὲ καὶ τοὺς πρ[οδ]ρ[όμους, ὅσοι ἂν α]ὐτῇ δοκῶ‖σιν [Col. 26.] ἐπιτήδειοι προδρομεύειν εἶναι, κἄν τιν' ἀποχειροτονήσῃ, καταβέ-

3 ἀκολουθεῖν Wyse (K^3, B); τρέφειν K^1, τρέχειν Campbell, K-W, H-L. θέλουσι λΓ (vel λλ) K, B. ΜΕΝΕΙΝ ΑΝΑΓΟΥϹΙ; μένειν, ἀναγράφουσι Campbell; μένειν, ἐπιβάλλουσι R D Hicks; μένειν ἀναγ<ώγοις> οὖσι H-L (K^3); μένειν ἀλλ' ἀνάγουσι B (intrans. certe usurpatur in Arist. *Av.* 383, 400, 1720 et Xen. *Cyr.* vii 1, 45 ἀναγαγὼν ἐστρατοπεδεύσατο, sed non de equis dictum); (post θέλουσιν) σημεῖον ἐπιβάλλουσι K-W. **4** γνάθον Hicks coll. Hesych. s.v. τρυσίππιον; ἐπιβάλλουσι post μένειν posuit Hicks, post γνάθον H-L (K^3), sed (ut videtur) novem tantum litteris locus relictus; praestat igitur ἐπιβάλλει (B). [καὶ ὁ τ]οῦτο K, H-L, B: [καὶ ὁ ἵππος ὁ τ]οῦτο (post γνάθον) K-W. **5** οἵτινες K^1; οἳ ἂν K^2 (H-L); [κρίνουσα, οἳ ἂ]ν <αὐ>τῇ K-W sed spatium non sufficit: ὅσοι ἂν K^3 (B); inter προδρόμους et αὐτῇ sex septemve litterarum spatium superest. **6** ΤΙΝΑΠ[ΡΟ]Χ (ut infra, v. 7): τιν' ἀποχ. J B Mayor, Campbell, Wyse, Blass, etc. K-W, H-L, K^3.

TESTIMONIA. **XLIX 4** Hesych. τρυσίππιον et ἵππου τροχός, infra exscriptus. Phot. ἵππου τροχός: τὸ τρυσίππιον διὰ τὸ τοῖς διὰ γῆρας ἐκτρυχωθεῖσιν ἵπποις ἐκτυποῦσθαι τροχόν, ἀπολεγόντων αὐτοὺς τῶν στρατηγῶν.

---

represents three horsemen in *chlamys* and *petasus* leading their horses by the bridle past two standing figures who examine them as they pass. A third figure is seated and is entering memoranda on a scroll resting on his knees. In the centre is a ἱπποτοξότης standing beside his horse. The subject is doubtless a ἵππων δοκιμασία (*Archaeol. Zeitung*, 37, 1880, pl. 15; Duruy, *Hist. d. Grecs*, ii p. 177; Daremberg and Saglio, *s.v.* Dokimasia, p. 327; Schreiber's *Bilderatlas*, i 40, 7). On the δοκιμασία of the ἱππεῖς and their horses, see Martin, *Les Cavaliers Athéniens*, pp. 328—334.

τοῖς μὴ δυναμένοις ἀκολουθεῖν κτλ.] Xen. *Mem.* iii 3, 4, ἐὰν οὖν...παρέχωνταί σοι τοὺς ἵππους οἱ μὲν οὕτως κακόποδας ἢ κακοσκελεῖς ἢ ἀσθενεῖς ὥστε μὴ δύνασθαι ἀκολουθεῖν, οἱ δὲ οὕτως ἀναγώγους ὥστε μὴ μένειν ὅπου ἂν σὺ τάξῃς...τί σοι τοῦ ἱππικοῦ ὄφελος ἔσται; *Hipparch.* i 13, τοὺς...ἱππέας ἡ βουλὴ ἄν μοι δοκεῖ προειποῦσα ὡς...τὸν μὴ δυνάμενον ἵππον ἀκολουθεῖν ἀποδοκιμάσει, ἐπιτεῖναι ἂν τρέφειν τε ἄμεινον καὶ ἐπιμελεῖσθαι μᾶλλον τῶν ἵππων. **ἀνάγωγος** is also an epithet of 'unmanageable' dogs in *Mem.* iv 1, 3.

τροχὸν——ἐπιβάλλει] Hesych. *s. v.* τρυσίππιον· τὸν χαρακτῆρα τὸν ὑπὸ τῆς βουλῆς ἐν ταῖς δοκιμασίαις τοῖς ἀδυνάτοις καὶ τετρυμμένοις <τῶν ἵππων ἐπιβαλλόμενον addidit Petitus>, ἵνα μηκέτι στρατεύωνται, τὸ παλαιὸν ἐκάλουν τρυσίππιον· τροχὸς δ' ἦν ὁ ἐπιβαλλόμενος χαρακτὴρ τῇ γνάθῳ τῶν ἵππων. Hesych. ἵππου τροχός· τῶν γεγηρακόσιν ἵπποις ἐχάραττον ἐπὶ τὴν γνάθον σημεῖον, τροχοῦ σχῆμα ἔχον. ἐκαλεῖτο δὲ καὶ τρυσίππιον. Aelius Dionys. apud Eustath. ad *Od.* iv 562, p. 1517, 8, τρυσίππιον· ἔγκαυμα ἵππου γεγηρακότος ἐπὶ τῆς γνάθου, ὅμοιον τροχῷ. Crates, *frag.* 30 (Kock i 140), ἵππῳ γηράσκοντι τὰ μείονα κύκλ' ἐπίβαλλε, quoted by Zenob. iv 41,...μετῆκται δὲ ἀπὸ στρατιωτικῶν ἵππων, οἷς γηράσκουσιν ἐπέβαλλον τὸ καλούμενον τρυσίππιον· ἔστι δὲ τοῦτο σιδηροῦς τροχίσκος...ὃν ἐκπυροῦντες ἐπέβαλλον ταῖς σιαγόσι τῶν ἵππων. Eupolis 318 (Kock i 343) ἀλλ' ὥσπερ ἵππῳ μοι 'πιβαλεῖς τρυσίππιον; Cf. Photius *s.v.* τρυσίππιον and ἵππου τροχός, and Pollux vii 186. As suggested by Kaibel and Wilamowitz, most of the above explanations probably rest ultimately on a scholium on the *Taxiarchi* of Eupolis founded on the present passage.

προδρόμους] 'mounted skirmishers.' The term is applied by Hdt. to 'horsemen in advance of an army.' Xen. *Hipparch.* i 25, uses it of 'javelin-men' under the command of a cavalry officer: εἰ τοὺς ἀμφὶ σὲ προδρόμους κοσμήσαις μὲν ὅπλοις ὡς κάλλιστα, ἀκοντίζειν δὲ μελετᾶν ἐξαναγκάσαις ὡς μάλιστα, κτλ. In the march of Alexander to the Granicus, the Paeonians formed a special corps of πρόδρομοι for purposes of reconnoitring (Arr. *An.* i 12, 7; Droysen, *Kriegsalterthümer*, p. 117, 3).

προδρομεύειν] not found elsewhere.

καταβέβηκεν] 'dismounts' (as dis-

βηκεν οὗτος. δοκιμάζει δὲ καὶ τοὺς ἁμίππους, κἄν τιν' ἀποχειροτονήσῃ, πέπαυται μισθοφορῶν οὗτος.
2 τοὺς δ' ἱππέας καταλέγουσιν οἱ καταλογεῖς, οὓς ἂν ὁ δῆμος χειροτονήσῃ δέκα ἄνδρας· οὓς δ' ἂν καταλέξωσι, παραδιδόασι τοῖς ἱππάρχοις καὶ φυλάρχοις, οὗτοι δὲ παραλαβόντες εἰσφέρουσι τ[ὸν] κατάλογον εἰς τὴν βουλήν, καὶ τὸν πίνακ' ἀνοίξαντες, ἐν ᾧ κατασεσημασμένα τὰ ὀνόματα τῶν ἱππέων ἐστί, τοὺς μὲν ἐξομνυμένους τῶν πρότερον ἐγγεγραμμένων μὴ δυνατοὺς εἶναι τοῖς σώμασιν ἱππεύειν ἐξαλείφουσι, τοὺς δὲ κατειλεγμένους [κ]αλοῦσι, κἂν μέν τις ἐξομόσηται μὴ δύνασθαι τῷ σώματι ἱππεύειν ἢ τῇ οὐσίᾳ, τοῦτον ἀφιᾶσιν, τὸν δὲ μὴ ἐξομνύμενον διαχειροτονοῦσιν οἱ βουλευταί, πότερον ἐπιτήδειός ἐστιν ἱππεύειν

7 ΑΝΙΠΠΟΥϹ : ἁμίππους Newman, Wyse, Blass, K-W, H-L, K[3]. ΤΙΝΑΠΡΟΧ (ut supra, v. 6). **12** ΠΙΝΑΚΑΝΟΙΞΑΝΤΕϹ : πίνακ' ἀν. K-W, B ; πίνακα ἀν. K, H-L. Κ(ΑΤΑ)ϹΕϹΗϹΜ(ΕΝ)ΑϹΜ(ΕΝ)Α. **13** ΕΝΓΕΓΡ. **15** ΕΞΟΜΗϹΗΤΑΙ : ἐξομόσηται K, H-L ; ἐξομνύηται K-W (B).

---

qualified); used differently in [Dem.] 42 § 24 of giving up riding, καταβέβηκεν ἀπὸ τῶν ἵππων.

ἁμίππους] 'infantry fighting in the ranks of the cavalry.' Thuc. v 57, 2, (of the Boeotians at Delium) ὁπλῖται, ψιλοί, ἱππῆς and ἅμιπποι. Xen. *Hell.* vii 5, 24 (Epameinondas) ἁμίππους πεζοὺς συνέταξεν αὐτοῖς (= τῷ ἱππικῷ); the opposite side was ἔρημον πεζῶν ἁμίππων (23); the MSS have in both cases ἀνίππ., corrected by Morus. Xenophon recommends their use: *Hipparch.* v 13, ἀσθενὲς τὸ πεζῶν ἔρημον ἱππικὸν πρὸς τὸ ἁμίππους πεζοὺς ἔχον. Harpocr. *s. v.*...οἱ σὺν ἵπποις στρατευόμενοι...μήποτε (perhaps) πρόδρομοί τινές εἰσιν οἱ ἅμα τοῖς ἱππεῦσι τεταγμένοι· Φιλόχορος γοῦν ἐν τῇ ιϛ' φησὶ καὶ προδρόμους. Ar., in *Pol.* 1321 *a* 17, speaks of generals οἳ συνδυάζουσι πρὸς τὴν ἱππικὴν δύναμιν καὶ ὁπλιτικὴν τὴν ἁρμάττουσαν τῶν ψιλῶν. Cf. Martin, *Les Cavaliers Athéniens*, p. 410.

§ 2. **οἱ καταλογεῖς**] These officials (who bear the same name as the καταλογεῖς under the Four Hundred, Lys. 30 § 13, but are not mentioned elsewhere) are described as employed in drawing up the roll of the cavalry; they hand it over to the Hipparchi and Phylarchi, to be brought by them before the Council. The fact that the βουλὴ conducted the δοκιμασία of the ἱππεῖς was already known (Xen. *Oec.* ix 15). In Lys. 14 § 10, 'Αλκιβιάδης ἐτόλμησεν ἀναβῆναι... οὔτε ὑφ' ὑμῶν δοκιμασθείς, the pronoun loosely identifies the δικασταὶ with the βουλευταί. The text shews that no proceedings before a lawcourt were involved in a δοκιμασία ἱππέων.

The term κατάλογος is applied to the official list of the ἱππεῖς in Lys. 16 § 13 (of Mantitheus), προσελθὼν ἔφην τῷ 'Ορθοβούλῳ (doubtless his Phylarchus) ἐξαλεῖψαί με ἐκ τοῦ καταλόγου, *ib.* § 6, τοὺς φυλάρχους ἀπενεγκεῖν τοὺς ἱππεύσαντας. The Hipparchi, as well as the Phylarchi, were responsible for the κατάλογος, as had already been pointed out by Bake, *Scholica Hypomnemata*, v 150, 170: the text shews that it was drawn up in the first instance by the καταλογεῖς.

τὸν πίνακ'] The κατάλογος of the ἱππεῖς under the Thirty is described as drawn up on a σανίδιον (Lys. 16 § 6) or σανίδες, Lys. 26 § 10, ὡς ἱππευκότος αὐτοῦ ἐπὶ τῶν τριάκοντα τοὔνομα ἐν ταῖς σανίσιν ἐνεγέγραπτο.

κατασεσημασμένα] Plat. *Leg.* 756 E, (in the scheme proposed for the appointment of the βουλή) τὰ κατασημανθέντα ὀνόματα ἐξενεγκεῖν τοὺς ἄρχοντας ἰδεῖν πᾶσι τοῖς πολίταις.

ἐξομνυμένους] Pollux viii 55 (ἐξωμοσία) ὅταν τις ἢ πρεσβευτὴς αἱρεθεὶς ἢ ἐπ' ἄλλην τινὰ δημοσίαν ὑπηρεσίαν, ἀρρωστεῖν ἢ ἀδυνατεῖν φάσκων ἐξομνύηται αὐτὸς ἢ δι' ἑτέρου. Schol. on Arist. *Eccl.* 1026.

ἐγγεγραμμένων] Lys. 26 § 10, quoted above, and 16 § 6 (as emended by Markland). Arist. *Eq.* 1371, ὁπλίτης ἐντεθεὶς ἐν καταλόγῳ ἐγγεγράψεται.

ἐξαλείφουσι] Lys. 16 § 7, ἐκ τούτων (the lists of ἱππεῖς under the Thirty) ῥᾴδιον ἦν ἐξαλειφθῆναι τῷ βουλομένῳ.

ἢ οὔ· κἂν μὲν χειροτονήσωσιν, ἐγγράφουσιν εἰς τὸν πίνακα, εἰ δὲ μή, καὶ τοῦτον ἀφιᾶσιν.

ἔκρινεν δέ ποτε καὶ τὰ παραδείγματα καὶ τὸν πέπλον ἡ βουλή, 3 νῦν δὲ τὸ δικαστήριον τὸ λαχόν· ἐδόκουν γὰρ οὗτοι καταχαρίζεσθαι τὴν κρίσιν. καὶ τῆς ποιήσεως τῶν Νικῶν, καὶ τῶν ἄθλων τῶν εἰς τὰ Παναθήναια, συνεπιμελεῖται μετὰ τοῦ ταμίου τῶν στρατιωτικῶν.

δοκιμάζει δὲ καὶ τοὺς ἀδυνάτους ἡ βουλή· νόμος γάρ ἐστιν ὃς 4

20 ἔκρινε H-L. Κ(ΑΙ) ΤΟΝ K, K-W, H-L: τὰ εἰς τὸν B.

§ **4** *Harp. ἀδύνατοι:...οἱ ἐντὸς τριῶν μνῶν κεκτημένοι τὸ σῶμα πεπηρωμένοι [πεπηρωμένον codd. praeter E (Suid.), ubi οἱ πεπηρωμένοι τὸ σῶμα; τὸ δὲ σῶμα πεπηρωμένοι

---

§ 3. **παραδείγματα**] Of the architect's plan for the temple at Delphi, Hdt. v 62. The construction of such a παράδειγμα is illustrated by an inscr. cited by Homolle, *Les Archives de l'Intendance Sacrée à Délos*, p. 13, n. 4 : εἰς τὸ παράδειγμα τοῦ προπύλου πίνακα ἠγοράσαμεν παρὰ Χρησίμου ΔΗ. ἐπισκευάσαντι τὸν πίνακα Θεοδήμωι ΗΗ. λευκώσαντι τὸν πίνακα ἀμφοτέρωθεν ΗΗΗ. The wood used for the πίναξ is also mentioned: τοῦ φοίνικος τοῦ περιγενομένου ἀπὸ τοῦ παραδείγματος (Wyse, *Class. Rev.* v 275 *b*). Cf. CIA ii 807 *b* 101 (B.C. 330), παράδειγμα τῶν κεραμίδων τῶν ἐπὶ τὴν σκευοθήκην and *ib.* 126, π. ξύλινον τῆς τριγλύφου τῆς ἐνκαύσεως. The last item recurs in B.C. 325, *ib.* 809 col. *e* 8, and in B.C. 324, *ib.* 811 col. *b* 193.

τὸν πέπλον] woven by ἐργαστῖναι, under the superintendence of two ἀρρηφόροι and certain priestesses. In CIA ii 477 we have an inscr., ascribed to B.C. 98, referring to a proposal to dedicate to Athene a silver φιάλη with 100 *dr.* on the part τῶν παρθένων τῶν ἠργασμένων τῇ Ἀθηνᾷ τὰ ἔρια τὰ εἰς τὸν πέπλον. These were the ἐργαστῖναι αἱ τὸν πέπλον ὑφαίνουσαι (Hesych.). In CIA ii 956, 957, 957 *b*, we have lists of ἐργαστῖναι (one of them containing more than 100 names) arranged under their respective tribes, many of them belonging to the Εὐπατρίδαι (*Bull. Corr. Hellén.* xiii 170; *Mittheil.* viii 65). A new *peplus* was made every year (Schol. Arist. *Eq.* 566). The *loci classici* are collected in Michaelis, *Parthenon*, Anhang II §§ 151—164, 171—3, p. 328–9. Suidas, *s. v.* ἐπιώψατο, describes the ἀρρηφόροι as selected by the archon βασιλεύς, while Harpocr., *s. v.* ἀρρηφορεῖν, states that four ἀρρηφόροι ἐχειροτονοῦντο δι' εὐγένειαν, and two of these ἐκρίνοντο to superintend the πέπλος. The text shews that the appointment was ultimately transferred to a law-court to secure an impartial selection.

νῦν δὲ τὸ δικαστήριον] The date of this transfer to a law-court of duties formerly entrusted to the Council is uncertain. The παράδειγμα of the σκευοθήκη designed by Philo was expounded in public by the architect himself:—Cic. *de Or.* i 62, 'Philonem illum architectum, qui Atheniensibus armamentarium fecit, constat perdiserte *populo* rationem operis sui reddidisse'; Val. Max. viii 12, 2, 'Philonem...rationem institutionis suae in *theatro* reddidisse constat.' It was constructed between B.C. 347/6 and 330/29.

The fact that the exposition took place before the 'people,' 'in the theatre,' is suggestive of a meeting of the ἐκκλησία rather than one of the βουλή. It is certainly inconsistent with an appearance before a δικαστήριον. There is more evidence for the theatre being used for meetings of the ἐκκλησία (Müller's *Bühnenalterthümer*, p. 73) than for those of the βουλή. The only evidence for the latter is CIA ii 482, B.C. 39—32.

Thus, the above passages respecting Philo suggest that the duty of deciding on παραδείγματα was in his time not yet transferred to a law-court; on the other hand, they do not refer to any hearing before the Council.

Νικῶν] 47 § 1.

τῶν ἄθλων] The musical, gymnastic, and equestrian contests. Among the minor contests were those in εὐανδρία (60 § 3), the Pyrrhic dance and the Lampadedromia (see Michaelis, *Parthenon*, Anh. II §§ 46—130, and Smith, *Dict. Ant. s. v.* Panathenaea). The special officials were the ten *Athlothetae* (60 § 1), who received subsidies from the ταμίαι ἱερῶν χρημάτων τῆς Ἀθηναίας (CIA i 188, 1—7).

ταμίου τῶν στρατιωτικῶν] 43 § 1.

§ 4. **τοὺς ἀδυνάτους**] Schol. Aeschin.

κελεύει τοὺς ἐντὸς τριῶν μνῶν κεκτημένους, καὶ τὸ σῶμα πεπηρωμένους ὥστε μὴ δύνασθαι μηδὲν ἔργον ἐργάζεσθαι, δοκιμάζειν μὲν τὴν βουλήν, διδόναι δὲ δημοσίᾳ τροφὴν δύο ὀβολοὺς ἑκάστῳ τῆς ἡμέρας.

καὶ ταμίας ἐστὶν αὐτοῖς κληρωτός.

συνδιοικεῖ δὲ καὶ ταῖς ἄλλαις ἀρχαῖς τὰ πλεῖσθ', ὡς ἔπος εἰπεῖν.

50. τὰ μὲν οὖν ὑπὸ τῆς βουλῆς διοικούμενα ταῦτ' ἐστίν. κληροῦνται δὲ καὶ ἱερῶν ἐπισκευασταὶ δέκα ἄνδρες, οἳ λαμβά-

28 δύ' ὀβολοὺς K-W, B : δύο ὀβολοὺς cum pap. K, H-L. **31** συνδιοικεῖ—εἰπεῖν delet Herwerden utpote 'ex capitis 47 initio maximam partem repetita, hic autem incommoda': eadem recte idcirco retinet K, quod talia Senatus officia nondum omnia sint commemorata.

post Bekkerum Dind.]. ἐλάμβανον δὲ οὗτοι δοκιμασθέντες ὑπὸ τῆς βουλῆς δύο ὀβολοὺς τῆς ἡμέρας ἑκάστης [ἢ ὀβολόν], ὥς φησιν 'Αρ. ἐν 'Αθ. πολ. Bekk. *An.* 345, 15 (cf. 200, 3) : οἱ μέρος τι βεβλαμμένοι τοῦ σώματος ὡς μηδὲ ἐργάζεσθαι· οἱ καὶ ἐχορηγοῦντο τὰ πρὸς τὸ ζῆν παρὰ τῆς πόλεως, μισθοφορούντων αὐτῶν (αὐτοῖς cod.) ὡς (τῶν cod.) ἐντὸς τριῶν μνῶν (om. cod.) περιουσίαν κεκτημένων. ἐδοκιμάζοντο δὲ οἱ ἀδύνατοι ὑπὸ τῆς τῶν πεντακοσίων βουλῆς καὶ ἐλάμβανον τῆς ἡμέρας, ὡς μὲν Λυσίας λέγει, ὀβολὸν ἕνα, ὡς δὲ Φιλόχορος, πέντε, 'Αρ. δὲ δύο ἔφη. Hesych. οἱ ἐντὸς κεκτημένοι τριῶν μνῶν παρὰ 'Αττικοῖς. ἐλάμβανον δὲ παρὰ τῆς βουλῆς δύο ὀβολούς (Frag. 430^2, 470^3).

i 103, κατὰ μῆνα (πρυτανείαν?) ἐκ τοῦ δημοσίου δίδοται τοῖς ἀδυνάτοις πολίταις μισθός· ἀδυνάτους δὲ πάντας λέγουσι τοὺς ὁπωσδηποτοῦν ἠχρειωμένους πρὸς ἐπικουρίαν ἑαυτῶν. At first it was only citizens who were disabled in war that received relief from the state. This institution is ascribed to Peisistratus in Plut. *Sol.* 31, ὁ νόμος ὁ τοὺς πηρωθέντας ἐν πολέμῳ δημοσίᾳ τρέφειν κελεύων. This limitation was afterwards removed. It is clear that the speaker in Lys. 24, ὑπὲρ τοῦ ἀδυνάτου, had never seen any service in the field; otherwise he would have mentioned the fact (Gilbert, i 329). The speech is addressed to the βουλὴ on the occasion of an εἰσαγγελία. The βουλὴ are there described as having given the grant (§ 7, ἔδοτε, and in more general terms § 22, πάλαι κοινῇ πάντες ἔδοτέ μοι). The grant had to be confirmed by each successive βουλή, as implied in § 26, τὴν αὐτὴν ψῆφον θέσθε περὶ ἐμοῦ ταῖς ἄλλαις βουλαῖς. It rested ultimately on a decree of the people, § 22, ἡ πόλις ἡμῖν ἐψηφίσατο τοῦτο τὸ ἀργύριον, but it does not follow that the case of each recipient was settled by decree.

μὴ δύνασθαι μηδὲν ἔργον ἐργάζεσθαι] Lys. 24 § 6, τέχνην κέκτημαι βραχέα δυναμένην ὠφελεῖν ἣν αὐτὸς μὲν ἤδη χαλεπῶς ἐργάζομαι.

δοκιμάζειν] The fact is stated by Harpocr., Bekker's *Anecd. Gr.* 345, 18, and Suidas.

δύο ὀβολοὺς] Hence in Harpocr. *s. v.* ἀδύνατοι the words ἢ ὀβολὸν must be struck out (as was suggested by Hulleman, *Quaestiones Graecae*, p. 5). The text is correctly quoted in Bekker's *Anecd. Gr.* 345, 15.

ταμίας] In B.C. 343/2, CIA ii 114, there were two βουλῆς ταμίαι. They superintended τὰ κατὰ ψηφίσματα ἀναλισκόμενα τῇ βουλῇ (114 B 61). Early in the third century we have an inscr. mentioning only one; CIA ii 329 Νικοκράτης βουλεύειν λαχὼν—καὶ ταμίας αἱρεθεὶς ὑπὸ τῆς βουλῆς εἴς τε τὰς θυσίας τοῖς............σιν μεμέρικεν τοῖς ἱεροποιοῖς—καὶ ὑπὲρ ἁπάντων ὧν ᾠκονόμηκεν ἀπολελόγισται τῇ βουλῇ ὀρθῶς καὶ δικαίως (Gilbert, i 254); cf. ii 431, 36.

§ 5. **συνδιοικεῖ—πλεῖσθ'**] 47 init.; 57 § 1, ὡς δ' ἔπος εἰπεῖν—διοικεῖ οὗτος πάσας.

ὡς ἔπος εἰπεῖν] c. 2 *ult.*, ὡς εἰπεῖν, 57 § 1, ὡς ἔπος εἰπεῖν.

L—LIII. *On minor officials appointed by lot.*

L § 1. **ἱερῶν ἐπισκευασταί**] 'repairers of temples'; not mentioned elsewhere. The small sum allowed for this department (30 minae) implies that their duties were unimportant. The word is used in an unofficial sense in Dem. *Androt.* 69.

νουτες τριάκοντα μνᾶς παρὰ τῶν ἀπο[δε]κτῶν, ἐπισκευάζουσιν τὰ μάλιστα δεόμενα τῶν ἱερῶν, καὶ ἀστυνόμοι δέκα. τούτων δὲ 2
πέντε [μὲν] ἄρχουσιν ἐν Πειραιεῖ, πέντε δ' ἐν ἄστει, καὶ τάς τε αὐλητρίδας καὶ τὰς ψαλτρίας [καὶ] τὰς κιθαριστρίας οὗτοι σκοποῦσιν, ὅπως μὴ πλείονος ἢ δυεῖν δραχμαῖν μισθωθήσονται, κἂν πλείους τὴν αὐτὴν σπουδάσωσι λαβεῖν, οὗτοι διακληροῦσι καὶ τῷ λαχόντι μισθοῦσιν. καὶ ὅπως τῶν κοπρολόγων μηδεὶς ἐντὸς δέκα σταδίων τοῦ τείχους καταβαλεῖ κόπρον ἐπιμελοῦνται, καὶ τὰς ὁδοὺς κωλύουσι κατοικοδομεῖν, καὶ δρυφάκτους ὑπὲρ τῶν ὁδῶν

L 3 ἐπισκευάζουσι H-L. **5** ΠΕΙΡΑΕΙ (K-W, B): Πειραιεῖ K, H-L. **7** ΔΥΓΕΙΝ
ΑΙC
ΔΡΑΧΜ... (fortasse δραχμαῖν scriptum erat); δυεῖν δραχμαῖς idcirco retinet K quod in titulis Atticis δυεῖν cum plurali tantum iunctum sit, Meisterhans, p. 162[2]; δυεῖν
CΤΑ
δραχμαῖν K-W[1], B; δυοῖν δραχμαῖν H-L, K-W[2]. **9** ΕΝΤΟCΙΔΙωΝ: ἐντὸς ῑ σταδίων J E B Mayor (K-W, H-L, K[3], B), ἐντὸς ῑ σταδίων <ἀπὸ>malebat van Leeuwen. **10** ΚΑΤΑΒΑΛΗΙ? ante corr. ΕΠΙΜΕΛΟΝΤΑΙ.

TESTIMONIA. **L § 2** * Harp. ἀστύνομος:...δέκα φησιν εἶναι τοὺς ἀστυνόμους 'Αρ. ἐν τῇ 'Αθ. πολ., "πέντε μὲν ἐν Πειραιεῖ, πέντε δ' ἐν ἄστει." τούτοις δέ φησι μέλειν περί τε τῶν αὐλητρίδων καὶ ψαλτριῶν καὶ τῶν κοπρολόγων καὶ τῶν τοιούτων (Frag. 408[2], 448[3]). Heraclidis epitom. Rose, Frag. 611, 8, καὶ τῶν ὁδῶν ἐπιμελοῦνται ὅπως μή τινες κατοικοδομῶσιν αὐτὰς ἢ δρυφάκτους ὑπερτείνωσιν.

ἀποδεκτῶν] 48 §§ 1, 2.

§ 2. **ἀστυνόμοι**] *Pol.* 1321 *b* 18, ἑτέρα δ' ἐπιμέλεια... ἡ τῶν περὶ τὸ ἄστυ δημοσίων καὶ ἰδίων, ὅπως εὐκοσμία ᾖ, καὶ τῶν πιπτόντων οἰκοδομημάτων· καὶ ὁδῶν σωτηρία καὶ διόρθωσις καὶ τῶν ὁρίων τῶν πρὸς ἀλλήλους... καλοῦσι δ' ἀστυνομίαν οἱ πλεῖστοι τὴν τοιαύτην ἀρχήν, *ib.* 1331 *b* 9 τὴν καλουμένην ἀστυνομίαν. The fact that the ἀστυνόμοι were appointed by lot is stated in Dem. 24 § 112. Cf. Gilbert, i 245, and Häderli, *die Astynomen und Agoranomen* (Teubner) 1886.

αὐλητρίδας] Hyperides, ii 4, 3, πλείονος μισθοῦντες τὰς αὐλητρίδας ἢ ὁ νόμος κελεύει. Cf. Plato, *Protag.* 347 D (of the συμπόσια τῶν φαύλων καὶ ἀγοραίων ἀνθρώπων) οὗτοι τιμίας ποιοῦσι τὰς αὐλητρίδας, πολλοῦ μισθούμενοι ἀλλοτρίαν φωνὴν τὴν τῶν αὐλῶν.—ὅπου δὲ καλοὶ κἀγαθοὶ συμπόται καὶ πεπαιδευμένοι εἰσίν, οὐκ ἂν ἴδοις οὔτε αὐλητρίδας οὔτε ὀρχηστρίδας οὔτε ψαλτρίας. The αὐλητρὶς (as well as the κιθάρα) is to be seen at the symposium, in Schreiber's *Bilderatlas*, i 76, 2 and 4; and the κιθαριστρία and the ψαλτρία in the mural paintings from the Farnesina garden in Baumeister's *Denkmäler*, figs. 1605, 1609.

κοπρολόγων κτλ.] Arist. Frag. 662 Kock, κοπρολογεῖ κόφινον λαβών. Schol. Dem. *Timocr.* 735, 16, ἀστυνόμος ὁ τῶν δημοσίων ἐπιμελούμενος καὶ τοῦ καθαρὰν εἶναι τὴν πόλιν. Cf. Wachsmuth, *Stadt Athen*, ii 282.

τὰς ὁδοὺς] A decree relating to the Peiraeus which was proposed by Demades in B.C. 320 (Ditt. no. 337) assigns to the ἀγορανόμοι some of the duties of the ἀστυνόμοι—requiring them ἐπιμεληθῆναι τῶν ὁδῶν τῶν πλατειῶν... ἐπαναγκαζόντων δὲ καὶ τοὺς τὸν χοῦν (rubbish) καταβεβληκότας εἰς τὰς ὁδοὺς πάντας ἀναιρεῖν τρόπῳ ὅτῳ ἂν ἐπίστωνται...μὴ ἐξεῖναι μηδενὶ μήτε χοῦν καταβάλλειν μήτε ἄλλο μηδὲν μήτε κόπρον μήτε ἐν τῇ ἀγορᾷ μήτ' ἐν ταῖς ὁδοῖς μηδαμοῦ. Cf. Meier and Schömann, p. 105—8 Lipsius.

κατοικοδομεῖν] [Xen.] *de Rep. Ath.* iii 4, δεῖ δὲ... διαδικάζειν εἴ τις... κατοικοδομεῖ τι δημόσιον. The general superintendence of buildings has been ascribed to the ἀστυνόμοι on the analogy of the provisions suggested in Plat. *Leg.* 763 C, τῶν τε ὁδῶν ἐπιμελούμενοι... καὶ τῶν οἰκοδομιῶν. Cf. Polyaen. iii 9, 30, 'Ιφικράτης ἐν ἀπορίᾳ χρημάτων ἔπεισεν 'Αθηναίους τὰ ὑπερέχοντα τῶν οἰκοδομημάτων ἐς τὰς δημοσίας ὁδοὺς ἀποκόπτειν ἢ πιπράσκειν κτλ.

δρυφάκτους] Balconies projecting from the fronts of houses. (Lat. *maeniana*, like that of the *casa del balcone pensile* at Pompeii; forbidden at Rome in A.D. 368

ὑπερτείνειν, καὶ ὀχετοὺς μετεώρους εἰς τὴν ὁδὸν ἔκρουν ἔχον[τας] ποιεῖν, καὶ τὰς θυρίδας εἰς τὴν ὁδὸν ἀνοίγειν· καὶ τοὺς ἐν ταῖς ὁδοῖς ἀπογιγνομένους ἀναιροῦσιν, ἔχοντες δημοσίους ὑπηρέτας.

51. *κληροῦνται δὲ καὶ ἀγορανόμοι, πέντε μὲν εἰς Πειραιέα, πέντε δ' εἰς ἄστυ. τούτοις δὲ ὑπὸ τῶν νόμων προστέτακται τῶν ὠ[νίω]ν ἐπιμελεῖσθαι πάντων, ὅπως καθαρὰ καὶ ἀκίβδηλα πωλῆται.*

TESTIMONIA. **LI § 1** *Harp. ἀγορανόμοι: οἱ κατὰ τὴν ἀγορὰν ὤνια διοικοῦντες ἄρχοντες...'Αρ. δ' ἐν 'Αθ. πολ. κληροῦσθαί φησι "πέντε μὲν εἰς Πειραιᾶ, πέντε δὲ εἰς ἄστυ" (Frag. 409[2], 449[3]).

---

and again by Honorius and Theodosius.) Schol. Arist. *Vesp.* 386 δρύφακτοι· τὰ νῦν ταβλωτὰ (ταβλώματα Schol. *Eq.* 675) καλούμενα, τὰ τῶν οἰκοδομημάτων ἐξέχοντα ξύλα, cf. 349 and 830 with Schol.

ὀχετούς κτλ.] the λαῦραι of Arist. *Pax* 99; cf. Wachsmuth, *Stadt Athen*, p. 284–5.

θυρίδας εἰς τὴν ὁδὸν ἀνοίγειν] θυρίς is usually a 'window,' as in *de Anima* 404 *a* 4 and *Probl.* 913 *a* 10, αἱ διὰ τῶν θυρίδων ἀκτῖνες, also in Arist. *Vesp.* 379, and *Thesm.* 797, ἐκ θυρίδος παρακύπτωμεν, Plut. *Dion* 57, πρὸς ταῖς θύραις τοῦ οἴκου καὶ ταῖς θυρίσιν, and *Mor.* 522 (*de Curiositate* 13). The same meaning can be retained in Plat. *Rep.* 359 D, ἵππον χαλκοῦν, κοῖλον, θυρίδας ἔχοντα, καθ' ἃς ἐγκύψαντα ἰδεῖν ἐνόντα νεκρόν, cf. Lucian, *Hermotimus*, 20, τὸν ἀρχιτέκτονα ἐπέπληξε τὸν Ἥφαιστον, διότι μὴ καὶ θυρίδας ἐποίησεν αὐτῷ κατὰ τὸ στέρνον, ὡς ἀναπετασθεισῶν κτλ., and Plut. *Mor.* 2, 273 B, διὰ τί πύλην μίαν θυρίδα καλοῦσι (τὴν γὰρ φαινέστραν τοῦτο σημαίνειν) and *ib.* διὰ θυρίδος προκύψασα. I can find no passage in which θυρίς means the same as θύρα. In L and S θυρίς is defined as a diminutive of θύρα; but, of the two passages quoted, the first (Plato, *l. c.*) is inconclusive, and in the second (Plutarch *l. c.*) it certainly means a 'window.' In a Greek house the principal windows were in the *peristyle*, and any that looked into the street were on the upper storey. We must suppose that windows with shutters opening outwards on to the street were prohibited. Possibly such shutters were considered dangerous in the event of their being loosened by the wind and falling into the street.

The author of the *Oeconomica*, 2, 1347 *a* 6, says of Hippias, τὰ ὑπερέχοντα τῶν ὑπερῴων εἰς τὰς δημοσίας ὁδοὺς καὶ τοὺς ἀναβαθμοὺς καὶ τὰ προφράγματα, καὶ τὰς θύρας τὰς ἀνοιγομένας ἔξω ἐπώλησεν (taxed, cf. Wachsmuth, *Stadt Athen*, ii 286); and Plutarch, *Poplic.* 20, infers from the comic poets that in former days the doors of Greek houses usually opened outwards. Mr Kenyon, who regards θυρίς as synonymous with θύρα, supposes that the ἀστυνόμοι prohibited this. If so, it must have been in defiance of the ἀστυνόμοι that the doors of Athenian houses, in the time of the Attic comedy, 'habitually opened outwards.' The fact is far from certain, but it does not concern us here, unless θυρὶς is to mean the same as θύρα, an opinion which, in the light of the general usage of Greek authors, we can hardly accept.—θυρίδας and θύρας are, however, sometimes confounded in MSS (see *apparatus criticus* to Aesch. 1 § 74, συγκλῄουσι τὰς θύρας, where one MS has θυρίδας).

ἀναιροῦσιν] 'take up for burial,' Arist. *Vesp.* 386, Xen. *Anab.* vi 4, 9.

LI § 1. **ἀγορανόμοι**] *Pol.* 1321 *b* 12, πρῶτον μὲν οὖν ἐπιμέλεια τῶν ἀναγκαίων ἡ περὶ τὴν ἀγοράν, ἐφ' ᾗ δεῖ τινα ἀρχὴν εἶναι τὴν ἐφορῶσαν περί τε τὰ συμβόλαια καὶ τὴν εὐκοσμίαν, and 1299 *b* 17. Lys. 22 κατὰ τῶν σιτοπωλῶν, § 16, ἐπὶ μὲν τοῖς ἄλλοις ὠνίοις ἅπασι τοὺς ἀγορανόμους κατεστήσατε. In Dem. 24 *Timocr.* § 112 the ἀγορανόμος, as well as the ἀστυνόμος, is described as holding a κληρωτὴν ἀρχήν. Arist. *Vesp.* 1407, *Ach.* 724, 968 and Schol. on 896; Xen. *Symp.* ii. 20. Cf. Meier and Schömann p. 101—4 Lipsius; Schömann, *Ant.* p. 416; Büchsenschütz, *Besitz u. Erwerb*, p. 536; Gilbert, i 246; Häderli, *die Astynomen und Agoranomen.*

ἐπιμελεῖσθαι...ὅπως...πωλῆται] At the end of the next sentence the papyrus has ἐπιμελεῖσθαι followed by ὅπως χρήσωνται. In the inscriptions of the fourth century against 37 exx. of ὅπως ἂν c. subj. we have only one of ὅπως, CIA ii 115, 45 (Ditt. no. 106), ἐπιμελεῖσθαι...ὅπως... κομίσωνται: in the same inscr. ὅπως ἂν occurs twice (Meisterhans, p. 212[2]). Cf. 29 § 3. In this respect the usage of inκληροῦνται δὲ καὶ μετρονόμοι, πέντε μὲν εἰς ἄστυ, πέντε δὲ 2 εἰς Πειραιέα· καὶ οὗτοι τῶν μέτρων καὶ τῶν σταθμῶν ἐπιμελοῦνται πάντων, ὅπως οἱ πωλοῦντες χρήσονται δικαίοις.

ἦσαν δὲ καὶ σιτοφύλακες κληρωτοί, πέντε μὲν εἰς Πειραιέα, 3 πέντε δ' εἰς ἄστυ, νῦν δ' εἴκοσι μὲν εἰς ἄστυ, πεντεκαίδεκα δ' εἰς Πειραιέα. οὗτοι δ' ἐπιμελοῦνται, πρῶτον μὲν ὅπως ὁ ἐν ἀγορᾷ

LI 7 ΧΡΗϹΩΝΤΑΙ: *χρήσονται* Sidgwick, Rutherford, Blass, H-L, K-W, K^3. **8** *δὲ καὶ* <*δέκα*> B; *κληρωτοὶ* <*ι'*> ex Harp. addiderunt K-W. Quidni etiam in vv. 1, 5? ΠΕΡΑΙΕΑ: *Πειραιέα* K, K-W, B; *Πειραιᾶ* H-L. **9** ΕΙΚΟϹΙ (littera *ι* evanida) K, H-L, B: *εἰσὶ ι̅ε̅* K-W. **10** ΠΕΙΡΑΙΕΑ K, K-W, B: *πειραιᾶ* H-L.

§ **2** * Harp. *μετρονόμοι*: *ἀρχή τις Ἀθήνησίν ἐστιν ἡ τῶν μετρονόμων...ἦσαν δὲ τὸν ἀριθμὸν ι̅, ε̅ μὲν εἰς Πειραιᾶ, ε̅ δ' εἰς ἄστυ* (legebatur *τὸν ἀριθμὸν ι̅ε̅, εἰς μὲν τὸν Π. ι̅, ε̅ δὲ εἰς ἄστυ*: epitomes ope correxit Dind. collato Voemelio in Bergkii *Ephem. antiq.* 1852, p. 31): *εἶχον δὲ τὴν ἐπιμέλειαν ὅπως δίκαια ᾖ τὰ μέτρα τῶν πωλούντων, ὡς καὶ Ἀρ. ἐν τῇ Ἀθ. πολ. δηλοῖ.* Bekk. *An.* p. 278, 25: *ἀρχή τις Ἀθήνησι κληρωτὴ ἡ τῶν μετρονόμων, δέκα τὸν ἀριθμόν, ὧν πέντε μὲν ἦσαν ἐν τῷ Πειραιεῖ, πέντε δὲ ἐν ἄστει. οὗτοι δὲ τὴν ἐπιμέλειαν εἶχον ὅπως δίκαια ᾖ τὰ μέτρα τῶν πωλούντων.* Photius: *ἄρχοντες ἦσαν δέκα τὸν ἀριθμόν, ὧν πέντε μὲν ἐν ἄστει, πέντε δ' ἐν Πειραιεῖ· καὶ εἶχον τὴν ἐπιμέλειαν ὅπως—πωλούντων* (cf. Frag. 412^2, 452^3).

§ **3** * Harp. *σιτοφύλακες*: *ἀρχή τις ἦν Ἀθήνησιν, ἥτις ἐπεμελεῖτο ὅπως ὁ σῖτος δικαίως πραθήσεται καὶ τὰ ἄλφιτα καὶ οἱ ἄρτοι. ἦσαν δὲ τὸν ἀριθμὸν ι̅, ε̅ μὲν ἐν ἄστει* (*τὸν ἀριθμὸν ι̅ε̅ μὲν ἐν ἄστει*), *ε̅ δ' ἐν Πειραιεῖ, ὡς Ἀρ. ἐν Ἀθ. πολ.* Photius: *ἀρχή τις—ἄρτοι. ἦσαν δὲ τὸν ἀριθμὸν πάλαι μὲν πέντε καὶ δέκα ἐν ἄστει, πέντε δὲ ἐν Π. ὕστερον δὲ τριάκοντα μὲν ἐν ἄστει, πέντε δ' ἐν Π.* Bekk. *An.* 300, 19: *ἄρχοντες Ἀθήνησι κληρωτοί. οὗτοι δ' ἐπεμελοῦντο ὅπως —— οἱ ἄρτοι κατὰ τὰ ὡρισμένας τιμὰς καὶ τὸν σταθμόν* (Frag. 411^2, 451^3).

---

scriptions differs from that of ordinary literature. In the latter *ὅπως ἄν* is less common; *ὅπως* with the future indicative is frequent in both. See Goodwin's *Moods and Tenses*, §§ 339, 348, ed. 2; Madvig, *Gk. Syntax*, §§ 122—123.

§ 2. **μετρονόμοι**] The numbers given in the text, five for the city and five for the Peiraeus, confirm the account in Photius, *s.v.* art. 1, and Bekker's *Anecd.* 278, 25 (accepted by Voemel, and Gilbert, i 247). The MSS of Harpocr. have: *ἦσαν δὲ τὸν ἀριθμὸν ι'ε', εἰς μὲν τὸν Πειραιᾶ ι', ε' δ' εἰς ἄστυ.* Boeckh accepts 15 as the total, but assigns five to the Peiraeus and ten to the city. Dindorf corrects Harpocr. thus: *ἦσαν δὲ τὸν ἀριθμὸν ι', ε' μὲν εἰς τὸν Πειραιᾶ, ε' δ' εἰς ἄστυ*, and this is confirmed by the text.

τῶν μέτρων καὶ τῶν σταθμῶν] These are the subject of a long inscr. in CIA ii 476, early in first century B.C., discussed in Boeckh, *Staatsh.* ii 318—332 Fränkel. The *ἄρχοντες* mentioned in the inscr. are doubtless the *μετρονόμοι*.

ἐπιμελοῦνται...ὅπως...χρήσονται] The papyrus has *χρήσωνται.* 'Quicumque Codices Graecos paulo diligentius inspexit saepissime vidit librarios *ὅπως* et *ὅπως μή* cum coniunctivi aoristis [primis] coniungere, ubi veteres indicativi futurum posuissent' (Cobet, *Nov. Lect.* 266). Cf. l. 3.

§ 3. **σιτοφύλακες**] Harpocr. *s. v. ἦσαν δὲ τὸν ἀριθμὸν ι'ε'* (*ι'ε', ι'* Valesius) *μὲν ἐν ἄστει, ε' δ' ἐν Πειραιεῖ.* These numbers, as altered by Valesius, seemed to be confirmed by Photius, *ἦσαν δὲ τὸν ἀριθμὸν πάλαι μὲν πεντεκαίδεκα,* <*ι'*> *ἐν ἄστει, ε' δ' ἐν Πειραιεῖ*, and were accepted by Boeckh. But the text, which is Harpocration's authority for his statements, shews that *ι'ε'* must be separated in Photius, as well as in Harpocration, so that we get 10 in all, 5 in the city and 5 in the Peiraeus. In Lys. 22 § 8 (of the *σιτοφύλακες*), *οἱ μὲν τέσσαρες* (Bergk, for *δύο*, a corruption of *δ'*) are contrasted with another member of the board, Anytus. Cf. Boeckh, i 105 Fränkel; Gilbert, i 247.

κληρωτοί] Lys. 22 § 16, *σιτοφύλακας ἀποκληροῦτε.*

νῦν δ' εἴκοσι *κτλ.*] Photius, *ὕστερον δὲ λ' μὲν ἐν ἄστει, ε' δ' ἐν Πειραιεῖ.* Here the total is correct, but the text shews that Photius ought to have said: *κ' μὲν ἐν ἄστει, ι'ε' δ' ἐν Π.*

σῖτος ἀργὸς ὤνιος ἔσται δικαίως, ἔπειθ' ὅπως οἵ τε μυλωθροὶ πρὸς τὰς τιμὰς τῶν κριθῶν τὰ ἄλφιτα πωλήσουσιν καὶ οἱ ἀρτοπῶλαι πρὸς τὰς τιμὰς τῶν πυρῶν τοὺς ἄρτους, καὶ τὸν σταθμὸν ἄγοντας ὅσον ἂν οὗτοι τάξωσιν· ὁ γὰρ νόμος τούτους κελεύει τάττειν.

4 *ἐμπορίου δ' ἐπιμελητὰς δέκα κληροῦσιν· τούτοις δὲ προστέτακται τῶν τ' ἐμπορίων ἐπιμελεῖσθαι, καὶ τοῦ σίτου τοῦ καταπλέοντος εἰς τὸ Ἀττικὸν ἐμπόριον τὰ δύο μέρη τοὺς ἐμπόρους ἀναγκάζειν εἰς τὸ ἄστυ κομίζειν.*

52. *καθιστᾶσι δὲ καὶ τοὺς ἕνδεκα κληρωτούς, ἐπιμελησομέ-*

12 πωλήσουσι H-L. **17** CITIKON K, K-W, H-L: Ἀττικὸν ex Harp. Torr; ἀστικὸν quondam proposui coll. Bekk. *An.* 255, 208, 284, 456; accepit B: nunc unice verum arbitror Ἀττικόν, etenim σιτικὸν et ἀστικὸν oculi errore e proximis verbis σίτου et ἄστυ videntur irrepsisse.

LII 1 <τοὺς> ἐπιμελησομένους Rutherford, H-L; cf. Heracl. in Testimoniis.

§ **4** *Harp. ἐπιμελητὴς ἐμπορίου:...Ἀρ. "ἐμπορίου δ' ἐπιμελητὰς —— τοῦ σίτου τοῦ καταπλέοντος εἰς τὸ Ἀττικὸν ἐμπόριον —— κομίζειν" (Frag. 409², 449³). Bekk. *An.* 255, 22: ἐμπορίου ἄρχοντες ἦσαν κληρωτοί, δέκα τὸν ἀριθμόν, ἑκάστου ἔτους καθιστάμενοι, οἷς προσετέτακτο τῶν ἐμπορίων ἐπιμελεῖσθαι, καὶ τοῦ σίτου τοῦ καταπλέοντος εἰς τὸ ἐμπόριον τὸ ἀστικὸν τὰ δύο μέρη τοὺς ἐμπόρους ἀναγκάζειν (reliqua propter ὁμοιοτέλευτον omissa)...ib. 208, 26 ἀστικὸν ἐμπόριον· ὅπου οἱ ἀστοὶ ἐμπορεύονται. ἦν δὲ καὶ ἄλλο ξενικόν, ὅπου οἱ ξένοι (cf. 284, 6; 456, 3).

TESTIMONIA. **LII 1** Heraclidis epitoma; Rose, Frag. 611, 8: ὁμοίως δὲ "καθιστᾶσι καὶ τοὺς ἕνδεκα" τοὺς (secl. K-W; sed fortasse e κληρωτοὺς exortum) "ἐπιμελησομένους τῶν ἐν τῷ δεσμωτηρίῳ." Pollux viii 102: οἱ ἕνδεκα: εἷς ἀφ' ἑκάστης φυλῆς ἐγίνετο καὶ γραμματεὺς αὐτοῖς συνηριθμεῖτο...ἐπεμελοῦντο δὲ "τῶν ἐν τῷ δεσμωτηρίῳ" καὶ ἀπῆγον κλέπτας ἀνδραποδιστὰς λωποδύτας, εἰ μὲν ὁμολογοῖεν, θανατώσοντες, εἰ δὲ μή, εἰσάξοντες εἰς τὰ δικαστήρια, κἂν ἁλῶσιν, ἀποκτενοῦντες. Bekk. *An.* 310, 14: οἱ ἕνδεκα τοὺς κλέπτας καὶ τοὺς λωποδύτας καὶ τοὺς ἀνδραποδιστὰς ὁμολογοῦντας μὲν ἀποκτιννύουσιν, ἀντιλέγοντας δὲ εἰσάγουσιν "εἰς τὸ δικαστήριον" (Frag. 429³). Phot.

σῖτος ἀργὸς] 'unprepared corn,' Hippocr. *Vet. Med.* 12, πυροὶ ἀργοί. The position of ἀργὸς (after, instead of before, σῖτος) is defended by *Eth. Nic.* vi 4, 2, ἡ μετὰ λόγου ἕξις πρακτικὴ ἕτερόν ἐστι τῆς μετὰ λόγου ποιητικῆς ἕξεως, quoted by Dr Jackson to prove that part of a complex epithet may be placed after the article and substantive. Mr Newman adds *Pol.* 1252 *b* 27, ἡ ἐκ πλειόνων κωμῶν κοινωνία τέλειος πόλις ἤδη.

§ 4. **ἐμπορίου...ἐπιμελητάς**] All that is known of these officials apart from the statement in the text, is that they were the proper authority to receive legal notice (φάσις) of any infringement of the law forbidding citizens and resident aliens lending money on the security of a cargo bound for any other port than that of Athens. Dem. 35 §§ 50, 51, ἐάν τις... χρήματα δανείσῃ εἰς ἄλλο τι ἐμπόριον ἢ τὸ Ἀθηναίων; 58 §§ 8, 9 (Gilbert, i 248). Cf. Meier and Schöm., p. 98 Lips. The ἐμπόριον extended over the greater part of the east shore of the harbour of the Peiraeus; Wachsmuth, *Stadt Athen*, ii 96—esp. 114.

ἐμπόριον] After τοῦ σίτου the epithet σιτικὸν (which is first found in Polybius) is redundant. The variant Ἀττικὸν in Harpocration's quotation of this passage is supported by Dem. 34 § 36, Ἀθήναζε εἰς τὸ Ἀττικὸν ἐμπόριον σιτηγεῖν, and § 37, εἴ τις...ἄλλοσέ ποι σιτηγήσειεν ἢ εἰς τὸ Ἀττικὸν ἐμπ., 35 § 28 τοῦ ὑμετέρου ἐμπορίου (quoted by Mr Torr). ἀστικὸν is suggested by Bekk. *Anecd.* 208, ἀστικὸν ἐμπόριον· ὅπου οἱ ἀστοὶ ἐμπορεύονται. ἦν δὲ καὶ ἄλλο ξενικόν, ὅπου οἱ ξένοι, cf. 255, 284, 456. One of the parts of the ἐμπόριον in the Peiraeus was the στοὰ ἀλφιτόπωλις, also called the μακρὰ στοά (Dem. 34 § 37, cf. Thuc. viii 90, 5, Wachsmuth, *u. s.* p. 101); but I can find no authority for applying the epithet σιτικὸν to the ἐμπόριον, or to any part of it, at or before the date when the text was written.

LII § 1. **τοὺς ἕνδεκα**] c. 7 § 3. Schömann, p. 414; Gilbert, i 243; *Dict. Ant.* i 942.

νους τῶν ἐν τῷ δεσμωτηρίῳ, καὶ τοὺς ἀπαγομένους κλέπτας καὶ τοὺς ἀνδραποδιστὰς καὶ τοὺς λωποδύτας, ἂν μὲν [ὁμολογῶ]σι, θανάτῳ ζημιώσοντας, ἂν δ' ἀμφισβητῶσιν, εἰσάξοντας εἰς τὸ δικαστήριον, κἂν μὲν ἀποφύγωσιν, ἀφήσοντας, εἰ δὲ μή, τότε θανατώσοντας, καὶ τὰ [ἀ]πογραφόμενα χωρία καὶ οἰκίας εἰσάξοντας εἰς τὸ δικαστήριον, καὶ τὰ δόξαντα δ[ημ]όσια εἶναι παραδώσοντας τοῖς πωληταῖς, καὶ τὰς ἐνδείξεις εἰσάξοντας· καὶ γὰρ ταύτας εἰσάγουσιν οἱ ἕνδεκα. εἰσάγουσι δὲ τῶν ἐνδείξεών τινας καὶ οἱ θεσμοθέται.

κληροῦσι δὲ καὶ εἰσαγωγέας πέντε ἄνδρας, οἳ τὰς ἐμμήνους 2

2 <κακούργους, τούς τε> κλέπτας, K-W, coll. Etym. Mag. **3** τοὺς bis delent H-L. **3, 4** ἐὰν bis H-L. **4** ΖΗΜΙΩΘΗϹΟΝΤΑϹΕΝΔ corr K.

ἡγεμονία δικαστηρίου :...τοῖς ἕνδεκα ὅσαι λῃστὰς καὶ λωποδύτας καὶ ἀνδραποδιστὰς εἰσάγουσι. Etym. M. 338, 31: κληρωτοὶ ἄρχοντες ἦσαν οὗτοι, προεστηκότες τοῦ δεσμωτηρίου· καὶ τοὺς ἀπαγομένους κακούργους ἐπὶ θάνατον παραλαμβάνοντες ἐζημίουν· τοὺς δὲ ἀμφισβητοῦντας εἰσῆγον "εἰς τὸ δικαστήριον" καὶ τὸ γνωσθὲν περὶ αὐτῶν ἔπραττον. εἰσῆγον δὲ "καὶ τὰ ἀπογραφόμενα χωρία <καὶ Schleusner> οἰκίας" καὶ τὰ "δημόσια εἶναι" δόξαντα παρεδίδουν τοῖς πολίταις (πωληταῖς Schleusner). εἰσῆγον δὲ ἐνίας ἐνδείξεις. Bekk. *An.* 250, 4: ...καὶ τοὺς ἀγομένους ἐπὶ κακουργήμασι παρελάμβανον κλέπτας καὶ ἀνδραποδιστὰς καὶ φονεῖς. καὶ τοὺς μὲν ὁμολογοῦντας θανάτῳ ἐζημίουν, τοὺς δὲ ἀμφισβητοῦντας εἰσῆγον εἰς δικαστήριον. Schol. Arist. *Vesp.* 1108: ἡ τῶν ἕνδεκα ἀρχὴ τοὺς μὲν ὁμολογοῦντας καὶ ἀνδραποδιστὰς καὶ λωποδύτας θανάτῳ ἐκόλαζον, τοὺς δὲ ἀρνουμένους εἰς δικαστήριον εἰσῆγον. εἰσῆγον δὲ καὶ τὰς ἐνδείξεις. Schol. Patm. Dem. p. 11, 16, Sakkelion; Schol. Lucian. iv 170 Jacobitz.

§ 2 Pollux viii 101: εἰσαγωγεῖς οἱ "τὰς ἐμμήνους δίκας" εἰσάγοντες· ἦσαν δὲ

ἀπαγομένους κλέπτας...ἀνδραποδιστὰς...λωποδύτας] Isocr. *Antid.* § 90, τοῦτον ἀπαγαγὼν ἀνδραποδιστὴν καὶ κλέπτην καὶ λωποδύτην. Meier and Schöm. p. 273—6, Lips. Pollux ἀνδραποδιστής· ὁ τὸν ἐλεύθερον καταδουλούμενος ἢ τὸν ἀλλότριον οἰκέτην ὑπαγόμενος.

κλέπται, ἀνδραποδισταί and λωποδύται came under the general heading of κακοῦργοι; cf. [Dem.] 35 *Lacr.* 47, τοιχωρύχους καὶ κλέπτας καὶ τοὺς ἄλλους κακούργους τοὺς ἐπὶ θανάτῳ οὗτοι (*sc.* οἱ ἕνδεκα) εἰσάγουσιν, *Androt.* §§ 26—28. Cf. Meier and Schöm. p. 86 Lips.

ἂν μὲν ὁμολογῶσι κτλ.] Aeschin. 1 § 113, οἱ δὲ νόμοι κελεύουσι τῶν κλεπτῶν τοὺς μὲν ὁμολογοῦντας θανάτῳ ζημιοῦσθαι, τοὺς δ' ἀρνυμένους κρίνεσθαι, and Dem. *in Timocr.* § 65, τῶν...κακούργων τοὺς ὁμολογοῦντας ἄνευ κρίσεως κολάζειν οἱ νόμοι κελεύουσιν. Schol. Arist. *Vesp.* 1108, ἡ τῶν ἕνδεκα ἀρχὴ τοὺς μὲν ὁμολογοῦντας καὶ ἀνδραποδιστὰς καὶ λωποδύτας θανάτῳ ἐκόλαζον, τοὺς δὲ ἀρνουμένους εἰς δικαστήριον εἰσῆγον. These passages (quoted in *Class. Rev.* v 224) prove the incorrectness of the interpretation suggested in the *Saturday Review*, March 21, 1891, p. 359 'if (the Eleven) are *unanimous*...or if they *disagree.*' See also the passages quoted in the *Testimonia.*

θανάτῳ] Dem. 4 § 47, τὸν ἀνδραποδιστῶν καὶ λωποδυτῶν θάνατον...κακούργου μὲν γάρ ἐστι κριθέντ' ἀποθανεῖν.

τὰ ἀπογραφόμενα χωρία κτλ.] Our knowledge of this part of the duties of the Eleven has hitherto been derived from the Etym. Magn. 338, 35, which is obviously quoted from the text: see *Testimonia.* Meier and Schömann, p. 88 Lipsius.

πωληταῖς] 47 § 2.

τὰς ἐνδείξεις] Schol. Arist. *Vesp.* 1108, εἰσῆγον δὲ καὶ τὰς ἐνδείξεις. Bekker, *Anecd.* 250, 11, τῶν δὲ ἐνδείξεων εἰσέφερον εἰς δικαστήριον ἃς μὲν οἱ ἕνδεκα, ἃς δὲ οἱ θεσμοθέται. Etym. Mag. 338, 39, εἰσῆγον δὲ ἐνίας ἐνδείξεις (Meier and Schömann, p. 87 Lipsius). The text does not enable us to distinguish between the ἐνδείξεις under the control of the Eleven, and those under that of the Thesmothetae. The general statement, καὶ γὰρ ταύτας εἰσάγουσιν οἱ ἕνδεκα, is modified in the following sentence.

§ 2. **εἰσαγωγέας]** These officials are

εἰσάγουσι δίκας, δυοῖν φυλαῖν [ἕ]καστος· εἰσὶ δ' ἔμμηνοι προικός, ἐάν τις ὀφείλων μὴ ἀποδῷ, κἄν τις ἐπὶ δραχ[μ]ῇ δανεισάμενος ἀποστερῇ, κἄν τις ἐν ἀγορᾷ βουλόμενος ἐργάζεσθαι δανείσηται παρά [τι]νος ἀφορμήν· ἔτι δ' αἰκείας καὶ ἐρανικαὶ καὶ κοινωνικαὶ καὶ ἀνδραπόδων καὶ ὑποζυγ[ίων] καὶ τριηραρχίας καὶ τραπεζιτι-

13 ΑΠΟΔΩΙ (K) cf. Lys. 30 § 22 δύο τάλαντα ἀποδοῦναι: ἀποδιδῷ Blass, Kontos, K-W, H-L; cf. Dem. 34 § 13 οὐδ' ἀποδίδωσι τὸ δάνειον. ἐπὶ δραχμῇ: ὑπὲρ δραχμὴν H-L. **14** ἐν: ΕΑΝ. **15** ΑΙΚΕΙΑΣ (K, H-L, B): αἰκίας K-W. ΕΡΑΝΙΚΑΣ—ΚΟΙΝΩΝΙΚΑΣ (K[1], B): ἐρανικαὶ—κοινωνικαὶ Bury, K-W, H-L, K[3]. 'Desiderantur autem ἐμπορικαί, cf. Poll.' (B). **16** ΤΡΙΗΡΑΡΧΙΑΣ (K, H-L, B): τριηραρχικαὶ Bury (K-W). ΤΡΑΠΕΖΙΤΙΚΑΣ (B): τραπεζιτικαὶ Bury, K-W, H-L, K[3].

προικός, ἐρανικαί, ἐμπορικαί. Hesych. εἰσαγωγή (εἰσαγωγῆς = -εῖς Scaliger): ἀρχὴ Ἀθήνησι τῶν τὰ ἐγκλήματα (leg. ἔμμηνα K-W) εἰσαγόντων (cf. Schol. Dem. *Mid.* § 3).

---

mentioned twice in Pollux viii 93, ἀρχῆς κληρωτῆς ὄνομα, and 101, εἰσαγωγεῖς οἱ τὰς ἐμμήνους δίκας εἰσάγοντες, ἦσαν δὲ προικός, ἐρανικαί, ἐμπορικαί. But their existence was doubted by Meier. These doubts were dispelled in 1869 by the publication of an inscr. of B.C. 425/4 relating to the superintendence of judicial proceedings connected with the assessment of the tribute; CIA i 37, 47, ἐπὶ τῶν ἐσαγωγέων (Meier and Schömann, p. 94 Lips.; Gilbert, i 396). The text shews that their number was five; not ten, as had been conjectured.

Pollux is mistaken in placing ἐμπορικαὶ δίκαι under the control of the εἰσαγωγεῖς. These were under the Thesmothetae as is proved by passages in the Orators, and by c. 59 § 5, quoted elsewhere by Pollux himself. In CIA i 38, frag. *f*, certain ἐπιμεληταὶ are appointed to attend to cases of delay in the payment of tribute, ο[ἱ δὲ ἐπιμεληταὶ ἐσαγό]ντων ἔμμηνα ἐς τὸ δικαστήριον, thus shewing that at that time (probably shortly after 432 B.C.) there were some ἔμμηνοι δίκαι not under the care of the εἰσαγωγεῖς (Gilbert, i 358).

τὰς ἐμμήνους—δίκας] Lawsuits which had to be decided within a month (Meier and Schöm. p. 906 f.). They are first mentioned in B.C. 425/4, CIA i 38 (quoted in last note). The text mentions several varieties of such lawsuits that are omitted by Pollux.

προικός] actions for restitution of dowry. (1) If the husband divorced his wife, he was bound to return the dowry or to pay interest at the rate of 18 per cent. per annum (Dem. *Aph.* i 17, *Neaer.* 52). The κύριος might enforce these claims by a προικὸς δίκη (Isaeus 3 §§ 9, 78). (2) A similar action might be brought against the heirs who kept a widow out of her rights. The δίκαι προικός in the text are limited by the definition in the next clause, ἐάν τις ὀφείλων μὴ ἀποδῷ.

κἄν τις—ἀποστερῇ] The benefit of the expeditious process for recovery of debts is here limited to creditors who are satisfied with what in Athens was regarded as the moderate rate of 12 per cent. (Dem. *Aphob.* i 23, 35; Aesch. *Ctes.* 104; cf. Boeckh, i 156 Fränkel). Those who charge higher rates, such as 16, 18 or even 36 per cent., are excluded from this privilege. Lipsius in *Leipzig. Verhandlungen*, 1891, p. 57 n.

ἀφορμήν] 'capital.' The speech of Dem. *pro Phormione* is a παραγραφή to a δίκη ἀφορμῆς. The text refers to the case of a small tradesman setting up business in the market-place and refusing to repay the capital he had borrowed for the purpose.

αἰκείας] Meier and Schöm. p. 647 f. Lips. About B.C. 346/5, according to Dem. *c. Pantaenetum* 37 § 33, the tribunal in such cases was the Forty; cf. Schol. Plat. *Rep.* 464 E. The text implies that the tribunal had been changed.

ἐρανικαί] lawsuits for the recovery of friendly loans, or for the decision of disputes between various members of an ἔρανος (Meier and Schöm. p. 637—643 Lips.).

κοινωνικαί] suits against corporations (Meier and Schömann, p. 767 Lips.). In Dem. 14 § 16 κοινωνικὰ probably means property held by corporations (*ib.* p. 602, Lips. note 321).

ἀνδραπόδων] Dem. *Callicl.* 55 §§ 31, 34 (Meier and Schömann, p. 766). By the law of Solon quoted in Lys. *c. Theomnest.* i 19, (the owner was liable) οἰκῆος καὶ δούλης βλάβην ὀφείλειν, cf. Plat. *Leg.* 936 D. On **ὑποζυγίων** κτλ. see next page.

καί. οὗτοι μὲν οὖν ταύτας δικάζουσιν ἐμμήνους εἰσάγ[ον]τες, οἱ δ' 3
*ἀποδέκται τοῖς τελώναις καὶ κατὰ τῶν τελωνῶν, τὰ μὲν μέχρι δέκα
δραχμῶν ὄντες κύριοι, τὰ δ' ἄλλ' εἰς τὸ δικαστήριον εἰσάγοντες
ἔμμηνα.*

53. *κληροῦσι δὲ καὶ τετταράκοντα, τέτταρας ἐκ τῆς
φυλῆς ἑκάστης, πρὸς οὓς τὰς ἄλλας δίκας λαγχάνουσιν· οἱ*

18 *δέκα* <(=*δραχμῶν*).
LIII 1 <*τοὺς*> *τετταράκοντα* K-W. **1—2** ΕΚ ΤΗϹ ΦΥΛΗϹ (casu obliteratum) ΦΥΛΗϹ ΕΚΑϹΤΗϹ *ἐξ ἑκάστης φυλῆς* K[1]; *ἐκ τῆς φυλῆς ἑκάστης* K-W, H-L, K[3], B.
2 ΑΛΛΑϹ : *ἰδίας* Wyse.

§ 3 Pollux viii 97 : *ἀποδέκται δὲ ἦσαν δέκα, οἳ τοὺς φόρους καὶ τὰς εἰσφορὰς καὶ τὰ τέλη ὑπεδέχοντο, καὶ τὰ περὶ τούτων ἀμφισβητούμενα ἐδίκαζον. εἰ δέ τι μεῖζον εἴη, εἰσῆγον εἰς δικαστήριον.*

LIII § 1 * Harp. *κατὰ δήμους δικαστάς:...περὶ τῶν κατὰ δήμους δικαστῶν, ὡς "πρότερον μὲν—ἐδίκαζον," εἶτα ἐγένοντο τετταράκοντα, εἴρηκεν 'Αρ. ἐν τῇ* <*'Αθηναίων* addidit Meier> *πολιτείᾳ.* Pollux viii 101 : *οἱ δὲ τετταράκοντα "πρότερον μὲν ἦσαν τριάκοντα," οἳ περιιόντες κατὰ δήμους τὰ μέχρι δραχμῶν δέκα ἐδίκαζον, τὰ δὲ ὑπὲρ ταῦτα τοῖς διαιτηταῖς παρεδίδοσαν· "μετὰ δὲ τὴν τῶν τριάκοντα ὀλιγαρχίαν" μίσει τοῦ ἀριθμοῦ τοῦ τριάκοντα τετταράκοντα ἐγένοντο.* Phot.: *κληρωτή τις ἦν 'Αθήνησιν ἀρχὴ μ̄* (*μετὰ* cod.) *τὸν ἀριθμόν, οἳ τὰς ἰδιωτικὰς δίκας ἐδίκαζον· ἀλλὰ τὰς μὲν ἄχρι "δέκα δραχμῶν αὐτοτελεῖς" ἦσαν δικάζειν, τὰς δὲ ὑπὲρ ταύτας τοῖς διαιτηταῖς παρεδίδουν.* Bekk. *An.* 306, 15 : *ἀρχή τίς ἐστι κληρωτὴ τεσσαράκοντα τὸν ἀριθμὸν πρὸς οὓς αἱ ἴδιαι δίκαι ἐλαγχάνοντο καὶ τὰ "μέχρι δέκα δραχμῶν." "τὰ δ' ὑπὲρ τοῦτο τὸ τίμημα τοῖς διαιτηταῖς παραδιδόασιν"* (cf. p. 310, 22 ; Frag. 413[2], 453[3]).

---

l. 16. **ὑποζυγίων**] actions arising out of damage done by beasts of draught or burden. Cf. Solon's law in Plut. *Sol.* 24 ; and Plat. *Leg.* 936 E, *ἐὰν ὑποζύγιον ἢ ἵππος* (Dinarch. *c. Antiph. περὶ ἵππου*) *ἢ κύων* (Lys. *περὶ τοῦ κυνὸς* ap. Harpocr. *s. v. καρκίνος*) *ἤ τι τῶν ἄλλων θρεμμάτων σίνηταί τι τῶν πέλας, κατὰ ταὐτὰ ἐκτίνειν τὴν βλάβην* (*τὸν δεσπότην*). The special case of homicide caused by a *ὑποζύγιον ἢ ζῷον ἄλλο τι* is considered *ib.* 873 E (*inf.* c. 57 *ad fin.*).

τριηραρχίας] The speech delivered by Apollodorus against Polycles, [Dem.] *Or.* 52, belongs to this class. Polycles failed to join his ship for four months after the official year had expired, and his predecessor Apollodorus had incurred extra expenses for which he sues Polycles.

τραπεζιτικαί] In the *Trapeziticus* of Isocr. the banker Pasion is accused of repudiation and forgery.—*δίκαι μεταλλικαὶ* and *ἐμπορικαὶ* are not included in the list, probably because they came under the *ἡγεμονία* of the Thesmothetae (Dem. *c. Apol.* § 12, and *inf.* 59 § 5).

§ 3. **δικάζουσιν**] *i.e.* 'have the *ἡγεμονία τοῦ δικαστηρίου* in these law-suits,' Meier and Schöm. p. 43 Lips. Cf. c. 57 *ad fin.*

ἀποδέκται] c. 48 § 1.

τοῖς τελώναις] *e.g.* the farmers of the public taxes were allowed to bring a *φάσις* against any one suspected of defrauding the revenue. They might even arrest him and bring him before a magistrate. Cf. Gilbert, i 335.

LIII § 1. **τετταράκοντα**] a body of officials instituted by Peisistratus under the name of *οἱ κατὰ δήμους δικασταί* (16 § 5), revived in B.C. 453/2 (26 § 3), and (as stated in the text) increased in number from 30 to 40 after the time of the Thirty tyrants. They are mentioned in Isocr. *Antid.* 237, *ἐν δὲ ταῖς τῶν τετταράκοντα* (*σανίσιν ἀναγκαῖον ἐνεῖναι*) *τούς τ' ἐν τοῖς ἰδίοις πράγμασιν ἀδικοῦντας καὶ τοὺς μὴ δικαίως ἐγκαλοῦντας.* In Dem. *Pant.* 33 we are told that cases of *αἰκεία* and *τὰ τῶν βιαίων* came under their jurisdiction. They are described as appointed by lot in *Timocr.* 112, *εἰ μέν τις ἀγορανόμος ἢ ἀστυνόμος ἢ δικαστὴς κατὰ δήμους κλοπῆς ἐν ταῖς εὐθύναις ἑάλωκεν, ἄνθρωπος πένης καὶ ἰδιώτης καὶ πολλῶν ἄπειρος καὶ κληρωτὴν ἀρχὴν ἄρξας.* It was only in unimportant cases, where the matter in dispute was not above the value of 10 drachmas, that they were competent to decide on their own authority : other cases they referred, πρότερ[ον] μὲν ἦσαν τριάκοντα, καὶ κατὰ δήμους περιιόντες ἐδίκαζον, μετὰ δὲ τὴν ἐπὶ τῶν τριάκοντα ὀλιγαρχία[ν] τετταράκοντα [Col. 27.] 2 γεγόνασιν. καὶ τὰ μὲν || μέχρι δέκα δραχμῶν αὐτοτελεῖς εἰσὶ [κρίνει]ν, τὰ δ' ὑπὲρ τοῦτο τὸ τίμημα τοῖς διαιτηταῖς παραδιδόασιν. οἱ δὲ παραλαβόντες, [ἐ]ὰν μὴ δύνωνται διαλῦσαι, γιγνώσκουσι, κἂν μὲν ἀμφοτέροις ἀρέσκῃ τὰ γνωσθέντα [καὶ] ἐμμένωσιν, ἔχει τέλος ἡ δίκη. ἂν δ' ὁ ἕτερος ἐφῇ τῶν ἀντιδίκων εἰς τὸ δικαστήριον, ἐμβαλόντες τὰς μαρτυρίας καὶ τὰς προκλήσεις καὶ τοὺς νόμους εἰς ἐχίνους, χωρὶς μὲν τὰς τοῦ διώκοντος, χωρὶς δὲ τὰς τοῦ φεύγοντος,

3 ΠΕΡΙΟΝΤΕϹ retinent K-W[2] (et B) coll. Hyper. i 13, 6 et ii 2, 12: περιιόντες K, K-W[1], H-L. 4 ΕΠΙ supra versum, non habet Pollux. 7 ΓΙΓΝΩΙϹΚΟΥϹΙ γιγνῴσκουσι (coll. 54, 7 et Herondae papyro V 21) B: sed cf. Meisterhans, p. 141, 17[2]. 9 ἐὰν H-L.

§ 2 *Harp. διαιτηταί:...καὶ εἰ μὲν ἤρεσκε τοῖς ἀντιδίκοις, τέλος εἶχεν ἡ δίκη· εἰ δὲ μή, τὰ ἐγκλήματα καὶ τὰς προκλήσεις καὶ τὰς μαρτυρίας, ἔτι δὲ καὶ τοὺς νόμους καὶ τὰς ἄλλας πίστεις ἑκατέρων ἐμβαλόντες εἰς καδίσκους καὶ σημηνάμενοι παρεδίδοσαν τοῖς εἰσαγωγεῦσι τῶν δικῶν. λέγει δὲ περὶ αὐτῶν 'Αρ. ἐν 'Αθ. πολ. Pollux viii 126: ἡ δ' ἔφεσις αὐτῶν εἰ εἰς δικαστήριον γένοιτο, εἰς ἐχῖνον τὰς ψήφους (sic) ἐμβαλόντες ἰδίᾳ ἑκατέρας τὰς τοῦ φεύγοντος καὶ διώκοντος κατεσημαίνοντο. Bekk. *An.* 235, 20.

11 *Harp. ἐχῖνος: ἔστι μὲν ἄγγος τι εἰς ὃ τὰ γραμματεῖα τὰ πρὸς τὰς δίκας ἐτίθεντο... μνημονεύει τοῦ ἄγγους τούτου καὶ 'Αρ. ἐν τῇ 'Αθ. πολ.... Phot. i 240 Naber, ἐχῖνοι: οἱ μὲν χαλκοῖ, οἱ δὲ ἐκ κεράμου· εἰς οὓς καθιᾶσιν οἱ διαιτηταὶ τὰ γραμματεῖα τῶν μαρτυριῶν ἅ τινες ἐμαρτύρησαν, καὶ κατασημηνάμενοι μετὰ ταῦτα εἰ ἐγκληθείη ἡ δίαιτα τοῖς δικασταῖς ἐπεδίδουν (fere eadem habet *Schol. Arist. *Vesp.* 1436, additis τοῦ δ' ἄγγους τούτου καὶ Δημοσθένης μνημονεύουσι καὶ 'Αρ.). Phot. ἐχῖνος: καδίσκος τίς ἐστι χαλκοῦς, εἰς ὃν αἵ τε μαρτυρίαι καὶ αἱ προκλήσεις ἔγγραφοι ἐνεβάλλοντο ὑπὸ τῶν δικαζομένων καὶ κατεσημαίνοντο ἵνα μηδεὶς κακουργήσῃ περὶ τὰ ἐμβαλλόμενα (fere eadem Etym. M.; καὶ κατεσημαίνετο ὁ ἐχῖνος, ἵνα μηδεὶς κακουργήσῃ μετὰ τὸ ἅπαξ ἐμβάλλεσθαι, Bekk. *An.* 258, 6). Cf. Frag. 415[2], 455[3].

---

in the first instance, to the arbitrators, and, if necessary, to the law-courts. Cf. Gilbert, i 358.

Most of the cases concerned with the rights of property were supposed by Meier to come under the jurisdiction of the Thesmothetae. Lipsius, in his revised edition of Meier and Schömann, p. 93, (1) assigns them to the Forty; he also (2) identifies the δικασταὶ κατὰ δήμους with the δικασταί concerned with the several tribes (*ib.* p. 90 n.). Thus they could act in their several divisions of four for each of the ten tribes. Lastly, (3) he holds that after a time they ceased to go on circuit and held their court in Athens. The first of these opinions is opposed by Caillemer in Daremberg and Saglio, *Dict. Ant.* iii 200 f.; but all three are confirmed by the text. (1) is supported by τὰς ἄλλας δίκας, whereby they have jurisdiction over all causes not assigned to the Eleven, the εἰσαγωγεῖς and ἀποδέκται. (2) by c. 48 § 5, οἱ τὴν φυλὴν εἰσάγοντες, 58 § 2, οἱ τὴν φυλὴν δικάζοντες, and *inf.* § 2, οἱ τὴν φυλὴν τοῦ φεύγοντος δικάζοντες.

λαγχάνουσιν] *sc.* 'the suitors.'

§ 2. **μέχρι δέκα δραχμῶν**] In B.C. 445/4 (CIA i 29 and iv p. 12) we have mention of a court probably consisting of thirty members, appointed by lot from the κληροῦχοι of Hestiaia and Ellopia and competent to decide cases of this kind. In *Pol.* 1300 *b* 23 and 32, Ar. approves of the institution of two separate courts, according to the value of the matter in dispute: matters that are worth little more than five drachmas need not be referred εἰς δικαστῶν πλῆθος.

αὐτοτελεῖς] 3 § 5 *ult.*

διαιτηταῖς] Meier and Schöm. pp. 48, 1009—1015; Smith, *Dict. Ant. s.v.* The text shews that all private causes (except the ἔμμηνοι δίκαι, c. 52) were in the first instance tried by the διαιτηταί.

ἐμβαλόντες—ἐχίνους] Dem. 45 § 17, ἐχρῆν αὐτὸ τὸ γραμματεῖον εἰς τὸν ἐχῖνον ἐμβαλεῖν and *ib.* 57, also 48 § 48, ἀντίγραφα (συνθηκῶν) ἐμβαλέσθαι εἰς τὸν ἐχῖνον.

μαρτυρίας, Meier and Schöm. p. 873 ff. Lips.; **προκλήσεις**, *ib.* 871 ff.

καὶ τούτους κατασημηνάμενοι, καὶ τὴν [γνῶ]σιν τοῦ διαιτητοῦ γεγραμμένην ἐν γραμματείῳ προσαρτήσαντες, παραδιδόασι τοῖς τέτταρσι τοῖς τὴν φυλὴν τοῦ φεύγοντος δικάζουσιν· οἱ δὲ παρα- 3
λαβόντες εἰσάγουσιν εἰς τὸ δικαστήριον, [τὰ μὲν ἐ]ντὸς χιλίων εἰς ἕνα καὶ διακοσίους, τὰ δ' ὑπὲρ χιλίας εἰς ἕνα καὶ τετρακοσίους. οὐκ ἔξεσ[τι δ' οὔ]τε νόμοις οὔτε προκλήσεσι οὔτε μαρτυρίαις ἀλλ' ἢ ταῖς παρὰ τοῦ διαιτητοῦ χρῆσθ[αι ταῖς εἰς] τοὺς ἐχίνους ἐμβεβλημέναις. διαιτηταὶ δ' εἰσὶν οἷς ἂν ἑξηκοστὸν ἔτος ᾖ. τοῦτο δὲ 4

12 [γνῶ]σιν τοῦ B; [κρί]σιν τοῦ K, H-L; [κρίσ]ιν <τὴν> τοῦ K-W; in ectypo fere nihil dispici potest; γνῶσιν defendit Dem. 40 § 42 κατὰ γνῶσιν διαιτητοῦ, 21 § 92 διαιτητοῦ γνῶσιν, 33 § 22 γνῶσιν—διαίτης, 36 § 17 τῆς γνώσεως. **13** ΤΟΙϹΔ? τοῖς δ̄ K[3], B.: τοῖς ἐπὶ? K[1]; πάλιν K-W, -ν εὐθὺς H-L. **14** Τ(ΗϹ)ΦΥΛ(ΗϹ) K[1]: τὴν φυλὴν Wyse, K-W, H-L, K[3], B, coll. c. 48 § 5, c. 58 § 2.

§ **3** Pollux viii 48 infra laudatus.
§ **4** ἑξηκοστὸν ἔτος. Cf. Bekk. *An.* 235, 3, infra laudatum, § 5 τῆς ἡλικίας κτλ.

κατασημηνάμενοι, cf. 39 § 17, *σεσημασμένων τῶν ἐχίνων*, 47 § 16, *ἐσημάνθησαν οἱ ἐχῖνοι* (and *ib.* *προκλήσεως ἐμβεβλημένης σοι καὶ μαρτυρίας*), and 54 § 27, *τῷ μὴ σημανθῆναι τοὺς ἐχίνους*.

In Meier and Schöm. p. 904 Lips. it is assumed that the ἐχῖνος was used for the reception of documents handed in at the ἀνάκρισις. Thus Dem. 28 § 1, ἐνεβάλετο τηρήσας τὴν τελευταίαν ἡμέραν, is there referred to the 'last day of the ἀνάκρισις.' Mr Wyse suggests that there is no reason why it should not refer to the arbitration. It may be doubted whether in the Attic orators there is a single certain example of ἐχῖνος *except in connexion with arbitration*. To the passages above quoted may be added 39 §§ 22, 37; 34 § 46; 40 §§ 21, 28, 58; 45 §§ 8, 20, 31, 57, 58, 61; 49 §§ 19, 55, 65; 54 § 30. There is nothing in the lexicographers which refers to the ἀνάκρισις before the presiding magistrate: Harp. *s. v.* ἐχῖνος (= Phot. i, Suid. 1); Schol. Arist. *Vesp.* 1436 where οἱ διαιτηταί are named, (= Phot. 3, ἐχῖνοι—ἐπεδίδουν, and Suid. *s. v.* ἐχῖνοι); Photius, ἐχῖνος 2 (= Lex Seg. 258, 3, with trifling variants; cf. *Etym. Mag.* p. 404, 54); Harp. *s. v.* διαιτηταί; Pollux viii 127; Schol. Patm. Dem. 48 § 48.—It is clear from col. 31 l. 11 that Hesychius in ἐμπήκτης does not refer to the ἀνάκρισις as supposed in Meier and Schöm. *l. c.* (Wyse).

προσαρτήσαντες] used in several passages of *Hist. An.*

τοῖς τὴν φυλὴν τοῦ φεύγοντος δικάζουσι] 48 § 5; 58 § 2. Probably those of the Forty who belonged to the same tribe as the defendant.

§ 3. **ἐντὸς χιλίων κτλ.**] The number of the δικασταί varies with the value of the matter in dispute: for property under 1000 *dr.* the court consists of 201 δικασταί; for property above that amount, of 401. Pollux, viii 48, says of cases of φάσις: εἰσήγετο δὲ τὰ μὲν ἐντὸς χιλίων εἰς ἕνα καὶ διακοσίους, τὰ δὲ ὑπὲρ χιλίας εἰς ἕνα καὶ τετρακοσίους. This statement ultimately comes from the text which shews that the distinction was not confined to cases of φάσις. This conclusion had already been drawn by Heffter, *Att. Gerichtsverfass.* p. 55, and Fränkel, *Att. Geschworenengerichte*, p. 102. From Dem. *c. Mid.* 223 it has been inferred that the round number of 200 was the smallest number for a δικαστήριον: ἄν τε διακοσίους ἄν τε χιλίους ἄν θ' ὁπόσους ἂν ἡ πόλις καθίσῃ (Meier and Schöm. p. 170 Lips.).

οὐκ ἔξεστι κτλ.] In Dem. 45 § 57 Apollodorus charges Stephanus with having stolen an important deposition which the speaker expected to find in the ἐχῖνος. Cf. Meier and Schöm. p. 904 Lips.

§ 4. **ἑξηκοστὸν ἔτος**] *i.e.* on attaining the age of 59. As explained below, there was a cycle of 42 ἐπώνυμοι τῶν ἡλικιῶν. All who attained the age of 18 in any given year had an ἐπώνυμος assigned to them. After completing 41 years, during which they were liable to be called out on military duty, they reached the age of 59 and then served as διαιτηταί for one year,—their 'sixtieth year.' The ἐπώνυμος assigned to the ἔφηβοι in each year was the ἐπώνυμος of the διαιτηταί who had held office in the previous year.

δῆλον [ἐ]κ τῶν ἀρχόντων καὶ τῶν ἐπωνύμων. εἰσὶ γὰρ ἐπώνυμοι δέκα μὲν οἱ τῶν φυλῶν, δύο δὲ καὶ τετταράκοντα οἱ τῶν ἡλικιῶν· οἱ δ' ἔφηβοι ἐγγραφόμενοι πρότερον μὲν εἰς λελευκωμένα γραμματεῖα ἐνεγράφοντο, καὶ ἐπεγράφοντο αὐτοῖς ὅ τ' ἄρχων ἐφ' οὗ ἐνεγράφησαν καὶ ὁ ἐπώνυμος ὁ τῷ προτέρῳ [ἔτει] δεδιαιτηκώς, νῦν δ' εἰς στήλην χαλκῆν ἀναγράφονται, καὶ ἵσταται ἡ στήλη πρὸ τοῦ βουλε[υτ]ηρίου παρὰ τοὺς ἐπωνύμους. τὸν δὲ τελευταῖον τῶν

22 <οἱ> ἐγγραφόμενοι quondam Blass (H-L); οἱ etiam Harp. omisit. ΕΝΓΡΑΦ. **24** ὁ ἐπώνυμος: ἐπώνυμος Harp. ΠΡΟΤΕΡΩΙ (item Harp.): πρότερον K-W, Poland, B. ΔΕΔΙΑΙΤΗΚΩϹ (edd.): δεδεικτικῶς (Harp. codices plerique), δεδιητηκώς Aldum secutus Dind., δεδιῳκηκὼς Rose; ἐπιδεδημηκὼς Photius et Suidas. **26** 'π' (sc. περὶ) fortasse per errorem pro π̀ (sc. παρὰ)' K. περὶ dubitanter retinet K; παρὰ K-W, H-L, B.

20—25. *Harp. στρατεία ἐν τοῖς ἐπωνύμοις:...τίς ἦν ἡ ἐν τοῖς ἐπωνύμοις στρατεία δεδήλωκεν Ἀρ. ἐν Ἀθ. πολ. λέγων "εἰσὶ γὰρ ἐπώνυμοι—ἐνεγράφησαν (codd., item Phot. Suid., correxit Bekk.) καὶ ἐπώνυμος ὁ (καὶ ὁ ἐπώνυμος ὁ Aldum secutus Dind.; ὁ ἐπώνυμος καὶ ὁ Rose) τῷ προτέρῳ ἔτει δεδιητηκώς (Aldum secutus Dind.; δεδεικτικῶς G, -ῶς BD, δὲ δεικτικῶς AC; τῷ προτέρῳ ἐπιδεδημηκὼς Phot. et Suid.: δεδιῳκηκὼς Rose, *A. P.* p. 456)· νῦν δὲ εἰς τὴν βουλὴν ἀναγράφονται." Cf. Frag. 429^2, 469^3.

ἐπώνυμοι τῶν φυλῶν] 21 § 6.

τῶν ἡλικιῶν] It has been sometimes supposed that the archon ἐπώνυμος of the year, in which a citizen reached the age of military service, was deemed to be the ἐπώνυμος of that citizen and of all who came of age in the same year. Thus the 42 ἐπώνυμοι would be the series of 42 archons corresponding to the 42 groups of citizens who were at any given time between the ages of 18 and 60 (Schömann, *Ant.* p. 423; Gilbert, i 300). But in the text the ἄρχοντες are contrasted with the ἐπώνυμοι, and the latter divided into ἐπώνυμοι τῶν φυλῶν and τῶν ἡλικιῶν. As the ἐπ. τῶν φυλῶν derived their names from ten of the Attic heroes, selected out of 100 (21 § 6), the ἐπ. τῶν ἡλικιῶν were presumably selected out of the remaining 90. The period of military service was included within a cycle of 42 years, each of them probably bearing the name of one of the Attic heroes. When a youth attained the age of 18, he was enrolled under the archon of the year and also under the eponymous hero under whom those of the citizens who had just completed their 42 years had been originally entered. This is Mr Kenyon's view and it appears to be substantially correct, except that the 42nd year of service was really devoted to the duties of the διαιτηταί which occupied the sixtieth year of the citizen's life (ἑξηκοστὸν ἔτος). It was when he reached the age of 59 (not 60, as Mr Kenyon says) that the citizen served as an arbitrator.

The lists were unfortunately drawn up on perishable material, at first on wood and afterwards on bronze, and no example of the στήλη χαλκῆ of the writer's time has survived. Had marble been used instead, the result might have been different, and an interesting question might have been conclusively decided. We have indeed several lists of διαιτηταί, all on marble; but these are for another purpose. Thus for B.C. 325/4 we have no less than 103 names with the superscription: διαιτηταὶ οἱ ἐπὶ Ἀντικλ[έους ἄρχοντος] ἀνέθεσαν στεφανωθέντε[ς ὑπὸ τοῦ δή]μου (CIA ii 943); also (for an unknown year) a list of 88 names (*ib.* 944); and there are lists of a few such names for B.C. 330 and 329 (*ib.* 941—2). But none of these preserve any record of an ἐπώνυμος τῆς ἡλικίας.

λελευκωμένα] 47 §§ 2, 4.

ὁ ἐπ. ὁ—δεδιαιτηκώς] A brief expression for the eponymus of the citizens who served as διαιτηταί for the previous year.

δεδιαιτηκώς] In classic Attic this verb usually has the double augment in the pf. and plpf., *e.g.* pf. Dem. 33 § 31 δεδιῄτηκα, 21 § 85 κατεδεδιῃτήκει (Dind.) or καταδεδ- (Bekk.); Thuc. vii 77 δεδιῄτημαι, Dem. 21 §§ 85, 96 ἀπο-, 55 § 61 κατα-; plpf. ἐδεδιῄτητο, Thuc. i 132 ἐξ- (Veitch).

βουλευτηρίου κτλ.] Paus. i 5, 1, τοῦ β.... πλησίον Θόλος ἐστὶ καλουμένη...ἀνωτέρω

ἐπωνύμων λαβόντες οἱ [τεττ]αράκοντα διανέμουσιν αὐτοῖς τὰς
διαίτας, καὶ ἐπικληροῦσιν ἃς ἕκαστος διαιτήσει· καὶ ἀναγκαῖον ἃς
ἂν ἕκαστος λάχῃ διαίτας ἐκδιαιτᾶν. ὁ γὰρ νόμος, ἄν τις μὴ
γένηται διαιτητὴς τῆς ἡλικίας αὐτῷ καθηκούσης, ἄτιμον εἶναι
κελεύει, πλὴν ἐὰν τύχῃ ἀρχὴν ἄρχ[ω]ν τ[ιν]ὰ ἐν ἐκείνῳ τῷ ἐνιαυτῷ
ἢ ἀποδημῶν. οὗτοι δ' ἀτελεῖς εἰσὶ μόνοι. ἔστιν δὲ καὶ εἰσαγ- 6
γέλλειν εἰς τοὺς διαιτητάς, ἐάν τις ἀδικηθῇ ὑπὸ τοῦ διαιτητοῦ, κἄν
τινος καταγνῶσιν, ἀτιμοῦσθαι κελεύουσιν οἱ νόμοι· ἔφεσις δ' ἐστὶ
καὶ τούτοις. χρῶνται δὲ τοῖς ἐπωνύμοις καὶ πρὸς τὰς στρατείας, 7
καὶ ὅταν ἡλικίαν ἐκπέμπωσι, προγράφουσιν ἀπὸ τίνος ἄρχοντος
καὶ ἐπων[ύμου μ]έχρι τίνων δεῖ στρατεύεσθαι.

29 διαίτας (hiatu admisso) secl. K-W. ἐάν H-L. **31** τινὰ ἐν K-W, K[3], B; ἄλλην K[1], τις ἐν Burnet (H-L). **33** ΔΙΑΙΤΗΤΑϹ (K-W, K[3], B): δικαστὰς Harp. (K[1], et H-L qui alioquin εἰς τοὺς ἄλλους διαιτητὰς exspectarent). **36** Α<: ἀπὸ Harp. (K, K-W, H-L). **37** ΤΙΝΩΝ: τινος Harp.

§ **5** ἐπικληροῦσιν—ἄτιμον εἶναι. Pollux viii 126 infra exscriptus.
§ **6** Harp. εἰσαγγελία infra exscriptus.

δὲ ἀνδριάντες ἑστήκασιν ἡρώων, ἀφ' ὧν Ἀθηναίοις ὕστερον τὰ ὀνόματα ἔσχον αἱ φυλαί.

§ 5. **ἐπικληροῦσιν**] Pollux viii 126, ἐπεκληροῦντο αὐτοῖς αἱ δίαιται, καὶ ἀτιμία (cf. **ἄτιμον**) ἀφώριστο τῷ μὴ διαιτήσαντι τὴν ἐπικληρωθεῖσαν δίαιταν. In Dem. *Aphob.* iii 58 a public (as contrasted with a private) arbitrator is described as κληρωτός. Cf. Meier and Schöm. p. 1012 Lips.

ἐκδιαιτᾶν] not found in this sense elsewhere. Cf. ἐκδικάζειν in [Xen.] *Rep. Ath.* iii 2, δίκας καὶ γραφὰς καὶ εὐθύνας ἐκδικάζειν, and Lys. 17 § 5.

τῆς ἡλικίας—καθηκούσης] The age has hitherto been inferred from Bekker, *Anecd.* 235 (=Schol. Plat. *Leg.* 920 D), πάντες Ἀθηναῖοι οἷς ἑξηκοστὸν ἔτος ἦν (§ 4), and from the less precise statements in Pollux viii 126, ἐκ τῶν ὑπὲρ ἑξήκοντα ἔτη γεγονότων, and Hesych. οἱ περὶ ἑξήκοντα ἔτη γεγονότες. The age of 50 is wrongly given in Bekker *Anecd.* 186 and Suidas, *s. v.* διαιτηταί.

ἄτιμον] the severer form of ἀτιμία is probably meant.

ἀτελεῖς] 'exempt' from serving as διαιτηταί.

§ 6. **εἰσαγγέλλειν εἰς τοὺς διαιτητάς**] Harpocr. *s. v.* εἰσαγγελία· εἰ γάρ τις ὑπὸ διαιτητοῦ ἀδικηθείη, ἐξῆν τοῦτον εἰσαγγέλλειν πρὸς (εἰς K-W) τοὺς δικαστὰς (διαιτητὰς is Bergk's correction), καὶ ἁλοὺς ἠτιμοῦτο (cf. Bekk. *Anecd.* 235, 24=Schol. Plat. *Leg.* 920 D, and Lex. Dem. Patm. p. 13).

We have an example of this procedure in Dem. *c. Mid.* 86, φυλάξας τὴν τελευταίαν ἡμέραν τῶν διαιτητῶν—, κατηγορῶν ἔρημον οὐδενὸς παρόντος, ἐκβάλλει καὶ ἀτιμοῖ τὸν διαιτητήν, first explained in this sense by Bergk, *Zeitsch. f. Alt.* 1849, 273, supported by Fränkel, *Att. Geschworenenger.* p. 73 f., as quoted in Meier and Schöm. p. 334 Lips.; see also Daremberg and Saglio, iii 126. Cf. Dr Hager on εἰσαγγελία in Smith, *Dict. Ant.* i 710 *b*, where, however, it is accidentally stated that, in Harpocr. *l. c.*, Bergk 'rather needlessly' alters διαιτητὰς into δικαστάς: Bergk really altered δικαστὰς into διαιτητάς, and the text confirms his alteration. The διαιτηταί for any given year form a 'college,' or corporate body; they pass resolutions and decree rewards in the phrase ἔδοξεν τοῖς διαιτηταῖς (Hubert, *de Arbitris*, p. 25; Meier-Schöm. p. 1013 Lips.). It is their president who is described as πρυτανεύων in Dem. *Mid. l.c.* Hitherto it has been deemed uncertain whether the εἰσαγγελία of an arbitrator came before the διαιτηταί or before a body of δικασταί (Hubert, p. 55; Gilbert, i 371). The text is decisive for the former alternative: but it also shews that the sentence was subject to appeal. In the latter event it would come before a law-court.

§ 7. **προγράφουσιν—στρατεύεσθαι**] Lys. 14 § 6, σκέψασθε δὲ τίνες εἰσὶν οὓς δεῖ παρεῖναι. οὐχ οἵτινες ἂν τὴν ἡλικίαν ταύτην

54. *κληροῦσι δὲ καὶ τάσδε τὰς ἀρχάς· ὁδοποιοὺς πέντε, οἷς προστέτακται δημοσίους ἐργάτας ἔχουσι τὰς ὁδοὺς ἐπισκευάζειν·*
2 *καὶ λογιστὰς δέκα καὶ συνηγόρους τούτοις δέκα, πρὸς οὓς ἅπαντας ἀνάγκη τοὺς τὰς ἀρχὰς ἄρ[ξαντ]ας λόγον ἀπενεγκεῖν. οὗτοι γάρ εἰσι μόνοι <οἱ> τοῖς ὑπευθύνοις λογιζόμενοι, καὶ τὰς*

LIV 5 <οἱ> ins. J B Mayor, K-W, H-L, K[3], hiatu admisso.

TESTIMONIA. **LIV § 1** Schol. in Aeschin. 3 § 25 infra exscriptum.
§ 2 Bekk. *An.* 276, 17 *λογισταί: ἄρχοντές εἰσι κληρωτοί, δέκα τὸν ἀριθμόν, ἐφ' ὧν πάντες οἱ ἄρξαντες ἀρχὴν ἡντινοῦν λόγον ἀπέφερον τῶν διῳκημένων* (fere eadem Etym. M. 569, 32). *Ib.* p. 310, 6: *οἱ λογισταὶ τὰς εὐθύνας ἁπάσας εἰσῆγον* (cf. Phot. *ἡγεμονία δικαστηρίου*). Phot. *εὐθύνας: κυρίως ἃς εἰσάγουσιν οἱ λογισταὶ πρὸς τοὺς δόξαντας μὴ ὀρθῶς ἄρξαι τῆς πόλεως ἢ πρεσβεῦσαι κακῶς· καὶ τὰ δικαστήρια μὲν οἱ λογισταὶ κληροῦσι, κατηγορεῖ δὲ ὁ βουλόμενος· καὶ τοῖς δικασταῖς ἐφεῖται τιμᾶσθαι τοῖς ἁλοῦσιν* (eadem Bekk. *An.* 245, 6 et Lex. Dem. Patm. p. 142). *Lex. rhet. Cantab. *λογισταί*, infra exscriptum.

ἔχωσιν; Dem. *Ol.* 3 § 4, *ἐψηφίσασθε...καὶ τοὺς μέχρι πέντε καὶ τετταράκοντα ἐτῶν αὐτοὺς ἐμβαίνειν.* Aeschin. *F. L.* 133, *ψηφισαμένων ὑμῶν... τοὺς μέχρι τριάκοντα ἔτη γεγονότας ἐξιέναι*, *ib.* 168, *πρώτην δ' ἐξελθὼν στρατείαν ἐν τοῖς μέρεσι καλουμένην...καὶ τὰς ἄλλας τὰς ἐκ διαδοχῆς ἐξόδους τὰς ἐν τοῖς ἐπωνύμοις καὶ τοῖς μέρεσιν ἐξῆλθον* (Gilbert, i 302, and *Beiträge*, 51 ff.). Cf. Lycurg. *Leocr.* 39, *αἱ δ' ἐλπίδες τῆς σωτηρίας τῷ δήμῳ ἐν τοῖς ὑπὲρ πεντήκοντα ἔτη γεγονόσι καθειστήκεσαν.* For **προγράφουσιν**, cf. Arist. *Av.* 450, *(τοὺς ὁπλίτας) σκοπεῖν ὅ τι ἂν προγράφωμεν ἐν τοῖς πινακίοις.*

LIV § 1. **ὁδοποιοὺς**] mentioned in Aeschin. 3 § 25 (with Schol. *οἱ ἐπιμελούμενοι τῆς καθαρότητος τῶν ὁδῶν τῆς πόλεως*), and by a Comic poet quoted in Plut. *Praec. Reip. Ger.* 15 § 9, *Μητίοχος μὲν <γὰρ> στρατηγεῖ, Μ. δὲ τὰς ὁδούς, Μ. δ' ἄρτους ἐποπτᾷ, Μ. δὲ τἄλφιτα, Μητιόχῳ δὲ πάντα κεῖται, Μητίοχος δ' οἰμώξεται* (ascribed to Cratinus by Bergk; Meineke, *Frag. Com.* iv p. 675). Boeckh, II x, p. 257 Fränkel.

§ 2. **λογιστὰς**] 'Auditors'; *Pol.* 1322 *b* 11, speaking of *τὴν ληψομένην λογισμὸν καὶ προσευθύνουσαν (ἀρχήν), καλοῦσι δὲ τούτους οἱ μὲν εὐθύνους οἱ δὲ λογιστὰς οἱ δ' ἐξεταστὰς οἱ δὲ συνηγόρους.* It had already been proved by Boeckh (II viii, p. 239[3]) that the *λογισταί* and *εὔθυνοι* were separate bodies; and this is confirmed by the present treatise (cf. 48 § 4). Almost all the *ὑπεύθυνοι* had to send in their accounts to the *λογισταί* (Aeschin. *c. Ctes.* § 20, *ἐγγράφειν λόγον πρὸς τοὺς λογιστὰς καὶ εὐθύνας διδόναι*, § 22, *λόγον ἀποφέρειν πρὸς τοὺς λ.*, Schol. on §§ 9, 15). CIA ii 444, 446, (an *ἀγωνοθέτης*) *ἀπενήνοχεν λόγους εἰς τὸ μητρῷον καὶ πρὸς τοὺς λογιστὰς καὶ τὰς εὐθύνας ἔδωκεν.* In B.C. 454, 452, 435 they were 30 in number (CIA i 226, 228 and 32). The number was subsequently reduced to 10, possibly after the time of the Thirty. Gilbert, i 214.

συνηγόρους] mentioned in *Pol.* 1322 *b* 11, quoted above. The present passage is loosely paraphrased in *Lex. Rhet. Cant.* p. 672, 20: *'Α. ἐν τῇ 'Αθ. πολ. οὕτως λέγει· λογισταὶ δὲ αἱροῦνται [an κληροῦνται?] δέκα, παρ' οἷς διαλογίζονται πᾶσαι αἱ ἀρχαὶ τά τε λήμματα καὶ τὰς γεγενημένας δαπάνας· καὶ ἄλλοι δέκα συνήγοροι οἵτινες συνανακρίνουσι τούτοις· καὶ οἱ τὰς εὐθύνας διδόντες παρὰ τούτοις ἀνακρίνονται πρῶτον, εἶτα ἐφίενται εἰς τὸ δικαστήριον, εἰς ἕνα καὶ φ'* (Rose, *Frag.* 447[3]). Mr Kenyon, however, regards this notice as 'differing wholly from the present passage'; and Lipsius implies that the name of Aristotle is mentioned by mistake. Wilamowitz places it among the spurious fragments.

οὗτοι—τοῖς ὑπευθύνοις λογιζόμενοι] It was the *λογισταί* who received the accounts of outgoing officials; who examined them conjointly with the *συνήγοροι*; and brought the accounts before a law-court of 501 *δικασταί* under their own presidency (Meier and Schöm. pp. 257 ff. Lips.). These functions have sometimes been erroneously ascribed to the *εὔθυνοι* (*ib.* pp. 115, 208 and Lipsius in *Leipzig Verhandl.* p. 64). The procedure may be illustrated by the oath taken by the corresponding officials in the deme Myrrhinus, CIA ii 578, *ὀμνύναι δὲ τὸν ὅρκον καὶ τὸν λογιστὴν λογιεῖσθαι ἃ ἄν μοι δοκῇ ἀνηλωκέναι, καὶ τοὺς συνηγόρους συνηγορήσειν τῷ δήμῳ τὰ δίκαια καὶ ψηφιεῖσθαι ἃ ἄν μοι δοκῇ δικαιότατα εἶναι.*

εὐθύνας εἰς τὸ δικαστήριον εἰσάγοντες. κἂν μέν τινα κλέπτοντ' ἐξελέγξωσι, κλοπὴν οἱ δικασταὶ καταγιγνώσκουσι καὶ τὸ γνωσθὲν ἀποτίνεται δεκαπλοῦν· ἐὰν δέ τινα δῶρα λαβόντα ἐπιδείξωσιν, καὶ καταγνῶσιν οἱ δικασταί, δώρων τιμῶσιν, ἀποτίνεται δὲ καὶ τοῦτο δεκαπλοῦν· ἂν δ' ἀδικεῖν καταγνῶσιν, ἀδικίου τιμῶσιν, ἀποτίνεται δὲ τοῦθ' ἁπλοῦν, ἐὰν [πρὸ τῆς] ἐνάτης πρυτανείας ἐκτείσῃ τις, εἰ δὲ μή, διπλοῦται· τὸ <δὲ> δεκαπλοῦν οὐ διπλοῦται.

κληροῦσι δὲ καὶ γραμματέα τὸν κατὰ πρυτανείαν καλούμενον, 3

7 -ΓΙΝΩΙϹΚΟΥϹΙ: -γινω K-W; -γιγνω H-L, K^3; -γιγνῴ B, cf. 53, 7. ΓΝΩϹΘΕΝ (K, H-L): <κατα>γνωσθὲν K-W, B. 8 ΕΠΙΔΕΙΞ: ἀποδείξ. K-W. 10 ἐὰν H-L. 11 ΕΚΤΙϹΗΙ: ἐκτείσῃ K-W, H-L, K^3, B: cf. Meisterhans, p. 144^2, n. 1252. 12 <δὲ> ins. K (edd.).

10 ἀδικίου Harp. infra exscriptus.

§§ 3—5 Pollux viii 98: γραμματεὺς ὁ κατὰ πρυτανείαν κληρωθεὶς ὑπὸ τῆς βουλῆς ἐπὶ τῷ τὰ γράμματα φυλάττειν καὶ τὰ ψηφίσματα, καὶ ἕτερος ἐπὶ τοὺς νόμους ὑπὸ τῆς βουλῆς χειροτονούμενος. ὁ δ' ὑπὸ τοῦ δήμου αἱρεθεὶς γραμματεὺς ἀναγινώσκει τῷ τε δήμῳ καὶ τῇ βουλῇ. ἀντιγραφεὺς κτλ. (reliqua p. 195 *b* exscripta).

§§ 3, 4 *Harp. γραμματεύς:...ὁ γραμματεὺς πῶς τε καθίστατο καὶ τί ἔπραττεν, ὡς τῶν γραμμάτων τ' ἐστὶ κύριος καὶ τὰ ψηφίσματα τὰ γενόμενα φυλάττει καὶ τὰ ἄλλα πάντα ἀντιγράφεται καὶ παρακάθηται τῇ βουλῇ, δεδήλωκεν 'Αρ. ἐν 'Αθ. πολ. § 4 *Harp. ἀντιγραφεύς, p. 195 *b* exscriptus. § 5 Suidas (e lexico Photiano) γραμματεύς (1): οὗτος πράξεως μὲν οὐδεμιᾶς ἦν κύριος, ὑπανεγίνωσκε δὲ τῇ βουλῇ καὶ τῷ δήμῳ τὰ πραττόμενα. Bekk. *An.* 226 γραμματεύς: καὶ τὸν γραμματέα ὁ δῆμος χειροτονεῖ, "ἀναγνωσόμενον αὐτῷ καὶ τῇ βουλῇ· καὶ οὗτος οὐδενὸς" τὸ σύνολον ἄλλου "ἐστὶ κύριος" ἢ "τοῦ ἀναγνῶναι"... (Frag. 399^2, 439^3). Bekk. *An.* 185, 14. Suidas s.v. (2) κληρωτοὶ δὲ ἦσαν τὸν ἀριθμὸν τρεῖς, γράφοντες τὰ δημόσια. οὐδενὸς δὲ ἦσαν οἱ γραμματεῖς οὗτοι κύριοι, ἀλλ' ἢ τοῦ γράφειν καὶ ἀναγνῶναι.

τὰς εὐθύνας—εἰσάγοντες] Dem. *de Cor.* 117, ὅτε με εἰσῆγον οἱ λογισταί, and *F. L.* 211.

κλοπὴν] δημοσίων χρημάτων. Dem. *c. Timocr.* 112, εἰ μέν τις ἀγορανόμος ἢ ἀστυνόμος ἢ δικαστὴς κατὰ δήμους γενόμενος κλοπῆς ἐν ταῖς εὐθύναις ἑάλωκεν,—τούτῳ μὲν τὴν δεκαπλασίαν εἶναι, and 127, συνέδρου γενομένου κλοπὴν αὐτοῦ τὸ δικαστήριον κατέγνω καὶ δεκαπλάσιον ἀπέτισε.

καταγιγνώσκουσι] the compound verb, in the special sense, is followed by the simple participle τὸ γνωσθέν, which, although more general in itself, has its meaning necessarily coloured by the previous context. To repeat the preposition is no more necessary here than in 57, 7, where διατίθησι is followed in the next sentence by τίθησι. Cf. Dem. *Timocr.* 9, where τῆς βουλῆς κατεγνωκυίας is followed several lines later by τὰ γνωσθένθ' ὑπὸ τῆς βουλῆς. I may also refer to my note on Eur. *Bacch.* 1065, κατῆγεν, ἦγεν, ἦγεν, where *Hec.* 168, ἀπωλέσατ', ὠλέσατ', and *Med.* 1252, κατίδετ', ἴδετε, are quoted.

δῶρα...δεκαπλοῦν] This penalty is also mentioned in Dinarch. *c. Aristog.* 17. The penalty of death (unnoticed in the text) is mentioned *ib.* §§ 4, 20. The two penalties are contrasted as alternatives in Dinarch. *c. Dem.* 60 and *c. Philocl.* 5 (Meier and Schöm. p. 445, n. 723).

ἐπιδείξωσιν] *Pol.* 1259 *a* 16, ἐπιδεῖξαι ὅτι. Aeschin. 3 § 228, τῆς γὰρ αἰτίας αἰσχρὸν τὸν αἰτιώμενόν ἐστι τὸ ἔργον μὴ ἔχειν ἐπιδεῖξαι.

ἀδικίου] here of 'maladministration.' Plut. *Per.* 32, εἴτε κλοπῆς καὶ δώρων εἴτ' ἀδικίου βούλοιτό τις ὀνομάζειν τὴν δίωξιν. The term is not found in the Orators, but is mentioned in Harpocr. *s. v.* ἔστι δὲ ὄνομα δίκης. ἀποτίνυται δὲ τοῦτο ἁπλοῦν, ἐὰν πρὸ τῆς θ' πρυτανείας ἀποδοθῇ· εἰ δὲ μή, διπλοῦν καταβάλλεται. Meier and Schöm., p. 424—8; Lipsius, *Leipz. Verhandl.* p. 64.

δεκαπλοῦν οὐ διπλοῦται] This fact has been hitherto unknown.

§ 3. **γραμματέα**] The full title is ὁ κατὰ πρυτανείαν γραμματεὺς τῆς βουλῆς, with the shorter forms γρ. τῆς βουλῆς or γρ. κατὰ πρυτανείαν. The regular form before the year of Eucleides was ὁ γρ. τῆς βουλῆς. As an exception we find in B.C.

ὃς τῶν γραμμάτων ἐστὶ κύριος, καὶ τὰ [ψη]φίσματα τὰ γιγνόμενα φυλάττει, καὶ τἄλλα πάντα ἀντιγράφεται, καὶ παρακάθηται τῇ

14 ΓΡΑΜΜΑΤΕΩΝ: *γραμμάτων* ex Harp. et Polluce Burnet, Bywater, Blass, Naber, K-W, H-L, K³. <τ'> post *γραμμάτων* addidit B ex Harp. ΓΙΝ (K-W): *γεν*. Harp.

409/8, CIA i 61 (as restored by Köhler) *παραλαβόντες παρὰ [τ]οῦ [κατὰ πρυτανείαν γραμμα]τέως τῆς βουλῆς*. In the fourth century the title *ὁ γραμματεὺς ὁ κατὰ πρυτανείαν* is first found in an inscr. of B.C. 358/7 or of 354/3 (CIA ii 61, where the other title *ὁ γραμματεὺς τῆς βουλῆς* is also found, and where mention is made of *τοὺς ἄλλους γραμματέας τοὺς ἐπὶ τοῖς δημοσίοις γράμμασιν*). The two forms are interchanged with one another down to B.C. 322/1, when the short title *γρ. τῆς βουλῆς* appears for the last time (CIA ii 186), while the title *γρ. ὁ κατὰ πρυτανείαν* continues in use down to the Roman age (Gilbert in *Philol.* xxxix p. 131—6, and *Gr. St.* i 254; also Müller's *Handbuch*, IV i 167). This *γραμματεὺς* always belonged to a different tribe to that presiding at the time (CIA i 45, 46, 51, 61, 188; Gilbert, *Philol.* p. 133); but, in or after B.C. 322/1 (the date of the death of Aristotle), the *γρ.* so called belonged to the presiding tribe.

The 'full title' cited at the head of this note is not actually found except in CIA i 61 (as restored); and there is much to be said in favour of the restoration proposed by C. Schaefer: *παραλαβόντες παρὰ [τ]οῦ [βασιλέως μετὰ τοῦ γραμμα]τέως τῆς βουλῆς*. The special literature of the Athenian *γραμματεῖς* includes (in addition to the works already quoted) two dissertations of 1878 by C. Schaefer and C. A. Holle; and Hartel's *Studien*, published in the same year; also an article by von Wilamowitz (in *Hermes*, xiv 148—153), who, like Stoientin, in *Jahrb. f. Philol.* 1880, 189—202, rightly attributed to Aristotle the account which we find in Pollux. The dissertation by Kornitzer (1883) unfortunately receded from this position, which is now proved to be the only tenable one.

γραμμάτων—κύριος] 'is responsible for all public documents'. According to the law quoted in Dem. *c. Timocr.* 63, he delivered to the *θεσμοθέται* the decrees of the Council. **τὰ ψηφίσματα—φυλάττει**] 'has the (general) custody of the public archives' (in the *Μητρῷον*). In Dem. *F. L.* p. 381 these are described as under the (special) charge of a public slave: *ἐν τοῖς κοινοῖς τοῖς ὑμετέροις γράμμασιν ἐν τῷ Μητρῴῳ ταῦτ' ἐστίν, ἐφ' οἷς ὁ δημόσιος τέτακται*. This *γραμματεὺς* is mentioned by Aeschin. 3 § 15, *λόγον καὶ εὐθύνας ἐγγράφουσι πρὸς τὸν γραμματέα καὶ τοὺς λογιστάς*, and by Chamaeleon, ap. Athen. 407 C, (Alcibiades) *ἧκεν εἰς τὸ Μητρῷον, ὅπου τῶν δικῶν ἦσαν αἱ γραφαὶ καὶ βρέξας τὸν δάκτυλον ἐκ τοῦ στόματος διηλείψε τὴν δίκην τοῦ Ἡγήμονος· ἀγανακτοῦντες δὲ ὅ τε γραμματεὺς καὶ ὁ ἄρχων τὰς ἡσυχίας ἦγον δι' Ἀλκιβιάδην*.

τἄλλα ἀντιγράφεται] 'checks (or supervises) the transcription of all other public documents.' Thus, in the inventory of the *χαλκοθήκη* in CIA ii 61, ascribed to B.C. 358 or 354, *Εὐκλῆς ὁ δημόσιος* is to enter all the items and the *γρ. κατὰ πρυτανείαν* is to check them (*ἀντιγράφεσθαι δὲ τὸγ γραμματέα τὸγ κατὰ πρυτανείαν καὶ τοὺς ἄλλους γραμματέας τοὺς ἐπὶ τοῖς δημοσίοις γράμμασιν*), and lastly, the *γραμματεὺς τῆς βουλῆς* is to record the list on a tablet and to make a copy (*ἀντίγραφα*).

Pollux, viii 98, after describing the *γρ. ὁ κατὰ πρυτανείαν* and the *γρ. ἐπὶ τοὺς νόμους* in terms borrowed in part from the text, continues as follows: *ἀντιγραφεὺς πρότερον μὲν αἱρετὸς αὖθις δὲ κληρωτὸς ἦν καὶ πάντα ἀντεγράφετο παρακαθήμενος τῇ βουλῇ*. In Bekker's best MS the following words, *δύο δ' ἦσαν, ὁ μὲν τῆς βουλῆς ὁ δὲ τῆς διοικήσεως*, come after the next heading *λογισταί*, and this order is approved by Lipsius; but Harpocration *s. v.* agrees with the other MSS in making them apply to the *ἀντιγραφεῖς*:—*ὁ καθιστάμενος ἐπὶ τῶν καταβαλλόντων τινὰ τῇ πόλει χρήματα, ὥστε ἀντιγράφεσθαι ταῦτα* (Dem. *c. Androt.* p. 615 and Aeschin. *c. Ctes.* 25). *διττοὶ δὲ ἦσαν ἀντιγραφεῖς, ὁ μὲν τῆς διοικήσεως, ὥς φησι Φιλόχορος, ὁ δὲ τῆς βουλῆς, ὡς Ἀριστοτέλης ἐν Ἀθ. πολ.* Cf. Bekker's *Anecd.* p. 185, *ὁ δὲ καταγραφόμενος τὰ ἐν τῇ βουλῇ γενόμενα*. The present is the only passage in the treatise to which Harpocration can refer, but it is remarkable that the title *ἀντιγραφεύς* does not occur in the text.

*βουλῇ. πρότερον μὲν οὖν οὗτος ἦν χειροτονητός, καὶ τοὺς ἐνδοξο-
τάτους καὶ πιστοτάτους ἐχ[ειρ]οτόνουν· καὶ γὰρ ἐν ταῖς στήλαις
πρὸς ταῖς συμμαχίαις καὶ προξενί[αι]ς καὶ πολιτείαις οὗτος
ἀναγράφεται· νῦν δὲ γέγονε κληρωτός. κληροῦσι δὲ καὶ ἐπὶ τοὺς* 4
*νόμους ἕτερον, ὃς παρακάθηται τῇ βουλῇ, καὶ ἀντιγράφεται καὶ
οὗτος πάντας. χειροτονεῖ δὲ καὶ ὁ δῆμος γραμματέα τὸν* 5

17 Κ(ΑΙ)ΑΠΙΣΤ: corr. K. **19—20** ΕΠΙ ΤΟΥΤΟΙΣ Ν[Ο]ΜΟΝ ΕΤΕΡΟΝ: corr. K e Polluce (edd.).

§§ 4, 5. Cf. Testim. p. 194.

πρότερον] The date at which this official ceased to be *χειροτονητὸς* and became *κληρωτὸς* is unknown. The office became annual between B.C. 367 and 363. The last example of its being held for a *πρυτανεία* only is in 368/7; the first example of its being held for a year is in 363/2. Possibly appointment by lot was introduced about the same time.

τοὺς ἐνδοξοτάτους *κτλ.*] For the period between 450 B.C. and 403 B.C., about 28 names are known (Hille in *Leipz. Stud.* i 240); but only one is at all familiar, Ἀγύρριος Κ[ολλυτεὺς], CIA ii 1*b* (404/3 B.C.). In the fourth century, down to B.C. 322, we have 38 names, not one of them 'famous' (see Wyse in *Class. Rev.* v 276).

στήλαις] cf. note on Dem. *Lept.* § 36.

ταῖς συμμαχίαις] *e.g.* in B.C. 433/2, the treaties between Athens and Leontini (CIA iv 33 *a*) and Athens and Rhegium (CIA iv 13), *Χαρίας ἐγραμμάτευε*: also in B.C. 378/7, the second maritime Confederacy (CIA ii 17), *Καλλίβιος Κηφισοφῶντος ἐγραμμάτευε*. The latest example now known belongs to B.C. 356/5 (CIA ii 66).

προξενίαις] 'grants of the title of *πρόξενος*' (cf. note on Dem. *Lept.* 60, and Gilbert, i 173). As exx. we have (in B.C. 431/0) CIA i 45, *Προκλέης Ἀτάρβου Εὐωνυμεὺς ἐγραμμάτευε.—ἀναγραψάτω πρόξενον καὶ εὐεργέτην Ἀθηναίων* (*Ἀστίαν τὸν Ἀλεὸν*) *ἐστήλῃ λιθίνῃ ὁ γραμματεὺς ὁ τῆς βουλῆς καὶ καταθέτω ἐν πόλει.* *ib.* ii 29 (Echembrotos of Cleone)—*Πιστόξενος ἐγραμμάτευε*, and ii 3 (Amyntor, Eurypylus, &c) —*Δεξίθεος ἐγρ.—ἐπειδὴ καθῃρέθη ἡ στήλη ἐπὶ τῶν τριάκοντα ἐν ᾗ ἦν αὐτοῖς ἡ προξενία, ἀναγράψαι τὴν στήλην τὸν γρ. τῆς βουλῆς.* ii 21 (Eurytion) *Αἰσχύλος ἐγρ.*, ii 69 (Philiscus, B.C. 355) *ἐνάτης πρυτανείας ᾗ Πάνδιος Σωκλέους ἐξ Οἴου ἐγρ.—ἀναγράψαι τόδε τὸ ψήφισμα τὸν γρ. τῆς βουλῆς.* ii 119 (Apelles of Byzantium, B.C. 339)—*ἀναγράψαι αὐτοῦ τὴν προξενίαν τὸν γρ. τὸν κατὰ πρυτανείαν.* ii 124 (an officer of Philip in B.C. 337)—*ἀναγράψαι δὲ τὴν προξενίαν κτλ.* Cf. Monceaux, *Les Proxenies Grecques*, p. 83.

πολιτείαις] 'grants of citizenship. The oldest inscr. on this subject is that in Ἐφ. Ἀρχ. 1883, pp. 37, 38: *Ἵππαρχον* &c *Ἀθηναῖος ἐναι ἀνδραγαθίας ἕνεκα τῆς ἐς Ἀθηναίος καὶ φυλὴν καὶ δῆμον καὶ φρατρίαν ἐλέσθαι ἣν περ ἂν βόλωνται καὶ ἀναγράψαι αὐτὸς ἐστήλῃι λιθίνῃι τὸγ γραμματέα τῆς βολῆς.* CIA ii 243—*εἶναι Ὀξύθεμιν* (friend of Demetrius Poliorcetes)— —*Ἀθηναῖον—ἀναγράψαι δὲ τόδε τὸ ψήφισμα τὸν γραμματέα τὸν κατὰ πρυτανείαν.* *πολιτεία* is used of 'a grant of citizenship' in inscriptions of Ephesus, Ditt. no. 134, *ἀναγράψαι δὲ αὐτῷ τὴν πολιτείαν εἰς τὸ ἱερὸν τῆς Ἀρτέμιδος, οὗ καὶ αἱ λοιπαὶ πολιτε[ῖαι ἀν]αγεγραμμέναι εἰσίν*, and *ib.* 315, *ἀναγράψαι ὅπου καὶ αἱ λοιπαὶ πολιτεῖαι ἀναγεγραμμέναι εἰσί.* See Schömann, *Ant.* p. 355; Gilbert, i 175; *Dict. Ant.* i 443; Hartel, *Studien*, p. 271—3; Reinach, *l'Épigraphie Grecque*, p. 371.

ἀναγράφεται] Thus, in a decree in honour of Thrasybulus of Calydon, the first two lines are inscribed in large characters, CIA i 59: *[ἐπὶ Γλαυκί]ππου ἄ[ρ]χον[τ]ος. [Λόβων ἐκ] Κηδῶν ἐγραμμάτευε.* Then follows the decree in smaller characters and the name of the *γραμματεὺς* is repeated in the second line, *Λόβων ἐγραμμάτευε.* CIA ii 51 (decree of citizenship &c B.C. 369) l. 3—*Ἀζηνιεὺς ἐγραμμάτευε.* CIA ii 54 (do. B.C. 363)—*Παλληνεὺς ἐγρ.—τὸ δὲ ψήφισμα τόδε ἀναγράψαι τὸν γραμματέα τῆς βουλῆς.* Mr Wyse (*Class. Rev.* v 276 *a*) points out that this style is not found in any inscr. between 356/5 and 320/19.

§ 4. **ἐπὶ τοὺς νόμους**] Pollux viii 98, *καὶ ἕτερος ἐπὶ τοὺς νόμους ὑπὸ τῆς βουλῆς χειροτονούμενος.* The term *χειροτονούμενος* applies to the first *γραμματεὺς* of an earlier time, and not to the second *γραμματεύς*.

§ 5. **τὸν ἀναγνωσόμενον**] It is probably the same official that is meant in Dem. *Lept.* 94 (of a new law), *τῷ γραμματεῖ παραδοῦναι, τοῦτον δ' ἐν ταῖς ἐκκλησίαις ἀναγιγνώσκειν.* When the letter of Nicias was delivered in Athens (Thuc. vii 10) *ὁ γραμ-*

ἀναγνωσόμενον αὐτῷ καὶ τῇ βουλῇ, καὶ οὗτος οὐδενός ἐστι κύ[ρι]ος ἀλλὰ τοῦ ἀναγνῶναι.

6 *κληροῖ δὲ καὶ ἱεροποιοὺς δέκα, τοὺς ἐπὶ τὰ ἐκθύματα καλουμένους, [οἳ] τά τε [μαν]τευτὰ ἱερὰ θύουσιν, κἄν τι καλλιερῆσαι*
7 *δέῃ, καλλιεροῦσι μετὰ τῶν μάντε[ων]. κληροῖ δὲ καὶ ἑτέρους δέκα, τοὺς κατ' ἐνιαυτὸν καλουμένους, οἳ θυσίας τέ τινας θύουσι, [καὶ τ]ὰς πεντετηρίδας ἁπάσας διοικοῦσιν πλὴν Παναθηναίων.*

23 ἀλλα : ἀλλ' ἢ Blass, Richards, Gennadios (e Suida K-W, H-L); ἀλλὰ defendit K, sed ἀλλ' ἢ fortasse praestat. **28** διοικοῦσι H-L.

§§ **6, 7** *Etym. M. *ἱεροποιοί: κληρωτοὶ ἄρχοντές εἰσι δέκα τὸν ἀριθμόν, οἳ τά τε μαντεύματα ἱεροθετοῦσι* (*ἱεροθύτουν* cod. V; *ἱεροθυτοῦσι* cod. D, Bekk. *An.* 265, et Photius: *οἳ τὰ μεμαντευμένα ἱερὰ θύουσιν* Lex. Dem. Patm.), "*κἄν τι καλλιερῆσαι δέῃ καλλιεροῦσι μετὰ τῶν μάντεων,*" *καὶ θυσίας τὰς νομιζομένας ἐπιτελοῦσι* "*καὶ τὰς πενταετηρίδας ἁπάσας διοικοῦσι πλὴν Παναθηναίων.*" *ταῦτα δὲ 'Αρ. ἱστορεῖ ἐν τῇ 'Αθ. πολ.* Pollux viii 107 *ἱεροποιοί*, p. 198 *a* exscriptus.

ματεὺς [τῆς πόλεως] παρελθὼν ἀνέγνω τοῖς 'Αθηναίοις, where Herwerden, Stahl and Hude bracket *τῆς πόλεως*. The margin of M (the MS in the British Museum) has: *ὑπηρέτην τὸν εἰωθότα ἐν τῷ κοινῷ δήμῳ τὰ γράμματα ἀναγιγνώσκειν*. We should have expected to find him named in CIA ii 61, 26, *ἀκούσασαν δὲ τὴν βουλὴν ἀνταναγιγνωσκομένων τ[ῶν ἀναγεγραμμένων κτλ.]*. In CIA ii 114, 10 (B.C. 343/2) we read of a decree in honour of Phanodemus: *ἀναγνῶναι τόδε τὸ ψήφισμα τὸγ γραμματέα τῷ δήμῳ*. In [Plut.] ii 841 F, we learn that the orator Lycurgus required the *γρ. τῆς πόλεως* to see that the authorised text alone of Aeschylus, Sophocles and Euripides was adopted in the public performances of their plays, [Plut.] ii 841 F, *τὸν τῆς πόλεως γραμματέα παραναγινώσκειν τοῖς ὑποκρινομένοις*.

ἀλλὰ]=ἀλλ' ἢ in *Eth. N.* x 5, 1176 *a* 22, vii 13, 1152 *b* 30, *Rhet.* ii 23, 1402 *a* 27 (Index Ar.).

§ 6. **ἱεροποιοὺς**] 'Commissioners of sacrifices.' *Pol.* 1322 *b* 18, *ἄλλο δ' εἶδος ἐπιμελείας ἡ περὶ τοὺς θεούς. οἷον ἱερεῖς τε καὶ ἐπιμεληταὶ τῶν περὶ τὰ ἱερὰ τοῦ σῴζεσθαί τε τὰ ὑπάρχοντα καὶ ἀνορθοῦσθαι τὰ πίπτοντα τῶν οἰκοδομημάτων καὶ τῶν ἄλλων ὅσα τέτακται πρὸς τοὺς θεούς*—(*b* 24) *οἷον ἱεροποιοὺς κτλ.* The text is quoted in Etym. Magn., without any distinction between the two boards. The article adds a reference to Dem. p. 47, 13, *οἱ λογοποιοὶ τὰς πομπὰς ὑμῖν πομπεύουσι μετὰ τῶν ἱεροποιῶν.* The *ἱεροποιοί* are mentioned under the Four Hundred in 30 § 2. Cf. [Dem.] 58 § 29, *τὴν μὲν ἀρχὴν ἣν ἐκεῖνος ἄρχων ἐτελεύτησεν, ἱεροποιὸς ὤν, παρὰ τοὺς νόμους ἦρχεν οὗτος, οὔτε λαχὼν οὔτ' ἐπιλαχών.* CIA ii 741 (B.C. 334/3), *ἐκ τοῦ δερματικοῦ—ἐκ τῆς θυσίας τῇ 'Αγαθῇ Τύχῃ παρὰ ἱεροποιῶν —ἐξ 'Ασκληπιείων παρὰ ἱεροποιῶν—ἐγ Βενδιδέων, παρὰ ἱεροποιῶν.* (B.C. 333/2), [*ἐκ Πανα*]*θηναίων παρὰ* [*ἱεροποιῶ*]*ν.* B.C. 332/1 *ἐκ Παναθηναίων παρὰ ἱεροποιῶν, ἐξ 'Ελευσινίων παρὰ ἱεροποιῶν.* Certain kinds of *ἱεροποιοί*, however, were elected and not appointed by lot. Thus, Dem. *c. Mid.* §§ 115, 171 states that he had the honour of being 'elected' from among all the Athenians as one of the three *ἱεροποιοὶ τῶν σεμνῶν θεῶν*. In an inscr. published in *'Αθήναιον*, 6 p. 483, we find 10 *ἱεροποιοὶ οἱ αἱρεθέντες ὑπὸ τῆς βουλῆς* (out of the 10 tribes). Gilbert i p. 249; Müller's *Handbuch*, v 3, 34.

ἐκθύματα] The word is hitherto only known in the sense of 'pustule' (Hipp. *Epid.* 3, 1086 L and S). *ἐκθύω*, however, means in act. to sacrifice, in Soph. *El.* 572, and Eur. *Cycl.* 371; and, in middle, to expiate. In the text *ἐκθύματα* (if genuine) means 'expiations.' The corresponding phrase in an inscr. of B.C. 329/8, in 'Εφ. 'Αρχ. 1883, 110—126, B 82, is *εἰς τὰ ἐπιθύσιμα*.

μαντευτὰ] 'appointed by oracle.' Xen. *Anab.* vi 1, 22, *ἐθύετο τῷ Διΐ, ὅσπερ αὐτῷ μαντευτὸς ἦν.* Sacrifices are enjoined in the *μαντεῖαι* quoted by Dem. *c. Mid.* 52—54.

καλλιερῆσαι] [Xen.] *Vect.* vi 3, *τούτοις (τοῖς θεοῖς) καλλιερήσαντας ἄρχεσθαι τοῦ ἔργου.*

§ 7. **τοὺς κατ' ἐνιαυτὸν**] possibly corresponding to the *ἐπιμελητάς* of 30 § 2.

πεντετηρίδας] These festivals are also enumerated in Pollux viii 107 (as cor-ϵ[ἰσὶ δὲ] πεντετηρίδες μία [μὲν ἡ εἰ]ς Δῆλον (ἔστι δὲ καὶ ἑπ[τε]τηρὶς ἐνταῦθα), δευτέρα δὲ Βραυρώνια, τρίτη [δὲ Ἡράκλει]α,

29 ϵ[ἰσὶ δὲ] K, K-W, ε̄ (sc. πέντε) [δ' εἰσὶ] H-L (B). πεντετηρίδες <δ'> K-W.

---

rected by Rose), ἱεροποιοί· δέκα ὄντες οὗτοι ἔθυον θυσίας τὰς <νομιζομένας καὶ (τὰς added by Kenyon)> πεντετηρίδας <διοικοῦσι>, τὴν εἰς Δῆλον, τὴν ἐν Βραυρῶνι, τὴν τῶν Ἡρακλείων (Ἡρακλειδῶν codd.; corr. Jungermann), τὴν Ἐλευσῖνι.

πλὴν Παναθηναίων] At this festival the procession was marshalled by the δήμαρχοι: Suidas, *s. v.* οὗτοι δὲ διεκόσμουν τὴν ἑορτὴν τῶν Παναθηναίων, and Schol. Arist. *Nub.* 37, οὗτοι δὲ τὴν πομπὴν τῶν Παναθηναίων ἐκόσμουν. In CIA ii 741 ἱεροποιοὶ are twice mentioned in connexion with a Panathenaic festival: *a* 34, [ἐκ Πανα]θηναίων παρὰ [ἱεροποιῶ]ν, and *c* 8, [ἐκ Πα]ναθηναίων παρὰ ἱερο[ποιῶν]. The former refers to B.C. 333/2, the latter to 332/1, and, as neither of these is the 3rd year of an Olympiad, the lesser Panathenaea must be meant, and not the 'penteteric' festival mentioned in the text. The difficulty is more serious in CIA i 188, 74 (Ditt. no. 44): ἀθλοθέταις παρεδόθη ἐς Παναθήναια τὰ μεγάλα (such and such a sum), ἱεροποιοῖς κατ' ἐνιαυτόν, Διύλλῳ Ἐρχιεῖ καὶ συνάρχουσιν ἐς τὴν ἑκατόμβην (5114 dr.). Boeckh, II p. 8 Fränkel, supposes that, in the Panathenaea, it was the ἀθλοθέται who undertook the duties connected with the games, which were undertaken by the ἱεροποιοὶ in the other festivals, while the ἱεροποιοὶ were only concerned with making arrangements for the hecatomb.

εἰς Δῆλον] The ancient πανήγυρις at Delos was revived by the Athenians in the spring of B.C. 425, Thuc. iii 104, 2, τὴν πεντετηρίδα τότε πρῶτον μετὰ τὴν κάθαρσιν ἐποίησαν οἱ Ἀθηναῖοι, τὰ Δήλια. Besides the πεντετηρὶς mentioned in the text there was an annual θεωρία (Plat. *Phaedo* 58 B, *Crito* 43 C). Hermann, *Gottesdienst. Alt.* § 65, 31—34.

It was formerly supposed that the Delian festival was held on the 6th and 7th of Thargelion = May-June (Boeckh, II p. 72 Fränkel). The Delian inscriptions point to its having been really held in the month known at Delos as Ἱερὸς, corresponding to the Attic Anthesterion = Feb.-March (Robert in *Hermes* xxi 161, approved by A. Mommsen in Bursian's *Jahresb.* 1886, 3 p. 335—8). It included musical (Plut. *Nic.* 3; Lucian *de Salt.* 16) and gymnastic competitions, as well as horse-races (Thuc. iii 104; Dittenberger, 121, 16).

M. Homolle (*Bull. Corresp. Hellén.*, 1891, pp. 149—155) remarks that 'the inventories from Delos for 279 B.C. mention 30 of the cups that the Athenians gave every year, and 23 of the wreaths that they gave every four years... He also remarks that the inventories for 334 B.C., which come next in date, mention 11 of these cups and 20 of these wreaths, so that the last cup would have been given in 315 B.C., and the last wreath in 322. He argues that, as the Athenians certainly left Delos before 310 B.C., the cessation of their gifts after 315 B.C. is attributable to their departure and marks the exact date. But then one would like to know why there was not a twenty-fourth wreath for 318 B.C. The new treatise suggests the reason. It states that the Athenians held a festival at Delos every four years; but adds parenthetically *and every six years also*, and then alludes obscurely to the archonship of Cephisophon in 329 B.C. Suppose that [after the festival in 330] the interval was increased in 329 from four years to six: the twenty-second and twenty-third wreaths would then belong to 324 B.C. and 318 B.C. and would probably complete the series; for there is no other record of festivals at Delos every six years, and such festivals would presumably have been recorded, had they existed for any length of time' (Mr Torr in *Class. Rev.* v 277).

Βραυρώνια] The festival originally held at Brauron in honour of Artemis is mentioned in Hdt. vi 138 (cf. Arist. *Lysistr.* 646 and Schol.). It was afterwards held in the Brauronion on the Acropolis (Paus. i 23, 9; Wilamowitz, *Aus Kydathen*, 128 n. 47 f.). We have lists of dresses dedicated to Artemis by Athenian ladies (CIA ii 751 ff., p. 113), one of whom actually bears the name of Πεντετηρὶς (*ib.* 756, 15, B.C. 345).

There was also a festival held at Brauron in honour of Dionysus, Arist. *Pax* 874 with Schol. ἐκεῖ δὲ καὶ τὰ Διονύσια ἤγετο, καὶ καθ' ἕκαστον δῆμον. Hence the Dionysia are described by Suidas i 454 as having been held every four years at Brauron. But the country Dionysia were celebrated annually through-τετάρτη δὲ Ἐλευ[σίνι]α, [πέμπτη] δὲ Παναθήναια· καὶ τούτων οὐδεμία ἐν τῷ αὐτῷ ἐγγί[γνεται]. *[ἆθλα] δὲ πρόκειται [*κατὰ τὰ ψη]φίσ[ματα τὰ*] ἐπὶ Κηφισοφῶντος ἄρχοντος.

31 Ἐλευ[σίνι]α, [ε̄] δὲ Wyse (K³, qui ε̄ pro πέμπτη scribi potuisse ostendit, coll. c. 47 § 4 ubi [θ̄] pro ἐνάτης recte datum; 'dispiciuntur vestigia litterae ϵ, et super eam ductus transversus qui numerum indicat' (B). Ἐλευσίνια. τὰ δὲ K-W. **32** ΟΥΔΕΜΙΑ ΕΝ? legit K; ΟΥΔΕΤΡΙΑ H-L; equidem puto primitus fuisse οὐδέτερα. ΕΝΤΩΙΑΥΤΩΙΓΙΝΕΤΑΙ: ἐν τῷ αὐτῷ ἐγγί[νεται] K¹; ἐν τῷ αὐτῷ ἔτει γίνεται J B Mayor; ἐν τῷ αὐτῷ ἐνιαυτῷ γίγνεται Blass (H-L). [τ]ὰ δὲ Παναθήναια ⟦καὶ⟧ τούτων οὐδεμιᾷ ἐν τῷ αὐτῷ ἐν[ιαυτῷ] γίνε[ται] K-W; καὶ τούτων οὐδεμία ἐν τῷ αὐτῷ ἐν[ιαυτῷ] γίγνε[ται] B. **32** . . . . . δὲ πρόκειται . . . . αις . . . . ἐπὶ Κηφισοφῶντος ἄρχοντος K, qui ante αις aut φ,

---

out Attica; and it is more probable that the festival under the control of the ἱεροποιοί was the distinctive Brauronian festival of *Artemis*. Hemsterhuys, Corsini and others refer the Brauronian πεντετηρίς (cf. Pollux viii 107) to the Dionysia. K. O. Müller points out that the existence of a ἱέρεια τῆς Ἀρτέμιδος τῆς Βραυρωνίας (Dinarch. *Arist.* 12) does not prevent the festival being under the management of the ἱεροποιοί, and Rinck, *die Religion der Hellenen*, ii 105, refers it to the festival of Artemis. Hermann *l. c.* § 62, 14—20.

Ἡράκλεια] Dem. *F. L.* § 125, παῖδας καὶ γυναῖκας ἐκ τῶν ἀγρῶν κατακομίζειν ἐψηφίζεσθε... καὶ τὰ Ἡράκλεια ἐν ἄστει θύειν. Harpocr. *s. v.* πολλῶν ὄντων τῶν κατὰ τὴν Ἀττικὴν Ἡρακλείων νῦν ἂν ὁ Δημοσθένης μνημονεύοι ἤτοι τῶν ἐν Κυνοσάργει, ταῦτα γὰρ μάλιστα διὰ τιμῆς εἶχον Ἀθηναῖοι. The festival referred to by Dem. was probably held about midsummer, apparently in the month Hecatomboeon, at the same time as the Panathenaea: Steph. Byz. *s. v.* Ἐχελίδαι·—τοῦ τετρακώμου Ἡρακλείου, ἐν ᾧ τοὺς γυμνικοὺς ἀγῶνας ἐτίθεσαν τοῖς Παναθηναίοις (Böhnecke, *Forschungen*, p. 655). On the Ἡράκλεια at Marathon, cf. Paus. i 15, 4; Pind. *Ol.* ix 95, Schol. Pind. *Ol.* xiii 110. See also Hermann *l. c.* § 62, 21—24.

Ἐλευσίνια] A festival held (as the context shews) once in four years and therefore distinct from the *Eleusinia* in the ordinary sense of the term. A. Mommsen, *Heortologie*, 1864, p. 243, doubted its existence. Cf., however, inscr. from Eleusis in Ἐφ. Ἀρχ. 1883, pp. 110—126 β 50, σύμπαν κε[φάλαιον ἱερεῦσι καὶ] ἱερείαις εἰς τὴν τριετηρίδα τῶν Ἐλευσινίων καὶ εἰς τὴν πεντετηρίδα, cf. *ib.* 1887, p. 3, v. 25, τῆς πανη[γύρε]ως τῶν Ἐλευ[σι]νίων τῶν μεγάλων. It has been conjectured that the τριετηρίς and πεντετηρὶς fell in the second and fourth year respectively of the Olympiad. If the inscr. in CIA ii 741 (Ditt. 374) is correctly restored, the ἱεροποιοί, presumably οἱ κατ' ἐνιαυτόν, were concerned with the *annual* celebration of the Ἐλευσίνια, cf. *c* 66 [ἐξ Ἐλε]υσινίων παρὰ ἱεροποιῶ[ν—], B.C. 432/1, the *first* year of an Olympiad, and *d* 74 ἐ[ξ Ἐλευσινίων παρὰ] ἱεροπ[οιῶν—], B.C. 331/0, the *second* year of an Ol. For the fourth year of an Ol., 333/2, the inscr. *b* 39, as restored in the *Corpus*, has [ἐκ τῆς θυσ]ίας [τῇ Δήμητρι καὶ τῇ Κόρῃ] τῇ Δαείρ[ᾳ παρὰ ἐπιμελητῶ]ν. (Wyse, in *Class. Rev.* v 335 *b*.)

The inscr. in Ἐφ. Αρχ. 1883, mentioning the πεντετηρὶς τῶν Ἐλευσινίων, refers to B.C. 329/8, the very year in which Cephisophon was archon. Payments are there made to the ἱεροποιοὶ οἱ κατ' ἐνιαυτόν, β 8 and 38 (κατὰ ψήφισμα δήμου [τ]ὸ [εἰς θ]υσ[ίας]), and to the ἱεροποιοὶ ἐγ βουλῆς β 67, 72, 76, 82 (εἰς τὰ ἐπιθύσιμα), γ 4 (Wyse, *ib.*).

Παναθήναια] the great Panathenaea; c. 60.

ἐν τῷ αὐτῷ] probably means 'in the same place,' which is true, the festivals being associated with Delos, Brauron, Marathon, Eleusis and Athens respectively. 'At the same time' is in itself a less likely interpretation. It is not at all probable that the festivals would actually clash in respect of date; but there would be no point in drawing attention to this. The Delian festival and the great Panathenaea were alike in the third year of an Olympiad (Thuc. iii 104). The *Delia* of 334 fell in the third year; those of 279 in the second year of an Ol. The Delia were probably held in the month of Anthesterion; the Panathenaea (and probably the Heracleia) in Hecatomboeon; the Eleusinia possibly in the fourth year of an Olympiad, and probably in the same month as the annual Eleusinia, *i.e.*

κληροῦσι δὲ καὶ εἰς Σαλαμῖνα ἄρχοντα, καὶ εἰς Πει[ραι]έα 8
δήμ[αρχ]ον, οἳ τά τε Διονύσια ποιοῦσι ἑκατέρωθι καὶ χορηγοὺς

aut fortasse ρ, scriptum fuisse arbitratus, conicit [τοῦτο] δὲ πρόκειται [γραφ]αῖς [ταῖς] ἐπὶ κτλ. .....δὲ πρόκειται [ἐν γρα]φαῖς (ΦΔΙ B) [ταῖς] ἐπὶ κτλ. K-W. [νόμος] δὲ πρόκειται [περὶ τούτων τεθεὶς] ἐπὶ κτλ. H-L, invita papyro. equidem tentavi [ἆθλα] δὲ πρόκειται [πάσ]αις [καθάπερ] ἐπὶ κτλ.; vel [ἐν ταῖς γρα]φαῖς [ταῖς] ἐπὶ κτλ., coll. Plut. ii 1134 A, ἡ τῶν Παναθηναίων γραφὴ περὶ μουσικοῦ ἀγῶνος; vel [κ(ατὰ) τὰς σ(υγ)γρα]φὰς [τὰς] ἐπὶ κτλ. (coll. Dittenb. *Sylloge*, p. 24); vel potius [ἆθλα] δὲ πρόκειται [κ(ατὰ) τὰ ψη]φίσ[ματα τὰ] ἐπὶ κτλ.; sed Cephisophon Olympiadis in anno quarto archon erat, nec video cur in anno proximo post Panathenaea, potius quam ante ludos illos, nova praemia decreta fuerint; eo meliore igitur iure πέμπτη δὲ Παναθήναια delenda putat B.
34 ΠΕΙ...ΕΑ, Πειραιέα K, K-W, B: Πειραιᾶ H-L. **35** ποιοῦσι etiam H-L.

---

in Boedromion. The month (and even the year) of the Brauronia is unknown. (A. Mommsen, *Heortol.* 409, assigns it to the 16th of Munichion.)

The insertion of ἐνιαυτῷ is only possible if we disconnect the Panathenaea from the four penteteric festivals. The text, as edited by K-W, implies that not one of these four is in the same year as the Panathenaea; which is only possible if the Delian festival had already been transferred to the second year of the Ol., and the Heracleia to the first year, leaving the Brauronia (and possibly the Eleusinia) in the fourth year.

l. 32. **ἆθλα δὲ πρόκειται**] The suggestion ἆθλα is confirmed (in point of sense) by the context, and (in point of expression) by *Pol.* 1330 *a* 33, τοῖς δούλοις ἆθλον προκεῖσθαι τὴν ἐλευθερίαν, Hdt. ix 101, ἄεθλα πρόκειται, viii 93, ἄεθλον ἔκειτο, *ib.* 26, τὸ ἄεθλόν σφι κείμενον, Plat. *Rep.* 638 C, προκείμενα ἆθλα, Xen. *Cyr.* ii 3, 2, ἆθλα πρόκειται, i 6, 18 ἆθλα προτιθείς. Cf. inscr. found at Sestos, in Dittenberger, 246, 78 (before 120 B.C.), τιθεὶς ἆθλα πάντων τῶν ἀθλημάτων τοῖς τε νέοις καὶ τοῖς ἐφήβοις. It is a welcome confirmation of this suggestion to find that ἆθλα has been independently proposed by Mr Newman, *Class. Rev.* v 117 *b*.

The inscr. already quoted from 'Εφ. 'Αρχ. 1883, pp. 110—126, describes the payments made to the ἱεροποιοὶ οἱ κατ' ἐνιαυτόν, β 8 and 38 κατὰ ψήφισμα δήμου [τ]ὸ [εἰς θ]υσ[ίας], and γ 7 καὶ τοῦτο (more than 1000 *dr.*) ἱεροποιοῖς κατεβάλομεν κατὰ ψήφισμα δήμου ὃ Λυκοῦργος εἶπεν. The date of the inscr. is the archonship of Cephisophon, B.C. 329/8. It is clear that in that year, on the proposal of Lycurgus, there was a special decree of the people affecting the πεντετηρὶς of the 'Ελευσίνια. The same decree added a horse-race to the contests, and we are told that the prize in that contest was 70 medimni, β 38, 48, εἰς τὴν ἱπποδρομίαν τὴν προστεθεῖσαν κατὰ ψήφισμα ἆθλα μέδιμνοι ΡΔΔ. The suggestion in the text assumes that, under the active administration of Lycurgus (cf. Dürrbach, *Lycurgue*, pp. 99—102), prizes for the other festivals as well were the subject of decrees in the same year, but there is no evidence on this point. It may also be admitted that the 4th year of an Olympiad is not a very likely year for a decree to be passed affecting the Panathenaic and Delian festivals, which would not be held till three years later, in the 3rd year of an Olympiad.

ἐπὶ Κηφισοφῶντος] B.C. 329/8, the latest date mentioned in this treatise.

§ 8. **εἰς Σαλαμῖνα ἄρχοντα**] CIA ii 594 (127 B.C.?), v. 1, ἐ[πὶ] 'Επικλέους ἄρχοντος ἐν ἄστει, ἐν Σαλαμῖνι δὲ 'Ανδρονίκο[υ], v. 31, Διονυσίων τῶν ἐν Σαλαμῖνι τραγῳδοῖς. *ib.* ii 469 (somewhat before 69 B.C.), v. 75 and 80, ἐπὶ Πυθέου ἄρχοντος ἐν Σαλαμῖνι, ἐν ἄστει δὲ 'Ιππάρχου, v. 82, Διονυσίων τῶν ἐν Σαλαμῖνι τραγῳδῶν ἐν ἀγῶνι (cf. n. 470, v. 58). Before the discovery of this treatise there was nothing to shew how the archon in Salamis was appointed. Cf. de Schoeffer, *De Deli Insulae Rebus*, p. 201: 'Archon Salaminis insulae fueritne ab Atheniensibus constitutus an a cleruchis electus, prorsus ignoramus; nomen archontis minime obstat quominus illud verisimilius videatur,' Dittenberger, *Syll. Inscr. Graec.* n. 383, n. 2, on an 'archon' in a decree of Scyros posterior to 196 B.C. (Wyse in *Class. Rev.* v 335.)

Salamis was not reckoned as a regular Attic deme, but as a community dependent on Athens. Hence (like Athens) it had an archon at its head (Hermann, *Staatsalt.* § 117, 4).

εἰς Πειραιέα δήμαρχον] In CIA ii 573 *b* we have a decree, of the second half of the fourth century, placing the θεσμοφόριον in the Peiraeus under the protection of the δήμαρχος. In ii 573 the δήμαρχος is mentioned in connexion with a theatre in the Peiraeus. In an inscr.

*καθιστᾶσιν· ἐν Σαλα[μῖνι] δὲ καὶ τὸ [ὄν]ομα τοῦ ἄρχοντος
ἀναγράφεται.*

55. *αὗται μὲν οὖν αἱ ἀρχαὶ κληρωταί τε καὶ κύριαι τῶν
[εἰρη]μένων [πραγμάτ]ων εἰσίν. οἱ δὲ καλούμενοι ἐννέα ἄρ-
χοντες, τὸ μὲν ἐξ ἀρχῆς ὃν τρόπον καθίσταντο [εἴρη]ται· [νῦν]
δὲ κληροῦσιν θεσμοθέτας μὲν ἓξ καὶ γραμματέα τούτοις, ἔτι δ'
ἄρχοντα καὶ βασι[λέα] καὶ πολέμαρχον, κατὰ μέρος ἐξ ἑκάστης
2 <τῆς> φυλῆς. δοκιμάζονται δ' οὗτοι πρῶτον μὲν ἐν τῇ [βουλῇ] τοῖς
πεντακοσίοις, πλὴν τοῦ γραμματέως, οὗτος δ' ἐν δικαστηρίῳ*

LV 1 'an *κληροῦνται καὶ κύριαι?*' K-W. **3** *[εἴρη]ται [ἤδη· νῦν]* K, K-W, H-L: *[εἴρη]ται· [νῦν]* B, cum versus proximi in spatio eodem non plus quam tres exstent litterae. **4** *κληροῦσι* H-L. **5** *ἑκάστης <τῆς>* B. **7, 10** *<τῷ> δικαστηρίῳ* hic et in c. 45, 7 K-W; idem in c. 46, 13 et c. 55, 10 articulum omissum non inserunt.

TESTIMONIA. **LV §§ 1, 2, 4** Heraclidis epitoma; Rose Frag. 611, 8: *εἰσὶ δὲ καὶ ἐννέα ἄρχοντες. θεσμοθέται ς'* (Coraes; *θεσμοθέται καὶ* vel *θεσμοθετικοὶ καὶ* codd.) *οἳ δοκιμασθέντες ὀμνύουσι δικαίως ἄρξειν καὶ δῶρα μὴ λήψεσθαι ἢ ἀνδριάντα χρυσοῦν ἀναθήσειν.*

§§ 2, 3 Pollux viii 85, 86, p. 202 *b* exscriptus. *Lex. rhet. Cantab. *θεσμοθετῶν ἀνάκρισις: κατὰ Ἀριστοτέλην οἱ θεσμοθέται ἐκ τῶν θ̄ ἀρχόντων, αὐτοὶ ἓξ ὄντες. οἱ δὲ λαχόντες ὑπὸ τῆς βουλῆς τῶν πεντακοσίων καὶ τοῦ δικαστηρίου "δοκιμάζονται" "πλὴν τοῦ γραμματέως" ἐρωτώμενοι τίνες αὐτῶν πατέρες, ὁμοίως καὶ δήμων τίνων εἰσί, καὶ "εἰ ἔστιν" αὐτοῖς "Ἀπόλλων πατρῷος καὶ Ζεὺς ἕρκειος," καὶ εἰ τοὺς "γονέας" εὖ ποιοῦσι, καὶ εἰ "τὰ τέλη" τελοῦσι, καὶ εἰ τὰς ὑπὲρ τῆς πατρίδος στρατείας ἐστρατεύσαντο* (Frag. 375^{2}, 414^{3}).

---

ascribed to the beginning of the 3rd cent., *ib.* 589, one Callimedon has a place of precedence assigned him *ἐν τῷ θεάτρῳ ὅταμ ποιῶσι Πειραιεῖς τὰ Διονύσια—καὶ εἰσαγέτω αὐτὸν ὁ δήμαρχος εἰς τὸ θέατρον.* Lastly, in ii 1059, a lease granted by the *Πειραιεῖς* is superscribed *ἐπὶ Ἀρχίππου ἄρχοντος* (B.C. 321/0), *Φρυνίωνος δημαρχοῦ[ντος]*. Cf. Wachsmuth, *Stadt Athen*, ii 5. While, in the other demes, the *δήμαρχος* was elected by the members of the deme, in the important deme of the Peiraeus he was appointed by lot. Otherwise he would have become too powerful a personage.

Διονύσια] *τὰ κατ' ἀγρούς*, celebrated in the month Poseideon, and on the grandest scale in the Peiraeus. CIA ii 589 (quoted above), *ib.* 741 (Ditt. 374), 6, 72, 79, *ἐγ Διονυσίων τῶν ἐν Πειραιεῖ*. Cf. Müller's *Handbuch*, v 3, 162, and Wyse in *Class. Rev.* v 276 *b*.

LV—LVI § 1. *On the nine Archons.* Hermann, *Staatsalt.* § 138; Schömann, *Ant.* p. 410—414; Gilbert, i 239—243; *Dict. Ant. s. v.*

LV § 1. **ἐξ ἀρχῆς**] c. 3 §§ 2—4; 8 § 1; 22 § 5; 26 § 2.

κληροῦσιν *κτλ.*] The process is described in c. 8 § 1, *ταῖς φυλαῖς τὸ δέκα κληροῦν ἑκάστην, εἶτ' ἐκ τούτων κυαμεύειν.*

θεσμοθέτας—ἓξ ἑκάστης τῆς φυλῆς] It has hitherto been uncertain whether, in the annual appointment of archons, the holders of the office were taken from different tribes. Those who (like Schömann, p. 410) accepted this view, supposed that one of the ten tribes was unrepresented. We now learn that the tenth tribe supplied the *γραμματεὺς* to the *θεσμοθέται*.

γραμματέα] The existence of a *γρ.* to the *thesmothetae* has hitherto been unknown. Pollux, viii 92, after stating that the three first archons select two *πάρεδροι* each, adds: *προσαιροῦνται δὲ καὶ γραμματέα, ὃς ἐννόμῳ δικαστηρίῳ κρίνεται*, but says nothing of any such secretary to the other six archons.

§ 2. **δοκιμάζονται**] Harpocr. *s. v. δοκιμασθείς·—Λυκοῦργος δ' ἐν τῷ περὶ διοικήσεως "γ' δοκιμασίαι κατὰ τὸν νόμον," φησί, "γίνονται, μία μὲν ἣν οἱ θ' ἄρχοντες δοκιμάζονται κτλ."* Bekk. *Anecd.* 235, 11. Dem. *Lept.* 90 describes the six *thesmothetae* as undergoing a double *δοκιμασία*, *ἔν τε τῇ βουλῇ καὶ παρ' ὑμῖν ἐν τῷ δικαστηρίῳ* (cf. Lys. 15 § 2). Dem. 57 §§ 66, 70 refers to the *δοκιμασία* of all the nine archons. Gilbert, i 208; Schömann, p. 406.

μόνον, ὥσπερ οἱ ἄλλοι ἄρχον[τες] (π[άντες γὰρ καὶ] οἱ κληρωτοὶ
καὶ οἱ χειροτονητοὶ δοκιμασθέντες ἄρχουσιν), οἱ δ' ἐννέα [ἄρχ]οντες
[ἔν] τε τῇ βουλῇ καὶ πάλιν ἐν δικαστηρίῳ. καὶ πρότερον μὲν οὐκ
ἦρχεν ὅντ[ιν' ἀ]ποδοκιμάσειεν ἡ βουλή, νῦν δ' ἔφεσίς ἐστιν εἰς τὸ
δικαστήριον, καὶ τοῦτο κύριόν ἐστι τῆς δοκι[μα]σίας. ἐ[πε]ρωτῶ- 3
σιν δ', ὅταν δοκιμάζωσιν, πρῶτον μὲν 'τίς ‖ σοι πατὴρ καὶ πόθεν [Col. 28.]
τῶν δήμων, καὶ τίς πατρὸς πατήρ, καὶ τίς μήτηρ, καὶ τίς μητρὸς
πατὴρ καὶ πόθεν τῶν δήμων;' μετὰ δὲ ταῦτα, εἰ ἔστιν αὐτῷ
Ἀπόλλων πατρῷος καὶ Ζεὺς ἕρκειος, καὶ ποῦ [τ]αῦτα τὰ ἱερά
ἐστιν, εἶτα ἠρία εἰ ἔστιν καὶ ποῦ ταῦτα, ἔπειτα γονέας εἰ εὖ ποιεῖ,
[καὶ] τὰ τέλη τελεῖ, καὶ τὰς στρατείας εἰ ἐστράτευται. ταῦτα δ'

9 ἐννέ' K-W, B. **12** ἐπερωτῶσι H-L. **16** ἑρκεῖος edd. **18** <εἰ> τελεῖ K-W e Lex. Cantabr. coll. Dinarch. ii 18.

πάντες—δοκιμασθέντες ἄρχουσιν] Aeschin. *c. Ctes.* §§ 14, 15; Lysias 26 §§ 6, 12. Pollux viii 44, *δοκιμασία δὲ τοῖς ἄρχουσιν ἐπηγγέλλετο καὶ τοῖς κληρωτοῖς καὶ τοῖς αἱρετοῖς, εἴτ' ἐπιτήδειοί εἰσιν ἄρχειν εἴτε καὶ μή*. The text states that, whereas the nine archons were examined by the Council and by the law-court, all the other officers (whether appointed by lot or by show of hands) were examined by the law-court alone. This is in exact agreement with the view put forward by C. Schaefer in *Jahrb. f. class. Phil.* 1878, 821 (the other views are stated in Gilbert, i 208, n. 3).

The passages bearing on the *δοκιμασία* of the *ἀρχαὶ χειροτονηταί* are Dem. 40 § 34, *χειροτονησάντων ὑμῶν ἐμὲ ταξίαρχον ἧκεν αὐτὸς ἐπὶ τὸ δικαστήριον δοκιμασθησόμενος*, and Aesch. *Ctes.* 15, *χειροτονητὰς ἀρχὰς...ἄρχειν δοκιμασθέντας ἐν τῷ δικαστηρίῳ*. In the latter passage it is added that the *κληρωταὶ ἀρχαὶ* are *οὐκ ἀδοκίμαστοι*, but nothing is stated about the law-courts. Cf. c. 45 § 3.

§ 3. **πρῶτον μὲν** κτλ.] Dinarchus, *Aristog.* 17, *ἀνακρίνοντες τοὺς ὑπὲρ τῶν κοινῶν τι μέλλοντας διοικεῖν, τίς ἐστι τὸν ἴδιον τρόπον, εἰ γονέας εὖ ποιεῖ, εἰ τὰς στρατείας ὑπὲρ τῆς πόλεως ἐστράτευται, εἰ ἱερὰ* (*ἠρία* Baiter and Sauppe, coll. § 18 *πατρὸς μνῆμα*) *πατρῷα ἔστιν, εἰ τὰ τέλη τελεῖ*. Xen. *Mem.* ii 2, 13, *ἐὰν δέ τις γονέας μὴ θεραπεύῃ, τούτῳ δίκην τε ἐπιτίθησι καὶ ἀποδοκιμάζουσα οὐκ ἐᾷ ἄρχειν τοῦτον... καὶ ἐάν τις τῶν γονέων τελευτησάντων τοὺς τάφους μὴ κοσμῇ, καὶ τοῦτο ἐξετάζει ἡ πόλις ἐν ταῖς τῶν ἀρχόντων δοκιμασίαις*. Lys. 16 § 9 (of the *δοκιμασία* of a *βουλευτής*), *ἐν ταῖς δοκιμασίαις δίκαιον εἶναι παντὸς τοῦ βίου λόγον διδόναι*. Pollux, viii 85, 86, gives a summary of the text, *ἐκαλεῖτο δέ τις θεσμοθετῶν ἀνάκρισις* (Dem. *Eubul.* 66), *εἰ Ἀθηναῖοί εἰσιν ἑκατέρωθεν ἐκ τριγονίας καὶ τὸν δῆμον* (corrected in margin of Cobet's copy into *τῶν δήμων*, which is proved to be right by the text) *πόθεν, καὶ εἰ Ἀπόλλων ἔστιν αὐτοῖς πατρῷος καὶ Ζεὺς ἕρκειος, καὶ εἰ τοὺς γονέας εὖ ποιοῦσι, καὶ εἰ ἐστράτευνται ὑπὲρ τῆς πατρίδος καὶ εἰ τὸ τίμημα ἔστιν αὐτοῖς*. In the quotation in *Lex. Rhet. Cant.* the clause last quoted is in closer accordance with the text, *εἰ τὰ τέλη τελοῦσι*: though the form in Pollux has been supposed to be the older form (Gilbert i 210, n. 1).

πατρὸς πατήρ...μητρὸς πατὴρ] Pollux viii 85, *Ἀθηναῖοι—ἐκ τριγονίας*, not necessarily part of an earlier formula.

Ἀπόλλων πατρῷος—Ζεὺς ἕρκειος] The gods of the Athenian's home. Dem. 57 § 54, *παιδίον ὄντα μ' εὐθέως ἦγον εἰς τοὺς φράτερας, εἰς Ἀπόλλωνος πατρῴου ἦγον*, and § 67 quoted below. Cf. Harp. *s. v.* *τὸν δὲ Ἀπόλλωνα κοινῶς πατρῷον τιμῶσιν Ἀθηναῖοι ἀπὸ Ἴωνος· τούτου γὰρ οἰκίσαντος τὴν Ἀττικήν, ὡς Ἀριστοτέλης φησί, τοὺς Ἀθ. Ἴωνας κληθῆναι καὶ Ἀπόλλωνα πατρῷον αὐτοῖς ὀνομασθῆναι*, and *s. v.* *ἕρκειος Ζεύς· Δείναρχος ἐν τῷ κατὰ Μοσχίωνος "εἰ φράτορες αὐτῷ καὶ βωμοὶ Διὸς ἑρκείου καὶ Ἀπόλλωνος πατρῴου εἰσίν." ἑρκ. Ζεύς, ᾧ βωμὸς ἐντὸς ἕρκους ἐν τῇ αὐλῇ ἵδρυται.—ὅτι δὲ τούτοις μετῆν τῆς πολιτείας οἷς εἴη Ζεὺς ἕρκειος, δεδήλωκε καὶ Ὑπερείδης κτλ.*

ἠρία] Dem. 57 § 66, *ὥσπερ γὰρ τοὺς θεσμοθέτας ἀνακρίνετε, ἐγὼ τὸν αὐτὸν τρόπον ἐμαυτὸν ὑμῖν ἀνακρινῶ.* (67)—*οἰκεῖοί τινες εἶναι μαρτυροῦσιν αὐτῷ; πάνυ γε· πρῶτον μέν γε τέτταρες ἀνεψιοί,—εἶτ' Ἀπόλλωνος πατρῴου καὶ Διὸς ἑρκείου γεννῆται, εἶθ' οἷς ἠρία ταὐτά* (cf. Dinarchus, quoted above).

ἀνερωτήσας, 'κ[ά]λει,' φησίν, 'τούτων τοὺς μάρτυρας.' ἐπειδὰν δὲ παράσχηται τοὺς μάρτυρας ἐπερωτᾷ, 'τούτου βούλεταί τις
4 κατηγορεῖν;' κἂν μὲν ᾖ τις κατήγορος, δοὺς κατηγορίαν καὶ ἀπολογίαν, οὕτω δίδωσιν ἐν μὲν τῇ βουλῇ τὴν ἐπιχειροτονίαν, ἐν δὲ τῷ δικαστηρίῳ τὴν ψῆφον· ἐὰν δὲ μηδεὶς βούληται κατηγορεῖν, εὐθὺς δίδωσι τὴν ψῆφον· καὶ πρότερον μὲν εἷς ἐνέβαλλε τὴν [ψ]ῆφον, νῦν δ' ἀνάγκη πάντας ἐστὶ διαψηφίζεσθαι περὶ αὐτῶν, ἵνα, ἄν τις πονηρὸς ὢν ἀπαλλάξῃ τοὺς κατηγόρους, ἐπὶ τοῖς δικασταῖς
5 γένηται τοῦτον ἀποδοκιμάσαι. δοκιμασθέν<τες> δὲ τοῦτον τὸν τρόπον, βαδίζουσιν πρὸς τὸν λίθον ἐφ' ο[ὗ] τὰ τόμι' ἐστίν, ἐφ' οὗ καὶ οἱ διαιτηταὶ ὀμόσαντες ἀποφαίνονται τὰς διαίτας, καὶ οἱ μάρτυρες ἐξόμνυνται τὰς μαρτυρίας. ἀναβάντες δ' ἐπὶ τοῦτον ὀμνύουσιν δικαίως ἄρξειν καὶ κατὰ τοὺς νόμους, καὶ δῶρα μὴ λήψεσθαι τῆς ἀρχῆς ἕνεκα, κἄν τι λάβωσι, ἀνδριάντα ἀναθήσειν χρυσοῦν. ἐντεῦθεν δ' ὀμόσαντες εἰς ἀκρόπολιν βαδίζουσιν καὶ πάλιν ἐκεῖ ταὐτὰ ὀμνύουσι, καὶ μετὰ ταῦτ' εἰς τὴν ἀρχὴν εἰσέρχονται.

56. λαμβάνουσι δὲ καὶ παρέδρους ὅ τε ἄρχων καὶ ὁ βασι-

20 ΒΟΥΛΕΥΤΑΙ: corr. K. **25** ἵν' ἐὰν H-L. **27** ΔΟΚΙΜΑΣΘΕΝ (K): *δοκιμασθέν<τες>* Rutherford, Richards, Blass, K-W, H-L. **28** ὑφ' ᾧ τὰ ταμεῖά (ΤΑΜΙ?) ἐστιν K[1]; ἐφ' οὗ τὰ τόμι' ἐστίν van Leeuwen (H-L, K[3]); ἐφ' ᾧ κτλ. B; ὑφ' ('ΕΦ an ΥΦ incertum; utrumque libri Pollucis') ῳ τὰ τόμι' ἐστίν K-W. mihi quidem littera Υ cum Φ connexa potius quam Ε scripta videbatur (sed Ε posse legi censent K et K-W); sequitur ο potius quam litterae ω initium. **31** ὀμνύουσι H-L. **32** λάβωσιν H-L. **33** βαδίζουσι H-L.
LVI 1 καὶ ὁ βασιλεὺς om. Harp.

§ **5, 28** *Harp. λίθος (cf. Testim. ad c. 7, 5).
TESTIMONIA. **LVI § 1** Pollux viii 92: *πάρεδροι δ' ὀνομάζονται οὓς αἱροῦνται ἄρχων καὶ βασιλεὺς καὶ πολέμαρχος, δύο ἕκαστος οὓς βούλεται. δοκιμασθῆναι δ' αὐτοὺς ἐχρῆν ἐν τοῖς πεντακοσίοις, εἶτ' ἐν δικαστηρίῳ. προσαιροῦνται δὲ καὶ γραμματέα, ὃς ἐννόμῳ δικαστηρίῳ κρίνεται.* *Harp. πάρεδρος: 'Αρ. δ' ἐν τῇ 'Αθ. πολ. φησι "λαμβάνουσι δὲ καὶ παρέδρους ὅ τε ἄρχων <καὶ ὁ βασιλεὺς Rose, coll. Meier *Att. Proc.* p. 57; *Bull. de Corr. Hell.* vii 158> καὶ ὁ πολέμαρχος, δύο ἑκάτερος (ἕκαστος Rose) οὓς ἂν βούληται, καὶ οὗτοι—παρεδρεύσωσιν" (cf. Suid. s. v.). Frag. 389[2], 428[3].

---

§ 4. **ψῆφον**] Meier and Schöm. p. 635 ff. Lips.

ἀπαλλάξῃ] Dem. *c. Timocr.* § 37, ἂν ἀπαλλάξῃ τις τὸν ἐπιστάντα, and ἀπαλλάξας καὶ διαφθείρας, also And. *de Myst.* 122, *supra* c. 27 *ad fin.*

§ 5. **πρὸς τὸν λίθον**] Dem. 54 § 26, πρὸς τὸν λίθον (Harpocr.; βωμὸν MSS) ἄγοντες καὶ ἐξορκίζοντες. Plut. *Sol.* 25, ὤμνυεν ὅρκον ἕκαστος τῶν θεσμοθετῶν ἐν ἀγορᾷ πρὸς τῷ λίθῳ.

ἐφ' οὗ τὰ τόμι' ἐστίν] Dem. 23 *c. Aristocr.* 68 (the prosecutor in a case of homicide before the Areopagus) ὄμνυσιν... στὰς ἐπὶ τῶν τομίων κάπρου καὶ κριοῦ καὶ ταύρου. Arist. *Lys.* 186, καί μοι δότω τὰ τόμιά τις. The archon's oath was taken (Pollux viii 86) πρὸς τῇ βασιλείῳ στοᾷ, ἐπὶ τοῦ λίθου ὑφ' ᾧ τὰ ταμεῖα (ita codex Schotti; ἐφ' ᾧ τε ceteri: ἐφ' οὗ τὰ τόμια ὑός corr. Bergk, *Ep. crit. ad Schiller.*, p. 131).

ἀνδριάντα ἀναθήσειν] 7 § 1. Gilbert, i 211, n. 3.

LVI § 1. **παρέδρους**] In [Dem.] 59 § 72, and in CIA ii 597, the πάρεδρος to the archon βασιλεὺς is mentioned. Gilbert, i 218, n. 4.

λεὺς καὶ ὁ πολέμαρχος δύο ἕκαστος, οὓς ἂν βούληται, καὶ οὗτοι δοκιμάζονται ἐν τῷ δικαστηρίῳ πρὶν παρεδρεύειν, καὶ εὐθύνας διδόασιν ἐπὰν παρεδρεύσωσιν.

καὶ ὁ μὲν ἄρχων εὐθὺς εἰσελθὼν πρῶτον μὲν κηρύττει, ὅσα 2
τις εἶχεν πρὶν αὐτὸν εἰσελθεῖν εἰς τὴν ἀρχήν, ταῦτ' ἔχειν καὶ κρατεῖν μέχρι ἀρχῆς τέλους. ἔπειτα χορηγοὺς τραγῳδοῖς καθίσ- 3
τησι τρεῖς, ἐξ ἁπάντων Ἀθηναίων τοὺς πλουσιωτάτους· πρότερον δὲ καὶ κωμῳδοῖς καθίστη πέντε, νῦν δὲ τούτους αἱ φυλαὶ φέρουσιν. ἔπειτα παραλαβὼν τοὺς χορηγοὺς τοὺς ἐνηνεγμένους ὑπὸ τῶν φυλῶν εἰς Διονύσια ἀνδράσιν καὶ παισὶν καὶ κωμῳδο[ῖ]ς, καὶ εἰς Θαργήλια ἀνδράσιν καὶ παισὶν (εἰσὶ δ' οἱ μὲν εἰς Διονύσια κατὰ

2 ἕκαστος: ἑκάτερος Harp. (K[1]). ἂν: ΕΑΝ. **4** ΕΠΑΝ: ἐπειδὰν H-L. **9** ΤΟΥΤΟΙΣ K et H-L, 'i.e. τοῖς κωμῳδοῖς χορηγοὺς φέρουσιν': τούτους Wyse coll. Dem. 39 § 7 (K-W, B). **11—12** ἀνδράσι—παισὶ—ἀνδράσι H-L.

§ **3** Lex. rhet. Cantab. ἐπώνυμος ἄρχων :...ἔχει δὲ ἐπιμέλειαν χορηγοὺς καταστῆσαι "εἰς Διονύσια" καὶ "Θαργήλια," ἐπιμελεῖται δὲ καὶ τῶν "εἰς Δῆλον" καὶ τῶν ἀλλαχόσε πεμπομένων Ἀθήνηθεν χορῶν...

ἕκαστος] ἑκάτερος is found in the citation in Harpocr., where, however, καὶ ὁ βασιλεὺς is omitted. It was conjectured by Meier (*Att. Proc.* p. 71 Lips.) that it was owing to this omission that ἕκαστος had been corrupted into ἑκάτερος. We now see that this was actually the case (Lipsius, *Leipz. Verhandl.* p. 53, n. 3, was accidentally led to state the contrary by the reading in Mr Kenyon's first edition, ἑκάτερος).

§§ 2—7. *The Archon.*

§ 3. **χορηγοὺς**] Dem. *Lept.* Introd. p. iv—vii; Haigh's *Attic Theatre*, p. 71—75; Albert Müller's *Bühnenalterthümer*, p. 193.

τραγῳδοῖς] Lys. 24 § 9, κατασταθεὶς χορηγὸς τραγῳδοῖς, 19 § 29, τραγῳδοῖς δὶς χορηγῆσαι. Cf. Kühner, § 426, 2.

τρεῖς] In tragedy the number of competitors was limited to three. In the extant notices we never find more than three tragic poets competing, *e.g.* B.C. 467, (1) Aeschylus, *S. C. T.* &c, (2) Aristias, (3) Polyphradmon. B.C. 431, (1) Euphorion, (2) Sophocles, (3) Euripides, *Medea*, &c. B.C. 428, (1) Euripides, *Hippolytus*, &c, (2) Iophon, (3) Ion. Cf. Haigh, *Attic Theatre*, p. 19.

κωμῳδοῖς—πέντε] In comedy the number of competitors during the fifth century was three, as in tragedy: thus Aristophanes, in producing at the City Dionysia the *Clouds*, the *Peace* and *Birds*, during the latter part of the fifth century, had in each case two competitors. The same was the rule at the Lenaea. With the beginning of the fourth century the number was raised to five at both festivals (cf. Arg. Arist. *Plut.* and CIA ii 972, Haigh, *l.c.* p. 30—31).

τούτους—φέρουσιν] Dem. p. 996, 22, οὐκοῦν...οἴσουσί με, ἂν χορηγὸν ἢ γυμνασίαρχον ἢ ἑστιάτορα ἢ ἐάν τι τῶν ἄλλων φέρωσιν; It is only in the case of comedy that the φυλαὶ nominate; and even here it is a recent innovation. The χορηγοὶ concerned with the production of tragedies were not nominated by the tribes; cf. Lipsius, *Leipz. Verhandl.* 1885, p. 411.

Διονύσια] ἐν ἄστει. Elaphebolion 9-13.

ἀνδράσιν καὶ παισὶν] At the City Dionysia, besides the dramatic contests, there were choral competitions, between choruses of men and boys respectively. There were five choruses of men and five of boys, each chorus being provided by one of the ten tribes, each tribe being represented by one of its members as χορηγός. Haigh, *l. c.* pp. 14, 15.

Θαργήλια] On the second day of the festival, about May 25, there was a competition among the cyclic choruses of men and boys. Lys. 21 § 1, Θαργηλίοις νικήσας ἀνδρικῷ χορῷ, Ant. *de Chor.* §§ 11—13, of a χορὸς παίδων, CIA ii 553, εἴ τις ἄλλος νενίκηκεν ἀπ' Εὐκλείδου ἄρχοντος παισὶν ἢ ἀνδράσιν Διονύσια ἢ Θαργήλια κτλ. Dem. *Mid.* § 10 (lex), Θαργηλίων τῇ πομπῇ καὶ τῷ ἀγῶνι. Cf. A. Mommsen, *Heortol.*, 414—424.

φυλάς, εἰς Θαργήλια [δὲ] δυοῖν φυλαῖν εἷς· παρέχει δ' ἐν μ[έρει] ἑκατέρα τῶν φυλῶν), τούτοις τὰς ἀντιδόσεις ποιεῖ καὶ τὰς σκήψεις εἰσ[άγει, ἐά]ν τις ἢ λελητουργη[κέ]ν[αι] φῇ π[ρό]τερον ταύτην τὴν λῃτουργ[ίαν, ἢ ἀ]τελὴς εἶναι λελῃ[τουργηκὼς ἑ]τέραν λῃτουργίαν καὶ τῶν χρόνων αὐτῷ [τῆς ἀτελ]είας μὴ ἐξελη[λυ]θό[των, ἢ τὰ τετταράκοντα] ἔτη μὴ γεγονέναι· δεῖ γὰρ τὸν τοῖς παι[σὶν χορη]γοῦντα ὑπὲρ τετταρά[κον]τα ἔτη γεγονέναι. καθίστησι δὲ καὶ εἰς Δῆλον χορηγούς, καὶ ἀρχ[ιθ]έω[ρον τ]ῷ τριακοντορίῳ τῷ τοὺς

13 δέ, quod in lacuna absorptum censet K, in codicis imagine videre sibi visi sunt H-L, B: idem a librario omissum putant K-W. ΔΥΕΙΝ K[1], B: δυοῖν K-W, K[3], B (coll. Meisterhans, p. 162[2], ubi in titulis δυεῖν cum plurali tantum coniungi dicitur). **14** τούτοις), τὰς ἀντιδόσεις ποιεῖ K[1]; τούτοις τὰς κτλ. K-W (K[3], B); τοῦτον), τὰς κτλ. Richards (H-L). **15** λε......η π[ρὸς] ἕτερον K[1]; λεληιτουργηκέναι φῇ πρότερον scripsi (K[3], B); ΛΕΛΟΥΤΗΡΓ pr.? (Blass); λεληιτουργη[κέναι λέ]γῃ
H
π[ρ]ότερον K-W. **16** ΛΕΙΤΟΥΡΓΙΑΝ (vel ΛΟΥΤΗΡΓΙΑΝ pr.). ἢ ἀ]τελὴς εἶναι· λεληιτουρ[γηκέναι γὰρ] K-W; ἢ ἀ]τελὴς εἶναι λελῃ[τουργηκὼς K[3] (B). **17** τῶν χρόνων αὐτῷ [τῆς ἀτελ]είας μὴ ἐξελη[λυ]θό[των, ἢ τὰ $\bar{\mu}$] ἔτη K[3]; eadem (omisso $\bar{\mu}$ quod olim protuli) B; ἐξεληλυθότων non accipiunt K-W. Locum totum **15—19** ita constituunt H-L: ἐάν τις ἢ λέγῃ πένης εἶναι ἢ πρὸς ἕτερον ταύτην τὴν λῃτουργίαν μᾶλλον ἀνήκειν ἢ λῃτουργεῖν ἤδη ἑτέραν λῃτουργίαν ἢ τῶν χρόνων αὐτῷ ἕνεκα...είας μὴ ἐξεῖναι, διὰ τὸ τὰ νόμιμα ἔτη μὴ γεγονέναι. Melius K-W: ἐάν τις ἢ λεληιτουργηκέναι λέγῃ πρότερον ταύτην τὴν λῃτουργίαν, ἢ ἀτελὴς εἶναι· λεληιτουργηκέναι γὰρ ἑτέραν λῃτουργίαν καὶ τὸν χρόνον αὐτῷ τῆς ἀτελείας μὴ ἐξελθεῖν, ἢ τὰ νόμιμ' (incertum) ἔτη μὴ γεγονέναι. **18** παισὶ H-L. **20** ἀρχιθεώρους Torr coll. CIG 158 *a* 33 (H-L, K[3]); ἀρχιθέωρον Lipsius, Fränkel, K-W, B. Cf. Boeckh, ii 84[3], n. 391.

19 *Harp. ὅτι νόμος ἐστὶν ὑπὲρ τεσσαράκοντα τη γενόμενον χορηγεῖν παισὶν Αἰσχίνης τε ἐν τῷ κατὰ Τιμάρχου φησὶ καὶ Ἀρ. ἐν τῇ Ἀθ. πολ. (Frag. 431[2], 471[3]).

δυοῖν φυλαῖν εἷς] Ant. *de Chor.* 11, χορηγὸς κατεστάθην εἰς Θαργήλια καὶ ἔλαχον Κεκροπίδα φυλὴν πρὸς τῇ ἐμαυτοῦ. Schol. Dem. *Lept.* 27, ἐν τοῖς Θαργηλίοις δυοῖν φυλαῖν εἷς μόνος καθίστατο χορηγός.

ἀντιδόσεις] Lys. 24 § 10, εἰ—κατασταθεὶς χορηγὸς—προκαλεσαίμην αὐτὸν εἰς ἀντίδοσιν. Dem. *Lept.* §§ 40, 130, and *Or.* 42 *adv. Phaenippum*. [Xen.] *de Rep. Ath.* iii 4, χορηγοῖς διαδικάσαι εἰς Διονύσια καὶ Θαργήλια. Cf. Boeckh, IV xvi, Meier and Schöm. p. 738 Lips.; *Dict. Ant. s. v.*

τὰς σκήψεις εἰσάγει] CIA ii 809 (of the στρατηγοί, who dealt with ἀντιδόσεις in the case of the trierarchy and property-tax, just as the archon did in that of the χορηγία), ὅπως δ' ἂν καὶ αἱ σκήψεις εἰσαχθῶσι. Meier and Schömann, p. 743 n.

λεληιτουργηκὼς ἑτέραν λῃτουργίαν] Dem. 50 § 9, τούτων ἐγὼ οὐδεμίαν πρόφασιν ποιούμενος ὅτι τριηραρχῶ, καὶ οὐκ ἂν δυναίμην δύο λῃτουργίας λῃτουργεῖν, οὐδὲ οἱ νόμοι ἐῶσιν.

καὶ τῶν χρόνων—μὴ ἐξεληλυθότων] 'or owing to the period of his exemption having not yet expired.' The obligation to perform a λῃτουργία recurred only every other year, Dem. *Lept.* 7.

ὑπὲρ τετταράκοντα ἔτη] Aeschin. *c. Timarch.* § 11, κελεύει τὸν χορηγὸν τὴν οὐσίαν τὴν ἑαυτοῦ ἀναλίσκειν ὑπὲρ τετταράκοντα ἔτη γεγονότα τοῦτο πράττειν, ἵν' ἤδη ἐν τῇ σωφρονεστάτῃ αὑτοῦ ἡλικίᾳ ὤν, οὕτως ἐντυγχάνῃ τοῖς ὑμετέροις παισίν.

εἰς Δῆλον χορηγοὺς] lex. Cantab. 670; Ἀθήν. vii p. 480, no. 3 (Gilbert i 240); Thuc. iii 104, §§ 3, 6; Xen. *Mem.* iii 3, 12, χορὸς... ὁ εἰς Δῆλον πεμπόμενος, Lucian *de Saltat.* 16, ἐν Δήλῳ δέ γε οὐδὲν αἱ θυσίαι ἄνευ ὀρχήσεως, ἀλλὰ σὺν ταύτῃ καὶ μετὰ μουσικῆς ἐγίγνοντο· παίδων χοροὶ συνελθόντες ὑπ' αὐλῷ καὶ κιθάρᾳ, οἱ μὲν ἐχόρευον, ὑπωρχοῦντο δὲ οἱ ἄριστοι προκριθέντες ἐξ αὐτῶν. On the Delian πεντετηρίς, cf. 54 § 7.

ἀρχιθέωρον] Plut. *Nic.* 3 § 5.

τῷ τριακοντορίῳ κτλ.] Xen. *Mem.* iv 8, 2, ἕως ἂν ἡ θεωρία ἐκ Δήλου ἐπανέλθῃ, Plat. *Phaed.* p. 58 A; Plut. *Thes.* 23, τὸ πλοῖον, ἐν ᾧ μετὰ τῶν ἠϊθέων ἔπλευσε καὶ πάλιν

21 ἠθέους ἄγοντι. πομπῶν δ' ἐπιμελεῖ[ται τῆς τε] τῷ Ἀσκληπιῷ 4
γιγνομένης, ὅταν οἰκουρῶσι μύ[σ]ται, καὶ τῆς Διονυσίων τῶν
[μεγά]λων μετὰ τῶν ἐπιμελητῶν, οὓς πρότερον μὲν ὁ δῆμος

ἠιθέους K. **22** ΓΙΝ (K-W). <οἱ> μ. K-W, -ν <οἱ> μ. H-L.

§§ **4—7** Pollux viii 89: *ὁ δὲ ἄρχων διατίθησι μὲν Διονύσια καὶ Θαργήλια "μετὰ τῶν ἐπιμελητῶν," δίκαι δὲ πρὸς αὐτὸν λαγχάνονται "κακώσεως," "παρανοίας," "εἰς δατητῶν* (*διαιτητῶν* codd.) *αἵρεσιν," ἐπιτροπῆς ὀρφανῶν, ἐπιτρόπων καταστάσεως, "κλήρων καὶ ἐπικλήρων ἐπιδικασίαι. ἐπιμελεῖται δὲ καὶ" "τῶν γυναικῶν" αἳ ἂν φῶσιν ἐπ' ἀνδρὸς τελευτῇ κύειν, καὶ τοὺς οἴκους ἐκμισθοῖ τῶν ὀρφανῶν.* § **6** Lex. rhet. Cantab. *ἐπώνυμος ἄρχων:...λαγχάνονται δὲ πρὸς αὐτὸν* (Dobree: cod. *παρ' αὐτῶν*) *καὶ γραφαί· καὶ δίκας εἰς τὸ δικαστήριον εἰσάγει.* Bekk. *An.* 310: *πρὸς τὸν ἄρχοντα κακώσεως ἐλαγχάνοντο γραφαὶ καὶ τῶν γονέων, εἰ τούτους τις αἰτίαν ἔχοι κακοῦν, καὶ τῶν ὀρφανῶν* (*ib.* 269). *ἔτι δὲ παρανοίας καὶ ἀργίας,* (*κλήρων* add. K-W) *ἐπιδικασίαι καὶ ἐπικλήρων γυναικῶν.* Phot. *ἡγεμονία δικαστηρίου: τοῖς ἄρχουσιν οὐ πάσας πᾶσιν ἐφεῖτο δίκας εἰσάγειν· ἀλλὰ τῷ μὲν ἄρχοντι τὰς τῶν ὀρφανῶν καὶ τὰς τῆς παρανοίας καὶ τὰς τῶν ἐπικλήρων ἐπιδικασίας.* Harp. *ἡγ. δικ.: ...πρὸς μὲν τὸν ἄρχοντα αἱ τῶν ὀρφανῶν καὶ τῶν ἐπικλήρων* (*ἐλαγχάνοντο δίκαι*). Frag. 381², 420³.

ἐσώθη, τὴν τριακόντορον. Cf. Boeckh, *Seeurkunden*, pp. 76—79; A. Mommsen, *Heortologie*, p. 402. In the *Class. Rev.*, v 123 *a*, *τριακοντόριον* is described as an 'entirely new word'; but it is actually found in a contemporary inscr. of B.C. 325/4, CIA ii 811, p. 261, col. 2, 180, *τριακοντορίων κώπας*.

ἠθέους] trisyllabic in Attic, Eur. *Phoen.* 945, *οὐ γάρ ἐστιν ἤθεος*, and Eupolis *Incert.* 332 Kock, *εἰ μὴ κόρη δεύσειε τὸ σταῖς ἤθεος.* The Homeric form *ἠΐθεος* is retained by editors in Plat. *Leg.* 840 D, 877 E.

§ 4. **τῷ Ἀσκληπιῷ** κτλ.] Philostr. *Vit. Apoll.* iv 18, *τὰ δὲ Ἐπιδαύρια μετὰ πρόρρησίν τε καὶ ἱερεῖα δεῦρο μυεῖν Ἀθηναίοις πάτριον ἐπὶ θυσίᾳ δευτέρᾳ, τουτὶ δ' ἐνόμισαν Ἀσκληπιοῦ ἕνεκα, ὅτι δὴ ἐμύησαν αὐτὸν ἥκοντα Ἐπιδαυρόθεν ὀψὲ μυστηρίων.* The night of the 18th Boedromion, the eve of the festal march to Eleusis, was probably spent by the devout in sleeping in the temple of Asclepius, S. of the Acropolis (Mommsen, *Heortologie*, p. 253, ap. *Dict. Ant.* i 718 *b*).

Διονυσίων] The *πομπὴ* was on the 9th of Elaphebolion (about March 28). In it the statue of Dionysus Eleuthereus was carried from his temple in Limnae to another of his sanctuaries, near the Academy (Paus. i 29, Philostr. *Vit. Soph.* ii 15); and then brought back again and placed in the theatre. The procession included the priests and civil officials, the knights and the citizens in their tribes, as well as the *ephebi*, and the *canephori* (Schol. Arist. *Ach.* 242). Daremberg and Saglio, iii 242.

τῶν ἐπιμελητῶν] *sc.* *τῆς πομπῆς.* In Dem. *c. Mid.* 15, they are described as elected by open voting, (*Μειδίας*) *κελεύων ἑαυτὸν εἰς Διονύσια χειροτονεῖν ἐπιμελητήν.* In *Phil.* 1 § 35, Dem. implies that the functionaries concerned with the Dionysia were appointed by lot: *τὴν μὲν τῶν Παναθηναίων ἑορτὴν καὶ τὴν τῶν Διονυσίων ἀεὶ τοῦ καθήκοντος χρόνου γίγνεσθαι ἄν τε δεινοὶ λάχωσιν ἄν τε ἰδιῶται οἱ τούτων ἑκατέρων ἐπιμελούμενοι.* The first Philippic falls in the first half of B.C. 351. The speech against Midias is assigned by Dionys. Hal. *Epist. Ammon.* i 4, 4 (A. Schaefer, *Dem.* ii 103) to B.C. 349/8; the Dionysia at which Midias insulted Dem. fell two years before, early in April 351 or 350; and Midias must have been elected *ἐπιμελητὴς* either for 352/1 or 351/0. As the appointment of the *ἐπιμεληταὶ* by lot had come into force in the first half of 351, Midias must have been elected *ἐπιμελητὴς* for 352/1, and the change was probably made between the Dionysia, early in April, and the end of the civil year, about June.

After the time when the text was written, the appointment by lot was apparently given up. In B.C. 281/0 (*Ἀθήν.* vii 480, no. 3) we have 10 *ἐπιμεληταὶ τῆς πομπῆς τῷ Διονύσῳ* representing only 6 or 7 of the tribes, and therefore probably elected out of the whole body of citizens, instead of being taken by lot, one from each tribe. After B.C. 265 (CIA ii 420) they are described as *οἱ χειροτονηθέντες ἐπιμεληταὶ τῆς πομπῆς* and their number is 24 (two for each of the 12 tribes of that time). Daremberg and Saglio, *s. v.* iii 682—4.

ἐχειροτόνει δέκα ὄντας, [καὶ τὰ] εἰς τὴν πομπὴν ἀναλώματα παρ'
αὑτῶν ἤν[εγκ]ον, νῦν δ' ἕνα τῆς φυλ[ῆς ἑκά]στης κληροῖ, καὶ
5 δίδωσιν εἰς τὴν κατασκευὴν ἑκατὸν μνᾶς. ἐπιμελ[εῖται] δὲ καὶ
τῆς εἰς Θαργήλια καὶ τῆς τῷ Διὶ τῷ Σωτῆρι. διοικεῖ δὲ καὶ τὸν
ἀγῶνα τῶ[ν Διον]υσίων οὗτος καὶ <τὸν> τῶν Θαργηλίων. ἑορτῶν
6 μὲν οὖν ἐπιμελεῖται τούτων. γραφαὶ δ[ὲ καὶ δ]ίκαι λαγχάνονται
πρὸς αὐτόν, ἃς ἀνακρίνας εἰς τ[ὸ δι]καστήριον εἰσά[γει, γο]νέων
κακώσεως (αὗται δέ εἰσιν ἀζήμιοι τῷ βουλομένῳ δ[ιώκ]ειν),
ὀρφανῶν κ[ακώ]σεως (αὗται δ' εἰσὶ κατὰ τῶν ἐπιτρόπων), ἐπι-

25 ΗΝ[ΕΓΚ]ΟΝ ? (K, H-L), ΑΝΗΛΙϹΚΟΝ ? (K-W), [ἀ]νήλ[ισκ]ον B. 28 τῶ[ν Διον] H, K-W, B: τὸ[ν τῶν Διον] H-L sed spatium non sufficit. <τὸν> τῶν Θ. K-W. 30 εἶτ' [εἰς] K; εἶτ' [εἰς <τὸ>] H-L; εἰς τ[ὸ] K-W (B): scriptura incerta. γο]νέων Wyse, Blass, K-W, H-L, K[3].

ἑκατὸν μνᾶς] Probably the sum granted to the whole body.

§ 5. **τῆς εἰς Θαργήλια]** *sc.* πομπῆς. On the second day there was a procession, as well as a cyclic chorus.

τῆς τῷ Διὶ τῷ Σωτῆρι] This festival, which included a public sacrifice, was held on the 14th day of Scirophorion, the last month of the Attic year, either in Athens in the Cerameicus (so Hermann-Stark, *Gottesdienst. Alt.* § 61, 21; Boeckh, ii 117, 125 Fränkel; A. Schaefer, *Dem.* iii 337, n. 2; A. Mommsen, *Heortol.* p. 453), or in the Peiraeus (see esp. Wachsmuth, *Stadt Athen*, ii 143). The text does not help to decide the dispute as to the place where the festival was held. It should probably be distinguished from the θυσία to Ζεὺς Σωτὴρ on the last day of the year (Lys. 26 § 6), which was also superintended by the archon. Shortly before B.C. 268 the sacrifice of the εἰσιτήρια for the βουλὴ and δῆμος was offered not by the archon, but by the priest of Ζεὺς Σωτήρ (CIA ii 325—6).

§ 6. **γραφαὶ** κτλ.] The *archon eponymus* succeeded to many of the judicial functions of the ancient kings, and was specially regarded as the public protector of those who were unable to defend themselves. This is shewn by the duties here assigned to him. Cf. Dem. 25 *Lacr.* 48, ἐπικλήρων καὶ ὀρφανῶν καὶ τῶν τοκέων τῷ ἄρχοντι προστέτακται ἐπιμελεῖσθαι, and the Law quoted in Dem. 43 *Macart.* 75. In the following list we have no clear distinction drawn between γραφαί and δίκαι.

ἀνακρίνας] Dem. *Olymp.* 31, ὁ ἄρχων ἀνέκρινε πᾶσιν ἡμῖν τοῖς ἀμφισβητοῦσιν. Meier and Schöm. pp. 43, 823 Lips.; Dict. Ant. *s. v. Anakrisis.*

γονέων κακώσεως κτλ.] In Bekker's *Anecd.* p. 269, *s. v.* κακώσεως, the three kinds of κάκωσις are all mentioned in the same order, and in the same terms, as in the text: ἡ τοιαύτη δίκη οὕτως ἀπεφέρετο γονέων κακώσεως, ὀρφανῶν κακώσεως ἢ οἴκου ὀρφανικοῦ κακώσεως. On the various forms of κάκωσις cf. Meier and Schöm. p. 353—360 Lips.

'κάκωσις γονέων was committed by those who struck or reviled their parents, or even were disobedient to them; by those who refused them the means of support... or did not bury them after their death and pay them proper honours' (*Dict. Ant. s. v.*); Xen. *Mem.* ii 2, 13, ἐάν τις γονέας μὴ θεραπεύῃ, τούτῳ δίκην τε ἐπιτίθησι καὶ ἀποδοκιμάζουσα οὐκ ἐᾷ ἄρχειν τοῦτον... ἐάν τις τῶν γονέων τελευτησάντων τοὺς τάφους μὴ κοσμῇ, καὶ τοῦτο ἐξετάζει ἡ πόλις ἐν ταῖς τῶν ἀρχόντων δοκιμασίαις. Dem. *Timocr.* 107, (the laws) οἳ καὶ ζῶντας ἀναγκάζουσι τοὺς παῖδας τοὺς γονέας τρέφειν, καί, ἐπειδὰν ἀποθάνωσιν, ὅπως τῶν νομιζομένων τύχωσιν. Diog. Laert. i 55 (lex Solonis), ἐάν τις μὴ τρέφῃ τοὺς γονέας, ἄτιμος ἔστω. Isaeus 8 § 32, (the law of κάκωσις) κελεύει τρέφειν τοὺς γονέας. Hyperides, *pro Eux.* c. 21, φαῦλός ἐστι πρὸς τοὺς ἑαυτοῦ γονέας· ὁ ἄρχων ἐπὶ τούτου κάθηται.

ἀζήμιοι] Dem. 37 *Pant.* 46 (in a case of ἐπικλήρου κάκωσις), τῷ ἐπεξιόντι μετ' οὐδεμιᾶς ζημίας ἡ βοήθεια.

ὀρφανῶν κακώσεως] committed by those who wronged orphans. Dem. *Macart.* § 75, ὁ ἄρχων ἐπιμελείσθω τῶν ὀρφανῶν καὶ τῶν ἐπικλήρων. Schol. ad Dem. *Timocr.* ὁ ἄρχων ἐπεμελεῖτο...τῶν ὀρφανῶν.

κλήρου κακώσε[ως] (αὗται δέ εἰσι κατὰ [τῶν] ἐπιτρόπων καὶ τῶν συνοικούντων), οἴκου ὀρφανικοῦ κακώσεως (εἰσὶ δὲ καὶ [αὗται κατὰ τῶν] ἐπιτρό[π]ων), παρανοίας, ἐάν τις αἰτιᾶταί τινα παρανοοῦντα τὰ [ὑπάρχοντα ἀ]πολλύν[αι], εἰς δατητῶν αἵρεσιν, ἐάν τις μὴ 'θέλῃ [κ]οινὰ [τὰ ὄντα νέμεσθαι], εἰς ἐπιτροπῆς κατάστασιν, εἰς ἐπιτροπῆς διαδικασίαν, εἰς [ἐμφανῶν κατάστασ]ιν, †ἐπίτροπον

36 τὰ [ἑαυτοῦ κτήματα] K, decem tantum litterarum spatium relictum confessus; τὰ [πατρῷα] Wyse (H-L), τ[ὸν οἶκον] K-W, sed plures litterae flagitantur et τὰ fortasse legi potest; fortasse recte igitur τὰ [ὑπάρχοντα] B. ΔΙΑΙΤΗΤΩΝ: δατητῶν K (K-W, H-L, B) ex Harp. et lex. Cantabr. **38—39** εἰ [πλείονες τῆς αὐτῆς

36 *Lex. rhet. Cantab. εἰς δατητῶν <αἵρεσιν>:...ἐπὶ τῶν διανεμόντων τὰ κοινά τισιν, ὡς Ἀρ. ἐν τῇ Ἀθ. πολ. "δίκαι λαγχάνονται πρὸς" τὸν ἄρχοντα ἄλλαι τε (Dobree; ἀλλ' εἴ τις cod.) καὶ "εἰς δατητῶν αἵρεσιν," ὅταν "μὴ θέλῃ κοινὰ τὰ ὄντα νέμεσθαι. *Etym. M. δατητής: παρ' Ἀττικοῖς ὁ διανεμητής. Ἀριστοτέλης. *Harp. δατεῖσθαι...τὸ δὲ εἰς δατητῶν αἵρεσιν εἶδός τι δίκης ἐστίν. ὁπότε γὰρ κοινωνοῖέν τινες ἀλλήλοις καὶ οἱ μὲν βούλοιντο διανέμεσθαι τὰ κοινά, οἱ δὲ μή, ἐδικάζοντο οἱ βουλόμενοι τοῖς μὴ βουλομένοις προσκαλούμενοι εἰς δατητῶν αἵρεσιν. Λυσίας ἐν τῷ πρὸς Ἀλεξίδημον εἰ γνήσιος, καὶ Ἀρ. ἐν τῇ Ἀθ. πολ. (Frag. 383^{2}, 422^{3}). Addit Suidas, s.v. δατεῖσθαι: δατηταὶ κυρίως οἱ τὰ κοινὰ διανέμοντες τοῖς μὴ βουλομένοις.

38 aut hic aut alibi in eodem capitulo (velut v. 37, ante εἰς ἐπιτροπῆς κατάστασιν) excidit εἰς ἐμφανῶν κατάστασιν. Cf. *Harp. s.v. infra exscriptum (Frag. 382^{2}, 421^{3}).

ἐπικλήρου κακώσεως] committed by the guardians of poor heiresses; or by their nearest relatives, who either declined to marry them or give them a dowry, or who kept them out of their wedded rights. Law in Dem. *Macart.* 54, 75. Isaeus 3 § 46, οὐκ ἂν εἰσήγγελλες πρὸς τὸν ἄρχοντα κακοῦσθαι τὴν ἐπίκληρον...ἄλλως τε καὶ μόνων τούτων τῶν δικῶν ἀκινδύνων τοῖς διώκουσιν οὐσῶν καὶ ἐξὸν τῷ βουλομένῳ βοηθεῖν ταῖς ἐπικλήροις; and *ib.* 47 (cf. Meier and Schöm. p. 333 Lips.).

κατὰ τῶν ἐπιτρόπων κτλ.] These are the ordinary cases, but the statement is not exhaustive. Dem. 37 *Pant.* 45, ᾐτιάσατο ἐκεῖνον—ἐπὶ τὰς ἐπικλήρους εἰσελθεῖν καὶ τὴν μητέρα τὴν αὐτοῦ.

οἴκου ὀρφανικοῦ] 'an orphan's *estate*,' the regular technical sense of οἶκος, Xen. *Oec.* i 5, = ὅσα τις ἔξω τῆς οἰκίας κέκτηται, and vi 4, = κτῆσις ἡ σύμπασα. Thus, in Dem. 27 § 15, οἶκον μισθοῦν is 'to let the orphan's estate,' whereas in § 16 we have οἰκῶν οἰκίαν in a different sense.

παρανοίας] This suit might be instituted by a son (or other relative acting on his behalf), against one who had become mentally incapable of managing his own affairs. Plat. *Leg.* 928 D; Arist. *Nub.* 844 ff.; Xen. *Mem.* i 2, 49; Aeschin. *c. Ctes.* 251. Meier and Schöm. p. 566 Lips.

εἰς δατητῶν αἵρεσιν] If, in a business held in partnership, any one or more of the partners wished to retire, and the partners could not agree, those who insisted on the winding up of the concern might bring an action for the appointment of liquidators (Harpocr. *s. v.* δατεῖσθαι). It has been conjectured that δατηταί might be appointed even in cases not involving partnership in business, *e.g.* in disputes as to the division of an inheritance, and that this was the original object of the legal process (Meier and Schöm. p. 483 Lips.). This is confirmed by the context, which refers to matters of family property and the duties of guardians. Probably it was only in the case of the inheritance of a citizen that the archon eponymus was the responsible official. Daremberg and Saglio, *s. v.*

ἐπιτροπῆς κατάστασιν] 'constituting a wardship.' In the absence of directions by will, the next of kin acted as ἐπίτροποι if authorised by the archon (*e.g.* the elder brother, Lys. *c. Theomn.* i 5; or the uncle, Isaeus, *Cleonym.* § 9). Failing relatives suitable for the duty, the archon selected some one from the general body of citizens. Dict. Ant. *Epitropus*, i 751 *b*; Meier and Schöm. p. 552.

ἐπιτροπῆς διαδικασίαν] 'deciding between rival claims to a wardship.' Meier and Schöm. p. 471 ff. Lips.; and Lipsius, *Leipzig Verhandl.* p. 50.

εἰς ἐμφανῶν κατάστασιν] This clause

7 αὐτὸν ἐγγράψαι†, κλήρων καὶ ἐπικλήρων ἐπι[δικασίαι. ἐπιμελεῖτ]αι δὲ καὶ τῶν [ὀρφ]ανῶν καὶ τῶν ἐπικλήρων, καὶ τῶν γυναικῶν ὅσαι ἂν τελευ[τήσαντος τοῦ ἀνδρ]ὸς σκή[πτω]νται κυεῖν· καὶ κύριός ἐστι τοῖς ἀδικοῦσιν ἐπιβάλ[λειν, ἢ εἰσάγειν εἰς] τὸ δικα[στή]ριον. μισθοῖ δὲ καὶ τοὺς οἴκους τῶν ὀρφανῶν καὶ τῶν ἐπι[κλήρων, ἕως ἂν τις τετταρ]ακαιδε[κέ]τις γένηται,

θέλωσ]ιν ἐπίτροπον αὐτὸν ἐγγράψαι K²; *ἐὰν πλείους ἅμα ἐθέλωσ]ιν ἐπίτροπον* <*τὸν*> *αὐτὸν ἐγγράψαι* H-L: *ἐ[άν τις ἀμφισβητῇ δε]ῖν* Lipsius (Poland). *εἰς [ἐμφανῶν κατάστασ]ιν* ex Harp., *ἐπίτρ[οπ]ον αὐτὸν ἐγγράψαι* K-W, K³, verba tria ultima non intelligi posse confessi (B); *εἰ* fere certum, etiam *εἰς* vix ambiguum. **39** ΕΝΓΡΑΨΑΙ. **42** *ἢ εἰσάγειν* Lipsius, K-W, K³, B: *ζημίαν ἢ ἄγειν* K¹ (H-L) sed spatium vix sufficit.
Η
44 post *ἐπικλήρων* lacunam indicant K-W. ΑΚΑΙΔ...ΤΕΙC; *δ[ατη]τὴς* K; *δ...της* K-W; *ἐὰν μὴ αὐτὸς ὁ ἐπίτροπος διοικητὴς γένηται* aut simile aliquid expectabat Herwerden. [*ἕως ἂν τις τετταρ]ακαιδε[κέ]τις γένηται* optime B.

---

is suggested by Harpocr. *s. v.*, *ὁ δὲ Ἀρ. ἐν τῇ Ἀθ. πολ. πρὸς τὸν ἄρχοντά φησι λαγχάνεσθαι ταύτην τὴν δίκην, τὸν δὲ ἀνακρίναντα εἰσάγειν εἰς τὸ δικαστήριον.* It is placed here by Kaibel and Wilamowitz, by Mr Kenyon (ed. 3), and by Blass. But there is something to be said in favour of placing it (with Lipsius) before *εἰς ἐπιτροπῆς κατάστασιν*, and filling up the lacuna with words that agree with the sequel, *ἐπίτροπον αὐτὸν ἐγγράψαι.*

Isaeus, 6 § 31, *ἀπῄτει τὸν Πυθόδωρον τὸ γραμματεῖον καὶ προσεκαλέσατο εἰς ἐμφανῶν κατάστασιν. καταστήσαντος δὲ ἐκείνου πρὸς τὸν ἄρχοντα κτλ.* Dem. 53 § 14, *ἐξ ἐμφανῶν καταστάσεως.* A man in possession of goods or documents, which another person either owned or had a legal right to inspect, might be required by the latter to produce them, *ἐμφανῆ καταστῆσαι.* If he refused, he might be fined; on the other hand, the party summoned might disclaim possession of the things required or decline to admit the obligation of producing them. In either case the person demanding their production might bring an action *εἰς ἐμφανῶν κατάστασιν.* Meier and Schöm. p. 478 Lips.

In the present context, the phrase can only refer to procedure connected with cases of inheritance (*ib.* p. 59).

κλήρων καὶ ἐπικλήρων ἐπιδικασίαι] Dem. 43 *Macart.* 16. When a person claimed an inheritance or heiress adjudged to another, the former summoned the latter before the archon, who brought the case into court. Meier and Schöm. pp. 603—617 Lips.

§ 7. **τῶν ὀρφανῶν** κτλ.] The archon is *ἐπικλήρων καὶ ὀρφανῶν κύριος* (Lysias, 26 *Evand.* 12). Cf. Dem. 43 § 75 (lex), *ὁ ἄρχων ἐπιμελείσθω τῶν ὀρφανῶν καὶ τῶν ἐπικλήρων καὶ τῶν οἴκων τῶν ἐξερημουμένων καὶ τῶν γυναικῶν, ὅσαι μένουσιν ἐν τοῖς οἴκοις τῶν ἀνδρῶν τῶν τεθνηκότων φάσκουσαι κυεῖν. τούτων ἐπιμελείσθω καὶ μὴ ἐάτω ὑβρίζειν μηδένα περὶ τούτους. ἐὰν δέ τις ὑβρίζῃ ἢ ποιῇ τι παράνομον, κύριος ἔστω ἐπιβάλλειν κατὰ τὸ τέλος.* [Dem.] 35 § 48; Aesch. 1 § 158.

μισθοῖ] Isaeus 3 § 36, *μισθοῦν ἐκέλευον τὸν ἄρχοντα τοὺς οἴκους ὡς ὀρφανῶν ὄντων, ὅπως ... τὰ ἀποτιμήματα κατασταθείη καὶ ὅροι τεθεῖεν*, 2 § 9, *μετασχὼν τοῦ οἴκου τῆς μισθώσεως τῶν παίδων τοῦ Νικίου*, and 11 § 34, Lys. 32 *c. Diog.* 23, *ἐξῆν αὐτῷ κατὰ τοὺς νόμους οἳ κεῖνται περὶ τῶν ὀρφανῶν... μισθῶσαι τὸν οἶκον.* Dem. 27 *Aphob.* A 58, *ἐξῆν (τῷ ἐπιτρόπῳ) μηδὲν ἔχειν τούτων τῶν πραγμάτων μισθώσαντι τὸν οἶκον*, and 29 § 60. The income was often more than 12 per cent.

The lessees had to give security (*ἀποτίμημα*) for the property leased to them. The archon sent certain persons (*ἀποτιμηταί*) to value the security and determine whether it was a fair equivalent for the property leased (Harpocr. *s. v.* *ἀποτιμηταί· οἱ μισθούμενοι τοὺς τῶν ὀρφανῶν οἴκους παρὰ τοῦ ἄρχοντος ἐνέχυρα τῆς μισθώσεως παρείχοντο· ἔδει δὲ τὸν ἄρχοντα ἐπιπέμπειν τινὰς ἀποτιμησομένους τὰ ἐνέχυρα. τὰ μὲν οὖν ἐνέχυρα τὰ ἀποτιμώμενα ἐλέγοντο ἀποτιμήματα κτλ.*). On land thus offered as security a *ὅρος* was placed, with an inscr. stating the person for whose property it served as security, CIA ii 1135, *ὅρος χωρίου καὶ οἰκίας ἀποτίμημα παιδὶ ὀρφανῷ Διογείτονος Προβα[λισίου].* Meier and Schöm. p. 362—3 Lips.; Schulthess, *Vormundschaft*, pp. 139—173.

τετταρακαιδεκέτις] If this restoration is correct (and none better has been pro-

καὶ τὰ ἀποτιμήματα λαμβάν[ει· καὶ τοὺς ἐπιτρόπους], ἐὰν μ[ὴ ἀπο]δῶσι τοῖς παισὶν τὸν σῖτον, οὗτος εἰσπράττει.

57. *καὶ ὁ [μὲν ἄρχων ἐπιμελεῖτ]αι τούτ[ων. ὁ δὲ] βασιλεὺς πρῶτον μὲν μυστηρίων ἐπιμελεῖ[ται μετὰ τῶν ἐπιμελητῶν οὓς] ὁ δῆμ[ος χ]ειροτονεῖ, δύο μὲν ἐξ Ἀθηναίων ἁπάντων, ἕνα δ' <ἐξ> [Εὐμολπιδῶν, ἕνα] δ' ἐ<κ> Κηρ[ύκω]ν. ἔπειτα Διονυσίων τῶν ἐπὶ*

45 *καὶ τοὺς ἐπιτρόπους* E H Brooks (K-W, H-L, B); *καὶ οἱ ἐπίτροποι* (hiatu admisso) quondam conieci. ЄΑΝ (K, K-W, B): *οἱ ἂν* (ex *οἱ ἐὰν*) van Leeuwen (H-L). **46** [*ἀπο*]*δῶσι* et Wysio et mihi olim placuit (K[3]): [*δι*]*δῶσι* K-W, B, *ἀποδιδῶσι* H-L.
LVII 1 *ὁ μὲν ἄρχων* Blass et Herwerden (K-W, H-L, K[3]): *οὗτος μὲν οὖν* K[1]. **3** *ἐχειροτόνει* Harp. (K[1]). **4** *Εὐμολπίδων* K ex Harp.: *ἐξ Εὐμολπίδων—ἐκ Κηρύκων* Gertz (K-W, H-L, B).

TESTIMONIA. **LVII § 1** *Harp. *ἐπιμελητὴς τῶν μυστηρίων: παρ' Ἀθηναίοις ὁ λεγόμενος βασιλεύς...Ἀρ. ἐν Ἀθ. πολ. φησὶν οὕτως· "ὁ δὲ βασιλεὺς—τῶν μυστηρίων—χειροτονεῖ* (Bekker et Müller; *ἐχειροτόνει* codd.) *ἕνα δ' ἐξ Εὐμολπιδῶν, ἕνα δ' ἐκ Κηρύκων.* Suid. et Etym. M. *τέσσαρες δὲ ἦσαν, δύο μὲν ἐξ...εἷς δὲ ἐκ...καὶ εἷς ἐκ* (Frag. 386[2], 425[3]). Pollux viii 90: *ὁ δὲ βασιλεὺς μυστηρίων προέστηκε "μετὰ τῶν ἐπιμελητῶν" καὶ Ληναίων καὶ ἀγώνων τῶν ἐπὶ λαμπάδι* (cf. Lex. Dem. Patm. p. 11) *καὶ* (add. Schol. Pl. *Euthyphr.* p. 325) *τὰ περὶ τὰς πατρίους θυσίας διοικεῖ* (cf. Heraclidis epitom., Rose Frag. 611, 8, *ὁ δὲ βασιλεὺς τὰ κατὰ τὰς θυσίας διοικεῖ.* Schol. in Plat. *Phaedr.* 235 D, *ὁ δὲ βασιλεὺς μυστηρίων προνοεῖται καὶ τὰς θυσίας τὰς πατρίους διοικεῖ*). Bekk. *An.* p. 219, 14: ...*ὁ δὲ βασιλεὺς "μυστηρίων ἐπιμελεῖται μετὰ τῶν ἐπιμελητῶν οὓς ὁ δῆμος" ἐχειροτόνησε.* Phot. *ἡγεμονία δικαστηρίου*, ad fin. *ὁ βασιλεὺς καὶ τῶν μυστηρίων ἅμα τοῖς ἐπιμεληταῖς προΐσταται.* Cf. Frag. 385[2], 422[3].

posed), we here have the age at which the *ἐπίκληρος* ceased to be under the care of the archon. Nothing has hitherto been known on this point (Schulthess, p. 177). Isaeus (6 § 14) simply tells us that one Callippe would naturally have ceased to be under an *ἐπίτροπος* at the age of 30 (*τριακοντοῦτις*).

ἀποτιμήματα] here of lands offered as security by persons who had the estates of minors leased to them. The term is also applied to the security which a husband gives the *κύριος* of his wife as a guarantee that her marriage-portion (of which he has the usufruct) will remain intact (Meier and Schöm. p. 518). [Dem.] 49 § 11, *ὁ...ἐν πεδίῳ ἀγρὸς ἀποτίμημα τῷ παιδὶ τῷ Εὐμηλίδου καθειστήκει.* Cf. Schulthess, *l.c.* p. 157, and see note on *μισθοῖ*, above.

σῖτον] Pollux viii 33, *σῖτος δέ ἐστιν αἱ ὀφειλόμεναι τροφαί.* Cf. Harp. in *Testim.*, and Meier and Schöm. p. 525—6 Lips.

LVII. *The archon basileus.*

§ 1. **βασιλεὺς**] The archon basileus succeeded to the religious duties of the ancient kings. Gilbert i 241; Meier and Schöm. p. 61 Lips.

μυστηρίων] [Lys.] 6 *c. Andoc.* 4, *ἂν... λάχῃ βασιλεύς, ἄλλο τι ἢ ὑπὲρ ἡμῶν καὶ θυσίας θύσει καὶ εὐχὰς εὔξεται κατὰ τὰ πάτρια, τὰ μὲν ἐν τῷ ἐνθάδε Ἐλευσινίῳ, τὰ δὲ ἐν τῷ Ἐλευσῖνι ἱερῷ, καὶ τῆς ἑορτῆς ἐπιμελήσεται μυστηρίοις;*

ἐπιμελητῶν] *sc. τῶν μυστηρίων.* Dem. 21 § 171, *ἐχειροτονήσατε τοῦτον* (Midias) *μυστηρίων ἐπιμελητήν.* We have decrees in honour of these *ἐπιμεληταί* in CIA ii 315 (= Ditt. 386, 26; B.C. 283/2 or 282/1), and 376 (before end of 3rd cent. B.C.). In each of these decrees the compliment is paid to the two *ἐπιμεληταί* elected out of the whole body of the citizens, and not to those belonging to the *Κήρυκες* and *Εὐμολπίδαι*. Cf. CIA ii 741 (= Ditt. 374, 10), B.C. 334/3, [*ἐγ*] *Διονυσίων τῶν* [*ἐπὶ Λ*]*ηναίω*[*ι π*]*αρὰ μυστηρίων ἐπιμελητῶν.*

Κηρύκων] CIA ii 597 (a decree of the *Κήρυκες*, about the age of Alexander): *ἐπειδὴ Εὐθύδημος ὁ πάρεδρος τοῦ βασιλέως καλῶς καὶ φιλοτίμως μετὰ τοῦ βασιλέως καὶ τοῦ γένους τοῦ Κηρύκων ἐπεμελήθη τῶν περὶ τὰ μυστήρια κτλ.*

τῶν ἐπὶ Ληναίῳ] held in the district called *Λίμναι*, S. E. of the Acropolis, about Jan. 28—31 (Dict. Ant. i 638). It was the festival at which Comedies were generally produced, *e.g.* the *Acharnians*, *Equites*, *Vespae* and *Ranae*.

Ληναίῳ· ταῦτα δ' ἐστὶ [πομπὴ καὶ μουσικῆς ἀγών. τὴν] μὲν οὖν
[Col. 29.] πομπὴν κοινῇ πέμ||πουσιν ὅ τε βασιλεὺς καὶ οἱ ἐπιμεληταί· τὸν δὲ ἀγῶνα διατίθησιν ὁ βασιλεύς. τίθησι δὲ καὶ τοὺς τῶν λαμπάδων ἀγῶνας ἅπαντας· ὡς δ' ἔπος εἰπεῖν [[καὶ]] τὰς πατρίους
2 θυσίας διοικεῖ οὗτος πάσας· γραφαὶ δὲ λαγχάνονται πρὸς αὐτὸν ἀσεβείας, κἄν τις ἱερεωσύνης ἀμφισβητῇ πρός τινα· [διαδι]κάζει δὲ καὶ τοῖς γένεσι καὶ τοῖς ἱερεῦσι τὰς ἀμφισβητήσεις τὰς ὑπὲρ [τῶν γε]ρῶν ἁπάσας οὗτος. λαγχάνονται δὲ καὶ αἱ τοῦ φόνου δίκαι πᾶσαι πρὸς τοῦτον, καὶ ὁ προαγορεύων εἴργεσθαι τῶν

5 ΛΗΝΑΙΩΝ. [πομπὴ καὶ ἀγών. τὴν] H-L, K[3], B: [πομπὴ καὶ μουσικῆς ἀγών. τὴν] K-W. Supplementum illud parum multas, hoc parum paucas, litteras habere arbitratur K, sed (nisi fallor) fere viginti litteris spatium aptum est, ut ΠΟΜΠΗΚΜΟΥϹΙΚΗϹΑΓΩΝΤ litteras undeviginti continere possit. **7** ΤΙΘΗϹΙ (K, B): <δια>τίθησι Richards, Gertz, K-W, H-L. **8** καὶ del. K-W, H-L. **9** 'quidni οὗτος διοικεῖ?' B. **10** ΙΕΡΩϹ ἱερεωσύνης K-W, Meisterhans, p. 36[2]. ΠΡΟϹΤΙΝΑ (K-W, H-L, K[3], B); διαδικάζει addendum putat B: προστιμᾷ Bekk. *Anec.* (K[1]). **12** γε]ρῶν K e Bekk. *An.* 219 (K-W, H-L, B): ἱερῶν (quod etiam in ectypo videt B, coll. Bekk. *An.* 310), Richards.

§ **2** Pollux viii 90: δίκαι δὲ πρὸς αὐτὸν λαγχάνονται ἀσεβείας, ἱερωσύνης ἀμφισβητήσεως. καὶ τοῖς γένεσι καὶ τοῖς ἱερεῦσι (e schol. Pl. Bekk.: ἱεροῖς libri) πᾶσιν αὐτὸς δικάζει. Bekk. *An.* p. 219, 16: "γραφαὶ δὲ λαγχάνονται πρὸς αὐτὸν ἀσεβείας. καὶ ἄν τις ἱερωσύνης" ἀμφισβητήσῃ προστιμᾷ. "διαδικάζει δὲ καὶ τοῖς γένεσι καὶ τοῖς ἱερεῦσι τὰς ἀμφισβητήσεις τὰς ὑπὲρ τῶν γερῶν. λαγχάνονται δὲ—πρὸς τοῦτον." Phot. ἡγεμονία δικαστηρίου:...τῷ μέντοι γε βασιλεῖ τάς τε φονικὰς καὶ τὰς τῆς ἀσεβείας καὶ ἄν τις ἱερωσύνης ἠμφισβήτει, πρότερον δὲ καὶ τὰς περὶ τῶν γερῶν (ἱερῶν codd., corr. Meier) τοῖς ἱερεῦσιν ἀμφισβητήσεις. προηγόρευε δὲ καὶ τῶν νομίμων εἴργεσθαι τοὺς ἐν αἰτίᾳ. Pollux viii 90 προαγορεύει δὲ τοῖς ἐν αἰτίᾳ ἀπέχεσθαι μυστηρίων καὶ τῶν ἄλλων νομίμων κτλ. Bekk. *An.* 310, 6: ὁ βασιλεὺς εἰσάγει τὰς φονικὰς ἁπάσας, ἐπεὶ καὶ προαγορεύει τὸν ἀνδρόφονον εἴργεσθαι τῶν νόμων (leg. νομίμων), καὶ περὶ τῶν ἱερῶν (leg. γερῶν) καὶ τοῖς γένεσι δικάζει.

πομπὴ κτλ.] 'law of Euegoros' in Dem. *c. Mid.* 10, ἡ ἐπὶ Ληναίῳ πομπὴ καὶ οἱ τραγῳδοὶ καὶ οἱ κωμῳδοί. Cf. Plat. *Protag.* 327 E, and Schol. Arist. *Eq.* 547. The mistake in the MS (Ληναίων for Ληναίῳ) possibly arose out of such phrases as ἐνίκα δὶς ἐπὶ Ληναίων (Schol. Aeschin. 2 § 15).

διατίθησι...τίθησι] See note on 54 § 2, καταγιγνώσκουσι...τὸ γνωσθέν.

λαμπάδων ἀγῶνας] At the Panathenaea (Mommsen, *Heortol.* p. 169 f.) and Thesea (*ib.* 282), and the festivals of Hephaestus (*ib.* 311 f.), Prometheus and Pan. Plut. *Sol.* 1 *ad fin.* The expenses connected with the torch-race were borne by a γυμνασίαρχος. In CIA ii 606 we have a decree in honour of a γυμνασίαρχος reciting the names of certain λαμπαδηδρόμοι (about 350 B.C.). Law-suits concerning the γυμνασίαρχοι came before the archon basileus (Dem. 35 § 48).

ὡς ἔπος εἰπεῖν] here modifying πάσας. Cf. 49 § 5; and 2 § 3, ὡς εἰπεῖν, with οὐδενός.

πατρίους θυσίας] *Pol.* 1285 *b* 16, αἱ πάτριαι θυσίαι κατελείφθησαν τοῖς βασιλεῦσι μόνον, Plat. *Politicus*, 290 E, τῷ λαχόντι βασιλεῖ φασι τῇδε (at Athens) τὰ σεμνότατα καὶ μάλιστα πάτρια τῶν ἀρχαίων θυσιῶν ἀποδεδόσθαι. Athen. 234 F, κἀν τοῖς τοῦ βασιλέως δὲ νόμοις γέγραπται· θύειν τῷ Ἀπόλλωνι τοὺς Ἀχαρνέων παρασίτους.

§ 2. **γραφαὶ** κτλ.] Meier and Schöm. p. 61—64 Lips.

ἀσεβείας] Hypereides, *pro Eux.* c. 21, ἀσεβεῖ τις περὶ τὰ ἱερά; γραφαὶ ἀσεβείας εἰσὶ πρὸς τὸν βασιλέα. Meier and Schöm. pp. 62, 367 Lips.

ἱερεωσύνης] a hereditary priesthood. Cf. c. 42, 36, κἄν τινι κατὰ τὸ γένος ἱερεωσύνη γένηται.

τῶν γερῶν] Bekk. *Anec.* 219, 16 (τῶν ἱερῶν, *ib.* 310, 6, and Photius), quoted in *Testim.*). Cf. Aeschin. *c. Ctes.* 18, τοὺς ἱερεῖς τοὺς τὰ γέρα μόνον λαμβάνοντας.

εἴργεσθαι τῶν νομίμων] *inf.* § 4, εἴργεται τῶν ἱερῶν. Soph. *O. T.* 236 ff.; Dem.

νομίμων οὗτός ἐστιν. εἰσὶ δὲ φόν[ου] δίκαι καὶ τραύματος, ἂν μὲν 3
ἐκ προνοίας ἀποκτείνῃ ἢ τρώ[σ]ῃ, ἐν Ἀρείῳ πάγῳ, καὶ φαρμάκων, ἐὰν ἀποκτείνῃ δούς, καὶ πυρκαϊᾶς· [ταῦ]τα γὰρ ἡ βουλὴ μόνα δικάζει· τῶν δ' ἀκουσίων καὶ βουλεύσεως, κἂν οἰκέτην ἀποκτείνῃ

14 ἐὰν H-L. **15** ἢ τρώ[σ]ῃ K-W, quod fortasse legi posse recte (ut videtur) censet K: ΕΝΓΡ? ἐγγρ[άφεται] K; <τις>, γράφεται H-L. ΦΑΡΜΑΚΟΝ (K, H-L, B): φαρμάκων K-W Pollucem secuti. **16** πυρκᾳᾶς B. μόνη van Leeuwen (H-L).

§ 3 Pollux viii 90: καὶ τὰς τοῦ φόνου δίκας εἰς Ἄρειον πάγον εἰσάγει. ib. 117 Ἄρειος πάγος: ἐδίκαζε δὲ φόνου καὶ τραύματος ἐκ προνοίας, καὶ πυρκαϊᾶς, καὶ φαρμάκων, ἐάν τις ἀποκτείνῃ δούς. Bekk. *An.* 311, 9 περὶ Ἀρείου πάγου: αὕτη κρίνει τὰς φονικὰς δίκας καὶ φαρμάκων καὶ πυρκαϊᾶς.

17—18 *Harp. ἐπὶ Παλλαδίῳ...δικαστήριον οὕτω καλούμενον, ὡς καὶ Ἀρ. ἐν Ἀθ. πολ., ἐν ᾧ δικάζουσιν ἀκουσίου φόνου οἱ ἐφέται. Hesych. δικαστήριον ἔνθα ἐδίκαζον οἱ ἐφέται τοῖς ἀκουσίων φόνων δικαζομένοις. Eust. in *Od.* p. 1419, 53: ἐδίκαζον δὲ κατὰ Παυσανίαν ἐκεῖ ἀκουσίου φόνου οἱ ἐφέται. Bekk. *An.* 311, 8: δικάζουσι δ' ἐν τούτῳ οἱ ἐφέται (Frag. 417[2], 457[3]). Schol. in Aeschin. 2 § 87: ἐπὶ τούτῳ ἐκρίνοντο οἱ ἀκούσιοι φόνοι. οἱ δὲ ἐν τούτῳ τῷ δικαστηρίῳ δικάζοντες ἐκαλοῦντο ἐφέται, ἐδίκαζον δὲ ἀκουσίου φόνου καὶ βουλεύσεως καὶ οἰκέτην ἢ μέτοικον ἢ ξένον ἀποκτείναντι. Cf. Poll. viii 118.

17 *Harp. βουλεύσεως, infra exscriptus (Frag. 418[2], 458[3]).

Lept. 158, (Δράκων) γράφων χέρνιβος εἴργεσθαι τὸν ἀνδροφόνον, σπονδῶν κρατήρων ἱερῶν ἀγορᾶς, Ant. *de Chor.* 34, 40, *Herod.* 10. Pollux viii 66, εἴργονται ἱερῶν καὶ ἀγορᾶς οἱ ἐν κατηγορίᾳ φόνου, ἄχρι κρίσεως· καὶ τοῦτο προαγόρευσις ἐκαλεῖτο. Dem. *Macart.* 1069, προειπεῖν. The text shews that we are not justified in restricting the πρόρρησις to the next of kin, to the exclusion of the archon basileus (as urged by Philippi, *Areop.* p. 70).

§ 3. **φόνου δίκαι**] *Pol.* 1300 *b* 24, φονικοῦ μὲν οὖν εἴδη, ἄν τ' ἐν τοῖς αὐτοῖς δικασταῖς ἄν τ' ἐν ἄλλοις, περί τε τῶν ἐκ προνοίας καὶ περὶ τῶν ἀκουσίων καὶ ὅσα ὁμολογεῖται μὲν ἀμφισβητεῖται δὲ περὶ τοῦ δικαίου, τέταρτον δὲ ὅσα τοῖς φεύγουσιν ἐπὶ καθόδῳ ἐπιφέρεται φόνου, οἷον Ἀθήνησι λέγεται καὶ τὸ ἐν Φρεαττοῖ δικαστήριον. Meier and Schöm. p. 376—387 Lips.

τραύματος] Dem. p. 1018, 9, τραύματός με εἰς Ἄρειον πάγον προσεκαλέσατο, 54 § 18, τραύματος γραφαί. Aeschin. *F. L.* 93, *Ctes.* 51 and 212, τραύματος ἐκ προνοίας γραφὰς γραφόμενος. It was only 'wounding with intent to kill' that was classed with φόνος; in the absence of proof of such intent, the case was one of unlawful wounding (αἰκεία, 52 § 2).

ἐκ προνοίας κτλ.] Dem. 23 *c. Aristocr.* 24, γέγραπται γὰρ ἐν μὲν τῷ νόμῳ τὴν βουλὴν δικάζειν φόνου καὶ τραύματος ἐκ προνοίας καὶ πυρκαϊᾶς καὶ φαρμάκων, ἐάν τις ἀποκτείνῃ δούς. Lucian, *Anacharsis* 19.

φαρμάκων] Philippi, *Areop.* pp. 41, 51. Meier and Schöm. p. 382 Lips.

ἐὰν ἀποκτείνῃ δοὺς] Ant. *de Chor.* 17, εἰ τὸν δόντα τὸ φάρμακόν φασιν αἴτιον εἶναι, ἐγὼ οὐκ αἴτιος. It was probably essential that actual death should ensue, and that the poison should have been administered by the person charged before the Areopagus: 'etenim qui *per alium* curasset ut venenum daretur, eum oportuit βουλεύσεως accusari' (Forchhammer, *de Areop.*, p. 30). Similarly Antiphon, *Or.* 1, κατηγορία φαρμακείας, is really a case of βούλευσις, which would be tried by οἱ ἐπὶ Παλλαδίῳ.

ἐκ προνοίας applies to φαρμάκων as well as to φόνου κ.τ.λ.: *Magn. Mor.* i 16 (17), φασί ποτέ τινα γυναῖκα φίλτρον τινὶ δοῦναι πιεῖν, εἶτα τὸν ἄνθρωπον ἀποθανεῖν ὑπὸ τοῦ φίλτρου, τὴν δ' ἄνθρωπον ἐν Ἀρείῳ πάγῳ ἀποφυγεῖν· οὗ παροῦσαν δι' οὐθὲν ἄλλο ἀπέλυσαν ἢ διότι οὐκ ἐκ προνοίας.

πυρκαϊᾶς] Meier and Schöm. p. 387 Lips.

ἀκουσίων κτλ.] Schol. Aeschin. *F. L.* § 87, ἐδίκαζον δ' ἀκουσίου φόνου καὶ βουλεύσεως καὶ οἰκέτην ἢ μέτοικον ἢ ξένον ἀποκτεῖναι (MSS; ἀποκτείναντι Sauppe; κεἴ τις οἰκέτην—ἀποκτείνειε Wyse).

βουλεύσεως] 'conspiracy (against life).' Harpocr. (and Suidas) *s. v.*—ὅταν ἐξ ἐπιβουλῆς τίς τινι κατασκευάσῃ θάνατον, ἐάν τε ἀποθάνῃ ὁ ἐπιβουλευθεὶς ἐάν τε μή.—μάρτυς Ἰσαῖος ἐν τῷ πρὸς Εὐκλείδην, ἐπὶ Παλλαδίῳ λέγων εἶναι τὰς δίκας, Δείναρχος δὲ ἐν τῷ κατὰ Πιστίου ἐν Ἀρείῳ πάγῳ. Ἀριστοτέλης δ' ἐν τῇ Ἀθ. πολ. τῷ Ἰσαίῳ συμφωνεῖ. Hesych. τὸ ἐπιβεβουλευκέναι θάνατον οὕτως Ἀθήνησιν ἐλέγετο. And. *de Myst.* 94, Ant. *de Chor.* 16. Meier τις ἢ μέτοικον ἢ ξένον, [οἱ ἐπὶ Π]α[λλ]αδίῳ· ἐὰν δ' ἀποκτεῖναι μέν τις ὁμολογῇ, φῇ δὲ κατὰ τοὺς νόμους, ο[ἷον] μοιχὸν λαβὼν ἢ ἐν πολέμῳ ἀγνοήσας ἢ ἐν ἄθλῳ ἀγωνιζόμενος, τού[τῳ] ἐπὶ Δελφινίῳ δικάζουσιν· ἐὰν δὲ φεύγων φυγὴν ὧν αἴδεσίς ἐστιν, αἰ[τίαν ἔχῃ] ἀποκτεῖναι ἢ τρῶσαί τινα, τούτῳ δ' ἐν Φρεάτου δικάζουσιν· ὁ δὲ [ἀπολογ]εῖται προσορμισάμενος ἐν πλοίῳ.

18 ΟΙΕΠΙΠΑΛΛΑΔΙ|ΩΙ? K versus prioris parte ultima litteris evanidis scripta. *τούτ[ῳ μὲν ἐπὶ] Π.* K-W, sed neque spatium sufficere neque litteras *τουτ* cerni posse censet K. [*οἱ ἐφέται ἐπὶ Π.*] Brooks, H-L, sed ne his quidem verbis satis spatii relictum. **20** *τού[τῳ ἐν τῷ] ἐπὶ* K[1]; *τού[τῳ] ἐπὶ* Brooks, H-L, K[3], B: *τούτ[ῳ] δ' [ἐπ]ὶ* Lipsius (K-W), sed neque Δ cerni posse neque spatium litterae aptum superesse putat K. **21** ΑΙΔ(supra scr. Ρ)ΕCIC. **22** *αἰτίαν ἔχῃ ἀποκτεῖναι* K-W (K[3], B, coll. Dem. 23 § 77): *αἰτίαν προσλάβῃ κτεῖναι* K[1] (H-L). ΦΡΕΑΤΟΥ K-W, B coll. Dem. 23 §§ 77, 78, ubi *φρεαιτου* pr. S; nomen *ἀπό τινος Φρεάτου ἥρωος, καθά φησι Θεόφραστος,* deducit Harp.; *Φρεατοῖ* Harp., Ar. *Pol.* 1300 *b* 29 codex Ambrosianus, Helladius in Phot. *Bibl.* 535 *a* 28, Suidas; *ἐς Φρεάτου* et *ἐν Φρεάτ..* Hesychius: *Φρεαττοῖ* Pollux, Bekk. *Anec.* 311, 20 (K, H-L).

18—21 *Harp. *ἐπὶ Δελφινίῳ:...δικάζονται δὲ ἐνταῦθα οἱ ὁμολογοῦντες μὲν ἀπεκτονέναι δικαίως δὲ πεποιηκέναι τοῦτο λέγοντες, ὡς Δημ. ἐν τῷ κατ' Ἀριστοκράτους δηλοῖ καὶ Ἀρ. ἐν τῇ Ἀθ. πολ.* Pollux viii 119:...*οὓς ὡμολόγει μὲν ἀποκτεῖναι, δικαίως δ' ἔφη τοῦτο δεδρακέναι.* Eustath. in *Il.* p. 1221, 30: *δικαστήριον Ἀθήνησιν ἐπὶ τῶν ὁμολογούντων φασὶ δεδρακέναι μὲν φόνον, κατὰ νόμους δέ.* Bekk. *An.* 311, 13. Suid. ex Phot. *ἐπὶ Δ.*, Hesych. (Frag. 419[2], 459[3]).

22 *ἐν Φρεάτου.* Cf. Poll. viii 120 infra exscriptum.

---

and Schöm. p. 384—6 Lips.; Philippi, *Areopag*, p. 29—50; Dict. Ant. *s. v.*

ἐπὶ Παλλαδίῳ] Dem. 23 § 71, *δικαστήριον τὸ τῶν ἀκουσίων φόνων... τὸ ἐπὶ Παλλαδίῳ... ἐνταῦθ' ὑποκεῖται πρῶτον μὲν διωμοσία, δεύτερον δὲ λόγος, τρίτον δὲ γνῶσις τοῦ δικαστηρίου... τὸν ἁλόντ' ἐπὶ ἀκουσίῳ φόνῳ ἔν τισιν εἰρημένοις χρόνοις ἀπελθεῖν τακτὴν ὁδὸν καὶ φεύγειν ἕως ἂν αἰδέσηταί τινα τῶν ἐν γένει τοῦ πεπονθότος.* Paus. i 28, 8. Philippi, *Areopag*, p. 23.

The Palladium and the Delphinium were probably S. E. of the Acropolis, near the Olympieum (Milchhöfer in Baumeister's *Denkm.* p. 179 f.).

μοιχὸν λαβὼν κτλ.] Dem. 23 § 55, *ἄν τις ἐν ἄθλοις ἀποκτείνῃ τινά, ἂν ἐν πολέμῳ ἀγνοήσας, ἢ ἐπὶ δάμαρτι ἢ ἐπὶ μητρὶ ἢ θυγατρί, ἢ ἐπὶ παλλακῇ ἣν ἂν ἐπ' ἐλευθέροις παισὶν ἔχῃ.* Cf. Lys. 1 § 31. Philippi, p. 55.

ἐπὶ Δελφινίῳ] Dem. 23 § 74, *ἄν τις ὁμολογῇ μὲν κτεῖναι ἐννόμως δὲ φῇ δεδρακέναι.* Paus. i 28, 10, Pollux viii 119, *ἱδρῦσθαι ὑπὸ Αἰγέως λέγεται Ἀπόλλωνι Δελφινίῳ.*

ἐὰν δὲ φεύγων—τινα] Dem. 23 § 77, *δικαστήριον τὸ ἐν Φρεαττοῖ. ἐνταῦθα... κελεύει δίκας ὑπέχειν ὁ νόμος, ἐάν τις ἐπ' ἀκουσίῳ φόνῳ πεφευγώς, μήπω τῶν ἐκβαλλόντων αὐτὸν ἠδεσμένων, αἰτίαν ἔχῃ ἑτέρου φόνου ἑκουσίου.* Meier and Schöm. p. 379 f.

ἐν Φρεάτου] *l.c.* § 78, *ἐπὶ θαλάττῃ* (near the harbour of Zea). Paus. i 28, 11, *ἔστι δὲ τοῦ Πειραιῶς πρὸς θαλάττῃ Φρεαττύς.* Philippi, *Areop.* p. 48. There can be little doubt that the place derived its name from *φρέαρ*, and was so called long before the invention of the eponymous hero *Φρέατος*. Ulrichs puts it *west* of the entrance to the harbour of Zea, at a point where there is a very small bay with a landing-place to the S.W.; near the latter is an oval depression, resembling a slipper-bath, hewn out of the rocky shore, with a small round pit in front of it, both of them filled by a spring of fresh water, called *τὸ Τζιρλονέρι* (*Reisen*, ii 173). Milchhöfer, with perhaps more probability, prefers assigning it to the southern extremity of the tongue of land *east* of Zea (Baumeister's *Denkmäler*, p. 1200 *a*).

ἐν πλοίῳ] Dem. 23 § 78, *ὁ μὲν ἐν πλοίῳ προσπλεύσας λέγει, τῆς γῆς οὐχ ἁπτόμενος, οἱ δ' ἀκροῶνται καὶ δικάζουσιν ἐν τῇ γῇ.* Paus. i 28, 11, *οἱ πεφευγότες... πρὸς ἀκροωμένους ἐκ τῆς γῆς ἀπὸ νεὼς ἀπολογοῦντα.* Harpocr. *s. v.* *ἐν Φρεαττοῖ* (*φρεάτου* libri). Pollux viii 120, *τὸν ἐν*

24 δικάζουσι δ' οἱ λαχόντες τα[ῦτα ἐφέται], πλὴν τῶν ἐν Ἀρείῳ 4

24 τα[ῦτα ἐφέται] ex Harp. K, K-W: τα[ῦτα δικασταὶ] Paton (H-L, B); τα[ῦτα πάντα] Lipsius.

24 Harp. ἐφέται infra exscriptus.

αἰτίᾳ προσπλεύσαντα τῆς γῆς οὐ προσαπτόμενον ἀπὸ τῆς νεὼς ἐχρῆν ἀπολογεῖσθαι, μήτ' ἀποβάθραν μήτ' ἄγκυραν εἰς τὴν γῆν βαλλόμενον. Helladius in Photius, *Bibl.* 535 *a* 28,...ἐν Φρεατοῖ·—(ὁ κρινόμενος) ἐπὶ νηὸς ἔξωθεν τοῦ Πειραιῶς ἀπολογούμενος ἄγκυραν καθίει. Bekker, *Anecd.* 311, 17, ἐν Ζέᾳ· τόπος ἐστὶ παράλιος. ἐνταῦθα κρίνεται ὁ ἐπὶ ἀκουσίῳ μὲν φόνῳ φεύγων, αἰτίαν δὲ ἔχων ἐφ' ἑκουσίῳ φόνῳ.—ἐν Φρεαττοῖ· οἱ ἐπ' ἀκουσίῳ φόνῳ φεύγοντες, ἐπ' ἄλλῳ δέ τινι κρινόμενοι· οἱ ἐπὶ πλοίῳ ἑστῶτες ἀπολογοῦνται.

ἐφέται] Harpocr. *s. v.* οἱ δικάζοντες τὰς ἐφ' αἵματι κρίσεις ἐπὶ Παλλαδίῳ καὶ ἐπὶ Πρυτανείῳ καὶ ἐπὶ Δελφινίῳ καὶ ἐν Φρεαττοῖ (φρεάτοις *libri*; Φρεατοῖ *Epitome*) ἐφέται ἐκαλοῦντο. It is agreed that Harpocr. derived his information from this treatise (Philippi, *Areopag*, p. 210), and this is the only passage where the term can be inserted.

The ἐφέται were 51 in number (law in Dem. *Macart.* 57); they were more than 50 years of age and were selected from noble families, ἀριστίνδην αἱρεθέντες (Pollux viii 125). The ἐφέται and the Areopagus were probably among the primitive institutions of Attica, being certainly earlier than Solon (Plut. *Sol.* 19) and perhaps earlier than Dracon. According to Lange, *die Epheten*, the 51 ἐφέται and the 9 archons formed the pre-Solonian Areopagus. But (as has been shewn by Mr J. W. Headlam, *Class. Rev.* vi 249—252) all our evidence respecting the ἐφέται is derived from legal and judicial documents, and there is no proof that they ever held any constitutional position outside the law-courts. The ἐφέται are named in CIA i 61 (B.C. 409), in a quotation from a law of Dracon incorporated in those of Solon: ἐὰμ μὴ 'κ προνοίας κτ[είνῃ τίς τινα, φεύγειν. δι]κάζειν δὲ τοὺς βασιλέας αἰτιῶν φόνου ἢ [ἐάν τις αἰτιᾶται τὸν βου]λεύσαντα, τοὺς δὲ ἐφέτας διαγνῶναι (cf. Dem. *Macart.* 57 and *Aristocr.* 37). Solon reserved the φονικαὶ δίκαι for the Areopagus, leaving the ἐφέται to preside in the four courts held in the precincts of the Palladium, Delphinium and Prytaneum, and 'in Phreatto.'

One of Solon's laws quoted in Plutarch's *Solon* 19, runs as follows:—ἐπιτίμους εἶναι πλὴν ὅσοι ἐξ Ἀρείου πάγου ἢ ὅσοι ἐκ τῶν ἐφετῶν ἢ ἐκ τοῦ πρυτανείου καταδικασθέντες ὑπὸ τῶν βασιλέων ἐπὶ φόνῳ ἢ σφαγαῖσιν ἢ ἐπὶ τυραννίδι ἔφευγον. Here ἐπὶ φόνῳ refers to cases under the cognisance of the Areopagus, σφαγαῖσιν to those under that of the ἐφέται, and ἐπὶ τυραννίδι to those under that of the court sitting *in* the Prytaneum to try offences against the Constitution. This law is incorporated in the decree of Patrocleides (Andoc. *de Myst.* 78) after the time of the 400, where we find excluded from the privilege of ἄδεια all the names ὁπόσα ἐν στήλαις γέγραπται τῶν μὴ ἐνθάδε μεινάντων ἢ ἐξ Ἀρείου πάγου ἢ τῶν ἐφετῶν ἢ ἐκ πρυτανείου δικασθεῖσιν ὑπὸ τῶν βασιλέων ἐπὶ φόνῳ τίς ἐστι φυγὴ ἢ σφαγαῖσιν ἢ τυραννίδι. (So Droysen and Lipsius. The MSS, followed by Blass, have: ἢ ἐκ πρυτανείου ἢ Δελφινίου ἐδικάσθη ἢ ὑπὸ τῶν βασιλέων, ἢ ἐπὶ φόνῳ τίς ἐστι φυγή, ἢ θάνατος κατεγνώσθη, ἢ σφαγεῦσιν ἢ τυράννοις. But ἢ Δελφινίου must have been added by some one who confused the court for trial of Constitutional offences held *in* the Prytaneum, with that for trial of inanimate things held in its precincts; and, since the archon basileus presided in the Areopagus and Prytaneum, as well as in the four courts, the βασιλεῖς cannot be contrasted with these courts as is implied by ἤ.) In Dem. *Aristocr.* 38 it is stated that, in the event of a banished manslayer being killed, the ἐφέται were to have cognisance of the matter, διαγιγνώσκειν,—a term not necessarily implying that they acted as judges, but not inconsistent with it.

In Isocr. *c. Callim.* §§ 52, 54, a trial for homicide, held ἐπὶ Παλλαδίῳ, is stated to have come before a tribunal of 700 dicasts: (μάχης γενομένης) ἐκ τοῦ τραύματος φάσκοντες ἀποθανεῖν τὴν ἄνθρωπον λαγχάνουσιν αὐτῷ φόνου δίκην ἐπὶ Παλλαδίῳ. Similarly in [Dem.] *c. Neaeram* § 10 a trial ἐπὶ Παλλαδίῳ came before 500 dicasts. Hence it has been inferred that the ἐφέται had been deprived of their jurisdiction in that court (Gilbert, i 360 n). The first speech of Lysias is connected with a case of justifiable homicide, but there is nothing to shew whether it was delivered before δικασταί (Schömann, Scheibe, Frohberger, Blass, Philippi), or before ἐφέται (Forchhammer and others) in the court of *πάγῳ γιγνομένων· εἰσάγει δ' ὁ βασιλεὺς καὶ δικάζουσι[ν *ἐν ἡλι]αί[ᾳ]* καὶ ὑπαίθριοι, καὶ ὁ βασιλεὺς ὅταν δικάζῃ περιαι-*

25 [Ν]....ΑΙ[Ο]Ι K[3]: *δικάζουσι σκοταῖοι* olim conieci (H-L), coll. Luciani locis infra exscriptis. Ceterum *σκοταῖοι* cum litterarum evanidarum vestigiis non congruere nunc confiteor, et hac certe in clausula Areopagitarum iudicium excludi videtur. *τριταῖοι* Lipsius; cf. Schol. Aeschin. I § 188, *τρεῖς που τοῦ μηνὸς ἡμέρας τὰς φονικὰς*

§ **4, 26** Pollux viii 118 (*Ἄρειος πάγος*): *ὑπαίθριοι δ' ἐδίκαζον.*
26—27 Pollux viii 90: *καὶ τὸν στέφανον ἀποθέμενος σὺν αὐτοῖς δικάζει.*

---

the *Δελφίνιον*. The text implies that the *ἐφέται* had not lost the privilege of trying such cases; possibly they retained it only in a formal sense as a kind of presiding committee, while the actual voting was in the hands of the dicasts. This is consistent with the statement of Pollux viii 125, *κατὰ μικρὸν δὲ κατεγελάσθη τὸ τῶν ἐφετῶν δικαστήριον.*

δικάζουσι *κτλ.*] To restore the missing word is a difficult task. According to Lucian, one of the courts of homicide, that of the Areopagus, held its sittings during the night:—*Hermotimus* 64, *Ἀρεοπαγῖται ἐν νυκτὶ καὶ σκότῳ δικάζουσιν*, and *de Domo*, 18, *εἴ τις...ἐν νυκτὶ ὥσπερ ἡ ἐξ Ἀρείου πάγου βουλὴ ποιοῖτο τὴν ἀκρόασιν.* This suggests the emendation *σκοταῖοι*, proposed by me in the *Academy*, Feb. 6, 1891, and accepted in the Dutch edition; but this proposal assumes either that the writer now reverts to the description of the procedure before the Areopagus, or that, if (as is more probable) he refers to all the courts of homicide, this particular detail in the trials before the Areopagus was also adopted in the three courts which have just been mentioned.

Again, if we refer to the account in Pollux viii 117, we find that the court of the Areopagus sat for three consecutive days before the last day in each month, *τριῶν ἡμερῶν ἐδίκαζον ἐφεξῆς, τετάρτῃ φθίνοντος, τρίτῃ, δευτέρᾳ* (cf. Schol. Aeschin. I § 188). Then (after a sentence stating that the court of the Areopagus was composed of those who had been archons) he continues: *ὑπαίθριοι δ' ἐδίκαζον.* This suggests *τριταῖοι*, which has independently occurred to Lipsius and Mr T. Nicklin: the sense would then be 'they give sentence on the third day'; but *δικάζειν* naturally means 'to try a cause' and not 'to pass a sentence,' *ψηφίζεσθαι.*

Both the above suggestions are open to the objection that they do not suit the faint traces still visible in the MS. These traces point to some word beginning with *αλ* or *ελ* followed by something resembling *ιη* preceding the termination. Such a word is *ἀλεεινοί* (from *ἀλέα*). Hdt. ii 25, *ἀλεεινῆς τῆς χώρας ἐούσης*, opp. to *ψυχεινὸς* Xen. *Cyr.* x 6; epithet of *ἐσθής* in *Pol.* ii 8, 1, *ἐσθῆτος εὐτελοῦς μὲν ἀλεεινῆς δὲ οὐκ ἐν τῷ χειμῶνι μόνον ἀλλὰ καὶ περὶ τοὺς θερινοὺς χρόνους.* Cf. Hesych. *ἀλεάζω* (*ἀλίζω* Kuster)· *ἀθροίζω. ἀλεάζων· δικαζόμενος*, and *ἡλιαία* either from *ἀλεάζεσθαι* (*ἀθροίζεσθαι*) or from *ὕπαιθρον εἶναι τὸν τόπον καὶ ἡλιοῦσθαι.* This assumes that an epithet usually meaning 'lying open to the sun, warm, hot,' can here be applied to a tribunal holding its meetings in the sunlight, as well as in the open air. If so, the three courts are *contrasted* in this respect with the court of the Areopagus. But such an application of the epithet is quite unprecedented.

As a better alternative one might suggest *ἐν ἡλιαίᾳ*, [ΕΝΗΛΙ]ΑΙ[Α]Ι, which is found without the article in Arist. *Eq.* 897 *ἐν ἡλιαίᾳ*, Posidippus ap. Athen. 591 C *εἰς ἡλιαίαν ἦλθε*, and Diog. Laert. i 66. If this is right, the collocation of *ὑπαίθριοι* supports the view of those who connect *ἡλιαία* with *ἥλιος*: Et. Mag. *s. v.* 1: *εἰς τὸ ὕπαιθρον προσκαθημένων τῶν δικαστῶν· ἢ παρὰ τὸ ὑπαίθριον· καὶ προϋποτίθεται ἥλιον εἶναι παρὰ τὸ ἡλιοῦσθαι τοὺς ἐκεῖ ἀθροιζομένους*, and at end of art. 2: *ἡλιάζεσθαι καὶ ἡλίασις ἐστὶ τὸ ἐν ἡλιαίᾳ δικάζειν* (Welcker, *Gr. Götterlehre*, i 403, and Wilamowitz, *Aus Kydathen*, p. 90). The term *ἡλιαία* is indeed suggestive of a large body of *δικασταί*, and it is so explained by the grammarians. Harp. *s.v.* mentions 1500 or 1000; and Pollux, 500 (at least). Cf. Paus. i 28, 8, *τὸ δὲ μέγιστον καὶ ἐς ὃ πλεῖστον συνίασιν Ἡλιαίαν ἐκάλουν*, where it is *contrasted* with the courts for the trial of homicide. But we know of trials *ἐπὶ Παλλαδίῳ* coming before 500 to 700 dicasts (p. 214 *b*); and such a tribunal may well be called 'a heliastic court.'

ὑπαίθριοι] Antiphon, *de caede Herodis*, 11, *ἅπαντα τὰ δικαστήρια ἐν ὑπαίθρῳ δικάζει τὰς δίκας τοῦ φόνου.*

ρεῖται τὸν στέφανον. ὁ δὲ τὴν αἰτίαν ἔχων τὸν μὲν ἄλλον χρόνον εἴργεται τῶν ἱερῶν, καὶ οὐδ' εἰς τὴν ἀγορὰν δ[ίκαιον ἐ]μβαλεῖν αὐτῷ· τότε δ' εἰς τὸ ἱερὸν εἰσελθὼν ἀπολογεῖται. ὅταν δὲ μὴ εἰδῇ τὸν ποιήσαντα, τῷ δράσαντι λαγχάνει. δικάζει δ' ὁ βασιλεὺς καὶ οἱ φυλοβασιλεῖς καὶ τὰς τῶν ἀψύχων καὶ τῶν ἄλλων ζῴων.

δίκας ἐδίκαζον. Sed exspectares potius *τριῶν ἡμερῶν* (Poll. viii 117) vel *τρισὶν ἡμέραις*, aut *τετάρτῳ μηνὶ* (Ant. *De Chor.* 42) vel denique *ἐν μηνὶ τετάρτῳ* (ΕΝΜΗΝΙΔ'). Litteram secundam Ζ vel Ξ fuisse suspicantur K-W, sed in papyro litterae neutrius apparet vestigium. ΑΛΙΗ vel ΕΛΙΗ aegre discerni posse putat G F Warner; post *δικάζουσι[ν]* litterarum vestigia evanida hanc fere speciem habere testatur Kenyon:—ΕΛΙΙΙ..ΑΙ.Ι, prima praesertim littera obscure scripta. Legendum fortasse *ἐν ἡλιαίᾳ* sc. [ΕΝ ΗΛΙ]ΑΙ[Α]Ι. **28** *εἴργεται* H-L. *οὐδ' εἰς τὴν ἀγορὰν* Wyse, Blass, van Leeuwen, Hartman, coll. Dem. 23 § 80 et 24 §§ 103, 165 (K-W, H-L): *οὐδεὶς τὴν αἰτίαν* K[1]. *δ[ίκαιον]* van Leeuwen (K[3]), vel potius *ἔξεστιν* (Wyse): *δ[ύναται]* K[1]; *δ[έδοται]* Gertz (K-W, H-L, B). ΕΜΒΑΛΕΙΝ (K, H-L, B): *ἐμβάλλειν* K-W. **29** ΜΗ (K, K-W, B:) *μηδεὶς* H-L, sed spatii non satis est. **30** *εἰδῇ* Wyse (K-W, H-L, K[3], B). Post *λαγχάνει* 'intercidit fere *ὁ προσήκων ἐπὶ πρυτανείῳ*' K-W. **31** ΖΩΩΝ. Desiderantur *οὗτοι δικάζουσι καὶ τὰ καταγνωσθέντα ὑπερορίζουσι*, coll. Poll. viii 120, K-W.

29—31 Pollux viii 120 infra exscriptus.

τὸν στέφανον] characteristic of the office of archon. Aeschin. 1 § 19, *ἄν τις Ἀθηναίων ἑταιρήσῃ, μὴ ἐξέστω αὐτῷ τῶν ἐννέα ἀρχόντων γενέσθαι, ὅτι οἶμαι στεφανηφόρος ἡ ἀρχή*, and Schol. *ad loc.*, *οἱ γὰρ ἐννέα ἄρχοντες στέφανον ἐφόρουν μυρρίνης*, with Hesych. *s. v. μυρρινῶν*, and Pollux viii 86, *μυρρίνῃ δ' ἐστεφάνωντο.* Hence in Photius, *s.v. ἡγεμονία δικαστηρίου ad fin.*, (of the archon *βασιλεὺς*), *ἔχει δὲ μόνος καὶ στέφανον* should be corrected into *ἔχει δὲ μυρρίνης στέφανον*. Cf. Lys. 26 § 8 (of the archon), [Dem.] 58 § 27 (of the *θεσμοθέται*). Hermann, *Staatsalt.* § 124, 12.

εἴργεται] § 2.

οὐδ' εἰς τὴν ἀγορὰν *κτλ.*] Aeschin. 1 § 164, *ἔπειτα ἐμβάλλεις εἰς τὴν ἀγορὰν ἢ στεφανοῖ ἢ πράττεις τι τῶν αὐτῶν ἡμῖν;* *F. L.* 148, *οὐ καθαρὸς ὢν τὰς χεῖρας εἰς τὴν ἀγορὰν ἐμβάλλεις.* Lycurg. *Leocr.* 5, *εἰς τὴν ἀγορὰν ἐμβάλλοντα καὶ τῶν κοινῶν ἱερῶν μετέχοντα.* Dem. 24 *c. Timocr.* 103, *ἐὰν ἁλοὺς τῆς κακώσεως τῶν γονέων εἰς τὴν ἀγορὰν ἐμβάλλῃ*, and 165, *εἰς τὴν ἀγορὰν φοβοῖτ' ἐμβαλεῖν*, also *ib.* 60 and *Androt.* 77.

ὅταν δὲ μὴ εἰδῇ *κτλ.*] [Dem.] 47 *c. Euerg.* 69, *συμβουλεύομέν σοι... ὀνομαστὶ μὲν μηδενὶ προαγορεύειν, τοῖς δεδρακόσι δὲ καὶ κτείνασιν.* Plat. *Leg.* 874 A, *ἐὰν δὲ τεθνεὼς μὲν αὖ τις φανῇ καὶ μὴ ἀμελῶς ζητοῦσιν ἀνεύρετος γίγνηται, τὰς μὲν προρρήσεις τὰς αὐτὰς γίγνεσθαι καθάπερ τοῖς ἄλλοις, προαγορεύειν δὲ τὸν φόνον τῷ δράσαντι καὶ ἐπιδικασάμενον ἐν ἀγορᾷ κηρῦξαι 'τῷ κτείναντι τὸν καὶ τὸν καὶ ὠφληκότι φόνον μὴ ἐπιβαίνειν ἱερῶν'* (Wyse). Pollux, viii 120, *τὸ ἐπὶ Πρυτανείῳ δικάζει περὶ τῶν ἀποκτεινάντων κἂν ὦσιν ἀφανεῖς.*

ὁ βασιλεὺς καὶ οἱ φυλοβασιλεῖς] Pollux, viii 90, says (of the *βασιλεύς*), *δικάζει τὰς τῶν ἀψύχων δίκας.* In § 120 he says (of the *φυλοβασιλεῖς*), *προειστήκεσαν δὲ τούτου τοῦ δικαστηρίου φυλοβασιλεῖς, οὓς δεῖ τὸ ἐμπεσὸν ἄψυχον ὑπερορίσαι.* These statements have hitherto been regarded as inconsistent with one another, and it has been supposed by Philippi, *Areop.* p. 18, that the duty of the *φυλοβασιλεῖς* was simply to cast the condemned object beyond the bounds of Attica. The text shews both the statements are correct and that the *βασιλεὺς* and the *φυλοβασιλεῖς* jointly presided over this court.

The trial was held in the precincts of the Prytaneum. Dem. *Aristocr.* 76, *ἐὰν λίθος ἢ ξύλον ἢ σίδηρος ἤ τι τοιοῦτον ἐμπεσὸν πατάξῃ, καὶ τὸν μὲν βαλόντα ἀγνοῇ τις, αὐτὸ δὲ εἰδῇ καὶ ἔχῃ τὸ τὸν φόνον εἰργασμένον, τούτοις ἐνταῦθα λαγχάνεται. εἰ τοίνυν τῶν ἀψύχων κτλ.* Pollux, viii 120, *τὸ ἐπὶ Πρυτανείῳ δικάζει... περὶ τῶν ἀψύχων τῶν ἐμπεσόντων καὶ ἀποκτεινάντων.* In the ceremony of the *βουφόνια*, the priest who slew the ox fled after flinging away the axe, *οἱ δὲ ἅτε τὸν ἄνδρα ὃς ἔδρασε τὸ ἔργον οὐκ εἰδότες ἐς δίκην ὑπάγουσι τὸν πέλεκυν* (Paus. i 24, 4, cf. 28, 11 and vi 11, 6).

καὶ τῶν ἄλλων ζῴων] Plat. *Gorg.* 473 C, *ὑπὸ τῶν πολιτῶν καὶ τῶν ἄλλων ξένων* (Kühner § 405 *b* n. 1).

The fact that animals could be tried has been hitherto unknown. But the

58. ὁ δὲ πολέμαρχος θύει μὲν θυσίας τήν τε τῇ Ἀρτέμιδι
τῇ ἀγροτέρᾳ καὶ τῷ Ἐνυαλίῳ, διατίθησι δ' ἀγῶνα τὸν ἐπιτάφιον
⟦καὶ⟧ τοῖς τετελευτηκόσιν ἐν τῷ πολέμῳ, καὶ Ἁρμοδίῳ καὶ Ἀριστο-
2 γείτονι ἐναγίσματα ποιεῖ. δίκαι δὲ λαγχάνονται πρὸς αὐτὸν ἴδιαι
μέν, αἵ τε τοῖς μετοίκοις καὶ τοῖς ἰσοτελέσι καὶ τοῖς προξένοις
γιγνόμεναι· καὶ δεῖ τοῦτον λαβόντα καὶ διανείμαντα δέκα μέρη, τὸ

LVIII 1 ΘΥΕΙΜΕΝ ? (K[3], K-W, B) : ΠΟΙΕΙΤΑΙ ? K[1] (H-L). *τήν τε τῇ* : *τῇ τε* K-W. ΕΝΥΩ
2 ΕΝΥΑΛΙΩΙΕΝΥΑΛΙΩΙ ? *Ἐνυαλίῳ* K (K-W, B) : *Ἐνυαλίῳ τὴν ἐνιαυσίαν* H-L. **3** ΚΑΙ secl. K (H-L, B); retinent K-W, commatis signo post *ἐπιτάφιον*, non post *πολέμῳ* posito. *τῷ* : *τῳ* Rutherford 'vix recte.' **5** Μ(ΕΝ) K, H-L, B : *μόνον* K-W. **6** ΓΙΝΟΜΕΝΑΙ (adscr. ΟΙϹ).

TESTIMONIA. **LVIII § 1** Heraclidis epitom. (Rose, Frag. 611, 8): *καὶ τὰ πολέμια.* Pollux viii 91: "*ὁ δὲ πολέμαρχος θύει μὲν*" *Ἀρτέμιδι* "*ἀγροτέρᾳ καὶ τῷ Ἐνυαλίῳ, διατίθησι*" *δὲ τὸν ἐπιτάφιον ἀγῶνα τῶν ἐν πολέμῳ ἀποθανόντων, καὶ τοῖς περὶ Ἁρμόδιον ἐναγίζει.* (§ **2**) *δίκαι δὲ πρὸς αὐτὸν λαγχάνονται μετοίκων, ἰσοτελῶν, προξένων. καὶ διανέμει τὸ λαχὸν ἑκάστῃ φυλῇ τι* (*τὸ* ? Bekk.: sine dubio leg. *τῇ φυλῇ*) *μέρος, τὸ μὲν διαιτηταῖς παραδιδούς,* (§ **3**) *εἰσάγων δὲ δίκας ἀποστασίου, ἀπροστασίου, κλήρων*

---

case is provided for in Plato's *Laws*, 873 E, *ἐὰν δ' ἄρα ὑποζύγιον ἢ ζῷον ἄλλο τι φονεύσῃ τινά... ἐπεξίτωσαν μὲν οἱ προσήκοντες τοῦ φόνου τῷ κτείναντι, διαδικαζόντων δὲ τῶν ἀγρονόμων οἷσιν ἂν καὶ ὁπόσοις προστάξῃ ὁ προσήκων, τὸ δὲ ὄφλον ἔξω τῶν ὅρων τῆς χώρας ἀποκτείναντες διορίσαι.* Then follows the case of things without life: *ἐὰν δὲ ἄψυχόν τι κτλ.*

LVIII. *The Polemarch.*

§ 1. **πολέμαρχος**] Hermann, *Staatsalt.* § 138, 8—10; Gilbert, i 242.

θύει—Ἐνυαλίῳ *κτλ.*] a survival of the duties performed in early times by the Polemarch in his military capacity. **Ἀρτέμιδι**] The sacrifice to Artemis was in memory of the battle of Marathon on the 6th day of Boedromion, Xen. *Anab.* iii 2, 12; Plut. *de malign. Her.* 26; Aelian, *V. H.* ii 25 (wrongly ascribed to the 6th of Thargelion); Schol. Aristoph. *Eq.* 660 (Hermann, *Gottesdienst. Alt.* § 56, 3 and 5; Mommsen, *Heortol.* p. 213).

ἀγῶνα τὸν ἐπιτάφιον] Plat. *Menex.* 249 B, *ἀγῶνας γυμνικοὺς καὶ ἱππικοὺς—καὶ μουσικῆς πάσης*, [Lys.] 2 § 80; Philostr. *Vit. Soph.* ii 30 *ad fin.* *ἐν τῇ ἀκαδημίᾳ, οὗ τίθησι τὸν ἀγῶνα ἐπὶ τοῖς ἐκ τῶν πολέμων θαπτομένοις ὁ πολέμαρχος.* Cf. Suidas, *s. v.* *Θεμιστοκλέους παῖδες.* See Mommsen, *Heortologie*, p. 281, and Daremberg and Saglio, s. v. *Epitaphia*, iii 727, where this commemorative festival is connected with the *Θησεῖα* and assigned to the 7th of Pyenepsion (end of October), cf. CIA ii 471, 22, *ἐποιήσαντο δὲ καὶ τοῖς ἐπιταφίοις δρόμον ἐν ὅπλοις—καὶ ἀπεδείξαντο ἐν τοῖς ὅπλοις τοῖς τε Θησείοις καὶ ἐπιταφίοις.* In this part of his duties the Polemarch was assisted by the *στρατηγοί*; Gilbert, *Beiträge*, p. 61.

ἐναγίσματα] *ὡς ἥρωϊ.* Cf. Paus. ii 11, 7 (of Achilles); and ii 10, 1 (of Heracles). The offerings consisted of libations of wine, oil, milk and honey. Hermann, *Gottesdienst. Alt.* § 16, 14; Müller's *Handbuch*, v 3 p. 98.

§ 2. **δίκαι...ἴδιαι**] Meier and Schömann, pp. 64—70, 619; Lys. 23 § 2, *προσεκαλεσάμην αὐτὸν πρὸς τὸν πολέμαρχον νομίζων μέτοικον εἶναι.*

προξένοις] the addition of *ξένων*, after *προξένων*, proposed by Meier in the corresponding passage of Pollux, is proved by the text to be unnecessary. *ξένοι* who were not resident in Attica, could only be concerned in *δίκαι ἀπὸ συμβόλων* or *δίκαι ἐμπορικαί*. By *πρόξενοι* we must here understand the privileged class of foreigners presented by Athens with rights such as those of *ἔγκτησις, ἀτέλεια* and *προεδρία*.

The privilege of the Polemarch's protection is expressly granted to a *πρόξενος* in CIA ii 42, *πρόσοδον αὐτῷ εἶναι πρὸς τὸν πολέμαρχον καθάπερ τοῖς ἄλλοις προξένοις.* In 131, we also have the grant of *ἀτέλεια καὶ γῆς καὶ οἰκίας ἔγκτησις.* Meier and Schöm. p. 70 Lips.

λαβόντα] *τὰς δίκας.* **διανείμαντα—μέρη**] 21 § 4.

λαχὸν ἑκάστῃ τῇ φυλῇ μέρος προσθεῖναι, τοὺς δὲ τὴν φυλὴν δικά-
ζοντας το[ῖς] διαιτηταῖς ἀποδοῦναι. αὐτὸς δ' εἰσάγει δίκας τάς τε 3
[[τοῦ]] ἀ[ποστασ]ίου καὶ ἀπροστασί[ου] καὶ κλήρων καὶ ἐπικλήρων
τοῖς μετοίκοις, καὶ τἄλλ' ὅσα τοῖς πολίταις ὁ ἄρχων, ταῦτα τοῖς
μετοίκοις ὁ πολέμαρχος.

59. οἱ δὲ θεσμοθέται πρῶτον μὲν τοῦ προγράψαι τὰ δικαστήριά εἰσι κύριοι, τίσιν ἡμέραις δεῖ δικάζειν, [ἔπ]ε[ιτα] τοῦ δοῦναι

7 μέρος secl. K-W. **9** τοῦ secl. K-W; habet Harp.

μετοίκων (Frag. 387², 426³). Bekk. *An.* 290, 28: "καὶ τῷ Ἐνυαλίῳ διατίθησι" τὸν "ἀγῶνα τὸν ἐπιτάφιον."

§ **3** *Harp. πολέμαρχος:...Ἀρ. δ' ἐν τῇ Ἀθ. πολ. διεξελθὼν ὅσα διοικεῖ ὁ πολέμαρχος, πρὸς ταῦτα, φησίν, αὐτός τε "εἰσάγει δίκας τάς τε τοῦ ἀποστασίου καὶ ἀπροστασίου καὶ κλήρων—ταῦτα τοῖς μετοίκοις ὁ πολέμαρχος." *Harp. ἀποστασίου:...Ἀρ. δ' ἐν Ἀθ. πολ. περὶ τοῦ πολεμάρχου γράφει ταυτί· "οὗτος δὲ εἰσάγει δίκας τάς τε τοῦ ἀποστασίου καὶ κλήρων καὶ ἐπικλήρων." Bekk. *An.* 310, 9: ὁ πολέμαρχος (εἰσάγει δίκας) ἀποστασίου "καὶ κλήρων καὶ ἐπικλήρων τοῖς μετοίκοις· καὶ τἆλλα ὅσα τοῖς" ἀστοῖς ὁ ἄρχων, οὗτος τοῖς μετοίκοις παρέχεται (Frag. 388², 427³). Phot. ἡγεμονία δικαστηρίου:...τῷ πολεμάρχῳ δὲ ὅσαι ἀποστασίου γραφὴν ἔφερον· ἔτι μὴν καὶ ὅσα ὁ ἄρχων ἐν τοῖς ἀστοῖς, ὁ πολέμαρχος τοῖς μετοίκοις διῄτα.

TESTIMONIA. **LIX** Pollux viii 87: § **1** ἰδίᾳ δὲ οἱ μὲν θεσμοθέται προγράφουσι πότε δεῖ δικάζειν τὰ δικαστήρια, (§ **2**) καὶ "τὰς εἰσαγγελίας εἰσαγγέλλουσιν εἰς τὸν δῆμον καὶ τὰς" χειροτονίας "καὶ τὰς προβολὰς" εἰσάγουσι καὶ τὰς τῶν παρανόμων γραφάς, καὶ εἴ τις μὴ ἐπιτήδειον νόμον γράψειεν, "καὶ στρατηγοῖς εὐθύνας" (cf. Schol. Aeschin. 1 § 1, p. 253 Schultz, ἡ δὲ εὔθυνα—οἷον πρεσβείαν, στρατηγίαν κτλ.).

*Harp. θεσμοθέται:...ὁ δὲ Ἀρ. ἐν τῇ (ᾱ addit codex Angelicanus) Ἀθ. πολ. διέρχεται ὅσα οὗτοι πράττουσιν. Phot. θεσμ.:...τὰς εἰσαγγελίας εἰσήγγελλον εἰς τὸν δῆμον καὶ τὰς χειροτονίας καὶ τὰς προβολὰς ἁπάσας καὶ γραφὰς παρανόμων... Schol. in Plat. *Phaedr.* 235 D εἶχον δὲ ἐξουσίαν τοῦ ὑπογράψαι τὰ δικαστήρια, καὶ τὰς εἰσαγγελίας εἰσῆγον καὶ τὰς χειροτονίας καὶ προβολὰς καὶ γραφὰς παρανόμων καὶ ἄλλων τινῶν. Cf. Schol. in Aeschin. 1 § 16 in p. 219 *a* exscriptum.

τοὺς τὴν φυλὴν δικάζοντας] *i.e.* the four δικασταί assigned to each tribe, who introduce private actions concerning members of that tribe. As resident aliens are not members of any tribe, the lawsuits in which they are concerned are distributed by lot among the ten groups of four δικασταί each. This shews that μέτοικοι were in no way enrolled in any particular deme, as once suggested by Wilamowitz, *Hermes*, xxii 211. Cf. 53 § 1.

The quotation of this passage in Pollux is unintelligible, and none of the various corrections (enumerated in Hubert *de Arbitris Atticis*, p. 29 f.) are satisfactory (Lipsius, *Leipzig Verhandl.*, p. 55).

§ 3. **ἀποστασίου καὶ ἀπροστασίου**] The former designation was applied to the case in which a μέτοικος deserted (or acted without the sanction of) the προστάτης under whom he had been enrolled; the latter, to that in which he had no προστάτης. Dem. 35 *Lacr.* 48, ἀλλ' ὁ πολέμαρχος εἰσάξει. ἀποστασίου γε καὶ ἀπροστασίου.

On the δίκη ἀποστασίου, see Meier and Schöm. p. 619—623 Lips.; on the γραφὴ ἀπροστασίου, *ib.* p. 388—391.

κλήρων καὶ ἐπικλήρων τοῖς μετοίκοις] [Dem.] 46 § 22, ἐπιδικασίαι εἶναι τῶν ἐπικλήρων ἁπασῶν καὶ ξένων καὶ ἀστῶν καὶ περὶ μὲν τῶν πολιτῶν τὸν ἄρχοντα εἰσάγειν καὶ ἐπιμελεῖσθαι, περὶ δὲ τῶν μετοίκων τὸν πολέμαρχον. Pollux, viii 91, has κλήρων μετοίκων, corrected by Meier into κλήρων ἐπικλήρων μετοίκοις (or μετοικικῶν). The general purport of this correction is confirmed by the text.

LIX. *The Thesmothetae.*

§ 1. **θεσμοθέται**] Meier and Schöm. p. 72—81 Lips.; Gilbert, i 243; and Dict. Ant. s. v. *Archon.*

τίσιν ἡμέραις δεῖ δικάζειν] *e.g.* Dem. *c. Mid.* 47 (of a γραφὴ ὕβρεως), οἱ δὲ θεσμοθέται εἰσαγόντων εἰς τὴν ἡλιαίαν τριάκοντα ἡμερῶν κτλ. (Meier and Schöm., p. 906 Lips.).

ταῖς ἀρχαῖς· καθ' ὅ τι γὰρ ἂν οὗτοι δῶσιν, κατὰ τοῦτο χρῶνται.
2 ἔτι δὲ τὰς εἰσαγγελίας εἰσαγγέλλουσιν εἰς τὸν δῆμον, καὶ τὰς καταχειροτονίας καὶ τὰς προβολὰς ἁπάσα[ς] εἰσάγουσιν οὗ[τοι], καὶ γραφὰς παρανόμων, καὶ νόμον μὴ ἐπιτήδειον θεῖναι, καὶ προεδρικὴν

LIX 4 εἰσαγγέλλουσιν εἰς τὸν δῆμον secl. K-W; retinent K, H-L, B; εἰσαγγέλλουσιν defendunt Pollux et Photius: εἰσάγουσιν Schol. ad Plat. *Phaedr.* 235 et ad Aesch. i 16 (Gomperz). **6** <τοῦ> νόμον J B Mayor (H-L).

---

§ 2. **εἰσαγγελίας**] The statement of Pollux, viii 87, that it was the θεσμοθέται who laid εἰσαγγελίαι before the popular assembly was doubted by Boeckh (*Kleine Schriften*, v p. 163); but it is now clear that the ultimate authority for the statement was the present passage. Cf. Schol. Aeschin. 1 § 16, οἱ θεσμοθέται ἄλλα μὲν ποιοῦσι κοινῇ, ἰδίᾳ δέ, πότε δεῖ δικάζειν τὰ δικαστήρια καὶ τὰς εἰσαγγελίας εἰσάγειν εἰς τὸν δῆμον, καὶ τὰς χειροτονίας καὶ τὰς προβολὰς εἰσάγουσι καὶ τὰς τῶν παρανόμων γραφὰς καὶ ἕτερα.

καταχειροτονίας] they bring forward all cases of 'removal from office by the votes of the people.' In Dem. *c. Mid.* 6, the noun is applied to the preliminary vote of condemnation called προβολή: καταχειροτονίαν ὁ δῆμος ἐποιήσατο, and similarly with the verb in §§ 2, 199 and twice in § 175. In 51 § 8, in a speech before the βουλή, it is applied to a case of προδοσία: παρεδώκατε εἰς τὸ δικαστήριον, καταχειροτονήσαντες προδεδωκέναι τὰς ναῦς καὶ λελοιπέναι τὴν τάξιν. In the text the reference is to sentences passed by the ἐκκλησία on the occasion of an εἰσαγγελία, and then referred to a court of law (Lipsius, *Leipzig Verhandl.* p. 48).

προβολάς] c. 43 § 5. Preliminary decisions of the ἐκκλησία directing public prosecutions to be instituted, Dem. *c. Mid.* §§ 9, 11. Isocr. 15 § 314, προβολὰς ἐν τῷ δήμῳ ἐποίησαν.

προβολαί were only resorted to in case of offences against religion (Dem. *c. Mid.*), complaints against magistrates (Harpocr. *s. v.* καταχειροτονία), and against συκοφάνται (43 § 5). Meier and Schöm. p. 335—344 Lips. The supposition that προβολαί could only be brought against magistrates at the ἐπιχειροτονίαι (Schömann, *de Comit.* p. 231 f.) is founded on passages of grammarians connecting προβολαί with καταχειροτονία, and this supposed connexion may have originated in a misunderstanding of the present passage. The statement that the ἡγεμονία δικαστηρίου belonged to the θεσμοθέται is confirmed by Dem. *c. Mid.* 32, τῶν θεσμοθετῶν τούτων.

γραφὰς παρανόμων] c. 29 § 4, Hyperides, *pro Euxenippo*, c. 21, 27, παράνομά τις ἐν τῇ πόλει γράφει; θεσμοθετῶν συνέδριον ἐστι. Dem. *Lept.* 98, 99.

νόμον μὴ ἐπιτήδειον θεῖναι] It has sometimes been supposed that a γραφὴ παρανόμων could be directed against ψηφίσματα, as well as against νόμοι, on the ground of *inexpediency*, as well as on that of *illegality*.

This opinion rests on passages such as (1) the spurious law quoted in Dem. *c. Timocr.* 33, ἐὰν δέ τις λύσας τινὰ τῶν νόμων τῶν κειμένων ἕτερον ἀντιθῇ μὴ ἐπιτήδειον τῷ δήμῳ τῷ Ἀθηναίων ἢ ἐναντίον τῶν κειμένων τῳ, τὰς γραφὰς εἶναι κατ' αὐτοῦ κατὰ τὸν νόμον ὃς κεῖται, ἐάν τις μὴ ἐπιτήδειον θῇ νόμον. (Here inexpedient and contradictory laws are confusedly blended together.) (2) Pollux viii 56, ὑπωμοσία δέ ἐστιν, ὅταν τις ἢ ψήφισμα ἢ νόμον γραφέντα γράφηται ὡς ἀνεπιτήδειον, and 44 (in a γραφὴ παρανόμων) διήλεγχεν ὅτι ἔστι παράνομον ἢ ἄδικον ἢ ἀσύμφορον.

It was urged by Madvig (*Kleine Schriften*, p. 378 ff.) that, in the case of νόμοι, no less than in that of ψηφίσματα, the argument from inexpediency was really irrelevant, the only legitimate ground of attack in both cases being that of illegality. This opinion has, however, been contested by Schöll (*Sitzungsber. d. k. b. Akad.*, München, 1886, p. 136). Relying partly on the passage in Pollux viii 87, which proves to be quoted from the text (see *Testimonia*), he contends that, under a γραφὴ παρανόμων, a ψήφισμα could only be impugned on the ground of illegality, whereas a νόμος might be formally attacked on the ground of inexpediency, as well as on that of illegality (Dem. *c. Timocr.* 61, 68, 108). Cf. Gilbert, i 284, n. 1; Meier and Schöm. p. 431 Lips.; Dict. Ant. ii 340 *a*.

Lipsius, who formerly supported Madvig, now holds that the text confirms Schöll's view (*Leipzig Verhandl.* p. 48). But it will be observed that in the text the reference to inexpedient laws is introduced by καί, which (unless it is merely epexegetic) makes the following clause an additional item in the enumeration.

καὶ ἐπιστατικὴν καὶ στρατηγοῖς εὐθύνας. εἰσὶ δὲ καὶ γραφαὶ 3
8 *πρὸς αὐτοὺς ὧν παράστασις τίθεται, ξενίας καὶ δωροξενίας, ἄν τις δῶρα δοὺς ἀποφύγῃ τὴν ξενίαν, καὶ συκοφαντίας καὶ δώρων καὶ*

8 '*ξενίας μέν, ἐάν τις κατηγορῆται ξένος εἶναι, δωροξενίας δὲ* lex. Cant.—*ἄν τις—ξενίαν* glossa?' K-W. **9** *τὴν ξενίας* Meier, *Att. Pro.* p. 73, H-L.

§ **3** *Harp. *παράστασις*:...'*Αρ. δ' ἐν 'Αθ. πολ. περὶ θεσμοθετῶν λέγων φησὶν οὕτως* "*εἰσὶ δὲ γραφαὶ—τὴν ξενίαν*," "*καὶ ψευδεγγραφῆς—μοιχείας*." *Harp. *δωροξενία*:...*καὶ 'Αρ. δ' ἐν τῇ 'Αθ. πολ. περὶ τῶν θεσμοθετῶν λέγων γράφει ταυτί* "*εἰσὶ δὲ καὶ γραφαὶ—ἀποφύγῃ τὴν*" *συκοφαντίαν* ('ex sequentibus errore arreptum pro *ξενίαν*' Rose). **Lex. rhet. Cantab. ξενίας γραφὴ καὶ δωροξενίας διαφέρει. 'Αρ. ἐν τῇ 'Αθ. πολ. φησὶ περὶ τῶν θεσμοθετῶν διαλεγόμενος* "*εἰσὶ δὲ καὶ γραφαὶ πρὸς* (*περὶ* cod.) *αὐτοὺς ὧν παράστασις* (*περιστάσεις* cod.) *τίθεται, ξενίας καὶ δωροξενίας.*" *ξενίας μὲν ἐάν τις κατηγορῆται ξένος εἶναι, δωροξενίας δὲ* "*ἐάν τις δῶρα δοὺς ἀποφύγῃ τὴν ξενίαν.*" Pollux viii 44: *δωροξενίας δὲ εἴ τις ξενίας κρινόμενος δῶρα δοὺς ἀποφύγοι* (Hesych. *δωροξενία· τὸ ἐπὶ ξενίαν καλούμενον ἀποφυγεῖν δῶρα δόντα*). Harp. *ἡγεμονία δικαστηρίου*:...*πρὸς δὲ τοὺς θεσμοθέτας αἱ τῆς ξενίας τε καὶ δωροξενίας* (*ἐλαγχάνοντο δίκαι*) *καὶ συκοφαντίας καὶ δώρων καὶ ψευδεγγραφῆς καὶ ὕβρεως καὶ μοιχείας καὶ βουλεύσεως καὶ ἄλλων.* Bekk. *An.* 310, 12: *οἱ θεσμ. εἰσῆγον ξενίας καὶ συκοφαντίας καὶ δώρων καὶ ψευδεγγραφῆς καὶ ὕβρεως καὶ μοιχείας καὶ βουλεύσεως.* Phot. *ἡγεμ. δικαστ.*:...*οἱ θεσμ. συκοφαντίας καὶ δώρων καὶ ὕβρεων καὶ μοιχείας καὶ βουλεύσεως* (cf. Frag. 379², 418³). Pollux viii 87: *γίνονται δὲ γραφαὶ πρὸς αὐτοὺς ξενίας, δωροξενίας, δώρων, συκοφαντίας, ψευδοκλητείας, ψευδεγγραφῆς, βουλεύσεως, ἀγραφίου, μοιχείας.* Cf. etiam Bekk. *An.* 238, 24 *δωροξενία*; 240, 33 *δωροξενίας δίκη*.

This fact is in favour of a separation of legal proceedings on the ground of inexpediency from the strict procedure of the *γραφὴ παρανόμων*. We may accordingly suppose that the *γραφὴ παρανόμων* was originally intended to be directed against *ψηφίσματα*, as well as *νόμοι*, on the sole ground of illegality; and that, subsequently, fresh powers were granted for the institution of formal proceedings against *νόμοι* alone, on the sole ground of inexpediency. This new kind of procedure is the subject of the additional clause *καὶ νόμον μὴ ἐπιτήδειον θεῖναι*.

προεδρικὴν] the later form of the *γραφὴ πρυτανική* which is mentioned together with the *γρ. ἐπιστατική* by Harpocr. *s. v. ῥητορικὴ γραφή*.—*ἡ κατὰ ῥήτορος γράψαντός τι ἢ εἰπόντος ἢ πράξαντος παράνομον, ὥσπερ λέγεται καὶ πρυτανικὴ ἡ κατὰ πρυτάνεως, καὶ ἐπιστατικὴ ἡ κατ' ἐπιστάτου.* Cf. c. 44.

στρατηγοῖς εὐθύνας] Lys. 9 § 11; 14 § 38; [Dem.] 49 § 25. Generals might even be called back to give account before the expiration of their office (Lys. 28 § 5). Meier and Schöm. p. 263 Lips.; Gilbert, *Beiträge*, pp. 26—28; Schöll, *de Synegoris*, pp. 12, 14; Wilamowitz, *Aus Kydathen*, p. 62; Hauvette-Besnault, *les Stratèges Ath.* pp. 56—63.

§ 3. **γραφαὶ**] Meier and Schöm. p. 437 ff. Lips.

παράστασις] the fee (probably a drachm) paid to the state by the prosecutor in certain public causes. The present passage (as quoted by Harpocr. *s. v.*) has been the authority for the causes in which it was paid; but the list is probably not exhaustive. The fee was *not* paid in an *εἰσαγγελία κακώσεως ἐπικλήρων* (Isae. 3 *Pyrrh.* 45). Meier and Schöm. pp. 799 f., 813—4 Lips.

ξενίας] a prosecution for usurping the rights of citizenship. Meier and Schöm. pp. 437—442 and 95—98, Lips.; Dict. Ant. *s. v.*

The *Lex. Rhet. Cant.* adds the needless explanation: *ἐάν τις κατηγορῆται ξένος εἶναι*.

δωροξενίας] If a person tried on the charge of *ξενία* was 'acquitted by fraudulent collusion with the prosecutor or witnesses, or by any species of bribery, he was liable to be indicted afresh by a *γρ. δωροξενίας*' (Dict. Ant. *s. v.*; Meier and Schöm. p. 441 Lips.).

συκοφαντίας καὶ δώρων] omitted by Harpocr. and the *Lex. Rhet. Cant.* in their list of causes in which *παράστασις* was paid. Lipsius (*Att. Proc.* p. 73) was led to propose the addition of these causes by Bekker's *Anecd.* p. 310, 14, where *συκοφαντίας, δώρων, ὕβρεως* are inserted. On the *γρ. συκοφαντίας*, see Meier and Schöm. p. 413 Lips.; on the *γρ. δώρων*, p. 444.

ψευδεγγραφῆς καὶ ψευδοκλητείας καὶ βουλεύσεως καὶ ἀγραφίου
4 καὶ μοιχείας. εἰσάγουσιν δὲ καὶ τὰς δοκιμασ[ία]ς ταῖς ἀρχαῖς ἁπάσαις, καὶ τοὺς ἀπεψηφισμένους ὑπὸ τῶν δημοτῶν, καὶ τὰς
5 καταγνώσεις [τ]ὰς ἐκ τῆς βουλῆς. εἰσάγουσι δὲ καὶ δίκας ἰδίας, ἐμπορικὰς καὶ μεταλλικὰς καὶ δούλων, ἄν τις τὸν ἐλεύθερον κακῶς λέγῃ. καὶ ἐπικληροῦσι ταῖς ἀρχαῖς οὗτοι τὰ δικαστήρια τὰ ἴδια
6 καὶ τὰ δημόσια. καὶ τὰ σύμβολα τὰ πρὸς τὰς πόλεις οὗτοι κυροῦσι,

11 *καὶ ὕβρεως* ante *καὶ μοιχείας* ins. Harp. s.v. *ἡγεμονία δικαστηρίου* (cf. Bekk. *An.*, Phot.); non inserit Harp. s.v. *παράστασις*. *εἰσάγουσι* H-L. **14** *ἐάν* H-L. **15—16** *καὶ ἐπικληροῦσι—δημόσια* secl. K-W; defendit Pollux viii 87. **15** ΟΥΤΟΙΤΑ (K-W, K[3], B): *πάντα* K[1], *πάντα τὰ* H-L. **16** ΚΥΡΟΥϹΙ (K, K-W, B); idem habet Pollux: <*κατα*>*κυροῦσι* Wyse (H-L).

§§ **4—6** Pollux viii 87: (§ **4**) *εἰσάγουσι δὲ καὶ δοκιμασίαν ταῖς ἀρχαῖς, καὶ τοὺς ἀπεψηφισμένους, καὶ τὰς ἐκ τῆς βουλῆς καταγνώσεις.* (§ **5**) *καὶ δίκας ἐμπορικὰς καὶ μεταλλικάς, καὶ ἐὰν δοῦλος κακῶς ἀγορεύῃ τὸν ἐλεύθερον, καὶ ταῖς ἀρχαῖς ἐπικληροῦσι τὰ δικαστήρια τὰ ἴδια καὶ τὰ δημόσια.* (§ **6**) *καὶ τὰ σύμβολα τὰ πρὸς πόλεις κυροῦσι, καὶ δίκας τὰς ἀπὸ συμβόλων εἰσάγουσι καὶ τὰς τῶν ψευδομαρτυριῶν τῶν ἐξ Ἀρείου πάγου.*

ψευδεγγραφῆς] a prosecution against a public officer for making a false entry in the list of debtors to the state. Meier and Schöm. p. 415 Lips.; Dict. Ant. *s. v.*

ψευδοκλητείας] a prosecution for falsely appearing as witness to a summons. Meier and Schöm. p. 414 Lips., and Dict. Ant. *s. v.*

βουλεύσεως] a prosecution instituted by one who was wrongfully inscribed as a state debtor against one who had so inscribed him. The distinction between this kind of *γρ. βουλεύσεως* and the cognate *γρ. ψευδεγγραφῆς* is stated as follows by Boeckh, p. 390 Lewis: 'whoever falsely declared that another had been registered was liable to the action for false registration (*ψευδεγγραφῆς*). If, on the other hand, a man who had been a state debtor had paid all that was due, but his name was not erased, or, having been erased, was re-entered, the action for conspiracy applied (*βουλεύσεως*).' Meier and Schöm. p. 415 Lips.; Dict. Ant. i p. 314 *a*.

ἀγραφίου] a prosecution for non-registration of a name in the list of state debtors, instituted in the event of the name being improperly *erased* before the debt was paid. This action might be brought either against the person whose name was improperly erased, or against the officer who omitted to register the debt. If the name of a debtor had not been registered at all, he could only be proceeded against by *ἔνδειξις*, and was not liable to the *ἀγραφίου γραφή* (Dem. *c. Theocrin.* 67), Meier and Schöm. p. 447—9 Lips.; and Dict. Ant. *s. v.*

μοιχείας] Meier and Schöm. p. 402—9 Lips.; Dict. Ant. i 29 *b*.

§ 4. **δοκιμασίας**] 55 §§ 2—4. Gilbert, i 210.

ἀπεψηφισμένους κτλ.] Those whose claims to citizenship were rejected at the *διαψήφισις*, held by the members of the deme, might appeal to a law-court. 13 § 5; 42 § 1; Meier and Schöm. p. 989 f. Lips.

καταγνώσεις] 45 § 1, *τὰς καταγνώσεις εἰσάγειν τοὺς θεσμοθέτας εἰς τὸ δικαστήριον.*

§ 5. **ἐμπορικὰς**] commercial law-suits heard during the winter, when the sea was closed to mercantile enterprise. These, as well as the *μεταλλικαὶ δίκαι*, belonged to the class of *ἔμμηνοι δίκαι*, which were decided within a month. Meier and Sch., p. 635 Lips.; Dict. Ant. i p. 730 *a*.

μεταλλικὰς] mining suits, Dem. *Pant.* 35. Boeckh, *On the Silver Mines of Laurium*, § 12; Meier and Sch., p. 634 Lips.

δούλων] It was only in the event of a *δίκη κακηγορίας* being brought by a freeman against a slave that the *θεσμοθέται* presided over the court. In other cases, it came before the Forty. Meier and Sch., pp. 80, 628 Lips.

ἐπικληροῦσι—δικαστήρια] CIA ii 567 *b* (in a decree in honour of a *θεσμοθέτης*) *ἐπιμελεῖται δὲ καὶ τῆς κληρώσεως τῶν δικαστηρίων.* Meier and Sch., p. 160 Lips.

§ 6. **τὰ σύμβολα τὰ πρὸς τὰς πόλεις**]

καὶ τὰς δίκας τὰς ἀπὸ τῶν συμβόλων εἰσάγουσι, καὶ τὰ ψευδομαρτύρια <τὰ> ἐ[ξ] Ἀρείου πάγου. τοὺς δὲ δικαστὰς κληροῦσι 7
πάντες οἱ ἐννέα ἄρχοντες, δέκατος δ' ὁ γραμματεὺς ὁ τῶν θεσμοθετῶν, τοὺς τῆς αὑτοῦ φυλῆς ἕκαστος.

60. τὰ μὲν οὖν περὶ τοὺς ἐννέα ἄρχοντας τοῦτον ἔχει τὸν τρόπον. κληροῦσι δὲ καὶ ἀθλοθέτας δέκα [ἄ]νδρας, ἕνα τῆς φυλῆς ἑκάστης. οὗτοι δὲ δοκιμασθέντες ἄρχουσι τέτταρ[α ἔ]τη,

17 τὰ ψ. ΤΑC mutatum in ΤΑΨ. **18** <τὰ> Bernardakis, K-W, H-L, B coll. Poll. τὰς τῶν ψ. τῶν K-W. **18—20** τοὺς δὲ—ἕκαστος secl. K-W, cf. 63 § 1; defendit Schol. Arist. *Vesp.* 775. **19** ΠΑΝΤΑC K-W: πάντες corr. K, H-L, B.

17 *Bekk. *An.* 436 ἀπὸ συμβόλων δικάζει infra exscriptum (Frag. 380², 419³); cf. Harp. infra laudatum.

18—20 Schol. Ar. *Vesp.* 775: θεσμοθέται καὶ δέκατος ὁ γραμματεὺς κληροῦσι τοὺς δικαστὰς τοὺς τῆς αὐτῆς φυλῆς ἕκαστος.

TESTIMONIA. **LX § 1** Pollux viii 93: ἀθλοθέται δέκα μέν εἰσιν, εἷς κατὰ φυλήν, δοκιμασθέντες δὲ ἄρχουσιν ἔτη τέτταρα ἐπὶ τῷ διαθεῖναι τὰ Παναθήναια, τόν τε μουσικὸν <add. ἀγῶνα> "καὶ τὸν γυμνικὸν" "καὶ τὴν ἱπποδρομίαν." *ib.* 87 (οἱ ἐννέα ἄρχοντες...ἔχουσιν ἐξουσίαν) κληροῦν δικαστὰς καὶ ἀθλοθέτας, ἕνα κατὰ φυλὴν ἑκάστην.

'international contracts.' Such agreements were finally ratified by a heliastic court. In [Dem.] 7 § 9, Philip claims that they shall be ratified οὐκ ἐπειδὰν ἐν τῷ δικαστηρίῳ τῷ παρ' ὑμῖν κυρωθῇ ὥσπερ ὁ νόμος κελεύει. Cf. [Andoc.] *in Alcib.* 18. They secured to the citizens of the contracting states the reciprocal right of suing and being sued; *Pol.* 1275 *a* 8, (among those who are not citizens are) οἱ τῶν δικαίων μετέχοντες οὕτως ὥστε καὶ δίκην ὑπέχειν καὶ δικάζεσθαι· τοῦτο γὰρ ὑπάρχει καὶ τοῖς ἀπὸ συμβόλων κοινωνοῦσι. The decision was given in the court of the defendant's city, and in accordance with laws agreed upon in the σύμβολα.

τὰς δίκας τὰς ἀπὸ τῶν συμβόλων] These were mainly commercial suits; but while, in the ordinary δίκαι ἐμπορικαί, the suit was tried in the state where the contract was made, and in accordance with the laws of that state; in the δίκαι ἀπὸ συμβόλων, it was tried in the defendant's state and in accordance with the laws agreed upon in the σύμβολα. Thus, on the reduction of Chalcis in B.C. 446/5, the inhabitants retained their own jurisdiction except in the case of offences punishable by disfranchisement, exile, or death. These were to be sent to Athens for trial: περὶ δὲ τούτων ἔφεσιν εἶναι Ἀθήναζε εἰς τὴν ἡλιαίαν τῶν θεσμοθετῶν.

In Bekker's *Anecd.* i 436 we read: Ἀθηναῖοι ἀπὸ συμβόλων ἐδίκαζον τοῖς ὑπηκόοις· οὕτως Ἀριστοτέλης, and similarly (so far as regards the first statement) Hesych. *s. v.* ἀπὸ συμβόλων δικάζειν; but it will be observed that the text says nothing of ὑπήκοοι. Cf. Pollux viii 63, ἀπὸ συμβόλων δέ, ὅτε οἱ σύμμαχοι ἐδικάζοντο. Harpocr. σύμβολα: τὰς συνθήκας ἃς ἂν αἱ πόλεις ἀλλήλαις θέμεναι τάττωσι τοῖς πολίταις ὥστε διδόναι καὶ λαμβάνειν τὰ δίκαια, and similarly Phot. and Etym. M. On this subject cf. Meier and Schöm. pp. 994—1006 Lips.; Goodwin in *American Journal of Philology*, i 1880, p. 1—16; Dict. Ant. ii 734—6.

τὰ ψευδομαρτύρια] this form has hitherto been found only in Plat. *Theaet.* 148 B, ἔνοχος τοῖς ψευδομαρτυρίοις. In the case of δίκαι ψευδομαρτυριῶν in general, the management of the suit was in the hands of the same authorities as the trial at which the alleged false witness was tendered: it was only in the event of false witness before the Areopagus, that the case came under the cognisance of the θεσμοθέται. Meier and Schöm. p. 485 f.

§ 7. **τοὺς δὲ δικαστὰς κληροῦσι**] 63 § 1. Meier and Sch., p. 160 Lips.

ὁ γραμματεὺς] 55 § 1; 63 § 1.

LX. *The Athlothetae.*

§ 1. **ἀθλοθέτας**] The lists of payments from the treasures of Athena for public purposes include the following items: CIA i 183 (Hicks, no. 53), 7 (in the British Museum), ἀθλοθέταις ἐς Παναθήναια, in B.C. 415, 9 talents; *ib.* 188 (Ditt. no. 44), 5 (in the Louvre), ἀθλοθέταις ἐς Παναθήναια τὰ μεγάλα, in B.C. 410, 5 talents, 1000 drachmae.

καὶ διοικοῦσι τήν τε πομπὴν τῶν Παναθηναίων καὶ τὸν ἀγῶνα τῆς μουσικῆς καὶ τὸν γυμνικὸν ἀγῶνα καὶ τὴν ἱπποδρομίαν, καὶ τὸν πέπλον ποιοῦνται, καὶ τοὺς ἀμφορεῖς ποιοῦνται μετὰ τῆς βουλῆς,
2 *καὶ τὸ ἔλαιον τοῖς ἀθληταῖς ἀποδιδόασι. συλλέγεται δὲ τὸ ἔλαιον*

LX 6 ΑΜΦΟΡΕΙϹ ΠΟΙΟΥΝΤΑΙ (K): *ἀμφορεῖς* Gennadios, (K-W, H-L); *ποιοῦνται* retinet B, commatis signo post prius *ποιοῦνται* addito, et coll. c. 49 § 3. **7** ϹΛΕΓΕΤΑΙ ΤΟΔ΄ ΕΛΑΙΟΝ: *συλλέγεται δὲ τὸ ἔλαιον* Gennadios, Richards, Gertz, H-L, K-W[1], K[3], B; *τὸ δ' ἔλαιον συλλέγεται* R D Hicks (K-W[2]).

§ 2 *Schol. Soph. *O. C.* 701: *ὁ δὲ* **'Αρ.** *καὶ τοῖς νικήσασι τὰ Παναθήναια ἐλαίου τοῦ ἐκ τῶν μοριῶν γινομένου* **δίδοσθαί** *φησιν.* Cf. Phot. s.v. *μορίαι* (Frag. 345[2], 383[3]). Schol. Arist. *Nub.* 1005.

πομπὴν τῶν Παναθηναίων] Thuc. vi 56—58. Michaelis, *Parthenon*, p. 327.

τὸν ἀγῶνα τῆς μουσικῆς] Plut. *Per.* 13, *φιλοτιμούμενος δ' ὁ Περικλῆς τότε πρῶτον ἐψηφίσατο μουσικῆς ἀγῶνα τοῖς Παναθηναίοις ἄγεσθαι καὶ διέταξεν αὐτὸς ἀθλοθέτης αἱρεθείς, καθότι χρὴ τοὺς ἀγωνιζομένους αὐλεῖν ἢ ᾄδειν ἢ κιθαρίζειν.* Phrynis of Mytilene won the prize with the *κιθάρα* in B.C. 456. The prizes for *κιθαρῳδοί* were a crown, together with 500, 300, 200, or 100 *dr.* (schol., Arist. *Av.* 11); and for the *ἄνδρες αὐλῳδοί*, a crown and 100 *dr.* This competition is mentioned in Plut. ii 1134 A, *de Musica*, 8, *ἐν ἀρχῇ γὰρ ἐλεγεῖα μεμελοποιημένα οἱ αὐλῳδοὶ ᾖδον· τοῦτο δὲ δηλοῖ ἡ τῶν Παναθηναίων γραφὴ ἡ περὶ τοῦ μουσικοῦ ἀγῶνος.* The prize for the *ἄνδρες κιθαρισταί* was a crown, or 200 or 100 *dr.*; there was also a prize for the *αὐληταί*, probably a crown (Michaelis, *Parthenon*, p. 322). A crown won at a *μουσικὸς ἀγὼν* is represented in an inscr. published in 'Εφημ. 'Αρχ. 1862, 219 (copied *ib.* p. 318).

γυμνικὸν ἀγῶνα] mentioned in documents quoted in Dem. 18 § 116 and Hippocrates iii 830 Kühn, also in CIA ii 331, 177 (c. B.C. 270), *Παναθηναίων τῶν μεγάλων τῷ γυμνικῷ ἀγῶνι.* The contests included running, wrestling, boxing, and the *πένταθλον* and *παγκράτιον* (Michaelis, *l. c.* p. 323).

ἱπποδρομίαν] The horse-races were held at Echelidae (*τόπος 'Αθήνησι σταδίων ὀκτώ, ἐν ᾧ αἱ ἱπποδρομίαι*, Etym. M.). The race is mentioned in Xen. *Symp.* i 2. Cf. Athen. p. 168, *νικήσαντος ἵπποις Παναθήναια* (cf. Michaelis, pp. 324—5).

πέπλον] 49 § 3. Schol. Arist. *Av.* 826, *τῇ 'Αθηνᾷ πολιάδι οὔσῃ πέπλος ἐγίνετο παμποίκιλος, ὃν ἀνέφερον ἐν τῇ πομπῇ τῶν Παναθηναίων.* Among the mythological subjects represented on it was the battle of Athene with the Giants. Michaelis, *l. c.* p. 328.

ἀμφορεῖς] In the athletic contests the prize was a garland from the sacred olive-trees, together with a vase filled with oil from the same. Pindar's ornate description of the prizes is well known: *Nem.* x 62—66, *ἀδεῖαί γε μὲν ἀμβολάδαν ἐν τελεταῖς δὶς 'Αθαναίων μιν ὀμφαὶ κώμασαν· γαίᾳ δὲ καυθείσᾳ πυρὶ καρπὸς ἐλαίας ἔμολεν Ἥρας τὸν εὐάνορα λαὸν ἐν ἀγγέων ἕρκεσιν παμποικίλοις* (with Schol.). Cf. Simonides in Anth. Pal. xiii 19, 3, *καὶ Παναθηναίοις στεφάνους λάβε πέντ' ἐπ' ἀέθλοις ἑξῆς* (*i.e.* in the Pentathlon) *ἀμφιφορεῖς* <*τ'*> *ἐλαίου.*

Many of the Panathenaic vases have been found in Italy, Sicily, Greece, and at Cyrene. They have the figure of Athene on one side, and a representation of the contest for which they were awarded on the other. The earliest Panathenaic vase, now extant, known as the "Burgon Vase" in the British Museum (Vase Room II B 1), is ascribed to the 6th century B.C., and there are 14 others in the same room; in Room IV there are 10 of the 4th century, to which the majority of such vases belong, varying in date from 368 to 313 B.C. One of those in the Museum, bearing the inscr. *τῶν 'Αθήνηθεν ἄθλων*, belongs to B.C. 328, about the date when the text was written. Many of these vases are reproduced in colours in *Monumenti dell' Inst. Arch.* x; and single vases in Birch's *Ancient Pottery*, p. 430, Duruy, *Histoire des Grecs*, i 762, and Murray's *Handbook of Gk. Archaeology*, p. 104.—A Panathenaic amphora, with a spray of olive rising out of it and with three crowns beside it, may be seen on a table in front of a gnarled olive-tree, represented in relief on the outer side of several marble stalls found at Athens (see cut in Michaelis, *Parthenon*, p. 29).

§ 2. **ἔλαιον—μοριῶν** *κτλ.*] Arist. *Nub.* 1005, *ἀλλ' εἰς 'Ακαδήμειαν κατιὼν ὑπὸ ταῖς μορίαις ἀποθρέξει*, and Schol. *περὶ αὐτὸν δ'*

[ἀ]πὸ τῶν μοριῶν· εἰσπράττει δὲ τοὺς τὰ χωρία κεκτημένους ἐν
οἷς αἱ μορίαι εἰσὶν ὁ ἄρχων, τρί' ἡμικοτύλια ἀπὸ τοῦ στελέχους
ἑκάστου. πρότερον δ' ἐπώλει τὸν καρπὸν ἡ πόλις· καὶ εἴ τις ἐξο-
ρύξειεν ἐλαίαν μορίαν ἢ κατάξειεν, ἔκρινεν ἡ ἐξ Ἀρείου πάγου
βουλή, καὶ εἴ του καταγνοίη, θανάτῳ τοῦτον ἐζημίουν. ἐξ οὗ δὲ τὸ
ἔλαιον ὁ τὸ χωρίον κε||κτημένος ἀποτίνει, ὁ μὲν νόμος ἐστίν, ἡ δὲ [Col. 30.
κρίσις καταλέλυται. τὸ δ' ἔλ[αιον] ἐκ τοῦ κτήματος, οὐκ ἀπὸ τῶν
στελεχῶν, ἐστὶ τῇ πόλει. συλλέξας οὖν ὁ ἄρχων τὸ ἐφ' ἑαυ[τοῦ] 3
γιγνόμενον, τοῖς ταμίαις παρ[αδίδ]ωσιν εἰς ἀκρόπολιν, καὶ οὐκ
ἔστιν ἀναβῆναι πρότερον εἰς [Ἄρε]ιον πάγον πρὶν ἂν ἅπαν παραδῷ
τοῖς ταμίαις. οἱ δὲ ταμίαι τὸν μὲν ἄλλον χρόνον τηροῦσιν ἐν ἀκρο-

9 ΤΡΙ ΗΜΙΚΟΤΥΛΙΑ (B); τρία ἡμ- K, H-L; τριημικοτύλιον K-W. 11 ἐλαίαν del. Rutherford, ἐλάαν (deleto μορίαν) H-L. ἐλαίαν (K, K-W); ἐλᾴαν B; ἐλαία habet Soph. *O. C.* 701; ἐλάα Aristophanes, cf. Eustathium p. 84, 9 τὴν ἐλαίαν ἐλάαν ἀττικῶς; formam utramque defendunt tituli (Meisterhans, p. 24[2]). 12 ΤΟΥ (H-L, K[3], B), omiserat K[1]; [[μὲν?]] K-W. 14 <τὸ> ἐκ τοῦ H-L. ΑΠΟ (correctum in ΕΚ) ΤΟΥ ΚΤΗΜΑΤΟϹ (K-W, B): ΚΛΗΜΑΤΟϹ legerat K (H-L). 16 ΓΙΓΝ (edd.).

ἦσαν αἱ ὄντως ἱεραὶ ἐλαῖαι τῆς θεοῦ, αἳ καλοῦνται μορίαι· ἐξ ὧν τὸ ἔλαιον τῶν Παναθηναίων. Lucian, *Anach.* 9; Schol. Plat. *Parm.* 127 A; Suidas *s. v.* μορίαι (Michaelis, *Parthenon*, p. 322).

εἰσπράττει—κεκτημένους κτλ.] Schol. Arist. *Nub.* 1005, ὑπὸ ταῖς μορίαις: διὰ τὸ πάντα ἄνθρωπον κεκτημένον ἐλαίας ἀναγκάζεσθαι μέρος τι παρέχειν εἰς τὰ Παναθήναια κτλ.

τρί' ἡμικοτύλια] ¾ pint; the κοτύλη being about ½ pint.

πρότερον δ' ἐπώλει τὸν καρπὸν ἡ πόλις] Lysias 7 *de Olea Sacra* § 2, τοὺς ἐωνημένους τοὺς καρποὺς τῶν μοριῶν. The speech is not earlier than B.C. 395 (Blass, *Att. Ber.* i[2] p. 591): thus πρότερον here refers to a time not earlier than the archonship of Eucleides.

εἴ τις ἐξορύξειεν—βουλή] Lys. *Or.* 7 is addressed to the Areopagus, who (besides attending to the sacred olives every month) sent overseers (γνώμονας) to examine them every year (§ 25). In § 7 the speaker states the charge on which he is being tried: τὴν δὲ <μίαν> μορίαν, ἣν οὐχ οἷόν τ' ἦν λαθεῖν ἐξορύξαντα, ὡς ἀφανίζων νυνὶ κρίνομαι.

θανάτῳ] The terms used in Lys. 7 § 3, περὶ πατρίδος καὶ περὶ τῆς οὐσίας ἀγωνίσασθαι, and § 41, πατρίδος—στερηθείς, imply that the penalty at that time was (as in other cases of ἀσέβεια) banishment with confiscation of property. This shews that, even before the time when the state, instead of selling the olives, exacted from the tenant the delivery of a certain quantity of oil, the capital penalty had already become obsolete.

κτήματος] The delivery of the oil has now become a regular tax on the *property*, *i.e.* either on the χωρίον or on the store of oil manufactured by the proprietor. The alternative reading κλήματος draws a distinction between the 'fresh shoots' (Xen. *Oec.* 19, 8, τὸν βλαστὸν τοῦ κλήματος), and the trunk of the tree, implying that the state insists that the oil supplied to it shall be from the former. But this proviso, even if intelligible in theory, would be difficult to insist upon in practice. Besides στέλεχος is the ordinary term applied to the tree as a whole.

στελεχῶν] Dem. 43 *Macart.* 69, ταύτας (τὰς ἐλάας) ἐξώρυττον καὶ ἐξεπρέμνιζον, πλεῖν ἢ χίλια στελέχη, ὅθεν ἔλαιον πολὺ ἐγίγνετο. Hdt. viii 55, βλαστὸν ἐκ τοῦ στελέχεος.

§ 3. **ἐφ' ἑαυτοῦ**] 'in his own year of office.'

ταμίαις] 4 § 2; 7 § 3; 8 § 1; and esp. 30 § 2 and 47 § 1.

οὐκ ἔστιν ἀναβῆναι κτλ.] the archon could not take his place among the members of the Areopagus at the close of his year of office until he had handed over to the treasurers (of Athene) the full amount of olive-oil due for the year. For **ἀναβῆναι** cf. [Dem.] *c. Neaer.* 80, ἐγένετο τὰ ἱερὰ ταῦτα καὶ ἀνέβησαν εἰς Ἄρειον πάγον οἱ ἐννέα ἄρχοντες ταῖς καθηκούσαις ἡμέραις.

πόλει, τοῖς δὲ Παναθηναίοις ἀπομετροῦσι τοῖς ἀθλοθέταις, οἱ δ' ἀθλοθέται τοῖς νικῶσι τῶν ἀγωνιστῶν. ἔστι γὰρ ἆθλα τοῖς μὲν τὴν μουσικὴν νικῶσιν ἀργύρια καὶ χρυσία, τοῖς δὲ τὴν εὐανδρίαν ἀσπίδες, τοῖς δὲ τὸν γυμνικὸν ἀγῶνα καὶ τὴν ἱπποδρομίαν ἔλαιον. — — —

61. χειροτονοῦσι δὲ καὶ τὰς πρὸς τὸν πόλεμον ἀρχὰς ἁπάσας, στρατηγοὺς δέκα, πρότερον μὲν ἀφ' <ἑκάστης τῆς> φυλῆς ἕνα,

21 ΑΡΓΥΡΙΑΚ'ΧΡΥϹΑ (K[1]): ἀργύρια καὶ χρυσία (H-L, K[3], B); ἀργύριον καὶ χρυσᾶ (K-W), ἀργυρᾶ καὶ χρυσᾶ (Rutherford). **23** 'interciderunt magistratus creati in quadriennium, cf. cap. 18' K-W; idem coniecerat Weil; c. 43 § 1 et c. 61 § 1 (χειροτ. δὲ καὶ) confert B, qui addit tamen nihil amplius Polluci notum fuisse.

LXI 2 Δ(ε)Κ(ΑΙ) K[1]; δέκα, Richards, Gertz, K-W, H-L, B, K[3]. ἑκάστης add. K (K-W, H-L); ἑκάστης τῆς B.

TESTIMONIA. **LXI** Pollux viii 87 (οἱ ἐννέα ἄρχοντες...ἔχουσιν ἐξουσίαν), (§ **1**) στρατηγοὺς χειροτονεῖν ἐξ ἁπάντων, (§ **2**) καὶ καθ' ἑκάστην πρυτανείαν ἐπερωτᾶν εἰ δοκεῖ καλῶς ἄρχειν ἕκαστος (τὸν δ' ἀποχειροτονηθέντα κρίνουσιν), (§ **4**) καὶ ἱππάρχους δύο, (§ **5**) καὶ φυλάρχους δέκα, (§ **3**) καὶ ταξιάρχους δέκα.

2 *Harp. στρατηγοί :...οἱ καθ' ἕκαστον ἐνιαυτὸν χειροτονούμενοι στρατηγοὶ δέκα ἦσαν, ὡς μαθεῖν ἔστιν ἔκ τε τῶν Ὑπερίδου κατ' Αὐτοκλέους καὶ ἐκ τῆς 'Αθ. πολ. 'Αριστοτέλους (Frag. 390[2], 430[3]).

τὴν μουσικὴν νικῶσιν ἀργύρια καὶ χρυσία] The prizes recorded in inscriptions are crowns and sums of money varying from 100 to 500 *dr.* (Dittenberger, no. 395: Michaelis, *Parthenon*, p. 322). **ἀργύρια**, in pl. of 'sums of money,' Arist. *Av.* 600.

εὐανδρίαν] This contest is mentioned in Andoc. 4 § 42, νενικηκὼς εὐανδρίᾳ, Xen. *Mem.* iii 3, 12, Athen. 565 F; also in Harpocr. *s. v.* and Bekker's *Anec.* p. 257, 13. Cf. Thumser, *de Civium Ath. Muneribus*, pp. 81, 97—9. **ἀσπίδες]** In the early part of the fourth century the prize was an ox; CIA ii 965 (Ditt. 395, 75), εὐανδρίαι φυλῆι νικώσει βοῦς. We do not know the date when the ox was superseded by the portable prize mentioned in the text. The 'shields' are not named elsewhere.

γυμνικὸν ἀγῶνα καὶ τὴν ἱπποδρομίαν] In the above inscr. ll. 23—70 we have the record of the number of ἀμφορῆς ἐλαίου awarded (1) to the boys, and (2) to the youths, who were victorious in running, wrestling, boxing, or in the pentathlum or pancratium; and (3) to the victors in the horse-races. The part enumerating the prizes given to the men is lost.

LXI. *Officials elected by open voting (Military Officers).*

§ 1. **χειροτονοῦσι—τὰς πρὸς τὸν πόλεμον ἀρχάς]** 43 § 1 *ad fin.*

ἀφ' ἑκάστης—φυλῆς ἕνα] This was the case on the occasion when Cimon and his colleagues were called upon to act as judges in the dramatic contest of B.C. 468, when Sophocles gained the prize against Aeschylus: Plut. *Cimon* 8, describes the generals as δέκα ὄντας, ἀπὸ φυλῆς μιᾶς ἕκαστον. At some later date, which is not specified, the generals were chosen out of all the citizens (ἐξ ἁπάντων) without distinction of tribe.

It was held by Schömann (*Ant.* p. 420), Boeckh (on *Antig.* 190, and CIG pp. 294, 906), Sauppe and others, that the generals were elected by the several tribes alone. A. Schaefer (*Dem.* ii 182) held that they were elected ἐξ ἁπάντων (as attested by Pollux). The view that in earlier times the generals were elected κατὰ φυλήν, and afterwards ἐξ ἁπάντων, was held by Bergk, Lugebil, Müller-Strübing and others (see Gilbert, i 220, and *Beiträge*, pp. 16—20). This is proved by the text to be right.

Gilbert (*Beiträge*, pp. 21—23) accepts the narrative in Plutarch's *Cimon*, but does not admit that on that occasion the 10 generals belonged to the 10 different tribes, although this is the obvious meaning, as in the phrase in Pollux viii 94, οἱ φύλαρχοι δέκα, εἷς ἀπὸ φυλῆς μιᾶς ἕκαστος. In 440/39 two of the 10 generals, Pericles and Glaucon (FHG iv 645), belonged to the same tribe, Acamantis; this is our earliest evidence for a departure from the older system; possibly the change was due to a desire to elect the ablest men, *νῦν δ' ἐξ ἁπάντων· καὶ τούτους διατάττουσι τῇ χειροτονίᾳ, ἕνα μὲν ἐπὶ τοὺς ὁπλίτας, ὃς ἡγεῖται τῶν ὁ[πλι]τῶν, ἂν ἐξίωσι, ἕνα δ' ἐπὶ τὴν χώραν, ὃς φυλάττει, κἂν πόλεμος ἐν τῇ χώρᾳ γίγνηται, πολεμεῖ οὗτος· δύο δ' ἐπὶ τὸν Πειραιέα, τὸν μὲν εἰς τὴν Μουνιχίαν, τὸν δ'*

4 Ο...Τ(ΩΝ) ὁπλιτῶν H-L (K[3], B): Δ(?)...Τ(ΩΝ) π[ολι]τῶν K-W; δ[ημο]τῶν K[1]. ἐὰν H-L. 5 ΓΙΝ (K-W). ΠΟΛΕΜΕΙ: ἡγεῖται K-W. 6 ΠΕΙΡΑΙΕΑ (K, K-W, B): Πειραιᾶ H-L. ΜΟΥΝΥΧ.

---

such as Pericles, independently of the tribe to which they belonged. But, even after the change, nearly all the tribes were in practice represented on the board. Thus in B.C. 433/2 out of seven generals, six belonged to different tribes; in 424/3, out of six whose demes are known, five; in 418/7, all the six whose demes are given; in 417/6, all the five; and in 357/6, six out of the seven. There is no example of more than one tribe being represented by two *στρατηγοί* in the same year (Hauvette-Besnault, *Les Stratèges Athéniens*, pp. 24—29).

διατάττουσι] The fact that about this time the duties of the *στρατηγοί* were distributed over several members of the board was already known. The five officers charged with specific duties had already been identified, but it was not known that there were only five. The date of this change was supposed to fall between 334 and 325. In 334 B.C. (CIA ii 804 A 63) the *στρατηγοί* are still acting as a body in reference to the *συμμορίαι*, whereas in 325/4 we hear of a *στρατηγὸς ἐπὶ τὰς συμμορίας*. Cf. Hauvette-Besnault, *Les Stratèges Ath.*, pp. 159 ff. (Gilbert, i 220, and Busolt in Müller's *Handbuch*, IV i 162). The latest date actually mentioned in this treatise is B.C. 329; but it does not follow that the change in question took place earlier than that date, as the treatise may have been written in any year between B.C. 329 and 325.

ἐπὶ τοὺς ὁπλίτας] In Lys. 32 § 5 we have what at first sight appears to be a mention of this officer: *χρόνῳ δὲ ὕστερον καταλεγεὶς Διόδοτος μετὰ Θρασύλλου τοῦ ἐπὶ τῶν ὁπλιτῶν* (B.C. 410); and we know that Thrasyllus was elected a *στρατηγὸς* in the spring of 411 (Thuc. viii 76) and held office for 410/9 (*ib.* 104); but the words *τοῦ ἐπὶ* are omitted in two MSS, *Florentinus* and *Ambrosianus*, and the construction is parallel to *καταλεγεὶς τριηράρχων* in Isaeus, *de Apoll. her.* 5.

The decrees in the *De Corona* mention *ὁ ἐπὶ τῶν ὅπλων στρατηγὸς* (§ 38), *τὸν ἐπὶ τῶν ὅπλων* (115) and *ὁ ἐπὶ τῶν ὁπλιτῶν* (116), but these are forgeries of a later date (Hauvette-Besnault, p. 160 f).

In CIA ii 302 (c. 294/3 B.C.) Philippides is described as *[χειροτονη]θεὶ[ς στρατ]ηγὸς [ἐ]πὶ το[ὺς ὁπλίτας ὑπὸ τοῦ δήμου]*. In ii 331 the career of Phaedrus is described: in 296/5 he was twice elected *στρατηγὸς ἐπὶ τὴν παρασκευήν*, and was often elected *στρ. ἐπὶ τὴν χώραν* and thrice *ἐπὶ τοὺς ξένους*. It was probably after 272 B.C. that he was elected *ἐπὶ τὰ ὅπλα στρατηγός* and was afterwards *χειροτονηθεὶς ἐπὶ τὰ ὅπλα πρῶτος ὑπὸ τοῦ δήμου στρατηγός*. After the end of the fourth century this *στρατηγὸς* was the foremost member of the board. Ultimately in the theatre of Dionysus the only stall reserved for any of the *στρατηγοί* was inscribed with the title of *στρατηγοῦ ἐπὶ τὰ ὅπλα*.—The *στρ. ἐπὶ τοὺς ὁπλίτας* probably acted as president of the *στρατηγοί* (cf. Gilbert, i 222).

ἐπὶ τὴν χώραν] Plut. *Phocion*, 32, *Δερκύλλου τοῦ ἐπὶ τῆς χώρας στρατηγοῦ* (B.C. 317). CIA ii 331 (quoted above), and 1195 (towards the end of the 3rd cent.).

φυλάττει] The *φυλακὴ τῆς χώρας* involved placing patrols at important points in the interior and along the coast; Thuc. ii 24, *φυλακὰς κατεστήσαντο κατὰ γῆν καὶ κατὰ θάλασσαν*. In Xen. *Mem.* iii 6, 10, *περὶ φυλακῆς τῆς χώρας*, mention is made of *φυλακαὶ* and *φρουροί*. In B.C. 445 this *φυλακὴ* extended as far as Euboea; CIA iv 27 *a*, *περὶ δὲ φυλακῆς Εὐβοίας τοὺς στρατηγοὺς ἐπιμελεῖσθαι κτλ.* In B.C. 342, [Dem.] 7 §§ 14, 15, it has expanded into a *τῆς κατὰ θάλατταν φυλακῆς* in a still wider sense. About B.C. 265, CIA 334, we find a decree in honour of those who *ἐπέδωκαν εἰς τὴν σωτηρίαν τῆς πόλεως καὶ τὴν φυλακὴν τῆς χώρας*. In the time of the text this duty, which had once been shared by all the *στρατηγοί*, was apparently divided between the *στρατηγὸς ἐπὶ τὴν χώραν* for the interior, and the two *στρατηγοὶ ἐπὶ τὸν Πειραιέα* for the coast,—assuming that *φυλακῆς* is the right reading in the passage referring to the latter.

ἐπὶ τὸν Πειραιέα] In B.C. 324/3, CIA ii 811 *c* 434, *Δικαιογένης ὁ στρατηγὸς* is

εἰς τὴν Ἀκτήν, οἳ τῆς φ[υ]λακῆς ἐπιμελοῦνται καὶ τῶν ἐν Πειραιεῖ· ἕνα δ' ἐπὶ τὰς συμ[μο]ρίας, ὃς τούς τε τριηράρχους καταλέγει καὶ τὰς ἀντιδόσεις αὐτοῖς ποιεῖ, καὶ τὰς διαδικασίας α[ὐτ]οῖς εἰσάγει·
2 τοὺς δ' ἄλλους πρὸς τὰ παρόντα πράγματα ἐκπέμπουσιν. ἐπιχει-

7 φ.λΗC: Φ[υ]λῆς (vel φυλακῆς) K[1], φυλακῆς K-W et B deleto καὶ (φυλῆς et φυλακῆς Thucydidis in codicibus saepe confusa esse monet Wardale, *Class. Rev.* v 273). χηλῆς Torr (H-L, K[3]). ⟦καὶ⟧ K-W (B), fortasse recte. **9** alterum αὐτοῖς secl. K-W[2]. **10** πράγματα supra scriptum delent H-L.

8—9 Phot. ἡγεμ. δικ.: τῷ στρατηγῷ περὶ τριηραρχίας καὶ ἀντιδόσεως.

---

mentioned in the same context as the overseer of the *νεώρια*. Between B.C. 318 and 229 the Peiraeus and Salamis were under an officer called the *στρατηγὸς ἐπὶ τοῦ Πειραιέως καὶ τῶν ἄλλων τῶν ταττομένων μετὰ τοῦ Πειραιέως* (*Bull. Corr. Hellén.* vi 526). About 100 B.C. we read of *three στρατηγοὶ ἐπὶ τὸν Πειραιᾶ* (CIA ii 1207), and the archon of B.C. 97/6 is described as Ἀργεῖος Ἀργείου Τρικο[ρύσιος] *στρατηγήσας ἐπὶ τὸν* Πειρα[ιᾶ], *ib.* 1206.

εἰς τὴν Μουνιχίαν] In B.C. 325/4 we find Philocles mentioned by Dinarchus, 3 § 1, as *στρατηγὸς ὑφ' ὑμῶν ἐπὶ τὴν Μουνιχίαν καὶ τὰ νεώρια κεχειροτονημένος*. On Munichia, cf. 19 § 2; 42 § 3.

εἰς τὴν Ἀκτήν] possibly identical with the officer called the *στρατηγὸς ἐπὶ τὴν χώραν τὴν παραλίαν* in CIA ii 3, 1194 (the son of an official of B.C. 382/1), and 1195 (B.C. 241). The latter inscr. was found at Sunium. On Ἀκτή cf. 42 § 3.

φυλακῆς] *sc. τῆς χώρας τῆς παραλίας*, the rest of the *φυλακὴ* being assigned to the *στρ. ἐπὶ τὴν χώραν*.

ἐπὶ τὰς συμμορίας] B.C. 325/4, CIA ii 809 *a* 205—210, *ὅπως δ' ἂν αἱ σκήψεις εἰσαχθῶσι, τοὺς θεσμοθέτας παρα[πλ]ηρῶσαι δικαστήρια εἰς ἕνα καὶ διακοσίους τῷ στρατηγῷ τῷ ἐπὶ τὰς συμμορίας ᾑρημένῳ*. The *σκήψεις* mentioned in this inscr., and in c. 56 § 3, are the pleas put forward by one who maintains that another is better able to bear the expense of a trierarchy and who therefore challenges him either to undertake it or to exchange properties. It may also refer to *any* plea of exemption. It is used elsewhere (CIA ii 804) of the reasons pleaded by a trierarch for being unable to restore to the state the vessel confided to his care (Hauvette-Besnault, p. 143). For the relations of the board of *στρατηγοὶ* to the *συμμορίαι* and the *τριηραρχία* before the distribution of offices among the members of the board, cf. Dem. 39 § 8, *τίνα δ' οἱ στρατηγοὶ τρόπον ἐγγράφουσιν, ἂν εἰς συμμορίαν ἐγγράφωσιν, ἢ ἂν τριήραρχον καθιστῶσιν*, and 35 § 48, (*οἱ στρατηγοὶ*) *τριηράρχους καθιστᾶσιν*.

ἀντιδόσεις—ποιεῖ] [Dem.] 42 § 5, (on the 2nd of Metageitnion, August) *ἐποίουν οἱ στρατηγοὶ τοῖς τριακοσίοις τὰς ἀντιδόσεις*. Suid. *s.v. ἡγεμονία δικαστηρίου*.

διαδικασίας] *e.g.* [Xen.] *de Rep. Ath.* 3, 4, *διαδικάζειν, εἴ τις τὴν ναῦν μὴ ἐπισκευάζει*. CIA ii 795 f 39, *τριήρεις αἳ ἐπὶ Διοτίμου ἄρχοντος* (B.C. 354/3) *διεδικάσθησαν καὶ ἔδοξαν κατὰ χειμῶνα διαφθαρῆναι*, *ib.* l. 60, *ἀριθμὸς τριήρων καὶ σκευῶν τῶν διαδεδικασμένων*. Boeckh, *Seeurkunden*, p. 214; Meier and Schöm. pp. 467 f. In [Dem.] 47 § 26 (B.C. 339) we read of the *ἀποστολεῖς* and the *νεωρίων ἐπιμεληταί*, that these were the officials who *εἰσῆγον τότε* (c. B.C. 344) *τὰς διαδικασίας περὶ τῶν σκευῶν*. Cf. Meier and Schöm. p. 475.

τοὺς δ' ἄλλους] This shews that the above list of special posts is complete by the time when the treatise was written.

In the spurious decrees quoted in Dem. *de Cor.* §§ 38, 115 an officer called *ὁ ἐπὶ τῆς διοικήσεως* is mentioned (in the former decree immediately after *ὁ ἐπὶ τῶν ὅπλων στρατηγός*, in the latter after *τὸν ἐπὶ τῶν ὅπλων*). It was once supposed that this was the title of one of the *στρατηγοί*, but it is now agreed that this was not the case (Boeckh, note 322 Fränkel; Schömann, p. 421 n. 3). Again, in CIA ii 331 Thymochares, the father of Phaedrus (who held office between B.C. 296 and 272) was *χειροτονηθεὶς στρατηγὸς ὑπὸ τοῦ δήμου ἐπὶ τὸ ναυτικόν*. In the same inscr. Phaedrus is described as *στρατηγὸς ἐπὶ τὴν παρασκευὴν* and *ἐπὶ τοὺς ξένους*. The *στρ. ὁ ἐπὶ τὴν παρασκευὴν* is mentioned in CIA ii 403—405 in connexion with melting down the *τύποι* dedicated to the *ἥρως ἰατρός* (2nd century B.C.); also *ib.* 839. The decree in Pseudo-Plutarch ii p. 852 describes Lycurgus as *χειροτονηθεὶς ἐπὶ τῆς τοῦ πολέμου παρασκευῆς*, but this does not prove that he was a *στρατηγός*; and, in any case, these last titles belong to a later date than the text.

§ 2. **ἐπιχειροτονία**] 43 § 4, at the *κυρία*

ροτονία δ' α[ὐ]τῶν ἐστὶ κατὰ τὴν πρυτανείαν ἑκάστην, εἰ δοκοῦσιν καλῶς ἄρχειν· κἄν τινα ἀποχειροτον[ή]σωσιν, κρίνουσιν ἐν τῷ δικαστηρίῳ, κἂν μὲν ἁλῷ, τιμῶσιν ὅ τι χρὴ παθεῖν ἢ ἀποτ[εῖσ]αι, ἂν δ' ἀποφύγῃ, [π]άλ[ιν] ἄρχει. κύριοι δέ εἰσιν, ὅταν ἡγῶνται, καὶ δῆσαί τιν' ἀτακτοῦντα καὶ <ἐκ>[κη]ρῦξαι καὶ ἐπιβολὴν ἐπιβάλλειν· οὐκ εἰώθασι δὲ ἐπιβάλλειν.

χειροτονοῦσι δὲ καὶ ταξ[ιά]ρχους δέκα, ἕνα τῆς φυλῆς ἑκάστης· 3
οὗτος δ' ἡγεῖται τῶν φυλετῶν, καὶ λοχαγοὺς καθίσ[τ]ησιν.

χειροτονοῦσι δὲ καὶ ἱππάρχους δύο ἐξ ἁπάντων· οὗτοι δ' 4

11 δοκοῦσι H-L. **13** αλλ(supra scr. ω)ωι. **14** ἐὰν H-L. πάλιν? K-W (K[3], B); τὰ [λοιπὰ] K[1]; [ἔτι] H-L. κύριοι δ' H-L. **15** ΤΙΝ: τιν' K, B: τὸν K-W, H-L. ΚΗΡΥΞΑΙ (K): <ἐκ>κηρῦξαι Blass, Lipsius (K-W, H-L). **16** δ' H-L.

§ **3** Bekk. *An.* 306, 12 ταξίαρχοι—: ἄρχοντες ἡγούμενοι τῶν πολιτῶν κατὰ φυλήν, χειροτονητοί, δέκα τὸν ἀριθμόν, οἷς ὑπετέτακτο τὸ πλῆθος κατὰ φυλήν.

§ **4** Pollux viii 94 ἵππαρχοι δὲ δύο ἐξ ἁπάντων Ἀθηναίων αἱρεθέντες ἐπιμελοῦνται τῶν πολέμων. *Harp. ἵππαρχος:...λέγεται δὲ παρ' Ἀθηναίοις ἵππαρχος καὶ ὁ τῶν ἱππέων ἄρχων· δύο δ' ἦσαν οὗτοι, ὡς Δημ. ἐν δ̄ Φιλιππικῶν φησὶ καὶ Ἀρ. ἐν Ἀθ. πολ. Phot. ἵππαρχοι: δύο ἦσαν, οἳ τῶν ἱππέων ἡγοῦντο, "διελόμενοι τὰς φυλὰς" ἑκάτερος ἀνὰ πέντε· ἐπιμεληταὶ δέ εἰσι τῶν ἱππέων <οἱ φύλαρχοι additum ex Poll. viii 94> καθάπερ οἱ ταξίαρχοι δέκα ὄντες εἷς ἐφ' ἑκάστης φυλῆς τῶν ὁπλιτῶν (Frag. 391[2], 431[3]).

ἐκκλησία, ἐπιχειροτονεῖν εἰ δοκοῦσι καλῶς ἄρχειν. This procedure must have been instituted with special reference to military officials; hence the fulness with which it is treated here in comparison with 43 § 4 (Lipsius, Leipzig *Verhandl.* p. 49).

τιμῶσιν] It was a *δίκη τιμητός* (Meier and Schöm. p. 213 f, Lips.).

δῆσαι] During the Sicilian expedition Lamachus put to death a soldier who was caught signalling to the enemy, Lys. 13 § 67; and Iphicrates at Corinth transfixed with his spear a sentinel whom he found asleep at his post (Frontinus iii 12, 2). In Dem. 50 § 51 even a trierarch fears he may be put into bonds by a *στρατηγός*: *φοβούμενος μὴ δεθείην.* Cf. Xen. *Mem.* iii 5, 19, *τοὺς ὁπλίτας καὶ τοὺς ἱππεῖς—ἀπειθεστάτους εἶναι πάντων.*

ἐκκηρῦξαι] One Simon, who arrived too late for the battle of Corinth and the march to Coroneia, had a scuffle with the taxiarch and struck him, *καὶ πανστρατιᾷ τῶν πολιτῶν ἐξελθόντων, δόξας ἀκοσμότατος εἶναι καὶ πονηρότατος, μόνος Ἀθηναίων ὑπὸ τῶν στρατηγῶν ἐξεκηρύχθη.* This implies that the offender was expelled from the army, after being publicly proclaimed unworthy to serve as a soldier. Lys. 3 § 45.

ἐπιβάλλειν] [Lys.] 15 § 5, *ἐχρῆν γὰρ αὐτοὺς (τοὺς στρατηγοὺς) εἴπερ ἀληθῆ λέγουσιν ἀνακαλεῖν μὲν Πάμφιλον ὅτι ἀφαιρῶν τὸν ἵππον ἱππέως ἀπεστέρει τὴν πόλιν, ἐπιβάλλειν δὲ τῷ φυλάρχῳ, ὅτι ἐξελαύνων Ἀλκιβιάδην ἐκ τῆς φυλῆς ἄκυρον ἐποίει τὴν τούτων τάξιν, κελεύειν δὲ τὸν ταξίαρχον ἐξαλείφειν αὐτὸν ἐκ τοῦ τῶν ὁπλιτῶν καταλόγου.*

§ 3. **ταξιάρχους**] commanders of the 10 *τάξεις* of hoplites corresponding to the 10 *φυλαί*. They were instituted after 490 B.C. Dem. 4 § 26, *οὐκ ἐχειροτονεῖτε δ' ἐξ ὑμῶν αὐτῶν δέκα ταξιάρχους καὶ στρατηγοὺς καὶ φυλάρχους καὶ ἱππάρχους δύο*; each of the taxiarchs commanded the hoplites of a single tribe, Dem. 39 § 17, *ταξιάρχων τῆς φυλῆς*, Aeschin. *F.L.* 169, *Τεμενίδου τοῦ τῆς Πανδιονίδος ταξιάρχου.* **ἡγεῖται τῶν φυλετῶν**] As a rule the taxiarch was a member of the tribe which he commanded, Thuc. viii 92, *ὁ Ἀριστοκράτης ἦν ταξιαρχῶν καὶ τὴν ἑαυτοῦ φυλὴν ἔχων*, CIA ii 444, 446 (Gilbert, i 225).

λοχαγούς] Isocr. 15 § 117, Isaeus 9 § 14. The text shews that they were appointed by the *ταξίαρχοι*, and not, as has been supposed (Gilbert i 225), by the *στρατηγοί*.

§ 4. **ἱππάρχους**] Their importance is implied by Lys. 26 § 20, *ἀντὶ τούτων αὐτοὺς ὁ δῆμος ταῖς μεγίσταις τιμαῖς τετίμηκεν, ἱππαρχεῖν καὶ στρατηγεῖν καὶ πρεσβεύειν ὑπὲρ αὐτῶν αἱρούμενοι.* **δύο**] Dem. 4 § 26 *supra*, CIA ii 445, 15.

ἡγοῦνται τῶν ἱππέων, διελόμ[ενοι] τὰς φυλὰς πέντε ἑκάτερος· κύριοι δὲ τῶν αὐτῶν εἰσὶν, ὧνπερ οἱ στρατηγοὶ κατὰ τῶν ὁπλι[τῶν. ἐπιχειρο]τονία δὲ γίγνεται <καὶ> τούτων.

5 χειροτονοῦσι δὲ καὶ φυλάρχους <δέκα>, ἕνα τῆς φυλῆς, τὸν ἡγ[ησό]μενο[ν] <τῶν ἱππέων>, ὥσπερ οἱ ταξίαρχοι τῶν ὁπλιτῶν.

6 χειροτονοῦσι δὲ καὶ εἰς Λῆμνον ἵππαρχον, ὃς ἐπιμ[ελ]εῖται τῶν ἱππέων τῶν ἐν Λήμνῳ.

7 χειροτονοῦσι δὲ καὶ ταμίαν τῆς Παράλου καὶ ἄλλον τῆς [τοῦ Ἄ]μμωνος.

21 ωΝΠΕΡΕΙCΙΝ : *εἰσὶν ὧνπερ* van Leeuwen (H-L, K-W, K^3, B); *ὧνπερ* Gertz. **22** ΓΙΝ (K-W). ΤΟΥΤωΝ K: *<καὶ> τούτων* Gertz, Lips., K-W, H-L, B. **23** post *φυλάρχους* add. *δέκα* Richards, K-W, H-L, B; post *δὲ καὶ* excidisse antea putabam. **24** *τῶν ἱππέων* Pollucem secutus add. K (K-W, H-L, B).

§ 5 Pollux viii 94 *οἱ δὲ φύλαρχοι δέκα, εἷς ἀπὸ φυλῆς ἑκάστης, τῶν ἱππέων προΐστανται, καθάπερ οἱ ταξίαρχοι τῶν ὁπλιτῶν.* *Harp. *φύλαρχος:...ὁ κατὰ φυλὴν ἑκάστην τοῦ ἱππικοῦ ἄρχων, ὑποτεταγμένος δὲ τῷ ἱππάρχῳ, ὡς Ἀρ. ἐν τῇ Ἀθ. πολ. φησί* (Frag. 392^2, 432^3).

§ 7 *Harp. *ταμίαι:...εἰσὶ δέ τινες καὶ τῶν (ἱερῶν) τριήρων ταμίαι, ὡς ὁ αὐτὸς φιλόσοφός* (sc. Ar.) *φησιν* (cf. Suid. *ταμίαι* art. 2). Phot. s.v. *εἰσὶ δὲ καὶ ἄλλοι ταμίαι, ἄρχοντες χειροτονητοὶ ἐπὶ τὰς ἱερὰς καὶ δημοσίας τριήρεις, ὁ μὲν ἐπὶ τὴν Πάραλον, ὁ δὲ ἐπὶ τὴν τοῦ Ἄμμωνος.* Pollux viii 116 *ταμίας ἐκάλουν τοὺς ταῖς ἱεραῖς τριήρεσι λειτουργοῦντας, ἄλλους ἢ τριηράρχους* (cf. Frag. 402^2, 442^3).

*Lex. rhet. Cantab. *Πάραλος καὶ Σαλαμινία: ταύτας τὰς τριήρεις εἶχον διὰ παντὸς πρὸς τὰς ἐπειγούσας ὑπηρεσίας, ἐφ' αἷς καὶ ταμίαι τινὲς ἐχειροτονοῦντο...Ἀριστοτέλης δὲ Ἀμμωνιάδα καὶ Πάραλον οἶδε.* Schol. in Dem. p. 636, 16 Dind....*καὶ Ἀμμωνιὰς ἐπειδὴ τῷ Ἄμμωνι δι' αὐτῆς τὰς θυσίας ἔπεμπον.* Cf. Phot. s.v. *Πάραλοι* et *Πάραλος*, Harp. s.v. *Ἀμμωνίς*, Lex. Dem. Patm. p. 150 (Frag. 403^2, 443^3).

τὰς φυλὰς πέντε ἑκάτερος] Xen. *Hipparch.* 3 § 11, *ὅταν οἱ ἵππαρχοι ἡγῶνται ταῖς πέντε φυλαῖς.*

κύριοι] The disciplinary powers of the *ἵππαρχοι* are illustrated by Hesych. *s.v.* *ἱππάρχου πίναξ· ἐπεὶ οἱ ἵππαρχοι ἐν πίναξι τὰ ὀνόματα τῶν ἀτακτούντων γράφοντες παρεσημειοῦντο.*

§ 5. **φυλάρχους**] In CIA ii 444, 445 the *φύλαρχοι* belong to the tribes which they command.

§ 6. **εἰς Λῆμνον ἵππαρχον**] This officer was in command of a corps of Athenian cavalry stationed in Lemnos. That island had long been in the possession of Athens and was held by Athenian *κληροῦχοι*. Athens had recovered possession of Lemnos, Imbros and Scyros before B.C. 387 and her right was recognised in that year by the 'peace of Antalcidas'. Hyperides, *pro Lycophrone*, c. 14, *ὑμεῖς γάρ με, ὦ ἄνδρες δικασταί, πρῶτον μὲν φύλαρχον ἐχειροτονήσατε, ἔπειτα εἰς Λῆμνον ἵππαρχον, καὶ ἦρξα μὲν αὐτόθι δύ' ἔτη τῶν πώποθ' ἱππαρχηκότων μόνος, προσκατέμεινα δὲ αὐτόθι τὸν τρίτον ἐνιαυτὸν οὐ βουλόμενος πολίτας ἄνδρας ἐπὶ κεφαλὴν εἰσπράττειν τὸν μισθὸν τοῖς ἱππεῦσιν ἀπόρως διακειμένους. στεφάνοις δὲ τρισὶν ἐστεφανώθην ὑπὸ τοῦ δήμου τοῦ ἐν Ἡφαιστίᾳ καὶ ἑτέροις ὑπὸ τῶν ἐν Μυρίνῃ.* Dem. 4 § 27, *εἰς μὲν Λῆμνον τὸν παρ' ὑμῶν ἵππαρχον δεῖ πλεῖν.* CIA ii 14 (B.C. 387/6), *[ἱππαρχ]οῦντος ἐν Λήμνῳ.* CIA ii 593 (a decree passed by the *κληροῦχοι* at Myrina after the third Macedonian war), *ἐπὶ δὲ Λῆμνον στρατηγοῦντος Φιλαρχίδου Παιανιέως ἱππαρχοῦντος τὸ δεύτερον Τελεσιδήμου τοῦ Ἀμινίου Ἑκαλῆθεν.* Cf. Gilbert, i 424—5; Hauvette-Besnault, pp. 169, 170.

§ 7. **ταμίαν τῆς Παράλου**] In Dem. *Mid.* § 173, Midias is described as saying: *ἱππάρχηκα, τῆς παράλου ταμίας γέγονα.* Demosthenes adds: *τῆς μὲν παράλου ταμιεύσας Κυζικηνῶν ἥρπασε πλεῖν ἢ πέντε τάλαντα.* § 174, Midias allowed the Paralus to be outstripped in speed by one of the ordinary triremes, *οὕτως εὖ τὴν ἱερὰν τριήρη παρεσκευάκει.* The *ταμίας Παράλου* is mentioned in CIA ii 804 B 66 (B.C. 334/3), and probably also in 808 A 79 (B.C. 326/5). The *ταμίας* provided for the sacred trireme at the cost of the state all that, in the case of ordinary vessels,

62. *αἱ δὲ κληρωταὶ ἀ[ρχ]αὶ πρότερον μὲν ἦσαν αἱ μὲν μετ' ἐννέα ἀρχόντων ἐ[κ] τῆς φυλῆς ὅλης κληρούμεναι, αἱ δ' ἐν Θησείῳ*

LXII 1 ΜΕΤ (K, K-W, B): *μετὰ τῶν* (*μ̀τ́*) Gennadios, H-L.

---

was provided by the trierarch himself. The ship was entirely manned by Athenians (Thuc. viii 73, 5) who were paid 4 obols a day (Harpocr. *s.v.*). Cf. Boeckh, 305 ff. Fränkel. The Paralos and Salaminia are mentioned in Arist. *Av.* 1207 and Thuc. iii 33, 2: the Salaminia was sent in pursuit of Alcibiades in vi 53, 1 and 61, 4 (cf. Arist. *Av.* 147). A statement in Photius (*s.v.* *πάραλοι*), *λέγεται δὲ ἡ αὐτὴ καὶ Σαλαμινία*, led Boeckh to accuse Photius of confounding the two triremes with one another, which is inconsistent with the same lexicographer's article on *πάραλος*. Mr Marindin, in *Dict. Ant.* ii 827 *a*, understands *ἡ αὐτή* as meaning 'of a similar character'; but I should prefer attributing the mistake to a careless citation from the Schol. on *Av.* 1204, where we are told that, if, instead of *Πάραλος ἢ Σαλαμινία*, we read *Πάραλος ἡ Σαλαμινία*: *ἔσται ἡ αὐτὴ Πάραλος καὶ Σαλαμινία*.

l. 28. **τοῦ Ἄμμωνος**] It follows from the passages quoted in the *Testimonia* that the state-trireme, formerly called the *Σαλαμινία*, was superseded by one named after *Ζεὺς Ἄμμων* and known as the *Ἀμμωνὶς* (Harpocr.) or *Ἀμμωνιάς* (Lex. Rhet. Cant.). It was specially intended to convey *θεωρίαι* to the coast of Cyrene, on their way to the shrine of *Ζεὺς Ἄμμων*. Cimon sent from Cyprus to consult the oracle shortly before his death (Plut. *Cim.* 18); in the *Aves*, 716 and 618, Ammon is mentioned by the side of Delphi and Dodona; and it is therefore possible that *θεωρίαι* may have been sent there as early as 415 B.C. In [Plat.] *Alc.* ii 148 E, the Athenians consult the oracle on the question why they were constantly being beaten by the Lacedaemonians. We have a record of a sacrifice to *Ἄμμων* on the part of the *στρατηγοὶ* in B.C. 333 (CIA ii 741, 32); Boeckh ii 118—121 Fränkel. Thus it seems probable that the oracle was originally consulted by Athens in connexion with military undertakings, and this custom may account, not only for the sacrifice offered by the *στρατηγοί*, but also for the connexion in which the vessel is mentioned in this chapter, at the close of a description of the military officers of Athens.—Hesych. *s.v.* *Ἀμμῶν* (*Ἀμμώνια?*) has *ἑορτὴ Ἀθήνησιν ἀγομένη*, and it would be natural that the general interest in the oracle should be increased by the visit paid by Alexander the Great in B.C. 331. The sacred trireme *Ἀμμωνὶς* was mentioned by Dinarchus in his speech against Himeraeus (Harpocr. *s.v.* *Ἀμμωνίς*), which may be assigned to B.C. 324 (Rose, *Ar. Pseud.* p. 397).

It has been suggested (by Rose, *l.c.*) that the name of the sacred trireme Salaminia was changed in consequence of the revolt of Salamis in B.C. 318 (Paus. i 35, 2; Polyaen. iv 11, 1; Diod. 18, 69; CIG i p. 418), but the text shews that the *Ἀμμωνὶς* superseded it at an earlier date.

The name Salaminia was in itself not uncommon. Thus, in B.C. 357/6 there were two ships bearing the name Salaminia (one belonging to the second class, CIA ii 793 *b* 33; the other, one of the *νῆες ἐξαίρετοι*, *ib.* *c* 32); a trireme named Salaminia foundered at sea shortly before B.C. 325/4 (CIA ii 809 *d* 29 and 811, 89); and a *τετρήρης* of the same name occurs in an inscr. of B.C. 323/2 or shortly after: CIA ii 812 *a* 123. In the same inscr., *a* 25 and 42, there are two triremes named *Παραλία* (not *Πάραλος*). All these, however, are *warships*. Not one of the sacred triremes is mentioned in the naval archives of Athens. Cf. Boeckh II xvi, vol. I p. 306—7, and note 448 Fränkel.

LXII. *Salaries.*

§ 1. **αἱ μὲν μετ' ἐννέα ἀρχόντων**] It is not known what offices are meant: Mr Kenyon suggests that the phrase included 'all the various boards of ten.' A similar phrase occurs in the *ὅρκος ἡλιαστῶν* in Dem. *c. Timocr.* 150, *τῶν ἐννέα ἀρχόντων καὶ τοῦ ἱερομνήμονος καὶ ὅσαι (ἀρχαὶ) μετὰ τῶν ἐννέα ἀρχόντων κυαμεύονται ταύτῃ τῇ (τῇ αὐτῇ?) ἡμέρᾳ, καὶ κήρυκος καὶ πρεσβείας καὶ συνέδρων.*

αἱ δ' ἐν Θησείῳ κληρουμέναι] 'the offices assigned by lot in the Theseum' (c. 15 § 4). In Aeschines, *c. Ctes.* § 13 (B.C. 336—330), the offices to which the people elect (*χειροτονεῖ*), such as those of the *στρατηγοὶ* and *ἵππαρχοι*, are contrasted with those *ἃς οἱ θεσμοθέται ἀποκληροῦσιν ἐν τῷ Θησείῳ*. It might be inferred from this that the Theseum was the only place in which the allotment was held; whereas the text implies that the archons were appointed elsewhere. The place is not known.

κληρούμεναι διῃροῦντο εἰς τοὺς δήμ[ο]υς· ἐπειδὴ δ' ἐπώλουν οἱ δῆμοι, καὶ ταύτας ἐκ τῆς φυλῆς ὅλης κληροῦσι πλὴν βουλευτῶν καὶ φρουρῶν· τούτους δ' εἰς τοὺς δ[ημότ]ας ἀποδιδόασι.

2 μισθοφοροῦσι δὲ πρῶτον [μὲν ὁ δῆμος] ταῖς μὲν ἄλλαις ἐκκλησίαις δραχμήν, τῇ δὲ κυρίᾳ ἐννέα <ὀβολούς>· ἔπειτα τὰ δικ[αστήρια] τρεῖς ὀβολούς· εἶθ' ἡ βουλὴ πέντε ὀβολούς. τοῖς δὲ πρυτανεύουσιν εἰς σίτησιν [ὀβολὸς π]ροστίθεται [[δέκα προστίθενται]]. ἔπειτ' εἰς σίτησιν λαμβάνουσιν ἐνν[έα ἄρχον]τες τέττα[ρας] ὀβολοὺς ἕκαστος,

3 <αἱ> *διῃροῦντο* Gertz, H-L. **7** *ἐννέα* <*ὀβολούς*> K-W, H-L. **9** *ὀβολὸς* Blass (et K[3]), deletis quae sequuntur *δέκα προστίθενται*: scilicet scriptum erat Ι ΠΡΟϹΤΙΘΕΤΑΙ, ubi Ι significat *εἷς ὀβολός*, sed male intellectum pro *δέκα* erat acceptum; inde exortum additamentum *δέκα προστίθενται*. *εἷς ὀβολὸς* Rutherford, H-L; satis spatii relictum si ΙΟΒΟΛΟϹ scriptum erat. **10** <*οἱ*> *ἐννέα* Gennadios, H-L; *ἐννέα* K, K-W, B, coll. v. 2.

διῃροῦντο] 'used to be distributed over' the demes.

πλὴν βουλευτῶν] This shews that the preliminary appointment of members of the Council was made by the demes. The fact that the demes lost the preliminary appointment to certain offices, owing to their being corrupt, makes us understand how it was possible for Aeschines to taunt Demosthenes with having secured his appointment as *βουλευτὴς* by bribery and intrigue, Aesch. *in Ctes.* 62, *οὔτε λαχὼν οὔτε ἐπιλαχὼν ἀλλ' ἐκ παρασκευῆς πριάμενος*, 73, *βουλευτὴς ὢν ἐκ παρασκευῆς*.

The lists of Prytanies for the fourth century (CIA ii 864—874) prove that the number of members of the Council belonging to each deme varies with the size of the deme, and that the number appointed from the same deme is constant. It was inferred from this that a certain number were appointed from each deme, and not from the whole tribe indiscriminately (Köhler in *Mittheil.* iv 97; Hauvette-Besnault in *Bull. Corr. Hell.* v 361; Headlam, *On the Lot*, pp. 55, 56). This inference is confirmed by the text. Probably each deme nominated twice the requisite number; half of these were appointed by lot, and the rest held in reserve to take their places if necessary (Headlam, p. 188). Even in the case of offices filled by lot something of the nature of candidature is implied by Lys. 31 § 33 (of one who had drawn the lot to be a *βουλευτής*), *προθύμως κληρωσόμενος ἦλθε*, 6 § 4, *ἂν ἔλθῃ κληρωσόμενος τῶν ἐννέα ἀρχόντων* (cf. 20 § 13), and Isocr. 15 § 82, *κληροῦσθαι τῶν ἀρχῶν ἕνεκα*.

φρουρῶν] possibly the 500 *φρουροὶ νεωρίων*, mentioned with the 500 *βουλευταὶ* in 24 § 3.

§ 2. **δραχμήν**] At the end of c. 41 the highest sum named as the *μισθὸς ἐκκλησιαστικὸς* was 3 obols. The text implies that this sum had been doubled. In Arist. *Vesp.* 691 and Schol. a drachma is the sum paid at that time to the *συνήγοροι*, but there is no probability that that is the fee here meant.

τρεῖς ὀβολούς] In 27 § 3 the institution of the *μισθὸς δικαστικὸς* by Pericles is mentioned; but the amount is not named. It was raised to three obols by Cleon. (Schol. Arist. *Vesp.* 88, 300; Gilbert i 325—6.)

πέντε ὀβολούς] one obol more is the amount named in Hesych. *s. v. βουλῆς λαχεῖν· τὸ λαχεῖν βουλευτὴν καὶ δραχμὴν τῆς ἡμέρας λαβεῖν*. Hesychius has probably confounded the five obols paid to the ordinary *βουλευτὴς* with the six paid to the *πρυτάνεις*. Thuc. viii 69 mentions the *μισθὸς* without naming the amount.

ἄρχοντες κτλ.] This shews that the archons, amongst others, actually received something of the nature of a stipend. It was supposed by Schömann (*Ant.* p. 402) that the 'executive functionaries' (*ἄρχοντες*) as well as the 'commissioners' (*ἐπιμεληταί*), as contrasted with the 'subordinates' (*ὑπηρεταί*), 'served without pay.' Boeckh, II xvi p. 304 Fränkel, more cautiously describes this as the 'original' distinction between an *ἀρχὴ* and a *ὑπηρεσία*. c. 24 § 3 mentions the 700 *ἀρχαὶ ἔνδημοι* as in receipt of pay; and in c. 29 § 5 the board of Thirty appointed in B.C. 411 propose *τὰς ἀρχὰς ἀμίσθους ἄρχειν ἁπάσας ἕως ἂν ὁ πόλεμος ᾖ, πλὴν τῶν ἐννέα ἀρχόντων καὶ τῶν πρυ-*

καὶ παρατρέφουσι κήρυκα καὶ αὐλητήν· ἔπειτ' ἄρχων [εἰς Σαλα]μῖνα δραχ[μὴν] τῆς ἡμέρας. ἀθλοθέται δ' ἐν πρυτανείῳ δειπνοῦσι τὸν ἑκ[ατομβ]αιῶνα μῆνα, ὅ[τ]αν ᾖ τὰ Παναθήναια, ἀρξάμενοι ἀπὸ τῆς τετράδος ἱσταμένου. ἀμ[φι]κτύονες εἰς Δῆλον δραχμὴν τῆς ἡμέρας ἑκάστης ἐκ Δήλου <λαμβάνουσι>. λαμβάνουσι δὲ καὶ ὅσαι ἀποστέλλονται ἀρχαὶ εἰς Σάμον ἢ Σκῦρον ἢ Λῆμνον ἢ Ἴμβρον εἰς σίτησιν ἀργύριον.

ἄρχειν δὲ τὰς μὲν κατὰ πόλεμον ἀρχὰς ἔ[ξεσ]τι πλεονάκις, τῶν 3
δ' ἄλλων οὐδεμίαν, πλὴν βουλεῦσαι δίς.

12 <τῷ> πρυτανείῳ H-L. **13** Ο[Τ]ΑΝ (K-W, K^3, B): ᾧ ἂν K^1, H-L. **15** <λαμβάνουσι> add. K (K-W, H-L): nihil addit B.

τανέων οἳ ἂν ὦσιν, τούτους δὲ φέρειν τρεῖς ὀβολοὺς ἕκαστον τῆς ἡμέρας. This implies (as observed by Mr Kenyon) that 'the magistrates named, and others who are not named, received pay.' [Xen.] *de Rep. Ath.* 1, 3, says that the δῆμος is not eager for offices like those of στρατηγός or ἵππαρχος, —ὁπόσαι δ' εἰσὶν ἀρχαὶ μισθοφορίας ἕνεκα καὶ ὠφελείας εἰς τὸν οἶκον, ταύτας ζητεῖ ὁ δῆμος ἄρχειν.

κήρυκα καὶ αὐλητήν] Both the κῆρυξ τῷ ἄρχοντι and the αὐλητής are mentioned in CIA iii 1005 and 1007 (Gilbert i 157 n. 4).

ἄρχων εἰς Σαλαμῖνα] 54 § 8.

ἀθλοθέται] 60. **ἑκατομβαιῶνα**] The principal day of the greater Panathenaea (54 § 7; 60 § 1) was the third from the end of Hecatombaeon. Probably the lesser Panathenaea were also held in the same month: in Dem. *c. Timocr.* 28, the Panathenaea (of Ol. 106, 4, B.C. 353) are at hand on Hecatombaeon 11th. In the text the greater Panathenaea alone appear to be meant.

ἀμφικτύονες εἰς Δῆλον] the Athenian Commissioners of the funds of the Delian temple, called ἀμφικτύονες because *in theory* they were the deputies of the Ἰώνων τε καὶ περικτιόνων νησιωτῶν (Thuc. iii 104). The 'Sandwich marble,' now in the library of Trinity College, Cambridge, records their accounts from B.C. 377 to 374, beginning τάδε ἔπραξαν ἀμφικτύονες Ἀθηναίων. Each Amphictyon administered the temple for one year, beginning with Hecatombaeon, the first month in the Attic civil year (Hicks, *Gk. Hist. Inscr.* p. 142—148; CIA ii 814).

ἐκ Δήλου, from the funds of the Delian temple.

Σάμον] Athenian κληροῦχοι were settled in Samos after its conquest by Timotheus in B.C. 365. κληροῦχοι were also sent in 361 and again in 352 (Aeschin. 1 § 53; A. Schaefer, *Dem.* i^{2} p. 99 n, p. 474 n).

After the autumn of 322 the Athenians were no longer in a position to send ἀρχαί to Samos; at that date the island ceased to be under their control, and the Samians banished by Athens were restored by Perdiccas, Diod. xviii 18 (F. Cauer in *Berl. Phil. Woch.* 9 April, 1892, p. 458).

Σκῦρον .. Λῆμνον .. Ἴμβρον] The γραμματεὺς τοῦ δήμου for each of these islands is mentioned in inscriptions published in *Bull. Cor. Hell.* 1879 p. 63, CIA ii 592: and Conze's *Reise*, p. 88, respectively: also, in Scyros, a ταμίας τοῦ δήμου (*Bull. Corr. Hell. l. c.*). Cf. Gilbert, i 424.

§ 3. **τὰς μὲν κατὰ πόλεμον—πλεονάκις**] Thus Pericles was general for 15 years, and Phocion 45 times (Plut. *Per.* 15, *Phoc.* 8).—In *Pol.* 1371 *b* 24, (it is characteristic of a democracy) τὸ μὴ δὶς τὸν αὐτὸν ἄρχειν μηδεμίαν ἢ ὀλιγάκις ἢ ὀλίγας ἔξω τῶν κατὰ πόλεμον. Dem. *Prooem.* p. 1461, 9, δεινότατοι γάρ ἐστ' ἀφελέσθαι μὲν ὅσ' ὑμῖν ὑπάρχει, καὶ νόμους περὶ τούτων θεῖναι, ἄν τις ἀστυνομήσῃ δὶς ἢ τὰ τοιαῦτα, στρατηγεῖν δ' ἀεὶ τοὺς αὐτοὺς ἐᾶν, *c. Timocr.* 149 (ὅρκος ἡλιαστικός), οὐδὲ δὶς τὴν αὐτὴν ἀρχὴν τὸν αὐτὸν ἄνδρα καταστήσω. *Pol.* 1299 *a* 10, μὴ τὸν αὐτὸν δὶς ἀλλ' ἅπαξ μόνον. 1275 *a* 25, δὶς τὸν αὐτὸν οὐκ ἔξεστιν ἄρχειν ἐνίας (ἀρχάς).

The effect of the rule forbidding more than one reappointment to the Council was to give every Athenian citizen at some period of his life a seat in that body. At the time when the number of citizens was at its highest (about 30,000 in 460 B.C.), it is probable that the number who reached the age of 30 in each year, and thus became qualified for the Council, was rather less than 1,000 (Headlam, *On the*

63. *τὰ δὲ δικαστήρια [κ]λη[ροῦσιν] οἱ ἐννέα ἄρ[χο]ντες κατὰ φυλάς, ὁ δὲ γραμματεὺς τῶν θεσμο[θετῶν τῆς] δεκάτης φυλῆς.*
2 *εἴσοδοι δέ εἰσιν εἰς τὰ δικασ[τή]ρια δέκα, μία τῇ φυλῇ ἑκάστῃ, καὶ κλη[ρωτήρια] εἴκοσι, δ[ύο τῇ] φυλῇ ἑκάστῃ, καὶ κιβώτια ἑκατόν,*

LXIII 1 ΤΑΔ(Ε)ΤΑ corr. K. πληροῦσιν Dareste. **2** <τοὺς> τῆς H-L, coll. c. 59 ult. **3** δικαστήρια: an κληρωτήρια?

TESTIMONIA. **LXIII** Schol. ad Arist. *Vesp.* 775 (v. Testim. c. 59 ult.). Schol. ad Arist. *Plut.* 277, p. 340 *a* 21 Dübner: (§ 4) ἔρχεται ἕκαστος εἰς τὸ <δικαστήριον> πινάκιον ἔχων "ἐπιγεγραμμένον τὸ ὄνομα" αὐτοῦ καὶ "πατρόθεν καὶ τοῦ δήμου" "καὶ γράμμα ἕν" τι "μέχρι τοῦ κ," διὰ τὸ πάλαι δέκα φυλὰς εἶναι Ἀθήνησι, διῄρηντο γὰρ "κατὰ φυλάς." (§ 1) εἶτα οἱ θεσμοθέται κατὰ φυλὴν ἕκαστος καὶ δέκατος ὁ γραμματεὺς ἐκλήρουν τὰ γράμματα μέχρι τοῦ κ καὶ τὰ λαχόντα ἴσα τὸν ἀριθμὸν τοῖς μέλλουσι κληροῦσθαι δικαστηρίοις, (§ 5) ὑπηρέτης φέρων ἐτίθει καθ' ἕκαστον δικαστήριον ἕν· εἶτα πάλιν ἀπεκληροῦντο οἱ τὰ εἰληχότα γράμματα ἔχοντες τίνες δικάσουσι καὶ τίνες οὔ. *ib.* 972 Ἀθηναῖοι γὰρ ἀπὸ τῶν φυλῶν ἐποίουν τοὺς δικαστὰς κατὰ γράμμα, οἷον ἡ πρώτη τὸ α ἔσχε σημεῖον, καὶ ἡ δευτέρα τὸ β, καὶ αἱ ἄλλαι ὁμοίως ἕως τοῦ κ.

Lot, p. 50 n). Each of these might be a member of the 500 twice in his life, but not oftener. In the few cases in which the names of the *βουλευταί* from the same deme are preserved for more than one year, only one case of reappointment is to be found, viz. *Διονύσιος Ἡφαιστίωνος* of the deme *Φιλαΐδαι*, (in the middle of the fourth century) CIA ii 870, 3, and (in B.C. 341) 872, 17.

Boeckh, ii 515 Fränkel, states his conviction that no one could be a member of the *βουλή* for two consecutive years: the text proves that it was possible.

As regards other offices, we know the names of a large number of *ταμίαι*, *ἑλληνοταμίαι* and *ἐπιμεληταί*; but we never find one man holding the same office twice (Headlam, p. 91).

LXIII to the end. *The Law-Courts.*

On the Athenian procedure for the distribution of the *δικασταί* over the several *δικαστήρια*, see Schömann, *De Sortitione Iudicum apud Athenienses*, Opusc. Acad. i 200—229; Schömann, *Ant.* p. 475 E. T.; *Att. Process*, pp. 146—162 Lips.; Fränkel, *Att. Geschworenengerichte*, 1877, pp. 92 ff.; Gilbert, i 374—7; Busolt in Müller's *Handbuch*, IV i 180; and Caillemer in Daremberg and Saglio's *Dict.* iii 191.

§ 1. **δικαστήρια κληροῦσιν**] Pollux, viii 87, mentions as one of the duties of the archons, *κληροῦν δικαστάς*. A distinction must, however, be drawn between *κληροῦν δικαστάς*, which refers to the original assignment of dicasts to a heliastic division by means of the lot (c. 59 § 7), and *κληροῦν δικαστήρια*, which refers to the allotment of the several law-courts to the dicasts so appointed (*ib.* § 5). [Dem.] 47 § 17, *κληρουμένων τῶν δικαστηρίων*, and 37 § 39, *τῶν δικαστηρίων ἐπικεκληρωμένων*. **κατὰ φυλάς** is not meant to imply that each *δικαστήριον* was allotted to a different tribe, but that representatives of all the tribes sat in each *δικαστήριον*. Hitherto it has generally been supposed that the daily allotment was not 'by tribes,' but by heliastic divisions or 'sections' (Schömann, *Ant.* p. 475).

§ 2. **εἴσοδοι** κτλ.] the separate entrances for the members of the several tribes would not only facilitate entrance and exit, but also make it easier to detect personation. It may perhaps be inferred that the members of each tribe sat together in the court.

It seems premature, however, to mention the entrances to the law-courts at this stage of the description; it may therefore be suggested that *δικαστήρια* has been written by mistake for *κληρωτήρια*. The *εἴσοδος* in l. 7 is clearly the entrance into the pair of *κληρωτήρια* assigned to each tribe.

κληρωτήρια] either (1) 'vessels for holding lots' (*urnes à lots*, Reinach); or (2) 'rooms in which the dicasts have their several courts allotted to them' (so Kaibel and Kiessling, Poland, and Haussoullier). Mr Kenyon gives in the text of his translation 'twenty vessels for holding votes,' adding in the note the alternative rendering, 'rooms in which the jurors are elected.'

(1) is the preferable sense in Arist. *Eccl.* 682, ΒΛ. τὰ δὲ κληρωτήρια ποῖ τρέψεις; ΠΡ. ἐς τὴν ἀγορὰν καταθήσω· κᾆτα στήσασα παρ' Ἁρμοδίῳ κληρώσω

δέκα τῇ φυλῇ ἑκάστῃ, καὶ ἕτερα κιβώτι[α δέκα, εἰς ἃ ἐ]μβάλλεται
τῶν λαχόντων δικα[σ]τῶν τὰ π[ινά]κια, καὶ ὑδρίαι δύο· καὶ βακ-
τηρίαι παρατίθενται κατὰ τὴν ε[ἴσοδον] ἑκάστην ὅσοιπερ οἱ δικα-
[σ]ταί, καὶ βάλανοι εἰς τὴν ὑδρίαν ἐμβάλλονται ἴσαι ταῖς βακτη-
ρίαις, [γ]έγραπται δὲ ἐν ταῖς βαλάνοις τῶν στοιχείων ἀπὸ τοῦ
ἐνδεκάτου, τοῦ λ [[τριακοστοῦ]], ὅσαπερ ἂν μέλλῃ [τ]ὰ δικαστήρια
πληρωθήσεσθαι. δικάζειν δ' ἔξεστιν τοῖς ὑπὲρ τριάκοντα ἔτη γε- 3

5 εἰς ἃ B: οἷς K etc. **6** ΒΑΚΤΗΡΙΑ corr. K. **7** ΟΥΣΟΙΠΕΡ corr. K. **8** ταῖς βακτηρίαις: an τοῖς δικαστηρίοις? **9** Τ(ΩΝ) ΣΤΟΙΧΕΙ$^{\omega(\nu)}$ Blass (K[3]): [ΤΑ] ΣΤΟΙΧΕΙΑ (K[1], K-W, H-L). τοῦ ἐνδεκάτου delet Rutherford (H-L). **10** τριακοστοῦ del. K (K-W, H-L, B). ΕΑΝ.

ἅπαντας (where the Schol. absurdly explains *κληρωτήρια* as *τὰς κληρωτὰς ἀρχάς*). *κληρωτρὶς* means an urn for holding votes in Schol. Arist. *Vesp.* 674, *κληρωτρίδι τῶν ψήφων*, and 752, *τοῦ κήρυκος τὴν κληρωτρίδα προσφέροντος, ἔβαλον τὰς ψήφους*. Both senses are recognised in Pollux x 61, *κληρωτήριον· εἰ γὰρ καὶ ἐπὶ τοῦ τόπου ἔοικεν εἰρῆσθαι τοὔνομα ἐν τῷ Γήρᾳ Ἀριστοφάνους, ἀλλὰ καὶ ἐπὶ τοῦ ἀγγείου ἂν ἐναρμόσειεν*. The sense is uncertain in Eubulus ap. Athen. 640 B, *κλητῆρες .. μάρτυρες .. δίκαι .. κληρωτήρια .. κλεψύδραι, νόμοι, γραφαί*, and in CIA ii 441, *[ἀνα]γράψαι δὲ τόδε [τὸ ψήφισμα – –] κληρωτήριον λιθ[ι – –]ιον*.

(2) is supported by Plut. ii 793 D, *πρεσβύτῃ—ἐπίπονος καὶ ταλαίπωρος ἡ πρὸς πᾶν μὲν ἀεὶ κληρωτήριον ἀπαντῶσα φιλαρχία, παντὶ δὲ ἐφεδρεύουσα δικαστηρίου καιρῷ καὶ συνεδρίου πολυπραγμοσύνη*, Pollux ix 44, *κληρωτήρια ἔνθα κληροῦνται οἱ δικασταί*, and Bekk. *Anecd.* p. 47, *κληρωτήρια: ἔνθα κληροῦνται οἱ δικασταί*. It certainly has this meaning in col. 31 l. 18, *ὁ ἄρχων τὴν φυλὴν κα[λεῖ εἰς τὸ κ]ληρωτήριον*, and it therefore seems best to understand it in the same sense in the present passage. It is not obvious why each tribe requires two *κληρωτήρια*, unless we are to suppose that one of them was merely an antechamber serving as a waiting-room for the other.

κιβώτια] 'small boxes,' Arist. *Plut.* 711. The number of the first set of *κιβώτια* is 100, 10 for each tribe, because the dicasts in each tribe are distributed over all the ten divisions into which all the dicasts are divided. In each tribe, all the tickets (*πινάκια*) bearing the names of the dicasts in division A are placed in the first *κιβώτιον*, those of division B in the second, and so on for all the ten divisions. According to the number of dicasts required, an equal number of tickets is drawn by lot from each of the 100 *κιβώτια*. Each ticket so drawn has a court assigned it by lot; and the tickets are now placed in the second set of 10 *κιβώτια*, all tickets of dicasts assigned to any given court being placed in the *κιβώτιον* which bears the letter corresponding to that court. The names of all the dicasts who are selected to serve are thus distributed over the several courts that are to sit on the day in question. The process is described in detail in col. 31.

πινάκια] see note on § 4.

βακτηρίαι] 'bâtons' serving the dicasts as badges of office. The *βακτηρία* was marked with the same letter and colour as the court assigned to the dicast, who gave it up on entering the court when he received a *σύμβολον* (or 'token') instead. This *σύμβολον* enabled him to claim the *τριώβολον*. See *infra* col. 32 l. 3—15, and cf. Dem. *de Cor.* 210, (*δεῖ*) *παραλαμβάνειν γ' ἅμα τῇ βακτηρίᾳ καὶ τῷ συμβόλῳ τὸ τῆς πόλεως νομίζειν ἕκαστον ὑμῶν, ὅταν τὰ δημόσια εἰσίητε κρινοῦντες*. Bekk. *Anecd.* p. 185, *βακτηρία καὶ σύμβολον: ῥάβδον κατεῖχον οἱ δικάζοντες, καὶ σύμβολον ἐλάμβανον ἀντιδιδόντες διὰ τὸ κομίσασθαι τὸ τριώβολον*. Pollux, viii 16, *σκεύη δὲ δικαστικά, σύμβολον, βακτηρία, <πινάκιον>, πινάκιον τιμητικόν*.

βάλανοι] either actual acorns or (more probably) ballot balls of metal shaped like them. In either case the *βάλανος* had the letter of the court scratched upon it.

πληρωθήσεσθαι] to be made up to their full complement of *δικασταί*. Dem. *c. Timocr.* 92, *δικαστήρια πληροῦτε*. *Mid.* 209; Lys. 26 § 6; Isae. 6 § 37; CIA ii 395 (of the *θεσμοθέται*) *ὅταν πρῶτον πληρῶσιν δικαστήριον εἰς ἕνα καὶ πεντακοσίους δικαστάς*. Cf. Meier and Sch. p. 156, note 18 Lips.

γονόσιν, ὅσοι αὐτῶν [μ]ὴ ὀφείλουσιν τῷ δημοσίῳ ἢ ἄτιμοί εἰσιν· ἐὰν δέ τις δικάζῃ οἷς μὴ ἔξεστιν, ἐνδείκνυται καὶ [εἰς] τὸ δικαστήριον εἰσάγετ[αι], ἐὰν δ' ἁλῷ, προστιμ[ῶσιν αὐτ]ῷ οἱ δικασταί, ὅ τι ἂν δοκῇ ἄξιος εἶναι παθε[ῖν] ἢ ἀποτεῖσαι. ἐὰν δὲ ἀργυρίου τιμηθῇ, δεῖ αὐτὸν δεδέ[σθαι], ἕως ἂν ἐκτείσῃ τό τε πρότερον ὄφλημ[α ἐ]φ' ᾧ ἐνεδείχθη, καὶ ὅ τι ἂν αὐτῷ προστιμήσῃ τ[ὸ δικ]αστήριον.
4 ἔχει δ' ἕκαστος δικαστὴς πινάκιον πύξινον, ἐπιγεγραμμένον

13 ΟΙΣ : ᾧ Richards (H-L). ΚΑΙ—ΕΙΣΑΓΕΤΑΙ K-W, K[3], B: *κατὰ τὸ δικαστήριον εἰσαγγελία* K[1] (*εἰσαγγελίᾳ* Fraenkel, H-L). **15, 16** ΑΠΟΤΙΣΑΙ—ΕΚΤΙΣΗ. **18** *ἕκαστος* <ὁ> B.

§ **4** Hesych. *χαλκοῦν πινάκιον*: *Ἀθηναῖοι εἶχον ἕκαστος πινάκιον πύξινον ἐπιγεγραμμένον τὸ ὄνομα τὸ* (*τοῦ* cod.) *αὐτοῦ καὶ τοῦ δήμου πατρόθεν.* Schol. Arist. *Plut.* 277. Photius *πινάκιον· σύμβολον δικαστικόν, χαλκοῦν ἢ πύξινον.*

---

§ 3. **τριάκοντα ἔτη**] Pollux viii 122, *ἐδίκαζον οἱ ὑπὲρ τριάκοντα ἔτη ἐκ τῶν ἐπιτίμων καὶ μὴ ὀφειλόντων τῷ δημοσίῳ.* Cf. Dem. *c. Timocr.* 123 and Law *ib.* 50.

The text lends no support to the opinion that the number of dicasts was limited to 6,000 annually appointed by lot from the general body of duly qualified citizens. On the contrary, it favours Fränkel's view that all duly qualified Athenians might be enrolled on the list of dicasts. At Ardettos, near the Panathenaic stadium, *δημοσίᾳ πάντες ὤμνυον Ἀθηναῖοι τὸν ὅρκον τὸν ἐκκλησιαστικόν* (Harp. *s. v.* *Ἀρδηττός*). Fränkel, *Att. Geschworenenger.*, esp. pp. 14—20. The number 6,000, however, occurs in c. 24, 13 with reference to the previous century.

ἐνδείκνυται] *ἔνδειξις* was primarily put in force against debtors to the state (Dem. *Androt.* 33, *Nicostr.* 14). In Dem. *c. Mid.* 182 Pyrrhus is prosecuted by *ἔνδειξις* for acting as dicast. Cf. *Dict. Ant.* i 734 *b*.

προστιμῶσιν οἱ δικασταί] In cases where a person illegally acted as dicast, it was left to the court to impose the penalty, Dem. *c. Mid. l.c.*; similarly in the event of a disqualified person speaking in the *ἐκκλησία* ([Dem.] *Aristog.* i § 92).

§ 4. **πινάκιον**] All the extant *πινάκια* are of bronze; those of boxwood, mentioned in the text, having presumably perished. The specimens from the British Museum are given in Hicks, *Hist. Inscr.* p. 202. Out of the 65 collected in CIA ii 875—940, seventeen are mere fragments: the remaining 48 exhibit in the upper left-hand corner one of the first ten letters of the Greek alphabet:—A(4), B(6), Γ(5), Δ(9), E(8), Ξ(4), H(2), Θ(6), I(3), K(1). Two of them (914—5) were found in the same tomb, both bearing the same letter and the same name (with a slight difference in spelling). Cf. 917—8. Apparently each dicast remained permanently in the division first assigned him; so that the annual *κλήρωσις δικαστῶν* only affected those citizens who on reaching the age of 30 were assigned to a particular division for the first time. The *πινάκια* are discussed by Dumont, *Rev. Arch.* 1868, p. 140; C. Curtius, *Rhein. Mus.* 1876, 281; Klein, *Jahrb. des Vereins von Alterthumsfreunden in Rheinland*, 1876, p. 57—; P. Girard in *Bull. Corr. Hell.* 1878, p. 523—; Fränkel, *Att. Geschworenenger.* pp. 94, 95, 105; Meier and Schömann, pp. 151—2, Lips.; and Caillemer in Daremberg and Saglio, iii 189 f. The *πινάκιον* reproduced (as fig. 1) at the head of the frontispiece bears the name of *Διονύσιος Διονυ[σίου] ἐκ Κοί[λης]*; in the upper left-hand corner is the letter of the division, A; below this, an owl between A and Θ, being part of AΘH, for *Ἀθηναίων*; towards the right are two owls between A and A, and to the right of this is a gorgon's head (CIA ii 876).

The use of the *πινάκιον* in drawing lots for certain public offices is mentioned in Dem. 39 (*adv. Boeotum de nomine*) § 12, *τί δέ, ἂν ἄρα...ἅτερος ἡμῶν πείσας τὸν ἕτερον, ἐὰν λάχῃ, παραδοῦναι αὐτῷ τὴν ἀρχήν, οὕτω κληροῦται; τὸ δυοῖν πινακίοιν τὸν ἕνα κληροῦσθαι τί ἄλλο ἐστίν;* That this *πινάκιον* was of bronze is proved by § 10, *ἂν δ' ἀρχὴν ἡντινοῦν ἡ πόλις κληροῖ, οἷον βουλῆς ἢ θεσμοθέτου ἢ τῶν ἄλλων, τῷ δῆλος ὁ λαχὼν ἔσται; πλὴν εἰ σημεῖον, ὥσπερ ἄλλῳ τινί, τῷ χαλκίῳ προσέσται.* The *πινάκιον* is sometimes called the *γράμμα* Arist. *Plut.* 277, *ἐν τῇ σορῷ νυνὶ λαχὸν τὸ*

τὸ ὄνομα τὸ ἑαυτοῦ πατρόθεν καὶ τοῦ δήμου, καὶ γράμ[μα] ἓν τῶν
στοιχείων μέχρι τοῦ κ· νενέμηνται γὰρ κατὰ φυλὰς δέκα μέρη οἱ
δικασταί, παραπλ[ησί]ως ἴσοι ἐν ἑκάστῳ τῷ γράμ[μα]τι. ἐπειδὰν 5
δὲ ὁ θεσμοθέτης ἐπικληρώσῃ τὰ γρ[άμ]ματα, ἃ δεῖ προσπαρατίθε-
σθαι τοῖς δικαστηρίοις, ἐπέθηκε φέρων ὁ ὑπηρέτης ἐφ' ἕκαστ[ον
τὸ δικ]αστήριον τὸ γράμμα τὸ λαχόν.

19 ΕΑΥΤΟΥ : *τ' αὐτοῦ* H-L. **22** ΠΡΟΣΠ(ΑΡΑ)ΤΙΘΕΣΘΑΙ Blass (K[3]) : —ΓΙΝΕΣΘΑΙ K[1] (K-W, H-L). **23** *ἕκαστον τὸ* B.

γράμμα σου δικάζειν, σὺ δ' οὐ βαδίζεις, ὁ δὲ Χάρων τὸ σύμβολον δίδωσιν. *Ib.* 1166, *γράμμα* is synonymous with the section of dicasts indicated by a particular letter: *οὐκ ἐτὸς ἅπαντες οἱ δικάζοντες θαμὰ σπεύδουσιν ἐν πολλοῖς γεγράφθαι γράμμασιν* (Meier and Schöm. p. 150, note 9 Lips.).

ἐπιγεγραμμένον—δήμου] Cf. Plat. *Leg.* 753 C (in the scheme for the election of magistrates), *εἰς πινάκιον γράψαντα τοὔνομα πατρόθεν καὶ φυλῆς καὶ δήμου ὁπόθεν ἂν δημοτεύηται.*

νενέμηνται γὰρ κατὰ φυλὰς δέκα μέρη] *i.e.* are divided into ten sections distributed over the tribes. The ten *μέρη* did not coincide with the ten tribes, but each *μέρος* had a nearly equal number of dicasts from all the tribes. The extant *πινάκια* prove that members of different tribes belonged to the same section (Benndorf, *Götting. gel. Anz.* 1870, p. 276—).

ἑκάστῳ τῷ γράμματι] A, B, Γ, &c to K.

§ 5. **θεσμοθέτης**] Pollux viii 88, (*οἱ θεσμοθέται*) *ταῖς ἀρχαῖς ἐπικληροῦσι τὰ δικαστήρια τὰ ἴδια καὶ τὰ δημόσια.* CIA ii 567 *b* (inscr. in honour of a *θεσμοθέτης*), *ἐπιμελεῖται—τῆς κληρώσεως τῶν δικαστηρίων*, *ib.* 809, 206 (B.C. 325/4), *τοὺς θεσμοθέτας παρα[πλ]ηρῶσαι δικαστήρια εἰς ἕνα καὶ διακοσίους.* The *θεσμοθέτης* draws lots assigning the letters (Λ, M, N, P, &c) to the several courts. The letter thus allotted was placed over the entrance of the court. Hence *γράμμα* is synonymous with *δικαστήριον* in Arist. *Eccl.* 683—, *κληρώσω πάντας, ἕως ἂν εἰδὼς ὁ λαχὼν ἀπίῃ χαίρων ἐν ὁποίῳ γράμματι δειπνεῖ.* In the next three lines the letters B, Θ and K can only refer to the ten heliastic divisions (A to K) severally marked on the dicast's *πινάκιον*. In line 688 we have another sense of *γράμμα*: *ὅτῳ δὲ τὸ γράμμα μὴ 'ξελκυσθῇ κτλ.* Here (as in *Plut.* 277) *γράμμα* is synonymous with the *πινάκιον*, which has the letter of the heliastic division stamped upon it.

Even the original allotment of the citizens to the several heliastic divisions was under the superintendence of the *θεσμοθέται* (cf. 59 § 7). This would involve the use of a set of balloting balls or counters marked with a letter indicating the several divisions (A, B, Γ, Δ, E, to K). It is probably specimens of these that have survived in two bronze counters having on the one side four owls arranged diagonally and encircled with the word *θεσμοθετῶν*, and on the other the letter A or E (Fränkel in Sallet's *Zeitschrift f. Numismatik*, iii p. 383 f, and Caillemer in Daremberg and Saglio, iii 191). See figs. 2 and 3 in frontispiece.

FRAGMENTA

ex papyri paginis ultimis.

[Col. 31.] τ]ὰ δὲ [κιβώτια *ταῖς φυλ]αῖς [κατατίθενται* πρόσθεν [*τῶν ἀρχόντων* κ]αθ' ἑκάστην τὴ[ν φυλήν. ἐπ[ι]γέ[γραπται δ'] ἐπ' αὐτῶν τὰ στο[ιχεῖα μέχρι τ[οῦ κ. ἐπ]ειδὰν δ' ἐμβάλωσιν [των δικαστ[ῶ]ν τ[ὰ πινάκ]ια εἰς τὸ κιβώτι[ον, ἐφ' οὗ ἂν ᾖ ἐπι[γεγρα]μμένον τὸ γράμ[μα τὸ αὐτὸ ὅπ[ε]ρ ἐ[πὶ τῷ π]ινακίῳ ἐστίν, ἀ[πὸ τῶν στοιχείω[ν δια]σείσαντος τοῦ ὑ[πηρέτου ἕλκει ὁ [θεσμο]θέτης ἐξ ἑκάστου τοῦ κιβωτίο[υ πινά]κιον ἕν. οὗτος δὲ

Fragmentorum in lacunis supplendis post editorem primum multum praestiterunt H-L et Haussoullier (*Revue de Philologie*, XV, 2); etiam plura contulerunt K-W et B, quem in rebus dubiis plerumque secutus sum; ipse nonnulla olim tentavi, quaedam nunc primum protuli.

Pag. **31, 1** (=pag. 32 K-W; sed non satis causae apparet, cur paginam unam pluresve intercidisse censeamus). Paginae huius partem sinistram et dextram, ectypi in editione prima ordine inverso separatim expressam, coniunxit K. τ]ὰ δὲ [κιβώτια K-W. in medio fere versu ΛΛΟC H-L; ΑΝΔ K-W, B: ΑΙC? [ταῖς φυλ]αῖς [κατατίθενται] πρόσθεν [τῶν ἀρχόντων] scripsi, coll. Plat. *Rep.* 618 A (animarum de sortitione) τὰ τῶν βίων παραδείγματα εἰς τὸ πρόσθεν σφῶν θεῖναι ἐπὶ τὴν γῆν, et pag. 31, 35. **2** προσθεν (sic) Hauss., K^3, B, litteris θεν obscure scriptis. **3** ἐπιγέγραπται K-W, Hauss., K^3; ἐπιγεγραμμένας K^1, -να H-L. **4** τοῦ κ supplevi coll. 63, 20; idem suppleverunt ceteri. ΔΕΜ ΒΛΑΒωCIN. [τῶν]|[[τι]] δικαστ[ῶ]ν K-W, [τῶ|ν δικαστ[ῶ]ν H-L, K^3, οἱ δικαστ[αὶ] B. **6** ἐπι[γεγρα]μμένον Hauss. (edd.). **7** ἀ[πὸ] supplevi cum K-W (?), H-L, K^3, B. **8** διασείσαντος K-W (Hauss., H-L, B).

---

col. **31, 1—7. τὰ δὲ κιβώτια**] These are the 100 boxes arranged in sets of ten; the boxes in each set being distinguished by the first ten letters of the alphabet; the first box contains all the tickets of the first heliastic division, the second those of the second, and so on. Each box is shaken in turn by the attendant, and the presiding official, the θεσμοθέτης, draws one ticket out of each box.

2. τῶν ἀρχόντων] the ten officials mentioned in c. 63, *init.*

7. ἀπὸ τῶν στοιχείων, *ex ordine litterarum* (Blass).

8. διασείσαντος] Cf. the Homeric κλήρους πάλλειν, *Il.* 7, 171—189; 15, 191; 23, 353—4, 861; 24, 400; *Od.* 10, 206.

9. ἕλκει] 'Εφ. 'Αρχ. 1888, p. 114, v. 35, ὁ βασιλεὺς ἑλκέτω τὸν κ[αττίτε]ρο[ν ἑκάτε]ρο[ν ἐ]μ μέρει. Cf. Eustath. p. 675, 53, ('Ερμοῦ κλῆρος) ἦν ὁ ῥηθεὶς κλῆρος φύλλον ἐλαίας ὃ κατὰ τιμὴν τοῦ θεοῦ εἰώθεσαν ἐμβάλλειν καὶ πρῶτον ἀνέλκειν, also Photius *s.v.* 'Ερμοῦ κλῆρος (Wyse, *Class. Rev.* V 335 *a*).

καλεῖ[τ]αι ἐμ[πήκτη]ς, καὶ ἐμπήγνυσι τὰ πινάκια [τὰ ἐκ το]ῦ κιβωτίου εἰς τὴν κανονίδα, [ἐφ' ἧς τὸ α]ὐτὸ γράμμα ἔπεστιν ὅπερ ἐπὶ τοῦ [κιβωτίου. κληροῦται δ'] οὗτος, ἵνα μὴ ἀεὶ ὁ αὐτὸς ἐμπ[ηγνύων] κακουργῇ. εἰσὶ δὲ κανονίδες [δέκα ἐ]ν ἑκάστῳ τῶν κληρωτηρίων. [ἐπειδὰν δ'] ἐμβάλῃ τοὺς κύβους ὁ ἄρχων, τὴν φυλὴν κα[λεῖ εἰς τὸ κ]ληρωτήριον. εἰσὶ δὲ κύβοι [ξύλινοι, μέ]λανες καὶ λευκοί· ὅσους δ' ἂν δέ[ῃ λαχεῖν] δικαστάς, τοσοῦτοι ἐμβάλλον[ται λευ]κοί, <οἷον> κατὰ πέντε πινάκια εἷς, οἱ δ[ὲ μέλ]ανες τὸν αὐτὸν τρόπον. ἐπειδὰν δ' ἐ[ξαιρῇ] τοὺς κύβους, καλεῖ

11 ΕΝ.....C et ΕΝΠΗΓΝΥCΙ: ἐνπήκτης K-W, B; ἐμπ. H-L, K^3. **13** ἐφ' ἧς scripsi cum H-L, Hauss. (K^2, B); ἐφ' ᾗ K-W. **14** κιβωτίου scripsi cum Hauss., K-W, H-L, K^3. κληροῦται δ' propter sententiam addiderunt K-W, vocis ante lacunam superscriptae vestigia agnovit K. **15** ἐμπ[ηγνύτης ὢν] K^1, ἐμπ[ήκτης ὢν] Bywater, (Hauss., H-L, K^3); ἐνπ[ηγνύων] K-W, B. **17** ὅταν δὲ H-L. **17, 21, 29** ΕΝΒ (K-W, B). **19** χα[λκοῖ K^3 litterarum vestigia valde obscura secutus, [ξύλινοι K-W (B), color talorum albus et ater cum ligno magis quam metallo congruit; [πολλοί H-L, [λίθοι Hauss. **20** λαχεῖν H-L (B), ἑκάστοτε K (Hauss.), εἶναι K-W. **21** <οἷον> κατὰ πέντε B. **23** ἐξαιρῇ B; ἐξέλῃ Hauss., K-W, K^3; an ἐξέλκῃ? Wyse, coll. Arist. *Eccl.* 688 ὅτῳ δὲ τὸ γράμμα μὴ 'ξελκυσθῇ καθ' ὃ δειπνήσει: ἐμβάλῃ H-L.

TESTIMONIA. Pag. **31, 11** Hesych. ἐμπήκτης· ὁ τὰ δικαστικὰ γραμματίδια (γράμματα διὰ cod., corr. Musurus) παρὰ τοῦ θεσμοθέτου (θεσμοφόρου cod., corr. K-W) λαμβάνων ὑπηρέτης καὶ πήσσων εἰς τὴν κανονίδα (κανευνίδα cod., corr. Iunius). 'errat grammaticus: nam decem sunt e tribulibus ἐμπῆκται' K-W. Bekk. *An.* 258 ἐμπήκτης ὁ θεσμοθέτης.

22 'hinc nati errores in scholio Iunt. ad Ar. *Plut.* 277 p. 339 *b* 47 (Dübner)' K-W:—(44) ἔθος οὖν ἀπὸ (45) πασῶν τῶν φυλῶν δικαστὰς καθίζειν· εἶτα ἀπὸ (46) μιᾶς ἑκάστης ἐλάμβανον ἄνδρας πέντε τοὺς ἐπισημοτέρους· (47) καὶ πάλιν ἐκ τῶν πέντε ἕνα τὸν κλήρῳ λαχόντα ἐποίουν δικάζειν.

---

11. ἐμπήκτης] This designation is here applied, not to the θεσμοθέτης (as supposed by Hesych. and Bekk. *An.*), nor to the ὑπηρέτης. There is a separate ἐμπήκτης taken by lot from each heliastic division.

13. κανονίδα] probably a wooden frame fitted with a number of 'straight rules' or parallel ledges (κανόνες), stretching horizontally across it. We may suppose that the upper surface of each of these ledges was grooved and that each πινάκιον, as it was drawn, was inserted with its lower edge in the groove. In each κληρωτήριον, or balloting chamber, there were ten of these frames, one for each of the heliastic divisions.

14. κληροῦται] not mid. but pass., 'is chosen by lot.' The object of this, as we are told, is to prevent the jobbery that might arise, if the ἐμπήκτης were always the same and were therefore known beforehand.

19. κύβοι] wooden dice (or lots) of two colours, black and white, but differing from ordinary dice by not being marked with any pips. One out of every five lots was white, the rest black. The number of white lots is equal to the number of dicasts required. The archon draws the lots in succession; if the first lot is white, the bearer of the name on the first πινάκιον is considered to have drawn the lot to serve as dicast, and so on; the names of these dicasts are then called out.

τοὺς εἰληχότας ὁ [ἄρχων]. ὑπάρχει δὲ καὶ ὁ ἐμ-
πήκτης εἰς [ὦ]ν [αὐτῶ]ν. ὁ δὲ κληθεὶς καὶ
εἰλη]χ[ὼς] ἕλ[κ]ει [βάλανο]ν ἐκ τῆς ὑδρίας,
*καὶ *[π]ρο[δεί]ξας αὐτὴ[ν *ἀνέχ]ων τὸ γράμμα, δ[εί-*
κνυσιν πρ[οσελθὼν] τῷ ἄρχοντι τῷ ἐ[φ]εσ-
τηκότι. ὁ δὲ [ἄρχων ἐπειδὰ]ν ἴδῃ, ἐμβάλλει τὸ
πινάκιον α[ὐτοῦ εἰς τὸ κ]ιβώτιον, ὅπου
ἂν ᾖ ἐπιγεγραμ[μέν]ον τὸ αὐτὸ στοιχεῖ-
ον ὅπερ ἐν τῇ βαλ[άνῳ, ἵ]ν' εἰς οἷον ἂν λάχῃ
εἰσίῃ καὶ μὴ εἰς ο[ἷον] ἂν βούληται, μηδ' ἐ[ν-
ῇ συνάγειν [εἰς] δικαστήριον οὓς ἂν
βούληταί τις. π[αράκει]ται δὲ τῷ ἄρχοντι κι-
βώτια, ὅσ' ἂν ἀεὶ [μ]έλλῃ τὰ δικαστήρι[α
πληρωθήσεσθαι, [ἔχο]ντα στοιχεῖον ἕ-
καστον, ὅπερ ἂ[ν ᾖ] τοῦ δικαστηρίου ἑκάσ-
[Col. 32.] *του]* ειχ — — — — — — — —
ὑ]πηρέτῃ ει — — — — — — — — — ΝΩ

24 *ἄρχων* K-W, K[3], B; *ὑπηρέτης* K[1], H-L, Hauss., adversante spatio. **25** *εἰς [ὦ]ν [αὐτῶ]ν* B; *εἰς αὐτῶν* vel *εἰς αὐτῶν ἀκλήρωτος* desideraverat Paton; *εἰς τὸν [τόπο]ν* K. **26** *[εἰλη]χ[ὼς]* B; non χ sed ΛΕ legebat K; *παρεστὼς* fortasse scribendum; omnia incerta putant K-W. *ἕλκει* dubitanter agnoscit K. **27** *καὶ .ρο.ξας* K[3], ΚΑΙΠΡΟ..ΞΑΣ K-W; fortasse *προδείξας* scribendum. ....*ων* edd.; *ἀνέχων* supplevi. **28** *πρῶτ[ον μὲν]* K, H-L; ΠΡΩΤ (*προτείνας?*) K-W; *πρ[οσελθὼν]* B. **29** *τοῦτο ἐπειδὰν* Hauss., H-L. ΕΝΒ (K-W, B). **30** *ὅποθεν* H-L. **31** restituerunt Hauss., K-W, K[3], B. ΑΥΤΟΥΣΤΟΙΧΕΙΟΝ: *αὐτὸ στοιχεῖον* Richards et Herwerden (edd.). **32** *ἵν'* Hauss. (K-W, K[3]). **33** ΕΙΣΕΙΗ. *[οἷο]ν ἂν* K-W (K[3], B). ΒΑΛΗΤΑΙ (suprascr. ΟΥΛΗΤΑΙ). post *μηδὲ* aliquid scriptum fuisse videtur; *μηδὲ [ἐν|ῇ* K, *μηδ' ἐ[ν|ῇ* malui; *μηδὲ ἐξ|ῇ* Hauss. *μηδὲ|ῇ* B. **34** ΣΥΝΑΓΑΓΕΙΝ (supra scr. ΓΑΓ); *συναγαγεῖν* K[1], B; *συνάγειν* K-W, K[3]. *εἰς* H-L, B; *εἰς τὸ* Hauss., K-W, K[3]. **36** *ἀεὶ* Herwerden, Hauss., (edd.); *ὅσαπερ* exspectabant K-W. **37** ΝΤΑΣΣΤΟΙΧΕΙΟΝΕ.

Pag. **32**. Etiam haec pagina in partes duas sinistram et dextram discerpta; in medio litterae complures exciderunt. **1** ΕΙΧ..ΠΛ.Υ (supra scr. Ε) K-W. **2** ΩΣ..ΝΩ K-W.

---

26. βάλανον *κτλ.*] The dicasts having now been determined, it has still to be settled in which court each is to sit; each of them, when called, draws out of the urn a ballot marked with a letter denoting one of the courts and shews it to the presiding official, who now puts the ticket of the dicast concerned into the box marked with the same letter as the ballot which the dicast has drawn. The number of these boxes is as many as the number of courts that are to sit on the day in question. This ensures the dicast's taking his seat in the court he has actually drawn, and makes it impossible for him to choose his own court or to arrange to sit in the same court with certain others who are drawn as dicasts.

36. ὅσ' ἂν—πληρωθήσεσθαι] See note on c. 63, 11. These passages shew that (as in Ar.) the future, as well as the present, is found after *μέλλειν* in the *'Αθ. πολ.*

. ωϲ ὁ δὲ ὑπηρ[έτης δίδωσιν αὐτῷ βα]κτηρίαν ὁ]μόχρων τῷ [δ]ικα[στηρίῳ ἐφ' οὗ τὸ αὐτὸ] γράμμα ὅ]περ ἐν τῇ βαλάνῳ, ἵ[να ἀναγ]καῖον ᾖ αὐτῷ ε]ἰσελθεῖν εἰς [τὸ] ἑαυ[τοῦ δικαστ]ήριον· ἐὰν γὰρ ε]ἰς ἕτερον εἰ[σίῃ, ἐξελέγχεται ὑπὸ τοῦ] χρώματ]ο[ς τ]ῆς βακτηρίας. [τοῖς γὰρ δικαστηρ]ίοις χρῶμ]α[τ]α ἐπιγέγραπτ[αι *πᾶσιν] ἐπὶ τῷ σφηκ]ίσκῳ τῆς εἰσ[όδ]ου. [ὁ δὲ λαβὼν τὴν] βακτηρίαν] βαδίζει εἰς [τὸ] δικα[στήριον τὸ] ὁμόχρων μὲν τῇ βακτ[ηρί]ᾳ, ἔ[χον δὲ τὸ αὐτὸ] γράμμα [ὅπερ] ἐν τῇ βαλάνῳ. ἐπ[ειδὰν δ' εἰσέλθῃ], παραλαμβάνει σύμβολον δη[μοσίᾳ] παρὰ τοῦ εἰλη-

3 ΟϹ Κ, Κ-W (?), H-L. **3—7** restituerunt K-W, coll. Bekk. *An.* 220. **4** [τῷ ἔχοντι] τὸ αὐτὸ γρ[ά]μμα K-W; [ἐφ' οὗ τὸ αὐτὸ γρ]άμμα B suadente spatio. **5** ᾖ: ην K. **6** αὐτοῦ K-W, ἑαυτοῦ B. **8** "rectissime Hemsterhusius pro χρῶμα rescribi vult γράμμα, id quod vel adiunctum verbum postulat. Quis enim, inquit, Graece sciens dicat ἐπιγράφειν χρῶμα?" Schömann, *Opusc. Acad.* i 208. **9** Μ]Α[Τ]Α: (χρώματα K); χρῶμα K-W (B) e schol. Ar. ἑκάστῳ propter spatium K-W (B): ἐφ' ἑκάστῳ K e schol. Ar.; propter hiatum scripsi πᾶσιν. **14** ϹΥΝΒΟΛΟΝ K-W, B.

Pag. **32, 3—15** Bekk. *An.* 220 βακτηρία: ὁμόχρωμοι τοῖς δικαστηρίοις ἐδίδοντο βακτηρίαι, ἵνα ὁ λαβὼν οἱουδὴ χρώματος βακτηρίαν εἰς τὸ ὁμόχρωμον εἰσέλθῃ δικαστήριον καὶ μὴ εἰς ἕτερον πλανᾶται διὰ τὸ πολλὰ εἶναι τὰ δικαστήρια.

Suidas ('e lexico Photiano') βακτηρία καὶ σύμβολον. οἱ λαχόντες δικάζειν ἐλάμβανον παρὰ τῶν δημοσίων ὑπηρετῶν σύμβολον καὶ βακτηρίαν καὶ οὕτως ἐδίκαζον. τὴν χρόαν δὲ ὁμοίαν εἶχε τῇ βακτηρίᾳ τὸ δικαστήριον. τὸ μέντοι σύμβολον μετὰ τὴν κρίσιν ἀποδιδόντες ἐκομίζοντο τριώβολον· ὅπερ καὶ δικαστικὸν γέγονεν. Cf. Bekk. *An.* 185, 4: ῥάβδον κατεῖχον οἱ δικάζοντες, καὶ σύμβολον ἐλάμβανον ἀντιδιδόντες διὰ τὸ κομίσασθαι τὸ τριώβολον. Lex. Dem. Patm. p. 144. Schol. Arist. *Vesp.* 1110 ἐδίδοντο δὲ καὶ βακτηρίαι τοῖς δικασταῖς ὁμόχροοι τοῖς δικαστηρίοις, ὅπου ἕκαστος εἰσελθόντας δικάζειν ἔδει, ἵνα τὸν διαμαρτάνοντα ἀπελέγξῃ τὸ χρῶμα. Pollux viii 16.

Pag. **32, 8—15** *Schol. Arist. *Plut.* 278 (om. cod. Ravennas et cod. Venetus) περὶ τοῦ παραδιδομένου τοῖς εἰσιοῦσιν εἰς τὸ δικαστήριον συμβόλου 'Αρ. ἐν τῇ 'Αθ. πολ. οὕτω

---

col. **32, 3.** **ὁ δὲ ὑπηρέτης**] The attendant gives the dicast a small staff of the same colour as that assigned to the court in which he is to sit. The colour on the staff is thus substituted for the letter on the ballot, as it is obviously easier for the doorkeeper to see that each dicast, as he files in, has a staff of the right colour than one marked with the right letter.

βακτηρίαν] Dem. *de Cor.* § 210 quoted on c. 63 § 2.

4. **ὁμόχρων**] Each of the courts is marked outside with the colour corresponding to that on the several staves. We read in Paus. i 28 of two courts that derived their name from their colour: τὸν (τὸ Schöm.) μὲν οὖν καλούμενον Παράβυστον καὶ Τρίγωνον, τὸ μὲν ἐν ἀφανεῖ πόλεως ὄν,—τὸ δὲ ἀπὸ τοῦ σχήματος ἔχει τὸ ὄνομα· Βατραχιοῦν δὲ καὶ Φοινικιοῦν ἀπὸ χρωμάτων. Cf. Schömann, *Opusc. Acad.* i 226.

9. **σφηκίσκῳ**] 'the lintel,' *supercilium januae*, Steph. *Thesaurus*, vii 1606 Paris. Cf. CIA iv 3, 225 *c*, p. 168, σφηκίσκοι ἀπὸ τῆς στοᾶς καθῃρημένοι (at Eleusis).

14. **σύμβολον**] Dem. *de Cor.* quoted on c. 63 § 2 βακτηρίαι, and Arist. *Plut.* 279 quoted *ib.* § 4 πινάκιον. Cf. Etym. Mag. *s. v.* ὃ ἐλάμβανον οἱ δικασταὶ εἰς τὸ δικαστήριον εἰσιόντες· εἶτα τοῦτο δόντες, τὸ δικαστικὸν ἐκομίζοντο.

It has been proposed to identify with these σύμβολα certain leaden counters stamped on the one side with a design resembling that used for the reverse of a *χό]τος ταύτην τὴν ἀ[ρχήν, *κα]τὰ [τ]ὴν τά[ξιν ἀποδοὺ]ς* τὴν βακτηρίαν* . . . . ΤΗϹ [**τὸν α]ὐ[τὸν] τρόπον* . . . . ΤΕϹΤΟΙϹΑ . . Ω — *λα]γ[χ]άνουσ[ι]* . . . . ΔΙ . . . . . . ΟΙΚΕΑΠΕΡΥΚΡ — *τὰ] πινάκια. οἱ δὲ ὑπηρέται οἱ δημοσίᾳ [*ὑπὲρ τῆ]ς φυλῆς ἑκάστης π[αραδι]δόασιν τὰ κ[ιβώτια, ἓν ἐπὶ τὸ δικα[στήρ]ιον ἕκαστον, ἐ[ν οἷς] ἐστὶν τὰ* . . . . *α* . . *[τῆς] φυλῆς τὰ ὄντ[α ἐν ἑκάστῳ τ[ῶν δι]κα[στηρί]ων. παραδιδόα[σι δὲ τοῖς εἰληχ[όσιν ἀποδι]δόναι τοῖς δι[κασ-*

15 versus in fine *ἔπει]τα [τ]ὴν τε*— B; . . *τα . ην τα*... K^3; scripsi *[κα]τὰ [τ]ὴν τά[ξιν ἀποδοὺ]ς* coll. 37, 1—4. **16** post lacunam ΡΑ . . . ΤΗϹ K^3; ΡΑΤΑΥΤΗϹ K-W. *τὸν* supplevi. **17** versus in initio *τὸν] αὐ[τὸν] τρόπον* . . ΙΠΕ K-W. **18** ΤΟΔΙ K^3. Post lacunam ΟΙΚ . . ΠΕΡ. Κ. Κ; ΟΙΚΠΕΠΕΡ K-W. **19** *πινάκια* agn. K-W (K^3). *οἱ δὲ ὑπηρέται* B (K^3). ΟΙΔΗΜΟϹΙΑ (deleto Α et suprascr. ω?) ΑΙ . . B; *δημοσίαις* K-W. Versus in fine *ὑπὲρ* scripsi, quod manus tertia per compendium *ὑ* indicat, cf. p. 21, 24, p. 23, 22. **20** *π[αραδι]δόασιν* B; *ἀ[ποδι]δόασιν* K-W, K^3; scriptura incerta. **20—21** *τὰ κιβώτια* B (K^3): *τα[ῖς]*... K^1, K-W. **21** *ἓν ἐπὶ τὸ* K-W (K^3, B). **21—22** *ὁ[π]όσ[α] ἐστὶν* K-W. **22** An *τὰ [πιν]ά[κια]*? *τὰ ὄντ[α* K-W (K^3, B). **23** restituerunt K-W (K^3, B). **24** *π]αρ[αδι]δόναι* K-W (K^3); *ἀποδιδόναι* B.

γράφει "τοῖς γὰρ—ἀρχήν" (8—15). Frag. 490^2, 460^3. Cf. Schol. Iunt. ad v. 277, p. 340 *a* 40 *τοῖς λαχοῦσι δικάσαι εἰσελθοῦσιν ἑκάστῳ σύμβολον δίδοται δημόσιον παρὰ τῆς ἐπὶ τούτῳ εἰληχυίας ἀρχῆς, ἵν' οἱ ἐξιόντες καὶ τοῦτο προσφέροντες λαμβάνοιεν τὸν δικαστικὸν μισθόν*, *b* 4 *ἐδίδου δὲ ὁ κῆρυξ αὐτοῖς ῥάβδον, ἥτις ἦν σύμβολον τοῦ δικάζειν, ἵνα ἕκαστος καθ' ἑσπέραν ἀποδιδοὺς τῷ πρυτάνει τὴν ῥάβδον τριώβολον λαμβάνῃ μισθὸν τῆς δικάσεως.*

τριώβολον, and on the other with one of the first ten letters of the alphabet (Benndorf, *Zeitsch. f. d. Oesterr. Gymn.*, 1875 p. 601). See figs. 4 and 5, frontispiece.

The fact that letters after Κ are not found on these counters shews that the letters do not indicate the courts, but the heliastic divisions. If the courts had ten entrances each, these would correspond to the heliastic divisions, and all who left the court by the proper exit would receive counters marked with the letters corresponding to their own division. They would take these to the place where they had had their court allotted to them, and there receive payment in the chamber in which the allotment took place (col. 37 *ult.*).—In c. 63, 3, if the text is correct, the courts are actually described as having ten entrances, each of them, however, corresponding to one of the tribes, and not to one of the heliastic divisions.

15. τὴν ἀρχὴν] The official's title is not given. According to an inscr. of B.C. 341/0 (*Mittheil. d. arch. Inst.* vii 103), the *διάδοσις τῶν συμβόλων* in the *ἐκκλησία* was entrusted to the *συλλογεῖς τοῦ δήμου* (Rose, Frag. ed. p. 299 n). Schömann, *Opusc. Acad.* i 206, suggests either the *κωλακρέται* or the officials presiding over the trial, inclining to the latter; but it seems more probable that the *σύμβολα* were distributed by a person of less importance than the presiding officials, perhaps by a 'public slave' (*Att. Proc.* p. 162 Lips.). In the time of Aristophanes it was the *κωλακρέται* who paid the dicasts their fee of three obols: Schol. *Av.* 1541; *Vesp.* 695; Bekk. *An.* 275, 22; *lex. rhet. Cant.* 672, 15. But there is no proof of the existence of the *κωλακρέται* after 403 B.C.

16. βακτηρίαν] This line must have stated something about the dicast's delivering up his *βακτηρία* in exchange for the *σύμβολον*.

19—24. The tickets belonging to the dicasts in each court have been sorted out into ten boxes; these boxes are taken by the attendants of each 'tribe,' and handed over to the proper officials at the ten entrances of the court, to be re-

ταῖς ἑκάστῳ — ᴀ — — — [τ]ῷ ἀριθμῷ τ[ῶ]ν
παρὰ τῷ ᴀ . . . τούτου . . . . . ʏɴ . . . ς ἀπο[δί-
δωσι τὸν [μισ]θόν. γ[ίγνεται] δὲ πάντα [ταῦτα
κατὰ δικαστήρια ΤΡ . . . . . ΕΝΤΩ — —
δικαστήριον [ἢ] δ[ι]κασ[τή]ρια καὶ — — ΩΝ
ἔ[π]ειτ' ἐπὶ τὰ — — — — — — — — Κ
καὶ ἕτεροι κύ[βο]ι ἐν οἷ[ς . . . . .] τῶν ἀρ[χ]ῶν Τ!
ΤΩΕ — — — — — — — — — — — το . . τῶν [θεσμο-
θετῶν — — — — — — — ΟΥϹ τοὺς κύ[βους
βάλλουσιν ὁ ΠΕΝΤ . . . . . ΠΟ — — [δικασ-
τήριον. ὁ δὲ τῶν ἀρχ[όντ]ων — —
. . . ΔΑ . . . . ΤΗ ᴀ . . . . ἀρχῶν Ε —
— — — ΚΗΡΥ — . — — —

[Col. 33.

(a) ἀρ]χων τ — — — — — — — — ρ . . (b)
δ]ευτερο . καὶ . — — — — — — να . .
δ]εμία ἡμέρ[α — — — — — — αλ . .
λ]ΙΑΝΑ . ΕΙΕΚΑ — — — — — — οδε .
μ]ὴ ὤσει . . . Ν — — — — — — σιν.
ὅταν ἡ ἀρχὴ ᴀ . ᴀ — — — — κλη[ρω-
τηρίῳ ἑκάστῳ — — — — — — κιβ[ω-
τίου πινάκιον — — — — — — εις [ἑ-
κάστης τῆς φυ[λῆς — — — — ια . .
ἕτερον κενόν — — — — — — — του . .
τους πρώτους δ — — — — — — ετο[ὕ-
δωρ τέτταρας — — — — — — — ους . .

25 ΕΚΑϹΤΩΙ vel ΕΚΑϹΤΩΝ. **26** *παρὰ τῷ α...τούτου.....υν...ς* K[3]; *παρὰ τῶν....το.το.....ουν..ν* (suprascr. C) K-W; versum intactum reliquit B. **27** *τὸν μισθὸν* K-W (K[3], B). post *πάντα* Τ K-W, Π K[1]. **28** versus in fine Ν dispexit K; **29** versus in fine Κ (K). **30** *κειν ειτ' ἐπὶ τὰ* K; ΕΙϹΙΠΕΠΙΤΑ K-W; *ἔ[π]ειτ' ἐπὶ τὰ* B. *...ται* (*και* K-W)*.....ε....καὶ......*K. **31** *τῶν ἀρχῶν* Τ! ? K-W; *τῶν ἀρχῶν τ....* K. **32** *τῷ ε....ξ..ετα......το..τῶν* [*θεσμο|θετῶν* K; **36** *...δαν...τηα....ν ἀρχῶν* K; .ΙΔΑ....ΘΗΑ.....ΩΝ ΑΡΧΩΝΕ K-W.

Pag. **33**. Fragmenta *a* et *b* una collocarunt K-W; in nonnullis certe versibus (6, 7, 18) litterae extremae cum subsequentibus congruunt. **3** *.εμια..σι* K[3]. **5** init. *.ως* K[3]. **6** ΤΑϹΠΑΡΑΛΑΜ K-W; *.ται ἡ ἀρχὴ* K. **12** *δωρ τέτταρας* K-W (K[3]); [*ὕ*]*δωρ τέτταρας* B.

turned by them to the dicasts to whom they belong.

26, 27. ἀποδίδωσι τὸν μισθόν] At this point we have mention of the official paying the *τριώβολον*.

27, 28. γίγνεται—δικαστήρια] Dem. 23 § 63, *ταῦτα πάντα ἐπὶ πέντε δικαστηρίοις γίγνεται προστεταγμένα τοῖς νόμοις* (Blass).

31. ἕτεροι κύβοι] The purpose of this fresh set of 'dice' or 'lots,' as distinguished from those of col. 31, 19, is not clear. Possibly they were used to distribute the superintendence of the courts among the thesmothetae (or some other officials).

μηδεὶς παραφυ̣ — — — — — *τον χ.*
ὕδωρ μήτε ΤΟΝ̣ — — — — *τω . .*
. . ΗΤΑ̣ ΠΟ̣Ρ̣ΙϹΑ . . — — — — *αμη . .*
. . . . *λαχοντ* *τουτ . .*
ἀπολαμβάνου[σι *ακαθο̣ . .*
τὸν μισθὸν *οὗ ἕκ[ασ-*
ται αἱ φυλαὶ [ἔ]λ̣α̣[χον — — — *[ἐ̣πει-*
δὰν δικάσωσι — — — — — — — *εκα*
ΔΙΑ . ΑΤΟΝ *νο* — — — — — — —
τοῦ τ̣ε̣ συνη — — — — — — — —
ταῦτα δ' ἐπι̣ — — — — — — — —
ὅταν μὲν τ̣α̣ — — — — — — — —
τ̣ῷ̣ ἀριθμῷ̣ — — — — — — *δ* — —
. . *τοῦ νόμο[υ* — — — — — *σ̣ι* — —
εἰς αὐτὸ τὸ π[ρᾶγμα — — — . *νοτι* — *[βα-*
σιλεὺς — — — — — — — *εμ[ι]α* —
ϹΙ . *εἰσι δ* — — — — — — — — — —
κ̣ρ̣ους τι — — — — — — — — — —
. . ΤΑϹ — — — — — — — — — —
(sequuntur versus fere sex prorsus evanidi)

[Col. 34.] (*a*) (desunt versus decem)
. . . Η — — — — — — —
. . ΚΥΡ — — — — — — —
— — — — — — — — — —
— — — (*b*) — — — —
. ΟΝΤΙ | ΚΑΙΟΠ — — — —

15 . . *ητα . . αρεσ* K, . . . ΗΤΑ . ΠΑΡ . ϹΑ (vel ΤΑ) K-W. **21** *δια τα τον* K[3]; ΔΙΑ . Λ . ΑΙΟΠ K-W (litteram tertiam et quartam inductam putat B, qui *διὰ τὸν νόμον* conicit). **22** *τοῦτο συν* K ; *τοῦ τε συνηγόρου* ? K-W. **23** ΤΑΥΤΑΥΠΟΤΟΥ K-W; *ταῦτα ὑπὸ* K[3].

Pag. **34**. Fragmentum *a* paginae 33 fragmento *b* adhaeret. Frustulum *b* ex incerta coniectura adiunxit B. **15—23** (B) = p. 78, col. 34 *b* 18—25, et p. 79 *b* 1—9 (K-W): illud non descripsit K ; hoc dedit in p. 199, col. 34, frag. 2 (K[3]).

---

col. **33** *a* 17—19. Cf. col. 37 *ult.*

27. εἰς αὐτὸ τὸ πρᾶγμα] Dem. 57 *Eubul.* 7, *εἰς αὐτὸ τὸ πρᾶγμα πάντα λέγειν*, and 60, *ἐρῶ δ' εἰς αὐτὸ τὸ πρᾶγμα*. As the archon *βασιλεὺς* is apparently mentioned in the next line, the present passage refers to the procedure before the Areopagus, in which irrelevant matter was excluded: *Rhet.* i 1, 5, *κωλύουσιν ἔξω τοῦ πράγματος λέγειν, καθάπερ καὶ ἐν Ἀρείῳ πάγῳ*, Lycurg. *Leocr.* 12, 13, *μὴ ἐπιτρέπειν τοῖς ἔξω τοῦ πράγματος λέγουσιν* (with Rehdantz, p. 126 and Meier and Schöm. p. 933 Lips.). On the other hand, the mention of *ὕδωρ* in ll. 12, 14 suggests that the text may refer to the procedure in a *γραφὴ παρανόμων*, Aeschin. 3, 197, *τὸ δὲ δεύτερον ὕδωρ τῷ τὴν γραφὴν φεύγοντι καὶ τοῖς εἰς αὐτὸ τὸ πρᾶγμα λέγουσιν*.

(*b*)
(*a*) τῷ δικ | αστηρ[ίῳ — — —
διαστά | ντες — — — — —
ε]ἰσι . . | ΜΗΠ — — — —
ἁπλ[ῶ] | ἐνοχ . . — — —
. . καλ | οῦσι τọ — — — (*c*) [ἀναγ-
κάζωσ | ι τοὺς — — — λ-
ὅταν [τ | ὸ]ν δικ[αστὴν — Ν . Ν
— — | . ΝΟΚ — — — Υ . . . ΟΝ
— — — — — — — ἰδίου
— — — — — — — ἀγ]ώνων
— — — — — — — ΕΝ . . . . .
— — — — — — — δὲ τὰ δημό-
σια] — — — — — — . ΚΔΙΚ —
— — — — — — — -άχους [δ]ὲ
— — — — — — — CΟΔΕΙ . ΤΕΑ
— — — — — — — ΗCΥΠ . ΟΠΕΡ
— — — — — — — ἑπτάχους δὲ
— — — — — — ΩΝ καὶ δίχους
— — — — — καὶ δίχο[υ]ς ἑξάχο[υ
— — — — — ερον λόγ[ο]ς ΟΥΩC
— — — — — ωc ἐπιλαμβάνει

(*a*) τὸν α[ὐλίσκον, ἐπειδὰν δέῃ μεταξὺ τῶν λ]όγων (*b*) [Col. 35.]
ἢ μαρ[τυρίας ἢ νόμους ὑπὸ τοῦ γραμμ]ατέως

a **18** ωCΙΚ K-W. **20** ΔΕΚΑΛ K-W. **21** ΑΖΗΜ K-W. *b* **18** ΜΗΤΕ K-W.

Fragmentum *c* cohaeret cum p. 35 frag. *d*. **34**, *c* 20—36 (B) = 35, 1—16 (K-W) = 34 frag. 4 (K³). *c* **23** ΥC..ωΝ K-W, το]ὺς .. δας K³, versus in fine suprascripto ΔΑC (K, K-W) vel ΑC (B). **24** ἰδίους K, ἰδιώ[τ]ης K-W. **25** ωΝΤωΝ K-W, ωντ[ω]ν K. **26** Λ...ΟΙ K³. **29** 'suprascriptum ε, legendum igitur χόες' K-W. **30** ὁ δ' εἰς τοῦ K-W; ΤΟΥ pr., ΤΕΑ superscr., inducta illa, B. **31** εις υ...περ K³; ἧς ὑπὲρ ? B. **34** ἑξάχους K, K-W. **35** ὕστ]ερον λόγος οὗ ὡς ? K-W. **36** an ωCΙΕΠΙ ? B.

Pag. **35**, **1**—**37** (B) = 36 *a* + *b*, p. 80, + fragmentum incertum p. 79 *a* (K-W) = 34 (3) + nil + 34 (1) (K). *a* **1** ΕΝΑ K-W; να K. **1**—**4** supplevit B. *b* **1** Ν]ΟΜΟΝ K³ (ap. B). *a* **2** μαρ[τυρίαι] vel μάρ[τυρες] K-W.

---

col. **34**, **32**—**34**. The terms ἑπτάχους, δίχους, ἑξάχους refer to different intervals of time as measured by the κλεψύδρα. The word δίχους is quoted from Posidonius by Athenaeus, Παναθηναϊκὰ μέγιστα τὰ μὲν δίχοα τὰ δὲ μείζονα (p. 495 A), and ἑξάχους is found in Plutarch (*Sol.* 23).

36. ἐπιλαμβάνει τὸν αὐλίσκον] The αὐλίσκος is the short neck of the κλεψύδρα. The attendant could stop the flow of the water by placing his hand on the top of this. Ar. *Probl.* 16, 8, p. 914 *b* 12, μὴ εἰσιέναι τὸ ὕδωρ ἐπιληφθέντος τοῦ αὐλοῦ, and *b* 14 and 27, ἐπιλαβὼν τὸν αὐλόν, p. 866 *b* 13, (τὸ πνεῦμα) κωλύει ἐξιέναι, ὥσπερ τὸ ὕδωρ τὸ ἐκ τῶν κλεψυδρῶν, ὅταν πλήρεις οὔσας ἐπιλάβῃ τις.

ἀναγι<γ>ν[ώσκεσθαι . ἐπειδὰν δὲ ᾗ πρὸς] δ̣ι̣αμε-
μετρη[μένην τὴν ἡμέραν ὁ ἀγών, τότ]ε δὲ οὐ[κ] ἐ-
πιλαμβ[άνεται — — — — — — — ν ὕδωρ
τῷ τε κα[τηγορ- — — — — — — — — —
διαμε̣τ̣[ρ — — — — — — — — — [Ποσι-
δεῶνος — — — — — — — — — — [μα-
κρῶν τῷ̣[ν — — — — — — — — — —
. τακτο — — — — — — — — — — αγρα . .
(c) *δι̣[κ]αι — — — — — — — — — ε]ἴσ[ὶ]ν δ̣ύ' [ἕ-*
καστοι λ — — — — — — κατήγ]ορος

6 *τῷ τε κατηγόρῳ ?* K-W. **8** ϵ suprascr. *Ποσιδεῶνος* K-W. In CIA *Ποσιδεών* (syllaba secunda brevi) quattuordecim in locis scriptum (Meisterhans, p. 42[2]). **9** ΧΡωΝΤ K, K-W.

Pag. **35** *a* **3** *Harp. *διαμεμετρημένη ἡμέρα: μέτρον τι ἐστιν ὕδατος πρὸς μεμετρημένον ἡμέρας διάστημα ῥέον. ἐμετρεῖτο δὲ τῷ Ποσειδεῶνι* (melius *Ποσιδεῶνι*) *μηνί· πρὸς δὴ τοῦτο ἠγωνίζοντο οἱ μέγιστοι καὶ περὶ τῶν μεγίστων ἀγῶνες. διενέμετο δὲ τρία μέρη τὸ ὕδωρ, τὸ μὲν τῷ διώκοντι, τὸ δὲ τῷ φεύγοντι, τὸ δὲ τρίτον τοῖς δικάζουσι. ταῦτα δὲ σαφέστατα αὐτοὶ οἱ ῥήτορες δεδηλώκασιν, ὥσπερ καὶ Αἰσχίνης ἐν τῷ κατὰ Κηφισοφῶντος* (§ 126). *'Αρ. δ' ἐν τῇ 'Αθ. πολ. διδάσκει περὶ τούτων*...(Frag. 423[2], 463[3]).

Schol. ad Aeschin. 2 § 126 "*πρὸς ἕνδεκα γὰρ ἀμφορέας ἐν διαμεμετρημένῃ τῇ ἡμέρᾳ κρίνομαι*": *φασὶν ὅτι τὰς ἡμέρας τοῦ Ποσειδεῶνος μηνὸς ἐπιλεξάμενοι* (*ἐκλεξ.* K-W) *οἱ 'Αθηναῖοι ὡς συμμέτρους καὶ δυναμένας κατέχειν ἕνδεκα ἀμφορέας, πρὸς αὐτὰς καὶ ταῖς ἄλλαις ἡμέραις* (*τὰς ἄλλας ἡμέρας* cod., corr. Sauppe) *ἐσκεύαζον τὴν κλεψύδραν, μεγάλου πράγματος δηλονότι ἀγωνιζομένου* (*γυμναζομένου* cod., corr. K-W). *ἀπενέμοντο δὲ οἱ ἕνδεκα ἀμφορεῖς κατὰ τὸ τρίτον τοῖς ἀντιδίκοις καὶ τοῖς δικασταῖς.* Aliud schol. *τοῖς περὶ τῶν μεγίστων ἀγωνιζομένοις διῃρεῖτο ἡ ἡμέρα καὶ ἐδίδοτο αὐτοῖς ἥμισυ μὲν τῷ κατηγόρῳ, ἥμισυ δὲ τῷ ἀπολογουμένῳ, καὶ διεμετρεῖτο τὸ ὕδωρ ὅσον ἐπαρκεῖ εἰς τὰς ὥρας τοῦ ἡμίσους μέρους τῆς ἡμέρας. τοῦτο δὲ ἀπὸ μιᾶς ὥρας.* Hesych. *διαμεμετρημένην ἡμέραν· ἐπὶ τῶν μεγάλων δικῶν τὴν ἡμέραν ἐμέριζον εἰς διαστήματα.*

---

col. **35, 3, 4.** **διαμεμετρημένην**] Dem. *F. L.* p. 378, *πρὸς διαμεμετρημένην τὴν ἡμέραν*, Aeschin. 2, 126, *πρὸς ἕνδεκα γὰρ ἀμφορέας ἐν διαμεμετρημένῃ τῇ ἡμέρᾳ κρίνομαι.*

6. **τῷ τε κατηγορ-**] Aeschin. 3, 197 (in a *γραφὴ παρανόμων* the day was divided into three parts), *ἐγχεῖται γὰρ τὸ μὲν πρῶτον ὕδωρ τῷ κατηγόρῳ καὶ τοῖς νόμοις καὶ τῇ δημοκρατίᾳ, τὸ δὲ δεύτερον ὕδωρ τῷ τὴν γραφὴν φεύγοντι καὶ τοῖς εἰς αὐτὸ τὸ πρᾶγμα λέγουσιν* (col. 33 *a* 27)... *τὸ τρίτον ὕδωρ ἐγχεῖται τῇ τιμήσει.*

7, 8. **Ποσιδεῶνος**] The use of the *κλεψύδρα* in courts of justice is mentioned in Arist. *Ach.* 692, *Vesp.* 93, 857, and in the Orators, Dem. *de Cor.* 139, *ἐν τῷ ἐμῷ ὕδατι*, *c. Leoch.* 45, *ἐὰν ἐγχωρῇ τὸ ὕδωρ.* *Steph.* i § 8, *c. Conon.* 36 *ἐπίλαβε τὸ ὕδωρ*, and (at the end of a speech) *pro Phorm.* *ἐξέρα τὸ ὕδωρ.* The structure of the *κλεψύδρα* is described in Ar. *Probl.* 16, 8.

It was observed that the length of a short day in one of the winter months was equivalent to the time in which eleven *ἀμφορεῖς* successively could be emptied of their water. The standard adopted was a day in the month of Posideon (Dec.—Jan.). To ensure perfect accuracy it would be necessary to make allowance for the fact that the rate at which the water flowed would depend on its temperature (cf. Athen. p. 42; Plut. *Quaest. Nat.* c. 7). I learn from Mr J. Larmor that, when the level of the water in a water-clock is maintained constant, the rate at which it percolates through narrow tubes or pores of any form depends only on the degree of viscosity of water. According to the experiments of Poiseuille (*Mémoires de l'Institut*, x), the rate of percolation is increased by about one-thirtieth for each degree Centigrade of rise in the temperature. Thus a rise of 1° C. should make a water-clock go faster by about two minutes every hour.

(*c*) σ̣πεύδοι — — — — — — — — ρος ἐξω- (*b*)
θεῖν τοὺς — — — — — — — — τ]ὸ ὕδωρ
λαμβαν — — — — — — — — — επει . . ε̣τ̣ε̣
ρος τοῖς δ — — — — — — — — ἀ]γῶ[σ]ιν
ἐν δὲ τοῖς — — — — — — — — — — —
τ]ῷ̣ διαψη̣[φι — — — — — — — — — ΔΑ . . . Α
ἐ]πὶ τοῖς — — — — — — — — τοις πρόσ-
ε]στι δεσμ[ὸς — — — — — — δ]ήμευσις
χ]ρημάτων — — — — — — ὅ]τι χρὴ πα[θε]ῖν
(*d*) ἢ | ἀποτεῖ[σαι — — — — — — δικ]αστηρίων
ἐστι — — — — — — — — ν τινι ὅταν
ΔΕΔΕ — — — — — — — εἰ]σαγαγεῖν
συν — — — — — — — — ΤΑ̣ΝΗΝΜ̣ —
ΤΑΛ̣ — — — — — — — — — — — —
ΤΡΙΑ̣ — — [ψῆφοι δέ εἰσι χαλκαῖ], αὐλίσ-
κον [ἔχουσαι ἐν τῷ μέσῳ, αἱ μὲν ἡ]μίσειαι τε-
τρυ[πημέναι, αἱ δὲ ἡμίσειαι πλήρεις· οἱ] δὲ λα-

c **14** Υ supra v. *b* **18** Δ et Α supra v. **20** ΕϹϹΙ pr. **22** ʻΗ est in *d*, ΑΠΟΤΙ in *c*ʼ B. **23** ʻpost ἐστι sequebatur numeri nota, bipartita ut vid.ʼ B. **23** *b* ΝΗΝΟ̣ΤΑΝ K-W. **25** *b* ΦΑΝΗΝΑΙ K-W, ενην μεν K. *d* **27—35** ex Harp. restituit K. **28** ΜΙϹΙΑΙ.

28 *Harp. τετρυπημένη: Αἰσχίνης κατὰ Τιμάρχου (1 § 79, τῶν ψήφων ἡ τετρυπημένη, ὅτῳ δοκεῖ πεπορνεῦσθαι Τίμαρχον, ἡ δὲ πλήρης, ὅτῳ μή). Ἀρ. ἐν Ἀθ. πολ. γράφει ταυτί· "ψῆφοι—λαμβάνωσιν." Codices meliores, ABCD, post πλήρεις in v. 29 inserunt μήτε ταύτῃ (ταῦτα A) ὑπομεῖνας: quae depravata esse ex μήτε πάντῃ τετρυπημένας (vel potius ex μήτε τετρυπημένας) in v. 34 indicat Dind. In v. 34 post πλήρεις habent A et B μήτε ταύτῃ (C ταύτας), in A etiam lacuna significata: in archetypo igitur erant μήτε ταύτῃ ......λαμβάνωσιν, unde in deterioribus codd. exorta μήτε πάντῃ τετρυπημένας (K-W). πάντῃ om. ETD et Photius; ταύτῃ apud Suidam in codd.

Phot. τετρυπημένη· τῶν ψήφων οὐσῶν χαλκῶν καὶ αὐλίσκον ἐχουσῶν αἱ μὲν ἦσαν τετρυπημέναι, αἱ δὲ πλήρεις [ἀτρύπητοι] ὅσαι ἠφίεσαν τοὺς κρινομένους. Bekk. *An.* 307 τετ. ψῆφος: τῶν ψήφων οὐσῶν χαλκῶν καὶ αὐλίσκον ἐχουσῶν αἱ μὲν ἦσαν ὅλαι τετρυπημέναι, ὅσαι κατεψηφίζοντο, αἱ δὲ πλήρεις [ἀτρύπητοι] ὅσαι ἠφίεσαν τοὺς κρινομένους... (Frag. 424², 464³). Pollux viii 123 ψήφους δ' εἶχον χαλκᾶς δύο, τετρυπημένην καὶ ἀτρύπητον. Bachmann *Anec.* ii 333, 15—25 et 373, 1—10.

---

27. ψῆφοι — τετρυπημέναι—πλήρεις] In Aeschin. *c. Timarch.* 79, the herald standing by the side of the orator is described as proclaiming that of the two votes given to each dicast, that which was perforated, τῶν ψήφων ἡ τετρυπημένη, ὅτῳ δοκεῖ κτλ., was the vote of condemnation; that which was not, the vote of acquittal, ἡ δὲ πλήρης, ὅτῳ μή (with Schol.). Cf. Plut. *Lyc.* 12, τῆς τετρημένης (ψήφου).

These ψῆφοι are identified with certain small discs of bronze which have been found at Athens, pierced with a short metal stem. In the two specimens given in figs. 6 and 7 this stem, the **αὐλίσκος** of the text, is in one case perforated, in the other not: the former is clearly a ψῆφος τετρυπημένη, the latter a ψ. πλήρης. On one side of the disc are the words ψῆφος δημοσία, on the other is punched a letter of the alphabet (Γ or K in the only two specimens at present known to us). These letters probably correspond to those of the heliastic divisions (A to K). Cf. Meier and Schöm. p. 936 Lips., and Daremberg and Saglio, iii 196.

(*d*) χόντες [ἐπὶ τὰς ψήφους, ἐπειδὰν εἰρημέ]νοι (*b*)
ὦσιν [οἱ λόγοι, παραδιδόασιν ἑκάστῳ τ]ῶν
δικαστ[ῶν δύο ψήφους, τετρυπημένη]ν καὶ
πλήρη, [φανερὰς ὁρᾶν τοῖς ἀντιδίκοις, ἵ]να μή-
τε πλή[ρεις μήτε τετρυπημένας] ἀ[μφο]τέρας
λαμβ[άνωσιν — — — — — — [λ]άχω[σιν
ΑΠΟΛΑ Ṃ . ΙΣΟṂ . .
ΨΗΦΙΖ ẠΚỌ . . .

[Col. 36.] . . . . . του γ̄ ἀποδιδ[ῷ· ἐὰν γ]ὰρ γ̄ λαμ[β]άνῃ, [γ̄] ψηφί-
ζοντα]ι πάντες· ο[ὐ γὰ]ρ ἔστι λα[μβάν]ει[ν] σ[ύ]μβολον
οὐδέν]ί, ἐὰν μὴ ψηφίζηται. εἰσὶ [δ'] ἀμφορεῖς
δύο κεί]μενοι ἐν τῷ δικαστηρίῳ, ὁ μὲν χ[α]λκοῦς,
ὁ δὲ ξύ]λινος, διαιρετοὶ [ὅ]πως [μ]ή [τινε]ς ὑπο[β]άλλων-
ται ψήφ]ους, εἰς οὓς ψηφίζονται οἱ δικαστα[ί], ὁ μὲν
χαλκοῦ]ς κύριος, ὁ δὲ ξύλινος ἄκυρ[ος]. ἔχ[ει δ' ὁ] χαλ-
κοῦς ἐ]πίθημα διερρ[ινη]μένον, ὥστ' αὐ[τ]ὴν
μόνη]ν χωρεῖν τὴν ψῆφον, ἵν[α μ]ὴ δύο [ὁ] αὐτὸς
ἐμβάλ]ῃ. ἐπειδὰν δὲ διαψηφί[ζεσθαι] μέλ[λ]ωσιν
οἱ δικασ]τα[ί], ὁ κῆρυξ ἀγορ[εύ]ει πρῶτον, ἂν ἐ[π]ισκή-

35 *b* ἂ]ν [λ]άχωσ[ιν K-W. **36** *b* Μ..ΠΟΛΙ... K-W.

Pag. **36, 1** .....τοῦ γ̄ ἀποδίδ[ω]σ[ι..γ]ὰρ γ̄ λαμ[β]άνει, ἵ[να] ψηφί[ζωντα]ι πάντες K-W. .....τοῦ γ̄ ἀποδιδοὺς [γ]ὰρ γ̄ λαμβάνει ..ψηφι.....πάντες K^3. **2** λα[μβά]ν[ειν K-W, λα[μβάν]ει[ν K^3, λα[β]εῖν B. versus in fine ΙΒΟΡΟΝ vel -ΒΟΙΟΝ K apud B. σ[ύ]νβολον B. **5** ὅ]πως μὴ [προ]υπο[β]άλλωνται K-W; ὅ]πως μὴ...ὑπ. K^3. **6** ψῆφο]ι, εἰς K-W; ...εις K^3; ψήφ]ους, εἰς B. **7—9** e schol. Arist. rest. K. **10** ἵνα μὴ δύο ὁ αὐτὸς ἐμβάλλῃ van Leeuwen;—ἐμβάλῃ B;—βάλλῃ K-W, K^3. **11** οἱ articulo spatium non superesse putat K. ΑΝ: [ἵ]ν' H-L. ΣΚΕ: correxit K-W.

Pag. **36, 3—9** Schol. Arist. *Eq.* 1150...ὕστερον δὲ ἀμφορεῖς δύο ἵσταντο ἐν τοῖς δικαστηρίοις, ὁ μὲν χαλκοῦς ὁ δὲ ξύλινος, καὶ ὁ μὲν κύριος ἦν, ὁ δ' ἄκυρος. ἔχει δὲ "ὁ μὲν χαλκοῦς," ὥς φησιν Ἀρ. διερρινημένον ἐπίθημα εἰς τὸ αὐτὴν μόνην τὴν ψῆφον καθίεσθαι. Pollux viii 123 καὶ κάδον (εἶχον) ᾧ κημὸς ἐπέκειτο δι' οὗ καθίετο ἡ ψῆφος· αὖθις δὲ δύο ἀμφορεῖς ὁ μὲν χαλκοῦς ὁ δὲ ξύλινος, ὁ μὲν κύριος ὁ δὲ ἄκυρος. τῷ δὲ χαλκῷ ἐπῆν ἐπίθημα μιᾷ ψήφῳ χώραν ἔχον (Frag. 426^2, 466^3).

col. **36, 1.** **γ̄ λαμβάνῃ**] γ seems to refer to the *βακτηρία* and the two *ψῆφοι* received by each dicast during the trial; not to the three obols paid him when it is over. 'γ̄ et *τρεῖς* et *τρίς* esse potest' (Blass).

3. **ἀμφορεῖς**] also called *κάδοι* or *καδίσκοι*; Pollux viii 17, *καδίσκος·...τὸ ἀγγεῖον ᾧ τὰς ψήφους ἐγκαθίεσαν*. Harp. *καδίσκος*: *Ἴσαιος ἐν τῷ περὶ τοῦ Ἁγνίου κλήρου* (*Or.* 11 § 21 *bis*), *ἀγγεῖόν τι εἰς ὃ ἐψηφοφόρουν οἱ δικασταί*...Bekk. *Anec.* 275 *καδίσκοι: ὑδρίαι χαλκαῖ, εἰς ἃς καθίεντο αἱ ψῆφοι τῶν δικαζομένων*. Schol. Arist. *Vesp.* 321 &c (Meier and Schöm. p. 938—942 Lips.). Lys. 13 § 37. Cf. the *ὑδρίαι* of Xen. *Hell.* i 7, 9, and CIA iv 1, 116 *h*, p. 24.

8. **ἐπίθημα**] also called *κημός* Arist. *Vesp.* 754 (Pollux viii 16 *δι' οὗ κατῄεσαν αἱ ψῆφοι ἐπικειμένου τῷ καδίσκῳ*), *ib.* 123 *κάδον, ᾧ κημὸς ἐπέκειτο, δι' οὗ καθίετο ἡ ψῆφος*. Cf. Meier and Schöm. p. 938, n. 492—3.

11. **ὁ κῆρυξ**] Arist. *Vesp.* 752, *κεῖθι γενοίμαν, ἵν' ὁ κῆρυξ φησί, τίς ἀψήφιστος; ἀνιστάσθω*.

ἐπισκήπτωνται] Plat. *Leg.* 937 B, *ἐπισκήπτεσθαι δὲ τῶν ἀντιδίκων ἑκάτερον ὅλῃ* πτων]ται οἱ ἀντίδικοι ταῖς μαρτυρίαις· [δε]ῖ γὰρ πρότερον] ἐπισκήψασθαι [αὐ]τα[ῖ]ς πρὶν [π]άντα[ς] διαψηφίσασ]θαι. ἔπειτα πάλιν [ἀνακη]ρύττε[ι] "ἡ τετρυπη]μένη τοῦ πρ[ό]τερον [λέγοντ]ος, ἡ [δὲ] πλήρης το]ῦ ὕστερον λέγο[ν]τος." [ὁ δὲ δι]καστ[ὴς] λαβὼν] . . . ἐ[κ] τοῦ λυχνείου τὰς ψήφους, πιέ[ζει] τὸ μέσον] τῆς ψήφου, καὶ οὐ δεικνύων [τ]οῖς ἀγωνιζο]μένοις οὔτε τὸ τετρυπημέ[ν]ον οὔτε τὸ] πλῆρες, ἐμβάλλει τὴν μὲν κυ[ρία]ν εἰς τὸν χαλ]κοῦν ἀμφορ[έ]α, τὴν δὲ ἄκυρο[ν] εἰς τὸν ξύλ]ινον. πλα. . . . . ω οἱ δὲ τεταγ]μένοι, λαβ[ό]ντες [δύ ὑ]πηρέτ[ας, τὸν ἀ]μφορέα τὸν κύριον [ἐπαφ]ιᾶσιν [ἐπ'] ἄβακα τρυ]πήματα ἔχοντα [ὅ]σ[αιπερ] εἰσὶ[ν] αἱ [ψ]ῆφοι] . . αυται . . . ηχ . ρ . . . . τοῦ ἀ[ρ]ιθμῆσαι . . .] καὶ τὰ [διάκ]ενα [αὐτ]ῶν [καὶ] τὰ πλήρη δηλ[οῖ τοῖς ἀν]τιδ[ί]κοις. οἱ δ[ὲ ἐπὶ] τὰ[ς] ψήφους [εἰ]ληχότες] δια[ριθμοῦσιν α]ὐτὰς [ἐπ]ὶ τοῦ ἄβακος,

12 ΤΑΣ ΜΑΡΤΥΡΙΑΣ corr. K-W (K^3, B). **13** ΑΤΑΙΣ scriptum fuisse videtur, B. αὐτοὺς] ἐπισκ. [αὐ]τα[ῖs πρὶν π]άντα[s K-W; —[αὐ]τα[ῖ]s πρὶν [π]άντα[s] K^3: —[αὐ]τα[ῖs ἢ ἅ]παντας B. **14** ὁ κῆρυξ κηρύττει K, K-W, adversante spatio. **16** in fine ταστ..στα K^3; Α.ΑΤΑΣ.ΣΤΑ (ατος μετὰ ?) K-W. **17** ἐ[κ] τοῦ B; πρόσθ]εν τοῦ K^3. ψήφους [ἐ]πὶ ἕ[καστ]ον K, ψήφους....ἕκαστον K-W. cum Ν supra ΤΟ scriptum sit, τὸ [μέσον] conicit B. **18** ΚΑΙΟΥΔΙΚ.ΥΩΝ B (K^3); καὶ ὁ δεικνύων K^1 (K-W). ..ΣΑ K^1, ὡς Α K-W, [τ]οῖς ἀ- B (K^3). **19** ΠΕΝΟΙΣΑΥΤΗΣ τό τε τ[ετρυ]πημένον K-W. **20** καὶ τὸ] πλ. K-W. βάλλει K-W; ΕΝ suprascr. detexit B (K^3). **22** supra ΠΛΑ scriptum esse ΠΑΛ testatur K (ap. K-W). ΗΛΑ.Τ et versus in fine ω οἱ δὲ B (....α K). **23** λαβεῖν τὰς ...ὑπηρέται K, K-W. **24** ....ασι K; ἑστήκ]ασι K-W; [ἐπαφ]ιᾶσι B. ἄβα[κα] B; ἀνὰ K, K-W. **26** φοι τὰ] αὐτὰ...αι..ρ.....ναπευ ἀ[ρ]ιθμοὶ K^3. ΑΥΤΑ Α.ΕΥΑ.ΙΘΜΟΙ K-W. **27** εἶ]τα [καὶ] τὰ πλήρη δηλ[οῖ τοῖς ἀν]τιδ[ί]κ[οις K^3; ἀν]τίδ[ι]κ[οι iam K-W. **28—29** ους [εἰ]λη|χότας] δια K; ΦΟΥΣ.ΛΗ|—ΔΙΑ K-W. **29** ΟΥΑ.ΑΚΑΣ K-W; ..του α.ακας K^3, [ἐπ]ὶ τοῦ ἄβακος B (quod nunc probat K).

τῇ μαρτυρίᾳ καὶ μέρει, ἐὰν τὰ ψευδῆ φῇ τινὰ μεμαρτυρηκέναι, πρὶν τὴν δίκην διακεκρίσθαι (Meier and Schöm. p. 488 Lips.).

15. **τοῦ πρότερον λέγοντος**, the plaintiff: **τοῦ ὕστερον**, the defendant. Cf. l. 32—33. Similarly in the trials of the generals after Arginusae, Xen. *Hell.* i 7, 9, the votes of condemnation are placed in what is briefly called the *προτέρα ὑδρία*; those of acquittal, in the *ὑστέρα*; cf. Lys. 13 § 37.

17. **λυχνείον**] a 'lamp-stand,' probably with two branches, each of them supporting a flat disk, or pan (*πινάκιον*, Pollux, x 115). In the ordinary use of the *λυχνεῖον*, the two pans would be the proper place for the *λύχνοι*; in its present use, or rather in the metaphorical application of the term to part of the machinery of the law-courts, the two pans are the place for the two sets of *ψῆφοι*. The contrivance probably resembled a very simple type of *epergne*.

18. **οὐ δεικνύων**] Cf. Dem. *F. L.* 239, *κρύβδην ψηφίζεσθαι*, Meier and Schöm. p. 937 Lips.

24. **ἄβακα**] 'a reckoning-board,' Pollux x 105—6, here used to count the votes. Cf. Arist. *Vesp.* 332, *ἢ δῆτα λίθον με ποίησον ἐφ' οὗ τὰς χοιρίνας ἀριθμοῦσιν.*

χωρὶς] μὲ[ν τὰ]ς πλήρεις, χω[ρὶ]ς δὲ τὰς τετρυπ]ημένας. καὶ ἀναγορεύ[ει] ὁ κῆρ[υξ] τὸν ἀριθ]μὸν τῶν ψήφων, τοῦ μὲν [δ]ιώκον]τος τὰς τετρυπημένας, τοῦ δὲ φ[εύγοντος τὰ]ς πλήρεις· ὁποτέρῳ δ' ἂν πλείω[ν γ]ένηται, οὗ]τος νικᾷ. ἂν δὲ [ἴσαι], ὁ [φεύγων]. ἔ[πε]ιτα [Col. 37.] πάλιν τιμῶσι, ἂν δέῃ τιμῆσαι, τὸν αὐτὸν τρόπον ψηφιζόμενοι, τὸ μὲν σύμβολον ἀποδιδόντες, βακτηρίαν δὲ πάλιν παραλαμβάνοντες. ἡ δὲ τίμησίς ἐστιν πρὸς ἡμίχουν ὕδατος ἑκατέρῳ. ἐπειδὰν δὲ αὐτοῖς ᾖ δεδικασμένα τὰ ἐκ τῶν νόμων, ἀπολαμβάνουσιν τὸν μισθὸν ἐν τῷ μέρει οὗ ἔλαχον ἕκαστοι.

30 versus in fine ΕΙϹΧΩ..Ϲ..ΔΕΞΑΜΕ K-W. **34** ἂν πλείω [γ]ένηται K; [ἂν πλείων γ]ένηται (sic) B; πλείους γένωνται e lex. Cant. K-W, H-L.

Pag. **37, 1, 4** ΤΕΙΜ. **5** ΕΚΑΤΕΡΩΝ pr. **6—8** claudit librum coronis ingens ante hos versus infraque porrecta; unde apparet hoc in loco opus ad finem fuisse perductum.

32—35 *lex. rhet. Cantab. ἴσαι αἱ ψῆφοι αὐτῶν· ἐγένοντο δὲ ἴσαι ψῆφοι, ὡς Ἀρ. ἐν τῇ Ἀθ. πολ.· καὶ ἦσαν "τοῦ μὲν διώκοντος" αἱ τετρυπημέναι, "τοῦ δὲ φεύγοντος" αἱ πλήρεις, "ὁποτέρῳ δ' ἂν πλείους γένωνται," οὗτος ἐνίκα, ὅτε δὲ "ἴσαι, ὁ φεύγων" ἀπέφυγεν (Frag. 425^2, 465^3). Harp. κἂν ἴσαι, Hesych. ἴσαι ψῆφοι et κἂν ἴσαι, Append. prov. iii 30, 42, Schol. ad Arist. *Ran.* 685.

---

35. ἴσαι] *Probl.* 39, 13, διὰ τί ποτε, ὅταν τῷ φεύγοντι καὶ τῷ διώκοντι φαίνωνται αἱ ψῆφοι ἴσαι, ὁ φεύγων νικᾷ; and 15. Aeschin. 3 § 252, Ant. *Herod.* 51, Arist. *Ran.* 685, Aesch. *Eum.* 732—3 (Meier and Schöm. p. 938, n. 495 Lips.).

col. **37, 1, 2. τιμῶσι—τὸν αὐτὸν τρόπον ψηφιζόμενοι]** [Dem.] *Aristog.* 1, 83, θανάτου πᾶσιν ἐτιμᾶτο...καὶ ταῦτα πρὶν τὴν πρώτην ψῆφον διενεχθῆναι. Aeschin. 3 § 197, Dem. *F. L.* § 290 (Meier and Schöm. p. 943 Lips.). In Plat. *Apol.* cc. 1—24 are supposed to have been spoken ἐπὶ τῆς πρώτης ψήφου, and 25—28 ἐν τῇ τιμήσει (Shilleto on *F. L.*, *l. c.*). Cf. Ar. *Probl.* 953 *a* 4, τίμησις τί χρὴ παθεῖν ἢ ἀποτῖσαι.

2. σύμβολον, col. 32, 14.

3. βακτηρίαν, *ib.* 3. The dicast has received the σύμβολον which entitles him to draw his pay; but, as a second voting is necessary and he is not entitled to his pay until this is completed, he gives up his σύμβολον and receives his βακτηρία instead.

4. ἡμίχουν] The χοῦς was equivalent to 5·76 pints.

7. ἐν τῷ μέρει κτλ.] *i.e.* in the κληρωτήριον, col. 31, 18. Cf. also col. 33 *a* 17—19.

HERACLIDIS EPITOMA.

1. Ἀθηναῖοι τὸ μὲν ἐξ ἀρχῆς ἐχρῶντο βασιλείᾳ· συνοικήσαντος δὲ Ἴωνος αὐτοῖς, τότε πρῶτον Ἴωνες ἐκλήθησαν (cf. frag. 1). Πανδίων δὲ βασιλεύσας μετὰ Ἐρεχθέα διένειμε τὴν ἀρχὴν τοῖς υἱοῖς. 2. καὶ διετέλουν οὗτοι στασιάζοντες. Θησεὺς δὲ ἐκήρυξε καὶ συνεβίβασε τούτους ἐπ' ἴσῃ καὶ ὁμοίᾳ (cf. frag. 2). οὗτος ἐλθὼν εἰς Σκῦρον ἐτελεύτησεν ὠσθεὶς κατὰ πετρῶν ὑπὸ Λυκομήδους, φοβηθέντος μὴ σφετερίσηται τὴν νῆσον· Ἀθηναῖοι δὲ ὕστερον μετὰ τὰ Μηδικὰ μετεκόμισαν αὐτοῦ τὰ ὀστᾶ (cf. frag. 4). 3. ἀπὸ δὲ Κοδριδῶν οὐκέτι βασιλεῖς ᾑροῦντο, διὰ τὸ δοκεῖν τρυφᾶν καὶ μαλακοὺς γεγονέναι. Ἱππομένης δὲ εἷς τῶν Κοδριδῶν βουλόμενος ἀπώσασθαι τὴν διαβολήν, λαβὼν ἐπὶ τῇ θυγατρὶ Λειμώνῃ μοιχόν, ἐκεῖνον μὲν ἀνεῖλεν ὑποζεύξας [μετὰ τῆς θυγατρὸς] τῷ ἅρματι, τὴν δὲ ἵππῳ συνέκλεισεν ἕως ἀπώλετο.

4. τοὺς μετὰ Κύλωνος διὰ τὴν τυραννίδα ἐπὶ τὸν βωμὸν τῆς θεοῦ πεφευγότας οἱ περὶ Μεγακλέα ἀπέκτειναν. καὶ τοὺς δράσαντας ὡς ἐναγεῖς ἤλαυνον (Ἀθ. πολ. c. 1).

5. Σόλων νομοθετῶν Ἀθηναίοις καὶ χρεῶν ἀποκοπὰς ἐποίησε, τὴν σεισάχθειαν καλουμένην (6 § 1). ὡς δ' ἐνώχλουν αὐτῷ τινες περὶ τῶν νόμων, ἀπεδήμησεν εἰς Αἴγυπτον (11 § 1).

6. Πεισίστρατος τριάκοντα καὶ τρία ἔτη τυραννήσας γηράσας ἀπέθανε (17 § 1). Ἵππαρχος ὁ υἱὸς Πεισιστράτου παιδιώδης ἦν καὶ ἐρωτικὸς καὶ φιλόμουσος, Θεσσαλὸς δὲ νεώτερος καὶ θρασύς (18 §§ 1, 2). τοῦτον τυραννοῦντα μὴ δυνηθέντες ἀνελεῖν Ἵππαρχον ἀπέκτειναν τὸν ἀδελφὸν αὐτοῦ (18 § 3). Ἱππίας δὲ πικρότατα ἐτυράννει (19 § 1).

7. καὶ τὸν περὶ ὀστρακισμοῦ νόμον εἰσηγήσατο, ὃς ἐτέθη διὰ τοὺς τυραννιῶντας. καὶ ἄλλοι τε ὠστρακίσθησαν καὶ Ξάνθιππος καὶ Ἀριστείδης (22 §§ 1, 3, 5, 6).

8. Ἐφιάλτης (25) τοὺς ἰδίους ἀγροὺς ὀπωρίζειν παρεῖχε τοῖς βουλομένοις, ἐξ ὧν πολλοὺς ἐδείπνιζε (27 § 3).

Ediderunt Schneidewin (Heraclidis politiarum quae extant, 1847), Carolus Mueller (FHG ii 208, 1848), Valentinus Rose (Ar. Frag. 611, ed. 1886, p. 370); item Ἀθ. πολ. in appendice K-W et B. **2** αὐτοὺς K-W, coll. Ἀθ. πολ. 41 § 2. **3** Cf. Strab. 392, schol. Arist. *Lys.* 58, 59. **4** c. 41 § 2. **5** μοίρᾳ sive τιμῇ in codd. additum delevit Schneidewin. **8** μετὰ K-W (B) coll. frag. 4: περὶ codd. **9, 10** Cf. c. 2 § 2. **10** Cf. schol. Aeschin. i § 182. **12, 13** μετὰ τ. θ. del. Koeler. **13** ἕως ἀπώλετο B; ἕως ἀπόληται codd.; ὅπως ἀπόληται K-W. **18** δὲ διώχλουν codd.; δ' ἐνώχλουν K-W (B) coll. c. 11 § 1.

9. Κλέων παραλαβὼν διέφθειρε τὸ πολίτευμα (28 § 3), καὶ ἔτι μᾶλλον οἱ μετ' αὐτόν (28 §§ 4, 5; 35 § 3), οἳ πάντα ἀνομίας ἐνέπλησαν, καὶ ἀνεῖλον οὐκ ἐλάσσους χιλίων φ' (35 § 4). τούτων δὲ καταλυθέντων Θρασύβουλος καὶ Ῥίνων προειστήκεσαν, ὃς ἦν ἀνὴρ καλὸς καὶ ἀγαθός (37 § 1; 38 § 4).

10. Θεμιστοκλῆς καὶ Ἀριστείδης (23 § 2). καὶ ἡ ἐξ Ἀρείου πάγου βουλὴ πολλὰ ἐδύνατο (23 § 1).

11. καὶ τῶν ὁδῶν ἐπιμελοῦνται, ὅπως μή τινες κατοικοδομῶσιν αὐτὰς ἢ δρυφάκτους ὑπερτείνωσιν (50 § 2). ὁμοίως δὲ καθιστᾶσι καὶ τοὺς ἕνδεκα τοὺς ἐπιμελησομένους τῶν ἐν τῷ δεσμωτηρίῳ (52 § 1). εἰσὶ δὲ καὶ ἐννέα ἄρχοντες, θεσμοθέται ς', οἳ δοκιμασθέντες ὀμνύουσι δικαίως ἄρξειν καὶ δῶρα μὴ λήψεσθαι ἢ ἀνδριάντα χρυσοῦν ἀναθήσειν (55 §§ 1, 2, 4). ὁ δὲ βασιλεὺς τὰ κατὰ τὰς θυσίας διοικεῖ (57 § 1). καὶ τὰ πολέμια (58 § 1 ?).

FRAGMENTA

ex prima libri parte

1 (Rose, Frag. 381^3)

τὸν Ἀπόλλωνα κοινῶς πατρῷον τιμῶσιν Ἀθηναῖοι ἀπὸ Ἴωνος· τούτου γὰρ οἰκήσαντος τὴν Ἀττικήν, ὡς Ἀριστοτέλης φησί, τοὺς Ἀθηναίους Ἴωνας κληθῆναι καὶ Ἀπόλλωνα πατρῷον αὐτοῖς ὀνομασθῆναι. Harp. Ἀπ. πατρ.

πατρῷον τιμῶσιν Ἀπόλλωνα Ἀθηναῖοι, ἐπεὶ Ἴων ὁ πολέμαρχος Ἀθηναίων ἐξ Ἀπόλλωνος καὶ Κρεούσης τῆς Ξούθου <γυναικὸς> ἐγένετο. schol. Aristoph. *Av.* 1527; cf. Bekk. *An.* 291 = schol. Plat. *Euthydem.* p. 369 Bk. Heracl. *epit.* 1.

2 (384^3)

ἔτι δὲ μᾶλλον αὐξῆσαι τὴν πόλιν βουλόμενος (Theseus) ἐκάλει πάντας ἐπὶ τοῖς ἴσοις, καὶ τὸ 'δεῦρ' ἴτε, πάντες λεῴ' κήρυγμα Θησέως γενέσθαι φασὶ πανδημίαν τινὰ καθιστάντος. οὐ μὴν ἄτακτον οὐδὲ μεμιγμένην περιεῖδεν ὑπὸ πλήθους ἐπιχυ-

---

32 οἱ πάντας (πάντα B) ἀνομίας ἐνέπλησαν codd.; om. K-W. **38** ἀνοικ. codd.; em. K-W (B). **40** ἕνδεκα [[τοὺς]] K-W; ἕνδεκα <κληρω>τούς, B. **41** θεσμοθέται ς', οἱ Coraes (K-W, B); θεσμοθέται καὶ οἱ, θεσμοθετικοὶ καὶ οἱ et similia, codd.

7 γυναικὸς add. Rose (B).

θέντος ἀκρίτου γενομένην τὴν δημοκρατίαν, ἀλλὰ πρῶτος ἀποκρίνας χωρὶς εὐπατρίδας καὶ γεωμόρους καὶ δημιουργούς, εὐπατρίδαις δὲ γινώσκειν τὰ θεῖα καὶ παρέχειν ἄρχοντας ἀποδοὺς καὶ νόμων διδασκάλους εἶναι καὶ ὁσίων καὶ ἱερῶν ἐξηγητάς, τοῖς ἄλλοις πολίταις ὥσπερ εἰς ἴσον κατέστησε, δόξῃ μὲν εὐπατριδῶν, χρείᾳ δὲ γεωμόρων, πλήθει δὲ δημιουργῶν ὑπερέχειν δοκούντων. ὅτι δὲ πρῶτος ἀπέκλινε πρὸς τὸν ὄχλον, ὡς Ἀριστοτέλης φησί, καὶ ἀφῆκε τὸ μοναρχεῖν, ἔοικε μαρτυρεῖν καὶ Ὅμηρος ἐν νεῶν καταλόγῳ (547), μόνους Ἀθηναίους δῆμον προσαγορεύσας. Plutarch. *Thes.* 25. Cf. Heracl. *epit.* 2; Ἀθ. πολ. 41, 10.

3 (385[3])

γεννῆται. πάλαι τὸ τῶν Ἀθηναίων πλῆθος, πρὶν ἢ Κλεισθένη διοικήσασθαι τὰ περὶ τὰς φυλάς, διῄρητο εἰς γεωργοὺς καὶ δημιουργούς. καὶ φυλαὶ τούτων ἦσαν δ', τῶν δὲ φυλῶν ἑκάστη μοίρας εἶχε γ', ἃς φατρίας καὶ τριττύας ἐκάλουν. τούτων δὲ ἑκάστη συνειστήκει ἐκ τριάκοντα γενῶν, καὶ γένος ἕκαστον ἄνδρας εἶχε τριάκοντα τοὺς εἰς τὰ γένη τεταγμένους, οἵτινες γεννῆται ἐκαλοῦντο, <ἐξ> ὧν αἱ ἱερωσύναι <αἱ> ἑκάστοις προσήκουσαι ἐκληροῦντο, οἷον Εὐμολπίδαι καὶ Κήρυκες καὶ Ἐτεοβουτάδαι, ὡς ἱστορεῖ ἐν τῇ Ἀθ. πολ. Ἀρ. λέγων οὕτως· φυλὰς δὲ αὐτῶν συννενεμῆσθαι δ' ἀπομιμησαμένων τὰς ἐν τοῖς ἐνιαυτοῖς ὥρας, ἑκάστην δὲ διῃρῆσθαι εἰς τρία μέρη τῶν φυλῶν, ὅπως γένηται τὰ πάντα δώδεκα μέρη, καθάπερ οἱ μῆνες εἰς τὸν ἐνιαυτόν, καλεῖσθαι δὲ αὐτὰ τριττῦς καὶ φατρίας. εἰς δὲ τὴν φατρίαν τριάκοντα γένη διακεκοσμῆσθαι, καθάπερ αἱ ἡμέραι εἰς τὸν μῆνα, τὸ δὲ γένος εἶναι τριάκοντα ἀνδρῶν. Lexicon Dem. Patm. p. 152 Sakkelion (*Bull. de Corr. Hellén.* i 1887). Cf. schol. Plat. *Axioch.* 371[d]: Ἀριστοτέλης φησὶ τοῦ ὅλου πλήθους διῃρημένου Ἀθήνησιν εἴς τε τοὺς γεωργοὺς καὶ τοὺς δημιουργούς, φυλὰς αὐτῶν εἶναι τέσσαρας, τῶν δὲ φυλῶν ἑκάστης μοίρας εἶναι τρεῖς, ἃς τριττύας τε καλοῦσι καὶ φρατρίας, ἑκάστης δὲ τούτων τριάκοντα εἶναι γένη, τὸ δὲ γένος ἐκ τριάκοντα ἕκαστον ἀνδρῶν συνεστάναι. τούτους δὴ τοὺς εἰς τὰ γένη τεταγμένους γεννήτας καλοῦσι.—Harp. τριττύς:

---

15 <τὸ>γινώσκειν K-W. <τοὺς> ἄρχοντας K-W. **17** πολίταις: τοὺς πολίτας K-W. **24** διῄρητο ex ceteris testibus em. K-W et B: διῃρεῖτο cod. εἰς <εὐπατρίδας καὶ> γεωργ. e frag. 2, 14, K-W, sed εὐπατρίδας et in schol. Plat. et in Moeride omissos esse monet B, cum de plebe tantum sermo sit. **29** <ἐξ> et <αἱ> ex Harp. K-W, B. **32** ἀπὸ τῶν μισθωσαμένων cod., ex Suida correctus.

τριττύς ἐστι τὸ τρίτον μέρος τῆς φυλῆς· αὕτη γὰρ διῄρηται εἰς τρία μέρη, τριττῦς καὶ ἔθνη καὶ φατρίας, ὥς φησιν Ἀρ. *ἐν τῇ* Ἀθ. *πολ.* Cf. Pollux viii 111; Moeris, Suid., Harp., *s. v.* *γεννῆται.*

4 (frag. Rosio ignotum)

Ἀριστοτέλης *ἱστορεῖ, ὅτι ἐλθὼν Θησεὺς εἰς Σκῦρον ἐπὶ κατασκοπὴν εἰκότως διὰ τὴν Αἰγέως συγγένειαν ἐτελεύτησεν ὠσθεὶς κατὰ πετρῶν, φοβηθέντος τοῦ Λυκομήδους τοῦ βασιλεύοντος* <*μὴ σφετερίσηται τὴν νῆσον*>. Ἀθηναῖοι *δὲ μετὰ τὰ Μηδικὰ κατὰ μαντείαν ἀνελόντες τὰ ὀστᾶ αὐτοῦ ἔθαψαν.* Schol. Vatic. ad Eur. *Hipp.* 11 Schwartz. Cf. Apollod. bibl. iii 15, 5, *ἔνιοι Αἰγέα Σκυρίου εἶναι λέγουσιν.* Plutarch. *Thes.* 35, *Cim.* 8; schol. Lycophr. 1326. Frag. attulerunt K-W, B.

dubia

5 (cf. 394[3])

λυκόποδας ἐκάλουν, ὡς μὲν Ἀριστοτέλης, *τοὺς τῶν τυράννων δορυφόρους κτλ.* (Schol. Arist. *Lys.* 665); cf. Phot. *λυκόποδας.* Quae scholiis in eisdem (*Lys.* 665—6) de Leipsydrio commemorantur, ex Aristotele (c. 19 § 3) revera hausta sunt; qua ex causa fortasse etiam *λυκόποδες* Aristoteli per errorem adscriptum.

6 (447[3])

Lex. rhet. Cantab., *s. v.* *λογισταί*, ad c. 54 § 2 laudatum.

7 (456[3])

τὸ δὲ παρακαταβαλλόμενον ἐπὶ τῶν ἐφέσεων, ὅπερ οἱ νῦν παραβόλιον καλοῦσι, παράβολον Ἀριστοτέλης *λέγει* (Pollux viii 62). Res prope finem libri fortasse commemorata erat; sed *παράβολον* nusquam alibi inventum et iure suspectum; *παραβόλιον* condemnat Phrynichus.

8 (389[3])

Photius, *s. v.* *πελάται* 2, *οἱ μισθῷ δουλεύοντες, ἐπεὶ τὸ πέλας ἐγγύς, οἷον ἔγγιστα διὰ πενίαν προσιόντες·* Ἀριστοτέλης (cf.

52, 53 suppletum ex Heraclidis epitoma, v. 7.

Testimonia ad c. 2, 5). Quamquam πελάται in libro scriptum est, Ἀριστοτέλης tamen K-W ex Ἀριστοφάνης corruptum putant, cuius inter glossas politicas haec inventa sit (61 Fresen., Miller, *Mél. de litt. Gr.* 433).

aliena

9 (382^{3})

picturam Aegypti (invenerunt) et in Graecia Euchir Daedalo cognatus, ut Aristoteli placet (Plin. *N. H.* vii 205).

10 (386^{3})

Epimenides qui postea Buzyges dictus est secundum Aristotelem (schol. Lemov. ad Vergil. *Georg.* i 19).

11 (392^{3})

ἡ δὲ δὴ διασπορὰ κατακαυθέντος αὐτοῦ (Σόλωνος) τῆς τέφρας περὶ τὴν Σαλαμινίων (*al.* -ίαν) νῆσον ἔστι μὲν—μυθώδης, ἀναγέγραπται δ' ὑπό τ' ἄλλων ἀνδρῶν ἀξιολόγων καὶ Ἀριστοτέλους τοῦ φιλοσόφου (Plut. *Sol.* 32).

12 (399^{3})

πέπυσμαι...κύνας γενέσθαι φιλοδεσπότας Ξανθίππου τοῦ Ἀρίφρονος· μετοικιζομένων γὰρ τῶν Ἀθηναίων ἐς τὰς ναῦς, ἡνίκα τοῦ χρόνου ὁ Πέρσης τὸν μέγαν πόλεμον ἐπὶ τὴν Ἑλλάδα ἐξῆψε, καὶ ἔλεγον οἱ χρησμοὶ λῷον εἶναι τοῖς Ἀθηναίοις τὴν μὲν πατρίδα ἀπολιπεῖν ἐπιβῆναι δὲ τῶν τριήρων, οὐδὲ οἱ κύνες τοῦ προειρημένου ἀπελείφθησαν, ἀλλὰ συμμετῳκίσαντο τῷ Ξανθίππῳ καὶ διανηξάμενοι ἐς τὴν Σαλαμῖνα ἀπέβησαν. λέγετον δὲ ἄρα ταῦτα Ἀριστοτέλης καὶ Φιλόχορος (Aelian. *Nat. Hist.* xii 35, ex Alexandro Myndio, ut putant K-W). ἐν οἷς ἱστορεῖται, κύων Ξανθίππου τοῦ Περικλέους πατρὸς οὐκ ἀνασχόμενος τὴν ἀπ' αὐτοῦ μόνωσιν ἐναλέσθαι τῇ θαλάττῃ καὶ τῇ τριήρει παρανηχόμενος ἐμπεσεῖν εἰς τὴν Σαλαμῖνα καὶ λιποθυμήσας ἀποθανεῖν εὐθύς· οὗ καὶ τὸ δεικνύμενον ἄχρι νῦν καὶ καλούμενον Κυνὸς σῆμα τάφον εἶναι λέγουσιν (Plut. *Themist.* 10, capite in eodem et Aristotele, c. 23 § 1, et Cleidemo nominato). Fortasse in zoico quodam libro Aristotelem haec narrasse putant K-W, 'sicut in *Hist. An.* Z 24 mulum ab Atheniensibus immunitate donatum commemorat, quem Plutarchus in eodem capite Catonis (*Cat. mai.* c. 5) cum cane Xanthippi componit'. Rectius fortasse narrationem Philochoro tribuit J. H. Wright (cf. *Introd.* § 3 init.).

13 (401³)

Ἀριστοτέλης δὲ παρὰ Πυθοκλείδῃ μουσικὴν διαπονηθῆναι τὸν ἄνδρα φησίν (de Pericle Plut. *Per.* 4).

14 (415³)

πάππου ἢ τήθης πατὴρ πρόπαππος·...τάχα δ' ἂν τοῦτον τριτοπάτορα Ἀριστοτέλης καλοῖ (Pollux iii 17, ex Aristophane Byzantio, ut putant K-W).

15 (frag. 436 Heitz, a Rosio consulto praetermissum)

πεζὰς μόσχους, ἀντὶ τοῦ ἑταίρας· ἐλέγοντο γάρ τινες οὕτως ὡς Ἀριστοτέλης ἐν τῇ Πολιτείᾳ τὰς χωρὶς ὀργάνων. Κάνθαρος Συμμαχίᾳ 'αὐλητρίδα πεζήν' καὶ Εὔπολις Κόλαξι. Photius, a Rosio (*Arist. Pseud.* p. 446) laudatus, coll. Hesych. *s. v.*, Etym. Magn. πεζαί, Schol. Eur. *Alc.* 447, Theopomp. ap. Athen. xii 532. Aristotelis nomen fortasse ex alio eiusmodi fonte defluxit, qui e capite 50 § 2 (τάς τε αὐλητρίδας καὶ τὰς ψαλτρίας καὶ τὰς κιθαριστρίας) erat derivatus.

FRAGMENTORUM IN PAPYRO LONDINENSI INVENTORUM INDEX.

Fragmentorum numeri e Rosii editione Teubneriana (1886) repetiti, editionis Berolinensis (1870) numeris in parenthesi praepositis.

1870 1886	'Αθ. πολ.	1870 1886	'Αθ. πολ.	1870 1886	'Αθ. πολ.
(345) 383	60 § 2	(378) 417	59	(404) 444	54 § 6
(349) 387	8 § 3	(379) 418	59 § 3	(405) 445	48 § 4
(350) 388	7 § 3	(380) 419	59 § 6	(406) 446	48, 54
(351) 389	2 § 2	(381) 420	56 §§ 5–7	(407) 447	54 § 2 (?)
(352) 390	7 § 1	(382) 421	56 § 6(?)	(408) 448	50 § 2
(353) 391	8 § 5	(383) 422	56 § 6	(409) 449	51 § 1
(355) 393	15 § 3	(384) 423	56 § 7	(410) 450	51 § 4
(356) 394	19 § 3	(385) 424	57	(411) 451	51 § 3
(357) 395	19 §§ 4, 5	(386) 425	57 § 1	(412) 452	51 § 2
(358) 396	19 § 6	(387) 426	58	(413) 453	53 § 1
(359) 397	21 § 5	(388) 427	58 § 3	(414) 454	53 § 2
(360) 398	23 § 1	(389) 428	56 § 1	(415) 455	53 § 2
(362) 400	30 § 2	(deest) 429	52 § 1	(417) 457	57 § 3
(363) 402	27 § 3	(390) 430	61 § 1	(418) 458	57 § 3
(365) 403	27 § 4	(391) 431	61 § 4	(419) 459	57 § 3
(366) 404	25 § 3	(392) 432	61 § 5	(420) 460	p. 32, 8–15
(367) 405	25 § 4	(393) 433	43 § 2	(421) 461	28 § 3; 62 § 2
(368) 406	28 § 3	(394) 434	43 §§ 3–6	(422) 462	28 § 3
(369) 407	28 § 5	(395) 435	43 §§ 3, 4	(423) 463	p. 35, 1–8
(370) 408	34 § 1	(396) 436	43 §§ 4, 5	(424) 464	p. 35, 27–35
(371) 409	27 § 5	(397) 437	44 § 1	(425) 465	p. 36, 32–35
(372) 410	33 § 1	(398) 438	44 § 2	(426) 466	p. 36, 3–10
(373) 411	34 § 3	(399) 439	54 §§ 3–5	(427) 467	42 § 2
(374) 412	55 §§ 3, 5	(400) 440	48 §§ 1, 2	(428) 468	42 § 5
(deest) 413	3 § 5	(401) 441	47 §§ 2, 3	(429) 469	53 § 7
(375) 414	55 §§ 2, 3	(402) 442	47 § 1	(430) 470	49 § 4
(377) 416	7 § 1; 55 § 5	(403) 443	61 § 7	(431) 471	56 § 3

GREEK INDEX.

Chapters 1—63 are quoted by chapter and line; columns 31 to 37, by column (col.) and line.

** The double asterisk denotes words not found elsewhere; * the single asterisk, words not found in the *Index Aristotelicus*, or only in the corresponding fragments of the Ἀθ. πολ.

*ἄβαξ col. 36, 24, 29

ἀγαθός· ἀγαθοῦ πολίτου 28, 38; ἄνδρας καλοὺς κἀγαθούς 28, 31; πολλῶν ἀγαθῶν 5, 16 (Solon); *v.* ἄριστος, βελτίων, βέλτιστος

ἄγαλμα τῆς Ἀθηνᾶς 47, 5

ἀγανακτῶν ἐπὶ τοῖς γιγνομένοις 36, 1

ἀγαπῶντας (?) τὸ αὐτόματον 8, 28

Ἀγγελῆθεν 34, 3

*ἀγηλατῶ· ἠγηλάτει 20, 8

ἀγητοί 12, 6 (Solon)

ἀγνοοῦσι 14, 10; ἀγνοῶν 16, 13; ἀγνοήσας 57, 20

Ἄγνων 28, 19

ἀγορά· ἐν ἀγορᾷ 51, 10; 52, 14; εἰς τὴν ἀγορὰν 38, 4; 57, 28; ταῖς ἀγοραῖς (τῶν φυλετῶν) 48, 16

ἀγοράζει 42, 27

ἀγορανόμοι 51, 1

ἀγορεύει col. 36, 11

ἄγος 1, 2; 20, 7

*ἀγραφίου 59, 10

ἄγροικοι 13, 9

ἀγρός· *pl.* 2, 6; 16, 16; 24, 3

*ἀγροτέρα 58, 2

Ἀγύρριος 41, 33 f

Ἀγχίμολος 19, 26

ἄγω· (1) ἀγαγὼν—οὗ διέτριβεν 25, 16; ἀγαγούσης ὡς τὸν δήμιον 45, 2. (2) νῆες φρουροὺς (?) ἄγουσαι 24, 19; τῷ τριακοντορίῳ τῷ τοὺς ἠθέους ἄγοντι 56, 21. (3) of weight 10, 5, 8; 51, 13. (4) ἄγουσιν τὸν ἐνιαυτόν 43, 10; τὴν πολιτείαν—ἄγειν εἰς αὐτούς 27, 6; εἰρήνην ἄγειν 34, 9; ἐπὶ πέρας ἤγαγε τὴν εἰρήνην 38, 24

ἀγώγιμοι 2, 7 (in different sense in *Meteor.* 359 *a* 8 τὸ τῶν ἀγωγίμων βάρος)

ἀγών· (1) μουσικῆς 57, 5; 60, 4; ἀγῶνα γυμνικὸν 60, 5, 22; διοικεῖ 56, 28; διατίθησιν 57, 7; 58, 2; λαμπάδων ἀγῶνας τίθησι 57, 7. (2) *ἀγῶνας ἐπιφέρων* 25, 7

ἀγωνιζόμενος, ἐν ἄθλῳ 57, 20; τοῖς ἀγωνιζομένοις col. 36, 18

ἀγωνιστής 60, 20

ἀδελφή 18, 11

ἀδελφός 18, 36; 19, 2

ἀδίκημα 48, 21

*ἀδικίου τιμῶσιν 54, 10

ἀδικῶ· ἀδικεῖν δόξῃ 46, 9; δοκῇ 48, 12; καταγνῷ 45, 8; καταγνῶσιν 54, 10; ἀδικοῦντα περὶ τὸν μερισμὸν 48, 11; τοῖς ἀδικοῦσιν 56, 42; παρ' ὃν ἀδικεῖται νόμον 4, 23; τῷ ἀδικουμένῳ 4, 21; τῶν ἀδικουμένων 9, 4; ἀδικηθῇ ὑπὸ τοῦ διαιτητοῦ 53, 33

ἀδίκως 12, 9 (Solon)

ἀδόκιμος 49, 4 (omitted in *Index Ar.*; found in [Ar.] *Oec.* ii 1347 *a* 8 τὸ νόμισμα—ἀδόκιμον ἐποίησε)

ἀδύνατοι 49, 25

ᾄδω· ᾖδον ἐν τοῖς σκολίοις 19, 14; 20, 21

*ἀδωροδόκητος 25, 5

ἀεί 5, 19 (*n. c.*); 13, 11; 16, 25; 19, 7, 10, 21 &c; ἀεὶ μᾶλλον 27, 23; τῶν ἀεὶ βουλευόντων 30, 11 (decree); ὅσ' ἂν ἀεὶ μέλλῃ col. 31, 36

ἀεικής 12, 7, 40 (Solon)

*ἀειφυγίαν, ἔφυγεν 1, 3

ἀζήμιος 56, 31 (*Rhet.* 1372 *a* 12)

Ἀθηνᾶ 14, 24; τῆς Ἀθηνᾶς, ταμίαι 47, 2; ἄγαλμα 47, 5

Ἀθῆναι 19, 22; Ἀθήνησι 28, 29

Ἀθηναῖοι 16, 39; 19, 32, 37; 20, 9; 21, 18; 22, 17, 33; 23, 9. τῶν Ἀθ. καὶ

τῶν μετοίκων 43, 25. 'Αθηναίων, οἱ ἐθέλοντες 29, 24; τοὺς βουλομένους 39, 2 (decree); τοῖς δυνατωτάτοις 29, 34. ἐξ ἁπάντων 'Αθ. 56, 8; ἐξ 'Αθ. ἁπάντων 56, 3
ἀθλητής 60, 7
ἀθλοθέται 60, 2, 19; 62, 12
ἆθλον· *pl.* 49, 22; 54, 32 (?); 60, 20
*ἆθλος· ἐν ἄθλῳ ἀγωνιζόμενος 57, 20
ἀθροίζω· τοὺς ἀθροιζομένους 25, 17; χρημάτων ἠθροισμένων 24, 2
ἀθυμεῖν 15, 29
αἰαῖ 19, 15 (scol.)
Αἰγεύς frag. 4
Αἰγὸς ποταμοί 34, 15
Αἴγυπτος 11, 5
*αἴδεσις 57, 21
αἰκείας (δίκη) 52, 15
αἰκισθείς, πολὺν χρόνον 18, 23
αἵρεσις τῶν ἀρχόντων 3, 37; 26, 14; (τῶν στρατηγῶν κτλ) 31, 10 and 15 (decree). εἰς δατητῶν αἵρεσιν 56, 36
αἱρετοί 22, 23
αἱρῶ· Νάξον ἑλών 15, 15. *mid.* αἱροῦμαι ('elect')· αἱροῦνται 38, 5; 42, 9, 15; αἱρεῖσθαι 30, 11 (decree); αἱρουμένων 3, 20; ᾑροῦντο 4, 5; 22, 8; εἵλετο 11, 14; εἵλοντο 5, 4; 30, 2; 38, 18; ἕλωνται 31, 4 (decree); ἑλέσθαι 13, 8; and (in decrees) 29, 10, 37; 31, 11, 14; 39, 113; ἑλομένη 46, 8. *pass.* ᾑρέθη 38, 32; ᾑρέθησαν 3, 19; 38, 7; αἱρεθεὶς ἄρχων 13, 6; τοὺς αἱρεθέντας τῆς βουλῆς 25, 16; οἱ αἱρεθέντες 29, 21; 30, 1, 3; 32, 1; 38, 18; and (in decrees) 29, 17; 31, 12; ᾑρημένων 47, 10
αἰτία· (1) 'cause', διὰ τὴν αὐτὴν αἰτίαν 13, 5;—τοιάνδ' αἰτίαν 19, 8;—ταύτην τὴν αἰτίαν 23, 8;—ταύτας τὰς αἰτίας 13, 1; τὴν *αἰτίαν ἀνάπτει* τοῖς πλουσίοις 5, 19. (2) 'charge', ψευδῆ τὴν αἰτίαν εἶναι 6, 21: αἰτίαν ἔχῃ 57, 22;—ἔχων 57, 27; τὰς περὶ τῶν προτέρων αἰτίας ἐξήλειψαν 40, 19
αἴτιος· ναυμαχίας αἰτία 23, 5; αἰτίων μάλιστα γενομένων 32, 9. αἰτιώτατοι 20, 18; 33, 9
αἰτιῶμαι· *c. inf.* αἰτιᾶται 56, 35; αἰτιῶνται 27, 22
αἰτοῦντος, Πεισιστράτου τὴν φυλακὴν 14, 9
"Ακαστος 3, 10 f.
*ἀκίβδηλος 51, 3 (*Rhet.* 1375 *b* 6 κίβδηλον δίκαιον)
*ἀκληρωτί 30, 30 (decree)
ἀκολουθεῖν 49, 3
ἀκοντίζειν 42, 23
*ἀκοσμοῦντας, ζημιοῦσα τοὺς 3, 36 (*Pol.* 1272 *b* 8 ἀκοσμία τῶν δυνατῶν)
ἀκούσιος 57, 17
ἀκούω· ἀκούσαντες *c. gen.* 37, 18; and (in decree) 29, 19
ἄκριτον ἀποκτεῖναι 40, 12 (*Meteor.* 361 *b* 31 ἄκριτος καὶ χαλεπὸς ὁ 'Ωρίων)
ἀκρόπολις· (1) with article, κατέσχε τὴν ἀ. 14, 6; τὸ πρόπυλον τῆς ἀ. 15, 19; κατέφυγον εἰς τὴν ἀ. 20, 13; τὴν ἀ. ἐφρούρουν 37, 19. (2) without article, ἐν ἀ. 7, 21; 18, 14; 60, 18; εἰς ἀ. 55, 33; 60, 16. See πόλις.
'Ακτή 42, 22; στρατηγὸς εἰς τὴν 'Α. 61, 7
ἄκυρος ἡ βουλή 45, 21; ἀμφορεύς col. 36, 7
ἄκων 27, 10; ἀκόντων 23, 12; ἄκοντας 40, 6
ἄλγεα 5, 7 (Solon)
'Αλεξίας ἄρχων (405/4) 34, 14
ἀληθής 18, 28
ἁλίσκομαι· ἁλῶναι 19, 34; ἁλῷ 61, 13 f
ἀλκή 12, 53 (Solon)
'Αλκμέων 13, 17
'Αλκμεωνίδαι· τὸ γένος ἔφυγεν 1, 3; (τῶν φυγάδων) προειστήκεσαν 19, 9; Κλεισθένης τοῦ γένους τῶν 'Α. 20, 3; 28, 8; τῶν ἐναγῶν 20, 7; αἰτιώτατοι τῆς ἐκβολῆς τῶν τυράννων 20, 19; πρότερον τῶν 'Α. Κήδων ἐπέθετο τοῖς τυράννοις 20, 20
ἀλλὰ occurs about 30 times, always with negative preceding. ἀλλὰ ἤ 53, 17; also 26, 14; 54, 23 (Blass); μήτε—ἀλλά 16, 8; cf. μήν
ἀλλήλων 21, 16; ἀλλήλοις 5, 4; πρὸς ἀλλήλους 23, 18
ἄλλος· τὸν ἄλλον λόγον 15, 23; εἰς τὸν ἄλλον (=μέλλοντα) χρόνον 31, 18 (decree); οἵ τε ἄλλοι 12, 1; τά τε ἄλλα 8, 21; τὰ μὲν ἄλλα καθάπερ—εἶπεν 29, 16 (formula of amendment); τῶν ἄλλων τῷ βουλομένῳ 29, 14 (decree); ἐν μὲν τοῖς ἄλλοις 6, 13; τοῖς τε ἄλλοις πᾶσι καὶ δὴ καὶ 2, 3
*ἄλλοσε δαπανῆσαι 29, 30 (decree)
ἀλλότριος 34, 6
ἄλλως 34, 21
ἄλφιτα 51, 12
'Αλωπεκῆθεν 22, 24; 45, 4
ἅμα 3, 23; 11, 7; 16, 11; προῆλθεν ἡ πόλις ἅμα τῇ δημοκρατίᾳ—αὐξανομένη 23, 1
ἁμαρτάνω· 8, 22; 16, 5; 41, 19
ἁμαρτίαν, ἔγνωσαν τὴν 34, 14
ἀμείνονες 12, 60 (Solon)
ἀμειψάμενος 7, 24 (anon.)
*ἄμιπποι 49, 7
ἀμίσθους ἄρχειν, τὰς ἀρχὰς 29, 39 (decree)
"Αμμωνος, ἡ 61, 28
'Αμπρακιώτης 17, 14
ἀμφιβαλών 12, 8 (Solon)
ἀμφικτύονες εἰς Δῆλον 62, 14
ἀμφισβήτησις 28, 34; *pl.* 9, 9; 57, 11
ἀμφισβητῶ· —τῇ 57, 10; —τῶσιν 52, 4
ἀμφορεῖς 60, 6; (in the lawcourts) col. 36, 3
ἀμφότερος· 11, 9, 12; 12, 55; 15, 4 &c. ἐξ ἀμφοτέρων—ἀστῶν 42, 2
ἀμφοῖν ἀστοῖν, ἐξ 26, 23
ἂν *passim*; ἄν τε—ἄν τε 48, 19; *v.* ὃς ἄν, ὅστις ἄν
ἀνὰ δισχιλίους 26, 10

ἀναβαίνω· ἀναβάντες ἐπὶ τοῦτον (τὸν λίθον) 55, 30; ἀναβῆναι—εἰς Ἄρειον πάγον 60, 17
ἀναβαλλομένων τὴν ἀπογραφήν 40, 3
ἀναγιγνώσκειν 43, 20; ἀναγνωσόμενον 54, 22; ἀναγνῶναι 54, 23. *Probl.* and (omitted in *Index Ar.*) *Poet.* 1462 *a* 12
ἀναγκάζειν 51, 18; ἠναγκάσθησαν—καταστῆσαι τὴν—πολιτείαν 29, 4; ὁ δῆμος ἠναγκάσθη χειροτονεῖν τὴν ὀλιγαρχίαν 34, 26
ἀναγκαῖον *c. inf.* 44, 5; 48, 16; 53, 28; col. 32, 5; cf. ἐπάναγκες. ἀναγκαίης ὕπο χρείους 12, 37 (Solon)
ἀνάγκη *c. inf.* 9, 9; 47, 24; 48, 5; 54, 4. ἐν ταῖς ἀνάγκαις ('under torture') 18, 24
*ἀναγορεύει, ὁ κῆρυξ col. 36, 31; ἀναγορεύωσι, τῶν δήμων 21, 18
ἀναγράφω· (1) *act.* τὰ θέσμια 3, 20; νόμους 41, 12; τοὺς νόμους εἰς τοὺς κύρβεις 7, 2; πολιτείαν 30, 23; 31, 1; 32, 2; τὰς μισθώσεις—ἐν γραμματείοις λελευκωμένοις 47, 26; τὰ χωρία 47, 21. *c. acc. pers.* 47, 18, and εἰς λελευκωμένα γραμματεῖα 47, 16. (2) *pass.* τὸ ὄνομα ἀναγράφεται 54, 37; ἐν ταῖς στήλαις ἀναγράφεται 54, 19; εἰς στήλην χαλκῆν ἀναγράφονται 53, 25; ἀναγεγραμμένα 47, 31
ἀνάγω· ἀνήγαγον 12, 36 (Solon); ἀνάγουσι (?) 49, 3 (Blass)
*ἀνάγωγος (?) 49, 3
ἀνάδαστα ποιήσειν, πάντ' 11, 11; τὴν χώραν ἀνάδαστον ποιοῦσιν
ἀναθήματα 7, 20
ἀναιρῶ· (1) ἀνελόντες τὰ ὅπλα 15, 20; (2) τοὺς—ἀπογιγνομένους ἀναιροῦσιν 50, 14; (3) τὰς προσκλήσεις ἀνεῖλον 29, 24; ὅρους ἀνεῖλον 12, 33 (Solon); (4) τοὺς συκοφάντας ἀνῄρουν 35, 20; ἀνεῖλεν πολλούς 25, 6; ἀνελόντες τοὺς ἀναιτίους 18, 31; ἀνέλωσιν 40, 15; πολλοὺς ἀνῃρηκέναι 19, 3; ἀνῃρήκεσαν 35, 26; *pass.* ἀνῃρέθη 25, 23; ἀναιρεθέντος 37, 14; (5) ἀνεῖλεν ἡ Πυθία 25, 6
ἀναιτίους, ἀνελόντες τοὺς 18, 31
ἀνακαλεσαμένη 8, 9
ἀνάκειται, εἰκὼν 7, 21; cf. ἀνατίθημι
[ἀνακη]ρύττει col. 36, 14
*ἀνακράζω· πρῶτος ἐπὶ τοῦ βήματος ἀνέκραγε (Cleon) 28, 17
Ἀνακρέων 18, 5
ἀνακρίνοντες (=ἐρωτῶντες) 11, 3; ἀνακρίνας (forensic term) 48, 23; 56, 30
ἀναλαμβάνω· (τὴν ἀρχήν) 16, 35
ἀναλίσκειν ἐκ τοῦ ναυκραρικοῦ ἀργυρίου 8, 17 (decree); εἰς τὸ δέον ἀναλίσκηται 30, 20 (decree). *met.* ὥστε ἀναλίσκεσθαι τοὺς ἐπιεικεῖς 26, 11
ἀναλογίζηται τὸν ἑκατέρου βίον, ἐάν τις 17, 7
ἀνάλογον τῷ μεγέθει τοῦ τιμήματος 7, 14
ἀνάλωμα 22, 34; 56, 24
ἀναμίσγεσθαι 21, 11; ἀναμεῖξαι 21, 4 (ἀναμιγνύναι *Rhet.*, ἀναμιχθῶσι *Pol.*)
ἀναμφισβήτητον τὴν πολιτείαν, ποιοῦντες 35, 13
ἀναξίοις, ἐν οὕτω μικροῖς καὶ 6, 18
ἀναπληρῶ· ἀνεπληρώθη 10, 6
ἀνάπτει, τὴν αἰτίαν 5, 19 (not thus used in Ar.)
ἀναρχίαν ἐποίησαν 13, 5
ἀνασώσασθαι—τὴν ἀρχὴν 15, 9
ἀνατίθημι· ἀναθήσειν ἀνδριάντα 7, 5; 55, 32; ἀνέθηκε 7, 23 (anon.)
ἀναφέρω· τὰς ἐκτίσεις εἰς πόλιν 8, 23
ἀνδάνει 12, 24 (Solon); ἥνδανεν 12, 50 (Solon)
ἀνδραποδιστής 52, 3; *Frag.* 504^2, p. 1560 *b* 35
ἀνδραπόδων (δίκαι) 52, 16
ἀνδρειότερος 14, 10, 12
ἀνδριάντα, ἀναθήσειν 7, 5; 55, 32
*ἀνερωτήσας 55, 19
ἄνευ μισθοφορᾶς 30, 5 (decree); προχειροτονίας 43, 41; δικαστηρίου γνώσεως 45, 4
ἀνέχων (?) col. 31, 27
ἀνήρ· ἀνδρὸς Ἀργείου 17, 13; τελευτήσαντος τοῦ ἀνδρός 56, 41; χορηγοὺς—ἀνδράσιν 56, 11, 12
Ἀνθεμίων, Διφίλου 7, 23
*ἀνθίστημι· ἀντέστη τοῖς γνωρίμοις ὁ δῆμος 5, 2; τῆς βουλῆς ἀντιστάσης 20, 12
ἄνθρωπος 16, 22; 27, 24
ἀνίεσθαι—τὴν πολιτείαν 26, 2; ἀνεθεὶς 12, 12 (Solon)
ἀνοίγειν, τὰς θυρίδας εἰς τὴν ὁδὸν 50, 13; τὸν πίνακα 49, 12
*ἀνοικοδόμησις, τειχῶν 23, 17
*ἀνοικοδομῶ· ἀνῳκοδόμησε (τὸ Ἐπιλύκειον) 3, 29
ἀνταποδοθεισῶν (?) 3, 13
ἀνταράξας 12, 14 (Solon)
*ἀντεγγράφω· ἀντενέγραφον 36, 15
ἀντὶ 7, 24 (anon.); τῶν τεττάρων 21, 4; τετρακοσίων 21, 7; τῶν ναυκραριῶν 21, 21
*ἀντιγράφεται 54, 15, 20
*ἀντιδημαγωγῶν 27, 12
ἀντίδικος 53, 9; col. 35, 33; col. 36, 28
ἀντίδοσις 56, 14; 61, 9
Ἀντίδοτος ἄρχων (451/0) 26, 21
*ἀντικαθημένων ἀλλήλοις 5, 3
ἀντιλαμβάνεσθαι τῆς ἡγεμονίας 24, 2
ἀντιλέξαι 14, 9
*ἀντιστασιώτης 14, 3; 28, 8
Ἀντιφῶν 32, 10
Ἄνυτος 27, 25; 34, 23
ἀνύτω· ἤνυσα 12, 12 (Solon); οὐδὲν ἤνυσεν 14, 16 (ἀνύειν *Rhet.* 1409 *b* 4)
ἄξιος 63, 14 &c.
ἀξιοῦν 14, 15; ἠξίουν 37, 18
ἀξίωμα 23, 8; *pl.* 18, 1; 35, 24
ἀπαγαγὼν—ἐπὶ τὴν βουλήν 40, 11; τοὺς ἀπαγομένους κλέπτας 52, 2

ἀπαγωγήν, ἔνδειξιν—καὶ 29, 26 (decree); not used thus in Ar.
*ἀπαλείφω (of debts) 47, 34; 48, 2
ἀπαλλάξῃ τοὺς κατηγόρους 55, 26
ἀπαντῶ· ἀπήντησεν ὡς ἀπολογησάμενος 16, 33
ἅπαξ ἄρξαι 31, 18 (decree); προεδρεύειν 44, 14
ἀπαρκεῖ 12, 4 (Solon)
ἅπας· ἅπαντες 3, 31; ἐξ Ἀθηναίων ἁπάντων (opp. ἀφ' ἑκάστης τῆς φυλῆς) 57, 3; ἐξ ἁπ. Ἀθ. 56, 8; ἐξ ἁπ. 56, 8 (?)
ἄπειμι (*absum*)· ἀπῇ 34, 8
ἄπειμι (*abibo*)· ἀπιέναι 34, 8; 42, 35
ἀπείρων τοῦ πολεμεῖν, στρατηγῶν 26, 9
ἀπέρχομαι· ἀπελθόντας 52, 25; πάλιν εἰς παῖδας ἀπέρχονται 42, 6
ἀπεχθάνεσθαι 11, 3; ἀπεχθέσθαι 6, 15; 11, 14; ἀπεχθόμενος 28, 39
ἀπέχω· οὐδενὸς ἀπείχοντο 35, 22
ἄπιστος, πᾶσιν ἦν 19, 3
ἁπλοῦν, ἀποτίνεται 54, 11
ἁπλῶς, ἀρχαϊκῶς καὶ λίαν 14, 23; μὴ ἁ. μηδὲ σαφῶς 9, 7
ἀπὸ *passim*. (1) 'beginning with', ἀπὸ Κλεοφῶντος 28, 25; ἀπὸ—τοῦ λ 63, 10; cf. ἀφ' οὗ *neut.* 17, 2; *masc.*? 18, 7; ἀφ' ὧν 27, 22. (2) the source from which, ἀπὸ τῶν φόρων 24, 11; τῶν γιγνομένων 16, 12. (3) the derivation of a name, τῶν τόπων κτλ 13, 25; 21, 22. (4) interchangeable with ἐξ, ἐκ τοῦ κτήματος, οὐκ ἀπὸ τῶν στελεχῶν 60, 14; ἀφ' <ἑκάστης τῆς> φυλῆς opp. ἐξ ἁπάντων 61, 2; ἀπὸ <τῆς> φυλῆς ἑκάστης 43, 6. (5) proleptic, μὴ κατελθεῖν τοὺς ἀπὸ Φυλῆς 38, 15.—ἀπὸ τοῦ κυάμου 24, 20; ὁ ἀπὸ τοῦ τυπάνου 45, 7; ἀποστήσας ἀπὸ τῶν ὅπλων 18, 27
ἀποβαλεῖν Πύλον 27, 26
ἀπογιγνομένους, ἐκ ταῖς ὁδοῖς 50, 14 (not in Ar. in this sense)
ἀπογιγνώσκω· *ἀπέγνωσαν ποιεῖν* 41, 30
*ἀπογραφή· (1) ἀπογραφὴν εἶναι 39, 13 (decree); ἀναβαλλομένων τὴν ἀ. 40, 3; τὰς ὑπολοίπους ἡμέρας τῆς ἀ. 40, 6; (2) τὰς ἀπογραφὰς τῶν δημευομένων 43, 20
ἀπογράφω· *mid.* πρὶν ἂν ἀπογράψηται πάλιν 39, 18; *pass.* τὰ ἀπογραφέντα καὶ πραθέντα 47, 22; τὰ ἀπογραφόμενα χωρία 52, 6
ἀποδειξάμενοι 42, 30
ἀποδέκται· esp. 48, 1—12; also 47, 32; 50, 3; 52, 18
*ἀποδημία· 11, 4; 13, 1
ἀποδημῶν 53, 32; τοῖς ἀποδημοῦσιν 39, 16 (decree); Σόλωνος ἀποδημήσαντος 13, 2
ἀποδίδωμι· ἀποδιδόασι 43, 33; 48, 4; 60, 7; 62, 5; col. 32, 20; ἀποδιδόναι 40, 21; ἀποδιδούς 7, 14; 20, 4; col. 36, 1; ἀποδιδόντες col. 37, 3; ἀποδώσειν 11, 12; ἀπέδωκεν 25, 10; ἀπέδοσαν 40, 20; ἀποδῷ 52, 13; ἀποδῶσι 56, 46; ἀποδοῦναι 39, 26; 47, 24; 58, 8; ἀπεδέδοτο 4, 4
ἀποδοκιμάσαι 45, 19; 55, 27; ἀποδοκιμάσειεν 55, 11
ἀποθνήσκειν 45, 3, 5; ἀπέθανε 17, 1, 18; ἀποθανεῖν 18, 33; ἀποθανόντος 40, 16
ἀπόκειται χωρὶς 47, 34
ἀποκοπή, χρεῶν 6, 11; 10, 2; 12, 26; 13, 13; *pl.* 6, 3; 11, 9 (ἀποκοπαὶ—ὀνομάτων *Poet.* 1458 *b* 1)
ἀποκρίνομαι· ἀπεκρίνατο 16, 22
ἀποκτείνω· ἀπέκτεινον 35, 23; ἀπέκτεινεν 39, 19; ἀπέκτειναν 18, 20; 38, 12; ἀποκτείνῃ 57, 15, 17; ἀποκτεῖναι 37, 7; 40, 12; 45, 2; 57, 18, 22
ἀπολαμβάνω· col. 33, 17; 37, 6
ἀπολαύειν, τῆς ὀπώρας 27, 18
ἀπολειπόμενος, ἀπολείπεσθαι, conj. for ἐπι-, *q.v.*
ἀπολλύναι, τὰ ὑπάρχοντα 56, 36; *mid.* ἀπόλλυσθαι 26, 11
Ἀπόλλων πατρῷος 55, 21; frag. 1
ἀπολογεῖται 57, 23, 29; ἀπολογησάμενος 16, 33 (only in *Rhet. ad Alex.*)
ἀπολογία 55, 21
*ἀπομετροῦσι (τὸ ἔλαιον) 60, 19
*ἀπομιμησάμενος, τὴν θεὸν 14, 27
ἀπονέμω· τὰς—ἀρχὰς ἀπένειμεν ἄρχειν 7, 11 (τὰς ἀρχὰς—τούτοις ἀπονέμειν *Pol.* 1309 *a* 21)
ἀπορία 13, 22
ἄπορος 16, 6
ἀποσεισαμένων τὸ βάρος 6, 5
*ἀποστασίου 58, 9
ἀπόστασις (*trans.*) τῶν Ἰώνων 23, 18
ἀποστέλλων τὴν πομπὴν 18, 16; ἐφ' ἑκάστῃ τῶν ἀρχῶν—ἀπέστελλεν 8, 11; ἀπέστειλαν, Ἀγχίμολον 19, 26; Καλλίβιον 37, 18; *pass.* ἀποστέλλονται ἀρχαὶ εἰς Σάμον 62, 16
ἀποστερῇ, δανεισάμενος 52, 14; ἀπεστερήθη τῆς ἐπιμελείας 26, 2
ἀποτίμημα 56, 45
ἀποτίνει 60, 13; ἀπέτινον 4, 18; παθεῖν ἢ ἀποτεῖσαι 61, 13; 63, 15; ἀποτίνεται 54, 8, 9, 10
ἀποτυγχάνοντες 19, 9
ἀποφαίνω· οὐσίαν 4, 8; νόμον 4, 22; τῷ δήμῳ 46, 9; *mid.* ἀποφαινόμενος 12, 10; 28, 35; ἀποφαίνονται τὰς διαίτας 55, 29. Cf. οὐκ ἀποφαίνοντος τὴν οὐσίαν *Pol.* 1303 *b* 35
*ἀποφέρω· λόγον ἀπενεγκεῖν 54, 4
ἀποφεύγω· of acquittal, ἀπέφυγεν 27, 27; 45, 6; ἀποφύγῃ 59, 9; 61, 14; ἀποφύγωσι 52, 5. Opp. ἀμύνεσθαι *de Part. An.* 663 *a* 13
*ἀποχειροτονῶ· 49, 6, 7; 61, 12
ἀποχωρήσαντες, κακῶς 37, 3
ἀποψηφίσωνται μὴ εἶναι ἐλεύθερον 42, 8; ἀπεψηφισμένους ὑπὸ τῶν δημοτῶν 59, 12

ἀπροβούλευτος 45, 22
*ἀπροστασίου 58, 9
ἄπωθεν τῆς τυραννίδος 22, 28
Ἀργεῖος 17, 13; *pl.* 17, 15; 19, 25. Ἀργείας (γυναικός) 17, 11; τὴν Ἀργείαν 17, 17
Ἀργινούσαις, ἐν 34, 3
Ἄργος 17, 13
ἀργός, σῖτος 51, 11
ἀργύριον 8, 18; 22, 31; 62, 17; ἐὰν ἀργυρίου τιμηθῇ 63, 15; ἀργύρια 60, 21
Ἀρείου πάγου, βουλὴ ἡ ἐξ 4, 20; ἡ ἐξ Ἀρείου πάγου βουλή 41, 16; 60, 11; Ἀρείῳ πάγῳ, βουλὴ ἡ ἐν 8, 9; 23, 3; ἐξ Ἀρείου πάγου 35, 11; 47, 13; 59, 18; ἐν Ἀρείῳ πάγῳ 57, 15, 24; εἰς Ἄρειον πάγον 16, 33; 60, 17
Ἀρεοπαγῖται 3, 38; 8, 19; 25, 3, 7, 12, 21; 27, 4; 35, 10; ἡ τῶν Ἀρεοπαγιτῶν βουλή 3, 34; 4, 22; 26, 1
*Ἀρεοπαγῖτιν βουλήν, τὴν 41, 8
ἀρέσκῃ, ἐὰν 22, 34; 53, 8
ἀρετή 36, 10
ἀριθμός 41, 6; col. 36, 26, 32
Ἀρίσταιχμος ἄρχων (621/0) 4, 2
Ἀριστείδης 22, 39; 23, 13, 19; 24, 10; 28, 11; 41, 17
ἀριστίνδην 1, 1; καὶ πλουτίνδην 3, 2, 37
Ἀριστίων 14, 4
Ἀριστογείτων 18, 13, 22; 58, 3
Ἀριστόδικος 25, 24
Ἀριστοκράτης 33, 10
Ἀριστόμαχος 32, 3
ἄριστον, ἵν' ἐξ ἁπάντων αἱρῶνται τὸ 29, 15; βουλεύσωνται τὸ 29, 19; ᾗ ἂν δοκῇ αὐτοῖς ἄριστα ἕξειν 30, 20; ὡς ἂν δύνωνται ἄριστα 30, 21 (all in decrees)
ἅρματος, ἐφ' 14, 29 (*de Mundo* 400 *b* 6, *de Xenoph.* 980 *a* 12)
Ἁρμόδιος 18, 8, 12, 13, 21; 58, 3
ἁρμόσας 12, 46 (Solon)
*ἁρμοστής 37, 19
ἁρπαγαῖσιν 12, 17 (Solon)
Ἁρπακτίδης ἄρχων (511/0) 19, 37
Ἄρτεμις ἀγροτέρα 58, 1
ἄρτιος 12, 14, 18 (Solon)
ἄρτος, ἀρτοπῶλαι, 51, 12, 13
ἀρχαϊκῶς καὶ λίαν ἁπλῶς 14, 23
ἀρχαῖος χαρακτήρ 10, 6; τῆς ἀρχαίας πολιτείας 3, 1; τὸ ἀρχαῖον 8, 9; τῶν ἀρχαίων 7, 21
ἀρχαιρεσίαι 44, 16
Ἀρχέστρατος 35, 10
ἀρχή (1) 'beginning', 5, 6; 41, 13; ἐξ ἀρχῆς 3, 6 (?); 16, 1; 28, 5; 41, 7; 55, 3; ἐν ἀρχῇ 5, 20; ἀρχὴν ('motive') καὶ πρόφασιν 13, 13; ἀρχὴν—κακῶν 18, 8; κατ' ἀρχάς 35, 18
(2) 'rule', 'office', 'official'; the last two combined in 3, 4, πρῶται τῶν ἀρχῶν ἦσαν βασιλεὺς κτλ· τούτων δὲ πρώτη μὲν ἡ τοῦ βασιλέως. *Sing.* 3, 18; 7, 15, 30; 8, 14; 13, 4, 7, 12; 14, 17, 18; 15, 9; 16, 25, 28; 16, 35 (?); 17, 1, 4, 9, 18; 18, 4; 24, 6, 8; 36, 11; 41, 20; 55, 34; τῆς ἀρχῆς ἕνεκα 55, 32; ἀρχὴν ἄρχων τινά 53, 31. *Pl.* ἀρχαὶ ἔνδημοι, ὑπερόριοι, 24, 16; αἱ πρὸς τὸν πόλεμον ἀρχαί 43, 5; 44, 17; 61, 1; αἱ κατὰ πόλεμον ἀ. 62, 18; ἀ. κληρωταί 8, 1, 5; 30, 13 (decree); 43, 2; 55, 1; 62, 1; κληρούμεναι, ἐκ τῆς ὅλης φυλῆς 62, 2; ἐν Θησείῳ 62, 2; ἀρχαὶ εἰς Σάμον κτλ 62, 16; τῶν ἀρχῶν 3, 38; 8, 10; ταῖς ἀρχαῖς 48, 8, 14; 59, 3, 11; τὰς ἀρχὰς καθίστασαν 3, 2; ἐποίησε κληρωτάς 8, 1; αἱρουμένων τὰς ἀ. 3, 20; διετήρει τὰς ἀ. 4, 21; περὶ τὰς ἀ. 3, 33; 9, 2; ἀρχὰς—ἄρχειν 7, 11; 54, 4; ἀμίσθους 29, 30 (decree)
*ἀρχηγέται, ἑκατὸν 21, 25
ἀρχιθέωρος, εἰς Δῆλον 56, 20 (οὐ τὸ αὐτὸ δαπάνημα τριηράρχῳ καὶ ἀρχιθεώρῳ *Eth.* 1122 *a* 24)
Ἀρχῖνος 34, 23; 40, 4
Ἀρχῖνος Ἀμπρακιώτης 17, 14
ἀρχιτέκτονες—ἐπὶ τὰς ναῦς 46, 4
ἄρχω· (1) 'begin', ἡγούμενοι τοῦτο πρῶτον ἄρχειν δεῖν τῆς ὁμονοίας 40, 23; *mid.* ἤρξατο 27, 24; 40, 11; ἀρξάμενοι 62, 13. (2) 'rule', or 'hold office', ἄρχει 47, 4; 61, 14; ἄρχουσι 43, 4; 50, 5; ἄρχωσι 4, 21; ἄρχειν 4, 16; 24, 9; 29, 31; 39, 17; 62, 18; ἦρχεν 55, 11; ἦρχον 3, 2; ἄρξειν 55, 31; ἦρξεν 13, 7; 19, 39; *pass.* τὴν ἀρχὴν—τῶν ἀρχομένων ἥττω 36, 11
ἄρχων esp. 56, 5—46; also 3, 5, 9, 13, 16, 27; 13, 6, 11; 14, 8; 17, 2; 17, 8; 55, 5; Solon 5, 4; Lygdamis 15, 15. ἐπὶ—ἄρχοντος about 20 times; Νικομήδους ἄρχοντος 22, 29; ἄρχοντος Ὑψηχίδου 22, 40. For list of archons, see *English Index.* (=εἷς τῶν ἀρχόντων) col. 31, 17, 24, 35; τῷ ἄρχοντι τῷ ἐφεστηκότι col. 31, 28
ἄρχοντες, οἱ ἐννέα 7, 4, 12; 8, 3, 8; 22, 21; 29, 31; 30, 6; 45, 18; 47, 15; 55, 2; 59, 19; 62, 2, 10; 63, 1; cf. 3, 11, 24. αἵρεσις τῶν ἀρχόντων 3, 37; 26, 13; ᾑροῦντο τοὺς—ἄρχοντας 4, 5; ἄρχοντας ἑλέσθαι δέκα 13, 8; ἐκ ζευγιτῶν 26, 15; τῶν ἀρχόντων καὶ τῶν ἐπωνύμων 53, 20.—ἄρχοντες εἰς τὰ φρούρια 30, 7 (decree); τοῦ Πειραιέως—δέκα 35, 6
ἀσαφεῖς 9, 11
ἀσεβείας, γραφὴ 57, 10
ἀσεβήσαιεν 18, 30
ἀσελγείας—παύσασθαι 36, 2
ἀσθενεῖς 18, 31
Ἀσκληπίῳ, πομπὴ 56, 21
ἀσκῶν 23, 14 (*n. c.*); ἀσκῆσαι 23, 10
ἀσπίς 42, 31; 60, 22
ἀστός· ἐξ ἀμφοῖν ἀστοῖν—γεγονώς 26, 23; ἐξ ἀμφοτέρων—ἀστῶν 42, 3

ἄστυ· οἱ ἐν τῷ ἄστει 14, 30; τὰ ἐν τῷ ἄ. 19, 5; εἰς τὸ ἄστυ 6, 15; 39, 7 (decree); 51, 18; τῶν ἐκ τοῦ ἄστεως 19, 13; περὶ τὸ ἄστυ 21, 13; ἐν τῷ ἄστει 16, 8 (opp. κατὰ τὴν χώραν); 24, 3 (opp. ἐκ τῶν ἀγρῶν); 27, 9; 39, 18; οἱ ἐκ τοῦ ἄστεως (opp. οἱ ἐκ Πειραιέως) 38, 3; 39, 7; 40, 22; τῶν ἐν ἄστει μεινάντων 38, 30; 39, 1 (decree); τῶν ἐν τῷ ἀ. 39, 17 (decree); τοὺς ἐν τῷ ἀ. 39, 24 (decree).—ἐν ἄστει 50, 5; εἰς ἄστυ 51, 2

ἀστυνόμοι 50, 4

*ἀτακτοῦντα 61, 15

ἅτε—ἔχων 27, 13

ἀτελής 56, 16; ἁπάντων 16, 24; πάντων 42, 34; ἀτελεῖς 53, 32.—ἀτελὲς χωρίον 16, 18

ἄτιμος 8, 30; 16, 44; 22, 42; 53, 30; 63, 12

*ἀτιμοῦσθαι (τὸν διαιτητὴν) 53, 34

Ἀττικήν, εἰς τὴν 19, 31; γλῶσσαν—Ἀττικὴν 12, 38 (Solon); Ἀττικὸν ἐμπόριον 51, 17

ἀτυχῶ· ἠτύχησαν—ναυμαχίαν 34, 15

αὐθημερὸν (*e conj.*) 45, 2

αὖθις 12, 51 (Solon). Not in *Index.*

αὐλητής 62, 11

*αὐλητρίδες 50, 6

αὐλίσκον ἔχουσαι, ψῆφοι col. 35, 27; ἐπιλαμβάνει τὸν αὐλίσκον (τῆς κλεψύδρας) col. 34, 36

αὐξανομένη, κατὰ μικρὸν 23, 2; -ου τοῦ πλήθους 25, 3; (ἀρχὴ) τοῖς ἐπιθέτοις αὐξηθεῖσα 3, 18

αὔξησις 10, 4

αὐτοκράτορας, ἄρχειν 31, 13 (decree); τῶν δέκα τῶν α. (411) 32, 13; α.—τοὺς τριάκοντα—ἀποκτεῖναι 37, 6; δέκα—αὐτοκράτορας 38, 5; α. ἑαυτῶν 39, 4 (decree)

αὐτόματον, τὸ 8, 28

αὐτός 6, 20; 12, 2; 14, 13; 15, 25; 16, 14, 33; αὐτοί 2, 4, 7; αὐτοὶ δι' αὐτῶν 19, 9.—αὐτὴν μόνην χωρεῖν τὴν ψῆφον col. 36, 8.—τοῦ αὐτοῦ 4, 12

αὐτοτελεῖς κρίνειν 3, 32; 53, 5

αὐτόχειρ 39, 19 (decree). *Frag.* 1553 *b* 32

ἀφαιρῶ· ἀφελὼν 12, 5 (Solon); τὰς προσούσας δυσκολίας—ἀφεῖλον 35, 16; *pass.* οἱ ἀφῃρημένοι τὰ χρέα 13, 22; τοὺς ἀφαιρεθέντας (?) 25, 16; *mid.* ἀφείλετο, 'deprived of' 34, 1; 45, 7; 'rescued' 45, 4

ἀφανίσαι, τοὺς νόμους 22, 3

*ἀφέσιμος (ἡμέρα) 43, 13

ἄφεσιν, εὑρόμενος 30, 33 (decree)

Ἀφιδναῖος 34, 37

ἀφίημι· (1) καταπαλτὴν ἀφιέναι 42, 24; (ἐκκλησίαν ἀφεῖναι 44, 13; (2) 'release', ἀφεῖσαν ὑποσπόνδους 20, 15; τοῦτον ἀφιᾶσιν 49, 16, 19; ἀφέντας τοῦτον 40, 14; ἀφήσοντας 52, 5; (3) 'cede', τὴν ἀρχὴν τῆς θαλάττης ἀφήσουσι 32, 17; ἀφῶσι τὰς πόλεις 34, 12

ἀφικέσθαι 38, 23; ἀφικομένου 38, 24; -ων 38, 26

ἀφίστημι· ἀποστήσας ἀπὸ τῶν ὅπλων τοὺς πομπεύοντας 18, 26; οὕτως ἀπέστησαν 32, 17; ἀποστάντος—τοῦ δήμου πρὸς αὐτούς 38, 16; Εὐβοίας ἀποστάσης 33, 4

ἀφνεόν, ἐλπίδ' 12, 17 (Solon)

ἀφορμήν, δανείζηται 52, 15

*ἄφρακτα, χωρία 27, 17

Ἀχερδούσιος 38, 22

ἀψύχων, δίκαι 57, 31

βαδίζει εἰς τὸ δικαστήριον col. 32, 11; βαδίζουσι πρὸς τὸν λίθον 55, 28; εἰς ἀκρόπολιν 55, 33

βακτηρία 63, 6, 8; col. 32, 3, 10, 16; col. 37, 3

βάλανοι, *sortes*, 63, 8, 9; col. 31, 32; 32, 5, 13 (not found elsewhere in this sense)

βάλλουσι, τοὺς κύβους col. 32, 33; βάλλῃ col. 36, 10

βάρβαροι 22, 38

βάρος 6, 5

βασιλεία 3, 12

*βασίλειος στοά, ἡ 7, 4

βασιλεύς, king of Persia, 29, 4, 8. ὁ βασιλεύς, archon, esp. 57, 1—31; also 3, 4, 5, 17, 24; 19, 7, 30; col. 33, 28; τῆς τοῦ βασιλέως γυναικός 3, 26. τῶν βασιλέων, early Attic kings, 3, 7; ὁ β. of Pausanias king of Sparta 38, 25. Ἡρακλείδης, ὁ β. ἐπικαλούμενος 41, 34

βασιλικῆς (πολιτείας) 41, 11

βεβαίως 15, 14; 38, 12

βελτίω, opp. χείρω 28, 1. τὸ βέλτιστον 9, 13; 35, 19; τοῦ βελτίστου χάριν 35, 21; βέλτιστοι (?) γεγονέναι 28, 28; μεταδοῦναι τῶν πραγμάτων τοῖς βελτίστοις 36, 3; βελτίστους 38, 19; 42, 16; τὰ βέλτιστα νομοθετήσας 11, 15; βέλτιστα—τῇ πόλει 29, 13 (decree)

*βῆμα 28, 17

βίᾳ 13, 7.; 15, 9

βιαζόμενος 12, 12 (Solon)

βίαιον τὴν ἀρχὴν 36, 11

βίος, ὁ ἐπὶ Κρόνου 16, 27; διὰ βίου 3, 3, 39; τῷ βίῳ θρασύς 18, 7; τὸν ἑκατέρου βίον 17, 8

βιώσας (?)=βιούς 17, 3

βλασφημεῖν 6, 9; cf. Ar. *Dial.* frag. 1481 *a* 35 (κατὰ τῶν τετελευτηκότων) βλασφημεῖν οὐχ ὅσιον

βλέποντες, πρὸς τὸ παραυτίκα 28, 28

βοήθειαν 19, 21; 38, 8; ταῖς εἰς τὰ ἴδια βοηθείαις 16, 38

βοηθῶ 14, 13; 19, 28; 37, 17; 38, 2

*βουκολεῖον 3, 25

βουλεύσεως 57, 17; γραφή 59, 10

βουλευτήριον 32, 14; 48, 3, 10; 53, 26 (only in corresponding frag. and in *Rhet. ad Alex.*)

βουλευτής 4, 17; 35, 4; 45, 17; 48, 13; 49, 17; 62, 4

βουλεύω· inf. 4, 13; 45, 18; (*ἔξεστι*) *βουλεῦσαι δὶς* 62, 19. (In decrees) 30, 4, 16, 19; 31, 2; and *ἐκ τῶν ἀεὶ βουλευόντων* 30, 12; also *mid. βουλεύεσθαι* (*e conj.*) 30, 19; *μετὰ πλειόνων βουλεύσασθαι* 30, 22; *βουλεύσωνται τὸ ἄριστον* 29, 19

βουλή, ἡ τῶν Ἀρεοπαγιτῶν, 3, 34; 4, 22; 26, 1; *ἡ ἐξ Ἀρείου πάγου* 4, 20; 60, 11; *ἡ ἐν Ἀρείῳ πάγῳ β.* 8, 9; 23, 3; *τὴν Ἀρεοπαγῖτιν βουλὴν* 41, 18; *ἡ βουλή* 25, 14; 57, 16; *τῆς βουλῆς* 25, 8; *τὴν βουλὴν* 25, 13; *βουλῆς ἕδρα* 4, 17; cf. 30, 24; *β.* (*τετρακόσιοι*) 8, 18; 20, 10 f; *β.* (*οἱ πεντακόσιοι*) esp. 43, 6 ff; and 45—49: 21, 7; 22, 7; 24, 14; *συναθροισθείσης τῆς β.* 25, 20; *αἱ τῆς β. κρίσεις εἰς τὸν δῆμον ἐληλύθασιν* 41, 27; *ἡ β. δοκιμάζει τοὺς ἐγγραφέντας* 42, 12; *κυρία—ζημιῶσαι, δῆσαι, ἀποκτεῖναι* 45, 1; (*μισθοφορεῖ*) *πέντε ὀβολούς* 62, 8.—*βουλὰς τέτταρας* 30, 14 (decree 411)

βούλησις 9, 14

βουλόμενος c. inf. 11, 3; 12, 16; 18, 18; 21, 5 f; 22, 17; 25, 12; *οἱ βουλόμενοι βλασφημεῖν* 6, 9; *τῷ βουλομένῳ* 9, 4; 27, 17; *τῷ β. Λακιαδῶν* 27, 15; *τῶν ἄλλων τῷ β.* 29, 14; *τοὺς β. Ἀθηναίων* 39, 2 (decree): *βούλεσθαι* 15, 4; *ἐβούλετο* 11, 13; *ἐβούλοντο* 16, 36

**βραβεύειν* 9, 9 (*βραβευτὴς Rhet.* 1376 *b* 20)

Βραυρωνία, πεντετηρίς, 54, 30

βραχέος, χρόνου 35, 25

βωμόν, καθίζει—ἐπὶ τὸν 25, 19

γαῖαν 5, 8 (Solon)

γάλα 12, 64 (Solon)

γαμετῆς γυναικὸς 4, 9; *ἐκ τῆς γαμετῆς* 17, 10 (*Frag.* 172^{2})

γάμος 3, 27

γαμῶ· ἔγημεν 17, 12; *γῆμαι* 17, 17

γάρ passim. After *σημεῖον δὲ* 7, 21; 8, 7. *καὶ γὰρ* 22, 2; 41, 27; *καὶ γὰρ—καὶ* 19, 2; 27, 4. In third place, *μὲν γὰρ—δὲ* 3, 9; 11, 10; 14, 10; 16, 37; 24, 12; 28, 5; 40, 14; 41, 6; 47, 2; *τε γὰρ—καὶ* 16, 4, 31; 19, 10; *κατὰ ταύτην γὰρ* 2, 25; *ἐπ᾽ ἐκείνου γὰρ* 10, 4; *ἐπὶ πέρας γὰρ* 38, 24. In fourth place *ἔτι καὶ νῦν γὰρ* 3, 25; *καθ᾽ ὅ τι γὰρ* 59, 3

γεγωνῶ· ἵνα γεγωνῇ μᾶλλον 15, 19

**γεννῆται* frag. 3

γένος 1, 3; 16, 44; 20, 3; 28, 8; *κατὰ τὸ γ.* 42, 36; *τῷ γένει μὴ καθαροὶ* 13, 22; *τῷ γένει—προέχοντες* 35, 23; *τὰ γένη* 21, 6, 23; *τοῖς γένεσι* 57, 11

Γεραιστός 22, 42

γέρας 12, 4 (Solon); *ὑπὲρ [τῶν γε]ρῶν* 57, 12

**γεωμόροι* frag. 2, 14

γεωργῶ· ἐγεώργουν 13, 26; *γεωργοῦντα* 16, 17; *-τας* 16, 7

γῆ 2, 6; 12, 15 &c. *κατὰ γῆν* 19, 30. *Γῆ μέλαινα* 12, 32 (Solon)

γήρως <*ἕνεκα*> 35, 16 (law of Solon)

γίγνομαι (often spelt *γιν-* in papyrus) 2, 8 *n. c.*; 16, 11; *τί γίγνεται*; 16, 20; *τοιαύτης ἐξόδου γιγνομένης* 16, 17; *τοῖς ὑπὸ τῶν τετρακοσίων γιγνομένοις* 33, 11; cf. 35, 21. *ἐγένετο* 15, 1; *γενέσθαι* 11, 10; *γεγενῆσθαι* 18, 8; *γεγενημένων εὖ* 32, 10. *γέγονε* 3, 18; 42, 7; 54, 19; *γεγόνασιν* 53, 5; *γεγονέναι* 13, 14 f; 28, 28, 31; 42, 5; 56, 18 f; *γεγονώς* 26, 23; *-ός* 15, 24; 25, 19; *-ότες* 42, 3; *-ότας* 29, 38; 30, 5; *-όσιν* 63, 11

γιγνώσκω (often spelt *γιν-* in papyrus) 5, 7 (Solon). *γιγνώσκουσι* ('decide') 53, 7; *ἔγνωσαν c. inf.* 26, 15, 22; 37, 3. *c. acc.* 34, 14; *ὅ τι ἂν γνῶσιν οἱ δικασταί* 48, 27. *τὸ γνωσθὲν* 54, 7; *τοὺς ἐγνωσμένους* 36, 14

γλῶσσαν—Ἀττικὴν 12, 38 (Solon)

γνάθος (*ἵππου*) 48, 4

γνησίους, παῖδας 4, 9

γνώμη—διαφέρειν 32, 11. *γνώμην, γράψαντος* 14, 5; 29, 7; *γνώμας ἐπιψηφίζουσιν* 48, 12

γνώριμοι ('friends') 6, 7; opp. to *δῆμος*, 2, 1; 5, 2; 11, 8, 11; 16, 36; 28, 7, 10; 34, 19

γνώσεως, δικαστηρίου 45, 5; *γνῶσιν διαιτητοῦ* 53, 12 (not used thus in Ar.)

γονέων κακώσεως 56, 30; *γονέας εἰ εὖ ποιεῖ* 55, 17

Γοργίλος Ἀργεῖος 17, 13

γράμμα 63, 19, 21, 22, 24; col. 31, 6, 13, 27; col. 32, 4, 12

γραμματεῖον 47, 16, 19, 20, 27, 30; 48, 2, 4; 53, 13, 22

**γραμματεὺς ὁ κατὰ πρυτανείαν* 54, 13. *ὁ ἐπὶ τοὺς νόμους* 54, 19. (*τοῦ δήμου*) 54, 21. *θεσμοθετῶν* 55, 4, 7; 59, 19; 63, 2. (*στρατηγῶν* in 411) 31, 12 (decree)

γραφαί· ἀγραφίου 59, 10; *ἀδικίου* 54, 10; *ἀσεβείας* 57, 10: *βουλεύσεως* 59, 10; *δωροξενίας* 59, 8; *δώρων* 54, 9; 59, 9; *ἐπιστατική* 59, 6; *κακώσεως* 56, 30—34; *κλοπῆς* (*δημοσίων χρημάτων*) 54, 68; *μοιχείας* 59, 11; *ξενίας* 59, 8; *παρανόμων* 29, 23; 45, 24; 59, 6; *καὶ νόμον μὴ ἐπιτήδειον θεῖναι* 59, 6; *προεδρική* 59, 6; *πυρκαϊᾶς* 57, 16; *τραύματος* (*δίκαι*) 57, 14; *συκοφαντίας* 59, 9; *φαρμάκων* (*δίκη*) 57, 15; *φόνου* (*δίκαι*) 57, 12, 14; *ψευδεγγραφῆς* 59, 10; *ψευδοκλητείας* 59, 10.—*γραφαὶ λαγχάνονται πρὸς αὐτὸν* 57, 9; 56, 29

γράφω· γράφειν 29, 15 (decree); *ἔγραψεν* 29, 17 (decree); 34, 27; *ἔγραψαν* 29, 21; *γράψας εἰς πινάκιον* 48, 20; *-αντος γνώμην* 14, 5; 29, 7; *-αντες* 48, 9;

γέγραπται 8, 17; ἐν ταῖς βαλάνοις 63, 9; γεγράφθαι 9, 7; κατὰ τὰ γεγραμμένα 11, 7. γραψάμενος τὸ ψήφισμα—παρανόμων 40, 8.
γυμνικὸν ἀγῶνα, τὸν 60, 5, 22
γυναῖκα μεγάλην καὶ καλήν 14, 25; ἔσχεν γυναῖκα 17, 14; γυναικός, γαμετῆς 4, 9; παραιβατούσης τῆς γ. 14, 29; γυναικὶ πιθόμενος 35, 16; αἱ γυναῖκες 2, 4; γυναικῶν ἐπιμελεῖται 56, 41

Δαμασίας ἄρχων (c. 582) 13, 6, 10
Δαμωνίδης Οἴῆθεν 27, 19
δανείζειν 6, 2; 9, 3; δανεῖσαι 22, 33; δανειζόμενοι 38, 8; ἐδανείσαντο 39, 25; δανείσηται 52, 14; δανεισάμενος 52, 13; -οι 6, 9; 22, 35
δανεισμοί 2, 8; 4, 23
δαπανή· 8, 15; 22, 35
δαπανῶ· δαπανῆσαι 29, 30 (decree)
* δατητῶν αἵρεσιν, εἰς, 56, 36
δὲ passim. διὰ τοῦτο δὲ 21, 8 f; μετὰ δὲ ταῦτα 2, 1 &c.; πρὸς δὲ τούτοις 26, 6 &c.; καὶ—δὲ 12, 15; 41, 20 (?)
*δεδοικέναι 5, 20 (δεδιότες Ar.)
δεῖ 12, 10; 16, 22; ἔδει 7, 10; (ἔτη) ἑνὸς δέοντα εἴκοσι 17, 4; ἑνὸς δεῖν (δεῖ MS) 19, 39; 27, 7; εἰς τὸ δέον 30, 20 (decree)
δείκνυμι· τὸ γράμμα δείκνυσι col. 31, 27; δείξει—συνισταμένους 25, 15; δείξουσιν εἰ βούλονται 40, 12; οὐ δεικνύων col. 36, 18
δεινός, τὰ πολεμικά, τὰ πολιτικά, 23, 15
δειπνοῦσι, ἐν τῷ πρυτανείῳ 62, 12
δέκα 8, 3 f; ἄρχοντας 13, 8; ἐτῶν 11, 5; εἰς δ. φυλάς 21, 4; δ. (μέρη) 21, 13.
οἱ δέκα· (1) under the Four Hundred, in 411, δ. αὐτοκράτορες 31, 10—12; 32, 13; (2) after the Thirty, in 404, αὐτοκράτορες ἐπὶ τὴν τοῦ πολέμου κατάλυσιν 38, 5; ἡ τῶν δέκα τυραννίς 41, 22 (39, 21); superseded by (3) another Board of Ten, τοὺς βελτίστους εἶναι δοκοῦντας, ἐφ' ὧν συνέβη καὶ τὰς διαλύσεις γενέσθαι καὶ κατελθεῖν τὸν δῆμον 38, 19 f. Other bodies of Ten (in 411), πρόβουλοι 29, 11; (καταλογεῖς) 29, 37; ταμίαι τῶν ἱερῶν χρημάτων and ἐπιμεληταί 30, 8—10 (decree): (in 404) τοῦ Πειραιέως ἄρχοντες δ. 35, 6; δ. διαλλακτῶν 38, 26. For official bodies of Ten under the normal constitution see ἀγορανόμοι, ἀθλοθέται, ἀποδέκται, ἀστυνόμοι, Διονυσίων ἐπιμεληταί, ἐμπορίου ἐπιμεληταί, εὔθυνοι, ἱεροποιοί (*bis*), ἱερῶν ἐπισκευασταί, ἱππέων καταλογεῖς, λογισταί (*bis*), λογιστῶν συνήγοροι, μετρονόμοι, πωληταί, στρατηγοί, σωφρονισταί, ταμίαι τῆς 'Αθηνᾶς, ταξίαρχοι, τριηροποιοί, φύλαρχοι.
* δεκαετίαν, ἦρχον 3, 4
* δεκάζειν 27, 25; δεκάσας τὸ δικαστήριον 27, 27
* δεκαπλοῦν, τὸ γνωσθὲν ἀποτίνεται 54, 8 f; τὸ δ. 54, 12
δεκάτη 16, 13, 22
δέκατος ὁ γραμματεύς 59, 19; τῆς δεκάτης φυλῆς 63, 2
Δεκέλεια 34, 8
Δελφινίῳ, ἐπὶ 57, 21
Δελφοί· ὁ ἐν Δ. νεώς 19, 20
δεξιά· δοῦναι τὴν δ. πίστεως χάριν 18, 35; τὴν δ. δέδωκε 18, 36
δέομαι· ἐὰν μὴ δέωνται πλειόνων 30, 24 (decree); κἄν τι δέωνται ἐπισκευάζουσι τὰ μάλιστα δεόμενα τῶν ἱερῶν 50, 4
δεσμωτηρίου φύλακες 35, 6: ἐν τῷ δ. 52, 2
δεσμωτῶν φύλακες 24, 20
δεσποτικωτέρως 24, 7
δευτέρα 3, 6; δευτέρῳ 14, 7. τὸ δεύτερον 15, 2. οὐδενὸς ὄντα δεύτερον 38, 11
δέχομαι· δέχονται τὰ χρήματα 48, 8; δεχόμενος—τὴν πομπήν 18, 15; ἐδέχοντο 14, 30
δέω· θανατοῦν καὶ δεῖν καὶ χρήμασι ζημιοῦν 45, 8; (ἡ βουλὴ) κυρία—δῆσαι 45, 2 (πρότερον); 48, 7; (στρατηγοί) κύριοι δῆσαι 61, 15; ἀνάγκη τὸ ἐλλειφθὲν καταβάλλειν ἢ δεδέσθαι 48, 6; cf. 63, 16
δή· διὰ ταύτην δὴ τὴν αἰτίαν 23, 8; πρὸς δὴ ταύτην τὴν χορηγίαν 27, 18. *κάλλιστα δὴ* καὶ πολιτικώτατα ἁπάντων 40, 17. καὶ δὴ καὶ 2, 3; 16, 5, 40
δήϊον 12, 21 (Solon)
δῆλον 13, 10; 53, 20
Δῆλον, ἀμφικτύονες εἰς 62, 14; πεντετηρὶς εἰς 54, 29; χορηγοὶ and ἀρχιθέωρος 56, 20
δημαγωγίαν, διεδέχοντο—τὴν 28, 26
δημαγωγός 22, 14
δημαγωγῶ· πρὸς τὸ δημαγωγεῖν ἐλθόντος Περικλέους 27, 1; διετέλουν οἱ ἐπιεικεῖς δημαγωγοῦντες 28, 5; τοὺς προθύμως δημαγωγοῦντας 26, 3
Δημάρετος 38, 11
* δήμαρχοι 21, 19; δήμαρχος, εἰς Πειραιέα 54, 34
δημευομένων, τὰς ἀπογραφὰς τῶν 43, 20
δημηγορῶν 15, 20; ἐδημηγόρησε 28, 18
δήμιος 45, 3
δημιουργοί 13, 9
δημοκρατία 23, 2; 29, 2, 5, 18; 38, 30; 40, 13; 41, 13, 21
δῆμος· (1) *pagus*, τὸ ὄνομα τοῦ δήμου 63, 19; ἐκ τοῦ δ. τῶν Παιανιέων 14, 26; ἐπώλουν οἱ δῆμοι 62, 4; δήμων 21, 16, 21; τῶν δ. ἀναγορεύωσιν 21, 18; καλοῦσιν τῶν δ. 21, 19; πόθεν τῶν δ. 55, 13, 15; δήμους ἀντὶ τῶν ναυκραριῶν 21, 20; κατὰ δήμους 21, 12; 48, 24; οἱ κατὰ δ. δικασταί 16, 3; 26, 21; 53, 3; διῃροῦντο εἰς τοὺς δ. 62, 3
(2) *populus*, 12, 4, 11, 29, 49, 57

(Solon). 5, 2; 6, 1; 9, 12; 11, 10; 15, 14, 16; 18, 29; 20, 4, 13, 16, 17; 21, 1; 25, 1, 10; 29, 10; 34, 1, 7, 19, 26; 35, 19; 36, 6; 38, 17, 20, 28; 41, 2, 4, 5, 25—7; 42, 2, 31; 43, 12, 28. (=ἐκκλησία) 44, 8; 45, 22; 46, 3, 9, 21; 56, 23; 57, 3. δήμου προστάτης 2, 9; 23, 13; 25, 4. θαρροῦντος τοῦ δ. 22, 12; τῇ εἰωθυίᾳ τοῦ δ. πρᾳότητι 22, 19; τοῦ δ. καὶ τῶν εὐπόρων 26, 11; Περικλῆς προειστήκει τοῦ δ. 28, 1; τοῦ δ. προειστήκει Ξάνθιππος 28, 10. ἐπαναστὰς τῷ δήμῳ 14, 6; τῷ δ. διανείμασθαι 22, 31; ἐν τῷ δ. 25, 22. συνέπεισε τὸν δῆμον 14, 3; *pl.* οἱ δῆμοι κρατήσαντες 40, 24

δημόσιος, ὁ 47, 31; 48, 4. ἴδιος and δημόσιος 6, 4; 43, 27; 48, 25; 59, 16. δημοσία σφραγίς 44, 5; τὸ δημόσιον 63, 12; δημόσιοι ἐργάται 54, 2; ὑπηρέται 50, 14; τὰ δόξαντα δημόσια εἶναι 52, 7. δημοσίᾳ 49, 28; col. 32, 14, 19

δημότης· 21, 16; 22, 22; 27, 14; 42, 3, 5, 9, 11, 13; 59, 12; 62, 5

δημοτικός· τῷ ἤθει 16, 30; δημοτικὴν—πολιτείαν 29, 19; δημοτικά 10, 1; δημοτικώτερα 22, 1; 27, 3; 41, 15; δημοτικώτατος 13, 20; 14, 1; τρία—δημοτικώτατα 9, 2. οἱ δημοτικοί 6, 8, 13; 16, 36; 18, 30; 34, 18

διά· *c. gen.* (1) duration of time, διὰ βίου 3, 3, 39. (2) interval of time, διὰ τῶν αὐτῶν χρόνων 13, 6; adverbial *διὰ τάχους* 34, 1 (διὰ ταχέων in *Rhet.* 1386 *b* 1 &c). (3) agent, δι' Ἀριστοδίκου 25, 24; τῶν φίλων 6, 8; δι' αὐτῶν 33, 12; ἑαυτῶν 35, 7; αὐτοῦ 41, 5. (4) means, διὰ τούτων 25, 1; δι' ὧν 25, 9. (5) distributed possession, ἡ γῆ δι' ὀλίγων ἦν 2, 6; 4, 29; ἐὰν δι' ὀλίγων ποιήσωνται τὴν πολιτείαν 29, 9.

c. acc. (1) *personae*, δι' ὃν 22, 16; διὰ Παυσανίαν 23, 20; τοὺς δημαγωγοῦντας 26, 3; τοὺς δημαγωγούς 41, 9; τοὺς παροργίσαντας 34, 7: (2) *rei*, διὰ τοῦτο 21, 8; ταῦτα 38, 31; τοιάνδ' αἰτίαν 19, 8; ταύτην τὴν αἰτίαν 23, 8; ταύτας τὰς αἰτίας 21, 1; τὰ ἀξιώματα 18, 1; τὴν ἀπορίαν 13, 22; τὰς τῶν χρεῶν ἀποκοπάς 11, 8; τὴν τῆς θαλάττης ἀρχήν 41, 19; τὰς πατρικὰς δόξας 26, 9; τὴν εὔνοιαν 38, 28; τὰς ἡλικίας 18, 2; τὴν παρρησίαν 16, 23; τὸ πλῆθος τῶν πολιτῶν 26, 21; τὴν ῥᾳθυμίαν 8, 28; τὴν σεισάχθειαν 12, 27; τὴν συμμαχίαν 29, 4; τὴν Ξέρξου στρατείαν 22, 40; τὴν φιλονικίαν 13, 16; τὸν φόβον 13, 23. *c. inf.* διὰ τὸ ἀνῃρηκέναι 19, 2; ἀποβαλεῖν Πύλον 27, 26; βοηθῆσαι 19, 28; γενέσθαι 3, 7; δοκεῖν 20, 7; 11, 9; θαυμάσαι 16, 19; μεγάλην γεγονέναι μεταβολήν 13, 15; μὴ βούλεσθαι 15, 3; μὴ γεγράφθαι 9, 7; μὴ δύνασθαι 9, 12; μὴ χρῆσθαι 22, 3; νομίζειν 29, 8; ποιήσασθαι 41, 4; στασιάζειν 13, 8; συμβῆναι 28, 33; τιμωρεῖν 19, 2

διαβάλλειν 6, 5; διαβάλλουσι 28, 36; διαβεβλημένους 23, 20

*διαβουλεῦσαι, (κατελύθη) ἡ βουλὴ πρίν, 32, 4

διαγίγνομαι· διαγεγένηται (ἡ πολιτεία) μέχρι τῆς νῦν *c. part.* 41, 23

διάγω· διῆγον ἐν ἡσυχίᾳ 13, 3; οὕτως διάγουσι 42, 29

διαδέχομαι· διαδεξαμένων (?) τῶν υἱέων 16, 28 (cf. *Pol.* 1293 *a* 29 τῶν τελευτώντων διαδέχεσθαι τοὺς υἱεῖς); διεδέχοντο συνεχῶς τὴν δημαγωγίαν 28, 26

διαδίδωμι· πορίσασα δραχμὰς ἑκάστῳ ὀκτὼ διέδωκε 23, 7; (διωβελία) διεδίδοτο (?) 28, 21

διαδικάζει τοῖς γένεσι—τὰς ἀμφισβητήσεις 57, 10 (only in corresp. frag. and *Oec.* 1347 *b* 28)

*διαδικασία· ἐπιτροπῆς 56, 38; *pl.* κλήρων καὶ ἐπικλήρων 56, 39; (τριηραρχῶν) 61, 9

*διαιρετοί, ἀμφορεῖς col. 36, 5

διαιρῶ· 'divide', τὰ τιμήματα διεῖλεν εἰς τέτταρα τέλη 7, 9; διῄρητο 7, 9; διῃροῦντο εἰς τοὺς δήμους 62, 3; διελόμενοι τὰς φυλάς, πέντε ἑκάτερος 61, 20; 'distinguish' τοῖς μέτροις διῃρῆσθαι 7, 26

διαίτας ἀποφαίνονται 55, 29; διανέμουσι 53, 28; ἐκδιαιτᾶν 53, 29

διαιτηταί· 53, 6; 55, 29; 58, 8; ἑξηκοστὸν ἔτος 53, 19; διαιτητοῦ γνῶσις 53, 12; παρὰ τοῦ δ. 53, 18

*διαιτῶ· διαιτήσει 53, 28; ἐπώνυμος ὁ—δεδιαιτηκώς 53, 24

[διάκ]ενα col. 36, 27

*διακληροῦσι 50, 8; διακληρῶσαι 30, 18 (decree)

διάκονε 20, 22 (scolium)

διακόσιοι 24, 14; ἕνα καὶ διακοσίους (δικαστάς) 53, 15; διακόσια (μέτρα) 7, 27

διακοσμοῦντα τὴν πομπήν 18, 20

*διακρίων (στάσις) 13, 20

διαλέγομαι· διελέγετο μετὰ σπουδῆς αὐτοῖς 25, 17; διαλέξεται πρὸς τὸν δῆμον 43, 28

διαλείπω· διαλιπόντες ἔτη δύο 22, 11

*διαλλακτὴν Σόλωνα, εἵλοντο 5, 4; τῶν (ἐκ Λακεδαίμονος) δέκα διαλλακτῶν 38, 26

διαλύσεις (ἐπ' Εὐκλείδου) 38, 20, 25; 39, 1; 40, 1

διαλύων τοὺς διαφερομένους 16, 14; διαλῦσαι 53, 7; διελύθησαν—πρὸς τοὺς Ἐλευσῖνι 40, 25

διαμαρτάνων τῆς πρὸς αὐτὸν φιλίας 18, 9

διαμένει τὸ δέκα κληροῦν 8, 4; ἐν τῇ ἀρχῇ διέμεινεν 17, 4; διέμεινεν ἡ πολιτεία 25, 2; 33, 1 διαμφισβητεῖ, ὑπὲρ ἀμφοτέρων μάχεται καὶ 5, 20

διαμφισβητήσεις εἶχον, τῶν Σόλωνος θεσμῶν ὅσοι 35, 11

διανέμω· διανέμουσιν—τὰς διαίτας 53, 27; διανειμάντων 31, 20 (decree); διένειμε τὴν χώραν τριάκοντα μέρη 21, 12; διανεῖμαι σφᾶς τε αὐτοὺς καὶ τοὺς ἄλλους δέκα μέρη 30, 17 (decree); διανείμαντα (τὰς δίκας) δέκα μέρη 58, 6. διανείμασθαι τὴν γῆν 12, 15; τὸ ἀργύριον 22, 31

διαπέμπω· διεπέμποντο πρὸς τοὺς ἐν Πειραιεῖ 38, 23

διαπεσόντος (?), χρόνου 35, 25

διαπραξάμενος, ταῦτα 20, 9

δια[ριθμοῦσιν] col. 36, 29

διαρπάζειν, τὰς οὐσίας 35, 25

**διαρρινῶ· ἐπίθημα διερρινημένον col. 36, 8

διασείσαντος τοῦ ὑπηρέτου col. 31, 8

διασημαίνω· διεσήμηναν 15, 22

διασπείρω· διεσπαρμένοι κατὰ τὴν χώραν 16, 8; διεσπάρησαν οἱ λόγοι πρὸς τὸ πλῆθος 36, 4

*διασφάλλομαι· ἐν—οἷς ἔπραττον διεσφάλλοντο 19, 11

διασῴζειν ἐπειρῶντο τὸν δῆμον 34, 18

διατάττουσι (τοὺς στρατηγούς) 61, 3; διέταξε τὴν πολιτείαν 7, 7; τὴν πολιτείαν διέταξαν 29, 28; διατάξας 11, 1; διατάξασα 8, 11

διατελοῦσιν, χρώμενοι 8, 6; διετέλουν νοσοῦντες 13, 12; διετέλουν—δημαγωγοῦντες 28, 4; στασιάζοντες διετέλεσαν 20, 19

διατηρεῖν τοὺς νόμους 3, 34; διετήρει τὰς ἀρχάς 4, 30; τὰ μέγιστα τῶν πολιτικῶν 8, 22

διατίθησιν, ἀγῶνα 57, 7; 58, 2

διατρίβω· *c. part.* διέτριβε δημηγορῶν 15, 20. οὗ διέτριβεν 25, 16; διατρίβωσιν ἐν τῷ ἄστει 16, 8; διατρίβουσιν ἐν τοῖς φυλακτηρίοις 42, 33

διαφάδην 12, 57 (Solon)

διαφέρων, δικαιοσύνῃ τῶν καθ' ἑαυτόν 23, 15; συνέσει καὶ γνώμῃ διαφέρειν 32, 11. διαφερόμενοι πρὸς ἀλλήλους 23, 17; τοὺς διαφερομένους 16, 15

διαφθεῖραι ('corrupt') τὸν δῆμον 28, 16. (2) 'kill', Θηραμένην διαφθεῖραι 37, 4; διέφθειρεν αὐτόν 18, 38

διάφορος *c. dat.* 11, 8

διαφυλάττω· τὴν δημοκρατίαν 29, 2

διαχειρίζωσι—χρήματα 30, 14 (decree); cf. 43, 13, and *Pol.* 1322 *b* 28

*διαχειροτονοῦσιν 49, 17

*διαψηφίζεσθαι 55, 25; col. 36, 10; διαψηφίζονται 42, 4; διαψηφίσασθαι col. 36, 13

*διαψηφισμός 13, 24

διδάσκαλοι (ἐφήβων) 42, 22

διδάσκουσιν 42, 24

*δίδραχμον 10, 7; *Oec.* 1353 *a* 17

δίδωμι· διδόναι τοῖς πολλοῖς τὰ αὑτῶν 27, 21; διδόναι δημοσίᾳ τροφήν 49, 28; δίδωσι—εἰς τροφήν 42, 24; δίδωσιν ἐπιχειροτονίαν—ψῆφον 55, 22 f; δίκην (42, 34), ἐπιχειροτονίαν (43, 24), εὐθύνας (56, 4) διδόασιν; οὐδεμίαν ἑαυτῷ πλεονεξίαν διδούς 16, 32; δοῦναι τὴν δεξιάν and τὴν δεξιὰν δέδωκεν 18, 35 f; δοῦναι τὰ ἑαυτοῦ 35, 14; δοῦναι ταῖς ἀρχαῖς (τὰ δικαστήρια) 59, 2; (φάρμακον) δούς 57, 16; δοὺς κατηγορίαν καὶ ἀπολογίαν 55, 21

*διεγγυᾶσθαι 4, 10

διελθεῖν (?) 4, 16; χρόνου διελθόντος 4, 2; διελθόντων—ἐτῶν 42, 36

δικάζω· of the officials presiding at a trial, (οἱ εἰσαγωγεῖς) ταύτας δικάζουσιν 57, 17, 21, 23—26, 30; 59, 2; ἐμμήνους εἰσάγοντες 52, 17; cf. 57, 27 and 30. *Abs.* 63, 11, 13. κατὰ δήμους ἐδίκαζον 53, 3; τοῖς τὴν φυλὴν—δικάζουσιν 53, 14; 58, 7; δεδικασμένα col. 37, 5

δίκαιος πρὸς τὴν πολιτείαν 25, 5; οὐ—δίκαιον 9, 13; 11, 64; δικαίοις (μέτροις καὶ σταθμοῖς) 51, 7. *Adv.* δικαίως· λαβεῖν τὴν ἐξουσίαν 41, 4; ἐγγράφεσθαι 42, 10; ὤνιος ἔσται 51, 11; ἄρξειν 55 31

δικαιοσύνῃ—διαφέρειν 23, 15

δικαστήρια (under Solon) 7, 15; 9, 5, 10; (Ephialtes) 25, 10; (Pericles) μισθοφόρα 27, 11; (Anytus) δεκάσας τὸ δικαστήριον 27, 27. εἰσάγειν εἰς δικαστήριον (29, 26), εἰς τὸ δ. 45, 10; 48, 26; 52, 4, 6, 19. ἐφίησιν (ἐφῇ 53, 9) εἰς τὸ δ. 42, 8; ἐφέσιμος εἰς τὸ δ. 45, 14; ἔφεσις εἰς τὸ δ. 45, 16, 19; 55, 11. ἐν δικαστηρίῳ 55, 7, 10; ἐν τῷ δ. 47, 22; 48, 18; 55, 22; 56, 3; 61, 12. τὸ δ. 63, 17; τὰ δ. 63, 23; προγράψαι 59, 1. δ. ἴδια καὶ δημόσια 59, 15. τὰ δ. τρεῖς ὀβολοὺς (μισθοφορεῖ) 62, 7; τὰ δ. κληροῦσιν οἱ ἐννέα ἄρχοντες 63, 1; εἴσοδοι εἰς τὰ δ. (?) 63, 3

δικαστής, ἕκαστος, 63, 18; δικασταὶ—ἑξακισχίλιοι 24, 12; κατὰ δήμους 16, 13; 48, 24; ὅ τι ἂν γνῶσιν οἱ δικασταί 48, 27; ἂν καταγνῶσιν οἱ δικασταί 54, 9; 63, 14; ἐπὶ τοῖς δικασταῖς 55, 20; τῶν λαχόντων δικαστῶν 63, 6; δικαστὰς κληροῦσι 59, 18

δίκη· Solon in c. 12, ἐν δίκῃ χρόνου l. 30; βίαν τε καὶ δίκην l. 43; εὐθεῖαν δίκην l. 46.

δίκην διδόασιν—λαμβάνουσιν 42, 34; δίκας λαγχάνουσιν 53, 2; δίκαι λαγχάνονται πρὸς αὐτόν 58, 4; δίκας κρίνειν 3, 32

δίκαι· αἰκείας 52, 15; ἀνδραπόδων 52, 16; ἀποστασίου, ἀπροστασίου, 58, 9; εἰς δατητῶν αἵρεσιν 56, 36; εἰς ἐπιτροπῆς διαδικασίαν 56, 38; εἰς ἐπιτροπῆς κατάστασιν 56, 37; δούλων ἐάν τις τὸν ἐλεύθερον κακῶς λέγῃ, 59, 14; ἔμμηνοι 52, 11—20; ἐμπορικαί 59, 14; ἐρανικαί 52, 15; ἴδιαι 58, 5; 59, 13; κλήρων καὶ ἐπικλήρων 43, 21; 56, 39; 58, 9; κοινωνικαί 52, 15; μεταλλικαί 59, 14; παρανοίας 56, 35; προικός 52, 12; ἀπὸ τῶν συμβόλων 59, 17; τραπεζιτικαί 52, 16; τριηραρχίας 52, 16; ὑποζυγίων 52, 16; (ψευδομαρτυριῶν) col. 36, 11—13; τὰ ψευδομαρτύρια τὰ ἐξ' Αρείου πάγου 59, 17. For δίκαι ἀδικίου, κακώσεως, κλοπῆς (δημοσίων χρημάτων), πυρκαϊᾶς, τραύματος, φόνου, see γραφαί

δίμηνον ἦρξεν 33, 2

διὸ καὶ 3, 17, 21, 38; 5, 19; 8, 16; 16, 13, 26, 34; 17, 4; 20, 21; 23, 15, 20; 27, 20; διὸ καὶ νῦν 7, 29

διοικεῖν, μηδὲν τῶν πατρίων τὸν ἄρχοντα, 3, 16; πάντα, 16, 31; 44, 12; τὴν πολιτείαν, 27, 11. διοικεῖ—ἀγῶνα 56, 27; τὰς πατρίους θυσίας 57, 9. διοικοῦσι, πεντετηρίδας 54, 28; πομπήν 60, 4. διῴκει τὰ πλεῖστα καὶ τὰ μέγιστα 3, 35; τὰ κοινὰ 14, 17; τὰ κατὰ τὴν πόλιν 16, 2; τὴν πόλιν 23, 3. τὰ ἄλλα πάντα διῴκουν 26, 12. διῴκησαν, τειχῶν ἀνοικοδόμησιν 23, 17. πάντα διοικεῖται ψηφίσμασι καὶ δικαστηρίοις 41, 25; τὰ ὑπὸ τῆς βουλῆς διοικούμενα 50, 1; περὶ τῶν διῳκημένων 25, 7

διοίκησις ἀπὸ τῶν κοινῶν 24, 21; ἐγκύκλιος 43, 1

Διονύσια 56, 11, 12, 28; Δ. τῶν μεγάλων 56, 22; τῶν ἐπὶ Ληναίῳ 57, 4; in Salamis and Peiraeus 54, 35

Διόνυσος 3, 26

διπλοῦν—καταβάλλειν 49, 5

διπλοῦται 54, 12

δὶς τὸν αὐτὸν μὴ ἄρχειν 4, 15; οὐκ ἔστιν (ἐπιστάτην) δὶς τὸν αὐτὸν γενέσθαι 44, 3; ἔξεστι βουλεῦσαι δὶς 62, 19

*δισμύριοι 24, 12

*δισχίλιοι 24, 18; ἀπὸ τοῦ κυάμου 24, 20; δισχιλίους 26, 10

Δίφιλος 7, 21, 23

*δίχους col. 34, 33 f

διωβελία 28, 20 (διωβολία *Pol.* 1267 *b* 2)

*διώβολον 41, 34

διώκειν, 'prosecute,' 56, 31; τοῦ διώκοντος, 'the plaintiff,' 53, 11; col. 36, 32. διώκειν τὴν μέσην πολιτείαν 13, 18; τὴν πάτριον πολιτείαν 35, 9

δόγμα· οὐδενὶ δόγματι λαβοῦσα τὴν ἡγεμονίαν 23, 4

δοκιμάζει (ἡ βουλὴ) τοὺς ἐγγραφέντας 42, 12; — βουλευτάς 45, 17; — θ' ἄρχοντας 45, 17; — ἵππους, προδρόμους, ἀμίππους, 49, 1, 5, 7; — ἀδυνάτους 49, 25, 27. δοκιμάζωσιν (τοὺς ἄρχοντας) 55, 13; δοκιμάζονται (οἱ ἄρχοντες) 55, 6; (οἱ πάρεδροι) 55, 3. δοκιμασθέντες (οἱ ἄρχοντες) 55, 27; (οἱ ἀθλοθέται) 60, 3; δοκιμασθῶσιν οἱ ἔφηβοι 42, 14

δοκιμασίας ταῖς ἀρχαῖς ἁπάσαις, εἰσάγουσιν (οἱ θεσμοθέται) 59, 11

δοκῶ *passim. c. inf.* 6, 12; 9, 2; 10, 1; 20, 7; 22, 17; 25, 5; 28, 35 &c. τὰ δόξαντα περὶ τῆς πολιτείας 35, 3

δολοφονηθεὶς 25, 24. δολοφονηθέντος Διομήδους, *de Admir.* 836 *a* 16; δολοφονία *Eth.* 1131 *a* 7

δόξαν, παρὰ 11, 10; τῇ φύσει καὶ τῇ δόξῃ 5, 12; διὰ τὰς πατρικὰς δόξας 26, 9

δόρυ 42, 31

δορυφόροι (of Hippias) 18, 22

δουλεύειν 2, 11; ἐδούλευον οἱ πένητες τοῖς πλουσίοις 2, 3; τῶν πολλῶν δουλευόντων τοῖς ὀλίγοις 5, 2; cf. 12, 26. Γῆ — δουλεύουσα 12, 34 (Solon)

δούλων δίκαι 59, 4; φανερῶς δοῦλοι 40, 10

Δρακοντίδης 34, 27

Δράκων 3, 1; 4, 3; 7, 2; 41, 11

*δραχμή· 3, 19; 10, 6; 23, 7; 42, 25; 50, 7; 62, 7, 12, 14. ἐπὶ δραχμῇ 52, 13. μέχρι δέκα δραχμῶν 52, 19; 53, 5. Omitted ἐντὸς χιλίων—ὑπὲρ χιλίας 53, 15 f. (συναλλάγματα) δραχμιαῖα καὶ πεντάδραχμα *Pol.* 1300 *b* 33

*δρύφακτος 50, 11

δρῶ· τοῦτ' ἔδρων καὶ ἐπὶ τῶν ἄλλων 35, 17; βουλόμενοί τι δρᾶσαι πρὸ τῆς συλλήψεως 18, 18; τῷ δράσαντι λαγχάνει 57, 30

δύναμιν, εἶχον 12, 6 (Solon); μεγίστην εἶχεν δ. 13, 11; τὴν ναυτικὴν δ. 27, 5; περιείλοντο τὴν δ. 25, 22; ἐπιλειπόμενος τῇ δυνάμει 19, 5; τῶν ἐν ταῖς δυνάμεσιν 22, 13 (cf. τῶν ἐν ταῖς ἐξουσίαις *Eth.* 1095 *b* 21)

δύνασθαι 9, 12; μὴ δ. τῷ σώματι ἱππεύειν ἢ τῇ οὐσίᾳ 49, 16; particip. 7, 19; 49, 3; ἐδύναντο 18, 25; 19, 9; δύνωνται διαλῦσαι 53, 7.

δυναστείαν, καταλύσῃ τὴν (of the Thirty) 36, 6

δυνατός, καθ' ὅσον ἦν 14, 14; μὴ δυνατοὺς εἶναι τοῖς σώμασιν ἱππεύειν 49, 14; τοῖς δυνατωτάτοις καὶ τοῖς σώμασιν καὶ τοῖς χρήμασιν λῃτουργεῖν 29, 34 (decree)

δύο 4, 19; 13, 7, 9; 20, 14; 22, 11; τὰ δύο μέρη 51, 17. *gen.* τῶν δυεῖν ἐτῶν 42, 37; δυεῖν δραχμαῖν 50, 7; δυοῖν χάριν 16, 7. *dat.* δυοῖν φυλαῖν 52, 12; 56, 13; πρὸς τοῖν δυοῖν ὀβολοῖν 28, 32. Cf. Kühner, ed. Blass, i p. 633

δυσκολίας, τὰς παρούσας 35, 15

δυσχεραίνοντες, τῇ πολιτείᾳ 13, 15 (οἱ ἐν τῇ πολιτείᾳ δυσχεράναντες *Pol.* 1306 *b* 4); ἐπὶ τοῖς ἄλλοις ἐδυσχέραινον 2, 12.

δώδεκα 8, 13; 21, 9

δωδεκάτῳ, ἔτει 22, 10

δωρεὰν οὐκ ἔστιν αὐτοῖς λαβεῖν 46, 6; δωρεῶν 3, 13

*δωροξενίας γραφή 59, 8

δῶρα δούς 59, 9; λαβόντα 54, 8; μὴ λήψεσθαι 55, 3. δώρων γραφή 59, 9; δώρων τιμῶσιν 54, 9 ἐάν 7, 6; 16, 42 (law); 17, 7; 22, 34 &c. Cf. ἄν

ἑαυτοῦ, αὑτοῦ, *passim*. νοσοῦντες τὰ πρὸς ἑαυτούς (=ἀλλήλους) 13, 12

ἑβδομήκοντα 10, 6

ἕβδομος 15, 2

ἐγγίγνεται 54, 32

ἐγγραφὴ τῶν πολιτῶν 42, 38

ἐγγράφονται—εἰς τοὺς δημότας 42, 3, 4; ἐγγράφειν 42, 11; ἐγγράψαντας 42, 13; δικαίως ἐγγράφεσθαι 42, 10; τοὺς ἐγγραφέντας 42, 12; οἱ δ' ἔφηβοι οἱ ἐγγραφόμενοι — εἰς λελευκωμένα γραμματεῖα ἐνεγράφοντο, — ἐνεγράφησαν 53, 22 f. (ἱππέας) ἐγγράφουσιν εἰς τὸν πίνακα 49, 18; (ἱππέων) ἐγγεγραμμένων 49, 13. τῶν ἐγγεγραμμένων (εἰς τὸν τῶν τρισχιλίων κατάλογον) 36, 15. ἐπίτροπον ἐγγράψαι 56, 39. κἄν τις ἐλλίπῃ καταβολήν, ἐνταῦθ' ἐγγέγραπται 48, 5; (cf. πράξεις τῶν προτιθεμένων κατὰ τὰς ἐγγραφάς *Pol.* 1322 *a*)

ἐγγυηταί 4, 12

ἐγκαλῇ, ὅ τι ἂν 48, 22; οὐδεὶς οὐδὲν ἐνεκάλεσεν αὐτοῖς 38, 30

*ἐγκατεγήρασε τῇ ἀρχῇ 17, 1

ἐγκρατέστερον ἔσχον, τὴν πόλιν 35, 22 (cf. ἐγκρατῶς ἔσχον τὴν ἀρχήν *Pol.* 1284 *a* 40).

ἐγκύκλιοι (ἀρχαί) 26, 18; τὰς ἀρχὰς τὰς περὶ τὴν ἐγκύκλιον διοίκησιν 43, 1

ἔγχει 22, 22 (scolium)

*ἐγχειρίδια 18, 27

ἕδρα βουλῆς ἢ ἐκκλησίας 4, 17; τὰς ἕδρας — τῆς βουλῆς 30, 24

ἔερδον 12, 23 (Solon)

ἐθέλω *passim*; in pap. saepe θέλω. μὴ 'θέλουσι 49, 3; μὴ 'θέλῃ 56, 37. οἱ ἐθέλοντες Ἀθηναίων 29, 24 (decree)

εἰ μή τι παρεωρᾶτο 26, 18; εἰ μὴ — ἀποδιδοῖεν 2, 7; εἰ — ἐκλείποι 4, 17; εἰ δὲ μή, after ἐὰν μέν, 22, 35 &c; after κἂν μέν, 52, 5. εἰ — ἤ (=πότερον — ἤ) 43, 23

εἰκός 6, 13; 9, 12 &c.

εἴκοσι 17, 4; 24, 19; 29, 11; 30, 10

εἰκών 7, 21

εἰμί *passim*. εἴη 14, 9. ἐπὶ τῶν ἰδίων εἶναι 15, 25; πρὸς τοῖς ἰδίοις ὄντες 16, 9. τὸ νῦν εἶναι 31, 9 (decree)

εἰπεῖν 2, 12; 14, 9; ὡς εἰπεῖν 2, 12; ὡς ἔπος εἰπεῖν 49, 31; 57, 8. ἂν — εἴποι 7, 30; εἰπών 10, 5; Περικλέους εἰπόντος 26, 22; εἰπόντος τὸν πρὸ τοῦ ψηφίσματος λόγον Μηλοβίου 29, 6. εἶπα 12, 22 (Solon). Cf. εἴρηται

εἴργεσθαι τῶν νομίμων 57, 13; εἴργεται τῶν ἱερῶν 57, 28

εἰρήνην ἄγειν 34, 9; παρεσκεύαζεν εἰρ. 16, 26; ἐπὶ πέρας ἤγαγε τὴν εἰρήνην 38, 25. τῆς εἰρ. γενομένης αὐτοῖς 34, 17

εἴρηται, καθάπερ 4, 24; ὥσπερ 16, 3; ὅνπερ εἴρηται τρόπον 11, 2. τῆς ἡλικίας τῆς εἰρημένης 30, 15 (decree); εἰρημένοι ὦσιν οἱ λόγοι col. 35, 30. Cf. εἰπεῖν

εἰς· (1) of place, εἰς Αἴγυπτον 11, 5; εἰς Πειραιέα, εἰς ἄστυ, 51, 1 f; ἡ εἰς τὸ δικαστήριον ἔφεσις 9, 5
(2) of time, εἰς ἐνιαυτόν 30, 19 (decree); τρία ἔτη 47, 12; ἑκατὸν ἔτη 7, 7; τὸν μέλλοντα χρόνον 31, 1; and (in decrees) τὸν λοιπὸν χρ. 30, 15; τὸν ἄλλον χρ. 31, 18. ἐκ Παναθηναίων εἰς Παναθήναια 43, 4.
(3) of measure, or limit, εἰς ἑπτακοσίους ἄνδρας 24, 16
(4) of relation to, ἧδον — εἰς τοῦτον 20, 21. τὰ εἰς τὸν πόλεμον 23, 10

εἷς *passim*. =ὁ μὲν εἷς — ὁ δ' ἕτερος 37, 6 f; ἑνὸς δεῖν 19, 39; 27, 27; ἑνὸς δέοντα 17, 4; ἕνα 4, 14; μία 13, 17; μίαν 4, 19

*εἰσαγγελία· Σόλωνος θέντος νόμον εἰσαγγελίας 8, 26; *pl.* 29, 23; 43, 19; 59, 4

εἰσαγγέλλειν, πρὸς τὴν τῶν Ἀρεοπαγιτῶν βουλὴν 4, 22; εἰς τοὺς διαιτητάς 53, 32; (οἱ θεσμοθέται) τὰς εἰσαγγελίας εἰσαγγέλλουσιν εἰς τὸν δῆμον 59, 4; ἔξεστι καὶ τοῖς ἰδιώταις εἰσαγγέλλειν ἣν ἂν βούλωνται τῶν ἀρχῶν μὴ χρῆσθαι τοῖς νόμοις 45, 14 (not found in Ar. in technical sense)

εἰσάγω· εἰς δικαστήριον 29, 26 (decree). εἰς τὸ δικαστήριον 45, 10 (law); 48, 26; 52, 4, 6; 53, 15; 54, 6; 56, 30, 42; 63, 14. δίκας 52, 12, 17; 58, 8; 59, 13, 17. διαδικασίας 61, 6. δοκιμασίας 59, 11. ἐνδείξεις 52, 8, 9. προβολὰς κτλ 59, 5. τοῖς δικασταῖς τοῖς τὴν φυλὴν—εἰσάγουσιν 48, 25.

*εἰσαγωγεῖς 52, 11

*εἰσελαύνω· ἐφ' ἅρματος εἰσήλαυνε 14, 29

εἰσέρχομαι· εἰς τὴν ἀρχὴν εἰσέρχονται 55, 35; εἰσελθεῖν εἰς τὴν ἀρχήν 56, 6. εἰσελθόντες εἰς τὸ βουλευτήριον 32, 13. εἰσελθεῖν εἰς τὸ δικαστήριον col. 32, 6; εἰσίῃ (εἰς δικαστήριον) col. 31, 33; col. 32, 7. εἰσελθεῖν εἰς τὸ ἱερόν 57, 29. *Abs.* εὐθὺς εἰσελθών 56, 5; εἰσῄεσαν and εἰσιέναι 32, 5 f. τὸν εἰσιόντα ἐνιαυτόν 31, 13 (decree)

εἰσηγήσατο, ὥσπερ Ἀριστείδης 24, 10

*εἰσηγητής 27, 20

εἴσοδος, εἰς τὰ δικαστήρια (?) 63, 3, 7; δικαστηρίου col. 32, 10

*εἰσπράττειν 8, 17; 48, 6; 60, 8; ἐπιτρόπους—εἰσπράττει 56, 46

εἰσφέρει—τὰς μισθώσεις 47, 26. εἰσφέρουσι γράψαντες ἐν σανίδι 48, 9; τὸν κατάλογον εἰς τὴν βουλήν 49, 11. νόμους εἰσήνεγκαν εἰς τὴν βουλήν 37, 5. εἰσφέρεται—εἰς τὴν βουλὴν τὰ γραμματεῖα 47, 30

εἰσφορά 8, 15

εἶτα· εἶτ' 8, 4; 22, 34. πρῶτον μὲν—εἶτ' 42, 20; πρῶτον μὲν—ἔπειτα—εἶθ' 62, 6—9.

εἴωθεν 28, 24; εἰώθασιν 40, 4; τῇ εἰωθυίᾳ—πρᾳότητι 22, 19

ἐκ· (1) place, ἐξ Ἄργους 17, 12; 'out of' ἐκ τούτων 8, 4; ἐκ τῆς φυλῆς ἑκάστης 8, 12 &c; πρῶτος ἦρξεν ἐξ αὐτῶν 26, 16; ἐκ καταλόγου 26, 8. (2) origin, ἐκ τῆς γαμετῆς 17, 10. *ἐκ (=ὑπὸ) τῶν ἄλλων* ὁμολογεῖται 5, 13. (3) inference, ἐκ τῶν νῦν γιγνομένων, ἐκ τῆς ἄλλης πολιτείας, θεωρεῖν 9, 13. (4) time, ἐξ ἀρχῆς (=ἐν ἀρχῇ) 16, 1; 28, 5; 41, 7; 55, 3; ἐξ ὑπαρχῆς, *denuo*, 4, 16 (*Pol.* 1293 *a* 2, *initio*); ἐξ οὗ 60, 12; ἐκ Παναθηναίων εἰς Π. 43, 4

ἕκαστος· ἕκαστον 11, 6. ἑκάστη—τῶν φυλῶν 8, 2.

The art. generally added, but sometimes omitted:—ἑκάστῃ τῇ ἡμέρᾳ 43, 15; τῆς ἡμέρας ἑκάστης 62, 15. τῆς πρυτανείας ἑκάστης 43, 14; κατὰ τὴν πρ. ἑκάστην 61, 11: κατὰ πρ. ἑκάστην 47, 18. ἐκ τῆς φυλῆς ἑκάστης 8, 12; 29, 37; 44, 8; 53, 1; τῆς φ. ἑκάστης 48, 17; col. 32, 20; ἀπὸ <τῆς> φ. ἑκάστης 43, 6; ἀφ' ἑκάστης τῆς φ. 61, 2; ἕνα τῆς φυλῆς ἑκάστης 42, 18; 48, 15; 56, 25; 60, 3; 61, 17; ἐξ ἑκάστης τῆς φ. 22, 9: ἐξ ἑκάστης <τῆς> φ. 55, 5; ἑκατὸν ἐξ ἑκάστης φ. 8, 19. ἑκάστῃ τῇ φυλῇ 58, 7; τῇ φ. ἑκάστῃ 63, 3, 4, 5. καθ' ἑκάστην τὴν φ. col. 31, 2

Art. without ἕκαστος: δύο ὀβολοὺς ἑκάστῳ τῆς ἡμέρας 49, 28 (law); τρεῖς ὀβολοὺς ἕκαστον τῆς ἡμέρας 29, 32; δραχμὴν τῆς ἡμέρας 62, 12. ἅπαξ ἐν τῷ ἐνιαυτῷ 44, 14. εἷς ἐκ τῆς φυλῆς 47, 3, 8; ἕνα τῆς φυλῆς 61, 23.

Pl. 7, 14; 13, 25; 21, 24 &c.

ἑκάτερος *passim*. ἑκατέρου βίον 17, 8; ἐφ' οἷς ἑκάτεροι τυγχάνουσιν ἔχοντες 32, 15; ἐφ' οἷς ἔχουσιν ἑκάτεροι 34, 8

ἑκατέρωθι 54, 35

Ἑκατομβαιών 62, 13

ἑκατὸν ἀρχηγετῶν 21, 25; ἐξ ἑκάστης φυλῆς 8, 19 (cf. 21, 8); ἄνδρας, τοὺς ἀναγράψοντας τὴν πολιτείαν 30, 3, 17; 31, 21; 32, 1. ἔτη 7, 7. μνῶν 4, 9; τάλαντα 22, 30; (δραχμαῖς) 10, 6

ἐκβάλλω· ἐξέβαλον (Πεισίστρατον) 14, 19; πολλοὺς—ἐκβεβληκέναι 19, 3; ἐκ τῶν τάφων ἐξεβλήθησαν 1, 2

ἐκβολή· τῶν τυράννων 20, 18

*ἐκδιαιτᾶν, διαίτας 53, 29

ἐκδίκως 12, 36 (Solon)

ἐκεῖ 55, 34; pap. 19, 6

ἐκεῖθεν 15, 6

ἐκεῖνος 15, 20; 16, 40 &c.

ἐκεῖσε 19, 6

*ἐκθύματα (?) 54, 24

*ἐκκηρῦξαι 61, 15

ἐκκλησία, under Dracon, 4, 18; under Solon, 7, 15. ἐκκλησίαι, esp. 43, 16 f. ἐ. κυρία 43, 17; 62, 7. ἐλθὼν εἰς τὴν ἐ. 35, 11. ἐ. ἐν τῷ θεάτρῳ 42, 30. (ἀρχαιρεσίαι) ἐν τῇ ἐ. 44, 17. μισθοφόρον ἐκκλησίαν—ἀπέγνωσαν ποιεῖν, and οὐ συλλεγομένων εἰς τὴν ἐ. 41, 30; μισθοφοροῦσι—ταῖς ἐκκλησίαις 62, 6

ἐκκλησιάζειν 15, 17

ἐκκομισάμενοι, τὰ ἑαυτῶν 19, 36

ἐκλείποι τὴν σύνοδον, εἰ δέ τις τῶν βουλευτῶν 4, 18

*ἐκμαρτυρῶν (?) 7, 25

ἐκπέμπω· Κλεομένην ἐξέπεμψαν 19, 29; ὅταν ἡλικίαν ἐκπέμπωσι 53, 36; τοὺς ἄλλους πρὸς τὰ παρόντα πράγματα ἐκπέμπουσιν 61, 10

ἐκπίπτω (τῆς ἀρχῆς)· ἐξέπεσε 15, 2; 19, 6; ὅτ' ἐκπέσοι 16, 35; ἐκπεσόντα 17, 17. ὡς ἐξέπεσον (ἐκ τῆς πόλεως) οἱ περὶ τὸν Ἰσαγόραν 28, 9

*ἐκπολιορκῶ· ἐξεπολιορκήθησαν ὑπὸ τῶν τυράννων 19, 13

ἔκρουν ἔχοντας, ὀχετοὺς μετεώρους εἰς τὴν ὁδὸν 50, 12

*ἑκτήμοροι, πελάται καὶ 2, 5

ἐκτίνω· ἐὰν—ἐκτείσῃ τις 54, 11: ἕως ἂν ἐκτείσῃ 63, 16 ([Ar.] *Rhet. ad Alex.* 1444 *b* 2)

ἐκτίσεις 8, 23

ἐκτός 22, 41 (ἐντός *pap.*)

ἕκτῳ ἔτει 14, 19; 26, 14

ἐκφανεῖν 12, 19 (Solon)

ἐκφέρειν, δόξειεν αὐτοῖς 36, 14; ἀνέγραψαν καὶ ἐξήνεγκαν 30, 4

ἑκών 27, 10

ἐλαίαν μορίαν 60, 11

ἔλαιον 60, 7 *bis*, 14, 23

ἔλαττον 4, 8; οὐκ ἐλάττω μοῖραν 19, 24

ἐλαύνειν τὸ ἄγος 20, 7. ἠλάσατε 5, 16 (Solon)

*ἐλεγείαν, ποιήσαντι τὴν 5, 6; cf. 5, 20

ἐλεύθερος 42, 7; ἄν τις τὸν ἐλεύθερον κακῶς λέγῃ 59, 14. οὐσίαν—ἐλευθέραν 4, 6, 9

ἐλευθεροῦν τὰς Ἀθήνας 19, 22; τὸν δῆμον ἠλευθέρωσε 6, 2; ἐλευθερωθέντων διὰ τὴν σεισάχθειαν 12, 27

Ἐλευσὶς 39, 3. Ἐλευσῖνι 39, 10, 17; 40, 26. Ἐλευσινόθεν, Ἐλευσίναδε, 39, 6 f. Ἐλευσίνια, πεντετηρίς, 54, 31. Ἐλευσινίων 39, 13

ἕλκει—πινάκιον col. 31, 9; βάλανον col. 31, 26

ἐλλείπω· κἂν τις ἐλλίπῃ καταβολὴν—ἀνάγκη τὸ ἐλλειφθὲν καταβάλλειν 48, 5 f

Ἕλληνες 23, 11

*ἑλληνοταμίαι 30, 9(?) and 13 (decree)

ἐλπίδ'—ἀφνέαν 12, 17 (Solon)

ἐμβάλλει (τὴν ψῆφον) col. 36, 20; εἰς ἐνέβαλλε τὴν ψῆφον 55, 24. (*b*) ἐμβάλλει τὸ πινάκιον col. 31, 29; ἐμβάλωσιν—τὰ πινάκια εἰς τὸ κιβώτιον col. 31, 4; ἐμβάλλεται—τὰ πινάκια 63, 5. (*c*) βάλανοι εἰς τὴν ὑδρίαν ἐμβάλλονται 63, 8. (*d*) ἐμβάλῃ τοὺς κύβους col. 31, 17; ἐμβάλλονται λευκοὶ (κύβοι) *ib.* 21. (*e*) ἐμ-

βαλόντες τὰς μαρτυρίας—εἰς ἐχῖνους 53, 10; μαρτυρίαις—εἰς τοὺς ἐχίνους ἐμβεβλημέναις 53, 18. *Mid.* εὔθυναν—ἐμβαλέσθαι 48, 20. *Intr.* εἰς τὴν ἀγορὰν—ἐμβαλεῖν αὐτῷ 57, 28
*ἐμβιβάζω· ἐνεβίβασεν 23, 7
ἐμμένειν, τοῖς ὅρκοις 40, 13; κἂν—ἐμμένωσι (τοῖς γνωσθεῖσι) 53, 8
*ἔμμηνοι δίκαι 52, 11—20
ἐμπήγνυσι τὰ πινάκια col. 31, 11; ἐμπηγνύων
*ἐμπήκτης col. 31, 11, 24
ἐμπορίαν, κατ' 11, 4
ἐμπορικάς, δίκας 59, 14
ἐμπορίου ἐπιμελητάς—τῶν ἐμπορίων ἐπιμελεῖσθαι 51, 15, 16
ἔμποροι 51, 17
ἐμφανῶν κατάστασιν, εἰς 56, 38
ἔμφρων 18, 3
ἐν *passim*. (1) of place, ἐν τῇ στοᾷ 7, 3; ἐν ὅπλοις ('under arms'), 31, 11 (decree); of trial before a court, ἐν τοῖς (ἐν Πειραιεῖ) 29, 23 (decree); with vb. of motion, τοὺς μύδρους ἐν τῷ πελάγει καθεῖσαν 23, 24. (2) of circumstances &c., ἐν τούτοις ὤν 19, 6; adverbial use, ἐν κόσμῳ 28, 18. (3) of time, ἐν ᾧ 15, 20; ἐν ('within') πέντε ἔτεσιν 47, 23.—ἐνὶ φρεσὶ 4, 15 (Solon)
*ἐναγῶν, εἶναι τῶν 20
*ἐναγίσματα 58, 4
ἐναντίον τι, *c. dat.* 37, 10; ἐναντιώτατα 36, 10
ἐναντίον τῆς βουλῆς 47, 6, 10, 14; 48, 3; and (in decree) 30, 28
ἐναντιωθέντες 36, 4; ἀμφοτέροις ἠναντιώθη 11, 13
ἐνδείκνυται 63, 13; ἐνεδείχθη 63, 17 (not in Ar. in technical sense)
*ἔνδειξιν—καὶ ἀπαγωγήν 29, 26 (decree); *pl.* 52, 8, 9
ἕνδεκα, οἱ 7, 13; 29, 27; esp. 52, 1—10. τοῦ δεσμωτηρίου φύλακας ἕνδεκα 35, 6
*ἑνδεκάτῳ—ἔτει 15, 8; ἑνδεκάτῃ 41, 5
ἐνδέχεται 17, 7
ἔνδημοι, ἀρχαὶ 24, 16
ἔνδοθεν 5, 7 (Solon)
ἐνδοξότατος 54, 16
ἐνδύω· θώρακα ἐνδεδυκώς 55, 32
ἕνεκα. τῆς ἀρχῆς 55, 32; γήρως <ἕνεκα> 35, 16
ἐνῇ (?) col. 31, 33
ἐνιαύσιος (ἀρχή) 3, 22 (ἀρχαὶ ἐνιαύσιαι *Pol.* 1299 *a* 7)
ἐνιαυτός· τρὶς τοῦ ἐν. 47, 19; ἐν—ἐνιαυτῷ 53, 31; τὸν ἐν. 13, 10; τὸν πρῶτον ἐν. 42, 29; εἰς ἐν. 47, 16; ἐπ' ἐνιαυτόν 8, 10; κατ' ἐνιαυτόν 3, 20; 30, 4
ἔνιοι 3, 10; 7, 18; 8, 27; 13, 15; 18, 32. ἔνια 27, 4
ἐνίοτε 43, 30
ἐνίστημι· ἐνέστη φιλία 17, 15; πόλεμος 27, 9. τὴν ἐνεστῶσαν φιλονικίαν 5, 11; ἔχθρας ἐνεστώσης 5, 22; τοῦ χειμῶνος ἐνεστῶτος 37, 1. ἐνεστήσαντο τὴν—πολιτείαν 41, 2
ἐννέα ἄρχοντες, οἱ, see ἄρχοντες
ἕνους, τοὺς ἱππάρχους τοὺς 4, 11 (cf. *Pol.* 1322 *a* 11)
ἐνοχλῶ· ἠνώχλουν 11, 2
ἔνοχος γραφῇ παρανόμων 45, 24
ἐνσημαίνομαι· ἐνεσημαίνετο πικρῶς 18, 10
ἐνταῦθα 3, 26; 48, 5; 54, 30 &c.
ἐντεῦθεν 55, 33
ἐντὸς χιλίων 53, 15; τριῶν μνῶν 49, 26; τριῶν ἡμερῶν 48, 18; δέκα σταδίων 50, 9
ἐντυγχάνοντα, φιλανθρώπως, *c. dat.* 18, 17
Ἐνυάλιος 58, 2
ἐξ, see ἐκ
ἐξάγω· στρατιάν 37, 3
ἐξαιρῇ (or ἐξέλῃ) τοὺς κύβους col. 31, 23. ἐξεῖλεν 12, 64 (Solon)
ἐξαίρω· ἐξαράμενος (an exceptional use) τὰ ὅπλα πρὸ τῶν θυρῶν 14, 13
*ἐξαλείφουσι, τοὺς ἐξομνυμένους τῶν—ἐγγεγραμμένων 49, 13; ἐξήλειφον, opp. ἀντενέγραφον 36, 15. *Met.* τὰς περὶ τῶν προτέρων αἰτίας ἐξήλειψαν 40, 19
ἐξαπατηθέντος τοῦ δήμου 34, 6; ἐξαπατηθέντες ὑπὸ Κλεοφῶντος 34, 10; κἂν ἐξαπατηθῇ τὸ πλῆθος 28, 24
*ἐξαπορῶ· ἐξαπορησάντων τοῖς πράγμασι 23, 5
*ἐξάχους col. 34, 34
ἐξελάσαι *abs.* 22, 17; ἐξηλάθη—τῆς ἀρχῆς 13, 7
ἐξελέγχεται col. 32, 7; ἵνα μὴ—ἐξελέγχωσι τοὺς νεοπολίτας 21, 17; κἂν—κλέπτοντα ἐξελέγξωσιν 54, 7
ἐξεργαζομένης τῆς χώρας 16, 12; ἐξειργασμένα 46, 5
ἐξέρχομαι· ἐξῄει πολλάκις εἰς τὴν χώραν 16, 14. (Of troops) τῶν ἐξιόντων 26, 10; ἂν ἐξίωσιν 61, 4; cf. ἔξοδος
ἔξεστι 44, 15; 45, 14, 22; 53, 17; 62, 18; 63, 11, 13. ἐξῆν 4, 21; 27, 15. ἐξῇ 27, 17; col. 31, 33 (?). ἐξόν 6, 14; 11, 13. ἐξεῖναι 9, 4; 29, 14, 29; 39, 6, 16, 21 (decree)
ἐξετάζειν τὰ γένη 21, 6; ἐξετάζει—τὰ οἰκοδομήματα 46, 8
ἐξέτασις ἐν ὅπλοις 31, 11 (decree)
ἐξευρών, γυναῖκα μεγάλην καὶ καλὴν 14, 25
*ἐξηγεῖσθαι, τοὺς νόμους 11, 6
ἑξήκοντα 10, 8
ἔξοδος 16, 6
ἐξοικεῖν ἔχειν Ἐλευσῖνα 39, 3 (decree); ἐξ. τοὺς ἐθέλοντας 39, 25 (*ib.*); τοῖς βουλομένοις ἐξ. 39, 14 (*ib.*); ἐπινοούντων ἐξ. 40, 3
*ἐξοίκησις 39, 15 (decree); 40, 26
*ἐξόμνυμι· τοὺς ἐξομνυμένους—μὴ δυνατοὺς εἶναι—ἱππεύειν 49, 13; ἐξομόσηται 49, 15; μὴ ἐξομνύμενον 49, 16. ἐξόμνυνται τὰς μαρτυρίας 55, 30. (ἐξόμνυσθαι τὴν ἀρχὴν *Pol.* 1297 *a* 20)

* ἐξοπλισία 15, 16 (ἐξόπλισις *Probl.* 922 *b* 14)

ἐξορύξειεν, ἐλαίαν μορίαν 60, 11 (ἐξορυσσόμενοι τόποι, [Ar.] *de Admir.* 833 *b* 4)

ἐξουσία 6, 19; 41, 4, 24

ἔξω—τῆς πολιτείας 37, 12

ἔξωθεν, τῶν 36, 16

ἑορτῶν ἐπιμελεῖται 56, 29

ἐπαγγειλάμενος ὡς ἄλλους μηνύσων 18, 34

ἐπαινουμένων, τῶν 16, 30; διὰ τὴν εὔνοιαν—ἐπῃνέθησαν 38, 28

* ἐπάν 42, 14; 56, 4

ἐπάναγκες ἐπιψηφίζειν 29, 21 (decree); ἐγγράφειν 42, 11

ἐπαναφέροντες τοῖς πεντακισχιλίοις, οὐδὲν 33, 12

* ἐπαναχωρήσαντες 38, 3

ἐπανίστημι· ἐπαναστὰς τῷ δήμῳ 14, 6. ἐάν τινες τυραννεῖν ἐπανιστῶνται 16, 43. (Used in literal sense in Ar.)

ἐπανορθοῦντες—τὴν πολιτείαν 35, 12 (ἐπανορθῶσαι πολιτείαν *Pol.* 1289 *a* 3)

ἐπεί 3, 28; 14, 12; 15, 23; 19, 4, 30; 24, 17 &c.

* ἐπειδάν 7, 29 &c.

ἐπειδή 11, 1; 62, 3

ἔπεστιν, τὸ αὐτὸ γράμμα col. 31, 13

** ἐπεισκαλεῖν, and ** ἐπείσκλητος, 30, 22 f (decree)

ἔπειτα 6, 7. Often after πρῶτον μὲν (*q. v.*), but never followed by δέ. Cf. εἶτα.

ἐπελαύνει (?) 5, 9

ἐπερωτῶσιν, ἐπερωτᾷ 55, 13, 20

ἐπί· *passim.* (1) *c. gen.* (*a*) of place &c., ἐπὶ τοῦ βήματος 28, 17; ἐφ' ἅρματος 14, 29; ἐφ' οὗ 55, 28. ἐπὶ τῶν ἰδίων εἶναι 15, 25. (*b*) 'in the case of', ἐπὶ τῶν ἄλλων 35, 17. (*c*) 'over', [ἐπὶ τῶν] ναυκραριῶν 8, 14. (*d*) of time, ἐπὶ τῆς ἕκτης πρυτανείας 43, 22; cf. 44, 15; 47, 21, 25, 28. ἐπὶ τῆς ὕστερον βουλῆς 46, 6; ἐπὶ Μέδοντος—'Ακάστου 3, 9 f; Δράκοντος 41, 11; Σόλωνος 3, 30; 41, 12; Πεισιστράτου 41, 13; τῶν τετρακοσίων 29, 5. ἐπ' 'Αντιδότου (*sc.* ἄρχοντος) 26, 21; ἐφ' οὗ ἄρχοντος 17, 8. ἐπὶ (τοῦ δεῖνος) ἄρχοντος (20 times) 4, 2; 14, 8, 20; 17, 2; 19, 37; 21, 3; 22, 6; 22, 11, 21; 23, 22; 25, 8; 26, 19; 27, 8; 33, 2; 34, 14; 35, 1; 40, 1; 41, 3; 54, 33; ἐπὶ omitted only twice:—Νικομήδους (?) ἄρχοντος 22, 29, and ἄρχοντος 'Υψιχίδου 22, 40. ἐφ' ὧν ('under the authority of') 38, 19.

(2) *c. dat.* (*a*) of place, 'upon', ἐφ' ᾗ 7, 21; 'at', or 'near', ἐπὶ Παλληνίδι 15, 13; 17, 16; ἐπὶ Ληναίῳ 57, 5; ἐπὶ Παλλαδίῳ 57, 18. (*b*) condition, ἐφ' οἷς 23, 24; 32, 15; 34, 8; ἐπὶ τούτοις 1, 3 (?); 23, 36; ἐπὶ τῇ σωτηρίᾳ 19, 35; ἐφ' ᾧ τε 14, 22; 34, 17. (*c*) ground or reason, ἐπὶ τοῖς ἄλλοις ἐδυσχέραινον 2, 12; χαλεπῶς φερόντων ἐπὶ τούτοις 38, 8; χαλεπῶς ἐνεγκόντες ἐπὶ τῇ συμφορᾷ 33, 5; ἀγανακτῶν ἐπὶ τοῖς γιγνομένοις 36, 2; ἐφ' οἷς ἔχαιρεν ἡ πόλις 35, 20; ἐφ' ᾧ 63, 17. (*d*) object, ἐπὶ καταλύσει τοῦ δήμου 8, 25;—τῆς πολιτείας 25, 15; ἐφ' οἷς 38, 6; 'for', ἐφ' ἑκάστῃ τῶν ἀρχῶν. (*e*) 'in the power of', ἐπὶ τοῖς δικασταῖς 55, 26. (*f*) 'on the security of', ἐπὶ τοῖς σώμασι 2, 8; 4, 33; 6, 2; 9, 3

(3) *c. acc.* 'upon', ἐπὶ τὸν βωμόν 25, 9. 'over', ἐπὶ πάντας 42, 19; τὸ θεωρικόν 43, 2; 47, 10; τὰ ἐκθύματα 54, 24; τοὺς ὁπλίτας, τὴν χωραν, κτλ 61, 4—8; τὰς ναῦς 46, 4. 'for', ἐπὶ τὸ νομοφυλακεῖν 8, 20; τὴν ἀπόστασιν 23, 18; τὴν τοῦ πολέμου κατάλυσιν 38, 5. 'to', ἐπὶ πέρας 38, 24; τὴν ναυτικὴν δύναμιν 27, 5; ἕκαστον τὸ δικαστήριον 63, 23. 'throughout', ἐπ' ἐνιαυτόν 8, 10; ἔτη τέτταρα 13, 3;—τρία 22, 25

ἐπιβάλλειν 56, 42; ἐπιβολήν 61, 15; *sc.* ζημίαν 56, 42; τροχόν 49, 4

* ἐπιβολή 61, 15

ἐπιγράφει, τοῖς θεσμοθέταις 48, 25. ἐπεγράφοντο (τοῖς ἐφήβοις) 53, 23. ἐπιγέγραπται 7, 21; col. 31, 3; πινάκιον ἐπιγεγραμμένον τὸ ὄνομα 63, 18; ἐπιγεγραμμένον τὸ γράμμα col. 31, 6; τὸ στοιχεῖον col. 31, 31. 'allege', πρόφασιν 8, 24. 'paint on', τοῖς δικαστηρίοις χρώματα ἐπιγέγραπται col. 32, 9

ἐπιδείξωσιν, τινα δῶρα λαβόντα 54, 8

ἐπιδημῶ 39, 14, 16 (decree)

* ἐπιδιανέμω· ἐπιδιενεμήθησαν 10, 8

ἐπιδίδωμι· ἐπέδοσαν πρὸς *c. acc.*, 37, 16

* ἐπιδικασίαι, κλήρων καὶ ἐπικλήρων 56, 39

ἐπιεικεῖς, οἱ 28, 5; τοῖς ἐπ. 36, 9; παρὰ τοῖς ἐπ. 28, 4; τῶν ἐπ. (opp. τῶν τυχόντων) ἀνθρώπων 27, 24. τοὺς ἐπ. καὶ τοῦ δήμου καὶ τῶν εὐπόρων 26, 11. τοὺς ἐπιεικεστέρους 26, 4

'Επίζηλος 29, 7

**ἐπιζημιώσεις 45, 9 (law)

ἐπίθετον 3, 17 f; 25, 9 (not found elsewhere in same sense)

*ἐπίθημα col. 36, 8

ἐπιθυμῶσι 16, 10; ἐπεθύμουν 34, 21

ἐπικαλούμενος, ὁ βασιλεὺς 41, 34. ἐπικαλεσάμενος *c. acc.* 20, 6

ἐπικατέστη 3, 6 (τὴν τῶν ἐφόρων ἀρχὴν ἐπικαταστήσας *Pol.* 1313 *a* 27)

ἐπικηρυκευσάμενος, πρὸς *c. acc.*, 14, 21. ἐπικηρύττειν ἀργύριον (ἐπιτίμιον) [Ar.] *Oec.* ii 1351 *b* 31

ἐπίκληρος 9, 8; 42, 35; 43, 21; 56, 33, 39, 40, 44

*ἐπικληροῦσιν (τὰς διαίτας) 53, 28; τὰ δικαστήρια 59, 15; ἐπικληρώσῃ τὰ γράμματα 63, 22; τούτοις ἐπεκλήρουν 8, 3

ἐπικρατῶ· ἐπεκράτουν τῷ πολέμῳ 38, 17 (ἐπικρατοῦσιν οἱ δῆμοι τῶν εὐπόρων *Pol.* 1321 *a* 19)
*ἐπικυρωθέντων τούτων ὑπὸ τοῦ πλήθους 32, 2; ἐπ. τῶν νόμων 37, 12
*ἐπικύρωσιν—χειροτονίας 41, 32
ἐπιλαμβάνει τὸν αὐλίσκον col. 34, 36
ἐπιλείπεσθαι, οὐδενὸς τῶν πολιτῶν 34, 22. ἐπιλειπόμενος τῇ δυνάμει 20, 5; τῇ οὐσίᾳ 27, 18 (*act.* in Ar.)
ἐπιλήθου 20, 22 (scolium)
*ἐπίλοιπος 33, 3
Ἐπίλυκος 3, 29; Ἐπιλύκειον 3, 28, 30
ἐπιμέλεια 21, 20; 26, 2; 38, 29
ἐπιμεληταί (under the 400) 30, 10 (decree); Διονυσίων 56, 23; ἐμπορίου 51, 15; μυστηρίων 57, 2, 7; κρηνῶν ἐπιμελητής 43, 3
ἐπιμελοῦμαι (1) *c. gen.* 15, 25; 16, 10; 39, 5; 42, 17, 28; 44, 11; 46, 1; 51, 3, 16; 52, 1; 56, 21, 26, 29, 39; 57, 1, 2; 61, 7, 25. (2) followed by ὅπως *c. fut.* 50, 10; 51, 10—12. (3) *Abs.* 39, 5 (decree)
ἐπιμελῶς 27, 23
Ἐπιμενίδης ὁ Κρής 1, 3. Βουζύγης frag. 10
ἐπινοούντων ἐξοικεῖν 40, 2 (the *Index Ar.* quotes περὶ κόσμου only)
ἐπισκευάζειν, τὰς ὁδοὺς 54, 2; τὰ μάλιστα δεόμενα τῶν ἱερῶν 50, 3
*ἐπισκευασταί, ἱερῶν 50, 2
*ἐπισκήπτωνται—ταῖς μαρτυρίαις col. 36, 11; ἐπισκήψασθαι *ib.* 13 (πρῶτος ἐποίησε τὴν ἐπίσκηψιν *Pol.* 1274 *b* 7)
*ἐπίσκοπος τῆς πολιτείας 8, 20
ἐπισκοπῶν 16, 14
*ἐπιστατεῖ 44, 2; ἐπιστατούσης 41, 16; ἐπεστάτει 18, 3; ἐπιστατῆσαι 44, 13 (only found in *Rhet. ad Alex.* 1422 *b* 17, and that in another sense)
ἐπιστάτης τῶν πρυτάνεων 44, 1; τῶν προέδρων 44, 9
*ἐπιστατική, γραφὴ 59, 7 (in this sense, here only)
*ἐπιστέλλω· ἐπέ[στελλον] conj. 38, 7 (only in *Rhet. ad Alex.* 1420 *a* 6 ἐπέστειλάς μοι)
ἐπιστολὰς φέροντες, οἱ τὰς 43, 32
*ἐπιστύλιον 47, 33
*ἐπιτάφιος, ἀγὼν 58, 2
ἐπιτελῶ· ἐπετέλεσεν (πολιτείαν) 41, 17; τὸν ἄλλον λόγον 15, 23
ἐπιτήδειος 8, 10; 42, 17; 49, 6, 17; 59, 6. τὰ —εια, 42, 27
ἐπίτηδες 9, 11; 18, 30
ἐπιτίθημι· ἐπιθήσειν (=προσθήσειν) πρὸς τοῖν δυοῖν ὀβολοῖν ἄλλον 28, 22. ἐπέθηκε—τὸ γράμμα 63, 23. *Mid.* ἐπιτιθέμενον τυραννίδι 14, 11; ἐπέθετο τοῖς τυράννοις 20, 20; τῇ βουλῇ 25, 6
*ἐπιτίμους καὶ κυρίους καὶ αὐτοκράτορας ἑαυτῶν 39, 3 (decree)
ἐπιτιμῶ· τὰ μὲν ἐπιτιμῶντες 11, 2. *c. dat.* ἐπιτιμᾷ καὶ τούτοις 36, 8
ἐπιτρέπω· τὴν πολιτείαν ἐπέτρεψαν (Σόλωνι) 5, 5; ἐπιτρέψαι—τοῖς δυνατωτάτοις 39, 33 (decree); οὐ φάσκων ἐπιτρέψειν 34, 12
*ἐπιτροπῆς κατάστασιν, εἰς 56, 37; εἰς ἐπ. διαδικασίαν 56, 38
ἐπίτροποι 56, 32 f, 35, 38, 45
ἐπιφανεῖς 18, 24; 28, 14
ἐπιφέρων, ἀγῶνας 25, 7
*ἐπιχειροτονεῖν 37, 6; 43, 17
*ἐπιχειροτονία 43, 23; 55, 22; 61, 10, 22
ἐπιχειρῶ· ἐπεχείρει 15, 10, 17; ἐπεχείρησε 19, 5
ἐπιψηφίζειν, τοὺς πρυτάνεις 29, 22 (decree); τὸν ἐπιψηφιοῦντα 30, 27 decree; ἐπιψηφίζουσιν, γνώμας 48, 12; ἐπιψηφίσαντος Ἀριστομάχου 32, 3
ἕποιτο, ἕπηται, 12, 11, 13 (Solon)
ἐπονομάσας 21, 14 (ἐπονομάσαι Ar. ap. Strab. 445; Rose, Frag. 601[3])
ἐπορεξάμενος 12, 5 (Solon)
ἔπος· ὡς ἔπος εἰπεῖν 49, 31; 57, 8
ἑπτὰ καὶ δέκα 25, 2
*ἑπτακόσιοι 20, 9; 24, 16, 17
**ἑπτάχους col. 34, 32
**ἑπτετηρίς 54, 29
ἐπωνυμία 13, 25; 45, 6
ἐπώνυμοι (φυλῶν) 21, 25; 48, 17; 53, 21, 26. (2) ἡλικιῶν 53, 21, 27; ὁ ἐπώνυμος ὁ—δεδιαιτηκώς 53, 24; χρῶνται τοῖς ἐπωνύμοις καὶ πρὸς τὰς στρατείας 53, 35 (found in περὶ κόσμου, and in a quotation in *Rhet.*)
*ἐρανικαὶ δίκαι 52, 15
ἐργάζεσθαι, μηδὲν ἔργον 49, 27; ἐν ἀγορᾷ βουλόμενος ἐργ. 52, 14; ἐργαζόμενον, πέτρας 16, 19; εἰργάζοντο τοὺς ἀγρούς 2, 5
ἐργασίας, πρὸς τὰς 16, 6
ἐργάσιμος 47, 12 (ἐργάσιμα χωρία *Probl.* 924 *a* 1)
ἐργάτας, δημοσίους 54, 2
ἔργον, ἀγαθοῦ πολίτου 28, 38; ἔργον ἐργάζεσθαι 49, 27; ἔργα(=μέταλλα) 22, 30
Ἐρετρία 15, 8. τῇ περὶ Ἐρετρίαν ναυμαχίᾳ 33, 4
Ἐρεχθεύς Heracl. Epit. l. 3
ἔρημον γενόμενον 43, 22
ἕρκειος, Ζεὺς 55, 16 (see Jebb on Soph. *Ant.* 487); only in περὶ κόσμου 401 *a* 20
Ἑρμοκρέων ἄρχων (501/0), 22, 6
ἔρομαι· ἔρηται 7, 29; ἐρέσθαι 16, 20 (ἐρομένην *Rhet.* 1391 *a* 10)
ἔρχομαι, *passim*. ἐλθὼν εἰς Ἐρετρίαν 15, 8; ἐλθόντες πρὸς—15, 22; πρὸς τὸ δημαγωγεῖν ἐλθόντος 27, 1; αἱ τῆς βουλῆς κρίσεις εἰς τὸν δῆμον ἐληλύθασιν 41, 27
ἐρώμενον 17, 5; ἐρασθεὶς 18, 8
ἐρωτικός 17, 4
ἐσθλούς 12, 25 (Solon)
ἐσορῶν 5, 8 (Solon)

ἐσχάτας ἡμέρας, εἰς τὰς 40, 3
ἑταιρεία 20, 4; 34, 19, 21
'Ετεοβουτάδαι frag. 3, l. 30
ἕτερος, *passim*. μηδὲ μεθ' ἑτέρων 8, 30. τῶν ἑτέρων (opp. τοῦ δήμου) 28, 13, 19
ἑτέρωθι 12, 15
ἔτι 8, 3; 21, 23 (?); 47, 4. ἔτι καὶ νῦν 3, 25; 7, 6; 8, 6; 22, 7. ἔτι δὲ καὶ 9, 7. ἔτι δὲ 15, 11; 24, 20; 27, 16; 52, 15; 55, 4; 59, 4. ἔτι δὲ πρότερον 20, 20. δημοτικωτέραν ἔτι 27, 3
ἔτος, *passim*. ἔτει δευτέρῳ 14, 7; τῷ ὑστέρῳ ἔτει 22, 20; τρίτῳ 22, 28; 23, 21; τετάρτῳ 19, 3; 21, 2; 22, 39; πέμπτῳ 22, 5; 26, 19; ἕκτῳ 14, 19; ἑβδόμῳ 15, 2; ἑνδεκάτῳ 15, 9; δωδεκάτῳ 22, 10. ἔτη δύο 22, 11; δέκα ἐτῶν 10, 5; ἔτη ἑπτὰ καὶ δέκα 19, 38; 25, 1; τριάκοντα καὶ τρία, ἑνὸς δέοντα εἴκοσι 17, 3 f; ἐπὶ ἔτη τρία 22, 25; εἰς ἑκατὸν ἔτη 7, 7; πολλοῖς ὕστερον ἔτεσιν 3, 19
εὖ ποιεῖ 55, 17
*εὐανδρία 60, 21
Εὐβοίας ἀποστάσης 33, 4
εὐγενής 28, 7
εὐδιαφθορώτεροι 41, 28 (ὁμονοοῦσα ὀλιγαρχία οὐκ εὐδιάφθορος *Pol.* 1306 *a* 10)
εὐδοκιμῆσαι, παρὰ τοῖς Ἕλλησιν 23, 11; πρῶτον εὐδοκιμήσαντος, ὅτε 27, 2; οὐκ εὐδοκιμοῦντα παρὰ τοῖς ἐπιεικέσιν 28, 3; σφόδρ' εὐδοκιμηκώς 14, 2
εὕδοντες 12, 59 (Solon)
εὔθυναν—ἐμβαλέσθαι 48, 20; εἰσάγουσι 48, 26, cf. 54, 6. εὐθύνας διδῶσιν and δοῦναι 39, 23 (decree); διδόασιν 56, 4; ἔδωκε 48, 19; ἔδοσαν 38, 29; δεδωκότων 48, 18. μέχρι εὐθυνῶν 4, 12; περὶ τῶν εὐθυνῶν 31, 7 (decree)
εὔθυνοι 48, 15, 23
εὐθύνω· τοὺς ἁμαρτάνοντας ηὔθυνεν 8, 22
εὐθύς 22, 20; 38, 32; 55, 23. εὐθὺς εἰσελθών 56, 5. εὐθέως 18, 21. εὐθεῖαν—δίκην 12, 46 (Solon)
Εὐκλείδης ἄρχων (403/2) 39, 1
εὐκοσμίας ἐπιμελοῦνται 44, 11
εὐλογώτερον *c. inf.* 7, 26
Εὐμηλίδης ὁ 'Αλωπεκῆθεν 45, 3
Εὐμολπίδαι 39, 6; 57, 4; frag. 3, l. 30
εὔνοια· εἰς τὸν δῆμον 38, 28
*εὐπατρίδαι 13, 9; 19, 17 (scolium)
εὐπορία τροφῆς 23, 10; τὴν Κίμωνος εὐπ. 27, 13
εὐποροῦντες τῶν μετρίων 16, 9; εὐπόρησαν χρημάτων 19, 20
εὐπόρων, τῶν (opp. τοῦ δήμου) 26, 12; 28, 12
εὑρόμενος ἄφεσιν 30, 33 (decree)
*εὐσημία 44, 19
*ἐφέσιμος (κρίσις) 45, 13
ἔφεσις 9, 6; 45, 15, 19; 55, 11 (not found in Ar. in technical sense)
*ἐφέται (?) 57, 24
ἔφηβοι 42, 14, 17, 20, 25, 38; 53, 22, 34 (ἐφήβων ἢ φρουρῶν τάξις *Pol.* 1322 *b* 28)
'Εφιάλτης 25, 4, 13, 17, 18, 21, 23; 26, 14; 28, 11; 35, 9; 41, 17
ἐφίησιν εἰς τὸ δικαστήριον 42, 8; ἐφῇ εἰς τὸ δ. 53, 9 (not found in Ar. in technical sense)
ἐφίστημι· στρατηγῶν ἐφισταμένων 26, 8; τῷ ἄρχοντι τῷ ἐφεστηκότι col. 31, 28
ἔφοδος, ὅπως μὴ ᾖ τοῖς συκοφάνταις 35, 17
ἔχθρα 5, 22
ἐχθρὸν εἶναι καὶ φίλον, ὥστε τὸν αὐτὸν 23, 23
ἐχῖνος 53, 11, 18 (not found in Ar. in technical sense)
ἔχω· *passim*. ἔσχεν γυναῖκα 17, 14; ἐγχειρίδια ἔχοντας 18, 28; χλαμύδας ἔχοντες 42, 33. With double acc. τούτους φύλακας εἶχον τῆς ἀρχῆς 24, 8. Of troops, ἔχοντα στρατιάν, ἱππέας, στόλον 19, 27, 28, 30. εἶχον τὸ θεσμοθετεῖον 3, 30; τὰ πράγματα βεβαίως εἶχον 38, 12; τὴν πόλιν ἐγκρατέστερον ἔσχον 35, 22; τῶν ἐχόντων τὴν πολιτείαν 15, 12
Intrans. ἔχει—τόνδε τὸν τρόπον 42, 1; τοῦτον εἶχε τὸν τρόπον 3, 33; 9, 1; τοῦτον τὸν τρόπον ἔσχεν 12, 1. With adv. ἄριστα 30, 20 (decree); καλῶς 28, 25; κακῶς 19, 5; οἰκείως 36, 5; ὁποτέρως 3, 14
ἐῶ· *c. inf.* εἴασεν 21, 24; εἴων 22, 18. ἐῶντες τὰς πολιτείας παρ' αὐτοῖς καὶ ἄρχειν ὧν ἔτυχον ἄρχοντες 24, 8. εἴασ' 12, 9 (Solon)
ἕως ἐθάρρησαν 40, 7; ἐξηλάθη 13, 7; ἦν 29, 1; περιείλοντο 25, 22; προειστήκει 28, 1; προὔτρεψε 19, 22. *c. opt.* ἕως μηδὲν παρανομοῖεν 28, 37. ἕως ἂν—ᾖ 29, 31, 35 (decree);—γένηται 56, 44;—ἐκτείσῃ 63, 16

*ζευγίσιον 7, 27
ζευγίτης 4, 19; 7, 10, 12; 26, 15, 18 (*Pol.* 1274 *a* 20)
Ζεὺς ἕρκειος 55, 16. Διὶ τῷ Σωτῆρι, πομπὴ 56, 27
ζημίαν, ἐπιβάλλειν 56, 42
ζημιῶ· κολάζουσα καὶ ζημιοῦσα 3, 36; ζημιοῦν καὶ κολάζειν 8, 23. ἡ βουλὴ—ζημιοῖ τοὺς δημότας 42, 13. *subj.* (*abs.*) ζημιοῖ 29, 25 (decree). θανάτῳ ζημιῶσαι 29, 28 (decree); θ. ζημιώσοντας 52, 4; θ. ἐζημίουν 60, 12. χρήμασιν ζημιῶσαι 45, 1; χρ. ζημιοῦν 45, 8; ζημιώσῃ 45, 9. ζημιοῖ τῷ σίτῳ 49, 2
ζητῶ· τὴν ὀλιγαρχίαν ἐζήτουν 13, 19; τὴν πάτριον πολιτείαν 34, 23 (ἰσότητα ζητεῖ ὁ δῆμος *Pol.* 1298 *a* 11)

ἤ *passim*; ('than') 2, 17 &c. ἢ—ἢ 11, 11 &c. ἢ ('or else') 22, 43 (law)
*ἦ μὴν συγγράψειν, ὀμόσαντες 29, 12

(decree); omitted by author in 2, 11; 7, 5; 55, 31
ἡγεμονία *abs.* 23, 4; 24, 2, 5; θαλάττης 23, 11
ἡγεμών 20, 17; 22, 9, 20; 26, 4. ἡγεμόνεσσιν 12, 11 (Solon)
Ἡγησίας ἄρχων 14, 20
Ἡγησίστρατος 17, 11, 16
ἡγοῦμαι, (1) 'lead', *c. gen.* 13, 19; 61, 4, 18, 20, 24; *abs.* 61, 14
(2) 'think', 29, 13 (decree); 35, 21; 40, 22; 42, 16 (ἡγήσασθαι *c. inf.* quoted only from *Meteor.* 339 *b* 22
ἤδη 3, 19; 14, 14; 15, 14; 18, 14; 28, 26; 42, 37 &c.
ἥδομαι· ἡσθεὶς διὰ τὴν παρρησίαν 16, 23
Ἠετιωνεία 37, 9
ἤθεος 56, 21
ἦθος· τὸ δημοτικὸν εἶναι τῷ ἤθει 16, 30. ἤθη δεσποτῶν 12, 41 (Solon)
ἥκω· οὐ[χ ἥξ]ει 11, 5
ἡλιαία (?) 57, 20 (cf. *Pol.* 1301 *b* 23)
ἡλικία· γεγονέναι τὴν ἡλικίαν τὴν ἐκ τοῦ νόμου 42, 5; τῆς ἡλικίας αὐτῷ καθηκούσης 53, 30; ἐκ τῆς ἡλ. τῆς εἰρημένης, τῶν ἐκ τῆς αὐτῆς ἡλ. 30, 15, 23 (decree); 'those of the military age', ὅταν ἡλικίαν ἐκπέμπωσιν 53, 36. *Pl.* ταῖς ἡλικίαις 17, 7; διὰ τὰς ἡλικίας 18, 2
ἡμέρα 19, 36; 20, 13. τῆς ἡμέρας 29, 33; 49, 29; 62, 12; τῆς ἡμέρας ἑκάστης 62, 15. νύκτα καὶ ἡμέραν 44, 2. ὅσαι ἡμέραι ('daily') 43, 13. τίσιν ἡμέραις δεῖ δικάζειν 59, 2
ἡμικοτύλιον 60, 9 (*Hist. An.* 573 *a* 7)
ἥμισυς· αἱ—ἡμίσειαι *bis*, col. 35, 28 f
ἡμίχους col. 37, 4 (*Hist. An.* 630 *a* 34)
Ἡράκλεια, πεντετηρὶς 54, 30
Ἡρακλείδης ὁ Κλαζομένιος 41, 33
*ἠρία (*pl.*) 55, 17
Ἡρόδοτος 14, 25
ἡσυχάσαντες 4, 15 (Solon)
ἡσυχίαν, ἐτήρει τὴν 16, 26; διῆγον ἐν ἡσυχίᾳ 13, 3 (ἡσυχίαν ἄγειν *Pol.* 1297 *b* 7)
ἦτορ 5, 15 (Solon)
ἡττώμενος ταῖς ἑταιρείαις 20, 3; τοῖς ἰδίοις ἡττᾶτο 27, 21; ἡττηθέντος αὐτοῦ 19, 27; ἡττηθέντες—ναυμαχίᾳ 33, 3
ἥττω, τὴν ἀρχὴν τῶν ἀρχομένων 36, 11

θάλατταν, κατὰ 19, 27; τὴν τῆς θαλάττης ἡγεμονίαν 23, 11,—ἀρχὴν 41, 20; τὴν ἀρχὴν τῆς θ. 32, 16
θάνατος 19, 4; 26, 14; 28, 23; 29, 28; 52, 4; 60, 12. ἀμφοτέρων θάνατον κατέγνωσαν 28, 13
θανατοῦν καὶ δεῖν καὶ χρήμασι ζημιοῦν 45, 7; κυρίους εἶναι θανατοῦντας 37, 4. θανατώσοντας 52, 5 (θανατῶσαι, opp. φυγαδεῦσαι, *Oec.* ii 1347 *b* 33; θανατωθῆναι *de Adm.* 836 *a* 6)
Θαργήλια 56, 12 f, 27 f. (Θ. μετὰ τὰ Διονύσια *Met.* 1023 *b* 11)
Θαργηλιών 32, 4 f
θαρροῦντος ἤδη τοῦ δήμου 22, 12; θαρρούσης ἤδη τῆς πόλεως 24, 1; θαρρήσαντας τοὺς πολλοὺς 27, 6; ἕως ἐθάρρησαν 40, 7
θαυμάζειν 15, 24; θαυμάζοντες 14, 30; θαυμάσαι 16, 19; θαυμασάντων πάντων 25, 19
θεάτρῳ, ἐκκλησία ἐν τῷ 42, 30
Θεμιστοκλῆς 22, 31; 23, 14; 25, 11, 13, 21; 28, 11
θεόκτιτον, πατρίδ' εἰς 12, 35 (Solon)
Θεόπομπος ἄρχων (411/0) 33, 2
θεός, ἡ 30, 8 (decree). θεοῖς 7, 23 (anon.); 30, 8 (decree)
Θερμαῖος κόλπος 15, 6
θέσιν, νόμων 14, 7 (*Pol.* 1289 *a* 22, 1298 *a* 18)
*θέσμια, ἀναγράψαντες τὰ 3, 20; θέσμια—καὶ πάτρια 16, 42 (law)
θεσμοθέται 3, 19, 30; 45, 10; 48, 25 f; 55, 4; esp. 59, 1—20; col. 32, 32. εἰσάγουσι τῶν ἐνδείξεών τινας 52, 9. γραμματεὺς τῶν θ. 63, 2. ὁ θεσμοθέτης 63, 22; col. 31, 9
θεσμοθετεῖον 3, 30, 31
θεσμοὺς ἔθηκεν (Δράκων) 4, 3; Δράκοντος θεσμοῖς 7, 12; τῶν Σόλωνος θεσμῶν 35, 11; θεσμοὺς—ἔγραψα 12, 45 f (Solon); only in περὶ κόσμου 401 *a* 10, τοῖς τοῦ θεοῦ θεσμοῖς
Θετταλοί 19, 30
Θετταλός 17, 12; 18, 6; 19, 28
θεωρεῖν τὴν ἐκείνου βούλησιν 9, 14
θεωρίαν, κατὰ 11, 5. θεωρία sent to Delos 56, 20 note
*θεωρικόν, τῶν ἐπὶ τὸ 43, 3; 47, 10
Θηβαῖοι 15, 11
Θηραμένης 28, 19, 30, 30—39; 32, 10; 33, 10; 34, 25; 36, 1
θής· θῆτα 7, 11
Θησεῖον 15, 16, 22
Θησεύς 41, 10
θητικόν, τὸ 7, 15; θητικοῦ—τέλους 7, 24 (anon.); θητικὸν (τελεῖν) 7, 28, 30
θόλος 43, 11; 44, 6 (not found in Ar. in this sense)
Θουκυδίδης κηδεστὴς Κίμωνος 28, 13, 30
Θρασύβουλος· καταλαβόντος Θ. Φυλὴν 37, 1; τὸ ψήφισμα τὸ Θρασυβούλου 40, 8
θρασύνεσθαι 28, 27 (opp. ὑπομένειν in *Eth.* 1115 *b* 33)
θρασύς 18, 7
Θρᾷττα 14, 27
θρυλλεῖν· ἐθ[ρυ]λλ[εῖ]το 16, 27
θυγάτηρ 14, 22; 15, 4; 17, 13
θυρῶν, πρὸ τῶν 14, 13
θυρίς 50, 13
θύει 58, 1; θύουσι 54, 25
θυσίας—θύουσι 54, 27; θύει 58, 1; διοικεῖ 57, 9
θώρακα ἐνδεδυκώς 34, 11

Ἰαονίας 5, 8 (Solon)

ἰδίᾳ καὶ κοινῇ 40, 17. ἴδιος καὶ δημόσιος 6, 4; 43, 27; 48, 19, 24 f; 59, 15. νόμον—ἴδιον 8, 29. ἴδια 9, 10; ταῖς εἰς τὰ ἴδια βοηθείαις 16, 37. ἐπὶ τῶν ἰδίων εἶναι 15, 25. πρὸς τοῖς ἰδίοις ὄντες 16, 9; τοῖς ἰδίοις ἡττᾶτο 27, 21

ἰδιώτην (opp. ἄρχοντα) 48, 12; ἰδιώταις (opp. βουλῇ) 45, 14

ἱερεῦσι 57, 11

ἱερεωσύνη 21, 24; 42, 36; 57, 10

ἱερομνήμων 30, 36 (decree)

ἱερόν, at Eleusis, 39, 5. τὰ ἱερά 55, 16; περιῆλθον 42, 20. τῶν ἱερῶν 44, 4; 57, 28; τῶν ἱερῶν ἐπισκευασταί 50, 2

*ἱεροποιοί 30, 10 (decree); 54, 24

ἱερῶν *adj.* 30, 29 (decree); 43, 29. τῶν ἱερῶν χρημάτων 30, 8 (decree)

ἱκετηρίαν θείς 43, 27; ταῖς ἱκετηρίαις 43, 26 (τὴν ἱκετηρίαν αἰσχυνθέντες ap. *Rhet.* 1411 *b* 7)

*Ἴμβρον, ἀρχαὶ εἰς 62, 16

ἵνα, usually *c. subj.* even after past tense (cf. Eucken, i 52), αἱρῶνται 29, 15 (decree); γεγώνῃ 15, 19; γένηται 55, 27; δείξῃ 25, 17; διατρίβωσιν 16, 8; μὴ—ᾖ 42, 35; μὴ—κακουργῇ col. 31, 14; μὴ προεξαλειφθῇ 47, 34

c. opt. ἀσεβήσαιεν—καὶ γένοιντο ἀσθενεῖς 18, 30

Ἰοφῶν 17, 11

ἱππάδα (τελεῖν) 7, 18; 7, 24 (anon.); 7, 25 (*Pol.* 1274 *a* 21)

*ἵππαρχος εἰς Λῆμνον 61, 25. ἵππαρχον ἕνα 31, 14 (decree in 411). ἵππαρχοι 4, 8, 11, 13; 30, 7; 44, 16; 49, 10; 61, 19 (ἱππαρχίαι καὶ ταξιαρχίαι *Pol.* 1322 *b* 3)

*Ἵππαρχος, son of Peisistratus, 17, 10; 18, 2, 4, 16, 19; 19, 4

*Ἵππαρχος Χάρμου Κολλυτεύς 22, 15, 20

ἱππεύς 4, 19; 7, 10, 12. ἱππεῖς 24, 14; 26, 17; 38, 14; 49, 8; 61, 20, 26. ἱππεῖς (ἐν Ἐρετρίᾳ) 15, 12. Thessalians 19, 29, 31

ἱππεύειν 49, 14, 16 f

Ἱππίας 17, 10; 18, 2 f, 15, 17, 26, 35, 37; 19, 32

*ἱπποδρομία 60, 5, 22

Ἱπποκράτης 22, 24

ἵππος, παρέστηκεν 7, 25. καλὸν ἵππον ἔχων 49, 22. δοκιμάζει τοὺς ἵππους ἡ βουλή 49, 1

*ἱπποτροφεῖν 7, 18 (ἱπποτροφίαι *Pol.* 1321 *a* 11)

Ἰσαγόρας ὁ Τεισάνδρου 20, 2, 5, 10, 13; 28, 9. ἄρχων (508/7) 21, 3

ἰσομοιρίαν ἔχειν 12, 25 (Solon)

ἰσόρροπα τὰ πράγματα 29, 1

ἴσος 63, 8, 21. ἴσαι (αἱ ψῆφοι) col. 36, 35

*ἰσοτελέσι, δίκαι τοῖς 58, 5

ἵστημι· ἔστησαν (τοὺς νόμους) 7, 3. ἔστην 12, 8 (Solon). ἵσταται ἡ στήλη 53, 25; (μηνὸς) ἱσταμένου 62, 14

ἰσχυρᾶς τῆς στάσεως οὔσης 5, 3; ἰσχυρότερα 29, 3

ἰσχυκέναι 9, 5; ἴσχυσεν 23, 3

ἴσως (= μάλιστα) τέτταρας μῆνας 33, 1 (seems not to occur in Ar. in this sense)

ἴχνος τῆς πράξεως, λαβεῖν 18, 26

*Ἴων 3, 8; 41, 7

Ἰώνων ἀπόστασις 23, 18; ὅρκοι 23, 23

καθαίρω· Ἐπιμενίδης—ἐκάθηρε τὴν πόλιν 1, 4

καθαιρῶ· τοὺς—νόμους καθεῖλον ἐξ Ἀρείου πάγου 35, 10; καθελὼν (τὰ γραμματεῖα) 47, 32

καθάπαξ, ἀτίμους εἶναι 22, 43 (law); κύριον ποιήσαντες καθάπαξ 35, 15 (*Pol.* 1259 *b* 36; 1332 *b* 23)

καθάπερ ἐπὶ Ἀκάστου quoted in 3, 11; κ. εἴρηται 4, 24; κ. πρότερον 7, 9; 8, 11; κ. τοὺς πεντακοσιομεδίμνους 7, 26. τὰ μὲν ἄλλα καθάπερ κτλ (formula of amendment) 29, 16

καθαρὰ καὶ ἀκίβδηλα 51, 3; τῷ γένει μὴ καθαροί 13, 23

καθήκων (νόμος) 16, 41. τῆς ἡλικίας καθηκούσης 53, 30; ὅταν καθήκῃ conj. in 43, 15 (ὅταν οἱ χρόνοι καθήκωσιν οὗτοι *Hist. An.* 591 *a* 8; cf. *ib.* 568 *a* 17, 573 *a* 30, 585 *a* 18)

καθῆσθαι 48, 17. καθήμενον *papyri lectio* 45, 3

καθίζει—ἐπὶ τὸν βωμόν 25, 18; καθίζειν (τὴν βουλὴν) 43, 15

καθίημι· τοὺς μύδρους ἐν τῷ πελάγει καθεῖσαν 23, 24

καθίστημι· χορηγοὺς καθίστησι 56, 7, 19; χ. καθίστη 56, 9; λοχαγοὺς καθίστη 61, 18; καθίστη τὴν δημοκρατίαν 29, 18 (decree), κυρίους καθιστάναι 20, 11. καθιστᾶσι τοὺς ἕνδεκα 52, 1; χορηγοὺς καθιστᾶσι 54, 36; καθίστασαν, ἀρχὰς 3, 2. πολιτείαν κατέστησε 7, 1; ἄρχοντα κατέστησε Λύγδαμιν 15, 5; βουλὴν—κατέστησεν 21, 7; κατέστησε—δημάρχους 21, 19; οὐ κατέστησαν ἄρχοντα 13, 4; κατέστησαν—εὐπορίαν τροφῆς 24, 9; καταστῆσαι τὴν—πολιτείαν 29, 5; τοὺς τριάκοντα 34, 16; τοὺς φυλοβασιλεῖς 41, 9; καταστήσαντες (ἀρχὰς) 35, 4. κατέστη 16, 1; 17, 2; 22, 15; κατέστησαν 26, 20; 35, 1; καταστῇ 31, 11 (decree). καθίσταντο 3, 38; 55, 3. πολέμου καθεστῶτος 33, 14.

κάθοδος 15, 13; 19, 10; 38, 24; 41, 5, 23

καθόλου 9, 12

καθ' ὅ τι ἂν 43, 7; 59, 3

καί *passim.* καὶ γὰρ 5, 9. καὶ δὴ καὶ 2, 3; 16, 5, 40

καινὰς τριήρεις 22, 3

καίπερ *c. gen. abs.* 19, 23. *c. part.* 23, 17; 25, 3 (*Pol.* 1269 *b* 1) καιρός· κατὰ τούτους τοὺς κ. 23, 9, 13; 33, 13; κατὰ τοὺς κ. τούτους 26, 4; κατ' ἐκείνους τοὺς κ. 16, 40. ἐν τούτοις τοῖς κ. 22, 39; ἐν τοῖς ὕστερον—κ. 41, 1

κακά 16, 20; κακῶν 16, 21; 18, 8

* κακοπράγμων 35, 19

κακουργῇ, ἵνα μὴ col. 31, 15

κακοφραδής 12, 48 (Solon)

κακῶς 19, 4; 37, 3; 49, 2; 59, 14

κάκωσις γονέων 56, 30; ὀρφανῶν 56, 32; ἐπικλήρου 56, 33; οἴκου ὀρφανικοῦ 56, 34 (σωμάτων—κακώσεις *Rhet.* 1386 *a* 8)

Καλλίας ἄρχων (412/1) 32, 3, 8

Καλλίας ὁ Ἀγγελῆθεν ἄρχων (406/5) 34, 3

Καλλίβιος ἁρμοστής 37, 18; 38, 13

* καλλιερῶ· κἄν τι καλλιερῆσαι δέῃ, καλλιεροῦσι μετὰ τῶν μάντεων 54, 25

Καλλικράτης Παιανιεύς 28, 21

καλὸς κἀγαθός 28, 31. τὸ καλόν 6, 16. καλὸν ἵππον 49, 1. γυναῖκα μεγάλην καὶ καλήν 14, 25

καλῶ· καλεῖ εἰς τὸ κληρωτήριον col. 31, 18; τοὺς εἰληφότας *ib.* 25. καλοῦσι 6, 4; 21, 18; 49, 15. κάλει τοὺς μάρτυρας 55, 19. καλεῖται 13, 16; ἐκαλεῖτο 3, 28. τὸ καλούμενον 19, 32; τὸν κ. 54, 13; καλούμενοι 55, 2; καλουμένους 14, 6; 54, 25. ἐκλήθη 3, 30; κληθέν 16, 18

καλῶς 16, 38; 23, 9; 28, 25; 33, 13; 34, 13; 40, 7; 43, 18; 61, 12. κάλλιστα δή* 40, 17

* κανηφορεῖν 18, 11

* κανονίς col. 31, 13, 16

καρπός 60, 10

* καρπουμένους, τὰ αὑτῶν 39, 4 (decree)

καρτερὸν ἦτορ 5, 15 (Solon)

κατά· *c. gen.* (1) καθ' ἱερῶν ὀμόσαντες 1, 1; ὀμόσαντες καθ' ἱερῶν τελείων 29, 39. (2) κατὰ τῶν ἐπιτρόπων 56, 33. (3) κύριοι—εἰσιν—κατὰ τῶν ὁπλιτῶν 61, 21

c. acc. (1) of place, (*a*) κατὰ θάλατταν, γῆν, 19, 26, 30; τὴν χώραν 16, 8; τὴν εἴσοδον 63, 7. (*b*) 'opposite', τὸν ἐπώνυμον 48, 17. (*c*) φυλάς 22, 21; δήμους 16, 14; ἑκάστην (τριττύν) 8, 15; αὑτήν, 'by itself', or 'on its own responsibility', 8, 10. (*d*) κατὰ πέντε πινάκια εἷς col. 31, 21. (2) of object, ἐμπορίαν καὶ θεωρίαν 11, 4. (3) 'according to', τοὺς νόμους 16, 31; τὰ πάτρια 21, 24; πάσας (τὰς πολιτείας) 28, 37; τὰ γεγραμμένα 31, 15; σελήνην 43, 10; καθ' ὅσον ἦν δυνατός 14, 14; καθ' ὅ τι ἄν—43, 7; 59, 3;—δοκῇ 44, 17; 'in respect to', τῶν κατὰ τὴν πολιτείαν 2, 11; nearly equivalent to διὰ in κατὰ τὸ γένος ἱερεωσύνη 42, 36; κατὰ αὐτὰ ταῦτα ἔνοχός ἐστιν—γραφῇ παρανόμων 45, 23; (of rent) ταύτην τὴν μίσθωσιν. (4) (*a*) of parts of time, ἐνιαυτόν 30, 4 (decree); ἑκάστην τὴν ἡμέραν 27, 16; 30, 27 (decree); cf. κατὰ μικρόν 23, 2; 25, 3. (*b*) of periods of time, ἐκείνους τοὺς καιρούς 16, 40; τούτους τοὺς κ. 23, 9, 13; τοὺς κ. τούτους 26, 4: τῶν καθ' ἑαυτόν 23, 15; πόλεμον 29, 1; 62, 18

καταβαίνοντες εἰς ἄστυ 16, 15; καταβάντας ἐκ τῶν ἀγρῶν 24, 3. *Abs.* καταβάντες (from the acropolis) 18, 19. καταβέβηκεν (*ex equo*) 49, 6

καταβάλλω· (1) *lit.* καταβαλεῖ κόπρον 50, 10. (2) of payment (esp. by instalment) 47, 19, 25, 28, 33; 48, 2, 6 (τιμὴν *Oec.* ii 1346 *b* 29, 1349 *b* 5)

καταβολή (of payment) 47, 20, 30, 32; 48, 5 (αἱ καταβολαὶ τῶν προσόδων *Oec.* ii 1351 *a* 9)

καταγιγνώσκω· κλοπὴν—καταγιγνώσκουσι 54, 7. τούτων—θάνατον κατέγνωσαν 28, 23 (cf. *Rhet.* 1380 *b* 13). ἄν τινος ἀδικεῖν καταγνῷ 45, 9; ἀδικεῖν καταγνῶσιν 54, 10. (αὐτῶν) καταγνῷ 45, 16; (τινὸς) καταγνῶσιν 53, 34; εἴ του καταγνοίη 60, 12. *Abs.* καταγνῷ 48, 23; καταγνῶσιν 54, 9; καταγνόντος (τοῦ δήμου) 46, 10. *Pass.* καταγνωσθέντος τοῦ ἄγους 1, 2

κατάγνυμι· ἐλαίαν—κατάξειεν 60, 11

* καταγνώσεις, εἰσάγειν 45, 9 (decree); cf. 59, 13

κατάγω· κατήγαγεν—καταγούσης 14, 23 f (*Pol.* 1311 *b* 19)

καταδείξαντος, πρώτου 27, 25 (κατέδειξεν ἐναργῶς Ar. 1583 *a* 15 in epigram on Plato)

καταδέχομαι· κατεδέξαντο — τοὺς ὠστρακισμένους 22, 39 (*de Respir.* 476 *a* 29 καταδέχεσθαι τὴν τροφήν)

κατακλῄω· κατακλῄσαντες εἰς τὰ — οἰκήματα 15, 21; κατακλῄσας — εἰς τὸ — τεῖχος 19, 31; κατακλῃσθεὶς—ἐν τῷ ἄστει 27, 9

κατακούειν *abs.* 15, 18. (ἐὰν κατακούσωσιν αὐλοῦντος *Eth.* 1175 *b* 4; κατακούεσθαι τὴν φωνὴν *Hist. An.* 614 *b* 23)

* κατακυρῶ· κατεκύρωσεν—τοὺς νόμους 7, 7; τὰ τέλη—κατακυροῦσιν 47, 10, 15

καταλαβόντος Φυλήν 37, 1; -λαβόντων Μουνιχίαν 38, 1; χρείας -λαβούσης 3, 8

καταλέγω· μερισμόν 48, 10; τοὺς ἱππέας 49, 8, 10; τοὺς πεντακισχιλίους 29, 37 (decree); τρισχιλίους 36, 7; τριηράρχους 61, 82. τοὺς κατειλεγμένους καλοῦσι 49, 15 (πληρωμάτων κατειλεγμένων εἰς ἑκατὸν ναῦς *Oec.* ii 1353 *a* 19, the only authority for this sense in *Index Ar.*)

* καταλογεῖς (ἱππέων) 49, 9; (in 411) 29, 38 note

κατάλογος· τῆς στρατείας γενομένης ἐκ καταλόγου 26, 8; τοῦ κ. μετέχοντας 37, 7; τὸν κ.—ὑπερεβάλλοντο 36, 12; εἰσφέρουσι τὸν κ. εἰς τὴν βουλήν 49, 10

κατάλυσις· τοῦ πολέμου 38, 6. τῶν τυράννων 13, 24; 41, 14; (τῶν τετρα-

κοσίων) 33, 10; 34, 2. ἐπὶ καταλύσει τοῦ δήμου συνισταμένους 8, 25; συνισταμένους ἐπὶ τῇ κ. τῆς πολιτείας 25, 15 (κατάλυσις τῆς ὀλιγαρχίας *Pol.* 1305 *a* 3; καταλύσεις τυραννίδων 1312 *b* 21)
καταλύω· τὴν τυραννίδα 19, 8 (καταλυθείσης τῆς τυραννίδος 20, 1; 28, 7). τὴν βουλήν 20, 10; 25, 13; 41, 18 (κατελύθη, *sc.* ἡ βουλή, 32, 4). πάσας τὰς πολιτείας 28, 36; τὴν δυναστείαν 36, 6; τὸ κῦρος 35, 12; τοὺς τετρακοσίους 33, 7; τοὺς τριάκοντα 38, 5; τοὺς δέκα 38, 18. κατέλυσε 28, 21.
Pass. ἡ κρίσις καταλέλυται 60, 14; *Mid.* κατελύοντο τὸν πόλεμον 32, 15.
c. gen. μὴ καταλυθῶσιν τῆς ἀρχῆς 38, 10
καταπάλτην ἀφιέναι 42, 24
καταπαύειν τὴν ἐνεστῶσαν φιλονικίαν 5, 10
καταπλέοντος, τοῦ σίτου τοῦ 51, 16
καταπλαγεὶς 25, 18; 34, 26. καταπλῆξαι 38, 10
* καταρρυπαίνειν 6, 18
* κατασεσημασμένα τὰ ὀνόματα 49, 12. (ἐχίνους) κατασημηνάμενοι 53, 12
κατασιωπῶσιν 14, 12
* κατασκήψαντες, τεῖχος 37, 9
κατασκευάζω· κατεσκεύαζε δικαστάς 16, 13. τὴν ἀρχὴν — κατασκευάζοντες 36, 12. κατεσκεύασε (τὸ πολεμαρχεῖον) 3, 29; τοῦτο 18, 29; μισθοφορὰν τοῖς δικασταῖς 27, 22. κατασκευάσασι τὴν—ὀλιγαρχίαν 37, 10
κατασκευή, πομπῆς 56, 26
κατάστασις· (1) τῆς πολιτείας 42, 1; τῶν τετρακοσίων 41, 20; cf. 11, 10; 14, 20; 16, 41; 22, 6; 41, 6. (2) ἐπιτροπῆς 56, 37. (3) ἐμφανῶν 56, 38
* κατατραυματίσας ἑαυτόν 14, 2
*καταφατίζω· *impf.* 7, 5 (κατάφασις, καταφατικός, Ar. *saepius*, *e.g.* *Categ.* 12 *b* 7 ἡ κατάφασις λόγος ἐστὶ καταφατικός)
καταφεύγω· κατέφυγον 20, 13
καταχαρίζεσθαι τὴν κρίσιν 49, 21 (πολλὰ τῶν κοινῶν *Pol.* 1271 *b* 3)
*καταχειροτονία 59, 5
κατελθεῖν τοὺς ἀπὸ Φυλῆς 38, 15; τὸν δῆμον 38, 20. τῶν φυγάδων οἱ κατελθόντες 34, 20; τῶν ἐκ Πειραιέως κατελθόντων 38, 31. τῶν κατεληλυθότων 40, 11
κατέχω· (1) 'restrain', οὐ κατεῖχε τὴν ὀργήν 18, 9; ἑαυτόν 18, 37. κατέσχε δῆμον 12, 49 and 63 (Solon). (2) 'retain', βουλόμενος κατασχεῖν αὐτούς 40, 5. (3) 'hold'; 'gain, or keep, possession of'; τὴν ἀκρόπολιν κατέσχε 14, 6; κατεῖχον τὴν ἀρχήν 17, 9; κατέχοντα τὴν ἀρχήν 17, 18; κατασχήσειν τὴν ἡγεμονίαν 24, 5; κατασχόντος τοῦ δήμου τὰ πράγματα 20, 16; κατεῖχον τὴν πόλιν δι' ἑαυτῶν 35, 7; κατεῖχεν τὴν τυραννίδα 15, 13; κατασχόντες τὴν τυρ. 19, 37; *abs.* κατεῖχεν 15, 3
κατηγορία 55, 21
*κατήγορος 42, 9; 55, 21, 26
κατηγορῶ· *c. gen.* 18, 23, 29; 25, 20; 37, 17; 55, 21, 23. κατηγόρησε τὰς εὐθύνας Κίμωνος 27, 2
*κατοικοδομεῖν, τὰς ὁδοὺς 50, 11
κατοικῶ· 22, 42; 39, 17 f (decree); 40, 26
κεῖται 5, 7 (Solon): ὄνομα-κείμενον 7, 20
κελεύει 8, 7; 49, 26; 51, 14; 53, 31. κελεύουσιν 43, 29; 53, 34. κελεύῃ 44, 7. ἐκέλευεν 16, 20. ἐκέλευσεν 15, 18. κελεύων 22, 32; κελεύοντες 37, 5; κελευουσῶν 40, 21
κενόν col. 33, 10
κέντρον 12, 47 (Solon)
κέρδει καὶ χάρισιν 41, 29
κηδεστής 28, 13
Κήδων 20, 20, 22
κῆρυξ (τῶν ἐννέα ἀρχόντων) 62, 11; (in the law-courts) col. 36, 11, 31. *pl.* κήρυξιν—πρεσβείαις 20, 29 (decree); 43, 30
Κήρυκες 39, 5; 57, 4
κηρυξάντων, τῶν στρατηγῶν 23, 6. ὁ ἄρχων—κηρύττει 56, 52
Κηφισοφῶν ἄρχων (329/8) 54, 33
κιβώτιον 63, 4 f; col. 31, 1, 5, 10, 12, 14, 30; col. 32, 20
*κιθαριστρία 50, 6
Κίμων 26, 5; 27, 1; his εὐπορία 27, 13; τυραννικὴν ἔχων οὐσίαν 28, 12
κίνδυνον, μετὰ τὸν 38, 3
Κινέας 19, 28
κινεῖν, ταῦτα 11, 3; τὴν αἵρεσιν οὐκ ἐκίνουν 26, 14; κ[ινήσα]ντες τὴν δημοκρατίαν 29, 4
Κλαζομένιος 41, 33
Κλεαίνετος 28, 15
κλεῖς τὰς τῶν ἱερῶν, τὰς 44, 3
Κλεισθένης 20, 3, 4, 8, 15, 17; 21, 2; 22, 4, 16; 28, 7; 29, 17, 20; 41, 15
Κλειτοφῶν 29, 15; 34, 24
Κλεομένης 19, 6, 29; 20, 6, 13, 14
Κλεοφῶν 28, 19, 26; 34, 10
κλέπτης 51, 2
κλέπτοντ' 54, 6
Κλέων 28, 15
κλῆμα (?) 60, 14 *n. c.*
κλήρου καὶ ἐπικλήρου 42, 35; κλήρων καὶ ἐπικλήρων 9, 8; 43, 21; 56, 39; 58, 9
κληρῶ· *act.* ἐξ ὑπαρχῆς κληροῦν 4, 17; (in appointment of archons) δέκα κλ. ἑκάστην (τὴν φυλήν), εἶτ' ἐκ τούτων κυαμεύειν 8, 4; κλ. τοὺς ταμίας ἐκ τῶν πεντακοσιομεδίμνων 8, 7; κλ. τὴν βουλὴν τοὺς ἐννέα ἄρχοντας 30, 25 (decree); κλ. τοὺς λαχόντας πέντε τοὺς ἐθέλοντας προσελθεῖν ἐναντίον τῆς βουλῆς 30, 27 (decree)
κληροῖ (ὁ ἐπιστάτης τῶν πρυτάνεων) προέδρους ἐννέα 44, 8. κλ. (ἡ βουλή)

ἱεροποιούς 54, 24; ἱεροποιοὺς τοὺς κατ' ἐνιαυτόν 54, 27; Διονυσίων ἐπιμελητάς 56, 25

κληροῦσι—ἀθλοθέτας 60, 2; γραμματέα τὸν κατὰ πρυτανείαν 54, 13; (γρ. τὸν) ἐπὶ τοὺς νόμους 54, 19; δικαστάς (πάντες οἱ ἐννέα ἄρχοντες δέκατος δ' ὁ γραμματεὺς τῶν θεσμοθετῶν) 59, 18; τὰ δικαστήρια (οἱ ἐννέα ἄρχοντες κτλ) 63, 1; εἰς Σαλαμῖνα ἄρχοντα καὶ εἰς Πειραιέα δήμαρχον 54, 34; εἰσαγωγέας 52, 11; εὐθύνους 48, 14; θεσμοθέτας 55, 4; λογιστάς 48, 13; ὁδοποιοὺς κτλ. 54, 1; (τοὺς) τετταράκοντα 53, 1

(τριττῦς) ἐκλήρωσεν τρεῖς εἰς τὴν φυλὴν ἑκάστην 21, 14

Mid. κληροῦσθαι (τὰς ἀρχὰς) τοὺς ὑπὲρ τριάκοντα ἔτη γεγονότας 4, 14; 7, 29; (of dicasts) κληρουμένων—μᾶλλον τῶν τυχόντων ἢ τῶν ἐπιεικῶν ἀνθρώπων 27, 23; τοὺς κληρωσομένους τῶν ἐννέα ἀρχόντων 26, 15

Pass. κληροῦσθαι—τὸν ἐπιψηφιοῦντα 30, 27 (decree). βουλὴ κληροῦται 43, 6. (τῶν πωλητῶν) κληροῦται εἷς ἐκ τῆς φυλῆς 47, 2; (τῶν ταμιῶν τῆς Ἀθηνᾶς) κλ. εἷς ἐκ τῆς φυλῆς 47, 7; (ἐμπήκτης) col. 31, 14. κληροῦνται ἀγορανόμοι 51, 1; ἱερῶν ἐπισκευασταί 50, 1; μετρονόμοι 51, 5. (ἀρχαί) μετ' ἐννέα ἀρχόντων ἐκ τῆς φυλῆς ὅλης κληρούμεναι 62, 2; (ἀρχαί) ἐν Θησείῳ κληρούμεναι 62, 2; (ἀποδέκται) κεκληρωμένοι κατὰ φυλάς 48, 1

*κληρωτήριον 63, 4; col. 31, 15, 18

κληρωτὸς (γραμματεὺς κατὰ πρυτανείαν) 54, 19; (ταμίας) 49, 30. κληρωτοί (οἱ ἕνδεκα) 52, 1; (σιτοφύλακες) 51, 8. ἀρχαὶ κληρωταί 8, 1, 5; 30, 13 (decree); 43, 2; 55, 1; 62, 1

κλοπὴν (δημοσίων χρημάτων) καταγιγνώσκουσι 54, 7

Κοδρίδαι 3, 13

κοινῇ 5, 4, 10; 23, 17; 40, 18, 21; 57, 6

κοινόν, μέτριον καὶ 6, 14 (of Solon). κοινόν, *c. gen.* 39, 5 (decree). εἰς τὸ κοινόν 42, 28. τὰ κοινά 9, 10; 14, 17; 15, 25; 16, 10; 24, 5; ἀπὸ τῶν κοινῶν 25, 21; 56, 37; τὰς κοινὰς λῃτουργίας 27, 14

κοινωνεῖν *c. gen.* 6, 9; 13, 24; τῶν κοινωνούντων τῆς πράξεως 18, 16; κοινωνεῖν τῆς—πολιτείας 37, 8; ἀμφοτέρων κεκοινωνηκώς 37, 11

κοινωνικαὶ δίκαι 52, 15 (not found in Ar. in technical sense)

κολάζουσα καὶ ζημιοῦσα 3, 36; ζημιοῦν καὶ κολάζειν 8, 23

Κολλυτός 14, 26; 22, 16

κόλπος, Θερμαῖος 15, 6

κομίζειν (σῖτον) 51, 18; κομίσαντος (of troops) 17, 16. *Mid.* κομίσασθαι τὰ χρήματα παρὰ τῶν δανεισαμένων 22, 35

Κόνων ἄρχων (402/1) 25, 8

κόπρος, 50, 10; *κοπρολόγοι 50, 9

κόρος 12, 13 (Solon)

*κορυνηφόροι 14, 5

*κοσμητής 42, 19

κόσμος· τὴν θεὸν ἀπομιμησάμενος τῷ κόσμῳ 13, 28; τὸν ἄλλον κόσμον (of the Parthenon) 47, 6. ἐν κόσμῳ λεγόντων 28, 18

κρατεῖν, ἔχειν καὶ 56, 7; ὁ δῆμός ἐστιν ὁ κρατῶν 41, 26; οἱ δῆμοι κρατήσαντες 40, 24

κρατερὸν σάκος 12, 8 (Solon)

κράτος 12, 42 (Solon)

κρηνῶν ἐπιμελητής 43, 3

κριθαί 51, 12

κρίνειν, δίκας 3, 32; αὐτοτελεῖς κρίνειν 53, 6; κρίνει τὰς ἀρχὰς ἡ βουλή 45, 12; κρίνουσιν (στρατηγόν) 61, 12; κρίνασα 8, 9; ἔκρινεν 8, 25; 60, 11; παραδείγματα—ἡ βουλή 49, 20; κρίνεσθαι Μηδισμοῦ 25, 12; κρινόμενος 27, 26

κρίσις, οὐ κυρία 45, 13; καταλέλυται 60, 14. κρίσεως—κύριος 9, 11; κρίσεως—γενομένης 45, 5; ἀμφισβήτησις κρίσεως 28, 34. πρὸς τὴν κρίσιν 3, 21; καταχαρίζεσθαι τὴν κρίσιν 49, 22. αἱ τῆς βουλῆς κρίσεις 41, 27

Κρόνος· ὁ ἐπὶ Κρόνου βίος 16, 27

κτῆμα 60, 14

κτίζω· ἀπὸ τῶν κτισάντων 21, 22 (*Pol.* 1275 *b* 33, 1310 *b* 38

κτῶμαι· οὐσίαν κεκτημένους 4, 6; συμπείθειν τὸν κεκτημένον 39, 10 (decree); ὁ τὸ χωρίον κεκτημένος 60, 8, 13

*κυαμεύειν, ἐκ τούτων 8, 4; ἐκυάμευσαν τοὺς—ἄρχοντας 22, 21

κύαμος· τοὺς ἀπὸ κυάμου δισχιλίους ἄνδρας 24, 20; τὴν εἰληχυῖαν τῷ κυάμῳ βουλήν 32, 6

κύβοι col. 31, 17 f; col. 32, 31

(Κύλων) 1, 1—3 notes

κύρβεις 7, 3 (only in *de Mundo* 400 *b* 30, τὰ ἐν κύρβεσιν ἀναγεγραμμένα)

κύριος· ὁ νόμος 47, 4; οὐ κυρία ἡ κρίσις 45, 13; κυρία ἐκκλησία 43, 17; 62, 7; ἀμφορεὺς κύριος, ἄκυρος, col. 63, 21; κυρίαν (ψῆφον) col. 36, 20; ὅ τι ἂν οἱ δικασταὶ ψηφίσωνται, τοῦτο κύριον εἶναι 45, 11; ὅ τι ἂν γνῶσιν οἱ δικασταί, τοῦτο κύριόν ἐστι 48, 27; ὄντες κύριοι 52, 19

c. gen. ἁπάντων 41, 25; τῶν αὐτῶν 61, 21; τῶν γραμμάτων 54, 14; τῆς δοκιμασίας 55, 12; ἑαυτῶν 39, 3; τῆς κρίσεως 9, 12; οὐδενός 54, 22; τῆς πόλεως 20, 11; 34, 16; 35, 2; τῆς πολιτείας 9, 7; τῶν πραγμάτων 6, 1; 18, 1; 41, 2; 55, 1; τῆς ψήφου 9, 6

c. inf. 3, 31; 8, 23; 29, 36 (decree); 44, 13; 45, 19; 56, 42; 58, 1; 61, 14

c. part. 37, 13 κυρίους εἶναι θανατοῦντας

κυρίως, ζημιοῦσα 3, 36

*κῦρος, ὃ ἦν ἐν τοῖς δικασταῖς· κατέλυσαν τὸ 35, 12

κυροῦσι τὰ σύμβολα τὰ πρὸς τὰς πόλεις 59,

16; *κυρωθέντων δὲ τούτων* 30, 1 (only *ἐν τῇ Τενεδίων πολιτείᾳ*, p. 1569 *a* 27, frag. 593[3], *ἐκύρωσε καὶ περὶ τοῦ ἰδίου παιδὸς τηρηθῆναι τὸν νόμον*)
Κυψελίδαι 17, 14
κυεῖν 56, 42
κυσὶν πολλαῖσιν 12, 54 (Solon)
* *κωλακρέται* 7, 13
κωλύω· ἐκώλυσεν 18, 11; 22, 32. *c. inf.* *γενέσθαι* 34, 10; *δανείζειν* 6, 2; *κατοικοδομεῖν* 50, 11; *κοινωνεῖν* 37, 8; *παριέναι* 19, 31; as in Ar. (*Index* p. 419 *b* 32) never followed by *μή*
Κωμέας ἄρχων (560/59) 14, 8
κωμῳδοῖς, χορηγοὺς 56, 9, 11 (*κωμῳδοῖς χορηγῶν* *Eth.* 1123 *a* 23; *χορὸν κωμῳδῶν ὀψέ ποτε ὁ ἄρχων ἔδωκεν* *Poet.* 1449 *b* 1)
κωτίλλοντα 12, 19 (Solon)

λαγχάνω· δίκας λαγχάνουσι (πρὸς) 53, 2; *τῷ δράσαντι λαγχάνει* 57, 30. *οὐ ἔλαχον* col. 37, 8. *τοῦ εἰληχότος* col. 32, 14; *τοὺς εἰληχότας* col. 31, 24; *τοῖς εἰληχόσιν* col. 32, 24. *ἃς ἂν λάχῃ διαίτας* 53, 29; *εἰς οἷον ἂν λάχῃ (δικαστήριον)* col. 31, 32; *καθ' ὅ τι ἂν λάχωσιν* 43, 7. *ὁ λαχών* 47, 4; *εἷς ὁ λαχών* 44, 1; *τὸ γράμμα τὸ λαχόν* 63, 24; *τὸ δικαστήριον τὸ λαχόν* 49, 21; *τὸ λαχὸν μέρος* 30, 16 (decree); 58, 7; *τῷ λαχόντι* 50, 9. *οἱ λαχόντες* 57, 24; *οἱ λ. ἐπὶ τὰς ψήφους* col. 35, 30; *τῶν λαχόντων δικαστῶν* 63, 6; *τοὺς λαχόντας* 4, 14; *(πέντε)* 30, 26, 28
Pass. *γραφαὶ καὶ δίκαι λαγχάνονται πρὸς αὐτόν* 56, 29; *γραφαὶ λ. πρὸς αὐτόν* 57, 9; *δίκαι λ. πρὸς αὐτόν* 58, 4; *λ. δίκαι* 57, 12
Λακεδαιμόνιοι 19, 7, 21; 23, 19; 29, 3; 32, 14; 34, 8; 37, 18; 38, 25; 40, 20
Λακεδαίμων 37, 17; 38, 7, 27
Λακιάδαι 27, 15
Λάκωνες 19, 7, 21, 25; 23, 20
λαμβάνει ἀποτιμήματα 56, 45; *δίκην λαμβάνουσιν* 42, 34; *λ. δωρεάν* 46, 7; *εἰς σίτησιν λ.* 62, 10. *λαμβάνων* 25, 26; *λαμβάνοντες ἀργύριον* 43, 11; *λ. τριάκοντα μνᾶς* 50, 3. *τὴν θυγατέρα αὐτοῦ λήψεται* 14, 23. *ἔλαβεν (τὴν δεξιάν)* 18, 35; *προστάτην ἔλαβεν ὁ δῆμος* 28, 3. *λαβεῖν (αὐλητρίδα)* 50, 8; *λ. τὴν δεκάτην* 16, 22; *λ. τὴν ἐξουσίαν* 41, 4; *τὴν ἡγεμονίαν λ.* 23, 11. *λ. ἴχνος* 18, 25. *λαβών* 22, 36; *λ. τὴν ἀρχήν* 14, 16; 15, 13; *δωρεὰν λ.* 46, 6; *λ. τὴν ἐπιμέλειαν* 38, 29; *λ. τοὺς κορυνηφόρους* 14, 5; *μοιχὸν λ.* 57, 19; *λαβόντες ἀσπίδα* 42, 31; *δῶρα λαβόντα* 54, 8. *δῶρα λήψεσθαι* and *λάβωσι* 55, 32. *ληφθέντων (=ἁλόντων)* 19, 34
λαμπάδων ἀγῶνες 57, 7
λαμπρῶς, ἐλῃτούργει 27, 14 (*χορηγεῖν λαμπρῶς* *Eth.* 1122 *b* 22)
λανθάνω· λάθῃ—ἔρημον γενόμενον 43, 22
λέγω· λέγει 12, 15; *λέγουσι* 6, 8. *λέγων* 14, 12; *ὁ πρότερον λέγων, ὁ ὕστερον λέγων*, col. 36, 15 f; *ἐν κόσμῳ λεγόντων* 28, 18. *λέγεται* *c. acc. et inf.* 14, 8. *ὁ λεγόμενος λόγος* 18, 26. *ἐλέχθη* 21, 5. *v.* *εἰπεῖν* and *εἴρηται*
Λειμώνη (Ἱππομένους) Heracl. epit. l. 12
λείπω· (δίκην) ἔλιπεν 16, 34 (retinet Blass, coll. Dem. 49 § 19, 59 § 60)
Λειψύδριον 19, 12, 15
λείως 12, 19 (Solon)
Λέσβιοι 24, 7
λευκοί, κύβοι col. 31, 19
λευκῶ· πινάκιον λελευκωμένον 48, 20; *λελευκωμένα γραμματεῖα* 47, 16, 27; 53, 22 (only in *Phys. Ausc.* 185 *b* 29 *ὁ ἄνθρωπος οὐ λευκός ἐστιν ἀλλὰ λελεύκωται*)
Λεωκόρειον 18, 20
Λῆμνον, *ἀρχαὶ εἰς* 62, 16; *ἵππαρχος εἰς* 61, 25; *τῶν ἱππέων τῶν ἐν Λήμνῳ* 61, 26
Ληναίῳ, *ἐπὶ* 57, 5
λῆξις· λήξεις κλήρων 43, 21; *νεῖμαι—τοὺς ἄλλους πρὸς τὴν λῆξιν ἑκάστην* 30, 17 (decree); *ἵνα νεμηθῶσιν εἰς τὰς τέτταρας λήξεις* 31, 19 (only in *de Mundo* 401 *b* 20 *ἡ κατὰ φύσιν λῆξις*)
**ληροῦσιν* 17, 5 (*λῆρος* *Pol.* 1257 *b* 10; *ληρώδης* *Rhet.* 1414 *b* 16; *Hist. An.* 579 *b* 3)
λῃτουργία 27, 14; 56, 16
λῃτουργῶ· 27, 14; 29, 35 (decree); 56, 15 f
λίαν 12, 12 (Solon); *ἀρχαϊκῶς καὶ λίαν ἁπλῶς* 14, 22 (*λίαν ἀρχαίως* *Pol.* 1330 *b* 33; *λίαν ἁπλοῦν* *Meteor.* 339 *b* 34; *ἁπλῶς* 365 *a* 26)
λίθος· ὀμνύντες πρὸς τῷ λίθῳ 7, 5; *βαδίζουσι πρὸς τὸν λίθον* 55, 28
λογιζόμενοι, οἱ τοῖς ὑπευθύνοις 54, 5; *τοὺς λογιουμένους ταῖς ἀρχαῖς* 48, 14
λογισταὶ δέκα (τῆς βουλῆς) 48, 13. *λογισταὶ δέκα καὶ συνήγοροι* 54, 3
λόγος· (1) 'speech', *τὸν ἄλλον λόγον ἐπετέλεσεν* 15, 23; *τὸν πρὸ τοῦ ψηφίσματος λόγον* 29, 6; in the law-courts, (*εἰρημένοι*) *οἱ λόγοι* col. 35, 31. (2) 'current account', *ὁ τῶν δημοτικῶν λόγος* 6, 13 (=*ὡς οἱ δημοτικοὶ λέγουσι* 6, 8); *ὁ λεγόμενος λόγος* 18, 26; 'rumour', 'report', *διασπείρας λόγον* 14, 24; *διεσπάρησαν οἱ λόγοι πρὸς τὸ πλῆθος* 36, 4. (3) 'in name alone', *λόγῳ μόνον* 32, 12. (4) 'accounts', *λόγον ἀπενεγκεῖν* 54, 4
λοιδορήσας 18, 12; *ἐλοιδορήσατο* 28, 17
λοιπός· τὸ λοιπὸν 22, 41; 31, 15 (decree); *εἰς τὸν λοιπὸν χρόνον* 30, 15 (decree); *τὰ λοιπὰ (ἔτη)* 17, 4
λοξὸν—ὁρῶσι 12, 21 (Solon)
λοχαγοί 61, 18 (*de Mundo* 399 *b* 6; *Oec.* ii 1350 *b* 11; *λοχαγίαι* *Pol.* 1322 *b* 4)
Λύγδαμις ὁ Νάξιος 15, 11, 15
Λυκομήδης Σκύριος Heracl. epit. l. 7

*λυκόποδες frag. 5
λύκος 12, 54 (Solon)
Λυκοῦργος 13, 20; 14, 19
λυμαίνομαι· τὴν ὅλην ἐλυμήναντο πρᾶξιν 18, 21
*λυροποιός, Κλεοφῶν ὁ 28, 20
Λύσανδρος, King of Sparta 34, 16, 25
Λυσικράτης ἄρχων (453/2) 26, 19
Λυσίμαχος, father of Aristides, 22, 39; 23, 13
Λυσίμαχος ὁ ἀπὸ τοῦ τυπάνου 45, 2–7
*λυχνεῖον col. 36, 17
λωποδύτης 52, 3

μαλακός 3, 7; 18, 12
μᾶλλον 14, 17; 15, 19; 16, 3; 29, 8 &c. ἀεὶ μᾶλλον 27, 23.—μάλιστα 9, 4; 13, 18; 16, 40; 18, 4; 22, 16; 25, 2. πολλῶν μὲν καὶ ἄλλων, μ. δὲ Θηβαίων 15, 11; αἰτίων μ. γενομένων Πεισάνδρου κτλ 32, 9; μάλιστα with numbers 32, 9; τῶν προγεγενημένων 33, 5.—μάλα does not occur.
μανιῶν <ἕνεκα> 35, 15 (law)
*μαντευτὰ ἱερά 54, 25
μάντεων, μετὰ τῶν 54, 26
Μαραθῶνι, ἐν 22, 10
μαρτυρίαι 53, 10, 17; 55, 30
μαρτυρεῖ 5, 14; 6, 19
μάρτυρες 55, 30. κάλει τοὺς μάρτυρας 55, 19; ἐπειδὰν παράσχηται τοὺς μ. 55, 20
Μαρωνεία 22, 30
*μαστιγοφόρους—ὑπηρέτας 35, 6
μάχαιραν, σπασάμενος τὴν 18, 38
μάχην, τὴν ἐπὶ Παλληνίδι 17, 16; τὴν ἐν Μαραθῶνι 22, 10. (τῶν ἀπὸ Φυλῆς) νικησάντων μάχῃ τοὺς μετὰ τῶν τριάκοντα 38, 2
μάχεται, πρὸς ἑκατέρους ὑπὲρ ἑκατέρων 5, 9
Μεγακλῆς (the slayer of Cylon) Heracl. epit. l. 15
Μεγακλῆς Ἱπποκράτους Ἀλωπεκῆθεν 22, 24
Μεγαρέας· ἐν τῷ πρὸς Μ. πολέμῳ 14, 2; (+περὶ Σαλαμῖνος) 17, 6
μέγας· γυναῖκα μεγάλην καὶ καλήν 14, 25.
μείζων ('too powerful') 22, 27; μείζω 10, 4; στόλον μείζω 19, 30
μέγισται καὶ πρῶται τῶν ἀρχῶν 3, 4; τὰ πλεῖστα καὶ τὰ μέγιστα 3, 35; 8, 22; πρῶτον καὶ μέγιστον 9, 3; μεγίστην εἶχεν δύναμιν 13, 11; μέγιστον πάντων ἦν 16, 29
μέγεθος τοῦ τιμήματος 7, 14
Μέδων (βασιλεύς) 3, 9
*μεθιδρυσόμενος, ἐκεῖσε 19, 6
μεθίστατο 22, 27
μεθύων 34, 11
μέλανες, κύβοι col. 31, 19
μέλλω c. inf. praes. 6, 6; 7, 29; 18, 11; 24, 12, 14; 45, 3; col. 36, 10
c. inf. fut. 63, 10 and col. 31, 36 μέλλῃ πληρωθήσεσθαι (not noted either by H-L, or in *Class. Rev.* v 185 *b*).
εἰς τὸ μέλλον 6, 2; εἰς τὸν μέλλοντα χρόνον 31, 1
μέμνηται 6, 20; 12, 2
μεμψιμοιρία· pl. 12, 55: (only in *de Virt.* 1251 *b* 25; μεμψίμοιρος in *Hist. An.* 608 *b* 10)
μὲν—δέ *passim*, 1, 2 f; 3, 2 f &c. μέν without δέ 19, 9; 48, 23. μέν in irregular position 48, 24; μὲν—δὲ—δέ 21, 13. μὲν οὖν *passim*, 2, 10; 3, 14, 33; 4, 1; 8, 8; 9, 1, 10; 10, 1 &c.
μέν<τοι> 28, 35
μένω· μένειν 44, 5; 49, 2; ἔμεινεν 16, 35; μεινάντων 38, 31; 39, 3. μεμένηκε διὰ βίου 3, 38
μερίζειν κατὰ τὰς—τριττῦς 21, 10; (τὰ χρήματα) μερίζουσι ταῖς ἀρχαῖς 48, 8
μερισμός 48, 9, 11 (*Met.* 1027 *b* 20 Bz μ. ἀντιφάσεως)
μέρος, κατὰ 55, 5; τὸ λαχὸν μέρος 30, 16 (decree); ἐν μέρει 43, 7; 56, 13; ἐν τῷ μέρει col. 37, 7. τὰ δύο μέρη 51, 17. διένειμε τὴν χώραν—τριάκοντα μέρη 21, 12; διανεῖμαι τέτταρα μ. 58, 6; νενέμηνται—δέκα μ. 63, 20
μεσόγειος, ἡ 21, 14
μέσος· Σόλων—τῇ οὐσίᾳ καὶ τοῖς πράγμασι τῶν—μέσων 5, 12; τὴν μέσην πολιτείαν 13, 18; ψῆφοι—αὐλίσκον ἔχουσαι ἐν τῷ μέσῳ col. 35, 28
μετὰ c. gen. τῶν Ἀθηναίων 19, 33; αὐτοῦ 20, 11; ὀλίγων 20, 18; ὁποτέρων 11, 13; τούτων 14, 6. μεθ' ὅπλων 18, 28. μετὰ σπουδῆς 25, 17
c. acc. τοὺς ἀρχαίους 28, 29; τὸν—θάνατον 19, 4; τὴν τῶν νόμων θέσιν 14, 7; τὴν κάθοδον 15, 2; τὴν τῶν τυράννων κατάλυσιν 13, 24; 21, 3; τὴν πρώτην κατάστασιν 14, 19; ταύτην τὴν κατάστασιν 22, 6; τὰ Μηδικά 23, 2; 25, 2; τὴν ναυμαχίαν 23, 22; τὴν νίκην 22, 11; οὐ πολύ 6, 10; οὐ πολὺν χρόνον 25, 24; 34, 13; ταῦτα 2, 1; 10, 3; 14, 20; 15, 1; 19, 1; 24, 1 &c; τὴν τοῦ πατρὸς τελευτήν 19, 38; τὴν τυραννίδα 22, 23
μεταβολή 13, 15; 16, 2; 41, 5
μεταδιδόασι 36, 9; μετεδίδου 40, 9; μετέδωκε 40, 9; μεταδοῦναι 36, 39. Constr. τινός τινι
μεταιχμίῳ, ἐν 12, 65 (Solon)
μετακινεῖν (τοὺς νόμους) 31, 9 (decree)
μέταλλα 22, 29; 47, 8, 11
*μεταλλικαὶ δίκαι 59, 14
*μεταπέμπομαι· 3, 8; 18, 6; 20, 16; 38, 8
μετατίθημι· τὰς στάσεις ἀμφοτέρας μεταθέσθαι 11, 9
μετέχω· ἀρχῆς 7, 29; τοῦ καταλόγου 37, 7; οὐδενός 2, 12; τῆς πόλεως 8, 30; 26, 22; τῆς πολιτείας 21, 5; 42, 2; πάντων τῶν τόπων 21, 15. μετεχόντων πολλῶν 18, 14
μετεώρους, ὀχετοὺς 50, 12

μέτοικος 43, 25; 57, 18; 58, 11. *δίκαι—μετοίκοις* 58, 5, 10
μέτριος· μέτριον γενέσθαι καὶ κοινόν 6, 14; *μέτριοι τοῖς πολίταις* 35, 8; *εὐποροῦντες τῶν μετρίων* 16, 9; *ἔχειν τὰ μέτρια* 27, 16. *ἐν μετρίοισι* 5, 17 (Solon)
μετρίως 16, 3
μέτρον 7, 17, 26; *πεντακόσια μέτρα* 10, 4; *μέτρων καὶ σταθμῶν* 10, 3
* *μετρονόμοι* 51, 5
μέχρι δέκα δραχμῶν 52, 18; 53, 5; *εὐθυνῶν* 4, 12; *Σόλωνος* 2, 9; *ἀρχῆς τέλους* 56, 7; *τίνων* 52, 37; *τῆς νῦν* (*sc. πολιτείας καταστάσεως?*) 41, 23 (*τοῦ νῦν* usurpat Ar.); *τοῦ κ* 63, 20; col. 31, 4; *τούτου* 23, 1; *τριῶν* 43, 25
μή, μηδέ, μηδείς, μήτε passim.
μηδὲ μεθ' ἑτέρων 8, 29 (law of Solon). *μὴ—μηδέ* 9, 7. *μήτε—μήτε* 11, 3; 16, 10; 39, 6 (decree); col. 35, 34. *μήτε—ἀλλὰ* 16, 8
Μηδικά, *μετὰ τὰ* 23, 2; 25, 2; 41, 16
* *μηδισμοῦ, κρίνεσθαι* 25, 12
Μηλόβιος 29, 6
μήν· οὐ μὴν ἀλλά 6, 12; 7, 20; + *καί* 2, 11. *οὐ μὴν εἰκὸς ἀλλά* 9, 12. *ἦ μήν* 29, 12 (decree)
μήν, ὁ· μηνός 32, 4; *μῆνα* 62, 13; *μῆνας* 13, 7
μηνύειν 18, 8; *ἐμήνυεν* 18, 33; *μηνύσων* 18, 34
μήτηρ and *μητρὸς πατήρ* 55, 14
μικρόν 3, 14; 11, 12; 15, 17; 25, 3; 41, 10. *ἐν οὕτω μικροῖς* 6, 17
Μιλτιάδης 26, 5; 28, 10
μισθὸς (*δικαστικός*) col. 33, 18; col. 37, 7; cf. *τρεῖς ὀβολούς* 62, 7. *μ.* (*ἐκκλησιαστικός*) 41, 29—35; 62, 6 f
μισθοφορά· κατεσκεύασε μισθοφορὰν τοῖς δικασταῖς (Pericles) 27, 22; *ἄνευ μισθοφορᾶς* 30, 5 (decree). *μισθοφορὰν πορίζειν Pol.* 1304 *b* 27
μισθοφόρα τὰ δικαστήρια, ἐποίησε 27, 11; *μηδεμίαν ἀρχὴν εἶναι μισθοφόρον* 33, 9; *μισθοφόρον* 33, 9; *μισθοφόρον ἐκκλησίαν—ἀπέγνωσαν ποιεῖν* 41, 29. Cf. *Pol.* 1303 *b* 1; *Rhet.* 1399 *b* 2.
μισθοφορεῖν, ἐν ταῖς στρατείαις 27, 10; *μισθοφοροῦσι δραχμήν* 62, 6; *πέπαυται μισθοφορῶν* 49, 8. Cf. *Pol.* 1317 *b* 35
μισθοῖ τοὺς οἴκους τῶν ὀρφανῶν 56, 42; *μισθοῦσι τὰ μισθώματα* 47, 8; *τῷ λαχόντι μισθοῦσι* 50, 9. *Pass. ὅπως—μὴ μισθωθήσονται* 50, 7. *Mid. στρατιώτας μισθωσάμενος* 15, 18; *ἐμισθώσαντο τὸν—νεὼν οἰκοδομεῖν* 19, 20
* *μισθώματα* 47, 8
μίσθωσις 47, 27; *μισθώσεις τῶν τεμενῶν* 47, 26. *κατὰ ταύτην τὴν μίσθωσιν* 2, 5; *τὰς μισθώσεις ἀποδιδοῖεν* 2, 7
μισῶ· μισεῖν 28, 24
μνᾶ 10, 5, 8, 9; *ἐντὸς τριῶν μνῶν* 49, 26; *τριάκοντα μνᾶς* 50, 3; *ἑκατὸν μνᾶς* 56, 26
Μνησιθείδης *ἄρχων* (457/6) 26, 16
* *μνησικακεῖν* 39, 20 (decree); 40, 11. *ἐμνησικάκησε* 40, 16 (*μνησίκακος Rhet.* 1381 *b* 4; *Eth.* 1125 *a* 5)
* *μοῖρα* (= *μέρος*)· *συνεβάλετο δ' οὐκ ἐλάττω μοῖραν* 19, 24
μοιχείας γραφή 59, 11
μοιχὸν λαβών 57, 19
μόνος c. gen. 3, 21, 38 &c. *οὐ μόνον—ἀλλὰ καί* 40, 18 &c. *ὥστ' αὐτὴν μόνην χωρεῖν τὴν ψῆφον* col. 36, 9. *τρισχιλίοις μόνοις* 36, 9
* *μονοχίτων* 25, 18
* *μορίαι* 60, 8, 9; *ἐλαίαν μορίαν* 60, 11
Μουνιχία 19, 5; 38, 1, 16; 42, 21. (*στρατηγὸς*) *εἰς τὴν Μ.* 61, 6
μουσικῆς ἀγών 57, 5; 60, 5. *τοῖς τὴν μουσικὴν νικῶσιν* 60, 21
μύδροι 23, 24 (only in *de Mundo* 395 *b* 23 *μύδρους διαπύρους*)
* *μυλωθροί* 51, 11
Μύρων 1, 1
* *μύσται, ὅταν οἰκουρῶσι* 56, 22
μυστήρια 39, 8; 57, 2

Νάξιος 15, 11
Νάξος 15, 15
* *ναυκραρίαι* 8, 13 f
* *ναυκραρικοῦ ἀργυρίου, ἐκ τοῦ* 8, 18 (decree)
* *ναύκραροι* 8, 14, 17; 21, 20
ναυμαχία, ἡ περὶ Σαλαμῖνα 23, 5; *ἐν Σαλαμῖνι* 23, 22; 27, 7. *ἡ περὶ Ἐρετρίαν* 33, 4. *ἐν Ἀργινούσαις* 34, 4. *ἐν Αἰγὸς ποταμοῖς* 34, 15. *ἠτύχησαν—ναυμαχίαν* 34, 15
ναυμαχῶ· ἐναυμάχησαν—πρὸς τοὺς βαρβάρους 22, 37
ναυπηγουμένου 22, 37; *ἐναυπηγήσατο* 22, 36 (only in *Oec.* 1349 *a* 25 *ναυπηγεῖσθαι τριήρεις μέλλων. ναυπηγός* and *ναυπηγία* in *Pol.*; *ναυπηγική* in *Eth.*)
ναῦς· ἐπ' ἀλλοτρίας νεώς 34, 6; *νῆες φρουρίδες* 24, 18; *ἄλλαι νῆες* 24, 19; *εἰς τὰς ναῦς* 23, 7
ναυτικὴν δύναμιν, τὴν 27, 5
νέμω· νεῖμαι—τοὺς ἄλλους πρὸς τὴν λῆξιν ἑκάστην 30, 16 (decree); *ἵνα νεμηθῶσιν—εἰς τὰς τέτταρας λήξεις* 31, 18 (decree); *ἐκ τῆς φυλῆς ἑκάστης νενεμημέναι τριττύες τρεῖς* 8, 13; *νενέμηνται κατὰ φυλὰς δέκα μέρη οἱ δικασταί* 63, 20. *Mid. ἐάν τις μὴ 'θέλῃ κοινὰ τὰ ὄντα νέμεσθαι* 56, 37
Νεοκλῆς 23, 14
* *νεοπολίτας, τοὺς* 21, 17
νέος ὤν 27, 3; *τῇ νέᾳ βουλῇ* 46, 5. *νεώτερος* 19, 6; *ν. ὀκτὼ καὶ δέκα ἐτῶν* 42, 13; *νεώτερον* (?) 26, 5
* *νεωρίων, φρουροί* 24, 15
νεὼς ὁ ἐν Δελφοῖς 19, 20
* *νεώσοικοι* 46, 2, 4
νεωστί 3, 18

νίκην, μετὰ τὴν 22, 11. Νῖκαι 47, 5
Νικίας 28, 15, 29
Νικόδημος (or Νικομήδης) ἄρχων (c. 483/2) 22, 29
νικῶ· νικᾶν 12, 9 (Solon). ἐνίκησεν (τοὺς ἱππεῖς) 19, 31. *c. acc. cogn.* νικήσας τὴν ἐπὶ Παλληνίδι μάχην 15, 12; τὴν ἐν Μαραθῶνι μάχην νικησάντων 38, 2; τὴν μουσικὴν νικῶσιν—τὴν εὐανδρίαν—τὸν γυμνικὸν ἀγῶνα καὶ τὴν ἱπποδρομίαν 60, 20 f. *c. dat.* νικησάντων μάχῃ 38, 2; τοὺς τῇ ναυμαχίᾳ νικῶντας 34, 5. ὁ νικήσας (of one who gets a decree passed) 45, 24. (In the law-courts) ἐὰν δὲ νικήσῃ 42, 11; οὗτος νικᾷ col. 36, 35
νομίζειν 6, 21; νομίσαντες 18, 18
νομίμων, εἴργεσθαι τῶν 57, 14
νόμισμα 10, 4, 7
νομοθεσία 10, 2
νομοθετῶ· ἐνομοθέτησεν 8, 8; νομοθετήσας 11, 15 (both of Solon)
νόμος 4, 23; 16, 41. ὁ μὲν νόμος ἐστὶν 60, 13. εἰσαγγελίας 8, 26; περὶ τοῦ ὀστρακισμοῦ 22, 5. νόμον ἔθηκε 8, 28; 22, 17; νόμους ἔθηκε 6, 3; 7, 1; νόμος ἐτέθη 21, 4; 22, 13, 26. νόμον μὴ ἐπιτήδειον θεῖναι 59, 6. ἀναγράψαντες—νόμους 7, 3; ἀσαφεῖς—νόμους 9, 11; μὴ γεγράφθαι τοὺς νόμους ἁπλῶς μηδὲ σαφῶς 9, 7; νόμους (διατηρεῖν) 3, 35; νόμους ἐξηγεῖσθαι 11, 6; νόμων θέσις 14, 7; ἐν τοῖς νόμοις 10, 1; κατὰ τοὺς νόμους 4, 21; τοὺς—νόμους τοὺς περὶ τῶν Ἀρεοπαγιτῶν 35, 10; ὑπὸ τῶν νόμων 51, 2; ἐχρήσαντο τῷ νόμῳ 22, 12. νόμοι quoted, περὶ τῶν ταμιῶν 8, 6; Σόλωνος 8, 16; περὶ τῶν τυράννων 16, 39
*νομοφυλακεῖν, ἐπὶ τὸ 8, 20 (νομοφύλακες and νομοφυλακία in *Pol.*)
νόον, τρέφεσθε μέγαν 5, 17 (Solon)
νοσήσας 17, 2. *Met.* τὰ πράγματα νοσοῦντα 6, 19; διετέλουν νοσοῦντες 13, 12
νύκτα καὶ ἡμέραν 44, 2
νῦν 3, 24 &c. τὸ νῦν εἶναι 31, 9 (decree). καὶ νῦν 3, 39; 7, 29. ἔτι καὶ νῦν 3, 25; 7, 6; 8, 6; 22, 7. νῦν δέ (opp. πρότερον μέν) 53, 24; 54, 19; 55, 11, 25; 56, 25; 61, 2; (opp. πρότερον δέ) 56, 9; (opp. ποτε) 49, 20; (opp. τὸ μὲν ἐξ ἀρχῆς) 55, 4; νῦν δ' after impf. 51, 9

Ξάνθιππος ὁ Ἀρίφρονος 22, 28; 28, 10
Ξεναίνετος ἄρχων (401/0) 40, 27
ξενίας γραφή 59, 8
ξένος 19, 23; 20, 6; 57, 18
Ξέρξου στρατεία 22, 40
ξηρὰ καὶ ὑγρά 7, 17
ξύλινος (ἀμφορεὺς) col. 36, 5, 7. ξύλινοι (?) κύβοι col. 31, 19
ξυνήγαγον 12, 28 (Solon)

ὁ. τὰ μὲν ἑκὼν τὰ δ' ἄκων 27, 10.—τὰ δύο μέρη 51, 17.

Article often found in periphrastic phrases, οἱ περὶ Ἀνακρέοντα 18, 5; οἱ περὶ τὸν Κλεομένην 20, 12; τῶν ἐν τῇ πολιτείᾳ 38, 9; τὰ περὶ τὰς ἀρχάς 3, 33; τὰ πρὸς ἑαυτούς 13, 13; τὰ εἰς τὸν πόλεμον 23, 10; τὰ τοῦ πολέμου 30, 30 (decree); τὰ κατὰ τὴν πολιτείαν 2, 10; 29, 1 f.

Sometimes omitted (1) before the names of officials, as θεσμοθέται 3, 30; στρατηγοὺς καὶ ἱππάρχους 4, 8; cf. 30, 7: (2) in certain set phrases, as ἐν ἀγορᾷ 51, 10; 52, 14; ἐν ἄστει 50, 5; ἐν ἀκροπόλει 18, 14; εἰς ἀκρόπολιν 55, 33; 60, 18 (but εἰς τὴν ἀκρόπολιν 20, 13); ἄνευ δικαστηρίου γνώσεως 45, 4; ἐκ καταλόγου 26, 8; ἐν μέρει 43, 7; κατὰ μέρος 55, 5; εἰς πόλιν 8, 24; μέχρι ἀρχῆς τέλους 56, 7; ἔτει δευτέρῳ 14, 7; 15, 9 &c; καὶ αὐτὸν καὶ γένος 16, 44; τίς πατρὸς (and μητρὸς) πατήρ 55, 14 f. Similarly with ἀρχή 5, 6, 20. (The exx. mainly from H-L, *s.v.* Articulus.) See also ὅδε, ἕκαστος and τρόπος.
ὀβολός· 41, 33; 62, 9. δύο ὀβολοὺς (τοῖς ἀδυνάτοις) 49, 28; δυοῖν ὀβολοῖν 28, 22; τρεῖς ὀβολούς 29, 32; 62, 7; τέτταρας 42, 26; 62, 10; πέντε 62, 7; ἐννέα 62, 7
ὅδε, article sometimes omitted in papyrus after, 7, 8; 29, 29; 37, 5; not omitted in 42, 1 τόνδε τὸν τρόπον.—νόμος—ὅδε 16, 42
*ὁδοποιοί 54, 1
ὁδός 50, 11—14; 54, 2
ὀδύναι 16, 21
ὅθεν (1) 'whence', (of place) 15, 7; (of origin &c) 6, 11 ὅθεν φασὶ γενέσθαι; 8, 3 ὅθεν ἔτι διαμένει; 18, 12 ὅθεν συνέβη; 19, 20 ὅθεν εὐπόρησαν χρημάτων; 21, 5 ὅθεν ἐλέχθη τὸ φυλοκρινεῖν. (2) 'wherefore', ὅθεν καὶ 3, 8; 17, 15; 21, 18; ὅθεν ἔτι καὶ νῦν 7, 6; ὅθεν ὕστερον 19, 13
οἶδα *passim*. οἶδεν ἀδικοῦντα 49, 11; μὴ εἰδῇ 57, 20; εἰδότες 14, 12
Οἰῆθεν 27, 19
οἰκείας, ἐκ τῆς 7, 17; τῶν οἰκείων 40, 24
οἰκείως εἶχον 36, 5
οἰκέτην ἀποκτείνῃ 57, 17
οἰκήματα 15, 21
οἰκία· ἐὰν—οἰκίαν λαμβάνωσιν 39, 10; οἰκίας 20, 9; τὰ χωρία καὶ τὰς οἰκίας 52, 6
οἰκοδομεῖν 19, 20
οἰκοδομήματα δημόσια 46, 8
οἴκου ὀρφανικοῦ κακώσεως 56, 34; οἴκους ὀρφανῶν 56, 43
*οἰκουρῶσι μύσται, ὅταν 56, 22
οἰκῶ· *c. acc.* οἰκεῖν τὴν πόλιν 22, 19; *c. praep.* τοὺς οἰκοῦντας ἐν ἑκάστῳ τῶν δήμων 21, 16; οἰκεῖν ἐν τῷ ἄστει 24, 3 &c. ᾤκησαν (?) 3, 23

οἰνοχοεῖν 20, 23 (scol.)

οἴομαι· οἴονται 9, 10; οἴεσθαι 10, 6; ᾤετο 11, 10

οἷον, 'for example', 35, 14; 57, 19. *οὐχ οἷον* *papyri lectio* 40, 23

ὀκτώ 23, 7. ὀκτωκαίδεκα ἔτη 42, 3, 13

ὄλβος 12, 13, 18 (Solon)

ὀλιγαρχία κατέστη 32, 7; ὀλιγαρχίας ἐπεθύμουν 34, 20; ἐν ὀλιγαρχίᾳ 38, 29; τὴν ὀλιγαρχίαν ἐζήτουν 13, 19; χειροτονεῖν τὴν ὀλ. 34, 26; τὴν προτέραν ὀλ. 37, 11; τὴν ἐπὶ τῶν τριάκοντα ὀλ. 53, 4

ὀλιγαρχική, ἡ πολιτεία 2, 2; προσθεμένου τοῖς ὀλιγαρχικοῖς 34, 25

ὀλίγος· δι' ὀλίγων ἦν 2, 6; 4, 24. οἱ ὀλίγοι 41, 28; τῶν πολλῶν δουλευόντων τοῖς ὀλίγοις 5, 2

ὀλιγωρῶ· τούτων μὲν ὠλιγώρησαν 36, 12

ὅλος· τὴν ὅλην—πρᾶξιν 18, 21; ἐκ τῆς φυλῆς ὅλης 62, 2

ὅλως 13, 12

ὁμιλίαις—προσήγετο, ταῖς 16, 37

ὁμιλοῦντας, πρὸς χάριν 35, 19

ὄμνυμι· ὀμνύουσι 3, 11; 7, 6; 22, 7; 55, 31; 55, 34. ὀμνύντες 7, 5; τοὺς ὅρκους ὤμοσε τοῖς Ἴωσιν 23, 23; ὤμοσαν χρήσεσθαι 7, 4; περὶ τοῦ ὅρκου ὅντινα χρὴ ὀμόσαι γράψαι 31, 6. ὀμόσαντες 42, 4, 15; 55, 29, 33; ἦ μήν 29, 12 (decree); καθ' ἱερῶν 1, 1; καθ' ἱερῶν τελείων 29, 39; ὀμόσωσιν 39, 15

ὁμοίως καὶ πρότερον 26, 12; ὁμοίως—καὶ ἐπὶ τῶν ἄλλων 35, 17

ὁμολογία 19, 35

ὁμολογῶ· ὁμολογοῦσιν 28, 31; ὁμολογῇ 57, 19; ὁμολογῶσι 52, 3; ὁμολογεῖται 28, 31

ὁμονοίας, ἄρχειν τῆς 40, 23

*ὁμοφρονήσαντες 14, 18

ὁμόχρων τῷ δικαστηρίῳ, βακτηρίαν col. 32, 4; δικαστήριον ὁμόχρων τῇ βακτηρίᾳ col. 32, 11

ὀνειδίζων 12, 55; ὀνειδίσας 18, 36; ὀνειδίσαι 12, 57 (Solon)

ὄνομα 7, 19; 14, 27; 17, 13; 48, 20; 54, 36; 63, 19

ὅπλα, ἀνελόντες 15, 21; ἐξαράμενος 14, 13; μὴ θῆται 8, 29; παρείλετο 15, 15; παρείλοντο 37, 14; παρελέσθαι 37, 4; παρελόμενος 15, 13; παρεχόμενοι 4, 47; ἀπὸ τῶν ὅπλων 18, 27; τοῖς ἐκ τῶν ὅπλων 33, 8; ἐκ τῶν ὅπλων τῆς πολιτείας οὔσης 33, 14; μεθ' ὅπλων 18, 28; περὶ τῶν ὅπλων 15, 24. ἐξέτασιν ἐν ὅπλοις 31, 11 (decree)

ὁπλῖται 24, 18; 61, 21, 24. (στρατηγὸς) ἐπὶ τοὺς ὁπλίτας 61, 4

*ὁπλομαχεῖν 42, 22

ὁπότερος ἂν 46, 3; ὁποτέρως ποτ' ἔχει 3, 14

ὅπου 43, 15

ὀπώρα 27, 17

ὅπως (1) with *subj. pres.* (*a*) after past tense, ἄρχωσιν 4, 21; ἐξῇ 27, 17; ᾖ 9, 11; μετέχῃ 21, 15; προσιστῆται 41, 31; φυλάττωσιν 3, 21; μήτ' ἐπιθυμῶσι μήτε σχολάζωσιν 16, 10; μὴ ᾖ 35, 16; μὴ παραμελῶσι 16, 15; μὴ συμβαίνῃ 21, 9. (*b*) after pres. inf. dependent on pf. ind. προστέτακται—ἐπιμελεῖσθαι, ὅπως πωλῆται 51, 2—4.

(2) with *subj. 2nd aor.* μετάσχωσι 21, 5; μηδένα λάθῃ 43, 22.

(3) ὅπως <ἂν>—βουλεύσωνται 29, 18 (decree); ἂν συμβουλεύωσι 29, 24 (decree); ἂν σῶα ᾖ 30, 20 (decree)

(4) with *fut. ind.* (after ἐπιμελοῦνται), ὅπως—ἔσται—, ὅπως—πωλήσουσι 51, 10 f; μηδεὶς καταβαλεῖ 50, 9; χρήσονται (χρήσωνται MS); (after σκοποῦσιν), ὅπως μὴ—μισθωθήσονται 50, 7

ὀργή· ὑπὸ τῆς ὀργῆς 18, 37; οὐ κατεῖχε τὴν ὀργήν 18, 9

ὀρθῶς, ποιεῖν 41, 28

ὁρίζω· ὥρισαν τοῖς ὀστρακιζομένοις—κατοικεῖν 22, 41; ὡς ἐν τούτῳ τῷ πλήθει τῆς ἀρετῆς ὡρισμένης 36, 10

*ὅρκια ποιήσειν (?) 3, 12

ὅρκον ἐποίησαν 22, 7; ὅρκους ὤμοσεν 23, 23; τοῖς ὅρκοις ἐμμένειν 40, 13

ὁρμή 19, 24; ὁρμαῖς (?) 28, 16

ὅρος 12, 23, 66 (Solon)

ὀρφανοί 24, 20; ὀρφανῶν, ἐπιμελεῖται 56, 39; ὀρφανῶν κακώσεως 56, 32; οἴκους ὀρφανῶν 56, 43

ὀρφανικός· οἴκου ὀρφανικοῦ κακώσεως 56, 34

ὁρῶ *passim*. ὁρῶν 8, 26; ὁρᾶν col. 35, 33; ἰδών 16, 18; ἰδόντες 18, 16

ὅς· ἐξ οὗ 60, 12. ἐφ' ᾧ τε 14, 22; 34, 17. ᾗ ἂν δοκῇ αὐτοῖς ἄριστα ἕξειν 30, 19; ᾗ ἂν ἡγῶνται συμφέρειν 31, 7 (decrees)

ὁσίων 43, 30; + χρημάτων 30, 9 (decree)

ὅσος· ὅσον ἂν 51, 14; καθ' ὅσον 14, 14; ὅσοι μή 22, 18; ὅσαι ἡμέραι 43, 13

ὅσοσπερ· ὅσοιπερ 63, 7; ὅσαπερ ἂν 63, 10

ὅσπερ· ἐκ τοῦ αὐτοῦ τέλους οὗπερ 4, 13; τὸ αὐτὸ ὅπερ 31, 7, 13, 31. ὅπερ ἐγένετο 38, 11; ὅπερ καὶ συνέπεσεν 40, 15; ὅπερ εἰώθασι ποιεῖν ἅπαντες 40, 4; ὅπερ ἐστὶν ἀγαθοῦ πολίτου ἔργον 28, 38

ὅστις· ὅ τι χρήσεται 22, 31. ὅ τι ἂν γνῶσιν 48, 27; δοκῇ 48, 22; 63, 15; ἐγκαλῇ 48, 21; προστιμήσῃ 63, 7; χειροτονήσῃ 47, 11; ψηφίσωνται 45, 10; μὴ προγράψωσιν 45, 22. οἵτινες καταλέξουσι 29, 38; ὅντιν' ἀποδοκιμάσειεν ἡ βουλή 55, 11

ὀστρακίζω 22, 15, 24, 25, 27, 38, 40, 41; 27, 20

ὀστρακισμός 22, 13

ὀστρακοφορία 43, 23

ὅταν *passim*. 4, 17 &c

ὅτε *passim*; *c. opt.* 16, 35; 36, 14

ὅτι *passim*; 6, 18 &c

οὐ *passim*; ἢ οὔ 49, 28. οὐχί 18, 32 (*Poet.* 1448 *b* 18, 1459 *a* 21 &c). οὐ

μὴν ἀλλά 6, 12; 7, 26; + καί 2, 11; οὐ μὴν εἰκὸς ἀλλά 9, 12
οὐδὲ and οὐδείς *passim*; οὐδ' ἂν εἷς εἴποι 7, 30
οὐδείς· οὐδεμιᾶς 7, 28; οὐδ'—εἷς 7, 30
οὐκέτι χρῶνται 8, 16 &c
οὕνεκα 12, 28, 53 (Solon)
οὔπω 14, 17
οὐσία 4, 8; 5, 12; 27, 13, 19; 49, 16. *Pl.* 35, 23, 25; 47, 13
οὔτε—οὔτε 38, 30 f
οὔτεροι 12, 51 (Solon)
οὗτος *passim*. τοῦτον <τὸν> τρόπον 12, 1. τούτων δ' εἶναι 30, 5 (decree)
οὕτω, οὕτως, *passim*. ἐν οὕτω μικροῖς 6, 17
* [ὀφειλε]τῶν (?) 47, 14
ὀφείλειν δραχμὴν τῆς ἡμέρας ἑκάστης 30, 33; ὀφείλων (προῖκα) 52, 13; ὀφείλουσι τῷ δημοσίῳ 63, 12
* ὄφλημα 63, 16 (ὀφείλημα *Eth.* 1162 *b* 28, 1165 *a* 3)
ὀχετοὺς μετεώρους—ποιεῖν 50, 12
ὀψέ 26, 6

Πάγγαιον 15, 7
πάγος, Ἄρειος· *v.* Ἄρειος
Παιανιεύς 14, 26; 38, 22
παιδιώδης 18, 4
παιδοτρίβης 42, 22
παῖς 16, 19; παῖδες 2, 8; 4, 9; 19, 35. ἐὰν μὴ ἀποδῶσι τοῖς παισὶν τὸν σῖτον 56, 46. χορηγοὺς—παισίν 56, 11 f; παισὶν χορηγοῦντα 56, 18
* παλαιόπλουτοι 6, 12
πάλιν 11, 11; 12, 55; 14, 21; 15, 9; 16, 35; 20, 6. πάλιν ἐξ ὑπαρχῆς 4, 16. πάλιν δέ 12, 10, 15, 26
Παλλαδίῳ, ἐπὶ 57, 18
Παλληνίδι, ἐπὶ 15, 13
Παναθήναια 18, 11, 15; 43, 4; 49, 23; 54, 28, 31; 60, 4, 19; 62, 13
Πανδίων Heracl. epit. l. 3
πάνυ πένης 47, 4
παρά· *c. dat.* ἐῶντες—παρ' αὐτοῖς 24, 8; παρὰ τοῖς Ἕλλησιν 23, 11
c. acc. ἐλθόντι παρ' αὐτόν 27, 16: παρὰ τὸ Λεωκόρειον 18, 20; τοὺς ἐπωνύμους 53, 26; δόξαν 11, 9; τὸ βέλτιστον 35, 19; παρ' ὃν ἀδικεῖται νόμον 4, 23
παράβολον p. 253 frag. dubium 7 (not found elsewhere in this sense)
παραβῶσι τῶν νόμων, ἐάν τινα 7, 6
παράδειγμα ποιήσειν 40, 15. *Pl.*, 'plans', 49, 20.
παραδίδωσι δικαστηρίῳ 46, 10; (τὰ γραμματεῖα) τοῖς ἀποδέκταις 47, 32; τὰ μὲν ἴδια τοῖς δικασταῖς 48, 24; τὸ πρόγραμμα 44, 10; (τὸ ἔλαιον) τοῖς ταμίαις 60, 16. παραδιδόασι (τὰ τέλη) τῇ βουλῇ 47, 17; (τὸν κατάλογον) τοῖς ἱππάρχοις 49, 10; τὸ τίμημα τοῖς διαιτηταῖς 53, 6; (τοὺς ἐχίνους) τοῖς—δικάζουσιν 53, 14; τὰ κιβώτια col. 32, 23; τοῖς εἰληχόσιν col. 32, 24; ἑκάστῳ τῶν δικαστῶν δύο ψήφους col. 32, 31. παραδώσοντας τοῖς πωληταῖς 52, 7. παρέδωκαν τὴν ἀκρόπολιν 19, 36. παραδῶσιν ἐξειργασμένα 46, 5; παραδοῦναι τοῖς ἕνδεκα 29, 27 (decree)
* παραιβατούσης τῆς γυναικός 14, 29
* παραινῶ· 5, 10, 14; 36, 2
παραιροῦμαι· τῶν Ἀρεοπαγιτῶν ἔνια παρείλετο 27, 4. (Of ὅπλα) παρελόμενος 15, 13; παρείλετο 15, 15; παρελέσθαι 37, 14; παρείλοντο 37, 14. Cf. περιαιροῦμαι.
παρακάθηται τῇ βουλῇ 54, 15, 20 (only quoted from *de Admir.* 845 *b* 28 ἐγείρειν τὸν υἱὸν παρακαθήμενον)
παρακαλῶν *abs.* 14, 16
παράκειται τῷ ἄρχοντι κιβώτια col. 31, 35
παραλαμβάνει σύμβολον col. 32, 14; παραλαμβάνουσι τὸ ἄγαλμα τῆς Ἀθηνᾶς 47, 5; βακτηρίαν πάλιν παραλαμβάνοντες col. 37, 3. ἐὰν παραλάβωσιν (τὰ δημόσια) 48, 26; (εὔθυναν) 48, 26. παραλαβὼν τοὺς χορηγούς 56, 10; παραλαβόντες τὴν ἀρχήν 38, 6; τὰ γραμματεῖα 48, 2; (τὰς δίκας) 53, 7, 14; (ἱππέων κατάλογον) 49, 11; (τὸ πρόγραμμα) 44, 10
παραλία, ἡ 21, 13. παραλίων (στάσις) 13, 17
παραλλάξειν 11, 12
Πάραλος 61, 27
παραμελῶσι τῶν ἀγρῶν 16, 15 (ἐνέργεια παρημελημένη *Eth.* 1175 *a* 10)
παρανοίας, δίκη 56, 35. Cf. *de Part. An.* 635 *b* 5
παρανομοῖεν 28, 37; παρανομούσαις 28, 38; παρανομούντων 3, 21
παρανόμων γραφή 45, 24; 59, 6; *pl.* 29, 23. γραψάμενος παρανόμων 40, 8 (*Pol.* 1255 *a* 9)
* παρανοοῦντα 56, 35
παραπλησίαν *c. dat.* 29, 20. *Adv.* παραπλήσιον 10, 5
παραπλησίως ἴσοι 63, 21
παρασκευάζω· παρεσκεύαζεν εἰρήνην 16, 25
παράστασις τίθεται 59, 8 (found in *Pol.* in different senses)
* παραστρατηγηθῆναι διὰ τῶν φίλων 6, 8
παρατηροῦντες 18, 14
παρατίθενται, βακτηρίαι κατὰ τὴν εἴσοδον 63, 7
* παρατρέφουσι κήρυκα καὶ αὐλητήν (of the archons) 62, 11
παραυτίκα· πρὸς τὸ π. βλέποντες 28, 28
παραχρῆμα 18, 25
παραχωρησάντων τῶν Κοδριδῶν—3, 13; παρεχώρουν αὐτῇ τοῦ ἀξιώματος 23, 8
παρεγκλίνουσα τῆς βασιλικῆς, μικρὸν 41, 10
* παρεδρεύειν 56, 3
* πάρεδροι (to the ἄρχων, βασιλεύς and πολέμαρχος) 56, 1; (to the εὔθυνοι) 48, 15
πάρειμι (εἰμί)· παρὼν 11, 4, 6; τῆς παρ-

οὔσης πολιτείας 37, 8; ἐν τῷ παρόντι 6, 2; + καιρῷ 31, 2; τῶν παρόντων (masc.) 38, 13; πρὸς τὰ παρόντα πράγματα 61, 10

πάρειμι (εἶμι)· εἰς τὴν Ἀττικὴν παριέναι 19, 31

παρέργως 28, 35

παρέρχομαι· παρῆλθεν εἰς τοὺς—τόπους 15, 7; τῶν παρεληλυθότων—μνησικακεῖν 39, 20 (decree)

παρέχει δ' ἐν μέρει ἑκατέρα τῶν φυλῶν τοῦτον 56, 13. *Mid.* τοῖς ὅπλα παρεχομένοις 4, 5; τῶν ὅπλα παρεχομένων 4, 7. ἐγγυητὰς παρασχομένους 4, 12; παράσχηται τοὺς μάρτυρας 55, 20; τιμήματα παρεχομένοις (?) 39, 24

παρίστημι· παρέστηκεν ἵππος 7, 25

Πάρνης 19, 12

παροξυνθέντα 18, 13; παρώξυνε 18, 36

παροργίσαντας, διὰ τοὺς 34, 7 (*Act.* hitherto found in Gk. Test. alone)

παρορῶ· τὰ δόξαντα—παρεώρων 35, 3; εἰ μή τι παρεωρᾶτο 26, 18

παροχλῶ· παρώχλει 16, 25

παρρησία 16, 23

*παρωνύμιον 17, 12

πᾶς, ἅπας, *passim*. πάντες 12, 2; πάντ' ἀνάδαστα ποιήσειν 11, 11; πάντα ποιῶν 18, 33

πάσχω· ὑπὸ τῶν ἀντιστασιωτῶν ταῦτα πεπονθώς 14, 4; παθεῖν ἢ ἀποτεῖσαι 61, 13; 63, 15; (ἵππος) ὁ ταῦτα παθὼν 49, 4

πατήρ 19, 39; 55, 13; πατρὸς πατήρ 55, 14

πατρικὰς δόξας, τιμωμένων διὰ τὰς 26, 9

πατρικῶς χρωμένους, τῇ πόλει πάσῃ 28, 32

πάτριος· πάτριον πολιτείαν 34, 18, 22; τῶν πατρίων 3, 16; πατρίους νόμους 29, 17 (decree); πατρίους θυσίας 57, 8; κατὰ τὰ πάτρια 21, 24 and (in decrees) 31, 3; 39, 6, 19

πατρίδα, σώσας 11, 14; βεβοηθηκέναι τῇ πατρίδι 14, 14

*πατρόθεν προσαγορεύοντες 21, 17; τὸ ὄνομα τὸ ἑαυτοῦ πάτροθεν 63, 19

πατρῷος, Ἀπόλλων 55, 16; p. 251 frag. 1 (only in *Pol.* 1303 *b* 34 ἡ τῶν πατρῴων νομή)

παττάλῳ (?) 16, 18

Παυσανίας, Spartan general in Persian war, 23, 20

Παυσανίας, Λακεδαιμονίων βασιλεύς 38, 23, 25

παύω· *Mid.* ἐπαύσαντο χρώμενοι 7, 1; πέπαυται μισθοφορῶν 49, 8. τῆς ἀσελγείας παύσασθαι 36, 2. ἐπαυσάμην 12, 29, 63 (Solon)

πεδιακῶν (στάσις) 13, 19

πεζὰς μόσχους p. 255 frag. alienum 15

πείθω· οὐκ ἔπειθεν 14, 12. πείσας 18, 34; 40, 12. πεισθέντες—ταῦτα 24, 6. γυναικὶ πιθόμενος 35, 16 (law of Solon). πεισόμεθ' 5, 18 (Solon)

Πειραιεύς. Πειραιέως· τοῦ Π. ἄρχοντας δέκα 35, 5; τῶν ἐκ Π. κατελθόντων 38, 31; τοὺς τοῦ Π. ἄρξαντας 39, 22; τοῖς ἐκ Π. συγκατελθοῦσιν 40, 9; τοὺς ἐκ τοῦ Π. 40, 22; τὴν ἐκ Π. κάθοδον 41, 23. Πειραιεῖ· 38, 23; 39, 23 f; 50, 5; 61, 7. Πειραιέα· 38, 16; 42, 21; 51, 1, 6, 8, 10; εἰς Π. δήμαρχος 54, 34; (στρατηγοὶ) ἐπὶ τὸν Π. 61, 6

πειρῶμαι· *c. inf.* 6, 5; 20, 10; 34, 19

Πείσανδρος 31, 9

Πεισιστρατίδαι 19, 24 f, 34

Πεισίστρατος 13, 20; 14 *passim;* 15, 22; 16 and 17 *passim;* 23, 14; 28, 5; 41, 13

πέλαγος 23, 24

Πελαργικὸν τεῖχος 19, 32

*πελάται 2, 5

Πελοποννησίους, πόλεμος πρὸς 27, 8; τῶν Π. 38, 13

πέμπτῳ (ἔτει) 13, 3, 5; 26, 19

πέμπω· οὐ γὰρ ἔπεμπον—μεθ' ὅπλων 18, 28; τὴν πομπὴν—πέμπουσιν 57, 6

πένης 47, 4; πένητες 2, 3; πένησιν 13, 14

*πενθήμερον, κατὰ 30, 24 (decree)

*πεντακισχίλιοι, οἱ 29, 35, 39 (decree); 30, 2; 31, 10 (decree); 32, 1, 12; 33, 8, 12

πεντακόσιοι, οἱ 21, 7; 22, 7; 25, 10. π. 22, 22; 24, 14 f, 18; 55, 6. π. βουλευτάς 35, 3; 43, 6. πεντακόσια 7, 17

πεντακοσιομέδιμνος 4, 18; 7, 10 f, 27; 8, 7; 26, 17; 47, 3. -ον τελεῖν 7, 16

πέντε 13, 8; 19, 36. πεντεκαίδεκα 51, 9

πεντετηρίδες 54, 28—32 (διὰ πενταετηρίδος *Pol.* 1308 *b* 1)

πεντήκοντα 19, 39; 21, 8; 24, 15

*πέπλος (of Athena) 49, 20; 60, 6

πέρας, ἐπὶ 38, 24

περί· *c. gen.* τῆς ἀποκοπῆς 12, 26; ταύτης τῆς ἀρχῆς 13, 11; αὐτῶν 8, 26; 12, 2; τῶν βουλομένων 12, 15; τῶν διῳκημένων 25, 7; κλήρων καὶ ἐπικλήρων 9, 8; τῶν νόμων 11, 2; τῶν ὅπλων 15, 23; τοῦ ὀστρακισμοῦ 22, 5; πλείονος ποιήσασθαι 6, 16; τοῦ πλήθους 12, 10

c. acc. (local) τὸ ἄστυ 21, 13; Σαλαμῖνα 23, 4; Πάγγαιον 15, 7; τὸν Θερμαῖον κόλπον 15, 6. τὰς ἀρχάς 9, 1; τὸν ὀστρακισμόν 22, 13; τὸν χρόνον τοῦτον 23, 10.—οἱ περὶ Ἀνακρέοντα καὶ Σιμωνίδην 18, 5; τὸν Κλεομένην καὶ Ἰσαγόραν 20, 12; τὸν Ἰσαγόραν 28, 9; τὸν Ῥίνωνα 38, 28

περιαιρῶ· περιαιρεῖται τὸν στέφανον 57, 26; ἅπαντα περιείλετο τὰ ἐπίθετα 25, 8; περιείλοντο αὐτῶν τὴν δύναμιν 25, 22. Cf. παραιρῶ

περιεγένετο τῇ πόλει τάλαντα ἑκατὸν 22, 30

*περιελαυνόμενος τῇ στάσει 14, 21

περιέρχομαι· τὰ ἱερὰ περιῆλθον 42, 20; κατὰ δήμους περιιόντες 53, 3

περιζωσάμενος ἐδημηγόρησε 28, 17 (περιεζῶσθαι τὴν φορβείαν *Pol.* 1324 *b* 16)

Περικλῆς· (law concerning citizenship) 26, 22; πρὸς τὸ δημαγωγεῖν ἐλθόντος Π. 27, 1; ἐποίησε μισθοφόρα τὰ δικαστήρια 27, 12; πρὸς ταύτην τὴν χορηγίαν ἐπιλειπόμενος 27, 18; ἕως Π. προειστήκει τοῦ δήμου 28, 1; τοῦ δήμου (προστάτης) 28, 12

περιλαβεῖν· καθόλου π. τὸ βέλτιστον 9, 13

περιπολοῦσι τὴν χώραν 42, 32 (not found in technical sense; occurs only in frag. 12^2, 1476 *a* 6, ἥλιον περιπολοῦντα)

πέτρας σκάπτοντα 16, 19

πήγνυμι· ὅρους—πεπηγότας 12, 33 (Solon)

πηρῶ· τὸ σῶμα πεπηρωμένους 49, 26

πῖαρ 12, 64 (Solon)

πιείρας χθονός 12, 24 (Solon)

πιθανώτερος ὁ τῶν δημοτικῶν λόγος 6, 12

πικρός 19, 3. πικρότατον 2, 10. πικρῶς 18, 10

πινάκιον λελευκωμένον 48, 20. (δικαστοῦ) π. πύξινον 63, 18; πινάκιον col. 31, 7, 10, 30; *pl.* 63, 6; col. 31, 5, 11; col. 32, 19; col. 33, 9. ἐν τοῖς δικαστηρίοις ...φέρειν ἕκαστον πινάκιον (of Hippodamus) *Pol.* 1268 *a* 2

πίναξ 49, 12 (πίναξ ὃν ἀνέθηκε—χορηγήσας *Pol.* 1341 *a* 36)

*πιπράσκω· τὰ πραθέντα μέταλλα 47, 11; μ. πεπραμένα 47, 12 f; τέλη πεπραμένα 47, 16 (πραθέντων ἢ μισθωθέντων *Rhet. ad Alex.* 1425 *b* 23)

πιστεύω· ἐπίστευεν 21, 1

πίστεως χάριν 18, 34

πιστότατος 54, 17

πλανωμένους 12, 39 (Solon)

πλαττόμενος 18, 32

πλεονάκις 62, 18

πλεονεκτεῖν 4, 15

πλεονεξία 7, 17; 16, 32

πλῆθος, τὸ 2, 2; 9, 5; 12, 10; 16, 24; 20, 5, 12; 21, 2, 12; 22, 4; 25, 4; 28, 24; 34, 9; 36, 4; 41, 24, 32. τὸ πλ. τῶν πολιτῶν 26, 21. πλῆθος, 'number', 36, 10; 40, 4

πλὴν *c. gen.* 7, 2; 24, 7; 29, 31. πλὴν ἐὰν 43, 13; 54, 31. πλὴν βουλεῦσαι 62, 19. πλὴν μυστηρίοις 39, 7 (decree)

πλήρης, ψῆφος col. 35, 29; col. 36, 20, 33

πληρωθήσεσθαι, δικαστήρια 63, 11; col. 31, 37 (not found in Ar. in this technical sense)

πλησίον *c. gen.* 3, 25. τὰ πλ. οἰκήματα 15, 21

πλοίῳ, ἐν 57, 23

πλούσιος· 2, 4, 6; 4, 14, 19; 22, 33. πλουσιωτάτους 56, 8

πλουτίνδην 3, 2, 37

πλουτῶ· *impf.* 6, 11

πόθεν τῶν δήμων 55, 13, 15

ποιήματα 5, 13; 6, 20

ποίησις τῶν Νικῶν 49, 22. ἐν τῇ ποιήσει 12, 2

ποιητής 18, 6

ποῖον τέλος τελεῖ 7, 20

ποιῶ· εὖ ποιεῖ 55, 17. ποιεῖν τὴν σεισάχθειαν 6, 6; ποιεῖν—μέτρα 7, 17 f, 28. πάντα ποιῶν 18, 33. τοῦτο—ἐποίει 16, 7. ἀνάδαστα ποιήσειν 11, 11. ἐποίησε 27, 11; βουλὴν ἐποίησε 8, 18; ἐποίησε—σταθμά 10, 7; ἀτελῆ—ἐποίησεν 16, 24; ἀσαφεῖς ποιῆσαι τοὺς νόμους 9, 11; ποιῆσαι—χρεῶν ἀποκοπήν 10, 2; τὰ γεγραμμένα ποιῆσαι 11, 7. *Mid.* ποιεῖται τὰς τριήρεις 46, 7. ἀποδημίαν ἐποιήσατο 11, 4; 13, 1. δι' ὀλίγων ποιήσωνται 29, 9; περὶ πλείονος ποιήσασθαι 6, 16 (cf. *Eth.* 1160 *b* 15). ἐξοπλισίαν ποιησάμενος 15, 17; ὁμολογίαν ποιησάμενοι 19, 35. ἀλκὴν—ποιεύμενος 12, 53 (Solon); ποιοίατο 12, 61 (Solon)

*πολεμαρχεῖον 3, 28

*πολεμαρχία 3, 6

πολέμαρχος 3, 5, 17, 27; 22, 9; 55, 5; esp. 58

πολεμαρχῶ· -χήσας 3, 29

πολεμικά, τὰ 3, 7; 23, 14

πόλεμος· πρὸς Μεγαρέας 14, 2; + περὶ Σαλαμῖνα 17, 6. πρὸς Πελοποννησίους ἐνέστη 27, 8; συνεστήσαντο τὸν πόλεμον 24, 17; τὰ εἰς τὸν πόλεμον 23, 10; τὰ κατὰ τὸν πόλεμον 29, 1. αἱ κατὰ π. ἀρχαί 62, 18; αἱ πρὸς τὸν π. ἀρχαί 43, 5; 44, 7; 61, 1. ἐν πολέμῳ 57, 20; τετελευτηκόσιν ἐν τῷ πολέμῳ 58, 3. π. ἐν τῇ χώρᾳ 61, 5

πολεμῶ· ἀπείρων τοῦ πολεμεῖν 26, 9. πολεμεῖ οὗτος 61, 5

πολιορκῶ 19, 32; 20, 14

πόλις· τῆς πόλεως, τυραννεῖν 6, 15; τὴν τῆς πόλεως σωτηρίαν 6, 16; στασιαζούσης τῆς πόλεως 8, 29; τῆς πόλεως μὴ μετέχειν 8, 30; κυρίους τῆς πόλεως 20, 11; θαρρούσης τῆς πόλεως 24, 1. τῶν ἐν τῇ πόλει 3, 35; τῇ πόλει, περιεγένετο 22, 30; τῇ πόλει πατρικῶς χρωμένους 28, 32. πόλιν—στασιάζουσαν 8, 27; οἰκεῖν τὴν πόλιν 22, 19; πρὸς τὴν πόλιν ὀψὲ προσελθόντα 26, 6. τὰ σύμβολα τὰ πρὸς τὰς πόλεις 59, 16
=ἀκρόπολις· εἰς πόλιν 8, 24; ἐν τῇ πόλει 24, 15

πολιτεία 2, 2, 11; 3, 1; 4, 15; 5, 1, 5; 7, 1, 7; 8, 21; 9, 2, 14; 11, 1; 13, 14, 18, 25; 15, 12; 20, 5; 21, 5; 22, 2; 25, 2, 9, 15; 27, 6, 11; 29, 28, 33. *Pl.* 24, 8; 28, 34, 36; ('grants of citizenship') 54, 18. τὰ κατὰ τὴν πολιτείαν 28, 2; τὴν ἐπὶ τῶν τετρακοσίων π. 29, 5; ἡ τῶν τετρακοσίων π. 33, 1; δι' ὀλίγων ποιήσωνται τὴν π. 29, 9; ἀναγράψοντας τὴν π. 30, 3; τῶν ἐν τῇ πολιτείᾳ 38, 9

πολιτεύεσθαι κατὰ πάσας (τὰς πολιτείας), δυνάμενος 28, 37; ἐφ' ᾧ τε πολιτεύσον-

ται τὴν πάτριον πολιτείαν 34, 18; δοκεῖ τοῦτο πολιτεύσασθαι καλῶς 40, 7; τῶν Ἀθήνησι πολιτευσαμένων 28, 29. *Pass.* ἐπολιτεύθησαν Ἀθηναῖοι καλῶς 23, 8; καλῶς πολιτευθῆναι 33, 13
πολίτης *passim.* ἀγαθοῦ πολίτου ἔργον 28, 38; τῶν πολιτῶν ἐνίους 8, 27
πολιτικός, τῇ φύσει 18, 3; ἄνδρας—πολιτικούς 28, 32; τὰ μέγιστα τῶν πολιτικῶν 8, 22; τὰ πολιτικὰ δεινός 23, 14; περὶ τῶν πολιτικῶν 31, 8; τῶν πολιτικῶν (*conj.*) εἰσηγητής 27, 20. πολιτικῶς 14, 17; 16, 14; πολιτικώτατα 40, 17
πολλάκις 8, 27; 16, 14, 26
πολλαχῇ 12, 33, 39 (Solon)
πολλαχοῦ μέμνηται 6, 20; π. γέγραπται 8, 17
πολύς· πολὺν χρόνον 2, 2; 5, 3; 16, 34; 18, 23; 36, 13; οὐ πολὺν χρόνον 15, 3. μετ' οὐ πολύ 6, 10. πολὺ πρὸς ὠμότητα—ἐπέδοσαν 37, 15; νεώτερος πολύ 18, 6; δημοτικωτέρα πολύ 22, 1. πολλῷ *c. compar.* 16, 28; 19, 1. οἱ πολλοί 2, 10; 4, 2; 27, 21; 28, 27; 29, 8; 36, 5. τῶν γνωρίμων—οἱ πολλοί 16, 37. πολλῶν—ἄλλων 15, 10; μετεχόντων πολλῶν 18, 14. πολλοὺς 11, 8; πολλὰς ἀμφισβητήσεις 9, 9. τὰ πολλά 21, 19.
πλείων ἢ ἐνιαύσιος 3, 22. πλέον ἢ ἅπαξ 31, 17; 44, 14. πλείονος 50, 7; περὶ πλείονος 6, 16. οἱ πλείους 3, 9; πλείους 21, 5; 24, 12; 50, 8.
τὰ πλεῖστα 3, 35; 8, 21; 49, 31
πομπεύω 18, 27
* πομπή 57, 5. τὴν πομπήν, ἀποστέλλων 18, 16; διακοσμοῦντα 18, 20; ἀναλώματα εἰς 56, 24; κοινῇ πέμπουσιν 57, 6; διοικοῦσι 60, 4. πομπῶν 56, 21
πονηρός 35, 20; 55, 26
πονηρία 37, 15
πορεύονται, εἰς Πειραιέα 42, 21
πορίσασα δραχμὰς ἑκάστῳ ὀκτὼ διέδωκε 23, 6; ὀβολὸν ἐπόρισεν 41, 33; τὴν διωβελίαν 28, 20
Ποσιδεῶνος col. 35, 7
ποτέ 16, 32; ποτε—νῦν δὲ 49, 20; ὁποτέρως ποτ' ἔχει 3, 14
πότερον—ἢ οὔ 49, 17
που, ἑτέρωθί 12, 15
ποῦ ταῦτα τὰ ἱερά ἐστι 55, 16 f
πράγματα· 'government', προάγοντες τὰ πράγματα 17, 10; κατασχόντος τοῦ δήμου τὰ πράγματα 20, 17; τὰ πρ. παρέδωκαν τοῖς πεντακισχιλίοις 33, 8; μεταδοῦναι τῶν πρ. τοῖς βελτίστοις 36, 3; τὰ πρ. βεβαίως εἶχον 38, 12; κύριοι τῶν πρ. 18, 1; κύριος ὁ δῆμος γενόμενος τῶν πραγμάτων 41, 2. 'Public affairs', τά τε πράγματα νοσοῦντα μαρτυρεῖ 6, 19; ἐξαπορησάντων τοῖς πράγμασι 23, 6. 'Occupation', *vitae studia ac negotia* (Herwerden), τῇ οὐσίᾳ καὶ τοῖς πράγμασι τῶν μέσων 5, 12
πρᾶξιν, πράττειν τὴν 18, 14; τὴν ὅλην ἐλυμήναντο τὴν πρ. 18, 21; κοινωνούντων τῆς πράξεως 18, 17; ἴχνος τῆς πρ. 18, 26
πρᾷος 16, 5; νόμοι πρᾷοι 16, 39
πρᾳότης, τοῦ δήμου 22, 19
πράττειν τὴν πρᾶξιν 18, 13; τὰ κοινά 24, 5; ᾗ ἂν ἡγῶνται συμφέρειν 31, 7; ἐφ' οἷς ᾑρέθησαν οὐκ ἔπραττον 38, 7; ἔπραττον 19, 11; ἔπραξε 25, 11
Mid. ἐπράττετο ἀπὸ τῶν γιγνομένων δεκάτην 16, 12; [τοῦ πράττ]εσθαι (τὰς ἐκτίσεις, or τὴν ζημίαν) 8, 24
πρεσβείαις 30, 29 (decree); 43, 30 (in another sense, κατὰ πρεσβείαν *Pol.* 1259 *b* 13)
πρέσβεις 37, 16; 43, 32 (not in this sense in *Index Ar.*; πρεσβευταὶ αἱροῦνται *Pol.* 1299 *a* 19)
* πρεσβευσάμενοι, πρὸς Λακεδαιμονίους 32, 14
πρεσβύτερος 18, 2. πρεσβυτάτην 5, 8 (Solon)
πρεσβύτης 14, 14
πρὶν τυχεῖν 12, 29; διαβουλεῦσαι 32, 4; &c. πρὶν ἂν ἀπογράψηται 39, 18 (decree); παραδῷ 60, 17. πρὶν ⟦ἢ⟧ ἀφικέσθαι 38, 22 (*de Part. Anim.* 668 *a* 35). Cf. Eucken, i 5—8. πρὶν—ἐξεῖλον 12, 64 (Solon)
πρό, (1) of place, τοῦ βουλευτηρίου 53, 25; τῶν θυρῶν 14, 13. (2) of time, τοῦ διελθεῖν 4, 16; τῆς ἐνάτης πρυτανείας 28, 37; τῆς νομοθεσίας 10, 2; τῆς συλλήψεως 18, 18; τούτου 26, 17. τὸν πρὸ (?) τοῦ ψηφίσματος λόγον 54, 11
προάγοντες τὰ πράγματα 17, 9; τούς τι προαγαγόντας ποιεῖν αὐτοὺς τῶν μὴ καλῶς ἐχόντων 28, 5; πάσας (τὰς πολιτείας) προάγειν 28, 37
προαγορεύων, (1) 'proclaim', 57, 13; (2) 'state beforehand', προειπεῖν 6, 7; τὴν ὥραν τὴν προρρηθεῖσαν 30, 32 (decree)
προαιροῦμαι· [προῃρεῖτο] πάντα διοικεῖν κατὰ τοὺς νόμους 16, 30; προῃρεῖτο τὴν πολιτείαν διοικεῖν αὐτός 27, 11
προανακρίνειν 3, 32
προβολή 43, 24; 59, 5 (not in Ar. in technical sense)
* προβούλευμα 44, 19
προβουλεύειν εἰς τὸν δῆμον 45, 21 (*Pol.* 1298 *b* 30, 1299 *b* 33, 1322 *b* 16)
πρόβουλοι 29, 11
προγεγενημένων, μάλιστα τῶν 33, 6; ταῖς -αις συμφοραῖς 40, 18
* πρόγραμμα 44, 10
προγράφουσι (οἱ πρυτάνεις), ὅσα δεῖ χρηματίζειν τὴν βουλὴν κτλ 43, 16; τὰς ἐκκλησίας *ib.* cf. 45, 23. (οἱ θεσμοθέται) τοῦ προγράψαι τὰ δικαστήρια κύριοι 59, 1. (Of the people) προγράφουσιν 53, 36. (Found only in the fragments, and in *Oec.* ii 1352 *a* 1)

*προδανείζω· τοῖς ἀπόροις προεδάνειζε χρήματα 16, 6
**προδιασπείρω· προδιασπείρας λόγον 14, 24
** προδρομεύειν 49, 6
πρόδρομοι 49, 5 (not in *Index* in this sense)
προδωσέταιρον, Λειψύδριον 19, 15 (scol.)
* προεδρεύειν 44, 14
** προεδρική, γραφὴ 59, 6
πρόεδροι 44, 8 (found in technical sense in the fragments only)
προειπεῖν 6, 7; *v.* προαγορεύων
** προεξαλειφθῇ 47, 35
* προεξαναστάντες τῶν [λοιπῶν] 18, 19
προέχουσιν ἀλλήλων 3, 23; ταῖς οὐσίαις κτλ προέχοντας 35, 24
προῆλθεν ἡ πόλις, μέχρι τούτου 23, 1 (μέχρι τινὸς προέρχονται *Pol.* 1280 *a* 10)
προθυμουμένων 38, 21
προθύμως 26, 3
προικὸς (δίκη) 52, 12
προΐστημι· προειστήκει 13, 17; 28, 1, 10, 14; 34, 24; προειστήκεσαν 19, 9; 38, 21. προεστηκώς 21, 2; προεστώτων 25, 2; προεστάναι 26, 5 (*Pol.* 1285 *a* 36, 1319 *b* 7)
πρόκειται 54, 32; περὶ τῶν προκειμένων 29, 25 (decree)
πρόκλησις 53, 10, 17
προκρίνω· προκρίνειε and προὔκρινεν 8, 2; προκρίνοντας 30, 12 (decree). προκρίνεσθαι 26, 15. ἐκ τῶν προκριθέντων 21, 25; 22, 22
προκρίτων, ἐκ 8, 1; 30, 11 (decree); 31, 4 (decree); 35, 4
πρόνοια· ἐκ προνοίας ἀποκτείνῃ ἢ τρώσῃ 57, 15 (*Pol.* 1300 *b* 26)
* προξενίαι 54, 18
προξένοις, δίκαι 58, 5
* πρόπυλον τῆς ἀκροπόλεως, πρὸς τὸ 15, 19
προρρηθεῖσαν, τὴν ὥραν τὴν 30, 32 (decree); *v.* προαγορεύων
πρός· *c. dat.* πρὸς τούτοις 23, 13; 24, 15, 17; 26, 6; τοῖν δυοῖν ὀβολοῖν 28, 22. τῷ λίθῳ 7, 5. τοῖς ἰδίοις ὄντες 16, 9
c. acc. πρὸς ἀλλήλους 23, 17; ἀμφοτέρους 11, 14; 16, 38; τοὺς Ἀργείους 17, 15; τοὺς Ἀρεοπαγίτας 15, 14; τῆς πρὸς αὐτὸν φιλίας 18, 9; πρὸς τὴν—βοήθειαν 19, 20; πρὸς τὴν βουλὴν εἰσαγγέλλειν 4, 22; πρὸς τὸ δημαγωγεῖν ἐλθόντος 27, 1; πρὸς ἑκατέρους μάχεται 5, 9; πρὸς τὸν Ἐφιάλτην ἔλεγεν 25, 13; τὴν κρίσιν 3, 21; τὰς μεμψιμοιρίας 12, 55; τὸ νόμισμα 10, 7; τὸ παραυτίκα 28, 28; τὰ παρόντα πράγματα 61, 10; τὸν Πεισίστρατον 14, 22; αἱ πρὸς τὸν πόλεμον ἀρχαί 43, 5; 44, 17; 61, 1; πρὸς τὴν πόλιν προσελθόντα 26, 6; τὰ σύμβολα τὰ πρὸς τὰς πόλεις 59, 16; δίκαιος πρὸς τὴν πολιτείαν 25, 6; πρὸς τὸ πρόπυλον 15, 19; τὰς τιμάς 51, 11, 13; πρὸς χάριν ὁμιλοῦντας 35, 19
προσαγορεύοντες, πατρόθεν 21, 17; προσηγόρευσε 21, 21
προσαγαγόντας τοὺς στρατηγούς, τὰ τοῦ πολέμου—ἀκληρωτί (decree). *Mid.* ταῖς ὁμιλίαις προσήγετο 16, 38; προσηγάγετο τὸν δῆμον 20, 4 (*Pol.* 1296 *b* 37, 1303 *b* 36)
* προσαιροῦμαι· προσελόμενοι σφίσιν αὐτοῖς ἄρχοντας 35, 53 (only quoted in *Index* from Pollux viii 92)
προσαναβῆναι 15, 18
** προσαναζητῆσαι 29, 16 (decree)
προσαρτήσαντες, τὴν γνῶσιν τοῦ διαιτητοῦ 53, 13
πρόσειμι (εἰμί)· τὰς προσούσας δυσκολίας 35, 15
πρόσειμι (εἶμι)· προσιόντες αὐτῷ 11, 2; τὰ χρήματα τὰ προσιόντα 29, 29 (decree); ἀπὸ τῶν προσιόντων 39, 8 (decree)
* προσεπιλαμβάνουσα τῷ πλήθει τὴν ἐξουσίαν 41, 24
προσέρχομαι· *c. dat.* 43, 31. προσελθεῖν ἐναντίον τῆς βουλῆς 30, 28 (decree). πρὸς τὴν πόλιν ὀψὲ προσελθόντα 26, 6. Cf. πρόσειμι (εἶμι)
προσέχοντες, τοῖς νόμοις 26, 13 (frag. 496[2])
προσῆκον, οὐ 13, 25
πρόσθεν (?) col. 31, 2
προσιστῆται τὸ πλῆθος, ὅπως 41, 31
* προσκαθεζόμενος ἐπολιόρκει 20, 14
προσκαθημένου δ' αὐτοῦ 19, 33
προσκαλοῦμαι· προσκληθεὶς φόνου δίκην 16, 32; ὁ προσκαλεσάμενος 16, 34; ἐὰν—προσκαλῆται 29, 25 (decree)
* προσκλήσεις 29, 23 (decree)
* προσκοσμῶ· προσεκεκόσμηντο 13, 21 (not found elsewhere in this sense)
προσκυνοῦντες 14, 30
προσόδους, τὰς 16, 11
* προσοργίζομαι· προσοργισθέντες 19, 29
* προσορμισάμενος ἐν πλοίῳ 57, 23
* προσπαρατίθεσθαι *c. dat.* 63, 22
προσποιοῦμαι· προσεποιοῦντο διώκειν τὴν πάτριον πολιτείαν 35, 8
προστάτης, ἡγεμὼν καὶ (of Hipparchus) 22, 20. προστάτης τοῦ δήμου 2, 9; 20, 18; 23, 12; 25, 4; 28, 6; 36, 6. προστάτην ἔλαβεν ὁ δῆμος 28, 3
προστάττω· προστέτακται 51, 2, 15; 54, 2
προστιθέασι τῶν οἰκείων 40, 24; προσθεῖναι 58, 7; ὀβολὸς προστίθεται 62, 9; προσθεμένου τοῖς ὀλιγαρχικοῖς 34, 25
* προστιμῶσιν αὐτῷ οἱ δικασταί 63, 14; προστιμήσῃ 63, 17 (Bekk. *Anec.* 219, 16 in Testimoniis, c. 57 § 2)
* προτεραίᾳ, τῇ 48, 8
πρότερον 3, 28; 7, 10; 8, 20; 10, 5; 12, 27; 17, 14; 20, 20; 62, 1; 63, 16. οὐ—πρότερον—πρὶν ἂν 60, 17. πρότερον μὲν—μετὰ δὲ— 53, 3. πρότερον—νῦν δέ, see νῦν. ὁ πρότερον λέγων, ὁ ὕστερον λέγων, col. 36, 15 f. τοῖς πρό-

τερον ναυκράροις 21, 20; ἐν τοῖς πρότερον χρόνοις 28, 4
πρότερος· τῷ προτέρῳ ἔτει 53, 24; τὴν προτέραν ὀλιγαρχίαν 37, 11; οἱ πρότεροι 22, 23
προτιθέασιν 44, 11; 48, 10
προτρέπω· προτρέψειν 40, 14; προὔτρεψε (εἰς) 19, 22; (ἐπὶ c. acc.) 27, 5; ὁ προτρέψας (ἐπὶ c. acc.) 23, 19
προϋπαρχούσας τριττῦς, τὰς 21, 10; τῶν προϋπαρχόντων δέκα προβούλων 29, 11
*προϋποβάλλωνται (?) col. 36, 5
πρόφασις τοῦ ἀπιέναι 42, 35; τὴν πρόφασιν τοῦ [πράττ]εσθαι 8, 24; ἀρχὴν καὶ πρόφασιν 13, 13
προφέρω· προὔφερεν, ἡ Πυθία 19, 21 (not in *Index* in this sense)
προχειροτονίας, ἄνευ 43, 31 (only in frag. 396²)
πρυτανεία 43, 14, 22; κατὰ πρυτανείαν 47, 18; (γραμματεὺς) κατὰ πρ. 54, 13; κατὰ τὴν πρ. 48, 14; + ἑκάστην 61, 11; ἐπὶ τῆς ἐνάτης πρ. 47, 21, 25, 28; πρὸ τῆς ἐνάτης πρ. 54, 11
πρυτανεῖον 3, 25, 27; 24, 20; 62, 12 (only in *de Mundo* 400 *b* 19)
πρυτάνεις 4, 11; 29, 21, 32; 41, 31; 43, 32; 44, 1; 45, 23
πρυτανεύει 43, 7; ἡ πρυτανεύουσα φυλή 44, 9; οἱ πρυτανεύοντες 43, 10; 62, 8; οἱ μετὰ τὴν ἕκτην πρυτανεύοντες 44, 18. (The *Index* refers to the fragments only)
πρῶτος 22, 27; οἱ πρῶτοι 5, 12; πρῶται τῶν ἀρχῶν 3, 4. πρῶτον μὲν—ἔπειτα (never ἔπειτα δέ) 9, 3; 21, 3; 24, 8; 25, 6; 27, 13; 29, 21; 34, 4; 36, 8; 43, 11; 51, 10; 56, 7; 57, 2; 59, 1.—εἶτα 42, 20.—ἐκεῖθεν δὲ 15, 6.—δεύτερον, τρίτον 30, 29 (decree).—μετὰ δὲ ταῦτα 55, 13 f; τὸ πρῶτον—μετὰ ταῦτα 3, 3. πρῶτον—τότε 28, 3; τότε πρῶτον 15, 9; 22, 12, 23; 41, 7
Πυθία, ἡ 19, 21; 21, 26
Πυθόδωρος ἄρχων (432/1) 27, 8
Πυθόδωρος ἄρχων (404/3) 41, 3; Π. Ἐπιζήλου 29, 7, 10, 16
Πυθοκλείδης frag. 13 p. 255
Πύλος 27, 25
*πύξινον, πινάκιον 63, 18
πυρκαϊᾶς (γραφή) 57, 16
πυροί 51, 13
πώ· οὔπω 14, 17; πώποτε apparently does not occur
πωληταί 7, 13; 47, 7; 52, 8. (*Index* refers to frag. 401² only)
πωλεῖ τοῦτον ἡ πόλις 42, 10; τὰ μέταλλα πωλοῦσι 47, 9; τὰς οὐσίας 47, 15; τὰ χωρία 47, 23. οἱ πωλοῦντες 51, 7. πωλήσουσιν—ἄλφιτα—ἄρτους 51, 12 f. ἐπώλει τὸν καρπὸν ἡ πόλις 60, 10; ἐπώλουν οἱ δῆμοι (τὰς ἀρχάς) 62, 3. *Pass.* ὅπως—πωλῆται 51, 3. τὰ πραθέντα 47, 11, 22. τὰ πεπραμένα 47, 12 f.

ῥᾳδίως 16, 36
ῥᾳθυμία 8, 28
Ῥαίκηλος 15, 6
ῥέζειν 12, 24, 44 (Solon)
ῥιζῶ· οὔπω τῆς ἀρχῆς ἐρριζωμένης 14, 18
Ῥίνων 38, 21, 28, 32

σάκος 12, 8 (Solon)
Σαλαμίς 17, 7; 22, 38; 23, 5, 22; 27, 7. ἄρχων εἰς Σαλαμῖνα 54, 34; 62, 11
Σάμιοι 24, 7
Σάμον, ἀρχαὶ εἰς 62, 16
σανίς 48, 9 (only in *de Admir.* 832 *a* 9)
σαφῶς, γεγράφθαι 9, 8
*σεισάχθεια 6, 4, 7; 12, 27
σελήνην, κατὰ 43, 10
σημαίνουσαν, ὡς—7, 25
σημεῖον δ' ἐπιφέρουσιν 3, 10; σ. δὲ φέρουσι 7, 19. ὅτι τελευταία—ἐγένετο τῶν ἀρχῶν, σ. καὶ τὸ—διοικεῖν 3, 15; σ. δ' ὅτι 13, 23; σ. δ' ὅτι—ὁ—νόμος 8, 5; σ. δὲ—γάρ 3, 25
Σικελία· ὁ ἐν Σ. τελευτήσας 28, 15; τὴν ἐν Σ. γενομένην συμφοράν 29, 2
Σιμωνίδης 18, 5
*σίτησιν, εἰς 62, 9 f, 17
*σιτικὸν (?) ἐμπόριον 51, 17 (*pap.*)
σῖτος ἀργός 51, 11; περὶ σίτου 43, 18; τοῦ σίτου 51, 16; ζημιοῖ τῷ σίτῳ 49, 2; ἐὰν μὴ ἀποδῶσι τοῖς παισὶ τὸν σῖτον 56, 46
σιτοφύλακες 51, 8 (*Index* quotes corresponding frag. only)
σκάπτοντα, πέτρας 16, 19
σκεύη, 'tackling' &c. 46, 23
*σκήπτωνται κυεῖν 56, 41
σκήψεις 56, 14 (οὐ δοτέον ἐπιτιμήσεως σκῆψιν *Top.* 131 *b* 11)
Σκιροφοριών 32, 7
σκόλιον 19, 14; 20, 21
σκοποῦσιν ὅπως μὴ *c. fut.* 50, 6
Σκυλλαῖον 22, 42
Σκῦρον, ἀρχαὶ εἰς 62, 16
σ[μικρόν] 12, 12 (*pap.*?); *v.* μικρός
Σόλων 5, 5, 11; 6, 1, 6; 8, 7, 16, 25; 9, 2; 13, 2 f; 14, 8, 15; 17, 6; 22, 1 f; 29, 20; 41, 12, 15; (appointment of ταμίαι) 47, 3. προστάτης τοῦ δήμου 28, 6. Σόλωνος θεσμῶν 35, 11
σοφιζομένων, πολλὰ 41, 31
Σοφωνίδης 25, 5
σοφώτερος 14, 10, 11
Σπαρτιᾶται 19, 23
σπουδάζω *c. inf.* σπουδάσωσι λαβεῖν 50, 8. ἐσπούδαζον μὴ κατελθεῖν τοὺς ἀπὸ Φυλῆς 38, 15; οὓς—ἐσπούδασεν ἐλθεῖν 38, 27. *Abs.* ἔνιοι μὲν ἐσπούδαζον 34, 9
σπουδῆς, μετὰ 25, 17
σπῶ· σπασάμενος τὴν μάχαιραν 18, 38
σταδίων, ἐντὸς δέκα 50, 10
σταθμός 51, 13; σταθμά 10, 7; σταθμῶν 10, 3; σταθμοῖς 10, 9
στασιάζειν, διὰ τὸ 13, 8. τὴν πόλιν—

στασιάζουσαν 8, 27; στασιαζούσης τῆς πόλεως 8, 29; στασιάζοντες 13, 11; 20, 19. ἐστασίαζον 20, 1. στασιάσαι 2, 1

στάσις· ἰσχυρᾶς τῆς στάσεως οὔσης 5, 3; τὴν αἰτίαν τῆς στάσεως 5, 19. περιελαυνόμενος τῇ στάσει 14, 21. διὰ τὴν στάσιν 13, 4; μετὰ τὴν στάσιν 41, 12. τὰς στάσεις ἀμφοτέρας 11, 9; 15, 5; στάσεις τρεῖς 13, 16

στατήρ 10, 9 (*Oec.* ii 1349 *a* 28, and fragments)

στέλεχος 60, 9, 15

*στεφανόπωλις 14, 27

στέφανος 57, 27

στήλη χαλκῇ 53, 25; ἐν ταῖς στήλαις 54, 17

στοά, ἡ βασίλειος 7, 3 (*Index* refers to fragm. only)

στοιχεῖον 63, 9, 20; col. 31, 3, 8, 37

στόλος 19, 30

στοχαζόμενον τοῦ πλήθους 22, 4

στρατεία, 'military expedition' 22, 41 (CΤΡΑΤΙΑΝ); 26, 7; 27, 10 (CΤΡΑΤΙΑΙC); 53, 35; 55, 18

στρατευομένοις 24, 4; στρατεύεσθαι 53, 37; τὰς στρατείας εἰ ἐστράτευται 55, 18 (ὅσας ἂν στρατεύσωνται στρατείας *Pol.* 1324 *b* 15)

στρατηγία 27, 26

στρατηγός 22, 14; 23, 16; 26, 8; 38, 32. στρατηγοί 4, 8, 11, 13; 22, 8; 23, 5; 29, 27; 30, 5; 34, 4; 44, 16; esp. 61, 2—16. ἐπὶ τοὺς ὁπλίτας 61, 3; ἐπὶ τὴν χώραν 61, 4; ἐπὶ τὸν Πειραιέα, εἰς τὴν Μουνιχίαν, 61, 6; εἰς τὴν Ἀκτὴν 61, 7; ἐπὶ τὰς συμμορίας 61, 8

στρατηγεῖν 17, 6

*στρατιά, (1) 'army' 19, 27; 22, 9. (2) 'expedition' κατὰ τὴν στρατιὰν (στρατείαν K-W) ἣν ἐξήγαγον 37, 2

στρατιώτης 15, 8; 37, 19

στρατιωτικῶν, ταμίας 43, 2; *c. art.* 47, 9 and 49, 23

στρέφω· ἐστράφην 12, 54 (Solon)

συγγενῶν, τῶν ἐκείνου 22, 15

συγγίγνεσθαι 15, 4

συγγνωμονικός 16, 5

συγγράφειν, συγγράψουσι, 29, 13 (decree); ταῦτα συνέγραψαν 30, 1 (only in *Eth. Eud.* 1214 *a* 2 and *Rhet. ad Alex.*)

*συγκαθιστῇ τὴν τυραννίδα 16, 44; συγκαθεστῶτες 34, 21

συγκατελθοῦσιν, τοῖς ἐκ Πειραιέως 40, 9 (*Pol.* 1300 *a* 18)

συγχωρῶν, παρανομούσαις οὐ 28, 39; τὰ συγκεχωρημένα 47, 12

συκοφάντης 35, 17 f; συκοφαντῶν προβολαί 43, 24

συκοφαντίας γραφή 59, 9

συλλαβόντες—ἀπέκτειναν 38, 11; τοὺς ἐφήβους 42, 19; ὕστερον συλληφθεὶς 18, 23

συλλέγεται, χρήματα 47, 29; τὸ ἔλαιον 60, 7; συλλέξας 60, 15. οὐ συλλεγομένων εἰς τὴν ἐκκλησίαν 41, 30; συλλεγέντες—κατὰ φυλάς 42, 14

συλλήψεως, πρὸ τῆς 18, 18 (not in Ar. in this sense)

συμβαίνω· *c. inf.* συμβαίνῃ 21, 9. συνέβαινεν 11, 7; 16, 11; 19, 1; 24, 10; 26, 2, 10; 37, 12. συνέβη 2, 1; 6, 6; 16, 28; 18, 7, 12; 22, 2; 23, 9; 26, 3; 27, 5; 34, 5, 16; 37, 19; 41, 1, 18. συνεβεβήκει 13, 14. συμβῆναι <εἶναι> 28, 33; *sine inf.* 16, 17. ἐὰν μὴ συμβαίνωσιν ἀλλήλοις 39, 11 (decree)

συμβάλλω· συνεβάλλετο—οὐκ ἐλάττω μοῖραν 19, 24

σύμβολον, παραλαμβάνει col. 32, 14; ἀποδιδόντες col. 37, 2. (2) τὰ σύμβολα τὰ πρὸς τὰς πόλεις 59, 16; τὰς δίκας τὰς ἀπὸ τῶν συμβόλων 59, 17

συμβουλεύειν 30, 14 (decree); συμβουλευόντων 22, 31; συνεβούλευεν 24, 2; συμβουλεύωσι 29, 24 (decree); συμβουλεύσαντος 27, 19. συμβουλεύεσθαι μετὰ τῆς βουλῆς 31, 3 (decree)

σύμβουλος 23, 16

συμμαρτυροίη 12, 30 (Solon)

συμμαχίαν, τὴν πρὸς βασιλέα 29, 4; ἀπὸ τῆς τῶν Λακεδαιμονίων συμμαχίας 23, 19; πρὸς ταῖς συμμαχίαις 54, 18

συμμαχικόν, τὸ 39, 9 (decree). Isocr. ἐν τῷ συμμαχικῷ (in another sense) *Rhet.* 1418 *a* 32

συμμάχομαι· συνεμαχέσαντο τὴν—μάχην 17, 15 (*Pol.* 1300 *a* 18, *Rhet.* 1396 *a* 18)

σύμμαχοι 24, 6, 11 (*Pol.* 1269 *b* 1, 1315 *a* 2, omitted in *Index Ar.*)

σύμμειξις 3, 26 (not in Ar. in this sense)

*συμμορία· (στρατηγὸς) ἐπὶ τὰς συμμορίας 61, 8

σύμπας· σύμπαντα 19, 39

συμπείθειν τὸν κεκτημένον 39, 10 (decree); συνέπεισε τὸν δῆμον 14, 3; συνέπεισεν *c. inf.* 20, 6. συμπεισθέντων τῶν πολλῶν 29, 8

συμπίπτω· *c. inf.* οὐ συνέπιπτεν ἂν 21, 11; συνέπεσε 19, 33; 26, 4

συμπολεμήσειν βασιλέα—ἑαυτοῖς 29, 9; μετὰ τῶν τριάκοντα συνεπολέμησαν 40, 2

*συμπροθυμουμένων αὐτῷ 15, 10

συμφέρειν, ᾗ ἂν ἡγῶνται 31, 7 (decree)

συμφορά 19, 14; 29, 3; ταῖς προγεγενημέναις συμφοραῖς 40, 18 (συμφοραῖς περιπεσεῖν *Eth.* 1100 *a* 7; word omitted in *Index Ar.*)

συμφωνοῦσι πάντες 12, 2 (frequent in genuine works; but the closest parallel is in the spurious *de Admir.* 838 *b* 34 συμφωνοῦσιν, *uno ore perhibent*)

σὺν οἷς ὁ πατὴρ ἦρξεν τὰ σύμπαντα (ἔτη) 19, 39

συνάγειν τὴν βουλήν—τὸν δῆμον 43, 12; 44, 7; συνάγειν (?) col. 31, 34
συναγωνιζομένου 38, 13; -ων 38, 20
συναθροισθέντος τοῦ πλήθους 20, 12; συναθροισθείσης τῆς βουλῆς 25, 20; συναθροισθέντες εἰς τὴν ἀγοράν 38, 4
συναιτίου γενομένου Θεμιστοκλέους 25, 11
συνάμφω 7, 17, 28
συναναγκασθῆναι μένειν 40, 6
*συναρεσκόμενοι τοῖς γιγνομένοις 33, 10
συναρμόσας 12, 43 (Solon)
συναρπάζειν 25, 14
*συνδιοικεῖ ταῖς ἄλλαις ἀρχαῖς τὰ πλεῖστα 47, 1; 49, 31
συνεθισθεὶς—μισθοφορεῖν 27, 10
*συνεισήγαγεν μετ' αὐτοῦ 14, 28
*συνεξαμαρτάνω· ὅσοι μὴ συνεξημάρτανον 22, 18
συνεξῆλθον, εἰς ὅ 19, 12
*συνεπιμελεῖται, τῶν ἄθλων—μετὰ τοῦ ταμίου 49, 23
συνέσει καὶ γνώμῃ—διαφέρειν 32, 11
συνεχῶς 28, 26
συνήγοροι, τοῖς λογισταῖς 54, 3
συνῆλθον, ἅπαντες εἰς τὸ θεσμοθετεῖον 3, 31
συνθήκας συντίθεσθαι 29, 36 (decree); κατὰ τὰς σ. τάσδε 39, 2; κελευουσῶν τῶν σ. 40, 21
συνίστημι· συνέστη φιλία, πόλεμος *conj.* van Leeuwen, for ἐνέστη, 17, 15; 27, 9. μεθ' ὁποτέρων ἐβούλετο συστάντι 11, 13. *Mid.* ἐπὶ καταλύσει τοῦ δήμου συνισταμένους 8, 25; ἐπὶ καταλύσει τῆς πολιτείας 25, 15. συνεστήσαντο τὸν πόλεμον 24, 17
*συνναυμαχήσαντας 34, 6
*συννέμω· συνένειμε πάντας εἰς δέκα φυλάς 21, 4; εἰς τὰς τέτταρας συνενεμήθησαν φυλάς 41, 8
σύνοδος 4, 18
σύνοιδα· τοὺς συνειδότας ἐμήνυεν 18, 33
συνοικεῖν 39, 13 (decree); τῶν συνοικούντων 56, 34; συνοικησάντων 41, 7
συνοικίζω 15, 5 (?)
συνομολογοῦσι 6, 20
συνορῶ· συνιδὼν τὸ πλῆθος 40, 4
συντάττω· οὐκ εἰς δώδεκα φυλὰς συνέταξεν 21, 9
συντελεῖν—εἰς τὸ συμμαχικόν 39, 8 (decree)
συντίθεσθαι, συνθήκας 29, 36 (decree)
συνωνοῦμαι· συνεπρίαντο πολλὴν χώραν 6, 8 (συμπρίασθαι πάντα τὸν σίδηρον *Pol.* 1259 *a* 24)
*συσπουδάζω· συνεσπούδασαν τὴν κάθοδον 38, 24
συσσιτοῦσι κατὰ φυλάς 42, 28; ἐν τῇ θόλῳ 43, 11
σφᾶς αὐτούς 21, 19; 30, 15. σφῶν αὐτῶν 30, 2
σφηκίσκος col. 32, 9 (only in corresp. frag.)
σφόδρ' εὐδοκιμηκώς 14, 1; σφόδρα πρεσβύτης 14, 14
σφραγῖδα, δημοσίαν 44, 5
σχεδόν 20, 18; 28, 31
σχολάζωσιν 16, 10
σῴζειν ἕκαστον ἑαυτόν 23, 6; τὴν δημοκρατίαν σῴζειν 40, 13. σώσας τὴν πατρίδα 11, 14. ἐπ' ἀλλοτρίας νεὼς σωθέντας 34, 6
σῶμα πεπηρωμένους 49, 26. φυλακὴν τοῦ σώματος 14, 4. ἐπὶ τοῖς σώμασιν 2, 8; 4, 23; 6, 3; 9, 3. σώμασιν—λῃτουργεῖν 29, 34 (decree). μὴ δυνατοὺς—τοῖς σώμασιν 49, 14
σῶα ᾖ, ὅπως ἂν 30, 20 (decree); only in *Oec.* ii 1347 *a* 24
σωτήρ, Ζεύς, 56, 27 (σωτὴρ ἁπάντων ὁ θεός *de Mundo* 397 *b* 20)
σωτηρίαν, τὴν τῆς πόλεως 6, 17; ἐπὶ τῇ τῶν παίδων σωτηρίᾳ 19, 35
Abs. περὶ τῆς σωτηρίας 29, 14, 22 (decree)
*σωφρονισταί 42, 18, 25, 27

τὰ μὲν ἄλλα καθάπερ 29, 16
τάλαντον 10, 8; 22, 30
ταμίας (τῆς βουλῆς) 49, 30. τ. στρατιωτικῶν 43, 2; *c. art.* in 47, 9; 49, 23. τ. τῆς Παράλου καὶ ἄλλος τῆς τοῦ Ἄμμωνος 61, 27
ταμίαι 4, 6; 7, 13; 8, 6, 7; 60, 16. οἱ ταμίαι τῆς Ἀθήνας 47, 2; τ. τῶν ἱερῶν χρημάτων τῇ θεῷ καὶ τοῖς ἄλλοις θεοῖς δέκα (411) 30, 8 (decree)
Ταναγραῖος 25, 24
ταξίαρχοι 30, 6; 61, 17 (*Oec.* ii 1350 *b* 10, *de Mundo* 399 *b* 7; ταξιαρχεῖν and ταξιαρχίαι in *Pol.*)
τάξις τῆς πολιτείας 3, 1; πολιτείας τάξιν 41, 10; τῆς τάξεως—ἐν τῇ πολιτείᾳ 5, 1; ἡ τάξις τόνδε τὸν τρόπον εἶχεν 4, 3; (ἡ βουλὴ) τάξιν εἶχε τοῦ διατηρεῖν τοὺς νόμους 3, 34; τὴν αὐτὴν τάξιν ἀποδώσειν 11, 12. *Pl.* τὰ περὶ τὰς τάξεις 42, 31
ταράττω· τῆς πόλεως τεταραγμένης 13, 2
ταραχαῖς, ἐν ταῖς 22, 18 (*Pol.* 1302 *a* 22)
ταραχώδεις τὰς πολιτείας 28, 33
τάττω· ἔταξεν ἐπὶ τὸ νομοφυλακεῖν 8, 20; τὰ περὶ τὰς ἀρχὰς τοῦτον ἔταξε τὸν τρόπον 9, 1; τοὺς φόρους οὗτος ἦν ὁ τάξας 23, 21; ἥντιν' ἂν—τάξωσιν τιμήν 39, 12 (decree); ὅσον ἂν—τάξωσιν—τάττειν (τὸν σταθμὸν) 51, 14. (στάσις) ἐφ' ᾗ τεταγμένος ἦν 13, 20; ἐπὶ τούτῳ τεταγμένοι 15, 21 (*Pol.* 1307 *b* 13); (ἀρχὴ) τεταγμένη πρὸς *c. acc.* 8, 15; οἱ τεταγμένοι col. 36, 23
τάφος 1, 2
τάχους, διὰ 34, 2
τε—καὶ *passim*
Τείσανδρος 19, 2
*τειχίζειν 19, 5; τειχίσαντες 19, 11
τεῖχος, τὸ Πελαργικὸν 19, 32; τὸ ἐν Ἠετιωνείᾳ 37, 9; τοῦ τείχους 50, 10; τὴν τῶν τειχῶν ἀποικοδόμησιν 23, 17

τέκνα 2, 4
τελείων, καθ' ἱερῶν 29, 39 (decree)
Τελεσῖνος ἄρχων (487/6) 22, 21
τελευταῖος 3, 9; 53, 26
τὸ τελευταῖον 18, 10
τελευτήν, μετὰ τὴν τοῦ πατρὸς 19, 38
τελευτήσας 28, 15; τελευτήσαντος 17, 8; 19, 27; 28, 2, 14; 56, 41; ἐτελεύτησεν 18, 22; τετελευτηκόσιν 58, 3
τέλος· ἔχει τέλος ἡ δίκη 53, 9; ἀρχῆς τέλους 56, 7. *adv.* 18, 33. *Classis, census*, τέτταρα τέλη 7, 9; ἐκ τοῦ αὐτοῦ τέλους 4, 12; τὸ ὄνομα τοῦ τέλους 7, 19; θητικοῦ ἀντὶ τέλους 7, 24 (anon.); ποῖον τέλος τελεῖ 7, 30. τέλη 24, 11; 47, 9, 15; 55, 18
τελῶ· τοῖς τὸ θητικὸν τελοῦσιν 7, 15; τελεῖν 7, 16, 27; ποῖον τέλος τελεῖ 7, 30; εἰ—τὰ τέλη τελεῖ 55, 18 (quoted in this sense from the fragments only)
τελῶναι 52, 18
τεμενῶν, μισθώσεις 47, 26
τετάρτῳ, ἔτει 19, 4; 21, 2; 22, 26
τετράδι ἐπὶ δέκα 32, 6 f; ἀπὸ τῆς τετράδος ἱσταμένου 62, 14
τετράκις 43, 14
τετρακοσίους καὶ ἕνα, βουλεύειν 4, 13; (βουλὴν) τετρακοσίους 8, 19: ἕνα καὶ τετρακοσίους (δικαστάς) 53, 16. οἱ τετρακόσιοι c. 29; 37, 10; 41, 20
τετρήρεις 46, 3 (frag. 558[2])
*τετταρακαιδεκέτις (?) 56, 44
τετταράκοντα (δικασταὶ κατὰ δήμους) 53, 1 f; 53, 27 (quoted from frag. 413[2]). τ. ἔτη γεγονότες 29, 12, 37; 56, 18
τέτταρες 4, 12; φυλοβασιλεῖς τ. 8, 12; ἀντὶ τῶν τεττάρων (φυλῶν) 21, 4; τέτταρας φυλάς 41, 8. τέτταρα τέλη 7, 9. τοῖς τέτταρσι τοῖς τὴν φυλὴν—δικάζουσιν 53, 13
τηρῶ· τὰ γραμματεῖα—τηρεῖ ὁ δημόσιος 47, 30; τὰς κλεῖς (ὁ ἐπιστάτης) 44, 3; (τὸ ἔλαιον) οἱ ταμίαι τηροῦσιν 60, 18. ἐτήρει τὴν ἡσυχίαν 16, 26. τηρήσας τοὺς Λάκωνας διαβεβλημένους 23, 19
τίθημι· νόμους ἔθηκε 6, 3; 7, 1; νόμον ἔθηκε 22, 16; + πρὸς αὐτοὺς ἴδιον 8, 28; (νόμους) θεῖναι 22, 4; ἐν τοῖς νόμοις ταῦτα δοκεῖ θεῖναι δημοτικά (of Solon) 10, 1; θεσμοὺς ἔθηκεν (of Dracon) 4, 3; Σόλωνος θεντὸς νόμον εἰσαγγελίας 8, 26. *Pass.* ἐτέθη (νόμος) 21, 4; 22, 13, 26; τοῖς νόμοις οἳ ἂν τεθῶσι περὶ τῶν πολιτικῶν 31, 8; παράστασις τίθεται 59, 8. *Mid.* νόμον ἔθετο 45, 8; μηδ' ἑτέρους (νόμους) θέσθαι 31, 9; ὃς ἂν μὴ θῆται τὰ ὅπλα μηδὲ μεθ' ἑτέρων 8, 29
τίκτει 12, 13 (Solon)
τιμήν, ἀποδοῦναι τὴν 47, 24; λαμβάνειν 39, 12 (decree); πρὸς τὰς τιμὰς τῶν κριθῶν τὰ ἄλφιτα καὶ πρὸς τὰς τιμὰς τῶν πυρῶν τοὺς ἄρτους (πωλεῖν) 51, 12. τιμῆς 12, 5 (Solon)
τιμήματα διεῖλεν 7, 9; μεγέθει—τιμήματος 7, 12; ἐκ τῶν τ. 8, 5. ἐν τοῖς τὰ τιμήματα παρεχομένοις (?) 39, 24 (decree). 'Penalty', τίμημα ἐπιγραψάμενος 48, 22; ὑπὲρ τοῦτο τὸ τίμημα 53, 6
τίμησις col. 37, 4
τιμητὰς ἑλέσθαι τρεῖς 39, 11 (decree). τιμηταὶ ζημίας οἱ δικασταί *Rhet. ad Alex.* 1427 *b* 6 (the only ref.)
Τιμοσθένης ἄρχων (409/8) 23, 22
τιμωμένων διὰ τὰς πατρικὰς δόξας 26, 9. *Litem aestimare*, δώρων τιμῶσιν 54, 9; ἀδικίου 54, 10; ὅτι χρὴ παθεῖν ἢ ἀποτεῖσαι 61, 13. πάλιν τιμῶσι, ἂν δέῃ τιμῆσαι, col. 37, 1. ἐὰν ἀργυρίου τιμηθῇ 63, 16
Τιμώνασσα 17, 13
τιμωρεῖν τῷ ἀδελφῷ 19, 2 (cf. *Pol.* 1311 *b* 21, *Rhet.* 1401 *a* 10); ὑπὲρ τῶν ἀδικουμένων 9, 4 (τιμωρεῖσθαι ὑπέρ τινος *Rhet.* 1372 *b* 4)
τίς, τινές, *passim*
τίς; τίς σοι πατήρ κτλ; 55, 13. τί γίγνεται; 16, 20
τιτρώσκω· ἔτρωσεν 39, 20 (decree); τρώσῃ 57, 15; τρῶσαι 57, 22
τοιόσδε· 3, 2; 29, 10
τοιοῦτος· 15, 1; 16, 15; 40, 1
*τόμια 55, 28
τοξεύειν 42, 23
τοξόται 24, 13
τόπος· ἀπὸ τῶν τόπων 13, 26; 21, 22; πάντων τῶν τόπων 21, 15; τοῖς τόποις 21, 23; τοὺς περὶ Παγγαῖον τόπους 15, 7
τόσον—ὅσσον 12, 4 (Solon)
τοσόσδε· not found (?) in 'Αθ. πολ.
τοσοῦτος· 16, 2
τότε 4, 16; 14, 16; 15, 9; 18, 28; 21, 2, 8; 22, 12, 22; 41, 7. τότε δ' after τὸν μὲν ἄλλον χρόνον, 57, 29; redundant after εἰ δὲ μή, 52, 5
τραγῳδοῖς, χορηγοὺς 56, 7
*τραπεζιτικαὶ (δίκαι) 52, 16
τραύματος, δίκαι 57, 14
τραχὺν—νόον 12, 19 (Solon). τραχυτέραν τὴν ἀρχήν 16, 29; τὴν τυραννίδα 19, 1
τρεῖς 4, 19; 8, 13; 13, 9, 16; 21, 14. τρεῖς καὶ ἑξήκοντα μνᾶς 10, 8. τρία ταῦτ' 9, 2; τρία μὲν ἱερῶν χρηματίζειν, τρία δὲ κήρυξι καὶ πρεσβείαις, τρία δ' ὁσίων 43, 29. μέχρι τριῶν 43, 25; ἐντὸς τριῶν ἡμερῶν 48, 18
τρέφειν (ἵππον) 49, 2; τῶν δημοτῶν ἔτρεφε πολλούς 27, 15. τρέφεσθε (νόον) 5, 17 (Solon); τρέφεσθαι 24, 12
τριάκοντα (δικασταὶ κατὰ δήμους) 26, 20; 53, 3. τρ. ἔτη 4, 15; ἔτη τρ. καὶ τρία 17, 3. τρ. μέρη 21, 12. οἱ τριάκοντα 34, 17; 35—37; 40, 20; 41, 22; 53, 4
*τριακοντόριον 56, 20; cf. p. xlvii, n. 4
τριακοσίους 20, 10; τριακόσια (μέτρα) 7, 18
*τριακοστῷ (ἔτει) 14, 7

τριηραρχίας (*δίκαι*) 52, 16
τριήραρχοι 61, 7
τριήρεις 22, 36; 46, 1—8
τριηροποιοί 46, 8
τρίς 47, 19
**τρισχίλιοι* 26, 10; 36, 7, 9, 13; 37, 8, 15
τρίτον 9, 4; *τρίτη* (*στάσις*) 13, 20; *τῇ τρίτῃ* (*ἡμέρᾳ*) 20, 14; *τρίτῳ* (*ἔτει*) 26, 21
**τριτοπάτωρ* frag. alienum 14 p. 255
τριττύς· τριττύες τρεῖς 8, 13; (*τὰς*) *τριττῦς* 21, 10, 14; *δώδεκα τριττύες* 21, 11. *τριττὺν τῶν πρυτάνεων* 44, 6 (reff. to *Frag.* only)
τριώβολον 41, 35 (reff. to *Oec.* ii 1347 *a* 35 and *Frag.* only)
τρομευμένους 12, 41 (Solon)
τρόπον, τὸν αὐτὸν 17, 10; 25, 22; col. 31, 22; col. 37, 1. *τοῦτον τὸν τρόπον* 3, 33; 9, 1; 12, 1; 16, 2; 26, 1; 32, 7; 42, 38; 55, 27; 60, 1. *τόνδε τὸν τρόπον* 7, 8; 15, 6; 29, 29; 37, 5; 42, 1. *ὅνπερ εἴρηται τρόπον* 11, 1. *ὃν τρόπον* 55, 3; *τρόπῳ τοιῷδε* 34, 17
τροφή 25, 1; *εὐπορίαν τροφῆς* 23, 10; *τροφὴν ἔσεσθαι πᾶσι* 24, 3; *δίδωσι—εἰς τροφὴν—δραχμήν* 42, 24; *διδόναι—τροφὴν δύο ὀβολούς* 49, 28 (law)
τροχὸν ἐπὶ τὴν γνάθον ἐπιβάλλει 49, 4
τρυπήματα col. 36, 25
τρυπῶ· ψῆφος τετρυπημένη col. 35, 29 f; col. 36, 14, 19, 30, 33
τυγχάνω· c. part. 2, 12; 18, 15; 24, 9; 37, 9, 11; 53, 31. *μᾶλλον τῶν τυχόντων ἢ τῶν ἐπιεικῶν ἀνθρώπων* 27, 24
τυπάνου, ὁ ἀπὸ τοῦ 45, 7 (not in Ar. in this sense; *ἀποτυμπανίζεσθαι* in *Rhet.* 1383 *a* 5)
τυραννεῖν 6, 15; 11, 4; 16, 43
τυραννικὴν ἔχων οὐσίαν (*Κίμων*) 27, 13. *τυραννικῶς*, opp. *πολιτικῶς*, 14, 17; 16, 4; 19, 8
τυραννίς 14, 11; 15, 14; 16, 1, 27, 41, 43; 19, 2, 37; 20, 1; 22, 3, 23, 28; 28, 7; 41, 14. *ἡ τῶν τριάκοντα καὶ τῶν δέκα τυραννίς* 41, 22
τύραννος 17, 3; *τ. κατέστη* 22, 14; *τῶν τοῦ τυράννου φίλων* 18, 30. *οἱ περὶ τῶν τυράννων νόμοι* 16, 39; *τοὺς τῶν τ. φίλους* 22, 18, 25; *ὑπὸ τῶν τ.* 19, 13; *ἐκβολῆς τῶν τ.* 20, 19; *τ. κατάλυσιν* 41, 14. *φίλοι τοῖς τυράννοις* 18, 25; *ἐπέθετο τοῖς τυράννοις* 20, 20

ὕβριν 12, 13 (Solon)
ὑβριστής 18, 17
ὑγρά, μέτρα—ξηρὰ καὶ 7, 17
ὑδρία 63, 6, 8; col. 31, 26
ὕδωρ col. 33, 14; *πρὸς ἡμίχουν ὕδατος* col. 37, 5
υἱός· υἱεῖς 17, 9; 19, 34; *υἱέων* 16, 28
Ὑμηττῷ, ἐν 16, 17
ὑπαίθριοι, δικάζουσιν 57, 26
ὑπακουσάντων, οὐχ 32, 16; *οὐχ ὑπήκουσεν* 34, 9
ὑπαρχῆς, ἐξ 4, 17 (*de Gen. Anim.* 745 *a* 18, *de Anima* 412 *a* 4, *Rhet.* 1355 *b* 24)
ὑπάρχει col. 31, 24; *ἡ—ὑπάρχουσα φιλία* 19, 25; *ὑπῆρχεν καὶ πρότερον* 8, 20; *ὑπῆρχον* 21, 23
ὑπεξαιρούμενοι τὸν φόβον 35, 24 (*ὑπεξαιρήσομεν τὰς ἐπιφερομένας δυσχερείας Rhet. ad Alex.* 1432 *b* 13, the only ref.)
ὑπέξειμι· ὑπεξιόντας 19, 34
ὑπεξέρχομαι· ὑπεξῆλθεν 15, 5; *ὑπεξελθόντος* 20, 8
ὑπέρ· c. gen. Πάρνηθος 19, 12; *τῶν ὁδῶν* 51, 11. *τῶν ἀδικουμένων* 9, 4; *ἑκατέρων* 5, 9. *τῶν γερῶν* 57, 12; *ὧν δεῖ χρηματίζειν* 44, 11
c. acc. ὑπὲρ δέκα ἔτη γεγονότες 4, 10; *—τριάκοντα—*4, 15; 30, 4 (decree); 31, 4 (decree);*—τετταράκοντα—*29, 12, 37 (decree); 42, 16; 56, 19; 63, 11. *τὰ ὑπὲρ τοῦτο τὸ τίμημα* 53, 6; *τὰ ὑπὲρ χιλίας* 53, 16
ὑπερβάλλομαι· τὸν κατάλογον—πολὺν χρόνον ὑπερεβάλλοντο 36, 13 (*Rhet. ad Alex.* 1420 *a* 8, 1438 *b* 6, the only reff.)
ὑπερηφανία 5, 21 (Solon)
ὑπερόριοι, ἀρχαί 24, 16
ὑπερτείνειν, δρυφάκτους ὑπὲρ τῶν ὁδῶν 50, 12
**ὑπεύθυνος* 54, 5
ὑπηρέτης 63, 23; col. 31, 8; col. 32, 2, 3, 19. *ἔχοντες δημοσίους ὑπηρέτας* 50, 14; *μαστιγοφόρους—ὑπηρέτας* 35, 7
ὑπισχνοῦμαι· ὑποσχόμενος ἐπιθήσειν 28, 22; *ὑποσχόμενός τι* 43, 26; *ὑπεσχόμην* 12, 44 (Solon)
ὑπὸ τῶν δορυφόρων 18, 22; *ὑπὸ τῆς ὀργῆς* 18, 37; *ὑπὸ τῶν τυράννων* 19, 13
ὑποβάλλωνται (?) col. 36, 5
ὑπογραφή 4, 1
ὑποδείκνυμι· ὑπέδειξεν, opp. ἐπετέλεσεν, 41, 17
ὑποζυγίων δίκαι 52, 16
ὑπόλοιπος 40, 5
ὑποποιησάμενον τοὺς ἑτέρους 6, 15. *τὸν ἐρώμενον* (*τοῦ ἑταίρου*) *ὑπεποιήσατο Pol.* 1303 *b* 24, the only ref.
**ὑπόσπονδος* 20, 15
ὑποφερομένη κατὰ μικρόν (*ἡ πολιτεία*) 25, 3; *τῆς πόλεως ὑποφερομένης* 36, 1
ὑποψία τῶν ἐν ταῖς δυνάμεσι 22, 13; only quoted from frag. and spurious works
ὑστεραίᾳ, τῇ 38, 4; 48, 9
ὕστερος· τῷ ὑστέρῳ ἔτει 22, 20; *τὸν ὕστερον ἐνιαυτόν* 42, 30; 45, 17; *αἱ ὕστεραι* (*φυλαί*) 43, 9
ὕστερον adv. 3, 19; 6, 12; 16, 18, 28; 18, 22, 29; 19, 13; 24, 18; 27, 21; 28, 24; 38, 26. *τῷ ὕστερον ἔτει* 34, 14; *ἐν τοῖς ὕστερον—καιροῖς* 41, 1. *c.*

gen. ἔτεσιν δ' ὕστερον τῆς τῶν τυράννων ἐκβολῆς μάλιστα ἑκατόν 32, 8
ὑφεῖλε τὰς ὑπολοίπους ἡμέρας 40, 5 (ὑφαιροίη *de Caelo* 294 *a* 18, the only ref.)
Ὑψιχίδης ἄρχων (481/0) 22, 40

Φαίνιππος ἄρχων (490/89) 22, 11
φαίνονται γὰρ ἀεὶ στασιάζοντες 13, 11; ἐφάνη τὰ μέταλλα 22, 29
φανερὰς ὁρᾶν (ψήφους) col. 35, 33. φανερῶς ληροῦσιν 17, 5; φ. ἦσαν δοῦλοι 40, 10
φάρμακον· φαρμάκων, δίκαι 57, 15
φάσκων *c. inf.*, after οὐ, 15, 18; 34, 12; 45, 4; οἱ φάσκοντες 17, 5
Φάϋλλος ὁ Ἀχερδούσιος 38, 22
Φειδώνεια μέτρα 10, 5
φέρω· (of pay) φέρειν τρεῖς ὀβολούς 29, 32 (decree); (of expenditure) τὰ ἀναλώματα—ἤνεγκον 56, 25. (of election) (χορηγοὺς κωμῳδοῖς) αἱ φυλαὶ φέρουσιν 56, 9; τοὺς χορηγοὺς τοὺς ἐνηνεγμένους ὑπὸ τῶν φυλῶν 56, 10. χαλεπῶς φερόντων ἐπὶ τούτοις 38, 9; χ. ἐνεγκόντες ἐπὶ τῇ συμφορᾷ 33, 5. ἐπέθηκε φέρων—τὸ γράμμα 63, 23
φεύγω· (of exiles) ἔφυγεν ἀειφυγίαν 1, 3; ἔφευγε τὰ λοιπά 17, 4; τῶν ἐξ Ἀρείου πάγου φευγόντων 47, 14; φεύγων φυγήν 57, 21; (of the defendant) 48, 21; 53, 11; col. 36, 32
φημί· φησιν 14, 25; 55, 19; φασὶ 6, 11; 7, 18; 9, 5; 16, 17; 17, 17; 18, 30, &c. ἔφη 14, 13; 16, 21. φῇ 56, 15; 57, 19
φθείρω· ἐφθάρθαι—κατὰ πόλεμον 26, 7
φθίνοντος Θαργηλιῶνος, ἐνάτῃ 32, 5
φιλάνθρωπος 16, 4, 30. *Adv.* 18, 17
φιλαργυρία (?) 5, 21 (Solon)
φιλεργία 16, 24 (*Rhet.* 1361 *a* 8)
φιλία 17, 15; 18, 9; 19, 26
φιλοκτήμων 12, 48 (Solon)
φιλόμουσος 18, 4 (*Eth.* 1175 *a* 34)
Φιλόνεως ἄρχων (527/6) 17, 2
φιλονικίαν τὴν ἐνεστῶσαν 5, 11; τὴν πρὸς ἀλλήλους φ. 13, 16
φίλος 23, 24; φίλοι τοῖς τυράννοις 18, 24; τῶν τοῦ τυράννου φίλων 18, 30; τοὺς τῶν τυράννων φίλους 22, 18, 25; φίλους 18, 32; φίλος τῶν τυράννων 20, 2; τῶν φίλων 20, 11; διὰ τῶν φ. 6, 8
φόβον, ὑπεξαιρούμενοι τὸν 35, 24
φοβούμενοι μὴ καταλυθῶσι τῆς ἀρχῆς 38, 9; φοβηθέντες μὴ—καταλύσῃ 36, 5; φοβηθεὶς 15, 4; 16, 34; φοβουμένων *abs.* 40, 1
*φονεύς 18, 36
φονικῶν (θεσμῶν) 7, 2 (*Pol.* 1269 *a* 1, 1274 *b* 24, 1275 *b* 10, 1300 *b* 24)
φόνου δίκην, προσκληθεὶς 16, 32; αἱ τοῦ φόνου δίκαι 57, 12; φόνου δίκαι καὶ τραύματος 57, 14
Φορμίσιος 34, 24
φόρος· τοὺς φόρους—τοὺς πρώτους 23, 21; ἀπὸ τῶν φόρων 24, 11 (*Pol.* 1272 *a* 18); φόρους (*pap.*) ἄγουσαι νῆες 24, 19
φράζω· ἐφρασάμην 12, 7, 20 (Solon); φρασαίατο 12, 51 (*id.*)
φρατρίαι 21, 23
Φρεάτου, ἐν 57, 22
φρενὸς ἔνδοθεν 5, 7 (Solon); ἐνὶ φρεσὶ 5, 15 (*id.*)
*φρούρια, ἄρχοντες εἰς τὰ 30, 7 (decree)
*φρουρίδες, νῆες 24, 18
φρουροί 24, 14, 19 (?); 62, 5
φρουρῶ *abs.* 24, 4; τὰ δύο ἔτη 42, 33; τὴν ἀκρόπολιν—ἐφρούρουν 37, 20; φρουροῦσιν τὴν Μουνιχίαν—τὴν Ἀκτήν 42, 21. (οἱ ἐκεῖ φρουροῦντες στρατιῶται *Oec.* ii 1351 *a* 28, the only ref.)
φυγάδες 19, 8; 20, 16; 34, 20; 37, 2
φυγήν, φεύγων 57, 21
Φύη 14, 27
φυλακή· 61, 7; τοῦ σώματος 14, 4, 9; ἡ τῆς πολιτείας φ. 25, 9; περὶ φυλακῆς τῆς χώρας 43, 18
φυλακτήρια 42, 33 (*Pol.* 1331 *a* 20, *b* 16; *Rhet.* 1360 *a* 9)
φύλαξ τῶν νόμων 4, 20; φύλακας τῆς ἀρχῆς 24, 8; δεσμωτῶν φύλακες 24, 21; τοῦ δεσμωτηρίου φύλακες 35, 6
φύλαρχοι 30, 7; 31, 14; 49, 10; 61, 23
φυλάττω· τὰ θέσμια φυλάττωσι 3, 20; τὰ ψηφίσματα φυλάττει 54, 15; φυλάττει (τὴν χώραν) 61, 5. παρ' αὑτοῖς ἐφύλαττον τοὺς ἐγνωσμένους 36, 14
φυλέται 31, 4 (decree); 42, 15, 26; 61, 18
Φυλή 37, 2; 38, 1, 15; 41, 23
φυλή· τοῖς δικασταῖς τοῖς τὴν φυλὴν ταύτην εἰσάγουσιν 48, 25; τοῖς τὴν φ. δικάζουσιν 53, 14; τοὺς τὴν φ. δικάζοντας 58, 7. τὴν φ. καλεῖ εἰς τὸ κληρωτήριον col. 31, 18. δυοῖν φυλαῖν 56, 13. φυλαὶ τέτταρες 8, 11; 41, 8; (χορηγοὺς κωμῳδοῖς) αἱ φυλαὶ φέρουσι 56, 9; (χορηγοὺς) ἐνηνεγμένους ὑπὸ τῶν φυλῶν 56, 10. ταῖς φυλαῖς 8, 4. διελόμενοι τὰς φυλάς 61, 20; κατὰ φυλὰς 22, 8, 22; 42, 15, 28; 48, 1; 56, 13; 63, 2, 20. ἐκ τῆς φυλῆς ὅλης 62, 2, 4. For τῆς φυλῆς ἑκάστης *et sim.*, and for εἷς ἐκ τῆς φυλῆς, *v.* ἕκαστος
*φυλοβασιλεῖς τέτταρες 8, 12; φ. 41, 8; 57, 31
*φυλοκρινεῖν 21, 6
φύσει, τῇ 5, 10; 18, 3, 24
φύω· πρὸς ἀμφοτέρους ἐπεφύκει καλῶς 16, 38
φωνῆς (?) 15, 17
φωρῶ· ἐφώρασεν 18, 27

χαίρω· ἐφ' οἷς ἔχαιρεν ἡ πόλις γιγνομένοις 35, 20
*χαλῶ· ἐχάλασεν (?) 15, 17
χαλεπώτατον—καὶ πικρότατον 2, 9

χαλεπῶς ἐνεγκόντες 33, 5; χ. φερόντων 38, 8
χαλκοῦς ἀμφορεύς col. 36, 4, 7; χ. ψῆφοι col. 35, 27; στήλην χαλκῆν 53, 25
χαρακτήρ, ὁ ἀρχαῖος 10, 7
χαρίζεσθαι τοῖς πολλοῖς 28, 27
χάρις· πρὸς χάριν ὁμιλοῦντας 35, 19
Adv. πίστεως χάριν 18, 35; τοῦ βελτίστου χ. 35, 21; τούτων χ. 29, 25 (decree); δυοῖν χ. 16, 7; ὧν χ. 22, 25
Pl. χάρισιν 41, 29
Χάρμος, father of Hipparchus, 22, 16
χαῦνα 12, 20 (Solon)
χειμῶνος, τοῦ χ. ἐνεστῶτος, 37, 1
χειροτονητός 54, 16 (*Rhet. ad Alex.* 1424 *a* 14 χειροτονηταὶ ἀρχαί, the only ref.)
χειροτονία· κριθῆναι μιᾷ χ. πάντας 34, 5; πρὸς τὴν ἐπικύρωσιν τῆς χειροτονίας 41, 32; τὰς χειροτονίας κρίνειν 30, 25 (decree); κρίνουσιν 44, 12. διατάττουσι τῇ χειροτονίᾳ 61, 3 (frag. and *Rhet. ad Alex.*, the only reff.)
χειροτονῶ· 34, 26; 42, 18, 22; 43, 3—5; 46, 3, 4; 49, 9, 18; 54, 17, 21; 56, 24; 57, 3; 61, 1, 17, 19, 23, 25, 27
χείρων· χείρους 27, 23; χείρω 28, 2
χηρῶ· ἐχηρώθη 12, 52 (Solon)
χίλιοι 17, 16; 19, 28; 24, 13, 14; 35, 5 (?); χιλίους πεντακοσίους 35, 26
Χῖοι 24, 7
χλαμύδας ἔχοντες 42, 33 (frag. 458^2, the only ref.)
χολούμενοι 12, 20 (Solon)
χορηγία *met.* 27, 18
χορηγοὺς τραγῳδοῖς καθίστησι τρεῖς—καὶ κωμῳδοῖς καθίστη πεντε 56, 7—9; χορηγοὺς καθιστᾶσιν 54, 35. εἰς Δῆλον χ. 56, 20
χορηγοῦντα, παισὶν 56, 18
χρείας καταλαβούσης 3, 8
χρειοῦς, ὑπὸ 12, 38 (Solon)
χρέα, οἱ ἀφῃρημένοι τὰ 13, 21. χρεῶν ἀποκοπαί 6, 3; 11, 8; χρεῶν ἀποκοπή 6, 11; 10, 2; 12, 26; 13, 13 (*Probl.* and *Oec.*, the only reff.)
χρή 6, 21; 15, 24
χρήματα, προεδάνειζε 16, 6; δανειζόμενοι 38, 8; διαχειριοῦσιν—διαχειρίζωσι τὰ χρήματα 30, 10, 14; χρ. συλλέγεται 47, 29; τὰ καταβαλλόμενα χρήματα 48, 3; τῶν ἱερῶν ἐν οἷς τὰ χρήματ' ἐστίν 44, 4. χρημάτων καταβολή 47, 31; χρημάτων εὐπόρησαν 19, 20; χρ. ἠθροισμένων πολλῶν 24, 1; τῶν ἱερῶν χρ., τῶν ὁσίων χρ. 30, 8 f. χρήμασιν λῃτουργεῖν 29, 34 (decree)
χρηματίζειν 43, 14, 29 f; 44, 11; περὶ σίτου καὶ περὶ φυλακῆς τῆς χώρας 43, 18. *Mid.* χρηματισάμενος 15, 7
χρησμῶν γιγνομένων 19, 7
* χρηστηριαζομένοις 19, 22
χρόνου τινὸς οὐ πολλοῦ διελθόντος 4, 2; χρόνου διαπεσόντος (?) βραχέος 35, 25. πολὺν χρόνον 2, 2; 5, 3; 16, 35; 18, 23; οὐ πολὺν χρ. 15, 3; χρ. τοσοῦτον 3, 23; χρ. τινὰ 28, 21; πλείω χρ. 44, 2 f; εἰς τὸν ἄλλον χρ. 31, 18 (decree); —λοιπὸν χρ. 30, 15 (decree); μετ' οὐ πολὺν χρ. 25, 24; 34, 13. *Pl.* διὰ τῶν αὐτῶν χρ. 13, 6; τῶν χρόνων—μὴ ἐξεληλυθότων 56, 17; ἐν τούτοις τοῖς χρ. 3, 14; ἐν τοῖς τότε χρ. 26, 8; ἐν τοῖς πρότερον χρ. 28, 4
χρυσίον· *pl.* 60, 21
χρυσοῦν, ἀνδριάντα 7, 5; 55, 33
χρῶμα, τῆς βακτηρίας col. 32, 7; χρώματα ἐπιγέγραπται, τοῖς δικαστηρίοις col. 32, 8
χρῶμαι· τοῖς Δράκοντος θεσμοῖς χρώμενοι 7, 2; (νόμῳ) χρώμενοι 8, 6; (νόμοις) οὐκέτι χρῶνται 8, 16; χρῶνται τοῖς ἐπωνύμοις καὶ πρὸς τὰς στρατείας 53, 35; ὡς (τῷ πλήθει) δεῖ χρῆσθαι 12, 10; χρώμενοι τῇ εἰωθυίᾳ—πρᾳότητι 22, 19; τῇ πόλει πάσῃ πατρικῶς χρωμένους 28, 32. ἐχρῶντο τῷ μὲν στρατηγῷ τῷ δὲ συμβούλῳ 23, 16; τοῖς συμμάχοις δεσποτικωτέρως ἐχρῶντο 24, 7. ὅ τι χρήσεται τοῖς χρήμασιν 22, 32. ἐχρήσαντο τῷ νόμῳ 22, 12; χρήσασθαι ταῖς—συμφοραῖς 40, 18; οὐ χρησάμενοι καλῶς τοῖς πράγμασι 34, 13
χώρα· ἡ χ. δι' ὀλίγων ἦν 4, 24. ἐξεργαζομένης τῆς χώρας 16, 12; φυλακὴ τῆς χ. 43, 18. ἐν τῇ χώρᾳ 19, 11. συνεπρίαντο πολλὴν χ. 6, 10; κατὰ τὴν χ. 16, 8; εἰς τὴν χ. 16, 14; (στρατηγὸς ὁ) ἐπὶ τὴν χ. 61, 5; τὴν χ. ἀνάδαστον ποιοῦσιν 40, 25
χωρεῖν τὴν ψῆφον, αὐτὴν μόνην col. 36, 9
χωρίον 15, 6; 16, 20; 60, 13; χ. ἀτελές 16, 18. *Pl.* 27, 17; 47, 21, 24; 52, 6; 60, 8
χωρίς 39, 26 (decree); χωρὶς μὲν—χωρὶς δέ 47, 18; 53, 11. Not found *c. gen.* in 'Αθ. πολ.

ψαλτρίαι 50, 6 (only in corresp. frag.)
ψευδεγγραφῆς γραφή 59, 10 (only in corresp. frag.)
ψευδῆ τὴν αἰτίαν εἶναι 6, 21
ψευδοκλητείας γραφή 59, 10 (only in corresp. frag.)
ψευδομαρτύρια τὰ ἐξ 'Αρείου πάγου 59, 17; cf. col. 36, 11, 13. Form ψευδομαρτυριῶν in *Pol.* &c.
ψηφιζόμενοι col. 37, 2; ἐὰν μὴ ψηφίζηται col. 36, 3; εἰς οὓς (*sc.* ἀμφορέας) ψηφίζονται οἱ δικασταί col. 36, 6. ὅ τι ἂν οἱ δικασταὶ ψηφίσωνται 45, 11; οὐκ ἔξεστιν οὐδὲν ἀπροβούλευτον—ψηφίσασθαι 45, 23; ψηφισάμενοι μηδεμίαν ἀρχὴν εἶναι μισθοφόρον 33, 9
ψήφισμα 29, 6, 10; 34, 27; 40, 8; 41, 26. τὰ ψηφίσματα φυλάττει 54, 14. ψηφίσματα quoted (Pericles) 26, 22 f.

B.C. 411 (Pythodorus) 29, 10—19 (with amendment); 29, 21—39; c. 30; c. 31. B.C. 403 (*αἱ διαλύσεις ἐπ' Εὐκλείδου*) c. 39
ψήφου, κύριος—τῆς 9, 6. *δίδωσιν—τὴν ψῆφον* 55, 23 f; *εἰς ἐνέβαλλε τὴν ψ.* 55, 24. *αὐτὴν μόνην χωρεῖν τὴν ψ.* col. 36, 9. *ψῆφοι χαλκαῖ* col. 35, 27; *τετρυπημέναι, πλήρεις, ib.* 29. *ψήφων, ἀριθμὸς* col. 36, 32

ὧδ' 12, 11
ὠμοτητα καὶ πονηρίαν, πρὸς 37, 16 (not in this sense in *Meteor*. the only ref.)
ὤνιος 51, 11. *ὤνια, καθαρὰ καὶ ἀκίβδηλα* 51, 13
ὠνοῦμαι· τόν τε πριάμενον καὶ ὅσου ἂν πρίηται 47, 17
ὥραν τὴν προρρηθεῖσαν 30, 32 (decree)
'Ωρεός 33, 5
ὡς· 'as', *ὡς λέγουσι* 6, 7 f; 14, 26; 18, 32; *φασίν* 18, 30; *φησιν* 14, 25; *ὁμολογεῖται* 5, 12
'how', *ὡς (τῷ πλήθει) δεῖ χρῆσθαι* 12, 10
'that', *ὡς οὐχ ἥξει* 11, 5; *οὐ χρὴ θαυμάζειν* 15, 24; *ἐφώρασε* 18, 26; *εἴη* 16, 27
'when', *ὡς ἐξέπεσε* 15, 2; *ἐξέπεσον* 28, 6; *οὐκ ἐδύνατο* 18, 33; *ἔλαβεν* 18, 35; *ἐφάνη* 22, 29; *εἶδεν* 25, 18; *ἐπεκράτουν* 38, 16
c. part. ὡς ἂν ἀπὸ τοῦ πράγματος κείμενον 7, 20 (*ὡς ἂν* not noticed elsewhere in Ar. in this sense); *δυνάμενος πολιτεύεσθαι* 28, 37; *πεπονθώς* 14, 4; *ὄντα* 18, 12; *ἐπανορθοῦντες* 35, 12; *ἀπολογησόμενος* 16, 33; *μηνύσων* 18, 34; *μεθιδρυσόμενος* 19, 5; *μεταδώσοντες* 36, 7
c. inf. ὡς εἰπεῖν 2, 12; *ὡς ἔπος εἰπεῖν* 49, 31; 57, 8
c. gen. abs. 6, 5; 13, 24; 36, 9
c. acc. abs. 7, 25; 29, 19
c. numeralibus, ὡς ἑπτακοσίους 37, 19
c. superl. ὡς ἰσαίτατα 30, 18 (decree)
ὡς=πρός, ὡς τὸν δῆμον 45, 3
ὥσπερ 8, 20; 9, 8; 16, 3; 24, 10; 61, 24. *ὥσπερ νῦν* 3, 32
ὥστε c. ind. οὐ κατεῖχεν ἑαυτὸν 18, 36; *οὐ συνέπιπτεν ἂν* 21, 11.—*c. inf. ἀπεχθέσθαι κτλ* 6, 14; *διατρέφεσθαι* 16, 6; *ἀναλίσκεσθαι τοὺς ἐπιεικεῖς* 16, 11; *τὸν αὐτὸν ἐχθρὸν εἶναι καὶ φίλον* 23, 23; *μὴ δύνασθαι* 49, 27
ὠφελούμενοι, ἐτύγχανον 33, 7

ENGLISH INDEX.

The numerals refer to the *pages*; *a* and *b* denote the first and second columns of the commentary.

For proper names not found here, see *Greek Index*.

Abbott's *History of Greece* quoted, 17 *a*, 45 *a*
abbreviations in the MS classified, xxxvi
Aegospotami, 132
Aeschines, *Schol.* on *F. L.* 150 corrected, 131 *b*; *Schol.* on ii 87 quoted, 212
Alcmeonidae 1, 72—76
altars as places of refuge, 103 *b*
Ambracia, Cypselidae in, 67 *a*
amendment, formula for, 117 *b*
Ammonias, state-trireme, 230 *a*, cf. Keil, *Solon. Verf.* 149
amnesty after the fall of the Thirty and the Ten, 143 *a*
Anaceum, 60 *b*
Anacreon, 68 *b*
Andocides, *de Myst.* 78; 214 *b* (cf. Keil, *Solon. Verf.* 110 f)
Androtion, lv; on Solon, 37 *a*; date of, 86 *a*; cf. Keil, *Solon. Verf.* 190 f
animals, damage done by, 188 *a*; judicial trial of, 216 *b*
Anthemion, 28, and *Addenda*, lxxvii
Antiphon, 127
Anytus, 110 *b*, 132 *b*
Apollonius Rhodius, *scholia* on, xxviii
arbitrators, 190—192
Archestratus, 134 *a*, and *Addenda*, lxxvii
Archinus of Ambracia, 67
Archinus, a leader of the moderate party, 404 B.C., 132 *b*, 144 *a*
archons, early history of, 6; official residences of, 8—11; mode of appointment before Dracon, 12, 31; under Dracon, 14; under Solon, 29—31; under Cleisthenes, 86; their appointment by lot, 29 *b*, 87 *a*; archonship opened to *zeugitae*, 106 *b*; oath of, 7, 25, 203; salaries of, 231 *b*; scrutiny of, 201 *b*; archons of same name, how distinguished, 129 *b*
chronological list of archons (*denotes those hitherto unknown)
621 *Aristaechmus, 12 *b*
594 Solon, 19 *a*, 49 *a*, 55 *a*
582 & 1 Damasias II, 50 f
560 Comeas, 55 *a*
555 *Hegesias, 57
527 *Philoneos, 65 *b*
511 *Harpactides, 75 *b*
508 Isagoras, 77 *b*
501 *Hermocreon, 84 *b*
490 Phaenippus, 85
487 *Telesinus, 86 *b*
483 Nicodemus, 88 *a*, 89 *a*
481 *Hypsichides, 91 *a*
478 Timosthenes, 94 *a*
462 Conon, 100 *a*
457 Mnesitheides, 106 *b*
453 Lysicrates, 106 *b*
451 Antidotus, 106 *b*
432 Pythodorus, 108 *a*
412 Callias, 126 *b*
411 Mnesilochus, 128 *a*
411 Theopompus, 128 *b*
406 Callias Ἀγγελῆθεν, 129 *b*
405 Alexias, 132 *a*
404 Pythodorus, 133 *b*, 146 *b*
403 Eucleides, 141 *a*
401 Xenaenetus, 146 *a*
329 Cephisophon, 200 *b*
Areopagus, before Dracon, 11 and 31 *b*;

under Dracon, 18; under Solon, 33; revival of its authority after Persian war, 92; attacked by Ephialtes, 100 f; privileges of, 101 *a*; attacked by Pericles, 107; under the Thirty, 142 *b*; trials before, 172 *b*, 212. Cf. Keil, *Solon. Verf.* 100 f, 120

Arginusae, 129 *b*; overtures of Sparta after, 131 *a*

Aristides, archonship of, 87 *a b*; ostracism and recall of, 91; προστάτης τοῦ δήμου, 93; co-operates with Themistocles in building the walls of Athens, 93; withdraws the Ionians from alliance with Sparta, 94; assesses the tribute, *ib.*; counsels the people to live in Athens and to assume the control of affairs, *ib.*; promoter of the seventh change in the constitution, 147

Aristides, *rhetor*, xxv, 20 *a*, 45 *a*, 49 *a*, 147 *b*. Cf. Keil, *Solon. Verf.* 196 f

Aristogeiton, 69 f

Aristophanes, *scholia* to, xxviii

Aristotle and Macedonia, 59 *a*; *Politics*, xii f, xl, xliii—xlvi, lviii, 63 *a*, 66 *a*, 67 *a*, 76 *a*, 78, 83 &c.; *Politicus*, xiv; περὶ βασιλείας, xiv (cf. Keil, *Solon. Verf.* 128—142); δικαιώματα πόλεων, xiv; νόμιμα βαρβαρικά, xiv; πολιτεῖαι, xiv—xxxi; style of, xlix; see 'Athenian Constitution'

assembly, public, under Dracon, 14; under Solon, 26; pay for attendance, instituted by Agyrrhius, 149; its final amount, 231. Number of meetings, 158; business at each, 159 f, 162 f

Athenaeus, xxvi

Athênê, statue of, 170 *a*; *peplus* of, 180 *a*, 223 *a*; treasurers of, 170, cf. 121

Athenian ascendancy, beginning of, 94

'Athenian Constitution', abstract of, lix—lxvii; authorship of, xxxix—liv; authorities followed in, liv (cf. Keil, *Solon. Verf.* 48, 51, 186, 205, 227, 231, and esp. 200 f); date of, xxxix; Berlin fragments of, xxxi f; British Museum papyrus of, xxxiv—xxxix; language and style, xlvi—l; literature of, lxvii—lxxv; relation to the *Politics*, xliii—xlvi; lviii; 57 *a*, 83 *a*; rhythm, l and *Addenda*, lxxvii

Atthides, writers of, lv f (cf. Keil, *Solon. Verf.* 200 &c.)

Attica; men of the 'Highlands', the 'Shore', and the 'Plain', 54 *a*

Attic lunar year, 157 *b*

auditors, 193 *a*

Bauer, Prof. A., quoted, 56 *b*, 58 *a*, 90 *b*, 130 *b*

beasts of burden, damage done by, 118 *a*

Bergk quoted, xxxii f

Berlin Fragments, the, xxxi f, liv

Blass, Prof. F., quoted, xxxi f, xxxviii, l, lxxviii, 82 *b*, and, in the critical notes, *passim*

Bouzyges, 254 frag. 10

bowmen, citizens serving as, 96 *b*

Brauronia, 198 *b*

British Museum *papyrus* described, xxxiv f

Busolt, Prof. G., quoted, 14 *a*, 15, 17 *b* &c.

Callixenus, 114 *a*

Cauer, F., criticised, 148 *b*

chiasmus, 124 *b*

Chios, 95 *a*

choregi, 204 f

chronology of rule of Peisistratus, 56

" of later years of Themistocles, 101—3

Cicero's mention of the Πολιτεῖαι, xxi

Cimon, 104 f; accused by Pericles, 107; his liberality, 108 f

citizens, revision of the roll of, 53; registration of, 150

citizenship, grants of, 196 *b*

Cleidemus, lv

Cleisthenes, 76—92

Cleitophon, 117 *b*

Clement of Alexandria, xxvi

Cleomenes, King of Sparta, 75—7

Cleon, 111 f

Cleophon, 112 f, 131

clerks, public, 194—6

cleruchi, 97 *b*

Cobet, marginal correction of Pollux viii 85, 202 *b*

Codrus, 6

coinage, Aeginetan and Euboic, 39

Comedy, *choregi* appointed for, 204

conflict of classes before Dracon and Solon, 3—5

conjectures proposed, (c. 2, 1) 4 *b*; (c. 3, 13) 7; (c. 4, 13 and 16) 16 *bis*; (c. 6, 19) 22; (c. 8, 24) 33; (c. 8, 28) 34; (c. 13, 24) 53; (c. 26, 5) 104; (c. 28, 16) 112 *a*; (c. 35, 9 f) 134 *b*; (c. 38, 7) 139; (c. 39, 24) 143; (c. 43, 15) 159 *a*; (c. 45, 3) 167; (c. 47, 14) 172; (c. 49, 24) 177; (c. 51, 17) 185; (c. 54, 32 f) 199; (c. 56, 46) 210; (c. 57, 26) 215; (c. 63, 3) 233 l. 3; (c. 63, 8) 234; (col. 31, 1 f) 237; (col. 31, 27) 239; (col. 32, 9) 240; (col. 32, 15, 16, 19) 241. *Schol.* on Aeschin. *F. L.* 150 corrected, 131 *b*. Photius, *s.v.* ἡγεμονία δικαστηρίου corrected, 216 *a*; mistake in Photius, *s.v.* πάραλοι, accounted for, 230 *a*

Council of 401 under Dracon, 16; 400 under Solon, 33. Council of 500, instituted by Cleisthenes, 79 *a*; appointed by lot, 157 *a*, 231 *a*; functions of, 168 f; their right of imprisoning, 166 *b*, 175 *b*; salary of, 231 *b*; scrutiny on appointment to, 168 *a*; transfer of some

of their duties to the Assembly 148 *b*, or the law-courts, 180 *b*
crown of *archon basileus*, 216 *a*
Crusius, Prof. O., quoted, 9 *b*, 44 *a*, 110 *a*, 149 *a*
Curtius, Prof. E., quoted, 9 *b*, 10, 54 *a*, &c.
Cylon, 1—3
Cypselidae in Ambracia, 67 *a*

Damasias II, 50 f
Damonides, 109
Dareste, M. R., quoted, 46 *a*
Deceleia, 131 *a*
Delos, festival at, 198, 199 *b*; *amphictyones*, 232 *a*; *choregi* and *architheoros*, 205 *b*
Delphi, temple at, 74 *a*
Delphinium, court in precincts of, 213 *a*
demagogues, 111
demes, names of, 82: number and distribution of, 80
Demetrius Phalereus, xlii
Dicaearchus, xxi, xliii
dicasts, 6000, 96 *b*; number of, 190 *b*, 235 *a*; pay, 241 *b*; procedure for their allotment to the several law-courts, 233 f; votes of, 246
Didymus, xxi f (cf. Keil, *Solon. Verf.* 59 f)
Diels, Prof. H., xxxiii, 3, 51 *b*
diobelia, 112 *b* (cf. Keil, *Solon. Verf.* 223)
Diogenes Laertius, xxv
Dionysia, 201 *a*, 204 *b*, 206 *a*
'district-judges', 63 *b*
dowry, restitution of, 187 *a*
Dracon, constitution before, 6—12; constitution of, 12—18 (defended by Keil, *Solon. Verf.* 96—98, 202); laws of, 12 *b*, 23 *b*

Edinburgh Review, 1891, p. 478 f, quoted, 18 *b*, 138 *b*
Eetioneia, 138 *a*
Eleusinia, 199 *a*
Eleusis, 141 f
Eleven, the, 99 *b*, 185 f
ephebi, 150—155
ephetae, 214; cf. Keil, *Solon. Verf.* 106 ff, 108
Ephialtes, 99—104; cf. Keil, *Solon. Verf.* 120, 213
Epimenides, 3
Erechtheus, 250, l. 3
Eretria, Knights of, aid Peisistratus, 59 *b*; battle of, 411 B.C., 128 *b*
Etymologicum Magnum, xxvii
Euboea, revolt of, 411 B.C., 128
Eucken, Prof. R., quoted, xlviii f, 3, 43 *a*, 76 *a*, 145 *a*
Euripides, *scholia* on, xxvii; 253 frag. 4
Eustathius, xxviii

Festivals, of Asclepius, 206; Brauronia, 198; Delian, 198, 205; Dionysia, 204; Heracleia, 198; Lenaea, 210 *b*; Panathenaea 223; Thargelia 204 f, 207
Five Thousand, the, 120, 126, 127, 128
fortresses of Attica, 123 *a*, 155 *a*
Forty, the, 188 *b*
Foucart, M., quoted, 97 *a*
Four Hundred, the, 115—128
Fragments, index of, 256

Gellius, xxv
generals, 85; election and duties of, 225 f; at Arginusae, 129 f
gennetae, 252 (cf. Keil, *Solon. Verf.* 64 f)
Gilbert, G., 7 *b*, 225 *b*, and *passim*
Giles, Mr P., quoted, 81 *b*
Girard, M. P., 151 *b*, 154 *b*
Gomperz, Prof., quoted, xlvii, 5 *a*, 14 *a*, 58 *a*
Goodwin, Prof. W. W., 164 *a*, 222 *b*
Grote, quoted, 26 *b*, 35 *b*, 36 *b*, 37 *b*, 42 *a*, 56 *a*, 59 *a*, 63 *b*, 79 *b*, 81 *a*, 85, 127 *b*, 128 *a*, 131 *a*, 135 *b*, 164 *b*; supported by text, 90 *b*, 117 *a*
guards, on the acropolis, 97 *a*; over the dockyards, *ib.*
guardships, 98 *b*

Hager, Dr H., 118 *b* &c.
Harmodius, 67—71; commemoration of, 217
Harpocration, xxvi
Hartel, Prof. von, quoted, 161 *b*
Haussoullier, M. B., quoted, 174 *b*, 237 f
Head, Mr B. V., quoted, 38 *b*, 39 *b*, 40
Headlam, Mr J. W., quoted, l, 13—18, 152 *a*, 156 *b*, 157 *b*, 214 *a*, 231 *a*, 232 *b*
Hegesistratus, 66 *b*, 67 *b*
heliaea, 215 *b*
Heracleia, 199 *a*
Heracleides of Clazomenae, 149 *b*
Heracleides Lembos, xxi, 250
Hermippus, xvi f
Herodotus, liv, 57 *b*; (v 66, 69) 78 *a*; (v 69) 79 *b*; (v 71) 1 *b* (cf. Keil, *Solon. Verf.* 96, 117)
Hesychius, xxvii
hiatus, l, lii (cf. Keil, *Solon. Verf.* 195)
Hicks, Mr R. D., 178 (*n. c.*)
Hipparchus, 68
,, son of Charmus, 85 *b*
holidays, Athenian, 158 *b*
Homer, *scholia* on, xxviii; Solon's reminiscence of, 48 *a*
homicide, law of, 23 *b*; the Areopagus and its cognisance of, 100 *b*, 142 *b*; trials for, 212—6
hoplites (2500), 98 *a*
horses and horsemen, δοκιμασία of, 177 f
houses, purchase-money of, 173; windows of, 183
Hultsch, quoted, 38 *b*

Ion, 146 *b*, 250 l. 2, 251 frag. 1
Ionisms in Solon's verses, 46 *b*, 47 *b*; in Cleidemus, 58 *a*
Isocrates, li, 12 *a*, 30 *a*, 93 *a*; (cf. Keil, *Solon. Verf.* 78 ff, 89 ff)

Jackson, Dr H., quoted, 185 *a*, and in critical notes 22, 41, 44 &c.
Jebb, Prof. R. C., quoted, 42 *b*, 44, 166 *a*

Keil, Prof. Bruno, quoted, lxxiv, lxxvii
Kenyon, Mr F. G., quoted, xxxiv f, 4 *a*, 14 *b*, 25 *b*, 47 *b*, 74 *a*, 78, 86 *b*, 102, 110 *a*, 120 *b*, 122, 134 *a*, 139 *a*, 146 *b*, 191 *a*, 193 *b*, and in the critical notes *passim*
Knights (1200), 96 *b*; (1000) 133 *b*; under the Thirty, 142. Of Eretria, 59 *b*
Köhler, Prof. U., quoted, lxxiv, 39 *a*

Larmor, Mr J., quoted, 245 *b*
law-courts, allotment of, 221 *b*, 233 f; Gk. Index, *s. v.* δικαστήρια, Ἄρειος πάγος, (ἐπὶ) Δελφινίῳ and Παλλαδίῳ, (ἐν) Φρεάτου
law-suits, see Gk. Index, *s. v.* γραφαί, and δίκαι
leases of mines, 171 f; of sacred enclosures, 173 f; property of minors, 209 *b*
Leeuwen, Prof. van, quoted, xxxvi f, and in critical notes *passim*
Leipsydrium, 72 *b*
Lemnos, ἵππαρχος sent to, 229 *a*
Leocorium, 70 *a*
Lesbos, 95 *a*
Liddell and Scott's *Lexicon*, 183 *a*
Lipsius, Prof. J. H., quoted, 150 *b*, 158 *a*, 189 *a*, 195 *b*, 219 *b* &c.
lot, appointment by, 16 *a*, 29 f, 87, 230 *b*, 236 *b*; Council appointed by, 157 *a*, 230 *a*. See also Gk. Index, *s. v.* κληρῶ and λαγχάνω
Lycurgus, administration of, 170 *b*, 200 *a b*
Lygdamis, 59 f

Macan, Mr R., quoted, lviii, lxvi, 30 *b*, 37 *a*
Mahaffy, Dr J. P., quoted, xv, 89 *b*
maladministration, fines for, 194 *b*
Marmor Parium, 50 *b* &c.
Maroneia, mines at, 89 *b*
Mayor, Rev. Prof. John E. B., quoted, 4 *a*, 55 *a*, 58 *a*, 154 *b*, 182 (*n. c.*) &c.
Mayor, Rev. Jos. B., quoted, xlvii (*n.*), 21 (*n. c.*), 67 (*n. c.*), 145 (*n. c.*) &c.
Megacles, son of Hippocrates, 87 *b*
Megarian war, 54
Meyer, P., quoted, 14 *a*
military discipline, 228 *a*; period of military service, 191 *a*
mines, 89 f, 171 f
Müller, Carl, xxix
Munichia, 72, 226 *a*

naucrari, 32 *b*, 81 *b*; cf. Keil, *Sol. Verf.* p. 93 ff
neutrals, Solon's law against, 34
Newman, Mr W. L., quoted, xlv, lvi, 13 *a*, 20 *b*, 34 *b*, 71 *b*, 83 *a*, 85 *b*, 95 *b*, 96 *a*, 103 *b*, 114 *b*, 167 *a*, 200 *a*
Nicias, 114
Nicodemus, or Nicomedes, 89 *a*
Nikê, figures of, 170

officials, home and foreign, 97 *b*; appointed by lot, members of Council, 157, 231 *a*; other officials so appointed, 170—5, 181—201, cf. Gk. Index, *s. v.* κληρῶ. Military officials, 225 f; elected by show of hands, 155 f; time of electing, 165 *b*. Scrutiny of, 202 *a*
oil from the sacred olive-trees, 223 f
Oncken, Prof. W., quoted, xxx
opisthodomos, 163 *a*
orthography; see critical notes on ἀεὶ 20 f; γίγνομαι 5; γιγνώσκω 19; ἐξοπλασία(?) 60; ἱερεωσύνη 83; λητουργία 108 *b*; Μουνιχία 72; σῴζειν 92; σῶος, σῶς 123
Ostracism, 84—92; 160 *a*; archeological evidence on, 88 *a b*

Palladium, court in precincts of, 213 *a*
Pallene, 60 *a*
Panathenaea, 71 *a*, 157 *a*, 198 *a*, 222 f
Panathenaic vases, 223 *b*
papyrus, xxxviii
Paralos, 229 *b* (cf. Keil, *Solon. Verf.* 149)
Paton, Mr W. R., quoted, 15 (*n. c.*), 83
Patrizzi, xxix
Patrocleides, decree of, 214 *b*
paupers, relief of, 181 (cf. Keil, *Solon. Verf.* 75)
Peiraeus, demarch of, 200 *b*; generals set over, 226 *b*; party of, 140—5
Peisander, 127
Peisistratus, chronology of, 56 (cf. Köhler, on p. lxxii, and Keil, *Solon. Verf.* 51); in Macedonia, 58
Pericles, 106—111; law of citizenship carried by, 106 *b*; his accusation of Cimon, 107; his successors, 111
petitions, 161 *a*
Phanodemus, lv
Pheidon, 37 *b*
Philochorus, xix, lvi; on ostracism, 84 *a*
Philon's σκευοθήκη, 168 *b*, 180 *b*
Philostephanus of Cyrene, xx
Phormisius, a leader of the moderate party 404 B.C., 132 *b*
Photius, xxvii; *s. v.* ἡγεμονία δικαστηρίου corrected, 216 *a*; mistake, *s. v.* πάραλοι, accounted for, 230 *a*
'Phreatto', 213 *b*

Phyle, 137
plans of buildings removed from cognisance of the Council, 180 *a*
Plato's *Republic*, *Politicus* and *Laws*, x, xi; *Rep.* 558 B, xliv *n*; *Gorgias* 515 E, 110; cf. Keil, *Solon. Verf.* 158, 218 f; *scholia* on, xxviii
Pliny the Elder, xxiii
Plutarch and the Πολιτεῖαι, xxiii f, 19 *a*; *Theseus*, 147 *a*, 251 frag. 2; *Solon*, xxiii f, 1—3, 21, 24 f, 33—37, 41—48 (cf. Keil, *Solon. Verf.* 40, 45, 55, 164, 173, 175, &c.); *Themistocles*, 102; *Cimon*, 104 f, 107 f; *Pericles*, 106—9; *Nicias*, 2, 114 *b*
Polemon, 27 *b*
Pollux, xxv f, 28, 176 *a*, &c., and in the *Testimonia*, *passim* (cf. Keil, *Solon. Verf.* 64); corected by Cobet, 202 *b*
Poole, Mr R. S., quoted, 39 *a*
Poste, Mr E., quoted, 14 *b*, 21 *a*, 97 *b*, 115 *a*, 123 *b*, 142 *a*
Postgate, Dr, 20 (*n. c.*)
proedri, 163
proxenos, grants of title of, 196 *a*
prytaneum, court in precincts of, 216 *b*
prytanies, duration of, 157 *b*
Pythocleides, 255 frag. 13
Pythodorus, archon 432/1, 108 *a*; archon 404/3, 116 *b*, 133 *b*

quadriremes, 169 *a*
Quarterly Review, Apr. 1891, quoted, 103 *a*

Reinach, Th., 13 *b*, 143 *b* &c.
Richards, Mr H., quoted, xlvii f, 19 *b*, 61 *b*, and in critical notes *passim*
Ridgeway, Prof., 40 *b*
Robertson Smith, Prof., xxxi
Rose, V., xxx, 74 *a* &c.
rotation in office, 16 f, 125 *b*
Rühl, F. xxi (*n*), lxxiii, 147 *b* &c.

sacrifices, commissioners of, 197 *a*
Salaminia, 230 *a b*
Salamis, battle of, 92; archon in, 200 *b*
salaries, 230 f
Samos, 95 *a*, 232 *a*
'Sandwich marble', 232 *a*
scholia, quotations from πολιτεῖαι in, xxviii
Schöll, quoted, 219 *b*
Schömann, quoted, 133 *a*, 148 *a*, 164 *b* &c.
Schvarcz, criticised, xlii f
scolia, 73, 77
seal of Athens, 163 *b*
Selden, xxix
Shute, Mr R., quoted, xl, lii f
Simonides, 68 *a*
slaves, damage done by, 187 *b*
Solon, liv, 18—48; date of his archonship, 49 f, 55 *a*; legislation of, 23; obscurities in his laws, 36 *b*, 134 *b*; law against neutrality, 34; limited power of testation granted by, 135 *a*; verses of, 19—21; 44—48; democratic tendency of his reforms, 34; reform of coins, weights and measures, 37 (cf. Keil, *Solon. Verf.* 70 f, 163—172); withdraws to Egypt, 41; opposes Peisistratus, 55; ashes of, 254 frag. 11; εἰσαγγελίαι, 34 *a*; κύρβεις 236 (Keil, *l. c.* 58); ὅροι 45 f; σεισάχθεια 21, 37 *b*
Solon and Peisistratus, 55, 66
Sophocles, his στρατηγία, 166 *a*; *scholium* on *O. C.* 701, 223.
Strabo and the Πολιτεῖαι, xxii
symmories, generals set over the, 226 *a*

taxes, Athenian, 95 f
Ten, the, appointed to succeed the Thirty, 139 *b*; their atrocities, *ib.*; superseded by another body of Ten, 140; excluded from the amnesty, 143 *a*; allowed to settle at Eleusis, *ib.* For other bodies of Ten, see Gk. Index, *s. v.* δέκα
Themistocles, brings about building of triremes, 90 f; date of his archonship, 90 *b*; co-operates with Aristides in building walls of Athens, 93 *b*; accused of Medism, 102; helps Ephialtes to overthrow the Areopagus (B.C. 462), 101 f
theoricon, 113 f, 156 *a*, 171 *b*
Theramenes, leader of aristocratical party, 114; character of, 115. A leader of the 400, 127; joins in subverting them, 128. Leader of moderate party after Aegospotami, 133; opposes extreme measures of the Thirty, 136; put to death, 137. Cf. lxiii *n*
Theseum, 61 *a*, 230 *b*
Theseus, 147 *a*, 251 frag. 2, 253 frag. 4
thesmothetae, 218 f; clerk to, 201 *b*
Thettalus, 66 *b*, 68 *b*
Thirlwall justified, 59 *a*, 63 *b*
Thirty, the, established by Lysander, 133; their rule, 133—6; defeated at Munichia and expelled from power, 139; excluded from amnesty, allowed to settle at Eleusis, 143
Thompson, Mr E. S., quoted, 13 *b*, 75 *b*
Thompson, Dr W. H., quoted, 25 *a*
Thrasybulus, occupies Phyle and defeats forces sent by the Thirty, 137; decree proposed by T. attacked by Archinus, 144
Three Thousand, privileged body under the Thirty, 137 *a*
Thucydides (i 126), 2 *a*; on Harmodius, liv, 69—71; (viii 67) 117 f, 125 *a*
Thucydides (son of Melesias), leader of aristocratical party, 111
Timaeus, xx
torch-races, 211 *a*

Torr, Mr Cecil, xxxix, 169 *a*, 185 *b*
treasurers, lxxvii, 121, 170; treasurer of the Council, 181 *b*
treaties, 196 *a*
tribes, four in early times, 31 *b*; ten instituted by Cleisthenes, 83 *b*
triremes, building of, 90 f, 169 *a*
'tyranny', law against, 65
Tyrrell, Prof. R. Y., quoted, 22 *b*, 103 *a*
Tzetzes, xxvii

verbs, compound followed by simple, 194 *a*
votes of dicasts, 246; reckoning-board for, 248 *b*

Walker, Mr E. M., quoted, 105 *a*
'war-king', 7
water-clock, 244 f
weights and measures, 184 *a*
Weil, Prof. H., quoted, 14 *n. c.*, 69 *a*
Wilamowitz, von, quoted, 97 f, 195 *a*, 218 *a*, and in critical notes *passim*
wills, 135 *a*
Wright, Prof. J. H., xix f, xxiv, lvii, lx
Wyse, Prof. W., quoted, 33 *b*, 62 *b*, 66 *b*, 85 *a*, 91 *b*, 97 *a*, 99 *a*, 103 *b*, 119 *b*, 126, 190 *a*, 199 *b* &c.; also in critical notes *passim*

Xanthippus, son of Ariphron, ostracised, 88 *b*; his dog, 254 frag. 12
Xenophon and the 'Αθ. πολ., lv; his political writings, ix, x; Pseudo-Xenophon, 'Αθ. πολ., ix (cf. Keil, *Solon. Verf.* 215)

year, lunar, 158 *a*

Zenobius, xxv; (vi 29) criticised, 113 *b*

CAMBRIDGE: PRINTED BY C. J. CLAY, M.A. AND SONS, AT THE UNIVERSITY PRESS.

BY THE SAME EDITOR.

Euripides.—Bacchae. With Critical and Explanatory Notes, and with numerous Illustrations from Works of Ancient Art. 1880, Third Edition, 1892, pp. clv + 275, crown 8vo, gilt top, 12*s*. 6*d*.*

Isocrates.—Ad Demonicum et Panegyricus, pp. xliv + 169, 1868, Second Edition, 1872, crown 8vo, 4*s*. 6*d*. Rivingtons (now Longmans), London.

Demosthenes.—Select Private Orations. With Introductions and English Notes.

Part II.—Containing Pro Phormione, Contra Stephanum I, II, Nicostratum, Cononem, Calliclem. 1875, New Edition, 1886, pp. lxxii + 271, crown 8vo, 7*s*. 6*d*.*

Demosthenes.—Speech against the Law of Leptines. With Introduction, Critical and Explanatory Notes, and Autotype Facsimile from the Paris MS. 1890, pp. xlviii + 122, demy 8vo, 9*s*.*

Cicero.—Ad M. Brutum Orator. A Revised Text. With Introductory Essays and Critical and Explanatory Notes, 1885, pp. xcix+258, demy 8vo, 16*s*.*

Aristotle.—The Rhetoric. With a Commentary by the late E. M. COPE, Fellow of Trinity College, Cambridge, revised and edited (with Indices) by J. E. SANDYS. With a biographical Memoir by the late H. A. J. MUNRO, 1877. 3 Vols, pp. xx+913, demy 8vo, 21*s*.*

Dictionary of Classical Mythology, Religion, Literature, Art, and Antiquities. Revised and Edited from the German of Dr OSKAR SEYFFERT, by Professor NETTLESHIP and Dr SANDYS. With about 500 illustrations. Second Edition, 1891, with new and full Indexes of Contents and Illustrations; pp. 706, double columns, crown 4to, 21*s*. Swan Sonnenschein and Co., London (Macmillan and Co., New York).

An Easter Vacation in Greece, with lists of books on Greek Travel and Topography, and Time-tables of Greek Steamers and Railways, by J. E. SANDYS, 1887, pp. 171, crown 8vo, 3*s*. 6*d*. Macmillan and Co., London and New York.

* *Edited for the Syndics of the Cambridge University Press;* Cambridge Warehouse, Ave Maria Lane, London (Deighton, Bell and Co., Cambridge; F. A. Brockhaus, Leipzig; Macmillan and Co., New York).